The Cambridge Primary Review Research Surveys

D1376187

The Cambridge Primary Review Research Surveys is the companion volume to *Children, their World, their Education: final report and recommendations of the Cambridge Primary Review.* Both are the outcome of England's biggest enquiry into primary education for over 40 years.

Fully independent of government, the Cambridge Primary Review was launched in 2006 to investigate the condition and future of primary education at a time of change and uncertainty and after two decades of almost uninterrupted reform. Ranging over ten broad themes and drawing on a vast array of evidence, the Review published 31 interim reports, including 28 surveys of published research, provoking media headlines and public debate, before presenting its final report and recommendations.

This book brings together the 28 research surveys, specially commissioned from 66 leading academics in the areas under scrutiny and now revised and updated, to create what is probably the most comprehensive overview and evaluation of research in primary education yet published. A particular feature is the prominence given to international and comparative perspectives. With an introduction from Robin Alexander, the Review's director, the book is divided into eight sections, covering:

- Children's lives and voices: school, home and community
- Children's development, learning, diversity and needs
- Aims, values and contexts for primary education
- The structure and content of primary education
- Outcomes, standards and assessment in primary education
- Teaching in primary schools: structures and processes
- Teaching in primary schools: training, development and workforce reform
- Policy frameworks: governance, funding, reform and quality assurance

The Cambridge Primary Review Research Surveys is an essential reference tool for professionals, researchers, students and policy makers working in the fields of early years, primary and secondary education.

Robin Alexander is Director of the Cambridge Primary Review, Fellow of Wolfson College, University of Cambridge, and Professor of Education Emeritus at the University of Warwick, UK.

Christine Doddington is Senior Lecturer in Education at the Faculty of Education, University of Cambridge.

John Gray is Professor of Education at the Faculty of Education, University of Cambridge.

Linda Hargreaves is Reader in Education at the Faculty of Education, University of Cambridge.

Ruth Kershner is Lecturer in Psychology of Education and Primary Education at the Faculty of Education, University of Cambridge.

York St John University

3 8025 00587697 7

The Cambridge Primary Review Research Surveys

Edited by
Robin Alexander

with
Christine Doddington, John Gray,
Linda Hargreaves and Ruth Kershner

YORK ST. JOHN
LIBRARY & INFORMATION
SERVICES

Routledge
Taylor & Francis Group

LONDON AND NEW YORK

Esmée
Fairbairn
FOUNDATION

First published 2010
by Routledge
2 Park Square, Milton Park, Abingdon, Oxon OX14 4RN

Simultaneously published in the USA and Canada
by Routledge
711 Third Avenue, New York, NY 10017

Routledge is an imprint of the Taylor & Francis Group, an informa business

© 2010 The University of Cambridge
The rights of each author to be identified as author of their individual chapter(s) have
been asserted in accordance with the Copyright, Designs and Patents Act 1988.

Typeset in Times New Roman
by Taylor & Francis Books

First issued in paperback 2013

All rights reserved. No part of this book may be reprinted or reproduced or utilised in
any form or by any electronic, mechanical, or other means, now known or hereafter
invented, including photocopying and recording, or in any information storage or
retrieval system, without permission in writing from the publishers.

British Library Cataloguing in Publication Data
A catalogue record for this book is available from the British Library

Library of Congress Cataloging in Publication Data
Cambridge Primary Review (Organization)
   The Cambridge Primary Review Research Surveys / edited by Robin Alexander.
      p. cm.
   Includes bibliographical references and index.
   1. Education, Elementary–Great Britain–Evaluation. I. Alexander, Robin J. II. Title.
   LA633.C36 2010
   372'.941–dc22
                                  2009022991

ISBN13: 978-0-415-54869-4 (hbk)
ISBN13: 978-0-415-84633-2 (pbk)

Contents

Figures

Tables

Contributors

EDITORS

Professor ROBIN ALEXANDER, University of Cambridge, UK
   (Director of the Cambridge Primary Review).

CHRISTINE DODDINGTON, University of Cambridge, UK.

Professor JOHN GRAY, University of Cambridge, UK.

Dr LINDA HARGREAVES, University of Cambridge, UK.

RUTH KERSHNER, University of Cambridge, UK.

AUTHORS

Professor MEL AINSCOW, University of Manchester, UK.

Dr MARIA BALARIN, University of Bath, UK.

Dr IAN BARRON, Manchester Metropolitan University, UK.

Professor PETER BLATCHFORD, Institute of Education, University of London, UK.

Professor MARK BRUNDRETT, University of Manchester, UK
   (now at Liverpool John Moores University, UK).

Professor PETER BRYANT, University of Oxford, UK.

Dr HILARY BURGESS, Open University, UK.

Dr RITA CHAWLA-DUGGAN, University of Bath, UK.

Professor JAMES CONROY, University of Glasgow, UK.

Dr JEAN CONTEH, University of Leeds, UK.

Dr ANDREA CREECH, Institute of Education, University of London, UK.

Dr PETER CUNNINGHAM, University of Cambridge, UK.

Professor HARRY DANIELS, University of Bath, UK.

Professor JULIE DOCKRELL, Institute of Education, University of London, UK.

Professor ALAN DYSON, University of Manchester, UK.

Professor MICHAEL FIELDING, University of Sussex, UK
(now at Institute of Education, University of London, UK).

Dr FRANCES GALLANNAUGH, University of Manchester, UK.

Professor USHA GOSWAMI, University of Cambridge, UK.

Professor KATHY HALL, Open University, UK
(now at National University of Ireland, Cork, Eire).

Professor SUSAN HALLAM, Institute of Education, University of London, UK.

Professor WYNNE HARLEN, University of Bristol, UK.

Dr RACHEL HOLMES, Manchester Metropolitan University, UK.

Professor CHRISTINE HOWE, University of Cambridge, UK.

Dr MOIRA HULME, University of Glasgow, UK.

Professor JUDITH IRESON, Institute of Education, University of London, UK.

Professor MARY JAMES, Institute of Education, University of London, UK
(now at the University of Cambridge, UK).

Professor LIZ JONES, Manchester Metropolitan University, UK.

Professor PETER KUTNICK, King's College London, UK.

Professor HUGH LAUDER, University of Bath, UK.

Dr JOHN LOWE, University of Bath, UK.

Professor STEPHEN MACHIN, University College, London, UK.

Professor MAGGIE MACLURE, Manchester Metropolitan University, UK.

Professor BERRY MAYALL, Institute of Education, University of London, UK.

Dr ELAINE MCCREERY, Manchester Metropolitan University, UK.

Dr SANDRA MCNALLY, London School of Economics and Political Science, UK.

Professor OLWEN MCNAMARA, University of Manchester, UK.

Professor IAN MENTER, University of Glasgow, UK.

Professor NEIL MERCER, University of Cambridge, UK.

Dr CHRISTINE MERRELL, University of Durham, UK.

Dr YOLANDE MUSCHAMP, University of Bath, UK.

SHARON O'DONNELL, National Foundation for Educational Research, UK.

Dr PHILIP NODEN, London School of Economics and Political Science, UK.

Professor KAMIL ØZERK, University of Oslo, Norway.

NICK PEACEY, Institute of Education, University of London, UK.

Dr ANDY PICKARD, Manchester Metropolitan University, UK.

Professor ANDREW POLLARD, Institute of Education, University of London, UK.

Dr JILL PORTER, University of Bath, UK.

Dr PHILIP RAYMONT, University of Cambridge, UK.

Dr TESS RIDGE, University of Bath, UK.

ANNA RIGGALL, National Foundation for Educational Research, UK.

Dr CAROL ROBINSON, University of Sussex, UK
  (now at University of Brighton, UK).

Dr GRAHAM RUDDOCK, National Foundation for Educational Research, UK.

Dr KATHERINE RUNSWICK-COLE, Sheffield Hallam University, UK
  (now at Manchester Metropolitan University, UK).

Dr MAHA SHUAYB, National Foundation for Educational Research, UK.

CAROLINE SHARP, National Foundation for Educational Research, UK.

Professor IAN STRONACH, Manchester Metropolitan University, UK
  (now at Liverpool John Moores University, UK).

Professor HARRY TORRANCE, Manchester Metropolitan University, UK.

LIZ TWIST, National Foundation for Educational Research, UK.

Professor PETER TYMMS, University of Durham, UK.

Dr KARL WALL, Institute of Education, University of London, UK.

Professor ROSEMARY WEBB, University of Manchester, UK.

Professor ANNE WEST, London School of Economics and Political Science, UK.

CHRIS WHETTON, National Foundation for Educational Research, UK.

Professor JOHN WHITE, Institute of Education, University of London, UK.

Dr FELICITY WIKELEY, University of Bath, UK.

Dr DOMINIC WYSE, University of Cambridge, UK.

Acknowledgements

All the chapters in this volume were specially commissioned and written for the Cambridge Primary Review. Chapters 2–29 were originally released as interim reports of the Review and in that form were widely circulated both electronically and in hard copy between November 2007 and May 2008. Most were then revised in preparation for their publication in this, the companion volume to the Review's final report. We are grateful to the authors for their contributions to this distinctive and essential strand of the Review's evidence, and for their stoicism in the face of the media exposure to which many of the reports were subjected. Any lingering doubts about the claim that education is an inherently political activity must surely have been dispelled by that first airing of these studies.

We thank the Trustees of Esmée Fairbairn Foundation for their generous financial support for the Cambridge Primary Review from 2006–8 and again from 2008–10, and the faith in the importance of this venture which that support represents. We thank the staff of the Foundation for their willing and sustained guidance from the moment when one of us first approached the Foundation in 2004; and members of the Review's Advisory Committee for being such generous and perceptive critical friends of the Review from May 2006 onwards. In the matter of wise guidance and ever-available support we owe a particular debt to Gillian Pugh, our Advisory Committee Chair, and Hilary Hodgson at Esmée Fairbairn Foundation.

Finally, we thank Anna Clarkson and the Education team at Routledge for taking on this unusual publishing project, the University of Cambridge for hosting the Review, and our Cambridge colleagues Julia Flutter, David Harrison and Catrin Darsley for their collaboration in the wider venture of which this book is part.

NOTE

The studies in this volume were commissioned as evidence to the Cambridge Primary Review. The views they express are those of their authors and are not necessarily shared by the Review, the University of Cambridge or Esmée Fairbairn Foundation.

Abbreviations

AAP	Assessment of Achievement Programme
ACCAC	Awdurdod Cymwysterau, Cwricwlwm ac Asesu Cymru (Qualifications, Curriculum and Assessment Authority for Wales)
ACfE	A Curriculum for Excellence (Scotland)
ACPC	Area Child Protection Committee
ADHD	Attention Deficit Hyperactivity Disorder
AfL	Assessment for Learning (England)
AifL	Assessment is for Learning (Scotland)
APU	Assessment of Performance Unit
ASD	Autistic Spectrum Disorder
AYP	Adequate Yearly Progress (USA)
BEST	Behaviour and Education Support Team
BIP	Behaviour Improvement Programme
CACE	Central Advisory Council for Education (England)
CAME	Cognitive Acceleration through Mathematics Education
CASE	Cognitive Acceleration through Science Education
CATE	Cognitive Acceleration through Technology Education
CATE	Council for the Accreditation of Teacher Education
CCEA	Council for the Curriculum, Examinations and Assessment (Northern Ireland)
CCEAM	Commonwealth Council for Educational Administration and Management
CICADA	Changes in Curriculum-Associated Discourse and Pedagogy in the Primary School
CIEA	Chartered Institute of Educational Assessors
CMT	Change Management Team
CNAA	Council for National Academic Awards
COSLA	Convention of Scottish Local Authorities
CPAL	Consulting Pupils on the Assessment of their Learning project (Northern Ireland)
CPD	Continuing Professional Development
CRE	Commission for Racial Equality
CSPAR	Class Size and Pupil Adult Ratio project
CSR	Class Size Reduction
DCELLS	Department for Children, Education, Lifelong Learning and Skills (Wales)

DCMS	Department of Culture, Media and Sport (England)
DCSF	Department for Children, Schools and Families (England)
DES	Department of Education and Science (England)
DES	Department of Education and Science (Ireland)
DfE	Department for Education (England)
DfEE	Department for Education and Employment (England)
DfES	Department for Education and Skills (England)
DfID	Department for International Development
DISS	Deployment and Impact of Support Staff in Schools project
DIUS	Department for Innovation, Universities and Skills (England)
DPEP	District Primary Education Programme (India)
DRC	Disability Rights Commission
DSG	Dedicated Schools Grant
DWP	Department for Work and Pensions
EAL	English as an Additional Language
EAZ	Education Action Zone
EBITT	Employment Based Initial Teacher Training
ECM	Every Child Matters
EFA	Education for All
EFSS	Education Formula Spending Share system
EGSIE	Education Governance and Social Inclusion and Exclusion in Europe project
EHP	Early Headship Programme
EiC	Excellence in Cities programme
EMAG	Ethnic Minority Achievement Grant)
EMIE	Education Management Information Exchange
EOC	Equal Opportunities Commission
EPA	Educational Priority Area
EPPE	Effective Provision of Pre-School Education project
EPPI	Evidence for Policy and Planning Information
ERA	Education Reform Act, 1988
ERO	Education Review Office (New Zealand)
ESG	Education Support Grant
ESL	English as a Second Language
ESRA	Extended Schools Remodelling Adviser
ESRC	Economic and Social Research Council
ESRT	Extended Schools Remodelling Trainer
ESSA	Education Standard Spending Assessment system
ESW	Education Social Worker
ETS	Educational Testing Service (USA)
EWO	Education Welfare Officer
EYFS	Early Years Foundation Stage
FACS	Families and Children Study
FSS	Formula Spending Share system
GBEP	Gansu Basic Education Project (China)
GDP	Gross Domestic Product
GEST	Grants for Educational Support and Training
GMR	Global Monitoring Report

GOI	Government of India
GRIST	Grant Related In-Service Training
GTC	General Teaching Council for England
HEADLAMP	Headteacher Leadership and Management Programme
HEI	Higher Education Institution
HIP	Headteachers' Induction Programme
HLE	Home Learning Environment
HLTA	Higher Level Teaching Assistant
HMCI	Her Majesty's Chief Inspector
HMI	Her Majesty's Inspector(ate)
HSKE	Home School Knowledge Exchange
IAEP	International Assessment of Educational Progress
IAQ	Indoor Air Quality
IBIS	Inspectors Based in Schools scheme
ICT	Information and Communications Technology
IE	Instrumental Enrichment
IEA	International Association for the Evaluation for Educational Achievement
IEG	Independent Evaluation Group
INCA	International Review of Curriculum and Assessment
IRT	Item response theory
IRU	Implementation Review Unit
ISB	Individual Schools Budget
ISC	In-School Centre
ITE	Initial Teacher Education
ITT	Initial Teacher Training
JAR	Joint Area Review
KBE	Knowledge-based economy
KS1 / KS2	Key Stage 1/2
LA	Local Authority
LEA	Local Education Authority
LGA	Local Government Association
LHTL	Learning How to Learn project
LMS	Local Management of Schools
LPSH	Leadership Programme for Serving Headteachers
LSB	Local Schools Budget
MA	Master of Arts
MDG	Millennium Development Goal(s)
MEd	Master in Education
MEN	Ministère de l'Education Nationale (France)
MFG	Minimum Funding Guarantee
MFL	Modern foreign language(s)
MLD	Moderate learning difficulties
MLE	Mediated learning experiences
MOTE	Modes of teacher education
NAB	National Advisory Board
NACCCE	National Advisory Committee on Creative and Cultural Education
NC	National Curriculum

NCC	National Curriculum Council
NCERT	National Council of Educational Research and Training (India)
NCLB	No Child Left Behind Act (USA)
NCSL	National College for School Leadership
NDC	National Development Centre for School Management Training
NEMP	National Education Monitoring Project (New Zealand)
NESS	National Evaluation of Sure Start
NFER	National Foundation for Educational Research
NI	Northern Ireland
NIEPA	National Institute of Educational Planning and Administration (India)
NLS	National Literacy Strategy
NNEB	National Nursery Examination Board
NNS	National Numeracy Strategy
NPD	National Pupil Database
NPQH	National Professional Qualification for Headship
NRCNA	National Research Council of the National Academies (USA)
NRT	National Remodelling Team
NUEPA	National University of Educational Planning and Administration (India)
NUT	National Union of Teachers
OECD	Organisation for Economic Co-operation and Development
Ofsted	Office for Standards in Education
Ofstin	Office for Standards in Inspection
ONS	Office for National Statistics
ORACLE	Observational Research and Classroom Learning Evaluation
OTTOs	One Term Training Opportunities
P4C	Philosophy for Children
PACE	Primary Assessment, Curriculum and Experience
PANDA	Performance and Assessment Data
PE	Physical education
PGCE	Post-graduate Certificate in Education
PICSI	Pre-Inspection Context and School Indicators
PIPS	Performance Indicators in Primary Schools
PIRLS	Progress in International Reading Literacy Study
PISA	Programme for International Student Assessment
PLASC	Pupil Level Annual School Census
PLC	Professional Learning Community
PLP	Primary Leadership Programme
PNS	Primary National Strategy
PPA	Planning, preparation and assessment time
PPP	Purchasing power parity
PROBE	Public Report on Basic Education (India)
PSCL	Primary Strategy Consultant Leaders
PSHE	Personal, social, and health education
PTA	Parent-teacher association
PTR	Pupil-teacher ratios
PwC	Philosophy with Children
PwC	PricewaterhouseCoopers
QCA	Qualifications and Curriculum Authority

QTS	Qualified Teacher Status
RAE	Research Assessment Exercise
RCT	Randomised controlled trial
RT	Reverberation time
SAD	Seasonal Affective Disorder
SAT	Standard Assessment Task/Test (England)
SAT	Scholastic Aptitude Test (USA)
SC	Scheduled Caste (India)
SCAA	School Curriculum and Assessment Authority
SCITT	School-Centred Initial Teacher Training
SCLN	Speech and language difficulties
SDP	School Development Plan(ning)
SEAL	Social and Emotional Aspects of Learning toolkit
SEBD	Social, emotional and behavioural difficulties
SED	Scottish Education Department
SEED	Scottish Executive Education Department
SEF	Self evaluation form
SEN	Special educational needs
SENCO	Special Educational Needs Co-ordinator
SENDA	Special Educational Needs and Disability Act
SES	Socio-economic status
SETF	Social Exclusion Task Force
SEU	Social Exclusion Unit
SEU	Standards and Effectiveness Unit
SIP	School Improvement Partner
SLANT	Spoken Language and New Technology project
SLD	Severe learning difficulties
SMT	Senior management team
SoA	Statement(s) of Attainment
SOED	Scottish Office Education Department
SpLD	Specific learning difficulties
SPRinG	Social Pedagogic Research into Group work project
SSA	Sarva Shiksha Abhiyan (Education for All) (India)
SSA	Scottish Survey of Assessment
SSA	Standard Spending Assessment system (England)
ST	Scheduled Tribe (India)
STAR	Student/Teacher Achievement Ratio (USA)
SWIPS	Social Work in Primary Schools project
TA	Teacher assessment
TA	Teaching assistant
TDA	Training and Development Agency for Schools
TGAT	Task Group on Assessment and Testing
TIMSS	Trends in International Mathematics and Science Study
TIPD	Teachers' International Professional Development
TLA	Teacher Learning Academy
TLRP	Teaching and Learning Research Programme
TPLF	Teachers' Professional Learning Framework
TRIST	Teacher Related In-Service Training

TSW	Transforming the Workforce Pathfinder
TTA	Teacher Training Agency
TTRB	Teacher Training Resource Bank
UDE	University department of education
UK	United Kingdom
UN	United Nations
UNCRC	United Nations Convention on the Rights of the Child
UNESCO	United Nations Educational, Scientific and Cultural Organization
UPE	Universal Primary Education
WAMG	Workforce Agreement Monitoring Group
WBO	Wet op het Basisonderwijs (Basic Education Act) (Netherlands)
WEI	World Education Indicators
WFTC	Working Families Tax Credit
WISC III	Wechsler Intelligence Scale for Children version 3
YOT	Youth Offending Team

1 Introduction

Research, the Cambridge Primary Review and the quality of education

Robin Alexander

This is the companion volume to the final report from the Cambridge Primary Review, a comprehensive and independent enquiry into the condition and future of primary education in England. Based at the University of Cambridge, the Review was supported from 2006–10 by Esmée Fairbairn Foundation. Details of its remit, processes and personnel appear in Appendices 1–3.

Children, their World, their Education – the final report – contains an account of why and how the Review was undertaken, what it investigated and what its findings indicate for future policy and practice. Structured loosely round the Review's ten nominated themes, the report discusses the evidence from four complementary strands of enquiry: written submissions received from individuals and organisations in response to an open invitation issued in October 2006; face-to-face regional and national 'soundings' with a wide range of groups and organisations both inside and outside education which were undertaken during 2007 and 2008; statistical and other official information held by government departments and national agencies; and commissioned surveys of published research prepared by the Review's 66 research consultants in 21 university departments in England, Scotland, the Republic of Ireland and Norway. The report culminates in a set of formally-framed conclusions and recommendations for future educational policy and practice.

This volume is rather different, and it serves three quite distinct purposes. The commissioned surveys of published research – the fourth of the Review's evidential strands referred to above – were such a substantial and distinctive component of the Review that we have always believed that they should be available separately and in full rather than serve merely as points of reference in a larger enterprise. Earlier versions were disseminated, mainly via the Review's website, between October 2007 and May 2008. The aim then was to encourage discussion which would feed back into the evidence-gathering process, and this was readily ensured by the added combination of unprecedented media coverage and an uncertain political climate. The final report refers to the research surveys alongside the other evidence mentioned above, and indeed draws on them heavily, but it does not and cannot convey a sense of the breadth and depth of each of the surveys as undertaken, nor of their combined scope and narrative power, nor of the sheer quantity of research surveyed: in all, across the 29 chapters nearly 3000 published sources are cited.

Our first purpose in presenting the research surveys here, therefore, is to ensure that justice is done to them as an important part of the Cambridge Primary Review as a whole and as a necessary adjunct to *Children, their World, their Education*.

The second purpose reflects a belief in the value of these research surveys in their own right, as a free-standing resource for teachers, students, researchers and policy-makers which is able powerfully to illuminate many of the most important problems in primary education and to help us to address some of its most urgent and difficult questions. With this in mind, *The Cambridge Primary Review Research Surveys* provides a reader or handbook of research relating to primary education, possibly the most extensive yet published. Of course, no such reader can claim to be comprehensive, and this is no exception; so we hope and expect that the book will be revised and added to from time to time in order to keep abreast of new research and of change in the educational, social and political conditions which provide its focus and context.

Our third purpose is less obvious and perhaps more controversial. Since the mid-1990s the prefixes 'evidence based' and 'research based' have been attached to the words 'policy' and 'practice' with increasing frequency in official circles (with academics and professionals dutifully following the trend), and the websites of British and American government departments confirm how inescapably the trend has become embedded in political and administrative discourse. For example, the Bush Administration's No Child Left Behind Act (2001) mentions 'research-based practice' no fewer than 111 times (Gamoran 2007). Sometimes 'evidence-based' or 'research-based' are uttered with discriminating and critical intent; sometimes they are used casually as to meaning though calculatedly as to intended impact. For although 'evidence-based' ought immediately to provoke methodological scrutiny, it may also seek to deflect it by brandishing 'evidence' or 'research' as a policy kitemark which forecloses further discussion. Sometimes, on closer inspection of the policies or practices in question, the 'evidence-based' claim can be sustained, but sometimes it cannot. Yet, along with the no less talismanic 'what works' and 'best practice', the phrase has become habitual among policy makers and their advisers in both Britain and the United States.

All three phrases are never less than problematic. There are questions about what kinds of evidence are appropriate, who decides, and whether their decisions are made on genuinely methodological grounds or relate more to ideology or expediency. In a value-laden field like education, the pragmatic criteria to which 'what works' so overtly appeals are not necessarily the only criteria that matter, and the claims to scientific rigour by which 'best practice' is ostensibly justified may not be in every case appropriate, let alone sustainable. We might also ask whether 'what works' necessarily and inevitably defines also what is educationally worthwhile; and whether the 'best' in 'best practice' accommodates the complex ethical and cultural questions which are intrinsic to educational debate properly conducted, and indeed which are semantically embedded in the word 'best' itself (for what is pedagogically efficient may not be best educationally); or whether all such questions are made subservient to pragmatic considerations. Meanwhile, cynics and even some serious commentators claim that for 'evidence-based policy' we should read 'policy-based evidence', on the grounds that policies are impelled more by the politics of power and electoral advantage than by a spirit of enquiry, and that the task is to find such evidence as will justify the policies, excluding meanwhile anything which is politically unpalatable. Such pessimism should itself be tested, though examples of policy-makers' resistance to or misuse of evidence come fairly readily to mind, and the problem surfaces at several points in the Cambridge Review's final report.

Similar claims are made in the arenas of professional training and practice, where intending and serving teachers are inducted into ways of thinking and acting which are purportedly underwritten by 'research'. Here the stakes are no less high than in the arena of policy, for the decisions taken by teachers affect, directly, profoundly and sometimes permanently, the lives and prospects of children. Again, therefore, the questions must be asked, and perhaps with added urgency, not just about the nature and reliability of the evidence but also whether its practical application is attended by proper understanding of its strengths and limitations. We should ask whether the full range of evidence pertaining to a given area of professional understanding and decision-making is drawn upon. We need to know whether trainees and serving teachers are initiated into the skills of critically evaluating the evidence in which their school and classroom decisions are purportedly grounded, or are merely expected to take it on trust. All such questions prompt a larger one about the trainers themselves, and the basis of their own claims to expertise in these matters.

This is not the place to pursue such questions. We mention them here to underline the third purpose of this collection, which is to invite discussion and debate not just about the purposes, content and outcomes of primary education but also about the evidential basis on which policies in relation to such matters are constructed and everyday decisions in primary schools and classrooms are made.

PERSPECTIVES, THEMES, QUESTIONS AND THEIR RATIONALE

Implicit in the questions above is a query about the authority and expertise of those who provide evidence in the expectation or hope that it will inform policy or practice; for nobody is immune to the intrusion of personal values in their professional activity. That being so, we should say something about the genesis and production of the studies in this volume.

The Cambridge Primary Review was formally launched in October 2006, but planning started nearly three years earlier, in January 2004. An essential task at that stage, once we had ascertained from consultations that an independent enquiry into the condition and future of English primary education was needed and supported, was to establish what it should investigate and how. From these deliberations came what were later refined and consolidated as the Review's ten themes and three overarching perspectives.

The themes and perspectives, and their attendant questions, were far from random. The paragraphs that follow quote, with minor amendments, from the summary of their rationale which we published at the outset.

A national system of primary education offers to an enquiry such as the Cambridge Primary Review, if that enquiry is properly conceived, a dauntingly vast canvas. It is *national*, so it raises questions about national values, national identity, the condition of English and indeed British society and the lives and futures of the groups and individuals of which that society is constituted. It is a *system*, so there are questions about policy, structure, organisation, finance and governance to consider. And being an *education* system, it raises a distinctively educational array of questions about the children whose needs, along with those of society, the system claims to address, and about schools, what goes on in them, and the contexts within which they operate.

Some earlier enquiries have claimed to be comprehensive but have in fact been restricted to the point where the discussion of even what they treat in detail loses some of its validity. This is because ostensibly bounded matters such as curriculum, teaching, assessment, leadership and workforce reform – to take some typical recent instances – raise larger questions of purpose, value and context. Thus, a curriculum is much more than a syllabus: it is a response to culture, the past and the future – and English culture today is complex, the pace of change renders our sense of history ever more fragile (yet essential), while even optimists concede that the future is highly problematic. Teaching is not merely a matter of technique, but reflects ideas about thinking, knowing, learning and relating. Assessment, for better or worse, has become as much a political as a professional activity. In turn, all of these are framed, enabled and/or constrained by policy, structure and finance. And so on.

Breadth of coverage in a national educational review is therefore essential. At the same time, no review can cover everything, choices must be confronted and made, and they must be argued rather than random. The Cambridge Primary Review responds to these imperatives of breadth and meaningful selectivity in its hierarchy of 'perspectives', 'themes' and 'questions'.

We start with three broad *perspectives*: children, the world in which they are growing up, and the education which mediates that world and prepares them for it. This is a variant on the more familiar opposition of the individual and society, but being triarchic it avoids the polarisation into which individual/society too readily slides, allows a more subtle interplay of connections and relationships, and accords education a mediating role between the development and learning of the young child and the culture and world in which he or she is growing up. These three perspectives – children, society and the wider world, primary education – have been the Review's core concerns and together they have provided the framework for its more specific themes and questions. They also provide the title for the Review's final report.

Next, ten *themes* unpack with greater precision aspects of the *education* perspective:

1. Purposes and values
2. Learning and teaching
3. Curriculum and assessment
4. Quality and standards
5. Diversity and inclusion
6. Settings and professionals
7. Parenting, caring and educating
8. Children's lives beyond the school
9. Structures and phases
10. Funding and governance.

Finally, for every theme there is a set of *questions* (listed in full in Appendix 2). These explicate the themes and indicate in more direct terms what the Review hoped to investigate in order that it might pronounce authoritatively and constructively on the condition and future of English primary education. Again, the questions were not random: under each thematic heading they fell into two groups: questions – to deploy the admittedly over-simple distinction – of 'fact' and 'value', of what is and what ought to be, of evidence and vision, of how (and how well) primary education is currently ordered and how it might be ordered better.

The relationship between the perspectives and themes is – as has been noted – hierarchical, but it is also permeative, for although the ten themes appear to elaborate the 'education' perspective in greater depth than the other two, the childhood and societal/global perspectives infuse that elaboration throughout.

With obvious justification and to widespread approval at the time, the Plowden Report of 1967 placed the child 'at the heart of the educational process'. However, it also drew the boundaries of that process somewhat narrowly, perhaps as a conscious echo of Froebel's garden: child, school, home and immediate community. One can see the rationale for this too, for if the child is at the heart of the educational process, this in a physical sense is the child's world. But even in 1967 this intimate nexus could never be enough. If the 1960s generation of children did not have the internet-driven global awareness which was so evident from the Cambridge Primary Review's community soundings forty years later, they were not necessarily any less aware of a world stretching far beyond the streets in which they lived; and if they and their parents were not as worried about global warming as those we talked to in 2007, they had their own nightmare of nuclear annihilation.

The failure meaningfully to locate children's lives and primary schooling in their wider social and global contexts led Plowden, when it came to define the aims of primary education, to capitulate to confusion, uncertainty and even a degree of banality about what it called 'society':

> All schools reflect the views of society, or of some section of society ... Our society is in a state of transition ... One obvious purpose [of primary education] is to fit children for the society into which they will grow up ... About such a society we can be both hopeful and fearful ... For such a society, children ... will need above all to be adaptable.
>
> (CACE 1967: 185)

The other characteristic of the Plowden view of the child's relationship to the wider world, at least in the chapter on aims, is its strong streak of fatalism or determinism. The child adapts to society and social change but appears powerless to influence them. For all its progressivism, there is more than a hint in Plowden of the old elementary school mission of 'fitting' the working class child for its pre-ordained 'station' in a society ordered by those who knew (and lived) considerably better. Readers of our final report will know that the Cambridge Primary Review rejects this 19th century legacy, and that the principles of childhood agency and empowerment are among its running themes, surfacing in the discussion of children's voice, aims, curriculum, learning, teaching, school culture and the relationship between children's lives inside and outside school.

Redressing historical tendencies to cultural determinism and educational parochialism required, when we came to translate the Review's themes and questions into topics for the surveys of published research, that they should have a strong orientation towards the world – and children's lives – outside the school, towards the condition of national life and towards international trends and comparisons. But this was not merely a corrective to Plowden: more fundamentally it represented a theoretical reassessment of the nature of childhood and the capacities of young learners, and a repositioning of childhood and schooling in relation to culture. In place of the old dualism of 'the individual' and 'society' and the reification of the latter as somehow apart from what goes on in schools, the Cambridge Primary Review's rationale was consciously shaped by the belief that

> No decision or action which one observes in a particular classroom, and no educational policy, can be properly understood except by reference to the web of inherited ideas and values, habits and customs, institutions and world views which make one country, or one region, or one group, distinct from another ... Life in

schools and classrooms is an aspect of our wider society, not separate from it: a culture does not stop or start at the school gates. The character and dynamics of school life are shaped by the values that shape other aspects of our national life. The strengths of our primary schools are the strengths of our society; their weaknesses are our society's weaknesses.

(Alexander 2001: 5 and 29–30)

This shift was assisted by changes in the policy arena itself. By the early 2000s, the simply-conceived duality of school and home had been replaced by multi-agency working, networking and 'extended' schools offering dawn-to-dusk provision, while the long-established local education authorities (LEAs) had been superseded by local authority children's services offering a range of purportedly 'joined up' provision of which primary schooling was just one.

Policy was also more obviously influenced by international considerations than hitherto. The expanding apparatus of international surveys of educational achievement – TIMSS, PISA, PIRLS and the rest (Chapter 18) – fuelled an obsession with international league tables and gave rise to often dubious claims about cause-effect relationships between particular patterns of teaching, pupils' educational achievement and nations' economic performance. Policy borrowing became the order of the day, much was made of the efficacy of pedagogic 'magic bullets' like interactive whole class teaching, and 'world class' joined 'what works' and 'best practice' in the policy-makers' rhetorical pantheon. One casualty was the proper use of evidence, and indeed a balanced sense of the value and limitations of international educational comparison in general. The second, of course, was the quality of children's primary education.

Meanwhile, policy thus re-armed was reaching ever further into those aspects of the work of schools which would have been deemed off limits at the time of Plowden or indeed before the 1988 Education Reform Act, not just as a matter of custom but because of the way the 1944 Education (Butler) Act had steered responsibility for the content and processes of education firmly towards the local authorities and schools. But the 1988 (Baker) Act, in the words of the then opposition (Labour) education spokesman Jack Straw, would 'centralise power and control over schools, colleges and universities in the hands of the secretary of state in a manner without parallel in the western world'. There were those who later suggested that Straw, as a future member of the New Labour Government of 1997, might more appropriately have said 'You ain't seen nothing yet', for the process initiated by the Conservatives was without doubt accelerated by their New Labour successors. But even when we allow for the political rhetoric of parties in opposition and the folk wisdom of weary voters, there is little doubt that by 2006, when the Cambridge Primary Review was launched, policy and its manifestation as a growing number of targets, initiatives and strategies had an impact on the work of teachers to an extent which at the time of Plowden would have been inconceivable.

THE RESEARCH SURVEYS

All these considerations and developments shaped both the Review's framework of perspectives and themes and the questions by which they were elaborated. With the research survey strand we also needed to respond to developments in the research arena itself. The expansion of comparative international enquiry is one field where we had access to evidence of a kind which was largely unavailable to Plowden (see

Chapters 11, 13, 14, 15, 16 and 18). Another is our exploitation of the coinciding of the Review with the final stages of the ESRC-funded Teaching and Learning Research Programme (TLRP), a constellation of research projects which together comprised Britain's biggest-yet programme of research on teaching and learning. It made sense to commission a review of relevant projects from TLRP and their implications (Chapter 20). It also made sense to register and investigate the fast-growing interest in children's voice (Chapter 2) and the educational applications of neuroscience (Chapter 6). Similarly, though the Review was not an audit of government policy, matters like testing, curriculum, standards and workforce reform had become so important that they could hardly be ignored in these surveys, for they now featured as prominently in the research literature as in professional and political discourse (see Chapters 14, 15, 17, 18, 19, 25, 26 and 29).

Out of thinking about matters such as this, then, came the list of intended research survey topics which appear in this volume's Appendix 3. In June 2006, four months before the Review's launch, this list was circulated to all British university departments of education and allied subjects which had been rated highly in the 2001 Research Assessment Exercise (RAE), and to the National Foundation for Educational Research (NFER), together with details of what would be involved in the research surveys and an invitation to tender. Once received, the research survey bids were circulated for peer assessment. By the time the Review was launched in October 2006 most of the contracts had been awarded, usually to groups of academics but occasionally to individuals. There were some gaps, and these were filled by direct invitation.

PROCEDURE

Each consultant group received, in addition to the brief scoping statements in Appendix 3, detailed notes of guidance on survey procedure, structure and presentation. All teams were also asked to submit outlines for approval before embarking on their surveys, and survey drafts, once received, were sent out for peer assessment. In some cases the surveys were finalised with little adjustment. In others there was considerable discussion before texts were eventually agreed.

There were changes to the remit of a few of the surveys as listed in Appendix 3. Survey 2/1 divided into two, one on children's cognitive development and learning (2/1a), the other on their social development (2/1b). One team (2/3) was forced by pressure of other work to withdraw, but this happened too late for us to commission an alternative, while another (2/2) faced similar problems but their findings (and, as it happens some of those from the missing survey 2/3) were incorporated directly into the relevant chapters (15 and 21) of the final report. It is hoped that these two surveys will be added to the next edition of this book. The two surveys on parenting, caring and educating (7/1 and 7/2) were merged as one. Beyond that, some teams interpreted their briefs more broadly or narrowly than indicated in Appendix 3.

Despite these adjustments and minor vicissitudes, the research surveys published between October 2007 and May 2008 remained close to the original list and the rationale for the exercise as a whole was sustained largely unimpaired from start to finish.

THE STRUCTURE AND SEQUENCE OF THIS COLLECTION

It may seem perverse to tie the commissioned research surveys so firmly to the ten Cambridge Primary Review themes and then to adopt a different basis for grouping them in this volume. In fact, the groupings used here are the same as when the earlier versions of the chapters were published as interim reports of the Review, though the actual sequence has been changed. Then and now, thematic grouping for publication has not been viable because while some Review themes have four surveys, others have three, two or only one. Once we took the decision to combine the themes we found some interesting cross-theme continuities – for example between parenting (Chapter 4), children's lives outside school (Chapter 3), children's voice (Chapter 2) and relationships between schools and other agencies (Chapter 5), all of which are brought together in Part 1; and the important meta-theme of national policy in Part 8 which links governance (Chapter 26), funding (Chapter 27) quality assurance (Chapter 28) and centrally-led educational reform (Chapters 26 and 29).

Cross-theme grouping also allowed us to give the sequencing of the surveys, both within sections of this volume and between them, what we trust is a reasonably convincing narrative coherence. In Part 1, as noted above, we start the sequence with children, their worlds inside and outside school, and the relationship between these worlds. Children's out-of-school lives are here defined much more broadly than through the usual focus on home and family, though this is certainly given an important place (Chapters 3, 4 and 5) and this approach opens up possibilities for an interesting discussion on the relationship between children's learning in the various worlds between which they daily move (Chapter 3).

Staying with both children and learning, Part 2 reviews research-led changes in the way development and learning are conceived (Chapters 6 and 7), concentrating particularly on the impact of cognitive and cultural psychology, neuroscience and socio-cultural research and on the necessity and power at the primary stage of purposeful and collaborative interaction between children and adults and among children themselves. If Chapters 6 and 7 consider evidence on what primary-age children have in common, Chapters 8 and 9 concentrate on some of the many dimensions of difference among them – and the problems of defining such difference – from cultural and ethnic diversity (Chapter 8) to variations in special educational need (Chapter 9).

With Part 3 we move from children and childhood to schooling, starting with aims and values and journeying via structure, content, assessment, outcomes and standards to teachers and teaching and, finally, national systems and policy. In considering evidence on aims and values, Part 3 moves well beyond the once-popular opposition of 'individual' and 'societal' aims to a more considered appraisal of the national and global, of social change, and what these might imply for a public system of primary education (Chapters 10 and 11). For good measure, Part 3 adds a comparison of officially-espoused aims in England and other countries (Chapter 13) and a historical survey and critique of such official statements as have been promulgated in the English context (Chapter 12).

Similar comparisons initiate Part 4, which consider research on the structure and content of primary education (Chapters 14 and 15), highlighting contentious issues like the school starting age, the scope of the curriculum and the incidence of testing before reflecting on alternatives which are available not just from international comparison but within England from outside the primary education mainstream (Chapter 16).

We return to testing in Part 5, and to the wider field of assessment, quality and standards of which testing is a part. In much public discourse testing and assessment are treated as synonymous, while educational standards, more often than not, are defined solely by reference to what can be tested, which of course is but a fragment of what is taught in school, and certainly of what is learned there. The discourse is thus doubly reductionist as well as highly politicised. Two carefully-balanced commissions (Chapters 17 and 18) consider first the national and then the international evidence on standards in primary education over time, while Chapter 19 looks much more broadly at what we mean by assessment and what we might mean if we want assessment to enhance learning as well as measure it.

Parts 6 and 7 concentrate on research on teaching and teachers, starting with findings and implications from the Teaching and Learning Research Programme (TLRP) referred to earlier (Chapter 20), and moving on to a detailed assessment of evidence on the different ways that children are organised for teaching and learning within the primary phase and how they fare as they move from one phase or stage to the next: from pre-school to primary, from primary to secondary, and within the primary phases from Key Stage 1 to 2 (Chapter 21). Noting that teaching and learning are framed physically as well as organisationally, Chapter 22 then considers evidence on the impact of the built environment.

From the built environment we move in Part 7 to the professional environment and the condition of the primary teaching profession and the impact on it of change and reform (Chapter 23) and the way teachers and support staff are recruited, trained and supported through their careers (Chapter 24). Both lines of enquiry have become the focus for recent government policy, and New Labour's drive for professional leadership and workforce reform is documented and assessed by reference to both official and independent evidence in Chapter 25.

Government policy remains the focus for Part 8, the book's final group of studies. Here we pair studies of the framing structures of governance (Chapter 26) and funding (Chapter 27), noting evidence about the impact of England's move since 1988, and especially since 1997, to a far greater degree of central control over those aspects of primary education which are deemed politically to matter most. These themes are also taken up in the remaining two chapters, one of which surveys changing mechanisms and procedures for national inspection and quality assurance from the patrician grand tours of HMI to Ofsted's ostensibly rougher and tougher or at least more intrusive and public regime (Chapter 28). The final chapter considers the trajectory of national reform in the primary phase since the 1988 Education Reform Act, attending particularly to the national curriculum and national testing introduced by the Conservatives and to New Labour's national literacy, numeracy and primary strategies and wider drives to raise educational standards (Chapter 29).

THE IMPORTANCE OF RESEARCH IN PRIMARY EDUCATION

There was a time not so long ago when educational researchers routinely ignored primary education, believing it to be not worth investigating. Their stance could be partly explained, though in no way justified, by the fact that until the late 1960s most primary teachers in England were non-graduates, and even after the introduction of the BEd degree in 1963 and the growth of postgraduate (PGCE) training during the 1980s, the majority of primary teachers were trained outside the university sector, though in colleges whose courses required university approval and whose staff perforce submitted to university paternalism (the word is used advisedly, for the gender divide was real and significant). The university departments of education (UDEs) themselves were primarily training rather than research institutions, and their twin and somewhat conflicting centres of activity were making the 'big four' disciplines of educational psychology, sociology, philosophy and history more or less digestible as theory for intending teachers, and the largely atheoretical secondary subject 'method' course. The disciplines also provided a passport to that academic respectability which, in the wider academic world, educational studies and education departments somewhat lacked. Thus, pedagogy was conceived as essentially a pragmatic activity which bore some kind of relationship to theory and research, though the structure of the course both discouraged proper examination of the nature of that relationship and implied that it didn't matter anyway. In as far as UDE staff had taught in schools, these were much more likely to be secondary than primary. Somehow, the significance of primary education and the fact that children spend half their educational careers in primary schools was forgotten or, more worry-ingly, ignored.

All – well, nearly all – of that has changed. From 1980, the PGCE became the majority route into teaching, increasingly for primary as well as secondary. Research in general began to be taken more seriously, the days of the research-light UDE were numbered, and successive Research Assessment Exercises (RAE) encouraged the belated confirmation of primary education as a field for research and scholarship. It was not long before primary began not only to challenge the secondary hegemony but also, in some fields, to establish superiority. One notable example was classroom research, where it was in primary rather than secondary classrooms that the main British observational, ethnographic and comparative studies of the 1980s, 1990s and early 2000s were undertaken.

Twenty years ago, the late Alan Blyth – himself an outstanding scholar and advocate of primary education since the 1960s – surveyed the scope and condition of research bearing on this phase. He identified seven areas in which significant research communities were by then at work: child development and learning, philosophical and critical analysis, the sociological analysis of primary schools, organisational and management studies, curriculum studies, pedagogy, and the lives and careers of teachers. Blyth was in no doubt that the most significant omission from his list was the comparative study of primary education and he argued forcefully, in the interests of both pure and applied research, for its inclusion (Blyth 1989).

It seems fair to claim that most or even all of Blyth's research communities have contributed in some way to this volume, including the hitherto absent comparativists and – a further group, not mentioned by Blyth – those working in the field of policy analysis. The latter is a vital addition, given the explosion and penetration of policy since the 1988 Act. We believe that this collection provides methodological and theoretical diversity as well as that thematic breadth which the coverage of the Cambridge Primary Review itself dictates.

During the 1980s and early 1990s some pretty disparaging things were said and written about the condition and relevance of British educational research, and there were those in politically high or extreme places who would happily have overseen the closure of the country's university departments of education, with teacher training moved to schools and – presumably – government as the sole arbiter of evidence about childhood, learning, teaching, curriculum, standards and all the other matters with which the surveys in this volume deal. That would have given real and potentially dangerous substance to the phrase 'policy-based evidence' to which we referred earlier. The relationship between research, policy and practice in English primary education is not always an easy one, and pursuing it as a serious mission – as opposed to under-taking research for what Blyth called 'Olympian' reasons regardless of its applications –

is a fairly recent preoccupation. But at least in England (and more widely in the UK) the relationship exists and the sharp debates provoked by some of these studies when they were first published in 2007–8 demonstrate that abundantly. Further, the Cambridge Primary Review has synthesised evidence generated not just by the researchers whose hundreds of studies feature in this volume and the professionals and members of the public whose voices are heard through the submissions and soundings, but also by government itself, for government data provide one of the four main strands of the Review, and government data and government-sponsored research, inspection and evaluation appear in this volume too. In combination, this wealth of material has the potential to provide foundations for future provision which are, indubitably, cemented by evidence.

Yet, we repeat, all evidential claims can and must be open to scrutiny, and both researchers and the agents of policy are sometimes too exclusive as to who and what they are prepared to admit to their respective evidential clubs. Researchers may be unjustifiably patronising towards inspection data; and policy makers have a tendency to presume – the richest of ironies – that only their own researchers are free from political bias. We owe it to children, their education and their future to welcome evidence from wherever it comes, to treat it with due seriousness and caution, to eschew the unthinking or cynical use of 'evidence-based', and to develop and sustain the mature and honest partnership between research, policy and practice on which progress in education surely depends.

REFERENCES

Alexander, R.J. (2001) *Culture and Pedagogy: international comparisons in primary education.* Oxford: Blackwell.

Blyth, W.A.L. (1989) 'The study of primary education in England: retrospect and prospect', in R.J. Alexander (Ed) *Primary Education and the National Curriculum: papers from the first national conference of the Association for the Study of Primary Education.* Cambridge: ASPE: 38–49.

Central Advisory Council for Education (England) (1967) *Children and Their Primary Schools* (the Plowden Report). London: HMSO.

Gamoran, A. (Ed) (2007) *Standards-Based Reform and the Poverty Gap: lessons from No Child Left Behind.* Washington DC: Brookings Institution Press.

Part 1

Children's lives and voices

School, home and community

Children and childhood are central to the Cambridge Primary Review. They constitute one of the three perspectives by which the entire inquiry is framed, together with these four foundational questions for those who submitted evidence:

- What do we know about young children's lives in and out of school, and about the nature of childhood, at the start of the 21st century?
- How do children of primary school age develop, think, feel, act and learn?
- To which of the myriad individual and collective differences between children should educators and related professionals particularly respond?
- What do children most fundamentally need from those charged with providing their primary education?

The first question reminds us that notwithstanding the contrasts between life at home and in school – for some children, parents and teachers an apparently unbridgeable gulf – childhood itself is seamless and the two worlds bear inexorably upon each other. That being so, teachers need as clear an understanding of children's lives outside school as of the more familiar canon embodied in the second question.

With the second question we are on the more familiar territory of child development and learning, which for many primary teachers of a certain age and older remains the bedrock of their professional knowledge. Familiar it may be, but just as the first question alerts us to the way that children's lives are changing, so we should be aware of how recent research, especially in psychology and neuroscience, is reshaping our understanding of children's minds. At the start of the 21st century this empirical revision yields a clearer apprehension of just how much children, including and especially very young children, can do, and how exceptionally fast, given the right conditions, they can learn. Through the intriguing interface between psychology and anthropology it also shows us something of the complexity of the relationship between mind and culture, a relationship about which 'socio-cultural models of learning' and 'cultural psychology' imply a greater degree of certainty than as yet actually exists. And whereas the professional mantra during the 1970s and 1980s was 'seven year olds aren't capable of that and we must wait until they are ready', now it is – or it certainly ought to be – 'seven year olds are probably capable of that and much more besides.' In each case, developmental research has been cited to legitimate the claim, first depressing educational expectations and now – it is to be hoped – raising them.

The developmental second question embodies something else. If children are acknowledged to be competent and active thinkers, then what they think should matter to us as much as how. That is where the relatively new research field of pupil/student voice comes in, and it provides a critically important interface between children's rights as embodied in the United Nations Convention on the rights of the Child (and indeed in the Children's Plan launched by the UK government in 2007) and the pedagogy of cognitive empowerment to which several chapters in this collection in different ways refer. Children's thinking deserves our respect.

Children – a truism which ought not to need re-stating – are individuals by virtue of both their genetic makeup and their familial and cultural circumstances. Again, the familiar professional territory of individual differences – which half a century ago was conceived largely in terms of assumptions about the nature and measurement of human intelligence, itself believed to be fixed – takes on a new gloss by virtue of our enhanced awareness of culture and cultural difference, for England in the early 21st century is a country of exceptional diversity. That being so, the third question above invites us to determine what differences, in the arenas of both policy and practice, most command our attention.

If the third question forces us to attend to diversity, the final one brings us back to what children have in common as individuals within a culture which is plural yet also shared. What, out of all this, should primary educators concentrate on, in order to do justice to children's needs now and in the future?

The eight chapters in Parts 2 and 3 survey research which in different ways bears on these four questions.

In *Children and their Primary Schools: pupils' voices* (Chapter 2), Carol Robinson and Michael Fielding examine research in an area of recent but rapidly increasing interest to practitioners and policy-makers as well as researchers themselves, that of children's voice. In view of what we have said above about competence and empowerment, it is assuredly the right place to begin. The chapter surveys representative research on what primary pupils and former pupils think of the purposes of primary schooling, the culture and organisation of primary schools, learning, teaching, assessment and the curriculum, and the transition to secondary education. The consistent sub-text is that children's voices matter, and in this the survey leads on to the emphasis on children's rights in Children's Lives Outside School (Chapter 3). In this respect, the chapter also looks forward to the next section, which deals with research on children's development, learning and educational needs.

Berry Mayall's *Children's Lives Outside School and their Educational Impact* (Chapter 3) focuses on children's out-of-school lives before and during the primary school years and their impact on their school activities and education more generally. The chapter is framed by changing perceptions of children's development and learning, and by the current emphasis on children's rights. It examines the relationship between what children know and do out of school and what takes place in school, and assesses the implications of – and warns against – the increasing 'scholarisation' of their home life as a result of recent government policy. The scope of Berry Mayall's survey is vast, and it is one of several in this collection to argue the need for teachers to balance their obligation to 'deliver' the national curriculum with teaching that respects and builds on children's non-school knowledge and experience – an old enough principle in the primary sector, but one to which recent psychological and neuro-scientific research, not to mention our obligations under the United Nations Convention on the Rights of the Child, gives renewed impetus.

Parenting, Caring and Educating (Chapter 4) takes a specific and central aspect of children's out-of-school lives and reviews research on changes in patterns of parenting and caring in the pre-adolescent years and their impact on children's primary education. Here, Yolande Muschamp, Felicity Wikeley, Tess Ridge and Maria Balarin examine changes in family structure and parenting practice, the complex and often demanding consequences of these for both parents/carers and schools, and the way home-school relations have featured in recent educational thinking and policy. They show how, for a much larger proportion of children than in many comparable countries, poverty remains the most challenging and intractable home circumstance of all, severely compromising children's health, well-being and capacity to engage with their schooling.

In *Primary Schools and Other Agencies* (Chapter 5) Ian Barron, Rachel Holmes, Maggie MacLure and Katherine Runswick-Cole shift the focus from school and home to the wider society. With Every Child Matters as its backdrop, their survey examines the shifting relationships over the past four decades between education and the various agencies with which primary school children may come into contact, especially in the areas of health, social care and the law. The authors pay particular attention to changing provision for children deemed to be in need of support or intervention from agencies other than the school. Like *Children's Lives Outside School*, they track changes in the way children and their needs have been perceived since the last big enquiry into primary education (Plowden, in 1967) and show how these perceptions have shaped the policy of the day. Yet they also show that while provision may change, attitudes are more resilient, and how concepts of childhood and family inadequacy or deficit continue to drive encounters between schools and other agencies, notwithstanding our supposed sensitivity to cultural diversity and plurality.

Each of these research surveys was independently conceived and undertaken. Yet, by taking the four surveys together we find that a number of major and subsidiary themes emerge with some consistency and are thereby reinforced. For example:

Childhood and family: changing ideas and practices

- Changing conceptions of children, childhood and children's needs (Chapters 2, 3 and 5), and the more pervasive tendency for views of children to become polarised; for example, children as victims versus children as threats (Chapter 3); children as innocent and suffering versus children as unsocialised and deficient (Chapter 5).
- Changing conceptions and practices of parenting and family life; changes in the way that the needs of children from problematic home circumstances are defined; but the challenges these changes pose for schools and statutory agencies (Chapters 4 and 5).

Childhood under pressure: children's lives and rights

- The considerable impact, for better or worse, of children's lives outside school on their learning within school (Chapters 3 and 4).
- The need for intervention to support vulnerable children and families, especially in the context of poverty (Chapter 4); but the tensions and possible policy contradictions which such support can generate (Chapter 5) and the dangers of an all-embracing 0–11 'scholarisation' of children's home lives which may belittle or crowd out those activities which are entirely independent of school yet are no less productive than school 'work' (Chapter 3).
- The pressures and constraints on both children's learning and the primary curriculum of the government's national testing policy at the primary stage, and the risk that

such demands will subvert the development of the broader life skills which are the goals of other policies, including *Every Child Matters* (Chapter 2).

- The overwhelming impact of inequality, and especially poverty, on many children's educational prospects (Chapter 4), and the risk that in some cases an otherwise laudable emphasis on parental involvement in schooling may aggravate rather than ameliorate such inequalities (Chapter 3), or stigmatise particular children and families (Chapter 5).
- The need to respect and build upon children's views, non-school lives and experiential learning and to respect and safeguard their rights (Chapters 2 and 3); yet the challenges such recognition may pose to traditional power relations in school and long-established assumptions about the relationship of teacher and learner (Chapter 2), especially if the UNCRC is taken to require genuine democratisation of school ethos and practices (Chapter 3).

2 Children and their primary schools

Pupils' voices

Carol Robinson and Michael Fielding

INTRODUCTION

The Cambridge Primary Review is the first major review of primary education in forty years since the publication of the Plowden Report in 1967 (CACE 1967). The Plowden Committee considered primary education in all its aspects as well as the transition to secondary school. However, since this time there have been various Acts and conventions which have had a significant impact on aspects of the primary curriculum. In particular, the Education Reform Act (ERA) of 1988 had a major influence on primary education in England and Wales. As a result of this Act the National Curriculum (NC) was introduced, resulting in significant changes being made within the curriculum, in teaching methods, and in forms of assessment. The Act introduced Standard Attainment Tests (SATs), a national system of assessment in the core subjects at the end of years 2 and 6 in primary schools (as well as years 9 and 11 in secondary schools). The introduction of SATs has allowed for comparison to be made between levels of pupil achievement in different schools and has led to many schools placing significant emphasis on pupils' achievement in the tests with the aim of reflecting the school in a favourable light. As well as significant changes in the school curriculum, there have also been major changes in the organisation of support for children and young people in England. Although the Plowden report committee argued for close collaboration between educational and medical services, this did not become a reality until The Children Act of 2004 and Every Child Matters (ECM) (Department for Education and Skills (DfES) 2004). ECM established a duty on Local Authorities to make arrangements to promote cooperation between agencies (including schools) in order to improve children's wellbeing.

There is a growing body of literature which focuses on the voices of pupils in schools. The recent publication of an *International Handbook of Student Experience in Elementary and Secondary Schools* is a significant contribution to this field (Thiessen and Cook-Sather 2007). There have been a number of UK-based research studies which have looked at pupils' perceptions of their experiences in primary school. However, much of the literature has explored pupils' experiences through the eyes of the teacher. In many cases the literature also stresses the value of listening to young people's views and details the processes implemented by schools to develop a deeper understanding of encouraging the voice of young people (for example, Fielding 2001; MacBeath et al. 2003; Rudduck et al. 1996; Rudduck and Flutter 2004). This chapter is concerned only with those studies which have explored pupils' experiences from the perspectives of the pupils themselves, and not with studies which have reported teachers' perspectives of pupils' experiences. It is primarily concerned with finding out about pupils' perspectives on specific areas of their primary experience; namely, the purposes of their primary education, their experiences of teaching, learning, the curriculum and assessment, and to a lesser extent the culture and organisation of their primary schooling. Some reference is also made to pupils' views on transfer from primary to secondary school and to their aspirations and preferences in respect of pupils' own futures. Very limited comparisons are made of pupils' views across different gender, social and cultural groups. These focus areas were identified at the outset of the research by those co-ordinating the various strands of the Primary Review and form the basis of this chapter. However, the chapter also outlines implications of the findings and raises more generic concerns about pupils' experiences of primary schooling in the UK.

In order to gather data for this survey, in the first instance a number of key people in the area of Pupil Voice were contacted, both UK-based and international. They were asked for any documentation, literature or references which discuss or outline what primary pupils and former pupils think of primary schooling: its purposes, culture, organisation, learning, teaching, curriculum and assessment; and pupils' aspirations in respect of these and their own futures. A specific request was made for evidence of comparisons in pupil voice across different social and cultural groups.

Electronic searching (which included ERIC, BEI, IngentaConnect, IBSS and PsycINFO) initially identified hundreds of references on pupils' experiences of primary school. After a first sift of titles and abstracts, 63 were selected. These, along with references and literature from colleagues, were explored in more detail. Many of the literature sources were rejected on one or more of the following grounds:

- they were found to relate to secondary pupils;
- they were based on teachers' perceptions of their pupils' experiences;
- they related to primary pupils in countries other than the UK.

A core body of literature based on findings from major research projects which looked at the perceptions of Key Stage 1 and 2 pupils in the UK emerged, along with several other literature sources which added to, and extended, the data within the 'core' literature. (See Appendix 1 for brief details of the 'core' literature and Appendix 2 for details of recent studies which, although not primarily concerned with eliciting pupils' perspectives of primary schooling, will serve to add to our understanding of children within primary school age).

In the vast majority of cases authors have published only one study which has detailed pupils' experiences, so there are very few studies which have built on earlier work. Most of the studies referred to involved between 30 and 150 pupils, although some involved considerably fewer pupils. Caution must, therefore, be exercised when considering the extent to which findings can be seen to be representative of the whole body of primary school pupils, as there are a large number of pupils whose opinions remain unknown.

A number of the studies were particularly concerned with curriculum development. Questionnaires and face-to-face interviews with individual pupils and groups of pupils were commonly used in the studies to elicit pupils' perspectives. In the write up of these studies there was, however, almost no mention of the methodological challenges of listening to and reporting on pupils' perspectives. Such challenges are discussed in work by Alderson and Morrow (2004) and need to be taken into consideration when involving children and young people in research projects.

This chapter is divided into nine main sections which reflect the views of pupils within various aspects of their primary schooling. The sections deal with primary pupils' views on the following:

1. The purposes of primary schooling;
2. The culture of primary schools;
3. The organisation of primary schools;
4. Learning within primary schools;
5. Teaching within primary schools;
6. The primary curriculum;
7. Assessment within primary schools;
8. Transfer from primary to secondary school;
9. Pupils' aspirations and preferences in respect of pupils' own futures.

Findings relating to each of these nine sections will be outlined in this chapter. At the end of each section key issues are summed up and considered in relation to current or recent work in the field of pupil voice. We do this for three reasons. Firstly, whilst the field of pupil voice has yet to produce extensive, robust research findings within the primary sector,[1] it has substantial national and international credibility at both primary and secondary levels. Its juxtaposition with the research evidence we foreground in this study may well suggest a lacuna in either body of work. Secondly, and more positively, the juxtaposition may well indicate considerable resonance between the two and thus help to further inform judgements. Thirdly, the values and perspectives underpinning most pupil voice work are those that animate the impetus behind the Cambridge Primary Review itself. For this reason the short dialogue between the research evidence and the pupil voice movement may well help us to frame and articulate what we have found out in a judicious and resonant way.

PUPILS' VIEWS ON THE PURPOSES OF THEIR PRIMARY SCHOOLING

As preparation for future employment

Pupils view the main purpose of their primary school as being to prepare them for getting a job in the future (Cullingford 1986; Silcock and Wyness 2000). Children in these studies assumed that the curriculum was given to them for the purpose of getting them jobs and to that extent did not question it, even if they subsequently discovered that there was no such direct connection. They knew their subsequent careers and employability depended on how well they did in exams and they understood this point fully before they left their primary schools. The following quote illustrates this point:

> If I didn't go to school I'd know nothing and wouldn't be able to get a job or nothing … it's really for people to learn things you didn't know before and when you are older you'll have so many 'O' levels you can get what you want … If you didn't go to school you wouldn't have no 'O' levels and you wouldn't ever get a job nowhere.
> (Cullingford 1986: 43)

Primary schooling tends to be viewed by pupils as less serious than secondary schooling; it is a kind of preparation for secondary school rather than a complete experience in itself, and the purpose of secondary school is seen as preparing pupils for a job when they leave the school (Cullingford 1986).

Interviews with people who had left school show the majority of those who are not employed felt their schooling was partly to blame, as the curriculum seemed to have nothing to do with the world in which they found themselves. Looking back, these pupils wished that what they had learned in school had been directed towards the skills they would need in employment, and more particularly directed towards an attempt to understand the political and social environment in which they now live (Cullingford 1986). Similarly, White and Brockington (1983) found the young unemployed whom they interviewed wished that school had been made more relevant to them, from the primary phase onwards.

As a way of meeting other people

For some, one of the purposes of primary schooling is to meet other people. They see school as the place where they can meet their friends and where there is, as a consequence, much more entertainment than at home (Cullingford 1986). Silcock and Wyness (2000) found Key Stage 2 pupils viewed the role of school as providing a context for social mixing; pupils liked the company of others and sought the benefits from wide acquaintanceship. Pupils were also aware of a school's capacity for providing the wider education that homes could not, or did not, provide.

To learn how to conduct yourself

Findings from studies also show that children realise they need to know how to conduct themselves outside of school, for example in restaurants and in interviews. They consider schools to help to equip them with these skills. In their eyes, the ability to gain a job does not depend solely on qualifications, but also on the way they behave in public (Cullingford 1986; Silcock and Wyness 2000).

Key issues

There is little reported evidence relating to pupils' views on the purposes of their primary schooling. In recent years, the ECM agenda suggests that one of the purposes of schooling is to equip learners for life in its broadest sense. However, this ideal is not reflected in the current emphasis on target setting and academic achievement in primary schools. This imbalance needs to be addressed. When thinking about the future of primary schooling in England, consideration needs to be given not only to what the prime purposes of primary schooling are but also to how the overarching purposes of primary schooling, their constituent parts and the interrelationship between them are conveyed to pupils, both formally and informally within schools, families and the communities they serve.

PUPILS' VIEWS ON THE CULTURE OF THEIR PRIMARY SCHOOLS

Authority within the primary school

Primary school children tend to be aware from the very first years that they are required to respond to and obey the head teacher and teachers without questioning.

Early in the school, children tend to believe the head teacher's authority goes unchallenged; however, as children move through the school they report a hierarchy of power of teachers and head teachers in the school organisation (Buchanon-Barrow and Barrett 1996; Elmer *et al.* 1987). In the PACE study, Pollard and Triggs (2000) found that from Years 1 to 6 there appears to be a steady decrease in pupils' perception that it is important to comply with teacher requirements and expectations. Buchanon-Barrow and Barrett (1996) reported that the essential difference in thinking displayed by older children is the emphasis on children themselves as being able to get rules changed and even being involved in running the school.

Children's happiness at school

Davies and Brember (1994) found that primary pupils show enthusiasm for all subjects in the curriculum, and Pollard (1990a), Lord and Jones (2006) and Newman (1997) found the years of primary education are often seen positively in retrospect. However, there is some indication that pupils' enthusiasm towards the curriculum starts to wane during the primary phase (for example Pell and Jarvis 2001).

In a study by Blatchford (1992), pupils aged seven years were asked whether they found being at school 'mostly interesting', 'mostly boring' or 'somewhere in the middle'. Forty two per cent found school 'mostly interesting', with boys being more positive than girls. This appeared to be, in equal proportions, because of the work conducted there and opportunities to play. Eight per cent found school 'mostly boring' and 50 per cent said 'somewhere in the middle' (*Ibid.*: 110). In a more recent study funded by The New Economics Foundation (Marks *et al.* 2004), which surveyed over 1000 children and young people aged 7 to 19 in Nottingham, findings showed that 65 per cent of primary school children rate their school experiences as positive.

Differences in the treatment of boys and girls

Myhill and Jones (2006) found that pupils consider that teachers expect more from girls than boys both in terms of achievement and behaviour. They found that underachieving girls tended to be the least likely to perceive girls as being favoured over boys, and only girls perceived that boys received more favourable treatment than girls. In Year 1, pupils considered that teachers treated boys in a less positive way than girls due to boys' poor behaviour; although boys tended to frame this as injustice.

In a study of 8-to 11-year-olds, girls considered that boys were more often punished than girls, and punished in different ways; boys were more likely to be sent to the head teacher, whereas girls may get shouted at by teachers (Morgan 1992: 194).

Key issues

The picture that emerges is one of primary schools as largely happy places, where girls and boys are treated differently from an early age and where issues of authority that effect the ambience and running of the school reside overwhelmingly with teachers and with the head teacher in particular. A number of schools have placed an increasing emphasis on listening to the voices of pupils in schools (Rudduck and Flutter 2004; Flutter and Rudduck 2004). One of the results of this is that rather than the teachers, and the head teacher in particular, being seen as having sole authority and power, decision making within the school moves towards being negotiated between teachers, the head teacher and pupils. One of the values underpinning pupil voice work is that of participation. In order to create a school in which there is a democratic inclusivity there need to be ways of allowing the whole student body to participate in school decision-making and a recognition that there are multiple voices to be listened to, regardless of ethnicity, disability, behaviour and social class (Robinson and Taylor 2007: 13). Where schools work towards creating a culture which thrives on the mutual respect of those within it, pupils become active participants and develop a sense of belonging to the school, rather than viewing school simply as a place they attend each day. Consideration needs to be given to the ways in which the recent move towards listening to the voices of pupils has changed the culture within some primary schools, and to the benefits that this change brings. However, when implementing such profound changes advocated within much of the pupil voice literature, consideration must also be given to staff apprehension about issues of control and to the perception by some that the basis of their professionalism is being eroded, not redefined.

PUPILS' VIEWS ON THE ORGANISATION OF THEIR PRIMARY SCHOOLS

The pressure of lack of time

Many primary pupils are aware that there is little time to spare in the school day and as a result, there is pressure to get through many work activities (Flutter and Rudduck 2004; Pollard and Triggs 2000). Within the PACE project (Pollard and Triggs 2000) this could be seen in some children in Key Stage 1 but became more apparent as children got older. The pressure on time results in many pupils placing more emphasis on performance in the form of work completed, than on understanding. Lack of time was also seen to have an important bearing on the presentational quality of pupils' written work, and 'getting things done' was perceived as being more important than producing work that was personally satisfying. Time pressure also had the effect of placing learning firmly in the domain of the teachers, who were perceived to be in possession of what had to be learned. Most children felt that it was wise to let teachers control learning or 'we won't know what to do' and 'if you did it yourself you'd go wrong' (*Ibid.*: 208).

Giving children more choice and control of their learning within the classroom

Findings from the PACE project (Pollard and Triggs 2000) also illustrated that children considered there to be more free choice in the infant years than in later years of primary school, largely because getting older means there is harder work and more to learn in order to progress through the educational system. Many pupils, however, would like a greater choice over the subjects and activities they do (Silcock and Wyness 2000; Pollard and Bourne 1994; Triggs and Pollard 1998). Almost two thirds of pupils in Years 1 and 2 within the PACE project indicated that they preferred to control their own activities. In Year 5, only 44 per cent said they preferred to choose, 37 per cent liked the teacher to choose and 13 per cent preferred the choosing to be shared. By Year 6 almost half of the children said they preferred the teacher to choose their work and activities as they trusted their teacher's judgment to know what had to be learned, and understood that the costs of following personal inclination could be high. As one Year 6 pupil commented:

> If the teacher chooses you get to learn more than when you're choosing.
>
> (Pollard and Triggs 2000: 113)

Where pupils wanted some control over what tasks and activities they did, the reasons given for this were: to avoid difficult work – pupils did not want to be faced with a challenge or be exposed to the risk of failure; to avoid things they did not like; to have more fun; to spend time on an activity of which they were getting less experience than they wished; and to get a broader curriculum with more of the things they enjoyed (Pollard and Triggs 2000).

Thus, where pupils have opportunities to make choices in the classroom, this is viewed as positive (Flutter and Rudduck 2004; Grainger *et al.* 2003; Lord and Jones 2006). However, there seems a common acceptance at both Key Stages 1 and 2 that too much choice might lead to pupils working hard at popular subjects at the expense of the least popular and they know that they have to study subjects because each has its own intrinsic merit (Silcock and Wyness 2000: 19).

Working arrangements within the primary classroom

Pupils know that they can learn from working with each other and recognise the value of peer support for learning in the classroom (Bearne 2002; Cullingford 1991; Demetriou, Goalen and Rudduck 2000; Flutter and Rudduck 2004; McCallum and Demie 2001). Pupils enjoy working with friends and consider that working in this way allows them to receive help, give help and exchange ideas. The following quotes illustrate this point:

> I'm sitting next to Jane and she helps me if I'm stuck and I help her. Sometimes she helps me know the answer but she doesn't actually, like, say 'Oh it's 36', she says 'Well, how may tens has it got … ? Now count the units … ' (Year 3)
>
> (Flutter and Rudduck 2004: 103)

> In my maths I can ask my friend and help my friends. And in my literacy, because I have got a quick mind, I can normally tell the others what to do and how to do it. (Year 3)
>
> (Demetriou, Goalen and Rudduck 2000: 31)

Flutter and Rudduck (2004) found that primary school pupils who have taken part in peer support strategies have seen the potential benefits of talking to others about their learning. A Year 6 pupil summed up his views of the advantages of taking part in peer tutorials:

> You are also helping yourself when you teach someone … you are kind of teaching yourself at the same time.
>
> (Flutter and Rudduck 2004: 124)

Cullingford (1991) found that the sense of feeling of achievement does not appear to diminish when pupils receive help from other pupils, and there seems to be some security in knowing that other children can help, which therefore results in fewer disturbances to the teacher.

Findings from the PACE project (Pollard and Triggs 2000) suggest that children generally prefer to sit with friends rather than with people they may not get on with; they are happier sitting with someone with whom they can relate as this makes classroom activities more enjoyable, interesting and fun. Where pupils were not happy with their groupings this was found to relate to being separated from friends; having to work with people pupils found uncongenial and uncooperative; and feeling they were misplaced by either having too much or too little demanded of them (*Ibid.*: 179).

Some pupils are aware that working with friends may not always have a positive effect on their learning as there can be a tendency to talk about non-work related topics and/ or to 'mess about' with friends, whereas this is less likely to happen when working with pupils they do not know so well. Thus, there is some recognition from children that the effort to work in unfamiliar and less preferred groups can be worthwhile (Flutter and Rudduck 2004; Pointon and Kershner 2000; Silcock and Wyness 2000). Many pupils can make a clear distinction between friends who help with their learning and those whom they enjoy being with but who are likely to have a negative effect on their work:

> I work best with Holly doing maths because she doesn't mess about and if I sit with Tom he always jumps up and takes the book all over the place. (Year 3)
> (Flutter and Rudduck 2004: 108)

Working with friends can also have a damaging impact on pupils' learning and confidence when the friendship goes wrong or when pupils are split from their friends. For younger pupils the loss of a friend or membership of a social group can be a devastating experience; for example, when pupils transfer from Key Stage 1 to 2, the social aspect of the classroom becomes of paramount concern and some pupils feel anxious and upset when separated from close friends (Flutter and Rudduck 2004).

Pupils are aware of 'ability' and 'attainment' as factors used to define groups, especially in Year 6 Mathematics where the majority of pupils are aware of being divided up in this way (Pollard and Triggs 2000). They consider there to be advantages and disadvantages of working only with pupils of a similar ability to themselves. Within the PACE project (Pollard and Triggs 2000), it was found that some pupils viewed 'setting' as positive because work was set at an appropriate level and pupils were able to work at a pace commensurate with their ability. However, pupils were also concerned that 'setting' results in stigmatisation of lower level pupils. Hallam *et al.* (2004) found pupils who prefer mixed ability teaching liked the fact that they can help, inspire and motivate each other, while avoiding stigmatisation of those in lower sets.

Key issues

Findings from studies concerned with the organisation of primary schools paint a largely bleak picture of pressured regimes that emphasise often personally unsatisfactory 'outputs' and partial understanding. Unsurprisingly, the desire for more control over aspects of their learning comes over very strongly. Together these studies resonate sympathetically with developing traits within the pupil voice movement that argue for increased attention to consulting pupils about teaching and learning, not just about matters of more general significance within schools.

The emphasis on peer support (for example through buddying schemes of various sorts, and peer teaching) is an important dimension of the pupil voice movement. The mixed message on 'setting' and 'ability' reflects the wider debate about attainment, personal identity and an inclusive society amongst professionals, parents and the wider community. These are matters the pupil voice movement is slowly beginning to address as it moves more overtly into territory previously occupied only by adults. One reading would suggest that, particularly in matters of such profound importance to the nurturing of a democratic society, pupil voice needs to connect more directly to intergenerational encounters in which the voices of adults and young people begin to develop a more deliberate dialogue.

PUPILS' VIEWS ON LEARNING WITHIN THEIR PRIMARY SCHOOLS

What motivates and demotivates pupils?

Pupils are motivated by interest, activity, challenge, success, the feeling that they are free to fail, gaining satisfaction in what they have produced and acknowledgement of their achievement (Blatchford 1992; Pollard and Triggs 2000). Pupils also like to feel that the work is useful and purposeful (Flutter and Rudduck 2004). In the PACE project (Pollard and Triggs 2000) pupils in Years 3 and 4 were pleased by the neatness and correctness of their work, by the quantity of work they produced and by their speed of working and their ability to finish work on time. Some pupils were pleased by being praised and rewarded, while a smaller group expressed intrinsic pleasure in work they perceived to have quality.

In contrast to this, pupils are demotivated by boredom with routine, repetitive tasks and lack of challenge (Cullingford 1991; Pollard and Triggs 2000). They dislike work that seems to be going over 'old ground' and do not understand the need to consolidate their learning with further practice in skills about which they already feel confident. They are quickly switched off learning activities they think are a waste of time (Flutter and Rudduck 2004). The following quote illustrates these points:

> I think that if there is something hard and it is like new, when I have never done it before, then I think, 'Yeah, I want to do this!' but sometimes if I have thought, if I have done it before and it was easy and I would go. 'Oh I don't have to do this work'. (Year 4)
>
> (Flutter and Rudduck 2004: 112)

Classroom activities that carry on for a long period without physical movement can also reduce pupils' engagement with learning, while classroom activities that don't involve writing are more likely to engage pupils' interests (Flutter and Rudduck 2004). In a study by Kinder *et al.* (1996: 16) they found 'uninteresting' lessons or 'being bored with work' ranked as a reason for truancy.

Key issues

The recent interest in pupil voice has resulted in pupils increasingly getting involved in processes that address issues of motivation and demotivation (for example pupils as researchers and surveys that ask questions such as 'What makes a good lesson?'). An area which these studies do not directly address, although it is beginning to come through in some of the pupil voice literature, is the importance of pupils developing an identity for themselves as a learner (Pollard 2007). As Pollard and Filer (1996) and Pollard (2007: 2) point out, pupils are more likely to 'become effective learners if they are able to manage their coping strategies and presentation of self in ways which are viable in relation to different teachers and classroom contexts, and in relation to their peers'. Pollard (2007) also acknowledges that pupils are more likely to become effective learners when they have sufficient self-confidence, capacity for self-reflection, and trust from their teacher to manage higher levels of risk and task ambiguity in classrooms. He considers relationships between teachers and pupils to be the basis of the moral order of the classroom, that this establishes the climate in which teaching and learning takes place, and that it is the relationship between the teacher and pupils which can help to develop a pupil's self-image and sense of identity as a learner. It is this emphasis on pupils developing a learner identity, as perceiving themselves as learners, and understanding their responsibility as a learner within the school which schools need to actively work towards.

PUPILS' VIEWS ON TEACHING WITHIN THEIR PRIMARY SCHOOLS

Teachers' expectations

Pollard and Triggs (2000) found that pupils were aware that teachers' expectations varied according to a range of factors, including the status or stage of the work, the teachers' views of what a pupil or group is capable of in terms of effort and achievement and, pupils suggest, the teachers' moods. The following quotes illustrate these points. Pupils were asked 'Does it matter if you don't do things the way your teacher wants them?'

> If he knows you're not very good at it then he doesn't mind, but if he knows you're being lazy then he doesn't like it so much.

> If she's in a good mood it's all right. But if she's not it all depends. I watch for her shouting at Simon most of the time.
>
> (Pollard and Triggs 2000: 166–70)

Teaching that helps learning

The use of clear learning intentions was found to help learning. For example, where teachers inform pupils of what they expect pupils to learn (WALT: 'we are learning to … ') and inform them of what they expect from them (WILF: 'What I am looking for … '), pupils tend to be clear about what they have to do and of the expected outcome, as the following quote illustrates:

> My teacher helps me learn by telling us what we're learning. (Year 1)
>
> (MacGilchrist and Buttress 2005: 114)

When pupils move to another class or school or when a different teacher takes their class, this often results in a lack of clarity about the work they should be doing, as one pupil commented:

I don't particularly like it with the student when we were doing topics because you did things one way and she did some things the opposite.

(Cullingford 1991: 102)

In MacGilchrist and Buttress' study (2005), Year 6 pupils found the use of both 'booster' groups and revision posters and knowledge boards helped their learning. The following quotes illustrate pupils' perceptions of the benefits of these:

I think my learning has improved for me because of the booster groups. Booster group teachers have taught me much more things than I was learning in the class, not because of the teacher, but because I couldn't concentrate as well in class with all my friends around me. Although in booster groups I have friends in them as well, they don't annoy me or talk to me about non-appropriate matters!

(MacGilchrist and Buttress 2005: 118)

When we go to school we have posters with useful information that we need to know on the walls. The posters go over the key things and by seeing them all the time we remember the information. They are bold and eye-catching that attracts our attention. They are also in our classrooms we can use them when we need help.

(MacGilchrist and Buttress 2005: 119)

On the other hand, pupils were found to lose interest in learning when sitting in front of a board. As one Year 6 pupil commented:

Pupils believe in my class that just sitting in front of a board may help you to work, but without fun, learning is not interesting – therefore children can lose interest in working.

(Pupils at Wheatcroft Primary School 2001: 51)

Key issues

The advent of pupil voice work in schools has seen an increasing interest in ways in which pupils can usefully and appropriately be consulted about matters to do with teaching, not just learning. These include those mentioned in the previous subsection and also, in some circumstances, classroom observations by pupils, although this tends to happen predominately at secondary level. Where time and space is made available in schools for pupils' voices to be heard on issues that affect their learning, teachers can gain insights into pupils' perceptions of teaching which helps, and teaching which hinders, pupils' learning. However, as cautioned earlier, as teachers move towards engaging in such dialogue, staff apprehension about issues of control and concern over aspects of their professionalism being eroded need to be addressed. The key generic point about consulting people about teaching and learning is one of substantial significance having been the focus of ESRC TLRP project *Consulting Pupils about Teaching and Learning* and a range of subsequent publications culminating in that by Rudduck and McIntyre (2007).

PUPILS' VIEWS ON THE PRIMARY CURRICULUM

Even the youngest pupils in primary schools recognise day-to-day patterns of teaching, although they may not use the word 'timetable'. However, some are confused about the notion of discrete 'subjects', for example, one pupil commented: 'We didn't do Literacy in Year 2. We do it in Year 3 ... ' (Flutter and Rudduck 2004: 85). Pupils are also often unsure what terms like 'geography' or 'science' entail (*Ibid.*).

Pupils tend to view the subjects they do in school as being for their own sake and the pleasure they derive from them are in the activities they do. In the absence of any analysis of the purposes underlying different parts of the curriculum, they accept what is given and then try to ascertain a purpose. For example, whether children like maths or not they find the subject 'necessary' or 'relevant' as it has a part to play in developing their long-term future. (Silcock and Wyness 2000).

Time spent on different areas of the curriculum

Pollard and Triggs (2000) found pupils to be vaguely aware of curricular imbalance but largely accepting of it. They recognise that core subjects are important for future jobs. Pupils at Key Stage 1 involved in the PACE project perceived a curriculum dominated by English ('stories', 'reading' and 'writing'). When asked 'Which of these sorts of things do you do in the classroom?', these activities accounted for 30 per cent of the nominations made. Maths accounted for 19 per cent. However, Science accounted for only 2 per cent of the nominations (*Ibid.*: 67). At Key Stage 2, Maths with sums was the most dominant of all the curriculum subjects and activities whilst English continued to play a significant role. Science, however, remained weak until Years 5 and 6 when there was a marked increase in the amount of time reported for 'writing about Science' and, to a lesser extent, for 'doing Science investigations' (*Ibid.*: 73–75).

With regard to the non-core subjects, in Key Stage 1 Physical Education (PE) received 24 per cent of the children's nominations (a little more than maths). However, in Key Stage 2, PE was perceived less strongly than Maths and English, but was seen as taking more time than any other non-core subject. In Years 3 and 4 half of the pupils thought they did 'a lot' of PE; however, this fell to a third in Years 5 and 6 (*Ibid.*: 76–77). There was also evidence in the children's accounts of varied access to the curriculum in Music and Information Technology (*Ibid.*: 83).

In the later stages of Key Stage 2 children reported a very subject-based and teacher-determined curriculum. They reported a curriculum in which the core subjects were powerfully present and which they experienced mainly through sitting, listening and writing rather than through activity (*Ibid.*: 83–84).

In a study by Ingram and Worrall (1990), six boys, six girls and their teacher were each asked to record the curriculum activities they did during morning and afternoon sessions at school over two five week periods, one at the beginning of the school year and one at the end of the school year. Their findings showed for the elected examples of Maths and English: there were large between-pupil variations in records; children were recording fewer lessons than the teacher supposed; and the discrepancy had increased by the last five week period (Ingram and Worrall 1990: 53).

Pupils' views on specific curriculum areas

Reading

Key Stage 2 pupils in the PACE project defined reading by a hierarchy of difficulty, as the following quotes illustrate:

I like it, I've got loads of books at home, I like big books and try to pick them out 'cos they've got lots of stories and it shows you can read well. (Year 3)

I don't like reading to the teacher. I don't know how to read and some words I get muddled up with other ones. When I get words muddled up I have to take them home to practise them. (Year 5)

(Pollard and Triggs 2000: 68)

Writing

Pollard (1996) found that whilst young pupils disliked writing (ranked in the last two places in Years 1 and 2 out of 12 possible activities), some Year 3 pupils enjoyed beginning to master the basic skills of handwriting. However, more recent research (Lord and Jones 2006) found pupils in Years 1 and 2 enjoyed writing and were positive about their achievements in joined-up writing, spelling, and marking and sharing stories; meanwhile those in Years 3 and 4 were negative about writing. A study of Year 3 pupils who found writing to be a particular area of difficulty found that some pupils enjoyed writing at home but seemed to find the classroom demands of Year 3 daunting, and the pressures of performance inhibited opportunities for improving and polishing writing (Bearne 2002: 126). However, Cullingford (1991) found children who enjoy writing discover a sense of personal ownership as writing stories allows them to pursue ideas of their own.

Mathematics

Pollard and Triggs (2000) found both very high and very low achievers tend to feel confident about their work in Maths. They found high achievers tend to be of the opinion that once the techniques are mastered, examples can be repeated. Very low attainers, on the other hand, enjoy the security of differentiated work which they can 'get right'. This contrasts with their feelings about writing activities where their shortcomings are clearly manifested. It tends to be those 'in the middle' who are more likely to experience Maths as problematic and worry about the demands it makes.

Science

There seems to be some disagreement in studies as to the popularity of science in primary schools. Several studies cite pupils' enthusiasm for science (for example Reid and Skryabina 2002; Harland *et al.* 1999), others indicate a decline in enthusiasm for science towards the end of primary school (for example Pell and Jarvis 2001), while others show that Science, and in particular writing in Science, is not liked amongst primary school pupils (Pollard 1996). Lord and Jones (2006) also found pupils' preference for practical activities within Science to be strongly evidenced in research (for example Pell and Jarvis 2001).

Areas of the curriculum liked and disliked by pupils

In a study by Blatchford (1992), when asked what the best thing about school was, 55 per cent of pupils gave answers relating to work, for example: 'studying'; 'learning work'; 'good lessons'; 'new subjects'; 'getting things right'; 'spelling'; and 'tests'. Fifteen per cent said PE, and 14 per cent playtime (*Ibid.*: 111).

Findings from the PACE project (Pollard and Triggs 2000) show that in the first two years of Key Stage 2 all the core curriculum subjects featured as favoured curriculum areas, with Maths, Reading and Writing appearing in the first three places. However, in Years 5 and 6 most children found little engagement in the core curriculum with its increasing categoric assessment. Children in Years 5 and 6 tended to revert to the activities, for example PE and Art, which they nominated as favourites in Year 1. Art was preferred because it was fun and interesting, because it was an activity where it was possible to exercise some autonomy over what you did and where it was easy to succeed. PE, on the other hand, was liked because it provided an opportunity to be active and have fun and where evaluation was not an issue. Silcock and Wyness (2000) found that, by Key Stage 2, pupils know their own curriculum strengths and weaknesses and, to an extent, gear their enthusiasm to those they can do well.

The most common criteria for explaining why pupils like particular curriculum areas are that they involve fun, activity and autonomy (Pollard and Triggs 2000: 103). Children appreciate different parts of the curriculum according to the amount of individual practical work they can carry out, rather than according to the importance of the work. Cullingford (1991) also found that pupils see Art as a welcome break from the taxing work of the central curriculum, as the following quote illustrates:

> I love doing art because I can take my time over it and enjoy it more than anything else and I like to do something out of my head.
>
> (Cullingford 1991: 153–54)

Lord and Jones (2006) reported that numerous science studies reveal that newness engenders the enthusiasm of pupils. In a study by Pell and Jarvis (2001), despite Science appearing difficult, young pupils' sense of novelty in doing Science raised their enthusiasm. Davies and Brember (1994), however, found that familiarity with the same equipment or teachers throughout primary school led to Key Stage 2 pupils becoming less keen on music, singing and PE than the infants. Pollard and Filer (1996) found in their study of four-to seven-year-olds that some children were motivated by 'new' work, while others found it worrying. The following quotes by pupils in Year 2 illustrate difference in pupils' thinking when asked how they feel when they are required to do some new school work. One pupil commented:

> I like anything new, 'cos it's exciting. If it's difficult, I listen really carefully and think hard. ...
>
> (Pollard and Filer 1996: 70)

Whereas another commented:

> I feel a bit worried, I think that I might get it wrong ...
>
> (Pollard and Filer 1996: 258)

In a study by Blatchford (1992), when asked what pupils thought to be the worst thing about school, nearly one third gave answers relating to work, for example: 'loads and loads of writing'; 'handwriting'; 'drama'; 'singing'; 'learning maths'; and 'just doing work' (*Ibid.*: 111).

Pollard and Triggs (2000) found that the explanations most frequently given by pupils for disliking a subject or activity were that pupils found them difficult to succeed at and they offered the experience of failure, or they were boring, physically constraining or lacking in opportunities for autonomy.

Dislike of an activity in primary schools is also associated with the constraints placed on physical activity (Pollard and Triggs 2000; Silcock and Wyness 2000). Key Stage 2 children, in particular, express a dislike of having to sit still for long periods; this is often associated with writing tasks or listening to the teacher reading stories. Pupils find certain kinds of work, like writing, particularly boring (Cullingford 1991; Pollard and Triggs 2000; Kinder *et al.* 1996). Even where pupils express an interest in subjects, the perceived burden of the pressure to recall and record, combined with the lack of opportunities for personal control, is demotivating for many. Pollard and Triggs (2000) found that low achievers in particular experience considerable anxiety and fear of their failure being exposed. They found that children in Key Stage 2 commented that they disliked Science, Geography, History and RE because of the weight of information presented to them which they had to learn. The experience of success was not necessarily associated with liking a subject or activity; many children expressed little enthusiasm for the core curriculum subjects in which they achieved high scores in the end of Key Stage 2 assessment tests.

Differences in boys' and girls' perspectives on the curriculum

Pollard and Triggs' (2000) findings suggest that there is no consistent pattern across all six years for positive preference which can be related to gender. However, some differences began to emerge in Years 5 and 6 as significantly more girls than boys preferred Art or Painting. More boys than girls selected Maths as a most liked subject in Year 6. This was a shift for the girls who, in Years 4 and 5, had nominated Maths as 'most liked' slightly more than the boys. The number of girls choosing Maths as 'most disliked' increased as they moved up the school; in Year 6 it was the subject mentioned most in this category. Boys in general disliked English activities more than girls; from Year 4 boys consistently disliked writing. However the general dislike of English, and of writing in particular, was less evident among the higher-achieving boys. Girls were found to consistently dislike Science more than boys until Year 6, when there was a more even divide between the sexes. In Years 5 and 6 girls disliked geography much more than boys did – in Year 6 it shared the top place as 'most disliked' with Maths – and boys consistently disliked singing more than girls, who did not mention this negatively after Year 3 (*Ibid.*: 98).

In a study by Blatchford (1992), boys were more likely than girls to say that the best thing about school is playtime (21 per cent boys, 6 per cent girls). He found that black boys were more likely than white boys, or black or white girls, to say that Maths was their favourite subject (black boys 82 per cent; white boys 58 per cent; white girls 63 per cent; and black girls 66 per cent) (*Ibid.*: 113).

Key issues

Findings from these studies suggest that it is increasingly difficult for schools to meet the aims of the Education Reform Act (1988), which hoped to establish a 'broad and balanced curriculum', as teachers place emphasis on the teaching of core subjects at both Key Stages 1 and 2 at the expense of other subjects. What comes over particularly strongly from research studies of pupils' perspectives on the curriculum are the pressures underlying external performance demands on teachers. This is a matter of considerable political as well as educational importance and it is thus not altogether surprising that it has yet to appear significantly in the pupil voice literature.

PUPILS' VIEWS ON ASSESSMENT WITHIN THEIR PRIMARY SCHOOLS

School-based assessment – assessment of class work

Pupils involved in the PACE project (Pollard and Triggs 2000) were asked specifically: 'Do you like it when your teacher asks to look at your work?' Findings show that in Key Stage 1 most children felt unequivocally positive about their teachers looking at their work, they felt their work would be positively received and that this would please their teacher and earn their approval, as the quotes below illustrate:

> I like it when she says you done it good. I feel happy. (Year 1)

> Yes, I feel lucky cause she usually puts a tick and 'good'. (Year 3)
>
> (Pollard and Triggs 2000: 138)

There was a decline in the eagerness with which children welcomed teachers looking at their work in Years 3 and 4, and this trend continued even more strongly in Years 5 and 6. In Year 4 over 40 per cent of children were still feeling positive about the situation; however, in Year 5 this fell to 20 per cent, and in Year 6 to 13 per cent. In some cases, one or more of the following words were used to describe pupils' concerns about teachers looking at their work: 'worried', 'nervous', 'scared', 'upset', 'guilty', 'ashamed', 'embarrassed', 'shaky' and 'doubtful' (*Ibid.*: 134).

A large proportion of mixed and negative feelings stem from two sources. Firstly children's own assessment of their work: they apply criteria of quality, neatness and correctness that they assume would be applied by their teacher; their feelings also vary with their own assessment of the 'effort' they put into the work. The second source of negative feelings is a strange sense of uncertainty about whether they have done what was required, and about how their teacher is likely to react to whether they have 'understood'. The most negative responses reveal considerable fear and apprehension about the consequences of 'getting it wrong'. At best, this would mean the disappointment of the teacher that they had failed to meet expectations. At worst, it would involve teacher censure, public humiliation and embarrassment, or 'telling parents' or having to do the work again (*Ibid.*).

Pupils tend to be disappointed when they receive a mark for their work which does not reflect the effort they put into it and Flutter and Ruddock (2004) found that pupils do not always understand what is involved when a teacher uses phrases like 'you must try harder' and 'the work is not good enough'.

School-based assessment – testing in schools

When asked about their views of tests, pupils in both Key Stage 1 and 2 were found to tolerate tests as they saw them as a way in which teachers can determine whether pupils remember what they have been taught. In some cases pupils enjoy the challenge of testing and assessment and in others pupils are worried, fearful and anxious (Bearne 2002; Doddington *et al.* 2001; Silcock and Wyness 2000).

Doddington (2001) found children were most worried when they did not know or understand what the tests were for, or when they felt that assessment was being used to emphasise their shortcomings rather than identify their achievements.

A study of Year 3 pupils by Doddington and Flutter (2002) found that the way testing was explained to pupils could make a profound difference to their confidence, for example, in some schools the tests seemed to make children 'very conscious of what they did *not* do, rather than what they *could* do', while in other schools pupils understood that they were given tests to help make progress in their learning. The following quotes suggest that young pupils were able to see tests that were part of ongoing teacher assessment in a positive and constructive way:

> [Tests] are probably because teachers want to see how good we are and probably put us in a higher table. (Year 3)

> I think [tests] are good because they can tell your next teacher how good you are and what sort of things you know and what sort of things you need to work on. So that's tests. That's what you learn from. We learn from our mistakes. (Year 3)
> (Flutter and Rudduck 2004: 97–98)

Pupils' assessment of their work

Where pupils assess their own work, effort and time taken are generally foremost in their evaluations and their sense of pride and accomplishment are very clear. Pupils also tend to assess the quality of work in superficial ways such as its neatness and it having 'no rubbings out'. Flutter and Rudduck (2004) found younger pupils, in particular, think that working hard is about being quiet, producing large quantities of work and completing work on time. Similarly, Croll (1996) reported children consider 'effort' to be the most important factor in determining why some children do better at school work than others, with ability and skill being of far less importance.

National assessment tests

For pupils in Years 2 and 6 the notion of SATs looms large in pupils' minds. This is particularly true for Year 6 pupils. Some pupils feel that their learning is almost entirely focused on achieving good grades in SATs. They are aware of the importance of SATs, and find both the tests and the preparation for them difficult (Silcock and Wyness 2000). Similarly, Pollard and Triggs (1998) found that pupils were aware of the importance of 'good marks' and 'getting things right' in their Key Stage 2 SATs. A comment made by one pupil, in a study by Reay and Wiliam (1999) illustrates pupils' concern about SATs:

> I'm really scared about SATs, Mrs O'Brien [a teacher in the school] came and talked to us about our spelling and I'm no good at spelling and David [the class teacher] is giving us times table tests every morning and I'm hopeless at times

tables so I'm frightened I'll do the SATs and I'll be a nothing. ... 'cause you have to get a level 4 or a level 5 and if you're no good at spellings and times tables you don't get those levels and so you're a nothing.

(Reay and Wiliam 1999: 345)

Reay and Wiliam (1999) found that pupils felt a sense of unease about what SATs might reveal about themselves as learners, with some pupils indicating far-reaching consequences in which good SATs results are linked to positive life prospects and poor results linked to future failure and hardship. When talking about a pupil who is likely to gain a level 6 in their Year 6 SATs tests, one pupil commented:

He's heading for a good job and a good life and it shows he's not gonna be living on the streets and stuff like that ... [and if you get a level two, what does that say about you?] ... I might not have a good life in front of me and I might grow up and do something naughty or something like that.

(Reay and Wiliam 1999: 347)

The pressure on pupils at Key Stage 2 tends to be far greater and the assessment process is much more overt than at Key Stage 1. Overall, children seem only too aware that whilst 'trying' is worthy, 'achieving' is actually the required outcome. Pollard and Triggs (2000) found that where schools have created a secure, non-threatening environment, high attainers begin to feel more confident and even exhilarated during the test period. However, under pressure, other pupils become demotivated and dysfunctional as the difficulty of the SATs challenges overwhelms them. Pupils tend to associate the tests with measurement and accountability, as one Year 6 pupil stated:

They are to judge what we have done ... and to prove that we have done everything.

(Pollard and Triggs 2000: 217)

SATs are also associated with the provision of 'national' evidence, and pupils believe that the test results matter because they will be used by the schools they are going to in order to help make decisions about which groups or sets they will be placed in. The quote below, by a Year 6 pupil, illustrates this point:

If you don't do well the next school won't think you are good at some things when you really are.

(Pollard and Triggs 2000: 216)

The majority of children are aware that SATs results constitute some sort of 'official' judgement of them. Some pupils are also aware of teachers' own sense of pressure from SATs, as the results are also used in assessing teachers (Flutter and Rudduck 2004; Pollard and Triggs 2000; Reay and Wiliam 1999). As one pupil commented:

SATs are about how good the teachers have been teaching you and if everybody gets really low marks they think the teachers haven't been teaching you properly.

(Reay and Wiliam 1999: 346)

Key issues

Findings from the studies reported here imply that pupils are assessed primarily, if not solely, on skills that can be measured by pencil and paper testing, and assessment is generally seen as a way of testing what pupils don't know rather than as a means to developing learning. Pollard (2007) suggests narrow target setting tends to emphasise formal aspects of provision and to over-simplify teaching and learning processes. He states:

> Maximising the potential of children and young people calls for a more appropriate understanding of them as social actors within their cultures and communities, and of how education fits into, and contributes to, their lives as a whole.
>
> (Pollard 2007)

The pressures that begin to inform pupils' views about the curriculum and the effects of external judgements on themselves and their teachers appear in a more pronounced way with regard to assessment. As yet, there is little evidence of these issues featuring to any significant degree in the pupil voice movement.

PUPILS' VIEWS ON THE TRANSFER TO SECONDARY SCHOOL

Children look forward to the transfer from primary to secondary school with a mixture of enthusiasm and anxieties about features of their new schools (Blatchford 1992; Bryan 1980; Delamont and Galton, in Pollard 1990b). Cullingford (1991) found that, to a large extent, children's views about specific features of secondary school stem from stories they hear from people they know and what they have seen and heard about secondary school on television programmes. Similar findings were reported by Measor and Woods (1984) who looked at pupils transferring from middle to secondary school at the age of 12.

In particular, pupils look forward to subjects they think will be covered more specifically at secondary school; for example science, biology, chemistry, computer studies, music, and some look forward to social opportunities such as making or renewing friendships (Blatchford 1992: 111). Aspects of secondary school which pupils tend not look forward to include a fear of bullying, being picked on and teased, and the general demands of work (Blatchford 1992; Cullingford 1991; Delamont and Galton, in Pollard 1990b; Measor and Woods 1984). Pupils also tend to be anxious about the large size of the school, movement between classes, and getting used to having different teachers for different subjects (Delamont and Galton, in Pollard 1990b). There is also some concern over whether pupils will lose their friends from primary school and whether they will be able to make new ones (Delamont and Galton, in Pollard 1990b). Measor and Woods (1984) found pupils to be anxious about new forms of discipline and authority, and to be concerned about the fact that they may find it difficult to evolve close personal relationships with their new teachers as they would no longer be taught by a single teacher who knew them well. Measor and Woods (1984) also found concern was raised over the prospect of homework. It was not so much the nature of the work, but the possibility of large amounts of it which could encroach into their private time. The following comments express some of these concerns:

> It's going to be much harder work. Very big. I'll get lost. I'll probably end up in the wrong class. It will be a bit scary at first.
>
> (Cullingford 1991: 41)

Will they teach me or just expect me to do it?

(Measor and Woods 1984: 11)

Measor and Woods (1984) also found pupils to be anxious about moving from a female-dominated to a male-dominated world, as one pupil commented:

I've never had a man teacher before, so I don't know what it's like.'

(Measor and Woods 1984: 10)

In some cases, what was mentioned as a fear by one pupil was seen positively by another, for example, one pupil viewed a cross-country final as a fantastic opportunity for training, whereas another pupil expressed concern about it (Delamont and Galton, in Pollard 1990b: 237).

Although some of the literature referred to in this section is fairly dated, for example, Measor and Woods (1984), findings from more recent research conducted by the principal author of this report suggests that primary school pupils today continue to have similar enthusiasms and anxieties about their transfer to secondary school as those described by Measor and Woods (1984).

Blatchford (1992) found that boys were generally happier about the transfer to secondary school than girls because of the work (boys 41 per cent; girls 22 per cent), and because of PE (boys 19 per cent; girls 2 per cent). He reported that white girls seemed more likely than black girls, or black or white boys, to say that they were not looking forward to secondary school because of the work. Measor and Woods (1984) found there to be some differences in the friendship behaviour of girls and boys. Boys tended to belong to large groups, and although girls also had a circle of friends they also tended to have 'best friends' to whom they felt close. In some instances pupils had 'contingency friends' in case the best friend or friends were absent, thus the prospect of losing friends and 'contingency friends' on transfer threatened the pupils' self-support system.

In a more recent study funded by the DfES, Galton *et al.* (2003) measured pupils' attitudes to school immediately before transfer and in the November and July following the move to secondary school. Their findings suggest that the current Year 7 curriculum is not sufficiently challenging or different from that of Year 6. The project also explored the difficulties pupils had in dropping particular persona that had been adopted in their primary schools. Some pupils reported that they wanted to change from 'dosser' to 'worker' but didn't know how to, thus they found it difficult to alter their reputation and to have a 'fresh start'.

It is not just the process of transferring to secondary school that can cause anxiety; it is also the process of choosing and being accepted in the preferred secondary school. As Urquhart (2001: 83) acknowledges, for many children the experience of choosing a school is one of protracted anxiety and ultimate disappointment that can last from the November of Year 6 to the start of secondary school the following September. Urquhart argues that such anxiety affects children's motivation to learn. As one pupil stated:

It kind of makes my work go down because it's like because … I don't really care I've got a school that's rubbish. I don't really care.

(Urquhart 2001: 84)

Key issues

One of the most significant changes pupils will experience as they move from primary to secondary school is the different types of relations they will have with staff. At primary school pupils are likely to have been taught by one main teacher and to have built a close relation with this person, and it is the class teacher who will most likely have dealt with both curriculum and pastoral issues. The person-centred tradition of education sees such academic and pastoral care as inextricably linked (as with the Schools-within-Schools Approach to Education on a Human Scale, Fielding *et al.* 2006). However, in the vast majority of mainstream secondary schools, the current way of working is to separate pastoral from academic and curriculum care. In such circumstances it is unlikely that pupils will build close relations with many, or any, of the staff. This lack of such a close relationship can lead to pupils feeling as though they don't 'belong' to the school or to them not identifying with the school. As Evans (1983) stated:

> It is the quality of the relationship between the tutor and the tutee that is most important. … The quality of this relationship is not achieved through 'pastoral care' alone but through its integration with the 'academic' function of the relationship.
> (Evans 1983: 30)

In order to ease the transition of pupils from primary to secondary schools, such profound changes in the pupils' relationships with staff need to be considered.

ASPIRATIONS AND PREFERENCES IN RESPECT OF PUPILS' OWN FUTURES

In a study by Roberts and Dolan (1989), primary school children were found to perceive 'work' as 'the usual thing' adults do. They also realised that different work attracts different rewards, and that rewards are hierarchically determined. Of the 60 pupils in the study, most felt that people should not simply be paid more for doing more work but should receive additional rewards if what they are doing is more 'valuable' or more 'unpleasant' (*Ibid.*: 23–24). Ninety-six per cent of pupils in the study believed that there was a direct link between working hard at school and getting 'good work' in the future; the same proportion of pupils considered that school learning would be important to them when they came to 'start work' (*Ibid.*: 25). However, 90 per cent of the children in the study considered it may be difficult to find paid employment after leaving school.

Pupils in Roberts and Dolan's study were from two different schools: significantly more of the pupils from the school in a relatively affluent area wanted to follow the work paths of their parents compared to children from the less affluent area. This may reflect the professional, relatively affluent and, therefore, satisfactory careers of many of their parents. However, for some in the latter school, paid work might be characterised by low pay, difficult and unsocial conditions and relatively limited opportunities (*Ibid.*: 26).

CONCLUSION: KEY FINDINGS

Although the findings presented in this chapter tell us something about the perceptions pupils have of their experiences during their time in primary school, it must be remembered that the studies referred to here are relatively small scale and, therefore, may not be truly representative of the primary school population. In addition, the studies referred to report pupils' perspectives on specific aspects of primary school life identified by the researcher. There seems to be a lack of data which reports on areas of primary school life identified as important by pupils. Thus the studies, whilst reporting on pupils' answers to questions posed to them, do not specifically elicit data reflecting what is important to pupils from the pupils' perspective.

The findings presented here raise questions and concerns around the following areas in particular:

- the purposes of primary schooling;
- the importance of listening to the voices of pupils in schools;
- the importance of pupils developing a learner identity;
- the change in teacher–pupil relationships experienced by pupils as pupils move from primary to secondary school.

The purposes of primary schooling

As suggested by the *Every Child Matters* (ECM) agenda, one of the purposes of schooling is to equip learners for life in its broadest sense. However, the current emphasis on target setting and testing does not reflect this. Since the introduction of the National Curriculum in 1988, and SATs in Years 2 and 6, there has been an increasing pressure for primary teachers to cover large quantities of work in order to help pupils gain their highest possible marks in SATs. Thus it is not uncommon for teachers to experience constraints in their freedom to teach a broad curriculum, and instead place emphasis on the teaching of the core subjects at both Key Stages 1 and 2 at the expense of other subjects. These findings suggest that teachers' decisions about what to teach are influenced by the pressure on them to teach pupils information that they are likely to need in order to perform well in these tests. Consideration needs to be given to ways in which systems of public accountability can develop forms of assessment that value more than academic ability. This again leads us to question what schools are trying to achieve for the children within them.

If children are to develop their full potential in all areas of their lives, there needs to be a clear vision within the primary sector of what its purposes are and how these are communicated to pupils. As Pollard suggests (2007), in order to maximise the potential of children there needs to be a more appropriate understanding of children as social actors within their cultures and communities, and of how education fits into and contributes to their lives as a whole.

The importance of listening to the voices of pupils in schools

The existence of power relations between staff and pupils in schools significantly affects the degree to which pupils participate in school decision making, and the degree to which they feel valued as a member of the school community. The recent move towards listening to the voices of pupils in schools has resulted in the power relations between teachers, the head teacher and the pupils in some schools becoming more equal, and decision making within these schools moving towards a more negotiated process. It is the normative goal of pupil voice work to challenge those structures and processes of power which curtail the opportunity to embed equality of voice for all in the life of the school (Robinson and Taylor 2007: 14). Schools developing a listening culture and ways of allowing students to become active participants in the school often resulted in pupils developing a sense of belonging to the school; school becomes a place where pupils want to be, where they feel valued and where their views are taken seriously. Within the pupil voice movement schools are increasingly listening to pupils about teaching and learning issues, as well as more general matters. Where pupils' voices are heard on teaching and learning, teachers can gain an insight into what helps and what hinders pupil' learning. Consideration needs to be given to how the cultures within some primary schools have changed as a result of listening to pupils, and to the benefits this brings to the pupils, the staff and to the school generally.

The importance of pupils developing a learner identity

A pupil's identity can affect the degree to which they engage themselves in opportunities for learning. If learning is to take place, pupils need to develop a learner identity. There needs to be further work on factors which help pupils develop and retain such an identity. The current emphasis on testing, and the large amount of work activities which need to be completed, result in pupils seeing the value of trusting teachers to decide what has to be learned, thus moving away from pupils being independent learners. The recent inclusion of Citizenship Education within the primary curriculum, which encourages pupils to play an active role in the life of their school and to take responsibility for their learning, is slowly beginning to filter into some schools. But this is a long process and in some cases there is little evidence of this happening on any significant scale. One important aspect of Citizenship Education is to develop a sense of responsibility in pupils, and to make pupils aware of their rights and responsibilities as learners, as well as their rights and responsibilities beyond the classroom and the school. The school council, a body comprised of pupil representatives, has long been recognised as a useful approach for enhancing pupils' sense of responsibility. Although not compulsory in English schools, there are increasing numbers of school councils in primary schools and, as Whitty *et al.* (2007) recently noted, school councils are now being offered more opportunities to take an active role in school decision-making.

The change in teacher – pupil relationships experienced by pupils as they move from primary to secondary school

One of the most significant changes that pupils will experience as they move from primary to secondary school is the different types of relations they will have with staff. As Pollard reminds us, relationships between teachers and pupils are the basis of the moral order of the classroom (2007). This establishes the climate in which teaching and learning takes place. It is the relationship between the teacher and pupils which can help to develop a pupil's self-image and sense of identity as a learner. Consideration needs to be given to whether the current organisation within secondary schools best serves the needs of pupils within them. Currently most secondary schools are organised around existing pastoral and academic structures and their vision is based around outcome, with little emphasis placed on the learner as a 'whole' person. It may be that pupils could benefit from an emphasis on a more person-centred education, with the development of pupils being at the fore.

With the Every Child Matters agenda being prominent in the minds of head teachers, teachers and those who are involved in services which help to meet the needs of children and young people, this could be seen as an opportune time to reconsider the purposes and aims of both primary and secondary schooling. This report has outlined findings from UK-based studies which have detailed pupils' perspectives on various aspects of their primary schooling. The overall findings suggest that the voices and views of pupils are not always heard in their schools, and that many schools still have a long way to go if they are to take pupils' perspectives into consideration. If schools are to create a culture of mutual respect and trust of members within it, where pupils are aware of their rights and responsibilities as learners and as members within and beyond the school community, there needs to be a move towards including pupils as active participants in the school in ways that allow their voices to be listened to. Such schools would recognise and celebrate the success of those within it; they would be a place where pupils want to be, where they are engaged and motivated to learn, and where pupils feel a sense of belonging. In such cases, the vision of the school should be driven by the development of the individual within the context of a caring, worthwhile community (a) in which they are valued and respected, and (b) to which they contribute. There should be a greater emphasis placed on widely conceived notions of learning and on commensurately imaginative forms of accountability, and pupils should no longer be moulded to fit into existing systems and structures but should be members of a school which is built around listening to and providing for their needs.

Implications of the research surveyed for the future of primary education

(i) National policy

- We understand the pressures on policy-makers to set clear agendas that are seen to break new ground and address compelling issues of the day. However, we would urge those concerned with the formulation and review of national policy to find ways of locating their work within longer time trajectories that, amongst other things, bring to their attention relevant work that has been done in the past.
- Secondly, we welcome some growing evidence (Alexander 2007) that there is a desire to return to the importance of clarifying the purposes of education in general and primary education in particular. Without such clarification and engaged debate, the 'how' becomes little more than mechanisms devoid of moral or educational legitimacy.
- Pupil voice will never be seriously supported by other than a small proportion of teachers and other staff unless there are clear messages that this new approach is not a covert way of trying to control, 'discipline', or reform teachers.
- There is surprisingly little evidence about the nature, experience and success of primary education that is rooted in data from pupils themselves. This suggests that, longer term, more extensive exploration of pupils' perspectives on primary education might usefully be sought through academic research.

(ii) National agencies

- For pupil voice to be embedded more successfully in daily teaching and learning practices we would recommend that initial teacher education and training engage seriously and imaginatively with new developments and research. Those universities currently pioneering this work, for example, Nottingham University, are an important and useful resource.

- Continuing Professional Development (CPD) might also usefully engage with these matters and draw on the experience of organisations; for example the Specialist Schools and Academies Trust are supporting Student Voice through national hubs, and there is imaginative and ground breaking work currently going on in Futurelab in Bristol.
- In all this work it is vital that the research and development link with universities be part of the means of engagement, evaluation and future development, otherwise there is a danger that we will end up nationally in much the same position as we currently are with 'learning styles' (that is to say, where some enthusiastic teachers develop aspects of the work in a wholehearted and unquestionable way and ignore the highly dubious nature of its evidence base).

(iii) Local authorities

- A number of local authorities, for example, Bedfordshire, Bolton and Portsmouth, have been supporting pupil voice work over substantial periods of time (in the region of 5 years). Lessons need to be learned about how this kind of innovation can be supported and developed, what obstacles are typically faced, and what can be learned from this kind of sustained work (often under difficult and pressured circumstances) and applied more widely.
- Similar lessons can also be learned from the four-year National College for School Leadership Networked Learning Communities programme, a central strand of which was concerned with the development of work on pupil voice.
- Note might usefully be taken of recent pioneering approaches like the Research Forum developments at Bishops Park College, Clacton (see Fielding *et al.* 2006). Here young people were at the heart of a process in which the school and the community developed shared understanding of what the purposes of the school were and how they could be imaginatively and effectively evaluated. Useful lessons about an intergenerational approach are particularly apposite here.

(iv) Primary schools

- Drawing from (iii) above, a number of innovative and sustainable approaches to involving teachers and staff in the day-to-day process of encouraging pupil voice might usefully be learned. These include things like having a pupil voice strand for staff with co-ordinating and leading 'teaching and learning' responsibilities within the school.
- Better use should be made of the practice of exemplary head teachers.

Emerging opportunities to listen to pupils' perspectives on aspects of their schooling are continuously presenting themselves. For example, largely as a result of *Every Child Matters*, there is now a move to consult young people in a more integrated way. In addition there is wide range of school-based research being conducted, often involving direct evidence from pupils, in PGCE and MA or MEd programmes of study. It seems a wasted opportunity to ignore such work, and there may be a case for using such sources of data imaginatively at local, regional and national levels.

Suggestions for further research

It is suggested that research be undertaken to explore in more depth the following areas:

- What the prime purposes of primary schooling are and how these are conveyed to pupils, families and the communities they serve.
- The ways in which the recent move towards listening to the voices of pupils has changed the cultures within some primary schools, and the benefits that this change brings. In particular, a focus on consulting pupils about teaching and learning issues (including issues of motivation and demotivation), as well as matters of more general significance. Consideration must also be given to staff apprehension about issues of control, and to the perception by some that the basis of their professionalism is being eroded rather than redefined.
- The profound change in teacher–pupil relationships as pupils move from primary to secondary school and the effect such a change has on the extent to which pupils feel they 'belong' to or identify with the school, and whether there are resultant changes in a pupil's sense of identity as a learner. There needs to be further work on factors which help pupils develop and retain such an identity.
- How former pupils perceive aspects of their primary schooling and its 'usefulness' for life beyond primary school.
- Pupils' views of the general experiences of primary schooling. Comparisons could be made across gender, social and cultural groups and, in view of the move towards 'inclusion', comparisons could also be made across specific groups which are now 'included' within mainstream primary schools. There appears to be a distinct lack of data relating to pupils' aspirations and preferences in respect of their own futures.

APPENDIX 1

'Core' literature referred to throughout the report

Research by Jean Rudduck. Jean Rudduck led a number of key research projects exploring pupils' experiences of teaching and learning and was a leading proponent of the pupil voice movement. Her initial longitudinal study, 'Making Your Way Through Secondary School' (with Gwen Wallace, Susan Harris and Julia Flutter) (Rudduck, Chaplain and Wallace 1996) highlighted the valuable contribution that consulting pupils about their experiences as learners could make to school improvement. Subsequent projects explored pupil consultation and pupil participation in primary and secondary schools, drawing attention to the importance of giving children and young people greater responsibility and autonomy in schools. From 1999–2002, Jean Rudduck co-ordinated 'Consulting Pupils about Teaching and Learning' project, (part of the ESRC Teaching and Learning Research Programme) (Rudduck and Flutter 2004), which explored the transformative potential of pupil voice through a national network of primary, secondary and special schools.

The Primary Assessment, Curriculum and Experience (PACE) project. The PACE project was funded by the Economic and Social Research Council (ESRC) and ran from 1989 to 1997. The project focused on the first full cohort of pupils to have been taught through the National Curriculum, and aimed to monitor the impact of the ERA on primary schools. 54 pupils were involved in the project, and interviews with these pupils throughout the duration of the project focused on their views of the curriculum, pedagogy and assessment.

The National Foundation for Educational Research (NFER) review of research on pupils' experiences of, and perspectives on, the curriculum between 1989 and 2005. The review was based on 314 publications and is reported in 'Pupils' experiences and perspectives of the national curriculum and assessment' (Lord and Jones 2006).

Research by Blatchford (1992), which reports on a study of 175 children from 33 inner London junior schools. Pupils were interviewed at 7 and 11 years, they were asked specifically about what they liked and disliked about their schooling.

A study by Buchanon-Barrow and Barrett (1996) which explored primary school children's understanding of the school. One hundred and forty four pupils aged 5 to 11 years from four schools in the London borough of Richmond were involved in the study. The pupils were interviewed and responded to a questionnaire which probed their understanding of the three following areas: functions of school rules; organisation of the power structure; their own role in school life. Children were also interviewed individually.

Work by Cullingford (1986 and 1991) which reports on a study of pupils' experiences of school. One hundred and ten pupils were involved in the study; they were divided equally between those in their last year of primary school and those in the first year of secondary school.

Research by Silcock and Wyness (2000) which focused on asking pupils: Which subject do you like best? Do you take tests? Do you like taking tests? A total of 75 pupils from three schools were included in the study, comprising 24 boys and 17 girls at Key Stage 1 and 17 boys and 17 girls at Key Stage 2. Of the three schools, one had a middle class intake, one largely a working class intake and one was a socio-economically mixed school.

Limited reference is made to **The Observational Research and Classroom Learning Evaluation (ORACLE) project**; a large scale observational study of primary school children in the UK funded by the Social Science Research Council from 1975 to 1980. The project aimed to provide a representative picture of the classroom experiences of teachers and pupils in English primary schools based on observation (Croll 1996, p. 4). As a result of the wide scale use of observation throughout the project to describe pupils' experiences, the extent to which data from this project could be used in this report, which focuses on the pupils' perspectives, has been limited.

APPENDIX 2

Recent research projects the findings from which are likely to add significantly to our understanding of primary age children

Mention should also be given to three research projects which, although not directly related to eliciting pupils' views of their primary schooling, add greatly to our understanding of children within the primary school age range.

A research project funded by the New Economics Foundation (NEF), in which over 1000 children aged 7–19 in Nottingham participated. In this project, questionnaires were designed to enable scales of life satisfaction and curiosity (used as an indication of children's capacity for personal development) to be calculated. Other scales used included those that assessed children's satisfaction with different aspects of their lives such as their families, friendships, neighbourhoods and schools. The project sought the views of children directly and measured the wellbeing of those involved in the project in terms of two dimensions: life satisfaction (capturing satisfaction, pleasure, enjoyment and contentment); and personal development (capturing curiosity, enthusiasm, absorption, flow, exploration, commitment, creative challenge and also, potentially, meaningfulness). Findings are written in a report entitled 'The Power and Potential of Wellbeing Indicators, measuring young people's wellbeing in Nottingham' (NEF, 2003).

Two DfES / DCSF funded longitudinal studies: The Effective Provision of Pre-School Education (EPPE) (1997–2003) and Effective Pre-School Education 3–11 (EPPE 3–11) (2003–8). These studies focus on the progress and development of 3,000 children from entering pre-school to the end of Key Stage 2 in primary school (from age 3 to 11 years old). Although the studies do not aim to gain the opinions of pupils directly, the EPPE Project is the first major study in the UK to focus specifically on the effectiveness of early years education. The studies are intended to explore the characteristics of different kinds of early years provision. EPPE (1997–2003) examined children's development in pre-school education, and progress in infant school up to the National Assessment at age 7 (end of Key Stage 1). EPPE 3–11 provides a five year extension to the EPPE (1997–2003) study. It follows the same cohort of children to the end of Key Stage 2. Findings from the studies will help to identify the aspects of pre-school provision which have a positive impact on children's attainment, progress and development, and so provide guidance on good practice.

A report by UNICEF, *Child Poverty in Perspective: An overview of child wellbeing in rich countries* (Innocenti Report Card 72007) provides a comprehensive assessment of the lives and wellbeing of children and young people in 21 nations of the industrialised world. Its purpose is to encourage monitoring, to permit comparison and to stimulate the discussion and development of policies to improve children's lives. The report measures and compares child wellbeing under six headings: material wellbeing; health and safety; education; peer and family relationships; behaviours and risks; and young people's subjective sense of their own wellbeing. The overall findings show the UK to be the lowest ranked of the 21 countries included in the study.

NOTES

1 The book by Jean Rudduck and Donald McIntyre (2007) *Improving Learning through Consulting Pupils* (London: Routledge) draws only on secondary school evidence from the ESRC TLRP research project, *Consulting Pupils about Teaching and Learning*.

REFERENCES

Alderson, P. and Morrow, V. (2004) *Ethics, Social Research and Consulting with Children and Young People*. London: Barnardo's.

Alexander, R.J. (2007) 'Where there is no vision … ', *Forum* 49 (1 and 2): 187–99.

Bearne, E. (2002) 'A good listening to: Year 3 pupils talk about learning', *Support for Learning* 17(3): 122–27.

Blatchford, P. (1992) 'Children's attitudes to work at 11 years', *Educational Studies* 18(1): 107–18.

Bryan, K. (1980) 'Pupil perceptions of transfer between middle and high schools', in A. Hargreaves and L. Tickle (Eds) *Middle Schools: origins, ideology and practice*. London: Harper and Row.

Buchanon-Barrow, E. and Barrett, M. (1996) 'Primary school children's understanding of the school', *British Journal of Educational Psychology* 66(1): 33–46.

Central Advisory Council for Education (CACE) (1967) *Children and Their Primary Schools: a report of the Central Advisory Council for Education (England)* (the Plowden Report). London: HMSO.

Cullingford, C. (1986) '"I suppose learning your tables could help you to get a job" – children's views on the purpose of schools', *Education 3–13* 14(2): 41–46.

——(1991) *The Inner World of the School: children's ideas about school*. London: Cassell Educational.

Croll, P. (Ed) (1996) *Teachers, Pupils and Primary Schooling: continuity and change*. London: Cassell.

Davies, J. and Brember, I. (1994) 'Attitudes of Year 2 and Year 6 children to school and school activities', *Curriculum* 15(2): 86–95.

Delamont, S. and Galton, M. 'Anxieties and anticipations: pupils views of transfer to secondary school', in A. Pollard (1990) *Children and Their Primary School: a new perspective*. London: The Falmer Press.

Demetriou, H., Goalen, P. and Rudduck, J. (2000) 'Academic performance, transfer, transition and friendship: listening to the student voice', *International Journal of Educational Research* 33 (4): 425–41.

Department for Education and Skills (DfES) (2004) *Every Child Matters: change for children*. London: The Stationery Office.

Doddington, C., Bearne, E., Demetriou, H. and Flutter, J. (2001) 'Testing, testing, testing … can you hear me? Can Year 3 pupils tell us anything we don't already know about Assessment?' *Education 3–13* 29(3): 43–46.

Doddington, C. and Flutter, J. (2002) *Sustaining Pupils' Progress at Year 3*. Cambridge: Faculty of Education, University of Cambridge.

Elmer, N., Ohana, J. and Moscovi, S. (1987) 'Children's beliefs about institutional roles in a cross-national study of representations of the teachers' role', *British Journal of Educational Psychology* 57: 26–37.

Evans, B. (1983) 'Countesthorpe College, Leicester: towards the "minischool"', in B. Moon (Ed) *Comprehensive Schools: challenge and change*. Windsor: NFER/Nelson: 5–32.

Fielding, M. (2001) 'Beyond the rhetoric of student voice: new departures or new constraints in the transformation of 21st century schooling?', *Forum* 43(2): 100–109.

Fielding, M., Elliot, J., Burton, C., Robinson, C. and Samuels, J. (2006) *LESS IS MORE? The development of a schools-within-schools approach to education on a human scale at Bishops Park College, Clacton, Essex*. Report submitted to Department for Education and Skills Innovation Unit, October 2006.

Flutter, J. and Rudduck, J. (2004) *Consulting Pupils: what's in it for schools?* London: RoutledgeFalmer.

Galton, M., Gray, J. and Rudduck, J. with Berry, M., Demetriou, H., Edwards, J., Goalen, P., Hargreaves, L., Hussey, S., Pell, T., Schagen, I. and Charles, M. (2003) *Transfer and Transition in the Middle Years of Schooling (7–14): continuities and discontinuities in learning.* London: DfES publications.

Grainger, T., Goouch, K. and Lambirth, A. (2003) 'Playing the game called writing: children's views and voices', *English in Education* 37(2): 4–15.

Hallam, S., Ireson, J. and Davies, J. (2004) 'Primary pupils' experiences of different types of grouping in school', *British Educational Research Journal* 30(4): 516–33.

Harland, J., Kinder, K., Achworth, M., Montgomery, A., Moor, H. and Wilkin, A. (1999) *Real Curriculum: at the end of Key Stage 2: report one from the Northern Ireland Curriculum Cohort Study.* Slough: NFER.

Ingram, J. and Worrall, N. (1990) 'Varieties of curricular experience: backmarkers and frontrunners in the primary classroom', *British Journal of Educational Psychology* 60(1): 52–62.

Kinder, K., Wakefield, A. and Wilkin, A. (1996) *Talking Back: pupil views on disaffection.* Slough: NFER.

Lord, P. and Jones, M. (2006) *Pupils' Experiences and Perspectives of the National Curriculum and Assessment: final report of the research review.* Slough: NFER.

MacBeath, J., Demetriou, H., Rudduck, J. and Myers, K. (2003) *Consulting Pupils: a toolkit for teachers.* Cambridge: Pearson Publishing.

MacGilchrist, B. and Buttress, M. (2005) *Transforming Learning and Teaching.* London: Paul Chapman Publishing.

Marks, N., Shah, H. and Westall, A. (2004) *The Power and Potential of Wellbeing Indicators: measuring young people's wellbeing in Nottingham.* London: New Economics Foundation.

McCallum, I. and Demie, F. (2001) 'Social class, ethnicity and educational performance', *Educational Research* 43(2): 147–59.

Measor, L. and Woods, P. (1984) *Changing Schools: pupil perspectives on transfer to a comprehensive.* Milton Keynes: Open University Press.

Morgan, G. (1992) 'Children are clients: what have primary pupils got to say about equal opportunities?' *Educational Management and Administration* 20(3): 193–97.

Myhill, D. and Jones, S. (2006) '"She doesn't shout at no girls": pupils' perceptions of gender equity in the classroom', *Cambridge Journal of Education* 36(1): 99–135.

Newman, E. (1997) *Children's Views of School: avehicle for developing teacher practice,* Paper presented at the British Educational Research Association Annual Conference, University of York, 11–13 September 1997.

Pell, T. and Jarvis, T. (2001) 'Developing attitudes to science for use with children aged from five to eleven years', *International Journal of Science Education* 23(8): 847–62.

Pointon, P. and Kershner, R. (2000) 'Making decisions about organising the primary classroom environment as a context for learning: the views of three experienced teachers and their pupils– the child's environment', *Teaching and Teacher Education* 16(1): 117–27.

Pollard, A. (2007) 'Education, schooling and learning for life: how meaning and opportunity build from everyday relationships', *Teaching and Learning Research Briefing,* March 2007, No. 23.

——(1996) 'Playing the system? Pupil perspectives on curriculum, pedagogy and assessment in primary schools', in P. Croll (Ed) *Teachers, Pupils and Primary Schooling: continuity and change.* London: Cassell.

——(1990a) *Learning in Primary Schools.* London: Cassell Educational Ltd.

Pollard, A. (Ed) (1990b) *Children and Their Primary School: a new perspective.* London: The Falmer Press.

Pollard, A. (1985) *The Social World of the Primary School.* London: Holt, Rinehart and Winston.

Pollard, A. and Triggs, P. with Broadfoot, P., McNess, E. and Osborn, M. (2000) *What Pupils Say: changing policy and practice in primary education.* London and New York: Continuum.

Pollard, A. and Bourne, J. (1994) *Teaching and Learning in the Primary School*. London: Routledge.

Pollard, A. and Filer, A. (1996) *The Social World of Children's Learning: case studies of pupils from four to seven*. London: Cassell.

Pollard, A. and Triggs, P. (1998) 'Pupil experience and a curriculum for lifelong learning', in C. Richards and P.J. Taylor (Eds) *How Shall We School Our Children? Primary education and its future*. London: Falmer Press.

Pupils at Wheatcroft Primary School (2001) 'Working as a team: children and teachers learning from each other', *Forum* 43(2): 51–53.

Reay, D. and Wiliam, D. (1999) '"I'll be a nothing": structure, agency and the construction of identity through assessment', *British Educational Research Journal* 25(3): 343–54.

Reid, N. and Skryabina, E.A. (2002) 'Attitudes towards physics', *Research in Science and Technology Education* 20(1): 67–81.

Roberts, R.J. and Dolan, J. (1989) 'Children's perspectives of "work": an exploratory study', *Educational Review* 41(1): 19–28.

Robinson, C. and Taylor, C. (2007) 'Theorising student voice: values and perspectives', *Improving Schools* 10(1): 5–17

Rudduck, J., Chaplain, R. and Wallace, G. (Eds) (1996) *School Improvement: what can pupils tell us?* London: Fulton.

Rudduck, J. and Flutter, J. (2000) 'Pupil participation and pupil perspective: carving a new order of experience', *Cambridge Journal of Education* 30(1): 75–89.

Rudduck, J. and Flutter, J. (2004) *How to Improve Your School*. London: Continuum.

Rudduck, J. and McIntyre, D. (2007) *Improving Learning Through Consulting Pupils*. London: Routledge.

Silcock, P. and Wyness, M.G. (2000) 'Diligent and dedicated: primary school pupils talk about the reformed curricula', *Curriculum* 21(1): 14–25.

Thiessen, D. and Cook-Sather, A. (Eds) (2007) *International Handbook of Student Experience and Elementary and Secondary School*. Dordrecht: Springer

Triggs, P. and Pollard, A. (1998) 'Pupil experience and a curriculum for lifelong learning', in C. Richards and P.H. Taylor (Eds) *How Shall We School Our Children? Primary education and its future*. London: Falmer Press.

Urquhart, I. (2001) 'Walking on air? Pupil voice and school choice', *Forum* 43(2): 83–86.

White, R. and Brockington, D. (1983) *Tales Out of School: consumers' views of British education*. London: Routledge and Kegan Paul.

Whitty, G., Wisby, E. and Diack, A. (2007) *Real Decision-making in Action? School councils in action*. London: Institute of Education.

3 Children's lives outside school and their educational impact

Berry Mayall

INTRODUCTION

The Cambridge Primary Review was carried out in the context of a number of theoretical and policy-relevant developments in the study of children and childhood. Whilst Plowden (CACE 1967) could confidently, it seems, rely on Piagetian concepts – a universalist vision of the child as individual explorer programmed to develop through identifiable stages – more recently other ideas within developmental psychology and sociology and the rights movement have come to prominence. All three conceptualise children as active participants in social relations and learning.

Thus psychologists stress that knowledge is actively constructed through social interactions (Goswami and Bryant in Chapter 6 of this volume). Socio-cultural theory focuses on the specificity of the concepts, language and patterns of action that children acquire in their earliest social environments – at home (for example, Bruner 1986); it is fashionable nowadays to study children 'in their cultures', rather than 'the child' in isolation (Greene 1999). We learn that children come to school with varying languages and varying linguistic styles, which may clash with those of the school (Bernstein 1971). We learn about the plurality of children's daily experiences and about cultural variation in the goals of socialisation across the world (Cole 1996; LeVine 2003). In relation to this, Penn (2002) has described and deplored the globalising of Western child-rearing ideas. In England, work on the varying cultural arenas within which children grow up has built on Bourdieu's work and has argued for the necessity for schools to recognise and respond to variation in children's lived experience.

Psychological paradigms which focus on children's own knowledge and perspectives – and which remain the dominant approach to children in England – are complemented by the sociology of childhood, developed over the last 25 years, where children are understood as social agents who contribute to social relational processes and to the construction of their own childhoods (Prout and James 1990; Hutchby and Moran-Ellis 1998b; Mayall 2002). Children are conceptualised as a social group, which contributes to the division of labour in a society, largely through the work they do in pre-schools and schools (Qvortrup 1985). Commentators within this paradigm draw attention to the power that adults hold over children and over childhood itself; to adult responsibilities to enable good childhoods; and to the difficulties adults and children face when adults try to reconcile adult power with respect for children (for example, Shamgar-Handelman 1994). These ideas challenge the idea of the teacher as benevolent but intrinsically superior, responding to the 'needs' and stages of development in their 'pupils'; instead, the educational endeavour is to be seen as a joint enterprise between citizens.

These ideas are further complemented by the growing strength of the children's rights movement. Whilst movements to respect children's rights go back over a hundred years, the 1989 UN *Convention on the Rights of the Child* (UNCRC) has most forcefully promoted these rights, through measures aimed at states' compliance (Franklin 2002). In response, a number of pressure groups have been formed (for example, Children's Rights Alliance). The articles of the Convention stress children's protection, provision and participation rights (the 3 Ps). In England, protection has traditionally been the priority in policy and practice (Hendrick 2003: Chapter 6). Child protection was an urgent priority in late nineteenth century England, in the work of voluntary bodies (such as Dr. Barnardos). After 1945, the welfare state took over many of their protective functions and provision for children has been central to policies. Adult responsibilities to protect and provide for children sit easily within the social history of the country. However, respecting children's participation rights (as outlined in Article 12 of the UNCRC), demands re-conceptualising children as citizens, rather than as objects of adult socialisation agendas (Lansdown 2001). It is notable – and consistent with English social history – that whilst health and welfare services have gone some way to recognising all 3 Ps, in education there has been considerable resistance, bolstered by traditional ideas about teacher-'pupil' relations and coupled with curricula handed down from government. Furthermore, children's citizenship rights in the here and now are not a prime focus of the UNCRC – an omission that encourages neglect of these rights (Freeman 2000), not least in education.

In connection with the above points, I note that over recent years ideas about home-school relations have changed, at least in the research literature. Thus at the outset of the state education system and for many years thereafter, educationalists worked on the assumption that school agendas were 'given'; the question then was how far children achieved within these agendas and how far their parents co-operated. We have a massive literature on how ethnicity, gender and social class help or impede children's academic progress; and on home-school relations (see Ainscow and Muschamp, Chapters 8 and 4 of this volume). There has been less research on the extent to which school staff recognise, respect and respond to what children bring from home and how such response may affect children's achievement within school agendas. Furthermore, school agendas themselves are up for re-consideration. For instance, some parents may challenge school education agendas and practices. Children's learning from new technologies may be in advance of teacher knowledge. And employers' demands of children when they grow up – for instance, flexible, computer-literate workers – may require school to reflect these demands. So whilst how children's learning before school may influence their learning in school is an interesting question, perhaps an equally interesting question relates to responsive behaviour by the school. How far do and should schools respond to and build on what children bring to school?

This point leads on to an undesirable feature of English life nowadays: the problematisation of children – as victims or threats – and of childhood itself. The adult tendency to consider children as inherently problematic goes back a long way (see Jenks 1996: Chapter 1), but reached new heights during the years of Conservative government (1979–97) when politicians responded to the huge increases in child poverty rates (to about 30 per cent) by demonising children and mothers (Pilcher and Wagg 1996). The 'New Labour' government (1997–) lifted some thousands of children out of poverty, although, in terms of justice between generations, it was more successful in reducing pensioner poverty (*The Guardian* 28.3.07: 38). Surveys have told us that childhood is worse in the UK than in other 'advanced' countries, and that our young people aged 11, 13 and 15 agree (Children's Society 2006; UNICEF 2007b), though an Ofsted report claimed that most say they are happy (Mansell 2007; Ofsted 2007a). As the authors acknowledge, there are many problems with the UNICEF data and with interpretation (see also Ansell, Barker and Smith 2007), but the media responded enthusiastically, reporting contentious findings as facts. In the weeks and months following the UNICEF report, *The Guardian* newspaper, for example, posted front-page headlines on the poor, risky and insecure lives of our children, and on bullying (14.2.07; 27.3.07). Politicians raised the game; a Commons select committee called for a national enquiry into bullying; and the Conservative party launched an enquiry into 'lost childhood in Britain' (*The Guardian* 26.3.07: 5); ministers proposed (following ASBOs) to assess every 11-year-old as to the risk of their turning to crime (*The Guardian* 28.3.07: 6). References to the UNICEF findings as fact continued into 2008, with, for example, the New Statesman giving major space to them (7.7.08). Commentators offered two basic causes for the 'facts' of this crisis in child welfare: stress arising from pressure on school-children and inequalities arising from child poverty (Toynbee 2007). The second of these issues is a running theme in this chapter.

A caveat. The remit for this report is to describe and discuss children's out-of-school lives and learning and how these relate to their experiences and the work they do in primary school. This is a huge topic and in most areas of their lives, there is unlikely to be any clear evidence on such links. Research has tended to be on what happens at school, or on what happens outside school, with little attention to linkages. And linkages are hard to prove. Further, to prove (almost) conclusively that there is no evidence of such links would require systematic reviews for each area of children's lives, of the kind carried out at the EPPI-Centre at the Social Science Research Unit, Institute of Education, University of London. For this chapter, given the limited time available and the wide range of topics that seem relevant, I have restricted the enquiry, in the main, to reviews of the literature, hand-searching journals and consulting experts. Whilst, therefore, there may be bias arising from these limitations, these three types of searches provide some triangulation.

This chapter has three main sections. I describe some aspects of children's out-of-school lives and learning firstly before they start school (under-fives); and secondly during the primary school years. Thirdly, I consider evidence for the impact of these lives and learning on activity at school, and for school responsiveness to these.

1 CHILDREN'S LIVES AND LEARNING IN THE PRE-SCHOOL YEARS

Children as social agents at home

Evidence from both psychological and sociological studies indicates that pre-school children are active agents in learning, through interaction with others at home and in the neighbourhood. The data reviewed here is mainly from small-scale studies which have mapped what happens within families, with emphasis on children's engagement and learning (Boulton 1983: Chapter 4; Mayall and Foster 1989; Mayall 1991; Ribbens 1994; Hutchby and Moran, Ellis 1998a; Ribbens Mcarthy and Edwards 2002).

Moral, cultural and cognitive learning

The sociable character of young children's behaviour is obvious to parents, but has also been studied by social scientists. In their early months, children respond to and initiate interaction with parents and siblings, imitate others' actions and interact playfully, angrily or aggressively (Alderson 2008: Chapter 2). Judy Dunn and colleagues (1988) studied children's learning at home (under-threes). She notes (1988: 5) that children quickly learn at home that when you take part in family dramas as actor, victim or observer, you also have to put the case from a particular perspective. Through interactions within the family, children learn about justice, fair shares, and other people's viewpoints. More generally, psychologists argue that children are 'prepared' to make moral judgments, in the same way as they are prepared, or programmed, to speak; and that feelings are the basis for moral development (Kagan 1986: xiii). 'Morality is a fundamental, natural and important part of children's lives from the time of their first relationships' (Damon 1990: 1). Brooker's study (2002) of children's learning at home, and how far this is acknowledged and responded to in school, is one of the few studies to span home and school experience and learning (see also Jackson 1979; Mayall 1994). Following Rogoff (1990), she notes that children learn by apprenticeship – they copy and later take on activities more autonomously. What they are learning is 'local knowledge' – what is relevant to their family and its cultural and moral norms and practices; this knowledge may or may not be resonant with 'official knowledge' – as Bernstein put it. It may or may not be recognised by school. Part of learning the moral codes of the family is learning about responsibility. Parents will vary in what they expect of their children here, from being responsible for self-care, or for 'good behaviour' to doing jobs around the home or helping with siblings (Brooker 2002: 49–51).

A critical aspect of what children learn at home is that they are persons. Indeed, parents find through interactions with children that they are not pre-social projects but people now – with their own specific characteristics and preferences. Whilst parents may be expected to 'socialise' their children, these child-adult interactions extend far beyond socialisation paradigms (Thorne 1993). Much of what parents do for and with their children is not future-oriented, but concerned with the present. For some parents children are companions: interesting, supportive, amusing, decision-makers. It can be confidently asserted (at least for England) that children stand more of a chance of respect as a person at home than anywhere else (Neale, Wade and Smart 1998; Neale 2002).

Children both inhabit and learn about the cultural and social worlds of their family. Studies have shown that at home 4-year-olds engage in discussions with adults far more than they do at pre-school (Tizard and Hughes 1984; Carr 2000); these discussions start from topical events – shopping, meeting other people, cooking – and range over the meanings of these events. Children also learn from hearing conversations between adults; these adult narratives, explanatory models and moral interpretations about what is happening locally serve also to tell children about their cultural and moral worlds (Bruner 1990: Chapter 3). Children also engage with media at home – a topic discussed later.

The Effective Provision of Pre-school Education (EPPE) study focused on 2,800 children aged 3 and 4 at entry to pre-school centres and over 300 children with no such experience. Interviews with parents (mostly mothers) indicated a wide range of activities they carry out with their children. From these, seven activities, high rates of which had significant effects on children's achievement at pre-school entry, were chosen: frequency read to, going to the library, playing with numbers, painting and drawing, being taught letters, numbers and songs/poems/rhymes. The researchers called this the home learning environment (HLE) (Melhuish *et al.* 2005). They found that high HLE scores were significantly related to children's achievement in reading and maths. An encouraging finding is that these relationships were much stronger for the HLE index than for parents' socio-economic status (SES) and qualifications. Indeed some who scored low on SES and qualifications scored high on the HLE index and some who scored high, scored low on the HLE index. What parents do is more important than their background (Siraj-Blatchford 2004). However, the study also found that parents communicated with their sons less than with their daughters on the HLE index.

Language

Children from all backgrounds learn speech that is adequate for communicating in the social environment in which they live. Bruner (1990: Chapter 3) refers to recordings of an 18-month to 2-year-old girl soliloquising about daily events – he calls it a drive to understand why things happen; and this drive pushes forward competence in grammatical construction and use of wider vocabulary. Tizard and Hughes (1984) suggest many reasons why children's conversations at home are so long, detailed and complex, far more so than at nursery school. An extensive array of activities takes place in and around the home and these provide food for thought and conversation. Mothers know their children intimately from birth – their interests, knowledge and concerns, so mothers can understand and tap into their children's opening gambits. Mothers have only a small number of children to interact with (compared to teachers). Children generally have a very close relationship with their mother, stay close to her and will share with her their concerns and questions. Margaret Carr (2000) supports these points and, following Rogoff, emphasises that teachers must seek children's own perspectives as a means of bridging the adult-child gap and of co-constructing learning with the children.

Participation in everyday household and neighbourhood activity

Studies of young children's lives (as listed at the start of this section) indicate that children enthusiastically participate in the activities of the home. This may include helping to clean the home, cooking and other food preparation, going shopping, visiting neighbours. The 'people work' that feminists have identified – caring for family members in both practical and emotional ways – is carried out by children too, who may fetch and carry, tidy up, care for and play with siblings, or comfort a sibling or parent. Thus children participate in the division of labour at home – as they do in pre-schools and schools (Mayall 1996: Chapter 4).

Health-related ideas and practices

An important kind of learning at home in the pre-school years is about what are appropriate health practices. Children learn about keeping themselves clean, brushing their teeth, maintaining their health through activity, rest, eating and drinking; restoring their health through resting, being comforted (Mayall 1994). They learn to follow family beliefs and customs in these matters and to take on some responsibility for their own health maintenance (Newson and Newson 1970: Chapter 4). Studies of health promotion within the family have noted that parents vary in how far they allow their children to engage with health-related decisions; some are authoritarian, others negotiate or strike trade-off bargains, and some allow children to decide (Holland, Mauthner and Sharpe 1996; see also Prout 1996).

In summary, evidence from psychologists and sociologists is that children by the age of five have acquired social and moral competence within their family setting. They have acquired a sense of who they are, in relational terms, an identity as a family member. They have learned enough language to function within their family. They are experienced in learning within relations with other children and with adults. They are active participants in family activities. They have acquired health-related knowledge about how to maintain their health.

Children who do not have enabling homes

High rates of relative child poverty continued through the New Labour years (1997–), with 22 per cent nationally and higher rates in some areas, such as London at 35 per cent (Hood 2004; DCSF 2008a). As Muschamp *et al.* show (Chapter 3), poverty severely compromises children's health, wellbeing and capacity to engage with schooling. Whether or not living in poverty, there are perhaps three main groups of children whose life in their early years and at school may be adversely affected by their living conditions: children in bad housing, children not living with parents and children whose parents cannot or will not look after them.

Children in bad housing

A Shelter report (Rice 2006) states that 1.4 million children in England live in bad housing (p. 9) – defined to include homelessness, overcrowding and unfitness. Ethnic minority families and families in poverty are especially likely to live in poor housing (Quilgars 2006). Bad housing is associated with poor experience and attainment in school, but it is not clear whether the housing problem causes difficulties for children, or whether housing problems exacerbate existing problems within the family. Thus children living in bad housing are nearly twice as likely as others not to attend school (some of this is to do with frequent house moves, and poor access to a school place) (Rice 2006: 12). They are nearly twice as likely as other children to leave school without any GCSEs (Rice 2006: 11). Poor housing conditions are associated with poor health in children, which in turn may affect school attendance (*Ibid.*: 21). Quilgars' (2006) review of the literature on health in relation to poor housing indicates poor health, especially respiratory problems, among the children, but she notes that identifying housing as the cause has not been proved.

'Looked after' children

In England (2003), 60,790 children were in the care of the local authority, with most (41,000) fostered, fewer (8,320) in residential accommodation, and 6,400 living with their parents. These children constitute 4.9 per thousand children (under 18s) (Gibbs *et al.* 2005: 204–6). DfES (2005) figures for 2005 give 23,600 0–9 year olds in care, again mostly in foster care. Whilst some ethnic minority groups (Asian families) probably use the care system less than others, 'dual heritage' and disabled children are probably over-represented (Gibbs *et al.* 2005: 218–19). 'Looked after' children have low educational attainment: for while 95 per cent of 16-year-olds gain one or more GCSEs/GNVQs, only 44 per cent of looked-after children do so; and they are less likely to gain A–C grades (13 per cent compared to 62 per cent of all young people) (DCSF 2008b).

Why 'looked after' children do relatively badly at school may relate to 'in care' factors, and/or to family factors. One study of 249 children in the care of six local authorities for over 12 months found that only 44 per cent remained in the same placement for the first 12 months; however, getting reliable and consistent data is difficult (Ward and Skuse 2001). Furthermore, the work parents (especially mothers) do to support and encourage their children throughout their school years is not easily replicated by carers and social workers who do not care for the child throughout those years (see Ward 1995: Chapter 3 for evidence that social workers have low educational expectations for 'looked after' children). Another analysis notes that 'looked after' children originate from the most disadvantaged social groups, characterised by 'family breakdown', poverty, poor parental support, maltreatment and high special educational need – and that these factors are strongly linked to low educational attainment – however this does not absolve local authorities from redressing social disadvantage (Berridge 2006). A Social Exclusion Unit report (2003) somewhat links 'in care' and home factors; it identifies five key reasons for under-achievement in education: instability of placement; time out of school; children lacking help at school with education; children lacking support and encouragement from some carers; children needing more help with emotional, mental or physical health and wellbeing (see also Jackson *et al.* 2003).

Children whose parents cannot or do not care for them

A small proportion of children have parents who, because of ill-health or disability, because of drugs or alcohol problems, or long stressful hours of work, cannot care for their children in ways which encourage and enable them at home and school. Clearly, it is difficult to put figures on these categories, because of definitional problems. For instance, it is alleged that about 50,000 children (under 18) are caring for an ill or disabled parent, providing substantial, regular care (Aldridge and Becker 2002). Another estimate puts it at 175,000 (Smithers 2005). Detailed research has suggested the desirability of considering the contributions, wishes and needs of all the people in a family, rather than simply deploring the inappropriateness of burdening children with caring responsibilities (Banks *et al.* 2001).

Pre-school care and education

This is another large topic and this survey cannot be exhaustive. Since 1997, care-and-education provision for pre-school children has been a government priority. The ten-year strategy for childcare (DfES 2005) sets out plans and aims thus: by March 2006 to reach 65 per cent of under-4s and their families in the 20 per cent most disadvantaged English areas; by 2010 all communities to have children's centres, offering integrated care, health and education, including family support and education. According to the Daycare Trust (2005), in 2005 there was a full-time registered childcare place for half of under-8s in England (compared to one place for every nine under-8s in 1997). This includes minders and nurseries; most of the expansion has been in the private sector. In terms of usage by parents, there was a rise of 10 per cent, from 31 per cent to 41 per cent, between 2001 and 2004, in the number of parents using childcare (Bryson *et al.* 2006).

In practice, the most common kind of childcare parents used was informal – relatives and partners. The Families and Children Study (FACS) shows that where mothers in two-parent families 'worked', partners and parents-in law were the commonest sources of care (27 per cent and 26 per cent respectively); and where the mother in lone-mother families 'worked', parents-in law and other relatives or friends were the commonest (27 per cent and 17 per cent) (Willitts *et al.* 2005). Sylva *et al.* (2007) similarly report that more socio-economically advantaged parents were more likely to use purchased childcare, whereas less advantaged parents tended to use relatives; and children who started in non-maternal childcare before the age of three months were more likely to come from disadvantaged families, whereas children who started non-maternal childcare between four and ten months were more likely to come from advantaged families. The Daycare Trust (2005) has found that many families cannot access 'high quality care' because services are inappropriate, too expensive or not available. It has been noted that the mix of government provided and 'market force' provision means that access is largely determined by ability to pay; and that consistent and substantial intervention at national and local levels is necessary to enable low-middle income families to access good daycare (NatCen 2005). A study of the quality of differing types of childcare for children aged ten and eighteen months, found that observed quality was lowest in nurseries, as compared to childminders, grandparents and nannies, except that nurseries offered more learning activities to the older children; cost was largely unrelated to quality of care, except in childminding, where higher costs were associated with higher quality (Leach *et al.* 2006).

Particular groups who are missing the benefits identified in the EPPE study (see below) are: children of lone parents (Daycare Trust 2007a), disabled children (Daycare Trust 2007b), some ethnic minority children, especially those in some Asian families (Daycare Trust 2007c), children living in workless households, in large families and with student parents, and children of parents working unsociable hours (Daycare Trust 2005) As regards ethnic minority children, it has been found that whilst they tend to enter pre-school with lower scores in pre-reading, they then make more progress than ethnic majority children on this (Siraj-Blatchford 2004). It may be particularly important to convey this message to parents, especially those of Black African, Indian, Pakistani and Bangladeshi origin who, reportedly, cite educational (rather than financial) reasons for using childcare (Bell *et al.* 2005).

As regards part-time provision, a DfES report (2006) said that all 3-and 4-year-olds were now entitled to free early education (12.5 hours per week for 38 weeks of the year), defined to include 'formal' provision in the maintained, private, voluntary and independent sectors, including registered childminder networks. The report claimed that 96 per cent of 3-year-olds and 'virtually all' 4-year-olds were taking up some free early years education (so defined); of 3-year-olds, 38 per cent were in maintained nursery schools and primary schools, with 55 per cent in private and voluntary provision and 3 per cent in independent schools; of 4 year-olds, most (79 per cent) were in maintained nursery and primary schools (DfES 2006). These percentages will include some children who also spend part of the day with other carers, given that many mothers 'work'. The Children's Plan (DCSF 2007) proposed to raise the free early education entitlement to 15 hours and to offer up to 15 hours for 20,000 two-year-olds in the most disadvantaged areas.

The Labour government set out a list of topics which should underpin 3-to 5-year-olds' experiences at educational establishments that receive grant funding (the Foundation Stage (DfES 2000)). This includes maintained, private and voluntary provision. One aim is to create 'a level playing field' for children attending a range of settings (DfES 2006). These topics include personal and social wellbeing and skills; activities designed to promote positive attitudes to learning; opportunities to talk and discuss with each other and with adults; and to explore reading, writing and mathematics. Knowledge and understanding of the world is to be promoted, and also physical and creative development.

Pre-school early education for 3-and 4-year-olds, as practised in playgroups, nursery schools and classes, private and local authority day nurseries and integrated centres, has been studied across England, in the EPPE study (Sylva *et al.* 2003, 2004). Their evidence is that early exposure to quality pre-school is more effective the earlier children start after they reach 2 years old, the higher the quality of the education provided, and amongst children from disadvantaged groups. It seems that regular attendance, sustained over time, leads to particularly positive intellectual development, improved independence, concentration and sociability. Such positive effects, whether children attend for a long or short time, were found to be significantly greater than for children who did not attend. (However, as the authors note, this was not a randomised controlled trial, and non-attenders may differ in various ways from attenders). A key finding is that better quality of provision happens where staff have higher qualifications, staff have leadership skills and there are long-serving staff; where trained teachers work alongside less qualified staff; and where there is strong parental involvement. Clearly, these features are expensive; and, as Sylva has noted (Gold 2006), it is critical for effective service-provision that early years centres are required to have trained teachers on the staff and to provide interlinked care and education. Currently, whilst 80 per cent of staff working with children in primary schools have degrees, only 20 per cent of those working with under-5s do (Morris 2007).

The EPPE children were followed to Year 5 of primary school (Sammons *et al.* 2007). The findings are complex. The quality of the home learning environment continued to relate to reading and mathematics attainment at school. Once this factor was taken into account, the quality of the pre-school experience continued to have a positive effect. School influences became more pronounced in their effects in Year 5, however; effective schools (measured by independent analyses of national assessment results) account significantly for variation in the children's reading and mathematics attainment in Year 5. These good schools compensated for children's early experience in poor quality pre-school provision or for having no pre-school experience at all. The Children's Plan (DCSF 2007: Chapter 4) has responded with plans to improve the qualifications of early years and school staff.

Also important are the studies of the impacts of Sure Start programmes (Melhuish, Belsky and Leyland 2005; National Evaluation of Sure Start [NESS] 2008). The authors were rightly cautious in their interim report, issued only a few months into the interventions and they found only limited, small effects on the 9-month-old children and their families (16,502 families in the first 150 Sure Start areas). The report suggested that the most disadvantaged families (defined as workless households, teenage mothers and lone mothers) were the 'hardest to reach' (or, to put it another way, least likely to use the services offered), whilst slightly more advantaged families, having 'greater human capital', were more likely to use the services. However, by the time the studied children were three-years-old, these differences had, in general, disappeared, which may be because services had improved (NESS 2008). The study also found that, compared to children in other, similar areas, the study children had better social development and there was better parenting and a better home learning environment.

A less encouraging picture is provided by an Ofsted (2007b) report: whilst standards were slowly improving, four in ten of the 27,000 childcare settings inspected were offering only 'satisfactory' or 'inadequate' care, and these nurseries and minders were caring for 215,000 of the 500,000 children involved.

All in all, given these expansions in childcare provision, whilst they are of varying quality, and whilst there are inequalities of access (favouring the well-to-do), primary schools today (compared to ten years ago) are receiving into their care more children with experience of out-of-home care, and therefore more children with experience of the Foundation Stage of the National Curriculum. The later findings of the EPPE study point to continued impacts of the home learning environment, and of high quality pre-school services on children's work in Year 5; the quality of the school itself is influential both in affecting attainment and in compensating for poor or no pre-school experience.

2 ACTIVITIES OUT OF SCHOOL DURING THE PRIMARY SCHOOL YEARS

Family life

Children's right to live with parents is emphasised in the UNCRC (Articles 7, 9 and 11). As noted above, some children do not have the benefits of family life in decent conditions with at least one supportive parent, and this section has to be considered in that context. Most children do live with at least one parent, and there are now several qualitative studies providing information on how primary-age children experience daily life in a range of family types (Ribbens 1994; Pollard and Filer 1996; Moore, Sixsmith and Knowles 1996; O'Brien, Alldred and Jones 1996; Kelley, Mayall and Hood 1993; Morrow 1998; Neale, Wade and Smart 1998; Christensen, James and Jenks 2000; Brooker 2002; Mayall 2002; Harden 2006. I have not given an exhaustive set of references below for each point.)

Some themes emerge across these studies. Home is not only a physical space, but is a social construct, almost synonymous with family. Home/family provides structures and continuity, rooted in past time – for eating, division of labour, routines, celebrations, contacts with wider kin. These structures and continuities in the activities of daily life can be seen as factors leading family members to feeling a sense of solidarity with the members of their family.

These points contextualise the finding that children talk about the home and family as reliable, with parents 'being there' for them. Children tend to be loyal in their talk about family members, especially parents. For children, home is a safe place, especially by contrast with the dangers of public space English children have learned about.

However, these same factors reflect how adults control what happens at home. For children, this control may explain the common finding that children value highly the short spaces/times which are their 'free time', within the home or nearby. Children note that they have no 'free time' at school, where every part of the day, including playtime, is under adult control.

Children's accounts indicate that their position in the family includes *dependence, interdependence* and *independence*. As noted above in respect of pre-school children, children learn moral codes at home. They are both *apprentices* in the social and moral world of the family, and *active participants* in its practices and in constructing their own identities and lives. The moral learning which begins in early childhood includes in the primary-school years increasing responsibilities, for self-care, organising school-related materials, caring for other members of the family, jobs around the home. Primary-age children are competent and experienced family members. As noted in respect of under-fives, it is within the family that children stand the best chance of respect for themselves as people. An important point here is that whilst psychological traditions stress that children move towards independence as moral beings, children themselves propose more complex understandings; they both seek independence and recognise the value of interdependence and reciprocity (Mayall 2002: Chapter 6; Holland *et al.* 2000; Thomson and Holland 2002).

Another theme in children's accounts is that family members, notably mothers, are reliable confidants. Children also, variously, report that other relatives, living close enough for interactive relations to develop, provide support and advice – grandparents, aunts, cousins (Morrow 1998; Mayall 2002). Some children derive great comfort and company from their pets. Mullender's work on children who live with domestic violence (1999; Mullender *et al.* 2003) shows that siblings often provide help, solidarity and comfort.

Relations with brothers, sisters and friends vary widely across families and are characterised by a wide range of feelings and social practices (Morrow 1998), but relational processes with siblings contribute importantly to how children see themselves as people, how they feel and act – their identity, both in the family and in wider social worlds (Edwards *et al.* 2006). This latter study makes the interesting and valuable point, too, that in an England where children are increasingly restricted to the home, older siblings can accompany and safeguard their younger siblings beyond its doors, and thus provide a way for young children to venture into the life of the neighbourhood. Children's accounts also indicate that older siblings will 'stand up for' their younger siblings in public places; and in school playgrounds. Having friends is a necessity at school, as defence as well as companionship, but friendships also allow children some independence from family life, and provide a shelter when life at home is stressful (Moore *et al.* 1996; Mayall 2002).

Coping

The above points contextualise children's comments on how they deal with hard times, including the 'breakdown' of family life. Studies note children's abilities to care for disabled parents and other family members, as well as maintaining their school work (Aldridge and Becker 2002). Children stress the importance of being informed and of participating in decision-making; what matters too is the quality of relationships, including those between adults. In cases where parents separate, continuity is important for children, which allows them 'psychological travelling time' towards the new arrangements, so that they have time to learn to cope (Moore *et al.* 1996: Chapter 9; Neale, Wade and Smart 1998; Piper 1999; Butler *et al.* 2002; Flowerdew and Neale 2003; Hogan *et al.* 2003; Smart 2003). A positive ethic of care – notions of interdependence, responsibility, respect, trust and commitment – can help children manage these transitions (Neale, Wade and Smart 1998: 42).

Food

Concern about obesity and related health problems has increased in recent years (Department of Health 2008) and government proposals to prioritise child obesity (DCSF 2008) include measures to improve school meals and increase time spent in sport and other physical activity at school. There is also current interest in whether nutrition may affect children's school work. A systematic review of the evidence for the effects of nutrition on learning, education and performance at school found no clear evidence. Of the 29 studies located that used a Randomised Controlled Trial (RCT), most were from the USA and none provided conclusive evidence. However, the reviewers assert that, whilst the impact of diet on educational attainment is still under consideration and UK studies are urgently needed, 'the evidence for promotion of lower fat, salt and sugar diets, high in fruits, vegetables and complex carbohydrates, as well as promotion of physical activity remains unequivocal in terms of health outcomes for all school children' (Ells, Hillier and Summerbell 2006: 5; see also NICE 2006 on obesity). Perhaps healthy children work better than unhealthy ones. Another review of studies focused on children with severe dietary deficiencies and asserts that children with iron deficiencies sufficient to cause anaemia are at a disadvantage academically and that their cognitive performance appears to improve with iron therapy. Academic disadvantage has not been found in children with zinc or iodine deficiency, and nor does therapy improve their performance (Taras 2005b).

Work

Old-style child development theory continues to be the dominant popular discourse about children in England (see Woodhead and Faulkner 2008 for discussion). Within this discourse children's contributions to the division of labour are not generally recognised. However, sociological approaches to children and childhood stress children as workers universally throughout history – in households, fields and factories, and nowadays, in Western industrialised countries, mainly at school (Qvortrup 1985). I have noted earlier that children can also be understood as contributors to household welfare, from an early age (Rheingold 1982; Mayall 1994, 2002; Moore *et al.* 1996; Mizen *et al.* 2001). But the psychological idea that activity at school should be seen as part of the socialisation process which turns pre-social young children into competent adult worker-citizens remains influential; and children themselves may accept their low social status as workers. Some children associate work with adults, whose housework and paid work keep the household afloat; other children identify both school work and homework (for school) as work (Mayall 2002: Chapter 5).

Belonging to groups

I have not found much evidence on the extent and character of children's out-of-school organised activities (but see below under 'Leisure, play and sport'). Most qualitative studies of daily life report that many children attend classes in, for instance, dance, music, religion and languages. But I think there is no large-scale data set on prevalence across a range of organised activities. I quote here some data from Woodcraft Folk, Scouts and Guides. Woodcraft Folk estimate that in 2006 about 3,750 children were members in the UK, almost all in England. This is a fall in membership by about a fifth since 2002. Data from Girlguiding UK says that currently one in seven 6-year-olds in the UK belongs to Rainbows, and a quarter of 8-year-olds are Brownies (80,000 girls are Rainbows and 250,000 are Brownies). There is a slight increase in Rainbows membership from 2005–6. As to the junior branch of the scouting movement, data about Cubs says that 132,302 girls and boys belonged in 2006, a decline from 150,108 in 2002. A small-scale study (Wikeley *et al.* 2007) with 26 Year 6 children and 29 Year 9s found that children from more affluent homes tended to belong to a rich and varied range of groups away from the school site, whereas those from poorer homes relied on clubs at school. This difference increased for the older children, and points to cultural and social disadvantages for the poorer children. During their participation in group work, the children enjoyed friendships and learned responsibility and the ability to discuss what they learned.

Leisure, play and sport

Work and leisure

It has been observed that children's lives in England (and in other European countries) have become increasingly 'scholarised' (Qvortrup 2001): that time children spend doing school-related work has increased and their leisure time has consequently decreased (Edwards 2002; Alldred, David and Edwards 2002). English children attend school for six hours a day and are also asked to do homework for school, even in the first years of primary schooling (DfES 1999; Smith 2000). Further, mothers are asked to convert the home into an overtly educational establishment, by helping children with their homework (Edwards and Alldred 2000). Children's time outside formal schooling is increasingly spent under adult supervision in environments which can be described as 'more school'. Thus in order (principally) to facilitate mothers' paid work (and thus decrease family poverty), more children now spend time in 'wraparound childcare': breakfast clubs and after-school care centres (Smith and Barker 2000a, 2000b; Holloway and Valentine 2000; Blatchford and Baines 2006). This expansion has been interpreted as part of a general move to ensure that children are supervised and controlled by adults at all times (McKendrick *et al.* 2000; James and James 2001). It has also been noted, through surveys in 1995 and again in 2006, that children's opportunity for play at school has been progressively reduced to the extent that 'playtimes' have been pushed aside, mainly, as teachers argue, to give more time for the basics of the National Curriculum and to obviate poor behaviour by children at playtimes (Blatchford and Sumpner 1998; Blatchford and Baines 2006). A Daycare Trust study (2008) elicited 88 children's views on attending wraparound childcare: children noted that they were there because of parental work hours; they thought the best things were friendships, doing new fun activities and getting independence from family; a minority said bad things were bullying and feeling scared. They wanted staff to be young, fun, caring and keen to interact with the children.

These developments are accompanied by decreases in children's access to public space. Thus in terms of independent mobility fewer primary-school children (in 1990 as compared to 1970) were allowed, without an adult, to go to school, to go to leisure facilities, and to use public transport (Hillman 1993; see for more recent data Harden 2000; O'Brien *et al.* 2000; Mayall 2002: Chapter 6; Hillman 2006). Parents have reduced their children's opportunities for play in the neighbourhood (under the influence of traffic-danger and 'stranger-danger').

These changes in themselves provide cause for concern – in particular that children should be given opportunities for physical activity and play. This theme has been taken up by the government, which notes that children have a right to play; and that provision of safe playspaces will help children learn social skills, keep fit, and avoid obesity

(DCMS 2006b; DCSF/DCMS 2008). These views and associated interventions come in the wake of the establishment of training courses for pre-school workers, and also the development of a relatively new profession – playworkers, who have to work out how best to relate to children and to enable but not dominate their activities in organised play environments (Brown 2003a and b).

Play

Academic and professional concern about increases in adult control over children's use of time and space is one factor that accounts for moves to promote children's play outside immediate adult control. But deeper factors are implicated too. Sutton-Smith and Kelly-Byrne (1984) propose that psychological interest in play developed in industrialised societies out of distinctions made between 'work' and 'play', adulthood and childhood; in societies where adults are obliged to do clock-controlled work, play becomes idealised and seen as children's principal, valued activity. Play is the work of little children, says D. W. Winnicott.

The idea that children have rights to both education and leisure time, including the right to play, and that they should not be exploited if they also 'work' can be seen as rooted in historical formulations of the proper activities of childhood. The UNCRC both reflects and promotes that view. Article 31 expressly describes children's right to 'rest and leisure, to engage in play and recreational activities appropriate to the age of the child and to participate freely in cultural life and the arts.' In their turn, States Parties must respect and promote these rights.

There has been little public pressure for children's rights to engage in 'cultural life and the arts' outside school. Whilst children generally do learn the cultures of their family and wider kinship structures, the proposition that adults should enable children to engage more broadly with the cultural life of the nation has been low on the agenda, either in general thinking or in social policies and programmes. I give a note later on cultural participation at school. However, increasingly theatres, galleries and museums offer child-friendly activities.

However, and in line with traditional psychological concepts of childhood, there is a huge literature on play, with emphasis on how it helps children develop; play is presented as an important arena for learning cognitively, physically and socially. This mainstream view has been proposed by some very eminent scholars, including Piaget. Play 'is a means ... of learning ... in a less risky situation'; and play also provides an excellent opportunity to try combinations of behaviours that would, under functional pressure, never be tried (Bruner 1976). Anthropologists, folklorists and sociolinguists are more interested in socio-cultural aspects of play, such as the communicative meaning of play in varying contexts. For them, play is particularly important in the years 0 to 12, but it continues through life (Fromberg and Bergen 2006: xv; Smith and Simon 1986). Meanwhile, cultural studies of childhood across the world have drawn attention to varieties of childhoods (Super and Harkness 1986; Cole 1996); across the world children both play and work – for their household's welfare; and learning takes place during children's ordinary activities, including building and maintaining relations with other children and adults. Yet child development textbooks devote much space to play and virtually none to work (Woodhead 2000).

A cautious summary of research evidence suggests that whilst children do seem to learn during play, or perhaps consolidate learning through play, they may (also) learn those things elsewhere (Sutton-Smith 1979). Recent reviews of the literature are similarly cautious (Cole-Hamilton *et al.* 2002; Manwaring and Taylor 2006). There are grave difficulties in proving that play leads to learning: what to include within 'play', how to separate play from other activity (Strandell 2000). We learn from a wide variety of activities and relations, and to single out the effects of play is difficult if not impossible.

A current impetus for critical work on play is precisely the theoretical presentation of children as active agents, who participate in the construction of their own lives and their relations with other people. Studies point to interactions between children and other people as key arenas for learning (Faulkner, Littleton and Woodhead 1998; Greene 1999). As noted earlier, studies have focused on how children make sense of the environments they find themselves in, such as families and childcare centres where they learn local norms and adults' expectations, as well as how to make good relations with each other. It has been argued that children have a right to participate in the structuring and delivery of playspaces – including those at school, and that this participation may encourage their feelings of ownership (Burke 2005; Davis 2007; DCSF/DCMS 2008). As more children spend more time on school premises, both before and after the main school day, the quality of school playgrounds matters more.

Research on the lives of disabled young people, aged 11 to 16 (Barnes *et al.* 2000) found that many problems reported by children and parents were the result of social barriers rather than the impairment. For example, many local playspaces were inappropriate, other children were unfriendly, attendance at a special school led to isolation from other children in the home neighbourhood. Similarly, Lewis *et al.* (2007) in a study of young people aged 9–19 found that they spent most of their out-of-school time at home and had poor opportunities for participating in informal neighbourhood networks with other young people. Unsuitable local facilities, other children's attitudes, adults' perception of the need to accompany their children, and adult fears for their children's safety and welfare were all implicated.

Participation in sport

Sport England (2003a) has studied trends in school-aged children's participation in sport, using data from three surveys (1994, 1999 and 2002). In 2002 (compared to 1994) fewer primary schools were dedicating two or more hours a week of curriculum time to PE. But some schools were compensating for this reduction by offering sports outside school time; thus 41 per cent of children in 2002 took part compared to 31 per cent in 1994. The three sports most popular among children, across all three surveys, are swimming, cycling and football; but involvement in cycling, walking and cricket has declined over the eight years; probably this relates to parental fears for children's safety. In compensation, perhaps, there were small increases in membership of clubs – slightly more primary-aged children belonged to a youth club or similar (55 per cent in 2002 compared to 51 per cent in 1994), and slightly more were members of sports clubs (41 per cent compared to 38 per cent). As to sports and exercise during the summer holidays, whilst 43 per cent of children in 2002 (compared to 42 per cent in 1994) claimed to do ten or more hours a week, a constant small proportion – 8 per cent – did less than an hour a week. Overall, it seems that slightly more children are involved in sports and physical activities nowadays than formerly, but that this takes place, less in free use of the neighbourhood and more in organised spaces.

In this connection, Sport England (2003b) identified an increase in numbers of leisure centres between 1995 and 2002, from 1492 to 1718. On the other hand, the National Playing Fields Association (2005) notes that 45 per cent of playing fields/sports pitches (34,000) in England have disappeared in the 13 years 1992 to 2005.

In summary the case for physical activity, including play, rests on long traditions that it is both natural to children and therefore a good thing and also that it is a means of learning; proving the latter has been difficult. The case can also be made (tentatively) that exercise has health benefits; it may help children be more alert and active in learning (see later). Current trends to restrict children's free activity in the neighbour-hood, coupled with increases in adult control of children's time in school-related environments, provide important contexts for initiatives aimed at offering children better access to time and space where they can act outside immediate adult control. The case for play is reflected in the UNCRC, and promoted by it.

Media

Nowadays virtually all children have acquired some media literacy before they start primary school. Whilst most, but not all, children have experience of stories in books, virtually all will have watched TV extensively and many will have worked – probably with a parent or sibling – on computer games (Marsh and Millard 2000: Introduction). These experiences mean that by the time they enter nursery education they already know a good deal about how a story works (that it has a plot, a beginning, middle and end, that it has characters, that often there is a problem to be resolved, that it may end happily). Children also know there are differing ways of presenting a story; it can be told through pictures – unmediated by words, or there may be a narrator; there may be 'real' people, or cartoon characters, or both; it may present ordinary life familiar to the children, or it may be sited outside the bounds of ordinary life, impossible but fascinating.

During the years when children attend primary school, television will continue to be the most important cultural medium for them at home. And the connection between television and other aspects of children's consumer culture – notably toys, books and videos – is also important. But most children will also interact with computers, again, mainly not for formal learning, but for engaging with popular culture. Varying figures on home ownership are given by varying agencies (Facer *et al.* 2003: Chapter 2); perhaps 75 per cent of children (under-18s) have internet connections in their homes, but family ownership will depend largely on affluence; it is poorer families which currently lack the internet. Family ownership is also related to children's age; a study of 14 UK nurseries found that 40 per cent of children had a computer at home (Siraj-Blatchford and Siraj-Blatchford 2001). Further, access to these technologies will be mediated by children's own wishes and competencies, by parental and family beliefs, negotiations and practices, and also by the siting of the computer (Facer *et al.* 2001; 2003). Children access the internet mainly at home and school; small proportions of children report using the internet elsewhere, for instance in libraries or at friends' houses (Livingstone and Bober 2004). A key point is that these technological resources for learning operate in social environments where children interact with other children and/or with adults. Children's use of computers (for fun and learning) will be mediated by the help ('scaffolding') given by other children and adults.

As the media diversify and interlink, through TV series, games, toys and books, the technologies now available to children are changing their experience, knowledge and social relations, as compared to pre-TV and-computer days (Sefton-Green 2004; Silvern 2006). This point has implications for how schools respond (see later). However, Facer *et al.* (2003: Chapter 9) argue that, although some 'armchair theorists' (p.156) propose (on the basis of speculation) that the new technologies are revolutionising children's lives and identities, detailed analysis of children's daily lives (aged 9–10 and 12–13) suggests that usage varies widely and traditional activities with family and friends are more important. As the newer technologies become commonplace in households, they will take their place alongside, but not dominate the range of family activities (Facer *et al.* 2003: Chapter 4).

3 EVIDENCE ON IF/HOW CHILDREN'S OUT-OF-SCHOOL LIVES AND LEARNINGS ARE RECOGNISED AND INCLUDED WITHIN SCHOOL AGENDAS IN PRIMARY SCHOOL

The question here is does out-of-school experience impact on school work? A complementary question is: does, and should, school respond to and build on children's out-of-school experience? In this section I draw together some evidence on these questions.

I note first that issues about the relations of gender, culture, ethnicity, class, faith and national origin to primary education are dealt with in Chapter 8 (Ainscow *et al.* 2007); and special educational needs in Chapter 9 (Daniels and Porter 2007). Relations between home and school are the main topic of Chapter 4 (Muschamp *et al.* 2007) but to the extent that children's and parents' interests are indistinguishable, I shall consider these briefly. But, as I understand it, my topic is mainly the experience and knowledge that most children acquire at home, and how that relates to school experience.

Home knowledge – its effects on learning at school and school responsiveness

The difficult question whether home knowledge and learning affects progress at school is addressed in Pollard and Filer's (1996) detailed study of five children over three years. The choice of this small number allows them to unravel the complexities of how children and their mothers worked through, more or less successfully, the challenges presented by school. The children, all 'white', came from 'relatively well-off and secure homes' (p. 306) where parents broadly shared the ideologies and practices of the school. Yet the cultures of the five homes varied and factors affecting children's trajectories through school life also varied; these points illustrate the difficulties of research in this area. Children faced two major challenges at school – making relations with other children, and coping with the curriculum – new sorts of learning and new sorts of teaching. The children varied in how successfully they faced these two sets of challenges, depending on the resources they brought to bear.

Ways in which schools can and should respond to children's knowledge acquired at home are explored by Fisher (1996: Chapter 1), using the Vygotskian idea of interactive, guided learning, where the more experienced (teachers) help to move the less experienced (children) onwards in learning. She usefully summarises what is entailed for teachers in their interactions with children. Thus children's learning at home before they go to nursery or school has important elements: children are active in their social and cultural context; they organise their own learning experiences; they use language to learn; and they learn through interaction with others. She argues that these points have clear implications for teachers: schools should provide meaningful and varied resources and experiences; teachers should capitalise on children's interests and knowledge; they should encourage conversations with children; and they should encourage interactions between children and between children and adults. Such a set of principles for schools and teachers can be seen as shifting responsibility and blame away from the home. Rather than conceptualise the home as the source of problems for which the school virtuously attempts to compensate, now the school is to value and build on the ways of learning children bring from home. The author argues that this strategy will help all children, regardless of social class and ethnicity, to achieve (cf. Christensen and Prout 2003).

The moral order of the school

However, other information suggests that this approach may be hard to implement. Reasons for variation in children's achievement may be profoundly rooted in school's social attitudes. Research has pointed to institutional racism in English schools, with teachers having low expectations of ethnic minority children, and failing to respect their linguistic patterns of speech (Ladson-Billings and Gillborn 2004). Furthermore, school agendas and parental views of what school should do may conflict. Some parents may want direct teaching of the basics, others an exploratory, child-based approach. An Ofsted study (2003: paras 64–70) about 6-year-olds in three countries indicated that whilst Finnish and Danish parents broadly agreed with their school that the main agenda was socialisation, English parents varied widely in their views: all wanted their children to enjoy school, but some favoured teaching in the 3Rs and homework (which the schools were providing) whilst others favoured more relaxed socialisation agendas. These varying views mirrored the difficulties the English teachers were having in combining EYFS guidelines with Key Stage 1 agendas.

The study by Brooker (2002), referred to earlier, focuses on children in one reception class, during 1997–98, and describes how these problems work their way through so that by the end of the year children of Bangladeshi origin were doing less well (in school terms) than the other children. Both racism and clashing theories of education were implicated. The teacher did not recognise the competencies they had learned at home and systematically devalued their 'readiness' (in Piagetian formulae) to learn. The school proposed that children were to be autonomous investigators, using a range of classroom resources to demonstrate to the teacher their readiness for more formal learning and teaching. But the Bangladeshi parents had told their children to sit quietly, be obedient and learn to read and write. So not only were the children bewildered by the school's social and physical environment, but the parents devalued what their children were doing at school.

I noted earlier that children by the age of five know a good deal about their family's health beliefs and practices and they monitor and maintain their own health. Very little research has studied relations between children's knowledge and school activities. My own research, in the 1990s, indicated that at school health maintenance was largely removed from children's control and instead lay with the teachers, who decided when children might carry out health-related activities. Staff also decided whether a sickness bid by a child was acceptable, and in some cases when asthmatic children might use inhalers. Children's competence was devalued at school. Standards of provision at many schools were poor – for instance buildings, playspace, food, lavatories (Mayall 1994; Mayall *et al.* 1996). However, since that time, there has been increased interest, sponsored by governments, in promoting healthy schools, mainly through voluntary effort by the schools themselves. A Healthy Schools programme launched in 1999 has encouraged schools to engage in a wide range of activities, and claims that 86 per cent of schools have signed up to a range of projects (Education Guardian 2007). The government has re-instated nutritional guidelines (abandoned by the government in 1980; see Mayall *et al.* 1996: 42). Schools' beliefs and practices will vary, however, and I believe there is no recent research evidence on the impact of children's knowledge on school practices, or on school responsiveness to this knowledge. Deficit models of family health practices may or may not prevail.

More generally, a crucial element in children's experience at school is the school's moral evaluations of them. As noted earlier, studies of children's daily lives indicate that whilst families vary, it is within the family that children stand the best chance of respect for themselves as persons. Studies of children's views of school consistently show that a key theme for children is respect; it is what children most want but find they do not get (Blishen 1969; Cullingford 1991; Mayall 1994; Pollard *et al.* 1994; Alderson 2000; Christensen and James 2001; Burke and Grosvenor 2003). Power relations between state school adults and children have remained virtually unaffected by years of reforms and initiatives. Indeed, current emphasis on competition and testing in the English education system may not only increase stress levels among children, but contribute, for those who do not come top, to their feeling devalued (Butterfield 1993; Davies and Brember 1999). Respect for children's right to express their views in matters that affect them, and to have those views taken seriously into account; their right to freedom of expression, and to seek, receive and impart information and ideas of all kinds – these are enshrined in Articles 12 and 13 of the UNCRC. These rights should be recognised on ethical grounds; and recognition may also help children to continue to value and benefit from their school experience as they get older (Lord and Harland 2000; UNICEF 2007a).

The school as learning community

With the aim of diminishing systematic variations in school achievement relating to home background, an important kind of intervention builds (in some cases implicitly) on the children's social and moral competence when they arrive in school. These interventions focus on how the school can provide collaborative learning environments, within which children are valued and value each other, are clear what the aims of the educational enterprise are, help each other and move forward together (Watkins *et al.* 2000). A recent review of the literature on classrooms as learning communities starts from their basic tenets. 'In a learning community, the goal is to advance collective knowledge and, in that way, support the growth of individual knowledge' (Scardamalia and Bereiter 1996, quoted in Watkins 2005: 43). This literature review indicates that as well as fostering children's happiness at school, the classroom as learning community boosts school achievement. Much of the research comes from the US, but UK practical experiments in changing the school towards a child-focused collaborative learning environment have also demonstrated that it raises achievement (as measured by national tests), as well as increasing happiness (Highfield Junior School 1997; Osler 2000; MacGilchrist and Buttress 2005). This work challenges the argument that the compulsory character of schooling militates against democratic practices in school (Cockburn 1998; Jeffs 2002; Devine 2002).

In this connection, the Ofsted (2003) study comparing 6-year-olds in three countries is instructive. The Danish and Finnish children, who were still (mostly) in pre-schools, were being prepared for school, with emphasis on a collective ethos, social development, co-operation, and respect for each other. Teachers encouraged discussions and collaborative work. In these respects (I note), the schools were building on the social and moral experience and knowledge which the children brought to their pre-school. By contrast, the English children were asked to engage with a more formal competitive curriculum, with emphasis on reading, writing and maths. In terms of academic success, the study notes that there are no simple pointers to what works best; in a comparative study across 31 countries, English children were doing better in the 3Rs at age 6 than the Danes and Finns, and at age 15 were still doing better than students in most countries; but at 15 the Finns outclassed all other countries; and the Danes did rather less well than the English and the Finns.

Teacher recognition of mothers' contributions to their children's education

The work of parents and especially mothers in providing emotional, intellectual and practical support for their children facing the challenges schools present to them has been described (David *et al.* 1993; Mayall 1994; Pollard and Filer 1996; Brooker 2002). Parents can be seen as mediators of the new world of school, and they also provide an emotional, physical and material infra-structure and a known secure base from which the children set out. Pollard and Filer argue (1996: Chapter 11) that teachers should be taught to value the contributions mothers make to their children's education, at home and at school, especially through supporting children's identities, self-confidence and learning.

But though parents – mainly mothers – are held responsible by schools, they lack power and will vary in how far they can negotiate with the school. Factors here are how far school and home share beliefs about school agendas, parents' social and cultural capital, their familiarity with the school system, school beliefs about parents.

The EPPE reports found that in pre-school centres that encouraged high levels of parent engagement in their children's learning, there were more intellectual gains for the children. 'The most effective centres shared child-related information between parents and staff, and parents were often involved in decision-making about their child's learning programme.' More particularly, children did better where the centre shared its educational aims with parents. This enabled parents to engage children at home with activities or materials that complemented those experiences in the Foundation Stage (Sylva *et al.* 2004: vii). An encouraging point here is that 'what parents do is more important than who they are' (as measured by social class or mother's qualifications). So they recommend that both pre-school and school settings should 'support' and educate parents (Sylva *et al.* 2004: 57) so that they can engage in productive relations and activities with their children.

An intervention study by MacGilchrist and Buttress (2005) in five schools in Redbridge also found that it was beneficial to children's learning if parents and children were fully in the know about what the school, using the National Curriculum, said was to be learned and how to learn it. Parents were given clear information about their children's progress as considered against national expectations, so that they could support or 'scaffold' their children's learning (p.107–10). Four of the schools did better than the borough average over two years, in terms of achievement in basic national curriculum topics (English, Maths and Science) (2005: 157).

Play, sport, and cultural activities

It has been noted that giving children opportunities to play in school playgrounds increases children's ability to concentrate on their school work (Pellegrini and Blatchford 2002). These may be only short-term effects; a review of the literature on associations between physical activity and school performance finds short-term effects, for instance on concentration, but long-term improvement of academic performance as a result of physical activity has not been well substantiated (Taras 2005a). However, there are other arguments – including rights-based arguments – in favour of playtime. Teachers think playtime gives children the chance to let off steam, get physical exercise and develop social skills (Blatchford and Baines 2006: 8). Children themselves almost all vote in favour of playtime at school. Work on socio-dramatic play by children in school suggests increases in self-confidence (Smilansky 1990; Turner *et al.* 2004)

Reduced play opportunities have been cited as a contributory factor in childhood obesity, and play opportunities are thought to increase both physical and social/mental fitness, according to the Children's Play Council (2006). Their review of five studies concludes that 'there is clear evidence that primary school children expend more energy per minute in free outdoor play than in any other activity except school PE lessons. They get more exercise during playtime than during the whole day put together'. So, as well as sports, opportunities for active play are important. Schools have to decide how far these playtimes should be adult-structured (Humphries and Rowe 1994) and how far children should be enabled to explore and make sense themselves of the space and the social relations inherent in it.

As regards children's right under Article 31 of the UNCRC to engage in 'cultural life and the arts' in school (as discussed previously), we may note that whilst education in arts topics is listed as part of the National Curriculum it has had considerably lower priority than 'core' topics. However, many schools aim to offer their children a rounded set of experiences, by giving them access to visual arts, music and drama through school trips and through importing arts groups (Downing *et al.* 2003; Turner *et al.* 2004).

Creativity can be seen as a motive force in both the arts and other areas of school activity. The arguments in favour of promoting creativity include helping children excel in work (difficult to prove), raising their self-esteem (Turner *et al.* 2004), preparing them for a future where flexibility, innovativeness and problem-solving will be valued by employers, and providing opportunities to follow their own interests and talents. It has been proposed that creativity can be a powerful contributing factor to achieving the five goals of Every Child Matters (DCMS 2006a). Over the last decade there has been a stream of publications urging the central relevance of recognising and fostering creativity in children at school (for example NACCE 1999; Sefton-Green and Sinker 2000; Roberts 2006). Government responses indicate acceptance of the point that active engagement fosters learning (DfES 2003; DCMS 2006a and b), and its establishment in 2002 of the Creative Partnerships scheme (Ofsted 2006) indicates support for cultural activities for children, both in and out of school (see also Arts Council 2005). In summary, whilst proving links between play, physical activity and school performance is difficult, it seems important on rights grounds (and on grounds of common sense) that primary schools should maintain and promote spaces and times for activity outside the classroom-based curricular activities. Children's active engagement in school activities, using their creativity, is accepted by government in principle, and increasingly in practice.

Media

Does children's engagement with the new media, in their early years and during their primary school years affect their work at school; do and should schools respond to and build on the experience and knowledge that children bring to school? If so, why?

Media-related work at nursery

Before children start primary school, many now go to nurseries and other centres. Nursery education is subject to guidance in the Foundation Stage on learning to use computers and on using them in other areas of the curriculum (QCA 2005). A study of one class, over three months, found no clear impact of children's experience with computers at home on their use of computers at nursery (Brooker and Siraj-Blatchford 2002); the finding that girls of Bangladeshi origin were learning less well at nursery than other children may reflect their low use of computers at home or other social and cultural factors affecting their behaviour. Children's activities round the computer at nursery had positive features: observation indicated five main types of group interaction – the activities supported language development; provoked enjoyable social interactions; led to scaffolding by more experienced children to help the less experienced; led to collaboration; and stimulated play not only round the computer but away from it, afterwards. Ways in which 7-to 8-year-old children 'scaffold' each other's computer-based work are also explored by Yelland and Masters (2007).

Media-related work at primary school

Does primary-age children's knowledge and experience out of school, in itself, make a difference to how they learn at school? A review of studies on the use of ICT (Information and Communication Technology) in teaching and learning about 'moving image literacy' at school found connections between the cultural experience of young people (aged 5–16) and their media literacy; these findings suggest that if the content of the curriculum recognises these cultural experiences then motivation towards high quality work may result, and young people may be enabled to actively determine meaning and to develop social identities in relation to their media cultures (Burn and Leach 2004). A second systematic review of studies on the use of ICT in literature work (CD-ROM story-books, multi-media software packages, interactive computer books) also identified improved student motivation among younger children, among those not initially motivated and among ESL children. This review pointed to the critical importance of the teacher as mediator of the technology, especially through influencing the discourse students use (Locke and Andrews 2004). A more recent study (Valentine, Marsh and Pattie 2005) found very high rates of home computer ownership among children in years 2, 6, 9 and 11 – 89 per cent, but usage of computers at home increased with age. There was a positive association between home use for school work and attainment in maths at years 6 and 9 and with attainment in English and maths at year 11. Children, teachers and parents reported that using ICT at home for school work raised children's confidence and motivation in their school work. But there was also a positive association between children's use of ICT at home 'for fun' and decreases in school attainment. This finding raises questions about the division of children's time at home between school-related activities and other activities (see also Selwyn 1998).

On the issue of school responsiveness, there is some evidence regarding primary and secondary schooling. A systematic review of the use of ICT in literacy learning (over the years 5–16) examined twelve randomised controlled trials (RCTs); these were all 'relatively small'. The evidence reviewed suggests that for the present there is 'little evidence of benefit' (Torgerson and Zhu 2003). A second systematic review of the impact of networked ICT on 5-to 16-year-olds' literacy in English found that the study authors assumed that networked ICT had a positive impact and explored how that impact was made; so the results should be considered as suggestive rather than conclusive (EPPI-Centre 2006). The authors of both of these reviews suggest that more and better studies are needed, and that until such time investment in the new technologies should be deferred.

At a less rigorous but still persuasive level, plenty of books and papers from the mid-1990s onwards offer information and examples about how ICT can be used across the curriculum. In many of the examples given it seems clear that use of ICT was an important factor leading to good quality work; examples are given for literacy, numeracy, science and technology, social and environmental studies and the creative arts (for example McFarlane 1997; Straker and Govier 1997; Grey 2001; Riley 2003; Sutherland 2004).

Article 17 of the UNCRC notes the rights of children to information and material that can be accessed through the mass media. Computer literacy can be seen as a (protection) right for all children, to help them cope with new technologies in their daily and working lives. This right to computer literacy is indeed enshrined in the National Curriculum, from the Foundation Stage onwards. And since ownership of the internet at home is structured by poverty – perhaps 10–15 per cent of children (all ages) do not have it – the school has a duty to compensate for these variations in home-ownership, in order to fit all children for a world where media literacy is important.

Media literacy

A further issue here concerns why (or not) schools should take serious account of children's popular culture – that is, encouraging children to develop critical and creative skills in thinking about and working with the media. Arguments in favour are presented by, for instance, Crook (1996); Marsh and Millard (2000: Chapter 10); Buckingham (2003, 2005). Broadly, they are to do with children's social relations with schooling. Thus:

- To do so respects children as people with knowledge and experience. In particular it respects their provision rights – that school should provide a curriculum that relates to the wider world; their protection rights, in helping them understand and so deal with the media (media education); their participation rights – collaborative, democratic working to make media; and to discuss media (see Merchant 2006). Media literacy work at school can help bridge the gap between children's lives at home and at school.

- Secondly, engaging with popular culture helps motivate children (as the systematic review quoted above found). Children are reported as responding with enthusiasm to teachers' willingness to engage with the cultures children experience at home (for example Greenhough *et al.* 2006: 66).
- Thirdly, children's knowledge of how stories work, derived from TV viewing and computer games, can be harnessed to help them compose their own stories, through multi-media methods (for examples see Rickards 1996; Greenhough *et al.* 2006: 66–69; Bearne and Wolstencraft 2006; Marsh and Millard 2000: Chapter 8).

Factors affecting schools' teaching of media literacy

However, many factors militate against schools taking an active part in media literacy work. First, teachers and schools are locked into national curriculum agendas, with their accompanying tests and competition between schools; this constraint is particularly acute at primary levels. These agendas leave little space for innovation; they emphasise old-style reading and writing (little oral work). Some teachers may not see media literacy as a proper topic for school attention. Some teachers resist the new technologies (Ofsted 2004) and some lack self-confidence in using and teaching media; they have no models from their own experience. Some may find it easier to opt for teaching technical skills, rather than to engage with the wider social dimensions of media use. Technologies are moving ahead so fast that schools cannot (or do not) keep up; there are many products on offer; it is difficult for schools to decide which to invest in; many are complicated and difficult to learn; and may not always work well (Marsh 2003). I also note that teachers (and the education system generally) have traditionally not been good at looking across the whole of children's lives and in thinking constructively about how home and school make up a whole for children.

POLICY, PRACTICE AND RESEARCH ISSUES

The government has a duty to respect children's protection, provision and participation rights. Part of this work is to counterbalance media hype which problematises and demonises children and childhood. Government should give high priority to reducing child poverty and to raising the social status of children, notably through recognition of children as the central resource for the future of the country.

If children's proper place up to age 5 is to be in 'early years' provision, then government should work towards a properly trained workforce, across the range of provision; and towards eliminating financial barriers to access.

Evidence from modern psychological, sociological and rights perspectives indicates the relevance of building on children's experiential knowledge. The education service should consider how to respond to and build on what children bring to school.

The above has implications specifically for the teaching profession – how to balance their duty to deliver the curriculum required by the government with the desirability of recognising, respecting and incorporating into school agendas the knowledge and experience that children acquire out of school. It may be that returning to earlier models in English education which assigned more autonomy to teachers (as in Nordic models) could help to deal with this dilemma.

Research on children's ideas about home suggests that children conceptualise their home as a private place, which offers some scope for 'free time'; many children see clear boundaries between home and school. As children find that more of their time is 'school time', their protective stance towards their home may increase. Whilst current moves to increase 'parental involvement' and to construct the home as a school-related environment may be productive in some ways, they may be counter productive if children – and their parents – resist them.

The scholarisation of childhood presents parents with dilemmas: how far to protect children from its incursions and how far to help them engage with its agendas. Parents have an important function in helping their children to have some free time. One issue here is whether and how far parents and their children consider use of the new technologies as constituting one kind of free time.

There is a long-running dilemma about parents as supporters of children's education, at home and school. Social policies may aim to educate parents in 'parenting skills' and in so doing may improve parenting, but also may imply that some parents are not doing well enough. This problem is exacerbated by two-faced thinking about mothers. For whilst mothers do most of the work for their children and are deemed responsible for outcomes, they are also a common target for denigration. In this respect, emphasis on parental support may inadvertently increase inequalities for children in access to education.

Democracy in schools is another important issue for policy, practice and research. Anti-democratic practices are likely to be challenged by children, especially as they get older, and not least to the extent that they have learned at home that democratic practices between children and adults are possible. Examples referred to earlier strongly suggest that within schools, and within the National Curriculum, teachers have found ways to respect children's participation rights. However a loosening of government control of the curriculum to allow teachers more scope for decisions about how best to work with children might help.

Finally, this chapter points to gaps in knowledge. I suggest a research programme of studies considering relations between children's out-of-school and school lives.

ACKNOWLEDGMENTS

I should like to express my gratitude to many who have offered guidance and information in this work: Robin Alexander, Liz Brooker, David Buckingham, Liesbeth de Block, Eva Lloyd, Jo Garcia, Ted Melhuish, Ginny Morrow, Peter Moss, Ann Oakley, Helen Penn, Sylvia Potter, Gillian Pugh, Iram Siraj-Blatchford and Kathy Sylva. I apologise to anyone whose work I have omitted to mention.

REFERENCES

Ainscow, M., Conteh, J., Dyson, A. and Gallanaugh, F. (2007) *Children in Primary Education: demography, culture, diversity and inclusion* (Primary Review Research Survey 5/1). Cambridge: University of Cambridge Faculty of Education. (Chapter 8 of this volume.)

Alderson, P. (2000) 'School students' views on school councils and daily life at school', *Children and Society* 14: 121–34.

——(2008) *Young Children's Rights: exploring beliefs, principles and practice.* 2nd edition. London: Jessica Kingsley.

Aldridge, J. and Becker, S. (2002) 'Children who care: rights and wrongs in debate and policy on young carers', in B. Franklin (Ed) *The New Handbook of Children's Rights: comparative policy, and practice.* London: Routledge.

Alldred, P., David, M. and Edwards, R. (2002) 'Minding the gap: children and young people negotiating relations between home and school', in R. Edwards (Ed) *Children, Home and School*. London: Routledge Falmer.

Ansell, N., Barker, J. and Smith, F. (2007) 'UNICEF: "Child Poverty in Perspective" report: a view from the UK', *Children's Geographies* 5(3): 325–30.

Arts Council England (2005) *Children, Young People and the Arts*. London: Arts Council.

Banks, P., Cogan, N., Deeley, S., Hill, M., Kiddell, S. and Tisdall, K. (2001) 'Seeing the invisible: children and young people affected by disability', *Disability and Society* 16(6): 77–814.

Barnes, C., Corker, M., Cunningham-Burley, S., Davis J., Priestley, M., Shakespeare, T. and Watson, N. (2000) *Lives of Disabled Children*. Research Briefing 8. Swindon: Economic and Social Research Council.

Bearne, E. and Wolstencraft, H. (2000) 'Playing with texts: the contribution of children's knowledge of computer narratives to their story-writing', in J. Marsh and E. Millard (Eds) *Literacy and Popular Culture: using children's culture in the classroom*. London: Paul Chapman Publishing Ltd.

Bell, A., Bryson, C., Barnes, M. and O'Shea, R. (2005) *Use of Childcare among Families from Minority Ethnic Backgrounds*. London: DfES.

Bernstein, B. (1971) *Class, Codes and Control Vol. 1: theoretical studies towards sociology of language*. London: Routledge and Kegan Paul.

Berridge, D. (2006) 'Theory and explanation in child welfare: education and looked-after children', *Child and Family Social Work* 12: 1–10.

Blatchford, P. and Baines, E. (2006) *A Follow-up National Survey of Breaktimes in Primary and Secondary Schools*. Final report to the Nuffield Foundation. London: Institute of Education.

Blatchford, P. and Sumpner, C. (1998) 'What do we know about breaktime? Results from a national survey of breaktime and lunchtime in primary and secondary schools', *British Educational Research Journal* 24: 79–94.

Blishen, E. (1969) *The School That I'd Like*. Harmondsworth: Penguin.

Boulton, M.G. (1983) *On Being a Mother: a study of women with pre-school children*. London and New York: Tavistock Publications.

Brooker, E. and Siraj-Blatchford, J. (2002) '"Click on Miaow!" How children aged 3 and 4 experience the nursery computer', *Contemporary Issues in Early Childhood* 3(2): 251–72.

Brooker, L. (2002) *Starting School: young children learning culture*. Buckingham: Open University Press.

Brown, F. (2003) *Play Theories and the Value of Play*. London: National Children's Bureau.

——(2003) 'Compound flexibility: the role of playwork in child development', in F. Brown (Ed) *Playwork: theory and practice*. Buckingham: Open University Press.

Bruner, J.S. (1976) 'The nature and uses of immaturity', in J.S. Bruner, A. Jolly and K. Sylva (Eds) *Play: its role in development and evolution*. Harmondsworth: Penguin.

——(1986) *Actual Minds, Possible Worlds*. London: Harvard University Press.

——(1990) *Acts of Meaning*. Cambridge, MA and London: Harvard University Press.

Bryson, C., Kazimirski, A. and Southwood, A. (2006) *Childcare and Early Years Provision: a study of parents' use, views and experiences*. London: National Centre for Social Research.

Buckingham, D. (2003) *Media Education: literacy, learning and contemporary culture*. Cambridge: Polity Press.

——(2005) *Schooling the Digital Generation: popular culture, the new media and the future of education*. London: Institute of Education.

Burke, C. (2005) 'Play in focus: children researching their own spaces and places for play', *Children, Youth and Environments* 15(1): 27–53.

Burke, C. and Grosvenor, I. (2003) *The School I'd Like*. London: RoutledgeFalmer.

Burn, A. and Leach, J. (2004) 'A systematic review of the impact of ICT in the learning of literacies associated with moving image texts in English, 5–16', in *Research Evidence in Education Library*. London: Institute of Education, University of London.

Butler, I., Scanlan, L., Robinson, M., Douglas, G. and Murch, M. (2002) 'Children's involvement in their parents' divorce: implications for practice', *Children and Society* 16(2): 89–102.

Butterfield, S. (1993) *Pupils' Perceptions of National Assessment: implications for outcomes.* London: Nuffield Education.

CACE (1967) *Children and Their Primary Schools: a report of the Central Advisory Council for Education (England)* (The Plowden Report). London: HMSO.

Carr, M. (2000) 'Seeking children's perspectives about their learning', in A.B. Smith, N.J. Taylor and M.M. Gallop (Eds) *Children's Voices: research, policy and practice.* New Zealand: Longman.

Children's Play Council (2006) *The Role of Play in Healthy Schools. Briefing paper.* London: National Children's Bureau.

Children's Society (2006) *Good Childhood? A question for our times.* London: The Children's Society.

Christensen, P., James, A. and Jenks, C. (2000) 'Home and movement: children constructing family time', in S.L. Holloway and G. Valentine (Eds) *Children's Geographies: playing, living, learning.* London: Routledge.

Christensen, P. and James, A. (2001) 'What are schools for? The temporal experience of schooling', in L. Alanen and B. Mayall (Eds) *Conceptualising Child-Adult Relations.* London: RoutledgeFalmer.

Christensen, P. and Prout, A. (2003) 'Children, place, space and generation', in B. Mayall and H. Zeiher (Eds) *Childhood in Generational Perspective.* London: Institute of Education.

Cockburn, T. (1998) 'Children and citizenship in Britain', *Childhood* 5(1): 99–117.

Cole, M. (1996) *Cultural Psychology.* Cambridge, MA: Harvard University Press.

Cole-Hamilton, I., Harrop, A. and Street, C. (2002) *Making the Case for Play: gathering the evidence.* London: National Children's Bureau.

Crook, C. (1996) 'Schools of the future', in T. Gill (Ed) *Electronic Children.* London: National Children's Bureau.

Cullingford, C. (1991) *The Inner World of the School.* London: Cassell.

Damon, W. (1990) *The Moral Child: nurturing children's natural moral growth.* New York: The Free Press.

Daniels, H. and Porter, J. (2007) *Learning Needs and Difficulties among Children of Primary School Age: definition, identification, provision and issues* (Primary Review Research Survey 5/2). Cambridge: University of Cambridge Faculty of Education. (Chapter 9 in this volume.)

David, M., Edwards, R., Hughes, M. and Ribbens, J. (1993) *Mothers and Education: inside out.* London: Macmillan.

Davies, J. and Brember, I. (1999) 'Reading and mathematics attainments and self-esteem in Years 2 and 6: an eight-year cross-sectional study', *Educational Studies* 25(2): 145–57.

Davis, L. (2007) *Primary Review: evidence submitted by Play England.* London: Play England.

Daycare Trust (2005) *Childcare for All? Progress report 2005.* London: Daycare Trust.

——(2007a) *Listening to Lone Parents about Childcare.* London: Daycare Trust.

——(2007b) *Listening to Parents of Disabled Children about Childcare.* London: Daycare Trust.

——(2007c) *Listening to Black and Minority Ethnic Parents about Childcare.* London: Daycare Trust.

——(2008) *Listening to Children about Childcare.* London: Daycare Trust.

Delpit, L. (1990) 'The silenced dialogue: power and pedagogy in educating other people's children', in N. Hidalgo, C. McDowell and E. Siddle (Eds) *Facing Racism in Education.* Cambridge, MA: Harvard University Press.

Department for Children, Schools and Families (DCSF) (2007) *The Children's Plan: building brighter futures.* London: DCSF.

DCSF (2008a) 'Ministers meet key players across London to tackle child poverty', Press release 14.05.08. London: DCSF.

——(2008b) '£56 million government fund for children in care to get personal tutors, homework support and theatre trips', Press release 28.05.08. London: DCSF.

DCSFs / Department of Culture, Media and Sport (DCMS) (2008) *Fair Play: a consultation on the play strategy*. London: DCSF/DCMS.

DCMS (2006a) *Government Response to Paul Robert's Report on Nurturing Creativity in Young People*. London: DCMS.

——(2006b) *Time for Play*. London: DCMS.

Department for Education and Science (DfES) (1999) *Homework: guidelines for primary and secondary schools*. London: DfES.

DfES (2000) *Aims for the Foundation Stage*. London: DFES.

——(2003) *Excellence and Enjoyment: a strategy for primary schools*. London: DfES.

——(2005) *Ten-Year Strategy for Childcare: guidance for local authorities*. London: DfES.

——(2006) *Provision for Children Under 5 Years of Age in England – January 2006*. London: DfES.

Devine, D. (2002) 'Children's citizenship and the structuring of adult-child relations in the primary school', *Childhood* 9(3): 303–20.

Downing, D., Johnson, F. and Kaur, S. (2003) *Saving a Place for the Arts? A survey of the arts in primary schools in England*. Slough: National Foundation for Educational Research.

Dunn, J. (1988) *The Beginnings of Social Understanding*. Oxford: Blackwells.

Education Guardian (2007) 'Healthier schools', *Education Guardian special supplement*, 27.02.07. London: The Guardian.

Edwards, R. (2002) 'Introduction: conceptualising relationships between home and school in children's lives', in R. Edwards (Ed) *Children, Home and School: regulation, autonomy or connection*. London: RoutledgeFalmer.

Edwards, R. and Alldred, P. (2000) 'A typology of parental involvement in education centring on children and young people: negotiating familialisation, institutionalisation and individualisation', *British Journal of Sociology of Education* 21(3): 435–55.

Edwards, R., Hadfield, L., Lucey, H. and Mauthner, M. (2006) *Sibling Identity and Relationships: sisters and brothers*. London: Routledge.

Ells, L.J., Hillier, F.C. and Summerbell, C.D. (2006) *A Systematic Review of the Effect of Nutrition, Diet and Dietary Change on Learning, Education and Performance of Children of Relevance to UK Schools*. Teesside: School of Health and Social Care, University of Teesside.

EPPI-Centre (2006) 'A systematic review of the impact of networked ICT on 5–16 year olds' literacy in English', in *Research Evidence in Education Library*. London: EPPI-Centre, Social Science Research Unit, Institute of Education, University of London.

Facer, K., Furlong, J., Furlong, R. and Sutherland, R. (2001) 'Home is where the hardware is: young people, the domestic environment and "access" to new technologies', in I. Hutchby and J. Moran-Ellis (Eds) *Children, Technology and Culture: the impacts of technologies in children's everyday lives*. London: RoutledgeFalmer.

——(2003) *Screen Play: children and computing in the home*. London: RoutledgeFalmer.

Faulkner, D., Littleton, K. and Woodhead, M. (Eds) (1998) *Learning Relationships in the Classroom*. London: Routledge.

Fisher, J. (1996) *Starting from the Child?* Buckingham: Open University Press.

Flowerdew, J. and Neale, B. (2003) 'Trying to stay apace: children with multiple challenges in their post-divorce lives', *Childhood* 10(2): 147–62.

Franklin, B. (2002) 'Children's rights and media wrongs: changing representations of children and the developing rights agenda', in B. Franklin (Ed) *The New Handbook of Children's Rights*. London: Routledge.

Freeman, M. (2000) 'The future of children's rights', *Children and Society* 14(4): 277–93.

Fromberg, D.P. and Bergen, D. (Eds) (2006) *Play from Birth to Twelve: contexts, perspectives and meanings*. Second edition. New York and London: Routledge.

Gibbs, I., Sinclair, I. and Stein, M. (2005) 'Children and young people in and leaving care', in J. Bradshaw and E. Mayhew (Eds) *The Wellbeing of Children in the UK*. London: Save the Children.

Gold, K. (2006) 'Sure start, sure finish', *Education Guardian*, 21.11.06: 13.

Goswami, U. and Bryant, P. (2007) *Children's Cognitive Development and Learning* (Primary Review Research Survey 2/1a). Cambridge: University of Cambridge Faculty of Education. (Chapter 6 in this volume).

Greene, S. (1999) 'Child development: old themes, new developments', in M. Woodhead, D. Faulkner and K. Littleton (Eds) *Making Sense of Social Development*. London: Routledge.

Greenhough, P., Yee, W.C., Andrews, J., Feiler, A., Scanlan, M. and Hughes, M. (2006) 'Mr Naughty Man: popular culture and children's literacy learning', in J. Marsh and E. Millard (2006) *Popular Literacies, Childhood and Schooling*. London: Routledge.

Grey, D. (2001) *The Internet in School*. London: Continuum.

The Guardian (2007) 'British children: poorer, at greater risk and more secure', 14 February; 'Cameron joins Willetts in lost childhood campaign' 26 March; 'Bullying: calls for national inquiry', 27 March; 'Every child to be screened for risk of turning criminal under Blair justice plan', 28 March; 'Poverty: One step back', 28 March.

Harden, J. (2000) 'There's no place like home: the public/private distinction in children's theorizing of risk and safety', *Childhood* 7(1): 43–59.

Hendrick, H. (2003) *Child Welfare: historical dimensions, contemporary debate*. Bristol: Policy Press.

HM Treasury and DfES (2007) *Policy Review of Children and Young People – a discussion paper*. London: HM Treasury.

Highfield Junior School (1997) *Changing our School: promoting positive behaviour*. Hampshire: Highfield School and Institute of Education, University of London.

Hillman, M. (1993) 'One false move: a study of children's independent mobility', in M. Hillman (Ed) *Children, Transport and the Quality of Life*. London: Policy Studies Institute.

——(2006) 'Children's rights, adults' wrongs', *Children's Geographies* 4(1): 61–68.

Hogan, D., Halpenny, A.-M. and Greene, S. (2003) 'Change and continuity after parental separation: children's experiences of family transition in Ireland', *Childhood* 10(2): 163–80.

Holland, J., Mauthner, M. and Sharpe, S. (1996) 'Family matters: communicating health messages in the family', in C. Hogg, R. Barker and C. McGuire (Eds) *Health Promotion and the Family*. London: Health Education Authority.

Holland, J., Thomson, R., Henderson, S., McGrellis, S. and Sharpe, S. (2000) 'Catching on, wising up and learning from your mistakes: young people's accounts of moral development', *International Journal of Children's Rights* 8(3): 271–94.

Holloway, S.L. and Valentine, G. (2000) 'Children's geographies and the new social studies of childhood', in S.L. Holloway and G. Valentine (Eds) *Children's Geographies: playing, living, learning*. London: Routledge.

——(2003) *Cyberkids*. London: RoutledgeFalmer.

Hood, S. (2004) *The State of London's Children Report*. London: Greater London Authority.

Humphries, S. and Rowe, S. (1994) 'The biggest classroom', in P. Blatchford and S. Sharp (Eds) *Breaktime and the School: understanding and changing playground behaviour*. London: Routledge.

Hutchby, I. and Moran-Ellis, J. (Eds) (1998a) *Children and Social Competence: arenas of action*. London: Falmer Press.

Hutchby, I. and Moran-Ellis, J. (1998b) 'Situating children's social competence', in I. Hutchby and J. Moran-Ellis *Children and Social Competence: arenas of action*. London: Falmer Press.

Jackson, B. (1979) *Starting School*. London: Croom Helm.

Jackson, S., Ajayi, S. and Garvey, M. (2003) *By Degrees: the first year, from care to university*. London: National Children's Bureau.

James, A.L. and James, A. (2001) 'Tightening the net: children, community and control', *British Journal of Sociology* 52(2): 211–28.

Jeffs, T. (2002) 'Schooling, education and children's rights', in B. Franklin (Ed) *The New Handbook of Children's Rights*. London: Routledge.

Jenks, C. (1996) *Childhood*. London: Fontana.

Kagan, J. (1986) 'Introduction', in J. Kagan and S. Lamb (Eds) *The Emergence of Morality in Young Children*. Chicago: University of Chicago Press.

Kelley, P., Mayall, B. and Hood, S. (1993) 'Children's accounts of risk', *Childhood* 4(3): 305–24.

Klugman, E. and Smilansky, S. (Eds) (1990) *Children's Play and Learning: perspectives and policy implications*. New York and London: Teachers College, Columbia University.

Ladson-Billings, G. and Gillborn, D. (Eds) (2004) *RoutledgeFalmer Reader in Multicultural Education*. London and New York: RoutledgeFalmer.

Lansdown, G. (2001) 'Children's welfare and children's rights', in P. Foley, J. Roche and S. Tucker (Eds) *Children in Society: contemporary theory, policy and practice*. Buckingham: Open University Press.

Leach, P., Barnes, J., Malmberg, L.-E., Sylva, K., Stein, A. and the FCCC team (2006) 'The quality of different types of child care at 10 and 18 months: a comparison between types and factors related to quality', *Early Child Development and Care* 178(2): 177–209.

LeVine, R.A. (2003) *Childhood Socialisation: comparative studies of parenting, learning and educational change*. Hong Kong: University of Hong Kong.

Lewis, A., Parsons, S. and Robertson, C. (2007) *My School, My Family, My Life: telling it like it is*. School of Education, University of Birmingham.

Livingstone, S. and Bober, M. (2004) *Children Go Online: surveying the experiences of young people and their parents*. E-Society: Innovative Research on the Digital Age.

Locke, T. and Andrews, R. (2004) 'A systematic review of the impact of ICT on literature-related literacies in English 5–16', in Research Evidence in Education Library. London: EPPI-Centre, Social Science Research Unit, Institute of Education, University of London.

Lord, P. and Harland, J. (2000) *Pupils' Experiences and Perspectives of the National Curriculum: research review*. London: Qualifications and Curriculum Authority.

McFarlane, A. (1997) *Information Technology and Authentic Learning*. London: Routledge.

MacGilchrist, B. and Buttress, M. (2005) *Transforming Learning and Teaching*. London: Paul Chapman Publishing.

McKendrick, J., Bradford, M. and Fielder, A. (2000) 'Time for a party!: making sense of the commercialisation of leisure space for children', in S.L. Holloway and G. Valentine (Eds) *Children's Geographies: playing, living, learning*. London: Routledge.

Mansell, W. (2007) 'Pupils *are* happy, says Ofsted poll', *Times Educational Supplement*, 23.2.07: 5.

Manwaring, B. and Taylor, C. (2006) *The benefits of play and playwork*, Birmingham: The Community and Youth Workers' Union, and Skills Active.

Marsh, J. (2003) 'One-way traffic? Connections between literacy practices at home and in the nursery', *British Education Research Journal* 29(3): 369–82.

Marsh, J. and Millard, E. (2000) *Literacy and Popular Culture: using children's culture in the classroom*. London: Paul Chapman Publishing Ltd.

Marsh, J. and Millard, E. (Eds) (2006) *Popular Literacies, Childhood and Schooling*. London: Routledge.

Mayall, B. (1991) 'Childcare and childhood', *Children and Society* 4(4): 374–85.

——(1994) *Negotiating Health: children at home and primary school*. London: Cassell.

——(1996) *Children, Health and the Social Order*. Buckingham: Open University Press.

——(2002) *Towards a Sociology for Childhood: thinking from children's lives*. Buckingham: Open University Press.

Mayall, B. and Foster, M.-C. (1989) *Child Health Care: living with children, working for children*. Oxford: Heinemann.

Mayall, B., Bendelow, G., Barker, S., Storey, P. and Veltman, M. (1996) *Children's Health in Primary School*. London: Falmer.

Melhuish, E., Belsky, J. and Leyland, A. (2005) *Early Impacts of Sure Start Local Programmes on Children and Families*. London: HMSO.

Merchant, G. (2006) 'A sign of the times: looking critically at popular digital writing', in J. Marsh and E. Millard (Eds) *Popular Literacies, Childhood and Schooling.* London: Routledge.

Mizen, P., Pole, C. and Bolton, A. (Eds) (2001) *Hidden Hands: international perspectives on children's work and labour.* London: RoutledgeFalmer.

Moore, M., Sixsmith, J. and Knowles, K. (1996) *Children's Reflections on Family Life.* London: Falmer.

Morris, E. (2007) 'Schools alone cannot sort out deprivation', *Opinion: Education Guardian*, 27.3.07: 4.

Morrow, V. (1998) *Understanding Families: children's perspectives.* London: National Children's Bureau.

Mullender, A. (Ed) (1999) *We are a Family: sibling relationships in placement and beyond.* London: British Agencies for Adoption and Fostering.

Mullender, A., Kelly, L., Hague, G., Malos, E. and Imam, U. (2003) '"Could have helped but they didn't": the formal and informal support systems experienced by children living with domestic violence', in C. Hallett and A. Prout (Eds) *Hearing the Voices of Children: social policy for a new century.* London: RoutledgeFalmer.

Muschamp, Y., Wikeley, F., Ridge, T. and Balarin, M. (2007) *Parenting, Caring and Educating* (Primary Review Research Survey 7/1). Cambridge: University of Cambridge Faculty of Education. (Chapter 4 in this volume).

National Advisory Committee on Creative and Cultural Education (NACCCE) (1999) *All Our Future: creativity, culture and education.* London: NACCCE.

National Evaluation of Sure Start (NESS) (2008) *The Impact of Sure Start Programmes on Three-Year-Olds and their Families.* London: Birkbeck College, University of London.

National Centre for Social Research (NatCen) (2005) *Local Childcare Markets.* London: NatCen.

National Playing Fields Association (NPFA) (2005) 'Lost–34,000 playing fields', *NPFA Press Release August 2005.* London: NPFA.

Neale, B. (2002) 'Dialogues with children: children, divorce and citizenship', *Childhood* 9(4): 455–76.

Neale, B., Wade, A. and Smart, C. (1998) *'I just get on with it': children's experiences of family life following parental separation or divorce.* University of Leeds: Centre for Research on Family, Kinship and Childhood.

New Statesman journal. (2008) 'Schools should not be stressing children' (7.7.2008: 12–13); 'British childhood: Our children need a new deal' (pp. 26–28).

Newson, J. and Newson, E. (1970) *Four Years Old in an Urban Community.* Harmondsworth: Pelican.

National Institute for Health and Clinical Excellence (NICE) (2006) *Obesity: the prevention, identification, assessment and management of overweight and obesity in adults and children.* London: NICE.

O'Brien, M., Alldred, P. and Jones, D. (1996) 'Children's constructions of family and kinship', in J. Brannen and M. O'Brien (Eds) *Children in Families: research and policy.* London: Falmer Press.

O'Brien, M., Jones, D., Sloan, D. and Rustin, M. (2000) 'Children's independent mobility in the urban public realm', *Childhood* 7(3): 253–77.

Ofsted (2003) *The Education of Six-Year-Olds in England, Denmark and Finland: an international comparative study. HMI no. 1660.* London: Ofsted.

——(2004) *ICT in Schools: the impact of government initiatives five years on.* London: Office for Standards in Education.

——(2006) *Creative Partnerships: initiative and impact.* London: Ofsted.

——(2007a) *TellUs2.* London: Ofsted.

——(2007b) *Getting on Well: enjoying, achieving and contributing.* London: Ofsted.

Osler, A. (Ed) (2000) *Citizenship and Democracy in Schools: diversity, identity, equality.* Stoke-on-Trent: Trentham Books.

Pellegrini, A. and Blatchford, P. (2002) 'Time for a break', *The Psychologist* 15(2): 60–62.

Penn, H. (2002) 'The World Bank's view of early childhood', *Childhood* 9(1): 119–32.

Pilcher, J. and Wagg, S. (1996) *Thatcher's Children: politics, childhood and society in the 1980s and 1990s*. London: Falmer.

Piper, C. (1999) 'The wishes and feelings of the children', in S.D. Sclater and C. Piper (Eds) *Undercurrents of Divorce*. Aldershot: Ashgate.

Pollard, A., Broadfoot, P., Croll, P., Osborn, M. and Abbott, D. (1994) *Changing English Primary Schools? The Impact of the Education Reform Act at Key Stage One*. London: Cassell.

Pollard, A. with Filer, A. (1996) *The Social World of Children's Learning*. London: Cassell.

Prout, A. (1996) 'Family beliefs and health promotion', in C. Hogg, R. Barker and C. McGuire (Eds) (1996) *Health Promotion and the Family*. London: Health Education Authority.

Prout, A. and James, A. (1990) 'A new paradigm for the sociology of childhood? Provenance, promise and problems', in A. James and A. Prout (Eds) *Constructing and Reconstructing Childhood: contemporary issues in the sociological study of childhood*. London: Falmer Press.

Qualifications and Curriculum Authority (QCA) (2000) *Curriculum Guidance for the Foundation Stage*. London: DfEE/QCA.

QCA (2005) *Curriculum Guidance for Early Years on How to Use ICT*. London: QCA.

Quilgars, D. (2006) 'Children, housing and neighbourhoods', in J. Bradshaw and E. Mayhew (Eds) *The Wellbeing of Children in the UK*. 2nd edition. London: Save the Children.

Qvortrup, J. (1985) 'Placing children in the division of labour', in P. Close and R. Collins (Eds) *Family and Economy in Modern Society*. London: Macmillan.

——(2001) 'School-work, paid work and the changing obligations of childhood', in P. Mizen, C. Pole and A. Bolton (Eds) *Hidden Hands: international perspectives on children's work and labour*. London: RoutledgeFalmer.

Rheingold, H. (1982) 'Little children's participation in the work of adults, a nascent prosocial behaviour', *Child Development* 53: 114–25.

Ribbens, J. (1994) *Mothers and their Children: a feminist sociology of childrearing*. London: Sage.

Ribbens Mcarthy, J. and Edwards, R. (2002) 'The individual in public and private: the significance of mothers and children', in A. Carling, S. Duncan and R. Edwards (Eds) *Analysing Families: morality and rationality in policy and practice*. London: Routledge.

Rice, B. (2006) *Against the Odds*. London: Shelter.

Rickards, H. (1996) 'Getting the best out of computer technology in primary schools', in T. Gill (Ed) *Electronic Children*. London: National Children's Bureau.

Riley, J. (Ed) (2003) *Learning in the Early Years*. London: Paul Chapman Publishing Limited.

Roberts, P. (2006) *Nurturing Creativity in Young People: a report to government to inform future policy*. London: DCMS.

Rogoff, B. (1990) *Apprenticeship in Thinking*. New York and Oxford: Oxford University Press.

Sammons, P., Sylva, K., Melhuish, E., Siraj-Blatchford, I., Taggart, B., Grabbe, Y. and Barreau, S. (2007) 'Influences on children's attainment and progress in Key Stage 2: cognitive outcomes in Year 5', *DfES Research Brief no: RB828*. London: DfES.

Sefton-Green, J. (1999) 'Media education but not as we know it: digital technology and the end of media studies?' *English and Media Magazine* 40: 28–34.

——(2004) *Literature Review in Informal Learning with Technology Outside School. Futurelab Report 7*. London: Futurelab.

Sefton Green, J. and Sinker, R. (Eds) (2000) *Evaluating Creativity: making and learning by young people*. London: Routledge.

Selwyn, N. (1998) 'The effect of using a home computer on students' educational use of IT', *Computers and Education* 31: 211–27.

Shamgar-Handelman, B. (1994) 'To whom does childhood belong?' in J. Qvortrup, M. Bardy, G. Sgritta and H. Wintersberger (Eds) *Childhood Matters: social theory, practice and politics*. Aldershot: Avebury.

Silvern, S.B. (2006) 'Educational implications of play with computers', in D.P. Fromberg and D. Bergen (Eds) *Play from Birth to Twelve: contexts, perspectives and meanings*. Second edition. New York and London: Routledge.

Siraj-Blatchford, I. (2004) 'Educational disadvantage in the early years: how do we overcome it? Some lessons from research', *European Early Childhood Education Research Journal* 12(2): 5–20.

Siraj-Blatchford, J. and Siraj-Blatchford, I. (2001) *Kidsmart: the phase 1 UK evaluation final report: unpublished white paper*. London: IBM United Kingdom Ltd.

Smart, C. (2003) 'Introduction: new perspectives on childhood and divorce', *Childhood* 10(2): 123–30.

Smilansky, S. (1990) 'Socio-dramatic play: its relevance to behaviour and achievement in school', in E. Klugman and S. Smilansky (Eds) *Children's Play and Learning*. New York and London: Teachers' College Press.

Smith, F. and Barker, J. (2000a) 'Contested spaces: children's experiences of out of school care in England and Wales', *Childhood* 7(3): 315–34.

——(2000b) '"Out of school" in school: a social geography of out of school childcare', in S.L. Holloway and G. Valentine (Eds) *Children's Geographies: playing, living, learning*. London: Routledge.

Smith, P.K. and Simon, T. (1986) 'Object play, problem-solving and creativity in children', in P.K. Smith (Ed) *Play in Animals and Humans*. Oxford: Basil Blackwell.

Smith, R. (2000) 'The politics of homework', *Children and Society* 14(4): 316–25.

Smithers, R. (2005) '175,000-strong hidden army of school-age carers', *The Guardian*, 13.04.05: 13.

Social Exclusion Unit (2003) *A Better Education for Children in Care*. London: Social Exclusion Unit.

Sport England (2003a) *Young People and Sport: trends in participation*. London: Sport England.

——(2003b) *Condition and Refurbishment of Public Sector Sports Facilities: update of 1995 study. Report by David Langdon Consultancy*. London: Sport England.

Straker, A. and Govier, H. (1997) *Children Using Computers. Second edition*. Oxford: Nash Pollock Publishing

Strandell, H. (2000) 'What is the use of children's play: preparation or social participation?', in H. Penn (Ed) *Early Childhood Services: theory, policy and practice*. Buckingham: Open University Press.

Super, C. and Harkness, S. (1986) 'The developmental niche: a conceptualisation at the interface of child and culture', *International Journal of Behavioural Development* 9: 545–69.

Sutherland, R. (2004) 'Designs for learning: ICT and knowledge in the classroom', *Computers and Education* 43: 5–16

Sutton-Smith, B. (1979) 'Epilogue: play as performance', in B. Sutton-Smith (Ed) *Play and Learning*. New York: Gardner Press.

Sutton-Smith, B. and Kelly-Byrne, D. (1984) 'The idealisation of play', in P.K. Smith (Ed) (1986) *Play in Animals and Humans*. Oxford: Blackwell.

Sylva, K., Melhuish, E., Sammons, P., Siraj-Blatchford, I. and Taggart, B. (2004) *The Final Report: Effective Pre-School Education*. London: Institute of Education, University of London.

Sylva, K., Melhuish, E., Sammons, P., Siraj-Blatchford, I., Taggart, B. and Elliot, K. (2003) 'Effective provision of pre-school education (EPPE) Project: findings from the pre-school period', *Research Brief No: RBX15–03*. London: Institute of Education, University of London.

Sylva, K., Stein, A., Leach, P., Barnes, J., Malmberg, L.-E. and the FCCC team (2007) 'Family and child factors related to the use of non-maternal infant care: an English study', *Early Childhood Research Quarterly* 22(1): 118–36.

Taras, H. (2005a) 'Physical activity and student performance at school', *Journal of School Health* 75(6): 214–18.

——(2005b) 'Nutrition and school-aged children's performance at school', *Journal of School Health* 75(6): 199–213.

Thomson, R. and Holland, J. (2002) 'Young people, social change and the negotiation of moral authority', *Children and Society* 16(2): 103–15.

Thorne, B. (1993) *Gender Play: girls and boys at school*. New Brunswick NJ: Rutgers University Press.

Tizard, B. and Hughes, M. (1984) *Young Children Learning: talking and thinking at home and school*. London: Fontana.

Torgerson, C. and Zhu, D. (2003) 'A systematic review and meta-analysis of the effectiveness of ICT on literacy learning in English, 5–16', in *Research Evidence in Education Library*. London: EPPI-Centre, Social Science Research Unit, Institute of Education, University of London.

Toynbee, P. (2007) 'The public worry more about Spanish donkeys than child poverty', *Leading article, The Guardian*, 30.3.07: 35.

Turner, H., Mayall, B., Dickinson, R., Clarke, A., Hood, S., Samuels, J. and Wiggins, M. (2004) *Children Engaging with Drama: an evaluation of the National Theatre's drama work in primary schools*. London: Institute of Education, University of London.

United Nations (1989) *Convention on the Rights of the Child*. Geneva: UN.

UNICEF (2007a) *Rights Respecting School Award Programme*. UNICEF website.

United Nations Children's Fund (UNICEF) (2007b) *Child Poverty in Perspective: an overview of child wellbeing in rich countries*. *Innocenti Report Card 7*. Florence: UNICEF Innocenti Research Centre.

Valentine, G., Marsh, J. and Pattie, C. (2005) *Children and Young People's Home Use of ICT for Educational Purposes: the impact on attainment at Key Stages 1–4*. Research Report no. 672. University of Leeds.

Ward, H. (1995) *Looking after Children: research into practice*. London: HMSO.

Ward, H. and Skuse, T. (2001) 'Performance targets and stability of placements for children long looked after away from home', *Children and Society* 15(5): 333–46.

Watkins, C. (2005) *Classrooms as Learning Communities*. London: Routledge.

Watkins, C., Lodge, C. and Best, R. (Eds) (2000) *Backing Tomorrow's Schools: towards integrity*. London: RoutledgeFalmer.

Wikeley, F., Bullock, K., Muschamp, Y. and Ridge, T. (2007) *Educational Relationships Outside School*. York: Joseph Rowntree Foundation.

Willitts, M., Anderson, T., Tait, C. and Williams, G. (2005) 'Children in Britain: findings from the 2003 Families and Children Study (FACS)', *DWP research report no. 249*. London: Department for Work and Pensions.

Woodhead, M. (2000) 'Towards a global paradigm for research', in H. Penn (Ed) *Early Childhood Services: theory, policy and practice*. Buckingham: Open University Press.

Woodhead, M. and Faulkner, D. (2008) 'Subjects, objects or participants? Dilemmas of psychological research with children', in P. Christensen and A. James (Eds) *Research with Children: perspectives and practices*. Second edition. London: Routledge.

Yelland, N. and Masters, J. (2007) 'Rethinking scaffolding in the information age', *Computers and Education* 48: 362–82.

4 Parenting, caring and educating

*Yolande Muschamp, Felicity Wikeley,
Tess Ridge and Maria Balarin*

INTRODUCTION

In this survey of published research we review changing patterns in the structure of families and identify trends in parenting and caring for today's generation of primary school children. We reveal how the reduction in the number of children born, the increase in the proportion of lone parents and the increasing age at which women have their first child have resulted in greater diversity of family forms, and parenting and caring practices. The impact of these changes on primary education is discussed through a review of the impact of government policy in relation to the role of parents and the home-school relationship. We conclude that the diversity in family structures brings with it complex administrative demands for home school communication and a complex array of family relationships for teachers to understand and engage with. The school remains a primary source of community-based support for working parents and carers, although the impact of complex employment arrangements adds to the demands for child care support beyond the school day.

The most challenging home circumstance, which cannot be viewed optimistically, is the increasing number of children living in relative poverty. Poverty remains a significant factor in the lives of many children with the inevitable impact in terms of health and wellbeing and a child's capacity to engage fully in school activities, both financially and emotionally.

Further research is needed into the lives of children and how their complex family relations, and the caring roles which many children undertake, impact on their education. In reality home-school relationships are between individual parents and individual teachers who both have the interests of the child at heart. Parents are not a homogeneous group but neither are teachers, and attempts to improve the relationship between both groups need to acknowledge the strengths and expertise of both. Teachers need to establish more dialogic links between home and school which build on the support for children's learning that already exists in the home and community. Further research as to how this can happen would be helpful.

The aim of this chapter is to provide a critical summary of the research which identifies the changes in patterns of parenting and caring in the pre-adolescence years over the past few decades. We examine roles and relationships of parents, carers and teachers in the home-school relationship and review the evidence on the efficacy and problems of different approaches. Part 1 focuses on the changes in the structure and formation of the family which reveal the diversity that now exists in parenting and child-care roles and practice. Part 2 focuses on parenting practices and assesses the impact of these on children's welfare and the conditions on which successful primary education may depend. Part 3 reviews the policy context of home-school relationships. Part 4 reviews the research into the home-school interface and the role of the home in supporting pupil learning. We conclude with a discussion of the main challenges for the primary school in managing their approaches to the relationship between parenting, caring and education, and highlight areas which would benefit from future research.

METHODS AND COVERAGE

We have drawn on a range of methodological approaches for this chapter. We have included both quantitative and qualitative data. The studies reviewed include large government sponsored surveys and independent research projects carried out by university research teams which range from longitudinal case studies of individual children to national surveys of schools and families. We draw on government surveys and data bases, for example the overviews and summaries provided by the Office for National Statistics (ONS), the Department for Work and Pensions (DWP) and the Department for Children, Schools and Families (DCSF)/Department for Education and Skills (DfES) in a range of publications and on their websites. We have used a range of bibliographic and research institute databases to review research reports and research findings reported in books and journal articles. The theoretical perspectives vary within these studies. We have worked within broad sociological perspectives in relation to the changing patterns of family structure, parenting practices and the policy context for an examination of the home-school relationship. Our research into learning in the home reflects the socio-cultural perspective taken in key studies. The literature in these fields is very extensive and our chapter is able to include only a small selection of what is available but we have used it to identify key trends in parenting, caring and education and provide a summary of research which illustrates and explains how the current context has changed since the review described in the Plowden Report (CACE 1967).

THE STRUCTURE AND FORMATION OF THE FAMILY

Demographic and social changes in the last half of the twentieth century have wrought considerable transformation in family formation and structure. Trends toward reduced fertility and later child bearing have led to an overall reduction in the number of children being born in economically developed Western societies. Increasing instability in family life and rising rates of family dissolution have resulted in greater diversity and complexity of family forms. Whilst the majority of children still live with both of their natural parents (married or cohabiting), one in four dependent children live in lone-parent families. Children in the twenty-first century have a higher probability of experiencing parental separation, lone parenting, step-families, visiting families, half-siblings or being an only child than children of 40 years ago (Bradshaw and Mayhew 2005: 34). As a consequence, children's lives are increasingly complex.

Statistics from the Office for National Statistics (ONS 2007) show the changing fertility and childbearing patterns in the UK. The last 40 years have been characterised by a fall in the number of children born, a rise in the average age of women at the birth of their first child and higher levels of childlessness. In 2005 the average age of women having their first child was 27.3 years. This compares with 23.7 in 1970. In 2005 the total fertility rate in the UK was 1.79 children per woman. Whilst this was at its highest level since 1992 (up from 1.77 children in 2004) (ONS 2007), fewer children being born means smaller families overall – although this trend is not reflected in some ethnic minority groups. These changes impact on family dynamics as parents have fewer children among whom to divide their attention and resources; children have fewer siblings; and many more children are an only child.

At the same time new family structures are emerging, creating a greater range of situations in which children are cared for. The proportion of households where dependent children live with a lone parent has doubled since 1970, reaching 6 per cent in 2002, and nine in ten lone parents are women (Spencer-Dawe 2005). Until the mid-1980s a large part of this rise was due to divorce, but more recently the number of single, lone mothers has grown at a faster rate. There are also more step-families, consisting typically of a couple living with one or more children from the woman's previous relationship. This reflects the tendency for children to stay with their mother following the break-up of a partnership. Cohabitation appears more unstable than marriage and is more likely to result in separation and lone motherhood. Greater diversity in the parenting environment can also be expected with the growing numbers of gay and lesbian families.

These trends are not confined to England and the United Kingdom. Although the UK now has the highest proportion of lone families in Europe, there is increasing diversity across Europe where many countries are also experiencing reduced fertility, later childbearing and increases in the proportion of smaller families, and numbers of lone parents.

PARENTING PRACTICES

The diversity of family structure is reflected in an increasingly wide range of parenting practices. For lone parents the double burden of work and care has impacted on the parenting role. As the majority of lone parents are women, who are already disadvantaged in the labour market, children may experience the impact of their mother's difficulties in balancing work and care. On a smaller scale, the increase in the number of gay parents has led to an increase in the number of children raised by two men or two women, as well as to an increase in diverse support networks, for example, two mothers with the involvement of a sperm donation father.

As the complexity of family forms grows, more children will experience shared care. Shared care may mean children experiencing parenting in different locations across time and space or two very different sets of living arrangements or parenting practices. The involvement of non-resident fathers in school and parenting may be a regular feature of children's experience but the non-resident father may also be an erratic presence. Children may spend very different amounts of time with the non-resident parent: for example, this could be regular weekend contact or only occasional holiday visits. Children may be living in two places over the week with different sets of siblings, both birth and step, in each. Schools in these circumstances may find it difficult to know which parent is the first point of contact, and children may have to reconcile different expectations relating to school work from their parents.

The proportion of women in employment has also increased in recent decades (McDowell *et al.* 2005) and this has led to an increase in complex child care arrangements. Increasing numbers of children attend some form of institutional care/education prior to going to school. The quality of this provision is known to be a key factor in later cognitive achievement at Key Stage 1 (Sylva *et al.* 2004; see also Chapter 3 of this volume). Despite this and the debates about the changing role of men, traditional assumptions about the seeming relationship between femininity and caring remain relatively fixed (McKie *et al.* 2002). The extent to which child care responsibilities affect labour market participation still varies considerably between men and women (Hatt 1997) and many women, especially those in working class households, still do not have a genuine choice between 'family work' and 'market work' (Walters 2005). Nevertheless women with partners have higher employment rates than lone mothers, although the gap closes as children get older (Holtermann *et al.* 1999). In coupled working families, employment opportunities have led to 'shift' parenting where an increasing number of mothers work when the father is at home (maybe evenings or weekends), and vice versa. With increased longevity and better health, this shared care now stretches to multi-generation or 'beanpole' families (Brannen 2004) which can be a potential resource for family support and learning (Kenner *et al.* 2007) but can also create increased demands for care. The national New Deal for Lone Parents programme aims to support lone mothers, who have the lowest rate of employment, into employment (Spencer-Dawe 2005). These mothers are encouraged to start work when the youngest child reaches school age and although there is no compulsion at present to work, the numbers of lone mothers at work is rising slowly.

Labour markets are now characterised by insecure employment, increased part-time work and shift work, which inevitably create problems for the work-life balance of families (Auer 2002). Fathers in England now work the longest hours in Europe and poor child care provision remains an issue, especially for parents who work unsocial hours. Thirty-two per cent of mothers and 46 per cent of fathers who worked unsocial hours said their job limited the time that they could spend reading with, playing with or helping their children with homework, compared with 12 per cent of mothers and 18 per cent of fathers who worked office hours (La Valle *et al.* 2002). Labour market inequalities have created a broad spectrum with dual wage earners at one end, through a large group of one and a half wage earners, to no-wage earners at the other. No wage means poverty and reliance on benefits, and the year 2006 saw the first rise in the number of children living in poverty since the Government's pledge to end child poverty in a generation. 3.8 million children now live below the poverty line (DWP 2007). Larger families are particularly vulnerable to poverty, and are often from ethnic minority communities. Large families in the UK are among the poorest in the OECD (Bradshaw *et al.* 2006).

These changes have a direct impact on the ways in which parents engage with their children's education.

THE POLICY CONTEXT OF HOME AND SCHOOL

In the past few decades, the relationship between parents and schools has been radically altered. While there is a long-standing acknowledgement of the value of parental involvement in schooling, the ways in which such involvement has been conceptualised have changed considerably. These changes followed the evolving conceptions of citizenship and civic participation in general (Vincent and Tomlinson 1997). From a post-war view that saw a clear separation between the public and private realms, 'the late 1960s and 1970s witnessed a shift in the hegemonic view of how parents should relate to schools' in which ' ... parental involvement became "good-practice"' (p. 363).

Although some emphasis on parental involvement was already present in the 1944 Education Act, it was during the late 1960s and 1970s that it became a central component of educational policies. In 1967 the Plowden Report set out what would become major concerns in relation to home-school relationships. The report was heavily influenced by research carried out by educational sociologists, who questioned the meritocratic ideals of the 1944 Act and highlighted the influence of socio-economic factors in school success (Douglas 1964; Bernstein 1970; Brown 1997). The acknowledgement of these issues within the report created a 'deficit model' of parenting. The report argued for the greater involvement of parents in schools in order to 'compensate for society' (Docking 1990). However, much of the policy emphasis during this time was on the provision of social welfare by schools through interventions such as free school meals and Educational Priority Areas that increased resources for schools operating in deprived neighbourhoods (Blackstone 1967). The Plowden Report also placed considerable emphasis on home-school communication, setting expectations of regular meetings, open days and parent-teacher associations. Whilst some criticised the report for not providing more specific guidelines for improving such communications (Blackstone 1967), there was a proliferation of small studies that promoted good practice. However, the rhetoric continued to place parents as a problem rather than as a support for schools. For example, schools still felt they needed to compensate for language deficit on entry to school (Tough 1976; Hughes 1994) despite evidence to the contrary (Tizard and Hughes 1984; Wells 1987).

In the 1980s the role for parents was recast as being that of 'consumers'. The Conservative government's rhetoric during this time put considerable emphasis on what it considered a crisis in family values, placing families at the centre of most educational and social policies. At the same time, their promotion of a market ideology for public administration in general entailed a much more active role for parents, who were now seen as 'clients' and 'consumers' of educational services (Hughes, Wikeley and Nash 1994, Crozier 2000). Parental choice, the main driver of 'excellence' in the educational market, was promoted by such policies as Grant-Maintained Schools (which allowed parents to vote for their school to opt out of local education authority control). The government also gave more voice to parents, by increasing their involvement in school decisions through greater representation on governing bodies, and promoting a monitoring role in relation to school practices through making those governors accountable at an annual meeting for parents, and during school inspections.

While the election of a Labour government in 1997 raised expectations of possible changes in the market ideology, there appeared to be strong continuities in terms of the actual policies. Some would even argue that in spite of considerable refinement in the government rhetoric concerning parental involvement, New Labour deepened some of the trends in home-school relations that were initiated by its predecessors (Cardini 2006). The shift in rhetoric moved from the ideology of parent-as-consumer to the creation of educational partnerships. With the publication of the White Paper, *Excellence in Schools* (DfES 1997) the government made a clear statement about the crucial role played by family-school partnerships in ensuring the improvement of educational standards. The government placed considerable emphasis on parental support for learning; for example the introduction of home-school agreements (DfEE 1998a) and the *Homework Guidelines for Primary and Secondary Schools* (DfEE 1998b). However this guidance was prescriptive as home-school agreements set out 'mutual responsibilities and expectations' (Smith 2000: 319) and guidelines provided specific instructions on the way in which homework should take place. The documentation made a clear case for focusing homework on the acquisition of literacy and numeracy skills, thus linking it to the government's literacy and numeracy strategies. There was also an indication of the number of hours per day that children of different ages should commit to homework, and schools were expected to provide clear guidance. Parents were only expected to monitor their children's completion of homework and there was little recognition of other educational activities already being encountered in the home.

The emphasis on partnership continued with the more recent *Every Child Matters: change for children* (DfES 2004) which re-stated the 'building of stronger relationships with parents and the wider community' as one of the government's central policy aims. Similarly the White Paper, *Higher Standards, Better Schools* (DfES 2005) placed considerable emphasis on the importance of home-school communication in securing greater pupil achievement. This White Paper stressed parents' rights to be regularly and adequately informed of their children's progress in school. These commitments have continued with the Children's Plan, published in December 2007, which declares that 'schools need to become better at working with parents' (DCSF 2007: 26). A version of the Children's Plan written for families highlights the role of parents as partners and acknowledges the variety of family structures through its reference to parents 'including those who do not live with their children'. The balance had shifted, at least in the rhetoric, to 'a notion of a home-school alliance that promotes the wider interests of children and the community' identified earlier by Wolfendale and Topping (1995: 2). This emphasis on home-school partnership had begun to address the problems of the deficit model of the previous decades but it did not remove the conflicting roles for schools. On the one hand teachers were to seek out partnership with parents in the education of their children, and on the other hand the detailed guidance and information that they were to provide for parents suggested that they were to continue to compensate for parental lack of ability or interest in education.

HOME-SCHOOL RELATIONS

The question of who retains power and control has remained central to much research into home-school relationships. Vincent (1996) questioned the idea that parents could be 'empowered' by teachers to play a more active role in the education of their children, as this ignored 'the considerable limitations imposed on agency by the contexts in which teachers and other education professionals work' (p2). It also ignored the active role parents take in the education of their children outside school. In this sense, the reality of parental participation suggests that parents from different backgrounds will enact and take advantage of the empowerment agenda in different ways. The work of Epstein (Epstein and Becker 1982; Epstein 1995; Epstein, Sanders *et al.* 2002) in the US takes an optimistic view, providing a typology of school-home relationships which has informed research in the UK (see David 1998; Hughes and Greenhough 2006). Epstein and her colleagues suggest that several strategies can be deployed to empower parents and improve home-school relationships. In particular, they highlight the importance of school initiatives which aim to promote parental involvement and provide clear guidelines on ways in which learning can be supported in the home. In this sense, much recent research into family-school relationships has focused precisely on understanding how relationships within homes, as well as those between home and school, might generate improved learning outcomes for children. While Epstein's work focuses on specific ways in which parents are involved in educational activities in the home, research emerging from the social capital perspective highlights the more general ways in which parents can establish 'positive relations with their children that reinforce school learning at home and provide opportunities, encouragement and emotional support for children's ongoing education' (Hao and Bonstead-Bruns 1998: 176).

The work of Lareau (1987, 2000) on family-school relationships, however, brings a further critical perspective to the possibilities of generating better educational results through improving children's home environment. Lareau places considerable emphasis on the importance of parents and children understanding 'the rules of the game' that operate in schools. She highlights how elements of social class, race and language can mediate relations between the family and school, but suggests that the deployment of adequate strategies can help 'activate' children's capital in educationally positive ways. In her extensive research into the different educational strategies deployed by parents, she shows that while both middle and working class parents have considerable interest in wanting to help their children succeed in school, middle class parents appear to have considerably more resources to do so effectively. Middle class parents deploy more strategies to actually influence their children's educational experience through, for instance, supporting homework and keeping close contact with school teachers (Lareau 2000). Working class parents, on the other hand, tend more often to believe that academic matters should be left to teachers, and in some cases even feel 'intimidated by teacher's professional authority' (Lareau 2000: viii). They often lack the knowledge of what information is relevant for them to follow their children's progress in school, and also 'lack confidence in their ability to address pedagogical issues. The structure of their family life often hinders more active involvement and they are ideologically inclined to view family and school as separate spheres' (Lareau 2000: xii).

Such findings are echoed by Crozier (1997) who, in the UK context, found that working class parents are less likely than middle class ones to get involved in their children's schooling, and that when they do it is generally in non-academic activities. Crozier and Davies (2006) found that there was also less involvement by some ethnic groups. They found that many Bangladeshi and Pakistani parents living in England, despite being concerned about education and willing to get involved, appeared to lack the educational knowledge appropriate for helping their children at home.

The longitudinal studies of Pollard and Filer (1996, 1999) give further insight to these arguments. Their detailed studies of children's development over the seven years of their primary schooling, recorded in both the home and school, show the influence of parents and teachers on the development of pupil identities. While the authors endorse the idea that pupils' learning experiences in school are influenced by their relations at home, they have a broader understanding of what the latter means, which includes not only relations with parents, but also with siblings, peers and teachers. Moreover, the authors show that the way in which these relations impinge on children's learning is in the way that they contribute to the development of children's identities, rather than through their more specific educational efforts. While this does not undermine the emphasis on improving parental support for learning or enhancing home-school relations, it does suggest that the understanding of parental roles has to be broader than it appears to be. Edwards and Warin (1999), for instance, have shown how many schools have a rather narrow view of what parental support for learning should comprise, with many schools seeing parents as 'support teachers' doing more of what is done in school.

A broader view of the parental role in learning is provided by Tizard and Hughes (1984, 2002) in their study of learning in the home. They argue that while many parents do not engage in activities such as play, games or stories that are educationally advantageous, many of the other simpler activities they do while caring for their children, such as merely talking, can be seen as being educationally advantageous. They show specific examples of useful learning outcomes which result from everyday parent-child activities such as making a shopping list, looking out of the window, living with babies, discussing past and future events, and watching television. They argue that 'learning at home occurs in a wide variety of contexts, and that there is no good reason to single out any one context, such as mother-child play, as especially valuable.' (p. 76). They warn however, that home life does not 'automatically' provide 'rich learning experiences', and acknowledge that 'very depressed mothers or some childminders ... may have little commitment to education' (p. 77). They also stress that most of the learning that takes place in the home is at the level of 'general knowledge' rather than the narrower focus of homework topics from the national curriculum and national tests. Moll *et al.* (1992), in their reflections within a study of household activities and their impact on learning, link this potential in the home to the school classroom when they argue that 'every household is, in a very real sense, an educational setting in which the major function is to transmit knowledge that enhances the survival of its dependants' (p. 320). They argue that the home is a 'fund of knowledge', which if mobilised 'can transform classrooms into more advanced contexts for teaching and learning' (p. 344). Crozier and Davies (2007) argue that developing better communication between parents and teachers can build on this.

Desforges and Abouchaar (2003) found that parental involvement takes place in various ways, ranging from providing role models and expectations for children, and sharing information with schools, to attending school events and participating in school governance. Their review, commissioned by the DfES, showed that forms of involvement are influenced by social class, maternal level of education, material deprivation, maternal psycho-social health, and single parent status and, to a lesser degree, by family ethnicity. The review also suggested that the level of involvement is related to both the child's age and attainment. The review's main finding however, suggested that 'parental involvement in the form of "at-home good parenting" has a significant positive effect on children's achievement and adjustment'. This is stronger than any other form of parental involvement, 'even after all other factors shaping attainment have been taken out of the equation' (2003: 4). This suggests that 'parenting has its influence indirectly through shaping the child's self concept as a learner and through setting high aspirations' rather than through working directly with schools (Desforges and Abouchaar 2003: 5; see also Pollard and Filer, above). The EPPE project (Sylva *et al.* 2004) also found that the quality of the home learning environment during the pre-school years had an effect on school achievement still visible at the end of Key Stage 1. Dunn, however, emphasises the importance of understanding the parent-child relationship and its impact on education, and argues that programmes developed to foster parental involvement should incorporate an understanding of the degree of complexity in parent-child relationships (Dunn 1993). However Hughes and Kwok (2007), in research conducted in the US, argue that it is the relationship between teachers and parents (and between teachers and students) that is the important factor in the home-school interface. They argue that the almost exclusive emphasis placed on increasing parental involvement can be at the expense of better home-school relations. They suggest that strategies for helping teachers connect with students and their parents are therefore fundamental.

While Desforges and Abouchaar documented a range of interventions to promote parental involvement (for example parent training courses, initiatives to promote home-school relations) their review found that there was insufficient evidence on the effectiveness of different modes of intervention and they identified the need for future research to focus on good practice. The ESRC Teaching and Learning Research Programme contains one such study, The Home School Knowledge Exchange (HSKE). Hughes and Greenhough (2006) argue that while much emphasis has been placed on two-way communication between schools and homes, in practice much of this is just 'one-way traffic' (p.72). 'While it is relatively common for schools to provide parents with information about school activities and events, it is much less common for schools to seek out parents' perspectives or knowledge' (p.472). The form and content of home-school communication appear to be largely determined by schools, and there are few mechanisms in place to discover parental concerns. While emphasis has been placed on giving 'voice' to parents, control over what they are told and what they can say is still largely with schools, which often have highly institutionalised mechanisms in place to communicate with parents. As part of their study, the researchers conducted activities to 'encourage communication between home and school'. The activities aimed to help parents understand better the demands that schools place on their children, and teachers to gain a better understanding of their students 'out of school interests and pursuits' (Hughes and Greenhough 2006: 481). The research highlighted the considerable variation in form that the activities took in the different schools, and drew the conclusion that context is highly important and has to be acknowledged when thinking about common strategies for generating better practices of home-school communication. In exploring their findings, the researchers used Moll and Greenberg's concept of 'funds of knowledge' (1992) to highlight the existence of relevant knowledge in the home which can be used positively in more formal in-school learning activities. The study highlights the need to understand home-school communication as a complex process in which issues of power and control are present and shape the forms of communication, but it also offers strategies that can be deployed to strengthen home-school communication.

Again drawing from a study carried out as part of the HSKE project, Feiler *et al.* (2006) show that when effective home-school communication is achieved 'the contribution that parents made to their child's learning was often rich and extensive' (p. 465). However, like Dunn (1993), they caution that there is considerable heterogeneity within the parental body. Even within class and ethnic groups, individual parents have different communicational needs. They suggest that schools need to deploy better strategies to find 'what kind of activities and support may be appropriate or helpful' (p. 464) for different parent groups. Such strategies should also take into account that often parents do not have a clear understanding of what they can do to support their children's learning at home or even what information they need. The authors stress that a 'one size fits all' approach to home-school communication is inadequate and they advocate what they describe as a 'layered patchwork' approach, 'a range of actions that will include different participants at different times in different ways' (p. 465). However, they warn of the risks of stereotyping through the use of such judgemental terms as 'hard to reach parents' (see also Crozier and Davies 2007).

This call for a 'patchwork approach' is at odds with the general view on the part of government which seems to be that 'more is better' in terms of homework, without much consideration of the complexities of the different conditions in the home and the possible effects of these on children's learning. This is evident for example in the attempts to ensure that the completion of homework 'becomes a matter for contractual agreement between schools and parents-as-consumers', in which the child appears to be a 'passive consumer' (Smith 2000: 322). Hoover-Dempsey *et al.* (2001) present a comprehensive discussion of studies carried out in recent years into the role of homework and of parents in relation to it. The studies include analyses of parental motivations to get involved in homework; student perceptions and feelings about homework; the influence of socio-economic variables on parents' involvement in homework; and home-school communications about homework. Drawing from the findings of such research, the authors identify three main reasons for parental involvement: parents believe that they should be involved; they think they can make a positive contribution to their children's learning; and they perceive invitations to become more involved. The authors highlight the importance of how parents construct their role in their children's education, which is done partly on the basis of personal experience. In this sense, greater parental confidence about the positive impact of their involvement makes them take a more active role in relation to homework. Supporting Epstein's ideas, the review argues that invitations from schools can have a stronger impact on involvement than parents' socio-economic status. It suggests that parental involvement in homework is varied and tends to fall within Epstein's categories of 'basic obligations' where parents merely comply with school requirements, although 'involvement' suggests more active participation. At the same time, there is evidence that the way in which parental involvement in homework influences student outcomes is by offering 'modelling, reinforcement, and instruction that supports the development of attitudes, knowledge, and behaviours associated with successful school performance' (Hoover-Dempsey *et al.* 2001: 203).

It has been suggested that increasing availability and access to technologies and educational materials in the future could make a distinct contribution to home-school relationships. Bauch (1997) suggests that new communications technologies can be positively used to enhance the flow of information between schools, students and their parents. However, in a study of computer use at home and in school, Kerawalla and Crook (2002) showed that while the increasing presence of computers in British homes has created greater expectations as to the contribution they can make to children's learning, in reality the home use of computers is more general than it is in schools and the contribution to school learning is small. The most common home use for computers is games playing, with educational uses being much less frequent. Similar findings have been encountered in the US context, where it was evident that many parents did not have the resources or the knowledge to promote better, more school-oriented uses of home computers. However, the authors were critical of how the surge of new technologies has been hailed as a 'potential resource for blending the activities of home life and school life' (Kerawalla and Crook 2002: 752). The reality that they found showed strong discontinuities between school and home in terms of computer use and the context in which computers are found. Availability was often greater at home than in school, and parents' use of computers as an educational tool was more limited. Many parents appeared to be uncomfortable in taking on a 'teaching' role with their children, and were concerned about the implications of 'importing the classroom into the home' (Kerawalla and Crook 2002: 769). At the same time, many parents seemed to expect that the educational effects of computers would occur 'spontaneously'. They comment on the apparent gaps between the ecologies of the home and the school with respect to computer use; consequently few schools promote initiatives for ICT use in fostering better home-school links. However, the authors cite some existing projects in the UK (such as at the Highdown School in Berkshire) and in the US where computers have successfully been used to foster better home-school links.

CONCLUSION

The changing patterns of parenting and child care present significant challenges for the primary school. The diversity in family structure brings with it complex administrative demands for home-school communication, and a complex array of family relationships for schools to understand and work with. Children living in mixed and 'beanpole' families may be ahead of their teachers in learning to manage different attitudes and expectations of their family members in relation to schooling. Further research is needed into the lives of these children and how their complex family relations, and the caring roles which many children undertake themselves, impact on their education.

The school remains a primary source of community-based support for working parents and carers, as the impact of complex employment arrangements adds to the demands for child care support beyond the school day. There are both constraints and opportunities within these changing circumstances for greater parental involvement in schools. Flexible working hours can mean either more or less time for involvement in school activities. Shared caring and the diversity of family structures can both impoverish and enrich the lives of children. Research has presented examples of good practice in these areas and there are optimistic projects on which to build, but more research is needed to reveal the impact of these changes. The most challenging home circumstance, which cannot be viewed optimistically, is the increasing number of children living in relative poverty. Poverty remains a significant factor in the lives of many children, with the inevitable impact in terms of health and wellbeing and a child's capacity to engage fully in school activities (both financially and emotionally). This is also an area where further research is needed in order to document and evaluate the many new initiatives in this area and the changing circumstances of children.

The policy rhetoric speaks of a changing relationship between parents and schools but the reality may be somewhat different. There is little evidence of real change. Whilst policy has shifted from viewing parents as problems, to parents as customers, and more recently to parents as partners, the home-school relationship is really between individual parents and individual teachers who both have the interests of an individual child at heart. Just as parents are not a homogeneous group, neither are teachers and attempts to improve the relationship between both groups by re-defining the role of parent may prove to be counter-productive. Whilst parents often welcome advice as to how to help their children with school-focused work, too high an expectation of what is achievable can lead to pressure and guilt for some and resentment for others. Neither emotion is likely to enhance the relationships between parents and their children's teachers. Similarly, there is a fine line between respecting teachers' professionalism and merely adding to their work load.

Ways in which teachers can establish more fruitful links between home and school, as a resource for learning which capitalises on the 'funds of knowledge' within the home, could provide new challenges for schools. There is a shortage of research into the ways in which families support children's learning within the community through leisure, and even work-related activities. Research and development would be useful in this area and would be in line with the government's personalised learning agenda. The increase in new technologies for learning, web-based information gathering, and changing perspectives of shared knowledge suggest that such research would be both relevant and timely.

REFERENCES

Auer, M. (2002) 'The relationship between paid work and parenthood–a comparison of structures, concepts and developments in the UK and Austria', *Community, Work and Family* 5(2): 203–18.

Bauch, J. (1997) 'Applications of technology to linking schools, families, and students', *Proceedings of the Families, Technology, and Education Conference*, http://ceep.crc.uiuc.edu/eecearchive/books/fte/ftepro.html

Bernstein, B. (1970) 'Education cannot compensate for society', *New Society* 387: 344–47.

Blackstone, T. (1967) 'The Plowden Report', *The British Journal of Sociology* 18: 291–302.

Bradshaw, J., Finch, N., Mayhew, E., Ritakallio, V. and Skinner, C. (2006) *Child Poverty in Large Families*. Bristol: Polity Press.

Bradshaw, J. and Mayhew, E. (2005) *The Wellbeing of Children in the UK*. London: Save the Children.

Brannen, J. (2004) *Working and Caring Over the Twentieth Century: change and continuity in four-generation families*. Basingstoke: Palgrave Macmillan.

Brown, P. (1997) 'The "third wave": education and the ideology of parentocracy', in A.H. Halsey, H. Lauder, P. Brown and A. Stuart Wells (Eds) *Education: culture, economy and society*. Oxford: Oxford University Press.

Cardini, A. (2006) 'An analysis of the rhetoric and practice of educational partnerships in the UK: an arena of complexities, tensions and power', *Journal of Education Policy* 21(4): 393–415.

Central Advisory Council for Education (England) (CACE) (1967) *Children and their Primary School: areport of the Central Advisory Council for Education (England)* (the Plowden Report). London: HMSO.

Crozier, G. (1997) 'Empowering the powerful: a discussion of the interrelation of government policies and consumerism with social class factors and the impact of this upon parent interventions in their children's schooling', *British Journal of Sociology of Education* 18(2): 187.

——(2000) *Parents and Schools: partners or protagonists*. Stoke-on-Trent and Sterling, USA: Trentham Books.

Crozier, G. and Davies, J. (2006) 'Family matters: a discussion of the Bangladeshi and Pakistani extended family and community in supporting the children's education', *The Sociological Review* 54(4): 678–95.

——(2007) 'Hard to reach parents or hard to reach schools? A discussion of home-school relations, with particular reference to Bangladeshi and Pakistani parents', *British Educational Research Journal* 33(3): 295–313.

David, M. (1998) 'Home-school relations or families, parents and education', *British Journal of Sociology of Education* 19(2).

Department for Children, Schools and Families (DCSF) (2007) *Building Brighter Futures: the Children's Plan*. London: DCSF

Department for Education and Employment (DfEE) (1997) *Excellence in Schools*. London: HMSO.

DfEE (1998a) *Home-School Agreements: guidance for schools*. London: HMSO.

——(1998b) *Homework Guidelines for Primary and Secondary Schools*. London: HMSO.

Department for Education and Skills (DfES) (2004) *Every Child Matters: change for children*. London: The Stationery Office.

DfES (2005) *Higher Standards, Better Schools for All – More Choice for Parents and Pupils.* London: The Stationery Office.

Department of Work and Pensions (DWP) (2007) 'New measures to lift thousands more children out of poverty announced', Press release March 27.

Desforges, C. and Abouchaar, A. (2003) *The Impact of Parental Involvement, Parental Support and Family Education and Adjustment: a literature review.* London: DfES.

Docking, J.W. (1990) *Primary Schools and Parents.* London: Hodder and Stoughton.

Douglas, J.W.B. (1964) *The Home and the School.* London: Macgibbon and Kee.

Dunn, J. (1993) *Young Children's Close Relationships: beyond attachment.* California: Sage.

Edwards, A. and Warin, J (1999) 'Parental involvement in raising the achievement of primary school pupils: why bother?', *Oxford Review of Education* 25(3): 325–40.

Epstein, J. (1995) 'School/family/community partnerships: caring for the children we share', *Phi Delta Kappan* 76: 701–12.

Epstein, J. and Becker, H. (1982) 'Teachers' reported practices of parent involvement: problems and possibilities', *The Elementary School Journal* 83(2): 103–13.

Epstein, J., Sanders, M., Simon, B., Clark Salinas, K., Rodriguez, Jansorn, N. and Van Voorhis, F. (Eds) (2002) *School, Family and Community Partnerships: your handbook for action* (2nd edition). Thousand Oaks: Sage.

Feiler, A., Greenhough, P., Winter, J., Salway, L. and Scanlan, M. (2006) 'Getting engaged: possibilities and problems for home-school knowledge exchange', *Educational Review* 58(4): 451–69.

Education Act 1994. London: HMSO.

Hao, L. and Bonstead-Bruns, M. (1998) 'Parent-child differences in educational expectations and the academic achievement of immigrant and native students', *Sociology of Education* 71: 175–98.

Hatt, S. (1997) *Gender, Work and Labour Markets.* Basingstoke: Macmillan.

Holtermann, S., Brannen, J., Moss, P. and Owen, C. (1999) *Lone Parents and the Labour Market: results from the 1997 labour force survey and review of research*, Employment Service Report 23. London: The Stationery Office.

Hoover-Dempsey, K., Battiato, A., Walker, J., Reed, R., DeJong, J. and Jones, K. (2001) 'Parental involvement in homework', *Educational Psychologist* 36(3): 195–209.

Hughes, J. and Kwok, O.M. (2007) 'Influence of student-teacher and parent-teacher relationships on lower achieving readers' engagement and achievement in the primary grades', *Journal of Educational Psychology* 99(1): 39–51.

Hughes, M. (1994) 'The oral language of young children', in D. Wray and J. Medwell (Eds) *Teaching Primary English: the state of the art.* London: Routledge.

Hughes, M. and Greenhough, P. (2006) 'Boxes, bags and videotape: enhancing home-school communication through knowledge exchange activities', *Educational Review* 58(4): 472–87.

Hughes, M., Wikeley, F. and Nash, T. (1994) *Parents and their Children's Schools.* Oxford: Blackwells.

Kenner, C., Ruby, M., Jessel, J., Gregory, E. and Arju, T. (2007) 'Intergenerational learning between children and grandparents in East London', *Journal of Early Childhood Research* 5(3): 219–43.

Kerawalla, L. and Crook, C. (2002) 'Children's computer use at home and at school: context and continuity', *British Educational Research Journal* 28(6): 751–71.

Lareau, A. (1987) 'Social class differences in family-school relationships: the importance of cultural capital', *Sociology of Education* 60: 73–85.

——(2000) *Home Advantage: social class and parental intervention in elementary education* (2nd edition). Rowman & Littlefield Publishers.

La Valle, I., Arthur, S., Millward, C., Scott, J. and Layden, M. (2002) *Happy Families? Atypical work and its influence on family life.* Bristol: Polity Press.

McDowell, L., Ray, K., Perrons, D., Fagan, C. and Ward, K. (2005) 'Women's paid work and moral economies of care', *Social and Cultural Geography* 6(2): 219–35.

McKie, L., Gregory, S. and Bowlby, S. (2002) 'The temporal and spatial frameworks and experiences of caring and working', *Sociology – The Journal of the British Sociological Association* 36(4): 897–924.

Moll, L.C., Amanti, C., Neff, D. and Gonzalez, N. (1992) 'Funds of knowledge for teaching: using a qualitative approach to connect homes and classrooms', *Theory into Practice* 31(2): 132.

Office for National Statistics website (2007) www.statistics.gov.uk.

Pollard, A. and Filer, A. (1996) *The Social World of Children's Learning*. London: Continuum.

——(1999) *The Social World of Pupil Career*. London, New York: Cassell.

Smith, R. (2000). 'Whose childhood? The politics of homework', *Children & Society* 14: 316–25.

Spencer-Dawe, E. (2005) 'Lone mothers in employment: seeking rational solutions to role strain', *Journal of Social Welfare and Family Law* 27(3–4): 251–64.

Sylva, K., Melhuish, E., Sammons, P., Siraj-Blatchford, I. and Taggart, B. (2004) 'The effective provision of pre-school education project: findings from pre-school to end of Key Stage One' [online http://www.ioe.ac.uk/schools/ecpe/eppe/eppe/eppepdfs/TP10%20Research%20Brief.pdf] (accessed 29.07.08)

Tizard, B. and Hughes, M. (1984) *Young Children Learning: talking and thinking at home and at school*. London: Fontana.

——(2002) *Young Children Learning* (2nd edition). Oxford: Blackwell.

Tough, J. (1976) *Listening to Children Talking*. London: Ward Lock.

Vincent, C. (1996) *Parents and Teachers*. London, Washington DC: Falmer Press.

Vincent, C. and Tomlinson, S. (1997) 'Home-school relationships: "The swarming of disciplinary mechanisms"?' *British Educational Research Journal* 23(3): 361.

Walters, S. (2005) 'Making the best of a bad job? Female part-timers' orientations and attitudes to work', *Gender Work and Organization* 12(3): 193–216.

Wells, C.G. (1987) *The Meaning Makers*. London: Hodder and Stoughton.

Wolfendale, S. and Topping, K. (1995) *Family Involvement in Literacy. Effective partnerships in education*. London: Continuum.

5 Primary schools and other agencies

*Ian Barron, Rachel Holmes, Maggie MacLure
and Katherine Runswick-Cole*

INTRODUCTION

This chapter examines the shifting relationships that have obtained over the past four decades between education and the various agencies with which primary school children in the UK may come into contact. Based on an analysis of key policy texts, legislation and research studies, the chapter describes the changing configurations of provision for children deemed to be in need of support or intervention from agencies beyond the school. It identifies major shifts of policy and practice, culminating in the wide-reaching reforms of the post-1997 Labour governments.

This chapter covers the period from the mid-1960s, around the time of the publication of the Plowden Report (CACE 1967), to the present. However the first two decades of the period, the 1960s and 70s, are dealt with more summarily than the remaining decades to allow for more detailed discussion of the significant volume of legislative and policy initiatives that have emerged since the early 1980s.

The scope of the chapter

The number of agencies potentially impacting upon schools is vast. In choosing to focus on agencies operating in the key areas of health, social care and the law, the chapter does not deal in detail with other agencies: for instance those which provide additional support for music or arts, or sporting organisations. It should also be noted that, especially in the current context of integrated services, boundaries between schools and other agencies may be blurred, both at the level of policy and of personnel. Boundaries may be becoming more permeable as a result of cross-professional arrangements, with responsibilities – for example, for children identified with special needs – distributed amongst a wide array of practitioners in different locations such as schools, local authorities, not-for-profit organisations, charities, etc. This brings implications in terms of finance, employment conditions and management. While some of these implications are discussed in the final section of the chapter, it must be acknowledged that relationships between schools and 'other agencies' may be nuanced and mobile in ways that cannot be fully represented here.

THE CHILD IN NEED OF SERVICES

The changing picture of engagement with agencies to be described below can be summarised, with inevitable over-simplification, in terms of changing constructions of the child in need of services. These include the '*deprived* child' of the 1960s and the Plowden Report, prevented from following her proper developmental path by adverse social circumstances; the '*vulnerable* child' of the 1970s and the Maria Colwell Inquiry (DHSS 1974), in need of protection from threat from within as well as outside her own family; the individualised '*market* child' of the 1980s and early 90s, whose opportunities are shaped for good or ill by the consumerist choices of her parents; and the '*distributed* child' of the present, hooked up to Labour's integrated services, her educational and economic potential linked to physical, mental and emotional well-being, protection from harm and neglect, and social and financial stability.

The 'insufficient' child

While constructions of the child in need of services have changed over time, all have relied to some extent on a notion of 'insufficiency'. In Western societies, the labels we learn to associate with the idea of childhood tend to define children as incompetent, unstable, credulous, unreliable, and emotional (Mayall 2002), and these are very often the same notions that lead agencies within and beyond the school into contact with children. For much of the twentieth century and beyond, developmental psychology has dominated the ways in which children (and provision for them) have been conceived. Lawyers, doctors, social workers, educationalists and academics have all come to depend on certain assumptions about child development as a basis for their work on, for, and with children. Whilst, within sociology, there is a growing awareness of the different ways in which agencies construct children, the image of the child as an 'incomplete' or 'inadequate' being, compared to adults, often persists within the agencies themselves and within schools.

Otherness in primary education

This means that recourse to services beyond the primary school is often characterised by a kind of '*otherness*', at least with respect to agencies concerned with health, social care and the law. The intervention of such agencies in the lives of primary schools and the children who attend them is almost always concerned with deviation from notions of 'norms', which have tended to be established through testing based on the developmental paradigm. Where pupils do not measure up to the assumed or tacit norm within a normative developmental paradigm, pupil effectiveness and well-being are called into question, and professionals other than teachers begin to enter children's lives: educational psychologists; health professionals; social workers; and those who provide support for children identified with special educational needs, children from the working and non-working classes, children from minority ethnic groups and children learning English as an additional language.

THE 1960S AND THE PLOWDEN REPORT

Introduction: the 'deprived' child

The child of the mid-1960s, depicted in the Plowden Report (CACE 1967), was the active, 'natural' child of Piagetian psychology and liberal humanism, who would find her own path to maturity and knowledge at her own rate, within the nurturing embrace of the school. Ideally, therefore, children in mainstream schools would have little need of other agencies: the discerning teacher would address the individual needs of each child and identify difficulties early enough to avoid the need for external support (paragraph 230). However the Report recognised that schools could not offer everything that certain children needed, and indeed envisaged *increased* funding and restructuring of the many agencies and personnel that such children might encounter. These included educational psychologists and psychiatrists, speech therapists, guidance officers, social workers, probation officers and education welfare officers, in addition to the health provision available to all children through the Schools Health Service. While identifying shortages across almost all services, the Plowden Report gave strong emphasis to a need for more social workers, to cope with the increasing school rolls, decrease in numbers of children in care, fragmentation of neighbourhood and family ties as a result of job mobility and slum clearance, and increasing numbers of children from immigrant families (paragraph 226).

The commitment to a broad array of services reflects one of the main emphases of Plowden, namely *social amelioration*, as reflected in its most notable outcome, the establishment of Educational Priority Areas (EPAs). The social improvement agenda of the Report, which envisaged education as a vehicle of redistribution, involved 'some unremarked conflict' with the progressive vision that the Report also championed (Kogan 1987: 14). The psychological notion of the child fulfilling her innate potential, nurtured by the school, did not entirely fit with the interventive project of 'positive discrimination' embodied in the EPAs and extra services for the needy. However a kind of bridge between the social and the progressive agendas of the Report was established in the notion of 'the environment' (Chapter 3). Children from certain kinds of background (or certain kinds of families) might be prevented from following their proper developmental path because of adverse social circumstances. Social interventions and additional services were needed to provide all children with 'an equal opportunity of acquiring intelligence' (paragraph 85).

Special educational needs

Attitudes to special education began to change in the 1960s (Evans and Varma 1990). Behavioural and developmental psychology suggested that modification of children's behaviour and potential was possible, and might be undertaken by teachers. This opened up the possibility of including greater numbers of children with educational difficulties in mainstream classrooms. By 1970, the Education (Handicapped Children) Act brought children who had previously been deemed 'ineducable', and therefore the responsibility of the health service, under the educational responsibility of local education authorities (LEAs). The Plowden Report, as noted, argued for increased provision of psychologists, psychiatrists, speech therapists and child guidance workers to support teachers in the education of children then described as 'slow learning', 'backward', 'maladjusted' and 'educationally sub-normal'.

Lack of co-ordination of services

Concern about the lack of co-ordination amongst agencies, and about barriers to communication amongst the professionals involved, were already being expressed at the time of the Plowden Report: as seen in the Seebohm Report (1968), Ingleby Report

(1960), and Younghusband Report (1959). The aspiration, as expressed in the Seebohm Report, was to provide 'one door to knock on'. Children's services were incorporated into Social Services in 1971. However, co-ordination remained an issue over the coming decades and provision continued to be patchy.

Parental involvement and a discourse of 'insufficiency'

A discourse of insufficiency or deficit runs through Plowden: the ideal child is one who does not need specialist support outside of what the school can provide for her individual needs. That ideal child is implicitly constituted as a white, middle-class child whose family are able to provide not only material and physical resources, but also the kind of emotional, intellectual and linguistic environment that the child needs to move smoothly along her developmental path. It is children from areas of social deprivation, or from immigrant families, who are generally seen to lack such support, and to be most in need of 'compensation' from school or extra services. 'The educational disadvantage of being born the child of an unskilled worker is both financial and psychological', the Report states (paragraph 85). The tendency to locate the deficit not only in social inequality, but in (associated) *family* practices is reflected in another of the Plowden committee's notable emphases: namely, the endorsement of parental involvement in education. Support for parental involvement, and the discourse of familial deficit which it frequently includes, has been a recurring feature of policy throughout the intervening years.

Culture and class

The Plowden Report demonstrated relatively little understanding of cultural and sub-cultural difference, and of the complex inflections of class and ethnicity, in shaping children's lives in the home and community. Broad assumptions about the family lives of children of unskilled or manual workers, broad characterisations of social deprivation by geographical area, and undifferentiated perceptions of the needs of 'immigrant families' proved insufficient to address complex and fast-developing social and economic conditions. 'On matters of race and culture in the inner city, it beat the drum tentatively and seriously underrated the issues' (Winkley 1987: 45).

THE 1970S: CRISIS AND BLAME

Introduction: the 'vulnerable' child

As the confidence and prosperity of the 1960s gave way to economic and political crisis, and the intensification of social problems associated with racial tensions and unemployment, Plowden's optimistic vision of child-centred education coupled with social intervention came under criticism from both the right (Cox and Dyson 1971) and the left (Simon 1985). The perceived success of the welfare reforms of the decade looked, in retrospect, exaggerated (Parton 1999). The fairly crude categorisations of Plowden, which associated class and ethnicity with geographical location, as reflected in EPAs, started to be replaced by 'positive discrimination in favour of special groups or those with special needs' (Smith 1987).

Among the agencies providing support for school-age children, *social services* became a focus of particular attention. In contrast to the empowered child (in principle at least) of the Plowden era, children increasingly came to be seen as *vulnerable*. Concern about 'child abuse' escalated, leading to a succession of circulars and guidance. (Cannan 1992; Hallett and Birchall 1992). This concern reached a peak with the inquiry into the death of Maria Colwell at the hands of her stepfather (DHSS 1974), which was strongly critical of social work practices, interagency working, and lack of communication between education and social services departments (Stevenson 1999).

Family practices

The location of a 'deficit' in certain families continued throughout the 1970s. Pringle (1974) argued that parental inadequacy was a key cause of delinquency, and was likely to be transmitted to successive generations. Parental attitudes were seen as key determinants of the child's progress (Cannan 1992). The tendency to identify family practices as integral to children's progress at school intensified with the move from Piagetian models of development, based on the notion of the staged progression of the individual child, to the interactional and ecological models of development that became influential in educational thinking in the 1970s and 80s (Bruner 1983; Vygotsky 1978; Bronfenbrenner 1979; Donaldson 1978). Theories of a 'mismatch' between cultural practices of home and school (for example Wells 1981; Bernstein 1971; Tough 1977) were frequently interpreted as deficits to be remedied by schooling or, at worst, by family services, social work or speech therapy. And, as critics have noted, the perceived deficits were often associated with differences of class, ethnicity or (later) gender (for example Brice Heath 1983; Edwards 1976).

Perceptions of children's vulnerability within their own families, coupled with class- or culture-based assumptions of deficit, tended towards a dichotomy between 'proper' and 'deviant' families, the latter falling under the scrutiny of welfare supervision (Cannan 1992).

Special educational needs

From 1971 disabled children were no longer placed in long-stay institutions, contributing to the need for more productive partnerships with parents, argued by the Warnock Report (DES 1978) and codified in the 1981 Education Act. The Warnock Report rejected the prevailing categories of 'handicap', and adopted a definition of 'special educational needs', recommending that provision for special education should 'wherever possible' occur within mainstream settings. These recommendations and their implications are discussed in more detail in the next section.

Lack of co-ordination of services

Ongoing concerns about poor co-ordination of services were, as noted, heightened by the death of Maria Colwell and the severe criticisms made by the ensuing inquiry. The report led to the development of Area Child Protection Committees (ACPCs) in England and Wales, to co-ordinate local efforts to safeguard children at risk. Despite attempts at improvements in communications with schools, Fitzherbert (1980: 349–50) characterised the involvement of social and health services as somewhat like 'rogue meteors diving in and out of the school atmosphere at odd times'.

THE 1980S AND BEYOND

Introduction: from the 'market' child to the 'distributed' child

The 1980s, 1990s and early twenty-first century are characterised by market-driven policies and practices in relation to the responsibilities of schools and their relationships with other agencies. These policies assume that state agents, whether they be central bureaucrats or individual teachers, tend to act in their own interests and against those of their clients (in this case usually conceived as parents rather than children themselves, because children are seen as 'deficient' by virtue of their immaturity). This is seen as the natural effect of state systems where market discipline is absent. Such systems across the 1980s, 1990s and early twenty-first century have been, and largely remain, underpinned by neo-liberal conservative ideologies. These have, latterly, incorporated some aspects of socialist and social democratic ideals, along with an integrative vision of the child, whose educational and economic potential is linked to physical, mental and emotional well-being, protection from harm and neglect, and social and financial stability.

Special educational needs: children with physical, sensory, learning, communication, emotional and behavioural difficulties

In 1974, as noted above, the Warnock Committee was established to look at the educational provision for 'handicapped' children in England, Scotland, and Wales (DES 1978). By 1974 the number of pupils attending special schools in England had risen to 128,410, representing 1.3 per cent of the school population. The Warnock Report, which shaped the 1981 Education Act, was ground-breaking in a number of ways. First, the report rejected the concept of eleven categories of 'handicap' and adopted instead a definition of special educational needs to take in all children who may have individual educational needs. Using this definition, it was suggested that 20 per cent of children were likely to need special educational provision of some kind at some time during their school careers. This figure has gone largely unchallenged since 1978 (Croll and Moses 2004), although there is a wide variation in practice.

The Warnock Report also recommended that provision for special education should 'wherever possible' occur within mainstream settings. This was a key change, as under the 1944 Education Act LEAs were expected to provide for 'handicapped' pupils in special schools and were only allowed to place children in mainstream schools if the 'circumstances permitted.' The 1981 Education Act was an exact reversal of the 1944 Act because the expectation, following the 1981 Act, was that special education provision should be in mainstream, not special schools, provided that certain basic conditions were met in responding to expressed wishes, educating children effectively and using resources efficiently.

The next key development in special education policy did not emerge until the 1993 Education Act, which brought about the creation of a key document for the practice of special education: *The Code of Practice for the Assessment and Identification of Special Educational Needs* (DfEE 1994). For the first time, practical guidance was given to LEAs, social services, health services and to the governing bodies of all maintained schools about their responsibilities for all children identified with special educational needs. Schools and LEAs and all those who are involved with children who have special educational needs, including the health service and social services, were obliged to have regard to 'The Code', although it did not carry legal force in itself.

In 2001, a revision of the *Code of Practice* replaced the original. The basic principles of the new *Code of Practice* remained the same but there were key differences between the old and the new versions. New rights and duties were introduced by the Special Educational Needs and Disability Act (SENDA) (2001). Changes as a result of SENDA include: a stronger right for children with special educational needs to be educated at a mainstream school; new duties on LEAs to arrange for parents of children with special educational needs to be provided with services offering advice and information and a means of resolving disputes; a new duty on schools and relevant nursery education providers to tell parents when they are making special educational provision for their child; and a new right for schools and relevant nursery education providers to request a statutory assessment of a child. In general, the aim of revising the *Code of Practice* was to streamline the process and make the responsibilities of different professionals and the roles of different agencies clearer.

Inclusion

The legislation and guidance which underpins the government's policy for inclusion is referred to as 'the inclusion framework' and has been in place since 2002 – this includes the 1996 Education Act, SENDA, *The Code of Practice for Special Educational Needs* (DfES 2001b), the National Curriculum Statutory Inclusion Statement (National Curriculum Online, no date), and statutory guidance *Inclusive Schooling: children with special educational needs* (DfES 2001a).

Removing Barriers to Achievement (DfES 2004b) is government guidance that aims to strengthen 'the inclusion framework'. The Audit Commission (2002) and Ofsted (2004) have found mixed responses to 'the inclusion framework' in their monitoring. Ofsted (2004) found that there was a growing awareness in schools of the benefits of inclusion, but that this had had little impact on the numbers of pupils in mainstream schools with special educational needs, nor on the range of entitlements the mainstream caters for. Indeed there has been an increase in the number of pupils in Pupil Referral Units and in independent special schools. The proportion of pupils in Pupil Referral Units rose by 25 per cent between 2001 and 2003 (Ofsted 2004). In 2004, 89,540 children had full-time special school places in special school and a further 2,200 children were attending special schools part-time (DfES 2006). The number of children with full-time places at special school represented 1.1 per cent of the school population in 2004.[1]

The Audit Commission Report (2002) also questions what is meant by the claim that provision for pupils with special educational needs in the mainstream is inclusive. Children with special needs may often be on the site of a mainstream school, but their opportunities for interaction with their peers are limited. Ofsted found that pupils at mainstream schools with units attached often had very limited opportunities for interaction with children in the mainstream. Ofsted also found that while most mainstream schools were now committed to meeting special needs, pupils with social and behavioural difficulties were still considered to be 'difficult' to include.

Armstrong (2005) claims that provision for children with SEN can be seen to be about controlling a part of the population and draws attention to Slee's contention (2001: 117) that New Labour's view of SEN involves 'a deep epistemological attachment to the view that special educational needs are produced through the impaired pathology of the child'. Armstrong goes on to argue that the proliferation of SEN initiatives was conceived by New Labour as a means of finding efficient and cost effective ways of managing individual pupils' needs.

> Nowhere does the strategy talk about the barriers that create educational disadvantage; nowhere does it talk about the institutional and social discrimination experienced by pupils from certain minority groups ... nowhere does it talk about the principles of an inclusive society and the role of education as a tool of social policy for supporting social cohesion and inclusion.
>
> (Armstrong 2005: 138–39)

Armstrong suggests that there was some sign of a shift in recognition from individual to school failure underlying New Labour's agenda, but that addressing individual deficit remained at the centre of government policy. Armstrong further suggests that the 2001 *Code of Practice* (DfES 2001b) continued to provide a convenient means of dealing with children who did not respond as expected to the demands of a centrally defined notion of suitable learning and behaviour and could perpetuate 'long standing and institutionally embedded practices such as racial and gender stereotyping' (p. 141). Armstrong argues that discrimination may arise from the Code, and that it has no provisions for supporting the rights of children in the face of such discrimination. In short, it does not recognise that SEN are socially constructed responses to behaviour and ways of being that are seen as problematic.

Removing Barriers to Achievement (DfES 2004b) locates SEN within a broader framework of disadvantages and seeks to intervene early, remove barriers to learning, raise expectations and achievement, and improve partnership. Armstrong argues that the model lacks an adequate theory regarding 'cultural and social formations in relation to the construction and negotiation of individual identities as "normal" or "abnormal" and of how social power is exercised' (2005: 145). Boys of primary school age account for 72 per cent of all statements, and ethnic differences are also strongly marked, with Irish–heritage Traveller and Roma/Gypsy children having the highest percentage of statements. *Ethnicity and Education* (DfES 2006b) does, however, suggest that poverty and gender have a strong correlation with SEN, but that the link with ethnicity is less significant.

Armstrong concludes that '... special education continues to fulfil its traditional function vis-à-vis the mainstream sector of containing troublesome individuals and depoliticising educational failure through the technologies of measurement and exclusion' (2005: 147). Armstrong goes on to contend that New Labour's concern to attach to SEN the notion of '*risk*' – whether it be around SEN, child protection, poverty or family circumstances – means that interventions are justified in order to address the needs of inadequate individuals to allow them to contribute to the greater social good.

Children from the working and non-working classes: poverty and lack of opportunity

In the late 1990s primary schools condemned as failing were overwhelmingly those in areas with high levels of poverty, according to figures from the Office for Standards in Education (Ofsted) (1998, cited on National Literacy Trust website[2]). In this respect the picture has changed little from the time of the Plowden Report. Poverty is still the best predictor of inspection grades, according to an analysis of more than two years of figures from Ofsted, which found that the poorest 10 per cent of schools in the country were eight times more likely to fail their inspections than schools with average levels of poverty or better. The poorest third of primaries account for 70 per cent of failing schools. The poorest tenth makes up nearly 40 per cent. Those who teach many pupils on free school meals are statistically unlikely to get a favourable inspection grade. The figures show that only 4 per cent of schools where more than a third of pupils received free school meals were given the top grade for quality of education.

This clear link between poverty and failure contradicts claims by Chris Woodhead, chief inspector at the time, that deprivation only affects a minority of schools placed under 'special measures' (*Times Educational Supplement*, 31 July 1998). The independent Rowntree Report on child poverty (1999) points to continuing, and possibly worsening, inequalities in education. The report's assessment of poverty and exclusion over the previous two years found 4.4 million children below the official poverty line (less than half of average income after housing costs). Two million children were living in houses where there was no one in paid employment. The report reveals significant differences in the performance of primary children in schools with 35 per cent or more of children on free meals, compared to pupils in all schools. It also points to an increasing concentration of poorer children in particular schools – leading to a polarisation within the primary sector (*TES*, 10 December 1999).

Loeber and LeBlanc (1990) and Loeber and Stouthamer-Loeber (1986) suggest that characteristics of human, social, and cultural capital include poverty, educational attainment, employment, family size, and family structure, and parental involvement in crime, deviance, and substance use. They claim that familial circumstances, typically denoted by characteristics of the parental life course, produce vastly different child-rearing environments that are commonly seen as either placing children at risk for, or insulating them from, antisocial behavior. Drawing on the notion of linked lives, a study undertaken by Macmillan, McMorris and Kruttschnitt (2004) examined the effects of stability and change in maternal circumstance on developmental trajectories of antisocial behavior in children 4 to 7 years of age. They conclude:

> The study demonstrated that early maternal circumstances influences early antisocial behavior, whereas stability and change in these circumstances both exacerbate and ameliorate behavior problems. Of particular note, meaningful escape from poverty attenuates antisocial behavior whereas persistence in poverty or long-term movement into poverty intensifies such problems.
>
> (Macmillan, McMorris and Kruttschnitt 2004: 205)

The findings highlight the importance of considering the dynamic features of family lives when trying to understand notions of disadvantage and deprivation, and the central role poverty and health issues seem to play in parenting and successful child development. They also suggest that important gains might emerge from programmes that limit children's exposure to poverty and enhance conditions, for example raising awareness of health issues, under which parenting can maximise positive child development.

Poverty and health

Mayall and Storey (1998) draw attention to a concern with children's health being evident from the very beginning of state education in the UK in the 1870s, because it was offered to the poorest children and made their health issues apparent. Initially the school health service was provided by education authorities, but from 1974 was made the responsibility of the health service. Finch (1984) describes three rationales offered over the years for the school health service: *efficiency* – in that health problems are seen as needing addressing so that children can benefit from education; *convenience* – a school–based service means it is accessible by all children; *complementarity* – because children are required to attend school and leave the care of the parents, the state has a duty to care for their health and welfare whilst they are there. The NHS Act 1977 placed a duty on the Secretary of State to provide for the dental and medical examination of children of school-age but the precise nature and extent of this was left to local determination. Mayall and Storey (1998) note a drift from universalist to selective services, based on the identification of particular needs. There was also a 20 per cent reduction in school nurses from 1979 to 1991 brought about by marketisation and devolved budgets.

In 1977 the then-Labour government had commissioned the Black Report (DHSS 1980), which was published in 1980. It identified many health inequalities as the result of social and economic circumstances, and called for elimination of child poverty during the 1980s. Whilst there was little coverage of child health issues according to Macintyre (1977), Blane (1985) suggests that Black explained differences in child health in terms of class inequalities. The report was rejected by the Conservative government as too costly and as irrelevant because they rejected the notion of health inequalities. Exworthy *et al.* (2003) argue that inequality was ignored or referred to as 'variation' under the Conservatives – the result of individual choices rather than structural inequality. The 1980 Education Act removed the nutritional requirements from the school meals service and the subsequent privatisation of school meals led to price and choice being the determinants of what children ate in school. Subsequent marketisation in the NHS led to school health services being the subject of purchase agreements. Saxena *et al.* (2002) note that death rates for children from the lower social classes were five times higher than those from the higher social classes in the 1970s and 1980s.

Health of the Nation: a strategy for health in England (DoH 1992) was concerned with reducing death from a range of diseases, and with reducing unhealthy lifestyle choices. It mentioned poverty and inequality only briefly. Liaison between health and education authorities was primarily focused on meeting the needs of children with special educational needs under the terms of the 1993 Education Act and the 1994 Code of Practice (DfEE 1994). Education authorities were encouraged to ensure that there was a health service contact for each school and to agree procedures for providing specialist equipment.

Mayall and Storey (1998) draw attention to the way in which education and health responsibilities were divided between different government departments until the late 1990s; this did not support collective responsibility for children's health and well-being. They also draw attention to the way that the *Health of the Nation* led to a view of child health promotion as an individual responsibility, without any clear means of providing children with the relevant skills and knowledge, and to a lack of co-ordination in the provision of services for children. Until 1996, joint service planning was seen as needed only for children in need. The Health Visitors' Association and the British Paediatric Association called for the school health service to move beyond screening and referral to health promotion work towards providing for children's rights to a healthy environment, in line with the UN Convention on the Rights of the Child (UN 1989) and the 1989 Children Act.

Mayall and Storey conclude that a centralised curriculum and testing system and the financial constraints of local management of schools meant that schools were no longer fulfilling the pastoral role as fully as they once had. They note that

> underlying debates on the character and functions of the school health service are issues about the appropriate division of labour between groups of adults for the health and welfare of children during their daily life at school and, more broadly, across their school career. The health care of children during their days at school has been neglected by policy makers ... parents remain the principal people deemed responsible for child health care.
>
> (Mayall and Storey 1998: 88)

Their research found that the school health service made very little contribution to health education. A key finding was that consultation between school and health staff was lacking.

The election of the Labour government in 1997 brought about renewed attention to child poverty and health inequalities. The Acheson Report (1998) recognised how individual characteristics, ethnicity, gender, early childhood, and social, economic and cultural contexts result in complex health outcomes and behaviours. It recommended: additional resources for schools serving children from less well-off groups to enhance their educational achievement; further development of high quality pre-school education to meet the needs of disadvantaged families in particular; the development of 'health promoting schools'; and further measures to improve school nutrition. A series of documents, such as *Saving Lives: our healthier nation* (1999), *Tackling Health Inequalities: cross-cutting review* (DoH 2002) and the Wanless Report (Wanless 2004) identified key policy themes that have had a bearing on the relationship between schools and health: lifestyle choices, life course factors (for example childhood experiences influencing adult behaviours), and health inequalities.

A particular focus, as noted earlier, has been on children perceived as being 'at risk'. This has included children whose health is affected by socio-economic and socio-cultural factors, as well as those with welfare and special educational needs. The inclusion of children with SEN in mainstream schools has meant those with special health needs becoming more prevalent than previously. Lightfoot *et al.* (2001) note that teachers, local education authority learning support staff, school care assistants, administrative and catering staff, school nurses and doctors, therapists and medical consultants may all have a role to play, which poses challenges of co-ordination. They refer to school staff not knowing whom to contact in the NHS and receiving variable responses from medical staff, usually because of concerns over confidentiality.

Sure Start developed as a major government programme aimed at closing the gap in outcome between children living in poverty and the wider population, and was set up after the 1998 Comprehensive Spending Review on services for young children. The Review found that children living in poverty were more likely to underachieve at school, to get involved in the criminal justice system as they went into adolescence, and to become parents as teenagers, and were less likely to be employed in young adulthood. Services for young children were found to be geographically patchy, uncoordinated, and of mixed quality (with most money spent on children over 4). It was concluded that early, co-ordinated and sustained support could make a difference to child outcomes (Eisenstadt 2002). Sure Start's objectives include to: improve health; improve the ability to learn; improve social and emotional development; and to strengthen families and communities. Emphasis is placed on the notion of co-ordination to add value, as the Spending Review had revealed that effort was wasted because providers did not talk to each other.

The Children Act (2004) seeks to increase co-ordination of health, social care and education. It enshrined five outcomes specified in the national *Every Child Matters* framework (DfES 2004c) in law. These outcomes are: being healthy, staying safe, enjoying and achieving, making a contribution to society and achieving economic well-being). The 2004 Act also gave wider roles for GPs, health visitors, school nurses and midwives in promoting child and family health. All services for children in England except for health are now the responsibility of one department in each local authority, Children's Services, and one central government department, the Department for Children, Schools and Families (DCSF).

Co-ordination of services related to health provision

At the time of writing in 2008, co-ordination is a key theme that runs through all current policy initiatives. The White Paper *Choosing Health: making healthy choices easier* (DoH 2004b) has a particular emphasis on health promotion, whole school approaches to health in all arrangements (including travel, meals and snacks), reducing health inequalities, and the co-ordination of services in one location as part of integrated services. It provides encouragement to schools to become extended schools and calls for the modernisation and expansion of school nursing services, intending by 2010 for every cluster of schools to have access to a team led by a qualified nurse. 'Healthy Schools' are expected to use a whole school approach involving the whole community. This involves providing for personal, social and health education; healthy eating; physical activity; emotional health and well-being.

A similar focus on multi-agency working, improving access to services for children and tackling health inequalities is at the heart of the *National Service Framework for Children, Young People and Maternity Services* (DoH/DfES 2004), a ten-year programme to stimulate long-term and sustained improvement in children's health. Further attempts at co-ordination are apparent in the *Chief Nursing Officer's Review of the Nursing, Midwifery and Health Visiting Contribution to Vulnerable Children and Young People* (DoH 2004a) which recommended: increasing the number of school nurses; strengthening the public health role of midwives and nurses; and greater integration and co-location of practitioners within children's centres. *Working Together to Safeguard Children* (DoH, HO and DfES 2006) sets out health service and health professional responsibilities in safeguarding children and promoting their well–being and welfare.

The *Common Assessment Framework for Children and Young People* (DfES 2006a) attempts to provide an integrated and holistic structure for assessing children's development. Key principles are to assess and intervene early. Assessments are to be undertaken by a range of specialists and be co-ordinated and shared. The Framework is designed to be used with unborn babies, children and young people with additional needs – covering areas relating to education, health, social care, behaviour and emotional development. Assessments cover three domains – how well a child is developing, including health and progress in learning; how well parents or carers are able to support their child's development and respond appropriately to his or her needs; and the impact of wider family and environmental elements on the child's development. Assessments are to be carried out by children's centres, schools and in health settings. Common assessments will enable health visitors and midwives to take a broad view of issues affecting unborn and new born infants as part of the Child Health Promotion Programmes and principles will be used at health drop-in centres in schools.

The Childcare Act (2006) places a duty on local authorities to improve the well-being of young children and to reduce inequalities in relation to the five outcomes of the *Every Child Matters* agenda, and provides the statutory basis for the Children's Centre model by combining childcare, education, health, some social services tasks and job centres on one site.

Exworthy *et al.* (2003) characterise recent health policy as concerned with the early childhood years as part of a life-course approach (as evidenced in Sure Start and a focus on the reduction of child poverty); with disadvantage in specific communities; with redistribution; and with the integration of health-supportive services. Primary Care Trusts have been given a central role in commissioning services, developing primary health care and tackling health inequalities. Exworthy *et al.* also note the development of target-setting and a performance culture in the health and other social services. Public service agreements determine the link between social policy and finance, within a framework that attempts to provide joined up government.

Exclusion, law and public order

The Social Exclusion Unit (SEU) was established in 1997, recognising that children and young people are especially vulnerable to the effects of social exclusion. The unit began with the premise that some children living in poverty are exposed to crime as victims, or drawn into early drug or substance misuse and offending. Such children may be faced with multiple problems, skip important stages of their education and face illiteracy and unemployment. Given this backdrop, it was assumed that some children's long-term prospects might include homelessness, mental health problems and chronic debt.

As social exclusion issues cross the boundaries of any one Department, a new Social Exclusion Task Force (SETF) was created in the Cabinet Office to coordinate the agenda across government. The SETF draws together the expertise of some staff from the former Social Exclusion Unit and policy specialists from the Prime Minister's Strategy Unit. The SETF was launched on 13 June 2006.[3]

The SEU and SETF have led a number of significant projects with the aim of breaking this cycle of disadvantage by providing support from the early years through to adulthood. The cross-departmental Green Paper, *Children at Risk* (2003) set out new arrangements for delivering an integrated and preventative approach to promoting the life chances of vulnerable children. The Paper looked at measures to reduce the levels of educational underachievement, offending, antisocial behaviour, teenage pregnancy and ill health among children and young people (aged 0–19). The SEU published a practice guide to coincide with the Green Paper, *A Better Education for Children in Care* (2003). This highlighted the issues that were raised through the SEU development work and gives good practice examples from local authorities.

The Excellence in Cities (EiC) programme was launched in September 1999 to raise standards and promote inclusion in inner cities and other urban areas (see DfES 2007). It focused on leadership, behaviour, and teaching and learning. Initially based only in secondary schools, the programme quickly expanded to include primary schools and worked closely with the Primary National Strategy. By April 2006, over 1,300 secondary schools and 3,600 primary schools in 57 local authorities had been involved in the EiC programme. The programme aimed to tackle underachievement in schools through specific Strands, including the development of Learning Mentors, the development of Learning Support Units, provision for Gifted and Talented pupils and the building of City Learning Centres. The programme also ran alongside the Leadership Incentive Grant and the Behaviour Improvement Programme.

EiC Action Zones were set up in urban areas where there was a mixture of social disadvantage and under-performance in schools, typically focusing on the needs of one or two secondary schools and their feeder primary schools. The Action Zones focused particularly on improving the quality of teaching and learning, on social inclusion, on the provision of support to pupil and families, and on working in partnership with businesses and other organisations. Eighty Excellence Clusters were also set up in smaller areas to focus on the provision for gifted and talented pupils, the development of Learning Mentors and Learning Support Units.

According to DfES (2007), there is continuing evidence of a 'partnership dividend' in EiC schools. Because of increased and sustained work with primary and secondary schools, the rate of increase in GCSE performance for EiC areas is around twice that of non-EiC schools for the fourth consecutive year. This means there has been a narrowing of the achievement gap between EiC and non-EiC areas from 12.4 per cent in 2001 to 6.9 per cent in 2005. Funding changes in April 2006 meant that the targeted funding and support for EiC partnerships that hitherto had come through local authorities changed. The funding now goes directly to schools within EiC areas as part of their School Development Grant. This gives schools the freedom to decide on the most appropriate and effective ways to address school improvement and pupil achievement, but also creates geographical variations in how, when and why schools engage with services and practices in different regions of England.

A report entitled *Tackling Truancy and Exclusion in School* (The Poverty Site, online[4]) suggested that the ways agencies were able to deal with truancy and exclusions from school had to change. The report identifies that changes were made in the form of the 1998 Crime and Disorder Act, which gave new powers to police. LAs set new targets for schools in 1999; in 2002 the national truancy sweeps began; and 2005 saw the introduction of new Education Regulations. In 1998 'Supporting families' was published, a government consultation paper drawn up by the Ministerial Group on the Family (Home Office 1998). The paper aimed to find ways of supporting all parents in their role to provide 'strong and stable families' and asserts that the policy of support for families will be assisted by 'measures to strengthen the institution of marriage' with its 'extra rights and also extra responsibilities'. This consultation paper contains 5 key themes: ensuring that all families have access to the advice and support they need; improving family prosperity and reducing poverty through the tax and benefit system; making it easier for families to balance work and home; strengthening marriage and reducing the risks of family breakdown; and tackling the more serious problems of family life, such as domestic violence, truancy, exclusions and school-age pregnancy.

Behaviour and attendance

Gallimore (1977) examines the role of Education Welfare Officers (EWOs), suggesting that schools have, historically, varied widely in their perceptions and definitions of their role and function, perhaps due to two major factors. Firstly, changing conceptions of the role of EWOs were successively introduced by the 1944 Education Act, the Plowden Report (CACE 1967) and the Seebohm Report (1968), accompanied by changes in nomenclature from 'board man' to 'truancy officer' to 'education welfare officer'. Secondly, Gallimore argues, there has been a lack of effective publicity from the education welfare service, which has meant that not only the general public but even head teachers are often unclear about the nature of the EWO's services. *Every Child Matters* (DfES 2003) brings the work of the EWO under the remit of multi-agency working, specifically within the Behaviour and Education Support Team.

Blyth and Milner (1997) discuss the role of Education Social Workers (ESWs) and suggest that, although practice varies considerably across local authorities, ESWs are always involved in a wide range of welfare activities, including child protection. However, there seems to be general agreement that dealing with school attendance is a central responsibility. Carlen *et al.* (1992) found head teachers critical of social services for seeming to lack action and continuity in relation to dealing with truancy. 'Circles of blame' emerged where agencies held other agencies responsible for problems encountered. Normington and Kyriacou (1994) suggest 'a general lack of understanding by each agency of the aims and roles of the other agencies [...] the records maintained by schools and agencies differ markedly, and none reflects the full picture of the child's problems nor gives a clear picture of the multi-disciplinary work occurring' (p. 14).

In December 2002 the government set out to improve children's behaviour and attendance in schools. The Behaviour Improvement Programme (BIP) is a key part of the National Behaviour and Attendance Strategy (DfES 2007b). It represents the government's commitment to tackling behaviour and attendance and targeting resources where they are needed most. Behaviour and Education Support Services have been established to work in partnership with schools, as part of the local authority and within a framework of inclusion, to help them promote positive behaviour, and to provide effective support to pupils, parents and schools where behaviour is a concern and may have an effect on achievement. The precise nature of the services provided by a local authority's behaviour support service will vary between authorities, as will the composition of staffing, contractual arrangements with schools and arrangements for local referral routes. However, all are likely to provide both preventative services and direct support services for children with behavioural difficulties.

Behaviour and Education Support Teams (BESTs) are multi-agency teams bringing together a complementary mix of professionals from the fields of health, social care and education. The aim of a BEST is to promote emotional well-being, positive behaviour and school attendance, by identifying and supporting those with, or at risk of developing, emotional and behavioural problems. BESTs work with children and young people aged 5–18, their families and schools to intervene early and prevent problems developing further. They are strategically placed in targeted primary and secondary schools, and in the community, alongside a range of other support structures and services. According to the DfES (2007b), successful BESTs bring together the skills, perspectives and experience of a range of practitioners, forming an effective multi-disciplinary team.

Also working more broadly to address the issue of antisocial behaviour is the youth justice system, as set out in section 37 of the Crime and Disorder Act 1998, which has the aim of preventing offending by children and young people aged 10 to 17. Youth Offending Teams (YOTs) are currently the main vehicle by which that aim and its supporting objectives are delivered. Working with young offenders aged 10 to 17, YOTs were introduced in April 2000 to coordinate action at a local level, bringing together professionals with a range of disciplines. Statutory involvement is required from local authority social services and education departments, the police, probation service and health authorities. Other agencies, such as housing and youth and community departments, are also encouraged to contribute resources to YOTs.

Sure Start is, as noted, another UK government initiative that aims to tackle child poverty and social exclusion through integration and co-ordination of services in early education, childcare and health and family support. It aims to 'deliver the best start in life for every child' (www.surestart.gov.uk). According to Edgley and Avis (2007), Sure Start has hitherto operated exclusively in neighbourhoods with high levels of deprivation, as measured by the Index of Multiple Deprivation (DETR 2000), attempting to find innovative ways of working, and providing additional services to improve the quantity and quality of services to disadvantaged families and preschool children (aged 0–4 years). According to McLaughlin (2004), Sure Start represents a central feature of government policy to modernise education, health and social care services through the promotion of inter-professional collaboration, via partnerships and interagency working. Local Children's Centre programmes draw together education, health and social care provision to move across professional and agency boundaries, between government departments, local authorities and professional groups, and across the private and the voluntary sector, working with those who deliver services and those who receive them.

Government policy is committed to further entrenching this collaborative model by 'mainstreaming' Sure Start services: that is, by ensuring that in future those planning early years childcare, health and family support services use the experience from Sure Start to adapt statutory services to become more integrated and responsive to children's and families' needs. A more collaborative and integrated model underpins a range of recent policy initiatives, from the Children Bill (House of Lords 2004), to *Every Child Matters* (DfES 2003), as well as the National Service Framework for Children, Young People and Maternity Services (DoH and DfES 2004), all of which aim to improve public services so that they better meet the needs of children and young people. Sure Start, then, is one element in a broader context of policy developments designed to cultivate collaborative and integrated service provision.

Children, race and ethnicity

Whilst the 1976 Race Relations Act established the Commission for Racial Equality (CRE),[5] which was concerned with eliminating racial discrimination, and promoting equality of opportunity and good relations between persons of different racial groups generally, it had comparatively little impact in schools. Gillborn (1997) argues that until the 1960s and 70s (and beyond) minority ethnic groups were seen largely as a 'problem'. Meeting their needs was conceived largely in terms of children needing to learn English as an additional language – a programme which was strongly advocated by the Plowden Report. Whilst, more recently, more attention has been paid to the value of diversity and to cultural and religious issues, 'multicultural education' for all children has often been seen in a negative light, being associated with a political correctness seen as unnecessary and a distraction (see, for example, Cole 1998). The National Curriculum statutory inclusion statement (National Curriculum Online, no date), which makes specific reference to the Race Relations Act 1976, sets out principles that are essential to developing a more inclusive curriculum. Teachers are required to 'ensure they meet the full range of pupils' diverse needs' and to 'be aware of the requirements of the equal opportunities legislation that covers race, gender and disability'.

Gillborn (2005) argues that the Thatcher government in the 1980s removed racial and ethnic equality issues from consideration, adopting a 'colour blind' approach on the grounds of supposed fairness. The Major administration in the early 1990s continued this approach. This led, Gillborn argues, to a lack of co-ordinated agency approaches to providing for the entitlements of minority ethnic groups. Such support as was available, through Section 11 funding, was short term and could be seen as exacerbating feelings of marginalisation. Gillborn (1997) also refers to the 'scaling down' of resources and support despite continued underachievement of certain groups – especially the (then) more recently established Bangladeshi communities. He also comments that the UK government had focused only on language issues without considering other factors.

Gillborn (1997) argues for social class as a key factor affecting the opportunities and achievements of children from minority ethnic groups. He notes that a study was set up to look at multicultural education within the National Curriculum but its findings were never published: 'Education reforms are posited in a deracialised discourse that, while never mentioning race, constructs a particular version of the nation, its heritage, and traditions that excludes any serious engagement with minority issues' (Gillborn 1997: 387). Little serious consideration has been given until recently to the complex relationship between ethnicity, race, socioeconomic circumstances and gender. Scott and Sylva (2002) suggest that studies often consider, individually, gender, ethnicity or age but rarely tackle the complexities of overlapping and interrelated aspects of disadvantage.

Leung (2001) points to the marginal place of English as an Additional Language (EAL) within the National Curriculum, where it is treated as being concerned with teaching strategies and approaches when, it could be argued, it should be a subject specialism. Over the past 20 years a key debate has been about withdrawal and in-class teaching. Government guidance has emphasised meaningful and interactive language situations and the need for audio-visual support for learning – in essence approaches that are seen as appropriate for all pupils. Pupils are expected to experience English as a subject in the National Curriculum at the same time as learning to speak and understand the English language. This is not the only approach: in the Australian state of Victoria (Department of Education, Victoria 1998), pupils follow a specific EAL curriculum before studying English as a curriculum subject.

The Plowden Report stressed the importance of immigrants learning English, but said little about how this was to be achieved. The Bullock Report (DES 1975) again emphasised the importance of teaching English to immigrants, at a time when this was usually achieved by withdrawal or special class or school methods with the pupils then being reintegrated. This, however, was at odds with the emphasis on first hand experience, discovery learning and language as a means to an end. Bullock warned of the dangers of separate teaching leading to children of immigrants being isolated from other pupils and of their teachers not communicating with those in mainstream education. Leung argues that this is when EAL as subject gave way to EAL as process. The Swann Report (DES 1985) argued for a pluralist and inclusive approach that brought EAL learning into the mainstream. Leung argues, however, that the low attainment of some minority ethnic groups suggests that this is not wholly successful, questioning whether it is appropriate to have as the only form of assessment of English one that has been developed to assess children speaking English as their first language.

Consistent with Conservative governments' denial of ethnicity as a factor in terms of achievement, little data exists regarding ethnicity prior to the election of the Labour government in 1997. If children did badly, then this had generally been seen as the fault either of the school or of the individual and so information about ethnicity was not systematically collected. Tikly (2004) argues that until 2003, when the DfES introduced the Pupil Level Annual School Census (PLASC) categories for recording ethnic groups, data collected varied between local authorities and between local and national government. Some groupings were very broad and there was little account of dual and mixed heritage in the recording. This could mean that differences within African, Middle Eastern and White minority ethnic communities may not have been evident, and data was missing for Somali, Tamil, Iranian, Turkish, Turkish Cypriot, Turkish Somali and Traveller and Gypsy/Roma pupils. Rarely was information available that dealt with ethnicity and gender despite evidence of differences in attainment. National data was difficult to collate until 2003 because of the differences in the categories used. Very little data was also available regarding nursery–aged children and the uptake of nursery education by ethnic group. The PLASC system is intended to standardise the collection of data. Scotland and Wales now have national systems but not Northern Ireland. Additional information is available from reports by Ofsted and Excellence in Cities projects.

Since 1997, more attention has been paid to ethnicity, race and EAL as factors which impact upon attainment. The government is, as noted, energetically pursuing an agenda of family-focused early intervention, with policy initiatives such as Every Child Matters (DfES 2004), and the Respect Action Plan (Home Office 2006) which proposes parenting classes to help families improve child behaviour and achievement. According to Scott, O'Connor and Futh (2006), parents from minority ethnic groups may have particular burdens to address. Those who are well established may experience discrimination across several contexts, while those who have arrived more recently may additionally struggle with language difficulties, lack of information about how to access services and benefits, and isolation.

The 2000 Race Relations (Amendment) Act meant that for the first time all schools were required to have a race equality policy and to pay attention to the rights and entitlements of all groups. Ofsted took on a major role as the agency responsible for monitoring the new legislative requirements. Tomlinson (2005) cites Figueroa (2003) who argues that Labour policy has emphasised 'citizenship', which 'does not include diversity, conflict resolution, international or global issues or gender and ethnic diversity and anti-racism' (page 166). Support for EAL and to improve the attainment of minority ethnic groups is provided through the Ethnic Minority Achievement Grant (EMAG), which replaced Section 11 funding in 1998. Tomlinson (2005) argues that whilst there had been resources for expert EAL teaching and research under Section 11 funding, this was dispersed by the EMAG. Gillborn (2005) comments that the Five Year Strategy (DfES 2004a) mentions minority ethnic pupils only once in a brief paragraph headed 'low achieving minority ethnic groups'.

The establishment of Education Action Zones (EAZs) was intended to support those in the inner city, with a focus on attainment (and special programmes for gifted and talented children) and behaviour (with the provision of learning mentors and more Learning Support Units for the disruptive). The success of EAZs has, however, been disputed by Power *et al.* (2003). Tomlinson (2005) states that Sure Start has been seen as more successful, but that there has been no substantial research to date that has looked at its effects on minority ethnic groups.

According to the publication *Ethnicity and Education* (DfES 2006b), pupils from groups including Travellers of Irish heritage, Gypsy / Roma, Black Caribbean, White and Black Caribbean, Black Other and Pakistani heritage pupils make less progress at primary school than White British pupils with the same prior attainment. Children of White UK heritage comprise the highest attaining group. Pupils of Indian and Chinese heritage perform above average. Bangladeshi, Pakistani and Black African children are the lowest attaining, but differences between groups are not as significant when account is taken of parents' education and occupation. There appears, again, to be a link between social class, deprivation, ethnicity and educational attainment.

Gypsy/ Roma and Traveller children are notably marginalised, reflecting the second-class citizenship status of the Gypsy/ Roma and Traveller communities. Although they are invisible in the statistics, there is evidence to suggest that this is a group of children at particular risk of poverty. This, Cemlyn and Clark argue, reflects their 'wider relationship with the dominant settled society and the discrimination and denial of human rights across a range of aspects of day-to-day living' (2005: 154). The children of asylum seekers constitute an even more neglected group. Save the Children have published a series of reports detailing the difficulties faced by children seeking asylum either with their parents or on their own. One of these reported on a study of children who had been detained for purposes of immigration control. It revealed the damaging effects on the children's health and education and particularly emphasised the point that 'the greatest negative impacts are on mental health' (Crawley and Lester 2005: ix).

The complex relationship between ethnicity, poverty, class and disability began to be recognised in legislation through the 2005 Equality Bill (House of Commons 2005), which makes provision for the establishment of the Commission for Equality and Human Rights. It dissolves the Equal Opportunities Commission (EOC), the Commission for Racial Equality (CRE) and the Disability Rights Commission (DRC). The Bill makes provision about discrimination on grounds of religion or belief and imposes duties relating to sex discrimination on persons performing public functions. It also amends the Disability Discrimination Act 1995.

Race relations, asylum and refugee families

There are many interesting questions continuing to emerge from the policies and practices of neo-liberal ideologies. For example, is the notion of 'class' beginning to be defined more widely to embrace other interwoven socio-cultural issues? If 'race', gender, religion and other factors are inscribed at the heart of class, how can government policies and practices sensitively support such complex sociological inter-relationships? Sayyid (2003) reviews current theoretical perspectives on diversity and the construction of identity. He acknowledges that the academic work on the nature of identity presents some difficulties in application to public services but notes that the way that we understand identity to be constructed has changed significantly from the 1970s, when there was a strong drive implicit within public policy and services to 'fit' people within a fixed, dominant cultural model. It is no longer possible to build public policy on this model in a world where belief systems, social codes, cultural allegiances and group identities are in a constant state of flux and change. According to Sayyid, individual narratives are constructed on difference – 'not on who we are but who we are not'. This model of the construction of identity is therefore a relative process with individuals living out the representational model of their own personal narrative in contrast to those who are different, drawing upon social and cultural tools that are available to them to do so.

Sayyid (2003) also claims that the emergence of a global culture has had a significant influence upon the construction of identity. Internet, television, ease of travel and increased methods of interaction across cultures and continents create societies in which there are not fixed, cultural identities and where one is more likely to find 'differences within differences within differences'. There is no universal model and to talk of a sharp distinction between the 'host' country and the 'immigrant' is no longer accurate. This complexity is a challenge for contemporary public policy, which needs to be flexible and responsive to change and diversity.

In contrast, practitioners work with individuals or families in contexts where discriminatory outcomes cannot be separated into separate strands labeled sexuality, race or class. Scott and Sylva (2002) suggest that this is an illustration of a significant gap between research and practice.

Scott, O'Connor and Futh (2006) suggest that parenting styles that fit familiar circumstances in the country of origin may be challenged by and found unacceptable in the new settings in Britain. For example, some disciplinary practices may be frowned upon, and might even instigate referral to social services. Equally, families from minorities may bring parenting styles that are considered advantageous in the new settings, for example greater social cohesiveness and closer supervision of children that helps the well-being of the parents and protects children in higher risk urban conditions.

Research undertaken by the Race Equality Foundation (2006) found inequitable experiences of black and minority ethnic communities in health, education and social care services. It also highlighted limited usage of mainstream services by these communities, and the reliance of many on services provided by BME (black and minority ethnic) voluntary and faith-based organisations. Scott, O'Connor and Futh (2006: 3) similarly state: 'many public services are under-used by minority parents – the services are failing them by not being acceptable and accessible. There is little information whether programmes based on Western ideas are acceptable to, and work for, minority families'. Voluntary, community and faith organisations provide a range of invaluable services to Asian, African and Caribbean communities, both directly and indirectly, as commissioned by mainstream providers. According to the research, there has been growing interest in including faith organisations in the development and delivery of local services, for example in urban regeneration, but there is little information about the extent of health and social care services provided by this sector or indeed by black and minority ethnic voluntary organisations in general.

There is now considerable national information on the experience of poverty of black and minority ethnic families and children. Outreach is important with all black communities, and may be the only way to contact newly-arrived communities. Black and minority ethnic mothers identify health visitors as a particularly valuable source of information. The research has shown that there is an association with black and minority ethnic workers being present in a service and the use made by these communities. Beyond being able to communicate effectively, workers' knowledge and skills in encouraging participation have been highlighted.

The Race Equality Foundation study concludes that any research concerned with gender, race and religion needs to place particular emphasis on the interrelationship of diversity rather than focusing on one single aspect of difference, beginning from the premise that inequality and prejudice will be prevalent. One of the challenges to the current research agenda is the need for future studies to be more multi-dimensional in their approach in order to have an impact on inequality and disadvantage. Finally there needs to be an emphasis on the integration of these research agendas into the existing processes that are part of the planning and provision of public social services.

Professional partnership with parents

Since the Warnock Report (DES 1978), the term 'partnership with parents' has become widespread in special education policy (DfES 2001a; DfES 2004b), and it has also been the focus of much debate within research (Dale 1996; Murray 2000; Todd 2003). The Audit Commission Report (2002) states that involvement of parents in the education of children with special needs in the United Kingdom is considered not only a right, but also a necessary component of the delivery of effective and efficient provision. Parents are seen to provide an important source of information on the working of the systems designed to meet their child's needs (Dockrell, Peacey and Lunt 2002).

Armstrong (1995: 18) states that partnership implies mutual respect, complementary expertise, and a willingness of partners to learn from each other. However, the term 'partnership' is often so loosely defined within policy and research that it tells us little. And despite the frequent rhetoric about the importance of parenting, little practical recognition has been given to the weight and, indeed, the usefulness of parents' expertise and experiences (Dale 1996). Dale puts forward an analysis of parent-professional relationships, which identifies different models of professionals working in partnership with parents in very different ways. The focus on partnership with parents can partly be understood as a government response to the increasingly confrontational relationships many parents experience as they engage with the special education system. Yet the vagueness of the rhetoric and the lack of commitment to minimum standards mean that a 'partnership model' can contribute to adversarial and conflict ridden relationships, which often result in partnership breakdown (Dale 1996).

The aim of recent policy has apparently been to soften the boundaries between parents and professionals by encouraging teachers to treat the concerns of parents in the same way as if they had been raised by a professional. The guidance in the DfES Code of Practice (2001b) asserts:

> Partnership with parents plays a key role in promoting a culture of co-operation between parents, schools, LEAs and others [...] All parents of children with special educational needs should be treated as partners.
>
> (DfES 2001b: 16)

However it remains the case that whoever makes decisions about the level of support available to a child in school is *de facto* in control of the relationship, and this is usually the education professional (Armstrong 1995). Armstrong has questioned whether the 'parents as partners' model should really be seen as a genuine attempt to work in partnership with parents. He suggests that the real intention is simply to incorporate parents into the bureaucratic procedure and so remove the 'genuine' power of parents. Some support for such an interpretation can be found in the Code of Practice, which implies that the key role envisaged for parents in this 'partnership' might be understood as that of 'informant':

> Parents hold key information [...] They have unique strengths, knowledge and experience to contribute to the shared view of a child's needs and the best ways of supporting them.
>
> (DfES 2001b: 16)

The notion of professional partnership with parents is therefore a contested one. It may represent a genuine desire to give parents a greater and more equitable share in decisions about their children's well-being and progress. But it may also be intended to recruit parents to the school's purposes, or to enable the smooth operation of 'bureaucratic' procedures. At times, partnership with parents may even function as a method of passing the child's 'problems' back to the parents.

Child protection and safeguarding children

The 1960s was the decade of the 'discovery of child abuse', according to Hendrick as cited in Boyden (1997). Subsequently, mounting concern about child abuse has led to a stream of circulars and guidance (Hallett, cited in Stevenson 1999a) and a number of high profile public inquiries such as the Maria Colwell Inquiry (DHSS 1974) and the Victoria Climbié Inquiry (Lamming 2003). According to Boyden (1997), child protection issues have been underpinned by theories of an adult society which is perceived to undermine childhood innocence, causing children to become segregated and protected from the adult world and the social dangers within it. Boyden suggests that as a consequence of this approach, child protection strategies have been both nurturing and constraining and have reflected particular images of children, childhood and the child.

Mayall (2002) argues that children in the UK are subsumed under 'family' and that policies for children are in fact targeted at families, often focusing on parents. Childhood is seen as a preparatory stage for adult life and, as such, the perceived dangers presented by unfamiliar adults justify the social exclusion of children from public places, and the measures that schools have undertaken in order to secure their premises and 'police' their staff. Mayall contrasts this situation with that in Finland, where children are seen not as citizens *in potentia* but as citizens in their own right, and children's rights to use public spaces override concerns about the perceived threats to their safety.

Policies for child protection in the UK also seem to reflect the wider tensions underpinning images of childhood (James and Prout 1997). On the one hand, children are seen as passive, suffering, innocent victims, and on the other they are seen as unsocialised, anti-social, deviant, and deficient (Boyden 1997). Research suggests that children themselves place a high priority on the importance of play and access to safe public spaces (Save the Children, cited in Lister 2006). However, in the UK's 'social investment state' (Lister 2006) where children are valued for what they will become and how they will contribute to the economy, rather than as citizens in their own right, play and access to safe public spaces is accorded relatively low priority.

The inquiry into the death of Maria Colwell (DHSS 1974) re-focused the spotlight on children's perceived needs (Stevenson 1999a). The report following Maria's death highlighted a serious lack of coordination among services responsible for child welfare.

The lack of interaction between education and social services departments emerged as particularly unsatisfactory, as it became clear that Maria's junior school teacher failed to get her concerns heard (Stevenson 1999a). The report into Maria's death resulted in the creation of Area Child Protection Committees (ACPCs) in England and Wales to coordinate local efforts to safeguard children. This led to a series of legislation in the 1980s, which included the Child Care Act 1980; Foster Children Act 1980; Children's Homes Act 1982; *Social Services Committee Report on Children in Care* (DHSS 1984); Child Abduction and Custody Act 1985; and Local Government Act 1988.

The Children Act (1989) marked the culmination of a period in which child welfare policy had become a major political concern. The central principles of the Act stressed the importance of an approach to working with families based on negotiation and involving parents and children in agreed plans. However, the Act focused the support of the state on those families considered to be 'in need'. The Children Act, then, made the assumption that 'normal' families should not need public services (Cannan 1992). The Act gave every child the right to protection from abuse and exploitation and the right to inquiries to protect their welfare within a new framework for care and protection of children. Part two of the Act stresses the importance of inter-disciplinary and interagency work as an essential process in the task of attempting to protect children from abuse. Within the Children Act, the education service is not considered to be an investigative or interventionist agency but it is considered to have an important role to play at the recognition and referral stages. All teachers are required to have an awareness of their duty to report concerns about a child's welfare.

Social services, social work and child protection

The Social Work in Primary Schools (SWIPS) project (Webb and Vulliamy 2001), carried out in schools in the north-east of England, sought to gain a detailed understanding of the extent and nature of the social work dimension of primary teaching. Earlier research undertaken by Webb and Vulliamy (1996) explored the impact of the Education Reform Act (1988) on primary schools, which revealed that an extremely time-consuming aspect of the role of many of their sample of head teachers was interaction with parents, involving the provision of counselling and social work. It also found that there was a neglect of a consideration of the primary head teacher as social worker.

In the 1989 Children Act, child protection was identified as a vital area of interagency responsibility, requiring schools and local education authorities (LEAs) to co-operate with social services. A number of agencies, including LEAs and their schools, were obliged to assist social services departments acting on behalf of children in need or investigating child abuse (David 1994). However, although school staff were deemed essential partners in ensuring both that children are properly protected from potential abuse and, when problems have arisen, that clear inter-agency plans are carried through to offer the child continued protection, there seems to be only minimal guidance written for schools. For example, Circular 10/95 (DfEE 1995) offered funding in the form of Grants for Education Support and Training (GEST) for child protection training for 1995–96, after which training requirements had to be met from mainstream funding.

Circular 10/97 (DfEE 1997b) introduced the requirement for specific coverage of child protection in initial teacher training. However Baginsky and Hodgkinson (1999) state that this provision varied between HE institutions, and was adversely influenced by the demands of the National Curriculum for primary initial teacher training, leading to increasingly reduced and more superficial coverage of the issues. The Teacher Training Agency (1997) suggested that training in child protection could be usefully included in a school's induction profile and/or identified as an area for development in a beginning teacher's career entry profile.

Government guidance (DoH 1991) and Circular 10/95 (DfEE 1995) specified that there should be a designated member of staff in every school who is responsible for child protection issues, and LEAs were required to keep a list of such named persons. According to the SWIPS project (Webb and Vulliamy 2001), some schools decided to conflate the roles of the Special Educational Needs Co-ordinator (SENCO) and the child protection co-ordinator as the situations and experiences that often rendered children 'at risk' were also likely to induce learning difficulties and/or behaviour problems, and so the two roles intertwined.

The Child Protection Register was established as a central record, usually maintained by social services, of all children in a given area for whom support is being provided via inter-agency planning. Generally these are children considered to be at risk of abuse or neglect. Child Protection Conferences were formal meetings attended by representatives from all of the agencies concerned with the child's welfare. Their purpose was to gather together and evaluate all of the relevant information about a child, and to plan any immediate action that might be necessary to protect them. Circular 10/95 (DfEE 1995) points out that every school should develop a child protection policy, which should reflect its statutory duties and pastoral responsibilities and refer to the procedures to be followed. LEAs are also required to identify a senior officer with responsibility for co-ordinating child protection policy and action across the authority's schools.

Other legislation also became involved in the relationship between education and social care in relation to child protection/safeguarding children, including the UN Convention on the Rights of the Child. This convention applies to all young people under 18 (or the age of majority if earlier). The UK is a signatory, but the Convention's provisions were not initially enforceable in UK courts. Signatories undertook to ensure that the courts and other public bodies make the best interests of the child a primary consideration in all actions concerning young people.

Despite the focus on Child Protection in policy, since the death of Maria Colwell another child death led to the publication of Lord Lamming's report into the death of Victoria Climbié in January 2003 (Lamming 2003). Lord Lamming found that police, health and social services had missed 12 opportunities to save her. In June 2003, Margaret Hodge was appointed the first children's minister and in September of that year the government's green paper *Every Child Matters* (ECM) was published. *Every Child Matters* (DfES 2003) defines 'child safety' as being safe from maltreatment, neglect, violence and sexual exploitation; being safe from accidental injury and death; being safe from bullying and discrimination; being safe from crime and anti-social behaviour in and out of school; having security, stability and being cared for; and ensuring that parents, carers and families provide safe homes and stability (DfES 2003: 9). *Every Child Matters* stated that 150 children's trusts needed to be set up by 2006, amalgamating health, education and social services, and involving a children's director to oversee local services, statutory local safeguarding boards to replace Area Child Protection Committees, and a children's commissioner for England. In 2005, Professor Al Aynsley Green was appointed as England's first children's commissioner.

DISCUSSION

Possibilities and tensions in the vision of integrated provision

The interaction of education, health services, law and social work has been conceptualised in this report as inter-agency intervention that seeks to connect previously disparate professional fields in order to engage, support and invest in particular 'types' of (problematic) families, and specific 'kinds' of 'insufficient' or 'incomplete' children, in an attempt to maximise each child's potential within the education system (and future market economy). Agencies are mobilised at different points, in different ways and for different reasons to provide guidance, resources and support for children and families constructed as being 'in deficit' and/or expressing aspects of 'otherness' within, and to some extent, across differing political ideologies. Both Thatcherism and New Labour's 'Third Way' seem to perpetuate notions of an 'ideal-typical', non-nuisance family that is sustained as 'productive' and therefore 'invisible' in terms of service engagement, one which arguably embodies traditional male/female roles, is white, middle-class and constituted by a heterosexual partnership.

The nature and thrust of differing interpretations of neo-liberal ideologies over the past three decades seems to form a shifting basis, upon which the provision for 'nuisance' families is premised. The extent to which different agencies construct the family, interact with each other and seek to offer 'seamless' provision differs between political eras, but also has elements in common. For example, interesting perspectives emerge from ways different agencies have become re-defined by their 'modernising' remits, their renewed roles and the changing responsibilities of the professionals working within them, as well as the ways agencies are mobilised in response to families and children who have become confined by their class, race and ethnicity, abilities and disabilities.

Market-driven policies and practices were precipitated by Thatcher's Conservative government and re-cast, 'resurrected but with new attitudes' (Freeden 1999: 43), by Blair's New Labour government. Movement across these entangled eras has involved some ideological shifts and tensions in relation to the family, accompanied by the more radical organisational re-configuration of services offered to the child 'in deficit' by different agencies. The Conservative neo-liberal position downplayed the barriers and complexities involved in enabling all children to access, and comprehensively participate in, education. Labour's Third Way orchestrated a shift in agencies' 'textures of contact and interactions with clients' (Jones 2001: 549), as the mantra of 'making a difference' intensified the politicisation and value-added commodification of inequalities. Agencies that proliferate support for families constructed as needing 'guided persuasion over coercion' (Freeden 1999: 46), or who were 'living in challenging circumstances' (Gewirtz 2001: 366) have become reorganised among market economies driven by the rhetoric and agendas of social inclusion.

According to Gilmour (1993), the Thatcher government started the neo-liberal transformation of the UK with its associated rise in inequality, social polarisation and increases in state centralisation and authority. Gilmour argues that 'the establishment of individualism and a free-market state is an unbending if not dictatorial venture which demands the prevention of collective action and the submission of dissenting institutions and individuals' (1993: 273–74). Thatcher took the position that economic and social phenomena can be explained by the actions of individuals:

> There is no such thing as society. There is a living tapestry of men and women and people and the beauty of that tapestry and the quality of our lives will depend upon how much each of us is prepared to take responsibility for ourselves and each of us prepared to turn round and help those who are unfortunate.
>
> (Thatcher 1987)

So, although the 1980s and 1990s were subsequent to and continued to embody mobilising social movements and collective action (including for example libertarian currents, women's equality, gay liberation, racial equality and disability politics), Thatcherism held that a child's 'belonging' to, or 'identifying' with different minority groups was relatively insignificant in terms of his or her opportunities to access, be included in and participate in mainstream education.

Certain tensions can be discerned within the flow of the 1980s and 1990s that pull between the appeal to traditional family ideals and to a market agenda. The concept of 'parental choice' straddles these two moments. Such tensions seemed to have promoted something of an individualised 'market' child, whose parents were perceived as consumers, and whose decisions were framed by the mantle of entitlement and rights. Inequalities in relation to class, poverty, race or ethnicity and special educational needs were primarily represented in terms of the inability to make the 'right' choices, or the propensity to carelessly fritter away equalities of opportunity offered to all. Issues of parenting and family 'responsibilities' towards children, and in support of the education system, were expressed in terms of choice, and policies advocated how the 'idealised' family *should* behave and *should* understand their roles and responsibilities. Given a national, standardised (and therefore seemingly 'equitable') curriculum, a child's inability to achieve, or behave, or progress was taken to indicate more about poor parental choices, inappropriate lifestyles and failing teachers than about other, more complex factors that permeate lived experiences within the education system.

From the late 1990s into the twenty-first century, the Labour government's policies and practices have carved out a 'third way'; drawing from aspects of neo-liberal conservatism and socialist components as well as ideational imports from the United States, they have also, however, implemented policies that deviate from all of these positions in crucial areas (Freeden 1999). Policies are characterised by tensions that move between community and professional cohesion on the one hand, understood in terms of services and agencies working together, and the quasi-market of parental choice and competition among schools and other services on the other. According to Jordan (2001), the Labour government has 'tackled the legacy of Thatcher-Major years – issues of inequality, division and conflict – by redefining social justice in terms of "opportunity" and "community"' (Jordan 2001: 527).

Freeden suggests that there has been a 'rediscovery of markets as tools of egalitarian choice, and an emphasis on the ethical virtues of participatory citizenship, dressed up in the mutually complementary and quasi-contractual language of rights and obligations' (1999: 44). According to Jordan (2001: 529), this 'involved a shift from generalised, mediocre, "one size fits all" public provision to an acknowledgement of the impact that social inequalities can have on a child's access to, and participation in the education system.' However this shift, according to Gewirtz (2001), nevertheless embodies an oversimplification of issues as a result of generalised and non-specific notions of community, and the homogenisation of particular groups. Labour's policies, according to Gewirtz, seem to be ideologically eclectic narratives of reinvention. Their particular imprint on social policy reform espouses 'tailor-made' services that have redefined the remits of statutory, non-statutory and voluntary agencies, involving new sets of qualificatory, regulatory and standard-setting systems to 'modernise' the whole approach to service delivery (cf DoH 1998).

Such an approach promotes public sector working in more cohesive and integrated ways, offering differentiated strategies of 'joined-up' services and intervention; constructing citizens as active, morally-autonomous individuals with high expectations of state services, but who in turn are expected to be self-responsible and hardworking (Crouch 2001). Blair (1996) claims that New Labour's policies and practices work to emancipate individuals from the vagaries and oppression of personal circumstance. According to Jordan, the 'promotion of "opportunity" and choice encourages mainstream citizens to be mobile in pursuit of "positive advantage" [...] including access to the best possible schools, clinics, care facilities' (2001: 528). However, as Jordan and Jordan (2000) point out, this programme has to balance measures for inclusion, equality and empowerment with ones for enforcement. The phrase 'tough love' captures the spirit of its culture shift (Jordan and Jordan 2000: Chapters 1 and 2). Freeden suggests that

> community is conjoined with an undertone of social sin, [where] failure is notably one of free will ... made all the more culpable in a cohesive society which offers opportunities to individuals as long as they embody what Blair has called 'common norms of conduct' in a 'strong and decent' community'.
>
> (Freeden 1999: 48)

As responsibilities for the child shift and compete between the family and the state, the courts and local authorities, education, social care and health, we witness the sustaining of market economy discourses among the rhetoric of the child as commodity, as low-cost or value-added, as in need of intervention and of parents as 'risk managers' (Ball 2004: 4). Children are seen as potentially irresponsible and as thoroughly commercialised. Government constructions of the child and of the family are articulated within policies and practices of integration and cohesion, producing the professionally 'distributed' child. 'Joined-up services', inter-professional and multi-professional working attempt to counteract the consequences of insular and non-communicative professional identities and practices.

These policies and practices rest on conceptualisations of an ideal-typical family which, according to Gewirtz (2001), is constructed as a middle-class family. Such practices may fail to recognise the postmodern child as complex and diverse, resistant to tendencies to be homogenised, to cohere or be complete. Rather than accommodating this fragmentation and diversity, inter-professional and inter-agency work seems still to be located within a compensatory discourse of cultural and social deficit. Ball (2004) suggests that this approach requires 'a disjunction between policy and preferred practice' (cf McNess, Broadfoot and Osborn 2003: 255). The result for many professionals and clients is a kind of 'bifurcated consciousness' or 'segmented self' (Miller 1983) or a struggle with 'outlaw emotions' (Jaggar 1989) as they try to live up to and manage 'the contradictions of belief and expectation' (Acker and Feuerverger 1997, quoted in Dillabough 1999: 382). There has, in Bauman's words, been a 'privatisation of ambivalence' (1991: 197).

Shifting notions and 'realities' of collaboration

The vocabulary of market economy and business, such as client, consumer, service user, manager and entrepreneur, increasingly has proliferated among education, health and social care services. Similarly, a shared inter-agency language has been developed in an attempt to shift sector-specific terminology. For example 'child protection' has been re-phrased as 'safeguarding children'; children who are 'at risk' are now constructed as potentially in danger of experiencing 'significant harm'; the 'EWO' (Education Welfare Officer) has become the 'BEST' (Behaviour and Education Support Team); EAZs (Education Action Zones) are now EICAZ (Excellence in Cities Action Zones); the 'Probation Officer' is now working within 'Youth Offending Teams' (YOTs); and 'inspections' are now referred to as 'JARS' (Joint Area Reviews).

This shifting language seems to have gone some way to addressing ways to think about issues that traditionally reside within insular and sector-specific practices. However Payne (2000) suggests that 'power struggles about objectives, roles and responsibilities are major impediments to collaboration' (2000: 26). Glendinning *et al.* similarly note the barriers to collaboration:

> inter-agency working is complex because professionals are differently situated and constrained institutionally by different policy frameworks. The notion of partnership is also problematic; partnerships are not always voluntary and there may be imbalances in the autonomy experienced by different partners.
>
> (Glendinning *et al.*, cited in Harris 2003: 303)

Interagency working was described in the Children Act (1989) as a complex process involving social services departments, police, medical practitioners, community health workers, the education service and others. *Every Child Matters: change for children* (DfES 2003) construes multi-agency working as essentially about bringing together practitioners with a range of skills to work across their traditional service boundaries, and claims that multi-agency working has been shown to be an effective way of supporting children and young people with additional needs, and securing real improvements in their life outcomes. ECM states that the lead professional is a key element of integrated support, whose role is to coordinate provision and act as a single point of contact for a child and their family when a range of services are involved and an integrated response is required.

Within the Children Act 2004, co-operation is identified as necessary for improving each child's well-being, specifically in relation to physical and mental health and emotional well-being; protection from harm and neglect; education, training and recreation; the contribution made by them to society; and social and economic well-being. Webb and Vulliamy cite the view of collaboration presented by Lupton and Khan, as 'existing on three levels: the interpersonal, involving the interaction of individuals; the inter-professional, determined by the training, knowledge and skills of each agency; and the inter-organisational, concerning the internal structures, finances, time-scales and priorities of agencies' (Webb and Vulliamy 2001: 68).

Over the last three decades therefore, policy, legislation and terminology have continued to shift between differing notions of co-operation, inter-agency working and collaboration. However, practical application in terms of 'joined up services' remains complex and highly problematic. Moran, Jacobs, Bunn and Bifulco (2006) suggest that the implementation of multi-agency working and the pace of service development still remain challenging for the agencies involved in frontline delivery.

Inter-organisational working

New Labour was clear that family support should be delivered on an inter-organisational basis. Guidance, such as *The Framework for the Assessment of Children in Need and their Families* (DoH, DfEE and HO 2000) and *Working Together* (DoH, HO and DfEE 1999), were intended to facilitate new opportunities for joint working between health, education and social services, formalised within the new children's services arrangements detailed in the 2004 Children Act. To strengthen the government's intentions to promote collaborative and inter-organisational working, the *Every Child Matters* programme now includes a Common Assessment Framework (CAF) together with improved practice in sharing information. As discussed earlier, this is intended to enable practitioners in schools, health settings, children's centres and other early years services to identify what additional services a child may need. Usually this will be through additional support delivered in universal or targeted services. The Children Act 2004 stated that, from April 2006, education and social care services for children were to be brought together under a director of children's services in each local authority, allowing local authorities more flexibility in organising their children's services. A National Service Framework was also established with integrated standards and inspection and, as noted above, England's first children's commissioner was appointed in 2005.

Inter-professional working

Since the 1980s, the government required agencies to work together in order to plan and implement 'joined-up solutions' to social problems (DfEE 1997a; 1998). However, despite this call for more integrated services and strengthened working relationships between schools, social services and parents or carers, the Children Act Report (DfES 2002) found that 'there was a reluctance of some agencies (including schools) to refer to social services and police' (p. 33). Hallet and Birchall (1992) found that, with the exception of the police, agencies considered the role of teachers in child protection to be important, but found schools to be isolated and difficult to co-operate with. In a seemingly reciprocal standoff, Hayden (1997) found that teachers were often critical of the lack of urgency on behalf of social services to effectively support children 'in need' and were angry at the lack of consultation and follow-up in cases where the school had raised child protection concerns.

The *Every Child Matters: change for children* programme (DfES 2003), as noted earlier, put in place a national framework to support the joining up of services so that every child can achieve the five ECM outcomes. Social services are identified as playing a central role in trying to improve outcomes for the most vulnerable. The functions of social services as specified in the Children Act 1989 remain unchanged, but how they are delivered at local level is set to change radically. The Children Act 2004 requires local authorities to lead on integrated delivery through multi-agency children's trusts, to develop a children and young people's plan, and to set up a shared database of children, containing information relevant to their welfare. *Every Child Matters: change for children in social care* states that,

Social workers and social care workers working with other agencies will have an important role in supporting universal services in meeting a wider range of needs. An example of how universal services can be strengthened is the development of a multi-disciplinary safeguarding children team in Sheffield, which provides advice on safeguarding children and young people to all services for children and young people in the city. This sort of initiative can, for example, help a school respond more confidently to children and young people affected by domestic violence. The duty on agencies to safeguard and promote children's welfare, Section 11 of the Children Act 2004, should help ensure safeguarding and promoting children's welfare becomes everyone's business.

(DfES 2004c: 4)

With reference to inter-professional working in early years, *The Five Year Strategy for Children and Learners* (DfES 2004a) set out the future direction of services for children, parents and families, including one-stop support at Sure Start Children's Centres, with childcare and education, health and employment advice and family support on offer together, within easy reach of every parent. The notion of 'extended schools' emerged, suggesting this service has an important role in addressing the needs of looked after children and children with disabilities:

Extended schools are one way of integrating service delivery and ensuring that services are delivered closer to where children and their families spend much of their time. Extended schools could play a greater role for example in supporting looked after children through the development of individual support programmes within their school, or by assisting disabled children to gain access to mainstream leisure and out of school activities so that they have less need for specialist services. We will see more effective earlier intervention by a range of agencies working with social workers and social care workers. This will help to ensure that any child or young person identified as having additional needs, such as substance misuse or serious behaviour problems, receives the right multi-agency intervention early on to prevent the development of longer term problem.

(DfES 2004c: 4)

Interpersonal partnerships

Freeden (1999) notes how Blair's vision of community, co-operation and cohesion are framed within an appeal to 'common norms of conduct' in 'a strong and decent community' (Freeden 1999: 48), as discussed above. By framing his vision around concepts of norms and decency, interpersonal partnerships become a vehicle of rectification for parents and those families who, for whatever reason, do not manifest these qualities. Interpersonal partnerships have become ways in which particular families are required to engage with different agencies as a result of their circumstances, lifestyle choices or predisposition to be labeled as, or fall into, the 'nuisance family' categories. Families are induced to engage (or not) with different professionals/individuals, including for example social workers, health practitioners or the police, and to access (or not) services that are informed and led by government policy and legislation.

In relation to parents/carers, there are mixed responses to the interpersonal partnerships engendered through inter-organisational and inter-professional working. Pugh, De'ath and Smith (1994) note that the use of groups to train or educate parents began in the

1970s, predominantly in the USA, and has grown in the UK in the last decade. Lloyd (1999) suggests that types of programmes include the Parent Plus programme developed in Ireland; Mellow Parenting based on the work of Newpin; and PEEP, an education focused pre-school project that covers highly disadvantaged areas. Bell (2007) points out that,

> New Labour have given parenting a high priority. [...] 'Good parenting' is seen as a solution to a range of social problems and its promotion is at the heart of preventive practice with children and families, as well as the focus of remedial and therapeutic interventions for families identified as problematic.
>
> (Bell 2007: 56)

The Children Act Report (DfES 2002) states that school-based interventions to support parents with young children at risk of behavioural problems can be effective. For example, a study commissioned under the Department of Health's Supporting Parents research initiative evaluated the SPOKES (Supporting Parents on Kids Education) Project in South London, which offered parents of five- and six-year-olds exhibiting early behavioural difficulties a combined parenting course and reading workshop (Scott and Sylva 2002). Children who were assigned to the intervention group moved from being within the worst 15 per cent of anti-social children to being outside the most anti-social 35 per cent, and showed a seven month improvement in reading age compared to the control group (p. 34). *Every Child Matters: change for children in social care* (DfES 2004c) acknowledges shortcomings in working with service users and the associated need for appropriate practice and relationships:

> A central part of the [...] programme is addressing the weaknesses in how we work together including with children, young people and their parents and carers. We know that the picture on working together is inconsistent. Too much is dependent on local relationships and there is too little implementation of what we know is good practice. For example disabled children and their families often need services from a number of agencies or providers. Whether or not they are successful in working together can either add to or reduce family stresses and strains.
>
> (DfES 2004c: 5)

Bell (2007) notes that parenting programmes 'command a good deal of political support', but argues for universal access to programmes, rather than access based on perceived need – that is to say, based on a deficit model of the needy family. Bell refers to evidence from Sanders *et al.* (2003), that

> universal population level approaches do contribute to preventing child maltreatment because they normalize and destigmatize attendance at parenting programmes, [...] because they provide opportunities for support networks to be established within communities and because they provide parents with a positive experience of professional help.
>
> (Sanders *et al.* 2007: 56)

Corporate parenting

The notion of 'corporate parenting' also brings the services and practices of social care, health and education together. 'Corporate parenting' emphasises the collective responsibility of local authorities to achieve good parenting for all children in their care – an essential part of which is to safeguard and promote their education. Section 4 of the joint DfES/DoH *Guidance on the Education of Children and Young People in Public Care* (2000) sets out some corporate parenting education principles, which include: prioritising education; high expectations and raising standards; inclusion and changing attitudes; early intervention and taking priority action; and listening to children. The joint guidance also sets out the range and number of individuals and agencies that may be involved in delivering 'corporate parenting'.

CONCLUDING REMARKS

From the 1960s to the twenty-first century, the interface between education, the law and social care has focused on the child or family with 'issues'. Notions of inter-organisational, inter-professional and inter-personal collaboration seem to be nurtured within a deficit model of the 'nuisance', 'incomplete' or 'insufficient' child, set against an increasingly demanding backdrop for schools to reach targets and standards. Webb and Vulliamy suggest that 'a great deal more opportunity is needed for contact with other agencies so that both schools and agencies can understand each other's working cultures, values and priorities' (2001: 73). However, they also point out that the government's inclusive education rhetoric is in danger of being submerged by the policy and practice of its Standards agenda: 'a strong emphasis is put on the academic side of the school at the expense of the pastoral side' (*Ibid.*: 74). In their Social Work in Primary Schools (SWIPS) project, Webb and Vulliamy suggest that their sample of schools felt under pressure to move from what Hargreaves (1995) terms a 'welfarist' school culture, with its focus on 'individual student development within a nurturing environment' (1995: 27) and child-centred educational philosophy, towards a 'formal' culture emphasising the achievement of 'learning goals', including homework, curriculum targets and test performance. Perhaps for all those who work on, for and with children, the pressing question is how these issues could be re-conceptualised, as well as re-thinking their potential for operating in practice, in ways that could begin to disturb notions of children as incompetent, unstable, insufficient, credulous, unreliable and incomplete.

NOTES

1. See also Chapter 9 of this volume (Daniels and Porter) for further SEN statistics.
2. www.nationalliteracytrust.org.uk/Database/stats/poorexam.html#ofstedfigures
3. http://www.cabinetoffice.gov.uk/facts/socialexclusion.aspx
4. http://www.poverty.org.uk/policies/truancy%20and%20exclusion.shtml
5. On 1 October 2007 the three equality commissions merged into the new Equality and Human Rights Commission: the Commission for Racial Equality (CRE), the Disability Rights Commission (DRC) and the Equal Opportunities Commission (EOC) (http://www.equalityhumanrights.com/).

REFERENCES

Acheson, D. (1998) *Independent Inquiry into Inequalities in Health* (Acheson Report). London: HMSO.

Acker, S. and Feuerverger, G. (1997) 'Doing good and feeling bad: the work of women university teachers', *Cambridge Journal of Education* 26: 401–22.

Akbar, A. (2007) 'Social workers condemned over parents' abuse of disabled girl', *The Independent,* 9th February 2007.

Armstrong, D. (2005) 'Reinventing "inclusion": New Labour and the cultural politics of special education', *Oxford Review of Education* 31(1): 135–51.

Audit Commission (2002) *Special Needs: a mainstream issue.* London: Audit Commission.

Baginsky, M. and Hodgkinson, K. (1999) 'Child protection in initial teacher training: a survey of provision in institutions of higher education', *Educational Research* 14: 173–81.

Ball, S. (2004). 'Education for sale! The commodification of everything?' Department of Education and Professional Studies Annual Lecture, Institute of Education, London (June 2004).

Barlow, J. and Stewart Brown, S. (2000) 'Behaviour problems and group-based education programmes', *Journal of Development Behaviour and Paediatrics* 21(5): 356–70.

Bauman, Z. (1991) *Modernity and Ambivalence.* Oxford: Polity Press.

Bell, M. (2007) 'Community-based parenting programmes: an exploration of the interplay between environmental and organizational factors in a Webster Stratton project', *British Journal of Social Work* 37: 55–72.

Bernstein, B. (1971) *Class, Codes and Control, Vol 1.* London: Paladin.

Blair, T. (1996) *New Britain: my vision of a young country.* London: Fourth Estate.

——(1997) 'Why we must help those excluded from society', *Independent,* 8 December.

——(1999) Speech to the Institute for Public Policy Research, London, 14 January.

Blane, D. (1985) 'An assessment of the Black Report's explanations of health inequalities', *Sociology of Health and Illness* 7: 423–45.

Blyth, E. and Milner, J. (1997) *Social Work with Children: the educational perspective.* London: Longman.

Board of Education (1931) *Report of the Consultative Committee on the Primary School* (The Hadow Report). London: HMSO.

Boyden, J. (1997) 'Childhood and the policy makers: a comparative perspective on the globalization of childhood', in A. James and A. Prout (Eds) *Constructing and Reconstructing Childhood: contemporary issues in the sociological study of childhood.* London: RoutledgeFalmer

Brehony, K.J. (2005) 'Primary schooling under New Labour: the irresolvable contradiction of excellence and enjoyment', *Oxford Review of Education* 31(1): 29–46.

Breslin, R., Brookes, H. and Marjolin, N. (2006) *Responding to Black and Minority Ethnic Children and Young People Affected by Domestic Violence.* A Conference Report organised by the NSPCC in partnership with Women's Aid; Ashiana Project; the Metropolitan Police; Centre for the Study of Safety and Wellbeing at the University of Warwick; and Women Acting in Today's Society. (4.10.06) NSPCC National Training Centre: Leicester.

Bronfenbrenner, U. (1979) *The Ecology of Human Development.* Cambridge, MA: Harvard University Press.

Bruner, J. (1983) *Child's Talk: learning to use language.* New York: Norton.

Butt, J. and Mirza, K. (2001) *Social Care and Black Communities.* London: HMSO.

Cannan, C. (1992) *Changing Families, Changing Welfare.* London: Prentice-Hall.

Carlen, P., Gleeson, D. and Wardhaugh, J. (1992) *Truancy: the politics of compulsory schooling.* Buckingham: Open University Press.

Cemlyn, S. and Clark, C. (2005) 'The social exclusion of Gypsy and Traveller children', in G. Preston (Ed) *At Greatest Risk. The children most likely to be poor.* London: Child Poverty Action Group.

Central Advisory Council for Education (CACE) (1967) *Children and Their Primary Schools: a report of the Central Advisory Council for Education (England)* (The Plowden Report). London: HMSO.

Cole, M. (1998) 'Racism, reconstructed multiculturalism and antiracist education', *Cambridge Journal of Education* 28(1): 37–48.

Cox, C.B. and Dyson, A.E. (Eds) (1971) *Black Papers on Education.* London: Davis-Poynter.

Crawley, H. and Lester, T. (2005) *No Place for a Child: children in immigration detention in the UK – impacts, alternatives and safeguards*. London: Save the Children www.savethechildren. org.uk/temp/scuk/cache/cmsattach/2414_no%20place%20for%20a%20child.pdf

Crime and Disorder Act 1998. C. 37. London: HMSO.

Croll, P. and Moses, D. (2004) *The Transmission of Educational Values*. End of Award Report to the ESRC.

Crouch, C. (2001) 'Citizenship and markets in recent British education policy', in C. Crouch, K. Eder and D. Tambini (Eds) *Citizenship, Markets and the State*. Oxford: Oxford University Press.

Dale, N. (1996) *Working with Families of Children with Special Needs*. London, Routledge.

Daniels, H. and Porter, J. (2007) *Learning Needs and Difficulties among Children of Primary School Age: definition, identification, provision and issues* (Primary Review Research Survey 5/2). Cambridge: University of Cambridge Faculty of Education. (Chapter 9 of this volume).

David, T. (1994) 'Introduction: multiprofessionalism–challenges and issues', in T. David (Ed) *Protecting Children from Abuse: multiprofessionalism and the Children Act 1989*. Stoke-on–Trent: Trentham Books.

Department of Education Victoria (1998) *ESL Students: assessment and reporting support materials*. Victoria, Australia: Department of Education.

Department of the Environment, Transport and the Regions (DETR) (2000) *Index of Multiple Deprivation*. London: DETR.

Department for Education and Employment (DfEE) (1994) *Code of Practice on the Identification and Assessment of Special Educational Needs*. London: DfEE.

DfEE (1995) *Protecting Children from Abuse: the role of the Education Service*. Circular 10/95. London: DfEE.

——(1997a) *Excellence for All Children*. London: HMSO.

——(1997b) *Teaching: high status, high standards*. Circular 10/97. London: DfEE.

——(1998) *Guidance on LEA Behaviour Support Plans*. Circular 1/98. London: DfEE.

——(1999) *Social Inclusion: pupil support*. Circular 10/99. London: DfEE.

Department of Education and Science (DES) (1975) *A Language for Life* (The Bullock Report). London: HMSO.

——(1978) *Report of the Committee of Enquiry into the Education of Handicapped Children and Young People* (The Warnock Report). London: HMSO.

——(1985) *Education for All: report of the Committee of Inquiry into the Education of Children from Ethnic Minority Groups* (The Swann Report). London: HMSO.

Department for Education and Skills (DfES) (2001a) *Inclusive Schooling: children with special educational needs*. London: DfES Publications.

DfES (2001b) *Special Educational Needs Code of Practice* (Ref: DfES/0581/2001). London: DfES Publications.

——(2002) *The Children Act Report 2002*. Nottingham: DfES Publications.

——(2003) *Every Child Matters*. Nottingham: DfES Publications.

——(2004a) *Five Year Strategy for Children and Learners: putting people at the heart of public services*. London: DfES.

——(2004b) *Removing Barriers to Achievement: the Government's strategy for SEN*. London: DfES Publications.

——(2004c) *Every Child Matters: change for children in social care*. Nottingham: DfES Publications.

——(2005) *Higher Standards: better schools for all*. London: DfES.

——(2006a) *Common Assessment Framework for Children and Young People*. Online. [Available: http://www.everychildmatters.gov.uk/deliveringservices/caf. Accessed 27 February, 2007].

——(2006b) *Ethnicity and Education: the evidence on minority ethnic pupils aged 5–16*. Nottingham: DfES Publications.

——(2007a) *Excellence in Cities*. Online. [Available: http://www.standards.dfes.gov.uk/sie/eic/. Accessed 29 January, 2007].

——(2007b) *Supporting Students Through Behaviour Improvement Programmes.* http://www.standards.dfes.gov.uk/research/themes/behaviour/Supportingstudents/ Accessed 28 March 2007.

DfES / Department of Health (DoH) (2000) *Guidance on the Education of Children and Young People in Public Care.* London: DfES.

DoH (1991) *The Children Act 1989 Guidance and Regulations.* London, HMSO.

——(1992) *Health of the Nation: astrategy for health in England* (Cmd 1986). White Paper. London: HMSO.

——(1998) *Modernising Social Services: promoting independence, improving protection, raising standards*, Cmd 4169. London: Stationery Office.

——(1999) *Saving Lives: our healthier nation.* White Paper Cmd 4386. London: HMSO.

——(2002) *Tackling Health Inequalities: summary of the 2002 cross-cutting review.* London: DoH Publications.

——(2004a) *Chief Nursing Officer's Review of the Nursing, Midwifery and Health Visiting Contribution to Vulnerable Children and Young People.* London: DoH Publications.

——(2004b) *Choosing Health: making healthy choices easier* (Cmd 6374). White Paper. London: HMSO.

DoH, Department for Education and Employment (DfEE), and the Home Office (2000) *Framework for the Assessment of Children in Need and their Families.* London: HMSO.

——(2004) *National Service Framework for Children, Young People and Maternity Services: executive summary.* London: DoH Publications.

DoH, Home Office and DfEE (1999/2006) *Working Together to Safeguard Children: a guide to inter-agency working to safeguard and promote the welfare of children* (2nd edition, 2006). London: HMSO.

Department of Health and Social Security (DHSS) (1974) *Report of the Committee of Inquiry into the Care and Supervision Provided in Relation to Maria Colwell.* London: HMSO.

DHSS (1980) *Inequalities in Health. Report of a research working group* (The Black Report). London: HMSO.

——(1984) *Children in Care. Government response to the second report from the Social Services Committee session 1984–4.* Cmnd. 9298. London: HMSO.

Dillabough, J.-A. (1999) 'Gender politics and conceptions of the Modern Teacher: women identity and professionalism', *British Journal of Sociology of Education* 20(3): 373–94.

Dockrell, J., Peacey, N. and Lunt, I. (2002) *Literature Review: meeting the needs of children with special educational needs.* London: Audit Commission.

Donaldson, M. (1978) *Children's Minds.* New York: Norton.

Easen, P., Atkins, M. and Dyson, A. (2000) 'Inter-professional collaboration and conceptualisations of practice', *Children and Society* 14: 355–67.

Edgley, A. and Avis, M. (2007) 'The perceptions of statutory service providers of a local Sure Start programme: a shared agenda?' *Health and Social Care in the Community* (Online Early Articles).

Edwards, A.D. (1976) *Language, Culture and Class: the sociology of language and education.* London: Heinemann.

Eisenstadt, N. (2002) 'Sure Start: key principles and ethos', *Child: Care, Health and Development* 28(1): 3–4.

Evans, O. and Varma, V. (Eds) (1990) *Special Education, Past, Present and Future.* Lewes: Falmer.

Exworthy, M., Blane, D. and Marmot, M. (2003) 'Tackling health inequalities in the United Kingdom: the progress and pitfalls of policy', *Health Services Research* 38: 1905–22.

Figueroa, P. (2003) 'Diversity and citizenship in England,' in J.A. Banks (Ed) *Diversity and Citizenship Education: global perspectives.* New York: Jossey-Bass.

Finch, J. (1984) *Education as Social Policy.* London: Longman.

Fitzherbert, K. (1980) 'Strategies for prevention,' in M. Craft, J. Raynor and L. Cohen (Eds) *Linking Home and School – a new review* (3rd edn.) Harper and Row: London: Ch. 23.

Foster Children Act 1980. C.6. London: HMSO.

Freeden, M. (1999) 'The ideology of New Labour', *The Political Quarterly* 70(1): 42–51.

Gallimore, C.C. (1977) 'The role of an Education Welfare Officer in two contrasting schools', *British Journal of Guidance and Counselling* 5(1): 102–5.

Gewirtz, S. (2001) 'Cloning the Blairs: New Labour's programme for the re-socialization of working-class parents', *Journal of Educational Policy* 16(4): 365–78.

Gillborn, D. (1997) 'Ethnicity and educational performance in the United Kingdom: racism, ethnicity, and variability in achievement', *Anthropology and Education Quarterly* 28(3): 375–93.

——(2005) 'Education policy as an act of white supremacy: whiteness, critical race theory and education reform', *Journal of Education Policy* 20(4): 485–505.

Gilligan, R. (1998) 'The importance of teachers in child welfare', *Child and Family Social Work* 3: 13–25.

Gilmour, I. (1993) *Dancing with Dogma*. London: Pocket Books.

Glendinning, C., Powell, M. and Rummery, K. (Eds) (2002) *Partnerships, New Labour and the Governance of Welfare*. Bristol: The Policy Press.

Great Britain (1970) *Education (Handicapped Children) Act 1970*. C.52. London: HMSO.

——(1976) *Race Relations Act 1976*. C. 74. London: HMSO.

——(1977) *National Health Service Act 1977*. C.49. London: HMSO.

——(1980a) *Child Care Act 1980*. C.5. London: HMSO.

——(1980b) *Education Act 1980*. C.20. London: HMSO.

——(1981) *Education Act 1981*. C.60. London: HMSO.

——(1982) *Children's Homes Act 1982*. C.20. London: HMSO.

——(1985) *Child Abduction and Custody Act 1985*. C.60. London: HMSO.

——(1988a) *Education Reform Act 1988*. C.40. London: HMSO.

——(1988b) *Local Government Act 1988*. C.9. London: HMSO.

——(1989) *Children Act 1989*. C.41. London: HMSO.

——(1993) *Education Act 1993*. C.35. London: HMSO.

——(1996) *Education Act 1996*. C.56. London: HMSO.

——(1999) *Protection of Children Act 1999*. C.14. London: HMSO.

——(2000) *Race Relations (Amendment) Act 2000*. C.34. London: HMSO.

——(2003) *Children at Risk* (2003) Green Paper. London: HMSO.

——(2004) *Children Act 2004*. C.31. London: HMSO

——(2006) *Childcare Act 2006*. C.21. London: HMSO

Hallet, C. and Birchall, E. (1992) *Co-ordination and Child Protection: a review of the literature*. Edinburgh: HMSO.

Hargreaves, D.H. (1995) 'School culture, school effectiveness and school improvement', *School Effectiveness and School Improvement* 6: 23–46.

Harris, S. (2003) 'Inter-agency practice and professional collaboration: the case of drug education and prevention', *Journal of Education Policy* 18(3): 303–14.

Hayden, C. (1997) *Children Excluded from Primary School*. Buckingham: Open University Press.

Heath, S. Brice (1983) *Ways with Words: language, life and work in communities and classrooms*. Cambridge: Cambridge University Press.

Hirsch, F. (1977) *Social Limits to Growth*. London: Routledge and Kegan Paul.

Home Office (1960) *Report of the Committee on Children and Young People* (Cmd.1191). London: HMSO.

——(1998) *Supporting Families: a consultation document*. London: HMSO.

——(2006) *Respect Action Plan*. London: Home Office Respect Task Force.

House of Commons (2005) *Equality Bill*. London: HMSO.

Jaggar, A. (1989) 'Love and knowledge: emotion in feminist epistemology,' in A. Jaggar and S. Bordo (Eds) *Gender Body/Knowledge*. New Brunswick, NJ: Rutgers University Press.

James, A. and James, A.L. (2004) *Constructing Childhood: theory, policy and social practice*. Basingstoke: Palgrave Macmillan.

James, A., Jenks, C. and Prout, A. (1998) *Theorizing Childhood*. London: Polity Press.

James, A. and Prout, A. (1997) 'A new paradigm for the sociology of childhood? Provenance, promise and problems,' in A. James and A. Prout (Eds) *Constructing and Reconstructing Childhood: contemporary issues in the sociological study of childhood*. London: RoutledgeFalmer.

Jenks, C. (2005) *Childhood*. London: Routledge.

Jones, C. (2001) 'Voices from the front line: state social workers and New Labour', *British Journal of Social Work* 31: 547–62.

Jordan, B. (2001). 'Tough love: social work, social exclusion and the Third Way', *British Journal of Social Work* 31: 527–46.

Jordan, B. and Jordan, C. (2000) *Social Work and the Third Way: tough love as social policy*. London: Sage.

Joseph Rowntree Foundation (1999) *Monitoring Poverty and Social Exclusion*. London: Joseph Rowntree Foundation.

Kogan, M. (1987) 'The Plowden Report: twenty years on', *Oxford Review of Education* 13(1): 13–22.

Lamming, H. (2003) *The Victoria Climbié Inquiry: report of inquiry by Lord Lamming*. London: HMSO.

Leung, C. (2001) 'English as an additional language: distinct language focus or diffused curriculum concerns', *Language and Education* 15(1): 33–55.

Lightfoot, J., Mukherjee, S. and Sloper, P. (2001) 'Supporting pupils with special health needs in mainstream schools: policy and practice', *Children and Society* 15(1): 57–69.

Lister, R. (2006) 'Children (but not women) first: New Labour, child welfare and gender', *Critical Social Policy* 26: 315.

Lloyd, E. (1999) *Parenting Matters: what works in parenting education*. Ilford: Barnados.

Loeber, R. and LeBlanc, M. (1990) 'Toward a developmental criminology', in M. Tonry and N. Morris (Eds) *Crime and Justice: a review of research* 12: 375–473. Chicago: University of Chicago Press.

Loeber, R. and Stouthamer-Loeber, M. (1986) 'Family factors as correlates and predictors of juvenile conduct problems and delinquency', in M. Tonry and N. Morris (Eds) *Crime and Justice: an annual review* 7: 29–151. Chicago: University of Chicago Press.

Macintyre, S. (1977) 'The Black Report and beyond: what are the issues?' *Social Science and Medicine* 44: 723–45.

Macmillan, R., McMorris, B.J. and Kruttschnitt, C. (2004) 'Linked lives: stability and change in maternal circumstances and trajectories of antisocial behavior in children', *Child Development* 75(1): 205–20.

Mayall, B. (2002) *Towards a Sociology for Childhood: thinking from children's lives*. Buckingham: OUP.

Mayall, B. and Storey, P. (1998) 'A school health service for children?' *Children and Society* 12(1): 86–97.

McLaughlin, H. (2004) 'Partnerships: panacea or pretence?' *Journal of Interprofessional Care* 18 (2): 103–13.

McNess, E., Broadfoot, P. and Osborn, M. (2003) 'Is the effective compromising the affective?' *British Educational Research Journal* 29(2): 243–57.

Miller, J.L. (1983) 'The resistance of women academics: an autobiographical account', *Journal of Educational Equity and Leadership* 3: 101–9.

Moran, P., Jacobs, C., Bunn, A. and Bifulco, A. (2006). 'Multi-agency working: implications for an early-intervention social work team', *Child and Family Social Work* 12(2): 143–51.

Murray, P. (2000) 'Disabled children, parents and professionals: partnership on whose terms?' *Disability and Society* 15(4): 683–98.

National Curriculum Online (no date) Statutory Inclusion Statement. Online. [Available: http://www.nc.uk.net/inclusion.html. Accessed 21 April, 2007].

New Policy Institute Poverty Site (2007) *Tackling Truancy and Exclusion in Schools*. [Available: http://www.poverty.org.uk/policies/truancy%20and%20exclusion.shtml. Accessed 21 April, 2007].

Normington, J. and Kyriacou, C. (1994) 'Exclusion from high schools and the work of the outside agencies involved', *Pastoral Care* 12(4): 12–15.

Ofsted (2004) *Special Educational Needs and Disability: towards inclusive schools.* London: Ofsted.

Parton, N. (1999) 'Ideology, politics and policy', in O. Stevenson (Ed) *Child Welfare in the UK.* Oxford: Blackwell.

Patterson, G.R. (1986) 'Performance models for anti-social boys', *American Psychologist* 41: 432–44.

Payne, M. (2000) *Teamwork in Multiprofessional Care.* London: Palgrave.

Power, S., Whitty, G., Gewirtz, S., Halpin, D. and Dickson, M. (2003) *Paving a Third Way: apolicy trajectory analysis of Education Action Zones.* End of Award to ESRC. London: Institute of Education, University of London.

Pringle, M.K. (1974) *The Needs of Children.* London: Hutchinson.

Prout, A. (2004) *The Future of Childhood.* London: Routledge Falmer.

Pugh, G., De'Ath, E. and Smith, C. (1994) *Confident Children: policy and practice in parent education and support.* London: National Children's Bureau.

Race Equality Foundation (2006) *Strengthening Faith Communities and Black and Minority Ethnic Voluntary and Community Sector's Capacity to Deliver Health and Social Care Services.* London: REF.

Sanders, M.R., Cann, W. and Markie-Dadds, C. (2003) 'The triple P positive parenting programme: a universal population-level approach to the prevention of child abuse', *Child Abuse Review* 12(3): 155–72.

Saxena, S., Eliahoo, J. and Majeed, A. (2002) 'Socioeconomic and ethnic group differences in self reported health status and use of health services by children and young people in England: cross sectional study'. *British Medical Journal* Vol. 325. Online. [Available: http://bmj.bmjjournals.com/cgi/reprint/325/7363/520.pdf. Accessed 25 March 2007].

Sayyid, S. (2003) 'Muslims in Britain: towards a political agenda,' in M. Seddon, D. Hussain and N. Malik (Eds) *British Muslims.* Leicester: The Islamic Foundation.

Scott, S., O'Connor, T. and Futh, A. (2006) *What Makes Parenting Programmes Work in Disadvantaged Areas? The PALS trial.* London: Joseph Rowntree Foundation.

Scott, S. and Sylva, K. (2002) *The 'Spokes' Project: supporting parents on kids' education.* Final report to the Department of Health.

Seebohm Report (1968) *Report of the Committee on Local Authority and Allied Personal Social Services* (Cmnd 3703). London: HMSO.

Simon, B. (1985) *Does Education Matter?* London: Lawrence and Wishart.

Social Exclusion Unit (2003) *A Better Education for Children in Care.* London: SEU.

Stone, J.E. (1996) 'Developmentalism: an obscure but pervasive restriction', *Education Policy Analysis Archives* 4(8). Online. [Available: http://epaa.asu.edu/epaa/v4n8.html. Accessed 11 January 2007].

Slee, R. (2001) '"Inclusion in Practice": does practice make perfect?', *Educational Review* 53(2): 113–23.

Smith, C. (1994) *Confident Parents, Confident Children: policy and practice in parent education and support.* London: National Children's Bureau.

Special Educational Needs and Disability Act 2001. C.10. London: HMSO.

Stevenson, O. (1999a) 'Children in need and abused: interprofessional and interagency responses', in O. Stevenson (Ed) *Child Welfare in the UK.* Oxford: Blackwell: 100–120

——(1999b) 'Social work with children and families', in O. Stevenson (Ed) *Child Welfare in the UK.* Oxford: Blackwell: 79–99.

Sure Start (no date) 'Welcome to Sure Start', http://www.surestart.gov.uk/ Accessed 12 April 2007.

Teacher Training Agency (1997) *Career Entry Profile for a Newly Qualified (Primary/Secondary) Teacher.* London: TTA.

Thatcher, M. (1987) Interview for *Women's Own* magazine, 31 October, 1987. Online. [Available: http://briandeer.com/social/thatcher-society.htm. Accessed 25 March 2007].

Tikly, L. (2004) *Analytical Report on Education: national focal point for United Kingdom.* London: Commission for Racial Equality.

Times Educational Supplement (1998) 'Ofsted figures support failing schools poverty link', N. Pyke, *TES,* 31 July 1998.

Times Educational Supplement (1999) 'Inspectors link poor results and poverty', G. Hackett, *TES,* 10 December 1999.

Todd, L. (2003) 'Disability and the restructuring of welfare: the problem of partnerships with parents', *International Journal of Inclusive Education* 7: 281–96.

Tomlinson, S. (2005) 'Race, ethnicity and education under New Labour', *Oxford Review of Education* 31(1): 153–71.

Tough, J. (1977) *The Development of Meaning: a study of children's use of language.* London: Allen and Unwin.

United Nations (1989) *Convention on the Rights of the Child.* Geneva: UN.

Vygotsky, L.S. (1978) *Mind in Society.* Cambridge, MA: Harvard University Press.

Wanless, D. (2004) *Securing the Health of the Whole Population* (The Wanless Report). London: HMSO.

Watson, D., Townsley, R. and Abbott, D. (2002) 'Exploring multi-agency working in services to disabled children with complex healthcare needs and their families', *Journal of Clinical Nursing* 11: 367–75.

Webb, R. and Vulliamy, G. (1996) *Roles and Responsibilities in the Primary School: changing demands, changing practices.* Buckingham: Open University Press.

Webb, R. and Vulliamy, G. (2001). 'The primary teacher's role in child protection', *British Educational Research Journal* 27(1): 59–77.

Wells, C.G. (Ed) (1981) *Learning through Interaction.* Cambridge: Cambridge University Press.

Whitney (1993) *The Children Act and Schools.* London: Kogan Page.

Winkley, D. (1987) 'From condescension to complexity: post-Plowden schooling in the inner city', *Oxford Review of Education* 13(1): 45–55.

Younghusband Report (1959) *Report of the Working Party on Social Workers in the Local Authority Health and Welfare Services.* London: HMSO.

Part 2

Children's development, learning, diversity and needs

Maintaining the focus on children and childhood, the research surveys in Part 2 were commissioned to support the Cambridge Primary Review's efforts to address the following questions from its Themes 2 and 5:

Development and learning

- What do we know about the way young children develop, act and learn – cognitively, emotionally, socially, morally, physically and across the full spectrum of their development?
- What are the pedagogical implications of recent research in, for example, neuroscience, cognition, intelligence, language and human interaction?
- What is the relationship between children's physical health, emotional well-being and learning?
- As children move developmentally through the primary phase how do they learn best? Judged against this evidence, how do current teaching approaches fare?

Diversity and inclusion

- Do our primary schools attend fairly and effectively to the different learning needs and cultural backgrounds of their pupils?
- Do all children have equal access to high quality primary education? If not, how can this access be improved?
- How can a national system best respond to the wide diversity of cultures, faiths, languages and aspirations which is now a fact of British life?
- How can primary schools best meet the needs of children of widely-varying abilities and interests?
- How can schools secure the engagement of those children and families which are hardest to reach?

These are formidable lists, and not all the questions were answered, either by the research surveys or by the Review's other evidence. Some of the questions, indeed, are less about research evidence than the confronting of value dilemmas, policy options and hard practical choices.

In *Children's cognitive development and learning* (Chapter 6) Usha Goswami and Peter Bryant draw on the substantial body of research evidence now available on children's cognitive development from birth to the end of the primary years. This was a major theme of the 1967 Plowden Report and this survey shows how much our understanding of children's thinking and learning has advanced since then. The survey highlights areas of consensus but also challenges some current beliefs about how children learn to think and reason, drawing on recent evidence from neuroscience and cognitive psychology. The authors stress the significance of language and pretend play for primary pupils as well as direct teaching and incremental, multi-sensory learning, and they highlight the importance of praise for effort rather than performance in order to sustain children's motivation for learning. Some of the implications of the research for children's learning experiences in the home as well as the school are considered, especially in the areas of reading and mathematics.

Children's social development, peer interaction and classroom learning, by Christine Howe and Neil Mercer (Chapter 7), focuses on one critical feature identified in the previous chapter, namely the social dimension of learning. It does so in the context of the classroom, which provides unique opportunities, seldom as fully exploited as they might be, for children to learn from each other. The chapter identifies the positive contribution that structured pupil-pupil interaction can make not only to learning but also to children's social development. While the educational value of collaborative learning can be clearly demonstrated, evidence also shows that factors and current practices in many primary classrooms militate against productive interaction between children and therefore constrain children's capacity to learn. On the basis of the research surveyed, the chapter identifies ideal features of peer collaborative learning and their implications for teaching.

In *Children in Primary Education: demography, culture, diversity, inclusion* (Chapter 8), Mel Ainscow and his colleagues take us beyond the classroom and the school to consider aspects of policy and practice as they relate to forms of provision made for particular individuals and groups of pupils. The chapter reviews research on the diversity of the English primary school population, by referring to official statistics, policy texts, and published research studies, as well as developments in school-based practice. It considers the implications of this evidence for policy, using the example of bilingual learners to identify alternative ways of understanding and responding to apparent differences between individuals and groups of pupils. Stressing that all accounts of pupil difference are constructs, and that these accounts both change over time and are shaped by the available procedures for defining them, the authors warn against the dangers of simplistic categorisation and the deficit thinking that seems to inform policy in respect of pupil difference. They propose approaches to capacity building in schools which include an enhanced role for the classroom teacher, based on dialogue and resources in order to generate new thinking about inclusive practice – in short, a policy-practice partnership that balances support and trust for teachers.

Learning Needs and Difficulties among Children of Primary School Age: definition, identification, provision and issues (Chapter 9) reviews the published research on children of primary age with special educational needs (SEN) and gives a particular focus to SEN identification and provision. Here, Harry Daniels and Jill Porter acknowledge the contested nature of special needs and the variety of interpretations that legislation and policy allow, and find that evaluation of provision is problematic because of the paucity of research. They examine the reasons that research can give for the system's relatively slow progress towards a broadly understood inclusive practice in primary schools. They find that, among other features, there are clear inequalities within the system in terms of gender and levels of socio-economic advantage, with some groups of children with comparable abilities and needs more likely than others to be statemented. They also highlight a tension, running through the system from policy to the level of school and classroom practice, between the pursuit of a broad agenda of inclusion and the use of league tables and narrowly-conceived measures of pupil assessment as levers to raise standards.

Although each of these research surveys was independently conceived and undertaken, collectively they raise a number of important general issues.

Ideas on thinking, learning and difference are complex

- Conceptions of thinking, learning and difference powerfully influence practice in schools, yet the complexity and socially constructed nature of these ideas are not always as well understood as they should be. If schools are to offer educational experiences through which all their pupils can learn and progress, some accepted practices and orthodoxies need to be revisited. For example: children think and reason largely in the same ways as adults, though without their experience, and popular educational assumptions such as developmental 'stages' and 'learning styles' are now clearly challenged by research data (Chapter 6); commonly or officially described differences between children are constructs and may be consistent neither with children as they are nor with the ways they learn, and therefore may not provide a reliable basis for teaching (Chapter 8).

Systemic tensions and the need for balance in policy and practice

- Valuable and productive educational ideas such as multi-sensory learning (Chapter 6), collaborative peer interaction (Chapter 7) and inclusion (Chapter 9) can stand in tension with narrow definitions of what counts as valid pupil learning outcomes and the apparatus of tests and league tables which drives such definitions (Chapter 9 and the chapters in Part 5 of this volume).
- Some policies and practices conceptualise learning in ways that generate constraints on the extent to which a school can be flexible and teachers are finding it increasingly difficult to support children identified with special educational needs in mainstream primary schools (Chapters 8 and 9).
- Teachers should be enabled to balance their attention to national policies and strategies with the need to base their classroom decisions on their unique local knowledge of contexts and children (Chapters 8 and 9). These judgements should be supported by knowledge and understanding of, for example: children's cognitive development (Chapter 6); the many contextual factors that affect learning (Chapter 9); the educational value of peer interaction (Chapter 7); the way teachers themselves talk and interact with children, which can powerfully influence children's conceptions of themselves and their ability to learn (Chapter 6).

A greater appreciation of children's lives and needs

- Children have complex lives, cultural backgrounds and needs, and these are not readily reducible to simple, statistically or demographically-led categorisations (Chapter 8). The experiences that children have at home and out of school are highly significant to their development and need to be properly understood (Chapter 8 and – in Part 1 – Chapter 3).

- A better understanding of how cognitive development occurs should inform both policy and practice. For example: learning is fundamentally a social activity that can be carefully and sensitively scaffolded and enhanced by adults from birth and throughout the primary years (Chapters 6 and 7); language development is fundamental to all learning so talk and collaborative activity and thinking about learning (metacognition) should be an intrinsic and integrated aspect of classroom life (Chapters 6 and 7); children are agents in making sense of their lives, taking action and shaping other people's understanding of their individuality and shared characteristics, so it is important to seek out children's views in both research and practice (Chapters 8, 9 and 2).

Persistent inequalities

- There is wide individual variation among children, for example, in language skills from an early age (Chapters 6, 7 and 9).
- Since children's experiences out of school inevitably vary, some children will need more guidance than others in engaging in important educational activities such as reading for enjoyment, using talk in their learning and collaborating with each other in pursuit of common learning goals (Chapters 6, 7 and 9).
- Targeting inequality is difficult because statistically-based constructions of diversity can conceal the extent to which children with similar characteristics and educational needs can be found clustered together in particular schools and areas (Chapter 9).
- Educationally relevant differences between children are best identified in their responses in school activities (Chapters 8 and 9).

6 Children's cognitive development and learning

Usha Goswami and Peter Bryant

INTRODUCTION

'At the heart of the educational process lies the child'. This observation from the Plowden Report (CACE 1967) remains as true at the time of writing in 2007 as it was in 1967. Since 1967, however, there has been an explosion of research on how children of primary age develop, think and learn. Some of this research contradicts basic conclusions from the Plowden Report. For example, it is no longer widely believed that there are different developmental stages in learning to think (Piaget's theory, CACE 1967: 50). Similarly, it is not believed that a child cannot be taught until she/he is cognitively 'ready' (CACE 1967: 75). Rather, it is important to assess how far a child can go under the guidance of a teacher (the 'zone of proximal development', Vygotsky 1978).

Given the enormous amount of empirical research into cognitive development since 1967, the survey provided in this chapter is necessarily selective. Fuller expositions can be found in Kuhn and Siegler (2006), Siegler *et al.* (2006), and Goswami (2002, 2008). We assume that the notion of 'foundational developmental domains' provides coherence across the field (Wellman and Gelman 1998). These foundational domains are naïve physics (knowledge about the physical world of objects and events), naïve biology (conceptual knowledge about the world of animates and inanimates) and naïve psychology (understanding and predicting people's behaviour on the basis of psychological causation). Cognitive developmental neuroscience is revealing powerful learning in all three domains from the earliest months of life. We focus here on key areas of consensus in the wider field, while highlighting current controversies (for example, in theory of mind research). We concentrate on *experiments* investigating how children develop cognitively, particularly in terms of learning, thinking, and reasoning, and how social/emotional development sets the framework for the child's learning with family, teachers and peers.

1. LEARNING

The infant brain has a number of powerful learning mechanisms at its disposal, even prior to birth. The foetus can hear through the amniotic fluid during the third trimester, and memory for the mother's voice is developed while the baby is in the womb (DeCasper and Fifer 1980). Foetuses can also learn to recognise particular pieces of music (such as the theme tune of the soap opera *Neighbours*, Hepper 1988). These responses seem to be mediated by the brainstem (Joseph 2000). Cortical activity is also present within the womb. For example, there are functional hemispheric asymmetries in auditory evoked activity (Schluessner *et al.* 2004).

The majority of the brain cells (neurons) comprising the mature brain form before birth, by the seventh month of gestation (see Johnson 2005 for overview). This means that the environment within the womb can affect later cognition. For example, certain poisons (for example excessive alcohol) have irreversible effects on brain development. Alcohol appears to have a specific effect on later mathematical cognition, via its effects on the development of the parietal cortex (the brain structure for spatial cognition, Kopera-Frye *et al.* 1996; and see Section 8 below, 'Cognitive prerequisites for reading and number').

1a. Statistical learning by neural networks

Recent research in visual and auditory learning has revealed that neural sensory *statistical learning* following birth is a crucial part of cognitive development. The brain learns the statistical structure of experienced events, building neural networks to represent this information using algorithms which have been discovered via research in machine learning (see Section 1e). This form of learning is unconscious and continues throughout life. Babies can distinguish simple forms (for example, cross versus circle, Slater *et al.* 1983) from birth, and can map cross-modal correspondences (when the same stimulus is experienced in different modalities) from the first month (Meltzoff and Borton 1979; Spelke 1976). Even 3-month-olds can detect which of two videos of kicking feet shows *their own* kicking feet (contingency detection, see Gergely 2002). Babies also seem to categorise what they see, forming a generalised representation or *prototype* against which subsequently-presented stimuli are then compared. This is statistical learning. Carefully-controlled experiments showing babies cartoon figures or pictures of real animals demonstrate that the babies learn statistical patterns in the input, such as which features co-occur together (for example, long legs and short necks, see Younger 1990). They learn about the features in different objects, and about the *inter-relations* between different features, thereby learning correlational structure. Rosch (1978) has argued that humans divide the world into objects and categories on just such a correlational basis. Certain features in the world tend to co-occur, and this co-occurrence specifies natural categories such as trees, birds, flowers and dogs. Babies' brains apply the same statistical learning mechanisms to dynamic displays, learning *transitional probabilities* between which objects or events follow each other (for example, Kirkham *et al.* 2002) and extracting *causal structure*.

The infant brain is equally skilled in the auditory domain. Infants track statistical dependencies and conditional probabilities between sound elements, and this is one basis of language acquisition. In language, we can think of prototypical sound elements, such as a prototypical 'P' sound, or a prototypical 'B' sound. Infant brains use auditory perceptual information about correlational structure to construct these prototypes (Kuhl 2004). They register the acoustic features that regularly co-occur, and these relative distributional frequencies yield phonetic categories like 'p' and 'b'. Although the brain of the neonate can distinguish the phonetic categories comprising all human languages, by around one year of age the brain has specialised in discriminating the phonetic categories used in the native language/s (Werker and Tees 1984). During the first year, infants also learn the statistical patterns (transitional probabilities) that govern the sequences of sounds used to make words in their language/s (Saffran *et al.* 1996). This statistical learning occurs in the context of communicative interactions with caretakers. Babies will not learn language from watching television, even if the 'input' is equalised to that offered by live caretakers (Kuhl *et al.* 2003). This is because social interaction plays a critical role in perceptual learning, as discussed later.

1b. Learning by imitation

Another important form of learning present from birth is learning by imitation. Meltzoff and Moore (1983) showed that babies as young as one hour old could imitate gestures like tongue protrusion and mouth opening after watching an adult produce the same gestures. By around 9 months, babies can learn how to manipulate novel objects such as experimenter-built toys by watching others manipulate them (Meltzoff 1988). Older babies can even imitate intended acts when the adult demonstrator has an 'accident'. For example, when an adult intends to insert a string of beads into a cylindrical container but misses the opening, the infant takes the beads and puts them in successfully (Meltzoff 1995). This shows that the babies attribute *goals and intentions* to the actor. Understanding the goals of another person transforms their bodily motions into purposive behaviour (Gergely *et al.* 2002).

1c. Learning by analogy

Learning by analogy is another important form of learning that is present early in life. Analogies involve noticing similarities between one situation and another, or between one problem and another. This similarity then becomes a basis for applying analogous solutions. Infants' ability to learn by analogy can be tested using simple problem-solving procedures. For example, an attractive toy might be out of their reach and behind a barrier (such as a box), with a string attached to the toy lying on a cloth (Chen *et al.* 1997). To get the toy, the infants need to remove the barrier, pull on the cloth to bring the string within reach, and then pull the string to get the toy. By presenting different problem scenarios with the common features of cloths, boxes and strings, Chen *et al.* demonstrated that 13-month-olds could use analogies to solve these problems. Toddlers can solve similar analogies in more complicated situations (Brown 1990) and, by the age of 3, children can solve formal analogies of the kind given in IQ tests (Goswami and Brown 1989). However, successful analogising depends on familiarity with the relations underlying the analogy. The multiple choice IQ test-type analogies given to 3-year-olds involved familiar causal relations (as in 'chocolate is to melting chocolate as snowman is to puddle'), in preference to more unfamiliar or abstract examples.

1d. Causal learning

Finally, causal or 'explanation-based' learning is also present in infancy. 'Explanation-based learning' is a concept drawn from research on machine learning. It depends on the machine's ability to construct causal explanations for phenomena on the basis of specific training examples. If the machine can explain to itself why the training example is an instantiation of a concept that is being learned, learning is rapid. Baillargeon *et al.* (2009) have argued that infants are faced with similar problems in learning about the physical world. For example, they see a variety of instantiations of a particular phenomenon, such as objects *falling*, and need to work out what causes them to fall. In a series of experiments, Baillargeon showed explanation-based learning at work in infants' physical reasoning about containment, support, occlusion and other events. The infants could also make predictions about novel events, demonstrating causal rather than associative learning. For example, they could work out which cover should conceal a tall object. The specific training examples that they received changed the age at which this ability emerged (these are described as 'teaching experiments'; see Wang and Baillargeon 2008).

1e. Connectionist models of learning and cognitive neuroscience data

All forms of learning important for human cognition are thus present in rudimentary form soon after birth. Statistical learning, learning by imitation, learning by analogy and causal learning underpin cognitive development. Developmental cognitive neuroscience is revealing how powerful these learning mechanisms are, for example, in rapid learning about social stimuli (like faces, Farroni *et al.* 2002), physical events (like grasping actions, Tai *et al.* 2004), and language (Dehaene-Lambertz *et al.* 2006). *Connectionism* is the computational modelling of learning via 'neural networks'. Each unit in the network has an output that is a simple numerical function of its inputs. Cognitive entities such as concepts or aspects of language are represented by patterns of activation across many units, just as cognitive representations are distributed in the brain. Connectionism has achieved some important *in principle* demonstrations of what simple networks can learn using statistical algorithms. For example, networks are very efficient at learning underlying structure (such as linguistic structure, conceptual structure). By recording statistical associations between features of the input, complex structure such as grammar can be learned without assuming innate knowledge (such as pre-knowledge about language via an innate 'Language Acquisition Device', see Section 4 following – 'Language'). Prior to connectionism, most cognitive theories assumed symbolic representations (the 'algebraic' mind, see Elman 2005). This is no longer the case.

Implications for education

The brain will learn from every experienced event, but because cognitive representations are distributed, cumulative learning is crucial. There will be stronger representation of what is common across experience ('prototypical') and weaker representation of what differs. It may be that direct teaching of what is intended to be prototypical (for example, reminding of the general principles being taught via specific examples) will strengthen learning. There will be multiple representations of experience (for example, in motor cortex and in sensory cortices). This supports multi-sensory approaches to education, but it does not support the idea that unisensory teaching approaches will have special benefits (for example, visual, auditory *or* kinaesthetic approaches). Learning depends on neural networks distributed across multiple brain regions: visual, auditory *and* kinaesthetic. Cognitive representations will be graded in terms of (for example) the number of relevant neurons firing, their firing rates, and the coherence of the firing patterns (Munakata 2001). This can lead to apparent 'gaps' in learning, when a network is not yet strong enough to support generalisation to every relevant context.

Connectionism has shown that a constant learning mechanism can yield learning effects previously considered developmentally special, such as 'critical periods' for learning (when a developmental time window appears particularly effective), 'U-shaped' learning curves (apparent mastery, then loss of a skill, followed by regaining mastery), and a 'novice' system that is very responsive to learning from errors followed by an 'expert' system which is more entrenched in its learning. All these effects can be modelled by statistical learning algorithms which are simple (for example tracking conditional probabilities) and incremental. The frequency with which learning events are experienced is therefore crucial to the acquisition of expertise. Motivation to learn is also important, as the emotional system can modulate sensory processing, for example, via attentional processes.

Connectionist models demonstrate that complex cognition can arise without assuming symbolic thought. However, as Vygotsky made clear (see Section 9 following – 'Theories of cognitive development and intelligence'), part of the input for human cognitive development is internal and symbolic. These internal mediators are also crucial for cognitive development; for example, inner speech, the imagination, and pretend play.

2. KNOWLEDGE CONSTRUCTION

Much of the knowledge that we think of as cognitive seems to develop initially via the way that our perceptual systems operate. For example, some types of motion typically specify mechanical agents (such as regular motion), and other types of motion typically specify biological agents (for example, self-initiated, erratic motion). Dynamic inter-relations between objects perceived in the everyday world give the impression of causality. This perceptual analysis of the dynamic spatial and temporal behaviour of objects and agents appears to be the basis of knowledge construction by the infant and child.

2a. Naïve physics

Infants and young children learn about mechanical causality from perceptual information (for example, Leslie 1994). Perception organises itself fairly rapidly around a core framework representing the arrangement of cohesive, solid, three-dimensional objects which are embedded in a series of mechanical relations such as *pushing*, *blocking* and *support*. Action is crucial to the development of these explanatory frameworks: as the child becomes able to manipulate different causes and observe the effects, further learning occurs. Causal principles such as temporal order, intervention in situations, and real world knowledge about likely causes and effects (for example, that a switch is probably a cause of something) are all important for inferring the causal structure of physical events, and can already be observed in two- and three-year-olds (for example, Bullock *et al.* 1982; Shultz 1982). Four-year-olds can use covariation data to induce causal structure (again, apparently using learning algorithms discovered in machine learning, such as causal Bayes nets; Gopnik *et al.* 2001). Causal reasoning is well-developed early in childhood. However, the ability to deal effectively with multiple causal variables – scientific reasoning – develops more slowly.

Scientific reasoning is usually understood as the kind of thinking that requires the co-ordination and differentiation of theories and evidence, and the evaluation of hypotheses (for example Kuhn 1989). Research suggests that children as young as 6 understand the goal of testing a hypothesis, and can distinguish between conclusive and inconclusive tests of that hypothesis in simplified circumstances (for example, Sodian *et al.* 1991). Young children are poorer at scientific reasoning in situations when they have to ignore their pre-existing knowledge and reason purely on the basis of the data, and when they have to keep multiple variables in mind at once (Kuhn *et al.* 1995). However, adults are poor at this too. There is a 'confirmation bias' in human reasoning – a tendency to seek out causal evidence that is consistent with one's prior beliefs. This is a major source of inferential error in fields as disparate as science, economics and the law, as well as affecting young children's thinking.

Naïve or intuitive physics, rooted in the perception of objects and events, in general yields reliable information about the structure and action of physical systems. However, in some cases naïve physics gives rise to misleading models of the physical causal structure of the world. For example, most children (and adults) employ a pre-Newtonian, 'impetus' theory of projectile motion (for example, Viennot 1979). Each motion must have a cause, and so we think that if a ball is dropped from a moving train, it will fall downwards in a straight line. In fact, it will fall forwards in a parabolic arc (Kaiser *et al.* 1985), as the moving train imparts a force (Newtonian physics). Newtonian physics requires direct instruction. Cognitive neuroscience studies suggest that when we learn particular scientific concepts, such as the Newtonian theory of motion, these concepts do not replace our misleading naïve theories. Rather than undergoing conceptual change, the brain appears to maintain *both* theories. Selection of the correct basis for reasoning in a given situation then depends on effective inhibition (metacognitive strategies – see Section 6 following, 'Metacognition and executive function').

2b. Naïve biology

Watching moving objects that change in their speed or direction gives important information about animacy. Children learn that things that move on their own are animate agents, and that their movements are not predictable but are caused by their own internal states (for example, Gelman and Opfer 2002). Biological entities can also grow taller or fatter, they can change their colour or form (for example, caterpillar to butterfly), and they can inherit the characteristics of their forebears. Much of this naïve biological knowledge is present by age 3 to 4. Perceptual similarity is another critical source of information, and is usually a reliable indication that objects share core properties such as blood, bones, or cellulose. When perceptual information is not reliable, even 2-year-olds prioritise structural similarity (for example, having bones) in categorising biological kinds. Via experience and observation, young children have learned that 'insides' are more important than 'outsides'. For artefacts, *function* is judged to be the most important shared feature (for example something can be 'a bag' as long as it can be used to carry other objects). Language helps young children to focus on structural and functional similarity, as consistency of labelling (for example 'bird' for robin *and* ostrich, 'animal' for cat *and* cow, 'plant' for tree *and* buttercup) denotes biological categories.

Again, children go beyond the perceptual learning of statistical information about shared features and so on, and construct causal explanatory frameworks concerning the structure and action of biological systems. Statistical co-occurrences (for example, that feathers reliably co-occur with wings, with flight, and with light body weight) help the child to distinguish a category like 'bird'. But adults have a 'theory' about why these features go together, which involves causal relations. Adults believe that there is a degree of *causal necessity* in the co-variation of low body weight, feathers and wings in birds, as these features facilitate flight. Children seem to construct similar causal explanatory systems. Gelman (2004) describes this as an 'essentialist bias', arguing that young children have an early tendency to search for hidden, non-obvious features that make category members similar. Children's implicit assumptions about the structure of the biological world, and about the underlying nature of categories, again depend on their *experience*.

2c. Naïve psychology and 'theory of mind'

The causal explanatory framework that children generate to explain human behaviour has been called 'theory of mind'. Infants and young children develop psychological understanding using the same learning mechanisms discussed earlier. They learn the correlations and conditional probabilities of the human behaviour around them, for example, the kinds of events that lead to happiness or to anger. They observe goal-directed actions and induce intentions, they follow the gaze of others and induce interest or intention, they engage in joint attention with caretakers, for example over shared toys (joint attention episodes are called 'hotspots' for learning, see Tomasello 1995), and they learn social contingencies. This perceptually-based social-cognitive learning is then enriched via imitation, pretend play and language. Developing a 'theory of mind' requires an understanding of the mental states of others, so that you can predict their behaviour on the basis of their beliefs and desires. Imitation and understanding others as being 'like me' is one source of knowledge about desires. For example, if another person is seen reaching for an object, the action can be imbued with goal-directedness because of the infant's own experiences with similar acts (Meltzoff 2002). The behaviour of others is also understood via pretend play. For example, socio-dramatic role-play helps children to gain insights into the beliefs, desires and intentions of other agents. Language is also important, as (for example) family discourse about emotions and their causes is linked to earlier development of 'theory of mind' (for example, Dunn *et al.* 1991). Conversations about psychological causality offer young children opportunities to enquire, argue and reflect about human behaviour. Deaf children born to hearing parents show delays in acquiring theory of mind (Peterson and Siegal 1995). This appears to be due to the absence of pervasive family talk about abstract mental states, as deaf children born to *signing* deaf parents do not show such delays.

A dominant view in the literature was that a 'theory of mind' did not develop until a watershed in psychological understanding occurred at the age of around 4 years (for example, Wimmer and Perner 1983). This view is no longer widely held. It was based on a philosophical argument that the only convincing evidence for the attribution of mental states to others was successful reasoning about *false* beliefs (Dennett 1978). Behaviour based on a false belief will differ from behaviour that depends on current reality. An example is the 'false location' task devised by Wimmer and Perner (1983). If Sally hides her marble in a box and goes out of the room, and Ann moves the marble into a basket, Sally will look in the *box* for her marble when she returns (Baron-Cohen *et al.* 1985). This is where she (falsely) believes the marble to be. Children younger than 4 years often say that she will look in the current location of the marble, in this instance in the basket. The reason for this error is still in dispute. However, babies who are shown an analogous 'false location' scenario spend significantly longer looking at the display when the Sally figure looks in the *basket* on her return, suggesting some awareness of her false belief (Onishi and Baillargeon 2005).

2d. Cognitive neuroscience: the mirror neuron system

Social cognition is currently an active area of research in developmental cognitive neuroscience. This is partly because of the discovery of a neural system called the 'mirror neuron system', which appears to be very important with respect to imitation and language. Mirror neurons were discovered in primate research examining how actions are represented in the brain, and how action, imitation and intention might be linked. Mirror neurons were found to activate when the monkey performed object-directed actions such as tearing, grasping, holding and manipulating, and the same neurons also fired when the animal observed someone else performing the same class of actions. Mirror neurons were even activated by the sound of an action, such as paper ripping or a stick being dropped (Rizzolatti and Craighero 2004). Rizzolatti and colleagues pointed out that action recognition has a special status, as action implies a goal and an agent. Further, mirror neurons are only activated by biological actions (for example, a human hand grasping), and not by mechanical actions (for example, a robot grasping, Tai *et al.* 2004). In humans, the mirror neuron system is active when participants imitate the motor actions of another human, or imitate their facial expressions. The mirror neuron system may therefore be a neural substrate for understanding the actions and internal states of others. Children with autism have great difficulty in identifying another person's emotions and thoughts, and are frequently described as lacking a 'theory of mind' (for example, Baron-Cohen *et al.* 1999). Adolescents with autism can imitate the facial expressions of others, but mirror neuron activity is absent (Dapretto *et al.* 2006). This is one illustration of how the new technologies in neural imaging are uncovering potential links between brain development and behaviour. Nevertheless, belief attribution involves other neural areas as well.

Implications for education

Cognitive development in the foundational domains of naïve physics, naïve biology and naïve psychology reflects the learning mechanisms discussed in Section 1 above, along with the active construction by the child of causal explanatory frameworks about the structure and action of systems. The idea that knowledge is actively constructed by the child is one of the central tenets of Piagetian theory. Piaget's related notion of stage-based change, that children think and reason in different ways according to their stage of cognitive development, has been undermined however. Nevertheless, his idea that action (physical interaction) with the world is a critical part of knowledge construction has been supported. The basis of cognition is indeed in sensory-motor learning, as Piaget proposed. However, sensory-motor representations are not *replaced* by symbolic ones. Rather, they are augmented by knowledge gained through action, language, pretend play and teaching. Cognitive neuroscience suggests that the entire cognitive system can be conceptualised as a 'loose-knit, distributed representational economy' (Clark 2006). There is no all-knowing, inner 'central executive' that governs what is 'known' and that orchestrates development. Rather, there is a 'vast parallel coalition of more-or-less influential forces whose ... unfolding makes each of us the thinking beings that we are' (p. 373).

3. MEMORY

Memory consists of a variety of cognitive systems. Chief among these are semantic memory (our generic, factual knowledge about the world), episodic memory (our ability consciously to retrieve autobiographical happenings from the past), implicit or procedural memory (such as habits and skills), and working memory (our short-term store). Memories that can be brought consciously and deliberately to mind (semantic and episodic memory) are called declarative, whereas knowledge that is usually indexed by changes in performance (for example, riding a bicycle) is called implicit memory. Associative learning and habituation (ubiquitous mechanisms of learning across species, see Section 1 above) are also implicit or procedural. Visual recognition memory is well-developed in young children. For example, Brown and Scott (1971) showed children aged from 3–5 years a series of 100 pictures, and found recognition memory on 98 per cent of trials. Declarative episodic memories develop more slowly. Children (and adults) *construct* declarative memories, and therefore prior knowledge and personal interpretation affect what is remembered.

3a. The development of episodic memory

Remembering is embedded in larger social and cognitive activities, and therefore the knowledge structures that young children bring to their experiences are a critical factor in explaining memory development and learning. Temporal and causal structures are particularly important. Very young children may not structure their experience in memorable ways, particularly if they do not understand particular experiences (for example, being abused), or if they do not have a clear temporal framework for organising the experience. Nevertheless, when tested with simple scenarios (for example 'giving teddy a bath'), even 18-month-olds retain memories that display temporal ordering and are arranged around a goal (Bauer 2002). Early event memory is not composed of a series of disorganised snapshots of individual components of the event. Nelson (1986) showed that younger children concentrate on remembering routines, as routine makes the world a predictable place. However, very young children also remember distinctive events. In one longitudinal study, Fivush and Hammond (1990) reported a 4-year-old who recalled that, when he was 2½, 'I fed my fish too much food and then it died and my mum dumped him in the toilet'. Young children rarely invent memories that have not occurred (Gilstrap and Ceci 2005). Intensive research on young children's eyewitness testimony shows that younger children are more susceptible to 'leading questions', but these increase inaccurate acquiescence (the child agrees that something happened which did not). Leading questions rarely cause children to invent false memories. Even pre-schoolers (3–5 year olds) make relatively few errors in response to misleading questions about abuse (16 per cent errors, see Eisen *et al.* 2002, who studied maltreated and abused children from low socio-economic status (SES) families).

The ways in which parents and teachers interact with children influences the development of episodic memory. Parents or carers who have an 'elaborative' conversational style have children with more organised and detailed memories (Reese *et al.* 1993). An elaborative style involves amplifying the information recalled by the child and then evaluating it. Mothers who tend to switch topics and provide less narrative structure, and who seldom use elaboration and evaluation, have children who recall less about the past. Longitudinal studies have shown that it is the experience of verbalising events *at the time that they occur* that is critical for long-term retention (Fivush and Schwarzmueller 1998). Language enables children to construct extended, temporally-organised representations of experienced events that are narratively coherent. Partaking in elaborative conversation facilitates the construction of a personal history.

3b. Working memory

The memory system for short-term recall is usually called working memory. Working memory is a limited capacity 'workspace' that maintains information temporarily while it is processed for use in other cognitive tasks, such as reasoning, comprehension and learning (for example, Baddeley and Hitch 1974). Although there are both visual and phonological (sound-based) working memory systems, most developmental research has focussed on the phonological system, as even visually-presented material is often translated into speech-based codes for short-term retention. The amount of material that can be stored temporarily in this speech-based system increases with age. The capacity of the system is also affected by factors such as word length (fewer words are retained if they are long words), phonological confusability (it is more difficult to retain words that sound similar, such as 'hat, rat, tap, mat'), and speech rate (children who articulate more slowly retain less information). Children who have well-specified phonological representations of words in semantic memory also have better working memories, as they can refresh ('redintegrate') verbal codes that are becoming degraded more efficiently. The development of working memory is important for the development of metacognition and the development of reading (see Sections 6 and 8, following).

Implications for education

Even young children have remarkably good memories. Children's memories for their own experiences are better when a carer or teacher adopts an elaborative conversational style to help them to make sense of temporal and causal aspects of their experiences. Adapting our dialogue with young children leads to more organised and detailed learning and memory. These findings are suggestive with respect to the kinds of dialogues in classrooms that will most aid retention and understanding. Children's autobiographical memories tend to be accurate, even for unusual events, and the invention of 'false memories' is rare. Work in cognitive neuroscience is currently focused on which brain structures are important for different types of memory. For example, the hippocampus is known to play a key role in consolidating memories and in recollection. Developmental aspects are not well-understood. For example, children with early hippocampal damage can acquire normal semantic memories and show age-appropriate working memory. However, they have enormous difficulty in remembering the events of their daily lives (Vargha-Khadem *et al.* 1997).

4. LANGUAGE

It is already clear that language plays a key role in cognitive development. Language aids conceptual development (Section 2b), the development of a theory of mind (2c), episodic memory development (3a) and is the basis of working memory (3b). It also plays a key role in Vygotsky's theory of cognitive development (see Section 9, following). Infants use the same abilities to acquire the phonological aspects of language that they use to acquire knowledge about the physical and psychological worlds, namely associative learning, tracking statistical dependencies, and tracking conditional probabilities (see 1a). Word learning is aided by the universal tendency of adults (and children) to talk to babies using a special prosodic register called infant-directed speech or 'Motherese'. This uses higher pitch and exaggerated intonation (for example, increased duration and stress) to highlight novel information, which appears perceptually effective in facilitating learning (for example, Fernald and Mazzie 1991). Children who are less sensitive to the auditory cues of the prosodic and rhythmic patterning in language may be at risk for developmental dyslexia and specific language impairment (for example Corriveau *et al.* 2007). Active production is also important for language acquisition, and babbling reflects early production of the structured rhythmic and temporal patterns of language and proto-syllables. Deaf babies do not show typical vocal babble, and babies born to deaf parents who sign 'babble' with their hands, duplicating the rhythmic timing and stress of hand shapes in natural signs (Petitto *et al.* 2004).

4a. Vocabulary development

The primary function of language is communication, and words are part of meaning-making experiences from very early in development. As discussed in Section 2, conceptual representations precede language development, being rooted in the perceptual experience of objects and events. Nevertheless, carers talk to babies before they can talk back, naming objects that are being attended to, commenting on joint activities or on the child's behaviour or apparent feelings. One study showed that toddlers hear an estimated 5000–7000 utterances a day, with around a third of these utterances being questions (Cameron-Faulkner *et al.* 2003). In a U.S. study, Hart and Risley (1995) estimated that children from high socio-economic status (SES) families heard around 487 utterances per hour, compared to 178 utterances per hour for children from families on welfare. Hence by the time they were aged 4 years, the high SES children had been exposed to around 44 million utterances, compared to 12 million utterances for the lower SES children. Word learning is also important for cognitive development because it is symbolic. Words are symbols because they *refer* to an object or to an event, but they are not the object or the event itself. Symbols allow children to disconnect themselves from the immediate situation. Gestures are also symbolic (for example, waving 'goodbye'). Gesture precedes language production in development, providing a 'cognitive bridge' between comprehension and production (Volterra and Erting 1990). Action is used to express meaning. Even later in cognitive development, gesture can provide important information about what the child understands in a given cognitive domain. These (frequently) unconscious gestures are sensed by their teachers, who alter their teaching input accordingly (for example, Goldin-Meadow and Wagner 2005). Gesture-speech 'mismatches' are often found when children are on the verge of making progress on a particular cognitive task.

Word learning (vocabulary development) is exponential in early childhood. Using the child language checklist (now translated into 12 languages), Fenson *et al.* (1994) showed that median English spoken vocabulary size is 55 words by 16 months of age, 225 words by 23 months, 573 words by 30 months, and 6000 words by age 6. Comprehension vocabulary at age 6 is around 14,000 words (Dollaghan 1994). However, the developmental range can be enormous. For example, at 2 years, the range in word production is from 0 words to more than 500 words. Fenson *et al.* also showed that there was no 'burst' in vocabulary acquisition at around 18 months for most children. The 'naming burst' had been important theoretically, as it suggested the sudden cognitive achievement of the 'insight' that words can name (Bloom 1973). This achievement at 18 months appeared to fit neatly with Piaget's theoretical view (now discounted, see Section 2a) that a symbolic understanding of the 'object concept' developed at the same time. However, infants as young as 4 months seem to have worked out that words can name. They already recognise their own names, and the word for 'mummy' (Mandel *et al.* 1995). New word learning is extremely rapid, with around 10 new words acquired daily at age 2. This rapid learning has been called 'fast mapping' (Carey 1978). Although first conceived as a dedicated language-learning mechanism, fast mapping is a powerful form of exclusion learning which is not special to humans (for example, intelligent dogs can use 'fast mapping' to learn novel words; Kaminski *et al.* 2004). Children use a combination of the context in which new words are encountered and their position in a sentence to eliminate potential candidates regarding word meaning.

4b. Grammatical development

The set of grammatical 'rules' that determine how words can be combined into sentences and phrases is called syntax. Morphology refers to the 'rules' governing the internal structure of words – we can say 'I'll undo it' but not 'I'll unmake it'. Whether grammatical development is a matter of acquiring rules or of reproducing pieces of heard language is the subject of intense debate. Rule-based views can be characterised by Chomsky's (1957) notion of a 'language acquisition device'; specialised innate knowledge about the general rules that all languages obey along with knowledge of permitted variations. Tomasello (2000, 2006) has suggested that grammatical development depends on the piecemeal acquisition of particular constructions that are good grammatical forms, and not on the acquisition of general syntactic categories. Children acquire utterances that represent a single relatively coherent communicative intention. By his account, children then build upon these piecemeal constructions by using the same pattern-finding mechanisms that underpin learning in other areas (statistical learning, categorisation, induction, analogy). Although it was previously believed that overt correction of grammatical errors by caretakers was rare, more recent research shows that extensive feedback is provided. Adults reformulate the child's utterance rather than overtly correcting it (Chouinard and Clark 2003). Again, we see the role of communicative interaction in language learning (see also Section 1a).

Implications for education

Language development is critical to cognitive development, and shows marked variation in the preschool years. Children can enter school having been exposed to significantly less language than their peers, and with very different-sized vocabularies. Gesture can be an important aspect of communication in the classroom. Children can reveal more knowledge via gesture than language. Both gesture and language are symbolic, enabling children to detach themselves from the immediate situation. This is important for enabling cognition itself to become the object of thought and reflection – metacognition (see Section 6).

5. PRETEND PLAY AND THE IMAGINATION

Pretend play may be the earliest manifestation of a child's developing ability to characterise their own cognitive relation to knowledge. Action (pretending) is another way to detach oneself from the immediate situation. In a famous paper, Leslie (1987) showed that in order to pretend that (for example) a banana is a telephone, the child must separate the *primary* representation of the banana (given by the sensory systems: yellow object with particular texture and smell) from the pretend representation (telephone receiver). The primary representation is the direct representation of the object, and it is crucial for cognition that our primary representations are veridical. During pretend play, this primary representation must be detached or 'quarantined' from the pretend representation of a telephone receiver. The pretend representation is not a representation of the objective world, rather it is a representation of a representation from that world. It is a *meta*representation. Thus the emergence of pretend play marks the beginning of a capacity to understand cognition itself – to understand thoughts as entities.

5a. The development of pretend play

Pretending develops during the second year of life, with early pretence typically tied to the veridical actions that people make on objects (for example a 12-month-old 'drinking' from an empty cup) and later pretence being more detached from object identities (for example a 2-year-old pretending a stick is a horse). Pretend play is usually carried out with others. Children show more advanced pretending when they imitate the pretence of others, and adult scaffolding of pretend play with toddlers facilitates symbolic development (Bigelow *et al.* 2004). Language is also important, as social partners can use language to help young children to understand pretend situations.

Pretend play is also linked to the development of a 'theory of mind'. However, different social partners offer different types of pretend play. Pretend play with siblings or friends differs from pretend play with the mother, and is more likely to be social pretence, because other children are usually in the drama themselves. Jenkins and Astington (1996) showed that children with siblings showed earlier development of a 'theory of mind' than children without siblings, and that having siblings had stronger effects for children with lower language abilities. One reason that pretend play with siblings and friends helps to develop psychological understanding is that shared pretend play makes high demands for imaginary and co-operative interaction. Shared socio-dramatic play provides a large number of opportunities for reflecting upon one's own and others' desires, beliefs and emotions. As children get older less time is spent in actual play, and more and more time is spent in negotiating the plot and each other's roles (Lillard 2002). This discourse about mental states enhances mind-reading skills. Hughes and Dunn (1998) showed in a longitudinal study of 4-year-olds that the rate of mental state talk between friends at nursery was significantly related to later performance on false belief and emotion understanding tasks. Mental state talk was also more advanced and more frequent in pairs of girls than in pairs of boys.

There are also large individual differences in pretending. Dunn and Cutting (1999) showed that some children share an imaginary world together with great skill and enjoyment, while others prefer to engage in boisterous games or even engage in 'shared deviance' (for example, killing flies together). However, greater skill in mind-reading does not always go with better prosocial behaviour. A study of 7-to 10-year-olds found that those who bullied others showed advanced performance in theory of mind tasks (for example, Sutton *et al.* 1999). It is unclear whether having advanced mind-reading skills enables a child to become a bully, or whether the experience of bullying *itself* aids children's social cognitive development.

5b. The role of the imagination in cognitive development

While Western psychology has focussed on the important role of imaginative play in enabling a deeper understanding of mind (social cognitive development), Russian psychology has emphasised effects on cognitive self-regulation (executive function, see Section 6). Vygotsky (1978) argued that the imagination represented a specifically human form of cognitive activity. According to his theory, a central developmental function of pretend play was that children had to act against their immediate impulses and follow the 'rules of the game'. This was thought to help them to gain inhibitory control over their thoughts and actions. The child's playmates exert an important regulatory function as well. For example, Karpov (2005) reports a study of children aged from 3 to 7 years who were required to stand motionless for as long as they could. The play context was 'being a sentry'. When the children had to stand motionless alone in a room without a play context, they were significantly less successful compared to the play context. However, when they had to be a sentry in a room full of their playmates, they were most successful. The playmates were monitoring the sentry, helping him to stand still for longer. Russian neo-Vygotskians argue that adult mediation is required to initiate or extend socio-dramatic play for learning purposes, so that it becomes 'a micro-world of active experiencing of social roles and relationships' (Karpov 2005: 140). Vygotsky regarded play as a major factor in cognitive development.

Implications for education

Pretend play is an early form of symbolic activity. In symbolic play, the meaning of things to the child depends not on their status as real objects in the perceptual world, but on their status in the imaginary world. Through pretend play, the child is manipulating her cognitive relations to information, and taking a representation as the object of cognition (forming metarepresentations – Leslie 1987). The child distinguishes veridical from non-veridical mental representations, and this is important for cognitive development. For example, the ability to reflect on and index one's own mental representations, tagging their internal source so that both current reality and past reality are kept in mind together, is metacognition (see Section 6). Pretend play with others is typically socio-dramatic play, and this is important for developing psychological understanding (mind-reading skills or 'theory of mind', Section 2c). The kind of language involved (mental state discourse) also provides a medium for reflecting on and knowing about our own thoughts and those of others. Pretending with others may also be important for developing cognitive self-regulation skills (executive function). Both language and imaginative pretend play share the core developmental functions of enabling children to reflect upon and regulate their own cognitive behaviour, and to reflect upon and gain a deeper understanding of the mind.

6. METACOGNITION AND EXECUTIVE FUNCTION

Metacognition is knowledge about cognition, encompassing factors such as knowing about your own information-processing skills, monitoring your own cognitive performance, and knowing about the demands made by different kinds of cognitive tasks. Executive function refers to gaining strategic control over your own mental processes, inhibiting certain thoughts or actions, and developing conscious control over your thoughts, feelings and behaviour. The assumption is that as children gain metaknowledge about their mental processes, their strategic control also improves. Developments in metacognition and executive function tend to be associated with language development, the development of working memory (which enables multiple perspectives to be held in mind) and non-verbal ability (Hughes 1998).

6a. The development of metamemory

Research in metacognition began with research on metamemory. Researchers studied children's awareness of themselves as memorisers, for example, their awareness of their strengths and weaknesses in remembering certain types of information. In general, children turned out to be quite good at monitoring their memories. They did not differ markedly from adults on measures like judging how well they had learned something (both groups tend to be over-optimistic about their learning). However, younger children were less good at planning, directing and evaluating their memory behaviour (see Schneider and Lockl 2002). For example, they were not very good at deciding how much study time to allocate to particular memory tasks. Younger children also had more difficulty in keeping track of the sources of their memories than older children. As metamemory skills develop, memory performance is enhanced (for example, children become increasingly skilled at applying appropriate mnemonic strategies). Schneider *et al.* (2000) suggested that developments in self-regulation (executive function) rather than in self-monitoring might explain developments in metamemory in children.

6b. The development of inhibitory control

The term 'executive function' derives from the 'executive deficits' that are exhibited by patients who have damage to frontal cortex. For example, when sorting a pack of cards according to a particular rule (for example, colour), frontal patients find it difficult to switch strategies when the sorting rule is changed (for example to shape). However, the patient is aware that 'this is wrong, and this is wrong, and this is wrong … ' (Diamond 1990). Frontal cortex turns out to be important for working memory, for strategic control over behaviour and for the inhibition of inappropriate behaviours. It also continues to develop into adolescence and early adulthood. In the last decade, there has been an explosion of developmental research into inhibitory control and cognitive flexibility (for example, Zelazo *et al.* 2003). Three-to 4-year-old children have considerable difficulty in rule shifting tasks, just like frontal patients, despite being able to verbally report new sorting rules (for example, Zelazo *et al.* 1996). If asked to re-label the cards verbally before sorting them, however, even 3-year-olds can sort correctly after the rule has been switched (Kirkham *et al.* 2003). This suggests that younger children have difficulty in flexibly shifting their attentional focus, but can be helped to overcome these difficulties via language and instruction.

In general, two types of tasks have been used to measure inhibitory control in young children (Carlson and Moses 2001). One requires children to delay gratification of a desire, for example, by suppressing a 'prepotent' response such as peeking at a gift. The second requires children to respond in a way that conflicts with a more salient response, for example, by labelling pictures of the sun 'night' and pictures of the moon 'day'. Performance in both types of inhibitory control task improves with age. When gender differences are found, girls outperform boys at all ages (for example, Kochanska *et al.*

1996). Hughes (1998) devised tasks to distinguish between inhibitory control, working memory and attentional flexibility. She found that all aspects of executive function developed together in preschoolers. Inhibitory control tasks are hence thought to tap a common underlying construct, with delay and conflict as key aspects. Planning is another important aspect of executive function, which also develops. Efficient planning and efficient inhibitory control are required for effective self-regulation. Performance in executive function tasks also correlates highly with performance in theory of mind tasks (for example, Carlson *et al.* 2004). This is not surprising, as one set of tasks measures what the child knows about his or her own mind, and the other what the child knows about somebody else's mind (Schneider and Lockl 2002).

6c. Cognitive neuroscience studies

The classic view of the development of metacognition and executive function is that development is related to maturational changes in frontal cortex (for example Zelazo *et al.* 2003). Brain imaging studies to date confirm significant correlations between structural developments in the brain and improved executive function, but the direction of cause and effect is unclear. Performance by children in conflict tasks such as the day/night task leads to strong activity in both dorsolateral and ventrolateral prefrontal cortex (for example, Durston *et al.* 2002). Response inhibition tasks also lead to strong activation in dorsolateral prefrontal cortex (for example Luna *et al.* 2001). In the adult literature, researchers distinguish between 'cool' and 'hot' executive function. The former refers to making purely cognitive decisions (for example, naming ink colour), whereas the latter involves making decisions about events that have emotionally significant consequences (for example, when gambling). 'Hot' executive function activates orbitofrontal cortex in adults. From experimental studies, Kerr and Zelazo (2004) argued that 'hot' executive function develops in a similar way to 'cool' executive function in young children. The key factor developmentally appears to be managing conflicting representations.

Implications for education

Metacognition and executive function both show important developments in the primary years. As discussed in Sections 1, 2 and 3, learning, knowledge construction and memory operate in similar ways in young children and adults. Self-regulation and inhibitory control do not. Gaining reflective awareness of one's own cognition is a major achievement of the primary years, as is cognitive self-regulation: hence learning in classrooms can be enhanced by developing self-reflection and inhibitory control in young children. Children with good metacognitive skills can improve their own learning and memory, for example, by adopting effective cognitive strategies and by being aware of when they don't understand something and seeking more guidance. This has been shown most clearly by metamemory research. It is also demonstrated by studies on 'learning to learn', which are reviewed in Section 7.

7. INDUCTIVE AND DEDUCTIVE REASONING

Contrary to what was believed at the time of the Plowden Report in 1967, inductive and deductive reasoning are available early in development and function in highly similar ways in children and in adults. Children do not gradually become efficient all-purpose learning machines, acquiring and applying general reasoning strategies across domains. In 1967, when Piaget's theory was more influential, it was thought that the development of reasoning and problem solving involved the acquisition of logical rules. It is now understood that inductive and deductive reasoning are influenced by similar factors and are subject to similar heuristics and biases in both children and adults.

7a. Deductive reasoning

Deductive reasoning problems have only one logically valid answer. An illustration is the logical syllogism. Given the premises:

> All cats bark
> Rex is a cat

the logically correct answer to the question 'Does Rex bark?' is yes. The plausibility or real-world accuracy of the premises does not matter for the validity of the logical deduction. When children are given syllogisms involving familiar premises, even if they are counterfactual (as in barking cats), they can make logically valid deductions (for example Dias and Harris 1988). Presenting the premises in play situations (for example pretending to be on a planet where cats bark) helps young children to reason logically, but 4 year olds can also succeed simply by being asked to think about the premises (Leevers and Harris 2000). When told, 'All ladybirds have stripes on their backs. Daisy is a ladybird. Is Daisy spotty?', one 4 year old commented, 'All ladybirds have stripes on their back. But they don't,' and then made the logically valid deduction. Even young children recognise that the premises, whatever they may be, *logically imply* the conclusions.

7b. Inductive reasoning

Although there is no logical justification of induction (Hume 1748/1988), inductive inferences are very useful in human reasoning. A typical inductive reasoning problem might take the form 'Humans have spleens. Dogs have spleens. Do rabbits have spleens?' (see Carey 1985). As all the animals named are mammals, one can 'go beyond the information given' and reason by analogy that rabbits probably do have spleens. However, if the problem takes the form 'Dogs have spleens. Bees have spleens. Do humans have spleens?', people are more reluctant to draw an inductive inference. This is because the most important constraint on inductive reasoning is similarity. Inductive generalisation depends on the similarity between the premise and conclusion categories, the sample size, and the typicality of the property being projected (Heit 2000). Successful reasoning by analogy also depends on similarity, with similarity of relations (for example, causal relations) being most important (Goswami 1991). As noted in Section 1d, very young children can make analogies involving causal relations. Encouraging metacognitive reflection improves analogical skills in young children. Brown (1989) demonstrated that children's inductive reasoning could be enhanced if they experienced a *series* of analogies, and if they were taught to look for analogies during problem-solving ('learning-to-learn'). For example, children aged 3, 4 and 5 years learned to transfer different solutions (stacking objects, pulling objects, swinging over obstacles) between problem pairs administered sequentially (A1-A2/B1-B2/C1-C2). By novel problem C2, 85 per cent of 3-year-olds were successfully solving the problem by using an analogy.

Implications for education

Young children do not acquire the 'rules of logic' as they get older, rather they reason both inductively and deductively in the same ways as adults. Developmental differences arise from having a smaller knowledge base and from having less expertise: young children are 'universal novices' (Brown and DeLoache 1978). Learning from examples (by analogy) is a powerful form of human learning. Research by Brown suggests that instructional analogies work best when teachers present a series of examples of a particular concept within an explicit framework that emphasises relational similarity, making the goals (causal structure) of the teaching transparent. A key factor in transfer of learning is recognition of underlying similarity at the level of structure.

8. COGNITIVE PREREQUISITES FOR READING AND NUMBER

The invention of orthographic systems (for example, the alphabet) and the number system (for example Arabic numerals) transformed human cognition, enabling the organisation of cognitive behaviour (learning, memory) by using symbols. These symbol systems require direct teaching, but for both reading and number there are cognitive prerequisites that facilitate learning. These prerequisites will be covered extremely briefly. Reading development builds on the cognitive representations for spoken language ('phonological representations'). Number builds on the cognitive representations for objects and quantities.

8a. Reading acquisition

Reading acquisition has several aspects: cognitive and metacognitive, motivational, communicative, sociocultural, and so on. The most important cognitive skills for reading are described by the term 'phonological awareness'. Phonological awareness refers to a child's ability to reflect upon the sound patterns of words in her mental lexicon at different 'grain sizes' (for example, syllable, rhyme). Phonological awareness is usually measured by tasks requiring the detection (for example, 'Which is the odd word out? "Hat, mat, fan?"') or manipulation ('What would "star" be without the "ss" sound?') of the component sounds that comprise words. As discussed earlier (Section 4a), an important part of language acquisition is phonological development. Children learn the sounds and combinations of sounds that are permissible in their language, forming 'phonological representations' for real words. Individual differences in the quality of these representations, measured by phonological awareness tasks, predict reading acquisition across languages (Ziegler and Goswami 2005). Awareness of syllables and rhymes develops prior to literacy across languages, but awareness of the smallest units of sound symbolised by letters (called *phonemes*) varies with orthographic transparency. Children learning languages with a 1:1 mapping from letter to sound (for example, Finnish, German) rapidly acquire awareness of phonemes. Children learning languages that lack a 1:1 mapping from letters to sounds (for example, English, French) acquire phoneme awareness more slowly. Phoneme awareness depends on teaching, because the phoneme is not a natural speech unit. Although the relative distributional frequencies of different acoustic features yield phonetic categories like 'p' and 'b' (see Section 4a), 'p' does not represent the same physical sound in words like 'pit' and 'spoon'. Hence the development of phonemic awareness depends in part on the consistency with which letters symbolise phonemes.

Providing training in phonological awareness at all grain sizes and in how phonological units link to letters enhances reading development across languages (for example, English: Bradley and Bryant 1983; Danish: Lundberg, Frost and Petersen 1988; German: Schneider, Roth and Ennemoser 2000). Nevertheless, reading efficiency is acquired at different rates in different languages (Seymour *et al.* 2003). Fluency is acquired fastest in languages where the mapping from letter to sound is 1:1, where syllable structure is simple (consonant-vowel syllables), and where there are relatively few phonemes (for example, Finnish has 21 phonemes, or 25 if foreign loan words are counted). It is slower in languages with inconsistent spelling systems, many phonemes (English has around 44), and where syllable structure is complex (English has relatively few consonant-vowel syllables). Similarly, developmental dyslexia manifests differently in different languages. Children with poor phonological skills are at risk for dyslexia in all languages. However, whereas dyslexic children learning to read a language like English continue to experience problems in reading accuracy, for languages like Finnish dyslexia manifests as extremely slow reading *speed* and poor spelling.

8b. The acquisition of number

Recently, the acquisition of number has become a 'hot topic' in cognitive neuroscience. Demonstrations that the physiological/cognitive structures in the parietal lobe upon which number knowledge builds are shared with other species has led to claims that number knowledge is innate (for example Feigenson *et al.* 2004). However, while there is convincing evidence for an approximate, analogue magnitude representation in the human brain that is shared with other species (for example Dehaene 1997), this does not mean that children have an innate understanding of symbolic number. An analogue representation implies that numbers are not stored mentally as discrete entities reflecting exact quantities, but are stored as approximations of quantity. As quantities get larger, the representations for numbers get less precise. Indeed, experiments with infants and young children show that the ability to make discriminations between quantities is ratio-sensitive (for example Jordan and Brannon 2006). For example, children are worse at comparing 8 with 12 (ratio 2:3) than 8 with 16 (ratio 1:2). For very small numbers (1–4), infants and young children rely on automatic perceptual processes called 'subitizing'. Subitizing is the fast perceptual enumeration of very small sets (the number is seen 'at a glance', Barth *et al.* 2005).

One critical factor for building a number system from these basic spatial and perceptual representations appears to be learning the count sequence. Counting appears to be learned first as a linguistic routine, like a nursery rhyme or the days of the week. The language of the count sequence captures number meaning in terms of both a distinctive individual quantity ('cardinality') and a quantity with a fixed place among other numerical quantities that is dependent on increasing magnitude ('ordinality'). This means that a number label in the count sequence, such as 'four', represents the fact that 4 cats is the equivalent amount to 4 biscuits, and that 4 has a magnitude between 3 and 5. Learning to count enables children to organise their cognitive structures for number (subitizing and the analogue magnitude representation) into a coherent system. Accordingly, certain cross-cultural differences in the set of number names have some cognitive consequences, although these are brief and occur around age 2 (for example, Hodent *et al.* 2005). By around 3 years, children are developing the expectation that even unmapped number words refer to exact numerosities (Sarnecka and Gelman 2004). Number knowledge such as the 'number facts' (for example the multiplication tables, 2 + 2 = 4 et cetera) are stored in the language areas of the brain, and not in the spatial area where the analogue magnitude representation is found (Dehaene *et al.* 1998). Other cognitive prerequisites for understanding mathematical operations, such as 1:1 correspondence for division, are reviewed by Nunes and Bryant (1996).

Implications for education

The cognitive prerequisites for reading and number depend on language development, perceptual development and spatial development. A child who enters school with poor phonological awareness will have more difficulty in learning to read, and a child with poor spatial skills will have more difficulty in acquiring symbolic number. The development of an awareness of syllables and rhyme is important for learning about phonemes. The ability to count accurately is important for learning about numbers. Developmental dyslexia and developmental dyscalculia are specific learning difficulties, thought to reflect specific problems with phonology and with the approximate analogue representation for quantity (for example, Snowling 2000; Molko *et al.* 2003).

9. THEORIES OF COGNITIVE DEVELOPMENT AND INTELLIGENCE

As noted earlier, Piaget's theory that children reason in qualitatively different ways at different developmental stages is no longer accepted (see Section 2). Whereas the Plowden Report assumed that children only became capable of logical thought based on symbolic and abstract material in adolescence (Plowden 1967: 50), today it is accepted that all the basic forms of learning and reasoning are available from baby- and toddler-hood. What develops is the child's knowledge base, metacognition, and self-regulation. However, Plowden was correct to note that the development of language is central to the educational process (Plowden 1967: 54–55). Language is a symbolic and abstract system, and via language, pretend play and the imagination, even very young children think logically with abstract material (for example, see Section 7a). This is most clearly demonstrated in Vygotsky's theory of cognitive development (Vygotsky 1978, 1986).

9a. Vygotsky

Vygotsky argued that language is the primary symbolic system and that, once acquired, language mediates cognitive development. As speech becomes internalised ('inner speech'), it becomes fundamental in organising the child's cognitive activities. 'Sign systems' or 'psychological tools' such as language, drawing and writing are culturally transmitted, and so the inter-relatedness of social and cognitive processes in the child is fundamental. Eventually, sign systems come to mediate psychological functioning *within* the child. The importance of learning from others is also highlighted by Vygotsky's notion of the 'zone of proximal development'. This differs between children, and essentially measures how much further a child can go when learning with the support of a teacher. Vygotsky's recognition that learning can change the child's developmental level suggests that teachers need to discover an individual child's zone of proximal development and teach to that in order for instruction to bring optimal benefits. Vygotsky also argued that play, in particular the creation of imaginary situations, plays a central role in cognitive development. Joint pretend play requires recognition of the 'rules of the game' and aids the development of self-regulation, as children have to play by the rules. Play in itself creates a zone of proximal development, and while children are highly motivated to play, teachers are thought to have an important role in creating zones of proximal development via play that support learning (Karpov 2005).

Russian neo-Vygotskyians (for example Karpov 2005) have also stressed the role of joint activity with adults for the effective use of the zone of proximal development in teaching. They argue that verbal mediation is not enough to optimise learning. Shared activity is required to mediate the child's acquisition, mastery and internalisation of new content. Mediation should begin with the adult explaining and modelling the procedure or material to be learned. The adult should then involve the child in joint performance of this procedure or material, thereby creating the zone of proximal development of a new mental process. The child's mastery and internalisation of the material should then be guided until the adult can begin to withdraw. Neo-Vygotskyians have also focused on an approach called 'theoretical learning'. This offers an alternative to the constructivist learning pedagogies based on Piaget's theory. Rather than being required to rediscover scientific knowledge for themselves, children taught by theoretical learning are taught precise definitions of scientific concepts. They then master and internalise the procedures related to these concepts by using the conceptual knowledge to solve subject-domain problems (Karpov 2005). Although claimed by Russian psychologists to be highly effective, Western psychology has not yet studied Vygotsky's ideas about theoretical learning or his ideas about the role of play in education in any detail.

9b. Neuroconstructivism

Neuroconstructivism is a theoretical framework for cognitive development emerging from cognitive neuroscience. It is based on a consideration of the biological constraints on the patterns of brain activity that comprise mental representations, for example, the biological action of genes (Mareschal *et al.* 2007; Westermann *et al.* 2007). Genetic activity is modified by neural, behavioural and external environmental events, and all of these interactions must be understood in order to describe cognitive development. Similarly, the ways in which the senses function will constrain the development of mental representations, as the senses will 'filter' information from the environment. Neuroconstructivism is important for understanding developmental cognitive disorders, as these are explained by altered constraints on brain development that in turn alter a child's developmental trajectory (for example, Karmiloff-Smith 2007). For example, altered sensory functioning (for example, in the auditory system) could explain why children with developmental dyslexia do not develop well-specified phonological representations (for example, Goswami 2003). However, our understanding of the biological constraints that affect the development of the neural structures that underlie cognitive processing is still very incomplete. Neuroconstructivism is not deterministic, as the progressive specialisation of neural structures is recognised to be driven by the environment experienced (and actively chosen) by the child. Whereas neuroconstructivism offers a biological perspective on cognitive development, connectionism (see Section 1e) offers a biological perspective on learning.

9c. Theories of intelligence

Intelligence received a lot of attention in the Plowden Report (CACE 1967: 56–64). The strong heritability of intelligence is now accepted, but the emphasis in research is on the key role of the environment for explaining variability (for example, Plomin and Spinath 2002). An influential idea in education has been that of 'multiple' or distinct intelligences (Gardner 1993, 1999; for example 'spatial intelligence', 'logical-mathematical intelligence', 'linguistic intelligence'). This theory grew from a modular view of the brain, which is less applicable developmentally (for example, Johnson 2005). The developing brain is a highly interactive system and knowledge will be distributed across neural networks in a number of regions (spatial and linguistic knowledge underpin mathematical performance, for example). The idea of multiple intelligences is a useful metaphor for emphasising that intelligence reflects a range of skills (note however that Gardner himself did not consider multiple intelligences to be an educational goal). Multivariate genetic research shows substantial genetic overlap between broad areas of cognition such as language, memory, mathematics and general cognitive ability (Kovas and Plomin 2006). Hence within the average child, genes are 'generalist' in their effects, and there are typically strong associations between ability in one area of cognition and ability in another. Dweck (1999, 2006) has emphasised the importance of children's self-theories of intelligence for their response to schooling. Her research shows that some children have an entity or fixed theory of intelligence, which leads them to consider effort as negative (if learning requires effort, they cannot be intelligent) and to adopt performance goals (for example, scoring well on tests). Other children have an incremental or growth theory of intelligence, seeing it as a malleable quality that can be changed by effort. These children adopt learning goals and feel that they need to work harder if they do not understand something. Dweck's research suggests that children's beliefs about intelligence can be altered by feedback from teachers, who should try and praise effort rather than performance. Dweck shows that receiving praise for effort rather than for performance increases the motivation to learn.

Implications for education

While the new theoretical frameworks of neuroconstructivism and connectionism are important for understanding how the brain creates cognitive representations from perceptual input, the older theoretical frameworks of Piaget and Vygotsky are important for understanding how the activities of the child and the parent/sibling/peer/teacher enrich and develop these cognitive representations into a sophisticated cognitive system. Given current levels of knowledge in these fields, the importance of language and imaginative pretend play, knowledge construction, direct teaching and being part of a community to cognitive development are probably more important for decisions about the education of the primary school child. The notion of multiple intelligences is important for flexibility in teaching, for example, approaching educational topics in different ways, using analogies from a variety of domains, and expressing key concepts in a variety of forms (for example, Gardner 2003). The kind of feedback offered in the classroom is very important for the child's self-esteem and view of themselves as a learner. Learning by children is primarily a social activity.

SOME CONCLUSIONS

This chapter documents some central aspects of child development, thinking and learning in the primary years. Some key conclusions are:

a. Learning in young children is socially mediated. Families, peers and teachers are all important. Even basic perceptual learning mechanisms such as statistical learning require direct social interaction to be effective. This limits educational approaches such as e-learning in the early years.

b. Learning by the brain depends on the development of multi-sensory networks of neurons distributed across the entire brain. For example, a concept in science may depend on neurons being simultaneously active in visual, spatial, memory, deductive and kinaesthetic regions, in both brain hemispheres. Ideas such as left-brain/right-brain learning, or unisensory 'learning styles' (visual, auditory *or* kinaesthetic) are *not* supported by the brain science of learning.

c. Children construct explanatory systems to understand their experiences in the biological, physical and psychological realms. These are causal frameworks, for example, to explain why other people behave as they are observed to do, or why objects or events follow observed patterns. Knowledge gained through active experience, language, pretend play and teaching are all important for the development of children's causal explanatory systems. Children's causal biases should be recognised and built upon in primary education.

d. Children think and reason largely in the same ways as adults. However, they lack experience, and they are still developing important metacognitive and executive function abilities. Learning in classrooms can be enhanced if children are given diverse experiences and are helped to develop self-reflective and self-regulatory skills via teacher modelling and guidance around social situations like play, sharing and conflict resolutions.

e. Language is crucial for development. The ways in which teachers talk to children can influence learning, memory, understanding and the motivation to learn. There are also enormous individual differences in language skills between children in the early years.

f. Incremental experience is crucial for learning and knowledge construction. The brain learns the statistical structure of 'the input'. It can be important for teachers to assess how much 'input' a child's brain is actually getting when individual differences appear in learning. Differential exposure (for example, to spoken or written language) will lead to differential learning. As an example, one of the most important determinants of reading fluency is how much text the child actually reads, including outside the classroom.

g. Thinking, reasoning and understanding can be enhanced by imaginative or pretend play contexts. However, scaffolding by the teacher is required if these are to be effective.

h. Individual differences in the ability to benefit from instruction (the zone of proximal development) and individual differences between children are large in the primary years, hence any class of children must be treated as individuals.

REFERENCES

Baddeley, A.D. and Hitch, G. (1974) 'Working memory', in G.H. Bower (Ed) *The Psychology of Learning and Motivation* 8: 47–90. London: Academic Press.

Baillargeon, R., Li, J., Ng, W. and Yuan, S. (2009) 'A new account of infants' physical reasoning', in A. Woodward and A. Needham (Eds) *Learning and the Infant Mind*: 66–116. New York: Oxford University Press.

Baron-Cohen, S., Cosmides, L. and Tooby, J. (1999) *Mindblindness: essay on autism and theory of mind.* MIT Press.

Baron-Cohen, S., Leslie, A.M. and Frith, U. (1985) 'Does the autistic child have a "theory of mind"?' *Cognition* 21: 37–46.

Barth, H., LaMont, K., Lipton, J. and Spelke, E.S. (2005) 'Abstract number and arithmetic in preschool children,' in *Proceedings of the National Academy of Sciences* 102: 14, 116–21.

Bauer, P.J. (2002) 'Early memory development', in U. Goswami (Ed) *Blackwell Handbook of Childhood Cognitive Development*: 127–46. Oxford: Blackwell.

Bigelow, A.E., MacLean, K. and Proctor, J. (2004) 'The role of joint attention in the development of infants' play with objects', *Developmental Science* 7(4): 419–21.

Bloom, L. (1973) *One Word at a Time.* Paris: Mouton.

Bradley, L. and Bryant, P.E. (1983) 'Categorising sounds and learning to read: a causal connection', *Nature* 310: 419–21.

Brown, A.L. (1978) 'Knowing when, where and how to remember: a problem of metacognition', in R. Glaser (Ed) *Advances in Instructional Psychology.* Hillsdale, NJ: Erlbaum.

——(1989) 'Analogical learning and transfer: what develops?' in S. Vosniadou and A. Ortony (Eds) *Similarity and Analogical Reasoning*: 369–412. Cambridge: Cambridge University Press.

——(1990) 'Domain-specific principles affect learning and transfer in children', *Cognitive Science* 14: 107–33.

Brown, A.L. and DeLoache, J.S. (1978) 'Skills, plans, and self-regulation', in R.S. Siegler (Ed) *Children's Thinking: what develops?*: 3–35. New York: Erlbaum.

Brown, A.L. and Scott, M.S. (1971) 'Recognition memory for pictures in preschool children', *Journal of Experimental Child Psychology* 11: 401–12.

Bullock, M., Gelman, R. and Baillargeon, R. (1982) 'The development of causal reasoning', in W.J. Friedman (Ed) *The Developmental Psychology of Time*: 209–54. New York: Academic Press.

Central Advisory Council for Education (England) (CACE) (1967) *Children and Their Primary Schools: a report of the Central Advisory Council for Education (England)* (the Plowden Report). London: HMSO.

Cameron-Faulkner, T., Lieven, E. and Tomasello, M. (2003) 'A construction based analysis of child directed speech', *Cognitive Science* 27: 843–73.

Carey, S. (1978) 'The child as word learner', in M. Halle, J. Bresnan and G.A. Miller (Eds) *Linguistic Theory and Psychological Reality.* Cambridge, MA: The MIT Press.

——(1985) *Conceptual Change in Childhood.* Cambridge, MA: MIT Press.

Carlson, S.M. and Moses, L.J. (2001) 'Individual differences in inhibitory control and children's theory of mind', *Child Development* 72: 1032–53.

Carlson, S.M., Moses, L.J. and Claxton, L.J. (2004) 'Individual differences in executive functioning and theory of mind: an investigation of inhibitory control and planning ability', *Journal of Experimental Child Psychology* 87: 299–319.

Chen, Z., Sanchez, R.P. and Campbell, T. (1997) 'From beyond to within their grasp: the rudiments of analogical problem solving in 10-and 13-month-olds', *Developmental Psychology* 33: 790–801.

Chomsky, N. (1957) *Syntactic Structures.* Berlin: Mouton de Gruyter.

Chouinard, M. and Clark, E. (2003) 'Adult reformulations of child errors as negative evidence', *Journal of Child Language* 30: 637–69.

Clark, E.V. (2006) 'La répétition et l'acquisition du langage', *La Linguistique* 42(2): 67–79.

Corriveau, K.C., Pasquini, E. and Goswami, U. (2007) 'Basic auditory processing and specific language impairment: a new look at an old hypothesis', *Journal of Speech, Hearing and Language Research* 50: 647–66.

Dapretto, M., Davies, M.S., Pfeifer, J.H., Scott, A.A., Sigman, M., Bookheimer, S.Y. and Iacoboni, M. (2006) 'Understanding emotions in others: mirror neuron dysfunction in children with autism spectrum disorders', *Nature Neuroscience* 9: 28–30.

DeCasper, A.J. and Fifer, W.P. (1980) 'Of human bonding: newborns prefer their mother's voices', *Science* 208: 1174–76.

Dehaene, S. (1997) *The Number Sense: how the mind creates mathematics.* New York: Oxford University Press.

Dehaene, S., Dehaene-Lambertz, G. and Cohen, L. (1998) 'Abstract representations of numbers in the animal and human brain', *Trends in Neuroscience* 21: 355–61.

Dehaene-Lambertz, G., Hertz-Pannier, L., Dubois, J., Meriaux, S., Roche, A., Sigman, M. and Dehaene, S. (2006) 'Functional organisation of perisylvian activation during presentation of sentences in preverbal infants', *Proceedings of the National Academy of Sciences* 103(38): 14240–45.

Dennett, D. (1978) *Brainstorms: philosophical essays on mind and psychology.* Cambridge: Bradford Books/MIT Press.

Diamond, A. (1990) 'Developmental time course in human infants and infant monkeys, and the neural bases of inhibitory control in reaching', *Annals of the New York Academy of Sciences* 608: 637–76.

Dias, M.G. and Harris, P.L. (1988) 'The effect of make-believe play on deductive reasoning', *British Journal of Developmental Psychology* 6: 207–21.

Dollaghan, C.A. (1994) 'Children's phonological neighbourhoods: half empty or half full?' *Journal of Child Language* 21: 257–71.

Dunn, J., Brown, J. and Beardsall, L. (1991) 'Family talk about feeling states and children's later understanding of others' emotions', *Developmental Psychology* 27: 448–55

Dunn, J. and Cutting, A.L. (1999) 'Understanding others, and individual differences in friendship interactions in young children', *Social Development* 8: 201–19.

Durston, S., Thomas, K.M., Yang, Y., Ulug, A.M, Zimmerman, R.D. and Casey, B.J. (2002) 'The development of neural systems involved in overriding behavioral responses. An event-related fMRI study', *Developmental Science* 5(4): F9–F16.

Dweck, C.S. (1999) *Self-Theories: their role in motivation, personality and development.* Philadelphia, PA: Psychology Press.

——(2006) *Mindset: the new psychology of success.* New York: Random House.

Eisen, M., Qin, J.J., Goodman, G.S. and Davis, S. (2002) 'Memory and suggestibility in maltreated children', *Journal of Experimental Child Psychology* 83: 167–212.

Elman, J.L. (2005) 'Connectionist models of cognitive development: where next?' *Trends in Cognitive Sciences* 9(3): 111–17.

Farroni, T., Csibra, G., Simion, F. and Johnson, M.H. (2002) 'Eye contact detection in humans from birth', *Proceedings of the National Academy of Sciences* 99: 9602–5.

Feigenson, L., Dehaene, S. and Spelke, E. (2004) 'Core systems of number', *Trends in Cognitive Sciences* 8: 307–14.

Fenson, L., Dale, P.S., Reznick, J.S., Bates, E., Thal, D. and Pethick, S. (1994) 'Variability in early communicative development', *Monographs of the Society for Research in Child Development* 59(5) Serial No. 242.

Fernald, A. and Mazzie, C. (1991) 'Prosody and focus in speech to infants and adults', *Developmental Psychology* 27: 209–21.

Fivush, R. and Hammond, N.R. (1990) 'Autobiographical memory across the preschool years: toward reconceptualising childhood amnesia', in R. Fivush and J. Hudson (Eds) *Knowing and Remembering in Young Children.* New York: Cambridge University Press.

Fivush, R. and Schwarzmueller, A. (1998) 'Children remember childhood: implications for childhood amnesia', *Applied Cognitive Psychology* 12: 455–73.

Gardner, H. (1993) *Multiple Intelligences: the theory in practice.* New York: Basic Books.

——(1999) *Intelligence Reframed.* New York: Basic Books.

——(2003) 'Multiple intelligences after twenty years', *Invited address to the American Educational Research Association, April 2003*, www.pz.harvard.edu/PIs/HG.htm.

Gelman, S.A. (2004) 'Psychological essentialism in children', *Trends in Cognitive Sciences* 8: 404–9.

Gelman, S.A. and Opfer, J.E. (2002) 'Development of the animate-inanimate distinction', in U. Goswami (Ed) *Blackwell Handbook of Childhood Cognitive Development.* Oxford: Blackwell: 151–66.

Gergely, G. (2002) 'The development of understanding self and agency', in U. Goswami (Ed) *Blackwell Handbook of Childhood Cognitive Development.* Oxford: Blackwell: 26–46.

Gergely, G., Bekkering, H. and Király, I. (2002) 'Rational imitation in preverbal infants', *Nature* 415: 755.

Gilstrap, L.L. and Ceci, S.J. (2005) 'Reconceptualizing children's suggestibility: bidirectional and temporal properties', *Child Development* 76: 40–53.

Goldin-Meadow, S. and Wagner, S.M. (2005) 'How our hands help us learn', *Trends in Cognitive Science* 9: 234–41

Gopnik, A., Sobel, D., Schultz, L. and Glymour, C. (2001) 'Causal learning mechanisms in very young children: two, three, and four-year-olds infer causal relations from patterns of variation and covariation', *Developmental Psychology* 37(5): 620–29.

Goswami, U. (1991) 'Analogical reasoning: what develops? A review of research and theory', *Child Development* 62: 1–22.

——(2002) 'Inductive and Deductive Reasoning', in U. Goswami (Ed) *Blackwell's Handbook of Childhood Cognitive Development.* Oxford: Blackwell: 282–302.

——(2003) 'Why theories about developmental dyslexia require developmental designs', *Trends in Cognitive Sciences* 7(12): 534–40.

——(2008) *Cognitive Development: the learning brain.* Hove: Psychology Press.

Goswami, U. and Brown, A. (1989) 'Melting chocolate and melting snowmen: analogical reasoning and causal relations', *Cognition* 35: 69–95.

Hart, B.H. and Risley, T.R. (1995) *Meaningful Differences in the Everyday Experience of Young American Children.* Baltimore, MD: Paul H. Brookes.

Heit, E. (2000) 'Properties of inductive reasoning', *Psychonomic Bulletin & Review* 7: 569–92.

Hepper, P.G. (1988) 'Foetal "soap" addiction', *The Lancet* 1: 1347–48.

Hodent, C., Bryant, P. and Houdé, O. (2005) 'Language-specific effects on number computation in toddlers', *Developmental Science* 8: 420–23.

Hughes, C. (1998) 'Executive function in preschoolers: links with theory of mind and verbal ability', *British Journal of Developmental Psychology* 16: 233–53.

Hughes, C. and Dunn, J. (1998) 'Understanding mind and emotion: longitudinal associations with mental-state talk between young friends', *Developmental Psychology* 34: 1026–37.

Hume, D. (1748/1988) *Enquiry Concerning Human Understanding.* Sections IV-VII (paras. 20–61): 25–79.

Jenkins, J.M. and Astington, J.W. (1996) 'Cognitive factors and family structure associated with theory of mind development in young children', *Developmental Psychology* 32: 70–78.

Johnson, M.H. (2005) *Developmental Cognitive Neuroscience* (2nd Edition). Oxford: Blackwell.

Jordan, K.E. and Brannon, E.M. (2006) 'The multisensory representation of number in infancy', *Proceedings of the National Academy of Sciences* 103(9): 3486–89.

Joseph, R. (2000) 'Fetal brain behaviour and cognitive development', *Developmental Review* 20: 81–98.

Kaiser, M.K., Proffit, D.R. and McCloskey, M. (1985) 'The development of beliefs about falling objects', *Perception & Psychophysics* 38: 533–39.

Kaminski, J., Call, J. and Fischer, J. (2004) 'Word learning in a domestic dog: evidence for fast mapping', *Science* 304: 1682–83.

Karmiloff-Smith, A. (2007) 'Atypical epigenesis', *Developmental Science* 10(1): 84–88.

Karpov, Y. (2005) *The Neo-Vygotskian Approach to Child Development*. Cambridge: Cambridge University Press.

Kerr, A. and Zelazo, P.D. (2004) 'Development of "hot" executive function: the children's gambling task', *Brain and Cognition* (Special Issue: *Development of Orbitofrontal Function*) 55: 148–57.

Kirkham, N.Z., Cruess, L. and Diamond, D. (2003) 'Helping children apply their knowledge to their behaviour on a dimension-switching task', *Developmental Science* 6: 449–67.

Kirkham, N.Z., Slemmer, J.A. and Johnson, S.P. (2002) 'Visual statistical learning in infancy: evidence for a domain general learning mechanism', *Cognition* 83(2): B35–B42.

Kochanska, G., Murray, K., Jacques, T.Y., Koenig, A.L. and Vandegeest, K. (1996) 'Inhibitory control in young children and its role in emerging internalization', *Child Development* 67: 490–507.

Kopera-Frye, K., Dehaene, S. and Streissguth, A.P. (1996) 'Impairments of number processing induced by prenatal alcohol exposure', *Neuropsychologia* 34: 1187–96.

Kovas, Y. and Plomin, R. (2006) 'Generalist genes: implications for the cognitive sciences', *TRENDS in Cognitive Sciences* 10(5): 198–203.

Kuhl, P.K. (2004) 'Early language acquisition: cracking the speech code', *Nature Reviews Neuroscience* 5: 831–43.

Kuhl, P. K., Tsao. F.-M. and Liu, H.-M. (2003) 'Foreign-language experience in infancy: effects of short-term exposure and social interaction on phonetic learning', *Proceedings of the National Academy of Sciences* 100: 9096–9101.

Kuhn, D. (1989) 'Children and adults as intuitive scientists', *Psychological Review* 96: 674–89.

Kunh, D., Garcia-Mila, M., Zohar, A. and Andersen, C. (1995) 'Strategies of knowledge acquisition', *Monographs of the Society for Research in Child Development* 60(4).

Kuhn, D. and Siegler R. (2006) *Handbook of Child Psychology*. New York: Wiley.

Leevers, H.J. and Harris, P.L. (2000) 'Counterfactual syllogistic reasoning in normal four-year-olds, children with learning disabilities, and children with autism', *Journal of Experimental Child Psychology* 76: 64–87.

Leslie, A.M. (1987) 'Pretense and representation: the origins of "theory of mind"', *Psychological Review* 94: 412–26.

——(1994) 'ToMM, ToBY and Agency: core architecture and domain specificity', in L.A. Hirschfeld and S.A. Gelman (Eds) *Mapping the Mind*. New York, NY: Cambridge University Press: 119–48.

Lillard, A.S. (2002) 'Pretend play and cognitive development', in U. Goswami (Ed) *Handbook of Cognitive Development*. London: Blackwell: 188–205.

Luna, B., Thulborn, K.R., Munoz, D.P., Merriam, E.P., Garver, K.E., Minshew, N.J., Keshavan, M.S., Genovese, C.R., Eddy, W.F. and Sweeney, J.A. (2001) 'Maturation of widely distributed brain function subserves cognitive development', *NeuroImage* 13(5): 786–93.

Lundberg, I., Frost, J. and Petersen, O.P. (1988) 'Effects of an extensive program for stimulating phonological awareness in preschool children', *Reading Research Quarterly* 23(3): 263–84.

Mandel, D.R., Jusczyk, P.W. and Pisoni, D.B. (1995) 'Infants' recognition of the sound patterns of their own names', *Psychological Science* 6: 314–17.

Mareschal, D., Johnson, M.H., Sirois, S., Spratling, M.W., Thomas, M.S.C. and Westermann, G. (2007) *Neuroconstructivism: Volume 1, How the Brain Constructs Cognition; Volume 2, Perspectives and Prospects*. Oxford: Oxford University Press.

Meltzoff, A.N. (1988) 'Infant imitation after a 1-week delay: long-term memory for novel acts and multiple stimuli', *Developmental Psychology* 24: 470–76.

——(1995) 'Understanding the intentions of others: re-enactment of intended acts by 18-month-old children', *Developmental Psychology* 31: 838–50.

Meltzoff, A. (2002) 'Imitation as a mechanism for social cognition: origins of empathy, theory of mind and the representation of action', in U. Goswami (Ed) *Blackwell Handbook of Childhood Cognitive Development*. Oxford: Blackwell: 6–25.

Meltzoff, A.N. and Borton, R.W. (1979) 'Intermodal matching by human neonates', *Nature* 282: 403–4.

Meltzoff, A.N. and Moore, M.K. (1983) 'Newborn infants imitate adult facial gestures', *Child Development* 54: 702–9.

Molko, N., Cachia, A., Riviere, D., Mangin, J.F., Bruandet, M., Le Bihan, D., Cohen, L. and Dehaene, S. (2003) 'Functional and structural alterations of the intraparietal sulcus in a developmental dyscalculia of genetic origin', *Neuron* 40(4): 847–58.

Munakata, Y. (2001) 'Graded representations in behavioral dissociations', *Trends in Cognitive Sciences* 1, 5(7): 309–15.

Nelson, K. (1986) *Event Knowledge: structure and function in development*. Hillsdale, NJ: Lawrence Erlbaum Associates.

Nunes, T. and Bryant, P.E. (1996) *Children Doing Mathematics*. Oxford: Blackwell.

Onishi, K.H. and Baillargeon, R. (2005) 'Do 15-month-old infants understand false beliefs?' *Science* 308(5719): 255–58.

Peterson, C. and Siegal, M. (1995) 'Deafness, conversation and Theory of Mind', *Journal of Child Pschology & Psychiatry* 36(3): 459–74.

Petitto, L.A., Holowka, S., Sergio, L.E., Levy, B. and Ostry, D.J. (2004) 'Baby hands that move to the rhythm of language: hearing babies acquiring sign language babble silently on the hands', *Cognition* 93: 43–73.

Plomin, R. and Spinath, F.M. (2002) 'Genetics and general cognitive ability (*g*)', *Trends in Cognitive Sciences* 6: 169–76.

Reese, E., Haden, C.A. and Fivush, R. (1993) 'Mother-child conversations about the past: relationships of style and memory over time', *Cognitive Development* 8: 403–30.

Rizzolatti, G. and Craighero, L. (2004) 'The mirror neuron system', *Annual Review of Neuroscience* 27: 169–92.

Rosch, E. (1978) 'Principles of categorisation', in E. Rosch and B.B. Lloyd (Eds) *Cognition and Categorisation*. Hillsdale, NJ: Erlbaum.

Saffran, J.R., Aslin, R.A. and Newport, E.L. (1996) 'Statistical learning by 8-month-old infants', *Science* 274: 1926–28.

Sarnecka, B.W. and Gelman, S.A. (2004) 'Six does not just mean a lot: preschoolers see number words as specific', *Cognition* 92(3): 329–52.

Schleussner, E., Schneider, U., Arnscheidt, C., Kähler, C., Haueisen, J. and Seewald, H. (2004) 'Prenatal evidence of left–right asymmetries in auditory evoked responses using fetal magnetoencephalography', *Early Human Development* 78(2): 133–36.

Schneider, W. and Lockl, K. (2002) 'The development of metacognition and knowledge in children and adolescents', in T. Perfect and B. Schwartz (Eds) *Applied Metacognition*. Cambridge: Cambridge University Press: 224–47.

Schneider, W., Roth, E. and Ennemoser, M. (2000) 'Training phonological skills and letter knowledge in children at risk for dyslexia: a comparison of three kindergarten intervention programs', *Journal of Educational Psychology* 92(2): 284–95.

Schneider, W., Visé, M., Lockl, K. and Nelson, T.O. (2000) 'Developmental trends in children's memory monitoring: evidence from a judgment-of-learning task', *Cognitive Development* 15: 115–34.

Seymour, P.H.K., Aro, M. and Erskine, J.M. (2003) 'Foundation literacy acquisition in European orthographies', *British Journal of Psychology* 94: 143–74

Shultz, T.R. (1982) 'Rules of causal attribution', *Monographs of the Society for Research in Child Development* 47: 194.

Siegler, R.S., Deloache, J.S. and Eisenberg, E. (2006) *How Children Develop*. New York: Worth Publishers.

Slater, A.M., Morison, V. and Rose, D. (1983). 'Perception of shape by the new-born baby', *British Journal of Developmental Psychology* 1: 135–42.

Snowling, M.J. (2000) *Dyslexia*. Oxford: Blackwell.

Sodian, B., Zaitchek, D. and Carey, S. (1991) 'Young children's differentiation of hypothetical beliefs from evidence', *Child Development* 62: 753–66.

Spelke, E.S. (1976) 'Infants' intermodal perception of events', *Cognitive Psychology* 8: 553–60.

Sutton, J., Smith, P.K. and Swettenham, J. (1999) 'Bullying and "Theory of Mind": a critique of the "social skills deficit" view of anti-social behaviour', *Social Development* 8(1): 117–27.

Tai, Y.F., Scherfler, C., Brooks, D.J., Sawamoto, N. and Castiello, U. (2004) 'The human pre-motor cortex is "mirror" only for biological actions', *Current Biology* 14: 117–20.

Tomasello, M. (1995) 'Joint attention as social cognition', in C. Moore and P.J. Dunham (Eds) *Joint Attention: its origins and role in development*. Hillsdale, NJ: Lawrence Erlbaum: 103–30.

——(2000) 'The item-based nature of children's early syntactic development', *Trends in Cognitive Science* 4: 156–63.

——(2006) 'Acquiring linguistic constructions', in D. Kuhn and R. Siegler (Eds) *Handbook of Child Psychology, 6th edition, Vol. 2*: 255–98.

Vargha-Khadem, F., Gadian, D.C., Watkins, K.E., Connelly, A., Van Paesschen, W. and Mishkin, M. (1997) 'Differential effects of early hippocampal pathology on episodic and semantic memory', *Science* 277: 376–80.

Viennot, L. (1979) 'Spontaneous reasoning in elementary dynamics', *European Journal of Science Education* 1: 205–21.

Voltera, V. and Erting, C. (1990) *From Gesture to Language in Hearing and Deaf Children*. Berlin: Springer-Verlag.

Vygotsky, L. (1978) *Mind in Society*. Cambridge, MA: Harvard University Press.

——(1986) *Thought and Language*. Cambridge, MA: MIT Press.

Wang, S. and Baillargeon, R. (2008) 'Can infants be taught to attend to a new physical variable in an event category? The case of height in covering events', *Cognitive Psychology* 56(4): 284–326.

Wellman, H.M. and Gelman, S.A. (1998) 'Knowledge acquisition in foundational domains', in W. Damon, D. Kuhn and R. Siegler (Eds) *Handbook of Child Psychology, 5th Ed., Volume 2, Cognition, Perception and Language*: 523–73. New York: Wiley.

Werker, J.F. and Tees, R.C. (1984) 'Cross-language speech perception: evidence for perceptual reorganization during the first year of life', *Infant Behavior and Development* 7: 49–63.

Westermann, G., Mareschal, D., Johnson, M.H., Sirois, S., Spratling, M.W. and Thomas, M.S.C. (2007) 'Neuroconstructivism', *Developmental Science* 10(1): 75–83.

Wimmer, H. and Perner, J. (1983) 'Beliefs about beliefs: representation and constraining function of wrong beliefs in young children's understanding of deception', *Cognition* 13: 103–28.

Younger, B.A. (1990) 'Infants' detection of correlations among feature categories', *Child Development* 61: 614–20.

Zelazo, P.D., Frye, D. and Rapus, T. (1996) 'An age-related dissociation between knowing rules and using them', *Cognitive Development* 11: 37–63.

Zelazo, P.D., Mueller, U., Frye, D. and Marcovitch, S. (2003) 'The development of executive function in early childhood', *Monographs of the Society for Research in Child Development* 68 (3, Serial No. 274).

Ziegler, J.C. and Goswami, U. (2005) 'Reading acquisition, developmental dyslexia, and skilled reading across languages: a psycholinguistic grain size theory', *Psychological Bulletin* 131(1): 3–29.

7 Children's social development, peer interaction and classroom learning

Christine Howe and Neil Mercer

INTRODUCTION

Within educational research a particular theoretical perspective has become influential over recent decades, from which classroom learning and cognitive development are seen as cultural processes. Here, knowledge is regarded not only as possessed individually but also as created and shared amongst members of communities, and the ways that knowledge is created and shared are seen to be shaped by cultural and historical factors. This *socio-cultural* perspective differs from other influential approaches to the study of education, such as those inspired by Piagetian stage theory or notions of inherited intelligence, by treating children's intellectual achievements as the product not just of their own efforts or discoveries but also of interaction in a cultural context. This does not mean that socio-cultural researchers believe that intellectual achievement is determined entirely by social experiences. Rather they share the view that, no matter what other factors are involved, one cannot fully understand the nature of thinking, learning and development without taking account of the intrinsically historical, social and communicative nature of human life. In the chapter that follows, we shall be adopting a socio-cultural perspective and therefore our focus too will be upon the social processes that shape children's growth. Equally though, we shall not be denying other influences and, from time to time (for example when discussing temperament), we shall consider these influences explicitly.

Detailed accounts of the socio-cultural perspective as applied to education can be found in Wells and Claxton (2002) and Daniels (2001). The assumption that is crucial for present purposes is that development and learning are shaped to a significant extent by social and communicative *interactions*. These interactions will inevitably reflect the historical development, cultural values and social practices of the societies and communities in which schools and other educational institutions exist, as well as the more local cultures and practices within particular schools and classrooms. An important implication is encouragement to look for the causes of educational success and failure in the nature and quality of the social and communicative processes in classrooms, rather than in the intrinsic capability of individual students, the didactic presentational skills of individual teachers, or the quality of the educational methods and materials that have been used.

In this chapter, we review a proportion of the research that this implication has stimulated. We have not attempted to cover everything, for the material is extensive. In any event, some aspects are dealt with elsewhere in the Primary Review, and we could not do justice to them while giving space to aspects which those other chapters do not cover.

This means, in particular, that we do not deal with interactions between teachers and children, or go into detail about interactions amongst children when they are not engaged in school work (both of which are important, but are dealt with elsewhere in this volume). Instead, we discuss the educational significance of classroom interaction amongst children, and consider which factors seem to be most important for their learning and cognitive development. We also review research which has attempted to improve the quality of collaborative activity, usually with the aim of improving both the productivity of that interaction and its learning outcomes for the individuals concerned. For reasons which we will explain, we give special attention to the quality of talk amongst children.

Classroom interaction amongst children has been studied from perspectives that contrast with the socio-cultural one that we shall be adopting. For instance, the *co-operative learning* tradition (for example Johnson and Johnson 2000; Slavin 1995) usually emphasises the goals that children pursue together, rather than the social and communicative processes through which this proceeds. Research into *peer tutoring* (for example Goodlad and Hirst 1989; Topping and Ehly 1998) involves instructing one child in how to assist another, but typically focuses on the outcomes of instructional exchanges rather than their content. In fact, there are, arguably, only two approaches to interaction amongst children that can be regarded as genuinely socio-cultural. The first approach stems from research reported in Vygotsky (1962, 1978), scarcely unexpected when Vygotsky's work provides the foundations for socio-cultural theory as a whole. The source of the second approach may be more surprising, for it is the early work of Piaget (1932, for example), who is more usually associated with a theory of individual development than with the effects of social interaction. In what follows, we shall start by outlining the Vygotskyan and Piagetian approaches to interaction amongst children, and the research that these approaches have inspired. This will allow us to draw conclusions about the nature of productive interaction.

With a clear conception of what productive interaction involves we shall then consider research which shows how rarely it occurs in classrooms. We shall acknowledge that the problem lies partly with the tasks that children are typically asked to perform, and we shall propose alternative approaches to task design. However, informed by our socio-cultural perspective, we shall emphasise that interaction amongst children does not take place in a vacuum, but is heavily influenced by the social histories that children bring to bear. After discussing how these histories should be conceptualised, we shall argue that as well as influencing classroom interaction, they are themselves constituted, in part at least, by social interaction, both within and outside the classroom. Thus, any attempt to promote interaction that is conducive to learning will of necessity have to acknowledge a contextual dimension. Our chapter will conclude by discussing the implications for classroom intervention.

THE WORK AND INFLUENCE OF VYGOTSKY AND PIAGET

Vygotsky's (1962, 1978) guiding assumption was that the acquisition and use of language transforms children's thinking. He described language as both a cultural tool (for developing and sharing knowledge amongst members of a community) and a psychological tool (for structuring the processes and content of individual thought). He also proposed that there is a close relationship between these two functions of language, which can be summed up in the claim that *inter-mental* (social, interactional) activity stimulates some of the most important *intra-mental* (individual, cognitive) capabilities. Since both forms of activity depend upon language, Vygotsky's emphasis upon inter-mental processes is implicitly an emphasis upon dialogue, and more specifically upon the co-ordination of meaning through talk. Thus, researchers following the Vygotskyian tradition emphasise reciprocity, mutuality and the continual (re)negotiation of meaning as interaction proceeds (as described, for example by Barron 2000; Nystrand 1986). Participants in effective social interaction may experience what Ryder and Campbell (1989) call *groupsense* – that is, a feeling of shared endeavour. Such co-ordinated activity depends upon the establishment and maintenance of what Rogoff (1990) and Wertsch (1991) have termed *intersubjectivity*. It will necessarily involve a shared conception of the task or problem. Partners will not only be interacting, but also *interthinking* (Mercer 2000).

For Piaget (for example 1932, 1985), the pathway to development and learning is the process of *equilibration*, a process that involves the reconciliation by individuals of conflict between prior and newly experienced beliefs. As such, equilibration implies that children need to encounter beliefs that differ from their existing ones but that, by virtue of not being too advanced, can be related to these. Since the beliefs of the children in a class are likely to be displayed through similar (although certainly not identical) levels of understanding, this implies that discussing beliefs with classmates ought to be productive, so long as beliefs differ and tasks are structured to draw these differences out. Although Piaget noted this implication himself (for example Piaget 1932), he did not elaborate it further, and his ideas remained largely undeveloped until the late 1970s. Piaget's colleagues (see, for example, Doise and Mugny 1984) then consolidated his ideas into the concept of *socio-cognitive conflict*, and initiated a programme of empirical investigation. The earliest studies were centred on Piaget's own classic tasks, with conservation and spatial transformation (that is, the famous 'three mountains' task) being particular favourites. Some of these studies (for example Doise, Mugny and Perret-Clermont 1975) compared children who worked on the tasks in groups with children who worked on them individually. Although these studies document greater progress in the 'grouped' children (as ascertained from pre-tests administered before the tasks to post-tests administered afterwards), the positive results do not necessarily stem from the expression of difference. Perhaps the mere fact of being part of a group was sufficient to stimulate progress. Other studies (for example Ames and Murray 1982; Bearison, Magzamen and Filardo 1986; Doise and Mugny 1979; Mugny and Doise 1978) have, however, focused directly upon difference, by comparing groups where members hold contrasting beliefs with groups where members hold similar beliefs, and/or by relating the extent to which differences are expressed in dialogue to pre- to post-test growth. These studies provide strong and consistent evidence for the relevance of differing beliefs.

Research with Piagetian tasks soon stimulated work in other contexts, with a particular focus upon children's understanding of the social domain. For instance, Damon and Killen (1982) and Kruger (1992) considered the relevance of group interaction to primary school children's reasoning about 'distributive justice', as exemplified in a scenario where four children were described as receiving ten candy bars for making bracelets and the task was to divide the bars fairly, bearing in mind, for instance, that one child had made the most bracelets, and another was younger and had made fewer bracelets. Leman and Duveen (1999) recorded pairs of children working on a moral reasoning task. This task, which has been employed in research with children working *individually* for over 50 years, requires judgments of who is naughtiest: a boy who breaks a large number of cups while engaged in routine behaviour (for example opening a door which the cups happened to be stacked behind) or a boy who breaks a small number of cups while engaging in forbidden behaviour (for example stealing food that he had been prohibited from touching). Using a specially designed board game entitled 'Conviction', Roy and Howe (1990) examined 9- to 11-year-old children's collaborative reasoning about legal transgressions that ranged from the relatively trivial, for example parking on a double yellow line, to the relatively serious, for example stealing from an elderly woman. In all of these studies, the exchange of contrasting opinions played a key role in effecting progress, although (importantly for material discussed later in our survey), Damon and Killen's data indicate that when contrast led to personal hostility the benefits were lost.

The research reviewed above is potentially significant for primary education: conservation and spatial transformation have long been recognised as relevant to mathematics, and the social topics relate to issues covered in citizenship education. Nevertheless, the research does not address the primary curriculum directly, and therefore it is encouraging that, from around 1990, studies began to be published that tested Piagetian ideas with standard school subjects. Literacy and the arts have been examined (for example Miell and MacDonald 2000; Pontecorvo, Paoletti and Orsolini 1989), but the focus has undoubtedly been upon mathematics and science. With mathematics, support for the Piagetian emphasis upon difference has been obtained in research on rational number (for example Damon and Phelps 1988; Schwarz, Neuman and Biezuner 2000) and matrices (Blaye 1990). With science, some of the clearest evidence comes from research conducted by one of this chapter's authors that involved groups (pairs or foursomes) working on tasks relevant to elementary concepts, for example whether small objects float or sink; the paths that objects trace as they fall through space; and the relative speeds of toy vehicles as they roll down slopes. In all cases, the groups jointly predicted outcomes, observed what happened, and jointly interpreted what they observed. The majority of the studies (for example Howe, Rodgers and Tolmie 1990; Howe, Tolmie and Rodgers 1992a) were with primary school children aged 8 to 12 years, although some studies included secondary- or tertiary-level students (for example Howe, Tolmie and Mackenzie 1995a; Howe, Tolmie, Anderson and Mackenzie 1992b). In every study, individual pre-tests prior to the group tasks allowed some groups to be comprised of participants with differing preconceptions about the subject matter, and other groups to be comprised of participants with similar preconceptions. Individual post-tests some weeks after the group tasks revealed consistently greater progress after working in differing groups. Sometimes the participants who worked in similar groups made no progress whatsoever, despite observing the same physical outcomes as the differing groups and being equally engaged in the tasks. Importantly, when the participants in the differing groups also had differing levels of understanding (which was not always the case), the more advanced individuals progressed as much as their less advanced partners.

Currently then, there is a sizeable body of research stimulated by the Piagetian approach, and producing broadly consistent results. Nevertheless, while this must be acknowledged, the results are not necessarily incompatible with the Vygotskyan emphasis upon inter-mental processes and the co-ordination of meaning. After all, these processes also seem to depend upon contrast of perspectives. Thus, questions are raised about the precise relation between the Piagetian and Vygotskyan approaches. Are their claims genuinely different? If they are, do the differences amount to incompatibilities, or are they matters of emphasis within a broadly consistent framework? In our view, there *are* fundamental differences between the Vygotskyan and Piagetian perspectives. However, these differences centre upon the role of language in *individual* cognition, and therefore, in effect, upon the sufficiency of a socio-cultural perspective. As noted already, few (if any) socio-cultural theorists believe that development and learning are purely the result of social and communicative processes, and Vygotsky would certainly not fall into this camp. Nevertheless, Vygotsky undoubtedly placed more emphasis on such processes than Piaget; and, unlike Piaget, Vygotsky believed that knowledge growth actually requires social experiences. On the other hand, insofar as both theorists believed that social and communicative processes are relevant, they appear to be carrying complementary implications about how these processes operate. Moreover, it is not simply that Vygotskyan theory implies the developmental importance of children's engagement with different views, as noted already; it is also that Piaget's account of such engagement seems to depend upon children establishing mutual goals and shared understanding of the task at hand. Note, for instance, that participants in the studies reported by Howe *et al.* (1990, 1992a, 1992b, 1995a) were required to predict and interpret *jointly.*

DIALOGUE AMONG CHILDREN IN THE CLASSROOM

Much of the research reviewed in the previous section did not simply examine the implications of having group members with differing ideas; it also considered the consequences of having these differences expressed during group interaction. As intimated already, progress has been consistently associated with the range of ideas expressed. It has indeed also been found in studies by Tolmie, Howe, Mackenzie, and Greer (1993), Howe, Tolmie, Greer, and Mackenzie (1995b), and Howe, McWilliam, and Cross (2005), which followed up the research outlined in the previous section and used similar tasks. More recently, Howe, Tolmie, Thurston, Topping, Christie, Livingston, Jessiman, and Donaldson (2007) have recorded the dialogue of primary school children aged 10 to 12 years, while they worked through extended (3+ weeks) programmes of teaching on evaporation and condensation, and force and motion. The programmes were delivered by classroom teachers, and although they incorporated group tasks modelled on those used in Howe and colleagues' earlier work, they also involved whole-class teaching and practical demonstration. They were, in fact, fully embedded in routine practice, and group work was only one component amongst many. Yet the expression of contrasting opinions during group work was the single most important predictor of learning gain. Crucially, this was gain that was detected not simply between pre-tests prior to the programme and post-tests a few weeks later, but also found to be sustained after an 18-month interval (Tolmie *et al.* 2007).

However, while the expression of differences is important, it should not be forgotten that the work of Howe and colleagues (as with much of the other research summarised above) explored dialogue in the context of tasks that constrained participants to joint activity. Thus, the tasks ensured that the expression of differences was co-ordinated and coherent, as illustrated in Transcript 1 (below). This transcript, which comes from data collected by Howe *et al.* (1992a), involves a group of 10- and 11-year-olds discussing the relative speeds with which a toy lorry and a toy car will roll down parallel slopes. The slopes had identical paper surfaces and were supported on pegs, whose height determined their angle.

Transcript 1: group work in science

Jonathon: Well, the lorry's heavier, and it gives more. See like it pulls down like. If it's light, it just moves down in its own time, but if it's got a lot of things it'll make it go faster. Also, it's on the higher peg.

Anna: But say it was like going down a water slide, and there was a great, big, heavy person getting down.

Chung: That's different. Skin's different to rubber, and you slide down in water.

Anna: I know, but cars are metal.

Chung: It's rolling on paper, so the lorry'll hit it, and it'll stop. But it's got weight to push it in the start, so I think it'll go faster.

The possible significance of the dialogic (perhaps not scientific!) coherence displayed in Transcript 1 can best be understood with reference to the work of Barnes and Todd. In one of the most important early studies of children's talk while working together in school, Barnes and Todd (1977) identified a form of dialogue that they regarded as particularly conducive to intellectual achievement. They termed this *exploratory talk*, and saw its key features as the effective sharing of information, the clear explanation of opinions, and the critical examination of explanations. Barnes (1977 – see Barnes 1992) had initially stressed the value of exploratory talk for learning and development in terms of it being a kind of thinking aloud that precipitates ideas, as the mind draws on previously unconnected reserves to come up with something new. But, as characterised by Mercer and Littleton (2007), exploratory talk is seen as beneficial because of its collaborative quality: it involves partners in a purposeful, critical and constructive engagement with each other's ideas. Statements and suggestions are offered for joint consideration. These may be challenged and counter-challenged, but challenges are justified and alternative hypotheses are offered. Partners all actively participate, and opinions are sought and considered before decisions are jointly made. Without doubt, the expression of differences is one component of exploratory talk, but it is not the only one. However, the emphasis upon joint activity in the research considered above may have guaranteed the presence of at least some of the other features. In which case, it is probably not difference *per se* that is important, but difference in the service of argumentation and, through this, mutually accepted goals.

Certainly, this contextualised sense of difference squares with other research. For instance, Anderson and colleagues (Anderson, Chinn, Waggoner and Nguyen 1998; Chinn and Anderson 1998) working in the USA have identified a kind of talk that they call *collaborative reasoning*, where 'children actively collaborate on the construction of arguments in complex networks of reasons and supporting evidence' (Kim, Anderson, Nguyen-Jahiel and Archodidou 2007). On the basis of data obtained through interventional studies, the researchers claim that the quality of children's reasoning is much higher during collaborative reasoning discussions than in usual classroom discussions.

Drawing on their own extended work, as well as that of several other cognitive scientists, philosophers and discourse analysts, Keefer, Zeitz, and Resnick (2000) identify the characteristics of the most productive classroom discussions about English literature. Two sets of characteristics resonate strongly with the concept of exploratory talk: a) *critical discussion*, which has the main goal of achieving shared understanding through accommodating divergent viewpoints and reconciling differences of opinion; b) *explanatory enquiry*, which, starting from a position of lack of knowledge, has the main goal of identifying correct knowledge, using cumulative discursive steps.

Finally, Berkowitz and colleagues (Berkowitz and Gibbs 1983; Berkowitz, Gibbs and Broughton 1980) have highlighted forms of dialogue that they term *operational transacts*. Operational transacts take reasoning and transform it in some way, as for example with 'I think the bottle will float because it's glass' followed by 'But it's got water in and that will make it sink'. The transformation can involve a justification for disagreement as in the example, but it can also involve a clarification or an elaboration. Operational transacts were shown by Berkowitz and Gibbs (and later Kruger 1992, 1993; Roy and Howe 1990) to promote understanding of moral and legal issues, and they have been found by Miell and MacDonald (2000) to support children's collaborative compositions in music.

There is, then, considerable consensus over the form of talk that supports learning and development at the primary school level. It is a form where children share knowledge, challenge ideas, evaluate evidence and consider options in a reasoned and equitable fashion. Children present their ideas as clearly and as explicitly as necessary for the ideas to become shared, jointly analysed and evaluated. For example, Transcript 2 below is an extract from a discussion in which a group of three Year 5 children are engaged in a computer-based activity called *Viking England*. In the roles of Vikings, they are planning a raid on the British coast.

Transcript 2: Viking England

Diana: Let's discuss it. Which one shall we go for?

All: (*inaudible–reading from instructions*)

Peter: 1 2 3 or 4 (*reading out the number of options available*) Well we've got no other chance of getting more money because

Adrian: And there's a monastery.

Diana: And if we take number 2 there's that (*inaudible*).

Peter: Yeh but because the huts will be guarded.

All: Yeh.

Adrian: And that will probably be guarded.

Diana: It's surrounded by trees.

Peter: Yeh.

Adrian: And there's a rock guarding us there.

Peter: Yes there's some rocks there. So I think I think it should be 1.

Adrian: Because the monastery might be unguarded

Diana: Yes 1.

Adrian: 1 yeh.

Peter: Yeh but what about 2? That, it might be not guarded. Just because there's huts there it doesn't mean it's not guarded does it? What do you think?

Diana: Yes, it doesn't mean it's not. It doesn't mean to say it's **not** guarded does it. It may well be guarded I think we should go for number 1 because I'm pretty sure it's not guarded.

Adrian: Yeh.

Peter: Ok, yes, number 1 (*he keys in 1 on keyboard*).

(Mercer 1995: 102)

As in the example above, children may use talk not only to express different views, but also to resolve their differences. Through resolution they may even find themselves converging upon ideas that go beyond what any of them were capable of achieving individually. However, work by Howe and colleagues (Howe 2006; Howe *et al.* 2007) suggests that the latter, in particular, is exceedingly rare at primary school level, at least in the context of discussions relating to the study of science. For instance, exchanges where two factors are co-ordinated into a superior account (for example 'I thought the flat box would sink because it's kind of heavy'; 'I know it's heavy, but it's spread across the water so it'll float') occurred only four times in the total of 1887 remarks that were included in the dataset analysed by Howe (2006). Fortunately though, the resolution of differences is not essential for learning. Groups that do not resolve their differences have been found to be as effective as groups that do resolve (Howe *et al.* 1990, 1992a, 2007), and groups that converge on ideas that are inferior to ideas held at pre-test have been found to be as effective as groups that take their participants forwards (Howe *et al.* 1990; Howe, Tolmie, Duchak-Tanner and Rattray 2000). Further work by Howe and colleagues (for example Howe *et al.* 1992a, 2005; Tolmie *et al.* 1993) indicates that, given dialogue that involves sharing, challenging, evaluating and so on, children will be motivated to reflect on the subject matter long after the group task is completed, perhaps using material that they experience afterwards. Thus, within-group resolution is beside the point. The key thing is that children experience the form of dialogue that we have been highlighting here, a form that from now onwards we shall refer to as *exploratory talk,* while recognising the short-hand nature of the term and its relation to alternative constructs.

THE QUALITY OF DIALOGUE AMONG CHILDREN IN THE CLASSROOM

Unfortunately, one of the strongest messages to emerge from work surveying classroom activity is that, at least in British primary schools, exploratory talk seldom occurs. On the contrary, much classroom-based talk amongst children is of limited educational value, when judged against the yardstick provided by the previous section. This conclusion was the alarming outcome of a large-scale research project carried out in the 1970s called ORACLE[1] (Galton, Simon and Croll 1980). The ORACLE team of researchers, observing everyday practice in a large number of British primary schools, found that just because several children were sitting together at a table (as was common), it did not mean that they were interacting. Typically, the children at any table were simply working, in parallel, on individual tasks. While they might well have talked as they worked, and while they might possibly have talked to each other about their work, they did not typically talk and work together. This problem of children working *in* groups but rarely *as* groups has also been underscored in a number of more recent studies, some of which have shown that even when children are set joint tasks their interactions are rarely productive (Bennett and Cass 1989; Galton, Hargreaves, Comber, Wall, and Pell 1999; Blatchford and Kutnick 2003; Kumpulainen and Wray 2002; Alexander 2008).

A specific example of the problem was detected in the Spoken Language and New Technology (SLANT) project, which was co-directed by one of this chapter's authors in the early 1990s. Here, researchers observed the interaction of children aged 8 to 11 years in 10 primary school classrooms, while they worked together in small groups at the computer (as described in Wegerif and Scrimshaw 1997). Detailed analysis of the joint sessions of work suggested that most of the interactions were not task-focused, productive or equitable. In some groups one child so completely dominated the discussion that the other group members either withdrew from the activity, becoming increasingly quiet and subdued, or else they participated marginally, for example as passive scribes of a dominant child's ideas. In other groups, the children seemed to ignore each other altogether, taking turns at the computer, each pursuing their own particular ideas when 'their turn' came round. Some groups' talk involved them in unproductive, often highly competitive, disagreements, a form of interaction referred to subsequently as *disputational talk* (Fisher 1993; Mercer 1995). From time to time these disagreements escalated, with the children becoming increasingly irritated with each other and engaging in vehement personal criticism. On the other hand, much group talk was relatively brief and somewhat bland. This latter form of interaction was termed *cumulative talk* by Fisher (1993) and Mercer (1995).

While the impoverished nature of classroom interaction can be taken for granted, it is unlikely to reflect a basic incapacity on the part of primary school children to engage in lively dialogue. Observational studies of children's off-task talk in primary school (notably by Maybin 2006) have shown that they use many varied language forms to discuss issues that concern them, to support their views, to report on events and generally make sense of the world (though Maybin did not report the natural incidence of discussion resembling exploratory talk). Further observational studies, this time in homes and in nurseries and playgroups, have demonstrated that even preschool children will justify opinions, suggest alternatives, and reach compromises during free play with their siblings or peers (see, for example, Dunn and Kendrick 1982; Eisenberg and Garvey 1981; Genishi and Di Paolo 1982; Orsolini 1993; Howe and McWilliam 2001). Take, for instance, Transcript 3, which presents a series of exchanges that took place amongst 4-year-olds when recorded playing together at nursery during the study reported in Howe and McWilliam (2001).

Transcript 3: Football

Scott: I'm sitting in the Celtic seat.
David: No, I'm Celtic.
Scott: But that's a yellow seat. I've got a Celtic seat (*points to green seat*).
Gerry: Let's swap stickers. I've got Celtic stickers (*moves stickers from seats*).
Scott: Yes, and we can be the Celtic team if we go outside.
David: No we're only talking about it, not doing it.
Gerry: I'm DiCanio; you can be the goalkeeper.
Scott: No, you can be Jorge Cadete.
Gerry: Okay.

In Transcript 3, the children justify (for example the mention of the yellow seat), suggest alternatives, and compromise. They even (by movement of stickers) make the otherwise contradictory evidence consistent with their claims. Thus, without doubt, Transcript 3 has many of the features associated in the previous section with exploratory talk, and there is no reason to believe that it is an isolated example. It is true that gender differences in usage of justifications, alternatives and/or compromises have been detected at the preschool level, with girls using the forms more frequently than boys (Hartup, French, Laursen, Johnston and Ogawa 1993; Howe and McWilliam 2001;

Miller, Danaher and Forbes 1986; Sheldon 1992). Nevertheless, research shows that the forms are far from unusual in boys' conversations. Similarly, although the frequency with which the features occur is positively correlated with socio-economic status (Bruck and Tucker 1974; Howe and McWilliam 2001; Tough 1973), preschoolers will use the forms on occasion regardless of social class. Transcript 3 comes from boys, who lived in one of the most deprived areas of Glasgow.

In addition to being associated with demographic factors like gender and socio-economic status, the incidence of justifications and other features of exploratory talk during pre-school interaction also varies with the kind of play activity that children are engaged in. In the work of Howe and McWilliam (2001), 82 per cent of the relevant forms occurred during symbolic or construction play, even though this kind of play was no more frequent overall than other activities, for example sand-and-water play. Similar results have been reported in Ervin-Tripp (1982), Garvey (1991), Orsolini (1993), and Sawyer (1996). As it happens, the effects of play activity turn out to be bound up with those of demography. Symbolic play is preferred by girls relative to boys (Johnson and Ershler 1981), with gender differences over construction activity being less marked. It is preferred by preschoolers of higher socio-economic status compared with preschoolers of lower status (Rubin, Fein and Vandenberg 1983). Nevertheless, the data indicate that play activity has an effect additional to that of demography; and when activity is a factor that teachers could, in principle at least, influence, it is worth asking about the relevance of play to primary school interaction, as well as to preschool. The activities that children engage in shift from play to more formal tasks at primary level, and they are less focused upon children's needs and wishes. Yet, when the form of activity has been found to exert such a significant influence at preschool level, it seems possible that this is one reason for the impoverished dialogue in primary schools.

TASK DESIGN AND THE BROADER CLASSROOM CLIMATE

Given our earlier discussion of Piagetian research, it can be anticipated that one requirement of group tasks at primary school level is that they are controversial; that is, amenable to different perspectives. This has been confirmed in research by Cohen (1994), which compares controversial with non-controversial tasks. However, granted the possibilities provided by controversy, further considerations are also relevant. First, research suggests that all group members must believe that both their own *and* their partners' contributions are important. As Meyers (1997) puts it, 'individuals exert less effort in groups when they believe that their work is not critical to the collective'. By contrast when students perceive their contributions to be original and significant, they continue to participate even if their work remains anonymous (Harkins and Petty 1982). In addition, individuals sometimes reduce their efforts to match the level at which they believe other group members are contributing (Chapman, Arenson, Carrigan and Gryckiewicz 1993; Jackson and Harkins 1985). Thus, children may withdraw their participation to avoid the possibility of being exploited by 'social loafers' within the group (Kerr 1983). Second, it is accepted (see Cohen 1994; Slavin 1996) that tasks should be inherently group-based, and not amenable to completion by individuals working independently. What is needed is 'a task that requires resources (information, knowledge, heuristic problem solving strategies, materials and skills) that no single individual possesses, so that no single individual is likely to solve the problem or accomplish the task objectives without at least some input from others' (Cohen 1994).

Third, tasks should be challenging relative to children's current level of understanding (Jackson and Williams 1985). With routine tasks, children tend to engage in fairly low-level thinking and interactions (Cohen 1994). Indeed social loafing may increase (and motivation decrease) when tasks are too easy (Harkins and Petty 1982).

While the need for controversy, challenge, mutual value, and group basis can be taken for granted, there is disagreement over the significance of group rewards. Slavin has argued repeatedly (for example 1983, 1987) that achievement is enhanced when group members are rewarded as a group. He believes that group goals and collective outcomes provide incentives for children to help each other and to encourage each other to put forth maximum effort. However, Slavin's research has been criticised on methodological grounds (Bossert 1988; Cohen 1994). It is accepted that reward can help some students, but it is not effective for all. Moreover, as Cohen (1994) points out, 'offering rewards on a competitive basis, although effective in increasing motivation of team members to work together, may have negative effects on inter-group relations, more specifically on the perceptions that team members have towards other teams'. It has been shown that 'the failure of one's team can have a negative effect on one's individual achievement in a way that is independent of prior achievement and individual outcome' (Chambers and Abrami 1991). Some researchers further believe that, whatever their short-term advantages, the use of rewards may have undermining effects on long-term motivation (Cameron and Pierce 1994). In a study of school children using computer tutorial packages, Fu-Yun (2001) examined the effects of competition between groups and found that co-operation without inter-group competition led to better attitudes to the subject matter and more positive inter-personal relationships than did co-operation with competition. The exchange of ideas and information within and among learning groups was also more effective and efficient when there was no competition. The author therefore concludes that it is preferable not to introduce competition into computer-based collaborative tasks. Slavin (1996) has attempted to address such points. He acknowledges that there are a few cases in which achievement gains (in comparison to control groups) have been found for small group learning interventions that lack group rewards, and suggests that there may be conditions under which such rewards are unnecessary. The tasks he specifies as not requiring rewards are controversial tasks without single answers, voluntary study groups and structured dyadic tasks.

The implication is perhaps that reward should not be seen as a factor additional to controversy, challenge, mutual value, and group basis, but rather as a factor that may be required when the latter have not been achieved. In fact, recent research suggests that insofar as controversy, challenge, mutual value, and group basis need supplementing, it will be via factors that are far more specific than issues like reward. For instance, in each of the four studies with 9- to 12-year-olds reported in Howe and Tolmie (2003), Howe *et al.* (1995b, 2000) and Tolmie *et al.* (1993), comparisons were made between four versions of a science group task. All versions used the basic *predict jointly – observe – interpret jointly* format outlined already, and by virtue of this (coupled with the considerable intellectual demand of the material) were challenging, amenable to several approaches, and inherently group-based. However, the versions varied in whether or not problem sequences were ordered by difficulty (that is to say easy first/hard later), whether or not group members were required to reach consensus, and whether and how consensual positions were to be recorded (that is to say multiple-choice versus open-ended). These differences had a significant impact upon both patterns of interaction and learning gain, confirming the relevance of controversy and so on, but suggesting that the way in which such factors operate is highly subtle.

Research into the nuances of task design is in its infancy at present, and as it develops it will undoubtedly help to clarify why classroom dialogue remains unproductive and how this can be addressed. However, few scholars believe that the answer lies purely with the specifics of task. Over twenty years ago, Wells (1986) drew attention to difficulties with the overall *climate* of British primary schools, arguing that the *normative environment* for talk in most classrooms is not compatible with children's active and extended engagement in using language to construct knowledge. This characterisation of the classroom environment for talk is also one that emerges from more recent work by Alexander (2008). According to Alexander, classroom discourse is 'overwhelmingly monologic' in form, as teachers typically offer children opportunities for making only brief responses to their questions:

> [...] if we are not careful, classrooms may be places where teachers rather than children do most of the talking; where supposedly open questions are really closed; where instead of thinking through a problem children devote their energies to trying to spot the correct answer, where supposed equality of discussion is subverted by [...] the 'unequal communicative rights' of a kind of talk which remains stubbornly unlike the kind of talk that takes place anywhere else. Clearly if classroom talk is to make a meaningful contribution to children's learning and understanding it must move beyond the acting out of such cognitively restricting rituals.
>
> (Alexander 2008: 9)

It is interesting that Wells was writing at a time when British primary education was still heavily influenced by Plowden philosophy (relating to the Plowden Report, CACE 1967), while Alexander was addressing a more recent context that is more curriculum- and assessment-led. It appears that the forces that oppose exploratory talk transcend policy changes.

However, the monologic climate of most classrooms does not fully explain why, when left to work together, children only rarely use talk of an 'exploratory' kind. As demonstrated some years ago now (Edwards and Mercer 1987), the norms or ground rules for generating particular functional ways of using language in primary school – spoken or written – are rarely made explicit. It is often simply assumed that children will pick these sorts of things up as they go along. But while picking up the ground rules and 'fitting in' in a superficial way with the norms of classroom life may be relatively easy, this may mask children's lack of understanding about what they are expected to do in educational activities and why they should do this. What is expected in terms of behaviour may be accepted without really being understood. The distinction between structures for classroom management (for example lining up in pairs or sitting rather than kneeling on chairs) and structures that develop learning (for example listening to a partner or asking a question) may not be apparent to children. Indeed, even when the aim of talk is made explicit – 'Talk together to decide'; 'Discuss this in your groups' – teachers rarely make explicit what kind of interactions they expect to take place, or discuss with their pupils ways of using talk to engage productively in joint activities. There may be no real understanding, on the part of at least some children, of how to talk together or for what purpose. Many children may not appreciate the significance and educational importance of their talk with one another. Moreover, in the 'monologic' environments described by Alexander (2006), they may frequently assume that the implicit ground rules in play in the classroom are such that teachers want 'right answers', rather than discussion.

THE SIGNIFICANCE OF CHILDREN'S SOCIAL HISTORIES FOR LEARNING IN CLASS

In general then, an anti-dialogic atmosphere pervades many English classrooms. This results in inappropriate task structures and confusing messages, and means that young children's formidable communicative competence is seldom on display. Change here is not going to happen overnight, but suppose change is wanted. Would it be merely a question of creating the requisite amount of classroom 'space', and providing appropriate tasks? Our socio-cultural perspective leads us to think not. As emphasised by Pollard and Filer (1996), children come to social encounters with histories, and there is evidence to suggest that these histories will influence how they respond.

To take the example of friendship, a series of studies have compared the manner in which children interact when working with *friends* with how they interact when working with other classmates. Examples include Azmitia and Montgomery's (1993) work with 11-year-olds solving a science reasoning task, Hartup *et al.*'s (1993) research with 9- to 10-year-olds using a board game, and Miell and MacDonald's (2000) study of 11- to 12-year-olds engaged in musical composition. Typically, children were asked to nominate their friends, and using these nominations, dyads were formed comprising friends (meaning mutually nominated individuals) or non-friends (that is, children who did not nominate each other). The studies are mainly couched in frameworks that emphasise *operational transacts* (for example Berkowitz and Gibbs 1983, as summarised earlier), rather than exploratory talk. Nevertheless, the message is clear: friends are more likely than non-friends to engage in interaction where knowledge is shared, ideas are challenged, evidence is evaluated, and options are reasoned about. As a result, nominated friends are more likely than non-friends to succeed with the task.

Although the message from the above research is consistent, there are a number of ambiguities surrounding its interpretation. First, research has revealed significant (albeit imperfect) positive correlations between the number of times that children are nominated as friends and: a) their centrality in broader classroom networks, as perceived by their peers; b) their popularity with their classmates, as revealed by the number of classmates nominating/rating them as liked, and not nominating/rating them as disliked (see, for example, Gest, Graham-Bermann and Hartup 2001; Lease, Kennedy and Axelrod 2002). Since the logistics of pairing mean that children who are frequently nominated as friends are more likely to be assigned to the friend dyads than the non-friend dyads in the above research, the results are as likely to be effects of centrality or popularity as friendship. The distinction is important, because centrality and popularity are matters of status, while friendship is a form of relationship. Certainly the dialogic features we are focusing upon have been found to be associated with popularity as well as friendship (see for example Cowie, Smith, Boulton and Laver 1994; Markell and Asher 1984; Murphy and Faulkner 2000, 2006). Second, the meaning of the link between friendship/centrality/popularity and social interaction is unclear. One possibility is that working with friends (and/or being central/popular) promotes exploratory talk. Another is that the ability to engage in exploratory talk promotes friendship (and/or centrality/popularity), and as a result the children who had relatively large numbers of friends (and/or were central/popular) and were therefore relatively likely to be assigned to friendship dyads in the above studies, were already predisposed towards exploratory talk. Popularity has been shown to *predict* use of the relevant dialogue features (Hay, Payne and Chadwick 2004), as opposed to being merely associated with this, and a predictive relation has yet to be demonstrated for friendship. However, longitudinal studies that allow effects to be teased out with any of these factors are currently few and far between.

Research also suggests that factors such as gender and temperament affect how children respond to activities designed to encourage exploratory talk and productive interaction at primary school level. As reported in Howe and McWilliam (2006), children from the first and third years of primary school were videotaped, while they engaged in groups of three in free play and three structured activities. The latter were designed to promote the expression and resolution of differences in problem-solving contexts, for example how to activate a robot, how to sequence a series of pictures so that they tell a story. The activities may therefore be relevant to the kind of tasks flagged in the previous section and, on one level, they were successful. In particular, there was no doubt that the focus upon difference promoted features that are associated with exploratory talk: for instance, justifications were used with about 25 per cent of oppositional responses, and only 5 per cent of non-oppositional. However, the focus also promoted physical aggression, with about 12 per cent of oppositional responses being accompanied with hitting, pushing, pinching and so on, as in Transcript 4 (below), and only 1 per cent of non-oppositional. Verbal aggression also occurred, for example name calling, abusive remarks, but not to an analysable extent. Importantly, the children who responded productively were not the children who responded aggressively; that is to say that the tasks elicited both kinds of responses, but not by the same children. Gender helped to differentiate: consistent with a vast literature (reviewed in Archer and Lloyd 1985; Maccoby and Jacklin 1980), boys were more aggressive than girls. However, the most important factor was temperament, defined by Rothbart, Ahadi and Hershey (1994) as 'constitutionally based individual differences in reactivity and self regulation'. Self-regulation (and particularly *inhibitory control* as assessed via Rothbart *et al.*'s *Child Behavior Questionnaire*) proved crucial: use of justifications was associated with high inhibitory control, and use of aggression was associated with low inhibitory control.

Transcript 4: opposition and aggression

(Leanne stabs Andrew in the back with a toy drill)
Andrew: Ow. Ow.
Leanne: Did that hurt? *(laughs sadistically and stabs again)*
Andrew: Ouch, give me that. You're done. *(tries to grab drill)*
Leanne: No. *(pulls drill away)*

At present, there is little additional research on the association between temperament and productive forms of interaction, although a doctoral thesis by Schroeter (2006) provides evidence that complements the above. However, the temperamental basis of aggression is well established (for example Caspi *et al.* 1995; Eisenberg *et al.* 1997; Rothbart *et al.* 1994), as is the association between aggression and opposition during peer interaction (Arsenio and Lover 1997; Calkins *et al.* 1999; Shantz 1986). Moreover, aggression displayed during peer interaction has serious long-term consequences.

It is probably the single most important predictor of peer *rejection* (for reviews see Deater-Deckard 2001; Newcomb, Bukowski and Pattee 1993). Rejection is usually operationalised as being disliked by many classmates and liked by few, and therefore is conceptually the opposite of popularity as discussed above. Defined in this way, rejection (especially when coupled with aggression) has proved to have negative implications for long-term adjustment. Apart from its known association with delinquency, criminality and mental illness (Bierman 2004; Deater-Deckard 2001), peer rejection has consistently emerged as a strong predictor of eventual school failure (Buhs and Ladd 2001; Coie *et al.* 1992; Gifford-Smith and Brownell 2002; Parker and Asher 1987).

An additional possible factor in children's social histories which might influence the quality of their discussion during collaborative activity in the classroom is a controversial one: the oral culture of their homes and communities. To be more precise, the issue is the extent to which their social experience outside school provides them with suitable guidance for using language as a tool for reasoning and learning in school. In the 1970s, the educational sociologist Bernstein (1971) argued that habitual patterns of spoken interaction differed between social classes in the UK, with more 'elaborated' forms (in which reasoning was made more explicit) being common only amongst the middle classes. He went on to argue that as those elaborated forms were a prerequisite for educational achievement, the educational opportunities for working class children were thus limited by their language experience. Bernstein was strongly criticised at the time for his views, and especially for his lack of strong observational evidence to support those claims. Some educational researchers have continued to argue, as did Bernstein's critics, that the problem is rather that schools expect children to employ middle class ways of using language, and that those privileged ways have no necessary association with learning and effective collaboration (for example Lambirth 2006). However, studies have identified relevant variation in the extent to which some forms of talk are used in the homes of children of different socio-economic background in the UK (for example Tizard, Hughes, Carmichael and Pinkerton 1983: see also the section above on 'The quality of dialogue amongst children in the classroom'). Furthermore, in recent research in such different societies as the USA and China, the variability in children's early language experience has been shown to be systematically related to maternal education, and so linked to observable differences in the language performance of pre-school children of different social backgrounds (for example Hoff and Tian 2005). Moreover, in a large-scale longitudinal study in the US, Hart and Risley (1995) found that the amount and quality of the dialogue children experience at home in the pre-school years correlated strongly with their eventual academic attainment. Though direct links have not been shown, it thus may be that children's social background influences the likelihood that they will spontaneously engage in reasoned discussion resembling exploratory talk in primary school, and this may impact on the benefit they gain from collaborative learning activity in class.

Overall then, a complex relationship seems to be emerging between children's social histories and exploratory talk. On the one hand, these histories will affect how children respond to attempts to promote exploratory interaction, albeit through the influence of some currently poorly understood combination of *relational* factors like friendship, and what might be called *status* factors like popularity and centrality in networks. Social class may also be relevant. On the other hand, it looks from the relation between opposition, aggression and rejection as if social histories could themselves be affected by promoting exploratory talk. Without sufficient care, promotional attempts may draw out aggression in those children who are temperamentally inclined, and increase the prospects of such children being eventually rejected. Obviously, we must be cautious about overplaying the significance of classroom experiences as contributors to rejection. Experiences in the playground and out of school are also important, for the forms of aggression that are typically referred to as 'bullying' are, surely, predominantly out-of-class phenomena. Nevertheless, classroom experiences are relevant, and it would be paradoxical indeed if, by virtue of prioritising activities that promoted exploratory talk in some children, contexts that contributed to rejection and eventual school failure were created for others.

IMPLICATIONS FOR INTERVENTION

The complexities sketched in the preceding section imply that great care needs to be taken about the design of interventions for promoting exploratory talk. Social histories need to be taken into account, but in a manner that recognises their complex nature (relations and status), and their bi-directional association (cause and effect) with social interaction. For this reason, we believe that more may be needed than improving social relations amongst members of a class, as for instance Kutnick and colleagues have attempted (see Kutnick 2005). This is not to say that relational interventions cannot be effective. Apart from Kutnick's own positive results, the successful interventions of Howe *et al.* (2007) and Tolmie *et al.* (2007), outlined earlier, were embedded in a broader programme that involved relational training. Specifically, attempts were made to promote empathy and trust amongst classmates. Nevertheless, we suspect that to optimise impact, it may also be necessary to address social interaction directly, in a fashion that promotes exploratory talk yet is responsive to its wider historical context. We believe, in short, that something that takes account of Edwards and Mercer's (1987) notion of 'ground rules' is what is required.

A series of classroom-based research projects involving one of this chapter's authors (Mercer) and colleagues has in recent years adopted a ground rules perspective to seek to improve the quality of collaborative activity in the classroom. The main aim has been to increase children's use of exploratory talk and then evaluate the effects of doing so on the quality of their talk, reasoning and learning. Children aged between 6 and 13 years have been involved, but we will here concentrate on the research with the age group 8–11 years, which has been the most substantial (as described in Wegerif, Mercer and Dawes 1999; Mercer, Dawes, Wegerif and Sams 2004; Wegerif and Dawes 2004; Mercer and Littleton 2007). An intervention programme called *Thinking Together* was designed in which teacher-led whole class dialogue and group activity were integrated. Within the programme, teachers worked with children to develop a shared conception of how they could talk and think together effectively (as set out in Dawes, Mercer and Wegerif 2003; Dawes and Sams 2004). The complete programme included activities related to specific curriculum subjects. It was implemented and evaluated using a quasi-experimental method in which children in intervention schools (those who followed the programme) were matched with children of the same age in 'control' schools with similar catchments (who pursued their normal curriculum activities). In order to evaluate changes in the quality of talk in groups, children were video-recorded carrying out activities in both the target classes and in the control classes. Effects of the intervention, over time, on children's curriculum learning and individual reasoning were also assessed. This research has produced three main findings. First, children in intervention classes came to use much more exploratory talk than those in control classes. Second, groups who began to use more exploratory talk also became better at solving reasoning problems together. The third main finding was that the children in intervention classes made gains in their *individual* scores on tests of reasoning and of curriculum attainment (in mathematics and science) which were significantly greater than those made by the children in control classes.

To illustrate the changes in the children's talk, below are two sequences from the group activity of children (aged 10 and 11 years) in the same target group. In both they are completing a test item from the Raven's Progressive Matrices test of non-verbal reasoning (Raven, Court and Raven 1995: this was the test used in the study to assess changes in both collective and individual reasoning). Transcript 5 was recorded before they were involved in the intervention programme, while Transcript 6 was recorded after they had completed it.

Transcript 5: Graham, Suzie and Tess doing Raven's test item D9 (before the Thinking Together lessons)

Tess: It's that
Graham: It's that, 2
Tess: 2 is there
Graham: It's 2
Tess: 2 is there Graham
Graham: It's 2
Tess: 2 is there
Graham: What number do you want then?
Tess: It's that because there ain't two of them
Graham: It's number 2, look one, two
Tess: I can count, are we all in agree on it?
(*Suzie rings number 2 – an incorrect choice – on the answer sheet*)
Suzie: No
Graham: Oh, after she's circled it!

Transcript 6: Graham, Suzie and Tess doing Raven's test item D9 (after the Thinking Together lessons)

Suzie: D9 now, that's a bit complicated it's got to be
Graham: A line like that, a line like that and it ain't got a line with that
Tess: It's got to be that one
Graham: It's going to be that don't you think? Because look all the rest have got a line like that and like that, I think it's going to be that because …
Tess: I think it's number 6
Suzie: No I think it's number 1
Graham: Wait no, we've got number 6, wait stop, do you agree that it's number 1? Because look that one there is blank, that one there has got them, that one there has to be number 1, because that is the one like that. Yes. Do you agree?
(*Tess nods in agreement*)
Suzie: D9 number 1
(*Suzie writes '1', which is the correct answer*)

In Transcript 5, the talk is not 'exploratory' but more aptly described as 'disputational' (as defined earlier), with cycles of assertion and counter assertion, forming sequences of short utterances which rarely include explicit reasoning. Tess does offer a reason – a good reason – for her view, but Graham ignores it. Suzie has taken the role of writer and she says little. At the end, having ringed the answer Graham wanted, she disagrees with it. It is not the right answer; but they all move on to the next problem anyway. In Transcript 6, the children's language clearly shows characteristics of exploratory talk. Graham responds to opposition from Tess by giving an elaborated explanation of why he thinks 'number 1' is the correct choice. This clear articulation of reasons leads the group to agree on the right answer. Such explanations involve a series of linked clauses and so lead to longer utterances. All three children are now more equally involved in the discussion. Compared with their earlier attempt, language is being used more effectively by the group as a tool for thinking together about the task they are engaged in. Significantly, there is no sign of aggression, despite the difference of opinions.

Overall the results of this research suggest that the intervention not only helped children learn more effective strategies for using language to think collectively (and so become better at collaborative working), but also the group experience of explicit, rational, collaborative problem-solving improved their *individual* reasoning capabilities. However, it not clear what children learned from their experience that made the difference. It may be that some picked up new, successful problem-solving strategies explained to them by their partners, while others may have benefited from having to justify and make explicit their own reasons. But a more radical and intriguing possibility is that children may have improved their reasoning skills by internalising or appropriating the ground rules of exploratory talk, so that they become able to carry on a kind of silent rational dialogue with themselves. That is, the *Thinking Together* lessons may have helped them become more able to generate the kind of rational thinking which depends on the explicit, dispassionate consideration of evidence and competing options. That interpretation is consistent with the claims of Vygotsky (1978, as discussed earlier) about the role of social activity in the development of children's thinking.

SUMMARY AND CONCLUSIONS

Research has shown that, under certain conditions, interaction with peers helps children's learning and development. This is consistent with both a Piagetian and Vygotskyan perspective. The expression of different views, such as alternative explanations or possible solutions to problems amongst children working together, seems to be particularly useful in stimulating learning and development: and it does not seem necessarily to matter if those differences are always resolved (or resolved productively) through discussion. Children can also develop important communicative skills through interaction with their peers, which again they would not learn through only taking part in conversations with adults. But, paradoxically, observational studies have shown that collaborative talk in classrooms is often unproductive and inequitable. There is no reason to believe that even young primary school children are incapable of using exploratory talk (as they have been observed to do this in informal contexts), but they often seem not to use their skills during classroom activities. Some studies have suggested that the design of tasks can promote the use of exploratory talk, and hence more productive interaction; but changing task design does not seem to be sufficient in itself.

Others suggest that the quality of collaboration can be improved if attention is given to developing an atmosphere of trust and mutual respect. There is evidence from intervention studies that this does lead to improved interaction and to improved learning, but the complexities of children's social histories suggest that it may not be sufficient. Other intervention studies support the view that the quality of interaction is significantly improved if children are helped to become more aware of how they use language as a tool for thinking together and taught some specific strategies for carrying on productive discussions. That research has recorded gains not only in children's use of exploratory talk and improved collaboration, but also in their individual skills in reasoning and academic attainment. Overall, it seems that children's social histories affect how they engage in collaborative learning activities, and those histories will embody their social learning both in and out of school. Although collaborative interactions and discussions are potentially very valuable for children's learning and development, that potential may only be realised if children are given structured guidance by their teachers on how to make the most of the opportunities that those activities offer.

In summary, then, our chapter has the following main implications for primary education:

- The educational value of collaborative learning has been clearly demonstrated by research from more than one line of enquiry. In particular, encouraging children to pursue joint goals, explain their understanding, express different points of view and attempt to reach consensus through discussion have all been found to help learning and understanding. The evidence relates to a range of curriculum subjects, across the arts, science and mathematics. Research supports the view that joint activity amongst pupils should be an intrinsic, integrated aspect of classroom life.
- However, observations in primary classrooms suggest that children commonly interact unproductively. It seems that group- and pair-based activity is rarely organised in ways that will best achieve productive interaction. For collaborative activity to be useful (and to be recognised as such by pupils), teachers need to do more than provide opportunities for children to work and talk together. They need to help children develop the necessary communicative skills for engaging intellectually with each other.
- For collaborative activity to be productive, children also need to be offered suitable activities. Some features of good task design have been identified. Generally speaking, tasks should be designed to encourage cooperation and group cohesion, rather than competitiveness.
- Factors such as gender, temperament and the social relations between members of class can affect the ways in which children engage in joint activity, as can situational factors like the existence of a competitive or cooperative environment.
- Social experience outside school may prepare children more or less well for the kinds of ways they are expected to talk and interact in joint educational activity. Some children may therefore need more guidance than others on how to engage productively in classroom dialogue.
- Research has helped identify some key qualities of successful collaboration and dialogue during problem-solving and similar activities. Research has also shown that children can be helped to interact more productively, and that this leads to more inclusive activity and to individual learning gains. This information could be used by teachers, to a greater extent than is presently common, to develop children's awareness of how they can use talk effectively as a tool for learning.

NOTES

1 Observational Research and Classroom Learning Evaluation.

REFERENCES

Alexander, R.J. (2008) *Towards Dialogic Teaching: rethinking classroom talk* (4th edition). York: Dialogos.

Ames, G.J. and Murray, F.B. (1982) 'When two wrongs make a right: promoting cognitive change by social conflict', *Developmental Psychology* 18: 894–97.

Anderson, R.C., Chinn, C., Waggoner, M. and Nguyen, K. (1998) 'Intellectually-stimulating story discussions', in J. Osborn and F. Lehr (Eds) *Literacy for All: issues in teaching and learning*: 170–86. New York: Guildford Press.

Archer, J. and Lloyd, B. (1985) *Sex and Gender*. Cambridge: Cambridge University Press.

Arsenio, W. and Lover, A. (1997) 'Emotions, conflicts and aggression during preschoolers' free-play', *British Journal of Developmental Psychology* 15: 531–42.

Azmitia, M. and Montgomery, R. (1993) 'Friendship, transactive dialogues and the development of scientific reasoning', *Social Development* 2: 202–21.

Barnes, D. (1992) 'The role of talk in learning', in K. Norman (Ed) *Thinking Voices: the work of the National Oracy Project*. London: Hodder and Stoughton.

Barnes, D. and Todd, F. (1977) *Communication and Learning in Small Groups*. London: Routledge and Kegan Paul.

Barron, B. (2000) 'Achieving co-ordination in collaborative problem-solving groups', *Journal of the Learning Sciences* 9: 403–36.

Bearison, D.J., Magzamen, S. and Filardo, E.C. (1986) 'Socio-cognitive conflict and cognitive growth in children', *Merrill-Palmer Quarterly* 32: 51–72.

Bennett, N. and Cass, A. (1989) 'The effects of group composition on group interactive processes and pupil understanding', *British Educational Research Journal* 15: 119–32.

Berkowitz, M.W. and Gibbs, J.C. (1983) 'Measuring the developmental features of moral discussion', *Merrill-Palmer Quarterly* 29: 399–410.

Berkowitz, M.W., Gibbs, J.C. and Broughton, J. (1980) 'The relation of moral judgement disparity to developmental effects of peer dialogue', *Merrill-Palmer Quarterly* 26: 341–57.

Bernstein, B. (1971) *Class, Codes and Action. Vol. 1: theoretical studies towards a sociology of language*. London: Routledge and Kegan Paul.

Bierman, K.L. (2004) *Peer Rejection: developmental processes and intervention strategies*. New York: Guilford Press.

Blatchford, P. and Kutnick, P. (2003) 'Developing groupwork in everyday classrooms', Special issue of the *International Journal of Educational Research* 39(1–2).

Blaye, A. (1990) 'Peer interaction in solving a binary matrix problem: possible mechanisms causing individual progress', *Learning and Instruction* 2: 45–56.

Bossert, S.T. (1988) 'Cooperative activities in the classroom', *Review of Research in Education* 15: 225–50.

Bruck, M. and Tucker, G. (1974) 'Social class differences in the acquisition of school language', *Merrill-Palmer Quarterly* 20: 205–20.

Buhs, E.S. and Ladd, G.W. (2001) 'Peer rejection as an antecedent of young children's school adjustment: an examination of mediating processes', *Developmental Psychology* 37: 550–60.

Calkins, S.D., Gill, K.L., Johnson, M.C. and Smith, C.L. (1999) 'Emotional reactivity and emotional regulation strategies as predictors of social behaviour with peers during toddlerhood', *Social Development* 8: 310–34.

Cameron, J. and Pierce, W.D. (1994) 'Reinforcement, reward and intrinsic motivation: a meta-analysis', *Review of Educational Research* 64: 363–423.

Caspi, A., Henry, B., McGee, R.O., Moffitt, T.E., and Silva, P.A. (1995) 'Temperamental origins of child and adolescent behaviour problems: from age three to age fifteen', *Child Development* 66: 55–68.

Central Advisory Council for Education (CACE) (1967) *Children and Their Primary Schools: a report of the Central Advisory Council for Education (England)*. London: CACE.

Chambers, B. and Abrami, P.C. (1991) 'The relationship between student team learning and achievement, causal attributions, and affect', *Journal of Educational Psychology* 83: 140–46.

Chapman, J.G., Arenson, S., Carrigan, M.H. and Gryckiewicz, J. (1993) 'Motivational loss in small task groups: free riding on a cognitive task', *Genetic, Social and General Psychology Monographs* 119: 57–73.

Chinn, C.A. and Anderson, R.C. (1998) 'The structure of discussions that promote reasoning', *Teachers College Record* 100: 315–68.

Cohen, E.G. (1994) 'Restructuring the classroom: conditions for productive small groups', *Review of Educational Research* 64: 1–35.

Coie, J.D., Lochman, J.E., Terry, R. and Hyman, C. (1992) 'Predicting early adolescent disorder from childhood aggression and peer rejection', *Journal of Consulting and Clinical Psychology* 60: 783–92.

Cowie, H., Smith, P., Boulton, M. and Laver, R. (1994) *Co-operation in the Multi-Ethnic Classroom: the impact of co-operative group work on social relationships in middle schools*. London: David Fulton.

Damon, W. and Killen, M. (1982) 'Peer interaction and the process of change in children's moral reasoning', *Merrill-Palmer Quarterly* 28: 347–67.

Damon, W. and Phelps, E. (1988) 'Strategic uses of peer learning in children's education', in T.J. Berndt and G.W. Ladd (Eds) *Peer Relations in Child Development*: 135–57. New York: John Wiley.

Daniels, H. (2001) *Vygotsky and Pedagogy*. London: Routledge/Falmer.

Dawes, L., Mercer, N. and Wegerif, R. (2003) *Thinking Together: a programme of activities for developing speaking, listening and thinking skills for children aged 8–11*. Birmingham; Imaginative Minds Ltd.

Dawes, L. and Sams, C. (2004) *Talk Box: speaking and listening activities for learning at Key Stage 1*. London: David Fulton.

Deater-Deckard, K. (2001) 'Annotation: recent research examining the role of peer relationships in the development of psychopathology', *Journal of Child Psychology and Psychiatry* 42: 565–79.

Doise, W. and Mugny, G. (1979) 'Individual and collective conflicts of centrations in cognitive development', *European Journal of Social Psychology* 9: 105–8.

——(1984) *The Social Development of the Intellect*. Oxford: Pergamon Press.

Doise, W., Mugny, G. and Perret-Clermont, A.-N. (1975) 'Social interaction and the development of cognitive operations', *European Journal of Social Psychology* 5: 367–83.

Dunn, J. and Kendrick, C. (1982) *Siblings: love, envy and understanding*. London: Grant McIntyre.

Edwards, D. and Mercer, N. (1987) *Common Knowledge: the development of understanding in the classroom*. London: Methuen/Routledge.

Eisenberg, A.R. and Garvey, C. (1981) 'Children's use of verbal strategies in resolving conflicts', *Discourse Processes* 4: 149–70.

Eisenberg, N., Fabes, R.A., Shepard, S.A., Murphy, B.C., Guthrie, I.K., Jones, S., Friedman, J., Poulin, R. and Maszk, P. (1997) 'Contemporaneous and longitudinal prediction of children's social functioning from regulation and emotionality', *Child Development* 68: 642–64.

Ervin-Tripp, S. (1982) 'Structures of control', in L. Wilkinson (Ed) *Communicating in the Classroom*: 27–47. New York: Academic Press.

Fisher, E. (1993) 'Distinctive features of pupil-pupil talk and their relationship to learning', *Language and Education* 7: 239–58.

Fu-Yun, Y. (2001) 'Competition within computer-assisted cooperative learning environments: cognitive, affective and social outcomes', *Journal of Educational Computing Research* 24: 99–117.

Galton, M., Hargreaves, L., Comber, C., Wall, D. and Pell, A. (1999) *Inside the Primary Classroom: 20 years on*. London: Routledge.

Galton, M., Simon, B. and Croll, P. (1980) *Inside the Primary Classroom (the ORACLE Report)*. London: Routledge and Kegan Paul.

Garvey, C. (1991) *Play*. London: Fontana.

Genishi, C. and DiPaolo, M. (1982) 'Learning through agreement in a pre-school', in L. Wilkinson (Ed) *Communicating in the Classroom*: 49–67. New York: Academic Press.

Gest, S.D., Graham-Bermann, S.A. and Hartup, W.W. (2001) 'Peer experience: common and unique features of number of friendships, social network centrality, and sociometric status', *Social Development* 10: 23–40.

Gifford-Smith, M.E. and Brownell, C.A. (2002) 'Childhood peer relationships: social acceptance, friendships, and peer networks', *Journal of School Psychology* 41: 235–84.

Goodlad, S. and Hirst, B. (1989) *Peer Tutoring: a guide to learning by teaching*. New York: Nichols.

Harkins, S.G., and Petty, R.E. (1982) 'Effects of task difficulty and task uniqueness on social loafing', *Journal of Personality and Social Psychology* 43: 1214–29.

Hart, B. and Risley, T.R. (1995) *Meaningful Differences in the Everyday Experience of Young American Children*. New York: Brookes.

Hartup, W.W., French, D.C., Laursen, B., Johnston, M.K., and Ogawa, J.R. (1993) 'Conflict and friendship relations in middle childhood: behaviour in a closed-field situation', *Child Development* 64: 445–54.

Hay, D.F., Payne, A., and Chadwick, A. (2004) 'Peer relations in childhood', *Journal of Child Psychology and Psychiatry* 45: 84–108.

Hoff, E. and Tian, C. (2005) 'Socioeconomic status and cultural influences on language', *Journal of Communication Disorders* 38: 271–78.

Howe, C.J., Rodgers, C. and Tolmie, A. (1990) 'Physics in the primary school: peer interaction and the understanding of floating and sinking', *European Journal of Psychology of Education* V: 459–75.

Howe, C.J., Tolmie, A. and Rodgers, C. (1992a) 'The acquisition of conceptual knowledge in science by primary school children: group interaction and the understanding of motion down an incline', *British Journal of Developmental Psychology* 10: 113–30.

Howe, C.J., Tolmie, A., Anderson, A. and Mackenzie, M. (1992b) 'Conceptual knowledge in physics: the role of group interaction in computer-supported teaching', *Learning and Instruction* 2: 161–83.

Howe, C.J., Tolmie, A. and Mackenzie, M. (1995a) 'Collaborative learning in physics: some implications for computer design', in C. O'Malley (Ed) *Computer-Supported Collaborative Learning*: 51–68. Berlin: Springer-Verlag.

Howe, C.J., Tolmie, A., Greer, K. and Mackenzie, M. (1995b) 'Peer collaboration and conceptual growth in physics: task influences on children's understanding of heating and cooling', *Cognition and Instruction* 13: 483–503.

Howe, C.J., Tolmie, A., Duchak-Tanner, V. and Rattray, C. (2000) 'Hypothesis testing in science: group consensus and the acquisition of conceptual and procedural knowledge', *Learning and Instruction* 10: 361–91.

Howe, C.J. and McWilliam, D. (2001) 'Peer argument in educational settings: variations due to socioeconomic status, gender and activity context', *Journal of Language and Social Psychology* 20: 61–80.

Howe, C.J., and Tolmie, A. (2003) 'Group work in primary school science: discussion, consensus and guidance from experts', *International Journal of Educational Research* 39: 51–72.

Howe, C., McWilliam, D. and Cross, G. (2005) 'Chance favours only the prepared mind: incubation and the delayed effects of peer collaboration', *British Journal of Psychology* 96: 67–93.

Howe, C.J. and McWilliam, D. (2006) 'Opposition in social interaction between children: why intellectual benefits do not mean social costs', *Social Development* 15: 205–31.

Howe, C.J. (2006) 'Group interaction and conceptual understanding in science: co-construction, contradiction and the mechanisms of growth', Paper presented at *Annual Conference of British Psychological Society Developmental Section*. Royal Holloway College, London.

Howe, C.J., Tolmie, A., Thurston, A., Topping, K.J., Christie, D., Livingston, K., Jessiman, E. and Donaldson, C. (2007) 'Group work in elementary science: organisational principles for classroom teaching,' *Learning & Instruction* 17: 549–63.

Jackson, J.M. and Harkins, S.G. (1985) 'Equity in effort: an explanation of the social loafing effect', *Journal of Personality and Social Psychology* 49: 1199–1206.

Jackson, J.M. and Williams, K.D. (1985) 'Social loafing on difficult tasks: working collectively can improve performance', *Journal of Personality and Social Psychology* 49: 937–42.

Johnson, D.W. and Johnson, F. (2000) *Joining Together: group theory and group skills (7th ed.)*. Boston: Allyn and Bacon.

Johnson, J. and Ershler, J. (1981) 'Developmental trends in preschool play as a function of classroom program and child gender', *Child Development* 52: 995–1004.

Keefer, M., Zeitz, C. and Resnick, L. (2000) 'Judging the quality of peer-led student dialogues', *Cognition and Instruction* 18: 53–81.

Kerr, N.L. (1983) 'Motivation losses in small groups: a social dilemma analysis', *Journal of Personality and Social Psychology* 45: 819–28.

Kim, I.-H., Anderson, R., Nguyen-Jahiel, K. and Archodidou, A. (2007) 'Discourse patterns during children's collaborative online discussions,' *Journal of the Learning Sciences* 16: 333–70.

Kruger, A.C. (1992) 'The effect of peer- and adult-child transactive discussions on moral reasoning', *Merrill-Palmer Quarterly* 38: 191–211.

——(1993) 'Peer collaboration: conflict, co-operation or both?', *Social Development* 2: 165–82.

Kumpulainen, K. and Wray, D. (Eds) (2002) *Classroom Interaction and Social Learning: from theory to practice*. London: Routledge-Falmer.

Kutnick, P. (2005) 'Relational training for group working in classrooms: experimental and action research perspectives', Paper presented as part of the *Educational Dialogue Research Unit Seminar Series*, The Open University, Milton Keynes, June.

Lambirth, A. (2006) 'Challenging the laws of talk: ground rules, social reproduction and the curriculum', *The Curriculum Journal* 17: 59–71.

Lease, A.M., Kennedy, C.A. and Axelrod, J.L. (2002) 'Children's social constructions of popularity', *Social Development* 11: 87–109.

Leman, P.L. and Duveen, G. (1999) 'Representations of authority in children's moral reasoning', *European Journal of Social Psychology* 29: 557–75.

Maccoby, E.E. and Jacklin, C.N. (1980) 'Sex differences in aggression: a rejoinder and reprise', *Child Development* 51: 964–80.

Markell, R. and Asher, S. (1984) 'Children's interaction in dyads: interpersonal influence and sociometric status', *Child Development* 55: 217–24.

Maybin, J. (2006) *Children's Voices: talk, knowledge and identity*. Basingstoke: Palgrave Macmillan.

Mercer, N. (1995) *The Guided Construction of Knowledge: talk amongst teachers and learners*. Clevedon: Multilingual Matters.

——(2000) *Words and Minds: how we use language to think together*. London: Routledge.

Mercer, N., Dawes, R., Wegerif, R. and Sams, C. (2004) 'Reasoning as a scientist: ways of helping children to use language to learn science', *British Educational Research Journal* 30: 367–85.

Mercer, N. and Littleton, K. (2007) *Dialogue and the Development of Children's Thinking: a sociocultural approach*. London: Routledge.

Meyers, S.A. (1997) 'Increasing student participation and productivity on small-group activities for psychology classes', *Teaching of Psychology* 24: 105–15.

Miell, D. and MacDonald, R. (2000) 'Children's creative collaborations: the importance of friendship when working together on a musical composition', *Social Development* 9: 348–69.

Miller, P., Danaher, D. and Forbes, D. (1986) 'Sex-related strategies for coping with interpersonal conflict in children aged 5 and 7', *Developmental Psychology* 22: 543–48.

Mugny, G. and Doise, W. (1978) 'Socio-cognitive conflict and structure of individual and collective performances', *European Journal of Social Psychology* 8: 181–92.

Murphy, S.M. and Faulkner, D. (2000) 'Learning to collaborate: can young children develop better communication strategies through collaboration with a more popular peer?', *European Journal of Psychology of Education* 15: 389–404.

——(2006) 'Gender differences in verbal communication between popular and unpopular children during an interactive task', *Social Development* 15: 82–108.

Newcomb, A.F., Bukowski, W.M. and Pattee, L. (1993) 'Children's peer relations: a meta-analytic review of popular, rejected, neglected, controversial and average sociometric status', *Psychological Bulletin* 113: 99–128.

Nystrand, M. (1986) *The Structure of Written Communication: studies of reciprocity between writers and readers.* London: Academic Press.

Orsolini, M. (1993) 'Dwarfs do not shoot: an analysis of children's justifications', *Cognition and Instruction* 11: 281–97.

Parker, J.G. and Asher, S.R. (1987) 'Peer relations and later personal adjustment: are low-accepted children at risk?', *Psychological Bulletin* 102: 357–89.

Piaget, J. (1932) *The Moral Judgement of the Child.* London: Routledge.

——(1985) *The Equilibration of Cognitive Structures: the central problem of intellectual development.* Chicago: University of Chicago Press.

Pollard, A. and Filer, A. (1996) *The Social World of Children's Learning.* London: Cassell.

Pontecorvo, C., Paoletti, G. and Orsolini, M. (1989) 'Use of the computer and social interaction in a language curriculum', *Golem* 5: 12–14.

Raven, J., Court, J. and Raven, J.C. (1995) *Manual for Raven's Progressive Matrices and Vocabulary Scales.* Oxford: Oxford Psychologists Press.

Rogoff, B. (1990) *Apprenticeship in Thinking: cognitive development in social context.* Oxford: Oxford University Press.

Rothbart, M.K., Ahadi, S.A. and Hershey, K.L. (1994) 'Temperament and social behaviour in childhood', *Merrill-Palmer Quarterly* 40: 21–39.

Roy, A. and Howe, C. (1990) 'Effects of cognitive conflict, socio-cognitive conflict and imitation on children's socio-legal thinking', *European Journal of Social Psychology* 20: 241–52.

Rubin, K., Fein, G. and Vandenbarg, B. (1983) 'Play', in E. Hetherington (Ed) *Handbook of Child Psychology: socialization, personality and social interaction. Volume 4*: 693–774. New York: Wiley.

Ryder, J. and Campbell, L. (1989) 'Groupsense: when groupwork does not add up to "groupwork"', *Pastoral Care in Education* 7: 22–30.

Sawyer, R.K. (1996) 'Role voicing, gender and age in preschool play discourse', *Discourse Processes* 22: 289–307.

Schroeter, B. (2006) 'Children's communication style in peer group interactions: variations according to temperament and sociometric status', Unpublished doctoral dissertation, University of Strathclyde.

Schwarz, B.B., Neuman, Y. and Biezuner, S. (2000) 'Two wrongs may make a right ... If they argue together!', *Cognition and Instruction* 18: 461–94.

Shantz, D.W. (1986) 'Conflict, aggression, and peer status: an observational study', *Child Development* 57: 1322–32.

Sheldon, A. (1992) 'Conflict talk: sociolinguistic challenges to self-assertion and how young girls meet them', *Merrill-Palmer Quarterly* 38: 95–117.

Slavin, R.E. (1983) 'When does cooperative learning increase student achievement?', *Psychological Bulletin* 94: 429–45.

——(1987) 'Developmental and motivational perspectives on cooperative learning: a reconciliation', *Child Development* 58: 1161–67.

——(1995) *Co-operative Learning: theory, research and practice. 2nd Edition.* Boston: Allyn and Bacon.

——(1996) 'Research on cooperative learning and achievement: what we know, what we need to know', *Contemporary Educational Psychology* 21: 43–69.

Tizard, B., Hughes, M., Carmichael, H. and Pinkerton, G. (1983) 'Language and social class: is verbal deprivation a myth?', *Journal of Child Psychology and Psychiatry* 24: 533–42.

Tolmie, A., Christie, D., Howe, C., Thurston, A., Topping, K., Donaldson, C., Jessiman, E. and Livingston, K. (2007) 'Classroom relations and collaborative groupwork in varying social contexts: lessons from Scotland', Paper presented at *American Educational Research Association* Annual Meeting, Chicago.

Tolmie, A., Howe, C.J., Mackenzie, M. and Greer K. (1993) 'Task design as an influence on dialogue and learning: primary school group work with object flotation', *Social Development* 2: 183–201.

Topping, K. and Ehly, S. (Eds) (1998) *Peer-Assisted Learning*. Mahwah, NJ: Lawrence Erlbaum.

Tough, J. (1973) *Focus on Meaning: a study of children's use of language*. London: Allen and Unwin.

Vygotsky, L.S. (1962) *Thought and Language*. Cambridge, MA: MIT Press

——(1978) *Mind in Society*. Cambridge, MA: Harvard University Press.

Webb, N.M. (1989) 'Peer interaction and learning in small groups', *International Journal of Educational Research* 13: 21–39.

Wegerif, R. and Dawes, L. (2004) *Thinking and Learning with ICT: raising achievement in primary classrooms*. London: Routledge.

Wegerif, R., Mercer, N. and Dawes, L. (1999) 'From social interaction to individual reasoning: an empirical investigation of a possible socio-cultural model of cognitive development', *Learning and Instruction* 9: 493–516.

Wegerif, R. and Scrimshaw, P. (Eds) (1997) *Computers and Talk in the Primary Classroom*. Clevedon: Multilingual Matters.

Wells, G. (1986) *The Meaning Makers*. London: Hodder and Stoughton.

Wells, G. and Claxton, G. (2002) (Eds) *Learning for Life in the 21st Century*. Oxford: Blackwell.

Wertsch, J.V. (1991) 'A sociocultural approach to socially shared cognition', in L.B. Resnick, J.M. Levine, and S.D. Teasley (Eds) *Perspectives on Socially Shared Cognition*. Washington, DC: American Psychological Association.

8 Children in primary education

Demography, culture, diversity, inclusion

Mel Ainscow, Jean Conteh, Alan Dyson and Frances Gallannaugh

INTRODUCTION

This chapter is concerned with reviewing the state of research on the 'diversity' of the English primary school population, and with understanding the implications of that research for present and future policy. It argues that differences between children are constructed rather than simply described, and that the constructs embodied in official statistics and policy texts currently tend to dominate discourse in primary education. Yet these constructions favour simplistic and evaluative categorisations which conceal as much as they reveal about diversity. Using 'bilingual learners' as an example, we show how other, more productive, constructions are possible, and that they can be found in the work of critical researchers and in the practice of some teachers and schools. We advocate a dialogue between national policy and practitioners in developing these constructions, and outline the policy directions that would be necessary to support such a dialogue.

At its simplest level, diversity refers to the self-evident differences between primary-aged children. These include differences in attainment, gender, ethnic background, family and social background, interests and aptitudes, social skills, amongst many others. Although many types of difference between children seem to have no educational implications, others are seen as shaping educational experiences and outcomes, and often as calling for policy and practice responses. To take an obvious example, a cluster of perceived differences around children's attainments and capacities for learning have called forth a range of practices in schools and classrooms (sometimes directed by national policy) in terms of streaming, setting by level of attainment, grouping by homogeneous attainment, grouping by differential attainment, social grouping, withdrawing low attainers, and providing adult support.

Understood in this way, our task is the rather straightforward one of mapping what is known about the most educationally-relevant differences between children. However, it is our contention that understanding difference is, in fact, anything but straightforward. The difficulties are illustrated by the example we have just cited. Although children's attainments self-evidently differ, the curriculum in relation to which attainments have been assessed has changed significantly over time, as have the forms of assessment in common use. Moreover, notions of 'capacities for learning' have also changed, though perhaps less coherently, and this has inevitably led to different understandings of the sorts of policy and practice responses that might be appropriate.

It is instructive to compare some of the explicit and implicit theories of why children attain differentially in policy texts from different periods. The Plowden Report (Central

Advisory Council for Education (CACE) 1967), for instance, was much concerned with explanations to do with children's developmental processes and stages, and with the interaction between these and their family and social backgrounds. 'Children,' it concluded,

> [...] are unequal in their endowment and in their rates of development. Their achievements are the result of the interaction of nature and of nurture.
>
> (CACE 1967: para. 1232)

Its recommendations were therefore couched in terms of the development of individually-appropriate, 'finding out' approaches to learning, unstreamed classroom provision, closer links between school and home, and favourable resourcing for schools serving disadvantaged populations. By the 1990s, however – in the 'three wise men' report (Alexander *et al.* 1992) and some of the work of Ofsted (HMI 1990; Ofsted 1996, 1999) – the focus had shifted to the role of teacher and school in generating attainment differences. The most important difference between children was not to do with their innate or environmentally-shaped capacities, so much as with whether they were for-tunate enough to go to a 'good' school. Policy and practice implications began to be couched in terms of ensuring that all schools and all teachers were 'good' in the sense of making fuller and more structured use of group and whole-class teaching, becoming more sceptical about 'finding out' approaches, and instead using teaching techniques of proven effectiveness.

In recent years, the emphasis arguably has shifted back somewhat to a Plowden-like concern with family and social background. However, there is a more distinct sense now that structured interventions by policy makers and practitioners – through the *Every Child Matters* (DfES 2003) agenda in particular – can overcome any negative effects generated by background factors. So Ed Balls, the first Secretary of State for Children, Schools and Families, argued:

> As the Every Child Matters department, our collective responsibility is to make this an age of opportunity for *all children,* not just some children. I am an optimist. I believe that that every child has talent. That children can rise above the worst of all possible starts and exceed even the highest expectations of those around them. We should reject the pessimism that would tell us that there has never been a worse time to be a child and that many children are doomed before they even start. This is not true.
>
> (Balls 2007; emphases in original)

What is clear from these examples is that the ways in which apparently self-evident differences between children are understood, the way those differences are explained, and the policy responses that are then deemed appropriate, are anything but fixed. The changing patterns we have identified here in terms of differences in attainment could equally well be found in relation to gender, ethnicity, social skills, aptitudes, or many other types of difference. Moreover, different types of difference seem to move in and out of focus over time. For instance notions from around the time of Plowden, that children could usefully be categorised straightforwardly in terms of their social class, or their access to particular linguistic codes, or their 'intelligence', have either disappeared or changed out of recognition. At the same time, more recent concerns with 'social exclusion' have generated different forms of categorisation, focusing on a wide range of groups – children in public care; children from Gypsy, Roma and Traveller communities; disabled children; children from particular ethnic groups – who are perceived to be encountering particular barriers to learning. Nor is this merely a temporal phenomenon. Understandings of difference in primary education may change over time, but they also vary between cultural contexts, whether that be at the national level or at the level of particular institutions (Artiles and Dyson 2005; Raveaud 2005).

The implication of all of this is that difference in the primary school population is not so much identified as constructed; that in different times and contexts, attention is paid to this or that form of difference; that these forms of difference are understood in particular ways and explained in particular ways; and that implications for policy and practice flow from these constructions. Our task in this chapter, then, cannot simply be to describe the important differences in the population. Rather, we must describe the ways in which difference is currently constructed in research, and how these relate to policy and practice.

With this in mind, we have chosen to interpret the term 'research' somewhat broadly. Much of what is known about diversity in the primary population comes currently not from scholarly research *per se*, but from the work of government and its agencies in collecting and analysing data about children – activities which have grown immeasurably in recent years. This government activity supports and is supported by research in academic institutions drawing on much of the same data and sharing many of the same assumptions about what diversity 'is'. The outcomes of these analyses are then used more or less directly to inform policy, which draws on them to sharpen its focus and to legitimate itself. There is a sense, therefore, in which policy both offers a further interpretation of the data and (as we shall see) constructs difference in ways that shape the further collection and analysis of data.

Beyond this there are, we suggest, two other broad approaches to diversity. First, there is a body of what we call here 'critical' scholarly research – critical in the sense that it rejects the assumptions of governmental and related analyses, and uses different kinds of data interpreted in different ways. Second, there are understandings of diversity which emerge in the work of at least some teachers and which, though often tacit, occasionally enter the public domain as practitioners collaborate with academic researchers to understand and develop their practice.

All of these activities generate constructions of diversity that have significant implications for policy and practice at the current time. We have, therefore, chosen to see them all as falling within the remit of this survey – though inevitably this means that we have to be selective in what we report. Moreover, given that the constructions generated by these different activities are themselves different and often in conflict with one another, it is our contention that no overview can be definitive, and that we must, therefore, take up a position in this contested field. Our own approach to diversity is based on a commitment to the promotion of equity (as we understand it) in the education system, and to a conviction that this is best achieved by adopting a stance of critical friendship towards practitioners and policy-makers. We are conscious that our own perspective is informed by discourses of 'diversity' and 'inclusion' that have their roots, amongst other places, in the racial politics of education in the USA (see, for instance, Baez 2004), and in the politics of the inclusion movement (if such it is) in England and elsewhere (see, for instance, Booth and Ainscow 2002). These origins will be evident throughout this chapter, as will the implications of our stated aims for our own understanding of diversity. We have no difficulty in acknowledging that reviewers operating from a different basis would have produced a very different chapter from the one that we offer here.

With this in mind we will begin the survey by considering the constructions of difference in official statistics and analyses, together with the constructions in policy that draw upon and drive these. We will then consider alternative constructions as they emerge in the work of critical researchers (and here we will use work on bilingual learners as a case that we can explore in more detail) and in some of the collaborative studies undertaken by practitioners and academic researchers together. Finally, we will consider how these alternative constructions might in turn inform alternative approaches to policy and practice.

CONSTRUCTIONS THROUGH OFFICIAL STATISTICS

The bases of official statistics

The English education system has become rich in official statistics in recent years. At the time of writing in 2007, most of those that are publicly available and relevant to understanding diversity in primary education may be accessed via the DCSF (Department for Children, Schools and Families) research and statistics gateway (http://www. dcsf.gov.uk/rsgateway/). However there are other portals, maintained, for instance, by the Office for National Statistics (http://www.statistics.gov.uk/) and the Neighbourhood Statistics Service (http://neighbourhood.statistics.gov.uk/dissemination/). There is, therefore, the capacity to bring together data on the primary school population from the national census, annual censuses of schools, and the performance of children in national assessments. In particular, the National Pupil Database (NPD) contains cumulative records for pupils in state schools, categorising them in relation to a wide range of characteristics, including age, gender, school placement, ethnicity, language status, entitlement to free school meals, attendance, special educational needs (SEN) status and levels of attainment. In this way, official statistics map out particular dimensions of difference within the student population.

Inevitably, these statistical constructions are constrained by the need to support large databases, and therefore have to focus on data that are easily quantifiable and easy to collect on a large scale. This has a number of consequences:

- Data are collected on some aspects of diversity, but not on others that are arguably just as significant in educational terms. For instance, NPD holds extensive data on children's attainments in national assessments, but says nothing about other outcomes that might be expected from education – notably, the majority of the outcomes in the *Every Child Matters* agenda (DfES 2003). Likewise, there are statistics on SEN and on ethnicity, but not on disability or on faith.
- Subtle and complex characteristics have to be reduced to whatever the most readily available measures make of them. So, for instance, socio-economic background is an important variable in relation to children's educational outcomes, but NPD uses the rather crude, binary proxy of entitlement or non-entitlement to free school meals (Hobbs and Vignoles 2007). Similarly, the categories used by the DCSF to collect information on ethnicity are characterised by a lack of internal consistency, confusing criteria based on racial characteristics, nationality and geographic origin (Buckler 2006).

- The allocation of children to some of the categories used by the databases is inherently unreliable. Ethnicity, for instance, is assessed by self-identification; entitlement to free school meals depends on the willingness of families to claim their entitlement; and SEN status depends on the highly variable assessments of different schools and local authorities.

In themselves these limitations are not necessarily fatal given that they derive from familiar problems of creating and handling large data sets, and that it ought not to be difficult to take them into account when interpreting the data. However, this is to overlook the powerful role that data of this kind play in informing policy and practice. At a time when government policy has focused on raising standards of attainment, NPD in particular makes it possible to relate the demographics of the student population to levels of attainment. As a result, diversity as constructed in national statistics is understood primarily in its relation to attainment, and a succession of government analyses via the research and statistics gateway document how some groups (as defined in the databases) do better than others. In turn, these somewhat uni-dimensional constructions feed into policy. If some groups do less well than others in terms of attainment, then policy interventions targeted at that group are seen to be called for. So, the low attainments of some minority ethnic groups call for an ethnic minorities achievement programme (http://www.standards.dfes.gov.uk/ethnicminorities/), the relatively low attainments of boys overall are seen as calling for responses by gender (http://www.standards.dfes.gov.uk/genderandachievement/understanding/), the low attainments of students identified as having SEN are seen as calling for efforts to 'remove barriers to achievement' (DfES 2004a), and so on.

Statistical constructions of diversity

Despite the caveats set out above, official statistics illuminate at least some aspects of diversity in the primary school population. Drawing on NPD (particularly when its data are combined with other national statistics, such as those from the national census), it is possible to characterise the primary school population in two ways. First, it is possible to describe the population and its sub-groups in terms of the individual categories within which data are collected. So, for instance, we know from the 2006 analyses (DfES 2006e), that:[1]

- The overall primary school population is something over 4 million and has been decreasing in size consistently over the last decade. There are marginally more boys than girls educated in maintained primary schools.
- About 16 per cent of the population comes from low-income families, as indicated by known entitlement to free school meals. This is more than in secondary schools, and is probably due to the greater take-up of the entitlement amongst primary children rather than to any differences in family income.
- Just over one fifth of the population is classified as of minority ethnic background. Since minority ethnic groups on the whole have a younger age structure than the White British group, this is a higher proportion than in secondary schools or amongst adults in the national population. National statistics recognise a range of different minority ethnic backgrounds, so that no single group constitutes more than 4 per cent of the population (the Pakistani group is largest at 3.3 per cent) and some

groups constitute a very small proportion (for instance, Irish Heritage Traveller at 0.1 per cent or Chinese at 0.3 per cent).
- The percentage of pupils in primary schools (of compulsory school age and above) whose first language is known or believed to be other than English is around 12.5 per cent.
- Around 20 per cent of children in the primary population are regarded as having SEN, with the large majority of these (about 19 per cent) being placed in mainstream rather than special schools (DfES 2006f).

Whilst figures such as these go some way towards indicating the diversity of the primary school population, they disguise both the distribution of and interaction between different characteristics. A second type of characterisation is necessary, therefore, to take these factors into account. In recent years, a veritable industry of statistical analysis has grown up both within DCSF and in the research community to explore distributions and interactions, and it is beyond the scope of this chapter to review all of the outputs from this work. However, there are some overarching findings that are of particular significance from our point of view.

For instance, the majority and minority characteristics that we have outlined above are not distributed evenly in geographical – and, therefore, in institutional – terms. So, the minority ethnic population in primary schools varies considerably by region as a proportion of the primary population as a whole – from about 4 per cent in the North East to nearly three quarters in Inner London (DfES 2005). These skewing effects are often magnified at school level as populations are concentrated in particular neighbourhoods and/or choose particular schools. As a result, there is a marked tendency for particular ethnic groups to be represented disproportionately in particular schools when compared to their presence in the school population as a whole. This applies as much, if not more, to White children as to those from minority groups (DfES 2006a; Johnston *et al.* 2006).

There are similar variations in the proportions of primary-aged children eligible for free school meals (DfES 2004b) or regarded as having SEN (DfES 2006f). The implication is that the primary school population in a particular region, local authority area or school may look quite different from the national population. In particular, it is not the case that children with particular characteristics are distributed evenly across the population, but that they are more concentrated in some places than in others. Another way to put this is to say that there are degrees of segregation within the population: the more the population of particular areas and schools is made up of children with similar characteristics, the less those children mix with peers whose characteristics are different.

These phenomena are compounded by the interactions between the characteristics that are recorded in national statistics. Again, these interactions are complex, but a few examples will suffice. There is, for instance, an interaction between ethnicity and entitlement to free school meals, with particularly high rates of entitlement amongst Travellers of Irish Heritage and Gypsy/Roma, Bangladeshi, Pakistani, and Black groups (DfES 2005). Similarly, variation is apparent in the SEN population by gender, ethnicity, free school meals status and age. The incidence of pupils with SEN without statements in primary and secondary schools is greater for boys (around one in every five boys) than for girls (almost one in every eight), as is the incidence of pupils with statements of SEN; members of certain minority ethnic groups (particularly Travellers of Irish heritage, Gypsy/Roma, Bangladeshi, Pakistani, Black, and White/Black Caribbean and African pupils) are most likely to be identified as having special educational needs, and White and Asian, Indian and Chinese pupils least likely; the proportion of pupils identified with SEN and known to be eligible for free school meals (28 per cent in primary schools) is much higher than for those pupils with no SEN; and the incidence of pupils with SEN without statements peaks at ages eight and nine (whilst the incidence of pupils with statements of SEN peaks at age 14) (DfES 2006f).

These interactions are also evident in relation to another key category used to characterise the primary population: level of attainment. Since national assessments are criterion-referenced, they tell us – in principle at least – something about the capabilities of the population. However, it is clear that attainment is impacted upon by other population characteristics. So, gender, ethnicity, entitlement to free school meals, and SEN status all impact upon attainment (DfES 2006c). Given that these factors interact with each other and are not distributed evenly in geographical or institutional terms, it follows that there is also an uneven distribution by attainment, and that there is some tendency towards the concentration of children with particular levels of attainment in particular schools. Low achievement, as observed by Cassen and Kingdon (2007), is a predominantly urban phenomenon, and, within that, is concentrated in particular urban areas. The corollary, of course, is that higher levels of achievement must also be concentrated outside these areas.

National statistics thus present a somewhat paradoxical picture of the primary school population. Viewed as a whole, that population is diverse in that children differ from each other in terms of a wide range of characteristics. The implication is that policies and practices are needed which are capable of responding to this diversity by educating children with different characteristics in the same system, schools and classrooms. This would seem to imply the sorts of individually-responsive forms of provision that lie at the heart of the Plowden recommendations, that have been integral to the development of inclusive education, and that have resurfaced more recently – and in a somewhat different form – in the call for 'personalisation' (Teaching and Learning in 2020 Review Group 2006). However, it is also clear that the diversity of the population as a whole is not necessarily reflected in full in every area or school. The tendency towards concentration, and hence towards segregation, is not necessarily a new one, or one that can be understood solely in relation to the policies of marketisation in recent years (Gorard 2000; Johnston *et al.* 2006). However, it does make the concept of diversity more complex than is sometimes supposed, and may call for very particular policy and practice responses.

CONSTRUCTIONS THROUGH POLICY TEXTS

In combination with these official statistics, or in addition to them, *policy texts* draw attention to particular aspects of diversity. In principle, such texts could offer quite different characterisations from those implied by official statistics. In practice, however, policy in recent years has been much concerned with what commentators have called 'performativity' (Ball 2003; Broadfoot 2001), and what government itself tends to call 'delivery'. Put simply, policy has focused on bringing about measurable changes, driven ultimately by Public Service Agreement Targets, to the performance of the education system as a whole, of individual authorities and schools, and of children (Dyson 2007). As a result, it has tended to characterise the primary population in ways that present it as susceptible to interventions aimed at raising performance. This in turn means characterising the population in terms of its current and desired performances, and of those characteristics that are likely to facilitate or inhibit those performances. The sorts of official statistics we set out above support just such a process.

Paradoxically, this process is often at its clearest when texts appeal to a different, perhaps more 'liberal', view of education, and where the contradiction between this and the inherent instrumentalism of official constructions rises to the surface. Take, for instance, the 2000 Ofsted published guidance to inspectors and schools to assist them, in the words of its title, in *Evaluating Educational Inclusion* (Ofsted 2000). The document is intimately concerned, as one might suppose, with the diversity of the school population and with the ways in which schools respond to that diversity. However, the meaning of diversity and inclusion is spelt out in a distinctive way:

> Educational inclusion is [...] about equal opportunities for all pupils, whatever their age, gender, ethnicity, attainment and background. It pays particular attention to the provision made for and the achievement of **different groups** of pupils within a school. Throughout this guidance, whenever we use the term **different groups** it could apply to any or all of the following:
> - girls and boys;
> - minority ethnic and faith groups, Travellers, asylum seekers and refugees;
> - pupils who need support to learn English as an additional language (EAL);
> - pupils with special educational needs;
> - gifted and talented pupils;
> - children 'looked after' by the local authority;
> - other children, such as sick children; young carers; those children from families under stress; pregnant school girls and teenage mothers; and
> - any pupils who are at risk of disaffection and exclusion.
>
> (Ofsted 2000: 4, emphases in original)

What is significant here is that the appeal to equal opportunities resolves itself into a focus on achievement, and that this in turn requires a search for groups in the school population who might not achieve as highly as possible without some form of careful attention. Many of these groups are the same as those constituted by the categories of official statistics. However, working at the school level, Ofsted is also able to identify other groups on whom such statistics are not collected.

A similar process is at work in the *Every Child Matters* agenda (DfES 2003). On the face of it, *Every Child Matters* signals a significant break from the intensive focus on standards of attainment that marked the first years of New Labour government. However, the structure on which the characterisation of the school population is based remains the same. Children are seen primarily in terms of the performances that might be expected of them, conceptualised in terms of the 'five outcomes' – being healthy, staying safe, enjoying and achieving, making a positive contribution, and achieving economic well-being. This in turn makes possible a further categorisation in terms of the barriers to which different groups of children are subject and which might prevent their achieving these outcomes:

> [...] certain factors are associated with poor outcomes including:
> -low income and parental unemployment
> -homelessness

-poor parenting
-poor schooling
-post-natal depression among mothers
-low birth weight
-substance misuse
-individual characteristics such as intelligence
-community factors, such as living in a disadvantaged neighbourhood.

Outcomes also vary by race and gender. Underachievement and school exclusion are particularly concentrated in certain ethnic groups. Boys have higher rates of offending and exclusion, while self-harm and eating disorders are more prevalent among girls.

(DfES 2003: 17–18)

Given the focus on performativity, policy-makers tend to provide mechanisms whereby these characterisations of the population can be brought directly to bear on practice. So, for instance, schools are encouraged to use a Pupil Achievement Tracker (http://www.standards.dfes.gov.uk/performance/pat/) to monitor the performance of individual pupils and whole populations in relation to the sorts of categories used by official statistics and articulated in these policy texts. Similarly, professionals working with children are encouraged to make use of a common assessment framework (http://www.everychildmatters.gov.uk/deliveringservices/caf/) in order to assess children's current performances and the potential facilitators and inhibitors of their achieving the desired outcomes.

Whilst such tools undoubtedly have their uses for practitioners and bring some benefits to children, they nonetheless reinforce a particular way of understanding the diversity of the school population. The emphasis on performativity means that the school population is relentlessly characterised in relation to outcomes. The aspects of diversity to which most attention is paid are those that are held to bear most directly on the achievement of these outcomes. As a consequence, differences are never neutral. Belonging to a particular ethnic group, or coming from a particular social background, or even having a particular gender, has a value insofar as it inhibits or facilitates the achievement of particular outcomes. Characteristics with a negative value are cast as obstacles to be overcome through policy and practice interventions. Given the tendency, outlined above, for poor outcomes to be associated with particular clusters of characteristics, and for these clusters to be distributed unevenly in geographical terms, this means that particular groups of learners in particular places are likely to be seen as overwhelmed by negative characteristics – as are the schools that serve them.

Again, an example may be useful. Primary schools have long prided themselves on what they see as their positive relationships with parents, and, indeed, the Plowden Report (CACE 1967) long ago recognised the importance of such relationships. However, recent policy has begun to cast these relationships in a particular light. Given the concern with performativity, a child's family background is to be judged in terms of its capacity to promote the achievement of desired outcomes. As the government's parenting strategy, *Every Parent Matters*, puts it:

Our vision is of responsive public services driven increasingly by ever greater numbers of parents with high aspirations and expectations for their children. Public services need to be respectful of parents as adults with expertise of their own and provide a personalised approach [...] That said, for a small minority of parents who have lost, or never had, the capacity to parent responsibly, public services must be ready to intervene promptly and sensitively [...] [W]e have to accept that this journey may be a long one and compulsion for the few, through measures such as parenting orders, may sometimes be required to ensure that responsibilities to the child (such as getting them to school every day) are being properly fulfilled.

(DfES 2007: 6–7)

The evaluative nature of this approach is clear. Some parents – those with 'high aspirations and expectations' – are able to facilitate their child's achievement of desired outcomes, and deserve a respectful approach from public services. Other parents – those who lack the 'capacity to parent responsibility' – demand intervention and, ultimately, compulsion. So, another set of evaluative categories is created through which the school population can be characterised. In this way, the rather minimalist information on families contained in official statistics is supplemented by a more qualitative set of categories around children whose parents are deemed to be more or less 'responsible', more or less 'aspirational', and more or less 'hard to reach'. These categories may never appear in official statistics, but they inevitably inform the ways in which schools view and approach their pupils' families, and may well make their appearance in pupil fields, pupil trackers and common assessment forms.

ALTERNATIVE PERSPECTIVES

We have suggested above that the constructions of difference in official statistics and policy texts are 'dominant' in the English primary system. Indeed they are, if by this we mean that they tend to inform policy as it emerges at national level and, in a centrally-directed system, tend therefore to create a framework within which practitioners and local policy-makers have to operate. However, this does not mean that such constructions are unchallenged. On the contrary, alternatives are formulated by researchers out of their critiques of official discourse and, as we shall see later, also emerge from the work of practitioners as they engage with the complexities of pupil diversity in classrooms.

In this part of the chapter, therefore, we wish to focus on these alternatives. Space does not permit us to deal with all of the critiques of official constructions that have emerged in recent years. We propose, therefore, to take a particular case – so-called 'EAL learners' – that has been the subject of considerable activity on the part both of policy-makers and of researchers, and explore how this category is used in official discourses and what alternative constructions have been advanced.

The EAL category

Official statistics use a category of 'pupils whose first language is known or believed to be other than English', into which some 12.5 per cent of primary children fall. It seems that the size of this group is growing and there is official concern that not only are their attainments lower than those of children for whom English is their first language, but that little progress has been made in closing the attainment gap, particularly in primary schools (DfES 2006a: 61). Until the mid-2000s (see DfES 2006e), data were not collected on the language(s) spoken by these children, and policy decisions about provision were often made on the grounds of ethnicity, following the categories developed for the

National Census in 2001, rather than specific language background. The implication presumably is that what matters is the perceived deficit they experience in not having English as their 'first' language.

In terms of policy texts, at the time of writing in 2007, the most widely used term for pupils who speak other languages than English in primary schools in England is 'EAL (English as an Additional Language) learners', though recent documentation has begun to use the term 'bilingual pupils' (DfES 2006b). 'EAL' has been used extensively through policy and pedagogical documents for the last 10 years, including – significantly for professional development and classroom discourses – in teacher training discourses. Among the standards required of newly qualified primary teachers is the requirement to

> Know how to make effective personalised provision for those they teach, including those for whom English is an additional language or who have special educational needs or disabilities, and how to take practical account of diversity and promote equality and inclusion in their teaching.
>
> (TDA 2008: Standard Q19, pp. 2–3)

'EAL learners' are almost always constructed as needing support (Bourne 2001; Conteh 2006, 2007a; Martin-Jones and Saxena 1995, 1996, 2003), and nowhere more emphatically than in the National Curriculum 2000 statement on inclusion (DFEE and QCA 1999), where it is suggested that 'learning English as an additional language' could constitute a 'barrier to learning', resulting in the need for special provision along the same lines as those required for learners identified as having SEN.

Such a deficit model seems to be embedded in teachers' expectations of their pupils with EAL, as suggested by the disparities between teacher assessment and test results at KS2 for EAL learners, particularly in English (DfES 2006a: 71–73). Indeed, the proportionality of these disparities by ethnicity matches the socio-economic status of the different groups, with Bangladeshi and Black African pupils showing higher percentage point differences than Indian and Pakistani. The problematising of bilingualism is made visible in primary classrooms with the deployment of 'bilingual support assistants' – the only bilingual professionals encountered by most primary pupils. The rationale for the support assistant's role can be traced back to the Swann Report, where it was characterised as:

> [...] providing a degree of continuity between the home and school environment by offering psychological and social support for the child, as well as being able to explain simple educational concepts in a child's mother tongue, if the need arises, but always working within the mainstream classroom and alongside the class teacher.
>
> (DES 1985: 407)

Bilingual assistants have been a key aspect in the construction of the 'transitional' model of bilingualism (Cummins 2001) in primary classroom practice over the years. Researchers such as Cummins argue that this model has a negative effect on bilingual pupils' attainments and potential for success.

In these ways, the 'EAL' category and accompanying policy discourses follow the pattern we have identified elsewhere: a category is created because of its apparent relevance to educational outcomes; the characteristics which it seeks to capture are evaluated in relation to their perceived tendency to facilitate or inhibit the achievement of those outcomes; and minority characteristics tend to be cast as deficits calling for policy and practice intervention. Policy thus comes to be based on a construction of difference that, as Leung *et al.* suggest in a seminal article (1997), makes two characteristic assumptions:

- pupils learning 'English as an additional language', while being linguistically and culturally diverse, constitute a distinct group with common characteristics and learning needs that are different from other pupils; and
- ethnicity and language are fixed concepts which have a neat one-to-one correspondence and which position 'EAL' learners as linguistic and social outsiders separate from the monolingual mainstream.

Leung *et al.* go on to argue that fluidity in language choice and use is hardly recognised in the mainstream education system. Official educational discourses view languages as individual attributes, as separate and hierarchical. National policies and pedagogical resources related to English primary classrooms use a wide range of terms and categories to define and describe language diversity. However, as a study by the VALEUR project (based at the European Centre for Modern Languages: http://www. ecml.at/mtp2/VALEUR/) is finding, although languages are categorised in multiple ways, the terms in use tend to be value-loaded in the ways they are perceived as mediating attitudes to language diversity by and for teachers, their pupils, and policy-makers.

Beyond EAL

It is, however, possible to construct differences around language in other ways. A growing body of qualitative research carried out in different British cities, usually of a sociolinguistic and/or ethnographic nature (for example Aitsiselmi 2004; Rampton 2005a, 2005b; Harris 2006) has shown how the conceptualisations of ethnic and language diversity described by Leung *et al.* (1997) are simplistic and unhelpful in understanding the complex nature of English society today. Bilingualism, indeed multilingualism, has been shown to be a natural and normal part of the lives and the personal and social identities of many second and third generation 'ethnic minority' pupils in English primary schools. For such pupils, moving across and between languages is a natural aspect of their daily lives (Conteh 2007a). For many of them, English is their dominant language and so to use the term 'EAL' to describe their language experiences and identities or to state that English is their 'second language' acknowledges only a small part of a complex whole. Aitsiselmi (2004: 34), in a case study conducted in Bradford, reported that while English has 'become the main language of communication among siblings, peers and friends for the younger generation', there is a clear consensus among informants of all ages that the heritage languages 'should continue to be used' for a range of purposes. Such qualitative findings are corroborated by national figures (DfES 2006a: 24) which show the flexible language use of minority ethnic pupils aged 5–16, particularly those of South Asian heritage.

Two linked and growing strands of research into language diversity in primary classrooms are beginning to challenge the prevailing monolingual ideologies and provide evidence for different conceptualisations of language and ethnicity from those described by Leung *et al.* (1997). These are the work in multiliteracies or 'simultaneous literacies' (Datta 2001; Kenner 2000; Gregory *et al.* 2004) and in children's learning in complementary settings (for example Martin *et al.* 2003; Conteh *et al.* 2007).

The work around multiliteracies has built on concepts which have come to the fore over recent years, mainly through anthropological research, of literacy as a social and cultural practice (Street 1984). Classroom- and home-based qualitative research also reveals the 'many pathways' (Gregory *et al.* 2004) along which children growing up in multilingual environments become confident users of the range of literacies available to them. While it is argued that such learning experiences are positive and have potential for benefiting children's learning in mainstream classrooms, they remain largely hidden from, and little understood by, mainstream teachers (Kenner 2000: 14). Indeed, as another manifestation of the deficit discourses discussed above, researchers such as Robertson (2007) show how children who are becoming multiliterate are sometimes categorised by their mainstream teachers as in need of extra support and even as having SEN.

Like multiliteracy, primary pupils' experiences in community-based settings (commonly called 'supplementary' or 'complementary' schools) are usually not well known outside the communities themselves. A large, ESRC-funded, research study in Leicester (Martin *et al.* 2003) has begun to reveal the philosophies, ethos and practices of such schools. It shows the importance of after-hours education in the maintenance of bilingualism, the enhancement of learning, and the widening of minority ethnic pupils' choices and uptake of identities. The importance of out-of-school learning for enhancing bilingual pupils' attainment is beginning to be recognised; for example, Tikly *et al.* (2002) have linked attendance at supplementary schools to enhanced attainment for pupils of African Caribbean heritage. It seems that the government has begun to recognise the potential value added nature of complementary schooling. In an edited collection, Conteh *et al.* (2007) provide several illuminative case studies from community-based settings in different regions of England, as well as an introductory chapter that describes the historical contexts and suggests theoretical and methodological frameworks to help shape future research.

These new perspectives point towards different kinds of policy and practice response. For instance, there is evidence that some of the problems around the deployment of teaching assistants for bilingual learners can be resolved where bilingual support assistants are able to use the full range of languages that they share with their pupils along with the knowledge they often have of local and cultural contexts. In this way, they are able to develop classroom interaction that differs from that which occurs with monolingual teachers in the kinds of affordances for learning it provides (Martin-Jones and Saxena 2003). There is evidence of similar processes at work where bilingual primary teachers use code-switching in mainstream and community-based primary classrooms (Conteh 2007a, 2007b).

Some wider implications

It seems to us that the case of bilingual learners offers some important pointers towards alternative ways of understanding diversity in the primary school population. In particular:

- The construction of difference in terms of fixed categories tends to conceal as much as it reveals about diversity. Constructing children as either having or not having English as a first language is useful in statistical terms for simplifying the process of data collection, and the formulation of targeted interventions. However, it conceals the actual fluidity of language use and the variations that exist across an identified population.

- The evaluation of difference in relation to sometimes narrowly-conceptualised outcomes tends to overlook the resources to which those differences give children access. So, seeing children's use of languages other than English as a 'barrier to learning' overlooks the educational and social resources that are embodied in multilingualism and 'multiliteracies' and the potential for capitalising on those resources through practices which recognise and respect them.
- Constructing diversity in terms of evaluative categories overlooks the role of the child as agent. Children effectively come to be seen as the sum of their categorised characteristics, some of which facilitate their achievement of outcomes, some of which act as barriers. They are then subject to increasingly powerful interventions (for which the successive 'waves' of the national strategies are paradigmatic examples) to overcome those barriers. However, this overlooks the sense in which children are using the resources at their disposal to make sense of and act within their worlds. Specifically, in the case of bilingual learners, it overlooks the ways in which children develop fluid language use and their identities as multiliterate learners.

In an interesting study of 'inclusion' and 'exclusion' in the classrooms of two apparently inclusive primary schools, Benjamin *et al.* (2003) show how such alternative understandings might be operationalised. They resist treating the categorised characteristics of children (their gender, ethnicity, attainments and so on) as fixed, as determining how children will perform educationally, or as calling for particular educational responses. Instead, they focus on the processes whereby the meaning of children's characteristics, the identities they achieve, and the responses that their peers and teachers make to them are subject to 'moment-by-moment negotiation and renegotiation':

> What we have shown in the paper is that children were active participants in those negotiations, but that the negotiations themselves were far from arbitrary. They were in part produced through a complex constellation of systemic indices of difference – primarily those of social class, 'race'/ethnicity, gender/sexuality and perceived academic ability. The children used this constellation of multiple and intersecting indices of difference, together with the schools' own formal curricular and policy cultures to produce moments of inclusion and exclusion.
>
> (Benjamin *et al.* 2003: 556)

This points to a much more situated and fluid understanding of diversity in terms, not of a fixed set of characteristics but of negotiated constructions, set in particular contexts, and shaped by underlying educational imperatives and social structures. Such an understanding does not yield the neat evaluative categorisations that currently dominate official statistics and policy texts. Indeed, it throws into doubt the project of characterising the diversity of the primary population in some definitive way, or of formulating policy and practice responses on the basis of such a characterisation. To that extent, it is less useful to, and more problematic for, policy-makers and practitioners than are currently dominant discourses. Whether it has any implications for these constituencies, or whether it is simply a powerful analytical tool for critical researchers is an issue to which we turn in the next section of this chapter.

Alternative policy and practice responses

In these final sections, we consider the extent to which different understandings of diversity are able to support adequate responses to diversity in policy and practice. This is, of course, something of a chicken and egg question since the adequacy of the response is likely to be judged in terms of the understanding that informs it. In our analysis, however, we take at face value the statement of purpose by Ed Balls, cited earlier in this survey:

> As the Every Child Matters department, our collective responsibility is to make this an age of opportunity for *all children*, not just some children.
>
> (Balls 2007, emphasis in original)

Whilst such a statement is capable of many interpretations, we take it as meaning – at the very least – that every child should be valued, that the particular characteristics of every child should be taken into account by the education system, and that the system should do all it can to enhance the life chances and improve the life quality of every child. We take it that, in broad terms, aims such as these are part of a long tradition in primary education, traceable at least as far back as Plowden, evident in the absence of selection by 'ability' in this phase, compatible with the notion of inclusive education as it has been developed in this country (Booth and Ainscow 2002). Perhaps most importantly, it is consonant with the avowed aims of very many primary practitioners.

Viewed in these terms, the dominant constructions we outline above are by no means entirely negative in their impact. The use of clear (if problematic) categorisations identifying groups whose characteristics are held to act as barriers to learning has proved particularly powerful in enabling practitioners and policy-makers to target their efforts on individual children deemed to be in need (for instance through the SEN system, or the national strategy 'waves' of intervention), on particular groups within the primary population (for instance through the ethnic minority achievement strategy, or the gifted and talented strand of the Excellence in Cities programme), or on schools where needy groups are concentrated (for example through the Schools Facing Challenging Circumstances programme). At the time of writing (August 2007), for instance, the Primary National Strategy website (http://www.standards.dfes.gov.uk/primary/) hosts lead items on a strategy for children who are newly arrived in the UK, on professional development materials to support gifted and talented education, on resources to support work with children whose social and emotional skills are deemed to be in need of development, and on developments for 'youngsters who have special educational needs, learning difficulties and/or disabilities'.

The analysis we have offered above, however, casts doubt on a response to diversity that relies on this categorise-and-intervene approach. Whatever the merits of such an approach, we suggest that it is inevitable that it will miss the complexity of diversity, reinforce the deficit view of those children (and families) deemed to be experiencing 'barriers to learning', and underestimate the role of children as agents in their own learning. Moreover, we saw above how different constructions of diversity are possible that appear to be less prone to these limitations and, therefore, hold out the promise of more equitable policy responses.

The work of critical researchers is, of course, essential in deconstructing dominant discourses and identifying alternatives in principle. However, if we want to know what those alternatives look like in practice, and how they can be operationalised in the complexities, contradictions and unequal power relations of schools then we suggest it is necessary to look towards the practices of some – perhaps many – schools and teachers. As Nias (1989) noted many years ago, the practice of primary teachers is not simply a straightforward matter of reproducing techniques acquired in training, nor of implementing policy devised elsewhere. Rather, teachers' practice emerges from the interaction of their identities as people, what they see as the aims of their work, and their need to build and sustain relationships with the children they teach. Nias predicted that, in this context, highly interventionist government policies act as a destabilising factor, creating a set of 'dilemmas' (Woods and Jeffrey 2002; Day *et al.* 2006) which teachers have to resolve. Whilst it is easy to view this situation negatively as the undermining of the supposedly 'child-centred' practices of primary teachers, it can also be seen in a more positive light. As teachers interact constantly with children, their struggles to reconcile their avowedly 'Plowdenesque' values with the very different constructions of recent policy creates a site in which new forms of practice can, potentially, emerge.

We say this particularly in the light of two potentially important recent studies, which have looked closely at how practices that respond effectively to learner diversity in primary classrooms develop. Both studies are located in the current policy context and see teachers struggling with the constructions of difference in that context. Significantly, perhaps, both studies also present teachers who have access to an external perspective – provided by researchers – and who may therefore have a better than usual chance of developing and sustaining practices outside current orthodoxies.

The first study, *Learning without Limits*, examined ways of teaching that are free from determinist beliefs about ability (Hart 2003; Hart *et al.* 2004). The researchers worked closely with a group of teachers, who had rejected ideas of fixed ability, in order to study their practice. They started from the belief that constraints are placed on children's learning by ability-focused practices that lead young children to define themselves in comparison to their peers.

Drawing on the ideas of Bourne and Moon (1995), Hart *et al.* argue that the notion of ability as inborn intelligence has come to be seen as 'a natural way of talking about children' that summarises their perceived differences. They go on to suggest that national policies reflect this assumption, making it essential for teachers to compare, categorise and group their pupils by ability in order to provide appropriate and challenging teaching for all. So, for example, inspectors are expected to check that teaching is differentiated for 'more able', 'average' and 'less able' pupils. In this context, what is meant by ability is not made explicit, leaving scope for teachers to interpret what is being recommended in ways that suit their own beliefs and views. However, it is noted that the emphasis on target setting and value-added measures of progress leave little scope for teachers who reject the fixed view of measurable ability to hold on to their principles.

Through examining closely the practices and thinking of their teacher partners, the researchers set themselves the task of identifying 'more just and empowering' ways of making sense of learner diversity. In summary, this would, they argue, involve teachers treating patterns of achievement and response in a 'spirit of transformability', seeking to discover what is possible to enhance the capacity of each child in their class to learn and to create the conditions in which their learning can more fully and effectively flourish.

The second study, *Understanding and Developing Inclusive Practices in Schools*, also pointed to the importance of inquiry as a stimulus for changing practices. Carried out by a research network that was part of the Economic and Social Research Council's Teaching and Learning Research Programme (Ainscow, Booth and Dyson 2004; Ainscow *et al.* 2003, 2006), the study involved 25 schools in exploring ways of developing inclusion in their own contexts, in collaboration with university researchers.

In broad terms, what was noted in the participating schools was neither the crushing of inclusion by the standards agenda, nor the rejection of the standards agenda in favour of a radical, inclusive alternative. Certainly, many teachers were concerned about the impacts on their work of the standards agenda and some were committed to views of inclusion that they saw as standing in contradiction to it. However, in most of the schools the two agendas remained intertwined. Indeed, the focus on attainment appeared to prompt some teachers to examine issues in relation to the achievements and participation of hitherto marginalised groups that they had previously overlooked. Likewise, the concern with inclusion tended to shape the way the school responded to the imperative to raise standards.

In trying to make sense of the relationship between external imperatives and the processes of change in schools, the study drew on the ideas of Wenger (1998) to reveal how external agendas were mediated by the norms and values of the communities of practice within schools and how they become part of a dialogue whose outcomes can be more rather than less inclusive. In this way, the role of national policy emerges from the study in something of a new light. This suggests that schools may be able to engage with what might appear to be unfavourable policy imperatives to produce outcomes that are by no means inevitably non-inclusive.

The common thread running through both studies is the way in which teachers who are required to work within the framework of categorical constructions are nonetheless capable of moving beyond those constructions and of developing new responses in a 'spirit of transformability'. An example may serve to illustrate this point. Dyson and Gallannaugh (2007) report how a primary school participating in the *Understanding and Developing Inclusive Practices* project faced a situation in which many of its pupils appeared unable to make adequate progress in writing using the strategies that were favoured by the then National Literacy Strategy. Faced with this situation, and with considerable external pressure to raise attainment, the school could have opted simply to intensify its existing approaches. Instead, it sought to understand why its pupils were not responding, and came to the conclusion that they lacked the life and language experience they needed to profit from established approaches. Instead, therefore, of intensifying its teaching of reading, the school opted to embark on an experiential approach in which children participated in activities designed to extend their experience, in which they were then encouraged to talk about those experiences and in which only then, if at all, were they expected to write.

The point here is not that the school had discovered some significant new way of teaching writing; the proposition that children learn by talking about their experiences is hardly new in primary practice (see, for instance, Tough 1977). Nor is it that the school had somehow escaped categorical and deficit-oriented thinking; as the researchers make clear, this was far from the case. However, the school was able to problematise the categorical and deficit-oriented thinking informing national policy by confronting its own experience of working with children to whom what was on offer did not readily apply. In this sense, the school entered into a 'negotiation' about how the characteristics of its pupils were to be understood, and about what responses were called for by those characteristics.

Some implications for policy

These studies open up interesting possibilities for the way policy responses to diversity in primary education might go in future. Currently, we suggest, policy is caught in something of a trap. Despite the occasional rhetoric about devolving decision-making, national policy-makers continue to believe that improvements in the system can be driven from the centre – the continual re-making of the Primary National Strategy being a case in point. In terms of responses to diversity, this assumption drives the categorisation of the primary population in ways that appear to be actionable from the centre. That categorisation in turn constructs the population in ways that tend to legitimate centrally-driven initiatives.

Any change in this situation, we believe, requires recognition that inclusive and equitable responses to diversity necessarily involve teachers working within their professional and institutional contexts to make sense of the complex situations they face. This in turn implies that the role of central policy is not to generate fixed categorisations and responses to those categorisations, but to support and facilitate responses that can be made at school and classroom level.

Whilst this may sound like a radical change of direction, we do not have in mind a return to a pre-1988 situation where schools and teachers had largely unlimited freedom – and very little by way of robust guidance – to respond to their diverse populations as they saw fit. Rather, we envisage something more like a dialogue between the broad generalisations, the overarching aims and the large-scale resources that national policy can bring to bear on the one hand, and the knowledge of detailed interactions that teachers can bring to the table. Whatever the limitations of national policy in recent years may have been, it has at least acknowledged difference as an issue and has tried to formulate responses that, for all their limitations, have aimed at least some version of equity and inclusion. With this in mind, national policy even now is able to act as a resource in providing teachers with conceptual tools, problematising their existing responses, and offering material resources and guidance frameworks within which their practices can be developed (Ainscow, Booth and Dyson 2006: 30ff.). Needless to say, the more policy pursued inclusive and equitable ends, the more productive it would be in this respect.

Beyond this, policy has much to do in building the capacity of schools and teachers to respond to diversity. Much of that capacity building depends on work done and led at school level. There is, therefore, an issue about the development of, and support structures for, school leaders who are concerned with diversity and know how to develop their schools in this respect. This may, of course, be a quite different task from developing school leaders who are able to implement national imperatives with maximum efficiency and fidelity. However, capacity building also depends on creating structures so that teachers have access to what practice actually looks like when it is being done differently, and exposure to someone who can help them to understand the difference between what they are doing and what they aspire to do (Elmore, Peterson and McCarthy 1996). It involves conceptualising teacher development in terms other than simply learning how to implement centrally mandated practices. In particular, it involves finding processes whereby teachers can be enabled to think through their shared experiences so that they can help one another to articulate what they currently do and define what they might like to do (Hiebert, Gallimore, and Stigler 2002). This means creating 'spaces' in schools and in the national agendas within which taken-for-granted assumptions about particular groups of learners can be subjected to mutual critique (Dyson *et al.* 2003).

SOME CONCLUSIONS

Characterising the diversity of the primary school population is far from the straight-forward task it may appear. It raises questions about what aspects of diversity are attended to, how those aspects are understood, and what educational responses they are seen as requiring. It cannot be divorced from questions about why the population is being characterised in a particular way – and these in turn lead to questions about how the purposes of education are understood. Finally, it raises questions about who is doing the characterising and the power that some constructions of diversity have to shape policy and practice.

In this survey, we have attempted our own characterisations – of the constructions informing official statistics and policy texts, of the critiques of and alternatives to those constructions proposed by critical researchers, and of the more implicit alternatives emerging in some forms of professional practice. This survey of evidence for our chapter is far from comprehensive. Critical work on dominant discourses is far more extensive and, in some cases, has proceeded at a far more theoretical level than we have attempted to show. Likewise, studies of practice and practitioner thinking go well beyond those we have been able to cite in this paper.

Instead, we have tried to formulate an argument that will have some purchase with researchers, practitioners and policy-makers who are concerned with how primary practice might move on from its current position. So, we have argued that currently dominant constructions conceal as much as they reveal, and mislead as much as they guide. We have argued that they rely on overly rigid forms of categorisation, that they are too simplistically evaluative, and that consequently they overlook both the complexities of and resources within the pupil population. We have argued that more fluid constructions of diversity are possible and that such forms can be found underpinning primary practice in some schools and classrooms. With this in mind we have argued for a reorientation of policy, from the generation of categories and categorical responses to providing a supportive framework for schools and teachers as they attempt to make sense of diversity in their own contexts.

Looking back at the history of primary practice over the past forty years, it is difficult not to see it in terms of a pendulum swinging first from faith in schools and teachers, to faith in central direction, and now, perhaps, beginning to swing back again. Our argument, however, is not for a return to the *status quo ante*. At the current time we see real potential for a partnership between reoriented national policy, and practitioners who are once again trusted but not simply abandoned to their own devices. Within such a partnership, we suggest, a more productive and equitable set of responses to diversity may well be possible.

NOTES

1 The figures below and elsewhere in this survey are deliberately given as approximations to indicate they should be handled with some caution. Amongst other issues, the figures reported in national statistics change year on year, some of the categories are rather crude, and different figures relate to slightly different populations. Readers are therefore advised to treat our figures as indicative and to refer to the original sources for a more detailed presentation.

REFERENCES

Ainscow, M., Booth, T. and Dyson, A. (2004) 'Understanding and developing inclusive practices in schools: a collaborative action research network', *International Journal of Inclusive Education* 8(2): 125–40.

Ainscow, M., Booth, T., Dyson, A., with Farrell, P., Frankham, J., Gallannaugh, F., Howes, A. and Smith, R. (2006) *Improving Schools, Developing Inclusion*. London: Routledge.

Ainscow, M., Howes, A.J., Farrell, P. and Frankham, J. (2003) 'Making sense of the development of inclusive practices', *European Journal of Special Needs Education* 18(2): 227–42.

Aitsiselmi, F. (2004) *Linguistic Diversity and the Use of English in the Home Environment: a Bradford case study*. Bradford, Department of Languages and European Studies: University of Bradford.

Alexander, R.J., Rose, A.J. and Woodhead, C. (1992) *Curriculum Organisation and Classroom Practice in Primary Schools: a discussion paper*. London: DES.

Artiles, A. and Dyson, A. (2005) 'Inclusion, education and culture in developed and developing countries', in D. Mitchell (Ed) *Contextualising Inclusive Education: evaluating old and new international perspectives*. London: Routledge.

Baez, B. (2004) 'The study of diversity: the 'knowledge of difference' and the limits of science', *The Journal of Higher Education* 75(3): 285–306.

Ball, S.J. (2003) 'The teacher's soul and the terrors of performativity', *Journal of Education Policy* 18(2): 215–28.

Balls, E. (2007) *The Every Child Matters Department: speech by Ed Balls, Secretary of State for Children, Schools and Families*. London: DCSF. Online.

Benjamin, S., Nind, M., Hall, K., Collins, J. and Sheehy, K. (2003) 'Moments of inclusion and exclusion: pupils negotiating classroom contexts', *British Journal of Sociology of Education* 24: 547–58.

Booth, T. and Ainscow, M. (2002) *Index for Inclusion: developing learning and participation in schools*. Bristol: Centre for Studies on Inclusive Education.

Bourne, J. (2001) 'Doing "what comes naturally": how the discourses and routines of teachers' practice constrain opportunities for bilingual support in UK primary schools', *Language and Education* 15(4): 250–68.

Bourne, J. and Moon, B. (1995) 'A question of ability?', in B. Moon and A. Shelton Mayes (Eds) *Teaching and Learning in the Secondary School*. London: Routledge.

Broadfoot, P. (2001) 'Empowerment or performativity? Assessment policy in the late twentieth century', in R. Phillips and J. Furlong (Eds) *Education, Reform and the State: twenty-five years of politics, policy and practice*. London: RoutledgeFalmer.

Buckler, S. (2006) *Final Report – Equality and Diversity in DfES Statistical Data*. Online. (Available: http://www.dfes.gov.uk/rsgateway/DB/STA/t000719/NSSQR_Final_report0705.pdf, accessed 1 August 2007).

Cassen, R. and Kingdon, G. (2007) *Tackling Low Educational Achievement*. York: Joseph Rowntree Foundation.

Central Advisory Council for Education (CACE) (England) (1967) *Children and Their Primary Schools: a report of the Central Advisory Council for Education (England)* (the Plowden Report). London: HMSO.

Conteh, J. (2006) 'Widening the inclusion agenda: policy, practice and language diversity in the primary curriculum', in R. Webb (Ed) *Changing Teaching and Learning in the Primary School*. Buckingham: Open University Press.

——(2007a) 'Bilingualism in mainstream primary classrooms in England', in Z. Hua, P. Seedhouse, L. Wei and V. Cook (Eds) *Language Learning and Teaching as Social Interaction*. London: Palgrave Macmillan.

——(2007b) 'Opening doors to success in multilingual classrooms: bilingualism, codeswitching and the professional identities of "ethnic minority" primary teachers', *Language and Education* 21(6): 457–72.

Conteh, J., Helavaara Robertson, L. and Martin, P. (2007) *Multilingual Learning Stories in Schools and Communities in Britain*. Stoke-on-Trent: Trentham Books.

Cummins, J. (2001) *Negotiating Identities: education for empowerment in a diverse society* (2nd edition). Ontario, CA: California Association for Bilingual Education.

Datta, M. (Ed) (2001) *Bilinguality and Literacy*. London: Continuum.

Day, C., Kington, A., Stobart, G. and Sammons, P. (2006) 'The personal and professional selves of teachers: stable and unstable identities', *British Educational Research Journal* 32(4): 601–16.

Department of Education and Science (DES) (1985) *Education for All – The Report of the Committee of Inquiry into the Education of Children from Ethnic Minority Groups* (the Swann Report). London: HMSO.

Department for Education and Employment (DFEE) and Qualifications and Curriculum Authority (QCA) (1999) 'Inclusion: providing effective learning opportunities for all pupils', in *The National Curriculum: handbook for primary/secondary teachers in England*. London: DfEE and QCA.

Department for Education and Skills (DfES) (2003) *Every Child Matters. Cm. 5860*. London: The Stationery Office.

DfES (2004a) *Removing Barriers to Achievement: the government's strategy for SEN*. London: DfES.

——(2004b) 'Statistics of Education: Schools in England', London: The Stationery Office.

——(2005) *Ethnicity and Education: the evidence on minority ethnic pupils. Research topic paper RTP01–05*. London: DfES.

——(2006a) *Ethnicity and Education: the evidence on minority ethnic pupils aged 5–16*. London: DfES.

——(2006b) *Excellence and enjoyment: learning and teaching for bilingual children in the primary years*. London: DfES.

——(2006c) *National Curriculum Assessment, GCSE and Equivalent Attainment and Post-16 Attainment by Pupil Characteristics, in England 2005*. London: DfES.

——(2006d) *Pupil Language Data: guidance for Local Authorities on schools' collection and recording of data on pupils' languages (in compliance with the Data Protection Act)*. London: DfES. Online.

——(2006e) *Schools and Pupils in England, January 2006 (Final)*. London: DfES.

——(2006f) *Special Educational Needs in England, January 2006. SFR 23/2006*. London: DfES.).

——(2007) *Every Parent Matters*. London: DfES.

Dyson, A. (2007) 'Department for Education and Skills', in C. Talbot and M. Baker (Eds) *The Alternative Comprehensive Spending Review*. Manchester: University of Manchester.

Dyson, A. and Gallannaugh, F. (2007) 'National policy and the development of inclusive school practices: a case study', *Cambridge Journal of Education* 37(4): 473–88.

Dyson, A., Gallannaugh, F. and Millward, A. (2003) 'Making space in the standards agenda: developing inclusive practices in schools', *European Educational Research Journal* 2(2): 228–44.

Elmore, P.L., Peterson, P.L. and McCarthy, S.J. (1996) *Restructuring in the Classroom: teaching, learning and school organisation*. San Francisco, CA: Jossey-Bass.

Gorard, S. (2000) 'Questioning the crisis account: a review of the evidence for increasing polarisation in schools', *Educational Research* 42(3): 309–21.

Gregory, E., Long, S. and Volk, D. (Eds) (2004) *Many Pathways to Literacy: young children learning with siblings, grandparents, peers and communities*. London: RoutledgeFalmer.

Harris, R. (2006) *New Ethnicities and Language Use*. Basingstoke: Palgrave Macmillan.

Hart, S. (2003) 'Learning without limits', in M. Nind, K. Sheehy and K. Simmons (Eds) *Inclusive Education: learners and learning contexts*. London: Fulton.

Hart, S., Dixon, A., Drummond, M.J. and McIntyre, D.I. (2004) *Learning without Limits*. Maidenhead: Open University.

Hiebert, J., Gallimore, R. and Stigler, J.W. (2002) 'A knowledge base for the teaching profession: what would it look like and how can we get one?' *Educational Researcher* 31(5): 3–15.

Her Majesty's Inspectorate (HMI) (1990) *The Teaching and Learning of Reading in Primary Schools.* London: DES.

Hobbs, G. and Vignoles, A. (2007) *Is Free School Meal Status a Valid Proxy for Socio-Economic Status (in Schools Research)?* London, Centre for the Economics of Education: London School of Economics.

Johnston, R., Burgess, S., Harris, R. and Wilson, D. (2006) *'Sleep-Walking Towards Segregation?' The changing ethnic composition of English schools, 1997–2003: an entry cohort analysis. Working Paper No. 06/155.* Bristol, Centre for Market and Public Organisation: University of Bristol.

Kenner, C. (2000) 'Biliteracy in a monolingual school system? English and Gujarati in South London', *Language, Culture and Curriculum* 13(1): 13–30.

Leung, C., Harris, R. and Rampton, B. (1997) 'The idealised native speaker, reified ethnicities, and classroom realities', *TESOL Quarterly* 31(3): 543–60.

Martin, P., Creese, A. and Bhatt, A. (2003) *Complementary Schools and their Communities in Leicester. final report for the ESRC for Project No: R000223949.* Online. (Available: http://www.uel.ac.uk/education/staff/finalreport.pdf, accessed 17 August 2007).

Martin-Jones, M. and Saxena, M. (1995) 'Supporting or containing bilingualism? Policies, power asymmetries and pedagogic practices in mainstream primary schools', in J. Tollefson (Ed) *Power and Inequality in Language Education.* Cambridge: Cambridge University Press.

——(1996) 'Turn-taking, power asymmetries, and the positioning of bilingual participants in classroom discourse', *Linguistics and Education* 8(1): 105–23.

——(2003) 'Bilingual resources and "funds of knowledge" for teaching and learning in multi-ethnic classrooms in Britain', *International Journal of Bilingual Education and Bilingualism* 6 (3&4): 267–81.

Nias, J. (1989) *Primary Teachers Talking: a study of teaching as work.* London: Routledge.

Ofsted (1996) *The Teaching of Reading in 45 Inner London Primary Schools.* London: Ofsted.

——(1999) *A Review of Primary Schools in England, 1994–1998.* London: The Stationery Office.

——(2000) *Evaluating Educational Inclusion.* London: Ofsted.

Rampton, B. (2005a) *Language in Late Modernity: interaction in an urban school.* Cambridge: Cambridge University Press.

——(2005b) *Crossing: language and ethnicity among adolescents* (2nd edition). Manchester: St Jerome Press.

Raveaud, M. (2005) 'Hares, tortoises and the social construction of the pupil: differentiated learning in French and English primary schools', *British Educational Research Journal* 31(4): 459–479.

Robertson, L.H. (2007) 'The story of bilingual children learning to read', in J. Conteh, P. Martin and L.H. Robertson (Eds) *Multilingual Learning Stories in Schools and Communities in Britain.* Stoke-on-Trent: Trentham Books.

Street, B.V. (1984) *Literacy in Theory and Practice.* Cambridge: Cambridge University Press.

TDA (2008) *Professional Standards for Qualified Teacher Status and Requirements for Initial Teacher Training.* Online (Available: http://www.tda.gov.uk/partners/ittstandards.aspx).

Teaching and Learning in 2020 Review Group (2006) *2020 Vision: report of the Teaching and Learning in 2020 Review Group.* London: DfES.

Tikly, L., Osler, A., Hill, J. and Vincent, K., with Andrews, P., Jeffreys, J., Ibrahim, T., Panel, C. and Smith, M. (2002) *Ethnic Minority Achievement Grant: analysis of LEA action plans. Research Report 371.* London: DfES.

Tough, J. (1977) *Talking and Learning.* London: Ward Lock Educational.

Wenger, E. (1998) *Communities of Practice: learning, meaning and identity.* Cambridge: Cambridge University Press.

Woods, P. and Jeffrey, B. (2002) 'The reconstruction of primary teachers' identities', *British Journal of Sociology of Education* 23(1): 89–106.

9 Learning needs and difficulties among children of primary school age

Definition, identification, provision and issues

Harry Daniels and Jill Porter

INTRODUCTION

This chapter is concerned with learning needs and difficulties among children of primary school age. This is an aspect of provision and policy where research is extensive and methodologically diverse. In a recent review, Dockrell, Peacey and Lunt (2002) outline the difficulties that are revealed in a close examination of the literature concerning attempts to meet the needs of children with special educational needs (henceforth SEN). They argue that intervention studies are limited in that they usually only consider one model of treatment, often without appropriate controls. They also suggest that: there is 'little focus on the reliability and validity of assessment measures used both in qualitative and quantitative research' (p. 2); that there has been very little research which has looked for features of schools which are both 'effective' and 'inclusive' (p. 38); that studies often involve small samples and there are few population-based perspectives on diversity and needs (p. 1); and that there are very few longitudinal studies that consider change over time (p. 1). Similar reservations were noted by the Evidence for Policy and Planning Information (EPPI) systematic review group which maintained a particular focus on pedagogical approaches and found only 68 out of 2095 reports that met its criteria (Nind *et al.* 2004) This finding acts as a note of caution with regard to the limitations of reviews such as the one we present here. Importantly, Davis and Florian (2004a) also note that reviews inevitably carry with them a cultural and historical specificity which renders them an important but incomplete part of any evidence base. They refer to the EPPI review conducted by Dyson, Howes and Roberts (2002), in which the authors acknowledge the constraints of rigid criteria for inclusion in a review.

With these cautions in mind, our intention is to provide an overview of trends that are seen to be emerging in policy and practice in English primary schools on the basis of a broadly based engagement with an extensive literature, which ranges from practitioner research to quasi-experimental designs. We have focused on the contested areas of how best to ensure equality of opportunity between those with special educational needs and those without, within a context of the changing agendas set by the *Every Child Matters* framework (DfES 2003b). In this chapter we have drawn on research concerning children for whom schools are seeking specialist support, as indicated by the reference to the stage of the SEN Code of Practice *School Action Plus* (DfES 2001a), as well as those whose learning needs have been formally recognised as requiring additional resources through the statementing procedure.

REGULATION OF THE FIELD: LEGISLATION, POLICY AND PRACTICE

The development of policy and practice in the field of special educational needs education has a long and convoluted history, and has often been (and remains) highly contested. The field has witnessed political struggles between single interest lobby groups, practitioners and their professional associations, economists and administrators, amongst others. The recent history of the legislation and official guidance bears testament to the continuing complexity of the field. Although by no means the starting point for the debate, the Warnock Report (DES 1978) is often taken as the moment at which the question of the location of provision for pupils with SEN was brought to the attention of a wide constituency of policy makers and practitioners. The international equivalent is the somewhat later Salamanca Statement (UNESCO 1994). The general move has been from policies and practices of segregation in special provision, through a phase where debates were concerned with the integration of individual children into existing systems, and on to the consideration of ways in which systemic responsiveness to a broad diversity of needs could be built in the name of inclusion. In English schools the *number* of pupils with statements[1] in maintained mainstream schools increased by over 95,000 from 1991 to 2000 (90 per cent of the total increase in pupils with statements). However, the number of pupils with statements in special schools stayed relatively constant. By 2000 the *proportion* of pupils with statements educated in special schools had fallen considerably, to around one third in 2000 from around a half in 1991. Both the actual numbers and proportions have since remained broadly constant in mainstream and special schools (House of Commons Education and Skills Committee 2006: 88).

By the time data were issued in January 2008 some 223,600 (or 2.8 per cent of) pupils across all schools in England had statements of SEN, a slight fall when compared to 2006. The percentage of pupils with statements of SEN placed in maintained mainstream schools (nursery, primary, and secondary) was 56.6 per cent – down 2.1 per cent from the previous year. The 2008 data also show a gradually increasing proportion of children with *new* statements of SEN being educated in special schools, and a decrease in the percentage of children with new statements in mainstream including a slight decrease in those in resourced provision (DCFS 2008). Although these changes might not be great they do appear counter to policy initiatives. In the 2008 data there were an additional 1,390,700 pupils with SEN but without statements, a growing number that now represents 17.2 per cent of pupils across all schools. Taking these two groups of pupils with SEN together they now constitute 22.4 per cent of the school population.

The meanings associated with the terms 'segregation', 'integration', and 'inclusion' have witnessed considerable variation over time, culture and context. The Organisation for Economic Co-operation and Development (OECD) (2000) has provided startling empirical evidence of variation in interpretation in rates of incidence, even across normative categories of sensory impairment. The field is marked by a profusion of documents that can easily confuse a lay reader or busy practitioner with regard to what is legally enforceable and what is either recommended or advisable. Parliamentary Acts introduce enforceable law. Sections of these are then articulated by enforceable regulations. However, the widely cited 2001 Code of Practice provides guidance. Local policy makers and practitioners must 'have regard to the provisions of the Code'. The latest version of this Code (DfES 2001a) came into effect in England in 2002, having replaced the original guidance (DfEE 1994). One clear change was with respect to the advice it provided on the Special Educational Needs and Disability Act (SENDA) 2001, which became legally enforceable at the same time that this new Code was published. SENDA brought the full force of anti-discrimination legislation to bear on education, which had been specifically exempt from such scrutiny in the past. Statutory guidance was issued in *Inclusive Schooling: children with special educational needs* (DfES 2001b) alongside the non-statutory guidance available in the *SEN Toolkit* (DfES 2001c).

There is, however, considerable scepticism from both official and academic perspectives about the effectiveness and efficiency of much of this guidance (Farrell 2001). In 1992 the Audit Commission noted a lack of consistency in the degree of need presented by a child who is taken to merit a statement, and the absence of a consistent threshold at which the LA takes over responsibility for the child's education. Both these factors create a number of difficulties, particularly for parents who move from one LA to another (Audit Commission/HMI 1992: note 23). Arguably this account witnesses the effects of a social circumstance which persists today. An extensive body of enforceable legislation and statutory and non-statutory guidance creates a complex set of requirements and suggestions, which allow for a considerable degree of local, highly situated interpretation (House of Commons Education and Skills Committee 2006; Ofsted 2004; Audit Commission Report 2002).

These interpretations often appear to arise as 'trade offs' made between contesting policy agendas, as witnessed in attempts to improve standards as well as to advance the development of inclusive practice. As Ainscow, Booth and Dyson note in their recent ESRC-funded policy analysis:

> From the ground-breaking work of Fulcher (1989) onwards, there has been a powerful tradition in the inclusion literature of scepticism about the capacity of policy to create inclusive systems, either because the policy itself is ambiguous and contradictory, or because it is 'captured' by non-inclusive interests as it interacts with the system as a whole.
>
> (Ainscow, Booth and Dyson 2006: 305)

Armstrong (2005) is also critical of New Labour policy, suggesting that interventions with technicist orientations have failed in their own terms to meet narrow performance criteria. He argues that the prevention of social exclusion requires a much broader view of risk and resilience than is embedded in policy. There is some empirical support for this argument. Wilkin *et al.* (2005) noted that school exclusion statistics for 2002–3 show that children with statements of their SEN were nine times more likely to be excluded than children without statements. Jacklin *et al.* (2006), with respect to children in public care, and the Audit Commission (2007), with respect to out of county placements, suggest the consequences: primary school children who embark on a marginal career involving multiple fixed term exclusions, and for whom home life is a significant challenge, face uncertain prospects in the provision that is made by the state for those who 'fall out' of systems.

This scepticism about the policy environment has been followed by concern about the practices that have arisen during this period. Mary Warnock (2005) herself has recently argued that the policy of inclusion and the associated practice of issuing statements need to be reviewed. The recently convened Select Committee noted significant concerns about the demands and tensions that had arisen in the field:

> The Warnock SEN framework is struggling to remain fit for purpose, and where significant cracks are developing in the system – most starkly demonstrated by the failure of the system to cope with the rising number of children with autism and social, emotional or behavioural difficulties (SEBD) – this is causing high levels of frustration to parents, children, teachers and local authorities.
>
> (House of Commons Education and Skills Committee 2006: 104)

In a controversial report funded by the National Union of Teachers (NUT), MacBeath *et al.* (2006) interviewed teachers, children and parents at 20 schools in seven local authorities and concluded that current practice placed far too many demands on teachers and schools. They make particular reference to the need for schools to work together in order to meet the diversity of needs that may be present in any particular community:

> Inclusion should not rely on individual schools struggling to contain children with special needs but should be conceived as a collaborative effort, sharing resources in a spirit of mutual support. Special schools should have a significant role to play as an expert resource for mainstream schools while they in turn have a supporting role to play in partnership with special schools.
>
> (MacBeath *et al.* 2006: 65)

In many ways MacBeath *et al.* echo the assertions made in the DfES report *Removing the Barriers to Achievement* (DfES 2004a), that integration with external children's services, earlier intervention, better teacher training and improved expectations would reduce educational difficulty (DFES 2004a: 133).

However, the House of Commons Education and Skills Committee (2006) suggest that the notion of 'flexible continuum of provision' being available in all local authorities to meet the needs of all children is not embedded in much of the guidance (p. 27). This suggestion is evidenced in the Croll and Moses (2000) study, which drew on interviews with special and mainstream head teachers and education officers to show that there was much support for inclusion as an ideal – but this was not evidenced in policy. They found evidence of significant concerns about feasibility, depending on the extent and severity of individual needs and structural constraints on the practices of mainstream schooling.

Prevalence of statementing

In the context of almost thirty years of legislation and government guidance, it is perhaps surprising that the level of statementing in primary schools is remarkably static with 1.6 per cent of pupils attracting additional resources. At one level this suggests that schools are, in general, fairly resistant to providing for larger numbers of pupils with SEN. This figure masks the variation between local authorities, with figures for 2008 data indicating a range of 0.3 per cent to 4.0 per cent (DCSF 2008). It is likely, given our discussion below, that this reflects not only differences in policies between authorities but also differences between the populations they serve.

Which children are most likely to receive a statement? Figures from the 2008 data release indicate that the most prevalent type of SEN continues to be 'Speech, Language and Communication Needs' (SLCN) (DCSF 2008), a group that challenge teachers to provide access to the curriculum but who typically also require input in the form of speech and language therapy (Lindsay *et al.* 2005). Statementing is therefore important for access to health resources and advice as teachers feel particularly unsupported to meet the needs of this group, and few authorities (less than 1 in 10) have dedicated specialist resources. The second largest group amongst those statemented in primary schools are children with autism, who constitute 19.7 per cent of statemented children; a higher proportion than children with moderate learning difficulties, or those with social, emotional and behavioural difficulties (SEBD). While the overall prevalence of moderate learning difficulties is higher, fewer children identified in this way will be statemented. Again it is important to recognise that there will be differences between regions; Scott *et al.* (2002) speculate that differences with respect to autism are likely to reflect levels of professional awareness, funding requirements, family migration as well as environmental factors. In addition, we might question whether it also reflects differences in the need for non-educational advice and support, the confidence and attitudes of teachers, along with an increased focus on whole class teaching.

Children with statements, however, constitute a relatively small proportion of children for whom teachers have concerns. Some authorities have as many as a further 30 per cent of children who have special needs but no statement, with an average across authorities of 17.8 per cent. In contrast to figures on statements, the proportion of children with SEN but no statements has steadily increased and is higher in primary schools than secondary. This group is particularly vulnerable when it comes to school admissions (Wilkin *et al.* 2005) as schools may recognise their legal obligation to accept pupils with statements but argue a lack of resources for those without. The largest group on School Action Plus are those with moderate learning difficulties, with similar proportions of children with SEBD as with Speech, Language and Communication Difficulties, and remarkably few (given the statementing level) of children with autistic spectrum disorder (ASD).

Research by Harris (2007) also sheds some light on the proportions of children identified, with the implication that we need to be cautious about the reliability of categories in school returns. Data from his local authority revealed inconsistencies and misinterpretations, including schools recording SLD (severe learning difficulties) for the children with the greatest cognitive difficulty rather than SpLD (specific learning difficulties); a further confusion in the distinction between this descriptor and that of MLD (moderate learning difficulties) and the assignment of undiagnosed (unstatemented) children with autism to the category of SLCN (speech, language and communication needs). A further factor appeared to be the availability of specialist help that conditioned which of the presenting difficulties were highlighted. The issue of linking assessment to funding of provision has been of particular concern (House of Commons education and Skills committee 2006) and not improved by LA devolvement of funding to schools that has led to a limiting of the provision of specialist support and advisory services (Wedell 2007).

On the basis of visits to 115 schools, Ofsted (2004) concluded that just as many school age children and young people were being educated outside the mainstream in 2003 as there were in 1999. This report also found that most schools had not taken appropriate steps to ensure that disabled pupils and pupils with SEN were included effectively in mainstream classes. In an IPPR discussion paper, Peacey (2005) notes the faltering progress towards inclusion and cites specific difficulties that have been understood for some time yet continue to cause problems. Examples include unrecognised language and communication difficulties (Redmond and Rice 1998); classroom acoustics (Shield and Dockrell 2004; Shields, Dockrell, Jeffrey and Tachmatzidis 2002); unfounded assumptions about the learning implications of specific impairments (Nunes and Moreno 1997); the quality of teacher talk and understanding (Dockrell and Lindsay 2001); and instructional planning / curriculum design for groups of children with diverse and often fluctuating needs (Dockrell and Lindsay 2001; Scruggs and Mastropeiri 1996; Wishart and Manning 1996).

Attitudes

There is a clear trend in a number of small-scale surveys and overviews towards an acceptance that the attitudes of teachers, parents and pupils are crucial in the development of inclusive practice (for example Rose 2001; Sebba and Sachdev 1997; Zigmond and Baker 1995). The SEN Review Group of Nind *et al.* (2004) found empirical support for inclusion in that it brought about changes in children's attitudes, including improved attitudes toward reading and writing and their own views of their competence, acceptance and self-worth in mainstream settings (p. 71).

The expectations and attitudes of all those involved when a child with special needs is placed in a mainstream classroom appear to be crucial. MacBeath *et al.* (2006) note the pressures that can arise, and suggest the need for adequate preparation, training and support. Talmor, Reiter and Feigin (2005) surveyed 330 Israeli primary school teachers and found that, contrary to the hypothesis of the research, the more positive attitudes to inclusion were associated with teacher 'burnout'. Additionally, the likelihood of burnout was influenced by the amount of social support the teacher received. Dolton and Newson (2003) surveyed 316 London primary schools and found an association between teacher turnover and pupil progress: the slower the pupil progress the higher the rate of turnover. On the basis of in-depth qualitative data collected from primary and secondary school teachers, pupils and parents, Mujherjee, Lightfoot, and Sloper (2000) note the strongly-felt need for more support when pupils with chronic health conditions are placed in mainstream schools.

DISCRIMINATION AND BIAS

An important question to be asked of primary schools in the light of the Disability Discrimination Act 2005 concerns equality of opportunity. All primary schools were required to have a Disability Equality Scheme in place by December 2007. Schools are expected to set out their plans for actively promoting disability equality, and for monitoring the impact of their actions on disabled pupils. Equally all authorities and other public bodies, including the DCSF and Ofsted, have a statutory duty to look more closely at children with special educational needs as well as those with a disability but no special educational needs. Recognition of procedures that lead to bias with respect to gender, ethnicity and poverty form an important part of this. Below we look in more detail at research that explores these issues.

The pervasiveness of gender bias is explored by Sacker *et al.* (2001), both with respect to identifying children with SEN and also in the provision of support. Their analysis of historical data is reflected in current figures which continue to confirm the higher incidence of boys than girls, both with and without statements, and with schools recognising difficulties earlier in boys than girls (DfES 2006a). Sacker *et al.* (2001) also report on biases with respect to class, revealing that – although more children from manual working class homes were receiving help in school – when scores in reading, mathematics and social adjustment were taken into account, children from professional homes were more likely to be receiving help than those from manual working class homes. They argue with respect to this secondary analysis of data from two cohort studies of children in 1969 and 1980 that schools in areas of deprivation are not given sufficient resources to meet their children's needs.

Croll (2002), analysing more recently collected data aggregated at school level, draws similar conclusions with respect to both bias and funding. He finds a moderately strong correlation between the level of poverty (as measured by free school meals) and levels of SEN in a school, and an even stronger correlation with achievement. He also finds a difference between children described as having learning difficulties, with those in the least deprived schools being on average one year behind their peers in reading compared to those in the most deprived being on average two to three years behind. Mittler (1999) and Riddell *et al.* (1994) have both noted the domination in provision for children of the most powerful and articulate parents who are supported by strong lobby groups and who, arguably, over-represent the case for children with dyslexia and autism compared to those of children with moderate learning difficulties. There is, therefore, a question over whether current funding arrangements for resource allocations perpetuate inequalities within the system. As Croll states:

> […] if resource allocation for special needs is to be based on audits at the level of such needs in schools, an audit based on schools' own characterization of their pupils will not fairly represent the distribution of such needs.
>
> (Croll 2002: 52)

His research makes a strong case for funding on the basis of social deprivation.

Turning now to look at the over-representation of other groups, Lindsay *et al.* (2005) found that, even after controlling for the effects of socio-economic disadvantage together with gender and year group, children from some ethnic groups were more likely to be identified as having SEN, particularly with respect to certain types of need. The small group of children with Irish Heritage are 2.6 times more likely to be identified than White British pupils and are more likely to have learning difficulties (specific, moderate and severe) and SEBD, but less likely to be identified with respect to ASD. While Black Caribbean pupils have a similar rate of identification, they are 1.5 times more likely to be identified as having SEBD. Sensory impairment is higher amongst Pakistani and Bangladeshi pupils, while pupils of Chinese origin have the lowest occurrence of identified SEN. Explanations for differences between groups are not simple and again there is considerable variation between LAs:

> 'an interaction between a number of inter-related and often self-perpetuating factors […] including: teachers' perceptions and expectations of ethnic minority pupils, their understanding of different cultures, pupils' responses and reactions to this, and teachers' reactions to behaviours they consider challenging.
>
> (Lindsay *et al.* 2005: 9)

It is perhaps unsurprising that research suggests no single or simple solution to raising achievement, but rather a package of measures designed to impact on ethos, curriculum organisation, teaching approaches and collaboration with parents and the wider community – all more general characteristics of effective schools (Lindsay and Muijs 2006).

SUPPORT

The SENCO[2] has long been seen as the school-based mainstay of support for teachers. This is recognised by the House of Commons Education and Skills Committee (2006), which proposes a number of conditions for effective SENCO functioning including training in order to support the work of their colleagues. Yet, as a number of studies have shown, this key role in the development of inclusive practice is highly pressurised and complex (Mackenzie 2007; Pearson and Ralph 2007; Szwed 2007) and new recruits are singularly under-prepared (Pearson 2008). Crowther *et al.* (2001) warn of the dilemma that exists for SENCOs as they seek to manage limited time resources between slavish compliance to external accountability demands and proactive support for classroom practice. On the basis of the responses of SENCOs in primary schools to a survey undertaken in three local education authorities in the north-east of England, Crowther, Dyson and Millward (2001) advocate the development of a more proactive role but despair at the 'lack of prospect of legislation or guidance creating the circumstances in which their anticipated role can be realized'. They outline a number of key elements in the transformation to a more proactive role, from a specific example in which a SENCO became:

- Instrumental in articulating a clear and forceful values position for the school, based on a commitment to inclusion and entitlement. As part of this, the language of special education was reconstructed to emphasize success, potential and achievement, rather than the traditional notions of failure, limited ability and underachievement.
- Focused on a role that stressed review and development of the processes of teaching and learning, rather than support for individual pupils. This involved using the 'resources' of special education in a direct way to develop pedagogy, rather than to spread them ever more thinly across increasing numbers of pupils experiencing difficulties.

(Crowther, Dyson, and Millward 2001: 96)

Four years later, Ellis and Tod (2005) argued that the recent initiatives on behaviour and attendance – for example the National Strategy's 'Behaviour and Attendance' strand (DfES 2003a, 2004b), and the 'Behaviour and Attendance' pilot materials from the Primary National Strategy (DfES 2003a, 2003c, 2003d and 2003e) provide an opportunity for SENCOs to move to adopt such a proactive position and take up a position which is oriented to added value rather than compensation. Cowne (2005) has also noted the need for time, school management and LA support for the development of the work of SENCOs. Webb and Vulliamy (2002) report the findings of the Social Work in Primary Schools (SWIPS) project, which involved qualitative research in 15 schools and a national questionnaire survey, and conclude that primary schools' growing social work responsibilities should be acknowledged by policy makers and resourced adequately, in part through the freeing of SENCO time from teaching responsibilities. As Dyson *et al.* (2004) concluded from their DfES-funded study of inclusion and pupil achievement:

Highly-inclusive and high-performing schools adopt a model of provision based on flexibility of grouping, customisation of provision to individual circumstances and careful individual monitoring, alongside population wide strategies for raising attainment.

(Dyson *et al.* 2004: 1)

They attribute this approach to a school level commitment, which in their earlier work they suggest can be promoted by SENCOs. In turn, this form of practice is commensurate with forms of distributed leadership that have been advocated elsewhere in the development of inclusive schools (Mayrowetz and Weinstein 1999).

Support from outside the school and interaction between specialist and mainstream provision has also been shown to be important for the prevention of exclusion from both primary and secondary schools. Hallam and Castle (2001) provide evidence that Multi-Disciplinary Behaviour Support Teams (MDBSTs), secondment of mainstream teachers to Pupil Referral Units, and In-School Centres (ISCs) all help to prevent exclusion. Davis and Hopwood (2002) have shown how the provision of additional support can lead to inclusive practice, and that this is most likely to occur when specialist and mainstream staff work in partnership to share their knowledge and diversify their roles.

Dyson and Ainscow (2003) have shown that the local context also influences the way teaching strategies are interpreted, adapted and implemented. Their experience is that evidence from research can be useful in stimulating teachers to reflect upon existing practices and to experiment with new approaches. Florian and Rouse (2001) also found school structures to have an important influence. Their study investigated teacher *knowledge and use* of the strategies thought to promote inclusive practice. They found that, contrary to the literature which suggests that teachers lack knowledge about inclusive practices, they were actually quite knowledgeable, but that *knowing* and *doing* were very different things.

Approaches to teaching

A number of recent reviews of the literature have questioned the assumption, inherent in the definition of 'Special Educational Needs', that some groups of children require a specialised approach to teaching. One of the impediments to such reviews is the paucity of research studies, both with respect to design (as noted in our introduction) and to coverage. Dockrell, Peacey and Lunt (2002) highlight in particular the small sample size of many studies and the lack of longitudinal studies. Davis and Florian (2004b), in a scoping study for the DfES entitled *Teaching Strategies and Approaches for Pupils with Special Educational Needs*, find that although certain teaching approaches are associated with specific categories of SEN they are not sufficiently differentiated from those which are used to teach all children. They acknowledge the importance of the work of Norwich and Lewis (Lewis and Norwich 2001; Norwich and Lewis 2001) on SEN pedagogy. The Lewis and Norwich analysis suggests that effective practice is 'not distinctively different teaching but [includes] more practice, more examples, more experience of transfer, and more careful assessment than their peers' (Norwich and Lewis 2001: 326).

A more extensive review followed (Lewis and Norwich 2005), underpinned by two key questions, asking firstly if differences between learners could be 'identified AND systematically linked with learners' needs for differential teaching?' They also asked an important second question 'What are the key criteria for identifying pedagogically useful groups?' Each of the contributors to this book cite the difficulty of definitions and the presence of co-occurring difficulties and in consequence heterogeneous groups. For most of the 15 groups there was no indication of need for specialised programmes with the exception of pupils with a sensory or dual-sensory loss. In two further chapters the respective authors argue for specific pedagogy – in relation to ASD (Jordan 2005) and Attention Deficit Hyperactivity Disorder (ADHD) (Cooper 2005), despite the acknowledged heterogeneity of the group. The commonality of notionally specialist strategies is also evident, with variations of strategies used for children with dyslexia, dyspraxia, moderate and severe learning difficulties, also being useful for other children.

Drawing together their review, Lewis and Norwich argue that there is still a value in seeing pedagogic strategies as a continuum with differentiation (or specialisation) being a process of intensification, albeit that strategies at the far end of the continuum may be seen as different in kind and reflect the viewer's stance about learning. The analysis of Lewis and Norwich (2005) also indicates the importance of teachers having relevant knowledge about the nature of the special needs group (particularly in relation to development) which acts as a kind of filter and interacts with knowledge about oneself as a teacher, particularly in relation to value positions; the psychology of learning (for example knowing about self-regulation); and knowledge of curriculum areas and general pedagogic strategies.

Davis and Florian (2004b) draw on Alexander's (2004) suggestion that pedagogy is best thought of in terms of knowledge as well as skill. Their attention is directed towards the ways in which an effective pedagogy may be developed. They conclude their report as follows:

> We found that there is a great deal of literature that might be construed as special education knowledge but that the teaching approaches and strategies themselves were not sufficiently differentiated from those which are used to teach all children to justify the term SEN pedagogy. Our analysis found that sound practices in teaching and learning in mainstream *and* special education literatures were often informed by the same basic research [...] The term special education is often used to refer to the process of making such accommodations [...] this process of making accommodations does not constitute pedagogy but is an element of it. Our view is that questions about a separate special education pedagogy are unhelpful given the current policy context, and that the more important agenda is about how to develop a pedagogy that is inclusive of all learners.
>
> (Davis and Florian 2004b: 33–34)

There is a common root here with the suggestion put forward by Gulliford (1985) more than 20 years ago when he advocated a problem-solving approach to teaching:

> It is easy, therefore, for teachers to be over-impressed by external influences or the latest new fashion and to underestimate the knowledge and understanding they acquire through the close experience of teaching individuals and classes. Much can be gained from the stimulus of other conceptions and the help of other expertise but the heart of the matter is trying to teach a child who is hard to teach – and learning from the experience.
>
> (Gulliford 1985: 32)

A conclusion that there is limited evidence to support the case for specialist pedagogy can refer to the lack of an evidence base as much as to no evidence, or to unsupportive evidence. As with other aspects of provision, the position taken by reviewers is underscored by the values and assumptions they perceive to underpin notions of specialist pedagogy. Despite differing positions of the reviews, one over-arching implication is that there is no simple response that can be made; no single toolkit that can be invoked to solve a particular group of children's difficulties in learning. Elsewhere, Florian and Kershner (2008) argue that teachers need to be able to draw on a combination of teaching strategies with multimodal responses to students whilst recognising the contextual nature of children's learning experiences. Teachers require a good knowledge base to do this.

Collaborative working

This problem-solving approach carries with it significant demands for an individual teacher working in isolation, and yet perhaps the greatest challenge that the move towards an effective form of inclusive education has presented is that of moving to a more collaborative form of practice in which individuals work together within and across professional boundaries. Norwich and Daniels (1997) and Creese *et al.* (1998) have shown that teachers value means by which they can support each other and be supported in their work concerning special needs matters within primary schools.

Effective collaboration between teachers and teaching assistants (TAs) has been cited as a well established and pervasive response to the demands of teaching in diverse classrooms (Lee and Mawson 1998). Despite the lack of clarity in the definition of the TA role (Kerry 2005), their work has been seen to be effective as part of the support for pupils with SEBD in primary schools (Groom and Rose 2005). TAs have developed their role from helper to assistant teacher during the period of rapid expansion of numbers of children with statements that occurred during the 1990s, and numbers of TAs expanded greatly after the publication of the first Code of Practice (Webb and Vulliamy 2006).

On the basis of a survey of 267 Key Stage 1 (KS1) and KS2 teachers, Galton *et al.* (2002) reported that more than half of the teachers received more than five hours help per week from a paid assistant. Smith *et al.* (2004) further suggested that the highest level of such support was to be found in KS1. Webb and Vulliamy (2006) summarise the work of TAs with respect to special needs support. They:

- gave individual pupils one-to-one support
- monitored individual pupils' attitudes, behaviours and approaches to learning
- developed IEPs
- explained tasks
- further differentiated tasks by providing additional resources and support

in order to:

- meet the needs of individual children
- helped pupils to remain on task
- improved pupil motivation and self esteem
- encouraged and reinforced positive behaviour.

All these activities are highly valued by head teachers, although a lingering concern remains about the additional management role that the presence of TAs in classrooms places on classroom teachers (Webb and Vulliamy 2006).

The *Every Child Matters* (ECM) agenda (DfES 2003b) introduces an emphasis on five broad outcome measures (being healthy, staying safe, enjoying and achieving, making a positive contribution to society, and achieving economic well-being). The desired practices of inter-agency working, establishing lead professionals and extended services demands a major effort to bring professionals together across the boundaries which have proved to be particularly resistant to change over the years (Leadbetter *et al.* 2007). Benefits have been shown to arise from collaborative work between Educational Psychologists and teachers (for example Atkinson *et al.* 2006), despite the challenges (for example Norwich and Kelly 2006); between teachers and Child and Adolescent Mental Health service professionals, educational psychologists and schools (for example Maddern *et al.* 2004); and, in general, between special and mainstream services (for example Mittler 2005). Mentors have been shown to add benefit to efforts to respond to children with behaviour problems in primary schools (St James-Roberts and Singh 2001) and collaborative work between a school-based family social work service and schools has been shown, through a broadly-based cost benefit analysis, to lead to a 250 per cent saving on interventions costs (Pritchard and Williams 2001). Given the concerns MacBeath *et al.* (2006) raise about children with mental health difficulties, which remain undiagnosed even in cases of anxiety and depression in very young children, it is important to note that Stallard (2002, 2005) has shown that collaboration with school nurses in schools in the delivery of short-term group administered cognitive behavioural therapy leads to reductions in both anxiety and depression in primary school children. This effective collaboration with the health services is also witnessed in the positive evaluation of parenting programmes as an intervention with conduct disordered children (National Institute for Health and Clinical Excellence, in collaboration with Social Care Institute for Excellence, 2005).

For many years, collaboration with parents has been discussed as a crucial element of education and as being of particular importance for pupils with special needs (for example Cunningham and Davis 1985; Mittler and Mittler 1982; Mittler *et al.* 1986). Croll (2001) reviewed progress over 20 years, and identified clear markers of improvement. Whilst cautions have been raised concerning the lack of an analysis of power in professional and parent partnerships (for example Todd and Higgins 1998; Riddell, Brown and Duffield 1994), Dockrell, Peacey and Lunt (2002) note that a lack of parental knowledge about specialist services may be ameliorated through community based intervention (see also Wesley, Buysse and Tyndall 1997). They also note that parents in relatively inclusive settings are more positive in their orientation to children with disabilities and difficulties than their counterparts in less inclusive settings (Bennett, DeLuca and Bruns 1997; Duhaney and Salend 2000; Guralnick *et al.* 1995), whilst parents of children identified with special needs remain concerned about attitudes of child peers and the quality of support available (Petley 1994; Riddell, Brown and Duffield 1994).

PERSONALISATION AND 'PUPIL VOICE'

Alongside the ECM agenda, the Primary Strategy (DfES 2003b) introduces the notion of personalisation of public services, which is being promoted as the next step in the modernisation of the welfare state (Leadbeater 2004). The proposal is that clients become co-producers of services and take a central part in the design and formulation of the particular service that is made available. Personalisation requires citizens who are capable of participating in dialogues about their needs and desires as well as about their own interpretations of their current situation. Just as Black and Wiliam (1998) argued that teachers and pupils should be prepared for self assessment in schools, so the personalisation agenda brings questions about the ways in which the most vulnerable are to be prepared for participating in dialogues about their futures. Policy has placed an increasing emphasis on the right of all children to have a 'voice' in educational decisions, both with respect to location of provision and, in the later educational years, in negotiating the curriculum. There is a growing body of literature that addresses the ways in which we elicit the voice of children and young people with difficulties in learning (including Lewis and Porter 2007). This has highlighted the dilemmas of providing a communication system or structure that does not constrain the message or infer a misplaced meaning for pupils with special needs (for example Porter *et al.* 2001; Grove *et al.* 2000) or, indeed, for other pupils (Fielding 2004). Participation, however, is more than the simple expression of choice and preferences. The ethos of provision where learners have the security and self-esteem to reflect on their relative strengths and difficulties in a process of self-determination has also been shown to be important (Porter, Robertson and Hayhoe 2001). Wedell (2005) argues that, whilst the continued emphasis on the 'standards agenda' and the assumption that this is best achieved through whole class teaching persists (p.5), it will fail to provide a context in which special educational needs can be effectively addressed.

SPECIAL EDUCATIONAL NEEDS AND EXCLUSION

Clearly the needs of some pupils are not being effectively addressed if we look at who gets excluded. Accurate figures on exclusion are particularly difficult to gather, with schools using a variety of (unofficial) responses including lunchtime exclusions, internal exclusions and offering parents the choice of taking their child out of school (Daniels *et al.* 2003; Pavey and Visser 2003; MacQuire *et al.* 2003; Vulliamy and Webb 2001; Wilkin *et al.* 2005). Taking account of these limitations, which indicate greater or lesser degrees of under-reporting, official figures suggest that children with special needs are more likely to be excluded than children without special needs. DfES figures for 2005/6 suggest they are more than three times more likely to be permanently excluded than the rest of the population (DfES 2007b). This is particularly true of children during the primary school years (Parsons *et al.* 2000), where overall levels of exclusion are generally low. Figures for 2005/6 indicate that both permanent and fixed period exclusions reach a peak at age 10 in the primary school, with the highest rates of permanent exclusion being attributed to disruptive, aggressive or threatening behaviour. It is therefore unsurprising that pupils with behavioural difficulties are most at risk (Wilkin *et al.* 2005), although other groups are also over-represented (including pupils identified with ADHD and ASD). Schools report that they tolerate a higher level of unacceptable behaviour from pupils with SEN and are reluctant to exclude them when there is no available alternative provision (Wilkin *et al.* 2005). Although exclusion may be drawing attention to the need for further assessment and additional support, it not only damages the child's self esteem but also slows the formal process of assessment (Hayden 1997).

Exclusion has been seen to exacerbate problems in circumstances that the child already finds difficult and can shape life trajectories. There is some evidence that pupils with SEN excluded from primary school are more likely to later have records of offending (Parsons *et al.* 2001). A number of factors have been cited reflecting the tensions that schools face between inclusion and raising standards, with the hard to reach being those who are more vulnerable to exclusion given an institutional emphasis on league tables and demonstrating 'value-added' in pupil performance (Hayden 1997; Hallam and Castle 2001; Maguire *et al.* 2003). Hayden aptly describes the children as being 'severely disadvantaged by the workings of the current education system' (Hayden *et al.* 1997: 40).

Follow-up studies of excluded children suggest that children continue to experience difficulties and in many instances require further additional support or changes in school placement (Hayden 1997; Parsons *et al.* 2001). This suggests that the primary school is key in determining a better future for these children. A range of interventions have been used in school, some geared towards individual skill development, for example anger management or anti-bullying techniques. Some of these have been more explicitly therapeutic, such as counselling or play therapy, and others focus on the wider context, such as 'Circle of Friends'. In an evaluation of DfES-funded pilot studies, Hallam and Castle (2001) suggest that successful intervention in school is likely to be a whole school issue, to include parents and to also give pupils the skills for managing their own behaviour. Parental contact has been found to be an essential aspect of managing exclusion (Wilkin *et al.* 2005). A review of parent-training programmes identified a number of characteristics that are common to successful programmes, including the use of social learning theory to inform a structured 'curriculum', and the inclusion of strategies to improve or enhance relationships (Gould and Richardson 2006).

EVALUATING PROVISION

In common with other areas of education, evaluation research has been driven by the simple question 'What works' (Sebba and Sachdev 1997) and has largely ignored a number of technical and conceptual issues (Florian *et al.* 2004). Typically the focus has been on outcome measures, often without explicit underpinning by a theoretical account of the mechanisms for change (Porter and Lacey 2005). A review of research on provision for children with SEN suggested that the focus has more typically been on evaluating interventions for children with SEN in relation to outcome measures such as cognitive gains, language and memory, attitudes, social acceptance, and friendship patterns (Porter *et al.* 2002).

Such evaluation studies could be described as naturalistic with at best quasi-experimental designs. Gersten *et al.* (2000) put forward a number of recommendations to improve the quality of research, with specific reference to evaluating specialist provision. They suggest a more explicit attention to providing more detail, both in relation to the sample and to the intervention, with explicit use of fidelity checks to ensure that the intervention is being implemented as described. They also point to the importance of control groups matched before assignment to conditions, with group sizes that are sufficiently large given the heterogeneity of the population. Elsewhere, others have criticised the lack of detail on teacher characteristics and on the subtleties of implementation (Nind *et al.* 2004).

The development of a national database collecting pupil data keeps the focus on a rather narrowly defined set of attainment outcomes. Theoretically, the data provided through the Pupil Level Annual School Census (PLASC) will enable comparisons to be made between groups of pupils receiving different types of provision over time so that schools are able to monitor their relative success compared to other schools. However, there are a number of technical issues that make the usefulness of this data problematic. Pupils are treated as a homogeneous group within their designated category. Evidence has already been cited to illustrate the considerable variation between authorities and schools in whether a pupil receives a statement. Although the statementing process is viewed as more straightforward for those with medical needs (Ofsted 2006), these categories still belie a wide range of needs. A simple look at the profile of children with autistic spectrum disorder reveals considerable variation (Jordan 2005), and that of children with ADHD reveals the co-occurrence of disability (Cooper 2005). The presence of additional needs within the populations of pupils with specified needs make for a group with diverse and complex needs. As Florian *et al.* (2004) ask, 'what does it mean to describe a student as having "moderate learning difficulties" as a primary need and "emotional and behavioural difficulties" as a secondary need, rather than the other way around?' (p.117).

From 2007 it is likely that schools will be required to record the achievement of pupils working below level one of the national curriculum using the 'P Scales'. Considerable concern has been raised about the sensitivity of these scales to provide a measure of progress in all children (Male 2000; Lewis *et al.* 2003). These scales are increasingly used in primary schools to inform the curriculum using commercially available database systems for recording.

In addition to quantifying progress, research has looked at ways of identifying the costs associated with services (Sleed *et al.* 2006; Romeo *et al.* 2006) owing much to the notion of 'best value'. A distinction to be made, between studies that compare the relative benefits of provision/services, the cost utility, and those of cost effectiveness, is how much it costs to produce a particular outcome. Crowther *et al.* (1998), looking specifically at the costs of resourcing provision for pupils with moderate learning difficulties, raise a concern that too little attention is paid to the question of efficiency, effectiveness and equity in the deployment of resources. Education may bear the lion's share of service costs in the primary school years (Knapp *et al.* 1999), with an equally high cost to those borne by the family (Knapp *et al.* 1999; Romeo *et al.* 2006), demonstrating the importance of involving all stakeholders in the evaluation process.

From 2007 schools will be producing schemes to demonstrate how they will be monitoring the impact of their policies and practices on children with disabilities. OECD interpret equity with respect to four measures:

- Equity of access or equality of opportunity;
- Equity in terms of learning environment or equality of means;
- Equity in production or equality of achievement; and
- Equity of realisation or exploitation of results.

(OECD 2004: 17)

A recent study by Ofsted (2006) found no difference between mainstream and special schools with respect to pupils with SEN making 'outstanding progress', but highlights the strength of resourced provision, particularly with respect to ethos, the provision of specialist staff and the provision of focused professional development for staff.

At a school level, we would argue, the process of evaluation should be informed through consultation with pupils. This opens out the possibility for schools of getting a clearer notion of what contributes to pupils' sense of well-being. Recognition of the importance of eliciting children's views is enshrined in legislation around the Code of Practice, echoing the torrent of global initiatives setting out children's rights (Lewis and Porter 2007). Caveats have often been given with respect to age and ability, and it is noticeable in the research literature how much has focussed on children of secondary school age. However, a recent study by Stafford *et al.* (2003) contrasts the enthusiasm with which primary age children respond to consultation to the more measured and perhaps cynical approach of pupils in the secondary years. The study highlights the importance of being aware of children's priorities and their agendas.

A number of methods have been developed for use with less articulate children, including those with language difficulties. Aubrey and Dahl (2006), in a review of the literature with reference to children who are vulnerable and have special educational needs, suggest the importance of activity-based methods and the attractiveness of computers. They highlight the relationship between question format and responsiveness, an issue pursued further by Dockrell (2004) in an exploration of the linguistic and cognitive demands placed on children through the use of interviewing techniques. Questions may not be the most useful format for children with special educational needs; Lewis (2002) suggests the value of using statements to prompt communication and Arksey *et al.* (2005) of using social stories – particularly with children with ASD. Research has pointed to the importance of the ethos of the school in facilitating consultation (Norwich and Kelly 2006), with a study by Woolfson *et al.* (2006) hearing from children about their need for an appropriate environment with approachable people and the availability of an advocate.

> Consultation should be a genuine attempt to listen seriously to young people's views and act on them, not just a window-dressing exercise conducted for the benefit of adults about issues already decided.
>
> (Stafford *et al.* 2003: 365)

It is important that the diversity of pupil views is heard.

CONCLUSION

This chapter has put forward the trends in emerging policy and practice, given a diverse and methodologically challenged literature on primary aged children with learning difficulties. Little has been stated specifically in relation to special schools, largely reflecting the tendency historically in the literature on special schools to make few distinctions between children of primary and secondary school age (until the point of transition from school). Instead we have focussed on the contested areas of how best to ensure equality of opportunity between those with special educational needs and those without, within a context of the changing agendas set by the *Every Child Matters* framework.

Despite the rhetoric of policy documents, nationally collected statistics suggest that there is a relatively stable proportion of children who are identified for additional resources and that the percentage of those pupils who are ultimately placed in specialist provision is also stable. This, however, belies an increasing number of pupils for whom teachers have concern, and who are placed at School Action stages of the Code of Practice. Two groups of pupils are more likely to be statemented in the primary school – those with Speech Language and Communication Needs and those with Autistic Spectrum Disorder – and we have no historic data on pupil categories to enable us to identify the extent to which this reflects an increased emphasis on speaking and listening and whole class teaching, or whether it simply reflects the procedures necessary to access non-educational support.

The current system allows for a local, highly-situated interpretation and it is apparent that the methodology for allocating resources privileges some children over others. Children with dyslexia and autism have powerful lobby groups and are well represented within the system. There is clear evidence that family background makes a difference with children from more affluent backgrounds receiving more help, and for less significant levels of difficulty, than those from poorer homes. There is a pervasive gender bias, with not only a higher incidence amongst boys than girls but earlier recognition of boys' difficulties. Children from certain minority ethnic groups are more likely to be identified as having SEN than others, controlling both for gender and socio-economic disadvantage. Finally, pupils with SEN are more likely to be excluded – particularly during the primary school years, exacerbating the child's difficulties and shaping their life trajectory.

As we have seen, categories of learning difficulty have different meanings in different settings and this variation is made more prominent when coupled with widely varied levels of statementing across authorities. Arguably this makes it difficult to place much reliance on the use of aggregated data. It also calls to question the system for allocating resources; Croll (2002) has argued powerfully for the advantage of an allocation system based on free school meals. The introduction of the Disability Equality Duty will further highlight these anomalies and the disadvantages faced by pupils with SEN.

The contesting policy agendas of raising standards in attainment and of inclusive schooling create considerable tensions within school. Data on the relationship between positive teacher attitudes and burnout are evidence of the challenges faced by teachers. It is perhaps unsurprising in this context that Ofsted (2006) favours resource centres, given a lack of difference in the progress of pupils in mainstream and special schools.

The mainstay of support for teachers in primary schools has long been the SENCO although in primary schools this role may well be taken on by the head or deputy, making the management of limited time and the demands of procedures for external accountability even more onerous. Research suggests that approaches for teaching pupils with difficulties in learning are not distinctively different, although the knowledge that underpins their use may be. This remains a contested finding in some areas of SEN. There is much to be gained from more collaborative forms of practice with individuals working together across professional boundaries in a problem-solving way. This has been found to be particularly effective with respect to children with conduct disorders and those at risk of mental health problems, two groups that are most at risk of exclusion.

Policy has placed an increasing amount of emphasis on 'children's voice'; indeed the importance of this is well represented by the requirement of schools to set out their plans for actively promoting equality of opportunity through consultation with disabled groups. This is highly consistent with the personalisation agenda and the increased participation of pupils in decisions about their learning. Primary schools play an important role in developing pupils' capacity for dialogues about their learning, including self-assessment and target setting.

We started this review with concerns about the quality of the evidence base and we finish with concerns about the national focus on narrowly-defined attainment outcomes that arguably marginalise further those pupils who experience difficulties in learning. Decision-making on the basis of single indicators, coupled with the use of a category system that assumes comparability, privileges some groups to the detriment of others – namely those identified with special educational needs. If the field is to move forward then research has to achieve a more decisive focus on the process rather than the outcome, with an identification of the mechanisms for change, for it to clearly inform policy and practice.

NOTES

1 A statement of SEN is a legal document which sets out a child's special educational needs as assessed by the Local Authority (LA); sets out the provision (support) which the LA feels is needed; and names the school, type of school or other provision which will give this support.
2 Special Educational Needs Co-ordinator

REFERENCES

Ainscow, M., Booth, T. and Dyson, A. (2006) 'Inclusion and the standards agenda: negotiating policy pressures in England', *International Journal of Inclusive Education* 10(4–5): 295–308.

Alexander, R.J. (2004) 'Still no pedagogy? Principle, pragmatism and compliance in primary education', *Cambridge Journal of Education* 34(1): 7–33.

Arksey, H., Kemp, P.A., Glendinning, C., Kotchetkova, I. and Tozer, R. (2005) *Carers' Aspirations and Decisions Around Work and Retirement*. Department for Work and Pensions Research Report, Vol. 290. Leeds: Corporate Document Services.

Armstrong, D. (2005) 'Reinventing "inclusion": New Labour and the cultural politics of special education', *Oxford Review of Education* 31(1): 135–51.

Atkinson, C., Regan, T. and Williams, C. (2006) 'Working collaboratively with teachers to promote effective learning', *Support for Learning* 21(1): 33–39.

Aubrey, C. and Dahl, S., (2006) 'Children's voices: the views of vulnerable children on their service providers and the relevance of services they receive', *British Journal of Social Work* 36: 21–39.

Audit Commission (2002) *Special Educational Needs – a mainstream issue*. London: HMSO.

——(2007) *Out of Authority Placements for Special Educational Needs*. London: HMSO.

Audit Commission / Her Majesty's Inspectorate (HMI) (1992) *Getting in on the Act: provision for pupils with special educational needs: the national picture*. London: HMSO.

Bennett, T., DeLuca, D. and Bruns, D. (1997) 'Putting inclusion into practice: perspectives of teachers and parents', *Exceptional Children* 64: 115–31.

Black, P., Harrison, C., Lee, C., Marshall, B. and Wiliam, D. (2003) *Assessment for Learning: putting it into practice*. Milton Keynes: Open University Press.

Black, P. and Wiliam, D. (1998) 'Inside the Black Box: raising standards through classroom assessment', *Phi Delta Kappan* 80(2): 139–48.

Cooper, P. (2005) 'AD/HD', in A. Lewis and B. Norwich (Eds) *Special Teaching for Special Children? Pedagogies for inclusion*. Maidenhead: Open University.

Cowne, E. (2005) 'What do special educational needs coordinators think they do?' *Support for Learning* 20(2): 61–68.

Creese, A., Norwich, B. and Daniels, H. (1998) 'The prevalence and usefulness of collaborative teacher groups for SEN: results of a national survey', *Support for Learning* 13(3): 109–14.

Croll, P. (2001) 'Teacher contact with parents of children with special educational needs: a comparison over two decades', *Journal of Research in Special Educational Needs* 1(2).

Croll, P. and Moses, D. (2000) 'Ideologies and utopias: education professionals' views of inclusion', *European Journal of Special Needs Education* 15(1): 1–12.

——(2002) 'Social deprivation, school-level achievement and special educational needs', *Educational Research* 44(1): 43–53.

Crowther, D., Dyson, A., Elliott, J. and Milward, A. (1998) *Costs and Outcomes for Pupils with Moderate Learning Difficulties (MLD) in Special and Mainstream Schools.* London: DfEE.

Crowther, D., Dyson, A. and Milward, A. (2001a) 'Supporting pupils with special educational needs: issues and dilemmas for special needs coordinators in English primary schools', *European Journal of Special Needs Education* 16(2): 85–97.

——(2001b) 'Supporting pupils with special educational needs: issues and dilemmas for special needs coordinators in English primary schools', *European Journal of Special Needs Education* 16(2): 85–97.

Cunningham, C. and Davis, H. (1985) *Working with Parents.* Milton Keynes: Open University Press.

Curtin, M. and Clarke, G. (2005) 'Listening to young people with physical disabilities' experiences of education', *International Journal of Disability, Development and Education* 52(3): 195–214.

Daniels, H., Cole T., Sellman, E., Sutton, J., Visser, J. and Bedward, J. (2003) *Study of Young People Permanently Excluded from School.* Nottingham: DfES.

Davis, P. and Florian, L. (2004a) 'Searching the literature on teaching strategies and approaches for pupils with special educational needs: knowledge production and synthesis', *Journal of Research in Special Educational Needs* 4(3): 142–47.

——(2004b) *Teaching Strategies and Approaches for Pupils with Special Educational Needs: ascoping study.* London: DfES.

Davis, P. and Hopwood, V. (2002) 'Including children with a visual impairment in the mainstream primary school classroom', *Journal of Research in Special Educational Needs* 2(3): 1–11.

Department for Children Schools and Families (DCSF) (2008) *Statistical First Release. Special Educational Needs in England: January 2008.* Online. (Available: http://www.dfes.gov.uk/rsgateway/ DB/SFR/s000794/index.shtml, accessed 30/6/08.

Department of Education and Science (DES) (1978) *Report of the Committee of Enquiry into the Education of Handicapped Children and Young People* (the Warnock Report). London: HMSO.

Department for Education and Employment (DfEE) (1994) *The Code of Practice on the Identification and Assessment of Special Educational Needs.* London: DfEE.

Department for Education and Skills (DfES) (2001a) *Special Educational Needs Code of Practice.* London: DfES.

DfES (2001b) *Inclusive Schooling: children with special educational needs.* London: DfES.

——(2001c) *SEN Toolkit.* London: DfES.

——(2003a) *Key Stage 3 National Strategy: behaviour and attendance training materials: Core Day 1.* London: DfES.

——(2003b) *Every Child Matters (Green Paper).* London: DfES.

——(2003c) *Primary National Strategy: behaviour and attendance: developing skills* (pilot materials). London: DfES.

——(2003d) *Primary National Strategy: developing children's social, emotional and behavioural skills: a whole-curriculum approach* (pilot materials). London: DfES.

——(2003e) *Primary National Strategy: developing children's social, emotional and behavioural skills: guidance* (pilot materials). London: DfES.

——(2004a) *Removing Barriers to Achievement: the Government's strategy for SEN.* Online. (Available: http://www.teachernet.gov.uk/senstrategy, accessed 14 April 2004).

——(2004b) *Key Stage 3 National Strategy: behaviour and attendance training materials: Core Day 2.* London: DfES.

——(2006) *First Release. Special Educational Needs in England, SFR 23/2006.* London: DfES.

——(2007a) *First Release. Special Educational Needs in England, SFR 20/2007.* London: DfES.

——(2007b) *Permanent and Fixed Period Exclusions from Schools and Exclusion Appeals in England, 2005/06 SFR 21/2007.* 26 June 2007. Online. (Available: http://www.dfes.gov.uk/rsgateway/ DB/SFR/s000733/SFR21–2007.pdf).

Dockrell, J.E. (2004) 'How can studies of memory and language enhance the authenticity, validity and reliability of interviews?', *British Journal of Learning Disabilities* 32(4): 161–65.

Dockrell, J.E. and Lindsay, G. (2001) 'Children with specific speech and language difficulties: the teachers' perspective', *Oxford Review of Education* 27(3): 369–94.

Dockrell, J., Peacey, N. and Lunt, I. (2002) *Literature Review: meeting the needs of children with special educational needs.* London: Institute of Education.

Dolton, P. and Newson, D. (2003) 'The relationship between teacher turnover and school performance', *London Review of Education* 1(2): 133–40.

Duhaney, L.M. and Salend, S.J. (2000) 'Parental perceptions of inclusive placements', *Remedial and Special Education* 21(2): 121–28.

Dyson, A. and Ainscow, M. (2003) *Standards and Inclusive Education: schools squaring the circle, unpublished paper.* University of Manchester, Faculty of Education.

Dyson, A., Farrell, P., Hutcheson, G. and Polat, F. (2004) *Inclusion and Pupil Achievement.* London: DfES.

Dyson, A., Howes, A. and Roberts, B. (2002) 'A systematic review of the effectiveness of school-level actions for promoting participation by all students', in *Research Evidence in Education Library.* London: EPPI-Centre, Social Science Research Unit, Institute of Education, University of London.

Ellis, S. and Tod, J. (2005) 'Including SENCOs in behaviour improvement: an exploration of the behaviour and attendance strands of the National Strategies', *Support for Learning* 20(2): 83–89.

Farrell, P. (2001) 'Special education in the last twenty years: have things really got better?' *British Journal of Special Education* 28(1).

Fielding, M. (2001) 'Target setting, policy pathology and student perspectives: learning to labour in new times', in M. Fielding (Ed) *Taking Education Really Seriously: four years hard labour.* London: RoutledgeFalmer.

——(2004) 'Transformative approaches to student voice: theoretical underpinnings, recalcitrant realities', *British Educational Research Journal* 30(2): 295–311

Florian, L. and Kershner, R. (2008) 'Inclusive pedagogy', in H. Daniels, H. Lauder and J. Porter (Eds) *Knowledge, Values and Educational Policy: a critical perspective.* London: Routledge: 173–183.

Florian, L. and Rouse, M. (2001) 'Inclusive practice in secondary schools', in R. Roseand and I. Grosvenor (Eds) *Doing Research in Special Education.* London: David Fulton.

Florian, L., Rouse, M., Black-Hawkins, K. and Jull, S. (2004) 'What can national data-sets tell us about inclusion and pupil achievement?' *British Journal of Special Education* 31(3): 115–21.

Fulcher, G. (1989) *Disabling Policies: a comparative approach to educational policy and disability.* Lewes: Falmer Press.

Galton, M. and MacBeath, J., with Page, C. and Steward, S. (2002) *A Life in Teaching? The impact of change on primary teachers' working lives.* London: National Union of Teachers.

Gersten R., Baker, S. and Lloyd, J.W. (2000) 'Designing high-quality research in special education: group experimental design', *The Journal of Special Education* 34(1): 2–18.

Gould, N. and Richardson, J. (2006) 'Parent-training/education programmes in the management of children with conduct disorders: developing an integrated evidence-based perspective for health and social care', *Journal of Children's Service* 4(4): 47–60.

Groom, B. and Rose, R. (2005) 'Supporting the inclusion of pupils with social, emotional and behavioural difficulties in the primary school: the role of teaching assistants', *Journal of Research in Special Educational Needs* 5(1): 20–30.

Grove, N., Porter, J., Bunning, K. and Olsson, C. (2000) 'Interpreting the meaning of communication by people with severe and profound learning difficulties: theoretical and methodological issues', *Journal of Applied Research in Intellectual Disabilities* 12(3): 190–203.

Gulliford, R. (1985) *Teaching Children with Learning Difficulties.* Windsor: NFER-Nelson.

Guralnick, M.J., Connor, R.T. and Hammond, M. (1995) 'Parent perspectives of peer relationships and friendships in integrated and specialised programs', *American Journal on Mental Retardation* 99(5): 457–76.

Hallam, S. and Castle, F. (2001) 'Exclusion from school: what can help prevent it?' *Educational Review* 53(2): 169–79.

Harris, R. (2007) *Special Educational Needs and Ethnicity: using the data in a London Local Authority.* Paper presented at the British Educational Research Association Annual Conference. Institute of Education, University of London, 5–8 September 2007.

Hayden, C. (1997) 'Exclusion from Primary School: children "in need" and children with "special educational need"', *Emotional and Behavioural Difficulties* 2(3): 36–44.

House of Commons Education and Skills Committee (2006) *Special Educational Needs: Third Report of Session 2005–06, Volume I.* London: The Stationery Office.

Jacklin, A., Robinon, C. and Torrence, H. (2006) 'When lack of data is data: do we really know who our looked-after children are?' *European Journal of Special Needs Education* 21(1): 1–20.

Jordan, R., (2005) 'Autistic spectrum disorders', in A. Lewis and B. Norwich (Eds) *Special Teaching for Special Children? Pedagogies for inclusion.* Maidenhead: Open University.

Kerry, T. (2005) 'Towards a typology for conceptualising the roles of teaching assistants', *Educational Review* 57(3): 20–30.

Knapp, M, Scott, S. and Davies, J. (1999) 'The cost of antisocial behaviour in younger children', *Clinical Psychology and Psychiatry* 4(4): 457–73.

Law, J., Dockrell, J.E., Castelnuovo, E., Williams, K., Seeff, B. and Normand, C. (2006) 'Early years centres for pre-school children with primary language difficulties: what do they cost, and are they cost-effective?', *International Journal of Language* 41(1): 67–81.

Leadbeater, C. (2004) *Personalisation Through Participation: a new script for public services.* London: Demos.

Leadbetter, J., Daniels, H., Brown, S., Edwards, A., Middleton, D., Popova, A., Apostolov, A. and Warmington, P. (2007) 'Professional learning within multi-agency children's services: researching into practice', *Educational Research* 49(1): 83–98.

Lee, B. and Mawson, C. (1998) *Survey of Classroom Assistants.* Slough: National Foundation for Educational Research.

Lewis, A. (2002) 'Accessing children's views about inclusion and integration', *Support for Learning* 17(3): 110–16.

Lewis, A., Lindsay, G. and Phillips, E. (2003) 'Assessment in special schools: national early assessment procedures and pupils attending special schools in England', *European Journal of Special Needs Education* 18(2): 141–53.

Lewis, A. and Norwich, B. (2001) 'A critical review of systematic evidence concerning distinctive pedagogies with pupils with difficulties in learning', *Journal of Research in Special Educational Needs* 1(1). Online. (Available: http://www.nasen.org.uk).

——(Eds) (2005) *Special Teaching for Special Children? Pedagogies for inclusion.* Maidenhead: Open University Press.

Lewis, A. and Porter, J. (2007) 'Research and pupil voice', in L. Florian (Ed) *Handbook of Special Education.* London: Sage.

Lindsay, G., Dockrell, J.E., Mackie, C. and Letchford, B. (2005) 'Local education authorities' approaches to provision for children with specific speech and language difficulties in England and Wales', *European Journal of Special Needs Education* 20(3): 329–45.

Lindsay, G. and Muijs, D. (2006) 'Challenging underachievement in boys', *Educational Research* 48(3): 313–32.

MacBeath, J., Galton, M., Steward, S., MacBeath, A. and Page, C. (2006) *The Costs of Inclusion.* London: National Union of Teachers.

Mackenzie, S. (2007) 'A review of recent developments in the role of the SENCO in the UK', *British Journal of Special Education* 34(4): 212–18.

Maddern, L., Franey, J., McLaughlin, V. and Cox, S. (2004) 'An evaluation of the impact of an inter-agency intervention programme to promote social skills in primary school children', *Educational Psychology in Practice* 20(2): 135–55.

Maguire, M., Macrae, S. and Milbourne, L. (2003) 'Early interventions: preventing school exclusions in the primary setting', *Westminster Studies in Education* 26(1).

Male, D. (2000) 'Target setting in schools for children with severe learning difficulties: head-teachers' perceptions', *British Journal of Special Education* 27(1): 6–12.

Mayrowetz, D. and Weinstein, C.C. (1999) 'Sources of leadership education: creating schools for all children', *Educational Administration Quarterly* 35(3): 423–49.

Mittler, P. (1999) 'Equal opportunities for whom?', *British Journal of Special Education* 26: 3–7.

——(2005) 'Building bridges between special and mainstream services', *Asia Pacific Disability Rehabilitation Journal* 16(1): 3–15.

Mittler, P. and Mittler, H. (1982) *Partnership with Parents*. Stratford-upon-Avon: National Council for Special Education.

Mittler, P., Mittler, H. and McConachie, H. (1986) *Working Together: guidelines for collaboration between professionals and parents of children and young people with disabilities*. Paris: UNESCO.

Mujherjee, S., Lightfoot, J. and Sloper, P. (2000) 'The inclusion of pupils with a chronic health condition in mainstream school: what does it mean for teachers?' *Educational Research* 42(1): 59–72.

National Institute For Health And Clinical Excellence/ Social Care Institute For Excellence (2005) *Overview Parent-training/education Programmes for Children with Conduct Disorders*. London: NICE.

Nind, M. and Wearmouth, J., with Collins, J., Hall, K., Rix, J. and Sheehy, K. (2004) *A Systematic Review of Pedagogical Approaches That Can Effectively Include Children with Special Educational Needs in Mainstream Classrooms with a Particular Focus on Peer Group Interactive Approaches*. EPPI-Centre: London.

Norwich, B. and Daniels, H. (1997) 'Teacher support teams for SEN in primary schools: evaluating a teacher focused support scheme', *Educational Studies*, 23(1): 5–23.

Norwich, B., Kelly, N. and Educational Psychologists in Training (2006) 'Evaluating children's participation in SEN procedures: lessons for educational psychologists', *Educational Psychology in Practice* 22(3): 255–71.

Norwich, B. and Lewis, A. (2001) 'Mapping a pedagogy for Special Educational Needs', *British Educational Research Journal* 27(3): 313–29.

Nunes, T. and Moreno, C (1997) 'Solving word problems with different ways of representing the task: how do deaf children perform?', *Equals: Mathematics and Special Educational Needs* 3 (2): 15–17.

Organisation for Economic Co-operation and Development (OECD) (2000) *Special Needs: statistics and indicators*. Paris: OECD.

——(2004) *Equity in Education: students with disabilities, learning difficulties and disadvantages*. Paris: OECD.

Office for Standards in Education (Ofsted) (2004) *Special Educational Needs and Disability: towards inclusive schools*. Manchester: Ofsted.

——(2006) *Inclusion: does it matter where pupils are taught?* Manchester: Ofsted.

Parsons, C., Godfrey, R., Howlett, K., Hayden, C. and Martin, T. (2001) *Excluding Primary School Children – The Outcomes Six Years On*. Oxford: NAPCE.

Parsons, C. and Howlett, K. (2000) 'Investigating the reintegration of permanently excluded young people in England', *INCLUDE*, online. (Available: http://www.include.org.uk/).

Pavey S. and Visser J. (2003) 'Primary exclusions: are they rising?', *British Journal of Special Education* 30(4): 180–86.

Peacey, N. (2005) *Are All Children Special? A discussion paper*. London: Institute for Public Policy Research.

Pearson, S. (2008) 'Deafened by silence or by the sound of footsteps? An investigation of the recruitment, induction and retention of special educational needs coordinators (SENCOs) in England', *Journal of Research in Special Educational Needs* 8(2): 96–110.

Pearson, S. and Ralph S. (2007) 'The identity of SENCOs: insights through images', *Journal of Research in Special Educational Needs* 7(1): 36–45.

Petley, K. (1994) 'An investigation into the experiences of parents and head teachers involved in the integration of primary aged children with Down's Syndrome into mainstream school', *Down's Syndrome: Research and Practice* 2: 91–96.

Porter, J., Downs, C., Morgan, M. and Ouvry, C. (2001) 'Interpreting communication of people with profound and severe learning difficulties', *British Journal of Learning Disabilities* 29(1): 12–16.

Porter, J, and Lacey, P. (2005) *Researching Learning Difficulties: a guide for practitioners.* London: Sage.

Porter, J. and Lacey, P., with Benjamin, S., Miller, O., Miller, C., Robertson, C., Sutton, J., and Visser, J. (2002) *The Role of Special Schools: a review of the literature.* London: DfES.

Porter, J., Robertson, C. and Hayhoe, H. (2001) *Self-Assessment and Learning Difficulties.* London: QCA

Pritchard, C. and Williams, R. (2001) 'A three-year comparative longitudinal study of a school-based social work family service to reduce truancy, delinquency and school exclusions', *Journal of Social Welfare and Family Law* 23(1): 23–43.

Redmond, S.M. and Rice, M.L. (1998) 'The socio-emotional behaviors of children with SLI [specific language impairments]: social adaptation or social deviance?', *Journal of Speech, Language and Hearing* 41: 688–700.

Riddell, S., Brown, S. and Duffield, J. (1994) 'Parental power and special educational needs: the case of specific learning difficulties', *British Educational Research Journal* 20(3): 327–44.

Romeo, R., Knapp, M. and Scott, S. (2006) 'Economic cost of severe antisocial behaviour in children and who pays it', *British Journal of Psychiatry* 18(8): 547–53.

Rose, R. (2001) 'Primary school teacher perceptions of the conditions required to include pupils with special educational needs', *Educational Review* 53(2): 147–56.

Sacker, A., Schoon, I. and Bartley, M. (2001) 'Sources of bias in special needs provision in mainstream primary schools: evidence from two British cohort studies', *European Journal of Special Needs Education* 16(3): 259–76.

Scott, F.J., Baron-Cohen, S., Bolton, P. and Brayne, C. (2002) 'Brief Report Prevalence of autism spectrum conditions in children ages 5–11 years in Cambridgeshire, UK', *Autism* 6(3): 231–37.

Scruggs, T. and Mastropeiri, M. (1996) 'Teacher perceptions of mainstreaming and inclusion', *Exceptional Children* 63(1): 59–74.

Sebba, J. and Sachdev, D. (1997) *What Works in Inclusive Practice?* London: Barnardos.

Shakespeare, T. (2000) *Help.* Birmingham: Venture Press.

Shield, B.M. and Dockrell, J.E. (2004) 'External and internal noise surveys of London primary schools', *Journal of the Acoustical Society of America* 115: 730–38.

Shield, B.M., Dockrell, J.E., Jeffrey, R. and Tachmatzidis, I. (2002) *The Effects of Noise on the Attainments and Cognitive Performance of Primary School Children.* Report to the DOH/DETR.

Sleed, M., Beecham, J., Knapp, M., McAuley, C. and McCurry, N. (2006) 'Assessing services, supports and costs for young families under stress', *Child: Care, Health and Development* 32 (1): 101–10.

Smith, P. Whitby, K. and Sharp, C. (2004) *The Employment and Deployment of Teaching Assistants* (LGA research report 5/04). Slough: National Foundation for Educational Research.

St James-Roberts, I. and Singh, C.S. (2001) 'Can mentors help primary school children with behaviour problems?' *Home Office Research Study 233.* London: Home Office Research.

Stafford, A., Laybourn, A., Hill, M. and Walker, M. (2003) '"Having a say": children and young people talk about consultation', *Children and Society* 17: 361–73.

Stallard, P. (2002) *Think Good – Feel Good: a cognitive behaviour therapy workbook for children and young people.* Chichester: John Wiley.

——(2005) *A Clinician's Guide to Think Good Feel Good: the use of CBT with children and young people.* Winchester: John Wiley.

Talmor, R., Reiter, S. and Feigin, N. (2005) 'Factors relating to regular education teacher burn-out in inclusive education', *European Journal of Special Needs Education* 20(2): 215–29.

Todd, E.S. and Higgins, S. (1998) 'Powerless in professional and parent partnerships', *British Journal of Sociology of Education* 19(2): 227–40.

UNESCO (1994) *Final Report: world conference on special needs education: access and quality.* Paris: UNESCO.

Vulliamy, G. and Webb, R. (2001) 'The social construction of school exclusion rates: implications for evaluation methodology', *Educational Studies* 27(3): 357–70.

Warnock, M. (2005) 'Special Educational Needs: a new look', *Impact No 11*. London: Philosophy of Education Society of Great Britain.

Webb, R. and Vulliamy, G. (2002) 'The social work dimension of the primary teacher's role', *Research Papers in Education* 17(2): 165–84.

——(2006) *Coming Full Circle? New Labour's education policies on primary school teachers' work*. London: Association of Teachers and Lecturers.

Wedell, K. (2005) 'Dilemmas in the quest for inclusion', *British Journal of Special Education* 32 (1): 3–11.

——(2007) 'How special is a need? Thresholds for statements. Points from the SENCo-Forum', *British Journal of Special Education* 34(3): 179.

Wesley, P.W., Buysse, V. and Tyndall, S. (1997) 'Family and professional perspectives on early intervention: an exploration using focus groups', *Topics in Early Childhood Education* 17: 435–56.

Wilkin, A., Archer, T., Ridley, K., Fletcher-Campbell, F. and Kinder, K. (2005) *Admissions and Exclusion of Pupils with Special Educational Needs*. London: DfES.

Wishart, J.G. and Manning, G. (1996) 'Trainee teachers' attitudes to inclusive education for children with Down's Syndrome', *Journal of Intellectual Disability Research* 40: 56–65.

Woolfson, R, Harker, M., Lowe, D., Shields, M., Banks, M., Campbell, L. and Ferguson, E. (2006) 'Consulting about consulting: young people's views of consultation', *Educational Psychology in Practice* 22(4): 337–53.

Zigmond, N. and Baker, J.M. (1995) 'Current and future practices in inclusive schooling', *The Journal of Special Education* 29(2): 245–50.

Part 3

Aims, values and contexts for primary education

The four research surveys in this section relate to the first of the Cambridge Primary Review's ten themes, *Purposes and Values*, which posed these questions, the first of them probably as fundamental as they come:

- What is primary education for?
- Taking account of the country and the world in which our children are growing up, to what individual, social, cultural, economic and other circumstances and needs should this phase of education principally attend?
- What core values and principles should it uphold and advance?
- How far can a national system reflect and respect the values and aspirations of the many different communities – cultural, ethnic, religious, political, economic, regional, local – for which it purportedly caters?
- In envisaging the future purposes and shape of this phase of education how far ahead is it possible or sensible to look?

Together, these four chapters offer historical, contemporary and international perspectives on the question of what, in a fast-changing and uncertain world, the central aims of England's system of primary education should be, and by what values that system might be underpinned.

The international focus of two of the four chapters is consistent with the stance taken by the Cambridge Primary Review as a whole, which is framed by the perspectives of education, childhood and – prominent in the present section – culture, society and the global context. Thus the questions about aims and values are predicated on some kind of prior response to another set:

- In what kind of society and world are today's children growing up and being educated?
- In what do England's (and Britain's) cultural differences and commonalities reside?
- What is the country's likely economic, social and political future?
- Is there a consensus about the 'good society' and education's role in helping to shape and secure it?
- What can we predict about the future – social, economic, environmental, moral, political – of the wider world with which Britain is interdependent?
- What, too, does this imply for children and primary education?
- What must be done in order that today's children, and their children, have a future worth looking forward to?

The last of these questions is undoubtedly stark, alarmist even, yet few now doubt that our habitual adult anxieties about the world in which children are growing up have been given a more urgent and even cataclysmic edge by the growing evidence on climate change, global warming and their environmental, economic and social consequences – if not for today's parents then for their children and grandchildren.

In such matters, the Review makes an important and decisive break with the more inward-looking, not to say parochial, discourse which has tended to dominate English primary education for much of the past half century. However, to say that national education systems can no longer afford to be exclusively national in outlook implies no reduction in the pre-eminence which this Review is giving to children and childhood – as the previous eight chapters demonstrate. Nor does an international outlook mean that local conditions and needs are ignored: they too feature prominently in the Review's other evidence. It is more a question of balance, of how we can do justice, simultaneously and in due measure, to individual, local, national and international considerations when formulating aims and curriculum for England's public system of primary education in the 21st century. There are other considerations and imperatives to be balanced – ethical as well as instrumental, cultural as well as economic. All this remains central to the Cambridge Primary Review's re-assessment of the proper character of England's system of primary education.

The issues covered by the chapters in this section are complex and in some instances contested, and the question of educational aims and values clearly requires measured and informed discussion rather than instant judgement. For that reason, this particular section introduction departs from earlier practice by adopting an explicitly interrogative format in drawing out selected issues from the four surveys.

In *Aims for Primary Education: the changing national context* (Chapter 10), Stephen Machin and Sandra McNally examine major economic and social trends in Britain which bear, or ought to bear, on discussion about educational aims and the future character of the curriculum. Working from a predominantly economic perspective they concentrate on three key issues: (i) the labour and broader social impacts of education, and their implications for educational standards, with particular reference to the question of the economic returns of education at different levels, including primary; (ii) recent trends in wage inequality, educational inequality and social mobility, and the relationship between them; (iii) the impact and viability in the educational context of the market theories and disciplines which since the 1980s have featured prominently in political discourse and government policy.

Aims for Primary Education: changing global contexts (Chapter 11), by Rita Chawla-Duggan and John Lowe, reviews the growing international prominence of primary education following the 1990 Jomtien World Declaration on Education for All (EFA), current efforts to achieve universal primary education (UPE) and the UN Millennium Development Goals (MDGs). It considers key tenets in the new international vocabulary of education: globalisation, the knowledge-based economy, lifelong learning and the benchmarking of standards, noting tensions between competition and equity and the growing international divergence of public and private schooling. The survey adds brief case studies of recent systemic primary education reforms in India and China, the world's two largest countries by population and two of its fastest-growing economies.

John White's *Aims as policy in English primary education* (Chapter 12) turns from considerations which shape aims to changing official views of what, in the case of English education, those aims have been and might be. He tracks developments over the past century or so up to and including the aims promulgated by QCA in 2007 and the values underpinning the 2004 Children's Act and the 2007 Children's Plan. White compares these with official statements of aims for primary education from Scotland and Northern Ireland, and sets them alongside critical consideration of aims and values from the theoretical literature. He finds the recent official aims statements more convincing than the 1980s and 1990s versions, though still lacking the vital ingredient of a clear rationale.

Finally, **Aims and Values in Primary Education: England and other countries** (Chapter 13), by Maha Shuayb and Sharon O'Donnell, expands the geographical frame of reference to include a detailed and systematic analysis of policy and published research on the aims and values of primary education from England, Germany, the Netherlands, New Zealand, Scotland and Sweden. It notes a recurrent and unresolved tension between goals to do with individual self-fulfilment and those which seek to address national economic need; it charts an increasing commitment to citizenship and, more recently, to healthy, safe and sustainable living; and it finds that despite variation in national emphasis there are more similarities than differences between the countries concerned in the way primary education is viewed.

Although these research surveys were independently conceived and undertaken, collectively they raise some important generic issues.

Determining aims for a national education system is a complex and sensitive task

- At the time of the last major report on English primary education (Plowden, in 1967) primary schools exercised considerable autonomy in the matter of educational aims and values. Now aims are determined by central government and its agencies and are likely soon to have statutory force (Chapter 12). This requires us to ask how viable is a single set of centrally-determined educational aims and values for a large and complex educational system – encompassing 17,300 primary schools and over 4 million children – in a country of such exceptional cultural diversity as England?
- Recent official statements of educational aims have become increasingly lengthy and comprehensive, yet they continue to lack a clear rationale and beg all kinds of questions about the society and world today's children will inherit and the lives they will lead (Chapter 11). Do aims presented without argument or justification have educational validity or practical use?
- In the matters of how educational aims should be determined and what they might be, how might England learn from Scotland and/or Northern Ireland, or indeed other countries? (Chapters 11, 12 and 13.)

Priorities and balance

- There is an often-noted tension between supposedly 'child-centred' aims to do with the development and needs of the individual and 'societally-centred' aims concerned with the economy and social cohesion (Chapters 11, 12 and 13). How real is this tension? How in a state education system can both kinds of aim be effectively pursued? Do centrally-determined aims tend to put the perceived needs of the state before those of the individual? Is there a risk that the entire process may become over-politicised?

- For the primary stage, the 'basics' of literacy and numeracy have always been regarded as pre-eminent, and this continues to hold not just in England but internationally (Chapters 12 and 13). Even for the young child who is still many years from adulthood and the workplace, numeracy and – especially – literacy can be shown to carry a lifelong premium which is economic as well as cognitive and social (Chapter 10). However, does this evident consensus once and for all settle the debate about the aims of primary education? With growing concern about equity (Chapters 10 and 11) and childhood well-being (Chapter 12 and much other Cambridge Primary Review evidence), not to mention creativity, citizenship, the sense of place and time, global understanding, moral development and spiritual awareness, how can a view of aims be arrived at which is not only educationally balanced but also viable as school and classroom practice?

Aims and equity

- The English education system now has aims which are expected to inform the work of all of its schools and are presumed to meet the needs of all the children who attend them (Chapter 12). Yet not all children are equally well served by what is provided (Chapter 13); the well-documented gap in pupil attainment at the top of the primary school conforms closely with social and economic inequalities and with measures of disadvantage and deprivation (see Parts 2 and 5 in this book); and some educational policies and practices may themselves even aggravate inequality (Chapters 10, 3 and 5).
- Marketisation, 'choice' and inter-school competition appear to be among the policies which exacerbate educational inequality because not all parents are equal in their capacity to access and interpret the information on which choice is based, or indeed to act on that information (Chapter 10 and, in an earlier section, Chapter 4). Parental inability to exercise choice may effectively lead to the educational segregation of their children. There are strong reasons to question the efficacy and fairness of 'choice and competition' as a school improvement strategy (Chapter 10).
- The no less pervasive notion of the 'knowledge-based economy' may lead to an overly instrumental view of education, elevating efficiency above equity and pursuing social cohesion without addressing the root causes of inequality (Chapter 11).
- In light of the above, is the pursuit of greater equity a matter of strategy alone, or does it imply a need to re-think schools' core purposes, values and priorities as well?

Educate locally, think globally

- Developed nations operate within a particular view of what globalisation entails: that is, international competition and the use of education to enable one national economy to outsmart another (Chapter 11). Globalisation may lead to tensions and even contradictions in national education policy as 'social justice' competes with 'social cohesion for the sake of stability' and 'individualism, the market and meritocracy' (Chapter 11).
- Understandably, the goal of national global competitiveness has given considerable impetus to the drive to raise educational standards. But it has also led to standards being defined largely and relatively unquestioningly in terms of what is marketable, even though what constitute standards and quality in education ought to be a matter for debate (Chapter 11).

- Has the prevailing view of globalisation produced the educational tensions and distortions claimed in Chapter 11? How far is this view compatible with the concern, now voiced with an increasing sense of urgency, that schools should educate for global awareness, interdependence and sustainability (Chapters 12 and 13, and the Review's *Community Soundings* report)?

10 Aims for primary education

The changing national context

Stephen Machin and Sandra McNally

INTRODUCTION

The nature of primary education in England has been subject to significant change in recent times. Part of this arises from government education policy, and part from changing demographic, economic and social structures. In this chapter we consider this changing national context of primary education.

Inevitably, we have had to be selective in how we address such a broad theme. We therefore focus on what we believe to be three of the major issues of relevance: the labour market and broader social consequences of education, and the implications for raising standards in primary education; inequality between socio-economic groups and changes in social mobility; and the application of 'market economics' to educational issues.

In the last few decades, there has been increasing awareness of the importance of education and skills to an individual's prosperity and well-being as well as to the competitiveness of the economy. The labour market has changed rapidly, in large part because of technological change. These changes are relevant to all stages of education and are an important part of the background to the increased emphasis on raising standards in education. The first part of our chapter deals with evidence on the consequences of education and skills for wages, among other outcomes (and the background to this). We relate this to the debate about raising standards.

Another major theme is inequality between socio-economic groups in educational performance and the decline in social mobility over time (at least up to the early 1990s). This means that children's incomes are more closely related to that of their parents than in the past. The causes of this inequality within and between generations, may be partly related to how the system of education operates – although this is difficult to pin down. Increasing equality of opportunity within education is certainly seen as part of the solution.

Finally, the application of 'market economics' to educational issues has happened since the 1980s. This manifests itself in the move to increase choice and accountability within the system, as well as efforts to incentivise schools and teachers. We discuss the implications of the 'market philosophy' both for raising standards and potentially for raising inequality.

THE CHANGING SOCIO-ECONOMIC CONTEXT

The 'value' of education

The 'value' of acquiring the basic skills acquired in primary school is evident even in the most routine tasks. However, even in a rich country like the UK, these skills cannot be taken for granted. It has been estimated that about one-fifth of adults in the UK are not functionally literate (Moser 1999). Numbers from the International Adult Literacy Survey of 1995 (OECD/Human Resources Canada 1995) show countries like the UK and US have very dense lower tails of their adult literacy skill distributions (including amongst younger adults) whereas in other countries, such as Sweden and Germany, hardly any adults are at these low levels. This clearly has serious implications for many aspects of individuals' well-being, as well as having important consequences for the rest of society.

McIntosh and Vignoles (2000) and Layard *et al.* (2002) consider the importance of basic literacy and numeracy skills for labour market returns in terms of wages and employment. They show that even acquisition of very basic skills in numeracy and literacy has an important effect on the probability of employment and on wages. The measure of literacy/numeracy, 'level 1', is equivalent to standards of literacy and numeracy that should be achieved by age 11 according to the National Curriculum (although 20 per cent of adults do not meet this standard[1]). Among the results reported is the finding that, controlling for other characteristics, acquisition of level 1 numeracy or literacy skills raises the probability of employment by about 5 percentage points, and, for workers, raises wages by about 9 percentage points in the case of numeracy skills and 7 percentage points in the case of literacy skills.

There are many studies that estimate the economic value of additional years of schooling or educational qualifications. In developed countries this normally pertains to secondary or post-compulsory schooling, as primary education is universal. However, some discussion of this is relevant to understanding the broader socio-economic context.

There is much good evidence of large average wage returns to additional years of schooling (see the reviews in Card 1999, 2001). The recent focus of this literature in the UK has been on returns to qualifications rather than years of schooling. Typically it is found that there are higher wage returns to academic qualifications than vocational qualifications and there is no return to low-level vocational qualifications (that is, defined as below 'level 2') – see, for example, Dearden *et al.* (2002) and Sianesi (2003).

Returns to individuals in terms of higher wages and employment are only one part of the story of how education affects individuals' livelihood and well-being. Social science researchers have considered the wider benefits of education by studying connections between education and outcomes like health, crime, civic engagement and intergenerational effects on children's outcomes. There is evidence of important effects of education on individual outcomes beyond the labour market. For example, education significantly improves health outcomes (Grossman and Kaestner 1997; Kitigawa and Hauser 1973; Lleras-Muney 2005), is associated with lower crime levels (Lochner and Moretti 2004; Feinstein and Sabates 2005; Machin and Vujic 2005), and enhances the extent of civic engagement and participation (Brehm and Rahn 1997; Bynner and Egerton 2001; Bynner and Parsons 1997). Moreover, there is evidence that raising the level of parental education benefits their children's educational outcomes (Black, Devereux and Salvanes 2005).

The changing labour market value of education

Over the last few decades, there has been a rapid upgrading of the educational status of the workforce (see, for example, Machin 2003). Other things being equal, one would expect this increase in the supply of more educated workers to depress wage gaps between more and less highly qualified workers. The logic here is that employers have more people with good qualifications to choose from; this increased competition should therefore lower the premia attached to 'good qualifications'. This has not happened because the demand for workers with good qualifications, especially higher level qualifications, has increased faster than the supply.

The pattern of change in the graduate wage differential in the UK, that is, graduates relative to non-graduates, has been well documented. The differential rose very sharply in the 1980s, and continued to rise at a lower rate in the 1990s and any growth had stagnated by the 2000s (Machin 1996, 1999, 2003; Machin and Van Reenen 2006). A number of studies document rising returns over time from the 1970s to the early 1990s (Harkness and Machin 1999; Gosling, Machin and Meghir 2000) and slightly rising or constant returns from the early 1990s to the early 2000s (Chevalier *et al.* 2004; Walker and Zhu 2005; O'Leary and Sloane 2004, 2005; McIntosh 2004).

The question arises as to why the returns to education in general, and higher education in particular, have increased so much over time. Various explanations are given but the weight of the evidence is behind what is known as 'skill biased technology change' (for reviews of possible explanations and discussions of the large body of evidence see, for example, Katz and Autor 1999, or Machin and Van Reenen 2006). This refers to the introduction of new technologies that are biased in favour of skilled workers. It comes from the hypothesis that employers' demand for skilled workers has been shaped by the kinds of technologies that are permeating into modern workplaces. In this changing environment, employers will be willing to pay more to workers who are skilled enough to operate these new technologies whereas less skilled workers will be less valued – and this will be reflected both in wages and in the employment probability. There is good evidence for the importance of skill biased technical change internationally as opposed to competing explanations such as increased globalisation (Berman *et al.* 1998; Machin and Van Reenen 2006).

How does this relate to primary education?

The major relevance of the above discussion to primary education is increased awareness of the importance of education to individuals and to the economy (and its rising value). There is still an economic premium to having 'basic skills', that is the expected levels of literacy and numeracy at age 11. This reflects the fact that many adults in the UK do not have these skills: if basic numeracy and literacy skills were universal, there would be no special 'wage premium' attached to them in the labour market. However, the economy as a whole would be expected to perform better. Indeed the UK has between 10 and 25 per cent lower output per hour than France, Germany and the US, and much of this can be explained by a poorer level of skills and a shortfall of capital investment (CEP[2] 2005).

A good primary education is important not only for imparting knowledge of basic skills to the next generation but also for enabling pupils to learn faster and more effectively as they go through the education system. Furthermore, it seems unlikely that pupils who perform poorly at primary education will be in a position to take advantage of opportunities that arise later in their educational career, such as going to university.[3]

In this context, it is not surprising that concerns about educational standards in primary school (and education more generally) have become a top priority. Furthermore, there have been long-held concerns about poor standards of education in UK schools. For example, as documented by Machin and Vignoles (2004), the proportion succeeding in their examinations at age 16 remained stagnant from around 1970 to the mid-1980s. In the 1980s, more than two thirds of the school leaver cohort did not achieve examination success at age 16 and while some pursued more vocational qualifications, many entered the labour market with no academic qualifications ('at all. Such statistics, along with international indicators, suggested to policy makers that the UK had a particular problem with a so-called 'long tail of low achievement'.

National statistics about the level of education in primary schools do not exist before the mid-1990s. However, reports document the state of primary education in particular local education authorities (LEAs). A particularly prominent report published by Ofsted in 1996 was *The Teaching of Reading in 45 Inner London Primary Schools* (Ofsted 1996). This report was very critical of the standards of teaching in the majority of these schools. Specifically, it included criticism of the following practices: free reading with little or no intervention by the teacher; too much time spent hearing individual pupils read; insufficient attention to the systematic teaching of an effective programme of phonic knowledge and skills. Such reports prompted concerns that standards in the teaching of reading varied widely from school to school, with many primary teachers not having had the opportunity to update their skills to take account of evidence about effective methods of teaching reading and how to apply them (Literacy Task Force 1997).

Thus, important parts of the changing national context of primary education include greater understanding of the value of education (especially to the economy); an increase in the value of education to individuals and to the economy over time; and growing awareness of poor performance and/or standards of education in English schools.

Recent performance and future prospects

In more recent times, available indicators suggest that educational performance has improved. There is always a debate about whether increases in KS SAT scores and other examination results, reflect a genuine improvement in standards as opposed to alternative explanations (such as easier examinations or 'teaching to the test'). However, it seems unlikely that the meaning of educational indicators has become completely distorted. Furthermore, recent international surveys such as the Programme for International Student Assessment (PISA) and the Progress in International Reading Literacy Survey (PIRLs) suggest that English school children perform well in literacy and numeracy compared to other countries (see Hansen and Vignoles 2005).

With regard to primary education, it seems likely that, even though progress seems to have hit a plateau in the last few years, some of this success has been due to the National Literacy and Numeracy Strategies. The background, implementation and evaluation of the National Literacy Strategy are discussed in detail by Stannard and Huxford (2007). The predecessor of the National Literacy Strategy ('the National Literacy Project') has been evaluated by Machin and McNally (2004). They find this to have been extremely effective in raising standards at low cost.

Another important development has been the increase in resources devoted to education in recent years. For example, expenditure on education and training as a percentage of GDP was 4.9 per cent in 1987/88 – and was still at that level in 1997/98. By 2005/06, it had increased to 5.6 per cent, which moved spending up close to the OECD (Organisation for Economic Co-operation and Development) average. Gordon Brown's aspiration is to match the resources of the state sector to current levels in the independent sector. This aim is extremely ambitious. For example, even though class sizes have fallen considerably in the state sector, pupil-teacher ratios are only half the size in the independent sector – on average 10 fewer pupils per class (Green *et al.* 2007). The future prospects of primary education may be viewed in a very positive light if expenditure really increases to meet this aspiration.

There is a debate in the literature about the extent to which resources matter for improving educational performance. For example, Hanushek (1986) reviews a large number of studies based on US data and concludes that increasing expenditure should not be expected to improve educational outcomes. However, these findings are challenged in other studies. For example, in a famous study, Krueger and Whitmore (2001) find positive effects of reduced class size (the Tennessee STAR (Student/Teacher Achievement Ratio) experiment). There are also examples in the UK where interventions involving the allocation of increased resources to schools have led to positive (and cost effective) outcomes (for example Machin *et al.* 2007a; Machin *et al.* 2007b). A reading of the literature might be that the effect of resources depends on how they are spent.

However, the quality and quantity of some school inputs are not entirely dependent on how much the government spends. Recruitment problems in the teaching profession are partly attributable to the rising wage return to other occupations. For example, there are substantial foregone earnings for a graduate with a Maths or Science degree entering the teaching profession. A consequence is that current teachers are being drawn from further down the educational achievement or ability distribution than they were in the past. There is some evidence for this in the UK (Chevalier *et al.* 2007; Nickell and Quintini 2002) as well as in the US (Corcoran *et al.* 2002; Lakdawalla 2001).

Machin and Vignoles (2005) draw a link between the teacher labour market and the introduction of the tightly prescribed national curriculum and daily lesson plan in primary schools. In the short run, it appeared that being more prescriptive in what teachers should be teaching (and teaching them how to teach it) might raise standards, at least in the absence of being able to recruit more effective teachers. They go on to argue that, in the longer term, it is of course important to try and re-establish teaching as an important and well-respected profession, which sits uneasily with policies that take away their autonomy. This longer run objective clearly requires policy makers to think seriously about improving the total compensation package for teachers, including their non-pecuniary conditions of work (Chevalier and Dolton 2005).

These concerns are accentuated by the fact that there is an ageing teaching population, especially in primary education. As documented by Chevalier and Dolton (2005), 40 per cent of all teachers are aged 45–55 and those aged above 55 account for another 6 per cent of the workforce. Within the next ten years, nearly 50 per cent of the current workforce would be expected to have retired. At the current level of recruitment into teaching, a large shortage of teachers is therefore predicted. Chevalier and Dolton (2005) explain that this could be partly mitigated by influencing the retirement plans of existing teachers – for example, by reforming pension rights. However, the challenges of recruiting more young people into the teaching profession clearly need to be addressed.

INEQUALITY

An important part of the socio-economic context of education in the UK is increasing inequality over several decades – as manifest in wages, education and social mobility.

Education is a mechanism in all of these phenomena and hence it is relevant to discuss these issues here.

Wage inequality

Changes in wage inequality since the 1970s are documented by Machin (2003) and Machin and Van Reenen (2006). From the late 1970s and through the 1980s, the inequality of earnings rose massively for both sexes. Post-1990, inequality at the upper end of the distribution continues to diverge whereas at the lower end it increased a little in the 1990s and decreased a little in the 2000s.[4] Another way to consider trends in wage inequality is to examine the growth of employment in high wage and low wage jobs (Machin and Van Reenen 2006). Since 1979, there has been a significant increase in well-paid jobs such as lawyers, senior managers, consultants, for example, and an increase in low-paid jobs such as cleaners, hair dressers, shop assistants. This is consistent with the 'polarisation of the labour market' (see also Goos and Manning 2003).

There have been many papers that have tried to explain these changes both in the UK and in other countries (especially the US, where patterns have been similar). There is no unique and simple explanation that is capable of fully explaining the patterns at different parts of the distribution. However, probably the most important contributory factor has been 'skill biased technology change' (see the discussion above, 'The changing labour market value of education'). Hence the high demand for highly skilled graduates has been an important mechanism for creating wage inequality over the last few decades.

Educational inequality

Although there have been increasing opportunities for those with good qualifications, access to good qualifications is not equal according to socio-economic background. Differences in educational progress start very early and then widen as children age. Feinstein (2003) finds significant gaps between children from a high and low socio-economic background in an index of development, which is derived from tests of ability (at 22 months) in cube stacking, language use, drawing and personal development. He then maps the development of children through from 22 months to 10 years old, and shows that the gaps between high and low socio-economic status children widen out slightly from 22 months to 5 years and then more substantially from age 5 to 10, the first years of school. These findings appear to be supported by school level information (see DfES 2002), which shows that the gap between average attainment at schools of low and high disadvantage (as measured by the percentage of pupils eligible for free school meals) rises as pupils move through the key stages.

The initial gap in early cognitive ability, combined with the growth in the attainment gap through the educational system, leads to substantial differences in final attainment levels between children from high and low socio-economic backgrounds. Machin and Vignoles (2004) analyse staying-on rates at age 16, broken down by parental income group for the cohorts finishing compulsory schooling in 1974 (the 1958 birth cohort), 1986 (the 1970 birth cohort) and 1996 (the 1980 birth cohort). At each point in time, there is a large gap between the staying-on rate of people from high-income backgrounds compared to people from low-income backgrounds. For example, in 1996 86 per cent of people from the richest fifth of families stayed on in education beyond the age of 16 whereas this is true for only 61 per cent of people from the poorest fifth of families. With regard to changes over time, although there was a rise in the staying-on rate for all children, the rate of growth was higher for those from high-income backgrounds in the earlier period (1974–86) and lower in the more recent period (1986–96). The result is that educational inequality (according to family income) was about the same for those at the end of their compulsory schooling in 1996 as it was back in 1974 (with much higher inequality in 1986).

Although the poorest groups have begun to catch up in terms of their chances of staying on in education beyond the age of 16 (at least relative to the 1980s), Blanden *et al.* (2005) report that a stubborn gap remains with regard to participation at university. Among cohorts of age 18 in the late 1990s, children of parents who are in the poorest fifth of the population compare unfavourably in terms of educational outcomes to children of parents in the richest fifth of the population. In the former group, only 9 per cent of children graduate from university by age 23. This compares to 46 per cent of children in the latter group.

Social mobility

Another aspect of inequality is the extent to which a person's income is related to that of their parents. A strong relationship suggests an immobile society and most likely indicates restricted opportunities for those born into poorer families. Evidence suggests that the level of mobility in the UK is low by international standards (for example Jantti *et al.* 2006; Corak 2006; Solon 2002).

Blanden *et al.* (2005) analyse the change in intergenerational income mobility over time using longitudinal studies of parents and their children. They find that intergenerational income mobility has fallen for those born in 1970 compared to those born in 1958. More specifically, adult earnings of the 1970 cohort were more strongly related to their parental income as teenagers than was the case for the 1958 cohort. Thus, social mobility declined across these cohorts. Moreover, the decline was substantial. Of course, things may well have changed since then. Data constraints make this a more difficult question to analyse, although it is the subject of ongoing research.[5]

Solon (2004) has developed a model about the determinants of social mobility. On this basis, factors that could potentially have a role in explaining the decline in social mobility include an increase in the earnings return to human capital and a shift towards less progressive public investment in human capital. In his words: 'an era of rising returns to human capital or declining progressivity in public human capital investment is also an era of declining intergenerational mobility'. In a UK context, Blanden *et al.* (2005) and Blanden and Machin (2007) find measures of education, at various ages through the education sequence, to be important in accounting for declining social mobility in the period when mobility fell.

The potential role of primary education

Wage inequality, educational inequality and social immobility are all inter-related and are all affected by education. The rising wage returns to education seems to be a likely mechanism in generating all these sources of inequality. Of course, a persistently high return for high-level qualifications is a reflection of the fact that demand continues to outstrip supply. If the overall level of education were to improve substantively, such that the 'long tail of underachievers' no longer existed, wage and income differentials between people with different levels of education would reduce and some of these social inequalities would be mitigated. Primary education has an important potential role to play in this process, both in equipping pupils with basic skills and in facilitating their progression to higher levels of education.

One would also want to address educational inequality directly by a particular focus on those from disadvantaged backgrounds. Of particular concern is that some aspects of primary education are geared in favour of helping higher income groups (in the context of Solon's model, they might be thought of as contributing to declining progressivity in human capital investment). For example, the admissions policy of most schools uses distance from the school as a criterion for admission in the case of over-submission. In a climate where parents know a lot about schools (for example from the Performance Tables), this encourages people to reside near what they perceive to be 'good schools'. Such a policy discriminates in favour of those who can afford to choose exactly where to live. Indeed there is evidence that high-income parents locate near high performing schools, and that house prices reflect this (Gibbons and Machin 2003; Rosenthal 2003). As discussed below, there is good cause for concern that choice and competition does not work in favour of those from low socio-economic groups.

A fundamental reform of admissions policy (for example, prohibiting schools to discriminate on the basis of residence) would do much to level the playing field in terms of educational opportunities. It would thereby reduce the large inequalities that appear later in terms of wages and intergenerational mobility. Another thing that could be done is to learn the lessons from successful area-based initiatives like Excellence in Cities and provide targeted funding to areas that need regeneration. There are many other initiatives that might potentially raise the educational performance of children from disadvantaged families (in other areas of policy like housing and benefits as well as in education). With regard to education, other important policies include the 'City Academy' programme and instructional programmes that are targeted at those with learning difficulties (such as Reading Recovery). In order to know what works for disadvantaged children, it is crucial to have a good evaluation strategy in place from the outset. Unfortunately, this is not always the case.[6]

APPLICATION OF MARKET ECONOMICS TO THE SCHOOL SYSTEM

The view that market disciplines should be applied to public services – including education – has been implemented in the UK since the 1980s. This is an important part of the changing socio-economic context that is relevant to education. In an education context, the implementation of 'market reforms' involves efforts to create competition between schools and other measures to incentivise teachers (such as an attempt to introduce Performance Related Pay). There are several contributory factors to a more competitive environment for schools: making information on school performance publicly available, such as in the School Performance Tables, and with Ofsted report; a tough regulatory regime; increasing choice over where parents may send their children to school; and linking funding to pupil numbers.

The idea behind a more competitive environment is that it would lead to improved productivity in the education system. There is a relevant literature in the US (for example Hoxby 2003), which shows that increasing competition among schools and decentralising school finance can increase pupil attainment. However, there is very little evidence in the UK. In a study concerning secondary schools, Bradley *et al.* (2001) found that schools with the best examination performance grew most quickly and that increased competition between schools led to improved exam performance. In a study concerned with primary schools, Gibbons *et al.* (2008) find little evidence of a link between choice and achievement and only a small positive association between competition and school performance (which is not causal). The only case where choice and competition seem beneficial is in faith primary schools which are attended by about 1 in 5 pupils. This may indicate that there could be more scope for improvement if choice and competition is coupled with other changes in governance and admissions arrangements.

However, an important concern is that choice and competition may exacerbate educational inequalities. Parents are not equal in the extent to which they can exercise choice or use information. For example, there is evidence (discussed above) that high income parents choose to live near high performing schools and pay a premium in the housing market. There is also evidence to suggest that high socio-economic groups have better information on and understanding of school performance, for example via 'league tables' (West and Pennell 1999) – although there is a large literature about the limitations of such information in assessing school effectiveness (for example Goldstein 1997; Kane and Staiger 2002). This inability to exercise choice could lead to educational segregation, with children from disadvantaged families having to make do with the schools that more advantaged parents do not want to send their children to. The extent to which segregation has changed over time is very controversial; different methods produce different results (Allen and Vignoles 2006; Goldstein and Noden 2003; Gorard and Fitz 1998).

The potential for choice and competition to lead to greater inequality is also a concern for the future. The projected fall in pupil rolls will only accentuate competition as schools struggle to maintain revenue. One of the problems with the application of quasi-market measures to the education sector is that schools are not like firms: they do not close down when they no longer make a profit and hence there is no automatic market mechanism to trigger the exit of failing schools. This means that pupils at failing schools that turn out to be very unpopular might be stuck there for a considerable period. A danger is that children from poor families are made to pay the price for a potential productivity gain elsewhere in the education system. This has a productivity cost in itself, as able pupils from poor families will not achieve their potential. Thus there are reasons to question the efficacy and fairness of 'choice and competition' as a school improvement strategy.

CONCLUSION

Important changes in the national context of primary education include a rising value of education in the labour market, increased inequality between socio-economic groups and the application of 'market economics' to educational issues.

It is difficult to say whether wage returns to education will keep on rising. This remains controversial and it is too early days to reach any strong conclusions. There is a little evidence of a decrease in O'Leary and Sloane (2005) and Walker and Zhu (2005), but Dickerson (2005) reports no change using the same data sources. However, whether or not wage returns to education will fall is not the most relevant issue. The important issue is that the wage return to education and skills is extremely high, and this is partly a reflection of the fact that many people leave school with either very low, or no educational qualifications. An important challenge for the primary education sector is to get more people to a level where they have the basic skills in literacy and numeracy, thus equipping them to learn when in secondary school and when they enter the labour market.

The rise in the return to education is one of the factors behind the increase in wage inequality and the decline in social mobility that has been observed over recent decades. There are indications that wage inequality is beginning to reduce (at least if one compares people at the middle of the wage distribution compared to the bottom). It would also appear that low-income groups are beginning to catch up with high-income groups with regard to the staying-on rate (beyond compulsory education). However, the inequalities are still extremely large. Furthermore, they remain persistently high for some indicators (for example, participation in university; wage inequality as measured at the top of the distribution relative to the middle). Improvements in the quality of primary education would help to reduce these inequalities in the long-term. This could happen by increasing the standard of achievement such that the 'long tail of underachievers' no longer exists. It is also important to address educational inequality directly by re-examining factors that discriminate against the poor (for example schools admissions policies) and targeting disadvantaged schools/families/areas for special assistance (both in the context of education and other areas of social policy).

Finally, many measures have been taken to enable parental choice and facilitate competition between schools. There is reason to express scepticism about the magnitude of productivity benefits that can realistically be expected from the latter strategy. The problem with parental choice is that better-off families have the freedom to exercise it whereas poorer families are faced with numerous constraints on their ability to make choices. Declining pupil rolls may aggravate this concern if this leads schools to become more competitive. For these reasons, policies to address the educational inequality between different socio-economic groups (including reform of admissions policies) would seem to be an important way forward in dealing with these concerns.

NOTES

1 (OECD/Human Resources Canada 1995.)
2 The Centre for Economic Performance, The London School of Economics and Political Science (LSE).
3 Performance at earlier stages of schooling have been identified as offering barriers to HE uptake and participation, though primarily in terms of shaping attitudes to education and learning (see, for example, Gorrard, Smith *et al.* 2006).
4 Inequality at the upper and lower ends of the distribution are defined here as the 90–50 wage ratio and the 50–10 wage ratio, respectively. If we rank individuals by level of pay, then the 10th percentile gives the pay of someone 10 percentage points from the bottom; the 90th percentile gives the pay of someone 10 percentage points from the top and the 50th percentile gives the pay of the person at the middle of the distribution.
5 For example, Blanden and Machin (2007).
6 One problem is where the proponents of particular strategies (for example some phonics programmes) do not allow researchers to know in what schools they operate, making it impossible to tell whether these programmes are effective. With regard to evaluation of public policy, granting funding to schools on a purely discretionary basis (like the Specialist schools policy) makes it very hard to construct a counter-factual. Therefore we cannot come up with a credible policy evaluation.

REFERENCES

Allen, R. and Vignoles, A. (2006) 'What should an index of school segregation measure?', *Centre for Economics of Education Discussion Paper No. 60*.

Berman, E., Bound, J. and Machin, S. (1998) 'Implications of skill-biased technological change: international evidence', *Quarterly Journal of Economics* 113: 1245–80.

Black, S.E., Devereux, P.J. and Salvanes, K.G. (2005) 'Why the apple doesn't fall far: understanding the intergenerational transmission of human capital', *American Economic Review* 95 (1): 437–49.

Blanden, J., Gregg, P. and Machin, S. (2005) 'Educational inequality and intergenerational mobility', in S. Machin and A. Vignoles (Eds) *What's the Good of Education?* Princeton, NJ: Princeton University Press.

Blanden, J. and Machin, S. (2007) *Early Age Test Scores, Education and Changes in Intergenerational Mobility*, mimeo.

Bradley, S., Johnes, G. and Millington, J. (2001) 'The effect of competition on the efficiency of secondary schools in England', *European Journal of Operational Research* 135(3): 99–122.

Brehm, J. and Rahn, W. (1997) 'Individual-level evidence for the causes and consequences of social capital', *American Journal of Political Science* 41: 999–1023.

Bynner, J. and Egerton, M. (2001) *The Wider Benefits of Higher Education*. London: Higher Education Funding Council For England.

Bynner, J. and Parsons, S. (1997) *It Doesn't Get Any Better: the impact of poor basic skills on the lives of 37 year olds*. London: Basic Skills Agency.

Card, D. (1999) 'The causal effect of education on earnings', in O. Ashenfelter and D. Card (Eds) *Handbook of Labor Economics* 3. Amsterdam: North-Holland.

——(2001) 'Estimating the return to schooling: progress on some persistent econometric problems', *Econometrica* 69(5): 1127–60.

Centre for Economic Performance (2005) 'Election analysis: business and the UK's productivity gap: policies to promote innovation, investment and skills', *CEP Election Analysis*. CEP: London School of Economics.

Chevalier, A. and Dolton, P. (2005) 'The labour market for teachers', in S. Machin and A. Vignoles (Eds) *What's the Good of Education?* Princeton, NJ, Oxford: Princeton University Press.

Chevalier, A., Dolton, P. and McIntosh, S. (2007) 'Recruiting and retaining teachers in the UK: an analysis of graduate occupation choice from the 1960s to the 1990s', *Economica* 74(293): 69–96.

Chevalier, A., Harmon, C., Walker, I. and Zhu, Y. (2004) 'Does education raise productivity or just reflect it?', *Economic Journal* 114: F499–F517.

Corak, M. (2006) 'Do poor children become poor adults? Lessons from a cross country comparison of generational earnings mobility', in J. Creedy and G. Kalb (Eds) *Research on Economic Inequality. Vol 13, dynamics of inequality and poverty*. The Netherlands: Elsevier Press.

Corcoran, S., Evans, W. and Swab, R. (2002) *Changing Labour Market Opportunities for Women and the Quality of Teachers, 1957–92*. Cambridge: National Bureau for Economic Research, Working Paper 9180.

Dearden, L., McIntosh, S., Myck., M. and Vignoles, A. (2002) 'The returns to academic and vocational qualifications in Britain', *Bulletin of Economic Research* 54: 249–74.

Department for Education and Skills (DfES) (2002) *Investment for Reform: 2002 spending review*. London: DfES.

Dickerson, A.P. (2005) *A study on rates of return to investment in Level 3 and higher qualifications*, Warwick Institute for Employment Research: University of Warwick (mimeo).

Feinstein, F. (2003) 'Inequality in the early cognitive development of British children in the 1970 cohort', *Economica* 70: 73–97.

Feinstein, L. and Sabates, R. (2005) *Education and Youth Crime: effects of introducing the Education Maintenance Allowance programme*, Research Report Number 14. Centre for Research on the Wider Benefits of Learning: Institute of Education, London.

Gibbons, S. and Machin, S. (2003) 'Valuing English primary schools', *Journal of Urban Economics* 53: 197–219.

Gibbons, S., Machin, S. and Silva, O. (2008) 'Choice, competition and pupil achievement', *Journal of the European Economic Association* 6(4): 912–47.

Goldstein, H. (1997) 'Value added tables: the less than holy grail', *Managing Schools Today* 6: 18–19.

Goldstein, H. and Noden, P. (2003) 'Modelling social segregation', *Oxford Review of Education* 29(2): 225–37.

Goos, M. and Manning, A. (2003) *Lousy and lovely jobs: the rising polarisation of work in Britain*, Centre for Economic Performance: London School of Economics (mimeo).

Gorard, S. and Fitz, J. (1998) 'The more things change … the missing impact of marketisation?', *British Journal of Sociology of Education* 19: 365–76.

Gorrard, S., Smith, E., May, H., Thomas, L., Adnett, N. and Slack, K. (2006) *Review of Widening Participation Research: addressing the barriers to widening participation in higher education*. A report to HEFCE by the University of York, Higher Education Academy and Institute for Access Studies. Bristol: Higher Education Funding Council for England.

Gosling, A., Machin, S. and Meghir, C. (2000) 'The changing distribution of male wages in the UK', *Review of Economic Studies* 67: 635–66.

Green, F., Machin, S., Murphy, R. and Zhu, Y. (2007) *The labour market for private school teachers*, Centre for Economic Performance: London School of Economics (mimeo).

Grossman, M. and Kaestner, R. (1997) 'Effects of education on health', in J. Behrman and N. Stacey (Eds) *The Social Benefits of Education*. Ann Arbor, MI: University of Michigan Press.

Hansen, K. and Vignoles, A. (2005) 'The United Kingdom education system in comparative context', in S. Machin and A. Vignoles (Eds) *What's the Good of Education?* Princeton, Oxford: Princeton University Press.

Hanushek, E.A. (1986) 'The economics of schooling: production and efficiency in public schools', *Journal of Economic Literature* 24(3): 1141–77.

Harkness, S. and Machin, S. (1999) 'Graduate earnings in Britain 1974–95', *DfEE Research Report 95*. London: DfEE.

Hoxby, C. (2003) 'School choice and school competition: evidence from the United States', *Swedish Economic Policy Review* 10: 9–66.

Jantti, M., Bratsberg, B., Roed, K., Raaum, O., Naylor, R., Osterbacka, E., Bjorklund, A. and Eriksson, T. (2006) 'American exceptionalism in a new light: a comparison of intergenerational earnings mobility in the Nordic countries, the United Kingdom and the United States', *IZA Discussion Paper Number 1938*. Bonn, Germany: Institute for the Study of Labor (IZA).

Kane, T.J. and Staiger, D.O. (2002) 'The promise and pitfalls of using imprecise school accountability measures', *Journal of Economic Perspectives* 16(4): 91–114.

Katz, L. and Autor, D. (1999) 'Changes in the wage structure and earnings inequality', in O. Ashenfelter and D. Card (Eds) *Handbook of Labor Economics* 3, North-Holland.

Kitigawa, E. and Hauser, P. (1973) *Differential Mortality in the United States: a study in socio-economic epidemiology*. Cambridge, MA: Harvard University Press.

Krueger, A. and Whitmore, D. (2001) 'The effect of attending a small class in the early grades on college-test taking and middle school test results: evidence from Project STAR', *Economic Journal* 111: 34–63.

Lakdawalla, D. (2001) *The Declining Quality of Teachers*. National Bureau of Economic Research, Working Paper No. 8263. Online (Available: http://ssrn.com/abstract=268344).

Layard, R., McIntosh, S. and Vignoles, A. (2002) *Britain's Record on Skills*. Centre for the Economics of Education, Discussion Paper No. 23.

Literacy Task Force (1997) *A reading revolution: how we can teach every child to read well*, London: The Literacy Task Force, University of London Institute of Education.

Lleras-Muney, A. (2005) 'The relationship between education and adult mortality in the United States', *Review of Economic Studies* 72: 189–221.

Lochner, L. and Moretti, E. (2004) 'The effect of education on criminal activity: evidence from prison inmates, arrests and self-reports', *American Economic Review* 94: 155–89.

Machin, S. (1996) 'Wage inequality in the UK', *Oxford Review of Economic Policy* 12(1): 47–64.

——(1999) 'Wage inequality in the 1970s, 1980s and 1990s', in P. Gregg and J. Wadsworth (Eds) *The State of Working Britain*. Manchester: Manchester University Press.

——(2003) 'Wage inequality since 1975', in R. Dickens, P. Gregg and J. Wadsworth (Eds) *The Labour Market Under New Labour: the state of working Britain*. London: Palgrave Macmillan.

Machin, S., McNally, S. and Meghir, C. (2007b) 'Resources and standards in urban schools', Centre for the Economics of Education, Discussion Paper No. 76.

Machin, S. and McNally, S. (2004) 'The Literacy Hour', *Discussion Paper No. 43*, Centre for the Economics of Education.

Machin, S., McNally, S. and Silva, O. (2007a) 'New technology in schools: is there a payoff?', *Economic Journal* 117(522): 1145–67.

Machin, S. and Van Reenen, J. (2006) 'Changes in wage inequality', in S.N. Durlauf and L.E. Blume (Eds) (2008) *New Palgrave Dictionary of Economics* (2nd Edition). London: Palgrave Macmillan.

Machin, S. and Vignoles, A. (2004) 'Educational inequality: the widening socio-economic gap', *Fiscal Studies* 25: 107–28.

——(2005) 'Education policy and the evidence', in S. Machin and A. Vignoles (Eds) *What's the Good of Education? The economics of education in the UK*. Princeton, Oxford: Princeton University Press.

Machin, S. and Vujic, S. (2005) *Crime and education in the United Kingdom*, Centre for Economic Performance: London School of Economics (mimeo).

McIntosh, S. (2004) 'Further analysis of the returns to academic and vocational qualifications', *Discussion Paper No. 35*, Centre for the Economics of Education.

McIntosh, S. and Vignoles, A. (2000) 'Measuring and assessing the impact of basic skills on labour market outcomes', *Discussion Paper No. 3*, Centre for the Economics of Education.

Moser, C. (1999) *A Fresh Start: improving literacy and numeracy*, The Report of the Working Group Chaired by Sir Claus Moser. London: DfEE.

Nickell, S. and Quintini, G. (2002) 'The consequences of the decline in public sector pay in Britain: a little bit of evidence', *Economic Journal* 112: F107-F118.

OECD / Human Resources Canada (1995) *Literacy, Economy and Society: results of the first International Adult Literacy Survey*. Paris: OECD.

Office for Standards in Education (Ofsted) (1996) *The Teaching of Reading in 45 Inner London Primary Schools: a report by Her Majesty's Inspectors in collaboration with the LEAs of Islington, Southwark and Tower Hamlets*. London: Ofsted.

O'Leary, N.C. and Sloane, P.J. (2004) 'The return to a university education in Great Britain', IZA Discussion Paper No. 1199. Bonn, Germany: Institute for the Study of Labor (IZA).

——(2005) 'The changing wage return to an undergraduate education', IZA Discussion Paper No. 1549. Bonn, Germany: Institute for the Study of Labor (IZA).

Rosenthal, L. (2003) 'The value of secondary school quality', *Oxford Bulletin of Economics and Statistics* 65: 329–55.

Sianesi, B. (2003) *Returns to education: a non-technical summary of CEE work and policy discussion*, Institute for Fiscal Studies (mimeo).

Solon, G. (2002) 'Cross-country differences in intergenerational earnings mobility', *Journal of Economic Perspectives* 16 (Summer 2002): 59–66.

——(2004) 'A model of intergenerational mobility variation over time and place', in Miles Corak (Ed) *Generational Income Mobility in North America and Europe 38–47*. Cambridge: Cambridge University Press.

Stannard, J. and Huxford, L. (2007) *The Literacy Game: the story of the National Literacy Strategy.* Routledge: London.

Walker, I. and Zhu, Y. (2005) 'The college wage premium, over-education, and the expansion of higher education in Britain', *IZA Discussion Paper No. 1627.* Bonn, Germany: Institute for the Study of Labor (IZA).

West, A. and Pennell, H. (1999) 'School admissions: increasing equity, accountability and transparency', *British Journal of Education Studies* 46: 188–200

11 Aims for primary education

Changing global contexts

Rita Chawla-Duggan and John Lowe

INTRODUCTION

Fuelled by an historic convergence of globalisation, knowledge driven economies, human rights-based development and demographic trends, the recognition of the key role of education is growing in countries around the world (OECD[1]/UNESCO[2] 2002). This chapter offers a comparative perspective that focuses upon the changing global context of primary education in terms of the emerging educational responses to globalisation. The analysis of the changing global context of primary education inevitably raises questions about aims, processes and purposes of education in the twenty first century. Such questions are underpinned by the social, economic and political transformations that confront education. The changes are complex, uneven and contradictory; where uncertainty and risk is a feature of the age (Lauder *et al.* 2006). This chapter begins by offering a brief historical overview of changes that have occurred in the last decade concerning primary education, leading to current priorities and trends; a conceptual understanding of the notion of globalisation and existing tensions that exist in relation to current educational concerns; the purposes of education in the context of globalisation, and its implications for and the place of primary education within those global goals. The final part of the chapter examines two case study countries, namely India and China, in order to illustrate and juxtapose some of the key issues that have arisen in those countries as a result of the characteristics of globalisation. The chapter concludes by considering future implications for primary education in light of the issues raised.

HISTORICAL OVERVIEW AND EMERGING TRENDS

From a global perspective, the 1990s was the decade of concern for 'basic' education. This by and large was interpreted as primary schooling. Within a framework of education as a human right, on the one hand, and an acceptance of the impact that basic education has on fundamental concerns in development, such as health, employability, agricultural productivity, and so on, on the other, a consensus emerged that the most important challenge to educational development was the achievement of 'Education for All' (EFA). This was formalised on a global scale at the beginning of the decade in the Jomtien Conference and the EFA Declaration, with its goal of achieving universal access to primary education by 2005. Interest in primary education was at its highest in a global sense in the 1990s, with the World Bank and other multilateral donor agencies acting as chief drivers to education and declaring primary education to be their major, sometimes sole, educational funding concern.

The decade did, however, see considerable failure to put these intentions into action. The follow-up Dakar Conference of 2000 can be seen partly as an attempt to breathe new life into the EFA ideal, with the realisation that progress had been disappointing and targets had to be revised. The focus and the agenda shifted, with a growing recognition that simply boosting primary school enrolment rates was an inadequate response to the demand for a more educated society that could meet the needs of development. The concern instead became the quality of the educational experience that was being offered. Although the notion of a 'quality education' had in fact been part of the Jomtien agenda, it had been displaced in subsequent policy and action in favour of apparently more easily measured, easily targeted quantitative enrolment concerns. Now, however, 'quality' is most firmly in the educational spotlight and the notion of what 'compulsory education' should be has also shifted to beyond the idea of 'basic education'. Whilst the rationale for focussing on quality in the *UNESCO EFA Global Monitoring Report 2005* (GMR) remains one that is firmly tied to the achievement of universal primary education (UPE), the understanding of education quality outlined in the *Report* takes us beyond the usual narrow quality indicators into discussions about what really matters in education, which includes notions of rights, equity and relevance (UNESCO 2005).

Globalisation has undoubtedly been a key part of the background to the changes outlined above, both in terms of increases in the scope, reach and depth of globalisation itself and also in terms of increasingly sophisticated analyses and understanding of the phenomena that inform policy initiatives. The ideology of globalisation has been used by a number of intergovernmental/multilateral organisations (such as, for example, the Organisation for Economic Co-operation and Development (OECD)) and has played an influential role in shaping current policy. Rizvi and Lingard (2006) state that these organisations speak consistently of the 'imperatives of globalisation' and of the need to reformulate educational purposes in line with the requirements of a global economy (p.248). The authors argue that the agenda of organisations such as the OECD has shifted so that their ideological view represents a set of aims linked to the requirements of the global economy. Policy concerns, in the past, were related to the economic and cultural ends of education, and between equity and efficiency concerns. Over the last ten years the shift has been a concern for social efficiency; it has promoted particular goals of education. Those goals are linked to the requirements of a global knowledge economy and economic growth.

One of the key global goals for governments remains 'Universal Primary Education' (UPE), by the revised year 2015. One way this is translated into policy terms is to equip all members of society with skills in literacy and numeracy that will allow them to function within their society. In order to achieve this aim, most countries have adopted a curriculum of five or six years of primary schooling which is considered sufficient to attain those objectives (UNESCO 2004).[3] However, existing trends suggest that compulsory education must extend beyond primary if it is to bring about a range of social and economic benefits to individuals and societies. Existing evidence on the relationship between human capital and the impact of education on the economic activity of individuals and a society has been explored by UNESCO/OECD in the 'world education indicators' (WEI) programme.[4] Their analysis has shown a consistently strong and positive association between improvements in the stock of human capital and economic growth among WEI countries, an association that is greater than among OECD countries (OECD/UNESCO 2002). Interestingly, the strongest correlations between schooling and economic growth occur in Argentina, Chile, Malaysia and Uruguay – suggesting that it is the higher levels of education (secondary and tertiary) that are important for human capital to translate into economic growth (*ibid.*). The point made is that human capital plays a stronger part in economic growth once it achieves a certain threshold, and that threshold lies beyond the primary phase.

The UNESCO review of education (2004), in focussing its attention beyond primary education, reflected a wider international change in educational focus. Their overview showed that no country has met the goals of universal primary enrolment without some critical mass of secondary participation. Others have also noted that no country has reached UPE without at least 35 per cent secondary net enrolment (Clemens 2004). With the emphasis on UPE, the EFA goals, and the United Nations Millennium Development Goals (MDG), notions of what should constitute 'compulsory education' and how it is expressed by national priorities have begun to change. Four in five countries now have regulations that define compulsory education beyond primary schooling. It is only in a minority of countries in Africa, North America and Asia where compulsory education is represented by the primary phase (UNESCO 2004).

There have also been changes in the supply of and demand for educational services which have been linked to the goal of UPE. A UNESCO review revealed that whilst the majority of countries have experienced growth in primary enrolment, increases at this level occurred in tandem with increases in secondary enrolment. This was the case for countries which had low levels of enrolment as well as those nearing UPE. The point made is that 'meeting demand for primary education can spur greater demand for schooling at secondary level. The costs of educational opportunity go beyond meeting UPE goals and imply the creation of additional opportunities at secondary level' (UNESCO 2004: 15).

GLOBALISATION: DEFINITIONS AND PERSPECTIVES

There is no consensus on a definition of globalisation, or its implications in terms of its consequences for individuals, groups and nations in different parts of the world (Lauder *et al.* 2006). The dominant view from the perspective of the developed nations is that it is about a competition among nations in which education plays a key role in outsmarting others in the search for scientific knowledge and technologies that enable innovation. National prosperity, justice and social cohesion are seen to rest on creating a highly skilled workforce with the knowledge, enterprise and insight required to attract the global supply of high skilled, high waged employment (*ibid.*). In other words the claim is that globalisation will bring widespread benefits, so long as education can produce the appropriately skilled workers. This rhetoric is taken as common sense or the 'education gospel' (Grubb and Lazerson 2006), but in reality it raises concerns for individuals and societies. The concerns are associated with growing inequalities and how education may be contributing to widening inequalities in the search for national prosperity.

Rizvi and Lingard (2006) outline three perspectives on globalisation. First, they define it as the ways in which the world is becoming increasingly interconnected and interdependent. As such, it is a set of social processes that imply 'inexorable integration of markets, nation states and technologies to a degree never witnessed before – in a way that is enabling individuals, corporations and nation states to reach round the world farther, faster, deeper and cheaper that ever before' (Friedman 1999: 9). In this way, globalisation is associated with technological revolutions in transport, communication and data processing. It is argued that such developments have transformed the nature of economic activity, changing the modes of production and consumption. From this perspective, the global economy is now characterised as informational, networked, knowledge based, post-industrial and service orientated (Porter 1990; Castells 2000).

Second, globalisation is perceived as a 'subjective ... awareness by people and states of recent changes in global economy and culture' (Rizvi and Lingard 2006: 251). This view of globalisation is reflected in changing values, where there is a common interest in collective actions to solve global problems (Albrow 1996: 34). It is a world of collective consciousness, where we see our problems as interconnected.

The final perspective of globalisation that Rizvi and Lingard (2006) outline is a critical one. It views globalisation as an ideological project of economic liberalisation that subjects states and individuals to market forces. In this ideology, power relations, practices and technologies play a 'hegemonic' role in organising how we understand the world (Schirato and Webb 2003). So, for example, the way in which the global economy operates and the manner in which culture, resources, crisis and power also operate are taken for granted by us as simply being the way the global economy operates.

Certainly globalisation is a fundamental change in the architecture of the world that, it is increasingly recognised, has implications for all countries and communities and that has changed our understanding of the nature of development itself and the options available to promote it. The growing complexity and sophistication associated with increased interconnectedness and mobilities of all sorts have immediate implications for the nature of an education appropriate to meet the needs of individuals, communities and nations in this era of globalisation. This alone would be one reason for an increasing concern with the quality of education, with this quality now being defined in terms of a preparation for a new set of economic, cultural and political conditions that are defined globally as much as locally.

CONSEQUENCES OF GLOBALISATION: TENSIONS IN POLICY

The consequences of globalisation have implications for education – and primary education, in particular – that may lead to tensions, if not contradictions, in policy emphases. There is, for example, considerable recognition in the literature that globalisation has commonly led to increased economic inequality, to the emergence of distinct 'winners' and 'losers' from globalisation, both in terms of differences between countries and communities and individuals within countries (as characterised by Hutton's 1996 description of a '30–40–30' society in the UK). The implications of this for education are themselves complex, depending for example on whether one approaches them from a perspective of 'social justice', 'social cohesion for the sake of stability' or 'individualism, the market and meritocracy'. The first of these leads to a concern for those who are disadvantaged and marginalised, treating education as a human right, and defining a quality educational experience in terms that recognise their communal and individual needs and differences, and which aims to open up possibilities for economic, social and political participation without a loss of identity. A 'social cohesion for stability' approach is concerned with the social and political destabilising effects of extreme inequalities and may also lead to a focus on the poor and the marginalised. The educational agenda that emerges from this approach, however, is one of greater assimilation to the dominant social norms and 'social pacification'. Both of these approaches do, however, generate a tension between educational policies that aim to engage with a global economic order that is inherently inequitable – because not to engage would be economic suicide – and their goal of either justice or cohesion that must challenge the structural roots of this inequity (Torres 2002).

The third perspective suggested above, characteristic of 'new right' politics and neo-liberal economics, essentially removes this tension from the government policy agenda by making success or marginalisation a matter for individual responsibility, with the market as the best possible arena for the management of competition. The potential consequences of this for education are illustrated in Ilon's (1997) mapping of educational provision onto a socio-economic stratification that derives from the individual's degree of participation in the global economy. At the upper end we see the growth of high-cost private schooling with standards defined internationally; at the bottom end we find sporadic attendance and low-quality schooling perceived to have minimal pay-offs.

THE GOALS OF EDUCATION AND THE PLACE OF PRIMARY EDUCATION

The need for a knowledge-based economy

Two characteristics associated with globalisation that have important implications for education in general, including primary education, are the growth of the so-called 'knowledge-based economy' (KBE) and the rapid pace of contemporary change (notably, though not exclusively, technological change). In particular, there is an issue which concerns the conflict between accelerating economic growth in some countries, such as India and China, and its implications for the provision of basic primary education and beyond. Brown and Hesketh (2004), amongst others, have challenged the significance, even the very existence, of the knowledge-based economy but it seems likely that a belief among policy makers in the growing importance of 'knowledge-work' for international competitiveness has driven much of their recent thinking. The essence of the KBE thesis is that the knowledge component of the modern global economy – ideas rather than material objects – is the greatest source of added value and, hence, of national and individual prosperity. The KBE is a high skills economy, based on leading-edge knowledge, research and creativity. One immediate consequence of this thesis is that tertiary education becomes a new focus of educational attention, exemplified by the World Bank's 'rediscovery' of this sector after years of neglect, but also visible in materials emerging from the OECD and national governments: for example, the OECD's strategic objective 4 is entitled 'Rethinking Tertiary Education in a Global Economy'. This speaks of the need for an appropriate balance of funding, both public and private, and also in terms of using indicators in relation to the individual and social returns of tertiary education. Returns to the individual are seen as labour market earnings, eschewing the broader liberal educational purposes once again, but in terms of tertiary education (Rizvi and Lingard 2006).

It would be difficult to prove that this increased concern with tertiary education has necessarily led to less policy attention being given to primary education, although presumably some sort of 'document count' might test this. What can be argued, however, on the basis of historical, national experiences around the world, is the likelihood of a 'backwash' effect: the greater the importance given to tertiary and higher education, the more that lower levels in the system are considered as a preparation for higher education rather than as useful ends in themselves (Dore 1997).

The knowledge economy and the associated changing purposes of education suggest a rather instrumental view of education. It serves the needs of a global knowledge economy where the economic framework and social efficiency, economic instrumentalism may be seen to usurp the goals of education associated with equity. Rizvi and Lingard (2006) illustrate how this is represented in the views of the OECD. For example, OECD strategic objective 5, 'Building social cohesion through education', speaks of improving equity and opportunities, but the focus is on special needs associated with being ethnically or culturally different as a result of the flows associated with globalisation. Equity is therefore associated with social cohesion. It is seen as essential to developing and maintaining cohesive societies and not about challenging existing definitions of how, for example, institutions may be reproducing inequalities in relation to class, caste or gender.

Education, technology and globalisation: lifelong learning

Economic, social and technological changes are now having a major impact on the nature and structure of educational institutions (Lauder *et al.* 2006). Economically, there have been three shifts: first, the increasing number of women entering the labour market has raised questions about the availability of early childhood education; second, the move to a knowledge-based economy has led to justifying more students entering higher education; and third, intensified global competition, linked to technological innovations, has meant that the shelf-life of skills is reducing, leading to constant retraining. Technological change combined with the emergence of new ideas and products leads to a need for continuous 'upskilling' or 'reskilling' throughout one's working life and therefore, a national and individual commitment to, and capacity for, continuous learning. (This argument can also be carried over into effectively coping with life outside the workplace as the pace of broader social change accelerates.) The more rapidly change takes place, the quicker that particular skills and knowledge become obsolete and must be replaced. These developments have led to a redefinition from 'education for life' to 'education through life' and a concept of lifelong learning, where the boundaries of education and life become blurred. The crucial question is how lifelong learning is interpreted.

> If students see it as a means to economic ends alone, then we produce clever, calculating pleasure machines. In contrast, if the outcomes of education are to produce students that are more conscious of what they owe to society and the environment, then we are one step towards understanding how the fundamental problems that confront us require collective solutions.
>
> (Lauder *et al.* 2006: 57–58)

During the 1990s, the notion of lifelong learning was underpinned by two emphases: one being a humanistic perspective that was about providing social democracy and opportunity, and the other being about the development of the neo-liberalist, self capitalising, individual (Rose 1999, cited in Rizvi and Lingard 2006). Rizvi and Lingard (2006) suggest that it is the latter purpose of lifelong learning that is currently emphasised; and this is reflected in shifts in educational policy goals of influential agencies such as the OECD. The goals are concerned with preparing people for the world of work and a life of self-capitalisation (*ibid.:* 253). They are indicated in a number of documents; for example, the OECD reports *The Knowledge-Based Economy* (OECD 1996a) and *Lifelong Learning for All* (OECD 1996b). In these documents education is perceived as being about developing dispositions for learning across the life cycle, rather than at a particular stage (Rizvi and Lingard 2006). Learners are expected to be flexible, mobile lifelong learners, who have cosmopolitan dispositions and are able to deal effectively with cultural diversity, endemic change and innovation. This view of learners places less emphasis on the purposes of education being social justice and social democracy, and more emphasis on a concern associated with a neo-liberal ideology and its relationship with economic development.

With children in primary schooling being many years away from the labour market, or indeed from full participation in society in general, the focus of learning (within a context of lifelong learning) here moves to generic and transferable skills, rather than the particular. Primary schooling becomes repositioned, in a continuum of education that is now of much greater span and which is concerned in its earlier stages with developing the capacity to learn – 'learning to learn' – as much as with the learning of any particular body of knowledge or narrow set of skills. The function of primary schooling in this lifelong learning scheme becomes one of developing 'core skills', primarily identified as literacy and numeracy although various degrees and forms of socialisation may also be seen as important. Knowledge of the particular does not disappear from the curriculum, but time devoted to it may be reduced and the teaching of it may be recast so as to emphasise increasing learner autonomy, the skills of independent learn- ing, and elementary metacognitive skills. In this context, strategies for effective and deep learning possibly replace transmission models of teaching.

In many countries in the world, however, the curricular simplification that is implied in the above account has not taken place. The backwash effect of selection examina- tions to higher levels of education, combined with increased quality differentiation among those higher level institutions that exacerbates competition for entry to the 'best' among them, leads to a content-cramming imperative in many schools. A further development associated with this highly charged competitive environment is the growth in private tutoring and 'cram' schools, outside the formal education system (Bray 1999). Traditionally this has been a phenomenon more associated with secondary schooling, but backwash effects are relentlessly driving further down the system.

At the other end of the education phase, improving early childhood education and childcare is linked to lifelong learning and a number of international policies where the rationales are those of economic development. Early education is now part of the process of globalisation (Woodhead 2001). Diverse programmes of family support, childcare and early education can now be found throughout the world, very often strongly influenced by models that originate in Europe or North America (Lamb *et al.* 1992). Moreover research evaluations increasingly take a cross national perspective, comparing quality in different country contexts (see, for example, Olmsted and Weikart 1989). The rationale forwarded in much of the documentation on the expansion of early years education, including the recent 'Education for All Global Monitoring Report' (UNESCO 2007), is one that constantly speaks about the economic and social returns to the individual and society of investing in early childhood care and education. There is also the view that examining European quality issues in global context (as well as in historical context) encourages a broader perspective on particular issues and constraints that determine what counts for early childhood quality in specific economic, cultural, educational and political contexts (Woodhead 2001).

Globalisation and the benchmarking of standards: quality as learning outcomes

Underpinning the doctrine of employability is that education will give the opportunity to make oneself employable. Reich (2006) argues that 'the fate of workers within their own country will depend on the value of their credentials, skills and knowledge in the global market' (Lauder *et al.* 2006: 35). This has led to a focus on raising educational standards, against a background of competition globally, because it is believed the best educated (that is those that are educated to a high standard) will be able to compete for high skilled, high waged jobs. A range of policies in all phases of education, through-out the world, have been introduced in attempts to raise standards, although what constitutes 'standards' is itself a matter of considerable debate. Standard setting, Room (2000) suggests, can be seen from two perspectives. 'From a consensus perspective, the trend towards global standard setting is seen as industrial progress from the national to the international level' (Lauder *et al.* 2006: 41), where international comparisons and league tables are seen as testament to the country's progress. 'From a conflict perspective, how standards are set will reflect the strategic interest of stake holders especially in relation to positional competition' (*ibid.*).

One important result of the focus on standards as a definition of quality has been an increased concern with the effectiveness of schooling and on the specification and measurement of learning outcomes. There are multiple strands to the responses to this that include attention to school management systems, the development of systemic education outcome indicators, the measurement of learning achievement, and the means to ensure teacher and school accountability.

The emphasis on evaluating and improving the outcomes of education is reflected in the OECD and in the independent evaluation of World Bank support to primary education (Independent Evaluation Group 2006). In both cases, the emphasis is on economics and social efficiency. For example, OECD strategic objective 2 states that: 'the prosperity of countries now derives to a large extent from their human capital and individuals need to advance their knowledge and competencies throughout their lives in order to succeed in a rapidly changing world' (cited in Rizvi and Lingard 2006). The IEG report for the World Bank stated that:

> primary education needs to focus on learning outcomes. The MDG push for uni-versal primary enrolment [...] will not suffice to ensure that children achieve the basic literacy and numeracy that are essential to poverty reduction. To reduce poverty, countries need to make improved learning outcomes a core objective in their primary education [...] recognising that improving learning outcomes for all will require higher unit costs than universal completion ... Improve the perfor-mance of sector management in support of learning outcomes [...] Improve monitoring and evaluation systems that track learning outcomes over time among different income and social groups [...]
>
> (IEG 2006: x)

The World Bank's 2005 'Education Sector Strategy Update' commits the Bank to maintaining momentum on 'Education for All' and the MDGs, whilst at the same time promoting 'education for the knowledge economy' (secondary, higher and lifelong learning). Few of the sample investment projects that were used in the IEG evaluation aimed to improve learning outcomes, but one of the countries showing the most improvement in learning outcomes was India, where national commitment to learning outcomes and their measurement is high. Even in countries where learning outcomes have improved however, absolute levels of student achievement remain low. For example, in Ghana, only 10 per cent of children reached the country's mastery levels in mathematics and 5 per cent in English. In India, half of the 7–10 year olds were unable to read fluently a short paragraph of grade one level (IEG 2006: xvi).

Equity and globalisation: promoting greater literacy and the debate over English

The idea of meritocratic competition is challenged by globalisation because nation states are losing control of some of the key features of selection (Lauder *et al.* 2006). In higher education, global consumerism raises questions about equality of opportunity in relation to access, since it is wealth that becomes the key determinant of access. In secondary schooling in England, much of the debate about educational opportunity has focused on the strategies adopted by the middle classes to sustain their advantage in domestic competition (Ball 2003). Lauder *et al.* (2006) ask 'what are the global routes to advantage now being laid?'

The issue of promoting greater literacy in an era of globalisation has, for some countries, raised the question of the language of instruction and the teaching of a second language. With the emergence of English as the global *lingua franca* in business, in science and technology, on the internet, and so on, the desire to learn English or to have one's children learn it, has exploded. In some contexts the issue is when to start teaching it, with tensions between the 'earlier the better' argument and that which emphasises the importance of a secure grounding in the child's first language. In other countries the debate is over whether to make English the language of instruction and at what age this should begin.

This debate over language of instruction must, in many countries, be located in the context of positional competition, where access to education through English is one of the key factors distinguishing elites in countries where English is not the official or national language. Fluency in English may act as a social marker domestically, as in India for example, and may also be a crucial skill for accessing the labour market associated with the higher skills end of the global economy. A further key element in this positional competition, and one which is closely linked to access to English, is the growth of private schooling.

The rise of private schooling

Private schooling has arisen in response to different contexts. One common context has been where it has met excess demand due to shortfalls in the public sector supply (UNESCO/OECD 2002), for example, in the area of early years' education. It has also arisen due to a response to differential demand – for example offering specific opportunities that are not provided by the state, such as English language schooling and pre-school education. How enrolment is distributed across types of educational institutions reflects how important the private sector is in providing education. In nine out of sixteen WEI countries, the proportion of private primary school enrolment exceeded 10 per cent (OECD 2004). In comparison to OECD countries, WEI countries had a higher proportion of primary school students enrolled in the private sector.

In some countries that allow or encourage the establishment of private schools, their popularity is closely linked to the issue of language of instruction. In countries as diverse as India, Taiwan and Tanzania, a significant market has arisen for private, English-medium primary schools. In some cases there is an ongoing struggle between government policy, which may try to prohibit English medium teaching, and parental demand. This demand may arise largely from an economic and social elite who see access to high quality private schooling and to English language instruction as part of the maintenance of an elite status for their children. In such cases it is more difficult for the government to sustain attempts to suppress such schools.

PRIMARY EDUCATION IN A GLOBAL CONTEXT: TWO CASE STUDIES

We now provide two case studies of recent primary level educational developments, India and China. These case studies provide examples of how the issues discussed above may appear in practice. It is also felt that there is particular significance in choosing these two countries, given that together they constitute some 40 per cent of the world's population and are both generating exceptionally high and sustained levels of economic growth that can be attributed largely to their engagement with the global economy. At the same time, the differences in their historical and contemporary ideologies add extra interest to any comparison between them.

Case Study 1: India

India is one of the fastest growing economies in the worlds, next to China. The British Government Department for International Development (DfID 2007)[5] informs us that the Indian economy is growing at 8 per cent per annum and, if this continues, it will become the fourth largest economy in 20 years. However, the same source also tells us that 30 million Indians still live with an income of less than a dollar a day and, while there is remarkable progress in education, with 83 per cent of children enrolled in primary school and infant mortality rates falling, nevertheless 47 per cent of under three year olds are malnourished. This is a mixed and general story. Information of this sort is essential of course, providing important data about progress and acting as a guide for general policy (Garrett 2007). A similar picture was portrayed in the earlier 2006 UN Human Development Report, which ranked India fairly low in terms of social indicators such as education, indicating that education for India's poorer majority has yet to catch up with the processes and benefits of wealth creation in which more affluent minorities are engaged. So what can we say of the primary level educational developments occurring in India to date?

Providing a highly significant example of a major national initiative to develop human capital, the Government of India (GOI) launched its District Primary Education Programme (DPEP) in 1994 with support from the World Bank, the European Union, UNICEF and the UK and Netherlands governments.

> DPEP aimed to universalize access, increase enrolment, maintain attendance and raise achievement in primary education; to give particular attention to equalising opportunity and provision for disadvantaged groups […] to maximize community involvement in education […] to upgrade school buildings, to raise levels of school resources and equipment; to support teachers and schools with training,

networking and resources centres; to strengthen and build capacity for planning, evaluation and management and to improve the quality of teaching itself.

(Alexander 2001a: 98)

Whilst DPEP gave primary education the attention and priority in Government, the models of pedagogy and pedagogical renewal enshrined in the DPEP were not without their problems. In terms of quality, as subsequently defined and developed in the context of EFA, the DPEP model made relatively uncritical use of child-centred pedagogy allied, somewhat paradoxically, to school effectiveness research (Alexander 2001a). Ramachandran (2003) argued that despite its explicit equity focus and considerable advances in this regard in many states and districts, access to primary schooling in rural areas continued to be a challenge for girls and children from scheduled castes and scheduled tribes.

A large number of documents and reports have been produced under the DPEP including the biannual progress reports written by the Government of India for the Joint Review Missions, and studies published by the National University of Educational Planning and Administration (NUEPA, formally NIEPA), Educational Consultants (New Delhi) and the National Council for Educational Research and Training (NCERT). Despite some encouraging responses to the programme, the work of Aggarwal (2001) suggested that improvements were marked during the first few years of the DPEP, but that student achievement levels were not sustained, that students from privately managed schools fared better than those in government schools, and that there was a long term concern over declining achievement in mathematics, which in turn had an adverse impact on secondary and senior secondary examination results (Aggarwal 2001). This has also brought attention to the issue of quality being addressed in programmes that not only existed within the DPEP but in the range of experimental projects and trailblazers in existence, designed to address the problem of access, retention and drop-out (ERU 2001). The prevailing view is that it is not enough to push children into school without considering the quality of the education they are likely to receive there.

DPEP has now been superseded by GOI's even more ambitious Sarva Shiksha Abhiyan (SSA) programme, which aims to universalise elementary education for all children in the 6–14 age group, a task which covers over 190 million children in well over one million schools (Ministry of Human Resource Development 2002). At the same time, the SSA retains the DPEP's policy of positive discrimination in favour of girls, children with special needs and those from scheduled castes and tribes. The emphasis on equity is combined, as more generally in the international EFA context, with a concern to move beyond access and enrolment and address the imperative of educational quality, and to do so in a more rounded and rigorous way than in the DPEP (Alexander 2007). The SSA has also sustained the attention given in the DPEP to securing a high level of local engagement and ownership of the reforms, especially where parents are concerned.

The concern for learning achievement, equity and learning outcomes

There has been progress in deed and commitment to UPE (universal primary education) in India. Census and Sample Surveys (National Family Health Survey, National Sample Survey Organisation, cited in Ramachandran 2005) indicate progress in literacy levels and primary school enrolment during the 1990s. Government sources indicate the allocation of substantial funds to elementary education, and reiterate commitment to social equity in access to quality education (*ibid.*). However, the hard to reach groups remain a challenge (ERU 2001; Ramachandran 2004). There are clearly lessons that other countries in the southern hemisphere may learn from India's experiences of mobilising hard-to-reach groups. Girls, with variations by region, caste, tribe and community remain two thirds of the unreached (ERU 2001), although specific pro-grammes focussing on girls have improved enrolment rates. The situation remains the same for those children from SC and ST communities.[6]

Ramachandran (2005) provides a forthright critique of the most recent situation, arguing that the statistics and commitments are not necessarily reflected in the reality of life in rural hamlets and urban slums. She explains how in the district of Udaipur in Rajasthan there have been numerous innovative projects over the last fifteen years, yet nearly all social development indicators (relating to immunisation, child mortality, infant mortality and maternal mortality) are well below the state average. Additionally, primary schools in those districts do not function; the actual teaching time is as low as twenty-five minutes a day and two thirds of the girls attend night schools, which run for two to three hours in dim light. Women in these areas perceive schools as dys-functional both for boys and girls. Ramachandran (2005) questions how many children will complete the primary cycle with the requisite skills. She also asks how much learning is actually happening when drop-out rates remain so high. For example, in Andhra Pradesh 96 per cent of children between the ages of 6 and 14 enrol in formal education, but the state drop-out rate is as high as 72 per cent between classes I and X. The rates may have changed since the figures cited by Ramachandran were collected, but the scale of the challenge undoubtedly persists. It is here that questions of quality and equity are brought to the forefront of the debate.

In terms of the way forward for India, a number of proponents (PROBE[7] 1999; Aggarwal 2001; Ramachandran 2005) have stressed the need to focus first and fore-most on learning outcomes but to do so in a context which links equity with quality:

> [...] access without quality is meaningless, and quality is the essence of equity. There is little point in pushing children into schools if we cannot simultaneously gear the system to ensure children acquire reading, writing and cognitive skills appropriate for each level of education. This necessitates [...] changes in curricu-lum, classroom transactions, teacher training, classroom environment, teacher attitudes and school community linkages. Working on any of these, without addressing related issues does not lead to significant improvement in the learning outcomes of children.
>
> (Ramachandran 2005: 172)

The case for providing educational opportunities beyond the primary phase

In line with this report's earlier discussion, Ramachandran argues that the goals of education in India need to extend beyond the primary years if children's prospects are to be significantly changed. Whilst the demand for education in India is high,

> huge classes and inadequately trained teachers may mean that investment, enthusiasm, demand and a hugely dynamic economy still leave the majority of children barely

literate and with no hope of continuing beyond the most elementary level to vocational or academic courses which might genuinely alter their future prospects.

(Ramachandran 2005: 167)

Educational statistics for 2002–3 show that there was only one upper primary school for every three primary schools and only one high school for every five primary schools. In this respect, educational opportunities were limited beyond the primary phase. In response to this concern Ramachandran (*ibid.*) suggests that, given that educational aspirations (especially amongst parents) have changed, the goals of education need also to change accordingly, with the development of post-primary education and training. It is an instrumental view of a changing world, with the overall goal being to address the whole system, rather than distinct phases of it:

> Ordinary middle and high school is not enough. Given the changing scenario in the country – especially with respect to the educational aspirations of people – we have to think seriously about and plan for post-middle school and post-secondary education and training opportunities. [...] Evidence from studies done in the last ten years clearly demonstrates that there is a tremendous demand in education – across the board and amongst all social groups. Wherever the government has ensured a well-functioning school within reach, enrolment has been high.
>
> (Ramachandran 2005: 172)

The emphasis on learning outcomes beyond the primary phase is to place the value on education as a preparation for work. Multiple exit points from high school onwards are one suggestion, where children access a range of technical and vocational skills that are context specific as a regional resource basis. Furthermore this link with education and training is envisaged to be working with business and the development community, thereby highlighting the increasing role that the private sector may take. This pragmatic view of education will no doubt sit uncomfortably with those educationalists who remain convinced of the value of education as a worthwhile activity in itself, where the basic objective of development is conceived as the expansion of human capabilities (Dreze and Sen 1995: 11) rather than a focus on the generation of economic growth.

It must be noted that since the publication of Ramachandran's critique, the SSA has made substantial progress towards the goal of universalising basic education to age 14, as shown by the recent data on access, enrolment, equity and attainment (NCERT 2006; NUEPA 2007).

Private schooling in India

Whilst there is undoubted evidence that there has been improvement in enrolment and access to primary education to date, class, caste and gender continue to be segregating variables (Aggarwal 2000; Krishnaji 2001; Anuradha*et al.* 2001). The expansion of private schooling in India has led to a situation where increasingly boys are being sent to private schools even in borderline SC and tribal families. The increase in the private sector is in response to the increase in demand for education. In Uttar Pradesh and Bihar (which have low literacy rates) almost every village and hamlet possesses a 'teaching shop' (Ramachandran 2005: 171). The demand for quality basic education and the perceived decline of the public educational system have in fact led to parallel increases in private and unaided schools (Anuradha *et al.* 2001; Reddy 2004). Children whose parents can afford to send them to private tuition classes and those with literate parents (especially mothers) have been found to be the ones most able to read (Ramachandran 2005), illustrating the way in which a range of factors arising from socio-economic status may facilitate or impede successful primary schooling.

The specific configuration of such factors must be analysed for each country and this is not the place to do this for India, but the huge diversity in educational access and quality of provision is an important national phenomenon. School attendance varies across states and age groups in India. The 1998 National Family Health surveys found that attendance was 90 per cent higher in Himachel Pradesh and Kerala than in Bihar (cited in Ramachandran 2005; again, though more recent figures may show that the gap is closing, the considerable regional disparities persist). Attendance declines further as children become older. This issue does not only apply to the disadvantaged states, but is symptomatic of India generally. The issue of transition is therefore raised as a problem, especially for girls and especially in rural areas. The real problem, however, is

> that as we go down the social and economic pyramid, access and quality issues become far more pronounced in India. The vast numbers of the very poor in rural and urban India have to rely on Government schools of different types. The relatively better off in rural and urban India either access better endowed government schools or opt for private aided and unaided schools.
>
> (Ramachandran 2005: 170)

Case study 2: China

Although one can legitimately query the accuracy of some of the official figures (Postiglione 2006), there is no doubt that the expansion of enrolment at all levels of education in China over the last twenty years or so has been a remarkable achievement. The quantitative aspirations within the 'quantity-quality' dilemma that had bedevilled Chinese educational policy-making for most of the twentieth century (Pepper 1996) had, in most of the country, been met by the early years of the twenty-first. By the late 1990s, therefore, attention began to be turned more fully to improving the quality of educational provision, and in 1998 the Ministry of Education announced an 'Action project for vitalising education for the 21st century'. The key component of this project in primary education was a major curriculum reform programme, designed to 'bring forth a new generation of high-calibre citizens, people who are competent enough to serve China's modernization drive' (Zhu, quoted in Wang 2005). The rhetoric here suggests this reform can be located within the wider post-Mao Chinese policies of opening up to the rest of the world and actively engaging with globalisation; but taking the longer view of Suzanne Pepper's (*op cit*) finely detailed study of 20th century educational reform in China, it can be seen as yet another twist in a protracted process of resolving multiple dilemmas within the Chinese context. Writing about higher education reforms in China, Mok (2005) has suggested that references to the demands of globalisation as a key reform rationale are at least partly a rhetorical device used by policy makers to justify actions designed to serve other, internally-driven ends, very much in line with Pepper's analysis. This argument might be extended to basic education reforms too but, given the general opacity of the policy-making process in China, such an extension would be difficult to defend and we must perhaps take the rhetoric at its face value. In that case, the reform described below may be seen as part of China's interpretation of the educational imperatives of globalisation.

The Primary Curriculum Reform Project

The Primary Curriculum Reform Project was launched in 2001 on a trial basis in 38 districts across the country but was rolled out rapidly thereafter so that by 2005 it was claimed that 95 per cent of grade one primary students were using the new curriculum (Wang 2005). The reform is much more than a change in the content of the curriculum; it demands 'new teaching methods and new mind-sets, from teacher-centred (*yi jiao shi wei zhong xing*) to learner-centred (*yi xue xi zhe wei song xing*)' (Robinson 2006). Official statements express the need for 'competence-oriented education' to meet the needs of the modern world, and criticise the earlier curriculum as being 'irrelevant to practical needs of society and meant for nothing but to prepare students for examinations' (Wang 2005); thereby continuing and yet seeking to end the long-running debate between reformers and traditionalists in Chinese education that Pepper (1996) documents.

The goals for the new mathematics curriculum provide an illustration of the overall orientation of the programme, with their reference to 'essential mathematical knowledge and necessary skills so that they will be prepared for future life development; students learn to apply mathematical thinking to everyday life [...] develop their creativity, practical abilities [...]' (Zhang undated). There is an emphasis on the reduction of content in favour of 'skills' and the solution of 'challenging and comprehensive problems with applications close to real life scenarios' (*ibid.*). It is interesting to observe, however, that even officially approved documents acknowledge that this content reduction has its critics, who see it as a dumbing-down and hence a loss rather than a gain in quality (Wang 2005).

Post-imperial Chinese education has a long history of borrowing educational models – curricular, pedagogical and systemic – from elsewhere, usually in the name of 'modernisation' and usually with accompanying backlashes (Pepper 1996), and it would be easy to see these reforms as just another chapter in that history. This is an over-simplification, however, and it is just as important to note how the new curriculum retains important aspects of much older indigenous models. There remains, for example, an explicit emphasis on moral education, designed 'to strengthen patriotism, collectivism and the socialist ideal in order to assist students in the development of correct values, outlooks on life, and views of the world' (Huang 2004: 105). It remains to be seen, however, whether the ideals of the new curriculum will survive the almost inevitable backwash from the highly competitive national examinations for entry into senior high school and university, exacerbated by the existence of elite 'key' high schools and universities that are in themselves a product of a concern to promote educational quality, though on a much narrower front.

Economic development and inequity in education

A concern about quality represents only part of the current basic education agenda in China, however. Concurrently, and highlighted by the concern over quality, the issue of equity is receiving much attention, both in the policy rhetoric and in some interesting development projects. Rapidly growing economic disparity in post-reform China has been widely noted and, not surprisingly, this is being accompanied by widening gaps in educational access and provision. Although new forms of social stratification – notably the emergence of an urban middle class – are appearing and bringing with them new bases for social inequality, the fundamental sources of such inequality remain as they have been for centuries: urban-rural, east-west, majority Han/non-Han minorities are the key axes of economic and educational inequality. It is not surprising that, in a country of China's size and geographic complexity, there are significant exceptions to these dichotomies, but it is a reasonably accurate generalisation to say that the minority peoples living in the rural areas of Western China are the most disadvantaged. These represent the last few per cent of the population who have yet to have access to 'compulsory' basic education and among whom girls remain much less likely than boys to attend school and complete the basic cycle; but they are also those who are most likely to lack teachers, materials and other inputs that contribute to a 'quality' education (Postiglione 2006). One of this report's authors has himself experienced the vast discrepancies when visiting a primary school in Beijing that would be the envy of many in the UK, with multimedia classrooms, magnificent buildings and a vast array of teaching materials; then, a short time later, visiting a two-room school in a remote Yunnan valley, where the children only had teachers when young volunteers from other parts of the country could be persuaded to go there for a few weeks or months and, as a result, remained illiterate in their own first language.

A further element emerging in Chinese education that is almost certainly adding to growing inequalities – as in India – is private schooling. Historically the means of delivering almost all education, private schooling rapidly disappeared from China after 1949, only to re-emerge in the post-1978 reform era. Lin (1999) points out how this emergence has paralleled ongoing changes in the country's social class structure and attendant new educational demands. Weak legislative structures and administrative confusion in relation to private schools has presented difficulties for their establishment and probably reflect a certain official ambiguity towards them. There is undoubtedly some concern over the emergence of elite private schools and their implications for equity (*ibid.*) but, given the growing economic and political significance of the new urban middle classes in China, their further expansion is almost inevitable.

There does appear to be a genuine concern in the government to address educational inequalities, although it is impossible to know from whence this concern arises: social justice, social cohesion and control, or more efficient human capital development. Thus, for example, the government has tried to increase the flow of qualified teachers to western areas by waiving university fees for those who train at 'normal' (teacher training) universities if they agree to seven years' service in the poorest western areas. Anecdotal evidence suggests that this scheme is meeting with very limited success. Hannum (2003) also points out that policies of decentralisation that have been a core component of reform in education and other spheres, and particularly the demand for greater local mobilisation of funds for education, have contributed significantly to the growing disparity.

Addressing equity: the Gansu Basic Education Project

More positively, the Gansu Basic Education Project (GBEP) is a major intervention which brings together various educational policy strands in an interesting approach to educational development in remote and disadvantaged communities (Robinson 2006). GBEP is a multi-component project but with two pivotal aspects, School Development

Planning and Participatory Approaches to Teaching, that define its shift of the emphasis in basic education towards a 'bottom up' approach that ultimately focuses on meeting the learning needs of the individual child (GBEP 2007). Important aspects in the project design include: teacher training and up-grading; a variety of access improvement strategies such as the provision of scholarships, posting of female teachers to remote areas, feeding programmes and the development of child friendly campuses; the development of locally relevant materials for teacher and manager training; and for classroom use.

A significant feature of the project is the considerable use it makes of ICT. To make use of an existing national infrastructure of satellite communications and educational television, resource centres were set up in 686 township central schools and in county-level in-service teacher training institutions. These are equipped with satellite dishes and a range of electronic hardware, including computers, printer, CD-player and re-writer, data storage items, television, digital camera and computer modem, plus a range of software. Not all of these centres have internet access but connectivity is rapidly increasing. The centres are used for teacher professional development activities but also for the production of print and video materials by local teams, to be relevant to local conditions and learning needs (Robinson 2006).

An unusual component of the programme has been the design and provision of 'Children's Schools', which start by asking: 'What is a child's school? What does a school look like that a child rather than an adult would design? What should a school be like when the child is placed at the centre of the picture?' (Smawfield and Du 2006). Important aspects of this design process include the provision, design and use of furniture to support participatory teaching methods and co-operative learning; the consideration of school and classroom displays; and the creation of a 'happy campus' by means such as the provision of sports and play space and facilities, and the general improvement of the appearance and functionality of school grounds, often with active community involvement.

A recent account of the progress of GPEP identifies changes in *relationships* – between the school and local authorities, between school and community and between teachers and pupils – as the project's greatest achievements to date (GPEP 2007). The last of these is perhaps most important in terms of identifying and then being able to meet the diverse needs of learners in a truly inclusive education that addresses the issue of equity at its most fundamental level.

CONCLUSION

This brief survey and its case studies of major educational interventions in two countries very different from England have identified some of the changes occurring in the last decade that have influenced the current priorities and place of primary education within the context of globalisation. There have been several drivers associated with the globalisation process, notably the development of technology and ideas about the knowledge economy. These, together with the influence of multilateral agencies on national education systems, have had implications for the role of education in general, and the place of primary education in particular. Existing trends suggest that the duration of compulsory schooling must be extended in all countries beyond the primary stage if it is to bring about social and economic development to individuals and societies. But there is a cost to expansion.

Many countries face constraints in meeting the cost of expanding educational opportunities. Systemic expansion entails a proportional increase in resources, but many governments are unable to cope with the higher costs (UNESCO/OECD 2002). Middle income countries have largely met the goal of universal primary education and now aim to widen access and improve secondary and tertiary levels of education. However, there are constraints in generating funds to meet the high cost of post-compulsory education. A further problem is that the national context may be one of considerable social and economic inequality, and inequalities in post-compulsory education may re-inforce social inequalities. It is therefore important that policies aiming to increase participation in education also share out the costs and benefits at all levels of education. Herein lie notions of equity – in terms of who is to cover the costs and who is to benefit. The case studies of India and China reflect this increasing concern with equity.

As more countries move towards knowledge-based economies, there will be an increase in the importance of human capital (OECD/ UNESCO 2002). The implication for attaining UPE, then, is that primary schooling can no longer usefully be considered in isolation, as a 'complete' educational experience in itself, but must be addressed on a continuum with other levels in education. On the whole, many non-OECD countries have achieved progress in raising access to and participation in education over the past generation (OECD/ UNESCO 2002). The translation of increased access to school into increased availability of human capital depends on participation in further and higher levels of education (*ibid.*). However, despite progress, more needs to be done in non-OECD countries, in order to attain the educational levels found in most OECD countries.

In a number of non-OECD countries, the issue of sharing costs among those that participate in the education system and society as a whole is currently being discussed (UNESCO/OECD 2002). The issue is relevant to the expansion of education at both ends of the spectrum – that is, pre-primary and beyond compulsory schooling, where public expenditure is less common than at other levels. The challenge will be to design policies that allow the new clients participating in education to share costs and benefits. Additionally, as the role of private sector funding increases, care needs to be taken that it does not create barriers for potential learners by denying access to opportunities.

Equity is clearly one of the dominant emerging issues in education worldwide, its significance highlighted by tendencies towards increased inequality within globalisation. But equity in education is no longer being interpreted in purely quantitative terms as in the past, in terms of the numbers of children from diverse backgrounds attending and completing school. Certainly, and sadly, these enrolment and retention issues remain a concern in far too many countries, but there is also an emerging view of equity in more qualitative terms, to be judged by the quality of the educational experience provided. The foundations of equity remain in the need to ensure that all children do receive an education, but now also there is a concern that this education will be of the highest possible quality for all. Inevitably, 'educational quality' will become a contested issue, with broad lines of division between an instrumentalist, purely human capital view of the role of education and an alternative position rooted in a more humanistic tradition. The examples of India and China presented here, though only brief snapshots, do suggest that any analysis of educational quality must retain sensitivity to contemporary and historical contextual differences; and this in an era when globalisation may be presented as an homogenising experience for all. We suggest that at heart, educational quality means meeting learners' diverse needs and opening rather than foreclosing opportunities to develop both as individuals, and as valuable members of local and global society.

NOTES

1 Organisation for Economic Co-operation and Development.
2 United Nations Educational, Scientific and Cultural Organization.
3 The International Standard Classification of Education (ISCED97) defines primary education as one that: 'gives students a sound basic education in reading, writing and mathematics, along with an elementary understanding of other subjects such as history, geography, natural science, social science, art and music. In some cases, religious instruction is featured. This level consists of education provided for children, the customary or legal age of entrance being not younger than five years, or older than seven years. This level covers in principle six years of full-time schooling' (UNESCO 2001).
4 Countries participating in the OECD/UNESCO World Education Indicators Programme (WEI) which has been examining the impact of human capital on economic growth relative to findings in OECD member states have included: Argentina, Brazil, Chile, China, Egypt, India, Indonesia, Jamaica, Jordan, Malaysia, Paraguay, Peru, the Philippines, the Russian Federation, Sri Lanka, Thailand, Tunisia, Uruguay and Zimbabwe. The findings show that demands for educational opportunities are growing across WEI countries, the higher rates of primary school completion and recognition of the positive gains to be realised to further levels of education (OECD/UNESCO 2002).
5 DfID (2007): www.dfid.gov.uk/countries/asia/india.asp (consulted 30/07/07).
6 'Scheduled Castes (SCs) and Scheduled Tribes (STs) are Indian population groupings that are explicitly recognized by the Constitution of India as previously "depressed". SCs/STs together comprise over 24% of India's population, with SC at over 16% and ST over 8%' (http://en.wikipedia.org/wiki/Scheduled_castes_and_scheduled_tribes).
7 PROBE: Public Report on Basic Education in India.

REFERENCES

Aggarwal, Y. (2001) *Quality Concerns in Primary Education in India: where is the problem?* Delhi: National University for Educational Planning and Administration.
——(2000) *An Assessment of Trends in Access and Retention*. New Delhi: National Institute of Educational Planning and Administration
Albrow, M. (1996) *The Global Age*. Cambridge: Polity.
Alexander, R.J. (2001a) *Culture and Pedagogy: international comparisons in primary education*. Oxford: Blackwell.
——(2001b) 'In pursuit of quality in elementary education: lessons from DPEP', in R.J. Alexander, P. Cohen, M. Mercer, V. Ramachandran and S. Shukla *Reflections on Equity, Quality and Local Planning in the District Primary Education Programme*. Delhi: The European Commission.
——(2007) *Education for All, the Quality Imperative and the Problem of Pedagogy*. Delhi: Department for International Development.
Albrow, M. (1996) *The Global Age*. Cambridge: Polity.
Anuradha, D., Noronha, C. and Sampson, M. (2001) *India: primary schools and universal elementary education*. India Education Team report No.3. New Delhi: World Bank.
Ball, S. (2003) *Class Strategies and the Education Market: the middle classes and social advantage*. London: Routledge.
Bray, M. (1999) *The Shadow Education System: private tutoring and its implications for planners*. Paris: International Institute for Educational Planning.
Brown, P. and Hesketh, A. (2004) *The Mismanagement of Talent: employability and jobs in the knowledge economy*. Oxford: Oxford University Press.

Castells, M. (2000) *The Rise of the Network Society* (2nd edition). Oxford: Blackwell.

Clemens, M. (2004) *The Long Walk to School: international education goals in historical perspective*, CGD working paper, No. 37. Washington DC: Centre for Global Development.

DfID (2007) Website: www.dfid.gov.uk/countries/asia/india.asp.

Dore, R. (1997) *The Diploma Disease: education, qualification and development* (2nd edition). London: Institute of Education.

Dreze, J. and Sen, A. (1996) *India: economic development and social opportunity*. New Delhi: Manzar Khan, Oxford University Press.

Educational Research Unit (ERU) (2001) *Backward and Forwards Linkages: ten case studies in primary education*. Report supported by DfID, on approval of DPEP Bureau, GOI.

Friedman, T. (1999) *The Lexus and the Olive Tree*. New York: Farrar Strauss Giroux.

Garrett, R. (2007) 'Foreword', in R. Chawla-Duggan (2007) *Children's Learner Identity as Key to Quality Primary Education: eight case studies of schooling in India today*. Lewiston, Queenston, Lampeter: The Edwin Mellen Press.

GBEP (2007) *The Gansu Basic Education Project (GBEP)*. Website: http://gbep.legend-net.cn/en/about.asp.

Grubb, W.N. and Lazerson, M. (2006) 'The globalisation of rhetoric and practice: the education gospel and vocationalism', in H. Lauder, P. Brown, J. Dillabough, and A.H. Halsey (Eds) (2006) *Education, Globalization and Social Change*. New York: Oxford University Press: 295–307.

Hannum, E. (2003) 'Poverty and basic education in rural China: villages, households, and girls' and boys' enrolment', *Comparative Education Review* 47(2): 141–59.

Huang, F. (2004) 'Curriculum reform in contemporary China: seven goals and six strategies', *Journal of Curriculum Studies* 36(1): 101–15.

Hutton, W. (1996) *The State We're In*. London: Vintage.

Ilon, L. (1997) 'Educational repercussions of a global system of production', in W.K. Cummings and N.F. McGinn (Eds) (1997) *International Handbook of Education and Development: preparing schools, students and nations for the twenty-first century*. Oxford: Elsevier Science.

Independent Evaluation Group (IEG) (2006) *From Schooling Access to Learning Outcomes: an unfinished agenda. An evaluation of World Bank support to primary education*. Washington DC: World Bank.

Krishnaji, N. (2001) 'Poverty, gender and schooling: astudy of two districts in Andhra Pradesh', in A. Vaidyanathan and P.R. Gopinathan Nair (Eds) (2001) *Elementary Education in Rural India: a grassroots view*. New Delhi: Sage Publications.

Lamb, M.E., Sternberg, K.J., Hwang, C. and Broberg, C. (Eds) (1992) *Child Care in Context: cross cultural perspectives*. Hillsdale, NJ: Lawrence Erlbaum.

Lauder, H., Brown, P., Dillabough, J. and Halsey, A.H. (Eds) (2006) *Education, Globalisation and Social Change*. New York: Oxford University Press

Lin, J. (1999) *Social Transformation and Private Education in China*. New York: Praeger.

Ministry for Human Resource Development (2002) *Sarva Shiksha Abhiyan: framework for implementation*. Delhi: Government of India Ministry of Human Resource Development.

Mok, K.-H. (2005) 'Riding over socialism and global capitalism: changing education governance and social policy paradigms in post-Mao China', *Comparative Education* 41(2): 217 – 242.

NCERT (2006) *Learning Achievement of Classes II, III and V: a baseline study*. Delhi: NCERT.

NUEPA (2007) *Elementary Education in India: where do we stand? District Report cards for 2003–4, 2004–5 and 2005–6, Volume Iand II*. Delhi: NUEPA.

OECD (1996a) *The Knowledge-Based Economy*. Paris: OECD.

——(1996b) *Lifelong Learning for All*. Paris: OECD.

——(2006) *Education At a Glance*. Paris: OECD.

OECD/UNESCO (2002) *Financing Education, Investments and Returns*. Paris: UNESCO/OECD Publications.

Olmsted, P. and Weikart, D. (Eds) (1989) *How Nations Serve Young Children*. Ypsilanti, MI: High Scope Press.

Pepper, S. (1996) *Radicalism and Education Reform in 20th-Century China: the search for an ideal development model*. Cambridge: Cambridge University Press.

Porter, M. (1990) *The Competitive Advantage of Nations*. London: Macmillan.

Postiglione, G. (2006) 'Schooling and inequality in China', in G. Postiglione (Ed) (2006) *Education and Social Change in China*. New York: M.E. Sharp.

PROBE (1999) *Public Report on Basic Education in India*. Delhi: Oxford University Press.

Ramachandran, V. (2003) *Snakes and Ladders: factors that facilitate/impede successful primary school completion*. Delhi: World Bank.

Ramachandran, V. (Ed) (2004) *Gender and Social Equity in Primary Education*. New Delhi, Thousand Oaks, London: Sage Publications.

Ramachandran, V. (2005) 'The best of times, the worst of times', *Changing English* 12(2): 167–75.

Reddy, S. (2004) *Status of Learning Achievements in India: a review of the empirical research*. Report Commissioned by the Azim Premji Foundation.

Reich, R.B. (2006) 'Why the rich are getting richer and the poor, poorer', in H. Lauder, P. Brown, J. Dillabough, and A.H. Halsey (Eds) *Education, Globalisation and Social Change*. New York: Oxford University Press: 308–16.

Rizvi, F. and Lingard, B. (2006) 'Globalisation and the changing nature of the OECD's educational work', in H. Lauder, P. Brown, J. Dillabough, and A.H. Halsey (Eds) *Education, Globalisation and Social Change*. New York: Oxford University Press: 247–60.

Robinson, B. (2006) 'Using ICT to improve teacher quality: dimensions of change and challenge in the context of rural China', paper presented at the conference *Preparing Teachers for a Changing Context*, Institute of Education, University of London, 3–6 May 2006.

Room, G. (2000) 'Globalisation, social policy and international standard setting: the case of higher education credentials', *International Journal of Social Welfare* 9: 103–19.

Schirato, A., and Webb, J. (2003) *Understanding Globalisation*. London: Sage.

Smawfield, D. and Du, Y. (2006) *Building Children's Schools: transforming the learning environment, Volume 1*. Lanzhou, Beijing, London and Cambridge: Gansu Basic Education Project/ Department for International Development/Cambridge Education.

Torres, C.A. (2002) 'Globalization, education and citizenship: solidarity versus markets?', *American Educational Research Journal* 30(2): 363–78.

UNESCO International Bureau for Education (2001) *World Data on Education*. Geneva: IBE (CD-ROM).

UNESCO (2004) *Global Education Digest: comparing education statistics across the world*. Canada: UNESCO Institute for Statistics.

——(2005) *Education for All Global Monitoring Report 2005 – The Quality Imperative*. Paris: UNESCO/OECD Publications.

——(2007) *Education for All Global Monitoring Report*. Paris: UNESCO/OECD Publications.

Wang, J. (2005) *Curriculum Reform of Elementary Education in China*. Online (Available: http:// www.chinese-embassy.org.uk/eng/zt/Features/t214562.htm).

Woodhead, M. (2001) 'Towards a global paradigm for research into early childhood', in H. Penn (Ed) *Early Childhood Services*. Buckingham: Open University Press: 15–35.

Zhang, L. (undated) *A Review of China's Elementary Mathematics Education*. Online Available: http://www.cimt.plymouth.ac.uk/journal/zhang.pdf).

12 Aims as policy in English primary education

John White

This chapter is divided into two parts. Section 1 looks at official accounts over the last century of what primary aims should be; while Section 2 surveys accounts by educational theorists across the same timespan. In each case, there is more emphasis on recent developments. The two sections are not wholly discrete, since educational theory has influenced policy and vice versa.

1. CHANGING POLICY ON PRIMARY AIMS

2007, the year in which the Primary Review reached its mid-point, may prove a milestone in the history of primary school aims in England. It saw the publication of the first ever set of detailed statutory aims for the school curriculum. As yet, in January 2008, these have only been applied to Key Stages 3 and 4, but there is every likelihood that they will soon be made mandatory for Key Stages 1 and 2 as well. This statement may not seem remarkable in itself. After all, we have had substantial national aims for eight years now – over two pages of them at the front of the *National Curriculum Handbook* (DfEE/QCA 1999 – see Appendix). As we shall see below, the 1999 aims have been largely ignored. What distinguishes the 2007 aims from their 1999 predecessors is that they now have the force of law behind them and have been designed so that curriculum subjects have to bring their own aims and programmes into line with them.

We will be coming back to these recent developments later. In order properly to understand them properly, we need to see them in their historical context.

Historical background up to 1988

Maintained primary education is a product of the inter-war period, when a division began to be made at eleven between primary and secondary schooling. Before then, all but the tiny minority of children who studied at selective secondary or central schools went to elementary schools catering for pupils of all ages.

Morant's introduction to the Code 1904

The public elementary school goes back to 1870. It was set up to provide basic education in the 3Rs for working class children. In 1904 Robert Morant, Permanent Secretary at the Board of Education, wrote an inspirational, six-paragraph statement of its purposes as an introduction to the elementary school Code. This was regularly reprinted in different editions of the *Handbook of Suggestions* for elementary school teachers until 1944. For several decades it was intended to give teachers of primary age pupils a sense of their mission. Since it is the most comprehensive, and indeed almost the only, statement of national aims for this age group before the 1999 ones, it is worth outlining in some detail.

In general terms, the aim of the elementary school was 'to form and strengthen the character and to develop the intelligence' of children, to assist 'both girls and boys, according to their different needs, to fit themselves, practically and intellectually, for the work of life.'

The intellectual side of this involved training in 'habits of observation and clear reasoning' so as to gain an acquaintance with 'some of the facts and laws of nature'; developing pupils' interest in the 'ideals and achievements of mankind' and giving them 'some familiarity with the literature and history of their own country'; improving their command over language and nurturing a lasting taste 'for good reading and thoughtful study'. The practical side covered practical/manual instruction, PE and games, and basic health education. In addition, 'an important though subsidiary object of the School' was to discover children of exceptional capacity and develop their special gifts so that they could transfer to secondary schools at the appropriate age.

The fifth of the six paragraphs was about character development. This picked out 'habits of industry, self-control, and courageous perseverance in the face of difficulties', learning to 'reverence what is noble, be ready for self-sacrifice', striving after purity and truth, 'a strong sense of duty', 'respect for others', 'unselfishness', an 'instinct for fair play and for loyalty to each other'.

The final paragraph was about a 'united effort' between school and home in enabling children 'not merely to reach their full development as individuals, but also to become upright and useful members of the community' and 'worthy sons and daughters' of their country.

There are many echoes of Morant's aims throughout the history of primary education in the twentieth century and into our own. We will come back to these.

Until 1926, the elementary curriculum was state controlled, and the aims have to be interpreted in that light. A keynote of Morant's policy was to draw a sharp line between elementary education and secondary, this line having been blurred since the 1890s. While the new, post-1904 maintained secondary schools, patronised largely by the middle classes, taught an academic curriculum, the accent of the elementaries was to be on the 3 Rs, rudimentary factual knowledge in various fields, and practical pursuits. This reinforced the nineteenth century conception of elementary education as suitable for the working classes. Helping pupils 'to fit themselves, practically and intellectually, for the work of life' is, after all, only a finger's breadth away from 'habituating them to a life of work'.

The paragraph on character development has to be read against this background. Its first mentioned virtue is 'habits of industry'. Its others are equally stoic qualities needed to sustain one through a hard life. There is nothing here about personal fulfilment as distinct from self-abnegation. For the poor in a still deeply Christian age, the former could exist, if at all, only beyond the rigours of this mortal life.

Although Morant deepened the gulf between an elementary and a secondary education, he also fashioned a ladder between the two, as the 'important though subsidiary' aim mentioned above indicates. This involved 'discover(ing) children of exceptional capacity and develop(ing) their special gifts so that they could transfer to secondary schools'. This is the origin of the *selective* aim of elementary/primary schools that has persisted into our own century. While it no longer appears – and in such an unambiguous form – in any national statement of aims, it exists *de facto* in a system like our own which embraces selective secondary schools of different types and also requires each school to identify its 5–10 per cent of gifted and talented pupils.

Morant's 'subsidiary' aim also continued to influence the system after the ending of state curriculum control in 1926. From the 1920s it began to receive a theoretical rationale in the shape of the eugenicist notion of intelligence testing associated particularly with Cyril Burt. The abilities embraced by Burt's notion of intelligence were abstract, logical and linguistic competences especially suited to the academic curriculum of the secondary school. Since he also believed that intelligence is innate and that there are individually differing ceilings of intelligence, adopting his perspective made it seem reasonable that most elementary pupils, being of indifferent and virtually unalterable intelligence, should receive a basic schooling of a non-academic sort, while those more gifted should be prepared for a more demanding régime. Burt himself suggested what he called 'a "treble-track" system – a series of backward classes for slow children, a series of advanced classes for quick children, both parallel to the ordinary series of standards for children of ordinary average ability' (Board of Education 1929: 422). This led to the widespread practice of streaming within the elementary school by the 1930s (Simon 1974: 244).

The Hadow Report (1931)

The inter-war period witnessed the emergence of the primary school from its elementary school chrysalis. The 1931 Hadow Report on *The Primary School* underlined the transition that had already occurred from a school 'for the children of the labouring poor' to a school which provided 'a basis for all types of higher teaching and training' (p. 91). In its section on 'The general aim and scope of the primary school', it stated that this should not 'be regarded merely as a preparatory department for the subsequent stage' but should be planned around 'the needs of the child at that particular phase in his physical and mental development' (pp. 70–71). 'It should arouse in the pupil a keen interest in the things of the mind and in general culture, fix certain habits, and develop a reasonable degree of self-confidence, together with a social or team-spirit' (p. 71). It is interesting how much shorter and more general this aims statement is than Morant's, and how much of it, even so, is about administrative arrangements to do with the emergence of the primary school rather than educational purposes.

Consonant with its emphasis on the needs of the child, Hadow questioned the centrality of the traditional aim of imparting knowledge, claiming, famously, that 'the curriculum is to be thought of in terms of activity and experience rather than of knowledge to be acquired and facts to be stored' (p. 93).

While Hadow and other inter-war developments can be seen, positively, as a breach with the elementary tradition as updated by Morant, they can also be interpreted as a subtle continuance of it. The middle classes expanded considerably during the twentieth century. As more and more of their children went to their local elementary/primary school, in the expectation that they would leave it for a secondary school at eleven, they must have found its working-class ethos, as defined by Morant, difficult to accept. The Hadow combination of a pre-age-eleven grounding for differentiated secondary schooling and of a more intrinsically enjoyable regime, freed from many of the mechanical exercises of the old one, must have suited them better.

Hadow described its 'main care' as the facilitation of children's growth – physical, intellectual and moral (p. 92). The terminology reflects the beginnings of a change in educational thinking, which reached its fullest expression in the Plowden Report of 1967 (CACE 1967). The conception of education as the inculcation of knowledge, habits and skills, exemplified in Morant's aims statement, was being replaced by the notion of it as a quasi-biological process of development. T.P. Nunn's book *Education: its data and first principles* (1920, frequently reprinted until 1963) was an influential text, advocating as it did 'securing for everyone the conditions under which individuality is most completely developed' (p. 13).

The radical change of perspective left its mark on thinking about the aims of education. In broad terms, they became less salient. Whereas Morant's aims were clearly intended to be an articulated guide to more specific planning, the general statement of aims in Hadow was, as we have seen, perfunctory. In Nunn, aims were played down even more. On the very first page of his book, he reviews different accounts of the universal aims of education – the formation of character, preparation for complete living, and so on – and dismisses them all as interpretable in so many, and often contradictory, ways as to be useless (p. 9). His own view is 'that there can be no universal aim of education if that aim is to include the assertion of any particular ideal of life; for there are as many ideals as there are persons' (p. 13). In place of universal aims imposed from without, he gives us his own picture of education as a process of biological growth leading to the most complete development of individuality. It is only nature that can set the goals, not politicians or educationalists.

Despite the sea-change in beliefs, Nunn's developmentalism fitted in well with the notion, already present in Morant's scheme, and developed under Burt, that one purpose of the primary school was to classify children according to their abilities and educate them according to their likely future destinations, academically and occupationally. Like Burt's notion of intelligence, the idea of education as a process of biological development carried with it the implication that there are individually varying ceilings of ability. Nunn, like his colleague Burt, believed that innate differences in capacity 'limit the possibilities of individuals with adamantine rigour' (p. 117). The emergence of the primary school from its elementary school chrysalis, accompanied by increasing middle-class pressure on it to prepare their children for transfer to secondary schools, had found its ideological rationale.

In all this we should keep in mind that from 1926 until 1988 state control of the primary curriculum had been relinquished. During this period it was schools and teachers who were responsible for what was taught and why. Like the *Handbook of Suggestions*, Hadow could only offer guidance, not prescribe. This may be a reason, apart from the ideological one just mentioned, why, over this period, an interest in formulating nationwide aims, as revealed in official pronouncements, was on the wane. This is very clear in the next milestone publication in the history of primary schools, the Plowden Report (CACE 1967).

The Plowden Report (1967)

Plowden (CACE 1967) has a short, four page, chapter on 'the aims of primary education'. It is hard to give a coherent account of it, given the way it swings this way and that.

It states at first that 'one obvious purpose is to fit children for the society into which they will grow up' (p. 185). This will be marked by rapid economic and social change, so children will need to be adaptable, responsive to others, able to withstand mass pressures, well balanced, willing to learn new skills, and aware of their obligations to the community.

Having said this, it then seems to endorse 'the view that general statements of aims were of limited value, and that a pragmatic approach to the purposes of education was more likely to be fruitful' (p. 185). By this it means encouraging schools and teachers to draw up their own aims so as to guide their activities, and to reflect on what aims might be implicit in their pedagogical practices.

It then veers back to general aims in its suggestion that the aims thus uncovered would tend to 'correspond to a recognisable philosophy of education, and to a view of society', which, among other things, underlines that schools must transmit values and attitudes, that children should learn to live with others in their school community, 'develop in the way and at the pace appropriate to them', have opportunities for individual discovery and for creative work, and become balanced and mature adults, able 'to live in, contribute to, and to look critically at' their society (pp. 187–88). Traditional virtues like 'neatness, accuracy, care and perseverance, and the sheer knowledge which is an essential of being educated' are also important (p. 188).

Plowden's chopping and changing is instructive. On the one hand, it reflects the fact that aims no longer emanated from the political community but were the province of professionals in the schools. On the other, it reveals how difficult it is in a national system to avoid national aims altogether. The result is its curious notion that national aims can be abstracted from what schools say they aim at, and its half-hearted attempt at spelling out such national aims, lazily dependent on an amalgam of traditional virtues and progressive nostrums rather than on a more considered and thorough investigation.

This discussion of aims in Plowden has concentrated on its brief chapter devoted explicitly to the topic. But as Dearden (1968: 50–54) pointed out, implicit references to aims lie scattered through the text, as in its familiar child-centred claim that no advances in educational policy can be effective 'unless they are in harmony with the nature of the child, unless they are fundamentally acceptable to him' (Chapter 2, para 9).

From Plowden to the National Curriculum 1967–88

The two decades between 1967 and 1988 are divisible, for our purposes, into two overlapping segments. The earlier years underlined the Plowden message that primary schools should review their own aims and their realisation in curriculum activities. This was understandable in an age when state control had not yet returned to the agenda (except for RE, which became statutory in 1944).

A study by Ashton *et al.* surveyed the most popular aims in primary schools. The first six were, in order:

- Children should be happy, cheerful and well balanced.
- They should enjoy school work and find satisfaction in their achievements.
- Individuals should be encouraged to develop in their own ways.
- Moral values should be taught as a basis of behaviour.
- Children should be taught to respect property.
- They should be taught courtesy and good manners.

(Ashton *et al.* 1975)

It is interesting that all six aims are about personal qualities, none about the acquisition of knowledge. It is also striking that the first three have to do with the pupils' own well-being, and the last three with their moral obligations. While these latter would not have been out of place in Morant's paragraph on character development, the first three reflect the more pupil-centred approaches favoured in the inter-war years.

In 1983 the Schools Council's working paper *Primary Practice* (Schools Council 1983) encouraged teachers, very much along Plowden lines, both to work out their aims and put them into practice, and also begin from their current practice and try to see what aims are implied in it. As in the Ashton study, personal qualities figured prominently in the discussion.

But by 1983 the post-1926 principle that schools, not the state, should determine aims was increasingly under challenge. In 1975–76 the excessively free régime at William Tyndale primary school in Islington caused a public furore. This was followed by Callaghan's speech at Ruskin College, Oxford in 1976, in which government first floated the idea of a national 'core curriculum'.

In 1981 the Conservative government's *The School Curriculum* proposed a set of aims in which 'the school curriculum needs to be rooted'. These were the first national aims in English history to be proposed for all maintained schools, primary as well as secondary. They were:

- to help pupils to develop lively, enquiring minds, the ability to question and argue rationally and apply themselves to tasks, and physical skills;
- to help pupils to acquire knowledge and skills relevant to adult life and employment in a fast-changing world;
- to help pupils to use language and number effectively;
- to instil respect for religious and moral values, and tolerance of other races, religions, and ways of life;
- to help pupils to understand the world in which they live, and the interdependence of individuals, groups and nations;
- to help pupils appreciate human achievements and aspirations.

(DES 1981)

What is striking about this list is the weight it gives to the acquisition of knowledge and understanding and related intellectual qualities. It does this with next to no indication of why this is important. Is knowledge a good thing for individual fulfilment, for democratic citizenship, for economic growth, or for some combination of all these? More fundamental questions about aims are ignored.

In putting knowledge first, and in paying so little attention to personal qualities more generally, the 1981 list is a departure from the tradition of thinking about aims for primary age children that goes back through the Ashton *et al.* data to Plowden, Hadow and even Morant. This is partly explicable, if not justifiable, in the light of media-fuelled anxiety about low educational standards, not least in primary schools, which were seen as in thrall to 'progressive' methods.

The National Curriculum and beyond

The National Curriculum 1988

When the National Curriculum appeared in 1988, it was built around ten foundation subjects, including the three core subjects of English, mathematics and science. But the only aims powering its complex system of programmes of study, attainment targets and level statements were that the curriculum:

- promotes the spiritual, moral, cultural, mental and physical development of pupils at the school and of society
- prepares pupils at the school for the opportunities, responsibilities and experiences of adult life

Apart from being minimal in the extreme, the aims were carelessly drafted, vapid and unclear. Taken literally, one job of the school was said to be the nonsensical one of promoting the physical development of society. Teachers did not have to be told that, among other things, they should be preparing pupils for adult life: they needed to know more about the *kind* of preparation, about the sorts of abilities and qualities young people should be acquiring. As for lack of clarity, the multiple ambiguities of 'spiritual' may have generated acres of published print over the last two decades, but have not been much help to schools, except the more religious of them, in knowing what they should be doing.

The aims give every impression of having been added as an afterthought. What the curriculum should consist of seems to have been the starting point, to judge from the battles, leading up to 1988, between Mrs Thatcher, who favoured a statutory core of English, mathematics and science, and the Secretary of State, Kenneth Baker, who stood out for the wider curriculum which prevailed.

If so, this was an extraordinarily illogical way to proceed. A school curriculum, whether in the narrower sense of timetabled activities or in one that goes wider, is, after all, not an end in itself. It is a vehicle for achieving certain purposes. These have to be determined first; the vehicles best suited to realise them, second.

This glaring defect in the 1988 scheme is worth commenting on for another reason. 1988 was an historic year. It marked the shift back from professional to political control of the content of school education. There was, and is, a powerful argument for political control of its broad framework, as distinct from its more detailed filling-in. The broad outlines of the curriculum and the aims on which they should rest should be inextricable from the kind of society which is thought desirable and which school education can help to bring about. What kind of society this should be is a political matter, something to be determined by all of us through the ballot box as democratic citizens and not by any sectional group. This is why teachers should not have a special voice. True, they have an expertise about how to implement a broad curriculum framework within the special circumstances of their school, its area, and its pupils. And this puts them in a better position than government when it comes to details. But they have no more authoritative a voice than postmen or doctors in deciding the larger directions.

In 1988 the government got its responsibilities relative to those of the professionals woefully back to front. Its first duty was to chart the direction of travel in the shape of substantive general aims; its second to work out in very broad terms what curricular vehicles were best suited to attain them. Neither of these things did it do. What it *did* do was what it had no moral authority to do. It imposed a curriculum framework which was literally almost aimless, and included in this innumerable detailed prescriptions, which fell not within its own province but in that of the professionals.

After 1988 all schools suffered, and still do suffer, from this constricting and arbitrary innovation. Primary schools were especially hard hit. A curriculum built around traditional subjects was the rule in most secondary schools. Indeed, as my colleague Richard Aldrich has shown, the subjects laid down in 1988 are almost identical with those made compulsory in the first maintained secondary schools when they came on stream in 1904. Over the course of the twentieth century they had become largely taken for granted in secondary circles. But primary schools had to make readjustments from their less subject-structured arrangements. Not that this was all bad. Any decent set of national aims would require pupils to have a good understanding of the scientific and technological basis of their own society and of others'. This is an area in which many primary schools were weak before 1988. The National Curriculum helped them to become stronger.

The 1999 aims

During the 1990s more and more teachers began to ask what the National Curriculum was *for*. Responding to their pressure, in the later part of the decade the government set about delineating the values, aims and purposes on which the school curriculum should rest. These drew on the statement of common values drawn up after widespread consultation by the National Forum for Values in Education and the Community in 1997. The aims and values were published, as was said at the start of this chapter, at the beginning of the *National Curriculum Handbook* (DfEE/QCA 1999). They covered more than two pages and are reproduced in this chapter's Appendix. Although they are presented under two headings, the second of which reiterates the minimalist aims of 1988, it is hard to discern much of a logical structure among them. They appear to be the product of a familiar pattern whereby a drafting committee gets hung up on minutiae but loses sight of the bigger structure. This said, there is much to be said for the *spirit* of these recommendations. They make a belief in the well-being of the individual the foremost of their values. Taken together, they are fitting aims for a tolerant, liberal democratic society concerned with its economic well-being and aware of its global responsibilities.

There is a marked difference of emphasis from the earlier national list of aims of 1981. (I am ignoring the 1988 non-aims). The 1981 precedence of knowledge over personal qualities is reversed. About 60 per cent of the 1999 items have to do with personal qualities, some 30 per cent with knowledge and understanding, and 10 per cent with skills. This kind of weighting is, after all, only what one might expect when aims begin to be taken seriously. For school education should have its sights on the kinds of persons it wishes its students to become, on the qualities of character, ethical as well as intellectual, with which they should be equipped. In order to be such people, they will need knowledge and understanding of all kinds of things. But acquiring knowledge and understanding is not a self-contained educational aim of its own, something self-evidently desirable without any need to ask for reasons. True, there is a sense in which acquiring knowledge *can* be seen as an end in itself, for example where someone is fascinated by science not for its extrinsic benefits but as something intrinsically interesting. But this is another matter. It is a defensible educational aim that pupils should be introduced to activities (like science) which can hold their attention in this intrinsic way. But there are good reasons behind this, for example, to do with the contribution this can make to personal fulfilment. It is not a self-evident truth that acquiring knowledge is a good thing. One must start further back, with wider concerns about people's well-being and the kinds of persons we would like pupils to become.

For all their raggedness, if the 1999 aims had been followed through and government had produced statutory and non-statutory guidance about what curricular vehicles were most suited to their realisation, the work of primary as well as secondary schools would have been transformed. Teachers' attention would have been constantly directed on to fundamental aims and values. Their imaginative powers would have been released as they were able to shape their activities with these in mind.

But this did not and could not happen, for the curricular vehicles had already been predetermined. Over 90 per cent of the 1999 *National Curriculum Handbook* was devoted to them. They were, with one or two additions, the foundation subjects of 1988.

This need not have been quite so much the impediment it proved to be if the specifications for the subjects had at least been brought into line with the new aims. But no attempt to do this seems to have been made. If you look at the paragraphs explaining the importance of the different subjects, at their programmes of study, and at their attainment targets and level descriptions, for the most part you find a massive mismatch with the overall aims. This is not true of the newly introduced subjects of Personal, Social and Health Education and Citizenship, which fit the aims very well – even though at primary level, as a combined subject, PSHE+Citizenship was not thought important enough to be of statutory status like the other subjects. It is not true, either, of Design and Technology. But most of the other subjects reveal a mismatch with the aims. Their programmes and purposes tend to follow inward-looking paths which two centuries and more of curricular history have worn smooth. For most, the main preoccupation emerging from their pages in the *Handbook* appears to be to lay the foundations of specialist knowledge in their subject so that learners can go more deeply into the field at a later stage (White 2004: 14–15, 182–83).

Given all this, it would have been surprising if the statement on aims and values had had much influence on the work of the primary school. There is no evidence, as far as I know, that it has had any. Teachers have used the *Handbook*, understandably enough, to see what they should be doing at their key stage in the different subjects. A few of them, judging from my own observations, do not seem to have known that the section on aims and values exists.

Recent developments: Northern Ireland

Since 2003 central education authorities in different parts of the UK have devised new aims statements for all maintained schools, intended to mesh more closely with curriculum activities. The first and best of these was drawn up in Northern Ireland by the Council for the Curriculum, Examinations and Assessment (CCEA). For the 'Big Picture' of the KS1&2 curriculum and for more specific features, including detailed aims, see (as at January 2008) http://www.nicurriculum.org.uk/key_stages_1_and_2/index.asp.

The central aim is 'to empower young people to achieve their potential and to make informed and responsible decisions throughout their lives'. This generates three groups of sub-aims, to do with young people as [1] individuals, [2] contributors to society, and [3] contributors to the economy and environment. These three are further subdivided as follows: [1] personal and mutual understanding, personal health, moral character, spiritual awareness; [2] citizenship, cultural understanding, media awareness, ethical awareness; [3] employability, economic awareness, education for sustainable development. Each of these sub-sections contains a number of more specific items.

What is impressive about this aims statement is its coherence. It is much better arranged, logically speaking, than the 1999 statement of aims and values in the English *Handbook*. It has a clear central aim and one can see without difficulty how the various sub-aims and sub-sub-aims mesh together as specifications of it. Take for instance, under 'media awareness' the item '[to help children to] become aware of the potential impact of media in influencing our personal views, choices and decisions'; or, under 'economic awareness', the item '[to help children to] learn to manage their money and to build up savings'. The bearing of these two items on the central aim of a life based on informed and responsible choices is not hard to discern. And although the language of any aims statement must be general and may be open to multiple interpretations, the CCEA document is, for the most part, clearly and unambiguously written, as the examples just given illustrate.

How well has CCEA succeeded in bringing curriculum activities into line with the aims? Here, as in England, it has had to treat as non-negotiable the continued existence of the traditional subjects as curriculum vehicles. This has massively restricted what it has been able to do, since one cannot assume that a subject framework always constitutes the most appropriate way of promoting aims. But it has managed to do something. Subjects are grouped at the primary stage into seven 'learning areas', some of these covering a single subject, like 'mathematics and numeracy', and some embracing two or more subjects, as in 'the arts' (art and design, and music) and 'the world around us' (geography, history, science and technology). The latter learning area is built around several interdisciplinary themes. A whole learning area is devoted to 'personal development'. Links between learning areas are stressed. There is also an emphasis on 'whole curriculum skills and processes' which curriculum activities are meant to foster. These fall under the headings of communication; managing information; thinking, problem solving and decision making; being creative; working with others; self management; and ICT skills. The various interconnected elements of the curriculum and its aims are presented graphically in the 'Big Picture' of the KS1 and 2 curriculum, already mentioned.

Given the constrictions within which CCEA has had to work, the match between curriculum and aims is reasonably good. In practice, much will depend on what weighting schools give to the areas of personal development and the world around us, as these reflect the general aims particularly well. The match is not as close as in the CCEA's 'Pathways' proposals for Key Stage 3, where the specific aims of the learning areas are each closely tied into one of the general aims.

I have dwelt on Northern Ireland developments as these have been especially imaginative and challenging to the status quo. They have also been influential in English curriculum reform, for instance in their use of 'Big Pictures' to present whole schemes.

Recent developments: Scotland

English developments, to which I turn soon, have also learnt from recent reforms in Scotland. Like the ones in Northern Ireland, these, as expressed in *A Curriculum for Excellence* (2004), have aimed at providing a less fragmented, more holistically designed curriculum for children of school age, due to come on stream in 2007. The purposes of the curriculum from 3–18 are included in the account of *A Curriculum for Excellence* at www.scotland.gov.uk/Publications/2004/11/20178/45862. In Scotland, guidelines on the curriculum are not statutory and schools need not follow them.

The Scottish aims are presented on a single page and neatly arranged under four headings: successful learners, confident individuals, responsible citizens, and effective contributors. The first three of these are identical to the ones in the new draft aims-statement for England and have plainly influenced the latter. I will describe the English version of the three below. According to *A Curriculum for Excellence,*

> The learning will take place through a wide range of planned experiences. These will include environmental, scientific, technological, historical, social, economic, political, mathematical and linguistic contexts, the arts, culture and sports. Sometimes the experiences may be linked to particular vocational or other specialised contexts. To achieve this breadth will require both subject-based studies and activities which span several disciplines. Children will also learn through the day-to-day experiences of the life of the school community, with its values and social contact, and from out-of-school activities, events and celebrations.

Recent developments: England

Since 2005 QCA has developed a new set of aims for all English maintained schools, intended, like the other schemes, to be easily mapped onto curriculum content. Programmes of study in the different subjects are to be slimmed down, leaving schools greater freedom to work out their own curricular arrangements. The three overall aims for all schools are found in the 'Big Picture' of the school curriculum at http://www. qca.org.uk/qca_5855.aspx.

They are very similar to the Scottish ones. They are that the school curriculum should enable all young people to become:

- successful learners, who enjoy learning, make progress and achieve
- confident individuals, who are able to live safe, healthy and fulfilling lives
- responsible citizens, who make a positive contribution to society.

Each of the three aims comprises a set of sub-aims. The three aims and their sub-aims are now being made statutory for Key Stages 3 and 4. It is expected that Key Stages 1 and 2 will soon follow suit.

The QCA description of the new aims, at http://curriculum.qca.org.uk/aims/index. aspx, says that the curriculum should enable all young people to become:

Successful learners who ...
- have the essential learning skills of literacy, numeracy and information and communication technology
- are creative, resourceful and able to identify and solve problems
- have enquiring minds and think for themselves to process information, reason, question and evaluate
- communicate well in a range of ways
- understand how they learn and learn from their mistakes
- are able to learn independently and with others
- know about big ideas and events that shape our world
- enjoy learning and are motivated to achieve the best they can, now and in the future

Confident individuals who …
- have a sense of self-worth and personal identity
- relate well to others and form good relationships
- are self-aware and deal well with their emotions
- have secure values and beliefs and have principles to distinguish right from wrong
- become increasingly independent, are able to take the initiative and organise themselves
- make healthy lifestyle choices
- are physically competent and confident
- take managed risks and stay safe
- recognise their talents and have ambitions
- are willing to try new things and make the most of opportunities
- are able to take the initiative and organise themselves
- are open to the excitement and inspiration offered by the natural world and human achievements

Responsible citizens who …
- are well prepared for life and work
- are enterprising
- are able to work cooperatively with others
- respect others and act with integrity
- understand their own and others' cultures and traditions, within the context of British heritage, and have a strong sense of their own place in the world
- appreciate the benefits of diversity
- challenge injustice, are committed to human rights and strive to live peaceably with others
- sustain and improve the environment, locally and globally
- take account of the needs of present and future generations in the choices they make
- can change things for the better.

Unlike the aims in the 1999 *Handbook*, these 2007 ones are more logically arranged, that is, under three headings picking out qualities of the successfully educated person. They are also meant to be more closely geared into the curriculum itself. In the revised Key Stage 3 curriculum they stand at the head of programmes of study in the different subjects and bear both on the subjects' self-descriptions under the rubric of 'The importance of … (history, science, and so on)', and on the now slimmed-down content of the programmes. (See again http://curriculum.qca.org.uk/aims/index.aspx).

How far is this new policy on aims an advance on what went before? Time will give a fuller answer, but already some things are clear.

- The most radical difference from the 1999 aims is that the 2007 ones are to be made statutory. This is the first time that English schools have had a detailed set of statutory aims to help them shape their curricula. The impact of this change on how twenty-first century schools, not least primary schools, will operate is potentially profound. It should mean that a school's success is to be judged not primarily in terms of test and exam results but by how far it meets the person-centred requirements embodied in the aims. There are big implications here about how a school's work can best be evaluated and inspected. In addition, obliging schools to construct their curriculum planning around aims with the force of law behind them should encourage them to be more imaginative in breaking away from conventional curriculum patterns. How far these desirable outcomes will in fact be realised is as yet unknown.

- It has been taken as read that the current school subjects – the National Curriculum subjects plus RE – are here to stay, at least for the immediate future. This puts a massive constraint on the system and raises doubts about how far a good match between aims and curriculum can be achieved. For the sensible way to plan these things would be to work out the aims first and then, without preconceptions, decide what kinds of curricular vehicles are best suited to promote them. This cannot now be done. The obstacle is the same one that has plagued developments since 1988 – that the subjects are the fixed point and everything else must fit round them. It is true that this still leaves room for interdisciplinary collaboration and QCA is actively promoting this, along with more devolution of detailed programming to the schools. This may be more easily realised in the primary than in the secondary sector, since there is more scope here for planning around projects and themes. We will have to see whether this strengthening of interdisciplinary activity in the QCA's new scheme avoids the fate of the cross-cultural themes introduced as part of the original National Curriculum in 1988. All sorts of hopes were pinned on these, but owing to pressures to confine thinking within subject boxes, they vanished without trace within a few years.

- While the 1999 aims were, as explained above, patently out of synch with most of the subjects, a problem with the 2007 ones is that, in one respect, there is now *too good a fit* with them.

  I have especially in mind the first of the three headline aims – that all young people should be helped to become successful learners. None of the traditional subjects need baulk at the prospect of aiming at successful learning. They all want that.

  The former mismatch between overall aims and curricular specifics is thereby reversed, at least for *Successful learners*. Traditional subjects can urge that they fit snugly and logically into the big picture of the curriculum.

- There are more charitable things to say about the other two headline aims – *Confident individuals* and *Responsible citizens* – and their specific items. Few of these can be hijacked by those wishing to keep subjects within traditional blinkers. True, the expression '*Confident individuals*' may be grist to their mill. *Any* teacher, including the least outward-looking, will prefer their pupils to be confident rather than diffident in their curriculum area – whether at solving geometrical problems, doing the high jump, or writing a letter to their MP.

  This qualification apart, most of the aims in these two categories are about desiderata in the world beyond traditional school subjects. They are about some of the qualities people need in order to lead a personally flourishing and morally decent life, and to become good workers and informed citizens. They are indeed genuine aims, not pseudo ones.

- Not that they are above criticism. A big drawback of the whole aims statement, the last two categories included, is that it is nothing but an ordered list. There is, so far, no indication of why the list has been constructed as it has – no stated rationale for it. (In this, the QCA can, once again, look to Northern Ireland's CCEA as a model. This takes very seriously the need to provide fuller reasons for its aims statement, as is evident in its current (2007) Key Stage 3 reforms).

Why is a rationale important? We need it in order to see how the items cohere together within a larger framework. Such a framework has been hinted at in many of the items, but not made explicit. For instance, something like the good of the pupil is a value embedded, but not presented as such, in the three fold list. There is a proto-picture at work in this of what a flourishing human life is ideally like. For many it will be an attractive picture. It emphasises self-confidence and self-awareness, taking the initiative, looking after oneself physically and emotionally, being independent, ambitious and making the most of opportunities. In terms of global perspectives on personal well-being, it is closer to what might be called a modern American ideal than to a traditional Indian or African one.

In other words, the picture is controversial. This is not to say it is indefensible. For twenty-first century England – as compared with, say, eleventh-century England – it may make a lot of sense. The problem for the QCA aims statement is that it is taken for granted, not argued for. Not only this. Half hidden behind the text, the picture is incomplete. Only a few features of the flourishing life have been sketched in. We need something more rounded, more satisfying to the understanding.

If we had this fuller account and rationale, we would, I suspect, be able to see gaps in the list not so evident before. The picture suggests, as I have said, that pupils should learn to look after themselves physically and emotionally. This is a defensible pre-requisite of leading a fulfilling life. As such, it belongs to a wider framework than the one presented. This has to do with the satisfaction of basic needs as a condition of human flourishing. Physical and emotional needs are certainly part of the story, but not the whole of it. Take money. Just as one needs to manage one's health – through exercise, diet and so on, so one needs to manage one's money – through income generation, control of expenditure, budgeting, and so on. There is nothing in the list of aims to do with money management, yet it is of basic importance in one's welfare. So is something else. Especially in a society like our own, with pressures from the media and advertisers to buy junk food, drink more than is good for one, gamble, worship celebrity, and spend too much time on television and computer games, young people need for their own good to be equipped with an understanding of such blandishments and the power to resist them. Again, there is nothing on this in the list of aims.

I have suggested that a fuller picture of personal well-being will enable us to identify gaps in the aims proposed. So far I have concentrated only on the necessary conditions of well-being, on basic needs. What well-being is goes wider than that. We can see this if we imagine someone whose basic needs are broadly met – she has food, shelter, clean air, a decent income, good health, and so on. How, given this, is she to lead her life so that it is a thriving one rather than a non-thriving one? Are some kinds of activities more conducive to this than others? How do relationships come into the frame? How far are good and bad luck significant? How far are success or failure in what one undertakes?

These are big questions – too big to explore in this survey. I just want to drive home how very sketchy is the portrayal of personal flourishing implicit in the new QCA document. A more rounded, fuller account would enable us to identify gaps – not only in the area of our basic needs, but also in the area of activities, relationships and experiences once these needs are met.

This lack of a fuller account affects not only aims which have to do with the well-being of the pupil, but also those concerned with the good of others in the community and in the wider world. For this notion, too, comes back to the same underlying question 'What is it for people to lead a flourishing life?'

Finally, I hope I have done enough to show why an aims statement like that from the QCA needs a rationale. But there are two further reasons for this, too – not entirely separate ones, but considerations closely connected with those already given.

The first is that, as we have seen with the *Successful learners* aims, an item may be interpreted variously. National aims have to be understood more or less in the same way by all parties, schools and teachers not least. The latter have to operationalise the aims, to embody them in programmes and whole school processes. They need more determinate guidance.

The second is this. A national aims statement needs a national gloss – a reasoned explanation of what is meant by the items it includes and of why they have been prioritised. This is for democratic reasons. Citizens in general, as well as those in the education system who apply the aims, have the moral right to know what vision of education government has in mind and how the details fit into this. If all they get is the details, however neatly organised under headings, all they can do is take them on authority, as pronouncements from on high.

I have produced a fuller critique of QCA thinking about aims in *What schools are for and why* (White 2007). This gives something of the historical background which has made subject-centredness so prominent a part of the English tradition. It also complements its critique of the lack of rationale in current arrangements by an alternative set of desirable aims and a discussion of the rationale for these. This focuses for reasons of shortage of space only on one central topic: the underlying notion of personal well-being, about which something has already been said above.

This is an appropriate point in this survey of the aims of primary education in England to leave the history of official aims over the last century and look at what educational theorists, especially philosophers, have said over the same period about what primary aims should be. Once again, the survey is weighted towards more recent developments.

But before we turn to aims theory in Section 2, it will be useful to summarise the main events in the story of aims policy.

SUMMARY SO FAR

It is now just over a hundred years since Morant drew up his aims for the precursor of today's primary school, the elementary school. He framed them in such a way as to sharpen the differences between the elementary and secondary systems, while at the same time making it a subsidiary purpose of the former to be a ladder of opportunity into the latter. The century between him and us has witnessed both continuities and discontinuities.

A major change occurred in 1926, when the elementary school curriculum passed from political to professional control. This remained the case for 62 years until the coming of the National Curriculum in 1988. It was early in this period that the primary school emerged from its elementary school chrysalis. By then the divide between secondary education aims and elementary aims was deeply entrenched; and the gulf persisted into the age of the primary school. With the demise of the tradition that non-secondary schools provided an education fitted to the destiny of the urban poor, in the age of Hadow and Plowden between the 1930s and the 1960s, the new primary schools became powered by more benign, child-friendly aims, more acceptable to an increasingly middle class clientele. Yet the wide gap between what secondary and non-secondary schools were taken to be about remained, if now in a different form. Throughout this whole period, from 1904 until the 1980s, it was taken as read that an education based on the study of a wide range of discrete academic disciplines belonged to the secondary school sector, and was not appropriate for elementary/primary schools.

Since the 1980s there have been radical changes in primary aims. The first national aims statement of 1981, the meagre aims of 1988, the fuller version of 1999, and the more streamlined aims set out by QCA in 2007 do not differentiate primary from secondary aims. For the first time in English history, there has been a single set of aims for the whole maintained system. Parallel to this development, the curriculum of the primary school has been brought into line with the traditional subject-based curriculum of the secondaries.

We are now within sight of a statutory aims-based curriculum for all schools that does not start from academic subjects but from more deeply embedded educational goods. If successful, this could well reverse the post-1988 assimilation of primary to secondary education and help to make both sectors more open to the more person-centred approaches found in the better primary schools before 1988.

Meanwhile, the 'important though subsidiary object of the School' which Morant proposed for his elementary system in 1904 is still with us in the primary sector. Now, as it was then, this object is

> To discover individual children who show promise of exceptional capacity, and to develop their special gifts (so far as this can be done without sacrificing the interests of the majority of the children), so that they may be qualified to pass at the proper age into Secondary Schools [we would say 'good' Secondary Schools], and be able to derive the maximum of benefit from the education there offered them.
>
> (Board of Education 1929: 9)

This aim is no longer in a national aims statement, but is implicit in the government's current Gifted and Talented Strategy as well as in that part of primary practice responsive to parents' pressure to get their children into 'good' schools. How justifiable this aim is is a further question.

Another interesting historical legacy is the re-emergence of the developmental approach introduced during the Hadow-Plowden period in the Early Years Foundation Stage (EYFS) for children aged 0–5, which overlaps the primary phase. 'Early Learning Goals' are specified for each of the six EYFS 'Areas of Learning and Development.' See Section 2 for Dearden's critique of developmentalist ideas.

2. WHAT SHOULD PRIMARY AIMS BE? THEORETICAL PERSPECTIVES

Views of educational theorists on what the aims of primary education should be are best understood against the background of policy changes discussed in Section 1. The 1960s are a major turning point. Before that time, in both policy and in theory, primary aims were in many ways conceived very differently from secondary ones. Since the late 1960s, it has become increasingly difficult to separate the two. The change began in the sphere of theory, as we shall see below. By the early 1980s, as we saw above, it had worked its way through into policy recommendations.

The primary school emerged, as we have seen, from the elementary school. At the beginning of the twentieth century there was, largely thanks to Morant, a clear cut division in function between the elementary and the secondary systems. Crudely speaking, elementary schools fitted working class children for blue collar jobs, while secondaries prepared middle class pupils and working class children on scholarships for white collar ones.

In 1911, drawing on his experience as Chief Inspector of elementary schools, Edmond Holmes published his influential cri-de-coeur *What Is and What Might Be.* This rejected 'the path of mechanical obedience' which these schools still obliged their pupils to follow, advocating in its stead 'the path of self-realisation'. 'The function of education,' he proclaimed in his very first sentence, 'is to foster growth'. In his view, we are all born with a number of instincts – communicative, dramatic, sympathetic, aesthetic, inquisitive and constructive. 'A good education will allow all [...] these to develop naturally into fully-fledged dispositions and thus enable each of us to achieve self-fulfilment'.

The metamorphosis of the elementary school into the primary school was propitious for growth theory, as we noted in Section 1. Nunn's *Education: its data and first principles* (1920) scarcely mentioned Holmes's text, but it reaffirmed its central idea, that education is a matter of biological development, while grounding it more firmly than Holmes did in the psychological sciences. Richard Selleck (1972) gives a readable account of the 'progressive' movement in English primary education from 1914 until 1939, in which the idea of education as growth, espoused also by Homer Lane and Maria Montessori, was pivotal.

By the 1960s, policy statements (Hadow and Plowden) had combined with the literature of educational theory to create a distinctive perspective on the aims of primary education. Hadow's (1931) formulation had enculated this well. The work of the primary school should be planned around 'the needs of the child at that particular phase in his physical and mental development' (pp.70–71).

The last years of the 1960s saw the apogee of this view of primary aims in the Plowden Report (CACE 1967). They also witnessed its wholesale undermining in Robert Dearden's *The Philosophy of Primary Education* of 1968, as well as in his and Richard Peters's essays in the latter's edited collection *Perspectives on Plowden* (1969). The luxuriant claims of 'child-centred' thinking were ripe for philosophical scrutiny and as a philosopher with extensive experience in primary classrooms Dearden in his 1968 book shows them no quarter. He makes it clear that primary aims cannot unproblematically be based on children's needs, what they are interested in, or their alleged mental growth. Human learning, as a socially-originating phenomenon, cannot be modelled on the biological unfolding of organisms from seed to mature specimen.

When Dearden turns from critique to his positive account of aims, concepts specific to the primary scene fall away. Primary education, like any stage of education, is largely about equipping learners to become autonomous persons, making independent, rational choices about how they are to live. Autonomy is a central value in much of the child-centred tradition, but it needs disentangling, in Dearden's view, from the growth ideology with which it has become enmeshed. Autonomy cannot be the only aim, however. We all also have moral obligations towards other people, and our education must prepare us to fulfil these too.

Dearden's positive account of aims is as applicable to secondary as to primary schools. After his book appeared, it became all but impossible to discuss what primary aims should be in a hived off way. The focus for philosophers, and from the early 1980s for politicians, too (as we saw in Section 1), became the aims of school education in general. Primary schools were assumed to need the same aims as secondary. As Dearden says of his later book *Problems in Primary Education* (1976), although he included the word 'primary' in the title, 'really much of the discussion would be equally relevant to secondary interests' (p.x). Part One of this book is about aims and principles.

Another philosophical book from the late 1960s also marked a watershed. This is Richard Peters's *Ethics and Education* (1966). In Chapter 5 Peters claims that the aims of education proper, and not some ersatz version of it, have to be intrinsic. Intellectual and aesthetic activities have to be studied for their intrinsic value and not, as in Dearden, as prerequisites of autonomous living. Although Peters' theory does not distinguish between different types of institution, it belongs to the tradition of thinking about secondary and university education based on the acquisition of academic knowledge for its own sake. For reasons which should now be clear, this aim had never been salient in the elementary/primary world.

The contrast between the 'growth' approach to education and the 'learning for its own sake' approach was never clearer than in the late 1960s, clarified as both positions were by contemporary philosophical treatments of them. To a large extent this contrast matched the fracture line in the English system between primary and post-primary institutions. Its echoes have persisted in defences of each of the two positions in later decades. In philosophy of education, David Cooper's *Illusions of Equality* (1980) argues for the ideal of educational excellence as manifested in an elite of scholars pursuing understanding and critical appreciation for their own sake. Colin Wringe's *Understanding Educational Aims* (1988), having reviewed aims focussed on the individual and others to do with society, comes down, Peters fashion, in favour of the pursuit of understanding for its own sake. On the other side, John Darling's *Child-Centred Education and its Critics* (1994) is, as its title suggests, a defence of the once-dominant perspective on primary aims against objections to it, not least from the Peters camp. In a more political context, conservative thinkers like Cyril Burt and other Black Paper authors of the 1970s, as well as their successors down to today, have repeatedly presented English schools as the site of a struggle between beleaguered champions of subject learning for its own sake and besieging devotees of child-centred ideology.

A critic of 'child-centred' thinking not in thrall to this latter polarisation has been Robin Alexander. His *Primary Teaching* (1984: Chapters 1, 2) includes a discussion of central concepts, dichotomies and assumptions in this area reminiscent of Dearden's approach but on a broader canvas than philosophy alone. But Alexander does not oppose the child-centred tradition to that of learning for its own sake. He is not centrally concerned in this book to spell out an alternative position on primary aims, but his generally approving remarks on making primary schools more responsive to a wider social and political world as well as to the child's well-being (pp. 32–35) clearly distance him from the advocates of knowledge for its own sake.

In this, Alexander belongs to a new mainstream. Beginning with Dearden, philosophical writings since the late 1960s on what school aims should be have tended to start from deeper bases than the polarised traditions just discussed. In doing so, they have become increasingly detached from an age-specific framework. Dearden (1968), as already stated, builds his account of primary aims around personal autonomy within a framework of morally appropriate behaviour. The non age-related framework in White 1973 is close to Dearden in this, but sees personal autonomy as an aspect of the more fundamental concept of a person's well-being. In White 1982, the canvas is wider. Four kinds of aim are discussed and relationships among them examined. The four have to do with: knowledge for its own sake, personal well-being/personal autonomy, morality, and economic demands. Preparation for work and its relationships with other aims is taken up in more detail in White 1997. It also figures in Wringe 1988, Chapter 6.

White 1990 takes up personal well-being and moral aims again and provides a new account of them. The treatment of morality reflects a shift in philosophical ethics in the 1980s, influenced especially by Alasdair MacIntyre's Aristotelian text *After Virtue* (1981), from seeing the basis of the moral life in following rules and principles to locating it in desirable personal dispositions, or virtues, like courage and generosity. This shift also casts doubt on the hard and fast line which many have drawn between one's own well-being, or self-interest, and morality. White's book explores the apparent inseparability of these two areas. At the same time, it argues now for the *separability* of the notions of personal autonomy and personal well-being, seeing the former as a value which has come to be embedded in the latter only with the rise of a modern, liberal kind of society. It is not prized, for instance, in societies based on a conception of personal well-being in which obedience to custom or to God is central.

The fact that personal autonomy has come to be seen, here as elsewhere, as a specifically liberal value rather than one more deeply associated with human nature as a whole is linked to the belief that defensible aims of education must be located within a specific kind of polity – that is, a liberal-democratic one. Educating for autonomy is inextricable from educating learners as citizens of such a society. This thought is not unconnected with the idea mentioned in the last paragraph, that an individual's well-being is inextricable from his or her moral relationships with others.

I am aware that the abstract argument of the last few paragraphs has made various connections and distinctions that need fuller explication to be more intelligible. But I hope it gives some indication of the direction in which thought about aims has been moving in recent decades. The trend from the 1980s onwards has been away from more piecemeal discussions of desirable aims towards intellectually satisfying accounts of how a whole array of aims hang together in a unified belief system. In this the notion of personal well-being, including the autonomous form this takes in modern societies, has become a central concept. Philosophical explorations of the concept are now becoming increasingly relevant to policy-making, given that well-being underpins the 2004 Children's Act, the five 'Every Child Matters' outcomes, and the 2007 Children's Plan.

In the 1960s Paul Hirst had produced a massively influential argument claiming that a liberal education should be built around seven or eight logically distinct forms of knowledge or understanding, all of which should be studied for their own sake (Hirst 1965). In the 1980s, influenced by MacIntyre, Hirst shifted his thinking away from this tradition. He now argued that education should be conceived as preparation for a good life via a critically reflective induction into a range of important social practices and the virtues which these bring with them, beginning with but not confined to those to do with the satisfaction of our basic needs.

A statement of Hirst's new theory is found in Roger Marples's 1999 collection *The Aims of Education*. This also includes several essays by leading philosophers of education about liberalism as a social framework from which aims are to be derived. Some of these pick up on John Rawls's account of liberalism in his *Political Liberalism* (1993) which marked a significant shift from his celebrated 1972 work *A Theory of Justice*. The relevance of this change to educational aims is that, while his earlier work suggested that personal autonomy should be a central value for any member of a liberal society, the 1993 book promoted a version of liberalism in which a view of the good life centred around autonomy is only one of many possible such views and should not be privileged over others. Discussions of which of Rawls's theories is to be preferred are still continuing. They are especially important in countries like Britain with their many cultural groups, for not all of which autonomy is a positive value: some religious groups, for instance. All this raises the question of whether a liberal-democratic state should impose autonomy as an educational aim on all learners, including those from communities which do not prize it.

Issues to do with autonomy and liberalism have also exercised Eamonn Callan, a particularly rigorous philosophical investigator of educational aims. His *Autonomy and Schooling* (1988) argues for a version of child-centred education built around the notion of autonomy and that is sensitive to learners' interests, while his *Creating Citizens* (1997) discusses problems from an egalitarian perspective with Rawls's 1993 account of liberalism, including the possibility of the liberal state's becoming complicit in oppressive cultural practices like the subordination of women to men. Callan also argues in favour of a non-chauvinist form of patriotism as a civic virtue, seeing it as a vital educational aim of the liberal state and one which helps to do justice to communitarian concerns about liberal values.

What civic aims should be in a liberal democracy and who should have the power to determine them have also been explored in Amy Gutmann's *Democratic Education* (1987). In the line of thought sparked off by MacIntyre 1981, Patricia White's *Civic Virtues and Public Schooling* (1996) is another manifestation of the shift over the last decades towards thinking of aims, first and foremost, in terms of the pupil's personal qualities, or dispositions, rather than in terms of the acquisition of knowledge, however necessary this is as a sub-aim required by more fundamental values. In her book she explores the role of virtues like courage, self-respect, decency, trust, hope and confidence in the education of the democratic citizen. Enslin and White's Chapter 6 in Blake *et al* (2003) gives a fuller conspectus of work on education for citizenship, including discussions of whether this should be within a national or a global framework.

Patriotism as an aim is also discussed, more dismissively than in Callan's book above, in Harry Brighouse's *On Education* (2005), again within the context of citizenship education in general. Chapters are also devoted to autonomy, human flourishing and economic participation. As with other writers on aims in recent years, Brighouse is especially interested in how such aims relate together and provides his own perspective on this. For instance, the importance he attaches to autonomous flourishing makes him wary of work-orientated aims premised on continuing economic growth. A central theme in Brighouse's earlier book *School Choice and Social Justice* (2000), as in several works mentioned earlier, is education for autonomy as a liberal requirement.

It is distressingly obvious to us in 2008 that there is no point in discussing the ethical foundations of aims in liberal-democratic societies unless such societies are ecologically viable. The promotion of dispositions and understanding in the area of sustainable development has now become a salient feature of contemporary discussions of aims. We saw this above in the latest aims statement from the QCA. Educational theorists are also increasingly engaged with this area. The topic is intimately connected with issues to do with education for global citizenship and education for economic participation, both mentioned several times above, and with notions of personal well-being giving less priority to conventional notions of 'success' as measured in financial and status terms (see Michael Bonnett's *Retrieving Nature* 2004, Chapter 9). Robin

Alexander's *Education as Dialogue* (2006) is also partly about education for sustainable development. (On another topic, for those wishing to compare recent official aims of education in England with those of France, Russia, USA and India, Alexander's *Culture and Pedagogy* (2001) is a valuable source.)

* * *

This section has looked at a range of theorists' views over the last century on what the aims of primary education should be. Since the late 1960s it has been increasingly difficult to treat this as a topic distinguishable from the aims of school education in general. In the last few decades writers on the topic, largely philosophers, have tended to move from a discussion of specific aims towards more comprehensive accounts. These have stressed interconnections among different types of aim and explored the liberal-democratic background implicitly assumed by so much writing in this area.

Theorists' writings on aims have influenced policy makers from the beginning of our period and continue to do so today. Official aims statements have tended in the past to be built around lists of items for which a rationale has rarely been provided. In forthcoming years we may hope that the increasingly holistic accounts of aims outlined in this section will encourage policy-makers to spell out more fully the reasons behind the aims they choose and the interrelationships between them.

APPENDIX

The school curriculum and the national curriculum: values, aims and purposes (DfEE/QCA 1999)

Values and purposes underpinning the school curriculum

Education influences and reflects the values of society, and the kind of society we want to be. It is important, therefore, to recognise a broad set of common values and purposes that underpin the school curriculum and the work of schools.

Foremost is a belief in education, at home and at school, as a route to the spiritual, moral, social, cultural, physical and mental development, and thus the well-being, of the individual. Education is also a route to equality of opportunity for all, a healthy and just democracy, a productive economy, and sustainable development. Education should reflect the enduring values that contribute to these ends. These include valuing ourselves, our families and other relationships, the wider groups to which we belong, the diversity in our society and the environment in which we live. Education should also reaffirm our commitment to the virtues of truth, justice, honesty, trust and a sense of duty.

At the same time, education must enable us to respond positively to the opportunities and challenges of the rapidly changing world in which we live and work. In particular, we need to be prepared to engage as individuals, parents, workers and citizens with economic, social and cultural change, including the continued globalisation of the economy and society, with new work and leisure patterns and with the rapid expansion of communication technologies.

Aims for the school curriculum

If schools are to respond effectively to these values and purposes, they need to work in collaboration with families and the local community, including church and voluntary groups, local agencies and business, in seeking to achieve two broad aims through the curriculum. These aims provide an essential context within which schools develop their own curriculum.

Aim 1: The school curriculum should aim to provide opportunities for all pupils to learn and to achieve.

The school curriculum should develop enjoyment of, and commitment to, learning as a means of encouraging and stimulating the best possible progress and the highest attainment for all pupils. It should build on pupils' strengths, interests and experiences and develop their confidence in their capacity to learn and work independently and collaboratively. It should equip them with the essential learning skills of literacy, numeracy, and information and communication technology, and promote an enquiring mind and capacity to think rationally.

The school curriculum should contribute to the development of pupils' sense of identity through knowledge and understanding of the spiritual, moral, social and cultural heritages of Britain's diverse society and of the local, national, European, Commonwealth and global dimensions of their lives. It should encourage pupils to appreciate human aspirations and achievements in aesthetic, scientific, technological and social fields, and prompt a personal response to a range of experiences and ideas.

By providing rich and varied contexts for pupils to acquire, develop and apply a broad range of knowledge, understanding and skills, the curriculum should enable pupils to think creatively and critically, to solve problems and to make a difference for the better. It should give them the opportunity to become creative, innovative, enterprising and capable of leadership to equip them for their future lives as workers and citizens. It should also develop their physical skills and encourage them to recognise the importance of pursuing a healthy lifestyle and keeping themselves and others safe.

Aim 2: The school curriculum should aim to promote pupils' spiritual, moral, social and cultural development and prepare all pupils for the opportunities, responsibilities and experiences of life.

The school curriculum should promote pupils' spiritual, moral, social and cultural development and, in particular, develop principles for distinguishing between right and wrong. It should develop their knowledge, understanding and appreciation of their own and different beliefs and cultures, and how these influence individuals and societies. The school curriculum should pass on enduring values, develop pupils' integrity and autonomy and help them to be responsible and caring citizens capable of contributing to the development of a just society. It should promote equal opportunities and enable pupils to challenge discrimination and stereotyping. It should develop their awareness and understanding of, and respect for, the environments in which they live, and secure their commitment to sustainable development at a personal, local, national and global level. It should also equip pupils as consumers to make informed judgements and independent decisions and to understand their responsibilities and rights.

The school curriculum should promote pupils' self-esteem and emotional well-being and help them to form and maintain worthwhile and satisfying relationships, based on respect for themselves and for others, at home, school, work and in the community. It should develop their ability to relate to others and work for the common good. It should enable pupils to respond positively to opportunities, challenges and responsibilities, to manage risk and to cope with change and adversity. It should prepare pupils for the next steps in their education, training and employment and equip them to make informed choices at school and throughout their lives, enabling them to appreciate the relevance of their achievements to life and society outside school, including leisure, community engagement and employment.

The interdependence of the two aims

These two aims reinforce each other. The personal development of pupils, spiritually, morally, socially and culturally, plays a significant part in their ability to learn and to achieve. Development in both areas is essential to raising standards of attainment for all pupils.

(DfEE/QCA 1999: 10–12)

REFERENCES

Alexander, R.J. (1984) *Primary Teaching*. London: Holt, Rinehart and Winston.
——(2001) *Culture and Pedagogy: international comparisons in primary education*. Oxford: Blackwell.
——(2006) *Education as Dialogue*. Hong Kong: Hong Kong Institute of Education.

Ashton, P., Kneen, P., Davies, F. and Holley, B.J. (1975) *The Aims of Primary Education: a study of teachers' opinions.* London: Macmillan.

Blake, N., Smeyers, P., Smith, R. and Standish, P. (Eds) (2003) *The Blackwell Guide to Philosophy of Education.* Oxford: Blackwell.

Board of Education (1929) *Handbook of Suggestions for the Consideration of Teachers and Others Concerned in the Work of Public Elementary Schools* (6th impression). London: HMSO.

Bonnett, M. (2004) *Retrieving Nature: education for a post-humanist age.* Oxford: Blackwell.

Brighouse, H. (2000) *School Choice and Social Justice.* Oxford: Oxford University Press.

——(2005) *On Education.* London: Routledge.

CACE (1967) *Children and Their Primary Schools: a report of the Central Advisory Council for Education (England).* London: HMSO.

Callan, E. (1988) *Autonomy and Schooling.* Kingston and Montreal: McGill-Queen's University Press.

——(1997) *Creating Citizens.* Oxford: Oxford University Press.

Cooper, D.E. (1980) *Illusions of Equality.* London: Routledge and Kegan Paul.

DES (1981) *The School Curriculum.* London: HMSO.

DfEE/QCA (1999) *National Curriculum Handbook for Teachers in England.* London: HMSO.

Darling, J. (1994) *Child-Centred Education and its Critics.* London: Paul Chapman.

Dearden, R.F. (1968) *The Philosophy of Primary Education.* London: Routledge and Kegan Paul.

——(1976) *Problems in Primary Education.* London: Routledge and Kegan Paul.

Gutmann, A. (1987) *Democratic Education.* Princeton: Princeton University Press.

Hadow Report (1931) *The Primary School,* Consultative Committee of the Board of Education. London: HMSO.

Hirst, P.H. (1965) 'Liberal education and the nature of knowledge', in R.D. Archambault (Ed) *Philosophical Analysis and Education.* London: Routledge and Kegan Paul.

Holmes, E. (1911) *What Is and What Might Be.* London: Constable.

MacIntyre, A. (1981) *After Virtue.* London: Duckworth.

Marples, R. (Ed) (1999) *The Aims of Education.* London: Routledge.

Nunn, T.P. (1920) *Education: its data and first principles.* London: Arnold.

Peters, R.S. (1966) *Ethics and Education.* London: Allen and Unwin.

Peters, R.S. (Ed) (1969) *Perspectives on Plowden.* London: Routledge and Kegan Paul.

Rawls, J. (1972) *A Theory of Justice.* Cambridge, MA: Harvard University Press.

——(1993) *Political Liberalism.* New York: Columbia University Press.

Raz, J. (2003) *The Practice of Value.* Oxford: Clarendon Press.

Schools Council (1983) *Primary Practice,* Working Paper No 75. London: Methuen.

Selleck, R. (1972) *English Primary Education and the Progressives, 1914–1939.* London: Routledge and Kegan Paul.

Simon, B. (1974) *The Politics of Educational Reform 1920–1940.* London: Lawrence and Wishart.

White, J. (1973) *Towards aCompulsory Curriculum.* London: Routledge and Kegan Paul.

——(1982) *The Aims of Education Restated.* London: Routledge and Kegan Paul.

——(1990) *Education and the Good Life.* London: Kogan Page.

——(1997) *Education and the End of Work.* London: Cassell.

——(2004) (Ed) *Rethinking the School Curriculum: values, aims and purposes.* London: Routledge/Falmer.

——(2007) *What schools are for and why,* IMPACT Paper No 14. Philosophy of Education Society of Great Britain.

White, P. (1996) *Civic Virtues and Public Schooling: educating citizens for a democratic society.* New York: Teachers College Press.

Wringe, C. (1988) *Understanding Educational Aims.* London: Unwin Hyman.

13 Aims and values in primary education

England and other countries

Maha Shuayb and Sharon O'Donnell

BACKGROUND

This chapter compares the stated aims, purposes and values of primary education in England with those of five other countries (Scotland, Germany, New Zealand, Sweden and the Netherlands), drawing on historical as well as contemporary sources. It covers the period from 1965 to 2008 and, in so doing, addresses the following two broad questions:

- what are the aims and values of primary education; and
- how have they changed over time?

The chapter defines primary education as the first phase of compulsory education, comparable with Key Stages 1 and 2 of the system in England – ages four/five to eleven.

STRATEGY AND METHODS

The chapter comprises an exploratory, predominantly descriptive, chronological review of literature on the stated purposes, values and priorities of primary education in England and Scotland (for the UK), Germany, the Netherlands, New Zealand and Sweden. It draws mainly on policy documents, key legislation, curriculum guidelines, policy guidance, and policy reviews and statements. Sources are placed in a historical perspective going back to the time of the publication, in 1967, of the Plowden Report in England (Central Advisory Council for Education (CACE) 1967).

The chapter reviews policy documents which were available to the research team as part of the documentary collection kept for the Eurydice at NFER[1] and INCA projects,[2] and available or accessible via the Eurydice Network or INCA databases. The review was further informed by some broader, international comparative literature and commentaries on the aims, purposes and values of primary education. A full list of references and websites consulted is attached.

THE SURVEY LIMITATIONS

As this review of the aims, purposes and values of primary education in the six selected countries covers documents available in English only, the authors are unable to make all-encompassing conclusions. It is also of note that few of the policy documents analysed and reviewed limited themselves to explicit statements of the aims, purposes and goals for primary education. Consequently, the authors analysed a range of documentation, drawing out the key points of reference relevant to the primary phase.

SUMMARY OF THE FINDINGS

In the last 40 years, primary education in England and the other countries of the study has witnessed considerable change and, in some cases, restructuring. Despite a large number of initiatives and system changes, the aims, purposes, values and priorities of primary education have continued, during the period, to be shaped by two main influences or theories. The first, put forward by advocates of a child-centred and progressive education[3] calls for a flexible and autonomous system of primary education (Boyce 1946; Marshall 1963; Schiller 1972; Marsh 1970; Armstrong 1980; Rowland 1984); the second, driven more by a country's political and socio-economic goals, emphasises centralisation and standardisation.

Aims, purposes and values in primary education: 1960 to 1979

Education during the sixties fell under the influence of humanist and child-centred philosophies. In England, a child-centred ethos was strongly manifested in the Plowden Report (CACE 1967) which advocated holistic and rounded education, care for children's diverse needs, and individualisation.

In Scotland, the influence of the child-centred philosophy was demonstrated in the publication of *The Primary Memorandum* (Scottish Education Department (SED) 1965), which set out a curriculum for the primary school designed to accommodate the interests of children of a wide range of abilities and interests.

However, attempts to implement these theories in primary education in England and Scotland proved challenging. In England, the escalating debate between advocates of child-centeredness and those on the side of educational conservatism resulted in the publication of contradictory policy documents, some disputing the principles of Plowden. In Germany, attempts to shift education towards a more child-centred approach were less successful than in England and Scotland and the teacher-centred system remained, whilst in New Zealand, school and teacher autonomy dominated the system. Perhaps the most significant effect of the child-centred approach expressed in the aims, values and purposes of education during this period was in the changing attitudes towards ethnic minority pupils and pupils with special educational needs. This resulted in a range of legislation and policy documents in England, published during the seventies, which related specifically to the needs of bilingual, ethnic minority, or 'handicapped' children. This movement was echoed in the education systems of the Netherlands, Scotland and Sweden, although the extent to which the values were applied varied between countries.

Towards the end of the period, child-centred education philosophies attracted considerable criticism, being deemed difficult to assess and a hindrance to economic growth.

Aims, purposes and values in primary education: the 1980s

During the eighties two main trends were identified in the majority of the countries surveyed: budgets allocated to education increased, and governments sought increased control over education. Education began to reflect governments' political, social and economic agendas. These factors contributed to the increasing centralisation and standardisation of education; particularly in England which, by the end of the decade, was described by some critics as one of the most centralised and undemocratic education systems in the western world.

This increased governmental control over education had a significant impact on the aims, purposes and values of primary education. Whilst some countries continued with, or began to adopt, child-centred aims and values, others focused on the economic outcomes of the educational process. In the Netherlands, for example, major restructuring of primary education took place in 1985 with the implementation of *The Primary Education Act 1981*, known as *WBO* (Netherlands. Statutes 1981). This stipulated that the main goal of primary education should be to provide a child-centred education and cater for pupils' emotional, social and cognitive needs.

In contrast to the Netherlands, other countries – including England, Germany and Scotland – became more concerned with the potential economic impact of education. This was partly due to the economic recession following the oil crisis of the seventies. England, for example, introduced its first National Curriculum which, although lacking detailed explicit aims and values statements, focused clearly on raising pupils' academic achievement in literacy, numeracy and science. The National Curriculum also emphasised the role of education, from the earliest phases, in preparing the next generation for a flexible job market, whilst acknowledging education's role in ensuring the spiritual, cultural and physical development of children.

With similar regard to the role of education in preparing pupils for their contribution to society as a whole, it was during this same period that Sweden introduced the teaching of citizenship as one of the aims of primary education. Although the Scottish action plan published in 1983 (SED 1983) adopted child-centred values, it also focused on the economic impact of the educational process (Hartley 1987). In Germany, attempts to modernise education and implement a more child-centred ethos were abandoned during the 1980s as neo-conservative values[4] continued to dominate the aims of the education system.

Similar to the changes in attitudes towards ethnic minority and disabled students which began in England during the seventies, the education systems in Sweden and New Zealand in the eighties began to highlight the need to cater for these groups. In Sweden, the *Skollagen (Education Act) SFS 1985:1100* (Sweden. Statutes 1985) emphasised access to education, freedom of belief and gender equality. Meanwhile, in New Zealand, a comprehensive review of the curriculum recommended a more equitable curriculum, particularly for those who had previously been disadvantaged including girls, multi-ethnic groups, and students with special needs.

Aims, purposes and values in primary education: the 1990s

The aims, purposes and values of primary education during the nineties focused on the restructuring and reorganisation of primary education and the introduction of school inspection in some of the survey countries. Emphasis on raising standards in literacy, numeracy and science persisted, whilst the rise of the importance of citizenship education also featured in most review countries during this period.

In England the new curriculum, published in 1999 (Qualifications and Curriculum Authority (QCA) 1999a), included an explicit statement of aims, values and purposes for the first time. These were dominated by the Government's desire to raise pupil performance in literacy, numeracy and science, but also reflected the aim of promoting pupils' spiritual, moral, social, cultural, and physical growth, and preparing pupils for the opportunities, responsibilities and experiences of life. The explicit statement of values (QCA 1999b) focused on the self, relationships, society and the environment.

In Scotland new guidelines for the curriculum for pupils aged five to fourteen, published in 1993 (Scottish Office Education Department (SOED) 1993), aimed to develop pupils' literacy, numeracy and science skills at the same time as their abilities to communicate, express feelings and ideas, think critically, solve problems, and live healthily.

Sweden, too, introduced a new curriculum for the compulsory phase of education in 1994 (Sweden. Ministry of Education and Science 1994). This focused on subject attainment in areas including literacy, numeracy, science, communication skills, citizenship education and history. It also included 'goals to strive towards' such as curiosity to learn, working independently and in groups, and critical thinking.

In New Zealand, the various policy documents published during the period encouraged students to become independent, lifelong learners and focused on the multicultural nature of New Zealand society. The curriculum (New Zealand. Ministry of Education 1993b) also emphasised a range of explicit values such as honesty; respect for others and the law; tolerance; caring; the rights of individuals, families and groups; non-sexism; and non-racism.

Whilst England, Scotland and Sweden were focusing on raising levels of achievement, both Germany and the Netherlands were emphasising the holistic development of the child – cognitive, social, and emotional. In Germany, the various educational reforms which were taking place emphasised a child-centred education and learning in a cross-disciplinary context. In the Netherlands similarly, the revised *Primary Education Act (WPO)* (Netherlands. Statutes 1998) stipulated that education should aim to develop children in a holistic manner, taking account of their cognitive, social and emotional needs.

The majority of the surveyed countries took an increasing interest in citizenship education and either introduced it as a separate subject, or embedded it throughout the whole curriculum.

The aims and values in primary education: 2000 to 2008

In the eight years of the 21st century, the aims, purposes and values of education expressed in the surveyed countries appear to be reflecting economic and social principles, at the same time as the philosophies of personalised teaching and learning. This 'hybrid' of economically driven, learner-centred, and society-influenced aims reflects the views expressed by various theorists on education and can, consequently, sometimes appear contradictory (Brehony 2005; Alexander 2004a, b; Hartley 2005).

At the turn of the 21st century, England developed its first curriculum for primary education which incorporated a clearly defined statement of aims, values and purposes for education. These embraced personalised learning, socio-economic and vocational philosophies. In Sweden and the Netherlands, the hybrid approach appears to be reflected in recent policy documents for primary education. These emphasise the key role of child-centred teaching and learning philosophies at the same time as the importance of education in preparing children for their place in society, and for their contribution to an ever-changing economy.

In England, *Excellence and Enjoyment: a strategy for primary schools* (DfES 2003) and *Every Child Matters* (HM Treasury 2003) emphasised that primary level education should be concerned with standards, but also with enjoyment and a child's individual needs. However there are those who argue that the focus appears to remain with standards and assessment, more than with enjoyment (Alexander 2004a, b). *The Children's Plan: building brighter futures* (DCSF 2007) continues this emphasis on personalising learning to ensure that all children, particularly those who are disadvantaged, fulfil their potential. At the same time, the aims of ensuring that children enjoy their childhood and education whilst achieving world class educational standards remain.

Academic standards are similarly highlighted in New Zealand, alongside the social, ethnic, and cognitive differences among students and the social and economic aims of education. In addition, the introduction of the new, 2007 curriculum (New Zealand. Ministry of Education 2007) emphasises the need to develop active, confident, creative, energetic, and enterprising young people. The 2007 curriculum also stresses the values of equality, diversity, community, integrity and ecological sustainability.

In Scotland, the development of *A Curriculum for Excellence* (Scottish Executive 2004b) (for all pupils from the age of three to eighteen years) focused on developing successful learners, confident individuals, responsible citizens, and effective contributors. It also emphasised that the values of wisdom, justice, compassion and integrity were important and that education should aspire to cultivate these to some degree in all children.

In the Netherlands and Sweden, the emphasis on child-centred education persisted into the new millennium and primary education continued to emphasise the cognitive, creative, social and emotional development of pupils.

In Germany, child-centred philosophies continued to influence the aims, purposes and values of primary education during this period, with the purpose of primary school education being defined as one of moving pupils on from play-oriented forms of learning; adapting the form and content of teaching programmes to the capabilities of individual pupils; developing pupils' social skills; and encouraging critical and independent thinking.

For the six countries reviewed, the aims, values and purposes of primary education in the last 40 years appear to have passed through distinct phases. In the first phase, the child was the main focus and this greatly influenced the aims and values of the curricula; in the second phase social and economic concerns began to come to the fore; whilst today's aims focus on raising standards of achievement, and on preparing children for life in a multicultural society and in an ever-changing economic and work environment in which they will require a wide range of skills. However, there appears to be a realisation across countries that in order to achieve excellence, academically and vocationally, education requires a degree of personalisation: emphasis on the individual, the child. Governments in the six reviewed countries have also begun to recognise what Sweden recognised many years ago: that citizenship education is vital as one of the aims of an all-round education if countries are to produce participative citizens for the future. Recent emphasis too has highlighted healthy, safe and sustainable living, and primary education's role in encouraging young children's awareness of such issues.

THE SURVEY

Introduction

This chapter compares and contrasts the chronological development of aims and values for primary education, from the 1960s to the present day, in England, Germany, the

Netherlands, New Zealand, Scotland and Sweden, and the influences on the development and content of these aims. This is against the background of philosophical debate on the place of aims, values and purposes in the education system, which appears to take one of two major lines.

There are those who feel that such clear manifestations of the philosophical thinking underpinning the educational process are essential to facilitate its assessment and evaluation. Standish (1999), for example, points out that one function of aims can be to assess the impact and effectiveness of the educational process, and that this accords with the principles of rational planning which characterise the modern world. He suggests further that, when education is provided on a large systematic scale, scepticism about providing aims could be regarded as political irresponsibility. Barrow (1999) supports this view, arguing that education systems, without their own intrinsic and explicit aims, risk being driven by extrinsic aims such as ideology or industry.

Others claim that an overemphasis on aims and values can reduce education to a technical and functional process; lead to indoctrination; limit the autonomy of the educational process; and emphasise ends and outcomes rather than the child as the focus or object of the educational process. Pring (1999), for example, whilst acknowledging that education can not but have objectives and aims, argues that endless lists of competences, which can be measured using different means, shift the focus of education from the aims to the means. As early as the turn of the twentieth century, Dewey (1916) was arguing that aims confine children's cognitive development to predetermined goals, which teachers receive from superior authorities and which the latter accept from whatever is current in the community. Like Pring, however, Dewey also recognises that general aims that are sensitive to context and individual needs are important.

In England, explicit statements of aims, values and purposes were not included in the curriculum documents for primary education until the publication of the revised National Curriculum in late 1999 (QCA 1999a). These came following a period of consultation and review of the National Curriculum, which took place from 1996 to 1999, and following a review commissioned by the QCA of values and aims in other countries' curricula (Le Métais 1997). That said, and as also noted in Professor John White's research survey for the Primary Review (White 2008, Chapter 12 in this book), the *Education Reform Act 1988* (Great Britain. Statutes 1988), which established the National Curriculum, had defined general aims for the new curriculum. These were:

- to promote the spiritual, moral, cultural, mental and physical development of pupils in school and of society; and
- to prepare pupils for the opportunities, responsibilities and experiences of adult life.

These curricular aims aside, however, some general aims and values had been expressed for primary education prior to 1988.

Aims, purposes and values in primary education: 1960 to 1979

Primary education in **England** during the 1960s and 1970s saw a move towards a holistic, child-centred system, aiming to cater for the individual's diverse needs regardless of ability or social background. Advocates of this philosophy argued that education should not only be concerned with a child's academic performance, but should also cater for his social, emotional and physical development.

This child-centred philosophy was strongly manifested in the Plowden Report (CACE 1967) which stated that 'at the heart of educational progress lies the child' (p. 7). The result of an investigation initiated in 1963 by the Conservative Education Secretary of the time, who requested the Central Advisory Council for Education to 'consider primary education in all its aspects', the Plowden Report advocated individualisation, learning by discovery, independent learning, an integrated curriculum and the involvement of schools in their local communities. It further recommended that, at the same time as fitting children for a society marked by rapid and far-reaching economic and social change, primary education should:

- care for children's diverse needs, including the needs of ethnic minorities and the handicapped, as well as the gifted;
- ensure the holistic and rounded development of the individual;
- emphasise, in addition to the acquisition of the basic skills of literacy, arithmetic and reading, that there are other skills which are necessary for those who are to live happily and usefully both as children and as adults;
- highlight the importance of cooperation between school and home; and
- transmit values and attitudes.

There was a backlash against the Plowden Report from the Conservatives, who claimed that the child-centred philosophy was a hindrance to economic growth as it did not allow for the development of skills necessary for a changing economy. Despite the considerable reaction to the Plowden Report, Her Majesty's Inspectorate (DES 1978a) reported that, by 1978, only five per cent of classrooms in England were espousing the child-centred philosophy, with three-quarters of schools continuing to adopt didactic teaching methods. Nonetheless, the values expressed in the Plowden Report had a far-reaching impact on education in England, in particular by bringing the issues of providing for the needs of ethnic minority pupils and for children with special educational needs to the Government's educational agenda. Following Plowden, various reports recognised, for example, that the multicultural and multilingual society that England had become needed to be taken into account when planning the school curriculum (DES 1975; Committee of Enquiry into the Education of Children from Ethnic Minority Groups 1981; Committee of Enquiry into the Education of Children from Ethnic Minority Groups 1985). Others (including the Committee of Enquiry into the Education of Handicapped Children and Young People, 1978) highlighted the need to develop a policy of inclusion for pupils with special needs.

The influence of this child-centred philosophy could also be seen in educational policy in **Scotland** with the publication, at around the same time, of *Primary Education in Scotland* (SED 1965), otherwise known as *The Primary Memorandum*. This too focused on providing a child-centred education system to accommodate children's varying interests and abilities. It advocated a curriculum which would capture the attention and interest of children of a wide range of abilities, and teaching methods suitable for mixed-ability classes which would enable children to proceed at different rates in the same class. This document had a very great influence in freeing teachers from some of the curricular and methodological restrictions which had grown up, a process which was aided by the disappearance of pupil streaming in primary schools and of formal selection for secondary school (Eurydice 2006).

Hartley (1987) argued that the socio-economic conditions of the time in England and Scotland promoted the augmentation of this child-centred educational philosophy.

He claimed that the economic expansion of the period, manifested in low unemployment rates, for example, made notions such as individual needs and choice relevant.

In the **Netherlands** also, where the education system is characterised by the two overarching principles of freedom of education[5] and equal state support for public and private schools[6] (Karsten 1994), the aims, purposes and values of primary education in the 1960s and 1970s were influenced by similar child-centred ideals to those being seen in England and Scotland. The emphasis was firmly fixed on the holistic development of the child, constructive education, widening access to education, and catering for ethnic minority pupils. A number of compensatory educational programmes targeting ethnic minority and disabled children, and children from the disadvantaged native working class were also implemented (Driessen 2000). During this period educational reform in the Netherlands aimed 'to construct a 'great society', in which life was good for everyone ... a society in which power, knowledge and income was equitably distributed' (Karsten 1999: 306).

In **New Zealand** at the time, although the aims and values of education also focused mainly on providing equal opportunities for education for all children, regardless of ethnicity or gender, the system was often criticised for an emphasis on uniformity to the extent of reducing teaching to a technical process. However, during this period, the influence of child-centred ideals could also be traced in several official documents, such as the official syllabus for reading:

> We must accept the fact that each child is a unique personality whose capacities differ from those of his classmates. A uniform standard of achievement throughout an ordinary class is a mistaken aim.
>
> (McLintock 1966)

One of the key documents published during this period was the Currie report (New Zealand Department of Education 1962). Although concerned essentially with the structure of the education system, rather than the specific aims and goals of education, the Currie report made a number of recommendations regarding teacher training, pedagogy, the development and piloting of a new curriculum, and equality and diversity.

Another important educational development during this period took place in 1972, when the third Labour government instigated an Education Development Conference. One of the outcomes of this was a paper on the aims and goals of education (New Zealand Education Development Conference 1974). This focused on four major concepts:

- the school as a professional unit;
- lifelong education as a continuing process beyond the formal school system;
- continuity throughout the educational system; and
- school community, cooperation and mutual support.

Within this framework, priority was placed on teacher training, strengthening school-based curricula, eliminating national exams, emphasising moral education as a planned part of the curriculum, and strengthening school-based assessment.

Against the background of a system characterised by local education board support for primary education and much school and teacher autonomy, the shift towards child-oriented primary education in New Zealand was, however, slow and some criticisms of education as technical and functional continued for the following 20 years.

In **Germany**, the more teacher-centred primary education of the 1960s and 1970s also focused, as in New Zealand, on equal rights to primary education, and on conformity to the extent of 'sameness' according to some commentators (Gruber 1985). Although, at the time, the Plowden Report received extensive media coverage in Germany and was of considerable interest to professionals, it had little impact on the aims of primary education partially due to the bureaucratic and highly politicised education system. As Gruber (*ibid.*) comments, the influence of neo-conservative values on education in Germany in the 1970s could be seen on many levels. The neo-conservatives opposed the child-centred philosophy, advocating a 'traditional' educational philosophy according to which children need pressure to learn; teachers should be authoritarian; and schools should be primarily concerned with children's academic achievement and preparing them for the hard reality of society. Although the traditional and functional educational practices dominating the German education system were increasingly criticised by parents, teachers and educationalists for overloading children, educational reform in Germany was limited (Mitter 1980). The heavily bureaucratic system was seen to be a major obstacle facing educational reform.

Education in Germany also continued to be economically driven. Marshall (1989), for example, argued that the German educational philosophy needs to be understood from an economic viewpoint.

> Education as a response to specific needs, the needs being economic, is at the crux of the German philosophy of education and is something about which Germans are in agreement. … Thus certification and achievement are increasingly important.
>
> (Marshall 1989: 314)

In **Sweden**, education during this period was also perceived as an important instrument for social change and equality. The 1960 Social Democratic political programme for education recommended that all education should be:

- free;
- directed towards the formation of independent and cooperative citizens who value the democratic way of life;
- balanced between the theoretical and practical aspects of education;
- job-oriented and available in schools and at places of work for everyone; and
- common to all citizens – in the form of a common compulsory school (*grundskola*) – for their educational development.

Interestingly, Sweden was the first of the six countries of this survey to emphasise the civic goals of education. The Social Democratic political programme (1960) also stipulated that there should be education on political and religious views (cited in Rusak 1977).

In 1962, nine-year compulsory comprehensive education was introduced, when the seven-year elementary school was combined with the four-year lower secondary school to form the compulsory school (*grundskola*). Similarly to New Zealand and Germany at the time, the *grundskola* was established under the fundamental principle underpinning the Swedish education system – that everyone should have access to equivalent education, regardless of his/her ethnic social background and place of residence (O'Donnell *et al.* 2007). Olof Palme, the Prime Minister of the newly elected Social Democrat Government following the 1969 elections, emphasised education for 'self-actualisation'. The aim was to enable individuals to develop their personalities and inner potential. Palme believed that these characteristics were essential components of democracy and social change. He also emphasised individualisation and schools' duty to support students with special needs to achieve their full potential. Palme also attacked the marking system at the primary stage, which he believed 'had no other function than to point out the loser' (Rusak 1977: 207).

In summary, in England, as in Scotland, the Netherlands and Sweden, education in the sixties and seventies was marked by an increasing interest in child-centred values (Maslow 1959; Rogers 1969). The aims, values and purposes of primary education were being influenced by demands for humanistic education, and by philosophies encouraging the adaptation of education to the needs of the individual child, and the needs of the individual child in society. They were also influenced by principles of equity and parity of opportunity for all which, in some cases, presented a challenge to the individual, child-centred philosophy. New Zealand, for example, struggled in shifting its functional, equal opportunity- and teacher-based system to a more flexible, child-centred one, while Germany continued to adopt an economically-driven education system.

Cunningham (1988) has argued that this apparent contradiction in the aims and values of primary education during the period was a manifestation of the clash between the pedagogical tradition of child-centred learning and, in England particularly, mounting political pressure for educational accountability, fuelled by concerns about education and economic performance. Certainly the child-centred philosophy received considerable criticism in subsequent years, particularly from those who argued that it was difficult to assess its effects and influence. This represented a major problem for many governments keen to measure the effectiveness of their investment in education. In England and Scotland, for example, Conservative (and some Labour) politicians claimed that the child-centred philosophy was a hindrance to economic growth, as it did not allow for the development of the skills necessary for a changing economy. The economic crisis of the seventies did indeed begin to shift the focus from the individual to society and to economic growth, as is evident from the discussion which follows on the values and aims of primary education during the 1980s.

Aims, purposes and values in primary education: the 1980s

The economic recession of the 1980s led many countries to reconsider and reform their education systems. Commentators argued that 'the idea of the market ... ousted the idea of rational planning and central government steering' (Karsten 1999: 309). Although such reforms aimed to dismantle centralised education bureaucracies, in some countries, including England, movements towards centralisation were also taking place.

In **England**, the eighties were characterised by increased centralisation and standardisation of the education system; the major aims and goals of which were raising standards and employability.

The Conservative Government headed by Margaret Thatcher came into power in 1979 and soon introduced the *Education Act 1980* (Great Britain. Statutes 1980). This introduced more centralised control over curriculum subjects, teacher training and other aspects of education, including the composition of school governing bodies.

In the 1985 White Paper *Better Schools* (Great Britain. Parliament. House of Commons (HoC) 1985), the Conservative Government's aims for education as a whole, including primary education, were stated as being to:

- raise standards at all levels of ability;
- promote enterprise and adaptability; and
- increase young people's chances of finding employment or creating it for themselves and others.

Better Schools also laid the foundations for the development of national objectives for the school curriculum in primary education, and for an examinations and assessment system which promoted the objectives of the curriculum.

The *Education Reform Act 1988* (ERA) (Great Britain. Statutes 1988) introduced the first statutory National Curriculum. ERA defined the general values underpinning the new curriculum as:

- promoting the spiritual, moral, cultural, mental and physical development of pupils at the school and of society; and
- preparing pupils for the opportunities, responsibilities and experiences of adult life.

These values appear to combine the main ideologies of child-centredness, educational conservatism, and social democracy which had dominated educational debate over the two previous decades. However, critics including Brehony (2005) and Alexander (2004a, b) argued that the 1988 curriculum abandoned many of the values expressed in the Plowden Report (CACE 1967), as the role of education shifted from child-centred education to an education based on the needs of society and the economy.

Similar educational developments to those in England during the 1980s were also taking place in **Scotland**. The increased emphasis on regulation and standards was, for example, reflected in the *Education (Scotland) Act 1981* (Great Britain. Statutes 1981b), which gave the Secretary of State powers to prescribe standards and regulations for schools. At the same time, whilst the Scottish action plan produced in 1983 (SED 1983) remained based on child-centred values, particularly in the primary stage, it shifted the focus from the child's personal development to an interest in his economic and social productivity (Hartley 1987).

In 1987, a consultation paper issued by the Secretary of State for Scotland, entitled *Curriculum and Assessment in Scotland: a policy for the Nineties* (SED 1987), focused on the need for a clear definition of the content and objectives of the curriculum; satisfactory assessment policies; and better communication between schools and parents. In 1988, working parties of teachers and educationists began working on developing a revised curriculum for the Education Department in a series of advisory documents. The resulting 5–14 Programme[7] is currently the basis of primary education in Scotland. Its overarching aims are to:

- satisfy the needs of the individual and society; and
- promote the development of knowledge and understanding, practical skills, attitudes and values.

In the **Netherlands**, the first phase of compulsory education was restructured during the 1980s with the implementation of *The Primary Education Act* (*WBO*) (Netherlands. Statutes 1981). Prior to 1985, when the 1981 Act was implemented, children aged four and five attended nursery school or kindergarten before entering elementary education at age six, where they remained until they were twelve years old. In 1985, *WBO* lowered the starting age for compulsory education from six to five years, abolished separate nursery schools and brought provision for four- and five-year-olds into primary education (*Basisschool*). (Although education is not compulsory until age five, nearly all children attend school from the age of four.)

WBO established the main goals of primary education as being to provide:

- an uninterrupted development process for pupils, which is adapted in accordance with the individual pupil's progress;
- an education geared towards emotional, intellectual and creative development; and
- the necessary knowledge and social, cultural and physical skills.

The Primary Education Act (Netherlands. Statutes 1981), in addition to listing the subjects to be taught to pupils in primary school,[8] also highlighted the need for primary level education to acknowledge and celebrate the multicultural nature of society.

In **New Zealand**, a comprehensive review of the curriculum and of assessment was carried out in 1984. The review described the aims of the curriculum as developing the child's intellectual, social and personal abilities. The intellectual goals of the 1984 curriculum review focused on developing the child's ability to communicate, calculate, think, and solve problems. The personal goals included fostering a sense of personal identity, self-worth, responsibility and independence. The social aims focused on developing the child's understanding of economy as well as developing his/her personal, social and participatory skills.

The review also recommended the development of a new, more coherent and integrated curriculum designed in consultation with all interested parties. It also called for a more equitable curriculum, especially for those who may previously have been disadvantaged such as girls, multi-ethnic groups and students with special needs. The review also proposed increased emphasis on culture and heritage to reflect the diverse ethnic groups of New Zealand.

Some argue that education in New Zealand during this period was marked by a move towards a market education system. In 1988, an investigation into the administration of education (chaired by a supermarket tycoon, Brian Picot) was published. The Picot Report (New Zealand. Department of Education 1988) emphasised choice. Commenting on the report, Gordon (1992) argued that it represented an uneasy compromise between neo-liberal imperatives and traditional Labour concerns with equity and community and that, whilst it established a new structure of education committed to neo-liberal theories, it did not emphasise competition and the market, which are both essential to transform education into the 'image of a private business' (Gordon 1992: 285).

> The uncertainty and ongoing struggle allowed educational interests to maintain many of the egalitarian functions of the educational system, albeit within a new structure of education which was clearly amenable to a neo-liberal 'market' mode.'
>
> (Gordon 1992: 286)

In 1988 the Department of Education published a draft National Curriculum Statement which described the aims of the curriculum as:

- providing learners with knowledge, skills and attitudes to enable them to grow in a changing world;

- developing knowledge, skills and attitudes to participate fully in everyday life;
- developing an awareness of cultural identity and traditions; and
- developing an understanding of and respect for oneself and others, and of the knowledge, skills and attitudes needed to live and work well with other people.

The draft, which was never implemented due to political change, also focused on equity and promoting citizenship. The **Swedish** education system, too, underwent major reform in the eighties. The *Skollagen (Education Act) SFS 1985:1100* (Sweden. Statutes 1985) stipulated that all children and young people should have access to education of equal value. This remained a principle of the system from earlier years (see the section on 'Aims, purposes and values in primary education: 1960 to 1979', above) whilst the Act further emphasised values including multiculturalism, citizenship, freedom of belief and gender equality. The Act determined that education should:

- provide students with knowledge and skills;
- ensure collaboration between school and home; and
- promote students' harmonious development so that they become responsible human beings and members of society.

In **Germany**, the process of updating the Global Plan for Education, which had begun in 1977, was abandoned in 1982. Neo-conservative values (see the section on 'Aims, purposes and values in primary education: 1960 to 1979', above) continued to dominate the aims of the education system in the 1980s. A survey of primary schools throughout Germany, carried out by the Max Planck Institute in 1984, revealed that the vast majority were following a traditional, didactic approach to education, with the teacher as the centre of the learning process (cited in Gruber 1985).

In response to the economic downturn during the 1980s, the aims and values of primary education in the majority of the countries reviewed were influenced by a particular desire to ensure that education provided children with the skills to participate economically in society. In addition to improving employability, systems' aims and goals during the period were also influenced by the developing standards agenda. As a result, child-centred ideals diminished. As Karsten (1999) comments:

> While in the 1960s and 1970s people spoke far more about pupils at schools in terms of promoting equality of opportunity, in the 1980s the emphasis began to shift towards improving pupils' performances.
>
> (Karsten 1999: 307–8)

Aims, purposes and values in primary education: the 1990s

The nineties witnessed continued restructuring and reorganisation of primary education and the introduction of school inspection in some of the surveyed countries. The rise of the importance of citizenship education also featured in most countries during this period. The influence of neo-liberalist values such as choice, competition and market-led education, which had begun to influence the aims, purposes and values of education in England during the eighties, was also reflected in some of the other countries of the review, notably New Zealand and the Netherlands, during this period.

When, in **England**, the then Department of Education and Science (DES) published *National Curriculum: from policy to practice* (DES 1989) as the first guidance document for teachers on the introduction of the new statutory National Curriculum, no explicit aims or values were included. The guidance was, however, based on the general values and principles of the National Curriculum which had been expressed in the *Education Reform Act 1988* (Great Britain. Statutes 1988) (see the section on 'Aims, purposes and values in primary education: the 1980s', above). These general values and principles were further reflected in the *School Inspections Act 1996* (Great Britain. Statutes 1996b), which determined that the role of Her Majesty's Chief Inspector of Schools in England should focus on assessing schools' performance in terms of quality and standards in developing children's cognitive abilities, alongside their social and personal skills, and their cultural and moral development.

There was increased emphasis on education from 1997 with the election of the first Labour Government for almost 18 years, and the new Prime Minister's declaration that his priority was to be 'education, education, education'. In this latter period of the nineties, the aims, purposes and values of primary education were dominated by the government's desire to raise pupil performance in literacy, numeracy[9] and science, and by the 'bedding down' of the National Curriculum, revised in 1995, in particular to reduce the amount of compulsory content.

Soon after the 1997 elections, the new Education Secretary, David Blunkett, published the White Paper *Excellence in Schools* (Great Britain. Parliament. HoC 1997). This, whilst defining education as the 'key to creating a society which is dynamic and productive, offering opportunity and fairness for everyone', did not make explicit references to the aims and values of primary education. It was primarily concerned with raising standards of literacy, numeracy and science. Brehony (2005) noted that the new Labour Government had adopted a neo-liberal position, along with the centralised policies it had inherited from the previous Conservative government.

In 1999, when the Department for Education and Employment (DfEE) and the QCA published *The National Curriculum: handbook for primary teachers in England Key Stages 1 and 2* (QCA 1999a), this included an explicit statement of values, aims and purposes.

> A belief in education, at home and at school, as a route to the spiritual, moral, social, cultural, physical and mental development, and thus the well-being, of the individual. Education is also a route to equality of opportunity for all, a healthy and just democracy, a productive economy, and sustainable development. Education should reflect the enduring values that contribute to these ends. These include valuing ourselves, our families and other relationships, the wider groups to which we belong, the diversity in our society and the environment in which we live. Education should also reaffirm our commitment to the virtues of truth, justice, honesty, trust and a sense of duty.
>
> At the same time, education must enable us to respond positively to the opportunities and challenges of the rapidly changing world in which we live and work. In particular, we need to be prepared to engage as individuals, parents, workers and citizens with economic, social and cultural change, including the continued globalisation of the economy and society, with new work and leisure patterns and with the rapid expansion of communication technologies.
>
> (QCA 1999a)

The handbook defined the two broad, interrelated and interdependent **aims** of the school curriculum as being to:

- provide opportunities for all pupils to learn and achieve; and
- promote pupils' spiritual, moral, social, cultural, physical and mental development and prepare all pupils for the opportunities, responsibilities and experiences of life.

It further identified the four main **purposes** of the school curriculum as being to:

- establish standards – to be used to set targets for improvement, measure progress towards targets, and monitor and compare performance between individuals, groups and schools;
- promote continuity and coherence – to facilitate the transition of pupils between schools and phases of education and provide a foundation for lifelong learning;
- promote public understanding of, and confidence in, the work of schools and in the learning and achievements resulting from compulsory education; and
- develop the school curriculum – so that it is responsive to the changing needs of pupils and the impact of economic, social and cultural change.

In addition, an explicit statement of **values** linked to the National Curriculum handbook (QCA 1999b) focused on four major factors:

- the self;
- relationships;
- society; and
- the environment.

With regard to the self, for example, the statement of values suggests that the curriculum should, amongst others, encourage pupils to understand their character and their strengths and weaknesses; develop self-respect and discipline; and take responsibility for their own lives. In respect of relationships, the values in the curriculum should encourage children to respect, care and value others; earn loyalty, trust and confidence; and work cooperatively. In relation to society, the curriculum should enable children to understand and carry out their responsibilities as citizens; respect the rule of law and religious and cultural diversity; and contribute to economic and cultural resources. The values in the curriculum regarding the environment should encourage children to accept their responsibility to maintain a sustainable environment for future generations and to understand the place of human beings within nature.

Similarly, in 1993, **Scotland**'s Scottish Office Education Department (SOED) published new guidelines for the 5–14 Curriculum (SOED 1993), reflecting on developments in the 5–14 Curriculum since 1989 and providing an overview of the whole curriculum. This guidance also stated that schools should specifically aim to help each pupil to acquire and develop:

- knowledge, skills and understanding in literacy and communication, and numeracy and mathematical thinking;
- an understanding and appreciation of themselves and other people and of the world about them;
- the capacity to make creative and practical use of a variety of media to express feelings and ideas;

- knowledge and understanding of religion and its role in shaping society and the development of personal and social issues;
- the capacity for independent thought through enquiry, problem solving, information handling and reasoning;
- an appreciation of the benefits of healthy living and physical fitness; and
- positive attitudes to learning and personal fulfilment through the achievement of personal objectives.

When *The New Zealand Curriculum Framework* (**New Zealand**. Ministry of Education 1993b) was launched, in addition to seven essential learning areas and eight groups of essential skills for students to learn, it determined the attitudes and values which should be an integral part of the school curriculum. As in England and Scotland, these values were neither specific to nor exclusive to the primary stage.

The curriculum framework addressed students' unique learning needs, and encouraged them to become independent and lifelong learners. It also focused on the multicultural nature of New Zealand society, recognising in particular the significance of the Treaty of Waitangi,[10] and emphasising the importance of second languages and gender equality.

It determined specifically that the school curriculum should encourage positive attitudes towards all areas of learning by providing challenging learning activities which are relevant to students' experiences and appropriate to their levels of achievement.

> Attitudes consist of the feelings or dispositions towards things, ideas, or people which incline a person to certain types of action. Attitudes to learning strongly influence the process, quality, and outcomes of both learning and assessment. Teachers' expectations, the support of parents and the community, and students' motivation are all significant factors. The school curriculum will encourage positive attitudes towards all areas of learning. It will provide challenging learning activities which are relevant to students' experiences and appropriate to their levels of achievement. Schools will give students ongoing constructive feedback about their learning and progress.
> (New Zealand. Ministry of Education 1993b)

A range of explicit values was also included in the curriculum framework document. Defined as the values which underpin New Zealand society, and which should consequently be reflected in the teaching of the curriculum, these are:

- honesty;
- reliability;
- respect for others and the law;
- tolerance;
- fairness;
- caring and compassion;
- non-sexism; and
- non-racism.

The New Zealand Curriculum Framework states specifically that:

> Values are internalised sets of beliefs or principles of behaviour held by individuals or groups. They are expressed in the ways in which people think and act. No

schooling is value-free. Values are mostly learned through students' experience of the total environment, rather than through direct instruction. The content of a school's curriculum reflects what is valued by a society and a school community. Although the values held both by individuals and by various groups in society may vary greatly, those which are reflected in the New Zealand Curriculum are supported by most people in most communities.

The school curriculum, through its practices and procedures, will reinforce the commonly held values of individual and collective responsibility which underpin New Zealand's democratic society ... The school curriculum will help students to develop and clarify their own values and beliefs, and to respect and be sensitive to the rights of individuals, families, and groups to hold values and attitudes which are different from their own. Students will examine the context and implications of their own values and those of others, and the values on which our current social structures are based.

(New Zealand. Ministry of Education 1993b)

In 1994, *Education for the 21st Century* (New Zealand. Ministry of Education 1994) set targets for education from 1995 to 2001. Whilst adopting the same aims and values as those of *The New Zealand Curriculum Framework*, this policy document further emphasised:

- a community of shared values;
- a sound foundation in the early years for future learning and achievement;
- high levels of achievement in essential areas and essential skills;
- success for those with special needs; and
- the full participation and achievement by Maori in all areas of education.

A number of social and economic factors contributed towards educational developments in New Zealand during the 1980s and 1990s. The labour market changed significantly – through rapid and comprehensive technological developments, the growth of the service sector, and increased trading relationships with non English-speaking countries, all of which increased demand for the education system to produce not only higher levels of skills, but also a broader range of them.

When **Sweden** introduced a new curriculum for compulsory phase education (seven-to sixteen-year-olds) in 1994 (Sweden. Ministry of Education and Science 1994), this expressed curriculum aims in two ways. The first focused on subject attainment (attainment targets) for individual subject areas including literacy, numeracy, science and so on; the second determined goals to strive towards and included aspects such as developing a curiosity to learn, working independently and in groups, and critical thinking. Importantly, this framework was also underpinned by the statement that school has an important role to play in imparting, instilling and forming in pupils those **values** on which Swedish society is based. It determined these values as:

- democracy;
- the inviolability of human life;
- the individual freedom of all people;
- gender equality; and
- tolerance.

Whilst governments and education departments in England, Scotland, New Zealand and Sweden were focusing much of their attention on aims and values as expressed via curriculum framework documents for school or compulsory level education, the situation was slightly different in Germany and the Netherlands, where there was renewed focus on child-centred education.

In **Germany**, for example, the extensive pedagogical reforms which took place during the nineties emphasised child-centred education and learning in a cross-disciplinary context (Textor 2003). In addition, a 1994 agreement of the Standing Conference of the Ministers of Education and Cultural Affairs of the 16 German Länder (federal states) determined the basic **function** and **objectives** of primary education as being determined by its position in the school system. These were to:

- carry children forward from more play-oriented forms of learning at pre-school level to more systematic forms of school learning;
- adapt the form and content of teaching programmes to suit the different learning requirements and capabilities of individual pupils;
- provide the foundations for the next level of learning (secondary education) and for lifelong learning;
- develop their social skills by providing students with a structured understanding of the impressions they gain from the world around them, and developing their psychomotor abilities and patterns of social behaviour;
- encourage critical and independent thinking, by educating children from different individual learning backgrounds and learning abilities in such a way as to develop the basis for independent thinking, learning and working and to provide experience of interacting with other people; and
- as a result, allow children to acquire a solid basis to help them find their way and act within their environment.

In the **Netherlands**, in 1998, a new *Primary Education Act (WPO)* (Netherlands. Statutes 1998) determined that the task of primary education was the continuous development of the children in its care, and that education should aim towards the holistic development of the child – cognitive, social, and emotional. *WPO* also introduced the concept of adaptive education; gearing education to a child's capabilities and needs, and focusing primarily on the child him or herself rather than on subject matter content or the formal structure of education.

Karsten (1999) noted that, in the Netherlands, the aims and values of education during this period were influenced by calls for a return to the basics of education; that is, an emphasis on the core subjects of literacy, numeracy and science, as had been happening in other countries at that time. However, Karsten commented further that these calls went unheeded by policy makers who favoured socio-cultural educational values, which emphasised equality.

Whilst curriculum framework documents introduced in England, Scotland, New Zealand and Sweden during the 1990s all began to refer explicitly to the aims and purposes of the school curriculum, and to the values (and, in some cases, attitudes) which the school curriculum could and should encourage in children to ensure their active participation in society and the economy, none of these framework documents referred to primary level education alone.

Many aspects of the overarching values of the self, relationships, and society, as expressed in the Primary National Curriculum Handbook in England (QCA 1999a) (quoted earlier), were reflected to some degree in similar framework documents for Scotland, New Zealand, Germany and Sweden. England, however, was the only one of the surveyed countries, in the late 1990s, to specifically include elements linked to the environment and towards ensuring a sustainable future in its aims and values statements. Sweden and New Zealand, in addition to the general values statements which all countries included with regard to respecting cultural diversity, also included explicit statements regarding gender equality.

The focus for primary education policy in the Netherlands during this period highlighted the need to ensure that primary level education catered specifically for individual needs in a child-centred, holistic educational environment.

Aims, purposes and values in primary education: 2000 to 2008

During the last eight years, the aims, purposes and values of primary education in the reviewed countries have continued to focus on raising standards, citizenship education and multiculturalism. There has also been increased emphasis on pupil enjoyment and participation, pupil safety, healthy eating and lifestyles, and sustainable development.

In **England**, primary education was particularly influenced by the publication, in 2003, of *Excellence and Enjoyment: a strategy for primary schools* (DfES 2003) (often known as 'The Primary National Strategy', or PNS) and by *Every Child Matters* (HM Treasury 2003).

The key message from *Excellence and Enjoyment* was that, whilst primary level education should continue to be concerned with standards, it should also emphasise enjoyment, partnership with parents, and a child's individual needs. The goal is for every primary school to combine excellence in teaching with enjoyment of learning. Commentators have argued (Alexander 2004a, b; Hartley 2005) that use of the terms 'excellence' and 'enjoyment' reveals attempts by the Government to distance itself from the increasingly target-focused culture of education during the 1990s and early years of the 21st century, which had been much criticised by educationalists. They argue further, however, that the strategy's focus remains one of standards, assessment and excellence in achievement, albeit through personalised learning. This seems to be evidenced by statements included in the strategy confirming, for example, that the Government will:

- support innovation and offer more scope for school autonomy;
- keep a strong focus on standards;
- change local target setting arrangements;
- provide primary schools with better performance data;
- maintain high national standards at key stage 1, but trial a new approach to assessing seven-year-olds;
- make sure that the achievements of all children, and of inclusive schools, are recognised; and
- examine ways in which an overall assessment of a school might be included in performance tables.

Hartley (2005) and Alexander (2004a, b) see major contradictions between the concepts of 'excellence' and 'enjoyment', with Hartley noting that the introduction of terms such as 'enjoyment' is a manifestation of the consumer and marketing culture of education in the 21st century. Alexander argues that enjoyment sits unconvincingly with the parallel requirement, which has been a significant feature of primary education in England for the last decade, that schools should continue to focus on raising standards. Indeed, a more recent strategy document for primary education, *The Primary Framework for Literacy and Mathematics* (DfES 2006) continues to focus on raising pupils' literacy and numeracy standards, and on improving the quality of learning and teaching in all schools.

Although *Excellence and Enjoyment* (DfES 2003) emphasised the personalisation of learning, in a speech in May 2004 (Miliband 2004), the then Minister of State for School Standards, David Miliband, stated that personalised learning does not mark a return to the theories of child-centred education, nor is it about pupils learning on their own or abandoning the National Curriculum. Miliband defined personalised learning as an educational aspiration reflecting moral purpose, excellence and equity, and as an educational strategy providing a focus for school improvement, an approach to teaching and learning using information and communications technology (ICT), and a commitment to making best practice universal. Hartley (2005) regards this approach to personalised learning as:

> ... personalised standardisation: a personalised pick-and-mix of pedagogy and curriculum, but only from the standard menu, which is drawn up by the Government.
> (Hartley 2005: 13)

The 2004 *Five Year Strategy for Children and Learners* (HM Government 2004b) also continued the focus on raising standards of achievement. For primary education, it aimed to ensure:

- high standards in reading, writing and mathematics and maximum progress for each individual child;
- personalised support for every child whatever their needs, including those with special educational needs, gifted and talented children, and children with English as an additional language;
- a richer curriculum;
- a closer relationship between parents and schools;
- extended services for parents outside school hours (through so-called 'extended schools');
- healthy and environmentally sustainable schools which teach children by example; and
- a robust approach to persistent failure in primary schools.

At the same time, *Every Child Matters* (HM Government 2004a) proposed re-shaping all services provided for children in England to help achieve the following outcomes for children and young people:

- being healthy;
- maintaining safety;
- enjoying and achieving;
- making a positive contribution; and
- achieving economic well-being.

The targets stipulated in *Every Child Matters* were given legal force in the *Children Act 2004* (England and Wales. Statutes 2004), which called for integrating front-line delivery, common processes and strategy, and inter-agency governance.

In 2007, with the division of the Department for Education and Skills (DfES) into the Department for Children, Schools and Families (DCSF) and the Department for Innovation, Universities and Skills (DIUS), the Government aimed to give centre stage to its commitment to placing the needs of families, children and young people at the centre of education. Following the restructuring, the DCSF published *The Children's Plan: building brighter futures* (DCSF 2007), the far-reaching aim of which – 'to make England the best place in the world for children and young people to grow up' – is underpinned by five key principles:

- government supporting parents and families in bringing up their children;
- all children having the potential to succeed and going as far as their talents can take them;
- children and young people enjoying their childhood as well as growing up prepared for adult life;
- 'joined-up' services being responsive to children, young people and families; and
- the prevention of failure as the key to avoiding crisis situations.

The plan sets out to secure the well-being and health of children and young people; safeguard the young and vulnerable; ensure individual progress to achieve world class educational standards; and close the gap in educational achievement for disadvantaged children. It seeks further to ensure that whilst young people both achieve their potential and enjoy their time in education, teaching is tailored to their needs and based on their 'stage not age'.

Linked to the *Children's Plan*, a review of the primary curriculum is ongoing. The review team is tasked with ensuring that there is:

- sufficient time in the primary curriculum for children to achieve a good grounding in reading, writing and mathematics;
- adequate and appropriate flexibility for other subjects;
- time for primary school children to learn a foreign language; and
- a smooth transition from play-based learning in the early years into primary school, particularly to help the youngest children entering primary school who can be at a disadvantage.

In **Scotland**, recent documents reflecting aims and values in primary education follow on from the national debate on the future of education, which began in 2000 when the Scottish Parliament approved five national educational priorities for debate. The *National Priorities in Education*[11] (Scottish Executive 2002) were intended to define priorities in educational objectives for the whole of school education, and were organised under five headings, further subdivided into outcomes. These were:

- Achievement and attainment, with the outcomes of:
  - Increased levels of numeracy and literacy;
  - Improved examination results (or other measures of achievement).

- Framework for learning, with the outcomes of:
  - Continuing professional development of teachers' skills;
  - Increased self-discipline of pupils;
  - Enhanced school environments which are more conducive to teaching and learning.
- Inclusion and equality, with the outcomes that:
  - Every pupil benefits from education;
  - Every pupil benefits from education, with particular regard paid to pupils with disabilities and special educational needs;
  - Every pupil benefits from education, with particular regard paid to Gaelic and other lesser-used languages.
- Values and citizenship, for which the outcomes were:
  - Increased respect for self and others;
  - Increased awareness of interdependence with other members of the neighbourhood and society;
  - Increased awareness of the duties and responsibilities of citizenship in a democratic society.
- Learning for life, with the outcomes of:
  - Pupils are equipped with the necessary foundation skills, attitudes and expectations to prosper in a changing society;
  - Increased levels of creativity and ambition in young people.

Following on from the national debate, the Scottish Executive published the policy document *Ambitious, Excellent Schools: Our Agenda for Action* in 2004 (Scottish Executive 2004a), and a series of publications have followed during the ongoing development work for a new curriculum framework (*Curriculum for Excellence*) covering the whole of education from age three to age 18.

Ambitious Excellent Schools set the agenda for the education system in Scotland from late 2004 onwards. Its principal influence for primary education was that it laid the foundations for the new 3–18 curriculum, with a greater emphasis on literacy and numeracy.

The document *A Curriculum for Excellence: the Curriculum Review Group* (Scottish Executive 2004b), in particular, established clear purposes, aims and values for the new curriculum. The essence of this was a unified set of purposes and principles for the whole curriculum in Scotland, throughout the early years, primary school and secondary school. Echoing to some degree the standards agenda in England, the overarching **aim** of the *Curriculum for Excellence* programme is to improve the learning, attainment and achievement of children and young people in Scotland. In addition there is an emphasis on ensuring that pupils achieve on a broad front, not just in terms of examinations, by ensuring that children and young people are acquiring the full range of skills and abilities relevant to growing, living and working in the contemporary world, and that they experience the choice and opportunity to help realise their individual talents.

The four overarching **purposes** of the new 3–18 curriculum, as illustrated in Figure 13.1, are to enable all young people to become successful learners, confident individuals, responsible citizens and effective contributors.

The new curriculum also aims to improve the learning, attainment and achievement of children and young people in Scotland. It defines successful learners as enthusiastic and motivated with a determination to learn, and as individuals who can use literacy, communication, numeracy and technological skills; think creatively and independently; and learn independently and as part of a group. Confident individuals have a sense of well-being, self-respect, secure values and beliefs, have ambition and are self-aware, pursue a healthy, active lifestyle, and relate to others and manage themselves; whilst responsible citizens show a commitment to participate in political, economic, social and cultural life, along with respect for others and their beliefs and cultures and can evaluate environmental, scientific, technological and ethical issues. Like successful learners, effective contributors can think and create, be enterprising, apply critical thinking and solve problems.

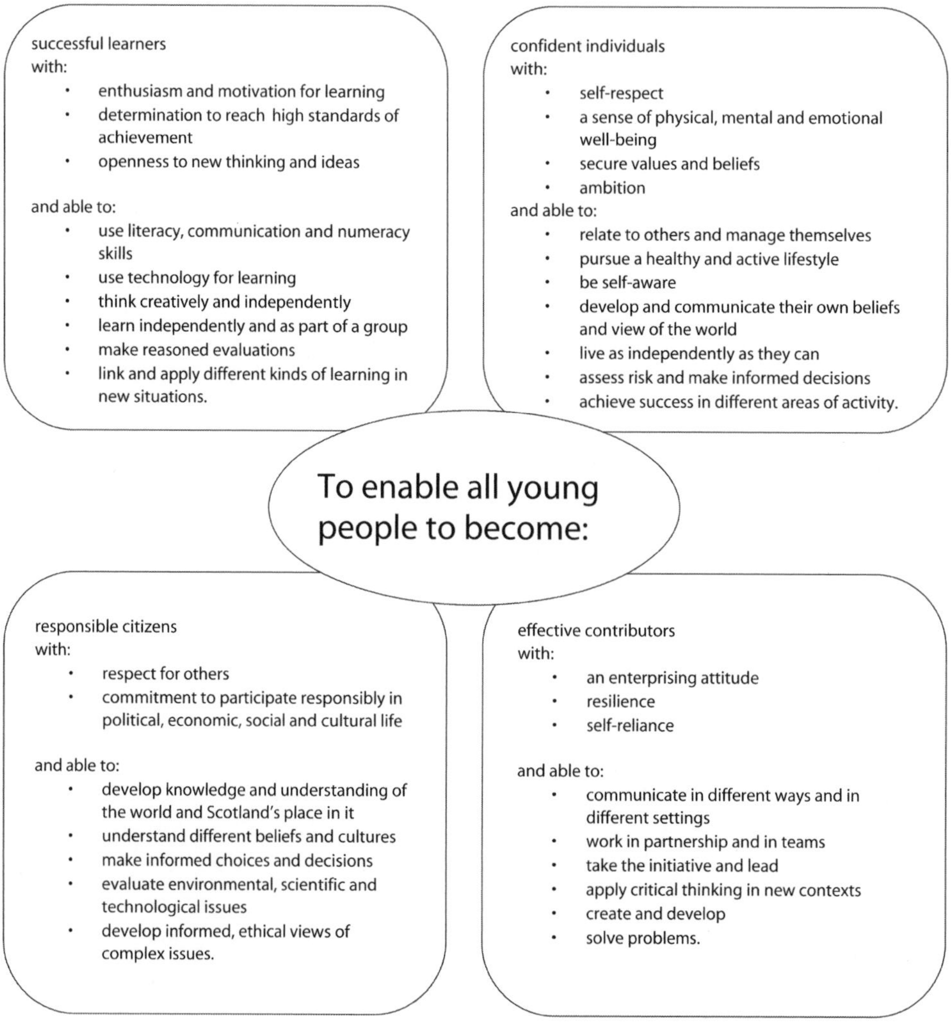

successful learners
with:
- enthusiasm and motivation for learning
- determination to reach high standards of achievement
- openness to new thinking and ideas

and able to:
- use literacy, communication and numeracy skills
- use technology for learning
- think creatively and independently
- learn independently and as part of a group
- make reasoned evaluations
- link and apply different kinds of learning in new situations.

confident individuals
with:
- self-respect
- a sense of physical, mental and emotional well-being
- secure values and beliefs
- ambition

and able to:
- relate to others and manage themselves
- pursue a healthy and active lifestyle
- be self-aware
- develop and communicate their own beliefs and view of the world
- live as independently as they can
- assess risk and make informed decisions
- achieve success in different areas of activity.

To enable all young people to become:

responsible citizens
with:
- respect for others
- commitment to participate responsibly in political, economic, social and cultural life

and able to:
- develop knowledge and understanding of the world and Scotland's place in it
- understand different beliefs and cultures
- make informed choices and decisions
- evaluate environmental, scientific and technological issues
- develop informed, ethical views of complex issues.

effective contributors
with:
- an enterprising attitude
- resilience
- self-reliance

and able to:
- communicate in different ways and in different settings
- work in partnership and in teams
- take the initiative and lead
- apply critical thinking in new contexts
- create and develop
- solve problems.

Figure 13.1 The aims of Scotland's 'Curriculum for Excellence'.
Adapted from http://www.ltscotland.org.uk/curriculumforexcellence/whatiscfe/purposes.asp [Accessed 03.11.2008].

The four **values** underpinning the new 3–18 curriculum are those which are inscribed on the mace of the Scottish Parliament and are regarded as the words which define the values for Scottish society. These are:

- wisdom;
- justice;
- compassion; and
- integrity.

In **New Zealand**, *Schooling in New Zealand: a guide* (New Zealand. Ministry of Education 2001b) defined the Ministry's main mission for all phases of education as:

- equipping students to play a full part in their community and the wider world through raising achievement and reducing disparity;
- ensuring high levels of access;
- ensuring participation in quality early childhood education; and
- ensuring effective transitions and pathways through school.

The Guide also highlighted the social, ethnic, and cognitive differences among students. It set a number of specific aims that target Maori and Pasifika[12] students such as:

- increasing their participation in education;
- improving the capability of schools to meet the needs of Maori pupils; and
- supporting Maori language teaching.

When, in 2003, the Ministry of Education published its key priorities for the next three years (New Zealand. Ministry of Education 2003a, b), the two main goals were to:

- build an education system that equips New Zealanders with 21st century skills; and
- reduce systematic underachievement.

In addition, *Education Priorities for New Zealand* (New Zealand. Ministry of Education 2003a) identified four key areas in which the education system was expected to deliver results, only the first of which relates specifically to primary level education:

- Providing all New Zealanders with strong foundations for future learning – these are the basic skills of literacy and numeracy; and the skills to be confident, motivated and healthy, and to have a strong sense of cultural identity.
- Ensuring high levels of achievement by all school leavers: in addition to school leaving qualifications, all school leavers need good skills in problem solving, creative thinking, interpreting information, reflecting on learning and knowledge and relating to others.
- Ensuring that New Zealanders engage in learning throughout their lives and develop a highly skilled workforce and consequently are motivated and self-directed lifelong learners.
- Making a strong contribution to New Zealand's knowledge base, particularly in key areas of national development; growing the knowledge base and supporting innovations. This supports tertiary education in particular.

In order to achieve these goals, the action plan set out in *Education Priorities for New Zealand* (New Zealand. Ministry of Education 2003a) identified key areas in which the education system was expected to deliver. These focused on providing all New Zealanders with a strong foundation for future learning, quality teaching, and strengthening family and community involvement. For the earlier years of education, there was a focus on the basic skills of literacy and numeracy; on cultivating confidence, motivation and good health; and on having a strong sense of identity.

Maori education continues to have a strong influence on the aims and values for the system in New Zealand and, in 2005, the Ministry of Education published the *Maori Education Strategy* (New Zealand. Ministry of Education 2005a). This focused on three main roles of education relevant to the Maori:

- enabling the Maori to live as Maori;
- facilitating their participation as citizens of the world; and
- contributing towards good health and a high standard of living.

Simultaneously, the Ministry published *The Schooling Strategy 2005–2010: making a bigger difference for all students* (New Zealand. Ministry of Education 2005b), which identified three priorities for education for the next five years:

- effective teaching;
- ensuring that children's learning is nurtured by their families; and
- ensuring that evidence-based practices are used by all involved in schooling

In November 2007, following a comprehensive consultation process, the Ministry of Education in New Zealand launched a new curriculum (New Zealand. Ministry of Education 2007). Applicable to the whole period of education in schools, this aims to develop young people who:

- are creative, energetic, and enterprising;
- seize the opportunities offered by new knowledge and technologies to secure a sustainable social, cultural, economic, and environmental future for New Zealand;
- work to create a New Zealand in which all cultures are valued for the contributions they bring;
- continue to develop the values, knowledge, and competencies that will enable them to live full and satisfying lives; and
- are confident, connected, actively involved and lifelong learners.

The 2007 curriculum further emphasises the values of:

- excellence, by aiming high and by persevering in the face of difficulties;
- innovation, inquiry, and curiosity, by thinking critically, creatively, and reflectively;
- diversity, as found in New Zealand's different cultures, languages and heritages;
- equity, through fairness and social justice;
- community and participation for the common good;
- ecological sustainability, including care for the environment;
- integrity, which involves being honest, responsible, and accountable and acting ethically; and
- respect for oneself, others and human rights.

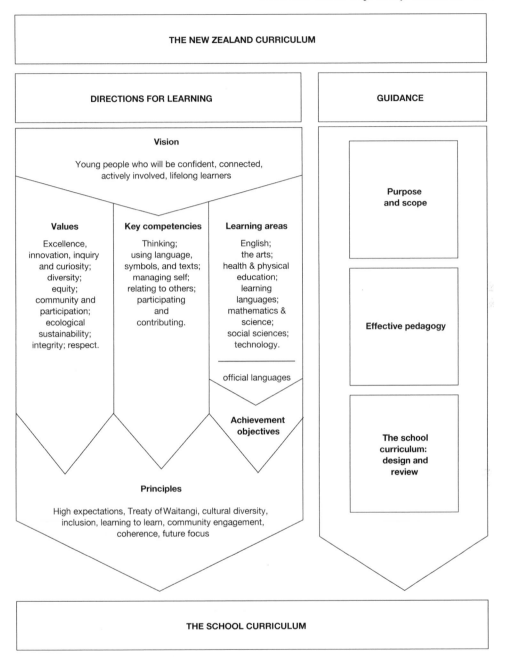

Figure 13.2 The New Zealand curriculum 2007.

Adapted from http://nzcurriculum.tki.org.nz/the_new_zealand_curriculum [Accessed 03.11.2008].

One of the key focuses of education in the **Netherlands** in recent years has been the change towards the adoption of a policy of inclusion of students with special needs in mainstream provision. Against this background and a continuing emphasis on child-centred education, *Primary School: a guide for parents and carers 2001–2002* (Netherlands. Ministry of Education 2001) defined the main aims of primary education as:

- acquiring knowledge;
- providing pupils with skills;
- understanding what pupils will need in modern society;
- highlighting the multicultural society of the Netherlands; and
- encouraging the intellectual, creative, social and emotional development of pupils.

Similarly to England, there is an increasing interest and emphasis on the school-community relationship in the Netherlands. 'Community school' in the Netherlands consists of

> a network in and around schools, ... based on the idea that teaching, youth care, sport and culture are all tailored to the needs of children and their parents in the neighbourhood ... [T]he aim of community schools is to prevent disadvantage, dropout, and learning and behavioural difficulties.
>
> (Eurydice 2008a)

The decentralisation of school management has also been a major feature of educational reform in the Netherlands during this period. On 1 January 2007 *The Education Participation Act* (*WMO*) (Netherlands. Statutes 1992) was replaced by *The Participation in School Decision-making Act* (*WMS*) (Netherlands. Statutes 2007), giving primary and secondary schools greater autonomy in devising their own policies. Finally, and in line with many other neighbouring countries, there have also been calls for compulsory standardised assessment across the entire country, for all pupils in the last year of primary school. This is with a view to facilitating national comparisons of school performance.

For the first time, in recent years policy documents published in **Germany** have begun to emphasise a similar national standards agenda to that reflected, to varying degrees, in the aims and values expressed for education in England, Scotland, and New Zealand. Publications such as *The Development of National Educational Standards* (Federal Ministry of Education and Research 2004) have highlighted that, since the publication of the results of recent international comparative surveys of pupil attainment, discussion in Germany has focused on the quality of schools and of teaching and learning. Although much of the focus has been on secondary education, changes are also being called for at pre-school and primary level, and education policy makers are beginning to introduce radical reforms, including the introduction of national, common educational standards in certain subjects in secondary education. Similar common standards are being developed for primary education, in particular for German and mathematics (literacy and numeracy).

At the same time as ensuring the sound development of a child's linguistic, mathematical and scientific skills, the role of primary schools remains one of developing independent, critical thinking, hard-working and socially active children. Current pedagogical reforms highlight a pupil-oriented approach to teaching and promote learning in a cross-disciplinary context. They also focus on reducing inequalities (Eurydice 2008b).

Primary education in **Sweden** in the 21st century continues to emphasise the values and goals established in the 1994 curriculum (Sweden. Ministry of Education and Science 1994), and to highlight the need for inductive learning methods and child-centred education.

During the first six years of the 21st century the aims, values, and purposes of primary education across the surveyed countries have addressed a number of economic, social, cultural, physical and political concerns. In an age of globalisation and rapidly changing economies and technologies, governments now more than ever are concerned with developing a generation equipped with the essential skills for their effective participation in a competitive economy. They are also increasingly aware of the importance, where possible, of tailoring learning to the personalised needs of the individual. The aims and values expressed in policy documents published during the period have, in addition, addressed issues of civic participation, social cohesion and identity, through an increasing emphasis on citizenship education and values of tolerance, equality and respect. They have also begun to highlight the value of healthy and sustainable living.

CONCLUSION

As this chapter has tried to illustrate, the aims and values of primary education in the six surveyed countries can be seen to have been driven by two sets of ideas: variants of child-centred education and social and economic progress.

Child-centred philosophies were most strongly manifested in the aims and values of primary education in the 1960s and 1970s, particularly in England, Scotland and the Netherlands, where there appeared to be great optimism in the ability of education to bring about equality and social change. The child-centred educational philosophy and its ethos of equality and individualism had a significant impact in changing attitudes towards students with special needs, and those from minority ethnic backgrounds in most of the surveyed countries.

During the eighties and nineties, the aims and values of education continued to reflect the importance of education in bringing about social change but, in addition, there was significant emphasis on education as a tool for economic improvement. This trend was particularly apparent in England, and was also reflected in New Zealand, as the influences of child-centred educational philosophies began to diminish, and standardisation and pupil performance in literacy, numeracy and science became an increasing priority at the primary stage.

In contrast, child-centred ideals flourished in Germany and the Netherlands during the late eighties and throughout the nineties. In Germany, although education continued to be driven by vocational goals, aspects of child-centred philosophies were incorporated into the aims and values of primary education. In the Netherlands, despite calls for a return to the basics of education (that is to say to an emphasis on the core subjects of literacy, numeracy and science), policy makers continued to emphasise holistic education.

In recent years a hybrid view of primary education seems to be emerging. This almost contradictory hybrid of child-centred and economically- and socially-motivated philosophies of education seems to be encapsulated in increasing references across the surveyed countries towards the personalisation of learning. The aims and values of primary education today combine the requirement to prepare children for their economic role in society with the need to identify their individual strengths and weaknesses, so as to provide them with the necessary support to achieve targets. The techniques of child-centred education are being adapted not only to ensure the individual child's growth, but also to prepare him or her to fulfil their economic role.

At the same time, the aims and values of primary education are also clearly focusing on preparing individuals for their wider role in society. Taking Sweden's lead from the 1960s, all the countries reviewed in this survey are placing an increasing emphasis on education for citizenship in its broadest form. This does not restrict itself to participation in civic, social and political life, an understanding of rights and duties, of other cultures and of life in often multi-ethnic, multilingual societies, but also increasingly involves an awareness of a responsibility for healthy, sustainable and environmentally responsible living.

In short, the aims and values of primary education today across the six countries reviewed appear to reflect more similarities than differences. Although recognising and incorporating some elements of child-centred techniques, they are expressed primarily in terms of economic and social goals.

ACKNOWLEDGMENT

Maha Shuayb and Sharon O'Donnell gratefully acknowledge the comments of Steve Benson, of the New Zealand Ministry of Education, on the first draft of this chapter.

NOTES

1 Eurydice at NFER is the Eurydice Unit for England, Wales and Northern Ireland in the Eurydice Network. Eurydice is the information network on education in Europe. Sharon O'Donnell, who assisted Maha Shuayb in the compilation of this report, is the Head of the Eurydice Unit for England, Wales and Northern Ireland.

2 INCA is the International Review of Curriculum and Assessment Frameworks Internet Archive. It provides a regularly updated online source of information on curriculum, assessment and initial teacher training frameworks in 20 countries. The project is funded by the Qualifications and Curriculum Authority (QCA) and the Training and Development Agency for Schools (TDA). It is managed and updated by the International Information Unit at the NFER. Sharon O'Donnell, who assisted Maha Shuayb in the compilation of this report, is the Project Leader for INCA at the NFER.

3 While in extreme forms child-centred and progressive education have sometimes been separated, in the opinion of Dewey (Dewey 1916) the two are regarded as being necessarily related to each other.

4 Neo-conservativism represented a return to a traditional point of view, in contrast to the more liberal or radical schools of thought of the 1960s. It advocated the preservation of the best in society and opposed radical changes.

5 This is a three-fold freedom – to establish schools, to administer them, and to determine the religion or other ideology on which they are based. This freedom has been laid down in the Constitution since 1848 (Netherlands. Statutes 1848 (article 23)), but is restricted by the requirements laid down in the Compulsory Education Act (Netherlands. Statutes 1969; Netherlands. Statutes 1994), which stipulate that children must attend an education establishment full-time until the end of the year in which they reach the age of 16, or have completed at least 12 full years.

6 Any group of parents or citizens may propose the establishment of a private school, which, if certain criteria are met, then receives state funding.

7 http://www.ltscotland.org.uk/5to14/index.asp

8 These were Dutch; arithmetic and mathematics; English; sensory coordination and physical exercise; a number of factual subject areas: geography, history, science (including biology), social studies (including civics), intellectual and religious movements; expressive activities: developing the use of language, drawing, music, handicrafts, play and movement; social and

life skills, such as road safety; and health education. The Act further recommended that these subjects should be taught in an interdisciplinary form where possible.

9 Amongst the conclusions of the government's 1992 'three wise men' enquiry into primary education (Alexander *et al.* 1992), which investigated the state of primary education in England, was a decline in standards of literacy and numeracy.

10 The Treaty of Waitangi is an agreement that formalises the relationship between the Maoris and the Crown. It was signed on 6th February 1840.

11 See http://www.nationalpriorities.org.uk/

12 New Zealand has a significant Pasifika population with its own particular needs. *Schooling in Zealand: a Guide* (New Zealand. Ministry of Education 2001b) defines the term Pasifika as people living in New Zealand who have migrated from the Pacific Islands, or who identify with the Pacific Islands because of ancestry or heritage. The term does not refer to a single ethnicity, nationality or culture and includes both those born in New Zealand and overseas.

REFERENCES

Ahlers, J. (1999) *Going to School in the Netherlands*. Den Haag: LDC.

Alexander, R.J. (2004a) 'Excellence, enjoyment and personalised learning: a true foundation for choice?' *Education Review* 18(1): 15–33.

——(2004b) 'Still no pedagogy? Principle, pragmatism, and compliance in primary education', *Cambridge Journal of Education* 34(1): 7–33.

Alexander, R.J., Rose, J. and Woodhead, C. (1992) *Curriculum Organisation and Classroom Practice in Primary Schools: a discussion paper*. London: DES.

Arbeitsgruppe am Max-Planck Institute für Bildungsforschung (1984) *Das Bildungswesen in der Bundesrepublik Deutschland*. Reinbek: Rowohlt.

Armstrong, M. (1980) *Closely Observed Children: the diary of a primary classroom*. London: Writers and Readers.

Barrow, K. (1999) '"Or what's a heaven for?" The importance of aims in education', in R. Marples (Ed) *The Aims of Education*. London: Routledge.

Boland, T., Letschert, J. and Van Dijk, W. (1999) *Primary Education in the Netherlands: a picture of a primary school*. Enschede: SLO.

Boyce, E.R. (1946) *Play in the Infant School*. London: Methuen.

Brehony, K.J. (2005) 'Primary schooling under New Labour: the irresolvable contradiction of excellence and enjoyment', *Oxford Review of Education* 31(1): 29–46.

Central Advisory Council for Education (CACE) (1967) *Children and Their Primary Schools: a report of the Central Advisory Council for Education (England)*. London: HMSO.

Committee of Enquiry into the Education of Children from Ethnic Minority Groups (1981) *West Indian Children in Schools* (Rampton Report) (Cm. 8273). London: HMSO.

——(1985) *Education for All* (Swann Report) (Cm. 9453). London: HMSO.

Committee of Enquiry into the Education of Handicapped Children and Young People (1978) *Special Educational Needs. Report of the Committee of Enquiry into the Education of Handicapped Children and Young People* (Warnock Report) (Cm. 7212). London: HMSO.

Cunningham, P. (1988) *Curriculum Change in the Primary School Since 1945: dissemination of the progressive ideal*. London: Falmer Press.

Department for Children, Schools and Families (DCSF) (2007) *The Children's Plan: building brighter futures* (Cm. 7280). London: The Stationery Office.

Department of Education and Science (DES) (1975) *A Language for Life* (Bullock Report). London: HMSO.

DES (1978a) *Primary Education in England: a survey by Her Majesty's Inspectors of Schools*. London: HMSO.

——(1978b) *Statistics of Education SS5: school building surveys 1975 and 1976*. London: HMSO.

——(1989) *National Curriculum: from policy to practice*. London: DES.

Department for Education (DFE) (1995) *The National Curriculum*. London: HMSO.

DFE (1992) *Choice and Diversity: a new framework for schools.* London: HMSO.

Department for Education and Employment (DfEE) (1997) *Excellence for All Children: meeting special educational needs* (Cm. 3785). London: The Stationery Office.

DfEE (1998) *The National Literacy Strategy: framework for teaching.* London: DfEE.

——(1999) *The National Numeracy Strategy: framework for teaching mathematics from reception to Year 6.* London: DfEE.

——(2001) *Schools: building on success* (Cm. 5050). London: The Stationery Office.

Department for Education and Skills (DfES) (2003) *Excellence and Enjoyment: a strategy for primary schools.* London: DfES.

DfES (2006) *The Primary Framework for Literacy and Mathematics.* London: DfES.

Dewey, J. (1916) *Democracy and Education.* New York: The Free Press.

Driessen, G. (2000) 'The limits of educational policy and practice? The case of ethnic minorities in the Netherlands', *Comparative Education* 36(1): 55–72.

England and Wales. Statutes (2004) *Children Act 2004. Chapter 31.* London: The Stationery Office.

Eurydice (2006) *Eurybase: the Information Database on Education Systems in Europe. The Education System in Scotland 2005/06.* Online [Available: http://www.eurydice.org/portal/page/portal/Eurydice/DB_Eurybase_Home, accessed 23 April, 2007]

——(2008a). *Eurybase: the Information Database on Education Systems in Europe. The Education System in the Netherlands 2006/07.* Online (Available: http://www.eurydice.org/ressources/eurydice/eurybase/pdf/0_integral/NL_EN.ppd, accessed 24 July, 2008).

——(2008b). *Eurybase: the Information Database on Education Systems in Europe. The Education System in Germany 2006/07.* Online (Available: http://www.eurydice.org/ressources/eurydice/eurybase/pdf/0_integral/DE_EN.ppd, accessed 24 July, 2008).

Federal Ministry of Education and Research (2004) *The Development of National Educational Standards: an expertise.* Berlin: BMBF.

Gordon, L. (1992) 'The New Zealand state and educational reforms: "competing" interests', *Comparative Education* 28(3): 281–91.

Great Britain. Parliament. House of Commons (1985). *Better Schools* (Cm. 9469). London: HMSO.

——(1997) *Excellence in Schools* (Cm. 3681). London: The Stationery Office.

Great Britain. Statutes (1980) *Education Act 1980. Chapter 20.* London: HMSO.

——(1981a) *Education Act 1981. Chapter 60.* London: HMSO.

——(1981b) *Education (Scotland) Act 1981.* London: HMSO.

——(1988) *Education Reform Act 1988. Chapter 40.* London: The Stationery Office.

——(1993) *Education Act 1993. Chapter 35.* London: The Stationery Office.

——(1996a) *Education Act 1996. Chapter 56.* London: HMSO.

——(1996b) *School Inspections Act 1996. Chapter 57.* London: HMSO.

Griffin-Beale, C. (Ed) (1979) *Christian Schiller in His Own Words.* London: A & C Black.

Gruber, K.H. (1985) 'Ignoring Plowden: on the limited impact of the Plowden Report in Germany and Austria', *Oxford Review of Education* 13(1): 57–65.

Hartley, D. (1987) 'The convergence of learner-centred pedagogy in primary and further education in Scotland 1965–85', *British Journal of Educational Studies* 35(2): 115–28.

——(2005) 'Excellence and enjoyment: the logic of a "contradiction"', *British Journal of Educational Studies* 54(1): 3–14.

HM Government (2004a) *Every Child Matters: change for children.* London: DfES.

——(2004b) *Department for Education and Skills: five year strategy for children and learners.* London: TSO.

HM Treasury (2003) *Every Child Matters* (Cm. 5860). London: The Stationery Office.

Karsten, S.J. (1994) 'Policy on ethnic segregation in a system of choice: the case of the Netherlands', *Journal of Education Policy* 9(3): 211–25.

——(1999) 'Neoliberal education reform in the Netherlands', *Comparative Education* 35(3): 303–17.

Le Métais, J. (1997) *Values and Aims in Curriculum and Assessment Frameworks* (International Review of Curriculum and Assessment Frameworks). Online (Available: http://www.inca.org. uk/pdf/values_no_intro_97.pdf, accessed 24 March, 2007).

Maclellan, E. (2004) *Assessment, Testing and Reporting 3–14: consultation on partnership commitments*. Strathclyde: University of Strathclyde.

Marsh, L. (1970) *Alongside the Child in the Primary School*. London: A & C Black.

Marshall, S. (1963) *An Experiment in Education*. Cambridge: Cambridge University Press.

——(1989) 'The German perspective', *Comparative Education* 25(3): 309–17.

Maslow, A. (1959) *New Knowledge in Human Values*. New York: Harper & Bros.

McLintock, A.H. (1966) 'Education, primary', in A.H. McLintock (Ed) *An Encyclopaedia of New Zealand*. Online (Available: http://www.teara.govt.nz/1966/E/EducationPrimary/ EducationPrimary/en, accessed 29 March, 2007).

Miliband, D. (2004) 'Personalised learning: building a new relationship with schools', Speech to the North of England Education Conference, Belfast, 8 January.

Ministerie Van Onderwijs (1998) *Attainment Targets 1998–2003: primary education*. Den Haag: Ministerie van Onderwijs, Cultuur en Wetenschap.

——(2006) *Primary Education*. Online (Available: http://www.minocw.nl/english/education/292/ index.html, accessed 4 January, 2006).

Mitter, W. (1980) 'Education in the Federal Republic of Germany: the next decade', *Comparative Education* 16(3): 257–65.

Netherlands. Ministry of Education (2001) *Primary School: a guide for parents and carers 2001–2002*. Zoetermeer: Ministry of Education.

Netherlands. Ministry of Education and Ministry of Health (1998) *Childcare and Education for Children Between the Ages of Two and Seven in the Netherlands*. Zoetermeer: Ministry of Education, Culture and Science and Ministry of Health, Welfare and Sport.

Netherlands. Statutes (1848) *Constitution of the Kingdom of the Netherlands*. Den Haag: Government of the Netherlands.

——(1969) *The Compulsory Education Act*. Den Haag: Ministry of Education.

——(1981) *The Primary Education Act (WBO)*. Den Haag: Ministry of Education.

——(1992) *The Education Participation Act (WMO)*. Den Haag: Ministry of Education.

——(1994) *The Revised Compulsory Education Act*. Den Haag: Ministry of Education.

——(1998) *The Primary Education Act (WPO)*. Den Haag: Ministry of Education.

——(2007) *The Participation in School Decision-making Act (WMS)*. Den Haag: Ministry of Education.

New Zealand. Department of Education (1962) *Report of the Commission on Education in New Zealand* (Currie Report). Wellington: Government Printer.

——(1988) *Administering for Excellence: effective administration in education* (Picot Report). Wellington: Government Printer.

New Zealand. Education Development Conference (1974) *Educational Aims and Objectives. Report of the Working Party on Aims and Objectives*. Wellington: Government Printer.

New Zealand. Ministry of Commerce (1999) *Bright Future: 5 steps ahead. Making ideas work for New Zealand*. Wellington: Ministry of Commerce.

New Zealand. Ministry of Education (1993a) *A Guide to the New Zealand Curriculum Framework*. Wellington: Learning Media.

——(1993b) *The New Zealand Curriculum Framework*. Wellington: Learning Media.

——(1994) *Education for the 21st Century*. Wellington: Learning Media.

——(1998) *Assessment for Success in Primary Schools* (Green Paper). Wellington: Ministry of Education.

——(1999a) *Information for Better Learning: national assessment in primary schools. Policies and proposals*. Wellington: Ministry of Education.

——(1999b) *Schooling in New Zealand: a guide*. Wellington: Ministry of Education.

——(2001a) *New Zealand's Educational Research and Development Systems: background report*. Wellington: Ministry of Education.

——(2001b) *Schooling in New Zealand: a guide*. Wellington: Ministry of Education.

——(2003a) *Education Priorities for New Zealand*. Wellington: Ministry of Education.

——(2003b) *Education Priorities for New Zealand: a summary*. Wellington: Ministry of Education.

——(2005a) *Maori Education Strategy*. Wellington: Ministry of Education.

——(2005b) *The Schooling Strategy 2005–2010: making a bigger difference for all students*. Wellington: Ministry of Education.

——(2007) *The New Zealand Curriculum for English-medium Teaching and Learning in Years 1–13*. Wellington: Learning Media.

New Zealand. Statutes (1964) *Education Act 1964. No. 135*. Wellington: Parliamentary Counsel Office.

——(1989) *Education Act 1989. No 80*. Wellington: Parliamentary Counsel Office.

——(2001) *Education Standards Act 2001. No 88*. Wellington: Parliamentary Counsel Office.

O'Donnell, S., Andrews, C., Brown, R. and Sargent, C. (2008) *INCA: The International Review of Curriculum and Assessment Frameworks Internet Archive*. Online (Available: http://www.inca.org, accessed 24 July, 2008).

Pring, R. (1999) 'Neglected educational aims: moral seriousness and social commitment', in R. Marples (Ed) *The Aims of Education*. London: Routledge.

Qualifications and Curriculum Authority (QCA) (1999a) *The National Curriculum: handbook for primary teachers in England Key Stages 1 and 2*. London: DfEE and QCA.

QCA (1999b) *The National Curriculum for England: statement of values by the National Forum for Values in Education and the Community*. Online (Available: http://www.nc.uk.net/nc_resources/html/values.shtml, accessed 25 March, 2007).

——(2000) *Curriculum Guidance for the Foundation Stage*. London: QCA.

Richards, C. (1999) *Primary Education – at a Hinge of History?* Abingdon: Routledge.

Rogers, C. (1969) *Freedom to Learn: a view of what education might become*. Columbus, OH: Merrill.

Rowland, S. (1984) *The Enquiring Classroom: an approach to understanding children's learning*. Lewes: Falmer Press.

Rusak, S.T. (1977) 'Sweden and Ontario under Palme and Davis: educational priorities', *Comparative Education* 13(3): 199–220.

Schiller, C. (1972) 'Introduction', in National Froebel Foundation (Eds) *Designing Primary Schools*. London: National Froebel Foundation.

Scottish Consultative Council on the Curriculum (1999) *The School Curriculum and the Culture of Scotland*. Dundee: SCCC.

Scottish Education Department (SED) (1965) *Primary Education in Scotland (The Primary Memorandum)*. Edinburgh: HMSO.

SED (1983) *16–18s in Scotland: an action plan*. Edinburgh: SED.

——(1987) *Curriculum and Assessment in Scotland: a policy for the 90s*. Edinburgh: SED.

Scottish Executive (2002) *National Priorities in Education*. Edinburgh: Scottish Executive.

——(2003a) *Educating for Excellence, Choice and Opportunity: the Executive's response to the national debate*. Edinburgh: The Stationery Office.

——(2003b) *A Partnership for a Better Scotland*. Edinburgh: Scottish Executive.

——(2004a) *Ambitious, Excellent Schools: our agenda for action*. Edinburgh: Scottish Executive.

——(2004b) *A Curriculum for Excellence: the Curriculum Review Group*. Edinburgh: Scottish Executive.

——(2004c) *A Curriculum for Excellence: ministerial response*. Edinburgh: Scottish Executive.

——(2005) *Education and Training in Scotland 2005: national dossier summary*. Edinburgh: Scottish Executive.

——(2006a) *A Curriculum for Excellence: building the curriculum 3–18 (1). The contribution of curriculum areas*. Edinburgh: Scottish Executive.

——(2006b) *A Curriculum for Excellence: progress and proposals*. Edinburgh: Scottish Executive.

Scottish Executive and Learning and Teaching Scotland (1999) *A Curriculum Framework for Children 3–5.* Dundee: LTS.

——(2000) *The Structure and Balance of the Curriculum: 5–14 national guidelines.* Dundee: LTS.

Scottish Office Education Department (SOED) (1993) *The Structure and Balance of the Curriculum 5–14.* Edinburgh: SOED.

Skolverket (1998) *The Swedish School System.* Stockholm: Skolverket.

——(2000) *Education for All: the Swedish education system.* Stockholm: Skolverket.

Standish, P. (1999) 'Education without aims', in R. Marples (Ed) *The Aims of Education.* London: Routledge.

Statistics Sweden (2000) *Sweden 2000: a knowledge society.* Stockholm: Statistics Sweden.

Sweden. Ministry of Education and Science (1992) *A New Curriculum for the Compulsory School.* Stockholm: Ministry of Education and Science.

——(1994) *1994 Curriculum for Compulsory Schools (Lpo 94).* Stockholm: Ministry of Education and Science.

——(1995) *Syllabi for the Compulsory School.* Stockholm: Ministry of Education and Science.

Sweden. Statutes (1985) *Skollagen (Education Act) SFS 1985:1100.* Stockholm: Ministry of Education and Science.

Taylor, P.H. and Richards, C.M. (1979) *An Introduction to Curriculum Studies.* Windsor: NFER.

Textor, M.R. (2003) *Elementary Education in Germany.* Online (Available: http://eric.ed.gov/ERICDocs/data/ericdocs2/content_storage_01/0000000b/80/31/b9/d7.pdf, accessed 2 March, 2007).

White, J. (2008) *Aims as Policy in English Primary Education* (Primary Review Research Survey 1/1), Cambridge: University of Cambridge Faculty of Education. (Chapter 12 in this book).

Wood, E. (2007) 'Reconceptualising child-centred education: contemporary directions in policy, theory and practice in early childhood', *Forum* 49(1 and 2): 119–35.

World Bank (2000) *Decentralization and School-based Management (SBM) Resource Kit: Case Studies. New Zealand's 'Self-managed Schools'.* Online (Available: http://www1.worldbank.org/education/globaleducationreform/pdf/new%20zealandf.pdf, accessed 2 April, 2007).

WEBSITES

Documents were retrieved from the websites of the following organisations:

England

Department for Children, Schools and Families (DCSF)
http://www.dcsf.gov.uk

(The former) Department for Education and Skills (DfES)
http://www.dfes.gov.uk/

DCSF Standards Site
http://www.standards.dfes.gov.uk/

Office for Standards in Education, Children's Services and Skills
http://www.ofsted.gov.uk/

Office of Public Sector Information: United Kingdom Legislation
http://www.opsi.gov.uk/legislation/uk.htm

Germany

Conference of the Secretaries of Cultural Affairs
http://www.kmk.org/

The German Parliament
http://www.bundestag.de/

Netherlands

Ministry of Education, Culture and Science
http://www.minocw.nl/

Ministry of Health, Welfare and Sport
http://www.minvws.nl/

New Zealand

Ministry of Economic Development
http://www.med.govt.nz/

Ministry of Education
http://www.minedu.govt.nz/

Scotland

A Curriculum for Excellence
http://www.acurriculumforexcellencescotland.gov.uk/

Learning and Teaching Scotland
http://www.ltscotland.org.uk/

Scottish Executive
http://www.scotland.gov.uk/

5–14 Curriculum
http://www.ltscotland.org.uk/5to14/index.asp

Sweden

Government Offices of Sweden
http://www.sweden.gov.se/

Swedish National Agency for Education
http://www.skolverket.se/

Statistics Sweden
http://www.scb.se/

And from the Eurydice and INCA websites

http://www.eurydice.org
http://www.inca.org.uk

Part 4

The structure and content of primary education

The chapters in this section relate to two of the Cambridge Primary Review's ten themes, *Structures and Phases* (Theme 9) and *Curriculum and Assessment* (Theme 3), for which the Review's remit posed the questions below.

The structures and phases of primary education

- How well do existing structures and phases – pre-school in its various forms, infant/ junior/primary, first/middle, foundation/KS1/KS2 – work?
- What are the salient characteristics, strengths and weaknesses of the various institutions and settings in which primary education takes place?
- Are there problems of coherence, transition and continuity within and between phases? How can these be overcome?
- What can the primary phase profitably learn from developments in the phases which precede and follow it?
- When should formal schooling start, bearing in mind that many other countries start later than we do and conceive of the relationship of pre-school and formal schooling somewhat differently?

The primary curriculum

- What do children currently learn during the primary phase?
- What should they learn?
- What constitutes a meaningful, balanced and relevant primary curriculum?
- Do notions like 'basics' and 'core curriculum' have continuing validity, and if so of what should 21st-century basics and cores for the primary phase be constituted?
- Do the current national curriculum and attendant foundation, literacy, numeracy and primary strategies provide the range and approach which children of this age really need?
- What kinds of curriculum experience will best serve children's varying needs during the next few decades?

Together these three chapters, while not necessarily answering all the questions above (several are examined elsewhere in this collection) continue the exploration, initiated in Chapters 10–13, of what primary education is for, how it should be organised and on what kinds of understanding and skill it should concentrate.

A second continuity from the previous section is the use of international comparison to illuminate both the distinctive features of English primary education and alternatives to current thinking and provision. Chapters 14 and 15 make explicit comparisons between arrangements in England and other countries in respect of system organisation, policy, school structure, school starting ages, curriculum and assessment, while Chapter 16 uses a more eclectic comparative approach, drawing on developments both within and outside the UK and from both state and private schooling, to identify alternative ways of thinking about the curriculum. Between them, Chapters 14 and 15 survey aspects of primary education in over thirty countries, and five of the section's seven authors work outside England.

The Structure of Primary Education: England and other countries (Chapter 14), by Anna Riggall and Caroline Sharp, describes the current structure of primary schooling in England, charts key changes since the publication of the Plowden Report in 1967, and then compares arrangements for primary education in six countries (England, Scotland, Germany, the Netherlands, Sweden and New Zealand). Its comparisons cover decision-making, the balance of control between national government, local government and schools, school starting ages, the length of the school year, the duration of primary schooling, school size and the relationship of pre-school and primary education. It notes, notwithstanding claims commonly made for distinctively English features like an early school starting age, the difficulty of proving a relationship between such features and standards of pupil attainment.

In *Primary Curriculum and Assessment: England and other countries* (Chapter 15), Kathy Hall and Kamil Øzerk provide a general overview of primary curriculum and assessment in over 20 countries including England, noting both general similarities, at least at the level of statutory requirements and formal curriculum labels, and areas where English curriculum and assessment requirements diverge from those elsewhere. They then look more closely at curriculum and assessment arrangements in England, the rest of the UK, France, Norway and Japan, noting as key areas of difference the degree of emphasis on the 'basics' of language and mathematics, the way those 'basics' are defined, the handling of cultural diversity, the dominance of the testing culture in England and the way tests there are used as instruments of school accountability.

Primary Curriculum Futures, by James Conroy, Moira Hulme and Ian Menter (Chapter 16) draws in a more eclectic way on the published education literature to identify alternative ways of thinking about the primary curriculum to those embodied in the National Curriculum which has been a statutory requirement for all schools since the 1988 Education Reform Act. It charts political, cultural and economic changes bearing on curriculum thinking and requirements and draws on alternative curricula that have emerged in recent years from both inside and outside the maintained education system, noting the particular influence of ideas from various schools and movements not subject to state control. It also assesses the efficacy of some of these approaches and identifies their shared principles.

From these three surveys we draw out a number of issues.

Similarity and difference: probing below the surface

Internationally, there are remarkable surface similarities between national systems of primary education. However, such similarities are very much at the level of officially-prescribed structures and the formal labels which are used to define what is taught, and below this level there may be more variation than is evident from a comparison of what is contained in the official literature. Yet even at the latter level, there are considerable differences in features such as the age of starting school, length of the school year, average size of school and length of primary schooling (Chapter 14). Similarly, apparent curriculum convergence in subject labels may mask substantial differences in the way individual subjects are conceived, as well as, naturally, in the way they are taught (Chapter 15).

Change, standardisation and flexibility

'Since the 1967 Plowden Report there have been a number of significant structural changes in English primary education, many of them initiated by or as a consequence of the 1988 Education Reform Act. These have resulted in an increased standardisation of primary school curriculum, teaching, assessment and inspection arrangements across the country' (Chapter 14). Yet 'education should become more fluid, with a greater emphasis on the dispositions of the learner than exclusively on what is to be known … Despite a changing landscape it is not easy to shift existing paradigms and long established practices' (Chapter 16).

When should children start primary school?

English children, as is well known, start compulsory schooling at a younger age than in many other countries. Notwithstanding the fact that in international achievement surveys (as shown later, in Chapter 18) pupils in some countries starting school as late as age 7 may outperform those in English primary schools by age 11, it is generally presumed that the earlier children start school the higher the educational standards they will achieve. However, 'the assumption that an early starting age is beneficial for children's later attainment is not well supported in the research and therefore remains open to question, while there are particular concerns about provision for four year olds in school reception classes' (Chapter 14).

Versions of the 'basics'

The international evidence shows that the 'basics' of language and mathematics are a consistently prominent feature of primary schooling. However, beyond that unanimity of commitment there are significant variations. Some countries treat language and literacy as pre-eminent rather than, as in the English '3Rs' tradition, giving literacy and numeracy parity. England includes science in the core curriculum alongside language and maths; many other countries do not, preferring to give more equal attention to science, humanities and the arts. Informing such differences are variations in the emphasis given to instrumental, developmental and cultural goals at the primary stage. (Chapter 15, but also Chapters 10, 12 and 13 in the previous section).

What about the rest of the curriculum?

The emphasis given to information technology varies, and England remains unusual in not – or not yet – making a modern foreign language compulsory at the primary stage. Another key difference is in the handling of culture, difference and identity. England's official curriculum documentation emphasises pluralism, diversity, tolerance and multiculturalism. In many other countries these are given relatively less emphasis than common values and shared national identity (Chapter 15).

Testing pupils and monitoring schools

'The scale of assessment for monitoring and accountability is of a quite different order in England compared to other countries' (Chapter 15). In England, there is more external, standard testing; it happens more frequently; it starts at a younger age; it occurs in more subjects; its outcomes are published in league tables ... Formal assessment in England, compared to our other review countries, is pervasive, highly consequential, and taken by officialdom to portray the actual quality of schools ... What distinguishes assessment policy in England is the degree to which it is used as a tool (a) to control what is taught, (b) to police how well it is taught, and (c) to encourage parents to use assessment information to select schools for their children' (Chapter 15).

Changing culture, changing curriculum

As shown in previous chapters (notably 10 and 11), reform of the primary curriculum cannot be separated from changes in the fabric of national life. 'We have seen a radical move away from a dependence on the historic resources of industrialization and towards a knowledge-based economy ... Migration has created new ways of looking at education which depend less than in previous ages on the transmission of a homogeneous culture, though this remains under review ... There is a perception that these shifts in population demography, together with the growing influence of mass media, have left youth bereft of the emotional resources to deal with an ever more complex culture' (Chapter 16).

Educational alternatives and pupil performance

'Educational alternatives range widely in their origins and motivations from the pragmatic to the principled and from left to right of the political and educational centres ... What appears to characterise all alternatives is that children's academic success in them is markedly better than in mainstream schooling ... These better than average performances are not simply explained by economic advantage ... However, they do share some tendencies, including ... less time spent using televisions and computers, more time spent on reading with and to children, greater emphasis on the life of the imagination, closer relationships between student and teacher ... continuing emphasis on literacy and numeracy, though interpreted more broadly than at present, more emphasis on generic teacher dispositions and skills than particular teaching methods, genuine partnership between student and teachers, a more intimate institutional – as opposed to class – environment' (Chapter 16).

14 The structure of primary education

England and other countries

Anna Riggall and Caroline Sharp

INTRODUCTION

This chapter aims to investigate the structure and phasing of the English primary education system. It considers issues of change in the years following the Plowden Report (CACE 1967) and draws comparisons between England and other countries. It sets out to address the following questions:

- What is the structure of the English primary education system?[1] How has this changed since 1967? How well do the structures work? What are the salient characteristics, strengths and weaknesses of the various institutions and settings in which primary education takes place?
- What is the evidence concerning the roles and relationships between pre-school and primary provision in England and other UK countries?[2]
- What is the structure of primary education in other countries? What is the evidence of effectiveness of different structures?
- What is the evidence on the impact of different primary phase structures and of different starting ages on learning and teaching? When should formal schooling start?
- What is the evidence that primary school structures influence results obtained in international comparative studies?

This chapter defines primary education as the first phase of compulsory education, comparable with Key Stages 1 and 2 of the system in England (ages four/five to 11). Pre-school education is defined as the period between birth and entry to formal schooling, although this evidence survey focused attention on the period immediately prior to school (ages three and four in England). Structure is defined as that which is decided for the schools by central or local government. It does not cover aspects of structure that lie mainly within the school's own control (such as management structures, timetabling or allocation of resources).

The survey comprised a review of relevant literature. It drew mainly on two types of information (descriptions of structures and research studies) and included different forms of literature (published articles, reports and conference papers). The parameters of the survey were as follows:

- Information from/including England between January 1967 – the date of publication of the Plowden Report (CACE 1967) – and December 2006.

- Information from other countries providing that it was readily available and written in English. The other countries included in the review were Scotland, the Netherlands, Sweden, Germany and New Zealand (further details concerning selection criteria for these countries are given in Appendix 1).

Details of the search strategy are given in Appendix 2. Decisions as to the relevance of the literature have been based on the following criteria:

- Whether it conformed to search parameters;
- Whether it was pertinent to the research questions;
- Its quality (any seriously flawed research has been excluded).

WHAT IS THE STRUCTURE OF THE ENGLISH PRIMARY EDUCATION SYSTEM?

This section seeks to describe the structure of primary education in England at the present time. In so doing it covers:

- who has control of and responsibility for the structure of primary education;
- different primary school types;
- key stages in primary school education;
- the structure of the National Curriculum;
- assessment in pre-school and primary years;
- length, structure and control of the school year;
- the structure of inspection in primary education.

Who controls the structure of primary education in England?

The control of education in England lies with the national government and central Department for Children, Schools and Families (DCSF). However, education in England is largely decentralised and many responsibilities lie with the Local Authorities (LAs), churches, voluntary bodies, governing bodies of schools and head teachers (O'Donnell *et al.* 2007).

The 150 English LAs take responsibility for area-wide aspects of educational provision. There are different types of local government structures: single-tier and two-tier configurations:

> Single-tier local government exists where a locality – usually a town, city or other urban area, is served by a single authority, which is responsible for all local service provision (…) and two-tier local government exists where, rather than all local services being provided by the local council, there is a division of responsibilities between a district (local) council, and a county council, which will cover a number of districts.
> (Labour Party 2007)

The duties of LAs in relation to the structure of education cover the appointment and support of governors; being the employer of teaching and non-teaching staff (although they may not have this right in respect of church, voluntary or foundation schools); coordinating school admissions processes; setting dates for the school year; and providing education, behavioural and finance plans for maintained schools. Governors and head teachers are responsible for what goes on within the school. For example, they decide on the use of the school premises (including extended school services); delegation of school budgets; performance target setting in relation to National Curriculum assessments, public examinations and unauthorised absence; pupil discipline and providing the LA with information about the school (Department for Education and Employment (DfEE) 2001).

In addition to overseeing primary education in maintained schools, LAs are required to provide a free, part-time place in some form of pre-school for every three- or four-year-old whose parents request it. This can be done through nurseries attached to primary schools or, outside the maintained sector, by parent groups, voluntary, private or independent bodies (for example private nurseries, nurseries attached to independent schools and pre-school playgroups). According to a recent Eurydice report (2006), most provision for children aged three to five years in England is in state-maintained nursery schools, classes in primary schools, and in voluntary and private settings.

Primary school types in England

The legal framework in England divides primary schools into three categories:

- Community schools, which are established and fully funded by LAs (and are often referred to as 'maintained' schools).
- Voluntary schools, which were originally established by voluntary or religious bodies (mainly churches). These bodies still retain some control over the management of these schools although the schools are now largely funded by LAs.
- Foundation schools, which are also funded by LAs but owned by school governing bodies or charitable foundations.

Primary schooling in England accommodates children aged from five to 11 years. Children must start full-time school the school term after they become five, although most children actually start school at age four (Eurydice 2006). There are a number of different school types that cover the age ranges relevant to this literature survey. They are:

- infant schools (typically age four to seven);
- first schools (typically age eight to 12 or nine to 13);
- junior schools (typically age seven to 11);
- middle schools (typically age eight to 12);[3]
- primary schools with pre-schools or nurseries[4] (typically age three to 11);
- primary schools without pre-schools or nurseries (typically age five to 11).

There are some other primary school types, including special schools that cater only for children with special educational needs which can be community, voluntary or foundation schools. Outside the mainstream primary school system there are Independent schools where parents pay for places.

The National Curriculum and 'Key Stages' in pre-school and primary education

The Education Reform Act of 1988 (GB Statutes 1988) set out a National Curriculum for every maintained school. This was made up of specified subjects and included the following:

- a set of attainment targets which specify the knowledge, skills and understanding which pupils of different abilities and maturities are expected to have reached by the end of each key stage;
- the types of matters, skills and processes which are to be taught to pupils of different abilities and maturities during each key stage;
- assessment for pupils at or near the end of each key stage for the purpose of ascertaining what they have achieved in relation to the attainment targets for that stage (Section 2).

The National Curriculum divides education up into 'key stages' of learning. In the primary years these are 'the Foundation Stage', 'Key Stage 1' and 'Key Stage 2'.

The Foundation Stage came into being as a distinct phase of education in 2000 and became part of the National Curriculum in 2002, 14 years after the National Curriculum for primary and secondary schools was introduced. The Early Years Foundation Stage became statutory in September 2008, combining curriculum guidance for the Foundation Stage with national standards for children in care and childminding. It set out six key areas of learning: personal, social and emotional development; communication, language and literacy; mathematical development; knowledge and understanding of the world; physical development and creative development (DCSF 2008). The Foundation Stage is delivered in pre-school settings for children aged from birth to five years old. This means that nurseries and reception classes in primary schools deliver the Early Years Foundation Stage curriculum, as do other pre-school settings such as playgroups, day nurseries, childminders and nursery centres (O'Donnell *et al.* 2007).

Key Stage 1 covers Year 1 and Year 2 of primary schools (ages five to seven) and Key Stage 2 covers Years 3 to 6 (ages seven to eleven). Compulsory National Curriculum subjects are the same for Key Stages 1 and 2. The 'core' subjects of English, Maths and Science are given relatively greater amounts of curriculum time. The other (Foundation) subjects that make up the curriculum are: Design and Technology, Information and Communication Technology (ICT), History, Geography, Art and Design, Music and Physical Education (DfES 2007a).

Assessment in the primary school years

As mentioned above, the Education Reform Act of 1988 set out a National Curriculum for all maintained schools to follow. A system of national assessment was designed to help ascertain how well pupils were performing. These assessments take place by means of the Early Years Foundation Stage Profile which is completed at the end of the Reception Year,[5] and through National Curriculum tests in core subjects at the end of Key Stage 1 and 2, at ages seven and 11 respectively.

Length and structure of the school year

In England, the school year comprises a minimum of 190 teaching days. The school year generally runs from September to July and schools are open five full days per week. Typically the year is divided into three terms, each with a half-term break. Term dates are determined by LAs or governing bodies (Eurydice 2006).

From 2004/5 there was a movement towards introducing a 'standard school year' in which the school year was divided into six terms of a more even length. In practice, the standard year represented a fairly subtle change to the existing school year pattern. The

Local Government Association (LGA)'s website states that the objective of the standard school year is to:

> Provide a model which allows for local flexibility, especially at the beginnings and ends to school terms, so as not to interrupt the integrity of smoother curriculum delivery, learning and assessment, and that teachers and parents with children at school in neighbouring authorities are not inconvenienced by differing term and holiday dates.
> (LGA 2007a)

'In principle decisions' to adopt the proposed standard school year were registered by 45 LAs and 17 London Boroughs at the time of writing (LGA 2007b).

A review conducted by Eames *et al.* (2005) considered the issue of school year patterns in more detail but found very little evidence that could answer questions about the impact of alternative school year patterns.

Inspection of primary education

Schools are inspected on a three-year cycle and inspections are carried out by the Office for Standards in Education (Ofsted). Schools are required to complete a Self Evaluation Form (SEF), and inspectors use this along with the school's Performance and Assessment (PANDA) report and any previous inspection reports to help inform their inspection. Inspection reports include the following:

- description of the school;
- overall effectiveness of the school;
- achievement and standards;
- quality of provision in terms of teaching and learning, curriculum and other activities and care, guidance and support;
- leadership and management;
- the extent to which schools enable learners to be healthy;
- the extent to which providers ensure that they stay safe;
- how well learners enjoy their education;
- the extent to which learners make a positive contribution;
- how well learners develop workplace and other skills that will contribute to their future economic well-being (Ofsted 2007).

HOW HAS THE STRUCTURE OF PRIMARY EDUCATION IN ENGLAND CHANGED SINCE 1967?

Since the Plowden Report (CACE 1967), a number of forces have influenced the structure of primary education in England. One of the major agents of structural change was the Education Reform Act of 1988 (GB Statutes 1988).

The influence of the 1988 Education Reform Act

The 1988 Education Reform Act introduced changes designed to encourage schools to behave competitively to attract pupils and strive to demonstrate their ability to improve standards through published league tables. As Gillard (2005) argues, the emphasis on parental rights to choose between schools was designed to stimulate a *market* to ensure quality by forcing failing schools to lose pupils and ultimately to close. In 1992, the introduction of a national system of school inspection was also introduced (GB Statutes 1992).

It has been argued that the 1988 Act emphasised structural divisions between different stages of pre-school and primary education. For example, Alexander (1995) suggests that divisions between infant, junior and adolescent education were deepened by the 1988 Education Act's creation of Key Stages. The division of separate Key Stages created a lack of continuity and flow in learning (starting in pre-primary and stretching into post-primary education). This served to compartmentalise early years, primary and adolescent curricula and practitioners. Alexander contrasts the organisation of education in England with that of other countries, asking whether primary structures that allow learning to flow more freely through infant, junior and adolescent stages (also known as 'all-through' schools) are of greater benefit to learners.

Bennett (1995) argues that the National Curriculum has become increasingly dominant in defining when progression takes place and what continuity is, but there remain tensions between the requirements of schools and readiness for meeting these requirements on the part of the child.

Changes in age of starting school

In England, the statutory school starting age (the term after a child's fifth birthday) is low in relation to that of other countries, most of which set six as the official starting age (Woodhead 1989; West and Varlaam 1990; Ball 1994; Sharp 2002). In practice, most English children start school at four because of the growing practice of admitting children to school at the beginning of the year in which they become five.

The term after a child's fifth birthday was established as the official school starting age in the 1870 Education Act. This decision was not taken on the basis of any developmental or educational criteria (see Woodhead 1989). Some MPs clearly favoured six as the school starting age. The main arguments in favour of setting the school starting age as early as five were related to child protection (from exploitation at home and unhealthy conditions in the streets). There was also a political imperative to appease employers because setting an early starting age enabled a relatively early school leaving age to be established, so that children could enter the workforce.

There was no legislation prohibiting children under five from attending schools, with the consequence that large numbers of under-fives were admitted to primary schools. Concerns about the welfare of children under five in schools (ranging from babies to four-year-olds) led to an official enquiry as early as 1908 (see Bilton 1993; Woodhead 1989).

By the time of the Plowden Report in 1967, the predominant pattern of entry to school was termly admission at statutory age (that is, there were three intakes each year for children to start school at the beginning of the term after they attained the age of five).

An effective lowering of the school entry age has taken place since 1967. The trend was identified in 1983, when the NFER surveyed all English and Welsh Local Education Authorities (LEAs, now LAs) (Cleave *et al.* 1985). At that time, there was a mixture of entry policies in evidence, including annual entry (one intake at the beginning of the year), biannual entry (two entry points, usually in the autumn and spring terms) and termly entry (three entry points a year). A majority of LAs admitted children to school before statutory school age, although fifteen LAs had a policy of admission at statutory school age in all or some of their schools. Many schools taking children under statutory school age formed separate 'reception' classes containing children aged between four and five years (although some children started in 'mixed age' classes, which included children of more than one year-group).

In 1986, a parliamentary select committee recommended the practice of annual entry to school before statutory school age:

> There should be no change in the statutory age of entry into school. However, we consider that local education authorities should, if they do not already do so, and under suitable conditions, move towards allowing entry into the maintained education system at the beginning of the school year in which the child becomes five.
> (GB Parliament, HoC ESAC 1986, para. 5: 44)

The 'suitable conditions' referred to by the committee were that infant classes should provide a similar environment, staffing and curriculum to nursery classes.

The following year another NFER survey confirmed the trend for lowering the age of entry to school, with ten LAs reporting recent changes in favour of earlier entry (Sharp 1987). Concerns were increasingly expressed that four-year-olds in reception classes were not experiencing 'nursery conditions'. These concerns were reflected in a Select Committee enquiry report of 1989, which proposed that: 'No further steps should be taken towards introducing four-year-olds into inappropriate primary school settings' (GB Parliament, HoC ESAC 1988, para. 7: 13).

Nevertheless, the trend was further accelerated during the 1990s following the introduction of the 1988 Education Reform Act. By 2002, 99 per cent of four-year-olds were attending some kind of educational provision, with 59 per cent of four-year-olds in infant classes[6] (DfES 2002).

There are a number of reasons for the trend towards lowering of age of entry to primary schools which began in the 1980s (see Sharp 1987; Daniels *et al.* 1995). Pre-school places were insufficient to meet parental demand, which was rising due to increasing female participation in the workforce. The 1988 Education Reform Act allowed schools greater control over their own budgets, which were largely based on the number of children on roll. This coincided with a reduction in the population of children starting school, giving schools both the incentive and capacity to take younger children. There was little inducement to create nursery classes because nursery education was governed by regulations stipulating the adult-child ratio (of 1:13) and staff qualifications required, making it a more complicated and expensive option. But these regulations did not apply to school reception classes, even though they catered for four-year-olds. Therefore, it was in schools' interests to lower the age of school entry by creating reception classes (but not nursery classes). Pressure built up on LAs to allow primary schools to accept four-year-olds. One of the immediate consequences of the increasing trend towards early entry to school was a removal of four-year-olds from pre-school settings, leading to concerns for the viability of nurseries and playgroups.

Changes in the size of English primary schools

One of the elements of school structure of potential interest to this survey is the size of primary schools. The Plowden Report (CACE 1967) contained information about the number of primary schools of different sizes in 1965. Table 14.1 reproduces this

Table 14.1 Number of primary schools in England

School size categories	January 1965	January 2004	Change
Up to 100	6,272	2,692	−3,580
101–200	5,153	5,566	+413
201–300	5,208	5,305	+97
301–400	2,703	2,615	-88
401–600	1,360	1,445	+85
601–800	87	132	+45
801–1000	6	7	+1
Total schools	20,789	17,762	−3,027
Total pupils (full-time)	4,003,934	3,972,690	−31,244

(Sources: Plowden Report (CACE 1967) Table 8, p. 114; DfES (2004) Table 20, p. 45).

information, placing alongside it the most recent figures available (derived from the Annual Schools Census that took place in January 2004).

Table 14.1 shows that in 1965 there were almost 21,000 primary schools, attended by just over four million pupils. These schools had an average (mean) size of 193 pupils. Forty years later, there has been a decrease of just over 3,000 primary schools although the population has decreased by just 31,224 pupils. The average school size has increased from 193 to 224 pupils during this period.

Table 14.1 shows that there has been a clear decline in the number of very small schools (those with under 100 pupils) and an increase in the number of larger schools (in all categories over 101 pupils, apart from a decline in the number of schools with 301–400 pupils).

Further scrutiny of the figures for the primary school population over the 40-year period (see DfEE 1998 and DfES 2004) shows a pattern of variation around the four million mark. The primary school population reached its highest point of 4,839,478 in 1973, although the number of schools did not peak until 1977. The lowest population figure was recorded in 1985 when there were 3,542,076 pupils in primary schools. The number of primary schools has declined every year since 1977.

The most likely explanation for the increase in school size is the formation of primary schools through the amalgamation of infant and junior schools (and first and middle schools in some areas). This has taken place for a variety of reasons, not least the need to rationalise school places in areas of declining population. The 1988 Education Reform Act also impacted on school expenditure and brought about greater alignment between school organisational structures and the National Curriculum key stages (see Wallace and Pocklington 2002).

These trends are further explored in the next section.

Changes in the types of primary schools

The Plowden Report (CACE 1967) recommended separate first and middle schools as the most suitable organisation of primary education; although it suggested combined (that is, combined first and middle) schools may be necessary in rural areas and some voluntary schools. Interestingly, the period since the Plowden Report appears to have seen a reduction in both first and middle schools.

Information provided by the DfES covering a ten-year period from 1997 to 2006 gives more details about the number of schools broken down by type (for example infant, first, primary) (DfES 2007c). During this period, the number of primary schools (that is, those taking children aged from four to 11) rose from 11,704 to 12,781. All other types of primary schools reduced in number. The greatest reduction took place in the number of combined first and middle schools, which reduced from 250 to 84 during this period. Separate middle schools declined from 206 to 95, and first schools from 1657 to 1180. The number of infant and junior schools also reduced during this period (infant schools from 2376 to 1752 and junior schools from 2199 to 1612).

The Local Authority's changing role

This section focuses on structural issues related to the role of the local authority. Blyth (1991) argues that the 1988 Education Reform Act has had a number of consequences for the role of the LA in primary education, including:

• the introduction of grant maintained schools and funding systems whereby schools received more money for more pupils;
• greater focus on management in primary schools;
• increased responsibility for financial affairs at the school level;
• greater political and financial pressures at the LA level;
• greater powers granted to governing bodies;
• greater involvement in the management of schools from teachers, governors and parents.

In *What is the LEA for?* Whitbourn *et al.* (2004) explain that the part played by the LA in the public education service is 'complex and varied'. They characterise the changes experienced by local authorities in the period between 1984 and 2004 as: 'A period of ambivalence, challenge and reductionism … followed by a new agenda which has set in hand a process of reformulation and clarification.' Local Education Authorities have since undergone a period of restructuring, whereby individual departments dealing with children's issues have been brought together to form Local Authority Children's Services. This took place following the Children's Act 2004 (England and Wales Statutes 2004). This move has not, however, substantively affected local authorities' responsibilities for the structure of primary education.

The formation of federations and collaborations

The Education Act of 2002 (England and Wales Statutes 2002) allowed groups of schools to establish federations or collaborations whereby they share some aspects of leadership and governance.

The distinction between these two new arrangements lies in the degree of formalisation. A federation involves specific arrangements for shared governance, as DfES (2007b) explains: 'The term federation describes a formal agreement by which up to five schools share a single governing body. … Each school retains its separate legal identity in respect of its budget, admissions and performance tables. … Each school is also subject to a separate inspection by Ofsted.'

A collaboration is based on the principle of allowing governing bodies and joint committees freedom to determine their own arrangements. They may carry out their functions jointly and delegate any of their functions to a joint committee with decision-making powers (except for the decision to appoint a head teacher).

Federations and collaborations can involve a mixture of primary and secondary schools. Most of the federations cited in the EMIE publication, *Schools in Collaboration: federations, collegiates and partnerships* (Arnold 2006) are at secondary level. However the report includes the following examples involving primary schools:

- Dumfries and Galloway – 'vertical' partnership between a secondary and its feeder primaries;
- Totnes Federation involving a primary, special and a community college (with specialist status for the performing arts);
- Glasgow Learning Communities which comprise secondary, associated primary and pre-five establishments;
- Cheshire – primary, secondary and special school clusters;
- Canterbury Federation, Kent – a 'hard' federation between a community primary and a foundation secondary.

Changes in the provision of early childhood education and care

One of the main structural changes to take place since the Plowden Report is a shift in the balance between education and care in the provision of group settings for children in the early years (from birth to age five).

There have been substantial recent changes in the structure of the curriculum and assessment in the early stages of education and care. The changes have been designed to ensure that all pre-school settings provide education rather than care and that delivery is equal and consistent across the country.

Since the Plowden Report, the debate has taken into consideration the variety of providers of pre-school settings and the balance of care versus education. Pugh (1990) summarised some of the main issues of concern in this field. She states that ensuring quality and equality in provision of services whilst sharing provision between central and local government, the private sector and parents has proved a major challenge. Pugh highlights the diversity in aims, value systems, hours of opening, admissions policies, level of fees, staff qualifications, staff pay and conditions of service that exist in such a wide variety of settings. In relation to the care versus education debate, Pugh questions the intention to emphasise the provision of education, given the lack of suitably-qualified staff.

WHAT IS THE EVIDENCE CONCERNING THE ROLES AND RELATIONSHIPS BETWEEN PRE-SCHOOL AND PRIMARY PROVISION?

In terms of the structure of primary education, there is little evidence upon which to base any assessment of the roles and relationships between pre-school and primary education. However, it is clear that changes in the structure of pre-school education in particular have placed greater importance on issues relating to transition and continuity between pre-school and primary education. Some research on transition has touched on aspects of structure such as the Foundation Stage Profile (see Sanders *et al.* 2005) but many studies focus specifically on transition practices and are therefore outside the remit of this study.[7]

Nevertheless, there has been some speculation as to the impact of the roles and relationships of pre- and post-primary education structures on the curriculum. For example, Beattie (1997) has questioned whether the structure of education could be viewed as a hindrance or liberator of the primary curriculum. He argued that the structure of the school system may determine the general characteristics of the curriculum. In other words, the relationship between pre- and post-compulsory levels of schooling affects the nature of what the primary and secondary school teach. He suggests that the young starting age for primary education in England has led to a focus on the needs of younger children within primary schools. He contrasts this with the situation in Germany, where high levels of selectivity in secondary schools and the brevity of primary education (only four years) restrict the curriculum in primary schooling.

WHAT IS THE STRUCTURE OF PRIMARY EDUCATION IN FIVE OTHER COUNTRIES?

Basic summaries about the education structures in the five selected countries are taken from the INCA database (O'Donnell *et al.* 2007). Further details are provided from additional literature sources, where available.

Control over the structure of education, curriculum and assessment in other countries

This section describes which bodies and individual post-holders have responsibility for the structure of education within each of the selected countries, including curriculum, assessment and the organisation of the school year. The countries included for comparative purposes were Scotland, Germany, the Netherlands, Sweden and New Zealand (see Appendix 1 for further information about the selection of comparator countries).

The First Minister for **Scotland** is responsible for the overall supervision and development of the education service with day-to-day responsibility delegated to the Minister for Education and Young People and the Minister for Enterprise and Lifelong Learning. The actual provision of education is the responsibility of the 32 unitary councils, known as the Scottish Local Authorities. The Scottish curriculum is guided by advice from the Scottish Executive Education Department (SEED) and Learning and Teaching Scotland (LTS). Assessment is carried out mainly through teacher assessment. There are no formal, compulsory national tests at primary level, although there are some assessment tools that teachers can use to support their professional judgement.

The Scottish school year starts in mid-August and runs to June with the dates of (usually three) terms being decided by the local authority. Schools must be open for a minimum of 190 days.

The education structure in **Germany** is largely determined by the federal structure whereby much educational legislation and administration is devolved to the 16 federal states (Länder). School districts have a large degree of autonomy and are responsible for the recruitment of staff and precise curricular content. There is no formal national curriculum or system of assessment in primary education. Germany uses a system of continuous teacher assessment as the main method of evaluating student progress.

The school year is divided into three terms starting in August and ending in July. Exact dates are decided by the federal states: there are 75 days of holiday plus about ten public and religious days (leaving about 176 days of schooling per year). Although half-day (morning only) schooling is traditional in Germany, there are moves to intro-duce more all-day schools in some areas.

In the **Netherlands** the education system is regulated by central laws and decen-tralised administration and management of schools. Central education policy, laid down by the Ministry of Education, Culture and Science governs teachers' qualifica-tions, funding and spending, examinations and inspections.

The overall curriculum in the Netherlands is determined by the Ministry of Educa-tion. Assessment is teacher-based in primary schools but there are national minimum attainment targets which students must meet. Progression in primary school is not automatic, but schools try to avoid pupils repeating years. There is a non-compulsory (but highly popular) primary school leaving test. The school year runs from August to July and must comprise a minimum of 200 instructional days.

Responsibility for the education system in **Sweden** lies with the National Ministry of Education and Science. Two independent agencies (the National Agency for Education and the National Agency for School Improvement) have been responsible for inspec-tion, evaluation and monitoring and supporting schools to achieve the national goals for education.[8] At the local level, municipalities make decisions on the running of schools, staffing and resources.

Sweden has a National Curriculum; assessment at the primary level is based on a combination of teacher evaluation and voluntary national tests. In Sweden, the school year generally runs from the end of August to early June and comprises a minimum of 178 days. The year is divided into two terms (dates vary between districts).

In **New Zealand** the Government is ultimately responsible for the structure of edu-cation. The Ministry of Education provides policy advice to government and develops the curriculum, allocates resources and monitors effectiveness. There is no local gov-ernment involvement in education in New Zealand; school governing boards have a degree of autonomy and control over the organisation and running of the school.

In accordance with the New Zealand Curriculum Framework, schools must cover the seven essential learning areas and eight groups of essential skills during the ten years of statutory learning. The learning areas cover languages, maths, science, tech-nology, social sciences, the arts, and health and well being. Skills include communica-tion, numeracy, information, problem solving, self management and competitive skills, social skills, physical, and work and study skills. Schools use a continuous, school-based assessment system. Many primary children are assessed on entry to school at age five. A randomly selected sample of three percent of children in Year 4 (aged eight to nine years) is involved in an annual assessment of all curriculum areas. This is known as the National Education Monitoring Project.

In New Zealand, the school year runs from late January through to December and is organised into four terms broken by two-week long holidays and a six-week summer break (during December and January). The primary school year comprises 394 half days.

Primary school ages and phases in selected countries

Table 14.2 shows the age groups for pre-school and primary education and the average primary school size in the five selected countries, with equivalent information for England provided for comparison.

In **England**, as noted earlier, pre-school focuses mainly on children aged three to five, whereas primary schooling focuses on children aged five to eleven. Most children start

Table 14.2 Pre-school and primary age groups in selected countries

Country	Pre-school age groups	Primary age groups	Average pupils per school
England	3–4/5	4/5–11	224
Scotland	3–4/5	4/5–12	128
Germany	3–6	6–10/12	185
Netherlands	0–4/5	4/5–12	222
Sweden	0–6/7	6/7–15/16	217
New Zealand	3–5/6	5/6–12/13	188

(Sources: O'Donnell *et al.* (2007); Eurydice (2006)).

school at four. The average size of primary schools in England was the largest among the selected countries at 224 children.

In **Scotland**, compulsory education starts at age five, although many children start school at four because schools have a single intake at the beginning of the school year. Local authorities set a cut-off date (normally 1st March) defining the cohort of children eligible to start school at the start of the following school year (normally in August). This means that children do not usually start school below the age of four years and six months. Primary education in Scotland continues to age twelve. The average primary school size in Scotland is the smallest among the six countries at 128 pupils.

In **Germany**, compulsory education starts at age six and primary schooling is only four years in length (in all but two federal states, where it is six years). Entry into compulsory schooling is based on the child having reached an appropriate level of development. In cases where the child is not deemed ready, he or she is required to attend preparatory classes known as Vorklassen or Vorschulklassen.

In the **Netherlands**, schooling is compulsory from age five, but virtually all children start school at four. Primary schools cater for children aged four to twelve. The compulsory age of starting school was changed from six to five years in 1985. The average size of primary schools in the Netherlands was second largest among the countries studied.

In **Sweden**, schooling is compulsory for nine years from age seven (although it is possible for children to start school at age six or eight). Most children attend all-through compulsory schools (Grundskola) which cover primary and lower secondary levels of education (O'Donnell et al. 2007). Sweden had a relatively large average school size among the selected countries, though it should be noted that these schools include children of secondary school age.

The decision to allow some discretion to Swedish parents to decide if their six-year-olds were ready for school was taken in the early 1990s. According to Pramling (1992), this raised a number of concerns, including that primary teachers were not well prepared to teach six-year-olds, the curriculum would be too structured and teacher-dominated, that children would be introduced too early to formal skills (reading, writing and maths) and that pre-schools would have their oldest children removed, resulting in too high a proportion of toddlers. Alvestad and Samuelsson (1999) explain the purpose of Sweden's pre-school curriculum, which was implemented in 1988: 'The purpose of the curriculum is to provide preschool educational opportunities based on the fundamental components of care, foster care, learning and education.'

In **New Zealand**, schooling becomes compulsory at age six but pupils can enrol in primary school from the age of five. Children do not start at the beginning of the school term – nearly all New Zealand children start school on their fifth birthday. A standard primary school caters for children aged five or six to twelve or thirteen. There are, however, some all-through schools which cater for children aged five or six right through to seventeen/eighteen.

THE IMPACT OF DIFFERENT SCHOOL STRUCTURES ON LEARNING AND TEACHING

It is difficult to comment on the impact of school structures because most of the available literature comprises descriptive accounts of the current structure of primary education and not research that has considered their relevance and appropriateness. It is evident that the structure of primary education has evolved over time and is largely taken for granted. The literature found in this survey did not identify evidence of any particular strengths or weaknesses related to the structural elements, although there are recurring questions posed about the appropriateness of the English primary school environment and curriculum for very young children.

This section considers two aspects of school structure which have been subject to research: age of starting school and school size. It ends with a consideration of evidence from international comparative studies in relation to attainment and these two aspects of school structure.

The impact of age of starting school

Two main educational arguments have been put forward in favour of the growing practice in England of children starting school at four. First, there is a body of research evidence demonstrating a correlation between being the youngest in the year-group (so called 'summer born') and doing less well than autumn- and spring-borns at school (see Sharp and Benefield 1995). One of the reasons suggested for this is that summer-borns may be disadvantaged in a termly or biannual entry system by spending less time at school than their older classmates.

Second, it has been suggested that it is an advantage for children to learn basic skills (such as reading, writing and counting) at an early age. For example, in 1999, the Chief Inspector of Schools argued that the inclusion of reading, writing and numeracy in the early years curriculum would help to overcome educational disadvantage experienced by children from poorer backgrounds (Ofsted 1999).

Research studies using sophisticated statistical analysis to consider the influence of length of schooling on pupils' school attainment have largely discounted differences in length of schooling as a major cause of underachievement among summer-born children (Sharp and Hutchison 1997; Tymms *et al.* 1997; Daniels *et al.* 2000). Tymms *et al.* (1997) studied the achievement of children at the end of the reception year and again in Year 2. Comparisons were made between summer-borns who had started school at the beginning of the autumn-term (annual entry) and those who entered school later in the year. The first assessment results (at the end of the reception year) showed evidence of poorer attainment among summer-borns who had started school after September, but by Year 2 their performance was similar to that of summer-borns who had started school one or two terms earlier. Two other large-scale research studies (Sharp and Hutchison 1997; Daniels *et al.* 2000) ruled out length of schooling as a causal factor for season of birth effects (concluding instead that being among the youngest when assessed, being the youngest in the year group and starting school at a young age were likely explanations for the observed differences in attainment levels of children born at different times of year).

There is no available evidence to show whether children from disadvantaged backgrounds are helped to achieve by an earlier school starting age. On the other hand, there has been a continuing concern about the quality and appropriateness of provision for four-year-olds in reception classes. It has been suggested that starting school at such a young age may be stressful for children (see Sharp 1988; Clark 1989; Woodhead 1989; Sharp and Hutchison 1997). There has also been much comment about the conditions and curriculum in reception classes, predicated on the theory that young children are best served by a 'nursery' environment, offering play-based learning, choice and independence.

Several qualitative research studies have shown that young children's opportunities to learn through play are curtailed in reception classes due to insufficient staff, lack of early years training, physical constraints (small classrooms, lack of facilities for outside play); lack of equipment (especially sand and water and large play equipment) and adherence to primary school timetables (see Barrett 1986; Sharp 1988; Sharp and Turner 1987; West *et al.* 1990; Cleave and Brown 1991; Bennett 1992). Many of these studies took place at the time of rapid increase in schools admitting four-year-olds to infant classes.

In 1993, Ofsted published a report based on a survey of primary schools focussing on the quality of education for four-year-olds in primary classes (Ofsted 1993). The report called for greater attention to be paid to the needs of four-year-olds in primary classrooms. Its recommendations included: improving staff development; increasing opportunities for teachers and other staff to work and plan together; deploying staff with National Nursery Examination Board (NNEB) qualifications to work with younger children in primary classes; increasing parental involvement; developing clear admissions policies at LA level; and improving the curriculum. The report concluded that having four-year-olds in primary classes was not in itself detrimental to good practice but was a challenge that required a better response from LAs and schools.

The introduction of the Foundation Stage in 2000 was intended to bring a parity of educational experience for three- and four-year-olds, irrespective of the type of educational 'setting'. Research into the quality of provision for four-year-olds in reception classes has, however, continued to raise some questions about provision for four-year-olds. For example, Adams *et al.* (2004) found evidence of pressure on reception class teachers from teachers in Key Stage 1 to prioritise the acquisition of academic skills (especially reading, writing and numeracy).

As well as a focus on four- and five-year-olds, there has been an interest in educational provision for six-year-olds, given that this is a common age for children to start formal schooling in many countries. In 2003, a comparative study considered the educational provision for six-year-olds in England, Denmark and Finland (Ofsted 2003). The comparison countries were chosen for study because the results of the first Programme for International Student Assessment (PISA) indicated different levels of attainment among 15-year-olds in their ability to apply their skills in reading, maths and science to real-life situations. England performed well, but Finland performed best of all 31 participating countries. Denmark was ranked some way below the other two countries. Whereas England and Denmark showed a wide variation between high and low scoring students, Finland had a relatively narrow range in scores. In both Finland and Denmark, children started school at the beginning of the year in which they became seven.

The study found that, compared with the other two countries, the English curriculum was more centralised and closely defined. Teachers in England were less secure about the nature and purpose of the curriculum in year 1. Much more was expected of English six-year-olds in terms of reading, writing and mathematics; less attention was paid to the development of pupils as people. English teachers made greater use of closed questions in whole-class teaching, with relatively little emphasis on speculation or extended interaction. English classrooms were comparatively cramped. Parents in England held diverse views about the kind of education their children should receive, and some expressed concerns about an abrupt change in curriculum following the reception year.

The impact of school size on attainment

There is relatively little research evidence on the impact of school size on learning and teaching. One fairly recent study which considered the performance of pupils in schools with different characteristics (Spielhofer *et al.* 2002) found no evidence of a relationship between primary school size and pupil progress in Key Stage assessments, although this may have been influenced by the relatively small number of primary schools included in the analysis.

In New Zealand, Harker (2005) conducted a similar study, examining the relationship between school size and pupil attainment. The author points out that most New Zealand primary schools would be considered 'small to medium' by international standards. The study found no evidence of a significant relationship between school size and academic attainment in primary schools.

Two other qualitative research studies have considered aspects of (large) primary school size and school amalgamation in England. Southworth and Weindling (2002) researched the views of school leaders on the benefits and limitations of large primary schools (those with over 400 pupils). They found that head teachers of large primary schools held mostly positive views of the impact of large schools on teaching and learning. Wallace and Pocklington (2002) studied the process of school amalgamation in two local authorities, documenting the complexity of the process for local authority and school staff and identifying the main change management processes and themes involved.

What is the evidence that primary school structures influence results obtained in international comparative studies?

This section is concerned with evidence on the extent to which primary school structures influence results obtained in large-scale international comparative studies of attainment in different subject areas.

The International Association for the Evaluation for Educational Achievement (IEA) measured reading standards in 32 educational systems (Elley 1992). The study assessed the reading standards of pupils aged nine and fourteen. At the time, children in most of the systems started school at age six, a few at five, and some (mainly those in Scandinavian countries) did not start school until the age of seven. The report included an analysis of the relationship between age of starting school and reading performance. Against expectations, this showed that the top ten scoring countries had a later starting age (the mean school starting age of these countries was 6.3, compared with a mean of 5.9 in the ten lowest scoring countries). But the top-achieving countries were also the most economically advantaged. When the researchers carried out a further analysis controlling for each country's level of 'development', the trend for older starting ages to be associated with better results was reversed. However, the author points out that the differences were small and that children in 'later starting' countries had largely caught up by the time they reached the age of nine.

The Programme for International Student Assessment (PISA) launched by the Organisation for Economic Co-operation and Development (OECD) in 1997 assesses the reading, mathematical and scientific literacy of fifteen-year-olds in all OECD and several other countries. Each PISA study focuses on a different area: PISA 2000 focused on literacy; PISA 2003 looked at mathematics; and PISA 2006 focused on science.

The PISA online database (OECD 2007) includes data for all of the countries featured in this study (bar Scotland for which there are no separate details). It shows that some countries perform better than others, but it is difficult to identify the underlying causes for this. None of the six areas covered by the OECD study (quality of learning outcomes, equity and distribution, learner characteristics, school resources or school policies and practices) can be categorised as elements of school structure as defined in this literature survey. Therefore the information from PISA cannot help answer the question set out above.

The Progress in International Reading Literacy Study (PIRLS) is a comparative study of the reading achievement of ten-year-olds that takes place every five years (the most recent published results are from the 2001 study). Over 140,000 pupils in 35 countries (including those focused on in this survey) participated in this study.

A report of the 2001 study data by Mullis *et al.* (2003) considered two issues relevant to the structure of primary education in a chapter on school curriculum and organisation for teaching reading: the number of years children spend in pre-primary education; and the age at which children start school. The report concludes that:

> Students in the PIRLS countries mostly began primary education when they were six or seven years old (...) although in England, New Zealand and Scotland almost all students began when they were five or younger. There is no clear relationship between age of entry to primary schooling and fourth-grade reading achievement. Among the top-performing countries on the PIRLS reading assessment, for example, the students in the Netherlands started primary school when they were six and those in England when they were five.
>
> (Mullis *et al.* 2003: 129)

The report went on to state that the more important issue from the schools' perspective was whether children were ready to learn in a formal environment.

A third international comparative assessment, Trends in International Mathematics and Science Study (TIMSS) is dedicated to improving teaching and learning in mathematics and science for students around the world. Carried out every four years at the fourth and eighth grades, TIMSS provides data about trends in mathematics and science achievement over time. Again, like PISA, the study is not concerned with the impact of structures on achievement.

However, one of the issues addressed in a report of TIMSS data by Martin *et al.* (2000) was the effect of school size on achievement (where schools were categorised as 'large' if bigger than the national average in that country). The report states: 'There seems to be a general tendency for greater percentages of students in high-achieving schools to be in the larger schools in each country.' (p.47).

The discussion so far has focused on the evidence of impact of school structures on assessment results in international comparative studies. However, it has also been suggested that primary school structures have themselves been influenced by results obtained in such studies. For example, Deckert-Peaceman (2005) referred to 'PISA-shock' in Germany following poor performance in the TIMSS and PISA studies. The author argues that this had a great impact and caused the German government to implement a number of countermeasures. Several of these concerned the structure of education, for example a move to all-day schooling (rather than half-day schooling) and the introduction of a flexible progression structure for pupils in the first two years of primary schooling (enabling pupils to progress through these years either quicker or slower than usual and introducing an earlier starting age for compulsory schooling). It is too early to tell if such measures will influence Germany's performance in future years.

There is little evidence to suggest that primary school structures influence the results obtained in international comparative achievement tests because the PISA, PIRLS and TIMSS studies do not routinely investigate this issue. The two studies that did investigate school starting age (Elley 1992; Mullis *et al.* 2003) found no strong evidence to support a causal relationship between school starting age and attainment levels.

SUMMARY AND CONCLUSIONS

This chapter aimed to investigate the structure of the English primary education system as a whole and its within-phase permutations. It included evidence on the roles and relationships of pre-school and primary provision and on starting ages for formal schooling.

The chapter described key features of the English primary education system, including its ages, phases, curriculum and assessment.

Changes in primary school structures since 1967

There have been a number of key changes to the education system since the publication of the Plowden Report in 1967. These include:

- The introduction of a National Curriculum, national assessment and a national system of school inspection;
- Local financial management of schools;
- The introduction of different kinds of schools, including Foundation schools (funded by LAs but owned by school governing bodies or charitable foundations); and group arrangements such as federations and collaborations;
- An entitlement to free part-time pre-school education for three- and four-year-olds;
- An adjustment to the pattern of the school year, with a trend towards adopting a 'standard' school year;
- A reduction in the school starting age (from five to four years) and a move from three entry points per year towards a system whereby all children in the age-group start school at the beginning of the school year (annual entry to school in the year before statutory school age);
- A reduction in the size of the primary school population by just over 31,000 pupils between 1965 and 2004; and

- A reduction of just over 3,000 in the number primary schools between 1965 and 2004, with a disproportionate reduction in the number of small schools. The average size of primary schools during this period has increased from 193 to 224 pupils.

Many of these changes have their origins in the Education Reform Act of 1988, although some resulted from separate pieces of legislation or a combination of economic and social forces.

Structural characteristics of primary schools in other countries

A consideration of the structures of primary education in six countries (England, Scotland, Germany, the Netherlands, Sweden and New Zealand) revealed considerable variations in the organisation of primary education. The following characteristics were apparent.

- There were differences in the extent to which decision-making about educational structures is delegated from central government to national agencies, local areas, or schools themselves.
- The length of the school year across the six countries ranges from 176 days in Germany to 200 in the Netherlands. (The school year in England comprises 190 days.)
- There are considerable differences in school starting ages (ranging from four to seven years old). Most systems make decisions on school entry based solely on chronological age, although Sweden allows parents to request an early starting age for their child and Germany requires children to be 'ready' for formal schooling.
- Although most countries take children into school at the beginning of the school year, children in New Zealand start school on their fifth birthday.
- Most of the six countries have lowered the age of entry to school in recent years.
- Pre-school provision is commonly available for children from the age of three, although Sweden and the Netherlands make pre-school education available for children under one.
- In most countries, primary schooling lasts for seven or eight years, although Germany has only four years of primary school and Sweden's schools encompass both primary and secondary ages. In four of the six countries, children transfer to secondary school at age 13.
- The average primary school size ranges from 128 in Scotland to 224 in England.

The impact of structures on teaching and learning

There was very limited evidence available to comment on the effectiveness or impact of different primary school structures. International comparative studies have not routinely considered the influence of primary school structures on assessment results. There is little evidence to support common-sense assumptions that spending longer in primary schools (due to a lower age of starting school, longer period of primary schooling and/ or a longer school year) results in higher attainment. However, it has been suggested that changes to primary school structures have been introduced in response to the findings of these 'high stakes' studies.

Two aspects of school structure have attracted more evaluative consideration in England and elsewhere: school size and starting age. The available evidence suggests that neither of these has a strong impact on children's attainment or progress at school.

There are however, some continuing questions raised by research into the appropriateness of the curriculum, pedagogy and environment offered to four-year-olds in English primary school reception classes.

Concluding remarks

This study has brought together evidence on the structures and phasing of primary education. There have been a number of structural changes in the years since the publication of the Plowden Report (CACE 1967), many of which took place as a result of the Education Reform Act of 1988 (GB Statutes 1988). There has been an increased standardisation of primary school curriculum, assessment and inspection arrangements across the country. There has been an increased participation in educational provision among younger children. Pre-school provision for three-year-olds has become an entitlement and more four-year-olds are attending primary schools. The number of small primary schools has decreased markedly during this period.

A comparison of structural features in other countries shows considerable variation in such features as age of starting school, length of the school year, average size of school and length of primary schooling. This diversity may be of potential interest to those wishing to consider alternatives to the prevailing structures in primary education in England.

While it has been relatively straightforward to collate information about elements of primary school structure, it is much more difficult to find evidence to evaluate their impact and effectiveness. One issue that has received greater attention from researchers is the impact of school starting age on attainment. The assumption that an early school starting age is beneficial for children's later attainment is not well supported in the research and there are concerns about the appropriateness of provision for four-year-olds in schools.

The general lack of evidence on impact does nothing to reduce the relevance of structural issues for children, parents, teachers and decision-makers. Further research may help to illuminate some of these issues. It is, however, inherently challenging to identify the influence of specific structural arrangements when considering the many different factors that influence learning and teaching in primary schools.

ACKNOWLEDGEMENTS

The authors would like to thank their colleagues in the NFER library, especially Hilary Grayson, Pauline Benefield and Alison Jones for their work in conducting the literature searches and checking all the references. We are grateful to our administrator, Jill Ware, for her work in preparing the manuscript and to Sharon O'Donnell and colleagues from NFER's International Unit for helping us to compile the information on primary education in other countries. Thanks are also due to those working on the DfES Statistical First Release in providing additional information on the types of English primary schools.

APPENDIX 1

Selection of comparison countries

In scoping this work, careful consideration was given to the inclusion of countries other than England. The selection criteria for the five countries (in addition to England) were as follows:

- Inclusion in the Eurydice and INCA databases, which not only gives access to quality-assured information, but also means that the team has the opportunity to check interpretations of data on structures and approaches with a named contact in each country.
- Inclusion in international comparative studies of educational performance (for example PISA, PIRLS, TIMSS). Such studies are highly influential and their results raise questions about the effects of educational structures and processes.
- Countries with particular characteristics of potential interest to the review (for example different approaches to pre-school/primary school structures and school starting ages).

The proposed sample and the reasons for selection are given in Table 14.3.

Table 14.3 Countries included in this study

UK countries	
England	Is included in PISA, PIRLS, TIMSS.
Scotland	Is included in PISA, PIRLS, TIMSS.
	Children may start school aged four years six months.
European countries (non-UK)	
Netherlands	Is included in PISA, PIRLS, TIMSS.
	The Netherlands is facing issues of cultural diversity and migration, similar to England and, although children must start school at age five, most start at four.
Sweden	Is included in PISA, PIRLS, TIMSS.
	Sweden has a comparatively late school starting age (seven years) and parents can negotiate a later school starting age if necessary.
Germany	Is included in PISA, PIRLS, TIMSS.
	Germany has school preparatory classes and school readiness checks. Selection for secondary school takes place when children are ten years old.
Rest of the world	
New Zealand	Is included in PISA, PIRLS, TIMSS.
	Compulsory school starting age is six years, although most start at five. There is a body of literature on education in New Zealand.

APPENDIX 2

Search strategy

A range of different educational and sociological databases were searched. Search strategies for all databases were developed by using terms from the relevant thesauri (where these were available), in combination with free text searching. The same search strategies were adhered to as far as possible for all the databases.

The key words used in the searches, together with a brief description of each of the databases searched, are outlined below. Throughout, * has been used to indicate truncation of terms, and (ft) to denote free-text search terms. All searches date from 2004 onwards.

A2.1 Applied Social Sciences Index and Abstracts (ASSIA)

ASSIA is an index of articles from over 600 international English language social science journals. The database provides unique coverage of special educational and developmental aspects of children.

#1	Primary education (ft)
#2	Primary schools (ft)
#3	#1 or #2
#4	Early childhood education
#5	Preschool education (ft)
#6	#4 or #5
#7	Structure*
#8	#7 and #3
#9	#7 and #6 (not #3)
#10	Learning
#11	Teaching
#12	#10 or #11
#13	#12 and (#3 or #6)

A2.2 Australian Education Index (AEI)

AEI is produced by the Australian Council for Educational Research. It is an index to materials at all levels of education and related fields. Source documents include journal articles, monographs, research reports, theses, conference papers, legislation, parliamentary debates and newspaper articles.

#1	Primary education
#2	School entrance age
#3	Early childhood education
#4	Nursery school education
#5	Preschool education
#6	Reception classes
#7	Infant school education
#8	Nursery schools
#9	Foundation stage (ft)

#10   Compulsory education
#11   #3 or #4 or #5 or #6 or #7 or #8 or #9
#12   England
#13   Scotland
#14   The Netherlands
#15   Sweden
#16   Germany
#17   New Zealand
#18   #12 or #13 or #14 or #15 or #16 or #17
#19   #1 and #18
#20   (#2 and #18) not #1
#21   (#10 and #18) not (#1 or #2)
#22   (#11 and #18) not (#1 or #2)
#23   Learning processes
#24   Teaching processes
#25   Teaching methods
#26   Pedagogy (ft)
#27   Teaching strategies (ft)
#28   #23 or #24 or #25 or #26 or #27
#29   #28 and #18
#30   School organisation
#31   School systems
#32   Structure* (ft)
#33   #30 or #31 or #32
#34   #33 and #18
#35   Role of education
#36   #35 and #18

A2.3 British Education Index (BEI)

BEI provides bibliographic references to 350 British and selected European English-language periodicals in the field of education and training, plus developing coverage of national report and conference literature.

#1   Primary education
#2   School entrance age
#3   Early childhood education
#4   Nursery school education
#5   Preschool education
#6   Reception classes
#7   Infant school education
#8   Nursery schools
#9   Foundation stage (ft)
#10   Compulsory education
#11   #3 or #4 or #5 or #6 or #7 or #8 or #9
#12   England
#13   Scotland
#14   The Netherlands
#15   Sweden

#16   Germany
#17   New Zealand
#18   #12 or #13 or #14 or #15 or #16 or #17
#19   #1 and #18
#20   (#2 and #18) not #1
#21   (#10 and #18) not (#1 or #2)
#22   (#11 and #18) not (#1 or #2)
#23   Learning processes
#24   Teaching processes
#25   Teaching methods
#26   Pedagogy (ft)
#27   Teaching strategies (ft)
#28   #23 or #24 or #25 or #26 or #27
#29   #28 and #18
#30   School organisation
#31   School systems
#32   Structure* (ft)
#33   #30 or #31 or #32
#34   #33 and #18
#35   Role of education
#36   #35 and #18

A2.4 British Education Internet Resource Catalogue

The Catalogue provides descriptions and hyperlinks for evaluated internet resources within an indexed database. The collection aims to list and describe significant information resources and services specifically relevant to the study, practice and administration of education at a professional level.

#1   Primary education
#2   School entrance age
#3   Early childhood education
#4   Nursery school education
#5   Preschool education
#6   Reception classes
#7   Infant school education
#8   Foundation Stage
#9   Compulsory education
#10   Learning processes
#11   Teaching processes or Teaching methods
#12   School organisation or School systems
#13   Role of education

A2.5 ChildData

ChildData is produced by the National Children's Bureau. It encompasses four information databases: bibliographic information on books, reports and journal articles (including some full text access); directory information on more than 3,000 UK and international organisations concerned with children; Children in the News, an index to press coverage of children's issues since early 1996; and an indexed guide to conferences and events.

#1 Starting school

A2.6 Current Educational Research in the United Kingdom (CERUK)

CERUK, which is sponsored by the National Foundation for Educational Research and the Department for Education and Skills and supported by the Eppi-Centre, covers current and recently completed research in education and related fields.

#1	Primary education
#2	School entrance age
#3	Early childhood education
#4	Nursery school education
#5	Preschool education
#6	Reception classes
#7	Infant school education
#8	Foundation Stage
#9	Compulsory education
#10	#3 or #4 or #5 or #6 or #7 or #8
#11	England
#12	Scotland
#13	The Netherlands
#14	Sweden
#15	Germany
#16	New Zealand
#17	#11 or #12 or #13 or #14 or #15 or #16
#18	#1 and #17
#19	(#2 and #17) not #1
#20	(#9 and #17) not (#1 or #2)
#21	(#10 and #17) not (#1 or #2)
#22	Learning processes and #17
#23	School organisation and #17

A2.7 The Educational Resources Information Center (ERIC)

ERIC is sponsored by the United States Department of Education and is the largest education database in the world. It indexes over 725 periodicals and currently contains more than 7,000,000 records. Coverage includes research documents, journal articles, technical reports, program descriptions and evaluations and curricula material.

#1	Primary education
#2	Early childhood education
#3	Preschool education
#4	Elementary education
#5	#2 or #3 or #4
#6	England

#7   Scotland
#8   The Netherlands
#9   Sweden
#10   Germany
#11   New Zealand
#12   #6 or #7 or #8 or #9 or #10 or #11
#13   #1 and #12
#14   (#2 and #12) not #1
#15   Plowden (ft)
#16   School entrance age
#17   School readiness not (#1 or #2)
#18   #17 and #12
#19   Learning process
#20   Teaching process
#21   (#19 or #20) and #12
#22   School organisation
#23   School systems
#24   Structure* (ft)
#25   #22 or #23 or #24
#26   #25 and #12
#27   Role of education and #13

A2.8 PsycInfo

This is an international database containing citations and summaries of journal articles, book chapters, book and technical reports, as well as citations to dissertations in
the field of psychology and psychological aspects of related disciplines, such as medicine, sociology and education.

#1   Primary education (Ti, AB)
#2   Early childhood education (Ti, AB)
#3   Preschool education (Ti, AB)
#4   Nursery school education (ft)
#5   Infant school education (ft)
#6   Reception classes
#7   Foundation Stage
#8   #1 or #2 or #3 or #4 or #5 or #6 or #7
#9   School starting age or School entrance age
#10   England
#11   Scotland
#12   The Netherlands
#13   Sweden
#14   Germany
#15   New Zealand
#16   #10 or #11 or #12 or #13 or #14 or #15
#17   #8 and #16
#18   #9 and #16
#19   School systems (Ti, AB) and #16
#20   School organisation and #16
#21   Role of education (Ti, AB) and #16

NOTES

1 This question excludes consideration of internal primary school organisational structure because this was the subject of Chapter 21 of this book.
2 This excludes consideration of transition issues because this was the subject of Chapter 21 of this book.
3 Middle schools may be deemed primary or secondary, depending on the number of pupils under and over the age of 11.
4 Pre-school education can also be provided in other 'settings', such as independent nurseries, day care and play groups. These typically take children from three months to school age (although this varies according to the provision in individual settings).
5 Following the introduction of the Foundation Stage in 2000, the Foundation Stage Profile was initiated in 2002/3 (QCA 2007).
6 Given that these statistics are collected in January, they represent an under-estimate of the number of children who were four years old when they started school, as many would have started in the previous September.
7 Transition is the focus of a separate research survey.
8 At the time of writing, the responsibilities of these two agencies were under review.

REFERENCES

Adams, S., Alexander, E., Drummond, M.J. and Moyles, J. (2004) *Inside the Foundation Stage: recreating the reception year. Final report*. London: Association of Teachers and Lecturers

Alexander, R.J. (1995) *Versions of Primary Education*. London: Routledge.

Alvestad, M. and Samuelsson, I.P. (1999) 'A comparison of the National Preschool Curricula in Norway and Sweden', *Early Childhood Research and Practice* 8(3): 265–84.

Arnold, R. (2006) *Schools in Collaboration: federations, collegiates and partnerships* (EMIE Report No. 86). Slough: EMIE at NFER.

Ball, C. (1994) *Start Right: the importance of early learning*. London: Royal Society for the Encouragement of Arts, Manufacture and Commerce.

Barrett, G. (1986) *Starting School: an evaluation of the experience. Final report to the Assistant Masters and Mistresses Association*. Norwich: University of East Anglia, Centre for Applied Research in Education.

Beattie, N. (1997) 'Contextual preconditions of open schooling: the English case in historical and comparative perspectives', *Cambridge Journal of Education* 27(1): 59–75.

Bennett, D. (1992) 'Policy and practice in teaching four-year-olds', *Early Years* 13(1): 40–44.

Bennett, S.N. (1995) *Progression and Continuity in Pre-School and Reception Classes*. Swindon: Economic and Social Research Council.

Bilton, H. (1993) 'Under-fives in compulsory schooling, 1908 and 1988. How far have we come?' *Early Child Development and Care* 91: 51–63.

Blyth, A. (1991) 'Managing change in British primary education: some European perspectives', *International Journal of Educational Management* 5(4): 8–13.

Central Advisory Council for Education (CACE) (1967) *Children and their Primary Schools: a report of the Central Advisory Council for Education (England)* (the Plowden Report). London: HMSO.

Clark, M.M. (1989) 'Continuity, discontinuity and conflict in the education of under fives', *Education 3–13* 17(2): 44–48.

Cleave, S., Barker-Lunn, J. and Sharp, C. (1985) 'Local education authority policy on admission to infant/first school', *Educational Research* 27(1): 40–43.

Cleave, S. and Brown, S. (1991) *Early to School: four year olds in infant classes*. Windsor: NFER-Nelson.

Daniels, S., Redfern, E. and Shorrocks-Taylor, D. (1995) 'Trends in the early admission of children to school: appropriate or expedient?' *Educational Research* 37(3): 239–49.

Daniels, S., Shorrocks-Taylor, D. and Redfern, E. (2000) 'Can starting summer-born children earlier at infant school improve their National Curriculum results?', *Oxford Review of Education* 26(2): 207–20.

Deckert-Peaceman, H. (2005) 'Starting school in Germany: the relationship between education and social inequality'. Paper presented at the Conference of the Australian Association for Research in Education, Melbourne, Victoria, 27 November-1 December.

Department for Children, Schools and Families (DCSF) (2008) *Statuary Framework for the Early Years Foundation Stage: setting the standards for learning, development and care for children from birth to five.* London: DCSF.

Department for Education and Employment (DfEE) (1998) 'Schools, pupils and teachers', in *Statistics of Education: schools in England 1998.* London: Department for Education and Employment.

——(2001) *Code of Practice on Local Education Authority–School Relations: Annexes 1–5.* Online (Available: http://www.standards.dfes.gov.uk/la/pdf/codeofpracannexes.pdf?version=1, accessed 23 April 2007).

Department for Education and Skills (DfES) (2002) *Provision for Children Under Five Years of Age in England: January 2002* (National Statistics First Release 09/2002). London: DfES.

——(2004) 'Schools, pupils and teachers,' in *Statistics of Education: schools in England 2004 Edition.* London: DfES.

——(2007a) *The National Curriculum for Five to 11 Year Olds.* Online (Available: http://www.direct.gov.uk/en/EducationAndLearning/Schools/ExamsTestsAndTheCurriculum/DG_4015959, accessed 24 April 2007).

——(2007b) *Federations and Collaborations.* Online (Available: http://www.teachernet.gov.uk/management/fallingschoolrolls/joiningup/federationcollaboration/, accessed 4 April, 2007).

——(2007c) *Maintained Primary Schools: number of schools and number (headcount) of pupils by mode of attendance.* Online (Available: http://www.dfes.gov.uk/rsgateway/, accessed 30 April, 2007).

Eames, A., Sharp, C. and Benefield, P. (2005) *Review of the Evidence Relating to the Introduction of a Standard School Year: final report* (LGA Research Report 17/04). Slough: NFER.

Elley, W.B. (1992) *How in the World Do Students Read? IEA study of reading literacy.* Hamburg: Grindeldruck GMBH.

England and Wales. Statutes (2002) *Education Act. Chapter 32.* London: The Stationery Office.

——(2004) *Children Act 2004. Chapter 31.* London: The Stationery Office.

Eurydice (2006) *Eurybase: the information database on education systems in Europe. The Education System in Scotland 2005/06.* Online (Available: http://www.eurydice.org/portal/page/portal/Eurydice/DB_Eurybase_Home, accessed 24 April 2007).

Gillard, D. (2005) 'The Plowden Report', in 'Informal education and lifelong learning', *The Encyclopaedia of Informal Education.* Online (Available: http://www.infed.org/schooling/plowden_report.htm, accessed 22 January 2007).

Great Britain. Parliament House of Commons. Education, Science and Arts Committee (1986) *Achievement in Primary Schools: third report. Volume 1, Report together with the Proceedings of the Committee.* London: HMSO.

——(1988) *Educational Provision for the Under Fives: first report. Volume 1. Report together with the Proceedings of the Committee.* London: HMSO.

Great Britain. Statutes (1988) *Education Reform Act 1988. Chapter 40. 53.* London: HMSO.

——(1992) *Education (Schools) Act. Chapter 38.* London: The Stationery Office.

Harker, R. (2005) 'School size and student attainment: some New Zealand data.' Paper presented at the CIES (West) Conference, Vancouver, BC, 29 September-1 October.

The Labour Party (2007) *What are the Different Types of Local Authority?* Online (Available: http://www.labouronline.org/councillors/different_types_of_local_authority, accessed 4 April, 2007).

Local Government Association (2007a) *Standard School Year.* Online (Available: http://www.lga.gov.uk/OurWork.asp?lsection=59andccat=420, accessed 3 April, 2007).

——(2007b) *Standard School Year – Recommended Calendar 2008–09*. Online (Available: http://www.lga.gov.uk/Briefing.asp?lsection=59andid=SX97BD-A783F3C5andccat=420, accessed 3 April, 2007).

Martin, M.O., Mullis, I.V.S., Gregory, K.D., Hoyle, C. and Shen, C. (2000) *Effective Schools in Science and Mathematics: IEA's Third International Mathematics and Science Study*. Chestnut Hill, MA: International Study Center, Boston College.

Mullis, I.V.S., Martin, M.O., Gonzalez, E.J. and Kennedy, A.M. (2003) *PIRLS 2001 International Report: IEA's study of reading literacy in primary schools in 35 countries*. Chestnut Hill, MA: International Study Center, Lynch School of Education, Boston College.

O'Donnell, S., Andrews, C., Brown, R. and Sargent, C. (2007) *INCA: the International Review of Curriculum and Assessment Frameworks Internet Archive*. Online (Available: http://www.inca.org.uk, accessed 24 April 2007).

Office for Standards in Education (Ofsted) (1993) *First Class: the standards and quality of education in reception classes. A report from the Office of Her Majesty's Chief Inspector for Schools*. London: HMSO.

——(1999) *The Quality of Nursery Education: developments since 1997–1987 in the private, voluntary and independent sector*. London: Ofsted.

——(2003) *The Education of Six Year Olds in England, Denmark and Finland: an international comparative study* (HMI 1660). London: Ofsted.

Pramling, I. (1992) 'To be six years old in Sweden in the 1990s', *Early Years* 12(2): 47–50.

Pugh, G. (1990) 'Developing a policy for early childhood education: challenges and constraints', *Early Child Development and Care* 58: 3–13.

Qualifications and Curriculum Authority (2007) *Foundation Stage 3–5*. Online (Available: http://www.qca.org.uk/160.html, accessed 27 March 2007).

Sanders, D., White, G., Burge, B., Sharp, C., Eames, A., McEune, R. and Grayson, H. (2005) *A Study of the Transition from the Foundation Stage to Key Stage 1* (DfES Research Report SSU/2005/FR/013). London: DfES.

Sharp, C. (1987) 'Local education authority admission policies and practices', in C. Sharp and G. Turner (Eds) *Four-Year-Olds in School: policy and practice. An NFER/SCDC Seminar Report*. Slough: NFER.

——(1988) 'Starting school at four', *Research Papers in Education* 3(1): 64–90.

——(2002) 'School starting age: European policy and recent research'. Paper presented at the LGA Seminar 'When Should Our Children Start School', LGA Conference Centre, Smith Square, London, 1 November.

Sharp, C. and Benefield, P. (1995) *Research into Season of Birth and School Achievement: a select annotated bibliography*. Slough: NFER.

Sharp, C. and Hutchison, D. (1997) *How Do Season of Birth and Length of Schooling Affect Children's Attainment at Key Stage 1? A question revisited*. Slough: NFER.

Sharp, C. and Turner, G. (Eds) (1987) *Four-Year-Olds in School: policy and practice. An NFER-SCDC Seminar Report*. Slough: NFER.

Southworth, G. and Weindling, D. (2002) *Leadership in Large Primary Schools*. Nottingham: NCSL.

Spielhofer, T., O'Donnell, L., Benton, T., Schagen, S. and Schagen, I. (2002) *The Impact of School Size and Single-Sex Education on Performance* (LGA Research Report 33). Slough: NFER.

Tymms, P., Merrell, C. and Henderson, B. (1997) 'The first year at school: a quantitative investigation of the attainment and progress of pupils', *Educational Research and Evaluation* 3(2): 101–18.

Wallace, M. and Pocklington, K. (2002) *Managing Complex Educational Change: large-scale reorganisation of schools*. London: RoutledgeFalmer.

West, A., Banfield, S. and Varlaam, A. (1990) 'Evaluation of an early entry to infant school pilot exercise', *Research Papers in Education* 5(3): 229–50.

West, A. and Varlaam, A. (1990) 'Does it matter when children start school?', *Educational Research* 32(3): 210–17.

Whitbourn, S., with Morris, R., Parker, A., McDonogh, A., Fowler, J., Mitchell, K. and Poole, K. (2004) *What is the LEA For? An analysis of the functions and roles of the Local Education Authority.* 2nd edition. Slough: EMIE at the NFER.

Woodhead, M. (1989) '"School starts at five … or four years old?" The rationale for changing admission policies in England and Wales', *Journal of Education Policy* 4(1): 1–21.

15 Primary curriculum and assessment

England and other countries

Kathy Hall and Kamil Øzerk

INTRODUCTION

This chapter offers a comparative analysis of primary curriculum and assessment policy in England compared to other countries. The purpose is to enhance understanding of England's curriculum and assessment priorities by providing an account of the ways in which primary curriculum and assessment policy in England conforms to and deviates from international trends.

The chapter is in three parts. The first part offers an overview of current curriculum and assessment policy in England and goes on to compare England with 21 other countries. The focus of analysis is curriculum orientation, subject headings and the official arrangements for primary assessment. This first part of the report draws primarily, though not exclusively, on secondary sources, specifically the International Review of Curriculum and Assessment Frameworks (INCA) Archive[1] which is an ongoing compilation of information on education in some 20 countries.

The second part attends more closely and in more detail to curriculum. It compares curriculum policy in England with policy in the other countries/parts of the UK: Wales, Northern Ireland and Scotland, and with three countries outside the UK: France, Norway and Japan. By comparing primary curriculum as detailed in government websites and other official sources of the respective countries, this part of the report enables a more penetrating exploration of differences and similarities in curriculum policy in England.

The third part of the chapter follows the pattern of the second but with reference to assessment.

The identification and discussion of the convergences and divergences may support policy makers as they deliberate about future reforms of curriculum and assessment in England.

ENGLAND IN INTERNATIONAL CONTEXT

Curriculum and assessment policy in England[2]

Schooling is compulsory in England from the age of 5 years, although most schools admit children from the age of 4 into 'reception' class which is part of what is called 'the foundation stage' of school. There is a 'foundation stage curriculum' which specifies 'early learning goals'. At the end of the foundation stage children take part in a compulsory school entry assessment scheme based on their performance throughout the phase known as the 'foundation stage profile'.

Our focus in this review is compulsory primary education. This comprises two 'Key Stages': Key Stage 1 (KS1) which spans ages 5 to 7, and Key Stage 2 (KS2) which spans ages 7 to 11. England has a statutory National Curriculum (NC), which is prescribed by central government. The NC is defined, for both Key Stages, in terms of subjects that are categorised as 'core' or 'foundation'. There are three core subjects: English, mathematics and science. There are seven foundation subjects: design and technology, information technology, history, geography, art, music, and physical education. In addition, all children in state primary schools are entitled to religious education and to be involved in a daily act of collective worship.

Furthermore, five cross-curricular elements are specified that are intended to provide a basis on which work in particular subjects is built, although these elements are non-statutory. These include creativity; information and communications technology (ICT) capability across all subjects; education for sustainable development; literacy across the curriculum; and numeracy across the curriculum. A further non-statutory element is personal, social and health education and citizenship. Modern foreign languages (MFL) is not yet a compulsory national curriculum subject, although it is government policy that by 2010 all children at KS2 should have the right to learn a language other than English.

All children in state schools are entitled to access the NC, including children with special educational needs (SEN). While access to a broad and balanced curriculum for all is expected, elements of the NC may be 'disapplied' for some children with SEN. While all state schools are obliged by law to implement it, they are also expected to cater for local circumstances by offering additional learning fitted to particular local needs. The school curriculum therefore is broader than the National Curriculum in that it consists of all the learning experiences that schools plan for their pupils' education.

The NC is designed to be used by schools as a framework and, as such, there are no time allocations laid down for the various subjects. Pedagogic recommendations are offered however and, as we will show later, policy provides a strong steer in relation to how to teach some aspects of the curriculum.

Curriculum-based, criterion-referenced assessments are a formal part of the curriculum in England. This means that unlike intelligence or aptitude tests, which seek to assess potential, the assessments seek to assess curriculum achievement against a) national curriculum criteria or national standards (level descriptions[3]), and b) expected standards of performance. Statutory teacher assessment and statutory testing take place in relation to national curriculum subjects although the tests cover only a limited range. At the end of each of the two Key Stages children's attainment in the curriculum is assessed in two ways: through teacher assessment and through external assessments, known as standard assessment tasks and tests (SATs).

At the end of KS1, when children are typically 7 years of age, teachers have to summarise their judgements of each child's attainments in reading, writing, speaking/listening, mathematics, and science, taking account of progress and performance throughout the KS. This summative teacher assessment (TA), which is distinct from ongoing day-to-day formative assessment, is an obligatory part of the National Curriculum assessment and is the main focus for end of KS1 assessment. It is carried out as part of teaching and learning in the classroom. The aim is to make a rounded judgement based on knowledge of how a child has performed over time and across a range of contexts. In addition to this summative assessment, children are assessed through external tests/tasks in reading, writing and mathematics. The purpose of these SATs is to help inform the final teacher assessment judgement. Schools do not have to report the results of the external tasks and tests separately.

At the end of KS2, when children are typically 11 years of age, they are assessed through an external testing programme in reading, writing, mathematics, and science. In addition, summative teacher assessment covers the full range and scope of the programmes of study within the various subjects, taking into account evidence of achievement in a variety of contexts. At the end of KS2, the results from teacher assessment are reported alongside the test results from the external tests (this is no longer obligatory at KS1). Both sets of results are supposed to have equal status and are intended to provide complementary information about a pupil's attainment.

In addition to the statutory assessment arrangements, there are optional English and mathematics tests available for schools to use during KS2. These are intended to support schools in monitoring progress during the Key Stage. Finally, so called 'world class tests' which measure performance in problem solving in mathematics, science and design technology have been made available recently for the most able nine-year-olds in primary education. In these tests children are expected to apply what they have learned to new situations and use their thinking skills to solve unfamiliar problems.

The statutory assessments at the end of KS2 are used to design performance tables of schools whereby a school's results can be interpreted against the results of all schools nationally and against other schools with a similar catchment profile. These results are reported in school prospectuses and websites and in the media generally. League tables rank schools in order of their success in the assessments, the intention being that parents are equipped with the necessary information on which to select the school which best suits their children.

England's primary curriculum and assessment arrangements in broad international context

This section provides an account of the primary curriculum and assessment arrangements in England with reference to provision in other parts of the UK and the Republic of Ireland, and selected countries worldwide for which relevant information is accessible. It allows a comparison, albeit at a cursory level at this stage, of curriculum and assessment arrangements in England and other countries. While the authors have sought to ensure the accuracy of the information provided, it is noteworthy at the outset that the tendency towards frequent and sometimes wide-ranging reform in matters of curriculum and assessment in many countries suggests that caution has to be exercised in the interpretation of summaries of provision. Moreover, there were some grey areas where establishing the status of a curriculum area was not straightforward and judgements had to be made (especially in relation to the information contained in Table 15.1 – see Appendix). Furthermore, we are concentrating on official curriculum as opposed to accounts of what happens in actual classroom practice. However, the official curriculum is an appropriate starting point for exploring how England compares and contrasts with other countries in the areas of study it endorses for its primary pupils. We are drawing primarily, though not exclusively, in this section on material from the International Review of Curriculum and Assessment Frameworks (INCA) Archive which is an ongoing compilation of information on education and structure and policy in about 20 countries. We supplement this information with details about Norway and other countries which is derived from official and other sources.

Table 15.1 (see Appendix), offers a visual display of the range of subjects in the primary curriculum, and Table 15.2 gives a visual display of the assessment arrangements. Together these two tables serve our purpose of identifying the extent to which England's approach is in line with, or deviates from, international curriculum and assessment trends. These tables are modified versions of the evidence presented in the comparative tables by Andrews *et al.* 2007; Le Metais 2003; and INCA/QCA. There is no attempt at this point to describe the relative status of different areas of study, to indicate time allocations, or to suggest anything about the integration or otherwise in teaching and learning.

The major point to note from Table 15.1 is the broad convergence in curriculum provision across all of these countries. England is in line with international trends in its provision of all the following: first language, mathematics, science, information technology, history, geography, physical education, art and craft, music, and religious education. All of these areas of study are now standard in the primary curriculum of all the countries listed in Table 15.1. However, England differs from many other countries in not as yet making PSHE, citizenship and a modern foreign language compulsory at the primary stage. There is also a grey area where matters like education for global awareness are concerned: they are increasingly encouraged though not obligatory.

Research conducted almost twenty years ago (Benavot *et al.* 1991) showed that first language, mathematics, science and social studies are not merely standard in primary curriculum internationally but the amount of time devoted to each is almost identical across nation states, regardless of a country's level of industrialization, urbanization or political structure. On the basis of their detailed analyses, these researchers demonstrated that national characteristics are only weakly linked with curricular emphases. In their words:

> The real surprise of our findings lies not in the unimportance of social influences, but in the relative unimportance of national influences on curricular structure. Similarities clearly outweigh differences. The few differences observed tend to be unstable and seem to arise as a matter of chance in national societies differing dramatically in wealth, political structure, and cultural and religious tradition. We may speak with some confidence about a relatively standard world curriculum.
>
> (Benavot *et al.* 1991)

It would seem that as countries have reformed their curricula over the past two decades greater convergence in curriculum provision is the result not only in Anglo-American countries and in Europe but in developing countries as well (Davies and Guppy 2007; Le Matais 2003).

All countries seek to adapt their curricula to fit their changing social, economic and political circumstances. More recent adaptations in most countries, including England, pertain to the higher status attributed to literacy and mathematics, but also even more recently to the emphasis on application of knowledge and understanding, and the development of individual capacity to learn (learning how to learn). England and Wales (also Sweden) have identified some subjects as 'core' and others as 'foundation'. France, too, has conferred higher status on literacy. Other countries have not weighted subjects in this way. In Ireland for instance all subjects are explicitly given equal standing. England is in line with several other parts of the world (for example Australia, Ireland, Singapore and Wales) in its emphasis on civics education (Le Metais 2003), although this is a relatively recent emphasis and, as noted, it is not compulsory.

As we noted above, our account in this section deals primarily with the specified curriculum. Intended subject content and pedagogy represent a deeper level of engagement with primary curriculum which we will return to in the next section with reference to a smaller number of specific countries against which we will compare England. We now place England's approach to assessment in the wider international context.

As in the case of curriculum, there is also convergence in assessment arrangements across countries although here convergence is far more limited than in the case of curriculum. In all countries teachers routinely assess and report on their pupils' progress over the primary phase. There has been a strong trend in the past ten years towards external assessment, both statutory and voluntary (Le Metais 2003). There are multiple purposes advanced for the increased emphasis on assessment: to help teachers plan their teaching, to identify underachieving pupils so additional support can be obtained, to assess pupil progress and to hold schools accountable. To support the realisation of these multiple purposes many countries (about half of those listed in Table 15.2 – see Appendix) now have attainment targets in various subjects against which judgements of progress and achievement can be made.

Table 15.2 shows that England is in line with the vast majority of countries insofar as a standardised assessment system (standardised across the country) or end of phase/ stage testing occurs in primary school. The USA and Australia operate external testing at the level of all and most states respectively, and several provinces in Canada implement provincial assessment programmes in the primary phase. England introduced its standard assessment tasks and tests earlier than many other European countries. Some countries are currently in the process of reviewing their assessment systems. For example, Ireland's Department of Education and Science (DES) is making standardised testing a requirement from 2008. Similarly in Switzerland there is some agreement across *Cantons* on new national standards and their assessment. In Spain national sample surveys of pupil attainment are undertaken on completion of primary education, when children are aged 12 years, and national testing for 9-and 11-year-olds is scheduled to begin in 2008/9 and 2009/10 respectively. Some countries, specifically Korea, Japan, New Zealand and Spain, limit external assessments by only requiring that samples of pupils rather than a full population be assessed.

It is noteworthy also that of the countries listed in Table 15.2 a dozen compulsorily assess primary achievement in literacy and numeracy and, less commonly, in science and/or social studies. Along with England, these countries are: Australia, Canada, France, Hungary, Japan, Korea, New Zealand, Spain, the USA, and Wales. However, as noted in the previous paragraph, some of these countries assess only a sample of a given population.

When we consider the state of assessment arrangements within the primary phase the pattern is considerably more diverse than it is for curriculum, with the UK in general – and England in particular – appearing to be unusual in the high incidence of assessment. Although it should be noted that assessment at ages 8, 9, and 10 in England is not obligatory, England still stands out as exceptional in its emphasis on statutory external standard assessment for children at ages 7 and 11. Other parts of the UK, specifically Northern Ireland and Wales, have abandoned the use of external testing of 7-year-olds in favour of annual teacher assessments only. These decisions were made in the wake of reviews of the National Curriculum and assessment policies. In Scotland, teachers decide when primary children should undertake national assessments.

In relation to assessment at the point of entry to compulsory schooling, England is again different to most other countries listed in that assessment is required. Baseline (school entry) assessment must also be carried out during the first year of compulsory primary education in Wales. Hungary, where there is assessment throughout the primary phase, requires children to be assessed before progressing to the compulsory phase of school to determine readiness for school. Readiness is also assessed in Sweden. In Germany the local doctor assesses children's readiness for school. School entry assessment is not the norm across the countries listed in Table 15.2.

An important purpose of assessment at compulsory school entry in England is to furnish baseline evidence for value added analyses. Wales, New Zealand, and some states in Australia, for example Victoria, also require school entry assessment for this purpose. However caution is necessary in the interpretation of national policies as some countries, while not requiring assessment at this point, do in fact typically assess children – a good example is France where a nursery school 'record of achievement' is kept and passed on to a child's first compulsory level school. In Scotland nursery schools pass on a record of achievement to schools with reference to literacy and oral language although this is not compulsory. The next section of our chapter will probe further the assessment regimes of selected countries, with a view to determining in more detail how England compares in assessment policies.

Finally, Table 15.2 indicates that England, like all countries with standardised assessment systems at primary level, makes the results available to various audiences but the nature of this publicity merits attention. It seems that England leads the emphasis on published league tables where individual schools are listed in relation to the aggregated attainments of their pupils, thus holding schools to account in a very public way. The USA and Norway are increasingly following this trend, but most other countries disseminate the results back to schools along with national aggregated results or they publish national trends only – the aim being to enable schools to compare their own school's performance with national trends and to alert schools to their relative weaknesses and strengths. Individual school results are not typically published in the form of league tables in the national press.

NARROWING THE COMPARATIVE FOCUS: CURRICULUM

We now turn to a more considered examination of curriculum policy in England by focusing on fewer countries but attending in more detail to the specific statements in relation to three aspects of curriculum: namely aims and principles, curriculum structure and subjects, and pedagogic directives. An analysis of England's curriculum compared to other parts of the UK is of interest on the grounds that traditionally England and the rest of the UK aligned in curriculum policy initiatives. For example, the Plowden Report in 1967 (Central Advisory Council for Education (CACE) 1967) and the Scottish Memorandum in 1965 (Scottish Education Department (SED) 1965) both endorsed so called progressivism in curriculum and teaching methods in England and Scotland respectively. Until recently England and Wales were administratively aligned educationally, but Wales has determined its education policies independently of England since the introduction of the Welsh Assembly. Northern Ireland (NI), while traditionally aligning itself with developments in England, determines its own curriculum policy. How England continues to compare with its nearest neighbours merits investigation.

We have also chosen to benchmark England against three other countries: France because of the historical and cultural links as well as its proximity; Norway because of its renowned emphasis on equity issues and early years education, like other

Scandinavian countries; and Japan, an Eastern country which is an economic competitor in the global market. In view of the increasing emphasis nations are placing on literacy, Japan is especially interesting as it has been described as one of the most literate societies in the world, despite the complexity of its language (Lessard-Clouston 1998; Crystal 1997; Akamatsu 1998). Like England (along with other parts of the UK), all three countries have centralised primary curriculum systems which means that what is expected to be taught is standardised and prescribed. It is noteworthy, however, that their centralising histories vary considerably in nature. In the case of Norway, the new national curriculum (Knowledge Promotion, see Øzerk 2006) is the first curriculum reform to have resulted in a common national curriculum for the 10-year basic school (6–16) (and upper secondary education (16–19) and training (16+)).

Table 15.3 in this chapter's Appendix draws on official sources in the case of each country to describe curriculum policy. The following text highlights and discusses key similarities and differences.

Curriculum aims and principles

It is noteworthy that when the National Curriculum (NC) was introduced in England in 1988 there was no explicit reference to a philosophical base. Several curriculum researchers commented on this lack, Lawton for instance, arguing that while '[s]ubjects may be useful as means to curriculum ends, they are not ends in themselves' (Lawton 1989). On its revision in 2000, however, there were explicit statements about educational opportunity, respect for the individual, as well as choice and diversity for parents.[4]

On the basis of official websites and curriculum policy texts there is considerable overlap and consistency in the stated goals and aims of the curriculum across all four parts of the UK and across our three selected comparator countries: France, Norway and Japan. Table 15.3 documents specified aims/purposes of, and rationales for, the curriculum in each country. Recurring in the various curriculum policy texts are all of the following foci:

- the development of all children's potential;
- the promotion of the rounded individual;
- the fostering of the good citizen;
- the cultivation of the lifelong learner; and
- the shaping of the flexible individual for life in a rapidly changing globalised world.

In the case of the four parts of the UK, the curriculum principles of breadth and balance ('breadth and depth' in the case of Scotland) accord with such wide-ranging aims. Thus far, England aligns with its immediate neighbours. Across the UK there now appears to be a desire to promote 'excellence' in learning in a way that combines cognitive and affective aspects, and that prepares the learner for a changing future (for England see DfES 2003). This is how Peter Peacock, the then Minister for Education and Young People in Scotland, expressed his views in 2004 in the context of the current revision of their curriculum:

> The curriculum in Scotland has many strengths ... However, the various parts were developed separately and, taken together, they do not now provide the best basis for an excellent education for every child. The National Debate showed that people

want a curriculum that will fully prepare today's children for adult life in the 21st century, be less crowded and better connected, and offer more choice and enjoyment.

(SEED 2007)

However, the curriculum documentation in England differs from that of Japan and France in two important interrelated emphases:

- the promotion of a shared common culture, and
- the promotion of basic skills, especially language, in the early years of compulsory primary schooling.

England's official documentation on curriculum endorses pluralism, diversity, tolerance and multiculturalism, themes which are especially evident in guidance for teachers in, for example, the programmes of study and schemes of work for RE, History, and Geography, and in the guidance on citizenship. It is more tentative, cautious and relativist than France or Japan in its statements and application of values.[5] In relation to the promotion of inclusion and enabling all children to participate fully in their learning, the principle of differentiation in the curriculum seeks to address diversity where the representation and accessibility of knowledge are to be considered by teachers. To exemplify, it is stated that teachers are expected to take 'account of pupils' specific religious or cultural beliefs relating to the representation of ideas or experiences or to the use of particular types of equipment, particularly in science, design and technology, ICT and art and design'.[6] With more particular reference to Religious Education, which is obligatory in England, the (non-statutory) national framework for RE of 2004 advises that all RE syllabuses must 'reflect the fact that the religious traditions of Great Britain are, in the main, Christian, while taking account of the teaching and practices of the other principal religions represented in Great Britain'[7] Difference is recognised and has to be taken into account, not only in curriculum content but also in pedagogic approach.

Japan, in contrast, seems to resist pluralism. A relatively homogeneous country, Japan has one large dominant ethnic group and one dominant language. As one travel book (Taylor *et al.* 1997) noted, Japan intends that only a small number of foreigners settle in the country. While several researchers question the assumed monoculturalism of Japanese society (Weiner 1997; Denoon *et al.* 1996), and while the Japanese Government is keen to promote internationalism and the ability of young people to understand other countries, there remains embedded in curriculum documents a strong emphasis on Japanese national consciousness – 'the traditions and culture of Japan' (Ministry of Education, Culture, Sports, Science and Technology 2005).

The themes of multiculturalism and diversity do not feature prominently in the new primary curriculum in France, whereas expressions like 'republican values' do (Ministère de l'Education Nationale (MEN) 2003). For example it is stated that the primary school system must adhere to republican principles of equal opportunity and effective integration into French society (MEN 2003: 46). The basis of state education in France is an initiation into a common culture through a single curriculum for all. Ten years ago President Jacques Chirac pronounced that 'The France we love and we want to preserve is not and never will be a mosaic of communities living alongside each other'.[8] France does not recognise difference in the way England does. As one commentator put it in relation to citizenship education, 'in France there is no 'multicultural citizenship' – just citizenship' (cited in Starkey 2000). Some education researchers in France are highly critical of what they see as an inadequate emphasis on cultural diversity and pluralism in the new elementary programme, particularly in relation to language, arguing that the approach endorsed is assimilationist rather than integrationist (Helot *et al.* 2005). The promotion of a shared culture and national identity is tightly bound to citizenship and French language and it is noteworthy that citizenship education or civic education features in relation to aims and curriculum rationale, as well as, of course, descriptions of curriculum structure.

While citizenship is now part of the English curriculum aims and rationale it is a relatively late component, having been added in the 2000 revision.[9] Scotland and Northern Ireland, for instance, have had a much longer history of the inclusion of civics education at primary level, thus highlighting children's responsibilities as future citizens. Citizenship has been a compulsory part of the NI curriculum from 2007. The traditional emphasis in Japan on equality of opportunity led its curriculum, through its courses of study, towards uniformity, self and group discipline, and rigidity with little or no role for differentiation or flexibility of provision. While the recent reforms of 2005 have oriented curriculum towards greater flexibility and concern for individual needs, for creativity, and for critical thinking, an orientation to group effort and social co-operation remain strong features expressed particularly in 'moral education' and 'special activities'.

France, Norway and Japan expect that the curriculum in primary education, particularly in the early years of compulsory primary education, should prioritise basic skills of language and arithmetic. These aims are a more explicit feature in the policy texts of these countries than in England or the other parts of the UK.

England also deviates from the other countries in this survey in the scale of its explicit references to the purpose of raising standards. No other country appears to be so preoccupied with national standards – a preoccupation which is manifested not only in the aims and curriculum rationale but also in the structure of the curriculum and in the nature of the assessment system. Indeed raising standards was the *raison d'être* of the introduction of the National Curriculum in England in 1988, following what was assumed by policy makers to be a period during which England's more decentralised curriculum and assessment policies led to an inadequate emphasis on products and outcomes. Interestingly, given its traditional emphasis on child-centred approaches, decentralisation and teacher/school autonomy (Hall *et al.* 1999), Norway now resembles England in the discourse of standards, although not nearly to the same extent. Norway, as already noted, has just introduced a national curriculum. It was worked out under its former coalition government in which the Ministry of Education and Research was dominated by the Conservative party, but it was introduced by a new coalition government in which the Minister of Education and Research is from the Socialist Left Party of Norway. The rationale advanced for the national curriculum, entitled 'Knowledge Promotion', is very similar to that advanced for the introduction of a National Curriculum in England in the late 1980s, incorporating as it does references to raising standards; accountability and evaluation; national assessment; basic knowledge and skills; clear objectives; free choice and competition; and consistency of provision (Telhaug 2005; Øzerk 2006).

The internationalisation of the curriculum, by which we mean the standardisation of curriculum rationale (and areas of study) in response to globalisation and the availability of information, especially assessment and evaluation information of attainment, means that continuity in aims and rationale is to be expected. However, research tells us that the curriculum policy changes made in response to common external pressures occur in culturally specific ways.[10] As we show in the next section, closer attention to the curriculum subjects and the status attributed to them, even at the level of national policy, more than hints at this cultural influence.

Curriculum structure, subjects, and cross-curricular elements

As already demonstrated there is considerable convergence internationally in curriculum policy, with all countries surveyed demonstrating a commitment to a similar range of areas of study. However, this more probing part of our analysis suggests some significant differences of emphasis within that range. Table 15.3 lists the curriculum areas and cross-curricular themes of each country.

The first point of difference to note is that England structures the curriculum in terms of subjects, while other parts of the UK (specifically NI and Scotland) have moved in their current reforms to broader domains of learning; for example, the Arts around Us (NI) and expressive arts (Scotland), compared to the two subjects of Art and Music in England. Similarly, England's non-core History and Geography are combined in Scotland and in Japan as 'social studies' and in Norway as 'social science'. In its most recent reforms France, too, stresses a more interdisciplinary approach. For instance, in the basic learning cycle, 'discovering the world' combines science, technology, and history and geography in one domain whilst 'artistic education' refers to music and art. In the consolidation cycle in France, covering the last three years of primary education, 'scientific education' covers experimental sciences, technology, and, interestingly, maths. It is possible that the subjects-focused arrangement of curriculum in England makes for less coherence in the learning experience and for reduced integration of subject matter in teaching and learning. The focus on raising standards and enhancing accountability generally in the English system is a key factor in explaining the emphasis on subjects rather than learning domains. To some extent the cross curricular areas of creativity, literacy across the curriculum and education for sustainable development temper this, along with the specified range of skills that are assumed to underlie all learning in the curriculum – although it should be noted that these are not compulsory.

The second noteworthy difference pertains to the status attributed to various areas of knowledge, and specifically the relative status accorded to language, natural science, citizenship and the status attributed to different language modes within the study of language.

The priority that England places on English, maths and science as core subjects is not matched by a similar priority in any other country in our survey, including other parts of the UK (Wales and NI having deviated from this model in their recent reforms). In England, English has equal status with maths and with science. In all of our other countries language has more significance in the curriculum than science, and in France, Norway and Japan language also has more significance than maths in the early phase of primary education. In the Preface to *The New Programmes* in France this is how the then (2003) Minister for Education, Jack Lang, expressed the significance of the French language in the elementary/primary curriculum:

> I will repeat it every day: the national language constructs and unites us. Every child should be equipped to enter this common house, and feel at ease and at home

there. A child who cannot achieve this aim or who reaches it imperfectly remains an outsider, is wounded and humiliated, and as a consequence, excluded. This feeling of exclusion generates aggressive or violent reactions in young people.

(MEN 2003: 8)

The New Programme itself states that 'competence in the national language is the fundamental objective. Feeling at ease in the French language is essential in order to access all types of knowledge. Throughout primary education, this requirement must be the permanent preoccupation of teachers' (MEN 2003: 95).

In Norway and Japan, as well as Scotland and NI, natural science and social science have equal status, whilst in France science is incorporated into the broad domain 'discovering the world' which includes science, technology, history and geography in the basic learning cycle. In the consolidation cycle 'scientific education', maths, experimental sciences and technology are incorporated. England is exceptional in its strong emphasis on natural science relative to social science. While all other countries in this part of our chapter include maths throughout the primary phase, it is singled out (along with science and English) as core in England. Interestingly, France places maths in the realm of scientific education along with other areas as we have noted.

The emphasis in England on natural science and maths, together with the attribution of equal status to English, maths and science, represents an orientation in English curriculum policy towards the economy and employment.[11] This orientation is further underlined when one considers the status of citizenship education which is part of the non-statutory 'Framework for Personal, Social, and Health Education (PSHE) and Citizenship'. As a non-obligatory element of the primary curriculum, unlike say in the case of NI ('Personal Development and Mutual Understanding') and Scotland ('Education for Mutual Understanding'), the social and civic dimension is comparatively weak in England. What is undoubtedly the case is that the curriculum in England, with its strong emphasis on maths and science, owes much to the perceived need of governments to make the education system align with the needs of the economy. Subjects perceived to be associated with economic advancement are therefore accorded higher status than subjects perceived to involve more personal interest, for example music and physical education. So strong is the emphasis on maths and science in some official reports that these subjects are sometimes viewed as synonymous with education. The Ofsted review entitled *Worlds Apart? A review of international surveys of educational achievement involving England* (Reynolds and Farrell 1996), for example, is about comparative achievement in maths and science but the title, as some commentators have pointed out, could be read as referring to educational achievement in general (Foster and Hammersley 1998). The authors of this officially-commissioned study justify their focus on both of these subjects, saying that 'mathematics and science are universally recognised as the key skills needed in a modern industrial society, and particularly in the new "information age" economies' (Reynolds and Farrell 1996: 1). It is taken as axiomatic that the greater economic success of the Pacific Rim countries is down to their superior performance in these subjects, as measured by international tests.

Also associated with the economy is Information Technology, which, in addition to being an obligatory subject in its own right in England, is expected to permeate the entire curriculum. Our judgement is that all countries are promoting IT in their curricula, but that Japan, rather surprisingly, places far less emphasis on it than Western countries.

The third point is about the status of elements within subjects. A content analysis of the documentation pertaining to language across our comparator countries suggests that within language (French, Norwegian, Japanese) the status attributed to literacy in England is higher than that attributed to oracy. Evidence for this stems from the Primary Strategy/Primary Framework for literacy and mathematics[12] and from the preoccupation of Government in England with the teaching of early reading – or, more precisely, with how to teach phonics. Although oracy (listening and speaking) has equal status with literacy in terms of the detail in the Programmes of Study and within the attainment targets and level descriptions (*English in the National Curriculum*), other official documents belie this apparent parity of esteem. Other parts of the UK do not exhibit this unequal emphasis on literacy and oracy – a situation that is further exacerbated by the assessment regime. Having said that, France, Norway and Japan all enhanced the status of literacy in their most recent curriculum reforms – a trend that began in the English-speaking world. In France and Japan literacy is expected to permeate all other aspects of the curriculum. Norway also raised the status of literacy but not at the expense of oracy – both are emphasised equally. Japanese is the most emphasised subject in curriculum policy in Japan, with almost twice as many hours devoted to it than to maths (the next most significant subject in terms of centrally-determined teaching time allocated) in the early years of compulsory schooling.[13] Moreover, the diversity of the spoken forms of Japanese means that oracy receives much attention at this early stage.

The introduction of a modern foreign language into England's KS2 curriculum from 2006,[14] albeit (still) non-statutory, represents a significant shift in curriculum policy towards a closer alignment with our European neighbours, or at least with Norway and France. By 2010 all children at KS2 will be entitled to learn a modern foreign language. Elsewhere in the UK, modern foreign language or regional language learning (apart from Welsh in Wales) has traditionally not been prioritised. However, in recent reforms Scotland introduced MFL in the final two years of primary school. France has recently introduced MFL or a regional language into the basic education cycle, while Norway has had a long tradition of endorsing the teaching of several languages from the beginning of primary schooling. Japan does not require primary schools to teach a language other than Japanese although its official documentation encourages the teaching of a modern foreign language (Ministry of Education, Culture, Sports, Science and Technology 2005).

Before leaving the issue of emphases within subject areas it is worth pointing out a further key difference between Japan and all other countries in our survey. Within the broad area of citizenship and social studies, there is a common theme of the democratic citizen and participation in a democracy alongside issues of multiculturalism in all our European countries. These themes are not nearly as strong in curriculum in Japan which (instead) prioritises moral education. The latter has four fundamental principles: self-control; living and communicating with others; respect for the environment, nature and beauty and the importance of life; respect for the rules by which people live, incorporating justice, equality and enjoyment of one's work.

All countries (Table 15.3) incorporate a range of elements into cross-curricular areas of study, thus broadening the base of curriculum in every country in our survey. There is some degree of similarity in the nature of these elements, typically including learning how to learn and lifelong learning, creativity and literacy across the curriculum. England, along with other countries, places additional emphasis on protecting the environment within cross-curricular themes. The elements included here apply across the curriculum and are deemed important for learning all school subjects. England is not dissimilar to other countries in highlighting within its cross-curricular themes those areas that policy makers have decided need to be given further emphasis. For example, the theme of creativity in England is a response to the many criticisms levelled against the curriculum in recent years, specifically that the inordinate emphasis on summative, high stakes assessment in narrow curriculum areas hinders the creative and more aesthetic aspects of the curriculum, thus challenging the curriculum principle of breadth and balance. Similarly, the rigidity of the Japanese curriculum in the recent past prompted the cross curricular elements, thinking skills, creativity, and problem solving to be introduced in the 2002 reforms.

Pedagogic prescription

Before leaving this part of our survey, some points about the extent to which policy determines the kind of teaching approach are appropriate. A common theme across all of our countries is flexibility in pedagogy. There are statements in all cases that the official curriculum is a framework and that there is an expectation that teachers will implement it as faithfully as their local circumstances allow. England, in line with other parts of the UK, does not prescribe the amount of time which is to be allocated to the teaching of any subject. Legislation prohibits the central prescription of time to be allocated to each subject in England. That said, and unlike other parts of the UK, literacy and numeracy are each recommended an hour per day through the (non-statutory) Renewed Primary Framework for Literacy and Maths (2006),[15] and the Qualifications and Curriculum Authority (QCA) offers guidance on timetabling the curriculum. It suggests, for example, that PE should be taught for two hours per week (QCA 2002). In addition, QCA's schemes of work for each curriculum subject guide pedagogy in particular ways.[16] The QCA invites teachers to 'customise your curriculum' and provides examples of how teachers 'have taken ownership of the curriculum, shaping it and making it their own', usually by integrating and combining units. France, Norway and Japan (Table 15.3) all specify how much time should be spent on each subject, although Norway can modify the specified times if the schools and homes agree that the 'competency aims' would be better served by doing so.[17] The subject syllabus, however, cannot be modified. In addition, the textbooks used in France and Japan need to be government-approved – there are no such restrictions in any part of the UK.

On the basis of our analysis of the pedagogic guidance available on official websites and other sources we conclude that there is a tendency across all of our countries towards greater specificity in how to deliver the curriculum. With the exception of the teaching of early reading in England, which is becoming increasingly prescriptive,[18] we suggest that the programmes of study (syllabuses) in non-UK countries – together with their pedagogic guidance – leave less room for teachers to decide on their own preferred methods and approaches.

NARROWING THE COMPARATIVE FOCUS: ASSESSMENT

What is and what is not assessed, the nature of assessment and how it takes place, as well as the purposes and effects of assessment all provide insights into what knowledge and skills are valued by a society. In this part of the chapter we develop our analysis beyond that offered in the first section, 'England in international context', to examine the extent to which England's primary assessment system aligns with that of its nearest neighbours and with that of three sample countries. To highlight similarities and differences and to avoid undue repetition of details already presented, we have selected two broad assessment purposes which suit this comparative analysis: firstly, assessment designed to monitor and hold to account; and secondly, assessment designed to support pupil learning. Table 15.4, which draws from the official sources in each country, presents the documentary evidence on which our analysis here is based.

Assessment designed to monitor and hold to account

All parts of the UK and France, Norway and Japan seek to monitor the quality of learning of their pupils at national level through assessment of pupil achievement against national norms or competencies within specific subjects. By doing so, national governments hold their education systems to account and obtain some degree of evidence about the health of their systems over time. Assessment of pupil achievement is a typical vehicle in our sample countries for monitoring standards and evaluating education systems.

Table 15.4 (see Appendix) shows that national policy in all countries specifies outcomes, competencies or curriculum criteria that pupils at given ages or stages would typically be expected to reach. Assessment is criterion- and curriculum-referenced. The specification of assessment expectations or criteria in terms of curriculum achievement fits with the emphasis in all of our review countries on opportunity to learn. In other words, assessment is focussed on the curriculum and not on attributes like potential or on aspects of learning that are not part of the official curriculum.

However, the scale of assessment for the purpose of monitoring and accountability is of quite a different order in England compared to our other review countries, confirming the conclusion drawn earlier when we took a broader approach. Assessment for accountability purposes features strongly throughout the English assessment policy documentation. It is significantly less stressed in other parts of the UK and in France, Norway and Japan. The following evidence (see Table 15.4) supports our conclusion about the uniqueness of England's assessment policy:

- there is more external, standard testing in England;
- external, standard testing occurs more frequently;
- external, standard testing begins at a younger age;
- external testing occurs in more subjects/subject areas;
- science is tested through external, standard tests;
- external test results are published in league tables that rank schools according to the success of their pupils in the tests;
- testing is 'high stakes'; and,
- external, standard testing is accompanied by obligatory summative teacher assessments at the end of each key stage, the results of which are reported to parents, and at KS2 also reported to government agencies and used to hold the system to account.

In summary, assessment in England, compared to our review countries, is pervasive, highly consequential, and is more generally assumed by the public to objectively portray the actual quality of primary education in schools. There are a number of features of the curriculum and assessment policy as a whole that facilitate this assessment regime. Firstly, the curriculum success criteria are detailed very explicitly for the various elements within subjects (attainment targets) and within a levelled scale, making it possible to design tests to align with the criteria. Secondly, statutory external tests are designed and administered at least twice during a pupil's life in primary school (that is to say, at the end of each key stage). Thirdly, schools have to predict the scale of their pupils' expected success in the tests (target setting) and report not just on their actual test results but also on the divergence between their targeted and actual results. Fourthly, every year their actual results are set not just against the national curriculum norms but also against the actual results of other schools of similar profile (in terms of pupil catchment), thus indicating a strong element of norm-referencing as well as criterion-referencing. Most significantly, the assessment results are used to monitor standards over time and to hold schools accountable to parents and prospective parents so that they can choose which schools best suit their children.

As a result of the foregrounding of assessment for accountability, there is a complex assessment industry and machinery within and without schools in England that is not paralleled at all in our comparison group of countries. Within schools, teachers administer and mark the externally-designed tests (with some external moderation and monitoring) within specified time frames, while externally there are various national and local agencies that design, monitor, collect, check, record and publish the results. Many researchers have demonstrated the negative impact on pupil learning of the priority accorded to assessment for accountability over assessment that is designed to support learning directly. This has been found to impact not only in terms of motivation and self esteem but also in terms of the principle of the broad and balanced curriculum, whereby the high stakes nature of assessment forces schools to privilege teaching in the areas that are tested (literacy, numeracy, science).[19] Such 'teaching to the test' prompts the criticism that while standards in tests might increase it may not follow that achievement in the relevant learning has changed at all (Broadfoot 2000).

Assessment designed to hold the primary system to account is not insignificant in other countries but it is less intrusive, less comprehensive, and considerably less frequent. This applies as much to other parts of the UK as to France, Norway and Japan. Interestingly, Wales and NI have significantly tempered their emphasis on testing in recent reforms such that they are now arguably as different from England as are other European countries in this regard. Scotland's approach was never as heavy-handed as England's, taking the line that national standards can be monitored by assessing national samples of a given population from time to time. The latter approach aligns with monitoring practices in France, Norway and Japan. Very recent reforms in Norway have resulted in the introduction, for the first time, of 'mapping tests' last year (2007) at 2nd and 5th grade in Norwegian reading while 5th graders are also tested in a modern foreign language (that is, English). The radical shift to testing in Norway stems from the country's concern about its standing in international assessments. While results in Norway are forwarded to government agencies, the results are not published or reported at school level. Individual pupil results are fed back to individual schools and parents; assessment in Norway is not high stakes (yet). Japan introduced national testing in Japanese and mathematics for all 12-year-olds from 2007.

To explain the divergence between England and other countries in our survey in relation to the prominence of assessment for accountability purposes, one has to revisit the aims of and rationale for the introduction of the English National Curriculum in the late 1980s. As shown in Table 15.3 (see Appendix), the need to raise standards and to provide evaluative information about the education system to the parent as tax payer (cast as consumer) was fundamental, a need which arose in turn from the perceived link between educational achievement and international economic competitiveness. This requirement meant that curriculum and assessment had to be framed in a manner that allowed learning to be reliably measured and monitored over time. The preoccupation with obtaining reliable measures of performances has continued since the advent of the National Curriculum and its original assessment framework.

So what distinguishes assessment policy in England is the degree to which it is used as a tool, a) to control what is taught; b) to police how well it is taught; and c) to encourage parents to use the resultant assessment information to select schools for their children. Unlike other countries in our survey, the concept of education as a commodity that can be traded in the market place is an explicit and officially endorsed feature of assessment policy in England. English, maths and science, as core subjects, are privileged by the assessment system insofar as these, or elements of these subjects, are selected for statutory assessment. Given the 'high stakes' nature of assessment, the plain message delivered by the assessment system is that these curriculum areas represent the knowledge that is most highly valued by society. In line with our analysis in this chapter's second section, 'Narrowing the comparative focus: curriculum', the emphasis on statutory assessment in maths and science fits with the assumption that the education system should privilege the needs of the economy over, say, personal or other social needs.

Assessment designed to support pupil learning

All countries, including England, refer to the procedures that they have in place to address this assessment for the purpose of supporting pupil learning. Whatever the nature and format of its assessments, the importance of using the assessment information to feed back into teaching and learning is highlighted. For example the new curriculum and assessment policy introduced in France in 2004 means that 8-year-olds do pencil and paper tests every second year in French, and maths at the point of entry into the second cycle – the consolidation cycle. These tests are intended to be diagnostic and to inform subsequent teaching and learning, as well as to aid national monitoring of achievement. That they occur at the beginning and not the end of the school year clearly raises their potential to aid learning. Teachers in Scotland select from a bank of available tests and administer these when they judge that children are ready. The results provide them with a measure of their pupils' achievement which they can use alongside their own teacher assessments to determine pupils' strengths and weaknesses.[20] Moreover, some local education authorities in Scotland don't require schools to use the standard national tests if they can show that they have a system of assessment that is equally robust and better fitted to their school context.

Assessment policy in France, Norway and Japan endorses on-going teacher assessment, including classroom-based, curriculum-oriented tests administered by teachers. Results are recorded and reported to parents to inform them about their children's progress. It is also assumed that this information will enable teachers to decide on next steps for learning and help them to plan suitable learning experiences. The emphasis throughout is strongly on the teacher as assessor. There is limited emphasis in France and Japan on assessment that involves negotiation with learners, on pupils as self and peer assessors, or on qualitative, prose descriptive accounts of learning and learning contexts. There is some evidence of this in Norway. In France, for instance, the pupil record, which is an elaborate account over the school years of a pupils' achievements, tends in the main to be based on numerical marks and grades, mostly the results of teacher-based tests.

However, policy in the UK in general explicitly recognises the role of the learner in the assessment enterprise and gives much attention in its guidance material to what is commonly called 'assessment for learning'. NI and Wales have scaled down their use of testing and now, like Scotland and England, prioritise assessment for learning. The official policy documents of all parts of the UK offer much guidance to teachers on the conduct of this kind of assessment. The language used and the strategies recommended are similar, something which is not altogether surprising since the recommendations stem largely from the work of a key group of researchers who come from all parts of the UK.[21] The recommendations place the learner at the centre of the assessment activities and the guidance is replete with references to negotiation with pupils about what they could do, and how they could go about bridging the gap between what they can do and need to be able to do. Self assessment and peer assessment are recommended for helping learners to understand, and sometimes frame, the criteria against which their work is judged.

Qualitative accounts and prose descriptions of performance, as opposed to marks or grades, are encouraged, the intention being to focus learner attention on descriptions of quality and understanding of success criteria rather than merely obtaining 'high marks'. Having learners assess themselves in relation to their own previous performance, rather than normative evaluations involving ranking with peers, is also encouraged. This approach to assessment invites learners to negotiate and discuss their learning, to set targets for themselves, to monitor and describe their own progress and to consider their achievements in relation to evidence. It privileges talk and discussion about learning and links well with the cross curricular theme of learning how to learn. In summary, it integrates learning and assessment. It is now recognised that this type of assessment is complex and difficult to do well, and therefore the guidance on it is extensive.

England is in line with the rest of the UK regarding its emphasis on assessment for learning. However, while policy in England promotes assessment for learning purposes, the high stakes nature of the assessments (designed to make the system accountable) compromises its potential benefits for learners. The very recently announced Government review of the primary curriculum in England (January 2008) makes quite clear that curriculum, and not assessment, will be its focus, suggesting that an overhaul of the assessment system in England is not likely to occur in the near future.[22]

SUMMARY AND CONCLUSIONS

Conclusions from comparing England and 21 other countries

There is strong convergence in curriculum provision across all 21 countries surveyed. England is in line with international trends in its provision of the following: first language, mathematics, science, information technology, design and technology, history, geography, physical education, art, music, and religious education. All of these areas of study are now standard in the primary curriculum of all the countries in our survey. However, England differs from many other countries in not as yet making PSHE, citizenship and a modern foreign language[23] compulsory at the primary stage. There is also a grey area where matters like education for global awareness are concerned: they are increasingly encouraged though not obligatory.

All countries surveyed seek to adapt their curricula to fit their changing social, economic and political circumstances. More recent reforms in most countries, including England, pertain to the higher status attributed to literacy and mathematics but also, more recently, to the emphasis on the application of knowledge and understanding, and on learning how to learn.

Teachers are expected to assess and report routinely on their pupils' progress in all of the countries surveyed. Assessment is expected to fulfil several purposes. England is in line with the majority of countries insofar as a standard assessment system or end of phase/stage testing occurs in primary school.

However, the pattern of arrangements for assessment is considerably more diverse than it is for curriculum, and England is unusual in its high incidence of assessment. It is exceptional in its emphasis on statutory external standard assessment for children at ages 7 *and* 11.

Conclusions from comparing England's primary curriculum with the rest of the UK and with France, Norway and Japan

There is considerable overlap and consistency in the stated goals and aims of the curriculum. Recurring in the various curriculum policy texts are the following foci:

- the development of all children's potential;
- the promotion of the rounded individual;
- the fostering of the good citizen;
- the cultivation of the lifelong learner; and
- the shaping of the flexible individual for life in a rapidly changing globalised world.

No other country appears to be so preoccupied with national standards.

The curriculum documentation in England differs from that of Japan and France in two key respects. Firstly, in relation to the promotion of a shared common culture: England's official documentation places more emphasis on pluralism, diversity, tolerance, and multiculturalism. Secondly, in relation to the promotion of basic skills, especially language, in the early years of compulsory primary schooling: France, Norway and Japan expect that the curriculum, particularly in the early years of compulsory primary education, should prioritise basic skills of language and maths. These aims are a more explicit feature in the policy texts of these countries than in England or in any other part of the UK.

England structures the curriculum in terms of subjects while other parts of the UK, specifically NI and Scotland, have moved in their current reforms to broader domains of learning, for example, the Arts around Us (NI) and expressive arts (Scotland).

England differs from the other countries surveyed in the status attributed to various areas of knowledge, and specifically in the relative status accorded to language, natural science, citizenship, and the status attributed to different language modes within the study of language. England's priority to English, maths and science as core subjects is not matched by a similar priority in any of the other countries surveyed, including other parts of the UK (Wales and NI having deviated from this model in their recent reforms). The emphasis in England on natural science and maths, together with the attribution of equal status to English, maths and science, represent an orientation in English curriculum policy towards the economy and economic advancement. This orientation is further evidenced in relation to citizenship education which is not obligatory, unlike say the case of NI or Scotland. The conclusion is that the social and civic dimension is comparatively weak in England.

The introduction of a modern foreign language into England's KS2 curriculum from 2006, albeit non-statutory, represents a significant shift in curriculum policy towards a closer alignment with our European neighbours.

Conclusions from comparing England's assessment policy with that of the rest of the UK and with France, Norway and Japan

All parts of the UK and France, Norway and Japan seek to monitor the quality of learning of their pupils at national level through assessment of pupil achievement against national norms or competencies within specific subjects. National monitoring is typically achieved through assessing the achievement of representative samples of pupils from a given population. The scale of assessment for the purpose of monitoring and accountability is of quite a different order in England compared to our other reviewed countries. It is significantly less stressed in other parts of the UK and in France, Norway and Japan. There is more external, standard testing in England; it occurs more frequently and starts at a younger age; more subjects are covered by the statutory assessments; test results are published in league tables; testing is high stakes; and external testing is accompanied by obligatory summative assessment carried out by teachers.

In summary, assessment in England, compared to our other reviewed countries, is pervasive, highly consequential, and taken by officialdom and the public more generally to portray objectively the actual quality of primary education in schools. Wales and Northern Ireland have significantly tempered their emphasis on testing in recent reforms such that they are now (along with Scotland) as different from England as are other European countries. What distinguishes assessment policy in England then is the degree to which it is used as a tool a) to control what is taught; b) to police how well it is taught; and c) to encourage parents to use assessment information to select schools for their children.

All countries, including England, refer to the procedures that they have in place to address assessment for the purpose of supporting pupil learning and, whatever the nature and format of its assessments, the importance of using assessments to feedback into teaching and learning is highlighted.

There is limited emphasis in France and Japan on pupils as self and peer assessors or on qualitative, prose descriptive accounts of learning and learning contexts. There is some evidence of this in Norway. Policy in the UK generally recognises the role of the learner in the assessment enterprise explicitly, giving much attention in its guidance material to what is commonly called 'assessment for learning'. NI and Wales have scaled down their use of testing and now, like Scotland, prioritise assessment for learning. England also emphasises assessment for learning and the official policy documents of all parts of the UK offer much guidance to teachers on the conduct of this kind of assessment.

While policy in England promotes assessment for learning purposes, the high stakes nature of the assessments designed to make the system accountable compromises its potential benefits.

APPENDIX

Table 15.1 Primary curricula compared[1]

	Language/ mother tongue	Alternative lang/ mother tongue	Foreign Lang	Maths	Science	Envir' ment	IT	Tech	History	Geog	Soc Studies Civics	Arts	Art	Craft	Music Dance	PE Sport	Health	Moral educ	Religious Ed	Home	Life Skills	Multi- cultural Ed
England	•	•		•	•	•	•	•	•	•	•	•	•	•	•	•	•	•	optional[2]	•	•	•
Ireland	•	•	•	•	•	•	•	•	•	•	•	•	•	•	•	•	•	•	optional	•	•	•
N. Ireland	•	•	•	•	•	•	•	•	•	•	•	•	•	•	•	•	•	•	optional	•	•	•
Wales	•	•		•	•	•	•	•	•	•	•	•	•	•	•	•	•	•	optional	•	•	•
Scotland	•	•	•	•	•	•	•	•	•	•	•	•	•	•	•	•	•	•	optional[3]	•	•	•
France	•		•	•	•	•	•	•	•	•	•	•	•		•	•	•	•		•	•	•
Germany	•	•	•	•	•	•	•	•	•	•	•	•	•	•	•	•	•	•	•	•	•	•
Hungary	•	•	•	•	•	•	•	•	•	•	•	•	•	•	•	•	•	•	some[4]	•	•	•
Italy	•		•	•	•	•	•	•	•	•	•	•	•	•	•	•	•	•	optional	•	•	•
Netherlands	•		•	•	•	•	•	•	•	•	•	•	•	•	•	•	•	•	optional	•	•	•
Norway	•	•	•	•	•	•	•	•	•	•	•	•	•	•	•	•	•	•	•[5]	•	•	•
Spain	•		•	•	•	•	•	•	•	•	•	•	•	•	•	•	•	•	optional	•	•	•
Sweden	•		•	•	•	•	•	•	•	•	•	•	•	•	•	•	•	•		•	•	•
Switzerland	•		•	•	•	•	•	•	•	•	•	•	•	•	•	•	•	•	optional	•	•	•
Australia	•		•	•	•	•	•	•	•	•	•	•	•	•	•	•	•	•	*some*	•	•	•
Canada	•	•	•	•	•	•	•	•	•	•	•	•	•	•	•	•	•	•	*some*	•	•	•
																			optional			
Japan	•	•	•	•	•	•	•	•	•	•	•	•	•		•	•	•	•	private	•	•	•
Korea	•	•	•	•	•	•	•	•	•	•	•	•	•		•	•	•	•	some	•	•	•
																			private			
New Zealand	•	•		•	•	•	•	•	•	•	•	•	•	•	•	•	•	•	some	•	•	•
Singapore	•	•	•[6]	•	•	•	•	•	•	•	•	•	•	•	•	•	•	•	some	•	•	•
USA	•	•	•	•	•	•	•	•	•	•	•	•	•	•	•	•	•	•	•	•	•	•

Notes:

1 Modified from Andrews et al. 2007: 27.

2 'Optional' means that a child's parents may request that the child does not study religious education.

3 Although public-sector schools in France are secular, which means that religious education is not taught as a subject in its own right, aspects of religious education are taught in other curriculum subjects to expand students' cultural knowledge and understanding of world events.

4 'Some' indicates that schools may choose whether to offer religious education within their programmes.

5 In Norway it is compulsory, but children have the right to get partial dispensation from some parts of teaching.

6 In Singapore English is regarded as an official/national language rather than as a foreign language.

Table 15.2 Primary assessment arrangements compared

	National standardised assessment system[1]	Attainment targets/ outcomes	During compulsory primary education	Published results	Assessment at school entry
England	*Yes*	*Yes*	*7, 8, 9, 10, 11*	*Yes (league tables)*	*5*
Ireland	Yes	Yes	No	Twice in primary phase	No
Northern Ireland	Yes	Yes	8, 11	No	4/5
Scotland	Yes	Yes	Teachers decide when children are ready to take national assessments	No	No
Wales	Yes	Yes	7, 11	Yes (for the country as a whole)	4/5
France	No	Yes	8	Trends only	No
Germany	Yes	Differs across states	No	No	6
Hungary	Yes	Yes	10	No	6
Italy	Yes	Yes	11	No	No
Norway	Some	Yes	7, 11	Yes	No
Netherlands	Yes	Yes	12 for some	Yes to schools	No
Spain	Yes	Yes	9, 11	No	No
Sweden	Yes	Yes	9	No	No
Switzerland	Under review	Differs between cantons	No	No	No
Australia	Yes	Yes	Varies	No	(No)
Canada	Some	Varies	Varies	Varies	No
Japan	Yes	Yes	12	No	No
Korea	Yes	Yes	SAT	No	No
New Zealand	Yes	Yes	8/9	Yes	5/6
Singapore	Yes	Yes	10, 12	Yes	No
USA	Yes	Yes	Varies	Yes (league tables increasing)	Varies

Note: 1 Ongoing teacher assessment occurs in all countries; this is not represented in the table.

(Modified from Andrews *et al.* 2007: 31; Le Metais 2003; and other sources.)

Table 15.3 Official curriculum foci compared

	England	Wales[1]	NI[2]	Scotland[3]	France	Norway	Japan
Compulsory starting age & Primary ages/stages	5 years Key Stage 1 (5–7) Key Stage 2 (7–11)	5 years Key Stage 1 (5–7) Key Stage 2 (7–11)	5 years Foundation Stage: yrs 1 & 2 KS1: yrs 3 & 4 KS2: yrs 5 & 6	5 years Primary 1– Primary 7	6 years Elementary education: 6–11	6 years 6–12/13	6 years 6–12
National Curriculum/	Yes	Yes	Yes	No[4]	Yes	Yes	Yes
Legally enforceable	Yes	Yes	Yes	No	Yes	Yes	Yes
Overall aims/goals of the curriculum	Two broad and interconnected aims of the school curriculum: to provide opportunities for all pupils to learn and to achieve; to promote pupils' spiritual, moral, social and cultural development and prepare all pupils for the opportunities, responsibilities and experiences of life. The NC aims reflect these: it promotes spiritual, moral, cultural, mental & physical development and prepares pupils for the opportunities, responsibilities and experiences of adult life.	To develop children's full potential. The new (revised) school curriculum aims to promote personal development and be responsive to individual needs (still being developed: more flexibility for local schools called for; concern being expressed about the challenge to breadth of the strong focus on literacy and numeracy and perceived overload at KS2[5]	The Revised Curriculum seeks to prepare young people for a rapidly changing world. Through opportunities to engage in active learning contexts across all areas of the curriculum the intention is to develop children's personal, interpersonal and learning skills and their ability to think both creatively and critically. Providing equality of opportunity for all children.	To enable all young people to become successful learners, confident individuals, effective contributors, and responsible citizens. A fundamental aim is to encourage a wide range of achievements and high levels of attainment. Aims to promote learning across a wide range of contexts and experiences; to promote high levels of literacy, numeracy and thinking skills, and high levels of health & well-being.	To provide children with the tools they need for life and future learning. In 2005 the Minister for Education proclaimed that the mastery of languages constitutes an absolute priority in primary education while new methods of science and technology teaching in school represent another priority in the primary school. The improvement of pupils' command of foreign languages is a further objective linked to the consequences of enlargement of the European Area.	A new NC-reform – Knowledge Promotion – aims of which are the cultivation of the following 5 basic skills in all subjects: *1. the ability to express oneself orally* *2. the ability to read* *3. the ability to express oneself in writing* *4. the ability to do arithmetic* *5. the ability to make use of information and communication technology* These basic skills have been incorporated into each of the subject curricula	Along with the former principles like development of 'individual dignity', 'full development of personality' and ensuring 'builders of a peaceful state and society', the new reforms aim to cultivate people who: a) are independent-minded and who seek personal development. b) are warm-hearted and enjoy physical well-being. c) are able to become creative leaders of Century of Knowledge.

Table 15.3 (continued)

	England	Wales[1]	NI[2]	Scotland[3]	France	Norway	Japan
	The 'Primary Framework' seeks to support and increase all children's access to excellent teaching, leading to exciting and successful learning.	The learning opportunities through the NIC help young people to develop as individuals, as contributors to society, and as contributors to the economy and environment.	Aims to develop children's full potential through a broad range of challenging experiences, to develop citizenship, enterprise and creativity.	Civic education continues to have a key place intending that pupils develop a sense of belonging to a national community.	(Norwegian, Maths, natural sciences, social studies, etc.) All teachers are therefore responsible for enabling pupils to develop basic skills through their work in various subjects.	d) are civic-minded. e) will actively participate in the formation of a state and society befitting the 21st century. f) are based on the traditions and culture of Japan. g) to live in a globalised world.	
Curriculum rationale/ principles	Balanced and broadly based. The specific purposes of the NC are to establish standards; to promote continuity and coherence; and to promote public understanding of schooling. Importance also of respect for the individual and choice for parents.	A focus on the learner. Skills development stressed. Continuity and progression. Flexibility. Relevance for twenty first century. Bilingualism. Access for all pupils.	Broad and balanced curriculum. Integration of learning across the areas of learning. Emphasis on the development of skills and capabilities for lifelong learning and for operating effectively in society. Coherence and progression. Ongoing integrated assessment. Active and hands on learning.	Challenge and enjoyment. Breadth. Progression. Depth. Personalisation and choice. Coherence. Relevance. Sees curriculum as a single framework from 3–18. Need to promote learning across a wide range of contexts and experiences.	Importance of equal opportunities and the building of a shared common culture emphasizing an essential base of a 'common core' of knowledge and basic skills: literacy and arithmetic. The common core established in 2006 is the basis for drafting curricula; it has 7 major skills: proficiency in French, knowledge of a foreign language, background in maths and science, openness to IT, knowledge of	Education for all. Curriculum needs to address 7 dimensions of the human being: spiritual, creative, working, liberally-educated, social, environmentally-aware, and integrated.	Curriculum to secure the improvement of 'academic ability' & the promotion of 'moral education'. Curriculum aims: a) to educate pupils to acquire basics firmly as well as the cultivation of the ability to learn and think independently. b) to develop personally. c) to enrich the experimental and problem-solving learning capacities of pupils.

Table 15.3 (continued)

the humanities; social and civic skills; independence & initiative.

	England	Wales[1]	NI[2]	Scotland[3]	France	Norway	Japan
Curriculum Structure: Curriculum areas/ subjects	For each subject and for each key stage, programmes of study set out what pupils should be taught, and attainment targets set out the expected standards of pupils' performance. The PsoS provide the basis for planning schemes of work. Basic Curriculum: RE and PSE NC core: English, maths, science; NC non-core: D+T, IT, history, geography, art, music and PE. Non-statutory guidance on Personal, social and health education and citizenship and modern foreign language at KS2.	KS1 (which is part of the Foundation Phase): Personal and social development; well-being and cultural diversity; Language, literacy and communication skills; Maths, Welsh language; Knowledge and understanding of the world; Physical development; Creative Development; RE; Sex Education KS2 Curriculum RE and PSE and sex education NC core: English[6], Welsh[7], maths, science; NC non-core: Welsh 2nd lang, D+T, IT, history, geography, art, music, PSE, and PE.	Curriculum structured in terms of 'areas of learning': RE Language & Literacy Maths & Numeracy The Arts The world around us Personal Dev & Mutual Understanding (which includes citizenship) PE	(Curriculum for excellence) 8 curriculum areas: mathematics; languages; expressive arts; health and wellbeing; religious and moral education; sciences; social studies; and technologies. Modern foreign language introduced in Primary 6 (10–11 years) and carried into Primary 7.	Curriculum structured in terms of domains. Basic learning cycle: last year of nursery & first two years of elementary: French maths, discovering the world (combining science, technology, and history and geography in one subject area); civics, PE and sport, artistic education (music and art); Foreign or regional language Consolidation cycle covering last 3 years of elementary school. French language; literary education and the humanities (combining literature – speaking, reading, writing, grammar, conjugation, spelling, vocabulary; a foreign	National Curriculum 'Knowledge Promotion' Norwegian, natural science, maths, social science, English, foreign languages, Christianity/ Religion/Ethics, arts and crafts, food and health, music, PE. Additional subjects in the Sami Knowledge Promotion: Sami (as a first language) Sami (as a second language) Sami arts and crafts	School Education Law determines the objective, goal, curricula, number of educational weeks and course subjects. Japanese, Social studies, Arithmetic, Science, Life environmental studies, Music, arts & handicrafts, homemaking, Physical education, Moral education and Extracurricular activities. English, as a modern foreign language, encouraged but not obligatory and no time allowances given (see below)

Table 15.3 (continued)

	England	Wales[1]	NI[2]	Scotland[3]	France	Norway	Japan
					or regional language; history and geography; and a weekly planned discussion on living together); Scientific education (covering maths, experimental sciences and technology); Artistic education (music and visual arts); Physical education and sport; Civics.		
Curriculum Structure: Cross-curricular areas/ themes/skills	Creativity, literacy across the curriculum, education for sustainable development. Thinking skills: enquiry, reasoning, information processing, creative thinking and evaluation; Economic awareness, environmental education, citizenship Key Skills: communication, application of number, IT, working with others, improving own learning and problem solving.	Development of communication, application of number, and ICT. Development programme for thinking skills in process the aim of which is improve pupil performance; increase engagement with learning; increase the frequency of creative lessons – this is linked with 'assessment for learning'.	Thinking skills and personal capabilities Communication Personal and interpersonal skills Managing information Problem solving and decision making Creativity Working with others Self-management IT Education for mutual understanding (EMU) and Cultural Heritage (CH) Health Education Economic Awareness	Organisational skills; creativity; teamwork; and the ability to apply learning in new and challenging contexts.	Literacy permeates all subject areas. IT as a tool for supporting all learning. Religious and moral education to be integrated into other subjects. Since public sector schools are secular, RE is not taught as a subject in its own right but since 2001 there is a move to expand children's cultural knowledge and understanding of world events and RE to be integrated into other subjects to support this aim.	5 basic skills to be integrated across the curriculum: oracy, reading, writing, arithmetic, ICT.	Reading, writing, problem solving, ability to think, creativity, academic ability and moral education.

Table 15.3 (continued)

	England	Wales[1]	NI[2]	Scotland[3]	France	Norway	Japan
Competency outcomes/ attainment targets	Attainment targets (ATs) set out the knowledge, skills and understanding which pupils are expected to have by the end of each key stage. Except in the case of citizenship. ATs consist of 8 Level Descriptions of increasing difficulty. Each LD describes the types and range of performance that pupils working at that level should characteristically demonstrate.	Attainment targets set out the knowledge, skills and understanding which pupils are expected to have by the end of each key stage. Except in the case of citizenship. ATs consist of 8 LDs of increasing difficulty. Each LD describes the types and range of performance that pupils working at that level should characteristically demonstrate. *Currently under review.*	Under review	Attainment outcomes For each curricular area there are broad attainment outcomes, each with a number of strands or aspects of learning that pupils experience. Most strands have attainment targets at five or six levels: A-E or A-F.[8] National tests are marked to criteria and levels.	Attainment targets (notions) are set for the end of each cycle.	NC contains competency outcomes on what children should know in each subject by end of 2nd, 4th and 7th grades.	Each school devises its own standards based on the national 'Courses of Study' – the latter specifies objectives for the various curriculum areas.
Pedagogical directives/ guidelines	Schools to choose how they organise their school curriculum to include the programmes of study. The national frameworks for teaching literacy and mathematics and the exemplar schemes of work show how the programmes of study and the attainment targets can be	Teachers can determine teaching methods. Teachers have flexibility to modify the curriculum. In many cases the action necessary to respond to an individual's requirements for curriculum access will be met through greater differentiation of tasks. Strong emphasis on skills especially learning how to learn.	Teachers to select from the curriculum areas that they consider appropriate; Integration of learning encouraged to make relevant connections for learners Flexibility to modify the curriculum to local and individual needs. Varied to suit learning style. Enquiry based.	Strong emphasis on flexibility Teacher choice in teaching methods Strong emphasis on the promotion of active learning and on learning how to learn.	Teachers select teaching methods. They are expected to organize the curriculum according to pupil needs and their own teaching style. Teachers are expected to take into account the 'learning rhythms' of each child and tailor teaching accordingly. Across the curriculum	The schools/teachers decide teaching methods, working activities, organisation of teaching. They are expected to design teaching activities to ensure 'adopted teaching' to every individual within their natural group setting.	Courses of study define the number of days and hours of instructional activity, the subjects to be taught and the sequencing of topics. Schools/teachers decide methods, working styles, teaching activities and the organisation of teaching.

Table 15.3 (continued)

	England	Wales[1]	NI[2]	Scotland[3]	France	Norway	Japan
	translated into practical, manageable teaching plans.				2.5 hours per day to be devoted to reading and writing for 6–8 year olds.		Replacement of social studies and science in the first 2 years of primary by 'Daily Life' intending to allow more integration and experienced-based learning
Curriculum time allocations	2 hours of physical activity per week within PE recommended Generally no times specified.	No times specified.	No time allocations specified.	No time allocations. Existing time allocations discontinued.	Defined by central government. Min/ Max weekly hour allocations, varying slightly for different grades. The following is for chn aged 6–8 Literature (speaking, reading, writing) 4.5–5.5 French language 1.5–2 Foreign or regional language 1.5–2 history and geography 3–3.5 living together/ collective life 0.5 maths 5 experimental sciences & technology 2.5–3 music & visual arts 3	Allocation of minimum total number of hours to each subject is done by the central government. Municipalities can increase the numbers, but they have to pay the extra costs by themselves. But the number of allocated hours to each subject can be changed up to 25%. This change must contribute to a better achievement of 'Competency aims'.	The number of hours per week in each subject is decided centrally. The following yearly hours allocation for year 2 (age 7) pupils illustrates the status accorded different subjects: Japanese 210 Maths 116 Life Environment Studies 79 Music 53 Art & Craft 53 PE 68.

Table 15.3 (continued)

	England	Wales[1]	NI[2]	Scotland[3]	France	Norway	Japan
					Physical education and sports 3 Cross disciplinary /integrated into different subjects: French lang 13 Civics 1		National 'Courses of Study' for elementary education in 2002.
Current curriculum reform	Revised in 2000 Government announced in December 2007 that the curriculum will be reviewed (Rose Review).	'Foundation phase' (Children's Learning) integrating 'Desirable Learning Outcomes for Children's Learning before Compulsory School Age' and the PoS for KS1 NC being trialled in 41 settings between 2004 and 2008.	Framework for the revised curriculum in place in Aug 06 being phased in from Sept 07. The Revised Curriculum includes a new Foundation Stage to cover P1 & P2 placing more emphasis on skills and confidence and introduction to more formal learning when children are ready.	The Scottish[9] 'Curriculum for Excellence' with the aim of developing a streamlined curriculum for 3–18 year olds and implementing new approaches to assessment.	Strengthened emphasis on literacy across the curriculum Foreign language at an earlier (in the basic education cycle) Civic education.	A National Curriculum was introduced under the name of: 'Knowledge Promotion' in the academic year 2006–2007.	

	England	Wales[1]	NI[2]	Scotland[3]	France	Norway	Japan
Most recent changes	Greater emphasis on creativity and the arts. Also on phonics in the early years of school; personalised learning; strengthening of emphasis on mental arithmetic.	Discontinuation of obligatory end-of-KS testing at KS2 from 2005 onwards. So phasing out of the statutory tasks and tests on grounds that they impact negatively on teaching and learning especially at KS2. Now teacher assessment to be the sole means of end of key stage assessment.	Greater emphasis on developing skills preparation for life and work and on a 'more appropriate' curriculum for the early years. KS1 now comprises Years 3 and 4 and KS2, Years 5, 6 and 7.	More emphasis on active learning; assessment geared to the promotion of learning and teaching; Fewer, more broadly spaced levels.	A common core curriculum established in 2006 specifying content of primary education officially at national level. Changes introduced in Sept 2002 brought in some new subjects. The major change is the strengthened status of literacy especially across the curriculum and the study of a foreign language from age 6 onwards.	Increased status to language, maths and science - Emphasising the importance of 'adopted teaching', 'inclusion' and promotion of basic skills in all subjects: 1. the ability to express oneself orally 2. the ability to read 3. the ability to express oneself in Writing 4. the ability to do arithmetic 5. the ability to make use of information and communication technology.	More emphasis on 'improving academic ability', 'moral education', 'enhancement of individual oriented instruction'.

Notes:

1 The curriculum in Wales in currently under review – the aim of the review is to establish a curriculum for the 21st century that meets the needs of individual learners whilst taking account of the broader needs of Wales. It is proposed that, following consultation in Spring 2007, revised versions of the Subject Orders will be available in Spring 2008 for implementation in September 2008. See http://www.accac.org.uk/uploads/documents/600.doc

2 See The Northern Ireland Curriculum Primary (2007) http://www.nicurriculum.org.uk/docs/key_stages_1_and_2/northern_ireland_curriculum_primary.pdf

3 At the time of writing, piloting of elements of 'A Curriculum for Excellence' is in process and guidance is being finalised along with CPD for teachers. The year 2007–08 will be a year of familiarisation, preparation and development and it will begin in August 2008. This report concentrates on the new curriculum (a Curriculum for Excellence) available at http://www.ltscotland. org.uk/5–14/about5to14/acurriculumforexcellence

4 There is no legally enforceable National Curriculum in Scotland and all curriculum and assessment guidelines are non statutory. There are 'national priorities' however which give a sense of direction for education and curriculum policy. Two of the five of these are especially relevant to the curriculum namely 'to raise standards of educational attainment for all in schools, especially in the core skills of literacy and numeracy, and to achieve better levels in national measures of achievement; and 'to equip pupils with the foundation skills, attitudes and expectations necessary to prosper in a changing society and to encourage creativity and ambition'. See http://www.nationalpriorities.org.uk/schools.html

5 http://old.accac.org.uk/uploads/documents/1507.pdf

6 There is no statutory requirement to teach English at Key Stage 1 in Welsh-medium schools.

7 In Welsh-speaking schools Welsh is a core subject in both Key Stages of primary education. In other schools Welsh is a non-core foundation subject.

8 See http://www.curriculumforexcellencescotland.gov.uk/index.asp and http://www.ltscotland.org.uk/5to14/about5to14/curriculumforexcellence/introduction.asp

9 This report draws on the existing official document about this Curriculum rather than the one it will replace.

Table 15.4 Official assessment foci compared

	England	Wales	NI[1]	Scotland	France	Norway	Japan
Stated purposes/ rationale	To raise standards. The purpose of end-of-key-stage summative assessment is to assess pupil achievement in relation to the expected, national standards. The aim overall is to provide schools and parents with evidence about achievement and to help parents and the public generally judge the quality of the education being provided. The purpose of ongoing formative assessment is to support teaching and learning.	Teacher assessment (ongoing) for diagnostic purposes, to support pupil progress, to record attainment, and to report to parents; Day-to-day teacher assessment seen as integral to teaching and learning. TA to record pupil attainment at end of KS2; to inform curriculum planning at school and class level; to monitor national performance.	The Annual Pupil Profile is designed to inform parents, teachers and pupils themselves.	The major emphasis is on assessment to support learning and teaching.	(With reference to national testing) to support teaching and learning through providing teachers with a tool to monitor pupil progress and to inform teaching decisions and planning; To monitor the education system; to provide comparisons of achievement over time.	At the primary level teacher assessment is for diagnostic purposes and to support pupil progress and provide information for parents. The use of marks is forbidden. A quality assessment system was introduced in 2003. Aims of this system are a) Contribution to an open dialogue about the school's activities b) Supply state authorities with information about the school system c) Supply data & information about the school. National mapping tests are seen as part of this system.	National standardized tests were introduced in 2007 in Japanese and mathematics The major emphasis is on assessment to support learning and 'evaluate the effectiveness of teaching'.

Table 15.4 (continued)

	England	Wales	NI[1]	Scotland	France	Norway	Japan
Assessment format	KS1 tests and tasks in English (reading, writing, spelling) and a maths test. These individual test results are not reported in isolation but are used to inform the teacher assessment levels. At KS2 three maths tests, two science tests, and three English tests (reading, writing and spelling). Optional tests available within Key Stages (i.e. years 3, 4 and 5) designed to help teachers raise standards by verifying their TA allocations.	Teacher assessment (informal, ongoing) used throughout primary; pupil self assessment encouraged. Statutory end of KS TA[2] Optional task/ testing material available to schools.	Statutory assessment suspended while the revised curriculum is being introduced from 2007 but an annual report in the form of a Pupil Profile report is being phased in and will be statutory for all children at KS2 from 2009/10. Emphasis on 'assessment for learning' involving: building a more open relationship between learner and teacher; clear learning intentions shared with pupils; shared/negotiated success criteria; individual target setting; taking risks for learning; advice on what and how to improve; peer and self assessment; and celebrating success.	Assessment for learning prioritised. Pupils sit national tests linked to levels in reading, writing and maths when the teacher judges them to be ready – these levels are now being revised.	Ongoing teacher assessment reported via report books. National diagnostic testing every alternate year for all 8 year olds as these children enter the consolidation cycle consisting of written tests in French and maths. National diagnostic testing at age 10 (on entry to final year of elementary ed) in some schools. End of year testing of samples for national monitoring.	National mapping tests are intended to provide feedback to the teachers, pupils, parents and the local decision makers. The results cannot be published in the media and the ranking of schools on the basis of results is prohibited.	Tests for 12 year olds in Japanese and maths.

Table 15.4 (continued)

	England	Wales	NI[1]	Scotland	France	Norway	Japan
Subject/areas assessed and range of evidence collected	National curriculum assessment is a formal part of the NC Assessment tasks/tests for English and maths for pupils at end of KS1 Tests in English, maths and science for pupils at end of KS2 (no science from 2010) + Teacher Assessment for both Key Stages.	Reading, writing and oracy in English (and Welsh), maths and science; Statutory TA covers the full range of the PoS in these areas and takes account of evidence in a range of contexts. Standard tests and tasks are now optional at both Key Stages.	Schools will be required to assess and report annually on each pupil's progress in: Areas of Learning; Cross-Curricular Skills; and Thinking Skills and Personal Capabilities. Assessment for learning as described above in all areas including attitudes and dispositions.	National standard assessments (see above)	Teachers have to record whether specific *notions* (attainment targets at cycle level) have been met, are in the process of being met, or have not been met.	National mapping tests are introduced in 2006–2007 aiming to determine whether the schools are succeeding in developing pupils' basic skills in reading 2nd grade and 5th grade. Mapping tests in English as a foreign language and maths at 5th grade.	See above. A document, 'Courses of Study', functions as National curriculum guidelines that serve as a national standard. It provides schools with the content and the objectives of each course. All though the elementary school students are not required to pass national tests in order to move on to the next level of schooling. Competition is strong because of the system of entrance exams for prestigious private high schools or colleges.

Table 15.4 (continued)

	England	Wales	NI[1]	Scotland	France	Norway	Japan
Grades/marks/ descriptions/ judgements	The level descriptions provide the basis for making teacher judgements (Teacher Assessment) about pupils' performance at the end of KS1&2. In deciding on a pupil's level of attainment at the end of a key stage, teachers should judge which description best fits the pupil's performance. When doing so, each description should be considered alongside descriptions for adjacent levels in an 8-level scale. Marks in the KS2 assessments are aggregated and pupils obtain a composite mark in each of English, maths, and science.	Teachers have to reach a rounded judgement. A level is allocated in reading, writing and oracy in English (and Welsh), maths and science; and an overall subject level in each of these subjects.	Teachers are expected to use a varied range of assessment techniques as an integral part of the learning and teaching process (including tests). These assessments are used to make judgements at the end of each year about the level at which children are working.	National tests are marked to criteria. Children can be awarded leve. Flexible approach in that level can be awarded without meeting every criterion for that level; emphasis on judgement.	Children are promoted from class to class within a cycle based on teacher assessments and in consultation with parents.	The use of marks/ grades at primary education level is prohibited (6–12/13).	Content of instruction and objectives in 'Courses of study' provide the basis for informal teacher assessment without grades or marks. There is no grade retention and no skipping of grades.

Table 15.4 (continued)

	England	Wales	NI[1]	Scotland	France	Norway	Japan
Ages/Stages/Time of year	End of KS1 at age 7, From Jan to June End of KS2 at age 11, usually May.	End of KS2 (11yrs) May/June.	Ongoing assessment throughout the year as described above.	National tests when the teacher deems that the children are ready to take them.	On entry to the consolidation cycle (age 8).	Mapping test for basic skills in reading in the middle of 2nd grade and 5th grade. Mapping test in English as a foreign language and maths at 5th grade.	Curriculum-based tests administered by teachers to inform teaching and learning decisions. At age 12 standardised tests Japanese and maths.
Reporting assessments/progress	Teachers are required to report annually to parents on pupils' progress. Results from summative end of KS tests and assessment tasks and TA are reported in relation to both national standards (i.e. NC criteria) and national performance (i.e. spread of results).		An Annual Pupil Profile Report (PP) which summarises all the assessment information available including any diagnostic assessment. Diagnostic assessments as part of the PP consists of Interactive Computerised Assessment System (InCAS) being phased in starting with Y5 in 07/08.	Schools are expected to report to parents on their children's strengths and weaknesses, including next steps in learning and on their child's level of attainment in the NC as well as information about personal and social development. Results of any tests are published annually for current parents in the schools and sent to the local authority. The LA uses the aggregated results to monitor progress in relation to national priorities.	The School Report Book is a link between home and school is used to show children's progress.	Schools are required to report the results of the tests to the local and central educational authorities. Parents get information about the results of their own child.	Internal curriculum-based tests for internal use. National test results communicated to schools and parents.

Table 15.4 (continued)

	England	Wales	NI[1]	Scotland	France	Norway	Japan
League tables	Published by school every year for end of KS2 aimed at enabling parents judge the most appropriate school for their child. The tables list a school's results indicating the % of pupils achieving at the expected level (L4) for that stage in each of English, maths, and science in the tests and in TA.	No league tables.	No league tables.	No league tables.	No league tables.	Yes, league tables are published every year. The tables list a school's results indicating the percentage of pupils achieving at three different achievement levels.	No league tables.
Assessment reforms and most recent changes	Changes at KS1	*Discontinuation of end-of-KS testing at KS2 from 2005 onwards. Currently being piloted: a programme linking thinking skills and assessment for learning, the aim of which is improve pupil performance; increase engagement with learning; increase the frequency of creative lessons.*	Order 2006 revokes previous legislation. From 06/07, end of KS1 and 2 TA are no longer statutory; The annual end-of-year school report to be replaced in 07/08 with a cumulative Pupil Profile for Year 5 pupils.	The Scottish curriculum is currently going through a national review called 'Curriculum for Excellence' with the aim of developing a streamlined curriculum for 3–18 year olds and implementing new approaches to assessment. Specifically, there will be greater. Emphasis on professional judgements made by teachers.	Reading, writing and maths achievement of 8 year olds were tested at the beginning of CE1 for the first time in October 2006.	Introducing national mapping tests for 2nd graders in reading and for 5th graders in reading in Norwegian and in English as a foreign language and in maths. The content of the mapping tests will be based on the subject syllabus goals for basic skills and competency aims as these are formulated in NC.	

Table 15.4 (continued)

	England	Wales	NI[1]	Scotland	France	Norway	Japan
National target setting	The Government has established national targets for the proportion of 11-year-olds achieving level 4 (the expected level for this stage) in English and maths NC tests at the end of KS2. Schools are required to set their own targets for the proportions of their pupils who will reach these national targets and their results have to be reported in school prospectuses and annual reports to school governors against their projected targets. Optional tests in English and maths are available to assist schools in monitoring pupils' progress towards these targets.			National standards in maths, science, reading and writing are surveyed on a 4-year cycle to monitor performance standards over time.		The new NC sets clear competency criteria. The new subject curricula contain clear competency aims for what pupils should know in each subject by the end of 2nd and 4th grade. The national mapping tests must be in accordance with these competency aims.	Concrete and clearly formulated objectives and content for instruction in national curriculum 'Courses of Study'.

Table 15.4 (continued)

	England	Wales	NI[1]	Scotland	France	Norway	Japan
	To support target setting for pupils who achieve significantly below age-related expectations, performance criteria have been developed in English and maths.						
Participation in International Studies of Achievement	UK-designed 'world class tests' (problem solving oriented) for the most able 9 year olds are designed to 'recognise, record and benchmark individual achievement and ability of the top 10% of 9 year olds.	PISA (15 year olds in maths, literacy and science); PIRLS (reading for 9 and 10 year olds) TIMSS (maths and science).	PISA (15 year olds in maths, literacy and science); PIRLS (reading for 9 and 10 year olds) TIMSS (maths and science).	PISA (15 year olds in maths, literacy and science); PIRLS (reading for 9 and 10 year olds) TIMSS (maths and science).	PISATIMSS	PISAPIRLS TIMSS	PISATIMSS

Notes:

1 Assessment policy is under review at the time of writing and all obligatory assessment suspended for 06/07 year and the assessment units (tests and tasks) are to be made available on a voluntary basis in 06/07 and 07/08 depending on the extent of demand from schools.

2 From 2005 teacher assessment is the only means of statutory assessment in Wales.

NOTES

1 The International Review of Curriculum and Assessment Frameworks Archive www.inca. org.uk
2 See http://nc.uk.net/ and http://www.standards.dfes.gov.uk/primary/about/
3 Level descriptions are summary prose statements that indicate the types and range of performance which children working at a particular level of the national curriculum should characteristically demonstrate. These descriptions are the basis for judging children's levels of attainment and teachers have to judge which level description 'best fits' a student's performance.
4 See http://www.nc.uk.net/about/values_aims_purposes.html
5 See Starkey (2000) in relation to citizenship.
6 http://www.nc.uk.net/nc_resources/html/inclusion.shtml
7 http://www.qca.org.uk/re and http://www.standards.dfee.gov.uk/schemes/
8 Cited in Starkey (2000).
9 See http://www.dfes.gov.uk/citizenship.
10 See, for examples, Alexander 2001; Osborn *et al.* 2003; Broadfoot 2000.
11 See Alexander 2001; Hamilton and Weiner 2000; Hall 2004.
12 http://www.standards.dfes.gov.uk/primary/about/
13 INCA (nd) Primary Education: an International Perspective http://www.inca.org.uk/pdf/ probe_japan.pdf
14 See http://www.dfes.gov.uk/languagesstrategy and http://www.dfes.gov.uk/languages/
15 See QCA 2006, available at http://www.standards.dfes.gov.uk/primaryframeworks/
16 See http://www.dfes.gov.uk/schemes/
17 In Norway the solo class teacher model no longer exists – a team of teachers is now responsible for classes of children.
18 See Hall 2006; also Hall 2007.
19 For examples see Hall *et al.* 2004; Harlen and Deakin Crick 2002; Reay and Wiliam 1999.
20 http://www.scotland.gov.uk/Publications/2005/06/2393450/34518
21 See Black and Wiliam 1998a; Black and Wiliam 1998b; Assessment Reform Group 2002; Black *et al.* 2003.
22 See letter from Secretary of State for Children, Schools and Families, Ed Balls, to Sir Jim Rose (dated 09.01.2008), available at http://www.dfes.gov.uk/pns/pnattach/20080003/1.pdf
23 The reference to the MFL in the proposed review of the curriculum in England hints at the possibility of increased status of MFL in the future. See http://www.dfes.gov.uk/pns/pnattach/ 20080003/1.pdf

REFERENCES

Akamatsu, N. (1998) 'L1 and L2 reading: the orthographic effects of Japanese on reading in English', *Language, Culture and Curriculum* 11(1): 9–27.

Alexander, R.J. (2001) *Culture and Pedagogy: international comparisons in primary education.* Oxford: Blackwell.

Andrews, C., Brown, R. and Sargent, C. (2007) 'INCA comparative tables, primary education', online. (Available: http://www.inca.org.uk/comparative_tables.html).

Assessment Reform Group (2002) *Testing, Motivation and Learning.* Cambridge: Cambridge University Press.

Benavot, A., Cha, Y.K., Kamens, D., Meyer, J.W. and Wong, S.W. (1991) 'Knowledge for the masses: world models and national curricula, 1920–86', *American Sociological Review* 98.

Black, P., Harrison, C., Lee, C., Marshall, B. and Wiliam, D. (2003) *Assessment for Learning: putting it into practice.* Maidenhead: Open University Press.

Black, P. and Wiliam, D. (1998a) 'Assessment and classroom learning', *Assessment in Education* 5(1): 7–74.

——(1998b) *Inside the Black Box: raising standards to classroom assessment* London: King's College.

Broadfoot, P. (2000) *Assessment and Society.* Maidenhead: Open University Press.

Broadfoot, P., Osborn, M., Planel, C. and Sharpe, K. (2000) *Promoting Quality in Learning: does England have the answer?* Cassell: London.

Central Advisory Council for Education (CACE) (1967) *Children and their Primary Schools: a report of the Central Advisory Council for Education (England)* (the Plowden Report). London: HMSO.

Crystal, D. (1997) *The Cambridge Encyclopaedia of Language* (2nd edition). Cambridge: Cambridge University Press.

Davies, S. and Guppy, N. (1997) 'Globalization and educational reforms in Anglo-American democracies', *Comparative Education Review* 41(4): 435–59.

Denoon, D., Hudson, M., McCormack, G. and Morris-Suzuki, T. (Eds) (1996) *Multicultural Japan: palaeolithic to postmodern.* Cambridge: Cambridge University Press.

DfCS (2008) 'Balls launches fundamental review of primary curriculum', online. (Available: http://www.dfes.gov.uk/pns/pnattach/20080003/1.pdf)

DfES (2003) *Excellence and Enjoyment.* Online (Available: http://www.standards.dfes.gov.uk/primary/publications/literacy/63553/pns_excell_enjoy037703v2.pdf).

Ellis, S. (2006) 'The Scottish context for the Curriculum', in J. Arthur, T. Grainger and D. Wray (Eds) *Teaching and Learning in the Primary School.* London: Routledge.

Foster, P. and Hammersley, M. (1998) 'A review of reviews: structure and function in review of educational research', *British Educational Research Journal* 24(5): 609–628.

Gipps, C. (1994) *Beyond Testing: towards at theory of educational assessment.* London: Falmer.

Hall, K. (2004) *Literacy and Schooling: towards renewal in primary education policy.* Aldershot: Ashgate.

——(2006) 'How children learn to read and how phonics helps', in M. Lewis and S. Ellis (Eds) *Phonics: Practice, Research and Policy*: 9–22. London: Sage.

——(2007) 'Literacy policy and policy literacy: a tail of phonics in early reading', in J. Soler and R. Openshaw (Eds) *Reading Across International Boundaries.* London: Routledge.

Hall, K., Collins, J., Benjamin, S., Sheehy, K. and Nind, M. (2004) 'SATurated models of pupildom: assessment and inclusion/exclusion', *British Educational Research Journal* 30(6): 801–17.

Hall, K., Øzerk, K. and Valli, Y. (1999) 'Curriculum reform in contemporary English and Norwegian official documents', *European Journal of Intercultural Studies* 10(1): 85–104.

Hamilton, D. and Weiner, G. (2000) 'Subjects, not subjects: curriculum pathways, pedagogies and practices in the United Kingdom', paper presented at the *Internationalisation of Curriculum Studies Conference,* Louisiana State University, USA.

Harlen, W. and Deakin Crick, R. (2002) 'A systematic review of the impact of summative assessment and tests on students' motivation for learning (EPPI-Centre Review, version 1.1)', in *Research Evidence in Education Library.* London: EPPI-Centre, Social Science Research Unit, Institute of Education, University of London.

Helot, C. and Young, A. (2005) 'The notion of diversity in language education: policy and practice in primary level in France', *Language, Culture and Curriculum* 18(3): 258–70.

Lai, M.-L. (1999) 'Jet and Net: a comparison of native-speaking English teachers schemes in Japan and Hong Kong', *Language, Culture and Curriculum* 12(3): 215–28.

Lawton, D. (1989) 'The National Curriculum', in D. Lawton (Ed) *The Education Reform Act: choice and control.* London: Hodder and Stoughton: 27–43.

Le Metais, J. (2003) 'International Trends in Primary Education (INCA/QCA Thematic Study No. 9)', online. (Available at http://www.inca.org.uk/thematic.asp).

Lessard-Clouston, M. (1998) 'Perspectives on language learning and teaching in Japan: an introduction', *Language, Culture and Curriculum* 11(1): 1–8.

Ministère de l'Education Nationale (MEN) (2003) *Qu'apprend-ton aL'Ecole Elementaire? Les Nouveaux Programmes Paris: CNDP, XO Editions.* Online (Available: http://www.cndp.fr/ecole/quapprend/pdf/755A0212.pdf).

Ministry of Education, Culture, Sports, Science and Technology (2005) *Japan's Education at a Glance 2005.* Tokyo: Ministry of Education, Culture, Sports, Science and Technology.

Osborn, M., Broadfoot, P., McNess, E., Planel, C., Ravn, B. and Triggs, P. (2003) *A World of Difference: comparing learners across Europe*. Buckingham: Open University Press.

Øzerk, K. (2006) *Opplæringsteori og læreplanforståelse*. Vallset: Oplandske Bokforlag.

QCA (2002) *Designing and Timetabling the Primary Curriculum: a practical guide for Key Stages 1 and 2*. QCA: London.

——(2006) *Renewed Primary Framework for Literacy and Maths*. London: QCA

Reay, D. and Wiliam, D. (1999) '"I'll be a nothing": structure, agency and the construction of identity through assessment', *British Educational Research Journal* 25(3): 343–54.

Reynolds, D. and Farrell, D. (1996) *Worlds Apart: a review of international surveys of educational achievement involving England*. London: Ofsted.

Scottish Education Department (SEED) (1965) *Scottish Memorandum Primary Education in Scotland*. Edinburgh: HMSO.

SEED (2007) *National Priorities in Education: achievement and attainment*. Online (Available: http://www.nationalpriorities.org.uk/schools/priority1.#outcome1).

Starkey, H. (2000) 'Citizenship education in France and Britain: evolving theories and practices', *The Curriculum Journal* 11(1): 39–54.

Taylor, C., Gonshcroff, N., Florence, M. and Rowthorn, C. (1997) *Japan – a travel survival kit*. Hawthorn, Vic: Lonely Planet.

Telhaug, A.O. (2005) *Kunnskapsløftet – ny eller gammel skole?: beskrivelse og analyse av Kristin Clemets reformer igrunnopplæringen*. Oslo: Cappelen akademisk forlag.

Weiner, M. (Ed) (1997) *Japan's Minorities: the illusion of homogeneity*. London: Routledge.

OTHER UK WEBSITES CONSULTED

http://www.standards.dfes.gov.uk/primary/about/
http://www.dfes.gov.uk/languages/
http://www.dfes.gov.uk/languagesstrategy
http://www.scotland.gov.uk/Publications/2005/06/2393450/34518
http://www.ltscotland.org.uk/5to14/about5to14/curriculumforexcellence/introduction.asp
http://old.accac.org.uk/uploads/documents/1507.pdf
http://www.nationalpriorities.org.uk/schools/schools.html
http://www.ltscotland.org.uk/5–14/about5to14/acurriculumforexcellence
http://www.nicurriculum.org.uk/docs/key_stages_1_and_2/northern_ireland_curriculum_primary.pdf
http://www.accac.org.uk/uploads/documents/600.doc

16 Primary curriculum futures

James Conroy, Moira Hulme and Ian Menter

INTRODUCTION

In this chapter we seek to address what the current trends in primary curriculum seem to indicate about the future, as well as exploring some of the possible curriculum developments that may be needed to enable primary schools to make an appropriate response to the shape of the future world.

There is little argument that developments since the time of the Plowden Report (CACE 1967) have been influenced as much by ideology and politics as by research evidence or a considered response to social and technological change. While there has never been a time when literacy and numeracy were not seen as key elements in the primary school curriculum, nevertheless the wider setting in which these were located has varied markedly. In the post-Plowden era there was a strong commitment, amongst educationalists at least, to a child-centred curriculum based on children's interests playing down the significance of subjects (especially when contrasted with the secondary school curriculum). The major 'turn' came as part of the 1988 Education Reform Act, when 'English' and 'mathematics' became the home of literacy and numeracy, respectively. These two subjects were joined by science to become the core subjects within the school curriculum from 5–16 and were to have priority treatment alongside the range of 'foundation subjects'. Since that time literacy and numeracy have re-emerged as skill-oriented curriculum components, with their prescribed pedagogies in the primary school, through the development of the literacy and numeracy strategies that emerged during the period of transition from Conservative to New Labour government in 1997.

However, the purpose of this chapter is not to engage with that interesting history but rather to assess current developments and what they may tell us about what is likely to emerge in the future. In so doing we will also comment on the wider policy context from which it is unwise to separate the primary school curriculum. We will also indicate some aspects of future scenarios that are worthy of attention. In setting about these tasks we offer a review of some of the recent alternatives that have been offered in part as a critique of dominant curricular approaches. These include schools that have established alternative curricula, new approaches that are being promoted within maintained (and other) schools, as well as reviewing recent developments in home schooling.

There are two trajectories evident within recent curriculum reform: (1) a stronger focus on individual 'capacities' and the development of core transferable skills (rather than subject content); and (2) a discernible 'affective turn' evidenced in renewed interest in the management of emotions. These developments do not take place in a vacuum but are shaped by broader political, cultural and economic influences and by the shifting relative influence of social and 'psy' disciplines in education. The changes described above intersect with two broader influences on teachers' work: the re-configuration or 're-professionalising' of teachers' work in the last two decades, and the challenges presented by the perceived needs of an emergent 'knowledge society'. The potential for reform of the primary curriculum cannot be dislocated from these complex contextual factors.

In the following section, we consider the implications of the 'learning society' for the formal school curriculum and suggest that the erosion of the transmission model has opened spaces for deliberation over the curriculum. We chart renewed interest in alternative approaches through a variety of forms – commissioned research reviews and targeted funding of a variety of local and national initiatives. We consider how alternative ('progressive') approaches with a long lineage are 'mediated' or 'refracted' in the contemporary policy field. In particular we identify elements of 'travelling' curriculum policy and suggest ways in which some of the enduring themes of primary education are blended with new approaches to serve the specific needs of the contemporary context. We conclude by suggesting that the curriculum of the future is likely to be constrained by a concern with responding to the political imperatives of the present, not least an enduring emphasis on performance. Whilst we note that the resurgence of interest in aspects of alternative approaches is in part a growing acknowledgement of the limitations of curricular prescription – for either the professional development of teachers or the advancement of children's learning – we suggest that transferring ideas from one context of practice to another is not straightforward. In the process of policy diffusion a re-ordering takes place in which the demonstration of individual competence is valued more highly than the processes of dialogue and collaboration involved in the social construction of understanding – core concerns of alternative approaches.

From the late 1990s teaching has been subject to successive waves of reform, with an explicit focus on classroom practice. The re-positioning of the teacher as 'pedagogical technician' has resulted in an emphasis on the acquisition of technical competence measured by compliance with performance criteria in professional standards. This reduction of the teacher's role and erosion of the professional knowledge base of teaching leaves the profession vulnerable to external intervention. In the drive to raise standards through the identification of 'what works', central government has strengthened its influence and drawn on the 'expert' knowledge of a ready pool of 'policy entrepreneurs' (Ball 1994). The 'what works' agenda has increased teachers' and Local Authorities' attraction to the problem solving skills traded by educational consultants and trainers. One consequence of this commodification of professional knowledge is the conflation of the affective and the performative; a process that has been referred to elsewhere as the 'instrumentalisation of the expressive' (Hartley 2003; Zembylas 2006). A loose coupling between emotion management and performance improvement has emerged from the intersection of child-centered education in the primary sector and outcomes driven assessment in the post-primary phase. We argue here that the contemporary 'affective turn' creates a backwards glance to child-centered pedagogies and alternative education, but it does so in a field where the management of the expressive is harnessed to equip individuals with the emotional resilience to cope in a system driven by the imperative of the 'examination'. From this perspective the primary curriculum of the future remains inextricably influenced by the performative culture prevalent in secondary schooling.

A CURRICULUM FOR THE 'KNOWLEDGE ECONOMY'

The modernisation of the curriculum has been a focus of education reform internationally in recent years. The traditional 'grammars of schooling' (Tyack and Tobin 1994) – linear progression by age and stage, fixed conceptions of knowledge, primary emphasis on outcomes measurement – are challenged by the emergence of the new discourses of the 'learning society'. The self-programmable 'knowledge worker' (Castells 2000) of the new work order is ill-served by a prescriptive curriculum driven by credentialism. The shift from 'mode one' to 'mode two' knowledge production (Gibbons, Limoges and Nowotny 1994) requires a reconfiguration of the curriculum: a move away from residual notions of the curriculum as a body of static 'knowledge-content' transmitted by teachers to an emphasis on creative 'application-in-use' (Kress 2000). Transmission models of learning, built on assumptions of learner compliance and passivity, are unlikely to realise either sustained economic success, or the social and civic outcomes pursued through the social justice and inclusion agenda. The curriculum of the future will need to focus on the evolving 'capabilities' needed by learners if they are to develop employability skills, live enriched lives and participate actively in democratic life. A future-oriented curriculum would focus on 'learning for understanding' and require a move away from 'assessment careers' towards 'learning careers' (Ecclestone and Pryor 2003). This implies a difficult shift from 'strongly classified' and 'strongly framed' traditional school subjects (Bernstein 1971) towards greater content integration. In this model the identification of explicit core and cross-curricular themes becomes an important strategy in reducing fragmentation and promoting higher levels of integration. Operationalising curriculum reform in this direction would clearly require expanded opportunities for teacher co-operation and collaboration and an extended view of teacher professionalism.

There is some evidence of an incremental move towards re-engaging with the profession in meeting these challenges. In a review of forces for change in England, the Qualifications and Curriculum Authority (QCA) (2005) has argued that changes in society and the nature of work, combined with advances in technology and new understandings about learning, require a more responsive pedagogy with greater opportunities for the personalisation of learning. The QCA and the National College for School Leadership (NCSL) have subsequently embarked on a programme of research to explore the future of the curriculum in collaboration with sixty schools within the NCSL's Leadership Network.

In Scotland, the 'Schools of Ambition' programme is leading practitioner engagement with a Curriculum for Excellence. The programme provides feedback to the policy community via school-based enquiry groups working within a school-university research partnership. While at present this scheme is limited mainly to secondary schools, there are some indications of similar approaches being opened up in relation to primary schools.

Such a willingness to engage in professional dialogue with stakeholders may represent a wider move across the UK towards a partnership model of curriculum development in contrast to the centre-periphery dissemination model of the recent past. Participation is also encouraged through professional consultation exercises that have drawn on the expertise of practitioners, school leaders, local government officers, members of the inspectorate and curriculum and qualifications bodies through a variety of mechanisms including key informant interviews, focus groups, online surveys, conferences and workshops. Examples include the QCA e-consultation (May–July 2006) on the proposed changes to the Key Stage One programme of study for reading following the Rose Report (2006) in England; and the consultation on the new Framework for Achievement (FfA) in Northern Ireland (Council for the Curriculum Examinations and Assessment 2005) and the Curriculum Review in Scotland (Scottish Executive Education Department 2004).

In summary, even a cursory review of curriculum reform cross-nationally reveals a stronger emphasis on goal-orientation, content integration and the development of transferable skills within curriculum documents, and some evidence of a greater willingness to engage with stakeholders in shaping the direction of curriculum reform. Reid (2005: 66), writing from an Australian perspective, describes a movement from "'teaching for subjects' to teaching *through* subjects *for* capabilities". The Scottish response to this challenge is found in the articulation of the 'four capacities' in 'A Curriculum for Excellence' (ACfE): successful learners, responsible citizens, effective contributors and confident individuals. Beyond the UK, educational goals are increasingly framed in terms of 'essential learnings' or 'new basics'. This terminology is woven through policy documents relating to curriculum reform in Australia, Canada, Finland and New Zealand (Halinen 2005; Hipkins *et al.* 2005). Significantly, essential learnings in this context extend beyond a 'restorationist' focus on basic skills to embrace new approaches to teaching and learning, particularly the significance of the learning community.

TRAVELLING POLICY: INFLUENCES FROM NON–OFFICIAL ALTERNATIVE APPROACHES

In the following section we consider the possible contribution of non-official alternative approaches to the modernisation of the curriculum in light of the challenges suggested above. Alternative approaches share characteristics with the model of a 'future-oriented' curriculum and pose significant challenges to current practice in UK schools. While clearly drawing on diverse philosophical, theoretical and political traditions, alternative approaches share a resistance to the outcomes-based regimes of assessment that are found in mainstream compulsory education, focusing instead on the *processes* rather than the product of learning. Many alternative approaches cohere around a rejection of teacher-controlled whole-class teaching and a concern with the promotion of learner autonomy. A commitment to developing young children's capacity to think and reason is a core concern threaded through a range of approaches that emphasise critical and creative thinking and the development of personal autonomy. Equally, many non-official approaches pose a challenge to narrow constructions of learning as primarily a cognitive act. For example, Krechevsky and Stork (2000: 61) have argued that, 'schools of the future ... need to honor affective, aesthetic and moral forms of knowing as valid modes of inquiry that are on a par with, and closely tied to, scientific analysis'. Alternative approaches, such as those adopted in Steiner Waldorf and Montesorri schools, address 'physical, behavioural, emotional, cognitive, social and spiritual maturation' (Rawson and Richter 2000, cited by Woods and Woods 2006: 317).

In the following section three challenges to mainstream schooling presented by alternative approaches are identified and some of the implications of pursuing these developments are discussed:

- The move away from teaching for subjects
- The role of the teacher as lead learner
- The 'affective turn'.

The move away from teaching for subjects

Building on the work of Piaget, Reuven Feuerstein's Instrumental Enrichment (IE) programme is a 'cognitive active-modification approach' that aims to equip learners with the cognitive skills needed to adapt to their environment (Feuerstein *et al.* 1980). As the emphasis is on cognitive development, IE is deliberately free of subject specific content and offers a radical alternative to the content-based curriculum. It differs from other thinking skills approaches in the centrality afforded to the role of a mediator within a programme of active intervention. IE programmes are based on the notion of 'structural cognitive modifiability', the idea that intelligence is not fixed. Through the provision of Mediated Learning Experiences (MLE), an adult mediator regulates the stimuli that are available to a child in order to support the development of transferable problem solving skills (Head and O'Neill 1999). Through a series of structured interventions the child develops the skills of reflective thinking that enable them to assess and deal appropriately with day-to-day problems and challenges. The Feuersteinian approach to mediated learning emphasises the involvement of the teacher as active agent in the design of appropriate learning materials and the provision of developmental learning opportunities.

The role of the teacher is also central to alternative approaches that advocate 'dialogic teaching' with the goal of creating authentic communities of enquiry (Alexander 2006). Philosophy for Children ('P4C') is a systematic thinking skills programme used with children over an extended period, between the ages of six and sixteen. The programme, originally developed by Matthew Lipman (2003), consists of seven 'novels' with accompanying support materials and manuals for teachers. Core themes within the texts are re-visited throughout the programme to develop deeper understanding. The problem-solving stories enacted by the central characters within each text are used to scaffold class discussion. The teacher acts as facilitator, promoting thinking through the use of open-ended questions. Stimulus material is used to generate questions that are then shared with the whole class operating as a supportive community of enquiry (Trickey and Topping 2004). Discussions are recorded using graphic mapping to aid reflection and development. The role of the teacher is considered to be vital in creating and sustaining the conditions within which productive and creative discussion can take place. P4C highlights the role of dialogue in the development of reasoning.

Philosophy with Children (PwC) is a similar approach promoted in the UK for primary age children by Joanna Haynes and Karin Murris (Haynes 2001; Murris 2000). *Storywise: thinking through stories* uses picture books and video animations as stimulus material or 'triggers' to promote thinking in a developed version of 'circle time'. The role of a trained facilitator is very important in supporting the development of reasoned discussion rather than just the sharing of ideas. In this strategy a facilitator helps the children to focus on a particular issue and build on each others' contributions. Questions generated by the children during 'thinking time' are recorded on a flip chart and revisited during the discussion. In addition to verbal responses, children are encouraged to offer a visual response by drawing a picture of their thoughts. PwC is grounded on the belief that thinking skills cannot be developed through the 'delivery' of de-contextualised knowledge.

There are clear links between these approaches and the recent attention to thinking skills promoted in the maintained sector by generic initiatives such as Assessment for Learning, Learning How to Learn (James *et al.* 2007), Activating Children's Thinking

Skills (McGuiness 2000) and subject-based initiatives such as Cognitive Acceleration through Science Education (CASE), Cognitive Acceleration through Mathematics Education (CAME) and Cognitive Acceleration through Technology Education (CATE) (Adey, Shayer and Yates 1995) or Thinking Through Geography (Leat and Chandler 2001). Thinking skills are given explicit attention in the English National Curriculum, and assessment for learning is firmly embedded within official discourse such as *Excellence and Enjoyment: a strategy for primary schools* (DfES 2003) and the Scottish Assessment is for Learning (AifL) initiative. Additional stand-alone thinking skills courses are widely available to schools through organisations such as the Cognitive Research Trust, which draws on the work of Edward de Bono (1991) and include the Somerset Thinking Skills Course (Blagg *et al.* 1993) and strategies such as Top Ten Thinking Tactics (Lake and Needham 1993). A meta-analysis of twenty-nine studies that investigated the impact of thinking skills on pupils found a moderate positive impact and some subject variation. Greater gains were found among programmes supporting mathematics and science than in reading (Higgins *et al.* 2005).

A commitment to dialogic teaching and the encouragement of 'learning talk' in the classroom represents a significant challenge to the legacy of 'direct instruction' in UK schools. The principles of 'collectivity', 'reciprocity' and 'support' proposed by Alexander (2006: 34) require a commitment from teachers to a more risky social pedagogy and the confidence and skills to support collaborative problem solving among pupil groups. A DfES review of effective grouping indicates that successful collaboration requires dedicated training for teachers and pupils in interpersonal interaction (Kutnick *et al.* 2005). In the absence of training in group work skills, pupils may be organised in groups but fail to learn through collaboration. Effective grouping requires careful attention to group size, composition, challenge of task and pupil characteristics. A significant barrier to expanding opportunities for active engagement through collaborative learning is the persistence of whole class, teacher-centered teaching. There are clear professional development implications in carrying forward the espoused commitment to collaborative, co-operative and problem-based learning contained in the Scottish *Curriculum for Excellence* (Scottish Executive Education Department (SEED) 2004) and the reduction in individual working proposed in the English National Curriculum.

The role of the teacher as lead learner

Classroom relations within mainstream schools would need to be reconfigured to draw lessons from alternative approaches to schooling. Most alternative approaches present a significant challenge to the conventional role of the teacher in relation to children's learning, positioning the teacher clearly as facilitator/mediator and lead learner in a shared enquiry rather than information giver (Feuerstein *et al.* 1980). The orientation is primarily towards shared learning, rather than the testing of individuals. Steiner schools, the Reggio approach and the democratic schools movement, whilst very different, share a common concern with avoiding some of the negative consequences associated with hierarchical relations within mainstream compulsory schooling.

Amongst these other significant alternatives are Steiner-Waldorf schools which, while private in Britain, are state-funded in the Netherlands and receive an ad-mixture elsewhere. While still small in number[1] their curricular and pedagogical philosophy has been influential in both alternative schools and at the margins of mainstream schooling. While the curriculum may differ quite significantly in Steiner schools located in different countries, the underpinning principles of using play, colour and music as the context and the readiness of children for particular topics has some resonances with La Fayette[2] (see below). Such subjects as philosophy, geology, astronomy and history of architecture sit alongside the more standard fare of literacy and numeracy.

There are currently twenty-three independent Steiner-Waldorf schools in the UK. There are several contrasts between Steiner schools and the maintained sector. Although pupils do not take national tests at Key Stages, Steiner-Waldorf schools do cover National Curriculum subjects and prepare learners effectively for external examinations. Classes are not, however, structured on the basis of subjects but are broadly based using project work to develop a range of skills and competences. Steiner schools have an explicit commitment to helping students become independent thinkers and are attentive to emotional influences on readiness to learn ('willing'). Congruence is sought between pace of learning and natural rhythms rather than age and stage edicts. Woods *et al.* (2005: 6) identify 'rhythm, rituals, symbols and ceremony' as defining features of Steiner education. Significantly, administration is organised through a collegiate system rather than a management hierarchy, which is designed to encourage greater levels of collegiality (between staff and between staff and pupils). The Steiner teacher occupies the role of 'pedagogical co-leader' (Woods and Woods 2006). Whilst some aspects of Steiner philosophy present very significant challenges to official education policy, the attention to the professional learning community has become embedded within the literature on leadership. The first state sector Steiner school, the Hereford Waldorf School, achieved academy status in 2007. By contrast in Scotland, in a somewhat peculiar appendix to a 2002 Convention of Scottish Local Authorities (COSLA) Executive update, the petition to *The Public Petitions Committee* from the Edinburgh Steiner school to become state funded is rejected on the grounds that such schools don't offer a curriculum that cannot be offered in mainstream funded schools, but admits to having 'bought into' students in the same school "[...] for children with a range of special educational needs, very often at the severe and complex end of the spectrum and which did not easily fit in to 'mainstream' SEN provision".[3]

Close attention to participatory processes is also evident in the Reggio approach, which promotes learning in small groups of between two and six children. The attention in Reggio Emilia (pre-school) education to *how* children make meaning is in contrast to the outcomes orientation embedded in summative forms of assessment. The Reggio approach gives greater priority to the learning of adults than conventional approaches, and positions teachers as theory builders as well as curriculum implementers. This conception of theorising, agentic educators has relevance for the formation of professional development programmes for the maintained sector. Children and adults form a community of learners engaged in collective projects (Krechevsky and Stork 2000).

The democratic or free schools movement shares this concern with inclusiveness, participation and dialogue. There are only two such democratic schools currently active in the UK: Summerhill in Suffolk, founded by A.S. Neill, and the Sands School, Devon. The popular notion of school/student councils is drawn from free schools, although in the maintained sector councils lack the power to effect the real change that is a feature of school meetings in democratic schools (Taylor and Johnson 2002). Although pupils exert negligible influence on decision making in the maintained sector, much greater attention is now afforded to the pupil perspective and to children's rights (Rudduck and Flutter 2003). The increasing attention given to pupil 'voice' in evaluating interventions and the introduction of citizenship education as a school sub-ject (in England) reinforces the notion of pupils as stakeholders within school and within society.

The 'affective turn'

Recent work on emotional literacy and the development of caring thought (as exem-plified within Philosophy for Children) draws attention to the affective domain in sup-port of learning and the promotion of responsible citizenship. There has been a great deal of attention focused on children's emotional literacy, emotional well-being and emotional resilience in policy circles in recent years. Sharp (2001: 1) defines emotional literacy as 'the ability to recognise, understand, handle and appropriately express emotions.' Much of this attention has been predicated on concerns around behaviour management in schools. Renewed interest in the affective domain has developed con-currently with the use of sanctions contained in the *Anti Social Behaviour Act* (2003) and the use of voluntary Parenting Contracts and civil Parenting Orders (DfES 2004). In 2002 the DfES commissioned a review of how children's emotional and social competence and well-being could most effectively be developed at a national and local level. The report by Weare and Gray (2003) recommended a holistic, whole school approach and the development of explicit teaching and learning programmes and cur-riculum guidance to support schools in this area. In June 2005 the DfES responded by circulating the Social and Emotional Aspects of Learning toolkit (SEAL), a curriculum resource to support the development of pupils' social and behavioural skills.

The enhancement of self-esteem or self-worth has long been a central tenet of primary education in UK schools. Self-esteem is associated with having the 'confidence to act' (Cigman 2001), feeling competent or possessing optimistic beliefs regarding self-efficacy. Many contemporary initiatives draw on the 'positive psychology' advanced by Martin Seligman (1990, 1995) in his work on 'the optimistic child'. There has been an expan-sion of interest in esteem within strategies to tackle exclusion, disaffection and under-achievement. Mental health professionals and psychotherapists have become the 'cultural retailers' of the self-esteem concept (Slater 2002) and trainers have engaged in lucrative 'policy entrepreneurship' (Ball 1994), advancing the merits of interventionist strategies to repair an 'esteem deficit'. The self-esteem movement developed from early interventions in the USA, such as the California Task Force, to promote self esteem and personal and social responsibility (Cruickshank 1999; California State Department of Education 1990). It is championed in the UK through commercial companies such as the Pacific Institute and Learning Unlimited. Following the discussion paper *Con-fidence in Scotland* (Scottish Executive 2005), the Glasgow-based Centre for Confidence and Well-Being, directed by Carol Craig, received £750,000 over three years (2004–7) to promote positive attitudes, confidence, individuality, creativity, innovation and well-being. Some of the discourse makes its way into funded national developments in Scotland such as Assessment is for Learning (AifL), and thence to the newly developing *Curriculum for Excellence 3–18*, which aims to take AifL as a model for implementation.

In both the USA and UK concerns have been voiced about these developments by commentators in higher education (Baumeister *et al.* 2003; Emler 2001) and in the media (Toynbee 2001; Slater 2002). Ecclestone (2004), drawing on Furedi's (1997, 2004) 'fear thesis', has expressed concern over the rise of a 'therapeutic pedagogy' which aims to 'empower' less confident learners to overcome (self-imposed) barriers to the achievement of learning goals. Fineman (2000) has pointed to the commodification of 'emotional intelligence' (EI) as a newly constructed competence to be traded by trainers. Research conducted by Emler (2001) found that low self-esteem was damaging to the individual, but did not promote anti-social behaviour. He also questions the positive relationship that is often assumed between self-esteem and academic attainment; arguing that both high and low achievers mediate results according to pre-existing views of themselves. Emler concludes that therapeutic approaches to tackle the self esteem deficit are little more than 'snake oil remedies.' Other writers have adopted a governmentality perspective and suggested that the self-esteem movement proceeds from a deficit model in which targets of intervention need to be worked upon to encourage 'care of the self', to re-make themselves as virtuous self-regulating subjects. Helsby and Knight (1998: 6) argue that the notion of empowerment here is one which 'appears to value atomized, technique-centred empowerment of execution, rather than holistic, critically-aware empowerment of conception'.

> Self esteem ... has much more to do with self-assessment than with self-respect, as the self continuously has to be measured, judged and disciplined in order to gear personal 'empowerment' to collective yardsticks ... a forever precarious harmony ... has to be forged between the political goals of the state and a personal 'state of esteem'.
>
> (Lemke 2001: 202)

The coupling of the affective with the performative is illustrated in the pervasive use of target setting to raise standards in mainstream schooling. Target setting is an integral aspect of the school improvement cycle. Measurable performance targets for age-related performance are monitored against performance outcomes at Key Stages and National Curriculum levels. The purpose of target setting is to encourage self-responsibility by moving from what has been achieved at a particular point in time (measurement), to what *can* be achieved in the future (enhancement). There has been a discernable shift from reliance on summative assessment towards a much stronger focus on formative and ipsative assessment. This is premised on the belief that dispositions to learning are not fixed but can be altered with appropriate feedback from skilled teachers (Black *et al.* 2003; Hayward *et al.* 2004). The self-monitoring of attainment operates at the level of overall pupil performance between institutions (for example, national comparisons using the Pupil Achievement Tracker), between teachers in the same institution, between pupils in the same classes to ipsative assessment of individual progress over time. By attending to the affective, a narrative unfolds in which it is possible to fail constructively; a process of 'failing forwards'. The skilled educator supports the learner in building emotional resilience and developing reflective self-esteem. Cigman (2001: 573) offers a composite of the 'good failure' who is 'motivated to struggle, to tolerate pain', and for whom '"I can" is supplemented (not as a prediction but as an intention) by "I will"'. From this perspective, educational failure is reconfigured as a problem of 'self-care'.

EDUCATIONAL ALTERNATIVES

As we suggest above, alternative provision has been and continues to be an enduring feature of British education, as indeed it is of other polities (most especially the United

States and Canada). Some of this has been controversial, with schools such as Summerhill having been subjected to substantial scrutiny. The continued existence and, more importantly the very significant growth of these alternatives (Davies *et al.* 2002), despite successive legislative encroachments, is testament to the maintenance of certain liberal impulses alongside the enduring strength of will which continues to motivate those who propose, sustain, support and make use of them. Of course there are other impulses governing the decisions of some parents to opt out of mainstream state and private provision which are more likely to be grounded in the negative emotions of fear. There are those (Ball 2003; Power *et al.* 2003) who see this drift as occasioned by the drive of middle class parents to seek positional advantage in an increasingly competitive era. But this is not a sufficient explanation for the many who clearly lack consumerist and political ambitions. As Davies *et al.* (2002) point out, while motivations vary, one set of issues is the sustainability and integrity of the family unit. Another sustaining factor is likely to be the existence in developed economies of a vast army of university-educated parents. Clearly the drivers of alternative provision are diverse. For some it is the claim that schools as institutions are not conducive to the developmental welfare of children; for others, the curriculum has become too rigid; for yet a third group there is a belief that the curriculum is insufficiently demanding. Each of these broad scripts embodies other sub-texts some of which would appear to be in conflict. For example, in the case of those who think that developmental welfare is the issue, some will argue that both curriculum and the governing rubrics are too harsh; for others they are too loose, failing to nurture substantial moral and intellectual character.

Still influential in the world of alternative curriculum are the writings of Rousseau and Dewey, as well as the children's rights inflected theories of John Holt (1983) who claims that late industrial forms of education stultify children's creativity and undermine their energies for learning. Children, Holt argues, should be much more self-determining with regard to the curriculum, pursuing those things which they find interesting. The underpinning belief here is that their 'natural' love of learning will not be undermined by having foisted upon them an education which in both style and content is constraining and ultimately alienating. These ideas find particular resonance in the growing number of private small schools. One of the most interesting and instructive examples from a curriculum development perspective is the Fayette Street Academy in Santa Fe, New Mexico (Chamberlain 2001),[4] which combines a profoundly child-centred and structurally informal approach with the study of a classical curriculum including, even in the elementary curriculum, consideration of classical languages and engagement with algebra, not to mention the continued use of traditional texts such as the McGuffy reader! Even more interesting is the way in which the texts are used to help students explore social and historical conditions and the attitudes that both inform and issue out of these. Moreover, in a world which has become simultaneously risk averse and deeply anxious that children do not play enough and take enough exercise, Fayette Street offers a robust outdoors environment.

Home schooling

What distinguishes what we might call these 'small schools' from mainstream state funded education is altogether more complicated than simply being a desire for an alternative curriculum. Rather, the distinction tends to centre on the belief that the more subtle environment and more comprehensive balance of the academic, practical and artistic is more carefully modulated than in mainstream schooling. Moreover, such approaches have become quite a significant shaper of certain strands in home school-ing. It is not long since home schooling or home education was considered the domain of two discrete groups. First, those who partook in the lifestyle and ambitions of advanced industrial democracies but who, for geographical or logistical reasons could not take advantage of formal communal schooling. Second, there are those who had, often for religious reasons, withdrawn from socio-political engagement. The Bob Jones University Press Testing and Evaluation Service[5] provides the largest home school testing service in the United States. Given its provenance as a robustly conservative religious institute this offers at least some indirect or circumstantial evidence of the motive power of religion in the early drive for home schooling. Both the numbers opting for home schooling and the range of motivations of those wishing to do so have expanded considerably in recent years. One substantial and growing group is comprised of those who have abandoned formal schooling because they believe it to be too con-strained by the imperatives of performativity, and the curriculum limitations imposed on the cultivation of the imagination in consequence thereof. In this group are parents who wish to see a greater emphasis on cultural and aesthetic engagements as well as those who want to see the world brought into learning in an unselfconscious way. What many home schooling families share across their political, religious and cultural dif-ferences (and indeed something shared with small school movements) is a significant emphasis on engagement with story. Moreover, there are many home school resource providers who offer curriculum materials that meet nationally determined targets. Most are values-based, some are professional and others emerge out of co-operative associations of home school organisations such as *Education Otherwise* in the UK[6] and *A to Z Home's Cool* in the US.[7]

Much of this material does not differ markedly from that to be found in the majority of state-funded primary or elementary schools. At this stage and given the growth in such alternatives as home schooling we might wish to explore some of the lessons to be garnered from its curriculum and pedagogic practices which might, in turn, inform more general questions about the shape and content of any putative future primary curriculum. But such lessons as there are may not be predicated on the growth of home schooling per se. Rather, if such provision makes a positive difference to children's achievement, there may be something to be learned in re-thinking a curriculum of and for the future. Such an enquiry is likely to begin by asking the basic question, 'do children educated in such environments significantly out-perform those in regular public and private schools irrespective of the curriculum adopted?' It is to this we now turn.

In the midst of the many differences in philosophy, outlook and practice of home schoolers, from those who follow the national curriculum pretty rigidly to those whose approach makes Summerhill seem like a model of mainstream pedagogical rectitude, home schooling appears to consistently offer children a more efficacious educational experience even as measured by the standards of normative performativity. One con-stant in the midst of much complexity is the better than average performance of home schooled children when compared to age cohorts in the general population. Rudner's (1998) study illustrated that those in grades 1–4 who are educated at home, on average, perform one grade level higher than their public and private school counterparts. Lest this be thought of as an effect of early nurture likely to dissipate later in the child's edu-cational development, it is striking that the performance gap expands as the student progresses so that by 8th grade such children are performing at four grades above the national average in the US.

Of course interpreting such outstanding performance is not uncomplicated and there are a range of pertinent factors apart from curriculum choice, not least of which is that in this study home schooled children typically come from families with relatively high incomes (although interestingly not very high), family stability and a strong commitment to education. Welner and Welner (1999) urge some caution in over-interpreting the performance gap; arguing that many of the students, by Rudner's own admission, come from families with slightly above mean national income. It is not clear how pupils from such backgrounds would have fared against the mean had they been educated within state or private schools or that home schooling is axiomatically superior. Nonetheless, and with rare exceptions, studies of home schooled children show clear and substantial evidence of high (and above average) performance (Ray 2000). Indeed, Rothermel's (2004) more recent study would suggest that students from lower socio-economic groups relatively outperform middle class peers. One reason for this, she suggests, is that children from poor socio-economic backgrounds who are home schooled are free from the stigma of poverty in the public space. Importantly she argues that while early intervention and pre-school attendance is increasingly seen as the future (on the basis of the Effective Provision of Pre-School Education Project, Sylva *et al.* 2004) that sample cohort was selected with a bias towards the 'under-privileged' and the sample did not include those intending to home school.

CONCLUSION

There are several salient features of the home schooling paradigm which may be of interest when considering the shaping of the curriculum into and for the future. These include a recognition that both television and computer use in home schooled environments was seen to be much lower than national patterns. In an educational and political climate which suggests that the future shape of the curriculum is likely to be dictated by shifts in technology (Hargreaves 1997) it is at least clear that having only moderate access to technologies is unlikely to be injurious to a child's educational attainment. Arguably, the reverse is the case so it may be that the imagined primary curriculum into the future need be rather less reliant on technology than the rhetoric would have us believe. A second consideration for curriculum development is whether or not the fashion for meta-cognitive exercises, which we have detailed earlier, need be as robustly sustained as is presently the case. Rather, reading would appear to be a more salient and potent educational stratagem. In this sense we might argue that we wish to go 'back to the future'. Perhaps more important than either of these is the clear intimation that what is at stake here is flexibility. What the growth of educational alternatives, from Reggio schools to home schools, amply demonstrates is that there is no single account of the effective curriculum. There are available a wide range of approaches which may need to be more carefully considered with respect to each child. In the structured and resource constrained environment of a public (or for that matter private) school, compromises are necessary but flexibility may need to represent the heart of any developments if we are to fit children to their own educational and developmental project while simultaneously recognising that public education (of both state and private varieties) represents not only individual achievement but the common good. Moreover, the experience of alternative forms of schooling would appear to go some way in vindicating our opening remarks that what appears to be emerging in mainstream curriculum thinking is indeed a stronger emphasis on individual capacities and a more significant focus on the affective.

Skills in literacy and numeracy and the ability to use available technologies to support those skills are likely to remain at the centre of the primary school curriculum for the foreseeable future. But the context within which those skills are developed may increasingly be one where the conventional organisation of knowledge is less important than ensuring that children become confident and independent learners. Thus it may be that curricular elements are increasingly determined at a local and regional level, with teachers and pupils themselves playing a significant part in their determination, thus ensuring that these young learners are developing experience of responsibilities for decision making and for collaborating with their peers and with adults. Such a curriculum would reflect diversity and the lived histories and geographies of the multiple communities which young people today find themselves to be a part of. If primary school is indeed a preparation for secondary education, then it is crucial that the primary students make that transition into secondary as prepared as possible to learn further and to act as a citizen of that particular community who can contribute to his or her own development and welfare as well as that of others.

NOTES

1 Currently around 894 worldwide.
2 See http://www.timsellers.net/steinerhomeschooling/thegradeyears.html
3 See http://www.cosla.gov.uk/attachments/execgroups/ed/edapr02item8.doc
4 It is interesting that the title, *The Heart of the Matter*, is the same as a 1995 discussion paper published by the then Scottish consultative Council for the Curriculum on education for personal and social development which emphasises culture and ethos as the foundational condition for effective learning.
5 See http://www.bjupress.com/
6 See http://www.education-otherwise.org/
6 See http://homeschooling.gomilpitas.com/

REFERENCES

Adey, P.S., Shayer, M. and Yates, C. (1995) *Thinking Science: the curriculum materials of the CASE Project*. London: Thomas Nelson and Sons.
Alexander, R.J. (2006) Towards Dialogic Teaching. York: Dialogos.
Ball, S.J. (1994) *Education Reform: a critical & post-structural approach*. Buckingham: Open University Press.
——(2003) *Class Strategies and the Education Market*. London: RoutledgeFalmer.
Baumeister, R.F., Campbell, J.D., Krueger, J.I. and Vohs, K.D. (2003) 'Does high self-esteem cause better performance, interpersonal success, happiness, or healthier lifestyles?', *Psychological Science in the Public Interest* 4: 1–44.
Bernstein, B. (1971) 'On the classification and framing of educational knowledge', in M.F.D. Young (Ed) *Knowledge and Control*. London: Collier-Macmillan.
Black, P., Harrison, C., Lee, C., Marshall, B. and Wiliam, D. (2003) *Assessment for Learning: putting it into practice*. Maidenhead: Open University Press.
Blagg, N.R., Lewis, R.E. and Ballinger, M.P. (1993) *Thinking and Learning at Work: a report on the development and evaluation of the thinking skills at work modules*. Sheffield: Department of Employment.
'Brain Gym' website: www.braingym.org/index.html (Accessed 10.12.07).

428   *James Conroy, Moira Hulme and Ian Menter*

CACE (1967) *Children and Their Primary Schools: a report of the Central Advisory Council for Education (England)*(the Plowden Report). London: HMSO.

California State Department of Education (1990) *Toward a State of Esteem: the final report of the California Task Force to promote self-esteem and personal and social responsibility.* Berkeley, CA: California State Department of Education.

Castells, M. (2000) 'Materials for an exploratory theory of the network society', *British Journal of Sociology* 51: 5–24.

Chamberlain, J. (2001) *The Heart of the Matter: diary of a school year.* Santa Fe, NM: Ginger Plum Press.

Cigman, R. (2001) 'Self-esteem and the confidence to fail', *Journal of Philosophy of Education* 35 (4): 561–76.

Council for the Curriculum Examinations and Assessment (2005) *Equality Impact Assessment on Reforming Qualifications and Promoting Learning for the 21st Century: a consultation on the development of a new framework for achievement.* Belfast: Council for the Curriculum Examinations and Assessment.

Cruickshank, B. (1999) *The Will to Empower: democratic citizens and other subjects.* Ithaca: Cornell University Press.

Davies, S., Aurini, J. and Quirke, L. (2002) 'New markets for private education in Canada', *Education Canada* 29(3): 39–42.

De Bono, E. (1991) *Teaching Thinking.* London: Penguin Books.

Ecclestone, K. (2004) 'Learning or therapy? The demoralisation of education', *British Journal of Educational Studies* 52(2): 112–37

Ecclestone, K. and Pryor, J. (2003) '"Learner careers" or "assessment careers"? The impact of assessment systems on learning', *British Educational Research Journal* 29(4): 471–88.

Emler, N. (2001) *Self-esteem: the costs and causes of low self-worth.* York: Joseph Rowntree Foundation.

Feuerstein, R., Rand, Y., Hoffman, M.B. and Miller, R. (1980) *Instrumental Enrichment: an intervention programme for cognitive modifiability.* Baltimore: Baltimore University Press.

Fineman, S. (2000) 'Commodifying the emotionally intelligent', in S. Fineman (Ed) *Emotion in Organizations* (2nd edition). London: Sage.

Furedi, F. (1997) *Culture of Fear: risk-taking and the morality of low expectation.* London: Cassell.

——(2004) *Therapy Culture: cultivating vulnerability in an uncertain age.* London: Routledge.

Gibbons, M., Limoges, C., Nowotny, H., Schwartzman, S., Scott, P. and Trow, M. (1994) *The New Production of Knowledge: the dynamics of science and research in contemporary societies.* London: Sage.

Halinen, I. (2005) *The Finnish Curriculum Development Processes, Finland in PISA-studies.* Online (Available: http://www.oph.fi/info/pisahelsinki/lectures/irmeli%20halinen.doc, accessed 15 May 2006).

Hargreaves, D. (1997) 'Education', in G. Mulgan (Ed) *Life After Politics.* London: Fontana.

Hartley, D. (2003) 'The instrumentalisation of the expressive in education', *British Journal of Educational Studies* 51(1): 6–19.

Haynes, J. (2001) *Children as Philosophers: learning through enquiry and dialogue in the primary classroom.* London: Routledge.

Hayward, L., Priestley, M. and Young, M. (2004). 'Ruffling the calm of the ocean floor: merging practice, policy and research in Assessment in Scotland', *Oxford Review of Education* 30(3): 397–416.

Head, G. and O'Neill, W. (1999) 'Introducing Feuerstein's Instrumental Enrichment in a school for children with social, emotional and behavioural difficulties', *Support for Learning* 14(3): 122–28.

Helsby, G. and Knight, P. (1998) 'Preparing students for the new work order: the case of Advanced General National Vocational Qualifications', *British Educational Research Journal* 24(1): 63–79.

Higgins, S., Hall, E., Baumfield, V. and Moseley, D. (2005) *A Meta-Analysis of the Impact of the Implementation of Thinking Skills Approaches on Pupils*. London: EPPI-Centre, Social Science Research Unit, Institute of Education, University of London.

Hipkins, R. and Vaughan, K. (2005) *Shaping our Futures: meeting secondary students' learning needs in a time of evolving qualifications. Final report of the Learning Curves project*. Wellington. New Zealand Council for Educational Research.

Holt, J. (1983) *How Children Learn*. London: Penguin.

James, M., McCormick, R., Black, P., Carmichael, P., Drummond, M.-J., Fox, A., Frost, D., MacBeath, J., Marshall, B., Pedder, D., Procter, R., Swaffield, S. and Wiliam, D. (2007) Improving *Learning How to Learn*: classrooms, schools and networks. London: Routledge.

Krechevsky, M. and Stork, J. (2000) 'Challenging educational assumptions: lessons from an Italian-American collaboration', *Cambridge Journal of Education* 30(1): 57–74.

Kress, G. (2000) 'A curriculum for the future', *Cambridge Journal of Education* 30(1): 133–45.

Kutnick, P., Sebba, J., Blatchford, P., Galton, M. and Thorp, J., with MacIntyre, H. and Berdondini, L. (2005) *The Effects of Pupil Groupings: literature review* (DfES Research Report 688). London: DfES.

Lake, M. and Needham, M. (1993) *Top Ten Thinking Tactics*. Birmingham: Questions Publishing Company.

Leat, D. and Chandler, S. (2001) *Thinking Through Geography*. London: Chris Kington Publishing.

Lemke, T. (2001) 'The birth of biopolitics: Michel Foucault's lecture at the Collège de France on neo-liberal governmentality', *Economy and Society* 30(2): 190–207.

Lipman, M. (2003) *Thinking in Education* (2nd edition). Cambridge: Cambridge University Press.

Long, F. (2005) 'Thomas Reid and philosophy with children', *Journal of Philosophy of Education* 39(4): 599–614.

McGuinness, C. (1998) *From Thinking Skills to Thinking Classrooms: a review and evaluation of approaches for developing pupils' thinking*. Nottingham: DfEE.

McGuinness, C. (2000) *Activating Children's Thinking Skills, GTCNI – Access to research resources for teachers*. Online (Available: http://demo.openrepository.com/gtcni/handle/2428/7566, accessed 10.12.07).

Murris, K. (2000) 'Can children do philosophy?', *Journal of Philosophy of Education* 34(2): 261–79.

Power, S., Edwards, T., Whitty, G. and Wigfall, V. (2003) *Education and the Middle Class*. Buckingham: Open University Press.

Qualifications and Curriculum Authority (QCA) (2005) *A Curriculum for the Future*. London: QCA.

Ray, B. (2000) 'Home Schooling: the ameliorator of negative influences on learning?', *Peabody Journal of Education* 75(1).

Reid, A. (2005) *Rethinking National Curriculum Collaboration: towards an Australian curriculum*. Canberra: Department of Education, Science and Training.

Rose, J. (2006) *Independent Review of the Teaching of Early Reading. Final report* (the Rose Review). London: DfES.

Rothermel, P. (2004) 'Home education: comparison of home-and school-educated children on PIPS baseline assessment', *Journal of Early Childhood Research* 2(3): 273–99.

Rudduck, J. and Flutter, J. (2003) *How to Improve Your School: giving pupils a voice*. London: Continuum Press.

Rudner, L.M. (1998) 'Scholastic achievement and demographic characteristics of home school students in 1998', *Education Policy Analysis Archives* 7(8). Online (Available: http://epaa.asu.edu/epaa/v7n8/, accessed 4 August 2007).

Scottish Executive Education Department (SEED) (2004) *A Curriculum for Excellence*. Edinburgh: Scottish Executive Education Department.

SEED (2005) *Confidence in Scotland: discussion paper*. Edinburgh: Scottish Executive.

Seligman, M. (1990) *Learned Optimism*. New York: Knopf.

——(1995) *The Optimistic Child*. New York: Harper Collins.

Sharp, P. (2001) *Nurturing Emotional Literacy*. London: David Fulton.

Slater, L. (2002) 'The trouble with self-esteem', *New York Times*, 03.02.02, Section 6, 44–47.

Sylva, K., Melhuish, E.C., Sammons, P., Siraj-Blatchford, I. and Taggart, B. (2004) *The Effective Provision of Pre-School Education (EPPE) Project:* Technical Paper 12 – The Final Report: Effective Pre-School Education. London: DfES/ Institute of Education, University of London.

Taylor, M. with Johnson, R. (2002) *School Councils: their role in citizenship and personal and social education*. Slough: NFER.

Toynbee, P. (2001) 'At last we can abandon that tosh about low self esteem: the psychobabblers' snake-oil remedies have been exposed as a sham', 28.12.08, London: *The Guardian*.

Trickey, S. and Topping, K.J. (2004) 'Philosophy for children: a systematic review', *Research Papers in Education* 19(3): 365–80.

Tyack, D. and Tobin, W. (1994) 'The grammar of schooling: why has it been so hard to change?', *American Educational Research Journal* 31(3): 453–80.

Weare, K. and Gray, G. (2003) *What Works in Developing Children's Emotional and Social Competence and Wellbeing?* Research Report 456. London: DfES.

Welner, K.M. and Welner, K.G. (1999) 'Contextualizing home schooling data: a response to Rudner', *Education Policy Analysis Archives* 7(13).

Woods, P., Ashley, M. and Woods, G. (2005) *Steiner Schools in England* (Research Report RR645/RB645). London: DfES.

Woods, P.A. and Woods, G.J. (2006) 'In harmony with the child: the Steiner teacher as co-leader in a pedagogical community', *Forum* 48(3): 317–25.

Zembylas, M. (2006) 'Challenges and possibilities in a postmodern culture of emotions in education', *Interchange* 37(3): 251–75.

Part 5

Outcomes, standards and assessment in primary education

We come now to three research surveys which, when first published as interim reports of the Cambridge Primary Review in November 2007, stirred up a hornet's nest of controversy, provoked heated television confrontations between our authors and government ministers, and propelled the Review to the top of the UK news story league table. All this demonstrated pretty convincingly that England's system of national testing may be 'high stakes' for children and teachers but the stakes for its political masters are higher still. After all, New Labour's first Secretary of State for Education said he would resign if the 2002 targets for literacy and numeracy were not met. They were not, but as by then he had moved to another department his successor had to resign instead.

The controversy persisted: the House of Commons Children, Schools and Families Committee launched its own inquiry into assessment and testing; in 2008 the Government rejected that inquiry's key findings and recommendations; and the year was crowned by the ignominious near-disintegration of the system for marking the test papers of children in their final year of primary schooling. Meanwhile, standards, tests and testing rarely left the headlines.

The research surveys in this section arose from questions posed as part of Cambridge Primary Review Themes 4 (*Quality and Standards*) and 3 (*Curriculum and Assessment*). They were particularly concerned with the national and international evidence on primary pupils' attainment, over time and by comparison with other countries; and with the form, impact and use of the assessment procedures through which such evidence is collected.

Quality and standards

- How good is English primary education?
- How consistent is it across the country as a whole?
- Have standards risen or fallen?
- How do they compare with those of other countries?
- How should 'standards' and 'quality' be defined for this phase?
- How should they be assessed?
- What is the available range of national and international evidence on these matters? How reliable is it?
- How well, and how appropriately, is it used?

Assessment

- How should children's progress and attainment be assessed during the primary phase?
- What is the proper relationship and balance of assessment for learning and assessment for accountability?
- What are the strengths and weaknesses of current approaches to assessment, both national and local?
- What assessment information should be reported, and to whom?
- What is the most helpful balance of national and local in curriculum and assessment?

Standards and Quality in English Primary Schools Over Time: the national evidence, by Peter Tymms and Christine Merrell (Chapter 17), and *Standards in English Primary Education: the international evidence*, by Chris Whetton, Graham Ruddock and Liz Twist (Chapter 18), examine evidence on the vital question of what has happened to standards of pupil achievement in English primary schools over time. While, in the context of a wider analysis, Chapter 17 focuses on the national evidence on attainment in mathematics and reading over time, Chapter 18 considers such evidence as is available on how English primary pupils compare with those from other countries. As new evidence is published, of course, the picture changes. The two surveys also assess the reliability of the evidence on which claims about national and comparative educational standards are based.

In *The Quality of Learning: assessment alternatives for primary education* (Chapter 19), Wynne Harlen considers assessment processes as well as outcomes. She reviews research on the forms and systems of assessment through which national standards are monitored, and the uses which are made of assessment results. She compares assessment systems in England with those in several other countries, raises questions about their validity, reliability and impact, and proposes radical changes to the way assessment is conceived, undertaken and used at the primary stage.

Each of these research surveys was independently conceived and undertaken, and it will be seen that care has been taken to look at the same undeniably contentious issues from different perspectives: national evidence compared with international; claims about test outcomes set carefully against examination of how far the testing procedures meet internationally accepted standards by which the reliability of such outcomes may themselves be judged; the imperative of public accountability weighed against the imperative of a rounded education; conventional political wisdom on the inevitability of high stakes testing compared with arguments for a rather different approach to assessment which is embedded in teaching rather than detached from it, and focuses on learning rather than accountability while not denying the need for the latter. For, as Wynne Harlen notes in Chapter 19, it is teaching, not testing, which 'drives up standards.' This simple but obvious truth is too often ignored.

Together, these three chapters raise important educational and political questions about procedures for assessing the performance of both pupils and their primary schools which were initiated by the Conservative governments of 1979–97 and were consolidated by the New Labour administrations of 1997–2009. Their findings, contrary to the sensationalising newspaper headlines of November 2007, were mixed.

Positive findings from the research surveys

- The essential stability of England's system of primary education over time (Chapter 17).
- Primary pupils' generally positive attitude towards their learning in the tested areas (though this appears to decline with age) (Chapter 17).
- From the national data: modest improvements in standards in primary mathematics over time, especially since 1995 (Chapter 17).
- From the international data: big improvements in primary mathematics from TIMSS 1995 to TIMSS 2003 (Chapter 18).
- From the international data: considerable improvements in primary science by comparison with other countries (Chapter 18).
- From the international data: high standards in reading skills among English primary pupils by comparison with those from other countries (Chapter 18).

Less positively, the surveys reveal

- The limited impact of the government's National Literacy Strategy, introduced in 1998, on readings standards since then (Chapter 17).
- Gains in reading skills at the expense of pupils' enjoyment of reading (Chapter 18).
- Increases in test-induced stress among primary pupils, and in pressure on their teachers (Chapter 17).
- A narrowing of the primary curriculum in response to the perceived demands of the testing regime (Chapter 17).
- The persistence of a much bigger gap between high and low attaining English pupils in reading, mathematics and science than in many other countries (Chapter 18).

The research surveys raise important methodological and procedural questions, for example

- The generally low level of dependability of the current national system of assessment in England (Chapter 19).
- The apparently misleading nature of the apparent dramatic improvements at Key Stage 2 between 1995 and 2000 (Chapter 17).
- A tendency to define 'standards' at the primary stage by reference to an excessively narrow range of educational outcomes (Chapter 17).
- The thinness of evidence about how English primary pupils compare with those from other countries (Chapter 18).

The research surveys question certain tenets of post-1997 government policy

- In terms of standards, the returns on a massive investment of public money in national strategies appear to be negligible for primary literacy and relatively modest for primary numeracy (Chapter 17; see also Chapter 29).
- Evidence does not support the claim that testing of itself 'drives up standards' (Chapter 19).

On the basis of the evidence examined the research surveys propose that

- Accountability of individual schools should be based not merely on pupil performance in the KS1 and KS2 tests but on the full contribution which the schools make to their pupils' education (Chapters 17 and 19).
- National standards of pupil achievement should be monitored through regular sample surveys which draw on a large bank of test items, rather than by the KS1 and KS2 tests (Chapter 19), and the process should be independent (Chapter 17).
- Greater use should be made of teacher judgement in the summative assessment of individual pupils (Chapter 19).
- The overall balance of assessment should be shifted away from testing and targets, because properly conceived and conducted formative assessment has greater impact than summative on the quality of pupil learning (Chapter 19).
- Policies and strategies in the domain of quality and standards should be more closely tied to the research evidence and should be more rigorously trialled and evaluated (Chapter 17).
- The research agenda relating to quality and standards in primary education should become both broader and more focused; more detailed information is needed on a broader range of educational outcomes (Chapter 17).

17 Standards and quality in English primary schools over time

The national evidence

Peter Tymms and Christine Merrell

INTRODUCTION

As the title indicates, this chapter is concerned with standards in primary education and it is as well at the outset to be clear about what we mean by that. The word can take on more than one interpretation. On the one hand, standards can be thought of as a level against which one tries to make a judgement. In high jumping terms that would be the height of the bar and the observations of individuals trying to jump over it. In educational terms it would involve ascertaining how many people met or exceeded a certain criterion; but another way of looking at standards is to take them as the level that one has reached. How high can an individual jump? It is that way of thinking about standards which is used in this chapter.

Educational standards and judgements about the quality of those standards can be approached by starting with a description of children. Such an approach might begin with what pupils know and can do when they start primary education, and then be followed with a description of how this progresses as they age. It might also include how their perceptions and attitudes change, as well as other variables. The educationalist can then be left to come to his or her own judgements about quality. Some may argue that the process of schooling is a vital part of quality and that standards and quality should be judged against processes. They would be quite right in pointing to processes as being at the heart of education but in the last analysis, in order to assess that quality, one must look at impact and therefore at change in children. And, of course, anyone's judgement about quality must involve making decisions, explicitly or implicitly, about what standards are expected or appropriate in order to decide whether what is seen is good or poor. In fact, whenever one makes judgements about quality or standards one makes them against a reference point. There will always be a comparison. This might be a comparison of change over time, or against other countries, other schools or against personal expectations, but the judgements are always comparative.

What might a description of what children know and can do when they start school look like? Figure 17.1 is taken from a study of Scottish children starting school (Merrell and Tymms 2007) and provides a graphical illustration of what we have in mind. It shows both the distribution of pupils and their abilities on the same scale. The enormous variation is apparent and differences between sexes, in social background, and other groupings readily follow. In the longer term it also becomes possible to take such a description and show how what children know and can do changes as they progress through their primary years. The parallel chart for England is almost identical once the half-year difference in the age of starting school is taken into account. However, the

Logits	Distribution of Children		Map of Items	Difficult
6		+	42 -17=?	
		|		
		|	What is 21 more than 32?	
		|		
5	|	+	What is 8 more than 13? What is a quarter of 8?	
	|	|		
	|	|	15+21=?	
	|	|	What is half of six?	
4	|	+		
	|	|	9-6=?	
	|	|	7+3=?	
	|	|		
3	|	+	What is 3 more than 8?	
	|	|	Point to some cosmetic.	
	|	|		
	|#	|	Read simple sentences, e.g. "The cat went for a walk".	
2	|##	+	Identify several two-digit numbers.	
	|###	|	Read high-frequency words e.g. dog, tree.	
	|####	|	Point to a capital letter.	
	|######	|		
1	|########	+		
	|#########	|	Point to a microscope.	
	|###########	|	Identify all letters.	
	|###########	|	Point to a hexagon.	
0	|###########	M+M	Identify approx half of letters.	
	|#########	|	Do informally presented subtraction problems.	
	|########	|	Repeat 3-syllable words correctly.	
	|#######	|	Identify all single digits.	
-1	|######	+	Understand meaning of maths concepts such as 'most' and 'least'.	
			Point to first letter of his/her first name.	
	|####	|	Detect some rhyming words.	
	|###	|	Count to 7 and recall counting 7 objects.	
	|##	|		
-2	|#	+	Identify half of single digits.	
	|#	|		
	|	|	Count to 4.	
	|	|		
-3	|	+	Point to some cherries.	
	|	|	Point to a kite.	
	|	|		
	|	|		
-4	|	+	Understand the meaning of maths concept of 'smallest'.	
	|	|	Point to someone writing and someone reading.	
	|	|	Point to a fork.	
-5	|	+	Point to some carrots.	Easy

Figure 17.1 What children know and can do when they start school in Scotland (Merrell and Tymms 2007).

statutory Foundation Stage Profile, which monitors the progress of children as they move through the Foundation Stage in England, could not be used to generate such detailed objectively based information.

TYPOLOGY AND STRUCTURE

Which aspects of the educational system are important? In writing about monitoring systems, Fitz-Gibbon and Tymms (2002) suggested that 'Multiple indicators[1] for complex organizations are a fairer representation of the multiple realities within each than is any attempt to assign a single label ... '. A similar point applies when considering standards in primary schools, and their description of the following typology of indicators (A–G) for monitoring educational domains (see also Fitz-Gibbon and Kochan 2000) is used as a structure for this chapter:

- Affective, for example attitudes, aspirations, quality of life. This can apply to both teachers and their pupils.
- Behavioural, for example skills, cooperation, initiative.
- Cognitive, for example achievement.
- Demographic descriptors, for example sex, socio-economic status.
- Expenditures, for example resources, time.
- Flow, for example who is taught what for how long, curriculum balance.
- Growth, for example physical, motor and health development.

The last item (growth, for example physical, motor and health development) was not included in the original list but it completes the key areas which are important when considering standards and quality in the primary years. Of course all the areas are connected, for example cognitive and motor development are interrelated (Diamond 2000); the quality of nutrition, both pre- and post-natal, impacts on cognitive development (Glewe and King 2001); birth weight is related to reading at the age of 11 (Corbett *et al.* 2007); and so on.

There is a certain amount of overlap between the above domains and the more recent 'Every Child Matters: change for children' framework (Department for Education and Skills (DfES) 2004), in which the five aims and outcomes are listed as being healthy, staying safe, enjoying and achieving, making a positive contribution, and achieving economic well-being.

Some of the A–G factors relate to input and output measures, whilst others are processes. In other words, some provide a source of factors (such as socio-economic status) against which standards can be assessed whilst some indicate the standards themselves (such as achievement in mathematics). This chapter presents an overview of standards and quality in English primary schools over time with respect to some of the factors described in the A to G typology. It is beyond the scope to cover them all in detail, and information is sorely missing in some areas. The report also discusses the findings in relation to some government initiatives, and concludes with a discussion of implications for the future.

BACKGROUND AND CONTEXT

The past twenty years have seen substantial changes in the English education system. The 1988 Education Reform Act, the aim of which was to raise standards, led to the introduction of a national curriculum and a statutory assessment framework. The National Curriculum was intended to provide a broad, balanced and coherent curriculum for children aged between 5 and 16. Key Stages were introduced, with Key Stage 1 including children aged 5–7 years and Key Stage 2 including children aged 7–11 years. The statutory assessments, conducted at the end of each key stage, were originally conceived to provide formative and diagnostic information to guide teachers' practice, as well as providing summative information about the levels of attainment reached (Task Group on Assessment and Testing (TGAT) 1988). However, this rapidly shifted and tests also became an accountability tool. The data enabled comparisons between children, schools and local authorities to be made and was in the public domain. The inspection system was reformatted into a body with quite a different purpose from its predecessor (Fitz-Gibbon 1995, 2001; Dunford 1998; Dunford *et al.* 2000) and again fed into the accountability model with the expressed purpose of monitoring the quality of teaching, management and children's attainment.

In 1997, following the election of the Labour party, the White Paper *Excellence In Schools* (DfEE 1997) placed emphasis on the importance of the basics of literacy and numeracy. The National Literacy Strategy's Framework and the National Numeracy Strategy's Framework were introduced into primary schools in 1998 and 1999 respectively. These frameworks provided teachers with a clear set of age-related outcomes linked to learning progression in literacy and mathematics (see DfES 2006 for current information). Meanwhile a variety of different ideas were brought in, an example being the more than 600 initiatives directed at raising achievement for 11-year-olds in statutory tests brought into the education system by 1999 (Sharp 1999). The *Every Child Matters* initiative is a new approach to the well-being of children, combining services with the aim of supporting children.

SOURCES OF EVIDENCE

A literature search was conducted in January 2007 using combinations of the following keywords: Behaviour, England, Literacy, Math, Mathematics, Primary, School, Skills, Standards and Trends. Relevant references were found on ERIC, WorldCat and ECO databases, and the Google Scholar search engine. Other relevant papers, not found through the literature search, have also been reviewed.

The studies in this chapter are not limited to nationally representative datasets. Some of the studies have small samples of just a few schools, which taken together provide a more comprehensive picture than relying solely on the findings of national statistics from statutory assessments. Take, for example, the work of Davies and Brember. They were assessing children at a time when very little other data were available; that was essentially just after it was decided to abandon the Assessment of Performance Unit (APU). Although their sample of schools was small, they collected data over a number of years and their work is very useful from a historical perspective. Other data collected from local education authorities and studies such as the Performance Indicators in Primary Schools (PIPS) project, filled in the gap between the end of the APU and the time-point at which the data from the statutory assessments could be regarded as reliable.

SUMMARY OF THE EVIDENCE: AFFECTIVE

Although, as stated earlier, this indicator can apply to both pupils and their teachers, this chapter will focus on pupils.

Pupils' attitudes: reading

Past studies have reported a positive relationship between attitude to reading and reading attainment or progress in the primary years (Twist, Gnaldi, Schagen and Morrison 2004; Tymms 2001; Baker and Wigfield 1999; McKenna, Kear and Ellsworth 1995). A positive attitude is widely regarded as desirable and important, and Sainsbury and Schagen (2004) stated that 'involvement in books allows children to experience through imagination other worlds and other roles, and this involvement contributes to their personal and social development as well as to their reading abilities'. However, attitude towards reading is just one aspect of the broader construct of motivation to read. Guthrie and Wigfield (2000) distinguished five aspects within the construct: learning orientation (a dedication towards understanding the content of what is being read); intrinsic motivation; extrinsic motivation; self-efficacy and social motivation (sharing of reading material). One study which included some of these aspects was a study of children's reading choices by Hall and Coles (1999). They surveyed the reading habits of 2,900 children aged 10 years during October 1994, investigating the type of material read, the number of books read, the amount of time spent reading books, and the children's perception of their own ability. The survey replicated a previous study conducted in 1971 by Whitehead *et al.*, enabling the authors to look at changes and similarities over time. There was a slight, but statistically significant, increase in the quantity of books read between 1971 and 1994 (excluding those read as part of lessons or homework) for both boys and girls of this age, and 90 per cent of the sample rated their own reading ability as being average or better in the 1994 survey. The 1994 study, not unexpectedly, found a clear relationship between socio-economic grouping and the amount of book reading, with children from more advantaged backgrounds tending to read more. Girls reported reading more books than boys and although few children reported reading non-fiction exclusively, those who did tended to be boys. Later Gorman *et al.* (1988) largely confirmed the findings, but by 1988 just 76 per cent of boys and 87 per cent of girls confirmed that they enjoyed reading stories. They also reported that 10 per cent of the sample 'hated writing'; this involved twice as many boys as girls.

Focusing more specifically on attitude towards reading, the Assessment of Performance Unit collected data from children aged 11 years between 1979 and 1983 (Gorman *et al.* 1988). They found that in 1980, 90 per cent of pupils indicated that they enjoyed reading stories. There was a change towards less positive attitudes over the five years of the study, however, and in 1983 a third of pupils agreed with the statement that they were 'not interested in books'.

The 1994 study by Hall and Coles surveyed children's attitudes as well as their reading habits. 77 per cent of 10 year-olds reported positive attitudes towards reading, with girls being more positive than boys. Brooks, Schagen and Nastat (1997) surveyed 5,229 eight-year-old children in England and Wales and found similar trends to Hall and Coles, with about a quarter of pupils reporting negative attitudes towards reading.

In 1998 Tymms (2001) analysed data collected from 21,000 pupils aged 7 years and found them to be generally positive towards reading. 68 per cent of the sample gave a very positive response to the statement 'I look forward to reading' and a total of 89 per cent were either neutral or positive. Just 11 per cent of children gave a negative response to the statement.

The Progress in International Reading Literacy Study (PIRLS) 2001 included a survey of attitudes to reading of children aged 10 years. Pupils were presented with a four-point scale to rate their attitudes to the following items: 'I read only if I have to'; 'I like talking about books with other people'; 'I would be happy if someone gave me a book as a present'; 'I think reading is boring'; and 'I enjoy reading'. The responses were averaged and then grouped into three bands (high, medium and low on the student attitude scale). The English pupils were generally less positive than children in other participating countries, placing them towards the bottom of the sample. This was in contrast to their reading abilities (Mullis *et al.* 2003). The high band included 44 per cent of pupils in the English sample, the medium band included 43 per cent and the low band 13 per cent. The international averages were 51 per cent of students in the high band, 43 per cent in the medium band and 6 per cent in the low band.

More recently, Sainsbury and Schagen (2004) assessed attitudes to reading of children aged 9 and 11 years in 1998 and 2003. They used the same questionnaire and the same 28 non-representative schools at the two time-points. 77 per cent of Year 4 pupils in 1998 reported that they enjoyed reading stories, but by 2003 the figure had fallen significantly to 71 per cent. The proportion of Year 4 children who reported that they were not interested in books remained virtually the same (20 per cent) over time. 77 per cent of Year 6 pupils reported that they liked reading stories in 1998 but this figure had fallen significantly to 65 per cent by 2003. The proportion of Year 6 pupils who were not interested in books decreased, although not significantly, from 19 per cent to 16 per cent over time. Girls were significantly more positive towards reading than boys.

Although the studies reviewed in this section surveyed samples of children at different ages and did not use common questionnaires, collectively they demonstrated pupils in primary schools are very positive about reading. There is evidence of attitudes to reading declining with increasing age, but this drop in attitude scores by age is not restricted to England (see for example Epstein and McPartland 1976). Reading enjoyment may have declined over time for pupils in the upper-primary age range but the evidence here is ambivalent. The possible changes could be related to policy changes, such as the National Literacy Strategy and National Curriculum, but Robertson *et al.* (1996) suggested that the impact of film and television offer children an appealing way to access stories without the need for reading. They also suggested the possibility that society now offers more distractions to children than were available in previous times.

Pupils' attitudes: mathematics

There are fewer studies of children's attitudes to mathematics than there are to reading. Tymms (2001) reported that children aged 7 years were less positive towards mathematics than towards reading and school. Only 52 per cent of children responded positively and 27 per cent neutrally to the statement 'I look forward to sums', compared with the statement 'I look forward to reading' to which 68 per cent of children responded positively and 21 per cent neutrally.

Albone and Tymms (2004) investigated changes in attitudes towards mathematics in children in Years 2, 4 and 6 (aged 7, 9 and 11 years respectively) between 1997 and 2003. A group of 56 English primary schools was used for the study and longitudinal data were available. They found that attitudes to mathematics declined with the increasing age of the pupils but, when they investigated trends over time, there was no change in the mean responses of pupils within each year group between 1997 and 2003. There were no differences between boys' and girls' attitudes to mathematics. Figure 17.2, taken from their paper, demonstrates the trends between 1997 and 2003.

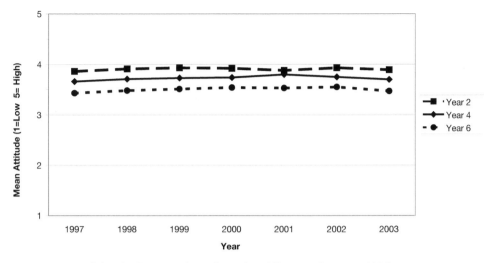

Figure 17.2 Pupils' attitudes towards mathematics (Albone and Tymms 2004).

Pupils' quality of life

In a review of testing and motivation for learning, Harlen and Deakin-Crick (2003) found several studies which focused on the effects of the statutory testing on pupils' self-esteem, behaviour and motivation to learn.

Davies and Brember (1998 and 1999) studied the self esteem of pupils in five schools over a period of eight years, beginning two years before the introduction of the statutory end of Key Stage tests (SATs). They saw a decline in the self esteem of pupils in Year 2 over the first four years, with the greatest decline coinciding with the introduction of SATs. As the assessment procedures were simplified and teachers became used to them, the self-esteem of successive cohorts of Year 2 pupils improved. The final cohort of children was more positive than any of the previous ones. The self-esteem of older pupils in Year 6 did not show the same decline but it should be noted that the study of those pupils did not begin until four years after the beginning of the study of Year 2 pupils.

Reay and Wiliam (1999) used a mixture of focus groups, individual interviews and classroom observations to investigate the views of pupils aged 11 years towards the statutory end of Key Stage 2 assessments. The sample consisted of a class of 20 pupils from a single London school. The authors noted considerable changes in the pupils over the course of an investigation that spread over the Spring term of 1998, the term leading up to the assessment. The pupils expressed an awareness of the consequences of the statutory assessment and anxiety about failure.

Pollard *et al.* (2000) reported negative behaviour and de-motivation in association with summative assessment.

More recently, the Briefing Paper published by the National Union of Teachers (2006) brings together evidence from previously published research and the results of a survey carried out on their behalf by Neill (2002). It points to an association between SATs and an increase in the stress and anxiety of pupils.

Despite the evidence outlined above for changes in self-esteem, stress, and quality of life, the situation is not clear. It must surely be true that pupils in Year 6 exhibit anxious behaviour as they prepare for, and sit, statutory assessments and that this must surely have held in Year 2 when there was statutory testing at the age of 7 (see for example McDonald 2001). However, there are a number of provisos that need to be set out.

Firstly, stress, self-esteem, attitudes and quality of life all relate to different constructs and should be broken down and discussed separately in serious investigations. For example, self-esteem is best construed as being composed of several factors (Marsh *et al.* 1988). Secondly, the evidence is based on small scale non-representative samples. Thirdly, any evidence for change should be seen against a background of 'a substantial rise in psychosocial disorders affecting young people over the last 50 years' (Collishaw *et al.* 2004). Finally, and perhaps most importantly, it is not clear what levels of stress are appropriate in our primary schools. Too much stress is clearly problematic but a complete absence of stress is not a perfect state of affairs either. Furthermore, optimum levels of stress vary from individual to individual (Eysenck 2006).

Perhaps the fairest conclusion is that testing in our schools causes anxiety and stress in pupils. This probably increased in the mid 1990s as statutory testing started to bed down.

SUMMARY OF THE EVIDENCE: BEHAVIOUR

Children learn key behaviours at school, and one of the more important functions of schooling is to mould behaviour. Some will start school with behavioural problems that significantly affect their ability to function academically and socially, for example those with severe problems of inattention, hyperactivity and impulsivity. Children who are identified with these behavioural problems by their class teachers tend to have significantly lower reading and mathematics attainment than those with no observed behavioural problems. This has been found in England as early as the start of school in Reception, and by the end of primary school they have fallen even further behind by as much as 1.2 standard deviation units (Merrell and Tymms 2001; Merrell and Tymms 2005). The proportion of such children has been estimated at 11 per cent (Merrell and Tymms 2001) and forms a significant group of children at risk of failure over time.

Naturally there are many other important issues associated with behavioural issues, but ADHD characteristics are common and important. Space does not permit further investigation here of this or other issues.

SUMMARY OF THE EVIDENCE: COGNITIVE (LITERACY AND MATHEMATICS)

This chapter is split into the two broad areas of mathematics and literacy. Literacy is further divided into reading, writing and spelling: spoken English and the comprehension of spoken language are also considered. Mainly for reasons of space other curriculum areas are not considered here.

The studies of mathematics and literacy are further separated into studies within the UK and international studies, and the UK studies naturally break down into three periods of time. The first covers the period from when reliable data were first collected up to the Education Reform Act of 1988. It draws on surveys with defined samples from primary pupils at different ages. There then follows an interim period before the third stage which runs from the large scale national test data collected in 1995 to the present.

Controversy

Before documenting details of the changing standards for mathematics and reading in England, it is appropriate to note the recent controversy surrounding the issue. The debate goes much deeper than an academic dispute as it links directly to public political claims. When the Labour party came to office they put great emphasis on standards, and the mantra 'Education Education Education' was translated into action. Far from reversing the Conservative administration's changes they accelerated them and by way of evidence of the impact of their policies they pointed to the rising statutory test scores at the end of primary schooling. For English, mainly reading, the results indicated that the percentage of children gaining a level 4 between 1995 and 2000 rose from 48 to 75 per cent. For mathematics the rise was from 44 to 72 per cent. Both of these are dramatic rises and it is hardly surprising that they were repeatedly cited as evidence for the efficacy of policies. Michael Barber, who was head of the Standards and Effectiveness Unit before moving to the Cabinet Office and who was the main architect of the National Numeracy and National Literacy Strategies, was keen to tell the rest of the world of the success and how to transform educational systems with comments such as 'Large scale reform is not only possible but can be achieved quickly' (Barber 2000).

The dramatic rises in scores were largely accepted uncritically. For example, in the £1 million evaluation of the strategies, headed by Canadian academic Michael Fullan, no mention was made of the possibility of problems with the figures. Even the National Audit Office (2001) used the National Literacy Strategy as an example of successful policy-making, using the test scores as evidence of efficacy.

In 1996 the rises started to seem very good and an Assistant Chief Executive of SCAA (School Curriculum and Assessment Authority, precursor to QCA) wrote: 'an independent benchmark could be useful in showing that standards have not slipped, *particularly if national performance improves over the year*' (Hawker 1996, emphasis added). Tymms and Fitz-Gibbon (2001) pointed to contradictory evidence, however, and private conversations were questioning the official figures. A little later, the abrupt change of a steep rise to a flat line in 2000 looked odd. It was also strange to see the English and mathematics results hugging each other so closely. It was time to review the evidence but taking on the establishment over such a key issue is no small matter. After demonstrating that the official rises misrepresented the way that standards had changed, Tymms decided that he had better seek independent authoritative support and sent his paper to the Statistics Commission asking for their comment. Very professionally they looked into the matter thoroughly and their report (2005) confirmed the finding that the official data has overstated the rise. QCA, the body responsible for maintaining standards in statutory testing, agreed. Only the DfES demurred, under the then Secretary of State of Education, Ruth Kelly. She asked the permanent secretary Sir David Normington to write a rebuttal, which he duly did.

Since then, Michael Barber has been knighted and the Statistics Commission has been disbanded.

What follows is a summary of the best evidence available relating to standards in English and mathematics in English primary schools. The statutory tests results from 1995 to 2000 are largely ignored because the mechanisms used to maintain the cut-scores for a level 4 were faulty. After 2000 the data become much more useful.

Mathematics: studies within the UK

Although it is convenient to review standards in mathematics as a whole, mathematics is, of course, composed of a number of sub-components. The APU, for example (The APU Experience 1990), divided mathematics into number, measures, algebra, geometry, and probability and statistics. The Trends in International Mathematics and Science Study (TIMSS)[2] also breaks its data collection down into similar, overlapping but not identical, categories. Unlike reading, where general tests measure the same underlying construct (see for example Stenner *et al.* 1988), mathematics differs (see, for example, Brown *et al.* 2003) and it is quite possible for an individual to be good at number but fail to understand aspects of geometry, or to be good at problem-solving but not good at mental arithmetic, for example. This means that the study of mathematics and its standards over time is complex. Nevertheless the various measures of mathematics are inevitably correlated with one another and it also makes sense to write about mathematics as a single measure whilst recognising that it can, and should, be broken down in some situations.

Mathematics: up to 1988

Conclusions of work between 1978 and 1982, from the APU and reported in Foxman (1990), indicated that 'Concepts and Skills' for 11-year-olds improved slightly by one or two percentage points. Over the same period Northern Ireland was ahead of England and Wales at the age of 11, and Wales was somewhat behind England and Scotland. Between 1982 and 1987 there was a general slight rise. For example, in geometry there was a rise of one to two per cent; in measurement the rise was about one per cent; for probability and statistics it was one per cent. But number had dropped by about two per cent and in one of its four sub-categories (fractions) by about 4.5 per cent. Algebra had risen by one per cent.

In conclusion, between 1978 and 1987 there had been a steady small improvement in the mathematics scores of children at the end of their primary education, although there had been a decline in Number.

Mathematics: 1990–95

Very little information is available during the interim period, from the abandonment of the APU in 1990 until 1995. The one study that stands out is that of Davies and Brember (2001). They reported the assessment of all Year 6 pupils in the same five randomly chosen schools in one Local Education Authority (LEA, now termed Local Authority (LA)) from 1989 to 1998. The mathematics scores remained constant.

Mathematics: since 1995

The information available for this period has been summarised in Tymms (2004). The main sources of data from within England are:

- The statutory end of Key Stage 2 assessment data
- The statutory end of Key Stage 1 data
- Performance Indicators in Primary Schools (PIPS) Project data for pupils in Year 6 (see for example Tymms 1999)

- Judy Davies and Ivy Brember (2001)
- The Leverhulme Five Year Longitudinal Study (Brown *et al.* 2003)
- The DfES/QCA/Ofsted data (Minnis and Higgs 2001)
- The QCA-commissioned comparability study (Massey *et al.* 2003)
- LEA data: Data collated from six authorities in Massey *et al.* (2003) and Tymms (2004).

This chapter concentrates on the results from the end of primary schooling, although key figures from earlier years are noted. This is partly because the attainment of children at this age can be seen as the result of all the schooling up to that time, but also because this is when most data are available. It is also generally the case that the older the child in primary school, the more reliable the test data. One clear reason for the improvement in reliability is that the reliability of a test is dependent on the number of questions asked and *ceteris paribus* older children can deal with more questions per half hour than younger children.

The statutory test data from the end of Key Stage 2 (age 11, Year 6, end of primary schooling) are reported as the percentage of students who obtained a level 4 or above. There was a steady rise in that statistic from 1995 to around 2000, with an uncharacteristic drop in 1998 and a very modest rise thereafter. The drop coincided with the introduction of the oral mathematics test but the following year the general upward trend was more than made up for. Tymms (2004) investigated this large rise by comparing the scores from statutory tests with data from the other independent studies, listed above, that had collected data over the same period.

For the purposes of the research they were all converted to a scale with a mean of 100 and a standard deviation of 15. The Davies and Brember study indicated that scores rose non-significantly over that period by 3.5 points. The PIPS mathematics data from Year 6 pupils are available from 1997 to 2002. Scores rose by 9 points. By contrast, the PIPS Year 4 data rose by just 1.6 points between 2001 to 2005. The Leverhulme study, which was carried out by Brown *et al.* between 1998 and 2002, suggested a rise of 2.7 points for Year 4 pupils although they found variation across different areas of mathematics. The QCA/DfES/Ofsted data collected between 1998 and 2000 rose by 5.2 points. The Massey *et al.* (2003) study was commissioned by QCA to replicate the English end of Key Stage 2 testing from 1997 and 2000, with equivalent samples in Northern Ireland. Massey *et al.* found that mathematics scores rose about 3.8 points between 1997 and 2000. Finally, independent assessment data collected by LEAs/LAs demonstrated a rise between 1996 and 1998 of 1.5 points and a rise between 1998 and 2000 of 1.5 points.

Overall, data from the studies reviewed consistently showed a rise in mathematics scores between 1995 and 2000. The rise was smaller than the statutory test data suggested and was equivalent to 7.7 standardised points or an effect size of 0.5, or a rise from 44 per cent gaining a level 4 or higher to 64 per cent. From 2000 to 2006 the statutory test results rose from 72 per cent gaining a level 4 or above to 76 per cent. This is equivalent to 1.9 standardised points or an effect size of 0.1.

Mathematics: international studies

Studies which compare achievement levels are always subject to criticism, and international studies are particularly vulnerable (see, for example, Prais 2007; Hilton 2006).

Despite this, of all curriculum areas, if it is possible to say something meaningful about standards across countries, it should be possible to do so in mathematics.

The International Association for the Evaluation of Educational Achievement (IEA) has been responsible for the TIMSS (formerly known as the Third International Mathematics and Science Study), which has conducted repeated surveys of mathematics in primary school for a number of years. Between 1995 and 1999 there was apparently no significant change in results for English pupils (Ruddock *et al.* 2005), but the results from 2003 were considerably higher. The rise was dramatic; between 1995 and 2003 the increase amounted to 47 standardised points on a scale with a standard deviation of 100, which is nearly half a standard deviation unit. However, there were problems with the sample and this has been the focus of significant criticism even though the rise parallels that reported in Tymms (2004).

England came tenth out of 25 participating countries in the 2003 TIMSS study. These were mostly industrialised countries in what is referred to as Grade 4 in the study (10-year-olds).

Literacy: studies within the UK – reading

As noted earlier, general tests of reading largely measure the same construct regardless of the format. This puts researchers in a stronger position when it comes to interpreting standards in reading over time from a range of studies than for mathematics, because both invariably involve a variety of tests.

As a general rule, children learn to read in primary school. Most cannot read before they start school and the vast majority of children are able to do so by the time they move to secondary school. The general consensus is that this process is a successful one and it has been ongoing for generations. There is, however, a small proportion of children who are not reading fluently by the age of 11, and this is often referred to as the 'tail of underachievement'. There is a particularly long tail for reading in the UK and this can clearly be seen clearly in the Progress in International Reading Literacy Study (PIRLS) 2001 results for children aged 9 years (http://timss.bc.edu/pirls2001i/pdf/P1_IR_Ch01.pdf) (Figure 17.3).

The very high position of England in the chart (third) is discussed later but it is the spread of scores to the left of the chart that is of focus here. The long tail of underachievement was also apparent for the United States, New Zealand, Scotland and Singapore. These are all English speaking countries and it is clear that a proportion of children have significant difficulty in learning to read English. This is worrying for it is the precursor to the existence of a group of students who find it hard to access the curriculum in secondary school and ultimately leads to illiterate adults whose ability to function in society is severely impaired. There is not the space here to discuss why this should be the case, however, and the focus now shifts to evidence for changes in reading standards over the years.

Reading: 1948 to 1988

Brooks (1997) provides a good account of work in this area. Between 1948 and 1979, there were a series of surveys of reading of 11-year olds in both England and Wales. The Watts-Vernon test was used in 1948, 1952, 1956, 1961, 1964 and 1970–71, whereas the National Survey 6 (NS6) test was used in 1955, 1960, 1970–71, 1976 and 1979. The

Countries	Average scale score	Years of formal schooling	Average age	Reading Achievement Scale score
Sweden	561	4	10.8	
Netherlands	554	4	10.3	
England	553	5	10.2	
Bulgaria	550	4	10.9	
Latvia	545	4	11.0	
Canada	544	4	10.0	
Lithuania	543	4	10.9	
Hungary	543	4	10.7	
United States	542	4	10.2	
Italy	541	4	9.8	
Germany	539	4	10.5	
Czech Republic	537	4	10.5	
New Zealand	529	5	10.1	
Scotland	528	5	9.8	
Singapore	528	4	10.1	
Russian Fed.	528	3 or 4	10.3	
Hong Kong, SAR	528	4	10.2	
France	525	4	10.1	
Greece	524	4	9.9	
Slovak Republic	518	4	10.3	
Iceland	512	4	9.7	
Romania	512	4	11.1	
Israel	509	4	10.0	
Slovenia	502	3	9.8	
International average	500	4	10.3	
Norway	499	4	10.0	
Cyprus	494	4	9.7	
Republic of Moldova	492	4	10.8	
Turkey	449	4	10.2	
Rep. of Macedonia	442	4	10.7	
Colombia	422	4	10.5	
Argentina	420	4	10.2	
Islamic Rep. of Iran	414	4	10.4	
Kuwait	396	4	9.9	
Morocco	350	4	11.2	
Belize	327	4	9.8	

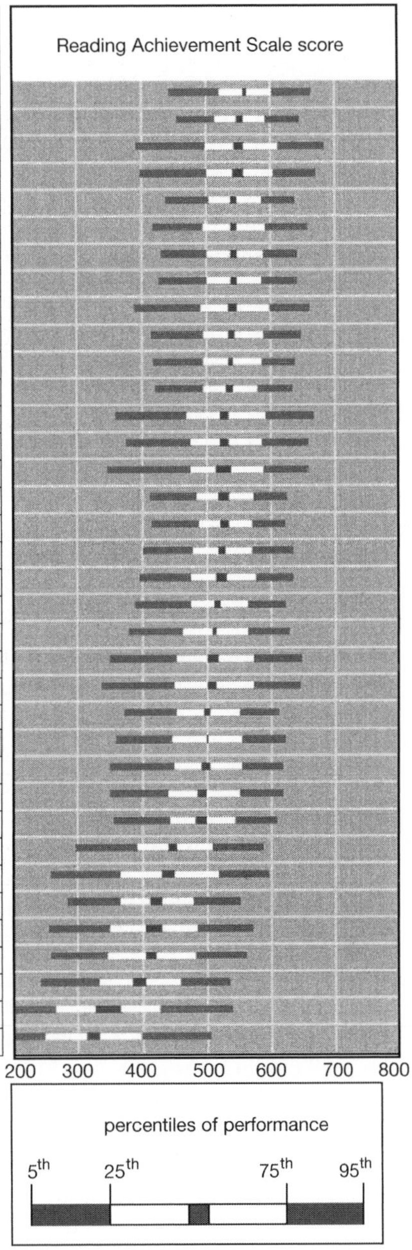

200   300   400   500   600   700   800

Source:
IEA Progress in International
Reading Literacy Study (2001)
Adapted from: PIRLS (2001)

percentiles of performance

5th   25th   75th   95th

Figure 17.3 Progress in International Reading Literacy Study (PIRLS) 2001 results.

APU Language Monitoring Project tests were used in 1979, 1980, 1981, 1982, 1983 and 1988.

The scores from the earliest of these tests, the Watts-Vernon, gradually rose between 1948 and 1964. This improvement took place in the years following the Second World War and it is thought that the post-conflict recovery period largely contributed to the rising scores. The results from the NS6 test series of 1955–79 remained largely stable.

The APU tests were different in content to the Watts-Vernon multiple choice test. They were based on 'authentic' tasks and the scores from them showed very little change between 1979 and 1988. There was a slight improvement, but it was so slight as to be of little educational importance. Surveys were carried out in Scotland between 1953 and 1963, and then 1978 to 1995. These used the Edinburgh Reading Test and then the Assessment of Achievement Programme (AAP) surveys in P4 and P7 (ages 9 and 11 years, respectively). There were slight changes in the survey results but nothing that could be said to be important educationally.

Reading: 1990–95

As noted earlier, the APU was disbanded in 1990 after the introduction of the National Curriculum and national testing because it was said that national testing would take over the monitoring of standards within England. This left a gap of five years without reliable assessment on a national scale because the new statutory End of Key Stage tests took some time to become established. It was 1995 before they were eventually considered to have overcome the inevitable 'teething problems' associated with the introduction of such a large-scale system. However, there are two sources of evidence in relation to reading during this time. One comes from Gorman and Fernandes (1992) which reports a study produced by the NFER of changes in reading standards between 1987 and 1991. Using the same test for 7-and 8-year-olds, they conducted two separate surveys in 1991, both producing very similar results. The sample consisted of 2,170 pupils in 61 schools in 1991. One of the surveys looked at pupils in the same 24 schools that were in the 1987 work and the second looked at a broader sample. Reading scores dropped between 1987 and 1991 by four to five standardised points on a scale with a standard deviation of 15 points. There was some discussion in the report as to why this drop should have occurred. It was suggested it may have been due to changes in home and school contexts, or perhaps something to do with the teachers' industrial dispute in the mid-1980s, or because of the introduction of a National Curriculum and heavy work-loads experienced by teachers.

A second source of information comes from the work of Davies and Brember (2001) in which they looked at the reading test scores of 5 randomly selected primary schools from one LA. They carried out assessments in those schools every year from 1989 onwards. Their results indicate a steady drop between 1989 and 1995 amounting to a fall of about 7 points on a scale with a standard deviation of 15 points. This finding corresponds to the findings of Gorman and Fernandes.

Reading: since 1995

The period from 1995 brings us into a different era because at that point national data from the statutory end of Key Stage assessments became available. As in the previous section on mathematics, this section will not use data from the end of Key Stage 1 assessments but will focus on the end of Key Stage 2 tests for 11-year-olds. The scores from these tests showed remarkable rises in English (reading and writing) between 1995 and 2000. The proportion of children who reached the standard of Level 4 (the standard which the DfES characterised as 'expected' for children of that age) rose from 48 per cent to around 75 per cent. This remarkable rise was challenged by Tymms (2004) who compared the end of Key Stage 2 results with a number of other datasets:

- The statutory end of Key Stage 3 assessment data
- The statutory end of Key Stage 2 data
- Performance Indicators in Primary Schools (PIPS) Project data for pupils in Year 6 and Year 4 (see for example Tymms 1999)
- Data from Judy Davies and Ivy Brember (2001)
- The DfES/QCA/Ofsted data (Minnis and Higgs 2001)
- The QCA-commissioned comparability study (Massey *et al.* 2003)
- LEA data: data collated from six authorities in Massey *et al.* (2003) and Tymms (2004).

All in all it was possible to look at 11 different studies, most involving the individual testing of thousands of pupils at different points in time, and to synthesise those results to produce a view of what happened to standards over the period in question. The report by Massey *et al.* (2003) to QCA concluded that the rise in reading had been 'illusory'. Tymms concluded that the results produced by QCA had exaggerated what had happened, but nevertheless found that there had been an improvement. Overall the data suggested that the proportion of children achieving Level 4 and above in reading had risen from 48 per cent to 58 per cent, which corresponds to an effect size of about 0.2 (3 points on a standardised reading test with a standard deviation of 15). This is a very small effect and could easily result from test practice.

In conclusion it can be said that the standards of reading have remained more or less the same over a very long time – since the 1950s. There was a rise following the immediate post-war period and there was a slight drop followed by a recovery after the introduction of the National Curriculum, but in essence standards have remained constant. Very little data specifically investigates the tail of under-achievement but the indications are that this has not improved, especially when the focus of effort of schools across the country has been on Level 4s, which is well away from the level of the under-achievers. Resources and effort were targeted at those pupils who were within range of achieving a Level 4 because that is the standard by which the success of schools was judged.

Reading: international studies

The major international study of reading is the Progress in International Reading Literacy Study (PIRLS), which was conducted in 2001 and involved tests of reading of 9-year-olds.[3] England came out extraordinarily well in this study (see Figure 17.3), coming third out of 35 countries and only behind Sweden and the Netherlands, although, as was noted earlier, there was a very wide range of achievement in the English sample. However, the study was not without its problems and Hilton (2006) itemised a series of issues. Challenged in particular was the idea that a single reading test could be translated into different languages and different cultures. The second major point had to do with the sampling, which showed England to be particularly advantaged. The tests themselves also have remarkable parallels to statutory tests used in England, but the most damning revelation was that England excluded a wider group of children with special needs than other countries.

Literacy: studies within the UK – writing

Perhaps because writing is harder and more expensive to assess than reading, it has been assessed far less often. Although there are numerous tests of reading which are regarded as reliable and valid, there are very few, if any, tests of writing of similar quality that can be bought off the shelf, and very few studies which have looked at writing standards over time. The APU made some considerable efforts in conceptualising and assessing writing but, although they produced some interesting findings, they did not report longitudinal studies (White 1986).

Writing has been tracked through the statutory end of Key Stage literacy tests but it is confounded with reading. Massey did investigate changes and the report indicated that the marking standards in relation to writing seemed to have been maintained (Massey *et al.* 2003: 63). It would seem that writing standards improved in primary schools between 1995 and 2000.

Spoken English and aural comprehension

The APU carried out some interesting and detailed work on speaking and listening, producing clear descriptions of abilities at age 11 and their relationships to other factors. They also created useful assessments in the area (MacLure and Hargreaves 1986) but no longitudinal results have been reported.

CURRICULUM-FREE COGNITIVE DEVELOPMENT

Although much effort is put into the curriculum-related cognitive development of children, they develop abilities in other areas as well and would develop cognitively even if school did not exist. This is an important area and worthy of extensive study, and covers non-verbal as well as verbal skills. Indeed it covers cognitive development generally and any proper treatment of the area would deal with changes over time for pupils of particular ages as well as growth trajectories for individuals. (For a recent theoretical perspective of the latter see Dickens 2007).

One part of this curriculum-free cognitive development involves vocabulary acquisition, which develops both inside and outside school time. Children learn new curriculum-related vocabulary in school, and as they learn to read this impacts on vocabulary acquisition. Vocabulary is also a reflection of the environment in which children find themselves and their ability to gain knowledge from the range of external sources available to them. In 2003 Alan Wells, who was at that time the director of the Basic Skills Agency, reported that the language skills of some young children were suffering. He suggested that the reasons for this decline in spoken language were due to some parents not devoting sufficient time to communicating with their offspring and other parents lacking the skills to develop the language of their children (Daily Telegraph 2003). This led the PIPS project, run by the Centre for Education and Monitoring (CEM) at Durham University, to analyse data on the vocabulary acquisition of children starting school in England between 1998 and 2002. The data were collected from an assessment of children at the start of Reception in the same 722 schools each year. The assessment remained unchanged over that period and thus enabled changes over time to be investigated. The researchers found that the vocabulary levels of these children had in fact remained stable over that period (PIPS Project 2003).

DEMOGRAPHIC DESCRIPTORS

It is often said that schools reflect society and that any complete consideration of standards should be carried out against a background of demographics. These have been changing. The average numbers of children per family has been falling; the proportion of twins and higher multiples has risen from around one in 90 live births to one in 30; parents are older; immigration has increased; ethnic diversity has widened along with the number or languages spoken in society; social boundaries are changing and so on.

Any or all of these factors could influence standards but they are simply noted as important in any holistic consideration of standards.

EXPENDITURE

Education takes up a noticeable proportion of the GDP (5.7 per cent in 2005–6) and this feeds, or should feed, directly into the quality of provision in our schools. In the financial year 2005–6, £10,908 million was spent on primary schools (excluding the cost of Ofsted) (Education and Skills Committee 2006). The cost for Ofsted in the 2005/06 financial year was just under £220 million (Ofsted 2006). Figures provided by the DfES indicate that the National Numeracy Strategy cost a total £553.05 million for the period 1998–05. The parallel figure for the National Literacy Strategy was £597.25 million. The two initiatives have now been combined into the Primary National Strategy and it is run by a private company.

It is vital that these vast sums of money are well spent and it makes sense to think in terms of cost effectiveness. The £500 million pounds spent on the NLS had a barely noticeable impact on reading.

The estimated cost of providing end of Key Stage 2 tests in 2007 is £33 per pupil. This includes production of test papers, transportation and marking. There are an estimated 573,000 pupils eligible for the assessment in 2007, making a total estimated cost of £18.9 million (National Assessment Agency 2007). To what extent is education in England better as a result of this expenditure? This is a hard question to answer, and to be able to do so one would need to include a consideration of alternatives as well as the many reasons for which national testing is carried out. Although this question could not be answered here it is vital that it be asked. Indeed, all educational initiatives should be evaluated and subjected to cost benefit analysis. All education managers, from the classroom teacher to the Secretary of State for Education, need to prioritise their time and resources, and judgements need to be made about the gains made in relation to the efforts made in order to do this efficiently.

FLOW

Other sections of this chapter have reported on attainment and attitudes over time, and this section will focus on classroom processes and how teaching and classroom management practices have changed in response to the implementation of the initiatives described in the introduction.

Broadly speaking, teaching in primary schools in the 1960s and 1970s was heavily influenced by the principles, attributed to Piaget, of the child investigating and learning independently within a stimulating environment. This theory and subsequent practice was challenged during the 1980s by the approach attributed to Vygotsky, which supported the view that a child's cognitive development requires verbal interaction with peers and adults. Thus cognitive development was seen as a social as well as a biological process. The common interpretation of Piaget's theories led to the child taking an active role as a learner and the teacher taking a more passive role in facilitating learning experiences, whereas the interpretation of Vygotsky's theories implied that the teacher was required to take a more active role in encouraging a learner to move beyond their current level of cognitive development. Alexander (2006) noted that the Vygotskian approach challenges the role of the teacher to move from a position of letting a child discover things for him/herself to a more interactive role between teacher and child, but he warned that it does not support a return to the traditional model of direct instruction from the teacher in order to pass on knowledge to the pupil. Through the studies reviewed in this section, we will consider how the implementation of national initiatives during the last 25 years has influenced teacher, pupil and peer interactions, and describe some of the changes witnessed in schools over this time.

Several studies were undertaken following the 1988 Education Act, some with longitudinal follow-ups. A study by Maurice Galton *et al.* (1999) spanned the time before and after the Act. They compared teaching and classroom management practices over two decades between the late 1970s and the late 1990s by replicating the ORACLE study (Observational Research and Classroom Learning Evaluation), which commenced in 1975. Over three years, beginning in September 1976, the study observed Key Stage 2 pupils in 58 primary school classrooms distributed over three local education authorities. The follow-up study was smaller-scale. The research team revisited 28 classrooms from the larger sample of original schools, where they then carried out the same kinds of classroom observations. Galton *et al.* concluded that, during the twenty-year period, very little appeared to have changed on the surface. The physical layout of the classrooms was similar, with children sitting together in mixed-sex groups. There was an observed increase in whole class teaching, much of which involved direct instruction, where pupils were seated around the teacher. In the 1970s this kind of activity typically lasted for 10 minutes at the beginning and the end of the morning, and for a quarter of an hour at the end of the day when the teacher read a story. In contrast, children were observed to spend up to half an hour in a single session in 1996. This led to more of them becoming distracted and consequentially to an increase in teacher-pupil routine feedback interactions. Differences in the way that subjects were presented were noted. In the 1970s, pupils spent most of the morning studying literacy and mathematics, similar to the 1990s, and the other curriculum subjects tended to be combined and studied through topics; however, there was a shift over time towards the study of these subjects becoming more discrete. It appeared that by teaching each subject in turn, teachers found it easier to provide evidence to inspectors that they were spending the statutory amounts of time on each subject. Writing and listening to the teacher were predominant activities at both time-points, accounting for 50 to 65 per cent of the lesson depending on the curriculum area, and the authors concluded that the cognitive demands placed upon pupils changed little. The pattern of teacher and pupil interaction, that is to say the amount of time spent by the teacher asking questions and making statements, remained stable. However, the content of those types of interactions changed over time with an increased proportion concerned with task and routine matters. They found less emphasis on active learning and more time devoted to direct instruction in the follow-up study. With a change in focus towards more class teaching, the combination of group-work coupled with individual attention has declined. From the 1990s study, Galton *et al.* identified a group of children who had different characteristics to children of the 1970s. These children neither seek nor receive attention, they do not display extended periods of off-task behaviour but neither do they demonstrate high levels of engagement. They liken these behavioural characteristics to those which have been observed in other studies of pupils in secondary schools who are exposed to direct instruction.

In 1991, five years before the follow-up to the ORACLE study described above, Cato *et al.* (1992) surveyed the teaching of literacy of pupils in Year 2 (aged 7 years) in 122 schools. These schools were predominantly combined infant and junior schools with only a few schools that taught infants alone. Of the schools visited by the research team, only two teachers used whole class teaching as their main strategy although it was widely used for shorter periods and specific activities such as story-telling and hand-writing. The majority of teachers organised their pupils into groups for most activities although this did not necessarily mean that the pupils in a group were working collaboratively. There was a discrepancy between the number of occasions the teacher reported listening to each pupil read and the frequency observed by the research team. Observations indicated that teachers spent far less time listening to their pupils read than was witnessed. Upon further investigation, teachers described how they managed to fit this activity into periods outside class time such as assembly and lunch time. For materials used to teach reading, most teachers reported using a combination of a reading scheme and 'real' books. For the method of instruction, almost all teachers said that their methods included a phonics approach and this was the main method for a quarter of the sample although these were not necessarily systematic. When asked about the impact of the National Curriculum, teachers reported a greater impact on the teaching of writing than reading. They had widened their teaching to include more work on variety of writing styles, punctuation and spelling. For reading, teachers described how they had increased their use of 'real' books, presumably to meet the demands of the curriculum which required them to introduce pupils to a wide range of reading material. The majority of teachers thought that their teaching methods had remained largely unchanged, but some felt the pressure of having to include all of the elements it contained and that this had led to a decrease in the flexibility to more in-depth study of topics which particularly interested pupils. Overall, the resource reported to be in most scarce supply following the implementation of the National Curriculum was time. Teachers were under pressure to fit all the statutory requirements into the school day. The finding that children were often grouped but within those groups actually worked independently echoed the findings of the ORACLE study.

A couple of years later, in 1992 and 1993, the CICADA study (Changes in Curriculum-Associated Discourse and Pedagogy in the Primary School) carried out interviews and observations of teachers and classroom practice. CICADA found that the 1988 legislation brought with it a change in terms of an increase in the management of curriculum planning, assessment and record-keeping but that pedagogy in the classroom remained relatively stable. Teachers reported four main areas of concern: the burden of statutory assessment; the demands of record-keeping; the unrealistic range and quantity, yet not necessarily appropriate content, of the National Curriculum – particularly at Key Stage 1; pressure to introduce more whole class teaching. This echoes the concerns found by other studies (Alexander *et al.* 1996).

The PACE project (Primary Assessment, Curriculum and Experience) was established in 1989 to monitor the impact of the changes occurring after the 1988 Education Act, and continued until 1997. More specifically, it sought to investigate changes in primary schools of teachers' practices, perspectives and behaviour during that period in terms of curriculum, pedagogy and assessment, using data collected from observations, questionnaires and interviews. The findings of the PACE project were reported by Osborn *et al.* (2000). They echoed the findings of Galton *et al.* in noticing an increase in the proportion of instruction and whole class teaching at the expense of more interactive pedagogy. There was a marked reduction in group work and an increase in individual work. Over the course of the study, this resulted in pupils becoming less independent in their use of space and their choice of activity, and this trend was more prevalent in Key Stage 2 than Key Stage 1. In fact Osborn *et al.* described how, as the study progressed and the pupils grew older, they preferred their teachers to choose their work for them, thereby avoiding risk of failure. It seemed as though the teachers had conveyed their own anxieties about the pressure to fit the work prescribed by the National Curriculum into the time available to their pupils. Integrated topic work was found to be increasingly difficult to sustain. Osborn *et al.* suggested that these changes in pedagogy were in part due to the implementation of the National Curriculum, which brought with it an increased pressure for teachers to deliver a broad curriculum and yet maintain a focus on improving standards of literacy and numeracy. Additionally, teachers were under pressure for pupils to meet expectations in the end of Key Stage statutory assessments, introduced during that period, and for their own teaching to meet the expectations of the inspection system.

The National Literacy Strategy began in English primary schools at the start of the Autumn term in 1998 with the aim of dramatically improving literacy standards. The National Numeracy Strategy was introduced a year later in Autumn 1999. The DfES (2003) claimed that the strategies had been successful at improving the quality of teaching and in raising standards in primary schools, and Ofsted also reported positive findings (2002). Other research that investigated the teaching processes and pupil-teacher interactions in the classroom were less positive. They found changes in teaching methods, classroom organization, use of time and resources in response to the introduction of the strategies but found fewer changes in pupil-teacher interactions. Whole class teaching was evident but this was a traditional, teacher-directed style rather than interactive. Teachers asked closed questions, pupils supplied brief answers which were not probed further, praise rather than diagnostic feedback was given and there was an emphasis on factual recall rather than higher-level activities (Alexander 2001; English *et al.* 2002; Hardman *et al.* 2003; Mroz *et al.* 2000; Moyles *et al.* 2003).

CHILDREN'S GROWTH

The primary school years are a time of rapid physical development. Not only are children getting taller and heavier, but they are developing physical skills and their health is being affected by everything around them. Physical development is important and intimately linked to other features of schooling. Bigger pupils can bully smaller pupils and physical appearance, including size, can influence the perceptions of peers and teachers alike. Similarly, fine motor coordination is linked to reading and there are concerns about the physical activity levels of school age children and their weight which may presage diabetes and heart problems. It has even been shown that physical growth spurts are associated with cognitive growth spurts (Andrich and Styles 1994).

Sadly there is neither the space nor the time to expand on this topic here. But any complete consideration of standards would need to consider this issue.

SUMMARY

The English education system has been subjected to major interventions, especially since the Education Act of 1988. It is difficult to be confident about direct causal links between changes in processes and changes in outcomes. However, it is interesting to look at quality and standards over time in relation to the implementation of national systems.

The attitudes of primary school children are generally very positive, although they decline with age and are more positive towards reading than mathematics. They are very positive towards school. Since the late 1980s the attitudes of children in the upper primary age range declined with respect to reading, whereas attitudes to mathematics appeared to remain stable.

Levels of reading have been more or less static since the 1950s. There was a small rise after the immediate post-war period, a small drop immediately following the introduction of the National Curriculum, and another slight rise after that.

The levels of mathematics have slowly but gradually risen over the years with some small regression here and acceleration there. The largest increases have been in the last dozen years.

Turning to the impact on processes, it seems that teachers felt under pressure to fit all the statutory requirements into the school day when the National Curriculum was introduced. This often led to more whole class teaching and direct instruction at the expense of interactive group work and the freedom of pupils to pursue topics of particular interest in greater depth. The statutory assessments at the end of each Key Stage, the reporting of those results in the media and the inspection system all increased the level of pressure on all levels of the education system, and coincided with changes in practice. Detailed research has found that the initial format of Ofsted inspections had a detrimental effect on pupils' exam performance in secondary schools (Shaw *et al.* 2003), and the overall effect of the changes, particularly league tables, was associated with a narrowing of the curriculum in primary schools. The literacy and numeracy strategies, which were introduced in 1998 and 1999 respectively, appeared to reinforce more traditional whole class teaching methods, and studies found that the discourse between teachers and pupils tended to be low level.

CONCLUSIONS AND IMPLICATIONS FOR THE FUTURE

Pupils in our primary schools get a good deal. Although it may seem strange to say it, average is good and it is our view that a typical pupil starting in Reception and moving up to Year 6 has a good quality of life in school, and learns to read well and to get on with fellow pupils. Of course the quality can be improved, particularly for those children who have persistent problems with reading and more generally for mathematics. For teenagers there is a problem with drunkenness and anti-social behaviour, and it may be that the issue could be addressed in primary schools.

In what ways could primary education have been better over the last 25 years? A significant amount of money has been invested in the English education system, and there are examples where more effective use could have been made of resources. Reading attainment has shown just a very slight improvement and attitudes to reading have declined. A clearer focus on those who have serious difficulty with reading would have made sense with less concentration on accountability in general and level 4s in particular. Five hundred million pounds was spent on the National Literacy Strategy with almost no impact on reading levels. Clearer trials of material before general release, more attention to the research literature, and serious consideration of cost effectiveness would all surely have helped.

We further suggest that standards over time should be monitored using assessment systems that operate outside an accountability framework, using samples rather than whole populations, and that such monitoring should include all of the areas outlined in the typology described in the introduction.

ACKNOWLEDGEMENTS

We are grateful to Professor Greg Brooks of Sheffield University for his advice and time in relation to standards and attitudes in reading.

NOTES

1 'An indicator can be defined as an item of information collected at regular intervals to track the performance of a system.' (Fitz-Gibbon 1990).
2 The International Association for the Evaluation of Educational Achievement (IEA) has been responsible for the TIMSS.
3 The study has since been repeated in 2006 but its reporting date fell outside the time frame adopted for this survey. (See also Chapter 18 of this book.)

REFERENCES

Albone, S. and Tymms, P. (2004) 'The impact of the National Numeracy Strategy on children's attitudes to mathematics', Paper presented at the British Educational Research Association annual conference, Manchester, September 2004.

Alexander, R.J. (2001) *Culture and Pedagogy: international comparisons in primary education.* Oxford: Blackwell.

——(1995) *Versions of Primary Education.* London: Routledge.

——(2006) *Towards Dialogic Teaching: rethinking classroom talk.* York: Dialogos.

Alexander, R.J., Willcocks, J. and Nelson, N. (1996) 'Discourse, pedagogy and the National Curriculum: change and continuity in primary schools', *Research Papers in Education* 11(1): 81–120.

Andrich, D. and I. Styles (1994) 'Psychometric evidence of intellectual growth spurts in early adolescence', *The Journal of Early Adolescence* 14(3): 328–44.

Baker, L. and Wigfield, A. (1999) 'Dimensions of children's motivation for reading and their relations to reading activity and reading achievement', *Reading Research Quarterly* 34(4): 452–76.

Barber, M. (2000) 'Large scale reform is possible', *Education Week* 15/11/00.

Brooks, G. (1997) 'Trends in standards of literacy in the United Kingdom', Paper presented at the Annual Meeting of the United Kingdom Reading Association, Manchester, July, and Annual Meeting of the British Educational Research Association, York, September 1997.

——(1998) 'Trends in standards of literacy in the United Kingdom', *TOPIC* Issue 19 Item 1. Slough: NFER.

Brooks, G., Schagen, I. and Nastat, P. (1997) *Trends in Reading at Eight.* Slough: NFER.

Brown, M., Askew, M., Rhodes, V., Denvir, H., Ranson, E. and Wiliam, D. (2003) 'Characterising individual and cohort progression in learning numeracy: results from the Leverhulme 5-year longitudinal study', Paper presented at AERA Annual Conference, Chicago, April 2003.

Cato, V., Fernandes, C., Gorman, T., Kispal, A. and White, J. (1992) 'The initial teaching of literacy: how do teachers do it?', *A Report on the Survey of the Teaching of Initial Literacy from the Centre for Research in Language and Communication.* Slough: NFER.

Collishaw, S., Maughan, B., Goodman, R. and Pickles, A. (2004) 'Time trends in adolescent mental health', *Journal of Child Psychology and Psychiatry* 45(8): 1350–62.

Corbett, S.S., Drewett, R.F., Durham, M., Tymms, P. and Wright, C.M. (2007). 'The relationship between birthweight, weight gain in infancy, and educational attainment in childhood', *Paediatric and Perinatal Epidemiology* 21: 57–64.

Daily Telegraph (2003) 'Ignored and grunted at: TV toddlers have to be taught to talk', online. (Available: http://www.telegraph.co.uk/education/main.jhtml?xml=/education/2003/06/05/tentalk01.xml, accessed 11 April 2007.)

Davies, J. and Brember, I. (1998) 'National curriculum testing and self-esteem in Year 2: the first five years: a cross-sectional study', *Educational Psychology* 18: 365–75.

——(1999) 'Reading and mathematics attainments and self-esteem in Years 2 and 6: an eight year cross-sectional study', *Educational Studies* 25: 145–57.

——(2001) 'A decade of change: monitoring reading and methematics attainment in Year 6 over the first ten years of the Education Reform Act', *Research in Education* 65: 31–40.

Department for Education and Employment (DfEE) (1997) *Excellence in Schools.* London: DfEE.

Department for Education and Skills (DfES) (2003) *Excellence and Enjoyment: a strategy for primary schools.* London: DfES.

DfES (2004) *Every Child Matters: change for children.* Nottingham: DfES Publications.

——(2006) *The Primary Framework for Teaching Literacy and Mathematics.* London: DfES.

Diamond, A. (2000) 'Close interrelation of motor development and cognitive development and of the cerebellum and prefrontal cortex', *Child Development* 71(1): 44–56.

Dickens, W. (2007) 'IQ-environment reciprocal effects and the meaning of general intelligence', Paper presented at the Annual Meeting of the American Educational Research Association, Chicago, April 2007.

Dunford, J.E. (1998) *Her Majesty's Inspectorate of Schools Since 1944: standard bearers or turbulent priests?* London: Woburn Press.

Dunford, J.E, Fawcett, R. and Bennett, D. (Eds) (2000) *School Leadership: national and international perspectives.* London: Kogan Page.

English, E., Hargreaves, L. and Hislam, J. (2002) 'Pedagogical dilemmas in the National Literacy Strategy: primary teachers' perceptions, reflections and classroom behaviour', *Cambridge Journal of Education* 32(1): 9–26.

Epstein, J.L. and McPartland, J.M. (1976) 'The concept and measurement of the quality of school life', *American Educational Research Journal* 13(1): 15–30.

Eysenck, H. (2006) *The Biological Basis of Personality.* New Brunswick: Transaction Publishers.

Fitz-Gibbon, C.T. (1990) *Performance Indicators: a BERA dialogue.* Clevedon, Avon: Multilingual Matters.

——(1995) 'Ofsted, schmofsted', in T. Brighouse and B. Moon (Eds) *School Inspection.* London: Pitman Publishing: 98–104.

——(2001) 'The future of inspection', *Education Review* 14(2): 82–84.

Fitz-Gibbon, C.T. and Kochan, S. (2000) 'School effectiveness and education indicators', in C. Teddlie and D. Reynolds (Eds) *The International Handbook of School Effectiveness Research.* London: Falmer Press: 257–82.

Fitz-Gibbon, C.T. and Tymms, P. (2002) 'Technical and ethical issues in indicator systems: doing things right and doing wrong things', *Education Policy Analysis Archives* 10(6). Online (Available: http://epaa.asu.edu/epaa/v10n6/, accessed 14 January 2007).

Foxman, D. (1990) *Assessment Matters: No 3 APU Mathematics Monitoring 1984–88 (Phase 2)*. London: SEAC.

Foxman, D., Hutchinson, D. and Bloomfield, B. (1991) *The APU experience 1977–1990*. London: SEAC.

Galton, M., Hargreaves, L., Comber, C., Wall, D. and Pell, A. (1999) *Inside the Primary Classroom: 20 years on*. London: Routledge.

Glewe, P. and King, E.M. (2001) 'The impact of early childhood nutritional status on cognitive development: does the timing of malnutrition matter?', *The World Bank Economic Review* 15 (1): 81–113.

Gorman, T. and Fernandes, C. (1992). *Reading in Recession: a report on the comparative reading survey*. Centre for Research in Language and Communication, Slough: National Foundation for Educational Research.

Gorman, T.P., White, J., Brooks, G., Maclure, M. and Kispal, A. (1988) *Assessment of Performance Unit: review of language monitoring 1979 – 1983*. London: HMSO.

Guthrie, J.T. and Wigfield, A. (2000) 'Engagement and motivation in reading', in M.L. Kamil, P.B. Mosenthal, P.D. Pearson and R. Barr (Eds) *Handbook of Reading Research: Volume III*. Mahwah, NJ: Lawrence Erlbaum Associates.

Hall, C. and Coles, M. (1977) *Children's Reading Choices*. London: Routledge.

Hardman, F., Smith, F. and Wall, K. (2003) 'Interactive whole class teaching in the National Literacy Strategy', *Cambridge Journal of Education* 33(2): 197–215.

Harlen, W. and Deakin Crick, R. (2003) 'Testing and motivation for learning', *Assessment in Education* 10(2): 169–207.

Hawker, D. (1996) 'Can we really trust the tests?', *TES* 16th February.

HM Treasury (2003) *Every Child Matters*, Green Paper. London: The Stationery Office.

Hilton, M. (2006) 'Measuring standards in primary English: issues of validity and accountability with respect to PIRLS and National Curriculum test scores', *British Educational Research Journal* 32(6): 817–37.

House of Commons Select Committee (2006) *Public Expenditure: government response to the Committee's fifth report of session 2005–06, first special report of session 2006–07*, House of Commons papers 2006–7 211. London: The Stationery Office

McKenna, M.C., Kear, D.J. and Ellsworth, R.A. (1995) 'Children's attitudes towards reading: a national survey', *Reading Research Quarterly* 30(4): 934–56.

MacLure, L. and Hargreaves, M. (1986) *Speaking and Listening: assessment at age 11*. Slough: NFER-Nelson.

McDonald, A.S. (2001) 'The prevalence and effects of test anxiety in school children', *Educational Psychology* 21(1): 89–101.

Marsh, H.W., Byrne, B.M. and Shavelson, R.J. (1988) 'A multifaceted academic self-concept: its hierarchical structure and its relation to academic achievement', *Journal of Educational Psychology* 80: 366–80.

Massey, A., Green, S., Dexter, T. and Hammet, L. (2003) *Comparability of National Tests Over Time: KS1, KS2 and KS3 standards between 1996 and 2001*. Final Report to QCA of the Comparability Over Time Project. London: Research and Evaluation Division of the University of Cambridge Local Examinations Syndicate.

Merrell, C. and Tymms, P.B. (2001) 'Inattention, hyperactivity and impulsiveness: their impact on academic achievement and progress', *British Journal of Educational Psychology* 71: 43–56.

——(2005) 'A longitudinal study of the achievements, progress and attitudes of severely inattentive, hyperactive and impulsive young children', Paper presented at the Annual Conference of the British Educational Research Association, University of Glamorgan, September 2005.

——(2007) 'What children know and can do when they start school and how this varies between countries', *Journal of Early Childhood Research* 5(2): 115–34.

Minnis, M. and Higgs, S. (2001) *Evaluation of the National Literacy and Numeracy Strategies, Technical report for the Testing Programme 1999–2001*. Online (Available: www.qca.org.uk).

Moyles, J., Hargreaves, L., Merry, R., Paterson, F. and Esarte-Sarries, V. (2003) *Interactive Teaching in the Primary School: digging deeper into meanings*. Maidenhead: Open University Press.

Mroz, M., Smith, F. and Hardman, F. (2000) 'The discourse of the literacy hour', *Cambridge Journal of Education* 30(3): 379–90.

Mullis, I.V.S., Martin, M.O., Gonzalez, E.J. and Kennedy, A.M. (2003) *PIRLS 2001 International Report: IEA's study of reading literacy achievement in primary school in 35 countries*. Boston, MA: Boston College, International Study Center.

National Assessment Agency (2007) Personal correspondence with Professor Peter Tymms under the Freedom of Information Act.

National Audit Office (2001) *Modern Policy Making*, Report by the Comptroller and the Auditor General. London House of Commons: TSO.

National Curriculum Task Group on Assessment and Testing (TGAT) (1988) *A Report*. London: DES.

National Union of Teachers (NUT) (2006) *NUT Briefing: the impact of National Curriculum tests on pupils*. London: NUT.

Neill, S.R. (2002) *National Curriculum Tests: a survey analysed for the National Union of Teachers, Leadership, Policy and Development Unit*. Warwick: University of Warwick.

Ofsted (2002) *The National Literacy Strategy: the first four years, 1998 – 2002*. London: Ofsted.

——(2006) *Resource Accounts 2005–06*. London: Ofsted

Osborn, M., McNess, E. and Broadfoot, P. with Pollard, A. and Triggs, P. (2000) *What Teachers Do: changing policy and practice in primary education, findings from the PACE project*. London: Continuum.

PIPS Project (2003) 'Words, words, words, PIPS and Baseline Assessment of Vocabulary', *PIPS Newsletter*, Issue 15, Spring.

Pollard, A. and Triggs, P., with Broadfoot, P. McNess, E. and Osborn, M. (2000) *What Pupils Say: changing policy and practice in primary education*. London: Continuum.

Prais, S.J. (2007) 'Two recent international surveys of schooling attainments in mathematics: England's problems', *Oxford Review of Education* 33(1): 33–46.

Reay, D. and Wiliam, D. (1999) '"I'll be a nothing": structure, agency and the construction of identity through assessment', *British Educational Research Journal* 25: 343–54.

Robertson, C. with Lovatt, P., Morris, D. and Nuttall, C. (1996) 'Reading: a pastime of the past?', *Reading* 30(2): 26–28.

Ruddock, G., Sturman, L., Schagen, I., Styles, B., Gnaldi, M. and Vappula, H. (2005) *Where England Stands in the Trends in International Mathematics and Science Study (TIMSS) 2003, National Report for England*. Slough: NFER.

Sainsbury, M. and Schagen, I. (2004) 'Attitudes to reading at ages nine and eleven', *Journal of Research in Reading* 27(4): 373–86.

Sharp, C. (1999) *Strategies to Raise Achievement at Key Stage 2: a process of educational change*. Slough: NFER.

Shaw, I., Newton, D.P., Aitkin. M. and Darnell, R. (2003) 'Do Ofsted inspections of secondary schools make a difference to GCSE results?', *British Educational Research Journal* 29(1): 63–75.

Statistics Commission (2005) *Measuring Standards in English Primary Schools*. Report by the Statistics Commission on an article by Peter Tymms. London: Statistics Commission.

Stenner, J., Horabin, I., Smith, D. and Smith, M. (1988) 'Most comprehension tests to measure reading comprehension', *Phi Delta Kappa* June: 765–67

Twist, L., Gnaldi, M., Schagen, I. and Morrison, J. (2004) 'Good readers but at a cost? Attitudes to reading in England', *Journal of Research in Reading* 27(4): 387–400.

Tymms, P. (1999) *Baseline Assessment and Monitoring in Primary Schools: achievements, attitudes and value-added indicators*. London: David Fulton Publishers.

——(2001) 'A test of the big fish in a little pond hypothesis: an investigation into the feelings of seven-year-old pupils in school', *School Effectiveness and School Improvement* 12(2): 161–81.

——(2004) 'Are standards rising in English primary schools?', *British Educational Research Journal* 30(4): 477–94.

Tymms, P. and Fitz-Gibbon, C.T. (2001) 'Standards, achievement and educational performance: a cause for celebration?', in J. Phillips and J. Furlong (Eds) *Education, Reform and the State*. London: Routledge Falmer.

White, J. (1986) *The Assessment of Writing and Attitudes to Writing*. Slough: NFER-Nelson.

Whitehead, F., Capey, A.C., Maddren, W. and Wellings, A. (1977) *Children and Their Books*. London: Macmillan.

18 Standards in English primary education

The international evidence

Chris Whetton, Graham Ruddock and Liz Twist

INTRODUCTION

This chapter examines international survey evidence on the performance of English children of primary school age in relation to those from other countries. It starts by setting out the context of these international surveys and specifies those which are discussed here. It examines the methodological basis of the surveys, noting criticisms and problems, before considering the survey findings in mathematics, reading and science. The strengths and limitations of the data are assessed, and implications for the future international monitoring of educational standards are identified.

THE CONTEXT

International comparative studies of educational achievement began in the early 1960s, in part as a cold-war reaction to the Soviet Union's launch of the first orbital satellite and the consequent concerns about levels of technical skills. The questioning of education systems which resulted lay behind the first international mathematics study in 1964. Early surveys were long, drawn-out studies held at irregular intervals and with methodological weaknesses (an early history is given in Husén and Tuijnman 1994). In contrast, modern surveys are tightly conducted, relatively rapid in reporting, involve more countries and are at regular intervals, allowing time sequences of information. They are also robust in methodological terms, though still not without critics of their operation and underlying philosophy (see, for example, Bonnet 2002 or Hilton 2006). Like the early studies, the current surveys operate in a political context but this is now that of global competition and a believed link to economic prosperity (Bonnet 2002). An overview of the purposes and conduct of surveys is given by Beaton et al. (1999).

There are currently two main sets of international surveys: those conducted by the International Association for the Evaluation of Educational Achievement (IEA) and those conducted by the Organisation for Economic Cooperation and Development (OECD) as a part of its activities, known as the Programme for International Student Assessment (PISA). The IEA is an international non-governmental organisation whose members are research centres and ministries of education. Its studies are designed to inform researchers, educators, policy makers and the public about educational achievement, and to relate this to contextual factors. The IEA studies have their roots in educational research and, since the founders of the organisation tended to be academic research centres, the approach tends to be bottom-up, defining the context of its tests through the communality of participating countries' subjects and curricula. The studies discussed here are currently conducted by an International Study Centre, based in Boston College, USA. A general description can be found at www.iea.nl.

PISA is overtly steered by the governments of the members of OECD, although other countries can participate. As such it is more reactive to the desires of national policy makers and this is reflected in its approach. This has been to define the skills needed for the populations of modern economically advanced countries and then to assess the extent to which these are present, independently of the countries' curricula. For this reason, PISA tests students at or near the end of schooling, and does so in three 'literacy' areas of reading, mathematics and science. The programme undertakes surveys every three years, rotating the subjects so that every nine years one particular area is the main focus and the others subsidiary. In 2000, the main focus was reading literacy; in 2003 it was numeracy; and in 2006 it was science. The sequence will then repeat from 2009 onwards. A general description can be found at www.pisa.oecd.org.

For a short time in two years (1989 and 1992) (Lapointe 1992a and b), there were also two large-scale international studies undertaken by the USA's Educational Testing Service, under the name 'International Assessment of Educational Progress' (IAEP). These covered mathematics and science, but only the second included primary schools. For this chapter, we have excluded other smaller international comparative studies. This is because they generally involve a single comparison with one other country and cannot provide a wide context, or because they were based on opportunity samples which would not meet the criteria of the full surveys, which utilise careful checks on samples and their attainment. (For examples see Martin *et al.* 2003, 2004a.)

Neither PISA, with its focus on school leavers, nor the IEA studies have concentrated on primary schooling, and hence the information for this age group from international comparative studies is relatively sparse.

To date, there have only been seven reputable international studies of primary-aged children in which England has participated. These were:

IEA	Reading	1971
IEA	Science	1984
IAEP	Mathematics and science	1991
IEA	Mathematics and science (TIMSS)	1995
IEA	Reading literacy (PIRLS)	2001
IEA	Mathematics and science (TIMSS)	2003
IEA	Reading literacy (PIRLS)	2006

Information is therefore rather sporadic and drawing strong conclusions is not advisable. A recent trend has been for the surveys to be held at regular intervals allowing more consistent data and a better understanding of changes taking place over time. It is likely, then, that better data will be available in the future.

For an earlier survey of England's (or the UK's) standards in literacy and numeracy to June 1994 see Brooks, Foxman and Gorman (1995). Reynolds and Farrell (1996) provide a summary of four major international comparisons covering 1960–91. A more recent review is Smithers (2004) for the Sutton Trust. None of these concentrated on primary education.

It should be stressed that measures of achievement are only part of these large international surveys. They also collect a great deal of contextual data. Included, for example, are information on children's attitudes, their home backgrounds, teachers' experience and qualifications; the nature of the school; the national educational system; and, in recent surveys, parents' views. As such the surveys offer huge opportunities for secondary analyses, and it is unfortunate that this expensively generated data has not been utilised to a greater extent. In part this may be because of the size and complexity of the data, but great efforts are now made to make it available for research scrutiny.

In examining achievement data, there are several issues to be considered. Of course most interest is immediately focused on the mean attainment measures, the absolute level, standing compared to other countries, and changes over time. However, other aspects are also important beyond these headline measures. The spread of attainment is of interest, for example. Is this narrow, indicating a cohesive education system in which all attain around the same level (whether high or low), or is the spread large, indicating a wide range of attainment and great disparities between the highest and lowest attainers? Related to this, the levels achieved by the highest attainers (these should be high for a high-value research and development led economy) and the levels achieved by the lowest attainers (the baseline levels of literacy and numeracy in a country) are both of interest.

METHODOLOGICAL LIMITATIONS

If conducting a survey on evidence of standards in one country is difficult, conducting one across many countries borders on the impossible. There are many sources of this difficulty which stem from the different underlying philosophies of education, the different structures of educational systems, the different curriculum emphases and, finally, the potentially different languages. International surveys adopt a series of techniques to attempt to make these as comparable as possible.

In essence, the approach taken by the various surveys is similar, though the language and precise processes may differ. A first stage agrees the content framework for the surveys and the approach to assessment to be taken: the modes of testing and style of items. These should be widely discussed by participants and agreed through processes involving their representatives. The tests themselves are usually the responsibility of a single agency, but the best practice is to draw on contributions from a wide range of participating countries, originated in many languages. The draft items are formed into several alternative forms and administered in field tests, usually the year before the actual survey. These field tests have the purpose of trialling the items to ensure that they function well psychometrically in each country and do not perform very differently in any of the countries. The field tests also allow a rehearsal of the processes to be used in the subsequent main survey. For both the field test and the main surveys, participating countries translate the tests into their own language(s) of education and submit these to a translation verification process, which involves independent scrutiny of the translation and the level of language adopted. Translations into the same language from different countries are compared and aligned. The samples of schools and children for the surveys are either drawn by an independent agency or have to be verified by a sampling referee. The numbers utilised are substantial, generally running to thousands of children in hundreds of schools. There is frequently random selection of pupils within schools rather than complete cohorts. Stringent criteria for inclusion are set for both school participation and the percentage of selected children to be achieved. Countries not meeting these are excluded or distinguished from the remainder in some way. Scrutineers from within or outside the countries observe the testing on an unannounced basis to ensure it is being conducted as required. (All of these processes are documented in comprehensive manuals.) Following the administration of the tests, they are marked within countries using common scoring systems, but with the operation supervised by people who have been centrally trained in consistency at international meetings. Proportions of the tests are double marked to check reliability and there may also be verification processes where some tests from one country are remarked in another country. The data capture is generally done using the same software in each country with the same embedded verification processes. There are many versions of the tests but arranged in systematic patterns so that they have some common questions, allowing the whole survey to be scaled together, the items to be calibrated on to one scale and the pupils to have their attainment measured in a comparable manner. This is done by a central analysis agency, which also examines the data for biases in any questions in particular countries or for questions which have performed differentially for reasons of the translation or otherwise. Finally the data are compiled into international and national reports, which include statements about the significance of the data, the differences between countries and the relationships to contextual variables. The processes of each survey are thoroughly documented in publications open to scrutiny.

Undertaking these operations is a detailed and onerous task, so international comparative studies of educational standards are large and expensive exercises. As such, it is reasonable to question the validity and reliability of the results they produce. There have been many critical examinations of these studies which to a greater or lesser extent suggest flaws in the methods adapted (Bonnet 2002, and Goldstein 2004 – of PISA; Clark 2004, and Hilton 2006 – of PIRLS; Galton 1998, and Winter 1998 – of TIMSS). Counter arguments have been put by Beaton *et al.* (1999), Whetton *et al.* (2007) and the studies themselves.

The criticisms can be grouped into four types: those that relate to the underlying conceptualisation of the studies as research enterprises; those that concentrate on cultural and linguistic factors; those that question the statistical and psychometric basis; and finally those which examine the sampling methodology.

The first set of criticisms relates to the conceptualisation of the studies. It is certainly the case that the recent motivation of many governments for participation in comparative studies is because of an assumed link between educational standards and economic success. Bonnet (2002) in particular has been critical of this assumption, arguing that the pursuit of causation is a chimera. Bonnet also suggested that the studies by their very nature accept a dominant model of schooling and enforce it on all even when the model does not apply, leading to incorrect conclusions. This viewpoint has been expressed most forcibly among French language commentators; see Lafontaine (2004) for example. The title of one paper sums up this view nicely: *Le bon (critique), la brute (médiatique) et les truands (Anglo-Saxons)* ['The critical good, the rough media and the Anglo-Saxon gangsters'] (Lafontaine and Demeuse 2002). There is probably no argument that can be used to overcome these objections, except to say that they are a counsel of despair and, if taken to their conclusion, mean that no cross-cultural educational comparisons are possible; a view which would not be accepted generally. In general those conducting the surveys are aware of the issues and strive to overcome them.

In an attempt to address such concerns, a study funded by the European Union Socrates programme (Bonnet *et al.* 2001, 2003) explored an alternative methodology for international comparative surveys. This study looked into 'the feasibility of implementing an internationally comparable survey of pupils' attainment in reading based on the use of indigenous untranslated test instruments in order to lessen linguistic and cultural biases' (Bonnet *et al.* 2001). The impetus for this work was doubt about the possibility of devising assessment instruments without cultural bias, in addition to a view that the English language was unduly dominant in original materials (from which translations were made) in previous studies. The study involved educationalists from England, Finland, France and Italy. The methodology adopted attempted comparative analyses whilst using assessment materials in their original language. The basis for the study was the construction of the national instruments according to a common framework of skills, levels of difficulty, text types and item types. It required the use of a common anchoring test, which was calibrated in each participating country. This was the vocabulary sub-test of the Wechsler Intelligence Scale for Children version 3 (WISC III). Those involved concluded that this approach offered some promise but that considerable further work was needed, including greater detail in test specifications in relation to sampling, item construction, and more sophisticated data analysis methods. However, they tended to overlook the contradictory fact that their methodology ultimately rested on intelligence tests, originating in an American context and subsequently translated, and therefore open to the same criticisms made of the standard survey methodology.

The next set of criticisms applies particularly to the tests of reading in PISA and in PIRLS, but also has some resonance in the testing of science. This argument is that linguistic and cultural factors make it impossible to compare countries fairly. The preexisting knowledge of students is said to be such that they bring different assumptions to the situation. Again, see Bonnet (2002) for this argument and Hilton (2006) for an English expression of it. Whetton *et al.* (2007) give a refutation in the context of PIRLS.

Bechger *et al.* (1998) go so far as to suggest 'validity within nations and comparability across nations may be conflicting aims' (1998: 101). In fact arguments are made for the cultural-specificity of texts, not only between but also within countries. Whilst acknowledging that the development process itself, including piloting of the PIRLS tests undertaken during this phase, made the tests 'as culturally fair as possible', Hilton suggests that the underlying methodology 'ignores deep cultural differences both between nations and between different groups in each nation' and that attempts to reduce this cultural specificity results in poorer assessment tools. The argument is raised both in relation to the texts themselves and also the items. Hilton argues that the texts are 'drained of cultural specificity through trialling and elimination, they are in fact also leached of intrinsic interest, comprehensibility, and vitality' (2006: 824). Whetton *et al.* (2007) provide a detailed refutation of these views.

Related to the cultural criticisms is the issue of translation. The demands of translation are substantial in these international comparisons and are discussed by Bechger *et al.* (1998), Bonnet *et al.* (2001) and Blum *et al.* (2001) in relation to literacy assessments. In the 2001 PIRLS cycle, for example, the tests were translated from English into 31 other languages. The translation and verification of the resulting translated texts in international comparisons is an extremely thorough and well-documented process, see for example Kelly and Malak (2003), and in general works well in modern studies. However, there can be problems to which the developers need to be alert. Investigations in relation to the IALS survey into adult literacy in the mid-1990s raised a number of concerns about equivalence, and Blum *et al.* (2001) illustrate these in relation to specific items.

All the international surveys utilise a statistical method generally known as item response theory (IRT) (see Van der Linden *et al.* 1997 for an overview). This technique scales the difficulty of questions in the tests and produces estimates of the ability of students. It is fundamental to the design of the studies, since it allows students to take different tests and their results to be combined through common or linking items. IRT is in general use throughout the world for psychometric studies but its use in international comparisons has been questioned, particularly by British critics (Goldstein 2004; Hilton 2006).

Goldstein criticises the international surveys for the lack of any systematic procedure for evaluating the IRT technique, and suggests that their data is in fact more complex than allowed for by IRT. He is particularly dubious about the assumptions of unidimensionality in IRT and the practice of removing items that do not fit the IRT models well. For reading, for example, this practice may serve to impose a pre-determined unidimensional model of reading achievement (Blum *et al.* 2001; Goldstein 2004; Hilton 2006). However, this may not actually occur. It is clear from the Technical Report for PIRLS 2001 (Mullis *et al.* 2003) that the items included within the final tests did support a unidimensional model in that just two items were identified as problematic, one because an incorrect mark scheme was applied in one country and one because of a translation error in one of the languages in one country. These particular items were removed from the analysis for these countries only. No other items displaying large item-by-country negative interactions were identified (that is to say when a country's performance on an item was unexpectedly low, given its overall performance and the performance of other countries on that particular item). Similar results have been found in TIMSS surveys (for example Martin *et al.* 2004b).

The final criticisms relate to the specification and achievement of the samples of students, with suggestions that these may not be representative of the individual countries. Winter (1998), for example, argued that international studies do not take sufficient account of sampling problems when comparing different countries.

The issue of sampling is of critical importance in international comparisons. It is essential that the sampling method adopted provides an accurate sample from which the data can be derived, whilst remaining manageable across all participating countries and education systems.

It is important to note that in the modern studies there are strict sampling targets that individual countries must achieve in order to be included in the main tables of the international report, and that the sampling framework adopted has to be approved by an independent organisation. In the case of IEA, this has been Statistics Canada. For PISA it has been WestStat. Both of these are substantial institutions with a great depth of expertise. The consequence of not meeting one or more of these targets was shown by the exclusion of the United Kingdom from the PISA 2003 reports (OECD 2004).

As an example, the sample design implemented in the PIRLS 2001 assessment is generally referred to as a three-stage stratified cluster sample. *The first-stage sampling units* consist of individual schools. Schools are selected with probabilities proportional to their size (PPS); size being the estimated number of pupils enrolled in the target grade, year 5 in PIRLS in England. The comprehensive national list of all eligible schools is called the school sampling frame. As the schools are sampled, replacement schools are simultaneously identified should they be needed to replace sampled schools which decline to participate. *The second-stage sampling units* are classrooms within sampled schools. Within each sampled school, a list of eligible classrooms from the target grade is prepared. A single eligible classroom per target grade is randomly selected from each participating school. *The third-stage sampling units* are pupils within sampled classrooms. Generally, all pupils in a sampled classroom will be selected for the assessment.

There are various participation targets which must be met, not all of which were fully met by England in PIRLS 2001: 85 per cent of initially sampled schools, 95 per cent of sampled classrooms and 85 per cent of sampled students and teachers; or a minimum combined school, classroom and student participation rate of 75 per cent, based on sampled and replacement schools (Joncas 2003).

To be included in the international report with annotation, as England was in 2001, the sample must meet the above targets with the inclusion of replacement schools and include at least 50 per cent of initially sampled schools and have a school participation rate of at least 50 per cent.

It is at the first and third stages of the sampling that concerns have been expressed about the representativeness of the achieved sample for PIRLS 2001 (Clark 2004; Hilton 2006). England's weighted participation rate of sampled schools (that is, 'first choice' schools) was 57 per cent; with replacement schools this increased to 88 per cent. At the third stage, the weighted pupil participation rate was 94 per cent. These participation rates led to England's inclusion in the international report with an annotation to indicate that replacement schools were required to meet sampling targets and that the proportion of pupils participating was less than 95 per cent of the national desired population. In PIRLS 2006, England met the sampling requirements in full (Twist *et al.* 2007).

Ultimately, each interested person must make their own view on the reliability and validity of these international surveys and of the methodological criticisms made of them. But this cannot be a single view of them all. The early studies did have weaknesses: in test specification (for example, IEA reading 1991); in sampling; in sample verification; and in analysis. These, though, have been learned from and addressed as far as possible in later surveys. The underlying constructs to be assessed are now published in framework documents (for example, OECD 2006 for PISA; Mullis *et al.* 2006 for PIRLS; Mullis *et al.* 2005 for TIMSS). The test developers attempt to draw on material from many participating countries and to cover a range of cultural approaches. Although the studies continue to work in English, the translations of tests are checked and verified carefully and sensitively. The samples are drawn by independent sampling organisations, not the countries themselves, and their achievement is monitored and checked. The final sample ratios required are high, and countries failing to meet them are excluded from the published results. Independent monitors view a selection of the test administrations in every country. The analysis techniques are agreed by technical committees and implemented with checks for dimensionality and the functioning of items. The reporting is careful to state the significance (or lack of significance) of differences. All of this is a considerable and expensive validation process, but whether it is sufficient has to be a personal view. For some it can never be. Bonnet (2002) considers the cultural model to be flawed. Goldstein (2004) considers the statistical model to be flawed. The authors of this review are involved in various ways in international surveys and need to declare that interest. It is our view that the methodology of the surveys presented here is sufficiently robust that their results can be considered to give a reasonable impression of the performance of the students in a participating country, compared to those in the other countries; we suggest, however, that the methodology adopted to measure the trend from one survey to another requires further investigation and validation.

MATHEMATICS

The IEA First International Mathematics Study, in 1964, was the first important international comparative study of this subject area. It did not, however, involve primary-aged pupils and this was also the case for the Second International Mathematics Study, in 1980–82. A different organisation, the International Assessment of Educational Progress, then mounted an international study of mathematics performance in 1988, but again this concentrated only on the secondary age range. A second study from this organisation did involve the primary age group and this study, in 1991, provides the first systematic information on how primary mathematics performance in England compared with that in other countries.

Mathematics: the 1991 IAEP study

The parent organisation of the 1991 IAEP study was Educational Testing Service (ETS) of the USA (Lapointe *et al.* 1992b). The target age group was 9-year-olds, and pupils from England were drawn from the two year groups containing pupils of this age.

The response rate for schools in England was 56 per cent, the lowest of all the participating countries, but not much below Scotland. The data for both countries were presented separately and annotated with cautions about the sample. The average percentage of questions correct for many of the participating countries were bunched around 60 per cent, including that for England. The large standard error for England's score contributes to this score not being significantly different from that of seven other participants including Spain, Ireland, Canada and the United States. Five countries, Korea, Hungary, Taiwan, the Soviet Union and Scotland outperformed England. The level of performance displayed by England could be described as poor. England did not outperform any of the participating countries to a significant level.

England's performance in mathematics was not as good as that for science in the same survey, as discussed below.

This first view of comparative mathematics performance predates the implementation of the National Curriculum in England, but the next international survey in 1995 came after it had been established. This was under the IEA banner and known as TIMSS.

Mathematics: the TIMSS studies

The 1995 survey of mathematics was run by IEA, and was originally entitled the Third International Mathematics and Science Survey (TIMSS) (Mullis *et al.* 1997; Harris *et al.* 1997), but once the survey was established as the baseline for a series of such surveys it changed to the Trends in International Mathematics and Science Survey, thus maintaining the TIMSS acronym. This series of surveys is important in establishing England's performance level in two ways. On each occasion, as with the earlier surveys already discussed, a measure of the performance of England compared with other countries was given. Additionally, the TIMSS series of studies is linked by common items used in consecutive studies. This allows country performance in different surveys to be placed on the same scale, allowing within-country trends in performance to be identified.

To date there have been three TIMSS surveys, in 1995 (Mullis *et al.* 1997; Harris *et al.* 1997), in 1999 (Mullis *et al.* 2000) and in 2003 (Mullis *et al.* 2004; Ruddock *et al.* 2004). The 1999 survey did not include the primary age group, and so comparisons over time can only be based on the period from 1995 to 2003. In order to gain trend information from these two studies, they are discussed here as a pair.

Both surveys had similar structures, items being grouped into 'blocks' with each block appearing in several different tests. Each test included both mathematics and science item blocks, thus allowing each pupil to be given both a mathematics score on the mathematics scale and a science score.

Mathematics: TIMSS 1995

The 1995 TIMSS survey involved two adjacent cohorts, which in England were Years 4 and 5. The results discussed below are from the older group since that was the cohort also tested in later TIMSS surveys. The data from the younger cohort gave a very similar picture.

In 1995 the following countries outperformed England:

Singapore, Korea, Japan, Hong Kong, Netherlands, Czech Republic, Austria, Slovenia, Ireland, Hungary, Australia, USA, Canada and Israel.

The countries generally performing at a similar level to England were:

Latvia, Scotland, Cyprus, Norway and New Zealand.

The countries outperformed by England were:

Greece, Thailand, Portugal, Iceland, Iran and Kuwait.

There are some similarities with the 1991 IAEP survey, in that Korea and Hungary again outperformed England. There were, however, several countries which had higher average scores than England in 1995 but had performed at a similar level in 1991 (USA, Canada and Ireland). Compared with 1991, England's performance was better against Scotland, which had outperformed England in the earlier survey, and against Portugal, outscored by England in 1995, but not in 1991.

Science is discussed in more detail below, but the comparison of mathematics performance with science is illuminating. The relationship showed a strong similarity to the 1991 IAEP study; the relative standing of England in mathematics was not as high as in science. An illustration of this is that in science only three countries, Japan, Korea and the USA, outperformed England, while in mathematics 14 countries had higher levels of performance. At the other end of the performance spectrum, England outperformed 13 countries in science but only six in mathematics. None of the six countries outperformed by England in mathematics would be regarded as key economic competitors.

The next TIMSS survey to involve primary age pupils was in 2003, and the data from this survey allowed England's performance against other countries to be quantified and provided a direct measure of any change in England's performance over time.

Mathematics: TIMSS 2003 and trends over time

The mathematics data from TIMSS 1995 was rescaled together with that from 2003 to give scores on the same scale (Ruddock *et al.* 2004).

In 2003 the following countries had higher average scores than England:

Singapore, Hong Kong, Japan, Chinese Taipei, Belgium (Flemish) and Netherlands.

The countries generally performing at a similar level to England were:

Latvia, Lithuania, Russian Federation and Hungary.

The countries outperformed by England were:

United States, Italy, Australia, New Zealand, Scotland, Norway and eight other countries.

In general terms, the countries outperforming England in 2003 were from the Pacific Rim or Dutch-speaking Europe. On this occasion the countries with higher mean scores than England included several obvious economic competitors and benchmarks. The performance demonstrated by English students appeared to be much better than that in previous international surveys, and this can be explored in two ways: by looking at England's relative standing against other important comparison countries and by analysing England's scores over time.

Fifteen countries tested the same primary age group in the 1995 and 2003 TIMSS. England's performance level increased significantly from 1995 to 2003, rising from a scaled score of 484 to 531. This increase, 47 scale points, was the largest change in performance in any of the 15 countries participating in both 1995 and 2003. Six countries increased their performance in mathematics, seven showed no change and two showed a decline in performance.

It is also possible to look at trends over time via the common items, meaning those used in both the TIMSS surveys in 1995 and 2003. In grade 4 mathematics there were 37 such trend items. The average success rate for these items in England rose from 63 per cent to 72 per cent, a rise of 9 per cent. This shows a clear and marked increase in performance from 1995 to 2003 in primary mathematics performance in England. To put this in further context, Table 18.1 shows how England's trend in performance compares with that of a range of other participating countries.

England's performance improved against five of these countries, two of which, the United States and Australia, had outscored England in 1995. In none of these five countries can the improvement in England's relative standing be attributed to a decline in performance in the comparison country.

In summary, in primary mathematics the international surveys show performance in England to have been mediocre in the 1991 and 1995 surveys. England's performance improved considerably from 1995 to 2003. This improvement is clearly shown

Table 18.1 Trends in England's mathematics performance compared with other countries

	1995	2003	*Relative to other country, England performance*	*Other country's performance 1995 to 2003*
Hong Kong	–	–		↑
Singapore	–	–		No change
Japan	–	–		No change
Netherlands	–	–		↓
Hungary	–	*	Improved	No change
United States	–	+	Improved	No change
Australia	–	+	Improved	No change
Scotland	*	+	Improved	No change
New Zealand	*	+	Improved	↑

+ England has higher level of performance than country shown.
* No significant difference between England and country shown.
– England has lower level of performance than country shown.

whether the change in England's score over this period is analysed or England's performance is compared with that of other participating countries. Nevertheless, the performance remains in the middle rank, below that of Pacific Rim and northern European countries, but significantly better than other English-speaking countries such as the USA, Australia, New Zealand and Scotland. It would be hard not to attribute this change in mathematics performance to the influence of the National Curriculum in England from 1989 and the associated Numeracy Strategy in the late 1990s, both of which formalised the requirements on teachers and perhaps raised their expectations of pupils. However, there are other possible explanations and the international surveys cannot easily attribute causation to the differences they disclose and the changes they highlight.

READING

In contrast to mathematics and science, the cycle of international surveys of literacy attainment has been sporadic. There were three IEA reading surveys in 1960 (Foshay *et al.* 1962), in 1971 (Thorndike 1973) and in 1991 (Elley 1992) and the written composition survey of 1983 (Purves 1992). To that list can now be added the Progress in International Reading Literacy Study (PIRLS) of 2001 (Twist *et al.* 2003; Mullis *et al.* 2003a) and 2006 (Twist *et al.* 2007; Mullis *et al.* 2007). The ages tested, as well as the number and nature of participating countries, has varied with each study.

The IEA survey in 1983 was the only international survey of writing attainment (Purves 1992). It involved 14 countries, including England and Wales (as one entity). The outcomes of this study differed from those of reading in that there was no comparative analysis of overall writing attainment between the countries, essentially due to the apparently insurmountable difficulties encountered in ensuring marking quality in writing in several different languages and from different education systems and curricula.

The 1960 IEA reading survey (Foshay *et al.* 1962) involved 12 countries, including England and Wales (participating jointly) and Scotland, and tested 13/14-year-olds. The

1971 IEA survey (Thorndike 1993) tested three age groups: 9-year-olds, 13/14-year-olds and 15/16-year-olds. England and Wales again jointly participated in this survey, and Scotland was also represented, each at all three age ranges.

The 1991 IEA reading survey (Elley 1992) again involved 9-year-olds. England was involved in the preparatory work for the study, including the pilot survey, but withdrew before the main survey took place. This was essentially because the model of reading being assessed was not thought by researchers at that time to adequately reflect the national curriculum, which was still a relatively recent innovation, or contemporary UK conceptions of the construct of reading:

> [the tests] consisted almost entirely of multiple-choice items, and focused almost entirely on literal comprehension – in short, they were felt to represent an out-moded and inadequate model of the reading process.
>
> (Brooks *et al.* 1996: 3)

A study conducted in 1996, by Brooks *et al.* (1996) provides some information about attainment at that point in relation to the attainment recorded in the 1991 survey, through the use of some of the IEA materials outside of the 'official' survey framework.

Results of international comparisons of reading (1960, 1971, 1991/96)

In the 1960 study of 13/14-year-olds, England and Wales performed relatively well, and comfortably in the top half of a sample of 12 countries (Brooks 1997). Scotland's overall attainment was even better and was second only to Yugoslavia. In the 1971 study, at the age of 9/10 the mean reading attainment of pupils in England and Wales, and Scotland, was exceeded only by pupils in Sweden, Italy and Finland (Thorndike 1973). Pupils in a further eight countries, including those in the Netherlands and the United States, achieved less well. In this study, the standard deviation for England and Wales, used to measure the spread of scores, was equal highest (with the United States), indicating a very wide range of scores.

For the age 13/14 group, the performance of England and Wales was just below the median score for all participating countries, with Scotland being just above. England and Wales had the second highest standard deviation, after Israel, and Scotland had the third greatest spread, out of the total of 15 participating countries (Belgium repre-sented twice, by French- and Flemish-speaking populations).

The results for the uppermost group being tested in this survey (15/16-year-olds) can be contrasted with those of the two younger cohorts. England and Wales had the third highest mean score of all 15 participating countries and a standard deviation of just 0.1 above the median. The highest scoring country at this age group, as at age 14, was New Zealand. Scotland was the second highest, and with a standard deviation below that of the median for all countries.

Perhaps the most interesting finding from the results for the three age groups asses-sed in 1971 is that, at least for the two younger groups, there is evidence for the wide range of attainment in England and Wales. This is one of the origins of the often asserted 'long tail of underachievement' in England. This phrase is used to describe the performance of less able pupils which is seen to 'tail off' dramatically and to lower the average score.

Following the introduction of the national curriculum in 1988 and its assessment in the early 1990s, attention turned once again to reading attainment in England relative to that of other countries. Brooks (1997) pointed out that there was evidence that reading attainment in England and Wales had been relatively stable in the years 1948–79. A study which utilised components from the IEA 1991 survey and also a reading test (*Reading Ability Series*) which had been standardised in England and Wales in 1987 was conducted (Brooks *et al.* 1996). The researchers had a sample of 1,817 9-year old pupils in 58 schools and used a split design with each pupil taking one of the two main parts of the IEA survey instruments (and all pupils taking the vocabulary test) used in the original survey. Brooks *et al.* (1996) suggested that attainment in England and Wales in 1996 would have resulted in a position in about the middle of the international table in 1991. As the survey involved pupils with a mean age of 9 years 0 months, compared to the mean age of 9 years 8.4 months of pupils in the IEA survey, an age adjustment was made, following the procedure described in the IEA report (Elley 1992). This led to a slight rise in the overall standing for England and Wales, but this result remained within the middle grouping of countries.

One notable aspect of Brooks *et al.*'s study was the reaffirmation of the 'long tail of underachievement'. Using data from the 1996 follow up to the 1991 survey, the standard deviation for England and Wales was greater than that of 23 countries, equal to that of New Zealand, and smaller than that of three countries (Denmark, Norway and Sweden). Brooks *et al.* also stated that the phenomenon of the 'long tail' was seen not only in literacy studies, but also in international comparisons of mathematics and science.

The study of Brooks *et al.* (1996), while providing the only link with the IEA study conducted in 1991, nevertheless has some limitations, several of which are acknowledged in the published report. The range of scores achieved was narrower than the range achieved in the international survey. This was a function of the survey design and the authors suggest that it may have led to a ceiling effect, that is to say that some pupils could not show the full achievement of which they were capable. In addition to this, of the six open-ended questions in the IEA instruments, the two requiring a longer written response were not included in the analysis. This is relevant when the findings from PIRLS 2001 are considered below.

Progress in International Reading Literacy Study (PIRLS 2001)

The results of the first of what is to be a five-yearly cycle of international comparisons of reading literacy, conducted under the auspices of the IEA, were published in 2003 and provided good evidence about England's reading standards in the 21st century (Twist *et al.* 2003; Mullis *et al.* 2003a).

Compared to earlier international surveys, great efforts were made to provide an explicit definition and framework for reading, within which the assessment instruments were conceived and the outcomes interpreted. The PIRLS 2001 definition of reading literacy was:

> The ability to understand and use those written language forms required by society and/or valued by the individual. Young readers can construct meaning from a variety of texts. They read to learn, to participate in communities of readers, and for enjoyment.
>
> (Campbell *et al.* 2001)

	Purposes for reading		
Processes of comprehension	Literary experience	Acquire and use information	
Focus on and retrieve explicitly stated information			20%
Make straightforward inferences			30%
Interpret and integrate ideas and information			30%
Examine and evaluate content, language and textual elements			20%
	50%	50%	

Figure 18.1 PIRLS assessment framework.

In the PIRLS assessment framework (Figure 18.1), two central purposes for reading are identified: reading for literary experience, and reading to acquire and use information. Each purpose is characteristically associated with certain types of texts: reading for literary experience tends to be associated with the reading of stories or poems; reading to acquire and use information with factual texts such as instructional or informational texts.

On these two purposes for reading, the PIRLS framework superimposes four 'reading processes'. It is these processes which determine the type of questions which are asked about each of the texts.

Within the 35 participating countries, England's scale score in PIRLS 2001 was significantly lower than that of Sweden, not significantly different from the scale scores of the Netherlands and Bulgaria, and significantly higher than those of all other participating countries, including France, Germany, Italy, Scotland, New Zealand and the United States. It was therefore evidence of extremely high standards of reading in English primary schools for children at the age of about 10.

The PIRLS assessment scaled the scores of the participating countries on the two different reading purposes. On the literary experience scale, England and Sweden scored significantly higher than all the other 33 participating countries. Nine countries scored significantly higher than Scotland, and 18 countries scored significantly less well. The performance of Scotland was not significantly different from that of another seven countries.

When the scale of reading to acquire and use information is considered, a slightly different picture emerges. England's scale score was significantly lower than Sweden, was not significantly different from a further seven countries and was significantly higher than the remaining 26 countries. Scotland's scale score was significantly lower than 12 countries, including England, was not significantly different from those of a further seven countries, and was significantly lower than the remaining 15 countries.

When relative performance on the two scales of reading purposes is compared, England had one of the largest differences between the two scale scores (14 scale points). Scotland had a difference of two scale points. All of the countries that tested in English (England, New Zealand, Scotland, Singapore and the United States) did better on the scale measuring reading for literary purposes, although for two countries – Singapore and Scotland – the difference was small, at one and two scale points respectively. In contrast, some other countries, for example France, did much better on reading and using information than on literary reading, perhaps reflecting different cultural and curricular emphases.

A striking finding in PIRLS 2001 was that girls scored significantly higher than boys in all participating countries, echoing the finding of various assessments of reading, and English more widely, in England annually. This finding also held for the two purposes separately.

In addition to the high average achievement, the other most notable feature of the results from England was the wide range in achievement, also a feature of earlier surveys of reading. This is most readily described when the attainment of pupils at different points on the distribution is compared across countries. Table 18.2 shows the scale score of pupils at the 5th, 25th, 50th, 75th and 95th percentiles for a subset of countries which participated in PIRLS 2001.

It is interesting to compare the range of scores from the Netherlands with those from England. Overall mean achievement was not significantly different in these two countries, but the pattern of performance across the ability range is very different. At the fifth percentile (that is, where 95 per cent of pupils in the country scored higher), children in the Netherlands had the highest scale score of all 35 countries (458), and those in England at the fifth percentile had a scale score which was 15th highest (395). At the other end of the distribution, the highest achievers at the 95th percentile, the scale score for pupils in England (685) was the highest of all countries whereas the scale score of pupils in the Netherlands at the 95th percentile was bettered by pupils at this percentile in 11 other countries. The range between the 5th and 95th percentiles was 187 scale points for the Netherlands, the smallest in the study, and for England was 290 scale points, one of the largest.

As well as measuring reading attainment, data concerning various other aspects of reading, including pupils' attitudes, was collected as part of PIRLS by means of pupil questionnaires. Evidence of the attitudes of an earlier generation was collected by the Assessment of Performance Unit in the 1980s, which found that at least nine out of ten pupils indicated that they enjoyed reading stories, the strongest response to any of the attitude items, and there were also clear indications that the majority of pupils were positive

Table 18.2 Scale scores of pupils at the 5th, 25th, 50th, 75th and 95th percentiles in PIRLS 2001

	5th percentile	25th percentile	50th percentile	75th percentile	95th percentile
England	395	501	559	612	685
France	403	481	528	573	636
Netherlands	458	517	556	593	645
New Zealand	360	472	537	593	668
Scotland	378	476	534	586	658
Sweden	445	521	565	605	663
United States	389	492	551	601	663

(Adapted from Mullis *et al.* (2003a), Exhibit B.1.)

about both reading independently and using books independently. Data collected for PIRLS 2001 gave a slightly less positive view of children's attitudes to reading but what raised greater concern was the fact that England had the second highest proportion of children who expressed clearly negative views about reading (13 per cent against an international average of 6 per cent). This was 18 per cent of boys in the sample and 8 per cent of girls. In the case of boys, just the Netherlands (23 per cent) and the United States (19 per cent) had a greater proportion in this 'low' category. Scotland came close behind England with 17 per cent. With respect to girls, the United States and England had jointly the greatest proportion of pupils expressing negative attitudes to reading, with Hungary, the Netherlands and Scotland in the next group (6 per cent).

Within all the participating countries, there was, unsurprisingly, a positive association between reading attainment and attitudes to reading. It is, though, interesting to note that that relationship did not exist between countries; the countries which had the highest overall attainment in PIRLS did not necessarily have the most positive attitudes to reading.

The results of the most recent study (PIRLS 2006) were published in November 2007. The most striking finding from this study was England's fall in performance in the published tables in both absolute terms (achieving an overall scale score of 539 compared to one of 553 in 2001) and in relative terms. In 2006, England had a mean score that was significantly lower than 11 countries, not significantly different from that of seven countries, and significantly higher than that of the remaining 22 countries (Twist *et al.* 2007). The three highest achieving countries in 2001 (Sweden, the Netherlands and England) all appeared to show significantly poorer performance in 2006. Three countries showed very large improvements in the years since the 2001 survey: the Russian Federation, Hong Kong and Singapore, each with a mean score 30 or more scale points higher than that achieved in 2001. These countries had scale scores that were significantly higher than all other participating countries. There was no significant change in the score for Scotland in the surveys.

As in 2001, scale scores for literary reading and for information reading were calculated. There was a fall in England's performance on the literary reading scale of 20 points, and on the information reading scale of 9 points; the difference between the scores on these two scales was much less in 2006 (2 points) than in 2001 (13 points).

Subsequent investigations into the measurement of the trend from 2001 to 2006 have shown that it is affected by the methodology adopted (Twist *et al.* 2007). What seems clear is that England's performance did not improve between 2001 and 2006, and may have fallen back slightly, whereas that of a number of other countries improved significantly.

Other features in the first survey were evident again in the 2006 survey. Girls continued to outperform boys in every country. The range of achievement in England between the most and least competent readers remained as wide in 2006, and this was again a feature of English-speaking countries. Attitudes to reading continued to be poor, relative to those held by children in many other countries.

SCIENCE

International comparative surveys in science have been mounted from the 1970s, starting with the IEA First International Science Study in 1970–71, but this did not involve primary age pupils. However, the Second IEA International Science Study, administered in 1984, did involve this younger age group. England participated in this second study of science performance, and this study gave a first view of England's primary science performance compared with that of other countries (Postlethwaite and Wiley 1992).

Science: the 1984 IEA study

The target population for the study was all students aged 10 on the date of testing, or all students in the grade where most 10-year olds were to be found on the date of testing. In England, the definition was all pupils in Year 5 in the age range 10:0 to 10:11 at the start of the school year. The mean age of pupils tested in England was 10:3, somewhat younger than in most participating countries. Special schools were excluded from the study, and the response rate for schools was 66 per cent. This was similar to the response rates in Italy, Norway and Sweden but lower than those achieved in the Pacific Rim countries or in Eastern Europe.

The core test for the study consisted of 24 science items and was taken by each pupil. Each pupil also took two of a further four 8-item tests, giving 40 items per student from a total pool of only 56 items, many fewer than in later surveys. The content covered was classified as biology (22 items), physics (21), earth science (8) and chemistry (5).

The participants (for the primary population) in the 1984 study included 16 complete countries, plus Canada split into English and French speaking components and a second age cohort tested in Sweden. The presentation of the results for these early studies differed from that for later studies, where the statistical significance of differences in scores between countries are indicated, and it has been necessary to estimate which differences in performance between England and other participating countries are significant.

On all the available measures in the 1984 survey the following countries outperformed England:

Japan, Korea, Finland, Hungary, Italy, Australia, USA.

The countries generally performing at a similar level to England were:

Singapore, Poland, Norway, Hong Kong.

The countries outperformed by England were:

Philippines, Nigeria.

Both Canadian language groups (English and French speaking) outperformed England, but the comparisons with Israel and the younger Swedish cohort were erratic. The older cohort in Sweden outperformed England on both measures.

The results of this survey do not suggest a high level of performance in science in England at that time. England did not, for example, outperform any of the developed countries in the survey. This set of data is important because it gives a picture of comparative performance by English pupils before the National Curriculum was introduced.

Science: the 1991 IAEP study

The next international science survey took place in 1988, organized by the IAEP, but did not involve primary age pupils. A further study was carried out by the same organisation in 1991, and this time primary students were involved (Lapointe *et al.* 1992a). The target age group was nine-year-olds, and pupils from England were drawn from the two year groups containing pupils of this age.

The response rate for schools in England was 56 per cent, the lowest of all the participating countries, but not much worse than Scotland. Again, estimates of the significances of the differences between countries have had to be made since these studies did not calculate them. The average percentage correct scores for many of the participating countries were bunched around 62 per cent. Treating the results with caution, it is reasonable to conclude that Korea and Taiwan outperformed England, while England outperformed Slovenia, Ireland and Portugal. England's results were similar to those for the USA, Canada, Hungary, Scotland, Spain, the Soviet Union and Israel.

Comparisons with the previous survey are hampered by the relative scarcity of countries participating on both occasions. Korea clearly outperformed England on both occasions. The USA and Canada had outperformed England in the 1984 IEA survey, but performed at a similar level in 1991. This survey took place during the initial stages of implementing the National Curriculum, noticeably so for the age group tested, but the next international survey, in 1995 does represent England's performance when the National Curriculum had just been established.

Science: the TIMSS studies

As explained above, the 1995 IEA survey included both maths and science and was originally entitled the Third International Mathematics and Science Survey but once the survey was established as the baseline for a series of such surveys it changed to the Trends in International Mathematics and Science Survey (TIMSS). In each subsequent survey, a snapshot of the performance of England compared with other countries was given and the country's performance in different surveys were placed on the same scale, allowing within-country trends in performance to be identified.

Science: TIMSS 1995

The TIMSS 1995 survey involved two adjacent cohorts, and in England these were Years 4 and 5. The science results discussed below are from the older group since that was the cohort also tested in later TIMSS surveys. In fact, the data from the younger cohort gave a very similar picture (Martin *et al.* 1997; Harris *et al.* 1997).

In 1995 the following countries only outperformed England:

  Japan, Korea and USA.

The countries generally performing at a similar level to England were:

  Austria, Australia, Netherlands, Czech Republic, Canada,
  Singapore, Slovenia, Ireland and Scotland.

The countries outperformed by England were:

Hong Kong, Hungary, New Zealand, Norway, Latvia, Israel, Iceland, Greece, Portugal, Cyprus, Thailand, Iran and Kuwait.

The picture of England's science performance obtained in 1995 was rather different from that shown in the earlier surveys. Only three countries outperformed England, two from the Pacific Rim and the USA. England performed at a similar level to several of its European neighbours, including Scotland and Ireland, and outperformed four others. Overall, the level of performance demonstrated by English students was high.

Looking back to the earlier studies, a number of common patterns can be identified in England's performance relative to other countries up to 1995. Japan and Korea consistently outperformed England, while the USA, Canada and Australia performed at a level higher than or similar to England. Singapore and Scotland performed at a similar level to England. It should be noted that changes in England's performance relative to other countries could have been caused by a change in performance in England, a change in performance in the country being compared with England, or a combination of the two. The TIMSS 2003 data allows judgements on which of these factors are involved and is discussed below.

Science: TIMSS 2003 and trends over time

The next full TIMSS survey was in 2003 (Martin *et al.* 2004b; Ruddock *et al.* 2004). The science data from TIMSS 1995 was rescaled together with that from 2003 to give scores on the same scale.

In 2003, only Singapore and Chinese Taipei outperformed England, with Japan, Hong Kong and the USA performing at a similar level. England's score was significantly higher than that of all the other participating countries. Again England showed a high level of performance, outscoring all the other European countries which participated.

Fifteen countries tested the same primary age group in the 1995 and 2003 TIMSS studies. England's performance level increased significantly from 1995 to 2003, rising from a scaled score of 528 to 540. Of the 15 countries, nine increased their performance, three showed no change and three showed a decline in performance. Most of the countries showing an increase in score from 1995 to 2003 had scores lower than England's in 1995. The increase in England's score, 13, was one of the smaller increases which occurred; large increases were made by, for example, Singapore (42) and Hong Kong (35). Norway showed the largest decline (38 scale points).

It is also possible to look at trends over time via the items used in both TIMSS 1995 and 2003. In grade 4 science there were 32 such items. The average success rate for these items in England rose by 4 per cent from 76 per cent to 80 per cent.

Table 18.3 examines England's change in performance relative to a range of other participants. England's performance improved against five of these countries, two of which, Japan and Scotland, had lower scores in 2003 than in 1995. In spite of England's improved performance, ground was lost against both Singapore and Hong Kong, countries with larger increases in score than England over this period.

In summary, the international surveys provide clear evidence of a rise in Year 5 performance for science from 1995 to 2003. The 1995 level of performance was already

Table 18.3 Trends in England's science performance compared to other countries

	1995	2003	Relative to other country, England's performance	Other country's performance 1995 to 2003
Japan	–	*	Improved	↓
United States	–	*	Improved	No change
Netherlands	*	+	Improved	No change
Australia	*	+	Improved	No change
Scotland	*	+	Improved	↓
Hungary	+	+		↓
New Zealand	+	+		↓
Hong Kong	+	*	Declined	↓
Singapore	*	–	Declined	↓

\+ England has higher level of performance than country shown.
* No significant difference between England and country shown.
– England has lower level of performance than the country shown.

high, amongst the highest in the participating countries, and this good performance in primary science has continued. Before 1995 it is more difficult to make comparisons with other countries. The available data is sparse and few countries participated in several of the surveys undertaken. It does, however, seem that England's performance in science in the surveys carried out before 1995 was not outstanding.

CONCLUSION

Direct evidence on the performance of primary school pupils in England from international surveys is sparser than might be expected. Prior to the 1990s, international surveys were irregular and methodologically weak. The number which included primary children was rather small. Recently, international organisations have established regular cycles of surveys which give the prospect of better examinations of trends over time. One series, the OECD's PISA, has thus far concentrated only on the outcomes of schooling and not directly addressed primary children. The other series, that of the IEA, has addressed the attainment of primary school children in mathematics, science and reading.

The available evidence is that the level of mathematics performance is currently in the middle rank, below that of Pacific Rim and northern European countries, but significantly better than some other English speaking countries such as the USA, Australia, New Zealand and Scotland. This middle ranking does though represent a slight improvement from earlier surveys in which England's performance was very poor.

There are greater cultural problems with the assessment for reading, and fewer surveys. In 2001, PIRLS indicated that the reading skills of English pupils were among the highest in the world, with good achievement in both literary and information reading. This does seem to have been an improvement on the standing in earlier surveys, though the reliability of the evidence from those is weak. There was some evidence that this high attainment was at the expense of enjoyment of reading. The 2006 PIRLS survey reported in November 2007 and suggested that there had been a fall in England's performance, although there is continuing investigation into the methods adopted to measure the trend from 2001. What is apparent is that a number of countries showed considerable improvement in the years since 2001 and that England did not.

Primary science represents something of a success story for England. There is clear evidence of a rise in performance from 1995 to 2003 even though England was amongst the highest in the participating countries in the 1990s. Before 1995 the available data is sparse but it does seem that England's performance in science in earlier surveys was at a lower level.

A consistent factor in England's results across all three subject areas is a high range of scores, compared to many other countries. High attaining English pupils are among the top ranking in the world in reading and science, but the greater spread of attainment means that the low attaining pupils are far below these in their attainment. For mathematics, the average performance is also poor by the standards of other English speaking countries and those of many European and international competitor countries.

International surveys now have a robust but not perfect methodology and are an important source of information on the relative performance of England's education system. Since their data is publicly available, they are also a resource for much secondary analysis, as yet relatively unused. The next survey to be published will be TIMSS 2007, which will continue the time series of comparative data.

REFERENCES

Beaton, A.E., Postlethwaite, T.N., Ross, K.N., Spearritt, D. and Wolf, R.M. (1999) *The Benefits and Limitations of International Education Achievement Studies*. Paris: International Institute for Educational Planning/UNESCO.

Bechger, T.M., van Schooten, E., De Glopper, C. and Hox-Joop, J.J. (1998) 'The validity of international surveys of reading literacy: the case of the IEA Reading Literacy Study', *Studies in Educational Evaluation* 24(2): 99–125.

Blum, A., Goldstein, H. and Guerin-Pace, F. (2001) 'International Adult Literacy Survey (IALS): an analysis of international comparisons of adult literacy', *Assessment in Education* 9 (3): 388–99.

Bonnet, G. (2002) 'Reflections in a critical eye: on the pitfalls of international assessment', *Assessment in Education* 9(3): 387–99.

Bonnet, G., Braxmeyer, N., Horner, S., Hannu-Pekka, L., Levasseur, J., Nardi, E., Remond, M., Vrignaud, P. and White, J. (2001) *The Use of National Reading Tests for International Comparisons: ways of overcoming cultural bias*. Paris: Ministère de l'Education Nationale, Direction de la Programmation et du Dévelopment.

Bonnet, G., Daems, F., de Glopper, C., Horner, S., Lappalainen, H.-P., Nardi, E., Remond, M., Robin, I., Rosen, M., Solheim, R.G., Tonnessen, F.-E., Vertecchi, B., Vrignaud, P., Wagner, A. K.H. and White, J. (2003) *Culturally Balanced Assessment of Reading (c-bar). A European Project*. Online (Available: http://cisad.adc.education.fr/reva/pdf/cbarfinalreport.pdf, accessed 6 August 2007).

Brooks, G. (1997) 'Trends in standards of literacy in the United Kingdom, 1948–96', Paper presented at British Educational Research Association conference, University of York, September.

Brooks, G., Foxman, D. and Gorman, T.P. (1995) *Standards in Literacy and Numeracy: 1948–1994* (NCE Briefing New Series 7). London: National Commission on Education.

Brooks, G., Pugh, A. and Schagen, I. (1996) *Reading Performance at Nine*. Slough: NFER.

Campbell, J.R., Kelly, D.L., Mullis, I.V.S., Martin, M.O. and Sainsbury, M. (2001) *Framework and Specifications for PIRLS Assessment 2001* (2nd edition). Chestnut Hill, MA: Boston College, TIMSS & PIRLS International Study Center.

Clark, M.M. (2004) 'International studies of reading, such as PIRLS–a cautionary tale', *Education Journal* 75: 25–27.

Elley, W.B. (1992) *How in the World do Students Read? IEA study of reading literacy.* The Hague: International Association for the Evaluation of Educational Achievement.

Foshay, A.W., Thorndike, R.L., Hotyat, F., Pidgeon, D.A. and Walker, D.W. (1962) *Educational Achievements of Thirteen Year Olds in Twelve Countries: results of an international research project, 1959–61.* Hamburg: UNESCO Institute for Children.

Galton, M. (1998) 'What do the tests measure?' *Education 3–13* 26(2): 50–59.

Goldstein, H. (2004) 'International comparative assessment: how far have we really come?' (Review Essay), *Assessment in Education* 11(2): 227–34.

Harris, S., Keys, W. and Fernandes. C. (1997) *Third International Mathematics and Science Study, Second National Report. Part 1: achievement in mathematics and science at age 9 in England.* Slough: NFER.

Hilton, M. (2006) 'Measuring standards in primary English: issues of validity and accountability with respect to PIRLS and National Curriculum test scores', *British Educational Research Journal* 32(6): 817–37.

Husén, T. and Tuijnman, A. (1994) 'Monitoring standards in education: why and how it came about', in A. Tuijnman and T.N. Postlethwate, *Monitoring the Standards of Education.* Oxford: Elsevier Science.

Joncas, M. (2003) 'PIRLS sampling weights and participation rates', in M.O. Martin, I.V.S Mullis and A.M. Kennedy, *PIRLS 2001 Technical Report.* Chestnut Hill, MA: Boston College, TIMSS & PIRLS International Study Center.

Kelly, D.L. and Malak, B. (2003) 'Translating the PIRLS reading assessment and questionnaires', in M.O. Martin, I.V.S Mullis and A.M. Kennedy, *PIRLS 2001 Technical Report.* Chestnut Hill, MA: Boston College, TIMSS & PIRLS International Study Center.

Lafontaine, D. (2004) 'From comprehension to literacy: thirty years of reading assessment', in J.H. Moskowitz and M. Stephens (Eds) *Comparing Learning Outcomes: international assessment and education policy.* London: RoutledgeFalmer.

Lafontaine, D. and Demeuse, D. (2002) 'Le bon (critique), la brute (médiatique) et les truands (Anglo-Saxons)', *Revue Nouvelle* 3–4(115): 100–108.

Lapointe, A.E., Askew, J.M. and Mead, M.A. (1992a) *Learning Science.* Princeton, NJ: Educational Testing Service.

Lapointe, A.E., Mead, M.A and Askew, J.M. (1992b) *Learning Mathematics.* Princeton, NJ: Educational Testing Service.

Martin, M.O., Mullis, I.V.S., Beaton, A.E., Gonzalez, E.J., Smith, T.A. and Kelly D.L. (1997) *Science Achievement in the Primary School Years: IEA's Third International Mathematics and Science Study (TIMSS).* Chestnut Hill, MA: Boston College, Center for the Study of Testing, Evaluation, and Educational Policy.

Martin, M.O., Mullis, I.V.S. and Kennedy, A.M. (2003) *PIRLS 2001 Technical Report.* Chestnut Hill, MA: Boston College, International Study Center.

Martin, M.O., Mullis, I.V.S., Gonzalez, E.J. and Chrostowski, S.J. (2004a) *TIMSS 2003 International Science Report: findings from IEA's Trends in International Mathematics and Science Study at the fourth and eighth grades.* Chestnut Hill, MA: Boston College, TIMSS & PIRLS International Study Center.

Martin, M.O., Mullis, I.V.S. and Chrostowski, S.J. (Eds) (2004b) *TIMSS 2003 Technical Report. Findings from IEA's Trends in International Mathematics and Science Study at the fourth and eighth grades.* Chestnut Hill, MA: Boston College, TIMSS & PIRLS International Study Center.

Mullis, I.V.S., Kennedy, A.M., Martin, M.O and Sainsbury, M. (2006) *PIRLS 2006 Assessment Framework and Specifications* (2nd edition). Chestnut Hill, MA: Boston College, TIMSS & PIRLS International Study Center.

Mullis, I.V.S., Martin, M.O., Beaton, A.E., Gonzalez, E.O., Kelly, D.L. and Smith, T.A. (1997) *Mathematics Achievement in the Primary School Years: IEA's Third International Mathematics and Science Study (TIMSS).* Chestnut Hill, MA: Boston College, Centre for the Testing, Evaluation, and Educational Policy.

Mullis, I.V.S., Martin, M.O., Gonzalez, E.O. and Chrostowski, S.J. (2004) *TIMSS 2003 International Mathematics Report: findings from IEA's Trends in International Mathematics and Science Study at the fourth and eighth grades.* Chestnut Hill, MA: Boston College, TIMSS & PIRLS International Study Center.

Mullis, I.V.S., Martin, M.O., Gonzalez, E.J., Gregory, K.D., Garden, R.A., O'Connor, K.M., Chrostowski, S.J. and Smith T.A. (2000) *TIMSS 1999 International Mathematics Report: findings from IEA's Repeat of the Third International Mathematics and Science Study at the eighth grade.* Chestnut Hill, MA: Boston College, International Study Center.

Mullis, I.V.S., Martin, M.O., Gonzalez, E.J. and Kennedy, A.M. (2003a) *PIRLS 2001 International Report: IEA's Study of Reading Literacy Achievement in Primary Schools in 35 countries.* Chestnut Hill, MA: Boston College, International Study Center.

Mullis, I.V.S., Martin, M.O. and Kennedy, A.M. (2003b) 'Item analysis and review', in M.O. Martin, I.V.S Mullis and A.M. Kennedy (Eds) *PIRLS 2001 Technical Report.* Chestnut Hill, MA: Boston College, International Study Center.

Mullis, I.V.S., Martin, M.O., Kennedy, A.M. and Foy, P. (2007) *PIRLS 2006 International Report: IEA's Progress in International Reading Literacy Study in primary schools in 40 countries.* Chestnut Hill, MA: TIMSS and PIRLS International Study Center, Lynch School of Education, Boston College.

Mullis, I.V.S., Martin, M.O., Ruddock, G.J., O'Sullivan, C.Y., Arora, A. and Erberber, E. (2005) *TIMSS 2007 Assessment Frameworks.* Chestnut Hill, MA: Boston College, TIMSS & PIRLS International Study Center.

Organisation for Economic Co-operation and Development (OECD) (2004) *Learning for Tomorrow's World: first results from PISA 2003.* Online (Available: http://www.oecd.org/dataoecd/1/60/34002216.pdf, accessed 2 August, 2007).

——(2006) *Assessing Scientific, Reading and Mathematical Literacy: a framework for PISA 2006.* Paris: OECD.

Postlethwaite, T.N. and Wiley, D.E. (1992) *The IEA Study of Science II: science achievement in twenty-three countries.* Oxford: Pergamon.

Purves, A.C. (1992) *Education and Performance in Fourteen Countries: the IEA study of written composition.* Oxford: Pergamon Press.

Reynolds, D. and Farrell, S. (1996) *Worlds Apart? A review of international surveys of educational achievement.* London: Ofsted.

Ruddock, G., Sturman, L., Schagen, I., Styles, B., Gnaldi, M. and Vappula, H. (2004) *Where England Stands in the Trends in International Mathematics and Science Study (TIMSS) 2003: national report for England.* Slough: NFER.

Smithers, A. (2004) *England's Education: what can be learned by comparing countries?* Liverpool: Centre for Education and Employment Research.

Thorndike, R.L. (1973) *Reading Comprehension Education in Fifteen Countries* (IEA International Studies in Education 3). Stockholm: Almqvist and Wiksell.

Twist, L., Hodgson, C. and Schagen, I. (2007) *Readers and Reading: the PIRLS 2006 national report for England.* Slough: NFER.

Twist, L., Sainsbury, M., Woodthorpe, A. and Whetton, C. (2003) *Reading All Over the World: Progress in International Reading Literacy Study (PIRLS). National report for England.* Slough: NFER.

Van der Linden, W.J. and Hambleton, R.K. (Eds) (1997) *Handbook of Modern Item Response Theory.* New York: Springer.

Whetton, C., Twist, L. and Sainsbury, M. (2007) 'Measuring standards in primary English: the validity of PIRLS – a response to Mary Hilton', *British Educational Research Journal* 33(6): 977–86.

Winter, S. (1998) 'International comparisons of student achievement', *Education 3–13* 26(2): 26–33.

19 The quality of learning

Assessment alternatives for primary education

Wynne Harlen

INTRODUCTION

Why and how we assess our pupils has an enormous impact on their educational experience and consequently on how and what they learn. This chapter provides a critical review of the assessment system in England in the light of evidence from research and practice. It begins by considering the 'why' and 'how' of assessment and then, in Section 3, describes how the various purposes and uses of assessment are met in England, in the other countries of the UK and in France, Sweden and New Zealand. In the fourth section alternative methods of conducting pupil assessment for different purposes are considered in relation to their validity, reliability, impact on learning and teaching and cost. The main points from this analysis are drawn together in the final section, indicating viable alternatives to tests and to the high stakes use of measures of pupil achievement.

Note on terminology

At the start it is perhaps necessary to make clear that the word 'assessment' is used here to refer to the process of making judgements about pupils' learning – and more generally about any learner's learning. In some countries, including the USA, the word 'evaluation' is used for this process and in many cases the two words are used interchangeably. Here we use the word 'evaluation' to refer to the process of making judgements about teaching, programmes, systems, materials, and so on. Both assessment and evaluation involve decisions about what data to use, how to collect the data in a systematic and planned way, the interpretation of the data to produce a judgement, and the communication and use of the judgement; it is the type of data that defines the difference. Different ways of collecting data for assessment include the use of tests, discussed in more detail later. The data, of whatever kind, is only ever an indication, or sample, of a wider range that could be used.

1. WHY ASSESS?

There are two main reasons for assessing pupils:

- to help their learning
- to report on what has been learned.

These are usually discussed as different purposes of assessment and sometimes, mistakenly, as different *kinds* of assessment and ones that are somehow opposed to one another. They are certainly different in several important respects, but what should unite them is the aim of making a positive contribution to learning. This impact on learning is one of the criteria to be used later in evaluating different answers to the question of how we assess.

Decisions that are involved in assessment, about the evidence to gather, how it is judged and by whom, how the results are used and by whom, follow from the reasons for the assessment. Assessment for the first of the two reasons above is called formative assessment or, alternatively, assessment *for* learning. It is defined as:

> the process of seeking and interpreting evidence for use by learners and their tea-
> chers to decide where the learners are in their learning, where they need to go and
> how best to get there.
>
> (ARG 2002a)

It is carried out as part of teaching and so involves the collection and use of evidence about the learning in relation to the specific activities and goals of a lesson. This is detailed evidence, interpreted by the teacher and pupil to decide where the pupil has reached and so what next steps are needed to help achievement of the goals, or to move on.

Assessment for the second reason is called summative, or assessment *of* learning, and is carried out for the purpose of reporting achievement of individual pupils at a particular time. It relates to broad learning goals that are achieved over a period of time. It can be conducted in various ways, as discussed later, including by tests or examinations at a certain time, or summarising achievement across a period of time up to the reporting date.

Uses of assessment results

Before going on to the question of 'how', it is necessary to consider the use made of the results since this influences decisions about how to gather and interpret evidence. For formative assessment there is, by definition, one main use of the data: to help learning. If the information about pupils' learning is not used to help that learning, then the process cannot be described as formative assessment. By contrast, the data from summative assessment are used in several ways, some relating to individual pupils and some to aggregated results of groups of pupils.

For individual pupils, the uses of summative assessment can be described as either 'internal' or 'external' to the school community:

- 'Internal' uses include using regular grading, record keeping and reporting to parents and to the pupils themselves; at secondary level, informing decisions about courses to follow where there are options within the school.
- 'External' uses include meeting the requirements of statutory national assessment, for selection, where selective secondary schools exist; at the secondary level, certification by examination bodies or for vocational qualifications, selection for further or higher education.

In addition to these uses, which relate to making judgements about individual pupils, results aggregated for groups of pupils are used for evaluating the effectiveness of the education provided by teachers, schools and local authorities. The main uses of aggregated results in England are:

- Accountability: for evaluation of teachers, schools, local authorities
- Monitoring: to compare results for pupils of certain ages and stages, year on year, to identify change in 'standards'.

Assessment systems

The use of individual pupil results for accountability and monitoring is strongly contested and is a matter to which we return later. However, at this point it is useful to note that any *system of assessment* has to identify the role that measures of pupil performance will take in the accountability of teachers and schools and in monitoring at local and national levels, as well as how evidence about individual pupils will be gathered and used for different purposes.

In any system its various parts are interconnected; how one part is carried out influences how other parts can function. In assessment a prime example of this interaction is seen when schools are held accountable for meeting targets set solely on the basis of the results of pupils' performance in external tests. There is evidence at the primary level from the PACE project that this is associated with teachers' own classroom assessment becoming focused on achievement rather than learning (Pollard *et al.* 2000; Pollard and Triggs 2000). Other interactions among elements within assessment systems become clear when we consider different systems in Section 3 of this chapter, 'Some examples of assessment systems'.

The 'stakes' of assessment

The term 'high stakes' has been adopted to refer to pupil assessment where the results are used to make important decisions, either for the pupil or for the teacher, or both. In the case of primary school pupils, the stakes are high in places where there are selective secondary schools and entrance to a preferred school depends on the outcomes of assessment. Even where the 11+ examination has been ended, as from 2009 in Northern Ireland, the assessment that replaces it takes on the high stakes. However, a far more widespread source of high stakes is the use of the results of national tests for the evaluation of schools. Although the results of national tests may not, in theory, have high stakes for pupils, the results are of considerable importance for teachers where, as in England, aggregated results are used to set targets which schools are held accountable for meeting. The consequences of pupils not achieving at certain levels can be severe, including the school being described as having 'serious weaknesses', being placed in 'special measures' or even closed. To avoid these consequences, inevitably teachers place emphasis on making sure that pupils' test results are maximised, with all that this implies for teaching to the test and giving practice tests (ARG 2002b).

As discussed further in Section 4, the optimistic view that a range of purposes can be served by using the data from a single source is the root cause of the negative impact of testing on the curriculum and pedagogy. The use of national test results for individual school accountability, for monitoring national standards and for reporting on individual pupils means that the information is not well matched to what is required for each of these purposes. Although this was, indeed, what the TGAT report (DES/WO 1988)

suggested, it was based on expectations that Black, the Task Group chair, later described as naïve: that 'the assessment results (would) be interpreted in a context of
interpretation so that they would not mislead those they were meant to inform' (Black
1997: 41).

2. HOW SHOULD WE ASSESS?

Decisions about how the evidence for assessment is gathered, about the basis for judgement and about what quality assurance procedures need to be in place, are made in
the light of how the results are to be used. Before looking at the criteria for evaluating
different ways of assessing pupils, some options in making these decisions are briefly
considered.

What evidence?

In theory anything that a pupil does provides evidence of some ability or attribute that
is required in doing it. So the regular work that pupils do in school is a rich source of
evidence about the abilities and attributes that the school aims to help pupils develop.
This evidence is, however, unstructured and varies in some degree from class to class,
even pupil to pupil. These differences can lead to unfairness in the judgements unless
the assessment procedures ensure that the judgements of equivalent work are comparable. One way to avoid this problem entirely is to create the same conditions and tasks
for all pupils; that is, to use tests.

Testing is a method of assessment in which procedures, such as the task to be
undertaken and often the conditions and timing, are specified. Usually tests are marked
using a prescribed scheme either by the pupils' teacher or by external markers, who are
often teachers from other schools. The reason for the uniform procedures is to allow
comparability between the results of pupils, who may take the tests in different places.
Tests are described as 'performance', 'practical', 'paper-and pencil', 'multiple choice',
'open book', and so on, according to the nature of the tasks that are prescribed.

Teachers regularly create their own tests for internal school use; in other cases they
are created by an agency external to the school. Tests are criticised on a number of
points, considered in more detail later, but it is the emotional reaction of many pupils
to them that is a considerable cause of concern. The specific tasks or items are
unknown beforehand and pupils have to work under the pressure of the allowed time.
This increases the fear that they will 'forget everything' when faced with the test; the
anticipation is often as unpleasant as the test itself. To counter this, and also to assess
domains that are not adequately assessed in written, timed tests or examinations,
assessment tasks may be embedded in normal work. The intention is that these tasks
are treated as normal work. It may work well where the use is internal to the school,
but the expectation of 'normality' is defeated when the results are used for making
important decisions and the tasks become the focus of special attention by teacher and
pupils.

How is evidence turned into a judgement?

Making a judgement in assessment is a process in which evidence is compared with
some standard. The standard might be what other pupils (of the same age or

experience) can do. This is *norm-referencing* and the judgement will depend on what others do as well as what the individual being assessed does. In *criterion-referencing* the standard is a description of certain kinds of performance and the judgement does not depend on what others do, but only on how the individual's performance matches up to the criterion. In *pupil-referenced*, or ipsative, assessment the pupil's previous performance is taken into account and the judgement reflects progress as well as the point reached. The judgements made of different pupils' achievements are then based on different standards, which may be appropriate when the purpose is to help learning but not for summative purposes.

Summative assessment is either criterion-referenced or norm-referenced. Criterion-referencing is intended to indicate what pupils, described as having reached a certain level, can do. Formative assessment is often a mixture of ipsative and criterion referencing, where pupils are given feedback that takes into account the effort they have put in and the progress made as well as what has been achieved.

Who makes the judgement?

It is the essence of formative assessment that the information is collected and used in relation to on-going activities. Thus it is the teacher, together with the pupil, who collects and judges the information about what is being learned. In some cases it may be possible for teacher and pupil together to decide on immediate action. In other cases, the teacher may take note of what is needed and provide for it at a later time.

In summative assessment where external tests are used, the judgements will be made by someone outside the school – usually a teacher who has been trained to apply a mark scheme or to use level descriptions (criteria) to decide the 'level' that can be awarded. Teachers can also take a more central role in the assessment of their own pupils by collecting evidence and making judgements about the levels achieved. Judging a range of work against criteria is not a straight-forward matter of relating evidence to description (Wilmut 2004). For example, the level descriptions of the National Curriculum assessment comprise a series of general statements that can be applied to a range of content and contexts in a subject area. Not all criteria will apply to work conducted over a particular period and there will be inconsistencies in pupils' performance – meeting some criteria at one level but not those at a lower level, for instance. Typically the process of using criteria involves going to and fro between the statements and the evidence and some trade off between criteria at different levels, all of which involve some value judgements. Quality assurance procedures come into play to minimise the differences between teachers' judgements of the same work.

How is quality of assessment assured?

Quality assurance, meaning procedures to minimise inaccuracy due to any of a range of causes, has a role in parts of all types of summative assessment. In the case of external tests, some quality assurance is built into the test development process when items and procedures are modified as a result of trials. Where teachers make judgements of pupils' work at the primary school level, quality assurance may take the form of group moderation, or the use of examples of assessed work to guide decisions, or the use of items from a bank of tests and tasks that have been calibrated in terms of levels of achievement. The purpose is to align the judgements of different teachers. When the process involves teachers meeting to review samples of pupils' work it has value beyond the reliability of the results (ARG 2006a). The rigour of the moderation process that is necessary depends on the 'stakes' attached to the results. Where the stakes are relatively low, as in internal uses of summative assessment, within-school moderation meetings are adequate, whilst inter-school meetings are advisable when the results are used for external purposes. However, the use of exemplification and items banks are sometimes employed to substitute for moderation meetings, thus reducing opportunities for inter-school discussions and for the professional development that these meetings can provide. (There is more discussion of these quality assurance alternatives in Section 5.)

At the secondary level where certification depend on teachers' judgements, in part or whole, the range of procedures used includes visits to the school of verifiers and moderators, inspection of samples of work and statistical adjustment of marks (Harlen 1994). It is too early for the impact of recent suggestions for accrediting schools (ACCAC 2004) or teachers, at the secondary level (ASCL 2006), or Chartered Institute of Educational Assessors (CIEA 2008), to be considered.

3. SOME EXAMPLES OF ASSESSMENT SYSTEMS

In this section we describe briefly some key aspects of the assessment system at the primary level in England and, for comparison, in the other countries of the UK and in New Zealand, Sweden and France. In each case we consider how the system provides for formative and summative use of individual pupil assessment, for school evaluation and for the national monitoring of standards.

England

Assessment begins in the 'foundation stage', the period when children may be in nursery education or in the reception year of a primary school. The foundation stage ends when children enter Year 1 of primary education in the September following their fifth birthday. In order to provide 'a way of summarizing young children's achievements at the end of the foundation stage' (QCA 2003), the Foundation Stage Profile (FSP) was introduced in the school year 2002/3. The FSP comprises 13 scales relating to personal, social and emotional development, communication, language and literacy, mathematical development, knowledge and understanding of the world, physical development and creative development. For each scale a judgement is made in terms of nine points, relating to the child's progress towards achieving the 'early learning' goals. It is intended that the profile is built up over the foundation stage so that the evidence can be used formatively and then summarised against the performance descriptions of the scales for reporting at the end of each term. The process is entirely teacher-based and the evidence for completing the profile is derived from on-going learning activities. Occasionally, additional observations (of behaviour in different contexts) may be required although these should still be situated within the normal curriculum provision.

At the time of writing in 2008, the FSP assessments cannot be used to make comparisons between schools in the same way as national test and examination results are used in England since only aggregated results are submitted to the DCSF by local authorities and results for specific schools cannot be identified. Nevertheless, local authorities are still able to produce comparative information for schools and the results from individual schools or settings can be compared with national data at the time of inspections. The FSP results at the end of reception year are part of the data collected by inspectors, but as there is no requirement to collected base-line data on entry to the foundation stage, there is no measure of progress made by the children.

The teacher-based, on-going, wide-ranging, low stakes assessment of the FSP contrasts in many ways with what pupils experience at the primary stage in England. At the end of Key Stage 1 (Years 1 and 2, pupils aged 5–7) and of Key Stage 2 (Years 3 to 6, pupils aged 7–11) there are external tests and tasks in English and mathematics (and in science at Key Stage 2 only). (Note: the DCSF announced that from 2010 Key Stage 2 tests in science will be replaced by teachers assessment and some special tasks). that teachers are required to administer in a strictly controlled manner. In addition to the core subject tests at the end of Key Stages 1 and 2, assessment by teachers is also required. For Key Stage 2 both test results and teachers' assessment results are reported and are said to have equal status. From 2005, at Key Stage 1 only the teachers' assessment results are reported but tests in English and mathematics still have to be given to inform the teachers' judgements.

Although it is only at the end of a Key Stage that pupils' performance must be reported in terms of National Curriculum levels, schools have a statutory requirement to provide a summative report for parents for each pupil and each subject studied at least once every year and schools often choose to include the levels judged to have been reached. This trend towards annual reporting in terms of levels has been reinforced by widespread use of the optional tests produced by QCA for the years between the end of Key Stages for the core subjects.

The frequency of testing appears set to increase further following the proposal of single-level tests in the consultation document entitled *Making Good Progress* (DfES 2007) and built into *The Assessment for Learning Strategy* (DCFS 2008: 4). The proposed new tests, for pupils in Key Stages 2 and 3, are designed so that each test assesses achievement at a particular level. These tests would be shorter than the current end of Key Stage tests and in mathematics, reading and writing only for levels 3–8. The intention is that pupils sit a test when their teacher judges them to be able to pass, with testing opportunities twice a year (December and June). Thus they are intended to confirm teachers' assessment of the level at which a pupil is working. It is proposed that the results of the tests would be the basis of 'progression targets' for teachers and schools, adding to the targets based on end of Key Stage tests. Schools will be given 'progression targets' measured by 'the percentage of pupils who make two levels of NC progress during Key Stage two' and a 'progression premium (to reward schools which help pupils who entered a Key Stage behind national expectations to make good progress)' (DCFS 2008: 4). Thus it is clear that these proposed new tests would be used in the evaluation of teachers and schools, adding considerably to the pressures felt by teachers and pupils. Trials of the tests were begun in about 500 schools in September 2007. Although the pilot trials are not due to end until 2009, the Children's Plan states firmly that 'It is our intention to implement new single level tests … at the earliest opportunity' (Children's Plan 2007: para 3.68). There is further discussion of these proposals and evidence of the impact of testing in Section 4.

The formative use of assessment at the primary level features prominently in the Primary Strategy where assessment for learning forms part of the new primary resource Excellence and Enjoyment: learning and teaching in the primary years (DfES 2004). The renewed Primary Framework for Literacy and Mathematics also urges better use of assessment. Financial backing for schools to implement assessment for learning is being provided from 2008 for three years (DCSF 2008). All schools receive this extra funding through the Standards Fund and will also be offered support from local authority National Strategy consultants. However, as long as national test results are used to create targets for schools and give rise to league tables, teachers are likely to feel that priority needs to be given to ensuring that the statutory test results are optimised. The results from the same end of Key Stage tests are used to evaluate the performance of schools, local authorities and also to monitor changes in the performance of pupils year on year in the country as a whole.

Scotland, Wales and Northern Ireland

In these three countries of the UK considerable changes are underway, or being considered, in the systems of assessment created in the early 1990s. Scotland, having begun major reforms with a review of assessment in 1999, has gone furthest in implementing change. In Wales a new curriculum is being phased in from 2008 and end of Key Stage assessment is based on teachers' assessment, with optional tests and tasks available. In Northern Ireland a new curriculum organised in new Key Stages is being phased in and a new Pupil Profile for reporting assessment by teachers will be statutory from 2009/10. However, while these countries are at different points in implementation of change and differ in the details of the change, there is sufficient in common in the direction of the changes, towards greater use of assessment by teachers and away from frequent testing, to warrant discussing them together.

Scotland

Scotland is the largest of the three countries, with some 2,200 primary, 385 non-selective secondary, 57 independent secondary schools and 190 special schools. Transfer from primary to secondary school takes place at the end of Year 7 (P7), so there are seven years of primary education and four of secondary education before the statutory school leaving age of 16. Neither the curriculum nor its assessment is governed by legislation in Scotland, as it is in the rest of the UK. In the absence of regulation, factors which ensure implementation of changes include a tradition of conforming with central policy and wide consultation on changes. Inevitably, achieving consensus is a slow process and often means that change is evolutionary.

The newly introduced system of assessment in primary schools in Scotland contrasts sharply with that across the border in England. This has come about in reaction to the practice that developed through the 1990s after the introduction of the national assessment. Despite the initial intention in the assessment guidelines introduced in 1991 (SED 1991) to give a strong role to teachers' professional judgement and the formative use of assessment, there was, as in other countries of the UK at that time, an increasing emphasis on standards, target-setting and accountability in the mid- to late-1990s that distorted the curriculum and moved the focus of assessment to measurement (Hutchinson and Hayward 2005). HMI reports showed that the intention that national tests should be used to moderate teachers' professional judgements was not being realised. Instead targets were dominating classroom assessment practice and tests were used to decide the level of pupils' achievements.

In response, the Minister for Education in the newly formed Scottish Parliament commissioned a national survey on Assessment 3–14. The report, arising from the analysis of responses from a wide group of stakeholders, identified several major areas for change (Hayward, Kane and Cogan 2000). As a result a major programme of reform in assessment, entitled *Assessment is for Learning,* was introduced in 2003. The programme was concerned with the whole system of assessment for the age range 3 to 14. It was recognised that major changes would only be possible if policy-makers, researchers and teachers worked together collectively to own the new procedures. Thus new procedures to promote and sustain change were developed collaboratively, with groups of schools working together. To this end, ten projects were set up, between them dealing with formative assessment, personal learning plans for pupils, moderation of teachers' assessment, the development of a bank of tests and tasks for moderation of teachers' judgements and a framework for reporting progress to parents and others. Almost all local authorities (30 out of 32) took part in the development of at least one project and by the end of 2004 over 1,500 schools were involved. On completion of the development programme, *Assessment is for Learning* was formally adopted as policy for the education of pupils aged 3–14 by ministers (SEED 2004) and the action proposed included ensuring the participation of all schools by 2007.

The main features of the programme are as follows:

- Formative assessment is in operation both for pupils and for staff, with particular emphasis on self-assessment, setting own goals and reflecting on learning.
- For summative assessment, teachers use a range of evidence from everyday activities to check on pupils' progress. There are no Key Stages in Scotland and pupils are assessed by their teachers as having reached a level of development (identified in the curriculum guidelines by criteria at six levels, A to F), using evidence from regular activities. Assessment against the level criteria is an on-going process; a pupil may be judged to have reached a level at any time. When confirmed by moderation, this is recorded and then reported at the appropriate time.
- Quality assurance of teachers' judgements of pupils' performance is through taking part in collaborative moderation within and across schools to share standards and/or using National Assessment. A circular (SEED 2005a), advising on practical implications of the implementation of the programme, described the use of tests as 'Another way for teachers to check their judgements against national standards'. Teachers can use an externally devised bank of assessments and tests, which they mark themselves, and compare the results with the results of their own classroom assessments, when they judge that children have reached a particular level (SEED Circular 02, June, 2005a).
- Assessment results in terms of number of pupils at each level are collected by the local authority to be aggregated and used in monitoring progress against national priorities. There are no league tables of primary schools; individual school results are known only to the school management and parents.
- For monitoring of national standards there is a separate rolling programme of assessment of a sample of pupils, now called the Scottish Survey of Achievement. Begun in 1983 as the Assessment of Achievement Programme, it was revised in 2003 to include four subjects, English, mathematics, science and social subjects, each assessed in turn once every four years. Samples of pupils in years P3, P5, P7 and S2 (8, 10, 12 and 14 years of age) are tested in each survey (SEED 2005b).
- For evaluation of schools, a school self-evaluation toolkit has been developed to support self-evaluation against quality indicators, which include, but are not confined to, pupil performance data (HMIe 2006).

A new curriculum, entitled *Curriculum for Excellence*, covering the whole age range 3–18 is being developed in partnership between the Scottish Government, Learning and Teaching Scotland, the Scottish Qualifications Authority and HM Inspectorate of Education. The aim of ensuring consensus among stakeholders means that revision and trial of the curriculum is taking several years. The statements combine experience and outcomes, arranged in five stages, the primary ones being for pre-school and P1, up to P4, and up to P7. Primary teachers will, as before, make judgements in relation to the new statements of experience and outcomes.

Wales

Wales has about 1,500 state primary schools for Years 1 to 6, from which pupils transfer at the age of 11 to the 230 non-selective secondary schools (there are no selective secondary schools and no middle schools). The curriculum and assessment in place until 2000 were established by the Education Reform Act of 1988 that applied to both England and Wales. In 2000, following several reviews of the curriculum, the Wales Curriculum 2000 was introduced and the decision was taken to end statutory tests and tasks at the end of Key Stage 1. From that date, statutory assessment by teachers was the only form of assessment at the end of Key Stage 1 and at the end of Key Stage 2 both teachers' assessment and results of tests, intended to be of equal status, were reported. Whilst it has not been the practice in Wales to publish performance tables based on test results for individual schools, the results of both teachers' assessment and national tests were published as summaries for each subject and for each LEA and for Wales as a whole. ACCAC (then the Qualifications, Curriculum and Assessment Authority for Wales, now within the Department for Children, Education, Lifelong Learning and Skills (DCELLS) of the Welsh Assembly Government) also published guidance materials to improve the consistency of teachers' assessment.

A review of the school curriculum and assessment arrangements, begun in 2003, recommended more sweeping changes in the assessment system (ACCAC 2004). These were largely accepted by the Minister of Education in the Welsh Assembly Government. The main changes brought about in assessment were the ending of tests at the end of Key Stage 2 from 2005 and the requirement for the assessment of levels reached by pupils to be based only on 'best fit' judgements by teachers in relation to national curriculum levels. Similar changes were also made at Key Stage 3. It was also established that the use of data about pupils' performance would be only one element used in school self-evaluation and in the monitoring of overall performance at local authority and national levels. In revising the curriculum the reception year and Key Stage 1 have been combined into a new Foundation Phase, followed by Key Stage 2 for years 3–6 (aged 7–11). Reporting in levels is required only from Key Stage 2 onwards. Results are not used to create league tables of schools.

There has been considerable effort in supporting schools in setting up procedures to assure quality in teacher assessment outcomes. This has included centrally-produced guidance for using professional judgements, which is intended to move teachers away from dependence on test-derived data. It is recognised that it will take time to build up trust in teachers' judgements and convince them that the different use of time is worthwhile. As in Scotland, the involvement and sense of ownership of new arrangements is acknowledged as being an important factor in helping teachers through the period of change.

Northern Ireland

Although a smaller country than Wales, Northern Ireland, like Scotland, has a long tradition as a separate education system. The body currently responsible for curriculum and assessment has, since 1994, been the Council for Curriculum, Examinations and Assessment (CCEA), a non-departmental body reporting to the Department of Education in Northern Ireland. However, an extensive reorganisation of the administration of education in Northern Ireland has been set in train, in which a single body (the Education and Skills Authority) will take over the functions of the existing Education and Library Boards (local authorities), the CCEA and the Regional Training Unit. The new authority will be the employing authority for teachers and non-teaching staff in schools. The Bain report, published in 2006, drew attention to a surplus of about 50,000 school places, left vacant by population decline. The restructuring required to remove these empty places will now also make provision for the end of selection to secondary schools.

The curriculum is described in terms of Key Stages, but these are different from the Key Stages in England. Children move from pre-school into Year 1 in the year in which they reach the age of 5, not after it, so they are on average younger than Year 1 children in the rest of the UK. Foundation stage refers to Years 1 and 2, Key Stage 1 to Years 3 and 4, and Key Stage 2 to Years 5 to 7, with pupils moving into secondary school at the age of 11/12. Secondary education is, until 2010, selective and the selection mechanism, the transfer test known as the 11+ examination, has been a defining feature of Northern Ireland education since 1947. The 11+ has not only dominated the curriculum in Years 6 and 7 but has both sustained and been sustained by the prevailing 'testing culture'. It is now the declared intention of the government to change this situation.

Several reviews of the curriculum and assessment (Harland *et al.* 1999a, 1999b, 2001, 2002) and of the selection system in particular (Johnston and McClune 2000; Leonard and Davey 2001; Gardner and Cowan 2005) between them highlighted a number of problems of the assessment system. These include the absence of quality assurance of teachers' judgements at the end of Key Stage 1, where there were no tests and reporting of performance was on the basis of assessment by teachers. In Key Stage 2 there were no national tests as such but teachers were required to use certain external Assessment Units provided by CCEA to moderate their assessment at the end of the Key Stage. However, instead of being used to confirm teachers' judgements, it was found that these tasks are frequently administered as tests and used to determine the level at which children were working. Moderation of teachers' judgements by CCEA was not felt to be sufficiently rigorous and teachers did not trust the judgement of other teachers and schools particularly where there was competition to attract pupils in a shrinking catchment area. Moreover, Key Stage 3 teachers put little faith in the assessment of the primary teachers. There was little use of assessment to help learning.

Recognition of these problems led to recommendations for change including the ending of the 11+ transfer tests and of selection to secondary school. This has now been accepted and the last transfer test will be in the autumn of 2008, for those entering secondary schools in 2009. The minister has proposed that all pupils transfer to secondary schools sharing the same, new curriculum and at the age of 14 take different paths. This has not merely moved the age of testing from 11 to 14, for it is intended that the decision on which path to take is based on records of progress, on teacher and parent guidance and career advice (Northern Ireland Education Minister 2007).

In new arrangements being planned, all summative assessment at Key Stages 1, 2 and 3 will be teacher based and moderated. Several approaches to quality assurance and quality control of teachers' judgements are being considered, including the accreditation of schools, moderation of procedures, and professional development in assessment techniques. There is an emphasis on using assessment for learning so that pupils are aware of the goals of their learning and how to assess their achievement of the goals; all part of a more open relationship between pupil and teacher.

A Pupil Profile has been developed by CCEA in collaboration with parents, teachers and other educational partners. The aim of the Profile is to provide a record of each individual pupil's achievements, from on-going assessment, in a way that provides consistency between schools and reflects the revised Northern Ireland curriculum. This was introduced in 2007 and becomes statutory in 2009/10. Achievements will be recorded for communication (reading, speaking, listening, responding and presenting), using mathematics, ICT, thinking skills and personal capability (being creative, problem solving, self management, working with others) as well as for subject areas of the language, mathematics, the arts, the world around, and so on. It should help to avoid the current narrow focus on reading, writing and mathematics.

Countries outside the UK

New Zealand

New Zealand, with a population of about four million, is quite similar to Scotland in having a high proportion of small primary schools. Most pupils attend primary school for six years, although there are some schools covering the first eight years of education. In 1991 the curriculum was restructured in some 'sweeping changes modelled on the curriculum and assessment changes in the late 1980s in England and Wales' (Crooks 2002: 239). Thus there are strands within subject areas and achievement objectives at eight levels within each strand. The first five levels are spaced about two years apart. This curriculum is now being reviewed and is likely to be replaced by a less detailed description of objectives.

The attempts by teachers, encouraged by the Ministry of Education and the inspectorate (the Education Review Office), to use the levels of the curriculum in recording and reporting their assessment of pupils met with similar problems to some of those encountered in England. The levels are too widely spaced to give a satisfying account of progress, teachers' judgements of similar work varied and there was a tendency to base judgements on too narrow a range of tasks. Making the objectives more specific by sub-dividing them into different components or by creating intermediate steps within levels may improve agreement between teachers but may reduce the validity of the assessment. These difficulties remain but various forms of help with assessment have been developed for teachers. One of these provides assessment materials to be used with pupils on entry to school. These individually administered tasks are designed to give diagnostic information about certain aspects of numeracy, oracy and written language. A second support takes the form of banks of tasks, freely available on the Internet, for assessing English, mathematics and science at primary level. Teachers use these in various ways to check their judgement of levels, as ideas for their own assessment tasks and to check their pupils' achievement against national norms. There are also exemplars of performance at the different levels for each strand and subject area.

Other free assessment materials for upper primary and lower secondary pupils are available from the internet.

To date the introduction of national tests for all pupils has been resisted, although it has been proposed by the National party (Government of New Zealand 1998). Instead, what pupils experience in terms of tests or tasks is a matter for their teacher and school. The assessment results are used within schools for monitoring progress and standards and by the inspectorate for external review, but these uses, according to Crooks, 'do not have a dominant influence on teachers' assessment practice' (Crooks 2002: 246). He concludes that the assessment in New Zealand primary schools

> is predominantly low stakes assessment focused on monitoring pupils' learning, improving learning through direct feedback to students or adjustments to teaching programmes. Written or oral reports to parents can be seen as complementing the formative role by giving guidance to parents and students, while also having a summative role.
>
> (Crooks 2002: 246)

The low stakes atmosphere is preserved by the existence, as in Scotland, of a quite separate programme for national monitoring. The National Education Monitoring Project (NEMP 2006), which has been in existence since 1993, assesses each year small samples of pupils using tasks that are administered by teachers seconded from other schools and trained to administer the tasks. Over a four year cycle, 15 different curriculum areas are assessed and reported. This wide range ensures that attention is not focused on areas of learning that are most easily assessed by tests.

Sweden

Sweden provides an interesting contrast with England in terms of trends over the last 20 years. While, in the late 1980s, England was moving from a decentralised to a centralised curriculum and assessment system, the reverse was the case in Sweden. Reforms, begun in 1980 and continued through the 1990s, gave more decision-making power and financial responsibility at the local level. The 290 municipalities now have freedom to decide the courses and curriculum they offer, while the central government provides guidelines and general regulations. Thus 'it is the responsibility of the municipalities and the school board of each municipality to formulate educational plans for their school district and ensure that these plans are carried out in practice (National Agency for Education 2005)' (Wikstrom 2006: 115). The National Agency for Education provided guidance to municipalities as to the implementation of government guidelines.

The population of about nine million in Sweden is relatively homogeneous and the schools and school outcomes are more evenly spread across the country than in many other OECD countries (Wikstrom 2006). School is optional at age six, but compulsory from age seven. Pupils are in comprehensive schools for the first nine years, and more than 90 per cent then move to upper secondary school at the age of 16.

As well as school autonomy, assessment changed radically in the 1990s. Until the reform of 1994, pupils' grades were norm-referenced:

> Objectives to be taught were described in centrally issued curricula that contained rather detailed descriptions of what type of knowledge should be the focus of each

subject. Students were then awarded a grade from 1 to 5, on a scale representing the overall achievement in the country.

(Wikstrom 2006: 117)

The usual problems of norm-referencing were experienced: teachers mistakenly assumed that each class should be graded according to a normal distribution; the meaning of each grade level could change from one year to another and so they could not be used for monitoring over time; grades gave no information about what pupils could do.

Although norm-referencing served the purpose of selection quite well at the end of upper secondary school, its use at earlier stages was out of line with the need for grades to be informative and was also in conflict with a society that values equal opportunities rather than competition for grades. From 1994, criterion-referencing was introduced into the comprehensive school. All assessment is carried out by teachers. In the early years grades are not assigned, although teachers report to parents at least twice a year. Only in the upper years of the comprehensive school are pupils graded according to how well their work meets the criteria at various levels for each subject. As in many statements of curriculum objectives, the description of the levels is in quite general terms and teachers are expected to collaborate in agreeing their operational meaning. Wikstrom comments that, 'since it is the teachers who assess and grade the students there has been no need for standardised examination tests, and the idea of using tests for such purposes has not been discussed for several decades' (Wikstrom 2006: 120–21), a logic that has escaped politicians and some commentators alike in England!

Nevertheless there are tests for 'scale calibration' available in Swedish, English and mathematics which are described as National Tests. Teachers use these tests in the upper comprehensive school as part of the evidence on which they base their grades. The tests are also intended to have a diagnostic function. However, the lack of clear moderation procedures for aligning grade judgements by teachers means that the results are of low reliability and so cannot be used to monitor standards over time. Recognition of these problems has led to plans to improve teachers' assessment practice through more effective teacher education in assessment. It is the role of the National Agency for Education to provide the municipalities with guidance for aligning grades. It is also responsible for monitoring the system and the inspection of schools.

France

With a population of about 60 million, France has a school structure of primary schools up to the age of 10/11, lower secondary schools for ages 11 to 15/16 and upper secondary (lycées) to the age of 17/18. School education is compulsory from the age of six to 16 years, although many children attend pre-primary education from the age of three. There is a national curriculum for all levels set out in terms of knowledge, capacities and attitudes. As in the English National Curriculum this is expressed in terms of learning objectives. The central government determines the curriculum and organises the inspectorate, while the responsibility for costs and running of schools is at three different levels: the cities for primary schools, the departments for lower second-ary schools and the regions for the lycées. Teachers are free to decide content and pedagogy, and in primary schools have more leeway in relation to the school timetable and programme than is commonly believed.

A comparison of French and English teachers of pupils in the first two years of primary education showed some interesting contrasts between their feedback practices and how they responded to pupils at different levels of achievement (Raveaud 2004). French teachers expected all pupils to tackle the same work and their 'discourse suggested that it was better for a child's self-esteem to struggle on the same task as their classmates than to be labelled a failure by being given easier work to do' (Raveaud 2004: 206). Thus in France written judgements of on-going work were made on the same basis as summative judgements. To the teachers in England, facing pupils with tasks they cannot do would be seen as damaging to their self-esteem, but this concern is over-ridden in France by a desire to give all pupils the same chance. There is little written feedback of a formative nature, although in their oral remarks to pupils teachers recognise effort and prior achievement. Thus teachers' own assessment, at least on paper, is criterion referenced and summative. The work of older primary pupils will often be given marks out of 20.

All pupils are tested on entering the third year of the primary school and the first year of the lower secondary school in French, mathematics and science. The tests are provided by the Ministry of Education but are administered and marked by teachers. The purpose is diagnostic for teachers and parents, which is why they are conducted at the beginning of the year. The tests are based on the national curriculum and the outcomes are used to identify pupils' educational needs. 'Each school is responsible for conducting the analysis of its own results using the specific computer software provided and for drawing up a 'success chart' for each pupil and each form' (Bonnet 1997: 300). There is no quality assurance of the teachers' marking of the tests (Broadfoot 1994). Because of the timing, the teachers cannot be held responsible for the results and there is evidence that teachers genuinely use them to inform their teaching (Bonnet quotes Thélot (1993) in this regard). The test results influence practice by drawing attention to areas of weakness across all schools which can be addressed by teachers, as well as guiding plans for individual pupils. To give further opportunity for teachers to use assessment to inform their teaching, a bank of test items covering most subjects has been made available at a variety of levels for both primary and secondary school.

Representative samples of the results from the compulsory diagnostic testing in the third year of primary and first year of lower secondary are collected and analysed centrally to provide a national picture of achievement and benchmarks for teachers. However, this is not the only data on national standards available to the Ministry. There is also a national survey of samples of pupils at the end of primary and of lower secondary school. As well as tests in all subjects, information is collected in these surveys about non-cognitive attainments, attitudes and values. Comparisons over time are made possible by including some common items from year to year.

Results for individual schools are not centrally reported; only the anonymous samples and the sampled survey findings are used centrally to report regional and national results. These results are widely distributed and used at regional level to identify those areas of the curriculum where schools may need help through professional development. At the national level resource allocation to regions takes into account the pupils' results in order to compensate for under-achievement which may have been caused by differential socio-economic factors (Bonnet 1996).

For school evaluation, the emphasis is on self-evaluation against a set of national standard indicators. These indicators fall into four categories: input indicators (characteristics of pupils); output indicators (pupils' achievements); resources; and school management and environment. Using the computer programs provided, schools are able to compare their profile with that of similar schools nationally or in the same region. This is considered to be a better approach to school evaluation than relying on pupils' performance in tests or examinations. School inspectors are concerned with the work of individual teachers rather the school as a whole.

Overall it is apparent that, in France, assessment is used as a tool for the improvement of education at the individual pupil level through regular testing used diagnostically, at the school level through the use of indicators, and at the national level through the central collection of information. There is an underlying belief that better assessment and evaluation and the dissemination of the information will support constructive criticism that leads to improved practice.

Themes running through the examples

Even across this limited selection of six countries outside England, there are some noteworthy themes that indicate the pros and cons of alternative assessment systems. These are considered in this section before proceeding, in Section 4, to suggest how different approaches to assessment at the primary level can be evaluated and compared. A convenient structure is to consider themes relating to how the various systems provide for assessment for the main purposes of helping learning, reporting learning, monitoring achievement at regional or national levels and contributing to the evaluation of teachers and schools.

Helping learning

All of the systems either implicitly or explicitly encourage the use of assessment to help learning. Formative assessment is built into the system in Scotland, where it has been spelled out in terms of the characteristics of teachers and schools that indicate the use of assessment to help learning (Learning and Teaching Scotland 2006). This serves to underline that formative assessment is integral to teaching and is not a matter for a formal requirement or even guidelines. All that can be done is for systems to provide opportunities for assessment to be used formative and to avoid those features that inhibit this use. Thus several countries include the 'expectation' that information that the system makes available will indeed be used to help learning.

In England, the DCSF published *The Assessment for Learning Strategy* in 2008, setting out guidance for schools in 'developing their assessment of pupils to enhance learning and improve the rate at which pupils progress' (DCSF 2008: 3). As part of this strategy is to give schools 'progression targets' measured by single level tests, as mentioned earlier, the thrust appears to have considerable summative as well as formative aspects. The formative and summative aspects are identified in terms of a time scale of assessment for different uses: day-to-day to help pupils engage with learning; 'periodic' for teachers to check on consistency of progress with national standards; and 'transitional', where levels are judged and tests and tasks used for reporting pupils' achievements.

In Wales and Northern Ireland the emphasis on the development of skills, including thinking skills, in their new curricula is linked to assessment for learning. (See, for instance, 'Why develop thinking and assessment for learning in the classroom' (Welsh Assembly Government 2007)). In a less structured way than in England, schools in Wales and Northern Ireland are expected to use assessment for learning strategies, such as sharing with pupils' learning intentions and criteria to judge quality, providing formative feedback to help improvement rather than marks or grades and encouraging pupil self-assessment.

In France, New Zealand and Sweden, teachers are provided with information that is described as 'diagnostic', raising the question of whether 'diagnostic' is the same as 'formative'. Diagnostic information has the prime purpose of alerting teachers to the needs of pupils, but catering for those needs requires action in the form of adjusting teaching (Black and Wiliam 1998a: 2) and establishing a classroom climate where teachers and pupils together decide how to take the next steps in learning (ARG 1999: 7). So it is difficult to compare systems in terms of how well they support formative assessment, since most of them claim to do so, except in considering the impact of other elements of the system. We consider this further in Section 4.

Reporting learning

In relation to internal school summative assessment, for school records and reporting to parents, the accounts of systems in France, Northern Ireland and Scotland make reference to procedures for using records of achievement to plan action and not merely to report progress. This active use of records may, as in Scotland, involve pupils in self-assessment and parents in taking action. There are, however, differences across the systems in relation to the practice of giving marks or grades. This is explicitly avoided in Sweden and in Scotland when the feedback to pupils is intended to be formative.

In all the cases considered summative assessment is criterion-based, using criteria related to the levels of achievement identified in the curricula. Apart from England, external standardised tests for individual summative assessment have not been introduced or are being phased out (as in the case of Wales and Northern Ireland). This does not mean that tests are not used; indeed it is clear that in France, for example, pupils will experience quite frequent testing. Tests that are given to all pupils at certain points in their schooling are being used for two main purposes. In France and New Zealand, teachers are required to administer tests to all pupils at the start of certain years to provide diagnostic information about achievements in core subjects as a basis for teachers to plan appropriate learning experiences. In France, New Zealand and Scotland, teachers can use items from banks of tests and tasks to check their judgements of pupils' work for summative purposes. This acknowledges that teachers' judgements need some form of moderation since they will be assessing different work conducted in differing contexts against the level description criteria. An alternative form of moderation is group discussion of examples and the creation of exemplars of the agreed operational meaning of the criteria, as proposed in Wales. Without either of these, as in the lower years of the Swedish comprehensive school, the results of teachers' assessment are of low reliability. In these early years, however, the results do not have any 'high stakes' use.

Monitoring and evaluation

Tests are also used in France, Scotland and New Zealand for the purpose of monitoring regional and national standards, but in all cases these are quite separate from tests used by teachers, as just discussed. These monitoring surveys involve a relatively small sample of pupils on each occasion and are part of an ongoing programme designed to show not only what pupils can do at any one time but also to monitor changes across the years. A large number of items can be used in a survey, with any one pupil taking only a few of them. Thus the survey can provide a good sample of the curriculum domains. Results at the class and school level are of value only when combined with others to report at regional or national levels and so cannot be used for school evaluation. These surveys are therefore described as having low stakes. In France, a sample of the tests given at the beginning of the year in the primary and first year of lower secondary school is also collected. However, as this is an anonymous sample, the results cannot be used to report on the performance of individual schools.

Wide reporting of results of the national sample surveys in France, New Zealand and Scotland enable the information to be used formatively at the system level, providing feedback that can be used to identify aspects of the curriculum that may need attention. The value of this information to schools is in focusing attention on their own practice and the performance of pupils in the areas identified as weaknesses. This use of the results encourages participation in the surveys. In this way national data are collected without adding high stakes to the assessment of pupils.

High stakes use of tests is also avoided by ensuring that the evaluation of teachers and schools for accountability is based on a range of indicators relating to the context, environment, curriculum provision and resources as well as pupil performance. In Scotland, France, and Wales, such varied indicators are provided for school evaluation and school self-evaluation. This reflects an overall aim of the systems, in these and many other countries, for the assessment of pupils and evaluation of schools to provide those in schools with tools to improve their practice rather than to be used by others to control teachers and schools.

4. EVALUATING ASSESSMENT SYSTEMS

An assessment system is made of various components which serve the main purposes and uses of assessment identified in Section 1. In this section the different ways in which assessment can be carried out are discussed in terms of criteria relating to the desirable properties of the information they provide. Each component of a system needs to provide information that is valid for its purpose. Another requirement is that it should provide reliable data. Also to be taken into account is the interdependence of the various system components and the impact that assessment for one purpose may have on other assessment practices and on the curriculum and pedagogy. Further, there is the practicability of an approach, including the use of resources. Assessment can be costly, both in terms of monetary resources and the time of pupils and teachers. These four qualities can be used as evaluation criteria in seeking assessment system components that are fit for purpose.

Validity

In the context of assessment, validity refers to how well what is assessed corresponds with the processes or outcomes of learning that it is intended should be assessed so that justified inferences can be based on the results. This is 'construct validity', which is generally regarded as being the overarching concept that contains within it concepts such as face, concurrent, and content validity (Messick 1989; Gipps 1994). Validity is generally considered in relation to summative assessment but it is also applicable to formative assessment.

Formative assessment

For construct validity in formative assessment the methods used should provide information about what pupils can do in relation to the detailed goals of a lesson and should be interpreted by the teacher in terms of progression in the development of more general ideas or skills to that next steps can be identified. The methods the teacher uses to gather the information are likely to be a combination of direct observation, including listening to pupils' discussion, and review of what they write or draw about their experiences.

Summative assessment

For summative assessment that is for internal school uses and is conducted by the teacher, validity will depend on the range of evidence that is used. Construct validity is likely to be greater when teachers use information from the full range of learning activities, which cover all the goals, than when the special tests or tasks are used which can only cover some of the goals of pupils' work (although such tasks and tests have a role in filling gaps in teachers' observations). The problem with relying entirely on internal tests is that teachers tend to emulate external tests in developing their own tests and their assessment practices are particularly subject to this influence when there are high stakes attached to external tests (Pollard *et al.* 2000).

When summative assessment is for external use, that is for grouping or selection of individual pupils or to meet requirements of national assessment policies, high validity is essential, since what is assessed contains strong messages about what is valued. When the stakes are high, however, as in England where the results of national tests are used for evaluation and accountability of teachers and schools, the requirement of high validity tends to be compromised by the need for high reliability of the results in the interests of fairness. What this means is that what is included in the test is restricted to those learning outcomes where performance can be most easily marked as correct or incorrect. This tends to exclude outcomes that are more difficult to judge unequivocally as right or wrong, such as application of concepts, reasoning, understanding (as opposed to factual knowledge) and attitudes that are likely to influence future learning. This interaction between validity and reliability is a key point that we return to in the discussion of reliability.

Accountability

Validity is also of great importance in relation to the information used for accountability. It can be argued that validity here means having information about the actions and outcomes for which teachers and schools can be held accountable. In the context of pupils' learning, teachers can be held accountable for what they do in the classroom, what learning opportunities they provide and the help they give to pupils, and so on. They are not necessarily responsible for whether externally prescribed learning outcomes are achieved, since this depends on other factors over which the teacher does not have control, such as the pupils' prior learning and the many out of school influences and conditions that affect their learning. Thus teachers and schools ought to be held to account for the programme of learning opportunities that is provided and the evidence of relevant learning, but not judged solely on the level of outcomes reached by their pupils.

When rewards or sanctions are attached to results, which then acquire 'high stakes', attention is inevitably focused on maximising the outcomes that are assessed. The consequence is to focus teaching content on what is assessed, and teaching methods on transmission of this content, narrowing pupils' learning opportunities. (The education service is not the only area where practices are distorted by naïve measures of accountability; the health service in England provides many examples of this impact.) For high validity, information used in accountability should include, in addition to data on pupils' achievements, information about the curriculum and teaching methods and relevant aspects of pupils' backgrounds and of their learning histories. Various school self-evaluation guidelines provide some good examples of what this means (HMIe 2006; DfES/Ofsted 2004; Estyn 2004a, 2004b)). The validity of these approaches to accountability, however, is infringed if undue weight is given to pupil performance measures.

System monitoring

For monitoring standards of pupil achievement at the regional or national levels, the most valid information describes what pupils are able to do across the full range of learning objectives in particular areas of the curriculum. The interest is not in the performance of individual pupils but in the population performance in each learning domain, such as different aspects of mathematics, or reading or other subjects. Thus validity resides in how well the domain is sampled. If the data used in monitoring is a summation of individual test results, as it is in England where national tests results are used to monitor change in national standards, then the sample of the domain is restricted to the questions that any individual pupil can answer in a test of reasonable length. This is not necessarily a good sample of the domain, and will depend quite heavily on the particular content of the test. A more valid approach is to use a far greater number of items, providing a more representative sample of the domain. Since the concern is not with the performance of individual pupils, there is no need for all pupils to be given the same items. All that is needed is for each item to be attempted by an adequate sample of the population. Sampling of this kind, where only a small proportion of pupils are selected and each only takes a sample of the full range of items, is used in international surveys (such as the OECD's PISA and the IEA surveys such as TIMSS) and in national surveys in the Scottish Survey of Assessment (SSA) (SEED 2005b) and the Assessment of Performance Unit (APU), when this existed in England, Wales and Northern Ireland (DES/WO/DENI 1989; Foxman, Hutchinson and Bloomfield 1991).

Reliability

While validity refers to the kind of information used in assessment and evaluation, reliability refers to the accuracy or consistency of the information. Any observation or measurement has some error; what inaccuracy is acceptable depends on the purpose. In the context of assessment reliability is often defined as, and measured by, the extent to which the assessment, if repeated, would give the same result.

Formative assessment

In formative assessment reliability is not of concern because the evidence is both collected and used by teacher and pupil and no judgement of grade or level is involved; only the judgement of how to help a pupil take the next steps in learning. The teacher can detect and correct any mistaken judgements in on-going interaction with the pupil (Black and Wiliam 2006).

Summative assessment

In relation to summative assessment it is necessary to keep in mind the trade-off between validity and reliability mentioned earlier. Striving for high reliability can reduce validity because of preference for items and procedures that provide responses that are easily measured or judged. In the case of summative assessment for internal purposes the trade-off can be in favour of validity, since no external decisions need hang on the reported data. This would suggest that, from the arguments given above, use of teachers' judgements based on the full range of work is to be preferred to the use of tests. If the evidence is derived from regular work and is gathered over a period of time, it covers a range of opportunities for pupils to show their learning without the anxiety associated with tests. Nevertheless internal summative assessment is used to record pupil achievement and report to parents and so there needs to be some consistency in the judgements made by teachers in the same school. The approach to optimising reliability of teachers' judgements that is considered of general benefit is through moderation meetings where teachers discuss and apply criteria to examples of pupils' work (Good 1988; Radnor 1995; Hall and Harding 2002).

Moderation is not merely desirable but necessary when summative assessment is for use outside the school. If the results have high stakes uses, either for selection of pupils or for evaluation of teachers and schools, reliability is of the essence. Teachers' judgements are known to have low reliability when no attempt is made to provide the structure or training to assure consistency in the use of criteria (Harlen 2004). By comparison with teachers' judgements, external tests are widely considered to be more reliable and therefore to be preferred for summative assessment. However, as Wiliam (2001) and Black and Wiliam (2006) have pointed out, this assumption is not justified.

Regardless of the consistency of individual test items, the fact that a test has to be limited to a small sample of possible items means that the test as a whole is a rather poor measure for any individual pupil. This is because a different selection of items would produce a different result. Wiliam (2001) estimated the difference that this would make for the end of Key Stage tests in England. With a test of overall reliability of 0.80, this source of error would result in 32 per cent of pupils being given the wrong level. The only way to reduce this error would be to increase the length of the test, but this has only a small effect. Black and Wiliam calculate that

> if we wanted to improve the reliability of Key Stage 2 tests so that only 10 per cent of students were awarded the incorrect level, we should need to increase the length of the tests in each subject to over 30 hours.
>
> (Black and Wiliam 2006: 126)

Thus the case for using tests for reporting achievement of individual pupils, based solely on grounds of reliability, falls apart. When we also recall that efforts to achieve high reliability of a test are at the expense of validity, then the balance of advantage falls heavily on the side of using teachers' judgements. There are several ways of raising the reliability of teachers' assessment (Harlen 1994). The examples of practice in various countries show that the most commonly used are group moderation and the use of special tests or tasks that have been tried out and calibrated as assessing certain levels of achievement for teachers to use to check their judgements. The danger of these tasks being used to replace teachers' judgements is avoided where assessment is seen as a tool for improvement and not a basis for school evaluation. Where the only purpose is to give a good account of pupils' learning outcomes, there is no incentive to inflate results or depart from intended procedures. Moreover, this use of teachers' judgement is in harmony with the practice of formative assessment, as we see in considering impact below.

Accountability

In the context of accountability, reliability refers to whether the information used is sufficiently accurate for sound and fair judgements to be made. Only part of the relevant information will be concerned with pupils' learning outcomes. For this part, the arguments above make a strong case for basing the information on moderated teachers' judgements as these can provide more accurate information than external tests. For the other information that is needed, about input and process variables and resources, the evaluation carried out in the school should have checks built into the process. In some systems external checks are provided by inspectors using the same criteria.

System monitoring

The reliability of national monitoring of pupil performance depends on the reliability of individual items and on the number that are included. Using only a small number of items, in tests designed for individual pupils, restricts the sample of the domain that is assessed; merely collecting the same data from a larger number of pupils at the national level will not increase the reliability of the assessment of the subject domain. Less reliably assessed, but important aspects of achievement, such as application of knowledge and skills, can be monitored. These are known to be highly context-dependent (Pine *et al.* 2006) but, because a number of such items spread across different contexts can be included in a survey, a more reliable measure can be achieved. In surveys, optimum design calls for a balance between adequate sampling of the student population and adequate sampling of the subject domain: in this perspective, blanket uniform national tests are far from optimum, being over-sampled on the population and under-sampled on the subject domain.

Impact

The word 'impact' is used here to refer to what has been identified as 'consequential validity' (Messick 1989), that is to say the intended and unintended consequences of an assessment (Stobart 2006).

Formative assessment

In the case of formative assessment, the purpose is to have a positive impact on learning and indeed, as suggested earlier, the process can hardly be called formative (assessment for learning) unless this is the case. There is a growing volume of evidence, mostly from studies at the secondary level, that formative assessment does raise levels of achievement. Black *et al*. (2003) report their own research with teachers of English, mathematics and science whose pupils achieved 'significant learning gains' following the use of assessment for learning. Black *et al*. (2003) also cite research by Bergan *et al*. (1991), White and Frederiksen (1998) and a review of research by Fuchs and Fuchs (1986) as providing evidence of better learning when formative assessment is built into teaching. Working with younger pupils, a positive impact of non-judgemental, 'no marks', feedback on levels of interest, effort and achievement was reported in studies by Butler (1988) and Brookhart and DeVoge (1999), while studies by Schunk (1996) have found positive impacts on achievement of self-assessment.

Summative assessment

The nature of the impact of internal summative assessment on pupils varies with its frequency as well as the range of information taken into account. In many cases grades, marks or even levels are assigned to pupils' work more often than necessary and when it would be more appropriate to provide formative feedback. Also, teachers sometimes use grades as motivation, but Brookhart and DeVoge (1999) make the point that exhorting students to work 'to get a good grade' is on the one hand motivating to pupils but on the other sets up 'a performance orientation that ultimately may decrease motivation' (p. 423). Good grades are sometimes given to reward effort or good behaviour rather than as an indication of the quality of the work. This practice amounts to using grades as rewards and punishments, as extrinsic motivation, incurring all the dis- advantages for students' motivation for learning that this entails (Harlen and Deakin Crick, 2003; Reay and Wiliam, 1999). Internal school moderation of teachers' judge- ments should discourage this practice and school policies should require summative assessment only when really necessary (ARG 2006a).

As well as avoiding the practices that lead to negative impact on classroom work (as reviewed by Crooks (1988); Black and Wiliam (1998b); Harlen and Deakin Crick (2003)) action can be taken that has a positive impact. There is evidence that changing teachers' assessment can encourage a richer curriculum experience for pupils. For example, Flexer *et al*. (1995) reported changes when teachers of third grade pupils in a school district in the USA were introduced to assessment methods using evidence from pupils' classroom performance instead of using tests. The researchers reported several effects on teachers and pupils after a year of using these methods. Teachers were using more hands-on activities, problem solving and asking pupils for explanations. They were also trying to use more systematic observations for assessment. All agreed that the pupils had learned more and that they knew more about what their pupils knew. The teachers reported generally positive feedback from their pupils, who had better con- ceptual understanding, could solve problems better and explain solutions.

Such experiences underline the reality that teaching will inevitably be focused on what is assessed. When conducted by testing this impact is bound to have a narrowing effect on what is taught because, as discussed earlier, tests only sample the learning outcomes and include those outcomes more easily assessed by tests. The impact can be positive, however, as the work of Flexer *et al*. (1995) shows, if teachers use a much wider range of assessment methods. Further evidence was provided by Hall and Harding (2002) and Hall *et al*. (1997), who reported that the introduction of teachers' assessment in the National Curriculum Assessment in England and Wales, was perceived by teachers as having a positive impact on pupils' learning. Their summative assessment was based on teachers' judgements across a range of pupils' work. The impact was enhanced by teachers working collaboratively towards a shared understanding of the goals and of the procedures to achieve these goals. Unfortunately the funding and opportunities for these meetings declined in the face of pressure to raise test scores and the ground that was gained (in quality of teacher assessment) in the early and mid '90s was lost (Hall and Harding 2002: 13).

Accountability

However, it is the use of test results for accountability and particularly for creating performance targets and league table of schools that puts teachers under pressure to increase scores by teaching to the tests. Evidence is that they do this by giving multiple practice tests and coaching pupils in how to answer test questions rather than in using and applying their understanding more widely (Harlen and Deakin Crick 2003). Other known consequences are the de-motivation of lower achieving pupils and, for all pupils, a view of learning as product rather than process (ARG 2002b). It also leads to undue attention being focused on those who are performing just below the target level, with less attention for those who are either too far below or are already above the target level. Other evidence of impact of testing on pupils was gathered in a survey of teachers conducted by the NUT (NUT 2006).

In consultation responses concern was expressed that the additional testing proposed in England in *Making Good Progress* (DfES 2007) and in the *Assessment for Learning Strategy* (DCSF 2008) (see Section 3) will inevitably increase the pressure on teachers and the stress on pupils. The Assessment Reform Group's response to the consultation on *Making Good Progress* pointed out the following:

> The status of schools will be measured by new 'progress' results as well as by their results on the existing tests. The proposal to supplement schools' income in the light or these single-level test results will further increase the pressure to give these tests priority. Thus it is clear that there is here a significant addition to existing high-stakes testing pressures. We agree that schools should be expected to aspire to improve upon the attainments of their pupils. We do not agree that this is best achieved by placing yet greater emphasis on test results.
>
> High-stakes uses of individual pupils' results are likely to distort teaching and learning. What is proposed in *Making Good Progress* is not a low-stakes 'assess when ready' model based essentially on teachers' judgements, but a high-stakes external assessment, conducted every six months in every school year, in which tests are seen as being 'underpinned' by teachers' assessment, but are nevertheless a mechanism for awarding levels without any use of such assessments. We consider that there is a grave risk that this will exacerbate the current narrowing influence that national tests have on teaching and learning … the frequency of testing will mean that the experience of pupils in every year will be dominated by these single-level tests which will be even narrower than those currently used at the end of Key Stages. The already considerable time spent on test-related activities (estimated at around 10% of teaching and learning time in year 6 for example) would no doubt increase.
>
> (ARG response to DfES 2007)

The House of Commons Children Schools and Families Committee in its report on *Testing and Assessment* (2008a) also noted concerns about the proposed single levels tests. These related not only to the policy but also to the rushed nature of the trials, recommending that 'the Government allow sufficient time for a full pilot of the single-level tests and ensures that any issues and problems arising out of that pilot are fully addressed before any formal roll-out of the new regime to schools' (House of Commons 2008a: 69/70). The publication of the *Assessment for Learning Strategy* does not suggest that this recommendation has been heeded. The Government's response to the Committee's report was to emphasise the formative function of the single-level tests. The Committee, however, had recommended that:

> ... if single-level tests are introduced, they are used for summative purposes only and that Assessment for Learning and personalized learning are supported separately by enhanced professional development for teachers, backed up with a centralised bank of formative and diagnostic materials on which teachers can draw as necessary on a regular basis.
>
> (House of Commons 2008a: recommendation 26)

The effects of setting targets based on tests are by now widely known and recognised by pupils themselves:

> Students are drilled to jump through hoops that the examiner is holding ... The mechanical exam process is moulding a mechanical education.
>
> (Tom Greene, a secondary school pupil, writing in *The Independent*, 17.8.06)

and by parents:

> For my son, and for most 10-year-olds in the country, the next nine months will be ... a sterile, narrow and meaningless exercise in drilling and cramming. It's nothing to do with the skills of his teacher, who seems outstanding. Nor do I blame the school. It's called preparing for Key Stage 2 SATs.
>
> (Alex Benaby, writing in *The Guardian*, 10.10.06)

as well as by teachers and researchers.

Unfortunately this awareness did not appear to extend to the Government, whose response to the concern expressed about this matter by House of Commons Children, Schools and Families Committee on Testing and Assessment (House of Commons 2008a: Recommendation 23) was to deny any responsibility for teaching to the test and to blame teachers:

> The breadth of the curriculum and the quality of teaching are both entirely within the control of the school and the teacher.
>
> (House of Commons 2008b: 4)

This is despite the acknowledgement of Her Majesty's Chief Inspector of Education, Children's Services and Skills, also in response to the Committee's report, that in Year 6 some schools emphasised the subject tested at the expense of other learning opportunities (House of Commons 2008b: Appendix 2: 12). So, in the face of so much evidence of impact on children's educational experience, clearly associated with government policy, it is important to ask why tests and targets based on them were introduced and what benefit they were intended to have.

System monitoring

The rationale for testing is embodied in the slogan that 'testing drives up standards'. Important evidence on this matter was collected in an extensive review by Tymms of test results in England from 1995 to 2003. Tymms (2004) made reference to data on test results from nine sources in addition to the statutory national tests for pupils at ages 11 and 13.[1] The data from five key sources (including international surveys of achievements) were analysed to show year on year changes. The pattern that was found in national test results for eleven-year-olds was a rise over the first five years (1995–99) followed by no change from 2000 to 2003. The pattern was the same for mathematics and English. While some other data supported a rise from 1995–99, it was noted that the data from the Trends in Mathematics and Science Surveys (TIMSS) showed no rise in mathematics over this period.

While Tymms (2004) could identify several reasons why standards of tests may have changed over this time (mainly related to how cut-off scores for levels are determined when tests change from year to year) he concluded that the effect of teaching test technique (new to pupils of this age in 1995) and of teaching to the test are very likely to have accounted for a good deal of the initial change. This conclusion is supported by trends over time in other test regimes. For example, in the USA Linn (2000) found 'a pattern of early gains followed by a levelling off' (Linn 2000: 6) to be typical across States where high stakes tests are used.

The trend continues in the figures for 2006, where end of Key Stage results for English show no change from 2005 and mathematics has improved by only 1 per cent. The Government's target of 85 per cent reaching the 'required standard' has still not been reached. The results have been prompted further required changes in the Government's literacy and numeracy strategies with the aim of 'driving up performance in the test in future years', while commentators have suggested that:

> a more relaxed atmosphere in schools with pupils given more time to enjoy their learning rather than being taught for the test might just be the recipe for success.
> (Garner 2006)

However, as noted earlier, using national test results to monitor standards provides a very limited view of pupils' achievement. So we cannot really tell whether or not standards are changing. A more useful picture would be obtained by a sample survey, where teachers do not know which pupils will be tested and pupils in the same class will not in any case all be given the same items, so results would not be distorted by practising what is to be assessed. Moreover, a wide ranging survey would be able to identify areas of weakness and so facilitate better targeted remedial action.

A sample survey, separate from national tests, was recommended by the House of Commons Children, Schools and Families Committee on Testing and Assessment (House of Commons 2008a: recommendation 23). The Government's response, however, was to defend the practice of using national tests for several uses, in particular 'measuring pupil attainment; school and teacher accountability; and national monitoring. It is the Government's clear view that test result data is fit to support each of these three important uses' (House of Commons 2008b: Appendix 1, 9).

Resources

The resources required for assessment are of two main kinds: direct costs of materials, postage, external marking, and analysis and reporting results; and indirect costs of teachers' and teaching assistants' time in preparing, giving practice and invigilating tests, and in moderating teachers' assessment. Pupils' learning time is also a key resource to be considered. In England, the direct costs of national testing are borne by the QCA but clearly, as with all other costs, these are ultimately costs to the system. The costs of summative assessment far outweigh those of implementing formative assessment.

Formative assessment

Here the main cost is in providing teachers with professional development and with good descriptions of progression in the understandings, skills and attitudes that are the goals of learning. Once in place the running costs of formative assessment are zero; time may be used differently than without formative assessment but its practice does not necessarily require more or less time overall.

Summative assessment

The resources needed for internal summative assessment are essentially those of teachers' time and pupils' learning time. When teachers' judgements are used, the process need not reduce pupils' learning time since the collection and selection of examples of work for assessment has a potential formative value as self-assessment. Teachers' time is needed, however, for moderation meetings, for keeping records, writing reports and talking with parents. If tests are used for external summative assessment there is a tendency for a school to use tests for internal assessment and to purchase commercial tests for practice, involving direct cost to the school and taking up learning time for practice tests.

It is useful to have some idea of the scale of time used for these summative assessment activities, although any figures have to be treated with great caution. The estimation of the amount of time used for various assessment activities, for both internal and external uses was attempted by the *Assessment Systems for the Future* project (ARG 2006a), drawing on figures from three surveys of assessment costs. These were a survey by PriceWaterhouseCoopers for the QCA (QCA 2004); a survey conducted by what was then the Secondary Heads Association (SHA 2004); and one focusing on science, carried out for the Royal Society by Sheffield Hallam University (2003). Table 19.1 combines information for 2003 for the six years of the primary school.

The peaks of time at the end of Key Stages are evident. But it is also clear that it is not the time spent on administering tests, but the preparation for them that is most demanding. The extra time used when external summative assessment is based on tests, over that required for all other assessment activities, is 100 hours in Year 2, 96 hours for Years 3–5 and 165 hours for Year 6. So, in Year 6, 165 hours, or about 5 weeks (at 33 hours per week) would be available for teachers to use in other ways. This figure is consistent with findings of NUT (2003) research that Year 6 teachers spend about 4.6 hours per week preparing for national tests.

Table 19.1 Key Stage 2 – teachers' time (in hours per year)

	Y1	Y2*	Y3	Y4	Y5	Y6
Teachers' assessment (including observation, discussion, marking)	45	53	105	105	157	157
Internal testing and preparation and use of any special tasks or commercial tests	n/a	80	96	96	96	150
National testing	n/a	20	n/a	n/a	n/a	15
Moderation	40	40	25	25	25	30
Report writing	30	30	20	20	20	20
Parents' evenings	15	15	15	15	15	15
Total	130	218	261	261	313	387

*Note that in 2003 tests were required and reported at the end of KS1.
(Source: ARG 2006b).

Estimates for pupil time spent on assessment suggest that practising and taking tests occupies the equivalent of about nine days a year in Year 5 and 13 days in Year 6 above time for all other assessment activities. Again most of this is time that could be used in other ways.

Accountability

Turning to resources used for accountability, it inevitably takes time to gather the kind of information that we have argued is necessary for schools to provide an account of their performance. However, when accountability is based on self-evaluation by those within the school, it serves the important function of formative evaluation that should be part of the practice of any institution. The alternative, of basing judgement of schools on the performance of pupils, leads to the negative impacts on teachers and pupils outlined earlier.

System Monitoring

In relation to system monitoring, the economical advantage of collating achievement data already available, as in using national tests for identifying national trends, must be judged against the extent to which such data provide useful and relevant information. As we have seen, using end of Key Stages test results for this purpose is of highly questionable value. Similarly the more costly process of establishing and running surveys covering a wide range of educational outcomes has to be judged against providing more detailed feedback that can be useful not only at the policy level, but also directly to practitioners. Separating monitoring from the performance of individual students would obviate the need for central collection of student assessment data. In turn, this would set student summative assessment free from the high stakes that tend to reduce what is taught to what is assessed, whether by tests or teachers' assessment.

5. DISCUSSION

Even if we do not wish to go so far as to claim that what is assessed determines what is taught, it cannot be denied that, as stated at the start of this paper, it does have a large impact on pupils' education experiences. For that reason, if we are concerned to have an assessment system that supports the aims of a modern education, we need to be quite clear about what we want pupils to learn.

Whilst it is not the role of this chapter to identify the curriculum objectives of primary education, it is necessary to keep in mind the kinds of goals that are needed in order to prepare our pupils for their part in a rapidly changing and increasingly technological world. For this, what they learn should include, but go beyond, basic skills and knowledge. Current thinking, world-wide, emphasises the importance of helping children to develop certain skills, attitudes, knowledge and understanding; characteristics that are regarded as more important than accumulating large amounts of factual knowledge. Content knowledge can be found readily from the information sources widely available through the use of computers and especially the internet. What are needed are the skills to access these sources and the understanding to select what is relevant and to make sense of it. So pupils need understanding of broad, widely applicable concepts and the ability to use them to solve problems and make decisions in new situations. Indeed, such outcomes of education appear in statements from government departments and other organisations urging the development of citizenship, creativity and economic productivity. The OECD points out that what pupils should learn in school are

> the prerequisites for successful learning in future life. These prerequisites are of both a cognitive and a motivational nature. Students must become able to organise and regulate their own learning, to learn independently and in groups, and to overcome difficulties in the learning process. This requires them to be aware of their own thinking processes and learning strategies and methods.
>
> (OECD 1999: 9)

Statements such as this have implication for pedagogy, as does the emphasis on talk and interaction among pupils and between pupils and teachers (Alexander 2006).

Given that what we assess will influence whether or not pupils have opportunities to achieve such goals, it's pertinent to ask: are these important learning outcomes being assessed by the system presently in place in primary education in England? Examination of what is assessed in the national tests suggests that this is not the case. Further, since teachers' own assessment tends to follow the form and context of external assessment, this also fails to reflect these goals.

This situation is made all the more serious in the assessment system in England by using the external test results for several different purposes. What is tested for each individual pupil (mathematics and English at Key Stage 1, with science added at KS2) is also used for evaluating the performance of teachers, schools and LEAs and for monitoring national standards over time. We have argued that the information from these tests is of low validity not only on account of marking and other errors, but because they fail to cover some important outcomes of primary education. We have also seen that, being test-based, the information is also of low reliability, because a different selection of test items would be likely to give different results for a significant proportion of pupils. Overall, then the current system provides information of only low dependability. Moreover, evidence of changes in standards of achievements over the years (Tymms 2004) does not support the claim that testing 'drives up standards'. Added to this is the negative impact of high stakes tests on the use of assessment to help learning, on pupils' motivation for learning, and on how the time of teachers and pupils is used. There is no indication from other countries, either, that testing improves learning; rather the reverse:

> Finland – the country with the highest standards and the smallest gap between those who do best and those who do least well – has no regular testing or inspection programme. Rather, it has a fully comprehensive, unstreamed system in which highly educated teachers ... are treated as responsible professionals.
>
> (Mortimore 2006)

Together these points lead to the unavoidable conclusion that the current assessment system in England is inadequate both in what is assessed and how it is being assessed. How can we do better?

The criticisms fall chiefly on the use of tests for external summative assessment and on the high stakes created by the use of results for accountability and monitoring. Given that these are separable features, since other countries make use of tests without incurring the high stakes impact, four possibilities for change are:

- Tests combined with high stakes
- Tests with no high stakes
- No tests, but other assessment, with high stakes
- No tests, but other assessment, without high stakes.

Of course there are numerous other combinations, but discussion of these somewhat crude alternatives serves to highlight the principles that have to be considered.

The first of these four is what already exists in England. The second would not avoid the problem of the low validity and reliability of external tests if the same whole tests are given to all the pupils. However, alternative models suggested by Green *et al.* (2007) would be capable of increasing the validity of the tests whilst at the same time avoiding the wash-back into teaching that narrows the curriculum. One model would create a large bank of items, thus giving greater curriculum coverage, of which every pupil would take a sample. The average score for a school (except in very small schools) would give a good measure of performance for accountability purposes while teachers' assessment would be used for reporting on individual pupils. The school test data would be used to moderate the teachers' assessment. In a second model, pupils would be sampled, as in APU surveys, reducing the impact of testing and giving good data at the national level. Again, moderated teachers' assessment would be used at the individual pupil level and the school accountability data secured through a 'new balance of regional/area inspection services and national inspection' (Green *et al.* 2007: 4).

The third possibility listed above runs the risk that the alternative to tests, using teachers' judgements, could acquire the same disadvantages as the use of tests if the results were used for high stakes evaluation and monitoring. Moderation procedures would be likely to become more formalised, over-elaborate and to constrain teachers to collecting evidence using 'safe' methods that are going to 'pass' the moderation procedures. (There is evidence that this happens at secondary level where teachers' judgements are used for some parts of GCSE examinations (Donnelly *et al.* 1993)).

So we are left with the fourth alternative, of not depending on test results and ensuring that the results of summative assessment for pupils do not acquire high stakes for the teacher and school. This would mean that information for accountability and for system monitoring would have to be provided in other ways, as recognised in the models suggested by Green *et al.* (2007).

The alternative to depending on test results must enable the full range of learning outcomes to be included. The use of teachers' judgements would enable this to happen since teachers can collect evidence during the numerous opportunities they have for 'observing, questioning, listening to informal discussion and reviewing written work' (ARG 2006: 9). At once this not only improves validity but removes the source of unreliability that tests cannot avoid since they can include only a narrow sample of the learning goals. A particular advantage is that teachers will be gathering this information in any case if they are using assessment for learning.

Evidence from on-going learning activities can be used both for formative assessment and for summative assessment but with an important condition – that it is reviewed and reinterpreted against the reporting criteria. The reason for this is that, as noted earlier, in formative assessment judgements are often both pupil-referenced and criterion-referenced, while for summative assessment achievement has to be criterion-referenced (that is to say, judged only against the reporting criteria). This review of the evidence needs to be done only at those times, usually twice a year, when reporting is required. Practical ways of using evidence both formatively and summatively are suggested by Harlen (2007). The point to be made here is that this approach to assessment meets the major objections to tests, assuming that effective ways of assuring quality are in place.

Several approaches to quality assurance are used in those systems that depend for summative assessment on teachers' judgements, as mentioned in Section 3. The use of a calibrated bank of tasks and test items is a common one. This provides a role for tests and tasks but carries the danger that they may become the main or only source of evidence. When used to supplement teachers' judgements they have value in providing operational definitions of certain learning goals, which is of special benefit to inexperienced teachers. They can also 'plug gaps' where regular activities have, for one reason or another, not provided opportunities for teachers to judge students' performance. This is a somewhat different role from using the results of tests to give a separate assessment which is compared with that from teachers' assessment. This happens in the end of Key Stage tests in England, where

> the teachers' judgements and test results in the core subjects are reported alongside each other and are said to have equal weight. The rationale for reporting both is that they are intended to assessment different types of performance. But evidence from QCA surveys shows that many teachers include the test results in the evidence they use to form their judgements and so the value of using separate sources of evidence is compromised. In any case, teachers know that it is only the test results that matter since these are used for setting targets and evaluating schools' performance.
>
> (Harlen 2007: 144)

In the Scottish system, the intention is that teachers use national tests as a means of moderating their judgements. If the results do not agree then the teacher may use evidence from the test (which he or she has administered and marked) to reconsider the decision about the level reached. But this is only one way in which teachers can moderate their judgement and without the high stakes attached to the results in Scotland, there is much less imperative to use tests.

Alternative means of quality assurance are group discussion of examples of pupils' work to align judgements, and the use of exemplars of assessed work (usually written but could include video clips of performance). Moderation meetings, although more difficult to implement than the use of exemplars by individual teachers, have benefits beyond the reliability of the outcome:

> A system of moderation of teachers' judgements through professional collaboration benefits teaching and learning as well as assessment. Moderation that affects the planning and implementation of assessment, and consequently teachers' understanding of learning goals and of the criteria indicating progress towards them, has more than a quality assurance function.
>
> (ARG 2006a: 6)

Other conditions that are known to increase the reliability of teachers' judgements are the provision of detailed criteria linked to learning goals, professional development that addresses the known sources of error and bias in teachers' judgements and a school culture in which assessment is discussed constructively and positively and not seen as a necessary chore (Harlen 2005).

A revised system must make provision for dependable school evaluation and national monitoring. This will involve assessment of pupils since pupil performance is undeniably an essential measure of the effectiveness of an education system. However, as argued here, there are many other influences that affect pupils' achievement and schools ought not to be judged solely on the levels of pupil performance, but on the wider range of provision they make for their pupils' education. For national monitoring, a far greater sample of performance in a domain is needed than is provided by collecting the results of individual pupils who have all taken the same test. Whilst it would be possible to collect this wider information from teachers' assessment of a sample of pupils, it would be less intrusive and more reliable for monitoring trends over time to use a regular survey. A small sample of the pupil population, between them answering a range of items, is all that is needed to provide a good estimate of pupils' performance in a domain and to identify where strengths and weaknesses lie to inform policy and practice.

Finally, an effective assessment system is an open one, where all involved know what evidence is used and how it informs judgements. Much of the emotion aroused by assessment is a result of fear or suspicion of the unknown. To take this away we need to be completely open about the need for and purpose of assessment and why it is carried out in particular ways. Even the youngest pupils can be given some explanation of what evidence they and their teachers can use to judge the progress they are making. This helps pupils to take part in assessing their own work, which is a key feature of using assessment to help learning. It is equally important for summative assessment so that there are no surprises (for pupils or parents) in the reports of the level reached at a particular time.

NOTES

1 Tymms updates this work in Chapter 17 of this volume.

REFERENCES

ACCAC (Qualifications, Curriculum and Assessment Authority for Wales) (2004) *Review of the School Curriculum and Assessment Arrangements 5–16*. Cardiff: ACCAC.

Alexander, R.J. (2008) *Towards Dialogic Teaching: rethinking classroom talk* (4th edition). York: Dialogos. (First edition 2004).

Assessment Reform Group (ARG) (2006a) *The Role of Teachers in the Assessment of Learning*. Online (Available: www.assessment-reform-group.org, and from the CPA office of the Institute of Education, University of London).

——(2006b) ASF Working Paper 3. Online (Available: http://k1.ioe.ac.uk/tlrp/arg/ASF-working paper3.htm).

——(2002a) *Assessment for Learning: 10 principles*. Online. (Available: www.assessment-reform-group.org, and from the CPA office of the Institute of Education, University of London).

——(2002b) *Testing, Motivation and Learning*. Online. (Available: www.assessment-reform-group.org, and from the CPA office of the Institute of Education, University of London).

——(1999) *Assessment for Learning: beyond the black box*. Online. (Available: www.assessment-reform-group.org, and from the CPA office of the Institute of Education, University of London).

Association for School and College Leaders (ASCL) (2006) *Chartered Examiners*, Policy Paper 13. Leicester: ASCL.

Benaby, A. (2006) 'Losing a year and gaining … nothing', *The Guardian,* 10 October 2006.

Bergan, J.R., Sladeczek, I.E., Schwarz, R.D. and Smith, A.N. (1991) 'Effects of a measurement and planning system on kindergarteners' cognitive development and educational programming', *American Educational Research Journal* 28: 683–714.

Black, P. (1997) 'Whatever happened to TGAT?', in C. Cullingford (Ed) *Assessment versus Evaluation*. London: Cassell.

Black, P., Harrison, C., Lee, C., Marshall, B. and Wiliam, D. (2003) *Assessment for Learning: putting it into practice*. Maidenhead: Open University Press.

Black, P. and Wiliam, D. (2006) 'The reliability of assessment', in J. Gardner (Ed) *Assessment and Learning*. London: Sage.

——(1998a) *Inside the Black Box*. Slough: NFER Nelson.

——(1998b) 'Assessment and classroom learning', *Assessment in Education* 5(1): 1–74.

Bonnet, G. (1997) 'Country profile from France', *Assessment in Education* 4(2): 295–306.

Brookhart, S. and DeVoge, J. (1999) 'Testing a theory about the role of classroom assessment in pupil motivation and achievement', *Applied Measurement in Education* 12: 409–25.

Butler, R. (1988) 'Enhancing and undermining intrinsic motivation: the effects of task-involving and ego-involving evaluation on interest and performance', *British Journal of Education Psychology* 58: 1–14.

CIEA (Chartered Institute of Educational Assessors) (2008) Website: www.ciea.org.uk.

Crooks, T.J. (1988) 'The impact of classroom evaluation practices on students', *Review of Educational Research* 58: 438–81.

——(2002) 'Educational assessment in New Zealand schools', *Assessment in Education* 9(2): 237–54

Department of Education and Science (DES)/ the Welsh Office (WO) (1988) *Task Group on Assessment and Testing: a report*. London: DfES/WO.

DES/WO/DENI (1989) *National Assessment: the APU science approach*. London: HMSO.

Department for Children, Schools and Families (DCSF) (2008) *The Assessment for Learning Strategy*. Nottingham: DCFS Publications

DfES (2007) *Making Good Progress*, Consultation. London: DfES.

——(2004) *Excellence and Enjoyment: learning and teaching in the primary years*. London: DfES.

DfES/Ofsted (2004) *A New Relationship with Schools: improving performance through school self-evaluation*. London: DfES/Ofsted.

Donnelly, J.F., Buchan, A.S., Jenkins, E.W., Welford, A.G. (1993) *Policy, Practice and Teachers' Professional Judgement: the internal assessment of practical work in GCSE science.* Driffield: Nafferton Books.

Estyn (2004a) *Guidance on the Inspection of Primary and Nursery Schools.* Cardiff: Estyn.

——(2004b) *Guidance on the Inspection of Secondary Schools.* Cardiff: Estyn.

Flexer, R.J., Cumbo, K., Borko, H., Mayfield, V and Maion, S.F. (1995) *How 'Messing About' with Performance Assessment in Mathematics Affects What Happens in Classrooms* (Technical Report 396). Los Angeles Centre for Research on Evaluation, Standards and Student Testing (CRESST).

Foxman, D., Hutchinson, D. and Bloomfield, B. (1991) *The APU Experience, 1977–1990.* London: Schools Examination and Assessment Council.

Fuchs, L.S. and Fuchs, D. (1986) 'Effects of systematic formative evaluation: a meta-analysis', *Exceptional Children* 53: 199–208.

Gardner, J. and Cowan, P. (2005) 'The fallibility of high stakes "11 plus" testing in Northern Ireland', *Assessment in Education* 12(2): 145–65.

Garner, R. (2006) 'Is a more relaxed atmosphere in our primary schools the key to better pupil performance?' *The Independent*, 7 December 2006.

Gipps, C. (1994) *Beyond Testing.* London: Falmer Press.

Good, F.J. (1988) 'Differences in marks awarded as a result of moderation: some findings from a teachers assessed oral examination in French', *Educational Review* 40: 319–31.

Government of New Zealand (1998) *Assessment for Success in Primary Schools.* Wellington: Ministry of Education.

Green, S., Bell, J., Oates, T. and Bramley, T. (2007) 'Alternative approaches to national assessment', unpublished paper.

Greene, T. (2006) 'There's more to education than exams', *The Independent*, Thursday 17 August 2006: 35.

Hall, K. and Harding, A. (2002) 'Level descriptions and teacher assessment in England: towards a community of assessment practice', *Educational Research* 44: 1–15.

Hall, K., Webber, B., Varley, S., Young, V. and Dorman, P. (1997) 'A study of teachers' assessment at Key Stage 1', *Cambridge Journal of Education* 27: 107–22.

Harland, J., Moor, H., Kinder, K. and Ashworth, M. (2003) *Talking 4: the pupil voice on the Key Stage 4 curriculum: report 4 of the Northern Ireland Curriculum Cohort Study.* Belfast: CCEA.

——(2002) *Is the Curriculum Working? The Key Stage 3 phase of the Northern Ireland Curriculum Cohort Study.* Slough: NFER.

Harland, J., Ashworth, M., Bower, R., Hogarth, S., Montgomery, A. and Moor, H. (1999a) *Real Curriculum at the Start of Key Stage 3: report two from the Northern Ireland Curriculum Cohort Study.* Slough: NFER.

Harland, J., Kinder, K., Ashworth, M., Montgomery, A., Moor, H. and Wilkin, A. (1999b) *Real Curriculum: at the end of Key Stage 2: Report One from Northern Ireland.* Slough: NFER.

Harlen, W. (2007) *Assessment of Learning.* London: Sage.

——(2005) 'Trusting teachers' judgements: research evidence of the reliability and validity of teachers' assessment used for summative purposes', *Research Papers in Education* 20(3): 245–70

——(2004) 'A systematic review of the reliability and validity of assessment by teachers used for summative purposes', in *Research Evidence in Education Library,* Issue 1, London: EPPI-Centre, Social Sciences Research Unit, Institute of Education.

——(1994) 'Towards quality in assessment', in W. Harlen (Ed) *Enhancing Quality in Assessment.* London: Paul Chapman.

Harlen, W. and Deakin Crick, R. (2003) 'Testing and motivation for learning', *Assessment in Education* 10(2): 169–208.

Hayward, L., Kane, J. and Cogan, N. (2000) *Improving Assessment in Scotland: report of the National Consultation on Assessment in Scotland.* Glasgow: University of Glasgow.

518   *Wynne Harlen*

HMIe (2006) *How Good is Our School? The journey to excellence.* Edinburgh: HMIe. Online (Available: http://www.hmie.gov.uk/documents/publication/hgiosjte.pdf).

House of Commons (2008a) *Testing and Assessment,* Third Report of Session 2007–8. Volume 1. London: The Stationery Office (TSO).

——(2008b) *Testing and Assessment,* Fifth Special Report. London: TSO.

Hutchinson, C. and Hayward, L. (2005) 'The journey so far: assessment for learning in Scotland', *The Curriculum Journal* 16(2): 225–48.

Johnston, J. and McClune, W. (2000) 'Selection project sel 5.1: pupil motivation and attitudes–self-esteem, locus of control, learning disposition and the impact of selection on teaching and learning', in *The Effects of the Selective System of Secondary Education in Northern Ireland,* Research Papers Volume II. Bangor, Co. Down: Department of Education: 1–37.

Learning and Teaching Scotland (2006) *What is an AIFL School?* Online (Available: http://www.ltscotland.org.uk/Images/aifl_triagram_tcm4–232905.pdf).

Leonard, M. and Davey, C. (2001) *Thoughts on the 11 Plus.* Belfast: Save the Children Fund.

Linn, R.L. (2000) 'Assessments and Accountability', *Educational Researcher* 29(2): 4–16.

Messick, S. (1989) 'Validity', in R.L. Linn (Ed) *Educational Measurement,* 3rd Edition. London: Collier Macmillan: 12–103.

Mortimore, P. (2006) 'Is "irreversible" reform really sensible?', *The Guardian,* 31 October 2006.

NEMP (National Education Monitoring Project) (2006) Website: http://nemp.otago.ac.nz/index.htm.

Northern Ireland Education Minister (2007) *Statement to the Assembly,* 4 December. Online (Available: http://www.deni.gov.uk/outling_a_vision_for_our_education_system).

National Union of Teachers (NUT) (2006) *NUT Briefing: the impact of National Curriculum testing on pupils.* (Sept 2006).

NUT (2003) *The Case Against National Curriculum Tests* (Sept 2003).

Organisation for Economic Co-operation and Development (OECD) (1999) *Measuring Student Knowledge and Skills.* Paris: OECD.

Pine, J., Aschbacher, P., Rother, E., Jones, M., McPhee. C., Martin, C., Phelps, S., Kyle, T. and Foley, B. (2006) 'Fifth graders' science inquiry abilities: a comparative study of students in hands-on and textbook curricula', *Journal of Research in Science Teaching* 43(5): 467–84.

Pollard, A. and Triggs, P. (2000) *Policy, Practice and Pupil Experience.* London: Continuum International Publishing Group.

Pollard, A., Triggs, P., Broadfoot, P., McNess, E. and Osborn, M. (2000) *What Pupils Say: changing policy and practice in primary education.* London: Continuum.

QCA (Qualifications and Curriculum Authority) (2004) *Financial Modelling of the English Examinations System, 2003–4,* report from PriceWaterhouseCoopers (PWC) for the QCA. London: QCA.

QCA (2003) *Foundation Stage Profile Handbook.* London: QCA.

Radnor, H.A. (1996) *Evaluation of Key Stage 3 Assessment Arrangements for 1995. Final report.* Exeter: University of Exeter.

Raveaud, M. (2004) 'Assessment in French and English infant schools: assessing the work, the child or the culture?', *Assessment in Education* 11(2): 193–212.

Reay, D. and Wiliam, D. (1999) '"I'll be a nothing": structure, agency and the construction of identity through assessment', *British Educational Research Journal* 25: 343–45.

Schunk, D. (1996) 'Goal and self-evaluative influences during children's cognitive skill learning', *American Educational Research Journal* 33: 359–82.

Scottish Education Department (SED) (1991) *Assessment 5–14.* Edinburgh: SED

Scottish Executive Education Department (SEED) (2005a) *Circular 02,* June, 2005. Edinburgh: SEED.

SEED (2005b) *Information Sheet on the Scottish Survey of Achievement.* Edinburgh: SEED.

——(2004) *Assessment, Testing and Reporting 3–14: our response.* Edinburgh: SEED.

SHA (Secondary Heads Association, now the Association of School and College Leaders) (2004) Online (Available: http://www.ascl.org.uk/datafiles/hostFiles/host-239/Policy%20paper%2013%20Chartered%20examiners%20FINAL%20priced.pdf).

Sheffield Hallam University Centre for Science Education (2003) *The Cost of Assessment. A report for the Royal Society.* Available from Centre for Science Education, Sheffield Hallam University.

Smith, E. and Gorard, S. (2005) '"They don't give us our marks": the role of formative feedback in student progress', *Assessment in Education* 12(1): 21–38.

Stobart, G. (2006) 'The validity of formative assessment', in J. Gardner (Ed) *Assessment and Learning.* London: Sage.

Thélot, C. (1993) *L'Évaluation du Système Éducatif.* Paris: Nathan.

Tymms, P. (2004) 'Are standards rising in English primary schools?', *British Educational Research Journal* 30(4): 477–94.

White, B.Y. and Frederiksen, J.T. (1998) 'Inquiry, modeling and metacognition: making science accessible to all students', *Cognition and Instruction* 16(1): 3–118.

Wikstrom, C. (2006) 'Education and assessment in Sweden', *Assessment in Education* 13(1): 113–28

Wiliam, D. (2001) 'Reliability, validity and all that jazz', *Education 3–13* 29(3): 17–21.

Wilmut, J. (2004) 'Experiences of summative teacher assessment in the UK. A review conducted for the Qualifications and Curriculum Authority', unpublished manuscript.

Part 6

Teaching in primary schools

Structures and processes

The three chapters in this section survey some of the vast body of published research on teaching, with particular reference to the primary phase. They approach this all-important topic from three standpoints:

- the teaching process itself (Chapters 20 and 21)
- the organisational context of teaching and learning (Chapter 21)
- the physical context of teaching and learning (Chapter 22)

The Cambridge Primary Review has ten themes, one of which is *Learning and Teaching* (Theme 2), but learning and teaching are synoptic and for that reason we find ourselves linking research surveys which have been commissioned under the themes *Structures and Phases* (Theme 9) and *Settings and Professionals* (Theme 6) as well as 'learning and teaching' itself. Context, then, is no less important a determinant of teaching quality than process.

The specific questions within the Review's remit under these themes are as follows:

- As children move developmentally through the primary phase how do they learn best and how are they most effectively taught?
- Judged against this evidence, how do current teaching approaches fare?
- How well do they capitalise on the findings of school and classroom research?
- What is the proper place of ICT and other new technologies in teaching and learning?
- How can teaching, and the system as a whole, most appropriately respond to differences in children's development, ways of learning and apparent capacities and needs?
- In what ways might teaching, and the organisation of classrooms and schools, change in order to enhance young children's engagement and learning and maximise their educational prospects?
- How are children grouped within the primary phase and what are the advantages and disadvantages of the different grouping arrangements?
- What are the physical and organisational characteristics of our best primary schools? How are they resourced and equipped?

Learning and Teaching in Primary Schools: insights from TLRP, by Mary James and Andrew Pollard (Chapter 20), is a special synoptic survey of evidence to date from the ESRC Teaching and Learning Research Programme (TLRP), the UK's biggest-ever programme of research on teaching and learning. 19 major projects within the TLRP portfolio relate to the primary phase and key findings from these are grouped within the following themes:

- learning and teaching in specific areas of the curriculum (spelling and number);
- learning and teaching across the curriculum (thinking skills and assessment for learning);
- the use of ICT to enhance learning;
- environments for better learning (pre-school, early years, group work, home and school);
- school conditions for the improvement of teaching and learning (pupil consultation and participation, classroom-focused enquiry and autonomous learning, educational networks, and teacher commitment).

The implications of the various project findings are then synthesised as ten 'principles for effective teaching and learning.'

Classes, Groups and Transitions: structures for teaching and learning, by Peter Blatchford, Susan Hallam, Judith Ireson and Peter Kutnick, with Andrea Creech (Chapter 21), examines evidence on the school and classroom conditions which frame the core processes of learning and teaching. It considers:

- different grouping arrangements, the factors that influence them and their impact on pupil learning;
- differences between grouping at the level of the class as a whole (for example, setting) and grouping practices within classes;
- the several transition points within the primary phase (year-on-year and between Key Stages);
- transitions from pre-school to primary and primary to secondary, the problems such transitions pose for pupils and how they can be minimised;
- the latest evidence on the long-running debate about the impact of class size on learning, teaching and attainment.

Primary Schools: the built environment, by Karl Wall, Julie Dockrell and Nick Peacey (Chapter 22), surveys research on the ways in which the physical properties of school buildings and grounds affect children's learning and development at the primary stage and the work of teachers. Read in conjunction with DCSF material relating to the Primary Capital Programme and the *Every Child Matters* outcomes, it provides systematic and detailed evidence on optimal conditions for the built environment of teaching and learning in respect of:

- noise and classroom acoustics;
- temperature, humidity, air quality and ventilation;
- natural and artificial classroom lighting.

These three surveys do not by any means tell the whole story. Even TLRP, vast, wide-ranging and current though it is, has gaps in respect of both the specific areas of learning and aspects of the primary curriculum in which different kinds of teaching are explored, and in the generic dimensions of teaching on which its projects concentrate. Nor do these chapters provide, either consciously or by virtue of their conjunction, a coherent map of the territory of teaching, still less of the larger field of pedagogy within which the act of teaching is located, though we show below how other chapters in this companion volume take us some way in that direction and in the final report we place the Primary Review's larger body of evidence on teaching and learning in what we hope is a useful pedagogical framework.

What is perhaps most striking about the TLRP evidence reported in Chapter 20 is the way it so strongly resonates with that from other studies in this book. There are many examples of this synergy:

- the benefits of high-quality pre-school experience and the conditions and practices which make that experience effective (Chapters 3 and 6);
- the centrality of interaction to children's learning and understanding, and especially of talk which is exploratory and dialogic, and which probes and provides reasons for ideas, suggestions and conclusions (Chapters 6, 7 and 21);
- the positive impact of properly-conceived group work on pupils' academic progress, their behaviour and personal relations (Chapters 7 and 21);
- the gains for teachers as well as pupils in involving the latter in consultation about their learning, not just about relatively peripheral school activities (Chapter 2);
- the evident need to shift the focus of assessment from testing to learning, yet the difficulty of making such a shift at the deeper levels of professional thinking and practice (Chapter 19);
- the importance of building on children's prior learning, paying as close attention to their personal and cultural experiences outside school as to what they have previously encountered in the classroom (Chapter 3).

Picking up the specific issue of grouping, Chapter 21 challenges claims about the benefits of setting pupils by their subject-specific attainment and argues instead – as does Chapter 20 – for within-class groups that are formed with a clear strategic purpose and capitalise fully on the group's communicative potential (something research going back to the early 1980s shows is rarely achieved).

Chapter 21 also maps the several transitions which primary pupils typically undergo as they move from pre-school to primary and thence to secondary, and within the primary phases from Key Stages 1 to 2. The number of such transitions exceeds those experienced by children in many other European countries and Blatchford and his colleagues show that while increasing efforts are being made to ease children's progress from one educational phase or stage to the next, there is as yet little overall coherence.

Chapter 22 is important not just as an adjunct to the school refurbishing and rebuilding programmes initiated during the early 2000s (for example, the government's Building Schools for the Future (BSF) initiative for secondary schools and the Primary Capital Programme), but because it is able to pinpoint such relatively scarce evidence as is available on the impact of the physical environment on pupils' learning. For example, Wall, Dockrell and Peacey report evidence confirming the common-sense observations that excessive noise adversely affects pupils' performance in tests and examinations; that elevated temperatures and humidity affect behaviour as well as attainment; that poor ventilation reduces concentration; and even that a good level of natural light in classrooms is associated with enhanced pupil performance as well as a sense of wellbeing.

Because the act of teaching is inseparable from the capacities of the teacher, these three chapters should be read in conjunction with those in Part 7 (Chapters 23, 24 and 25) which deal with research on the teaching profession, teacher training and development, and workforce reform. There are also necessary links with the chapters which examine evidence of the validity and impact of the ideas about learning and teaching embodied in government policy, notably the national literacy, numeracy and primary strategies whose impact is assessed by Wyse, McCreery and Torrance in Chapter 29 and which Balarin and Lauder (in Chapter 26) suggest amount to a 'state theory of learning.'

20 Learning and teaching in primary schools

Insights from TLRP

Mary James and Andrew Pollard

INTRODUCTION

This chapter has a very particular character. It provides an overview of the projects and thematic work of the UK's Teaching and Learning Research Programme (TLRP), insofar as this work relates to learning and teaching in the primary phase. In this sense the chapter is delimited by the themes, questions and issues covered by the TLRP. In the main overview, the chapter summarises the work of 19 projects, organised thematically. In the synthesis which follows the overview, some general principles, distilled from these projects, are described and discussed.

OVERVIEW

Scope and coverage

The Teaching and Learning Research Programme is funded from a number of UK government sources and managed by the Economic and Social Research Council (ESRC). Costing about £40 million spread over 12 years (2000–2012), it is the biggest programme of coordinated research in teaching and learning that the UK has ever known. The total number of projects within the TLRP is likely to exceed 70, and these are complemented by more than 20 cross-programme thematic analyses of various sorts. Projects cover issues ranging across the entire life course, from early years to old age, and involve research teams from all parts of the UK.

Twenty-two projects and fellowships within the TLRP's portfolio were based in schools or pre-school settings: two of these focused on early years, six on primary education, and eleven across all school phases. These nineteen (that is, excluding the secondary-only projects) will be the basis of this survey. The list below notes that three of these are 'associate projects'. These were funded from other sources but invited to become part of TLRP because of the significance of their work for teaching and learning. Many of these projects were established towards the beginning of the life of the Programme. It is certainly appropriate to take stock of what has been learned as a result of this work, although it holds some challenges because TLRP projects were not set up to investigate topics according to some map of the theoretical and substantive territory. They were selected, by a Steering Committee, from a large number of bids,[1] on the strength of their scientific quality and the extent to which they engaged with the core aims of TLRP:

- To work to achieve improvements in learning outcomes for identified groups of learners;
- To work in authentic settings of teaching and learning;
- To bring multi-disciplinary or interdisciplinary approaches to research;
- To enhance the capacity for a research-based approach to education and training practices;
- To work in partnership with practitioners, learners, policy makers and others in the research community, to achieve maximum impact through transformation of the research results into actionable strategies and practices;
- To make research-based contributions to the fundamental understanding of teaching and learning.

Each of these expectations was itself a response to concerns about the quality and impact of educational research which had been articulated in recent years, in the UK and elsewhere (see Pollard 2005 for more detail).

Thus, a diverse group of projects was funded: some dealing with learning in specific areas of the curriculum, some on learning across the curriculum, and others investigating environments for learning or school conditions for improvement. The projects that have involved primary schools, and are the particular focus of this survey, have been classified in the following way (see James & Pollard 2006):

1. *Learning in specific areas of the curriculum, notably English, mathematics and science*
   a. The role of awareness in the teaching and learning of literacy and numeracy in Key Stage 2 (Director: Professor Terezinha Nunes, Oxford University)
   b. 5–14 mathematics in Scotland: the relevance of intensive quantities (Director: Professor Christine Howe, University of Cambridge)
   c. Learning scientific concepts in classrooms at Key Stage 1 (Research Training Fellow: Stephen Hodgkinson, University of Brighton)
2. *Learning across the curriculum*
   a. ACTS II: Sustainable thinking classrooms (Director: Professor Carol McGuinness, Queen's University Belfast)
   b. LHTL: Learning How to Learn – In Classrooms, Schools and Networks (Director: Professor Mary James, Institute of Education, University of London)
3. *The use of ICT to enhance learning*
   a. INTERPLAY: play, learning and ICT in pre-school education (Professor Lydia Plowman, Stirling University)
   b. InterActive Education: teaching and learning in the information age (Director: Professor Rosamund Sutherland, University of Bristol)
   c. The use of ICT to improve learning and attainment through interactive teaching (Director: Dr Steve Kennewell, Swansea Metropolitan University)
4. *Environments for better learning*
   a. SPRinG: Social Pedagogic Research into Group work (Directors: Professor Peter Blatchford, Institute of Education, University of London (for KS2) and Professor Peter Kutnick, King's College London (for KS1))
   b. ScotSPRinG: Supporting group work in Scottish schools: age and the urban/rural divide (Director: Professor Donald Christie, University of Strathclyde)
   c. HSKE: Home-school knowledge exchange in primary education (Director: Professor Martin Hughes, University of Bristol)

    d.   Provision for gifted and talented pupils at secondary transfer (Research Training Fellow: Jenny Brookes)

    e.   Identity and Learning (Associate project) (Director: Professor Andrew Pollard, Institute of Education, University of London)

    f.   EPPE: Effectiveness of pre-school primary education (Associate project) (Director: Professor Iram Siraj-Blatchford, Institute of Education, University of London)

5. *School conditions for the improvement of teaching and learning*

    a.   Consulting Pupils about Teaching and Learning (Director: the late Professor Jean Rudduck, University of Cambridge)

    b.   CPAL: Consulting Pupils on the Assessment of their Learning (Director: Dr Ruth Leitch, Queen's University Belfast)

    c.   Understanding and developing inclusive practices in schools (Director: Professor Mel Ainscow, University of Manchester)

    d.   LHTL: Learning How to Learn – In Classrooms, Schools and Networks (Director: Professor Mary James, Institute of Education, University of London) (This project fell equally in two categories)

    e.   Lessons for learning: using research study lessons to innovate and transfer metapedagogy (Research Training Fellow: Pete Dudley, Capita)

    f.   VITAE: Variations in teachers' work and lives and their effects on pupils (Associate project) (Director: Professor Christopher Day, University of Nottingham)

The discussion of research findings which follows will be organised under these topics and, for brevity, the projects will be referred to mainly by their acronym or the relevant director's surname.

Each of these headings, and hence the foci of the projects, maps on to a simple conceptual framework that has been used to review the coverage of TLRP work (see Figure 20.1).

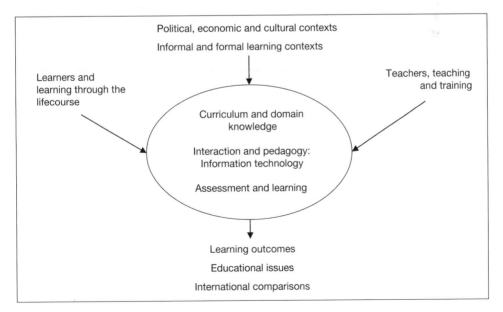

Figure 20.1 Reviewing TLRP: conceptual framework.

The coverage of projects is by no means comprehensive, and many of the relationships remain unexplored. This is not regarded as a fault; the field of education, even teaching and learning, is so broad and complex that no collection of projects could be expected to cover everything of potential interest. What projects promised to do was to investigate some important issues in some depth and with appropriate rigour.

In recognition that value could be added to project work by review and synthesis across projects, drawing in research and scholarship from beyond TLRP where relevant, the conceptual framework was also used as a device for identifying areas where useful cross-programme thematic work might be done. Thus, over time, a series of thematic initiatives was commissioned and these initiatives have produced, or are producing, research outputs in the form of commentaries, journal articles and special issues, annotated bibliographies and so on. Some of these thematic initiatives are relevant to this chapter's survey and will also be drawn upon, especially in the final section of this survey which synthesises findings. Of particular relevance is TLRP thematic work on:

1. Neuroscience, human development and teaching (Director: Dr Paul Howard-Jones, University of Bristol)
2. Teacher learning (Director: Professor Mary James, Institute of Education, University of London)
3. Changing teacher roles, identities and professionalism (Director: Professor Sharon Gewirtz, King's College London)
4. Curriculum, domain knowledge and pedagogy (Director: Professor Robert Moon, Open University)
5. Identifying learning outcomes (Director: Professor Mary James, Institute of Education, University of London)
6. Assessment of significant learning outcomes (Director: Professor Richard Daugherty, University of Cardiff)
7. Social diversity and difference: researching inequalities in teaching and learning (Director: Professor Miriam David, Institute of Education, University of London)

Methodological approaches

The methodological approaches adopted by projects were diverse, including: classroom experiments evaluating 'interventions' through pre- and post-tests compared with control groups; large-scale quantitative surveys; in-depth qualitative case studies of individuals, groups or schools; and combined approaches. Most projects combined approaches in some way, either by having separate survey and case study strands, for example, or by attempting to integrate quantitative and qualitative elements more formally.

The majority of projects funded through TLRP could be described as 'development and research'. In other words, they set out to stimulate some activity, innovation and change and to research the consequences. In some instances an action research approach, working collaboratively with teachers as researchers, was specifically adopted. Some such approach was regarded as necessary if projects were to fulfil the TLRP aim to 'work to achieve improvements in learning outcomes for identified groups of learners', which implied a developmental dimension. However, the further aim to 'work in authentic settings of teaching and learning' made the attribution of measured change to specific interventions rather difficult, except in those studies that were closely focused on very specific innovations in controlled settings. Even here the constraints of working in schools with whole classes of children precluded the use of fully randomised experiments. For this reason, TLRP researchers are cautious about claiming to have found unequivocal evidence of cause and effect relationships although they all examine, in some detail, the various and complex associations between teaching, learning and context.

In project research briefings, as elsewhere, TLRP researchers have been expected to make explicit the 'warrant' for the knowledge claims they make (see James *et al.* 2005). In most cases they make reference to the way their research builds on previous work, its theoretical underpinnings and justification, the extent to which it has fulfilled the empirical standards of the social scientific approach adopted, and the ways in which the work has been received by the user community.

Some TLRP project teams are composed of researchers working with a single, coherent theoretical position or framework: there are examples of cognitive constructivist psychological perspectives, symbolic interactionist sociological perspectives, and cultural historical activity theory perspectives. However, many teams attempted, with varying degrees of success, to view the subjects of their study through multiple lenses in order to 'bring multi-disciplinary or interdisciplinary approaches to research'. (See James 2006 for a discussion of the challenges of trying to meet TLRP's ambitious aims.)

The cross-programme thematic work also adopted a range of approaches although none could be characterised as systematic research reviews, in the style of EPPI[2] in the UK or the What Works Clearinghouse in the US. Much of this work was mostly carried out by a social, dialogic process involving a series of meetings or seminars, with contributions from researchers within and beyond TLRP and subsequent deliberation and synthesis by a core team or task group. (As part of its thematic work, the TLRP sponsored a 'Review of Reviews'. A summary can be found at http://www.tlrp.org/pub/documents/Rev%20Rev%20RB30%20FINAL.pdf).

Outputs from projects and thematic work have also taken various forms. In addition to books and journal articles, each project has produced a research briefing, for policy makers and practitioners, which summarises the research and findings. (These can be downloaded from the TLRP website at: http://www.tlrp.org/pub/research.html.) These summaries explain the focus of the research, identify key findings and their implications for policy and practice, and provide brief accounts of how the research was conducted and why we should have confidence in the conclusions. These research briefings are the main basis of the accounts in the next section of this survey. (All publications, from all projects, can be located via the TLRP website. As they are published, records are deposited in the TLRP DSpace repository which can be searched. Go to http://www.tlrp.org/search/all/.)

Cross-project thematic work has also produced a range of outputs, often in the form of journal special issues but, perhaps most importantly from the point of view of policy makers or practitioners, in a series of TLRP commentaries (also downloadable from the website).

SELECTED STUDIES

This section provides a very brief summary of the findings of each of the TLRP projects that carried out research in primary schools or pre-school settings. They are grouped according to the classifications outlined earlier.

Learning in specific areas of the curriculum

Two TLRP projects and one research training fellowship investigated specific areas of the curriculum in the primary phase. These involved the core areas of literacy, numeracy and science. The project on 'The role of awareness in the teaching and learning of literacy and numeracy in Key Stage 2' (Nunes) focused upon aspects of learning to spell and learning fractions. The project directed by Howe was an extension of this, based in Scotland, but researching aspects of mathematics only. The project conducted by Hodgkinson, as the focus of his research training fellowship, was linked to the SPRinG project on group work, summarised below. However, it is included in this section because its focus on primary science was particularly strong.

The two different subject foci of Nunes' project are summarised separately here although they were unified by similar experimental approaches to their investigations.

The teaching of literacy in primary and infants schools is a 'hot topic' and much current attention has been given to the role of phonics. Much less attention has been given to the potential value to junior age children of learning about the role of morphemes in spelling. The English language, with roots in many other languages, uses units of meaning called morphemes to form words. An understanding that spelling represents morphemes can help. For example, the correct spellings of 'magician' and 'infection' are not predictable from the way they sound. The ending of both sound the same. However, knowing that the suffix 'ian' is added to a noun denoting a person, but the suffix 'ion' is added to a noun denoting a concept, can help children make sense of the spelling of these kinds of words. Nunes' project on morphemes showed that literacy can be improved by increased awareness of how morphemes make words and are represented in spelling. Specifically they found that: i) primary school children of all ages have difficulties with spelling words when the spelling cannot be predicted from the way the word sounds; ii) children's difficulties with the spelling of many words can be reduced by making them aware of the morphemes that compose words; iii) making children aware of morphemes has a positive effect on their vocabulary growth. The implications of this study are that teachers should be made aware of the role of morphemes in spelling and that systematic teaching about morphemes should be introduced into primary schools.

Fractions were the other focus of Nunes' project. In this she and her team tackled the problem of teaching rational numbers. Quantities represented by natural numbers are easily understood: we can count and say how many oranges are in a bag. However, fractions cause difficulty to most people because they involve relations between quantities. For example, if two girls spend half of their pocket money on snacks, they may not each spend the same amount of money. As with the morphemes work, the project developed a teaching programme which boosted pupils' understanding of the relative nature of fractions. The team found that: i) most pupils in Years 4 and 5 have not grasped the relative nature of fractions as numbers, and their difficulty is primarily conceptual; ii) pupils have some intuitive understanding of the relative nature of fractions from their experiences with division; iii) teaching programmes that start from pupils' intuitions about sharing, and which establish connections to fractions as numbers, can have a positive impact on pupils' learning. The implications are that teaching pupils about fractions should include a focus on logical relations, but this should build on pupils' intuitions. Teacher education needs to help teachers become aware of pupils' intuitive understanding of the logic of fractions and the situations in which they are most easily understood.

The project conducted by Howe in Scotland, in collaboration with Nunes and her team, again studied the relations between quantities in mathematics. On this occasion the project was built on the observation that most mathematics teaching in the UK focuses on 'extensive quantities' involving one variable, such as distance or time, whilst 'intensive quantities' involving relationships between more than one variable (for example speed, which involves distance in relation to time) tend to be ignored or treated in piecemeal fashion. A survey of primary school children showed that this neglect leads to enduring difficulties and undermines children's mastery of fractions. A teaching programme was developed to remedy this and was found to boost understanding of intensive quantities as well as fraction usage. Moreover, the approach was compatible with current curricular demands and extended them in valuable ways. Specifically the project found that: i) primary school children of all ages have difficulties with intensive quantities, showing that mastery does not develop without teaching; ii) these difficulties are primarily conceptual; iii) primary school children of all ages have difficulties using fractions to name intensive quantities, but iv) a mere two or three hours of teaching can boost children's understanding and their use of fractions in these contexts. The implications are that intensive quantities, and the use of fractions to name them, should be explicitly taught in primary schools because children cannot be expected to generalise their knowledge from extensive contexts to intensive ones. However, this does not require major changes in the school curriculum because short teaching programmes have been found to be effective.

The studies summarised above were conducted in school contexts by researchers with backgrounds in psychology, using quantitative survey and experimental research designs and adopting cognitive constructivist theoretical perspectives. The study undertaken by Hodgkinson, as a fellowship towards a PhD, was of a very different kind. It adopted an ethnographic approach to the investigation of how young children come to understand the world as they interact in groups whilst undertaking science tasks. (This project is linked to the Key Stage 1 SPRinG project on group work which is summarised below.) The results of this project are yet to be evaluated or published; however, the narratives developed from contrasting ethnographic studies of classroom practice in England and Germany indicate two forms of classroom ritual – hegemonic and identity rituals – which shape the way children find meaning in classroom activities, or are excluded from doing so.

Learning across the curriculum

The two TLRP projects which we have classified under this heading focus on the development of skills and practices associated with analytical, critical and creative thinking, assessment for learning and learning how to learn. In both projects the approach to development was based on providing teachers with practical strategies that could be 'infused' across the curriculum. The project teams took the view that skills learned in separate lessons or courses would not easily transfer to different subject contexts without explicit attempts to integrate them across the curriculum. Previous research and scholarship had demonstrated that thinking skills and learning to learn are not separate psychological abilities but learnable practices that are used for learning different subject matter. Thus thinking skills and thinking something are inextricable, as are learning how to learn and learning something.

In the ACTS II project, McGuinness developed frameworks and classroom strategies with teachers, involving a curriculum topic and specific pattern of thinking being taught together. These methods were evaluated in a three-year study with Key Stage 2 pupils in schools in Northern Ireland. A particular focus was on the development and analysis of classroom talk that helped children to think about their thinking (meta-cognition). The findings indicated that: i) teachers were able to design and teach lessons using the 'infusion' approach; ii) children's thinking strategies were helped by such things as modelling thinking and using visual tools; iii) 94 teachers involved in the CPD programme reported changes in their classroom practices, in their perceptions of children's thinking and in their images of themselves as teachers; iv) on self-rating measures, children participating in ACTS reported positive changes in their learning, particularly their use of metacognitive strategies, which were related to effort.

However, these changes took time to build: those children who had participated for three years benefited most; and gains were not even across all learners. The 80 per cent of children with moderate to high developed abilities, as measured by verbal and non-verbal reasoning tests, benefited most. When the bottom 20 per cent were given problems to solve they showed positive changes in their strategies compared to control children, but these specific achievements did not translate into how the children rated themselves more generally. Children's self-evaluations were positively correlated with measures of attainment in reading and mathematics but effects were small compared to the impact of background factors such as social-economic circumstances, gender, prior attainment and age in class. This shows how powerful these background factors are. Nevertheless, the study showed that thinking skills and strategies are amenable to change and they can be a lever for improvement. As with the Nunes and Howe studies (above) the key seems to be to help children become aware of these strategies and how to use them. The implications are that developing children's capacity to learn takes time and special attention needs to be paid to children with poorer cognitive and social resources. This in turn requires teachers to develop both their practices and their beliefs about learners.

Making learning practices explicit was also a key theme in the Learning How to Learn project led by James. This project built on existing research which has demonstrated that assessment for learning (formative assessment) practices can lead to improved learning and achievement. This project was primarily concerned with the conditions in schools and networks that would allow such practices to become embedded and spread within and between schools. For this reason it is also included in the relevant section below. The strand of the project that focused on classrooms showed that assessment for learning helps teachers promote learning how to learn by providing ideas for practical strategies that enable pupils to become more autonomous learners. This enables classroom practice to be better aligned with the dominant values that 600+ teachers expressed in a questionnaire, and less driven by the culture of perfomativity. However, analysis of video evidence showed how difficult it is to shift from reliance on specific techniques, for example writing learning objectives on the board (the letter of AfL), to practices based on deep principles integrated into the flow of lessons (the spirit of AfL). Again, this project demonstrated that although advice on techniques is useful and important to teachers, longer term development and sustainability depends on professional development that encourages teachers to re-evaluate their fundamental beliefs about learning, the way they structure tasks, the nature of their classroom roles and their relationships with pupils.

The use of ICT to enhance learning

The use of ICTs in teaching and learning warrants a separate heading because three projects (one in secondary schools only) had this as a central focus, and a new set of large projects on technology-enhanced learning (TEL) was commissioned in Spring 2008. TEL work is therefore likely to continue into 2012.

The INTERPLAY project, led by Plowman in Scotland, investigated the challenges of introducing ICT into play settings involving very young children, and how practitioners can respond to changes to create opportunities for learning with ICT. Practitioners and researchers worked together to address these questions using the concept of 'guided interaction' to initiate small projects using different approaches. They found that: i) children's encounters with ICT are enhanced when practitioners use guided interaction (questioning, modelling, praising, supporting) and balance child-initiated and adult-led activities; ii) encounters with ICT accompanied by guided interaction can enhance dispositions to learn, knowledge of the world and operational skills, as well as hand-eye coordination; iii) providing a broad range of ICTs, including digital still and video cameras, mobile phones and electronic keyboards and toys, as well as computers, promotes more opportunities for learning. The implications are that professional development of practitioners is needed to develop a responsive, reflective pedagogy, and nurseries should broaden their focus beyond computers to other forms of ICT and be aware that children develop competence with ICTs at home.

The InterActive Education project (Sutherland) worked in partnership with primary and secondary school teachers to investigate ways in which ICT can be used to enhance learning in subject domains, particularly its value in helping children to enter new knowledge worlds. The approach was holistic and socio-cultural. The project found that: i) schools have interpreted enthusiasm for ICT in education as being largely about the acquisition of equipment; ii) effective teaching and learning with ICT involves building bridges between 'idiosyncratic' learning, arising from extended periods of individual engagement, and 'intended' learning that often needs to be supported by the teacher; for example, pupils are unlikely to develop knowledge of science from game-like simulation software; iii) there is a two-way exchange of knowledge between home and school use of ICT and this impacts on school learning; iv) the teacher remains key to the successful use of ICT for learning. The implications are that professional development is crucial so that teachers can put ICTs to good pedagogical use in the classroom, encouraging pupils to build on their out-of-school learning but helping them to construct 'common' knowledge which has currency in wider communities, as well as in the classroom.

The project led by Kennewell, in Wales, on the use of ICT to improve learning and attainment through interactive teaching, was an extension of the InterActive Education project. Kennewell's project focused particularly on deeply interactive or 'dialogic' teaching in schools and probed the role of ICT, particularly the use of interactive whiteboards, in this context. It also aimed to explore how engaging in reflective dialogue with researchers contributed to changes in teachers' thinking and practice. The project found that: i) good teachers use ICT to stimulate and support reflective and dialogic interaction; ii) ICT can help learners to engage with lesson content and influence the course of lessons, but not always in the way intended; iii) the potential of ICT to support group work is not widely recognised; iv) reflective dialogue with an observer concerning lesson activities and resource evaluation is valuable for teachers' professional development. The implications are that learning can be improved if resources and professional development encourage teachers to use ICT to support dialogic interaction, including forms of talk in group work. But teachers benefit from mentor support to explore resources, gain skills, develop the confidence to intervene, and to reflect on their teaching with ICT. More particularly, if interactive whiteboards are to achieve the claims made for them, there may need to be a new wave of professional development which takes account of the need to embed their affordances in teachers' pedagogical reasoning.

Environments for better learning

A group of TLRP projects investigated features of classroom settings and the wider environment that promote or inhibit learning. Two linked projects researched the effects of pupils working in groups in classrooms, and another three projects studied the interactions between learning in home and school. A further major 'associate' project has compared the learning benefits of different structures for provision in the early years.

The SPRinG (Social Pedagogic Research into Group work) project sought to develop a new approach to increasing engagement and learning in everyday classroom settings at Key Stage 1 (led by Kutnick), Key Stage 2 (led by Blatchford) and Key Stage 3 (led by Galton). The project team was aware of a wide gap between the potential of group work to enhance learning and their previous evidence of only limited use in schools. The problems that they identified were a lack of a strategic view of the purpose of groups and practical problems of formation and process. In response, the team embarked on a project to work with teachers to develop a programme of group work that could be successfully integrated into school life (the development stage) followed by a year-long intervention study to evaluate the success of the programme in terms of attainment, motivation and within-group interactions, compared to control groups (the evaluation stage). An applications stage was designed to apply group work to contexts known to be particularly problematic. The project found that: i) in contrast to views that group work may interfere with learning in mainstream curriculum areas, teachers successfully implemented effective group work in both primary and secondary and across the curriculum; ii) this had a positive effect on pupil's academic progress and higher conceptual learning (at KS1 effect sizes from 0.22 to 0.62 were recorded in reading and mathematics; at KS2, where science was a special focus of the project, effect sizes from 0.21 to 0.58 were recorded for conceptual understanding and inferential thinking); iii) there were positive effects on pupil behaviour, through increased on-task interactions, more equal participation, sustained interactions and higher level discussions; iv) there were improvements in personal relations between teachers and pupils and among pupils, provided that teachers took the time to train pupils in the skills of group working. The implications were that group work can be made to work with benefits to attainment, motivation and behaviour. However, this requires preparation and support. Group work skills need to be approached developmentally: social skills first, then communication skills, then problem-solving. Providing teachers with practical 'relational' strategies, based on principles, provides a successful approach to raising standards and improving behaviour.

The linked 'extension' project in Scotland (ScotSPRinG), led by Christie, had similar results. This project worked only in primary schools but investigated, especially, the effects of class composition in urban and rural school contexts where classes may be single age or a mix of year groups. As with the KS2 work in England, the team worked with upper primary school age pupils and focused upon the development of conceptual understanding in science, although a range of cognitive, affective and social measures were used to assess impact of innovations. Project findings showed: i) significant gains across a number of measures, attributable to the group work intervention; ii) cognitive gains were related to the quality of collaborative dialogue during group work; iii) there were no consistent differences between single age or mixed age classes, nor between urban and rural schools; iv) group work yielded significant gains in social relations, with collaborative engagement with tasks contributing most – however, socio-emotional gains were independent of the cognitive gains. The practical 'relational' strategies offered to teachers were highly valued and reported to benefit both teachers' professional practice and pupils' learning, which implies that the SPRinG approach is effective and sustainable.

The home-school knowledge exchange (HSKE) project, led by Hughes, investigated how the home and school environments for learning might complement each other. Focusing upon literacy and numeracy in these two worlds, the team helped teachers, parents and children to find new ways of exchanging knowledge between home and primary school, using videos, photographs, shoeboxes of artefacts and so on. They then investigated how this process of knowledge exchange could enhance learning and ease the transition to secondary school. The project found that: i) there are substantial 'funds of knowledge' embedded in national, ethnic and popular cultures of homes and communities that can be used to support learning in schools; ii) simple knowledge exchange activities can make teachers more knowledgeable about children's lives out of school, and parents more knowledgeable about what happens in school; iii) HSKE can have a positive impact on teachers, parents and children and on attainment, although gains were not statistically significant in mathematics and not uniform across the project in literacy (they were significantly better in Cardiff schools but not in Bristol). However, the implications are that policy-makers and school leaders should pay more attention to HSKE as a means of improving relationships and raising standards.

A research training fellowship, held by Brookes, is linked to the HSKE project but focuses particularly on provision for gifted and talented pupils at secondary transfer. Findings from this ethnographic study tracking 15 Year 5 children into Year 8 are yet to be evaluated and published. However, there are indications that school selection by parents, and the process of transfer, are experienced as multi-faceted, iterative, stressful and prolonged. Evidence from the HSKE project and this linked fellowship, focusing particularly on the social and emotional dimension of secondary transfer, has been the focus of an innovative dramatic representation of research findings which is now available on a DVD (see http://www.tlrp-archive.org/cgi-bin/tlrp/news/news_log.pl?display=1181220375 for details).

Both of the home-school projects outlined above drew to some extent on the methodological (longitudinal ethnography) and theoretical (symbolic interactionist) antecedents of work by Pollard. The interactions between pupils' experiences of schools, homes and communities in the formation of learner identities has been a focus of his longitudinal ethnography of two cohorts of children (ten in each of two primary schools contrasted by different social class settings). They were studied from ages 4 to 16 and tracked into secondary school. Although not funded by TLRP, this series of studies has been drawn into TLRP as an associate project, partly because Pollard's thinking, derived from this work, has informed the way the scope of the Programme has been conceptualised (see the framework above). Comparison and analysis of detailed case studies from this project revealed that: i) relationships between teachers and pupils remain the basis of the moral order of the classroom and underpin discipline and behaviour; ii) children develop their identities as learners through successive experiences as they move through schooling; iii) pupils actively negotiate their way through schooling, which, over time, can be conceptualised as a 'pupil career'; iv) the extent to which school provision matches learners' identities, social relationships and cultural resources strongly influences the outcomes of education. The implications are that attention needs to be given to the creation of positive classroom climates characterised by respect, trust and mutual exchange of dignity; the most fundamental form of education – the process of becoming a person – requires as much careful consideration as the acquisition of knowledge and skills; and personalised provision in schools should build on an understanding of the development of these strategic biographies, and respond to the social, cultural and material experiences of different groups of learners, which is challenging when inequalities between schools remain.

Another 'associate' project, funded by the DfES (now the DCSF), is the EPPE (The Effective Provision of Pre-School Education) project, the most significant European study to date on the impact of pre-school and the contribution of family background to children's development (3–11 years old). The findings from the pre-school study (3000 children and 141 pre-school settings) are that: i) high quality pre-school experience benefits children and these benefits remain evident at age 10; ii) children made more gains in settings combining education and care and in nursery schools where there were more highly qualified staff; iii) good early years staff provided direct teaching, instructive learning environments and 'sustained shared thinking' to extend children's learning; iv) a high quality early years home environment is associated with gains for children, but what parents do is more important than who they are. The implications of this project have already had a substantial impact on national early years policy including establishing free entitlement to pre-school for all children; pilot projects on an early (2 to 3 years) start for disadvantaged children with a greater emphasis on quality; expansion of Children's Centres under Sure Start and a funding framework to enhance staff qualifications; greater emphasis on adult/child interactions in the English Primary National Strategy and the Foundation Stage; and initiatives to increase parental involvement through joined up services, especially to disadvantaged families.

School conditions for the improvement of teaching and learning

A final cluster of TLRP projects focuses upon the conditions within schools, and across networks of schools, that support improvements in teaching and learning.

Consulting Pupils about Teaching and Learning, a network of six projects coordinated by the late Professor Jean Rudduck, built on the growing recognition that young people have a right to be heard and have something worthwhile to say about their school experiences. The UN Convention on the Rights of the Child (1989) included children's right to be heard as one of its four basic principles. Pupil consultation is also regarded as integral to the citizenship curriculum and lifelong learning. However, listening to and learning from pupils is a challenge to teachers and schools. The findings of the projects, drawn primarily from the testimony of pupils and teachers in 48 schools, provided evidence of benefits for: i) pupils, by enhancing engagement with learning, sense of agency and of self as learner; ii) teachers, by deepening insights into children's abilities and learning preferences, leading to more responsive teaching and a willingness to give pupils more responsibility; iii) schools, by strengthening school policy in substantive rather than marginal or tokenistic ways; and iv) national policy, by providing new insights and practical tools for school self-evaluation and development planning. Importantly, however, given the increasing status of 'pupil voice' as a 'movement', this research also cautioned that ingrained habits can prevent pupils being heard. Conditions for new ways of listening include: hearing the quiet voice in the acoustic of the school; avoiding the creation of a pupil voice elite; maintaining authenticity; sharing data and/or offering feedback to pupils; trust and openness as a pre-condition of dialogue and action.

This project has been extended by a subsequent project carried out in Northern Ireland with a particular focus on children's rights to be consulted on the assessment of their learning. This has particular relevance in Northern Ireland as policy makers introduce a Pupil Profile to record pupils' development and encourage the adoption of Assessment for Learning in classroom practice. Led by Leitch, the CPAL (Consulting Pupils on the Assessment of their Learning) project comprises three independent but interrelated studies in primary and post-primary schools. One of these asked (through focus groups, creative approaches and e-consultation) 80 Key Stage 2 pupils what they thought of the concept of the Pupil Profile, and another study investigated teachers' and parents' awareness of children's rights and their responses to key aspects of AfL pedagogy. Findings were that: i) KS2 pupils viewed Pupil Profiles as personal documents, useful for helping them improve their learning and helping them with decision-making about future schooling; ii) to fulfil these expectations, children thought that Profiles should provide feedback from teachers on how to improve, and should be attractive and readable, include a section contributed by pupils, have input from parents/carers, be inclusive of wider abilities and achievements, and enhance pupils' views of themselves; iii) teachers advocated children's rights, expressed by Article 12 of UNCRC and embodied in AfL practices, but viewed time, class size, curriculum coverage, need for control and school culture as constraining implementation. CPAL demonstrates that children can be consulted directly on significant matters of educational policy, and that, where principles of AfL are embedded in practice, pupils can experience high levels of participation. However, there is a need to promote greater consistency, among teachers, of what consultation means from a rights-based perspective.

The issue of children's rights was also implicit in the work of the project on inclusion, led by Ainscow. This collaborative action-research project in three local authorities addressed the question of how schools can include all children from the communities they serve and enable them both to participate fully and achieve highly. The findings were that: i) many barriers to participation and learning stem from teachers' misplaced assumptions about what pupils can do and how best to teach them; ii) 'interruptions' to established understandings and practices can be fostered when groups of staff engage with evidence about pupils' experience of school and their own practice; iii) it is not possible to improve outcomes for pupils simply by teaching the curriculum harder and longer; teachers have to strengthen pupils' pleasure in learning and their self-esteem. The implications are that teachers need to question their accepted ways of working; focusing on a specific issue for school enquiry is more productive than imposing whole school change; and the national focus on highly measurable outcomes needs to be broadened in addressing underachievement and inclusion.

The Learning How to Learn (LHTL) in Classrooms, Schools and Networks project has already been mentioned above. Its findings are also relevant to this section because it was principally concerned with the conditions in schools and networks that would enable the positive effects of assessment for learning to be scaled up and sustained without intensive and expensive support. Combining both quantitative and qualitative methods, this project worked with 40 infant, primary and secondary schools to investigate a 'logic model for a causal argument' that linked classroom practice to teachers' own learning practices and school management practices. It found that: i) classroom-focused inquiry by teachers is a key condition of promoting autonomous learning by pupils and that schools that embed AfL and LHTL make support for professional learning a priority; ii) educational networks are much talked about but little understood, and electronic tools for professional development purposes are not well-used – however, the intellectual capital of schools can be built on the social capital developed through teachers' personal networking practices. The implications are that school leaders need to create the structures and cultures that support collaborative classroom enquiry and the sharing of innovations in classroom practice, within and beyond the school, because a key aspect of teacher learning is 'knowledge creation' (That is, a third metaphor to add to the more familiar 'learning as acquisition of knowledge and skill' or 'learning as participation in communities of practice').

Linked to this project is another TLRP research training fellowship, awarded to Dudley to undertake an investigation of ways in which Japanese 'Lesson Study' might be adapted and used in UK schools. This provides a formal approach to collaborative classroom enquiry that emerged as a crucial factor in the LHTL project. Teachers work in groups to formulate hypotheses about adjustments to lessons to improve learning. These are tested in Research Lessons, which colleagues observe and discuss subsequently. New hypotheses and adjustments are tested in further iterations until the teachers feel ready to perform a public research lesson. This fellowship project has yet to be evaluated although there are early indications that: i) Research Lesson Study engages teachers at all levels of experience and sustains their interest over time; ii) it involves pupils directly in the analysis of teaching; and iii) leads to innovation in lesson design and improvements in pupil achievements. Partly because of the unique position of this researcher, who is also a policy maker (Director of the Primary National Strategy at the time of writing), he has been able to facilitate the dissemination of findings of this project, the LHTL project, and the TLRP more generally, through guidance materials produced by the National College for School Leadership and the Primary National Strategy.

Finally, the importance of teacher learning emerges again in the VITAE 'associate' project. This study of 300 teachers provides a new perspective on teachers' quality, retention and effectiveness over the whole of their careers. The findings are that: i) pupils of teachers who are committed and resilient are likely to attain more than pupils whose teachers are not; ii) teachers' sense of positive professional identity is associated with well-being and job satisfaction and this is a key factor in their effectiveness; iii) the commitment and resilience of teachers in schools serving more disadvantaged communities are more persistently challenged than others; iv) teachers do not necessarily become more effective over time – a minority risk becoming less effective in later years; v) sustaining and enhancing commitment and resilience is a key quality and retention issue. The implications are that head teachers, national associations and policy makers need to consider the connections between commitment, resilience and effectiveness and develop strategies for meeting the needs of teachers in different phases in their professional lives, and in different communities.

MAIN AREAS OF DIVERGENCE, DISAGREEMENT AND CONSENSUS

TLRP projects all share a concern with teaching and learning but they do not completely overlap in terms of focus, context, scale, methods or perspective. Therefore they cannot be compared directly and any ostensible areas of divergence, disagreement or consensus can be contested. As the synthesis below indicates, we have attempted to elicit some common themes and distilled these into principles for practice. However, they are at a very general level and some might say that they are self-evident truths. Even if this were true, TLRP evidence suggests that many are still some way from being operationalised, implemented and sustained in policy and practice. So they are worth reiterating.

At the level of detail some differences do emerge, for example, projects that focus on cognitive dimensions of learning (for example Nunes) might seem to contrast with those that emphasise emotional engagement, dispositions and motivation (for example Hughes and Pollard), or those that investigate learning as socio-cultural activity (for example Sutherland). However, surface differences usually disappear on further scrutiny because different projects ask different research questions. They do not necessarily refute the value of other questions or perspectives. All might be considered important and complementary in investigating the holistic experience of learning by children, in and out of school.

If there is one notable area of agreement in general, but divergence in detail, it concerns teacher learning. Most projects produced strong evidence that a key to improved learning and achievement by pupils is the learning of teachers. However, there are some differences implied by the evidence about how this learning is best achieved. Some projects (for example Nunes and Howe) argued strongly that research findings need to be translated into practical strategies and materials that teachers can use directly in classrooms, whilst others were more inclined to support classroom-based enquiry in which teachers have a greater say in identifying problems to work upon. However, even here, the differences are more of degree than substance. Those projects, such as Ainscow's, which adopted an action research approach still saw an important role for evidence from research in challenging the taken-for-granted assumptions that stand in the way of improvement in learning. As John Elliott pointed out in his contribution to the C-TRIP thematic seminar series,[3] Lawrence Stenhouse, who is often regarded as the father of teacher research in the UK, saw the transformation of schools as most likely to arise from a productive relationship between university researchers and classroom practitioners, who each have different but complementary roles in generating and testing new knowledge for practice.

SYNTHESIS OF KEY FINDINGS AND INSIGHTS

In 2006, the TLRP directors' team began work on looking across project findings to see whether any overarching messages were emerging. The TLRP Commentary, *Improving Teaching and Learning in Schools* (James and Pollard 2006), was the first statement of our tentative conclusions, including the ten principles for effective teaching and learning. We subsequently 'tested' their validity in discussion with various audiences. One such 'audience' was researchers working on TLRP post-school projects, who were interested in the extent to which such principles might generalise to their work. Discussions with them alerted us to some particular emphases and gaps in the school based work. For example, although the schools projects were interested in learning outcomes, and were underpinned by coherent conceptions of learning, they probably contributed more 'new' knowledge to our understanding of effective teaching than of learning per se. This is perhaps understandable given the nature of schools, which contrasts with post-compulsory settings where 'teachers', as such, do not always exist. Furthermore, whereas psychological, social-psychological or soiciological approaches were drawn upon, biological (neuroscientific) aspects of learning were not investigated in TLRP schools projects. As one respondent expressed it, 'Where is the brain in TLRP's model of learning?' TLRP has sought to redress this imbalance by funding a seminar series which has published a commentary on *Neuroscience in Education* (Howard-Jones 2007). In the first month after publication this commentary was downloaded 38,000 times. The object of this publication was to engender a formal dialogue between neuroscience and education because almost all teachers believe that knowledge of the brain is important in the design of educational programmes. Many programmes that claim to be 'brain-based' have been flourishing in the UK but, as this commentary makes clear, 'these programmes have usually been produced without the involvement of neuroscientific expertise, are rarely evaluated in their effectiveness and are often unscientific in their approach' (p.4).

Other criticisms of our attempt to synthesise our findings from school-based projects highlighted limited attention to issues of equity and transitions, including a need for greater clarity about the relationship of informal to formal learning because informal learning can occur within schools, as formal learning can occur in non-school settings. It is not the case that schools projects have nothing to say on these issues, as the summaries above make clear, but some of their data on these issues have yet to be fully analysed or written up. For this reason a further thematic group, led by Miriam David, is working on mining evidence across TLRP on *Social Diversity and Difference*.

Despite these reservations, our attempt to synthesise findings from school-based projects in the form of principles has been welcomed. In autumn 2007 we published them as a poster inside a magazine called *Principles into Practice: a teacher's guide*. This was sent out, with a DVD, to every school in the UK (electronic copies for download are available at: http://www.tlrp.org/findings/Schools%20Findings/Schools%20Findings.html). The poster has been included in guidance for head teachers and senior leaders, from the Primary National Strategy in England (DfES 2007), and translated into Welsh and distributed by the Welsh Assembly Government in a bilingual version (also available from the TLRP website).

Each of the ten principles is first expressed as a simple statement beginning with the stem: 'Effective teaching and learning. ... ' It is then expanded in a description of the practices that are seen as important. In the original version (in James and Pollard 2006) each principle was also mapped against the evidence that supported it. Such evidence comes from across school sectors. We have not reiterated all that evidence here because we have summarised project findings in the section above. However, we have added critical commentary with respect to some of these principles.

Principle 1. Effective teaching and learning equip learners for life in its broadest sense

Learning should aim to help individuals and groups to develop the intellectual, personal and social resources that will enable them to participate as active citizens, contribute to economic development and flourish as individuals in a diverse and changing society. This may mean expanding conceptions of worthwhile learning outcomes and taking seriously issues of equity and social justice for all.

As the first and most important aim of TLRP, all projects were expected to work to improve outcomes for learners. In the early days it was mostly assumed that this meant increasing attainment on tests and examinations. As the work progressed, researchers sought to broaden the concept of outcomes beyond those defined by the current standards agenda. The need to do this was emphasised by the work of the Inclusion projects, which saw engagement with learning as crucial. The projects on group work (SPRinG and ScotSPRinG), researched the affective dimension as an outcome of learning as well as a precondition for academic success. ACTS II found a positive relationship between attainment, effort and the development of metacognitive strategies, and the Learning How to Learn (LHTL) project concluded that a capacity for autonomous learning is possibly the most important outcome for students who will live and work in the fast moving world of the 21st century. The longitudinal studies carried out by Pollard emphasised the importance of the development of learner identities for personal fulfilment.

It is possible to argue that attempts to broaden the 'standards' debate were driven by a desire to promote educational values beyond those that focus narrowly on benefits to the economy. Education is driven by moral purposes (Pollard 2002) and educational research reflects this. Such values are contested and the way in which this principle is worded possibly understates the extent of the debate about the aims of education.

Within TLRP, this debate was acknowledged in the work of the cross-phase Learning Outcomes Thematic Group. Using the distinction made by Sfard (1998) concerning two metaphors of learning – learning as acquisition (of knowledge, skills and understanding) and learning as participation (in communities of practice) – and speculating on the need for a third 'knowledge creation' metaphor (Paavola *et al.* 2002), it became clear that there was a difference between the outcomes that were promoted in post-compulsory settings and those that are most obviously pursued in schools. As James and Brown (2005: 17) observed:

- The acquisition metaphor was used, and attainment/understanding/concepts and other cognitive outcomes were pursued, in all sectors of education, but especially in schools and HE.
- The participation metaphor was more characteristic of post-compulsory education (FE, HE, workplace learning, CPD, and lifelong learning) with strong emphasis on outcomes associated with social practice, dispositions, membership, access and inclusion.
- Only early years (pre-school and early primary) and HE appeared in the creative category to suggest a possible need for a 'knowledge creation' metaphor.

One implication of this analysis of the first 30 TLRP projects was that more focused attention needs to be given to the nature of the outcomes that are valued, promoted and assessed at every phase, and the degree of consistency and coherence that may, or may not, be needed in education across the life course and across diverse groups of learners.

Principle 2. Effective teaching and learning engage with valued forms of knowledge

Teaching and learning should engage learners with the big ideas, key processes, modes of discourse and narratives of subjects so that they understand what constitutes quality and standards in particular domains.

TLRP projects that focused on particular subjects showed that teachers need to possess both a good understanding of the subjects they teach and of the best ways to teach them. The literacy and numeracy projects carried out by Nunes and Howe emphasised the role of 'awareness' of this kind by teachers. They also showed that insights from research were readily used by teachers when they were transformed into worked examples.

Further cross-programme thematic work on curriculum, domain knowledge and pedagogy, led by Professors Moon and McCormick, has been undertaken and reported in a special issue of *The Curriculum Journal* in December 2007 (Volume 18, number 4). Within primary education the key question is often whether a primary teacher can successfully work across the whole of the primary curriculum even though his or her subject expertise may lie in one or two areas. This thematic group explored this and other questions using a heuristic model (see http://www.tlrp.org/themes/seminar/moon/papers.html) that examines the relationships between four perspectives: the subject knowledge perspective; the curriculum perspective; the learner perspective; and the pedagogical perspective. It also combines insights from the 'Anglo-American' research approach typical of the UK, with its focus on empirical work, with that of a more theoretical didactics approach more frequently found in the rest of Europe.

Principle 3. Effective teaching and learning recognise the importance of prior experience and learning

Teaching and learning should take account of what the learner knows already in order to plan their next steps. This includes building on prior learning but also taking account of the personal and cultural experiences of different groups of learners.

Pressures for 'delivery' and 'coverage' can work against the promotion of deep and secure learning, and enhanced motivation. Teachers need time to diagnose learning difficulties and help pupils to improve. This was a foundation principle of the LHTL project, which built on assessment for learning practice. The Inclusion project, the HSKE project and the EPPE project also encouraged teachers to challenge their taken-for-granted assumptions about the prior knowledge and experience of certain groups of children.

Principle 4. Effective teaching and learning require the teacher to scaffold learning

Teachers should provide activities and structures of intellectual, social and emotional support to help learners to move forward in their learning so that when these supports are removed the learning is secure.

The way teachers plan and structure activities in the classroom, and the role of classroom dialogue in scaffolding, was a theme in a number of projects. (The term 'scaffolding' acknowledged the seminal influence of educational thinkers such as Lev Vygotsky and Jerome Bruner.) The InterActive project found scaffolding learning, by teachers, to be crucial across ages and across the whole range of school subjects because it promoted sustained, mindful engagement. It was also found to be crucial in early years learning with ICT (Plowman's INTERPLAY project).

Principle 5. Effective teaching and learning need assessment to be congruent with learning

Assessment should be designed and implemented with the goal of achieving maximum validity both in terms of learning outcomes and learning processes. It should help to advance learning as well as determine whether learning has occurred.

Complex learning behaviours and outcomes (see Principle 1 above) need subtle measures which often require observation, by teachers, over time and across different contexts. However, the way in which the initial TLRP projects were commissioned did not easily permit new measures of wider learning outcomes to be developed and tested prior to the introduction of pedagogical innovations (see James and Brown 2005 for a discussion of this). In other words, most projects were 'development and research' rather than 'research and development', and assessments of outcome tended to be based on existing measures, such as national tests, rather than novel instruments. The problems raised were recognised as individual project teams sought to find adequate ways to assess the outcomes they wanted to promote, that is to say beyond conventional academic attainment.

These issues, identified by the Learning Outcomes Thematic Group (James and Brown 2005), have subsequently been revisited by another TLRP thematic seminar series, led by Daugherty, with support from the Assessment Reform Group. This 'Assessment of Significant Learning Outcomes' (ASLO) thematic series is exploring the ways in which the relationships between assessment and curriculum are conceptualised. It has become evident that the problems inherent in specifying a curriculum and in designing valid assessments have been compounded, even within one country (UK), by the use of different terminology in different sectors. The ASLO team has been investigating examples of work undertaken on maximising the extent of congruence of assessment practices with the full range of learning outcomes as specified in five contexts: national curriculum mathematics; the 'Learning to Learn Indicators Project' in Europe; workplace learning; higher education; and vocational education.

The aim of the seminars, and the publications arising from it, is to clarify the terms in which the alignment of assessment procedures to learning outcomes is discussed. This has involved exploring how, and by whom, control over programmes is exercised in each context, in order to identify insights that may have wider implications. It has also involved further consideration of the concept of validity, especially the issue of consequences, that is the impact of assessment. This takes analysis beyond the simple notion of assessed outcomes being aligned to a pre-specified curriculum; the relationship between learning and assessment is better understood as a complex, non-linear, interacting system which recognises synergistic relationships among curriculum, pedagogy and assessment. At the time of writing the ASLO group has yet to publish but working papers can be found at http://www.tlrp.org/themes/seminar/daugherty/index.html).

Principle 6. Effective teaching and learning promote the active engagement of the learner

A chief goal of teaching and learning should be the promotion of learners' independence and autonomy. This involves acquiring a repertoire of learning strategies and practices, developing positive learning dispositions, and having the will and confidence to become agents in their own learning.

Most TLRP schools projects emphasised the importance of developing learning awareness, explicit learning practices, positive learning dispositions, and learning autonomy. However, the LHTL Project found that, whilst teachers want to promote learning autonomy in their pupils, they find it difficult. Those who were most successful were those who took responsibility for what happened in their classrooms, and reflected on what they could do to improve matters, rather than blame external pressures or pupil characteristics.

Principle 7. Effective teaching and learning foster both individual and social processes and outcomes

Learners should be encouraged and helped to build relationships and communication with others for learning purposes, in order to assist the mutual construction of knowledge and enhance the achievements of individuals and groups. Consulting learners about their learning and giving them a voice is both an expectation and a right.

The TLRP group work projects demonstrated the benefits of efforts to improve the quality of group work and students' mastery of cooperation and collaboration. Pupils involved in these developments made significant academic gains, which were stable across schools in different social contexts. This confirms the importance of dialogue. Other projects examined the benefits of making space for teachers to consult students about their learning. The Consulting Pupils Project found that taking students' views seriously enhances self-esteem and agency and improves learning opportunities. However, these researchers also found that in the 'acoustic of the classroom' some pupils have more communicative competence, and are 'heard', more than others. Teachers need to be alert to social class and gender differences. The CPAL Project, which extended these themes, used the concepts of space, voice, audience and influence, from the UN Convention on the Rights of the Child (Article 12), as a framework for understanding the possibilities and challenges of encouraging student participation and consultation.

Principle 8. Effective teaching and learning recognise the significance of informal learning

Informal learning, such as learning out of school, should be recognised as at least as significant as formal learning and should therefore be valued and appropriately utilised in formal processes.

At classroom level, teachers can be encouraged and helped to value and build on informal learning. For example, projects investigating ICT in schools found that schools sometimes underestimate the extent of computer expertise derived out of school.

Explicit home-school knowledge exchange activities produced impact on outcomes but this was mediated by social class, gender and attainment factors, which underlines the importance of handling informal learning with sensitivity in order to avoid negative consequences for particular groups of pupils.

Principle 9. Effective teaching and learning depend on teacher learning

The need for teachers to learn continuously in order to develop their knowledge and skill, and adapt and develop their roles, especially through classroom inquiry, should be recognised and supported.

TLRP has produced very substantial evidence on the needs and character of teachers' professional development and learning, both through individual projects and through cross-programme thematic initiatives (for example, see http://www.tlrp.org/themes/ seminar/gewirtz/ and a special issue of *Research Papers in Education* 2005). That pupils' learning depends substantially on teachers' learning is perhaps the overriding finding from TLRP schools projects. In subject areas, as in relation to more generic approaches to learning, teachers were found to need opportunities to develop their own knowledge, beliefs and values, as well as their practical skills. Teachers need to possess frameworks of concepts and principles to guide the decisions they make in the unpredictable situations they often encounter in classrooms. Without this there is a danger of practice becoming ritualised and mechanistic. TLRP evidence suggests that this development is best achieved through teachers' critical inquiry, with colleagues, in classrooms contexts. The Research Lesson Study Project (Dudley) researched a model for CPD that is school-based, longer term, collaborative and inquiry-based. The Inclusive Project noted that visits from teachers in other schools were valued for questioning assumptions. Schools with cultures of participation and inquiry, and professional networks, are in a good position to support this but they benefit from help from local and national providers.

Specific, targeted professional development materials and courses were also valued. All TLRP development and research projects found that offering teachers practical strategies, based on principles and evidence, provided much needed support for setting up, managing and improving the effectiveness of innovations in everyday classroom settings.

Principle 10. Effective teaching and learning demand consistent policy frameworks with support for teaching and learning as their primary focus

Institutional and system level policies need to recognise the fundamental importance of teaching and learning and be designed to create effective learning environments for all learners.

A number of TLRP projects investigated the impact of policy on teaching and learning. Most noted that when senior management support innovation it becomes sustainable. However, LHTL Project head teachers revealed their concerns about leading learning in their schools within the context of prescriptive government policy. The greater the external pressure, the greater was the desire for flexibility, diversification and agency.

IMPLICATIONS FOR THE PRIMARY REVIEW AND FOR NATIONAL POLICY, NATIONAL AGENCIES, LOCAL AUTHORITIES, SCHOOLS AND OTHERS

In 1997 the New Labour government promoted 'standards not structures' as a new vision for the direction of education policy. After years of attempts to engineer improvements by changing the way the school system was structured and managed, this seemed at last to be recognition that, despite structural 'reforms', standards will only rise if core processes of teaching and learning are given priority. Although structures are necessary they are never sufficient to secure improvements in teaching and learning, and thereby higher standards. Structures should support these fundamental processes, including, and crucially, provision for professional development of teachers and leadership for learning.

UK governments have invested enormous amounts of financial and political capital in education in recent years. Many of the resulting initiatives are broadly consistent with the principles for teaching and learning which we have identified – certainly at a rhetorical level.

In England, the recent emphasis on 'personalised learning' in schools affirms the centrality of teaching and learning processes, and the DCSF ostensibly seeks to maintain this priority through the National Strategies and initiatives such as the Gifted and Talented programme. Taken as a whole, changes in curriculum, assessment and other elements of the *Five Year Strategy for Children and Learners* are designed to reduce prescription and increase flexibility, as is the increased integration of children's services and the *Every Child Matters* agenda. A similar emphasis is to be found in the new standards for teachers created by the Training and Development Agency for Schools. However, the benefits from such initiatives take time to be realised and political pressures sometimes press for more rapid outcomes, encouraging reversion to prescriptive models. Indeed, some commentators have suggested that the Education and Inspections Act, 2006, indicates that the government has reverted to structural change as a lever for raising standards, and others that the proposed single level tests in England will stimulate even more 'teaching to the test'. Current DCSF Select Committee inquiries into Assessment and Testing and the National Curriculum indicate that there is cross-party concern with the current level of prescription.

Policies have ultimately to be turned into practices which bring about improvements in learning and achievement for individuals and groups. The key challenge is to ensure that the various elements and contributions, at each level of the system and from each stakeholder, are as consistent as possible with what we know about effective teaching and learning. This is not always achieved, as practising teachers are often only too aware.

We hope that the ten principles which we have identified will be helpful in evaluating such policy proposals. They could be applied to the policies of any government department or agency, to a school, or to a classroom. We hope that they will generate debate. But they are offered with due humility. They are the result of an analysis of key findings across TLRP's projects, some of which were still active whilst the overall review was being conducted. Conclusions in this complex field will always be conditional. The learning of pupils, teachers, schools, communities, researchers and governments are bound up together. In various ways, all need to learn better if children are to succeed.

FURTHER RESEARCH NEEDED

Researchers will always say that further research is needed. There is justification in this in that knowledge is always provisional and needs to be constantly tested in new circumstances. However, as the preceding discussion has indicated, there are a number of areas in urgent need of further development:

- Further work on the contribution of neuroscience, on the one hand, and socio-cultural approaches, on the other, to our understanding of learning and the formation of learning identities;
- Further work on valid assessments of valued learning outcomes, following renewed public debate on the latter;
- Further work on how successful small scale innovations in teaching and learning can be effectively scaled up and rolled out across schools and across the system.

NOTES

1 The 'hit rate' was about one in ten.
2 The Evidence for Policy and Practice Information and Co-ordinating Centre (EPPI-Centre), part of the Social Science Research Unit at the Institute of Education, University of London.
3 See http://www.tlrp.org/themes/seminar/gewirtz/papers/seminar8/paper-elliott.pdf

REFERENCES

Department for Education and Skills (DfES) (2007) *Leading Improvement Using the Primary Framework: guidance for headteachers and senior leaders.* London: DfES,

Howard-Jones, P. (2007) *Neuroscience and Education: issues and opportunities.* TLRP Commentary. Swindon: ESRC.

James, M. (2006) 'Balancing rigour and responsiveness in a shifting context: meeting the challenges of educational research', *Research Papers in Education* 21(4): 365–80.

James, M. and Brown, S. (2005) 'Grasping the TLRP nettle: a preliminary analysis and some enduring issues surrounding the improvement of learning outcomes', *The Curriculum Journal* 16(1): 7–30.

James, M. and Pollard, A. (Eds) (2006) *Improving Teaching and Learning in Schools: a commentary by the Teaching and Learning Research Programme.* Swindon: ESRC.

James, M., Pollard, A., Rees, G. and Taylor, C. (2005) 'Researching learning outcomes: building confidence in our conclusions', *The Curriculum Journal* 16(1): 109–22.

Moon, B. and McCormick, B. (Eds) (2007) *The Curriculum Journal* 18(4).

Paavola, S., Lipponen, L., and Hakkarainen, K. (2002) 'Epistemological foundations for CSCL: a comparison of three models of innovative knowledge communities', in G. Stahl (Ed) *Computer-Supported Collaborative Learning: foundations for a CSCL community.* Proceedings of the Computer-supported Collaborative Learning 2002 Conference. Hillside, NJ: Erlbaum: 24–32.

Pollard, A. (2002) *TLRP: academic challenges for moral purposes.* Paper presented to the TLRP Annual Conference, Cambridge, September 2002.

——(2005) *Taking the Initiative? TLRP and educational research*, Annual Educational Review Guest Lecture, School of Education, 12th October.

Research Papers in Education. Special Edition (2005) 20(2).

Sfard, A. (1998) 'On two metaphors for learning and the dangers of choosing just one', *Educational Researcher* 27(2): 4–13.

21 Classes, groups and transitions

Structures for teaching and learning

Peter Blatchford, Susan Hallam, Judith Ireson and Peter Kutnick, with Andrea Creech

INTRODUCTION

In this chapter we are interested in ways in which pupils are organised into classes and into groups within classes, and whether transitions into, within and from the primary sector influence classroom teaching and pupils' progress. Educational reform as it relates to primary schools has mainly, and certainly since the Education Reform Act of 1988, been concerned with curriculum and assessment arrangements. In this chapter we argue that teaching and learning in schools take place in distinctive social contexts – classrooms and groups – that need to be recognised and studied carefully because of the effect they have on teaching and learning. Although some theorists, for example Bronfenbrenner (1979) and Doyle (1986), have been influential in identifying the contextual basis for school learning, there is still a strong tendency to see teaching, learning and classroom management in a kind of vacuum, separate from the school organisational contexts within which they are situated. At the same time, opinions can sometimes be strongly put, for example about grouping in schools, with many politicians at least now favouring some version of same-ability groupings, whether at the class or within-class level. There are also very strongly held views about the benefits of small classes in schools. But there are many complexities involved that require us to take an objective look at the research evidence available.

Much of this survey will cover research connected to grouping strategies in schools. It may be worth saying at the outset that we have considered this work at two main levels – the first concerns grouping at the class or school level and the second concerns pupil grouping within the classroom. With regard to the first level, various strategies have been used to group pupils into year groups, forms, and subject teaching groups. Throughout the chapter we refer to this type of grouping as 'structured/organisational grouping'. Topics covered include setting and streaming, mixed-ability and same-ability classes. The nature and composition of such groups has been the source of heated debates for many years. These debates have sometimes been unhelpfully polemical, with arguments raging between those defending ability grouping and those promoting mixed-ability teaching. The reality is more complex and less clear, and we aim to achieve a balanced account of what we know about grouping at this level, highlighting the reasons why schools adopt particular forms of grouping, and the impact of different forms of grouping on teaching and on pupil learning and attainment. But we also consider grouping in a second way, that is, groupings within classes. A focus on grouping at the class or school level may obscure what is happening in the groups within the class, in relation to teaching, learning and attitudes. One theme to emerge from our survey, which we might state at this early point, is that implications for practice are evident at both levels but perhaps clearer for the second compared to the first level. Another theme to emerge is that there is a gap between current practice and the potential for using pupil groups to enhance pupil learning while in school. Furthermore, the literature on transitions also emphasises differences in within-classroom processes between phases and years that may affect the child's move from one setting to another.

THE APPROACH OF THIS CHAPTER

Given that research in a number of areas covered in this survey of the evidence has been conducted over a number of years, this chapter seeks to offer an analytical and evaluative account rather than attempt a full summary of all the research in these fields. We have sought to draw out the main traditions of research, and situate the research covered in wider educational and policy contexts at the time. In a concluding section we aim to identify key findings, draw out implications for current policy and practice, and suggest areas for future research.

The chapter inevitably draws on the involvement of its authors in aspects of the research covered, not least because this work has contributed to recent publications and knowledge. Though this means that we are informed by (and some may feel over stress) our own work, our aim has been to be rigorous and even-handed about the research evidence covered.

In line with the overall purpose of the Primary Review, the approach has been to review research mainly, but not exclusively, from the UK. There are some research studies from overseas that warrant particular mention, for example the experimental USA STAR project on the effects of reduced class size on pupil attainment, because of its unique nature and the degree of impact it has had. We also refer to experimental studies of cooperative learning carried out by seminal researchers in the field (for example David and Roger Johnson, and Robert Slavin).

In line with the intended readership of this companion volume we have tried to make the text accessible to all in education; we have avoided technical terms and coverage and have sought to identify the key implications and messages.

The kinds of questions we address in this chapter include:

- What have been the main approaches and traditions of research in this area?
- How are pupils grouped in primary schools and what factors affect the adoption of different grouping arrangements?
- What is the impact on teaching and on pupil learning and adjustment of different forms of grouping?
- Are there problems of coherence, transitions and continuity within and between phases?
- What is the research evidence that small classes are important for learning and teaching?

OVERVIEW OF MAIN METHODOLOGICAL TRADITIONS AND ISSUES

In England and Wales there is a strong tradition of comparative studies of primary school organisation. Generally, research under this umbrella aims to identify features of schools and classrooms that have an impact on children's learning and achievement. Some studies are concerned with impacts on children's attitudes, behaviour and aspirations and a small number include these alongside children's academic achievement. Within this tradition there has been some interest in information on teaching and classroom practices that may be affected by school organisational factors such as school and class sizes, structured ability grouping through streaming and setting, and within-class grouping. Effort has gone into defining, measuring and evaluating the impact of these factors. In this section we concentrate on the main methodological traditions, including survey research, case studies, experiments and longitudinal studies.

Surveys and case studies

Survey research provides useful evidence on the extent of different forms of school organisation, such as school and class sizes and ability grouping practices in schools and classrooms. A number of research surveys are concerned with the nature and extent of grouping practices in schools and classrooms (Bealing 1972; DES 1978; Lee and Croll 1995; Hallam *et al.* 2003; Kutnick *et al.* 2006; Ofsted 1998b). Evidence is also available from primary school inspections undertaken by Ofsted. Comparisons between survey results help to establish trends over time and are most readily made when samples are based on large, randomly selected samples. Hallam *et al.* (2003) established the extent of setting, within-class grouping, vertical (mixed age) grouping and mixed ability grouping and were able to relate these to school size and age of pupils.

The UK also has a strong tradition of descriptive studies of primary schools and classrooms (for example, Galton, Simon and Croll 1980; Bennett *et al.* 1984; Tizard *et al.* 1988; Mortimore *et al.* 1988; Alexander 1995, 1997, 2001 (the latter comparing primary schools, classrooms and pedagogy in England and four other countries); Galton, Hargreaves *et al.* 1999). These provide detailed observations of teacher and pupil behaviour in classrooms, including teacher-pupil interactions, time spent on curriculum subjects and issues to do with the management of primary schools.

Descriptive evidence, such as that obtained in surveys and observations, is sometimes linked with other information and used to show relationships between two or more factors. Simple correlation studies provide useful indications of relationships but the design of these studies is not strong enough to draw reliable conclusions about effects of one factor on another; for example, an association between a measure of class size or pupil teacher ratios on the one hand and measures of pupil attainment on the other does not allow us to conclude that class size affects pupil attainment (Blatchford, Goldstein and Mortimore 1998). This is because we often do not know whether the results can be explained by another factor such as initial pupil attainment.

Case study research provides valuable insights into factors that might mediate, or moderate, the effects of school and classroom organisation on pupils, such as the curriculum and teachers' expectations, attitudes and classroom practice. Evidence is obtained from a variety of sources, including members of staff, pupils and other stakeholders, and from observations and secondary data. Compared with research in the secondary sector, where there are several highly influential case studies of ability grouping, there are fewer examples in the primary phase. In the past decade, two multisite case studies of primary schools have investigated school and classroom grouping practices. The first was a study of six schools of differing size and organisation, which obtained the perspectives of teachers, governors and pupils on the schools' grouping practices, how these groupings were implemented, resourced and evaluated and how they related to pupils' experience of learning (Hallam and Ireson 1999). This research highlighted school policy, ethos, the deployment of resources and classroom practice as factors that mediate the impact of structured grouping on pupils' attainment and their social development. A later set of 12 primary school case studies supplied additional information on the effect of grouping policy on teaching and learning strategies, the nature of tasks pupils undertook in the classroom and the impact on pupil learning (Kutnick *et al.* 2006).

Experimental and comparative studies

For practical reasons, very few randomised controlled trials of school organisation and structure have been reported, as few schools and parents are willing to allow children to be experimented on in this way. Those that exist tend to be of relatively brief duration. One exception is the Tennessee STAR project, in which students were randomly allocated to classes of different sizes (Finn and Achilles 1999; Nye *et al.* 2000).

As we show below there have been experimental studies of the effectiveness of various approaches to small groups. These are predominantly based in the USA and tend to arise from theoretical orientations that are predominantly social psychological. They include studies of co-operative learning (Slavin 1995; Johnson and Johnson 2003) and also include socio-constructivist studies of communication and collaboration (Mercer 2000; Webb and Mastergeorge 2003; Gillies and Ashman 2003). While these studies are insightful in identifying where groups are ineffective, they tend not to consider the whole classroom context within which group work takes place.

Though it is often assumed that experimental studies provide the most unambiguous evidence on causation, there have also been concerns that results are not necessarily valid (for example because control of the main independent variable necessary in experimental designs introduces changes that can make the situation differ from that found in everyday school life) and that alternative, longer term, more naturalistic quantitative methods may be preferable (Goldstein and Blatchford 1998). Recent advances in statistical modelling techniques, such as multi-level modelling, have made such approaches powerful and flexible.

Many studies capitalise on existing differences between schools and classrooms to compare the effects of various forms of organisation. This approach presents fewer practical difficulties but several methodological challenges remain to be confronted. It runs the risk of confounding variables that may co-exist with particular forms of organisation. A change in pupil grouping may be accompanied by changes in curriculum or teaching method for the new grouping, or special materials might be given to an intervention group, or teachers using an experimental approach receive special training whereas teachers in control classes do not. As a result of the co-existence of factors, it is very difficult, if not impossible, to disentangle the separate effects of each one individually.

A number of strategies may be used to control for such factors at various stages of the research process, when constructing the sample of schools or classrooms or manipulating aspects of the pedagogic environment. For example, when assessing the effects of ability grouping on mathematics achievement, Whitburn (2001) ensured that all students were given the same teaching materials, thus holding this factor constant across groups. Likewise, Slavin (1987) restricted his systematic review of ability grouping in primary schools to studies in which the curriculum remained the same for students in same ability groups and mixed ability groups. Control may also be exerted in the analysis stage through the use of sophisticated statistical techniques, which take account of prior differences between students in the specific variables of interest, such as prior academic achievement and socio-economic status (Blatchford *et al.* 2003; Ireson and Hallam 2001, 2009; Ireson, Hallam and Hurley 2005; Ireson, Hallam and Plewis 2001). Multi-level regression analysis provides simultaneous estimates of the strength of several school, classroom and individual factors.

Longitudinal studies

Three major longitudinal studies of ability grouping were undertaken in the 1960s (Barker Lunn 1970; Goldberg *et al.* 1966; Borg 1965). The study undertaken in New York schools by Goldberg *et al.* (1966) was unusual in that school principals assigned each pupil to one of 15 grouping patterns, ranging from extremely broad to extremely narrow, and pupils remained in these groups for two years. Borg (1965) compared two school districts in Utah, one of which had heterogeneous classes and the other of which had ability-grouped classes. Barker Lunn (1970) compared 36 streamed and 36 unstreamed schools in England and Wales and followed children through the four years of junior school, with a later follow up in secondary school by Ferri (1971).

More recent longitudinal studies evaluate the effects on pupils of different aspects of school organisation, teaching and classroom practice in the infant or primary phases. Good measures of pupil attainment, both on entry to the school and at a later stage, allow estimates of school and classroom effects to be made (Tizard *et al.* 1988; Mortimore *et al.* 1988). Classroom mapping is used to obtain information on the layout of classrooms and the composition of groupings (Alexander 1995, 2001; Mortimore, Sammons, Stoll and Ecob 1988) and to explore relationships between group size and composition, learning tasks and activities, interactions within pupil groups and the role of teachers (Alexander 1997; Kutnick, Blatchford and Baines 2002). Observations reveal a variety of groupings utilised by teachers within the classroom. They show that children may be in ability groups or mixed ability groups for the entire day or they may be regrouped for part of the day. Teachers may extract groups of similar ability from mixed groups to work on specific subjects or they may extract mixed groups from groups of similar ability. The size, number and composition of groups vary from one class to another, as does the amount of time that children spend in each type of group. Although seated in groups, a common observation is that children work independently rather than collaboratively or cooperatively (Galton, Simon and Croll 1980; Alexander 1997).

Longitudinal research on class size effects includes a large-scale UK study, which followed over 10,000 pupils in over 300 schools through the primary phase of education from age 4/5 to 11 years of age (for example Blatchford 2003). Longitudinal studies enable researchers to explore connections between variables at different points in time, and the use of sophisticated statistical methods help to unravel the direction of influence and establish reciprocal effects.

Methodological challenges

Several methodological challenges have been identified above, including those associated with the random allocation of pupils, eliminating or controlling confounding factors and defining, measuring and evaluating relevant school and classroom factors. In addition, the diverse structure and organisation of primary schools and classrooms presents a number of methodological challenges to those concerned with the effects of different forms of organisation on pupils. First, there may be variations from one year to the next in the school roll, intake, staffing, number of classes and grouping patterns. Within schools, pupils are grouped in a variety of ways, through streaming, setting, across age groups, mixed ability groups and within-class groupings. Within the classroom, individual teachers have their own grouping arrangements and these may change for different curriculum areas. Even within the same school, grouping arrangements vary for children of different ages (Baines, Blatchford and Kutnick 2003; Ireson and Hallam 1999, 2001; Hallam and Ireson 1999). Considerable care is needed to establish details of school organisation and pupil grouping arrangements.

A second issue concerns the nature of the educational outcomes that are considered. Two major groups of outcomes have been investigated; those relating to children's social and personal development and those relating to academic achievement. Recent research frequently makes use of national Key Stage test results, which provide a common, albeit limited, metric, whereas earlier research used a range of different standardised tests and examinations. In general, however, a narrow range of learning outcomes has been researched with little concern for critical thinking, creativity and meta-cognitive and transferable skills. Personal and social outcomes have also been assessed in a variety of ways, using interview techniques or self-completion measures of self-esteem, attitudes, motivation and alienation. The variety of measures presents challenges when making comparisons across studies.

Thirdly, findings show that within any single school the effects of class size and grouping are not consistent in size, over time, in different subject domains or between teachers (Baines, Blatchford and Kutnick 2003; Blatchford 2003; Ireson and Hallam 2001). This indicates that schools' unique characteristics and ethos, and teachers' classroom practices and processes mediate the effects of grouping arrangements (Ireson and Hallam 2001). Particular systems of pupil grouping are implemented differently by schools and even by different teachers within the same school.

A final issue is that the effects of school organisation are not consistent for different groups of pupils. Effects vary for pupils of differing ages and abilities. The issue is not merely whether particular forms of school organisation and grouping are effective, but for whom they are effective, in what ways and whether some children suffer as a result.

STRUCTURED GROUPING PRACTICES

Different types of structured groupings in primary schools

Classes in the primary school can be structured in a range of ways. They may include children of only one age cohort or many; up to four in the smallest primary schools. The classes may be mixed-ability or streamed (children put into classes on the basis of their measured or perceived ability). Whatever the arrangements for organising individual classes, children may be put into sets for some subjects. Sets differ from streaming in that children from more than one class are reorganised into groups based on attainment. Sets may be formed from within a year group or across year groups. Children may be in different sets for different subjects.

Changes in structured grouping practices over time

Historically, streaming was the dominant form of grouping adopted in the UK following the Second World War. Typically, children were placed in a class based on their ability by the age of seven. The top stream took the 11+ examination and were groomed to go on to grammar schools. The remaining children were set on a path towards the secondary modern school and low-level occupations for the rest of their lives. During the 1960s and 1970s, with the introduction of comprehensive education, the demise of the 11+, and an increasing emphasis on equal opportunities, streaming began to decline. This trend was encouraged by the Plowden report (CACE 1967), which advocated a more child-centred approach to primary education, and which was supported by research indicating that ability grouping had no significant effect on overall attainment and had negative personal and social consequences for pupils in the lower streams (Jackson 1964; Barker Lunn 1970, 1984). By the 1970s, of those schools that were large enough to stream, only about 20 per cent chose to do so (Bealing 1972; DES 1978). By the 1990s this had declined further to less than 3 per cent (Lee and Croll 1995). Streaming had almost disappeared, replaced by mixed-ability classes.

Following the Education Reform Act (1988), the 1990s saw the implementation of the National Curriculum and an emphasis on raising standards. Ability grouping in the form of setting pupils was perceived as a way to raise attainment and all primary schools were encouraged to introduce it (DfE 1993). This was reinforced by the White Paper *Excellence in Schools*, which suggested that 'setting should be the norm in secondary schools. In some cases it is worth considering in primary schools' (DfEE 1997: 38). The political interest in structured grouping led to a number of literature reviews being undertaken (Hallam and Toutounji 1996; Harlen and Malcolm 1997; Sukhnandan and Lee 1998). Ofsted also took an interest in ability grouping procedures, and annual reports for 1995/6 and 1996/7 both commented on the increase in teaching based on ability groups (Ofsted 1997, 1998a) particularly in Years 5 and 6 for mathematics and English. Against this background, Ofsted commissioned a survey of a random selection of 900 schools, of which 44 per cent responded (Ofsted 1998b), exploring the prevalence of setting and its effects. The findings indicated that, of those schools responding, about 60 per cent of junior schools set for at least one subject in some year groups, while over one-third of infant schools, and about one-half of combined infant and junior schools, did the same.

A subsequent survey, undertaken by the Institute of Education, University of London (Hallam *et al.* 2003) in 1999, and based on a random sample of 2000 schools (40 per cent response rate), took account of school size, the prevalence of mixed-age classes, grouping practices for all subjects, and year group. Within-class ability grouping was the most common grouping arrangement in the core subjects of mathematics and English, with mixed-ability groups within mixed-ability classes the most prevalent practice for all other subjects. The incidence of setting was relatively low (at most 24 per cent in mathematics in Year 6 in schools with same age classes) and the incidence of streaming was negligible. The incidence of setting increased as children became older. In schools with predominantly same-age classes, the incidence of cross-age setting was generally less than that of same-age setting, for example 15 per cent as opposed to 24 per cent in Year 6 in mathematics. In schools with mixed-age classes there was more cross-age setting. For example, 18 per cent in Year 5/6 mathematics compared with 12 per cent same-age setting. Other subjects showed the same pattern.

More setting occurred in mathematics than in any other subject, steadily increasing towards the end of Key Stage 2, although even here the most common form of organisation throughout both primary key stages was ability grouping within the classroom. There was much less setting in English than mathematics. In science, as in most other curriculum subjects, grouping was mainly mixed ability. There was a large number of mixed-age classes in the sample: 356 out of 765 schools had some or all mixed-age classes. Of those schools 91 per cent had under 100 pupils. The planning for mixed-age classes, particularly at Key Stage 2, was complex. Some had classes across Key Stages although this was relatively rare.

Ofsted primary school inspection data from 2003/04 indicated that 28 per cent of schools were setting for maths in KS2; 15 per cent for English; 2 per cent for science; and negligible percentages for other subjects. Overall, primary schools have tended to resist the introduction of structured ability grouping, preferring within-class groups.

Schools' rationales for the practices that they adopt

Studies which have explored head teachers' and teachers' rationales for adopting particular grouping strategies have suggested that these are pragmatic and not driven by dogma. Many schools have little option but to have multi-grade classes because of cohort sizes. A range of factors determine decisions about the organisation of classes and the groupings within them (Lee and Croll 1995). Hallam, Ireson and Davies (2002, 2004), in a large-scale survey following considerable policy changes that included the introduction of the literacy and numeracy hours and exhortations to introduce setting, found that 48 per cent of schools had made no changes in their grouping structures; 22 per cent had made changes because of the literacy hour; 2 per cent because of the numeracy hour; 7 per cent because of a combination of these; and 21 per cent for other reasons. Issues that schools considered when making decisions about grouping structures related to:

- learning (differentiation, raising attainment, developing pupil skills and good behaviour, flexibility);
- teaching (planning and delivery of the curriculum, use of more whole-class teaching);
- academic subject concerns (groupings for different subjects, making use of teacher expertise);
- introduction of the National Literacy Strategy;
- school and cohort size (issues relating to mixed-age classes, setting);
- resources (staffing, timetabling, space, teaching assistants/parents);
- as a result of evaluations of different grouping practices (perceived success, reduction in class teacher contact time, time lost in movement between sets).

The arrival of a new head teacher can facilitate change (Hallam *et al.* 2002) while parents can also be influential in the practices which schools adopt (Davies, Hallam and Ireson 2003).

When streaming was commonplace in the 1960s, Jackson (1964) found that policies were based on the assumption that ability was largely inherited and therefore immutable. Within streamed schools there was prejudice against pupils of below-average ability. Barker-Lunn (1970) noted a difference in ethos between streamed and non-streamed schools. The former were more systematic in their educational approach, concentrated more on the 3Rs, made greater use of tests, and had more authoritarian teachers. Teachers in non-streamed schools were more permissive, preferred more active methods of instruction, emphasised self-expression and personal experience and were critical of tests, selection and streaming. More recent research (Hallam *et al.* 2002) has indicated that while there may seem to be little difference in school ethos as defined by educational aims included in school documentation or as reported in interviews with teachers, in practice there are substantial differences in the way these aims are operationalised. In the six schools studied, similar aims to enable every child to fulfil their potential were pursued through streaming, different levels or types of setting, or mixed-ability teaching. These impacted on the pupils in very different ways, affecting the nature of the teaching, the allocation of teachers to classes, and pupil experiences. The pupils were socialised into the particular practices adopted within each school, although ethos differences emerged in the level of reported teasing related to ability, the particular pupils targeted, and the extent to which pupils were aware of their position in the pecking order. Grouping structures, while they did not define school ethos, clearly played a role in shaping shared attitudes within the school which in some cases valued some pupils more than others.

Historically, the allocation of pupils to ability groups was a somewhat arbitrary affair (Barker Lunn 1970; Jackson 1964). Recent research suggests that it is currently based on Cognitive Ability Tests, national attainment tests, or a combination of both, although many different factors influence the groupings that are formed in schools and classrooms including social relationships between pupils, gender and behaviour, physical aspects of the classroom and class size. Some pupils exhibiting poor behaviour are placed in low groups irrespective of their level of attainment. In other cases, teachers deliberately split up groups of potentially disruptive pupils into different ability groups in order to be better able to control their behaviour. Other factors such as group dynamics are also taken into account (Davies *et al.* 2003).

Although, in theory, movement between streams or sets is possible, in practice it is frequently restricted and children perceive that it is very difficult (Hallam *et al.* 2004). One problem is that there is often a gap between work that has been undertaken and what is required for the higher set (Jackson 1964). Where children do change group if the movement is in an upward direction they tend to do better, while in a downward direction they tend to do worse (Barker Lunn 1970). When streaming was widely adopted in the UK, there was clear evidence that the low streams tended to include disproportionate numbers of pupils of low socio-economic status, boys and those born in the summer (Barker Lunn 1970). More recently it has been demonstrated that pupils in certain ethnic groups are over-represented in low sets in some secondary schools (Gillborn and Youdell 2000), although data are not available for primary schools.

Mixed age classes

Data from the DfES (2002) indicates that about one in four classes in primary education are mixed age, with 25 per cent of pupils taught in such classes. Some of these are in small schools in rural communities where size constrains choice, while others are in urban communities. Research relating to small schools in rural communities tends to draw positive conclusions about the benefits of such groupings, frequently referring to the family atmosphere engendered (Cornall 1986; Galton and Patrick 1990; Francis 1992; Vulliamy and Webb 1995; Hargreaves, Comber and Galton 1996; Hayes 1999; Ofsted 2000).

In contrast to this, large schools where single-age year groups would have been possible have been criticised for adopting mixed-age classes because of the negative impact on attainment and the difficulty that teachers experienced in matching tasks to pupil needs (HMI 1978). Galton and Simon (1980) also found that children in mixed-age classes tended to achieve less but the differences were very small and the causes seem to be related to students concentrating less on their work, spending more time waiting for their teacher, and in routine interactions. In a large-scale study of multi-age teaching in a variety of contexts, Bennett, O'Hare and Lee (1983) found that multi-age groups were predominantly adopted out of necessity because of cohort size. Teachers typically grouped children within the class on the basis of ability, or individual assignments, but rarely age. Mixed-age classes put more stress on teachers and required greater preparation and more resources, but there were advantages in terms of flexibility of staff, children, and space. Case study interviews in selected schools (Lee 1984) revealed that heads and staff made conscious decisions to avoid having multi-aged classes. Teachers indicated that their approach to teaching remained the same as teaching a single-age class.

More recent research, undertaken since the introduction of the National Curriculum and testing at KS1 and KS2, has highlighted a number of challenges and advantages of mixed-age teaching. Berry and Little (2006) studied head teachers' and teachers' attitudes towards multi-age classes in 10 primary schools in London. Challenges associated with multi-grade teaching fell into three categories: curriculum organisation, ability range, and assessment. Opportunities included the adoption of a cognitive/stretching model, peer tutoring and behavioural stretching/modelling. These are very similar to the reported strengths and weaknesses of mixed ability classes. Most teachers expressed a preference for single-age classes, although almost as many had no preference. In relation to the National Curriculum and testing, teachers had to integrate curriculum frameworks, plan over a two year cycle, and plan up or down from one curriculum framework. Preparation for national testing also presented challenges. Hallam *et al.* (2002) found that schools sometimes adopted age-specific setting to allow pupils in Year 6 to prepare for their tests.

The impact of different types of structured grouping on attainment

Relatively few studies have explored the impact of different structured grouping strategies on attainment in primary schools in the UK. When streaming was common, Daniels (1961a) found a higher average level of attainment in schools that did not adopt streaming. This seemed to be caused by an increase in the attainments of the lower attaining pupils rather than the higher attaining pupils being held back. Blandford (1958) in a comparison of streamed and non-streamed schools found similar results with a greater spread of scores in streamed schools. The largest early study compared pupils in 36 streamed and non-streamed primary schools on a wide range of criteria (Barker Lunn 1970). The findings showed no difference in the average academic performance of boys and girls of comparable ability and social class in streamed or non-streamed schools. A follow-up study, two years later, showed no difference in performance at secondary school in relation to prior streaming in primary school (Ferri 1971). Daniels (1961b) compared achievement in streamed and unstreamed schools over a four-year period and concluded that lower ability pupils made better progress in unstreamed schools. International reviews of research on streaming in primary schools (Slavin 1987; Kulik and Kulik 1987, 1992; Kulik 1991) have also indicated that streaming has little impact on pupil attainment.

In the current context, where ability grouping tends to be based on setting for particular subjects rather than whole class streaming, Whitburn (2001) explored the effects of setting on mathematics in the primary school on the progress of over 1,000 pupils in a single education authority. When the same teaching materials were used for Key Stage 2 mathematics, the test results of pupils in mixed-ability classes were significantly better than those taught in sets. Lower-attaining pupils made better progress in mixed-ability classes, without hindering the progress of higher-attaining pupils. In case studies of 12 primary schools Kutnick *et al.* (2006) found that, where schools adopted setting, pupils rarely performed at KS2 levels higher than their local authority or national averages in the subjects which were setted. Value added for these schools was generally negative, while case study schools that used mixed-ability groupings tended to have positive value added although there were exceptions. Some studies have shown small positive effects, and some small negative effects. Overall, the effects have been negligible. Slavin (1987) reviewed seven studies which explored the impact of setting on elementary pupils' levels of achievement in either reading, mathematics, or a combination of the two. Five of the seven studies concluded that students placed in sets learned more than those in mixed ability classes, while the remaining two studies concluded that pupils in mixed ability environments learned more than those in sets.

Vertical or cross-age grouping is adopted of necessity when the intake of pupils to a school cannot be allocated to single-year group classes. In some cases, although rarely, it is adopted because of the perceived educational benefits arising from the social and family-like structure of classes where pupils are taught by the same teacher for several years (Veenman 1995). International reviews of attainment have shown no significant differences between vertical grouping and single-aged grouping in terms of pupils' academic achievement, although cross-aged setting where pupils of similar attainment are drawn from more than one age group for particular activities, for instance reading, can be positive (Slavin 1987; Kulik and Kulik 1992).

The most common grouping practice adopted in UK primary schools is within-class. International reviews have shown that within-class grouping in relation to ability or attainment can be effective in raising attainment (Lou *et al.* 1996). The effects seemed to be the greatest in mathematics and science. Pupils of low ability learned more in mixed-ability groups, whereas pupils of average ability learned more in groups of similar ability. High-ability pupils were unaffected by the type of grouping. Both mixed-ability and ability groups produced good results in mathematics and science, whereas ability groupings were better for reading. Working in groups seemed to support learning in mathematics and science regardless of the type of group (Kulik and Kulik 1987; Kulik 1991; Slavin 1987). More information is provided on p. 560.

The teachers' perspective and the impact on pedagogy

Studies of teachers' attitudes towards structured ability grouping in the UK and elsewhere have revealed generally positive attitudes towards teaching classes where pupils are grouped by ability (Daniels 1961a; Jackson 1964; Barker-Lunn 1970), although the grouping practices dominant in the school in which they teach are important mediators (Hallam *et al.* 2002). Historically, high ability groups in streamed systems were taught by those teachers who were perceived as the 'best'; usually the more experienced and better qualified. Low streams have tended to be allocated to the less experienced and less well-qualified teachers (Jackson 1964; Barker Lunn 1970). Recent research suggests that primary schools have perceived this as making best use of teacher expertise (Hallam *et al.* 2002).

A substantial literature now indicates the tendency for instruction in lower ability groups to have a different quality to that provided for high ability groups. At primary school, teachers and pupils expect top sets to undertake more difficult work at a faster pace. There is often differential access to the curriculum, the top groups benefiting from enhanced opportunities. An informal syllabus may also operate where, for the lower ability groups, topics are omitted and there are different expectations. Teachers tend to believe that they are matching instruction to the level of the students' ability but the evidence suggests that many pupils find that the work they are given in structured ability groups is inappropriate, and that often it is too easy (Hallam *et al.* 2002, 2004).

The impact of different types of structured grouping on children's personal and social development

Case studies of six primary schools in the UK, adopting different grouping practices, showed that pupils were aware of the grouping structures operating in their school, the reasons for them, and their advantages and disadvantages. They understood why and how they were grouped and accepted the rationales provided. Where streaming or setting was adopted these structures were perceived as providing work at the right level which would help pupils to achieve their full potential. In one school where mixed ability teaching was deliberately adopted to encourage the development of social skills and team work, the pupils were able to articulate this aim. In all cases pupils were socialised into the values of the school, as established by teachers and accepted by parents. Where structured ability groupings were adopted they legitimised, and made more transparent, differences in pupils' attainment. Some children, particularly those in the lower groups, experienced teasing and stigmatisation, although in the school where the emphasis was on working together it was the more able pupils who were more likely to be teased. Contrary to popular belief, pupils at primary level were not always aware of the extent of the differences between them. This was particularly true of the boys who tended to overestimate their ability, especially when they were in mixed-ability classes. The children's attitudes towards school did not appear to be affected by grouping structures, but pupils' awareness of their place in the pecking order and the nature of teasing in the school were. However, these were mediated by school ethos (Hallam *et al.* 2004).

International reviews of the impact of different grouping structures on self-concept have found no overall effect of ability grouping on self-esteem (Kulik 1991; Kulik and Kulik 1992). When pupils of different levels of attainment have been considered, ability grouping has tended to raise the self-esteem scores of lower ability pupils and reduce the self-esteem of the higher ability students. This suggests that structured groupings might have a levelling effect, with the more able children losing some of their self-assurance when they are placed in classes with children of similar ability. However, Devine (1993) found that the self-image of pupils of average and high ability remained similar regardless of type of grouping (sets or mixed ability) although only 3 per cent of pupils in low-ability groups held a high self-image compared with 29 per cent of similar ability pupils in mixed-ability groups. As with attainment outcomes, the effects of different kinds of grouping on pupils' self-esteem may be mediated by other factors; in this case, school ethos and the attitudes of teachers and peers.

In relation to social mixing and cohesion, the evidence suggests that primary school pupils tend to select those of similar social class, ability and ethnic grouping regardless of the grouping arrangements in the school (Barker Lunn 1970), although more social mixing occurs where pupils are not ability grouped. The recent adoption of setting procedures, where pupils regroup for different subjects as they progress through school, can split friendship groups and reduce the social support that pupils have developed. Some pupils report anxiety when groupings change and they have to work with different pupils and fit into new structures (Chaplain 1996). It has been suggested that mixed-ability teaching can lead to greater social cohesion because pupils help each other and the more able provide encouragement and support for the less able by their example (DES 1978; Scottish Office 1996). Pupils themselves perceive that this is the case (Hallam *et al.* 2004). However, in a study of the teaching of 9- to 11-year-olds, Peverett (1994) found little evidence that lower ability pupils benefited from the presence or support of higher ability pupils.

WITHIN-CLASS GROUPING

One of the few features of educational life that can be stated with certainty is that all pupils are grouped within classrooms. Consideration of 'grouping' in classrooms should not simply focus on what has traditionally been referred to as the 'small group' or the number of children that can sit around a table in the classroom (usually between four and six pupils). Classroom grouping, in terms of how the class is organised and taught, may consist of a whole class seated and working together, small groups, large groups of 7 plus, pairs of children, or individuals working alone. Descriptive research shows that, in both primary and secondary schools, any classroom may consist of a number of different sized pupil groups working simultaneously and group size may vary as a lesson progresses (Baines, Blatchford and Kutnick 2003; Kutnick *et al.* 2002). The number and type of pupil groups found in any classroom may be based on historic procedures and attitudes regarding teaching and learning.

In line with traditional classroom pedagogy, primary school teachers will often have responsibility for a whole class. However, it should be noted that a pupil will spend the majority of classroom time in the presence of peers (whether simply by being seated next to other children or actually working with other children). Thus, each pupil will have a very limited amount of time to interact with their teacher and we need to consider the role of within-class grouping in relation to the pupil's learning and the quality of interactions with peers as well as teachers.

Historical background

In England, consideration of pupil grouping in classrooms may be traced back to early recommendations of the Hadow Committee report on primary education (Board of Education 1931); yet recommendations for the use of pupil grouping have been most strongly linked to the Plowden Report (CACE 1967). Plowden's recommendations contained an assumption that teachers would gradually adopt a pupil-centred orientation to classroom pedagogy, and that this orientation would focus on developing individual children's understanding and interest. To allow the teacher to focus on particular children at any one time in the classroom, other children had to be occupied and group working tasks were recommended. Children in these groups would be differentiated by attainment within a particular curricular area or topic. Grouping in Plowden was conceptualised as of value in occupying the majority of the pupils in a class while the teacher focused attention on a few particular pupils. It was also a means of differentiating pupils by attainment for focused teaching. While Plowden's recommendations may have appeared radical in their day, research showed that very few teachers at that time (and – subsequently – over the next four decades) adopted the suggested teaching style (see, for example, Bennett 1976; DES 1978; Galton, Simon and Croll 1980; Kutnick 1988; Alexander 1997; Galton *et al.* 1999; Tizard *et al.* 1988). Research did find, however, that a dominant characteristic of a typical 'traditional' primary school teacher was their grouping of pupils within the classroom by attainment, especially in reading and mathematics (Barker Lunn 1984).

One distinct characteristic of primary school classrooms did develop between the 1950s and the 1990s; this was the physical seating of pupils. Until the 1960/70s, seating of pupils had been traditionally based at the individual desk, often set out in rows that faced the front of the room. This arrangement has been associated with didactic, rote/repetition and whole class teaching approaches (Hastings and Chantry 2002). Between the 1950s and 1990s, the traditional desk gave way to the large-scale adoption and incorporation of small tables (of various designs) around which between 4 and 6 children could sit (Galton *et al.* 1999; Hastings and Chantry 2002). Research has also shown that these groups of pupils rarely worked together.

The grouping of pupils in classrooms: findings from experimental and naturalistic research

Studies concerning group work in classrooms can be divided into two broad categories, representing naturalistic descriptions and experimental change of classroom activity (Kutnick, Blatchford and Baines 2002).

Experimental studies tend to arise from, or can be associated with, theoretical orientations that are predominantly psychological. Theories underlying co-operative learning (Slavin 1995; Johnson and Johnson 2003) have described their roots in the social psychological theories of Deutsch (1949) and Lippitt and White (1943), that stress the advantages of interdependence within heterogeneous groups, and Allport's (1954) operationalisation of 'contact theory' (that is to say that members of a group agree to seek a common goal and each member provides a unique, equally valued contribution towards that goal). When the social psychological focus on interdependence is applied to classroom studies (especially in comparisons of co-operative learning to traditional learning) findings show consistent enhanced relational and pro-school attitude development among pupils, and moderate learning gains (Johnson and Johnson 2003; Slavin, Hurley and Chamberlain 2003; Gillies 2003). While experimental studies are insightful in identifying where groups are ineffective, and recommending particular interpersonal and communicative methods to enhance group working, they tend not to consider the whole classroom context within which group work takes place. They also necessarily focus on singular aspects of behaviour within classrooms (for example communication) and take place over a limited duration of time.

Naturalistic studies, on the other hand, do account for the whole class context – often including a number of sociological concerns, for example regarding social inclusion and participation of all children within the classroom. For convenience, we divide naturalistic studies into two phases: studies between 1980 and 2000 that identify a range of problems associated with group work in classrooms, and recent studies that see classrooms as a 'social pedagogical' context within which pupil groups may be seen to promote or inhibit classroom learning and motivation.

From the first phase of naturalistic studies, three dominant themes arise: 1) while children experience classroom activity in groups, these groups may vary in size and phase of lesson; 2) children often do not work productively in groups; and 3) teachers are not confident in establishing and supporting group work. Descriptions of primary classrooms (see especially Galton, Simon and Croll 1980; and Galton, Hargreaves, Comber and Pell 1999) show that the children may be found in large groups (such as the whole class), in a range of small groups (usually about 4 to 6 children, seated around a classroom table), and in pairs or triads (sometimes sharing a table with other pairs). Additionally, pupils may be found working as individuals (often sharing table space with other individuals). These different group sizes are likely to be associated with phases of a lesson – with large groups/whole class coming together at the beginning and end of a lesson and smaller groups used in the middle of a lesson. Pedagogically, group sizes may relate to the variety of learning tasks that characterise a lesson; broad categories of learning task include new/cognitive knowledge, extension of existing knowledge and practice/revision of knowledge (from Norman 1978; and used in Bennett, Desforges, Cockburn and Wilkinson 1984, and Edwards 1994). These studies can be integrated to show a relationship between group size and learning task (Kutnick 1994). However, studies such as Galton *et al.* (1980), Alexander (1997), and Galton *et al.* (1999) identify a number of disparities such as children being most often found seated in small groups (for up to 80 per cent of their classroom time) while being assigned individual tasks, and the quality of talk within the small groups being likely to be at a low cognitive level. Other disparities found were: the assignment and use of small groups based on distribution of furniture in the classroom (Dreeben 1984); differentiation of pupils by ability-based seating (Ireson and Hallam 2001); teacher difficulties in the selection and design of tasks that legitimise group interaction (Bennett and Dunne 1992; Harwood 1995); and the fact that teachers tend not to move tables to accommodate individual, paired, small or large group seating for specific learning tasks (Hastings and Chantry 2002).

Importantly, many children, as well as their teachers, do not like working in groups (Cowie and Rudduck 1988). Galton (1990) found that children often feel insecure and threatened when told to work in groups – and pupils respond to this threat by withdrawal from participation or looking to the teacher to give legitimacy to their responses within groups. Teachers have expressed particular concern about: loss of classroom control, increased disruption and off-task behaviour (Cohen and Intilli 1981); children not being able to learn from one another (Lewis and Cowie 1993); group-work being overly time consuming, and the assessment of children when working in interactive groups as being problematic (Plummer and Dudley 1993); and that only the more academically able profit from group work. Teachers have also expressed the view that pupils, particularly boys, will misbehave during group work and that discussion within group work may cause conflict between pupils (Cowie 1994).

Findings from this first phase of naturalistic studies therefore make depressing reading for those who are aware of the success of experimentally-oriented studies of group work with school-aged pupils. The overall problem is that there is little coordination between the size of pupil groupings, their composition, pedagogic purpose of learning task and interactions among group members. In short, there is little awareness of social pedagogical relationships inherent in the classroom. It is of little surprise, therefore, if pupils and their teachers do not express confidence or liking of group work, and both feel threatened by group work.

In the second phase of naturalistic studies, a clearer understanding of the bases for success and failure of group work in the classroom is established. The social pedagogic approach drawn upon by Blatchford and Kutnick, for example, focuses on relationships between pupil groups (their size and composition), learning tasks, supportive interactions with peers and teachers, and whether pupils have received training for effective group working (see Blatchford, Kutnick, Baines and Galton, 2003, for more background to this approach). Evidence referred to in this phase arises, in the main, from 'mapping' classrooms while pupils engage in learning tasks, and from interviews with teachers (for a fuller discussion of mapping as a systematic, multi-dimensional description of grouping practices and more on data reported below see Baines, Blatchford and Kutnick 2003; Blatchford, Kutnick and Baines 1999; and Kutnick *et al.* 2002).

Mapping in primary schools showed that the majority of pupils were seated in small groups (50 per cent of mappings), and whole class groupings accounted for a further 20 per cent. In only 2 per cent of observations were individuals seated alone. Larger groups, as might be expected by their size, were mixes of boys and girls and ability. Smaller groups tended to be single-sex, single-attainment and friendship-based. The predominant learning task type used in classrooms was practice tasks, and the least likely task was new knowledge/cognition. While virtually all children were found seated in pairs or larger groupings, over 60 per cent of the assigned tasks asked children to work individually. Teachers and other adults in the classroom were only able to work with approximately one-third of the pupil groups in their classrooms at one time.

While most of the observations found children seated in pairs or larger groups, only a quarter of the (nearly) 200 teachers participating in the study stated that they prepared their classes for group working; and the majority of these teachers cited 'circle time' as their only form of group work preparation. Other social pedagogic concerns regarding group work found in this study included:

- The small groups that dominated classroom experience were likely to be composed of same-sex and same-ability pupils, providing contexts of social exclusion rather than inclusion in the classroom; this was especially true of low attaining boys (who were mainly assigned individual tasks where they were not asked to interact or discuss the task with others) and high attaining girls.
- In findings similar to the first phase of naturalistic research results, there was no clear relationship between the size of groups and the learning tasks/interaction assigned – most pupil groups were assigned practice tasks that required children to work alone.
- Adults in the classrooms tended to work with the whole class or large groups, or they worked with individuals, leaving most of the small groups to work autonomously from teacher or adult support.
- Adults were present in virtually all of the observations within which new knowledge/cognition was presented, thus inhibiting opportunities for pupils to co-construct and further develop their own new knowledge.

As a result of this systematic description of the range and use of pupil groupings in authentic primary school classrooms, three main concerns are identified (see Blatchford, Kutnick, Baines and Galton, 2003, for a full account).

- Relationships are fundamental for effective group working: pupils often feel threatened and do not understand how to work in a group of their peers. Teachers have not overcome this lack of group working 'skills' in their classrooms. On the other hand, we also know that teachers and pupils appreciated that supportive relationships are essential for the promotion of learning – relationships that build upon trust between peers and between children and teachers, and the ability to communicate effectively and jointly resolve problems with partners (Hall 1994; Kutnick, Blatchford and Baines 2005).
- Effective groupwork involves an effective classroom context: if group work is to be effective, pupils must be able to work in a socially inclusive manner with all other members of their class (and not be dominated by same-gender and friendship preference groups as noted in Kutnick and Kington 2005; Kutnick, Blatchford and Baines 2005). In order for pupils to be able to draw upon supportive relationships and be less dependent on their teachers in their learning, the physical (for example seating and furniture layout), interactional (for example group composition and size) and curriculum contexts of the classroom must be co-ordinated to support group work.
- Teachers are essential for the organisation of the learning experience of their pupils: but they rarely draw upon social pedagogic principles that relates pupil group size and composition to learning task and interaction, which would in turn promote effective group working.

How to make group work more effective: research findings

There are a number of studies that have explored ways in which group work and group work processes can be more effective. One set of studies explores group processes connected to cognitive and attainment progress (see Webb and Mastergeorge 2003; Webb and Farivar 1994; Mercer 2000; and others). Webb has argued that effective group working is dependent on effective communication among group members (including pupil-pupil explanations, pupil ability to help others in need and ability to ask for help from others). Pupils who undertake focused questioning, exploration of alternate answers and explanation for these answers are more likely to solve cognitive-based problems.

Researchers in England, especially Mercer (2000) and colleagues, have developed programmes to enhance 'exploratory' talk (a concept similar to explanatory or elaborative discussion). As part of a wide-ranging approach to transforming teaching and learning at Key Stages 1 and 2 in England, a National Strategy has produced a suite of training and guidance materials concerning teaching and learning approaches for classrooms, with some focus group work in application to numeracy and literacy and for group working generally (DfES 2003, 2004). These materials are based on the work of Mercer and colleagues, as well as other recent research such as Alexander's work on 'dialogic teaching' which proposes generic strategies and principles for improving the cognitive power of classroom interaction in whole class as well as small group settings (Alexander 2006). Materials focus explicitly on developing teachers' knowledge and understanding of a range of general group work issues such as benefits and drawbacks of various group sizes and pupil attainment grouping.

Other UK-based research focusing on cognitive processes includes that by Howe, working with Tolmie and others (see Howe and Tolmie 2003). Focusing particularly on the teaching of science in primary classrooms, these researchers note that group work is often 'used to support the integrated acquisition of conceptual understanding and testing procedures', and that this is promoted in current curriculum policies in Scotland and England. Children may encounter many problems in pursuing this approach unless they 'a) discuss conceptual material in small groups and reach consensus, and b) subject consensual positions to guided empirical appraisal'.

During the course of the 1990s, Howe and Tolmie conducted laboratory-based research on group work in science at all levels of the curriculum, with the object of trying to define the basic processes which led to productive outcomes for learning. This research established that:

- Tasks which uncover differences between group members' personal ideas about the topic in hand and lead to an exchange of views are central to growth in understanding (Howe, Rodgers and Tolmie 1990; Howe, Tolmie and Anderson 1991; Howe, Tolmie, Anderson and Mackenzie 1992; Tolmie, Howe, Mackenzie and Greer 1993).
- Discussion of this kind can have two effects: post-activity reflection and individual change, or on-task synthesis of different perspectives (Howe, Tolmie and Rodgers 1992; Tolmie and Howe 1993; Howe, Tolmie, Greer and Mackenzie 1995; Williams and Tolmie 2000).

Subsequent work focused on the design and support of group activities to promote the gathering, exchange and coordination of views. This research found that it is most productive to direct support at initial procedures for gathering information and achieving a consensus about which elements are important, and then leave group members to debate its wider meaning among themselves (Howe and Tolmie 1998; Howe, Tolmie, Duchak-Tanner and Rattray 2000; Howe and Tolmie 2003). Recently, tests of applicability of these basic findings to non-laboratory settings have confirmed the central influence on learning in classroom group work is the exchange of differing views, and also the importance of initial teacher resourcing and support of debate between pupils (Howe, Tolmie, Thurston, *et al.* 2007; Tolmie, Thomson, Foot, Whelan, Sarvary and Morrison 2002).

In Circle Time programmes (Bliss *et al.* 1995; Curry and Bromfield 1998) and PSE materials (Button 1981, 1982), trust and an associated willingness to discuss feelings are seen as a prerequisite for the examination of sensitive issues and activities designed to facilitate personal development. In these materials, the building of successful groups is addressed almost exclusively through an initial teacher-led training period and there is relatively little emphasis on important aspects of group structure within subsequent activities.

Programmes which are strongly grounded in the development of group dynamics (Stanford 1990; Kingsley-Mills, McNamara and Woodward 1992; Thacker, Stoate and Feest 1992) clearly specify particular attitudes and skills to be addressed and developed at each of the 'forming', 'norming' and 'storming' stages of group development (Tuckman 1965) in preparation for the productive work which should follow. A range of the materials emerging work activities (Johnson and Johnson 1987; Aronson and Patnoe 1997; Farivar and Webb 1991). Farivar and Webb give a particular order in which different attitudes and skills should be addressed: first 'class-building' activities, then group-work skills, then communication and co-operative skills, and finally helping skills.

Wilkinson and Canter (1982) list a further range of skills under the headings 'verbal', 'non-verbal' and 'assertiveness' which, together, are intended to constitute the building blocks of successful social interaction; these skills are to be developed depending upon an assessment of the needs of the particular individual(s) involved. Other skills that have been specified to aid general collaboration include role skills (Stanford 1990; Daniels 1994) such as leadership skills (Johnson and Johnson 1987); decision making (Stanford 1990; Kingsley-Mills *et al.* 1992); challenging or being critical (Lloyd and Beard 1995; Dunne and Bennett 1990; Johnson and Johnson 1987); supplementing ideas, improving work, compromising (Lloyd and Beard 1995); tutoring skills (Johnson and Johnson 1987); helping (Farivar and Webb 1991; Aronson and Patnoe 1997); and sharing (Aronson and Patnoe 1997).

Based on the understanding that skills in talk and discussion are likely to promote and support learning within the classroom, particular attention has been directed at 'argumentation'. Argumentation is the 'coordination of evidence and theory to support or refute an explanatory conclusion, model or prediction' (Suppe 1998, cited in Simon, Erduran and Osborne 2002). It functions to engage learners/coordinate understanding while allowing teachers to gain a range of insights into children's conceptual understanding, and may be linked to formative feedback. Exposition of children's alternative views has been developed in a range of argumentation techniques for use in the classroom (for example, see Johnson and Johnson 1994).

One of the few approaches to groupwork based on a large scale quasi-experimental study is that used in the SPRinG (Social Pedagogic Research into Group work) project (Blatchford, Galton, Kutnick and Baines 2005). This addressed the wide gap between the potential of group work, and its limited use in schools and the three main concerns given above. To do this successfully suggested that a new approach to conceptualising group work in classrooms was needed – an approach that would ground itself in the reality of everyday school life and the concerns of teachers and pupils, and integrate group work into the fabric of the school day.

The SPRinG project is distinctive in being a general programme that applies group work across the curriculum and over the school year. The team worked with teachers to develop a programme of group work that could be successfully integrated into school life, and which took on board the concerns and difficulties teachers can have with group work. The programme built on and extended previous research by stressing three key principles:

- First, it stresses supportive relationships between pupils through a 'relational' approach. Activities were designed to help pupils communicate effectively through listening, explaining and sharing ideas, but also to help them trust and respect each other, and plan, organise and evaluate their group work.
- Second, the programme provides guidance on the key role of the teacher in adapting grouping practices for different purposes and learning tasks and in supporting and guiding groups. The key aim is to encourage pupil independence rather than directly teaching pupils.
- Third, for group work to be successful the classroom and groups need to be organised and managed in supportive ways. There was guidance on classroom seating

arrangements, and the characteristics of groups such as their size, composition and stability over time.

The project was extensively evaluated (see Baines, Blatchford and Chowne 2007; Blatchford, Baines, Rubie-Davies, Bassett and Chowne 2006; Blatchford, Galton, Kutnick and Baines 2005; Kutnick, Ota and Berdondini 2008). Its effectiveness was tested by comparing pupils trained with the SPRinG programme with pupils who were not, but who were engaged in parallel educational research. The main research question was whether the group-work programme led to increases in learning and attainment, more 'favourable' behavioural and dialogue patterns supportive of learning, and motivational patterns and attitudes to learning. The study involved an intervention over a longer time frame than many such studies, taking a full school year rather than being performed just before and after the usual brief intervention period.

The research found that, far from impeding learning, group work led to raised levels of achievement. At KS2, for example, the programme concentrated on science activities and led to significantly higher attainment and higher conceptual understanding and inferential thinking (effect sizes 0.21–0.58). At KS1 in reading/literacy, children in the experimental condition improved more than those in the control group (effect size 0.23). In mathematics, children in the experimental group improved more than the control children (effect size 0.71). Despite some teachers' worries that group work might be disruptive, systematic classroom observations showed it actually improved pupils' behaviour in class. SPRinG groupwork raised pupil levels of engagement in learning, encouraged them to become more actively engaged in the learning process and facilitated more higher level, thoughtful learning processes. Other findings indicated that teachers' own professional skills and confidence were enhanced. They found their teaching repertoire was extended and there were unexpected benefits as, for example, pupils developed group working skills, and teachers found they were 'freed' from some procedural duties and classroom control and were now able to spend more strategic time on teaching. Group work seemed to be most effective when adopted by the whole school, rather than the individual teacher, so that there could be integration of principles of group learning between classes and across the school experience. Teachers working in areas of deprivation or in difficult circumstances found that group work could be used successfully and could aid classroom relationships and integration.

TRANSITIONS: PRE-SCHOOL TO PRIMARY, TRANSITION WITHIN THE PRIMARY PHASE AND TRANSITION FROM PRIMARY TO SECONDARY

During their primary school careers children in the UK pass through a number of important transition points. These include transition from Foundation Years to Key Stage 1, transition between Key Stages 1 and 2 and the transition to 'big school' between Key Stages 2 and 3. Much of the research in the UK has focused on this latter transition, providing qualitative and quantitative evidence supporting ways in which this crucial point of change may best be supported by school management teams, teachers, parents and carers. Relatively little research has been undertaken that is specifically concerned with the former two key transitions, nor has there been a great deal of research relating to transition between year groups in primary school. However, there is some evidence (Minnis, Seymour and Schagen 1998) that the effects of transition are cumulative; hence the importance of taking an overview of transition experiences throughout the primary years and their possible impact on outcomes for pupils. This brief review will highlight some of the recent key studies in the UK relating to transition across the primary years.

Transition from Early Years to Key Stage 1

Sylva *et al.* (2004) carried out a large scale investigation into the impact of pre-school settings on children's cognitive and social/behavioural development through the transition to KS1. This longitudinal (five year) project employed both quantitative measures and qualitative methods to examine the progress between ages three and seven of 3000 children from six different types of pre-school setting. (Further funding has allowed Sylva and her colleagues to track pupils through to the end of their primary school years.) The sample also included 300 'at home' children who had no pre-school experience before starting school. Pre-school experience, compared to none, was found to enhance all-round development in children, continuing to have a positive impact on the children's social and cognitive development throughout KS1. Issues of pre-school quality were raised, with the qualifications level of staff found to be significantly related to children's academic and social/behavioural development. The team also found that the quality of the home learning environment, only moderately related to parents' education and socio-economic status, was an important factor in facilitating the progression from pre-school through KS1 and was found to be a significant protective factor against risk of future special educational needs (SEN) (Sammons *et al.* 2003).

Sanders *et al.* (2005) added to the body of evidence relating to transition from Foundation Years to KS1, interviewing school staff from sixty schools as well as seventy children and their parents. The researchers conclude that transition is most usefully viewed as a process of change that is most successful when it is gradual and characterised by continuity and good communication. The salient point is made that in England, unlike most of the rest of Europe, children make the transition from pre-school environments into Reception classes and then just one year later undergo a second key transition. This second transition involves having to adapt from a play-based environment to more formal subject-based and teacher-directed learning. There is a suggestion that anxiety amongst children and parents relating to the transition from Reception to Year 1 may not have received the attention it warrants. The process was found to be made easier for teachers, parents and pupils alike when induction strategies were implemented, including visits from Reception to Year 1 as well as enhanced lines of communication between Foundation and KS1 teachers and between teachers and parents. Furthermore, when Year 1 children were given opportunities for play-based learning and for expressing their own expectations of Year 1 this was found to alleviate their anxiety.

Recommendations for good practice in transition from early years to KS1

Pre-school case studies (Sylva *et al.* 2004: vi) revealed six key strategies which would help to equip pre-school children with social/behavioural, as well as cognitive, skills to help them through key transitions. These were:

- Quality of adult-child interactions: encourage sustained one-to-one 'shared thinking' between adults and children, together with adult modelling and open-ended questioning.
- Child-initiated play and teacher-initiated group work: work towards an equal balance.

- Knowledge of the curriculum: ensure that pre-school workers have comprehensive curriculum knowledge.
- Understanding of child development: improve child development component of initial and CPD pre-school courses.
- Adult skills to support children and less-qualified staff: aim for a good proportion of trained teachers amongst the staff in pre-school environments.
- Parent engagement in children's learning: involve parents in decision making related to educational aims and learning programmes.

Sanders *et al.* (2005) identified specific transition strategies that could ease the passage for children moving from the play-based environment of Reception into the more formal Year 1:

- Communication between Foundation and Year 1 teachers, relating to meeting the needs of individual children.
- Continuity of pedagogical approach to routines, expectations and activities in Reception and Year 1.
- Additional support for children who are less mature or less able than their classmates, or who have SEN or English as an additional language (EAL).
- Opportunities for Year 1 children to engage in play-based activities.
- School-home communication in preparation for transition to Year 1.
- Guidance for parents on how to support children's learning in Year 1.
- Induction visits to Year 1 for Reception children.
- More provision for training about this transition, including support for teachers in how to introduce appropriate literacy and numeracy activities.
- Further research to broaden the evidence base on effective transition practices.

Transition during the middle years

Galton, Morrison and Pell (1999) suggest that more attention needs to be directed towards transitions from one year to another as pupils move through the middle years of each Key Stage. In particular, the views of the pupils need to be elicited regarding how they visualise the next year. It is suggested that at each year-to-year progression point pupils should be helped to visualise the next year in such a way that fosters excitement in relation to opportunities for extending learning and increasing responsibility.

Using the common baseline of KS1 assessments for a cohort of approximately 10,000 primary pupils, Minnis *et al.* (1998) estimated the progress pupils had made by the end of Year 3, the end of Year 4 and the end of Year 5. The evidence from this study suggests that patterns of performance vary considerably from school to school and are cumulative; the consequences of transition experiences may thus have far-reaching consequences for latter stages of schooling.

Attention has been drawn to the particular issues associated with transition from Year 2 to Year 3 (KS1–KS2), which potentially involves moving from an infant school site to junior school site and furthermore requires adaptation to a new pedagogical approach, particularly in respect of literacy (Doddington, Flutter and Rudduck 1999). It is suggested that in some schools priority is given to dedicating resources to Year 2, when National Curriculum tests are taken; pupils may thus perceive Year 3 as a less important year and respond accordingly by under-performing. Teachers in Doddington's study also put forward the view that Year 3 is a stage where pupils commonly engage in forming new social groups and that there is a danger such groups may develop anti-work norms. Furthermore, it was suggested that a dip in progression at Year 3 could be interpreted as a reflection of pupils reverting to their normal levels of attainment following artificially inflated Year 2 test results (*ibid*).

Transition from Key Stage 2 to Key Stage 3

Transition from primary to secondary school (KS2–KS3) can be particularly challenging as it involves transfer to new social contexts and physical school environments, together with transition from one pedagogy and curriculum to another (Bryon and Sims 2002; Capel, Zwozdiak-Myers and Lawrence 2004; Lucey and Reay 2000; Measor and Woods 1984). Galton *et al.* (2000: 341) suggest that, whilst many schools have successfully implemented induction strategies which alleviate anxiety amongst pupils and parents, it is still the case that around 40 per cent of pupils experience a 'hiatus in progression' at this point in their school careers. This hiatus, Galton claims, may be attributable to discontinuity in the curriculum and variations in teaching practice between KS2 and KS3. Bryon and Sims (2002) suggest that problems with progression may be addressed at least in part with collaborative networking amongst KS2 and KS3 teachers and the use of cross-phase bridging units of work. However, Galton *et al.* (2000) make the salient point that current educational systems, for example whereby parents may choose schools outside of their catchment area, undermine efforts to achieve continuity through liaison amongst pyramids or clusters of primary and secondary schools.

Four main problem areas related to the primary-secondary transition have been identified (Bolster, Balandier-Brown and Rea-Dickins 2004; Braund and Hames 2005; Lucey and Reay 2000; OfSTED 2002). These are:

1) insufficient increase in challenge of work tasks for pupils;
2) difficulties in adjusting to change in learning and social cultures;
3) failure to make use of pupils' previous learning and attainment; and
4) distrust amongst teachers of primary performance assessments gained through national testing.

There is some evidence that cross-phase units of work contributed to improving progression, continuity and positive pupil attitudes before and after transition (Braund and Hames 2005). However, some researchers (Bolster *et al.* 2004; Capel *et al.* 2004) suggest that liaison strategies between KS2 and KS3 tend to focus on literacy, numeracy and science, possibly to the detriment of subjects such as physical education and languages. In order for Year 7 teachers to capitalise on their pupils' previous learning, greater standardisation across the primary curriculum and collaboration and continuity between primary clusters and secondary schools are suggested.

Support for at-risk pupils

The transition from primary to secondary school can be a particularly difficult time for disaffected pupils or those who are at risk of exclusion from school (Hallam and Rogers 2008). At-risk groups include those on free school meals, pupils with special educational needs, pupils less fluent in English, and pupils from some ethnic groups (Galton *et al.* 1999; Minnis *et al.* 1998). Buddying schemes that link at-risk Year 6 pupils with Year 7 pupils have been implemented successfully in some UK local authorities (Galton *et al.* 2003). Furthermore, the use of Learning Mentors to support transition has become more widespread (Hallam and Rogers 2008). Hallam and Rogers (*ibid*) suggest that good practice in the support of pupils at risk of exclusion during the transition process includes interventions that begin prior to transition and continue for long enough to enable the pupil to settle in to the new environment. Furthermore, liaison between primary and secondary Special Educational Needs Coordinators (SENCOs) facilitates the setting up of support structures that meet individual needs from day one in the new school.

Key transition issues

There is much scope for further systematic evaluation of the impact of transition strategies on the progress and attitudes of pupils. Three broad areas have been identified: cumulative effects, communication, and continuity (Galton *et al.* 2003).

First, the possible cumulative nature of transition has been identified and demands further investigation. Research is needed that focuses on Early Years transitions as well as year-to-year transitions throughout primary school, with a view to developing effective transition strategies as well as strategies that could possibly interrupt established patterns of negative transition experiences and replace these with accumulated positive experiences. In particular, the impact of quality pre-school provision on successful transition needs to be further investigated, as does the role which home learning environments play in helping children negotiate transition from Early Years contexts through Key Stages 1 and 2.

Second, communication between pre-schools, primary schools and families have been shown to be a crucial factor in successful transition. School policies and practice relating to communication need to ensure that simple, reassuring messages are conveyed to pupils and parents/carers about key transitions and that pupils and parents/carers are involved in decision-making relating to possible actions to deal with challenging transitions.

A third but related issue is concerned with eliciting the views of pupils themselves. It has been suggested that, from the very earliest transition points, enhanced outcomes have been promoted when children have been encouraged to articulate their ideas about the upcoming year and when transition strategies have addressed the academic and/or social concerns of pupils as well as those of teachers and parents/carers. Research in this vein, giving attention to pupils' accounts of why they disengage or under perform at key transition points, has the potential to provide a valuable insight into how children approach and experience primary school transitions and could inform strategies that help to prepare pupils for significant changes in teaching approaches between Key Stages.

A further issue related to communication is that of continuity. It has been demonstrated that transition is a gradual process that is best negotiated by pupils when information transfers ahead of the pupil. In particular, pupils are helped to become professional in their approaches to learning when schools are able to respond to information relating to prior learning as well as special education needs or risks. Further research in this area has the potential to inform policies related to continuity of the curriculum and teaching at each of the identified primary transition points.

Finally, much transition work promoting curriculum continuity has focused on core subjects. Research is needed that would investigate the potential value in directing transition strategies at non-core subjects, potentially helping schools to engage in the development of inclusive teaching and learning strategies in particular subject areas that will help pupils sustain their excitement in learning.

THE EDUCATIONAL EFFECTS OF CLASS SIZE DIFFERENCES

Introduction

There has been a vigorous debate about the educational effects of class size differences in primary schools. Though there is consensus among many in education that smaller classes allow a better quality of teaching and learning, and that this a main reason why parents pay to send their children to private schools, others argue that the effects are modest and that there are other, more cost-effective strategies for improving educational standards (Slavin 1987; Rivkin, Hanushek and Kain 2000).

In a review for the National Commission on Education, Mortimore and Blatchford (1993) pointed out that, unusually in an international context, UK class sizes were larger on average in primary than in secondary schools, turning on its head what seems sensible educationally. Politically, in some countries at least, the policy tide has changed in favour of small classes. Current UK Government policy is for a maximum class size of 30 at Reception and KS1 in England and Wales. Class size reductions have been implemented by a number of US States, most notably in California where huge funds were made available. There have been initiatives involving class size or pupil to adult ratio reductions in the Netherlands, and in Asia Pacific countries as diverse as New Zealand and China.

It needs to be recognised that there is still a lot of variability in class sizes in the UK, even during the first three years of schooling. Many teachers would consider that 29 children in a class, especially when only 5–7 years of age, is still too many. Policy is still contentious, with opposition parties claiming that class sizes overall have increased. The Liberal Democrat policy at the time of the 2001 election was that the Government should go further and reduce the maximum class size to 25 children.

Despite the important policy and practice implications of the topic, the research literature on the educational effects of class size differences has not been clear (Blatchford and Mortimore 1994). However, recent research and reviews provide some answers, and in this section we summarise research evidence, and address whether class size differences affect children's educational attainment and learning, and classroom processes like teaching and pupil behaviour. It draws on main reviews of research: Anderson (2000); Biddle and Berliner (no date); Blatchford and Mortimore (1994); Blatchford, Goldstein and Mortimore (1998); Blatchford, Russell and Brown (2008); Cooper (1989); Ehrenberg, Brewer, Gamoran and Willms (2001); Finn, Pannozzo and Achilles (2003); Galton (1998); Grissmer (1999) and Hattie (2005), and also the CSPAR study (see below).

Do class size differences affect children's educational attainment and learning?

Overall, it has been concluded that much previous research has not had designs strong enough to draw reliable conclusions (Blatchford, Goldstein and Mortimore 1998). It has long been recognised, for example, that simple correlational designs, which examine associations between a measure of class size or pupil–teacher ratios on the one hand and measures of pupil attainment on the other, are misleading, because we often do not know whether the results can be explained by another factor, for example that poorer performing pupils are placed in smaller classes. To arrive at sounder evidence, two kinds of research design have been used. In this section we concentrate on two studies which represent each approach.

Experimental studies

It is often assumed that the problems of correlational research are best overcome by the use of experimental research or randomised controlled trials. This is one reason for the great attention paid to the Tennessee STAR project. A cohort of pupils and teachers at Kindergarten through to Grade 3 were assigned at random to three types of class within the same school: a small class (around 17 pupils), a 'regular' class (around 23 students) and a regular class with a teacher-aide. In brief, the researchers found that in both reading and maths pupils in small classes performed significantly better than pupils in regular classes, and children from minority ethnic group backgrounds benefited most from small classes (Finn and Achilles 1999; Nye *et al.* 2000). Although some aspects of the project are still contentious (see Goldstein and Blatchford 1998; Grissmer 1999; Hanushek 1999; Mitchell *et al.* 1991; Prais 1996), reanalysis of the data, using more sophisticated techniques, supported the central finding of a difference between small and regular classes (Goldstein and Blatchford 1998) but showed that the main effect was restricted to the first year of school. In fourth grade the pupils returned to regular classes and the experiment ended, but gains were still evident after a further three years, that is, Grades 4–6 (Word *et al.* 1990).

Longitudinal studies

There are some difficulties with experimental studies (see Goldstein and Blatchford 1998) and an alternative approach is to set up longitudinal studies, which measure the full range of class sizes and which account statistically for other possibly confounding factors (including pupil differences at an earlier point). This was the approach adopted in a large scale UK study; the Class Size and Pupil Adult Ratio (CSPAR) project, see for example Blatchford (2003), Blatchford, Bassett and Brown (2005); and Blatchford, Bassett, Goldstein and Martin (2003). This project tracked over 10,000 pupils in over 300 schools, from school entry (at 4/5 years) to the end of the primary school stage (11 years). It used a multi-method approach and sophisticated multi-level regression statistical analyses. In brief it found the following:

Class size and pupil progress. There was a clear effect of class size differences on children's academic attainment over the Reception year, in both literacy and maths, even after adjusting for other possible confounding factors. The effect is comparable to that reported by the STAR project, and this trend is therefore supported by both experimental and non-experimental research designs.

Who benefits? Small classes (below 25) worked best in literacy for children who were most in need academically, that is to say those with the lowest school entry scores and who had the most ground to make up. For the purposes of analysis, pupils were split into three ability groups, based on their pre-Reception year literacy scores (bottom 25 per cent, middle 50 per cent and top 25 per cent). There was a strong and statistically significant increase in attainment for all three groups, although below 25 in a class there was a larger effect for pupils with lower baseline attainment.

Benefits for how long? The effects of class size in the Reception year were still evident on literacy progress at the end of the second year of school (Year 1), though by the end of the third year the effects were not clear. There were no clear longer-term effects of class size differences on mathematics achievement. Though this indicates that the early benefits 'wash out' after two years in school, there were no restrictions in terms of which size of class they moved to from year to year (in contrast with the STAR project).

'Disruption' effect. The CSPAR's naturalistic design captured changes in class sizes from year to year. The biggest changes took place between Reception and Year 1 and an important 'disruption' effect on children's educational progress was found. The effect of small Reception classes carried over into Year 1 only when children moved into a similar or smaller class. Moving to a class of a different size, especially a larger class, had a negative effect on progress.

Do class size differences affect classroom processes like teaching and pupil behaviour?

Despite the widely held view that small classes will lead to a better quality of teaching and learning, the research evidence is not clear. One reason for this is the often anecdotal nature of the evidence collected. Overall, research suggests that class size effects are likely to be not singular but multiple and that it is difficult to capture all the possible complexities involved. But as a way of summarising and integrating data on classroom processes related to class size differences, we have prepared the following (see Blatchford, Russell and Brown (2008) for a more extended account). This again draws on the CSPAR because it is one of the few systematic UK studies on classroom processes available.

Within-class groups

For much of their time in UK primary schools children are seated and work in groups. The CSPAR results showed that larger classes led to more and bigger groups in the class. In class sizes over 25 there is more likelihood of a pupil being in a large group of 7–10. The qualitative analyses showed this had an adverse effect on the amount and quality of teaching and the quality of pupils' work and concentration in these groups. It is therefore important educationally to consider the mediating role of within-class groupings.

Effects on teachers

Perhaps the most consistent finding is that the most important classroom process, affected by class size, is individualisation of teaching. The smaller the class the more likelihood there is that a teacher will spend more time with individual pupils. In smaller classes there also tends to be more teaching overall, and large classes present more challenges for classroom management, pupil control, and marking, planning and assessment. Teachers are put under more strain when faced with large classes. Qualitative studies suggest that in smaller classes it can be easier for teachers to spot problems and give feedback, identify specific needs and gear teaching to meet them, and set individual targets for pupils. Teachers also experience better relationships with, and have more knowledge of, individual pupils.

Effects on pupils

Finn *et al.* (2003) conclude that students in small classes in the elementary grades are more engaged in learning behaviours, and that they display less disruptive behaviour than do students in larger classes. The CSPAR study found more disengagement in the case of 4/5 year old pupils when working on their own. However, it found no effects on pupil attentiveness in 10/11 year old pupils, possibly because of assessment and curriculum pressures at that age. The CSPAR study showed that in large classes pupils were more likely to simply listen to the teacher and not be singled out by her; they are one of the crowd. Conversely, in smaller classes pupils were more likely to interact in an active way with teachers through initiating, responding and sustaining contact.

It might be expected that in larger classes pupils would turn to each other and pupil-pupil interactions would increase. In the CSPAR there was more pupil-pupil interaction overall in larger classes in the early years of primary education but by the later primary school years there was no evidence for such an effect, probably because of the assessment and curriculum pressures just mentioned. Interestingly, the CSPAR did not find that pupils in smaller classes had better peer relations; indeed, if anything, peer relations were worse.

Curriculum effects

Research has begun to show a moderating role of school subject on relationships between class size and classroom processes. Rice (1999) found that in mathematics, but not science, as class size increased less time was spent on small groups and individuals, innovative instructional practices, and whole group discussions. In the CSPAR study, the overall effects of class size on individualised attention were found in all subjects but English. One direction for future research is to identify more precisely ways in which class size effects vary in relation to particular school subjects and student age.

Overall, results suggest that while small classes will not make a bad teacher better, they can allow teachers to be more effective; conversely, large classes inevitably present teachers with difficulties and the need for compromises. Small classes can offer *opportunities* for teachers to teach better (Anderson 2000) or, to use a different term, they can create *facilitating conditions* for teachers to teach and students to learn (Wang and Finn 2000).

DISCUSSION

In the survey of evidence for this chapter we have examined recent research, mainly in the UK, to identify what is known about different grouping arrangements in schools, the factors influencing these arrangements, and the impact they have on pupil learning and adjustment. It distinguishes between grouping at the class and the within-class level. In general it argues that both levels are important but that the latter is likely to be more directly important for pupil learning. It also addresses research on problems of coherence, transitions and continuity within and between phases, and research evidence on the educational benefits of small classes.

In this final section we summarise main points arising out of each section, and identify implications for policy and practice, and suggestions for future research.

Overview of main methodological traditions

In the UK there is a strong tradition of descriptive research within primary schools and classrooms. These studies include naturalistic observation in classrooms that reveals how teachers organise the class and interact with children.

Case studies provide useful information on factors that may mediate the effects of school and classroom organisation on teachers and pupils. They highlight school policy, ethos, the deployment of resources, teachers' classroom practice and the nature of tasks pupils undertake as factors that mediate the impact of pupil grouping on children's learning, adjustment and attainment.

Survey research provides evidence on the overall pattern of school and class sizes and the nature and extent of different forms of grouping in primary schools. This allows us to establish trends over time and draws attention to the constraints and opportunities imposed by school size, which tends to affect the extent of particular forms of organisation such as setting and cross-age grouping.

For practical reasons there are few randomised controlled experimental studies of school organisation or pupil grouping. Instead, many studies capitalise on existing differences between schools and classrooms. These studies run the risk of confounding variables that may co-exist with particular forms of organisation. However, sophisticated statistical techniques such as multi-level regression analysis can provide estimates of several school, classroom and individual factors simultaneously.

Strong research designs are able to provide evidence on the effects of school and classroom organisation on children's learning and other educational outcomes. Longitudinal studies are needed to explore links between variables over time and to establish reciprocal effects. In view of the complexity of schools and classrooms, research methods must be carefully designed to uncover and take account of multiple factors that may interact with, or mediate, the effects of different school structures and pupil grouping arrangements. As the effects of grouping practices may be cumulative, there is also a need for sustained investment in longitudinal studies that follow children through the primary phase of education. The reviews presented in this section show that there is now a firm evidence base to provide a platform for systematic, longitudinal research on the effects of pupil grouping and group work, and how they are mediated in schools and classrooms. Following children through transitions from one year group or Key Stage to another allows researchers to tease out the relative effects of several factors. Qualitative methods can be valuable, especially when they allow students' and teachers' voices to be heard, and may be fruitfully combined with quantitative methods. Future research should not focus solely on children's attainment but should consider other outcomes such as health and well-being, social adjustment, motivation and attitudes to learning.

Structured grouping practices

Overall, primary schools have tended to resist the introduction of structured ability grouping, preferring within-class groupings. Most primary school children are taught in mixed-ability classes with within-class ability groups for some subjects. Setting is relatively rare, tending to occur in the higher year groups and for those subjects which are subject to national assessment, particularly mathematics.

Approximately 25 per cent of pupils are taught in mixed-age classes. These offer similar challenges to teachers as mixed-ability classes in relation to curriculum organisation, ability range, and assessment.

Issues that schools consider when making decisions about grouping structures relate to:

- learning (differentiation, raising attainment, developing pupil skills and good behaviour, flexibility);
- teaching (planning and delivery of the curriculum, use of more whole-class teaching);
- academic subject concerns (groupings for different subjects, making use of teacher expertise);
- school and cohort size (issues relating to mixed-age classes, setting);
- resources (staffing, timetabling, space, teaching assistants/parents);
- evaluations of different grouping practices (perceived success, reduction in class teacher contact time, time lost in movement between sets).

The arrival of a new head teacher can facilitate change, while parents can also be influential. The ability-grouping structures adopted also tend to reflect the ethos of the school.

The evidence, nationally and internationally, regarding the impact of structured ability grouping on attainment suggests that there are no consistent effects. The quality of the teaching seems to be the most important factor in determining pupil outcomes, not whether they are taught in structured or mixed ability groups. Nevertheless, when structured ability grouping practices are adopted, the quality of the teaching in the different groups can vary. Children in the top groups tend to work at a faster pace, have differential access to the curriculum, benefit from enhanced learning opportunities, and teachers have high expectations of them. For children in the lower groups topics may be omitted, there are lower expectations, and activities may be restricted. Teachers believe that they are matching instruction to the level of the students' ability but the evidence suggests that many pupils find the work they are given is inappropriate; often it is too easy.

Pupils are aware of the grouping structures adopted in their schools, the reasons for them, their advantages and disadvantages, and accept the rationales provided. Pupils are socialised into the values of the school as established by teachers and accepted by parents. Structured groupings legitimise and make more transparent differences in pupils' attainment. Children in the lower and higher groups may experience teasing, and in the lower groups stigmatisation. There are no consistent effects on self-concept, or on social mixing, although pupils perceive that they help each other more in mixed ability settings.

The adoption of structured ability groupings therefore has no positive effects on attainment but has detrimental affects on the social and personal outcomes for some children. Moreover, the allocation of pupils to groups is a somewhat arbitrary affair and often depends on factors not related to attainment. In theory, movement between groups is possible but in practice it is frequently restricted. This limits the opportunities for some children. Grouping pupils within the class in different ways for different activities offers more flexibility, facilitates movement between groups structured by ability, and avoids limiting the opportunities for some children. It would help for teachers to tailor work more specifically to pupil needs, adopting within-class groupings to do this while also being mindful that pupils' attainment levels do not follow a stable trajectory. Groupings need to be constantly reviewed to take account of this. They should also vary groupings dependent on the nature of the task, avoiding children labelling themselves as being in one specific group. Future research needs to address how such flexibility can best be developed in classrooms and what its impact is on pupils and teachers.

Within-class grouping

In all British classrooms, pupils are grouped in some form but research has shown that, in general, little group work takes place and still less is of good quality. A number of studies suggest pupils are most likely to be seated in an arrangement that does not facilitate their learning of specific tasks – and may actually inhibit their learning. Pupils may sit *in* groups but rarely interact and work *as* groups. Importantly, groups in classrooms are often formed without a strategic view of their purpose, and there is little support for pupil–pupil interactions within groups. Pupils and teachers are not trained for group-work and have doubts about, and difficulties implementing, it in classrooms. Instead, pupils tend to work individually or as a whole class. There is then a wide gap between the potential of group work to affect pupil achievement, motivation and classroom behaviour, and its limited use in schools.

The size of classes, size of within-class groups, composition of within-class groups, nature of the assigned learning task, intended social interaction used in task completion and teacher intervention appear to be related. Planning for effective learning needs to take account of the social pedagogic relationships between these factors. Research indicates that group work can be successfully used and implemented into everyday primary classrooms, provided teachers are aware of social pedagogical principles and take time to train pupils in the skills of group working. It also shows that involvement in group work, with support provided for relational and other group working skills, has positive effects on pupils' academic progress. Results indicate that within-class grouping, rather than class-level organisational grouping initiatives, may have greater potential to raise standards.

These results have implications for educational policy and practice. There are three main contexts for learning in any classroom: teacher-led work, individual work and interactions between pupils. Pressures arising from the curriculum and the classroom context mean a heavy emphasis on whole-class teaching followed by individual work, with little room for group work. Teachers can feel unsatisfied with whole-class teaching, especially when they have a strong belief in the value of addressing the individual needs of pupils (Blatchford *et al.* 2006). We argue that the third context for learning – peer-based interactions, or 'co-learning' – has been neglected, certainly in the UK. We suggest that, given space and time to develop pupils' group working skills, teachers can bring about a transformation in the teaching and learning environment. It offers learning possibilities for pupils not provided by either teacher-led or individual work, and can contribute to national concerns with engagement in learning and attitudes to work and classroom behaviour. On the basis of evidence reviewed here, group work deserves to be given a much more central role in educational policy and school practice.

Research indicates that effective interventions may need to vary according to age of pupil and curricular area, and more research on these influences would be helpful. There is also a strong indication from the SPRinG research that implementation of good quality groupwork works best when part of a whole school initiative; future research could do well to examine more fully whole-school processes that can best support and sustain group work.

Transitions

Further research is needed that would investigate how knowledge and practices relating to communication and curriculum continuity at each of the primary transition points may be drawn upon to facilitate these transitions. Furthermore, the concept of the effects of transition as being cumulative suggests that there is much scope for further development of transition strategies targeting Early Years and Key Stage 1 to 2 transitions, as well as year-to-year transitions throughout primary school.

The potentially cumulative nature of transition suggests that directing research and resources at the earliest primary transitions could have long-term implications for pupils' successful negotiation of transition at subsequent stages of school careers. In particular, the impact of quality pre-school provision on successful transition has been identified and needs to be further investigated. Furthermore, the quality of home learning environments has been shown to comprise an important protective factor against the subsequent development of SEN, suggesting that initiatives whereby parents could be helped to improve the quality of the home learning environment would be valuable.

The extent and quality of communication amongst pre-schools, primary schools and families has been shown to impact considerably on successful transition. Research that would promote policy and good practice in the area of communication is needed. Specifically, pupils as well as professionals and parents/carers need to be involved in any such research, with a view to addressing the concerns of all parties and taking account of each perspective when formulating possible actions to deal with challenging transitions.

Finally, curriculum continuity has been shown to play a key role in successful transition. The development of consistent policies relating to the quality and quantity of transfer of information is needed, as are strategies to help teachers take account of pupils' prior learning and special needs. These strategies should not be restricted to core subjects; research is needed that would acknowledge the potential benefits, in terms of inclusion and sustaining interest in learning, in directing transition strategies at non-core subjects.

Class size

Policy implications

The STAR and CSPAR projects show we need to take account of the age of the child when considering class size effects. There is a clear case for small class sizes in the Reception year, but results show where resources could be further targeted; that is at classes smaller than 25 for those with the most ground to make up in literacy skills. Another policy implication is to maintain smaller classes across years where possible.

Age versus start-up effect?

Results also suggest that class size reduction initiatives are best seen as a policy of prevention but not remediation, in the sense that the evidence supports the use of small classes immediately after entry to school but there is little evidence that small classes introduced later in children's school lives are as effective. However, there is still the possibility that smaller classes may be advantageous at later strategic points of transition in students' school lives, for example in the first year of secondary education. Research evidence on this possibility is needed.

Alternatives to class size reduction (CSR)

Hattie (2005) argues that we should consider effects of class size not in relation to zero – that is, having no effect – but in comparison with other interventions, for example tutoring, phonics training, and 'Success for All'. In general, CSR does not do well in these comparisons. But is this a fair test? It should be no surprise that reducing class sizes in and of itself does not result in gains in student achievement as obvious as those stemming from involvement in a defined educational intervention. A fairer test is to compare it with effects of other, alternative classroom contextual changes. Blatchford, Russell and Brown (2008) have considered three alternatives: reduced pupil-teacher ratios (PTRs), an increase in teaching assistants (TAs), and flexibility in classroom grouping, and suggest that these are no better than CSR and involve difficulties not always taken into account. Overall, though, there is a need for studies to compare systematically different contextual approaches.

Implications for practice

It has often been pointed out that teachers do not necessarily change the way they teach when faced with smaller classes and that this might well account for the relatively modest effects of class size on achievement. Blatchford, Russell and Brown (2008) have suggested several ways in which CSR can be accompanied by pedagogical changes to enhance beneficial effects for students, for example taking advantage of the possibilities of increased individualisation; adopting more adventurous and flexible teaching; and implementing more effective collaborative learning between pupils. Some have argued that teacher professional development is a better investment than CSR, but it is better not to see them in opposition. Rather, professional development should be used to help teachers harness the opportunities of small classes, and help teachers develop strategies for realising educational objectives in large classes.

CONCLUSION

Over the long history of research into school structure and classroom grouping, there has been little transfer between research findings and widespread classroom application. One reason for this is the methodological difficulty of establishing clear effects, for example of grouping practices in schools. But another reason is that concerns about underachievement, lack of pro-school attitudes and exclusion have tended to be approached by calls for more differentiation by ability or attainment. This chapter has made it clear that such moves are not supported in the research literature. Indeed, differentiation by ability/attainment has been associated with limited access to knowledge by some pupils, domination of pedagogic practices by teachers, preferred teachers for 'elite' pupils and enforcement of social divisions among pupils.

A great amount of effort has gone into curriculum development and recommendations for school/classroom structure, but much more effort now needs to be directed to the consideration and development of classroom-based social pedagogy (including the effective use of pupil groupings). It is more important for teachers to prepare their pupils to work effectively together, for example in their classroom groups, and to use these within-class groups flexibly. When teachers put a long-term commitment (up to a year) into developing relational and other social pedagogic practices within their classrooms, pupils respond with improved attainment, classroom behaviours and pro-learning attitudes.

REFERENCES

Alexander, R.J. (1995) *Versions of Primary Education*. London: Routledge.

——(1997) *Policy and Practice in Primary Education: local initiative, national agenda*. London: Routledge.

——(2001) *Culture and Pedagogy: international comparisons in primary education*. Oxford: Blackwell.

——(2006) *Towards Dialogic Teaching: rethinking classroom talk*. York: Dialogos.

Allport, G. (1954) *The Nature of Prejudice*. Cambridge, MA: Addison Wesley.

Anderson, L. (2000) 'Why should reduced class size lead to increased student achievement?', in M.C. Wang and J.D. Finn (Eds) *How Small Classes Help Teachers Do Their Best*. Philadelphia, PA: Temple University Center for Research in Human Development and Education.

Aronson, E. and Patnoe, S. (1997) *The Jigsaw Classroom: building cooperation in the classroom*. Harlow: Longman.

Baines, E., Blatchford, P. and Chowne, A. (2007) 'Improving the effectiveness of collaborative group work in primary schools: effects on science attainment', *British Educational Research Journal* 33(5): 663–80.

Baines, E., Blatchford, P. and Kutnick, P. (2003) 'Changes in grouping practice over primary and secondary school', *International Journal of Educational Research* 39: 9–34.

Barker Lunn, J.C. (1970) *Streaming in the Primary School*. Slough: NFER.

——(1984) 'Junior school teachers: their methods and practice', *Educational Research* 26: 178–88.

Bealing, D. (1972) 'The organisation of junior school classrooms', *Educational Research* 14(3): 231–35.

Bennett, N. (1976) *Teaching Styles and Pupil Progress*. London: Open Books.

Bennett, N., Desforges, C., Cockburn, A. and Wilkinson, B. (1984) *The Quality of Pupil Learning Experiences*. London: LEA.

Bennett, N. and Dunne, E. (1992) *Managing Classroom Groups*. Hemel Hempstead: Simon and Schuster Education.

Bennett, N., O'Hare, E. and Lee, J. (1983) 'Mixed age classes in primary schools: a survey of practice', *British Educational Research Journal* 9(1): 41–56.

Berry, C. and Little, A. (2006) 'Multi-grade teaching in London', in A. Little (Ed) *Education for All and Multigrade Teaching: challenges and opportunities*. Dordrecht, the Netherlands: Springer.

Biddle, B.J. and Berliner, D.C. (undated) 'What research says about small classes and their effects', part of series *In Pursuit of Better Schools: what research says*. Online (Available: www. WestEd.org/policyperspectives or http://edpolicyreports.org).

Blandford, J.S. (1958) 'Standardised tests in junior schools with special reference to the effects of streaming on the constancy of results', *British Journal of Educational Psychology* 28: 170–73.

Blatchford, P. (2003) *The Class Size Debate: is small better?* Maidenhead: Open University Press.

Blatchford, P., Baines, E., Rubie-Davies, C., Bassett, P. and Chowne, A. (2006) 'The effect of a new approach to group-work on pupil-pupil and teacher-pupil interaction', *Journal of Educational Psychology* 98: 750–65.

Blatchford, P., Bassett, P. and Brown, P. (2005) 'Teachers' and pupils' behaviour in large and small classes: a systematic observation study of pupils aged 10/11 years', *Journal of Educational Psychology* 97(3): 454–67.

Blatchford, P., Bassett, P., Goldstein, H. and Martin, C. (2003) 'Are class size differences related to pupils' educational progress and classroom processes? Findings from the Institute of Education Class Size Study of children aged 5–7 Years', *British Educational Research Journal* 29 (5): 709–30.

Blatchford, P., Galton, M., Kutnick, P. and Baines, E. (2005) 'Improving the effectiveness of pupil groups in classrooms', *Final Report to ESRC* (L139 25 1046).

Blatchford, P., Goldstein, H. and Mortimore, P. (1998) 'Research on class size effects: a critique of methods and a way forward', *International Journal of Educational Research* 29: 691–710.

Blatchford, P., Kutnick, P. and Baines, E. (1999) 'The nature and use of classroom groups in primary schools', *Final report to ESRC* (R000237255).

Blatchford, P., Kutnick, P., Baines, E. and Galton, M. (2003) 'Toward a social pedagogy of classroom group work', *International Journal of Educational Research* 39: 153–72.

Blatchford, P. and Mortimore, P. (1994) 'The issue of class size in schools: what can we learn from research?', *Oxford Review of Education* 20(4): 411–28.

Blatchford, P., Russell, A., Bassett, P., Brown, P. and Martin, C. (2004) 'The effects and role of Teaching Assistants in English primary schools (Years 4 to 6) 2000–2003', *Results from the Class Size and Pupil-Adult Ratios (CSPAR) Project: final report*. London: DfES.

Blatchford, P., Russell, A. and Brown, P. (2008) 'Teaching in large and small classes', in A.G. Dworkin and L.J. Saha (Eds) *The New International Handbook of Teachers and Teaching*. Springer.

Bliss, T., Robinson, G. and Maines, B. (1995) *Developing Circle Time*. London: Lame Duck Publishing.

Board of Education (1931) *Report of the Consultative Committee on the Primary School* (the Hadow Report). London: HMSO.

Bolster, A., Balandier-Brown, C. and Rea-Dickins, P. (2004) 'Young learners of modern foreign languages and their transition to the secondary phase: a lost opportunity?', *Language Learning Journal* 30: 35–41.

Borg, W. (1965) 'Ability grouping in the public schools', *The Journal of Experimental Education* 34: 1–97.

Braund, M. and Hames, V. (2005) 'Improving progression and continuity from primary to secondary science: pupils' reactions to bridging work', *International Journal of Science Education* 27: 781–801.

Bronfenbrenner, U. (1979) *The Ecology of Human Development*. Cambridge, MA: Harvard University Press.

Bryon, A. and Sims, J. (2002) 'Key factors in ensuring successful school transition for youngsters at risk', *DfES National Training Programme for Learning Mentors*. Liverpool: DfES.

Button, L. (1981) *Group Tutoring for the Form Teacher. 1: lower secondary school*. London: Hodder and Stoughton.

——(1982) *Group Tutoring for the Form Teacher. 2: upper secondary school*. London: Hodder and Stoughton.

CACE (1967) *Children and Their Primary Schools: a report of the Central Advisory Council for Education (England)*. London: HMSO.

Capel, S., Zwozdiak-Myers, P. and Lawrence, J. (2004) 'Exchange of information about physical education to support the transition of pupils from primary and secondary school', *Educational Research* 46(3): 283–300.

Chaplain, R. (1996) 'Pupils under pressure: coping with stress at school', in J. Rudduck, R. Chaplain and G. Wallace (Eds) *School Improvement: what can pupils tell us?* London: David Fulton Publishers.

Cohen, E.G. and Intilli, J.K. (1981) *Interdependence and Management in Bilingual Classrooms* (Final Report No. NIE-G-80–0217). Stanford University, School of Education.

Cooper, H.M. (1989) 'Does reducing student-to-teacher ratios affect achievement?', *Educational Psychologist* 24(1): 79–98.

Cornall, J.N. (1986) 'The small school: achievements and problems', *Education Today* 36(1): 25–36.

Cowie, H. (1994) 'Co-operative group work: a perspective from the U.K.', *International Journal of Educational Research* (special issue on co-operative learning in social contexts).

Cowie, H. and Rudduck, J. (1988) 'Learning together – working together', in Vol. 1: *Cooperative Group Work – an overview*, and Vol. 2: *School and Classroom Studies*. London: BP Educational Service.

Curry, M. and Bromfield, C. (1998) *Circle Time In-service Training Manual*. Tamworth: NASEN.

Daniels, H. (1994) *Literature Circles: voice and choice in the student-centred classroom*. York, Maine: Stenhouse Publishers.

Daniels, J.C. (1961a) 'The effects of streaming in the primary schools: I – what teachers believe', *British Journal of Educational Psychology* 31: 69–78.

——(1961b) 'The effects of streaming in the primary schools: II – Comparison of streamed and unstreamed schools', *British Journal of Educational Psychology* 31: 119–26.

Davies, J., Hallam, S. and Ireson, J. (2003) 'Ability groupings in the primary school: issues arising from practice', *Research Papers in Education* 18(1): 1–16.

Department for Education (DfE) (1993) 'Improving primary education', Patten (DfE News 16/93). London: DfE.

Department for Education and Employment (DfEE) (1997) *Excellence in Schools* (Cm.3681). London: HMSO.

Department of Education and Science (DES) (1978) *Primary Education in England: a survey by HM Inspectors of Schools*. London: HMSO.

Department for Education and Skills (DfES) (2004) *Excellence and Enjoyment: learning and teaching in the primary years*. Nottingham: DfES Publications Centre.

DfES (2003) 'The Standards Site: time to talk … speaking and listening for learning'. Online (Available: http://www.standards.dfes.gov.uk/primary/features/literacy/818741/).

Deutsch, M. (1949) 'A theory of cooperation and competition', *Human Relations* 2: 129–52.

Devine, D. (1993) 'A study of reading ability groups: primary school children's experiences and views', *Irish Educational Studies* 12: 134–42.

Doddington, C., Flutter, J. and Rudduck, J. (1999) '"Exploring and explaining 'dips" in motivation and performance in primary and secondary schools', *Research in Education* 61: 29–38.

Doyle, W. (1986) 'Classroom organization and management', in M.C. Wittrock (Ed) *Handbook of Research on Teaching*. New York: Macmillan.

Dreeben, R. (1984) 'First-grade reading groups: their formation and change', in P. Peterson, L. Wilkinson and M. Hallinan (Eds) *The Social Context of Instruction*. Orlando, FL: Academic Press.

Dunne, E. and Bennett, N. (1990) *Talking and Learning in Groups*. London and Basingstoke: Macmillan Education.

Edwards, A. (1994) 'The curricular applications of classroom groups', in P. Kutnick and C. Rogers (Eds) *Groups in Schools*. London: Cassell.

Ehrenberg, R.G., Brewer, D.J., Gamoran, A. and Willms, J.D. (2001) 'Class size and student achievement', *Psychological Science in the Public Interest* 2(1).

Farivar, S. and Webb, N. (1991) *Helping Behavior Activities Handbook: cooperative small group problem solving in middle school mathematics*. Los Angeles, CA: UCLA.

Ferri, E. (1971) *Streaming Two Years Later: a follow up of agroup of pupils who attended streamed and nonstreamed junior schools*. London: NFER.

Finn, J.D. and Achilles, C.M. (1999) 'Tennessee's class size study: findings, implications, misconceptions', *Educational Evaluation and Policy Analysis* 21(2): 97–109.

Finn, J.D., Pannozzo, G.M. and Achilles, C.M. (2003) 'The "why's" of class size: student behaviour in small classes', *Review of Educational Research* 73(3): 321–68.

Francis, L.J. (1992) 'Primary school size and pupil attitudes: small is happy?', *Educational Management and Administration* 20(2): 100–104.

Galton, M. (1979) 'Systematic classroom observation: British research', *Educational Research* 21: 102–15.

——(1990) 'Grouping and groupwork', in C. Rogers and P. Kutnick (Eds) *The Social Psychology of the Primary School*. London: Routledge.

——(1998) 'Class size: a critical comment on the research', *International Journal of Educational Research* 29(8): 809–18.

——(2003) *The Effects of Class-size Re-education on Transfer: the Holywells experiment*. An Evaluation Report for Suffolk Local Education Authority. Cambridge University: Faculty of Education.

Galton, M., Gray, J. and Rudduck, J. (1999) *The Impact of School Transitions and Transfers on Pupil Progress and Attainment (RR131)*. London: DfES.

Galton, M., Gray, J., Rudduck, J., Berry, M., Demetriou, H., Edwards, J., Goalen, P., Hargreaves, L., Hussey, S., Pell, T., Schagen, I. and Charles, M. (2003) *Transfer and Transitions in the Middle Years of Learning (7–14): continuities and discontinuities in learning*. Nottingham: DfES.

Galton, M., Hargreaves, L., Comber, C., Wall, D. and Pell, A. (1999) *Inside the Primary Classroom: 20 years on*. London: Routledge.

Galton, M., Morrison, I. and Pell, T. (1999) 'Transfer and transition in English schools: reviewing the evidence', *International Journal of Educational Research* 33: 341–63.

Galton, M. and Patrick, H. (1990) *Curriculum Provision in the Small Primary School*. London: Routledge and Kegan Paul.

Galton, M. and Simon, B. (Eds) (1980) *Progress and Performance in the Primary Classroom*. London: Routledge and Kegan Paul.

Galton, M., Simon, B. and Croll, P. (1980) *Inside the Primary Classroom*. London: Routledge and Kegan Paul.

Gillborn, D. and Youdell, D. (2000) *Rationing Education: policy, practice, reform and equity*. Buckingham: Open University Press.

Gillies, R. (2003) 'Structuring cooperative group work in classrooms', *International Journal of Educational Research* 39: 35–49.

Gillies, R. and Ashman, A.F. (Eds) (2003) *Co-operative Learning: the social and intellectual outcomes of learning in groups*. London: Routledge Falmer.

Goldberg, M.L., Passow, A.H. and Justman, J. (1966) *The Effects of Ability Grouping*. New York: Teachers College Press.

Goldstein, H. and Blatchford, P. (1998) 'Class size and educational achievement: a review of methodology with particular reference to study design', *British Educational Research Journal* 24(3): 255–68.

Grissmer, D. (1999) 'Class size effects: assessing the evidence, its policy implications, and future research agenda', *Educational Evaluation and Policy Analysis* 21(2): 231–48.

Hall, E. (1994) 'The social relational approach', in P. Kutnick and C. Rogers (Eds) *Groups in Schools*. London: Cassell.

Hallam, S. and Ireson, J. (1999) 'Ability grouping in the primary school', *End of Award Report to ESRC.*

Hallam, S., Ireson, J. and Davies, J. (2002) *Effective Pupil Grouping in the Primary School – a Practical Guide.* London: Fulton.

——(2004a) 'Grouping practices in the primary school: what influences change?', *British Educational Research Journal* 30(1): 117–40.

——(2004b) 'Primary school pupils' experience of different types of grouping in schools', *British Educational Research Journal* 30(4): 515–34.

Hallam, S., Ireson, J., Lister, V., Andon Chaudhury, I. and Davies, J. (2003) 'Ability grouping in the primary school: a survey', *Educational Studies* 29(1): 69–83.

Hallam, S. and Rogers, L. (2008) *Improving Behaviour and Attendance in School.* Berkshire: McGraw Hill/Open University Press.

Hallam, S. and Toutounji, I. (1996) *What Do We Know About the Grouping of Pupils by Ability?* London: Institute of Education, University of London.

Hanushek, E.A. (1999) 'Some findings from an independent investigation of the Tennessee STAR Experiment and from other investigations of class size effects', *Educational Evaluation and Policy Analysis* 21(2): 143–63.

Hargreaves, L., Comber, C., and Galton, M. (1996) 'The national curriculum: can small rural schools deliver? Confidence and competence levels of teachers in small rural primary schools', *British Educational Research Journal* 22(1): 89–99.

Harlen, W. and Malcolm, H. (1997) *Setting and Streaming: a research review* (Using Research Series 18). Edinburgh: SCRE.

Harwood, D. (1995) 'The pedagogy of the world studies 8–13 project: the influence of the presence/absence of the teacher upon primary children's collaborative group work', *British Educational Research Journal* 21: 587–611.

Hastings, N. and Chantry, K. (2002) *Reorganising Primary Classroom Learning.* Buckingham: Open University Press.

Hattie, J. (2005) 'The paradox of reducing class size and improving learning outcomes', *International Journal of Educational Research* 43: 387–425.

Hayes, D. (1999) 'Organising learning in multigrade classes: a case study about a multi-task lesson', *Curriculum* 20(2): 100–109.

Her Majesty's Inspector of Schools (1978) *Primary Education in England.* London: DfES.

Howe, C.J., Rodgers, C. and Tolmie, A. (1990) 'Physics in the primary school: peer interaction and the understanding of floating and sinking', *European Journal of Psychology of Education* 4: 459–75.

Howe, C.J. and Tolmie, A. (1998) 'Productive interaction in the context of computer-supported collaborative learning in science', in K. Littleton and P. Light (Eds) *Learning with Computers: analysing productive interaction.* London: Routledge.

——(2003) 'Group work in primary school science: discussion, consensus and guidance from experts', *International Journal of Educational Research* 39: 51–72.

Howe, C.J., Tolmie, A. and Anderson, A. (1991) 'Information technology and group work in physics', *Journal of Computer Assisted Learning* 7: 133–43.

Howe, C.J., Tolmie, A., Anderson, A. and Mackenzie, M. (1992) 'Conceptual knowledge in physics: the role of group interaction in computer-supported teaching', *Learning and Instruction* 2: 161–83.

Howe, C.J., Tolmie, A., Duchak-Tanner, V. and Rattray, C. (2000) 'Hypothesis testing in science: group consensus and the acquisition of conceptual and procedural knowledge', *Learning and Instruction* 10: 361–91.

Howe, C.J., Tolmie, A., Greer, K. and Mackenzie, M. (1995) 'Peer collaboration and conceptual growth in physics: task influences on children's understanding of heating and cooling', *Cognition and Instruction* 13: 483–503.

Howe, C.J., Tolmie, A. and Rodgers, C. (1992) 'The acquisition of conceptual knowledge in science by primary school children: group interaction and the understanding of motion down an incline', *British Journal of Developmental Psychology* 10: 113–30.

Howe, C., Tolmie, A., Thurston, A., Topping, K., Christie, D., Livingston, K., Jessiman, E. and Donaldson, C. (2007) 'Group work in elementary science: organisational principles for classroom teaching', *Learning and Instruction* 17(5): 549–63.

Ireson, J. and Hallam, S. (1999) 'Raising standards: is ability grouping the answer?', *Oxford Review of Education* 25(3): 343–58.

——(2001) *Ability Grouping in Education*. London: Sage Publications.

——(2009) 'Academic self-concepts in adolescence: relations with achievement and ability grouping in schools', *Learning and Instruction*.

Ireson, J., Hallam, S. and Hurley, C. (2005) 'What are the effects of ability grouping on GCSE attainment?', *British Educational Research Journal* 31(4): 313–28.

Ireson, J., Hallam, S. and Plewis, I. (2001) 'Ability grouping in secondary schools: effects on pupils' self-concepts', *British Journal of Educational Psychology* 71: 315–26.

Jackson, B. (1964) *Streaming: an education system in miniature*. London: Routledge and Kegan Paul.

Johnson, D.W. and Johnson, F. (2003) *Joining Together: group theory and research*. Boston, MA: Allyn and Bacon.

Johnson, D.W. and Johnson, R.T. (1994) 'Collaborative learning and argumentation', in P. Kutnick and C. Rogers (Eds) *Groups in Schools*. London: Cassell.

Johnson, D. and Johnson, R.T. (1987) *Learning Together and Alone*. Englewood Cliffs, NJ: Prentice-Hall.

Kingsley-Mills, C., McNamara, S. and Woodward, L. (1992) *Out From Behind the Desk: a practical guide to group work skills and processes*. Leicestershire: Leicestershire County Council.

Kulik, J.A. (1991) *Ability Grouping. Research-based decision making series*. Storrs, CT: National Research Center on the Gifted and Talented, University of Connecticut.

Kulik, J.A. and Kulik, C.-L.C. (1987) 'Effects of ability grouping on student achievement', *Equity and Excellence* 23(1–2): 22–30.

——(1992) 'Meta-analytic findings on grouping programs', *Gifted Child Quarterly* 36(2): 73–77.

Kutnick, P. (1994) 'Use and effectiveness of groups in classrooms', in P. Kutnick and C. Rogers (Eds) *Groups in Schools*. London: Cassell.

——(1988) *Relationships in the Primary School Classroom*. London: Paul Chapman Press.

Kutnick, P., Blatchford, P. and Baines, E. (2005) 'Grouping of pupils in secondary school classrooms: possible links between pedagogy and learning', *Social Psychology of Education* 8(4): 349–74.

——(2002) 'Pupil groupings in primary school classrooms: sites for learning and social pedagogy?', *British Educational Research Journal* 28(2): 189–208.

Kutnick, P., Hodgkinson, S., Sebba, J., Humphreys, S., Galton, M., Steward, S., Blatchford, P. and Baines, E. (2006) 'Pupil grouping strategies and practices at Key Stage 2 and 3: case studies of 24 schools in England', *Research Report 796*. London: DfES.

Kutnick, P. and Kington, A. (2005) 'Children's friendships and learning in school; cognitive enhancement through social interaction?', *British Journal of Educational Psychology* 75: 1–19.

Kutnick, P., Ota, C. and Berdondini (2008) 'Improving the effects of group working in classrooms with young school-aged children: facilitating attainment, interaction and classroom activity', *Learning and Instruction* 18(1): 83–95.

Lee, J. (1984) 'Vertical grouping in the primary school: a report of a study by Lancaster University on behalf of the Schools Council', *School Organisation* 4(2): 133–42.

Lee, J. and Croll, P. (1995) 'Streaming and subject specialism at Key Stage 2: a survey in two local authorities', *Educational Studies* 21(2): 155–65.

Lewis, J. and Cowie, H. (1993) 'Cooperative group work: promises and limitations: a study of teachers' values', *Education Section Review* 17(2): 77–84.

Lippitt, R. and White, R.R. (1943) 'The social climate of children's groups', in R.G. Barker, J.S. Kounin and H.F. Wright (Eds) *Child Behaviour and Development*. New York: McGraw-Hill.

Lloyd, C. and Beard, J. (1995) *Managing Classroom Collaboration*. London: Cassell Education.

Lou, Y., Abrami, P.C., Spence, J.C., Poulsen, C., Chambers, B. and d'Apollonia, S. (1996) 'Within-class grouping: a meta-analysis', *Review of Educational Research* 66(4): 423–58.

Lucey, H. and Reay, D. (2000) 'Identities in transition: anxiety and excitement in the move to secondary school', *Oxford Review of Education* 26: 191–205.

Measor, L. and Woods, P. (1984) *Changing Schools*. Milton Keynes: Open University Press.

Mercer, N. (2000) *Words and Minds: how we use language to think together*. London: Routledge.

Minnis, M., Seymour, K. and Schagen, I. (1998) *National Results of Years 3, 4 and 5 Optional Tests*. Slough, NFER.

Mitchell, D.E., Beach, S.A. and Badaruk, G. (1991) *Modelling the Relationship Between Achievement and Class Size: a re-analysis of the Tennessee project STAR data*. Riverside, CA: California Educational Research Co-operative.

Mortimore, P. and Blatchford, P. (1993) *The Issue of Class Size*. National Commission on Education, Briefing No. 12, March.

Mortimore, P., Sammons, P., Stoll, L., Lewis, D. and Ecob, R. (1988) *The Junior School Project*. London: ILEA Research and Statistics Branch.

Norman, D.A. (1978) 'Notes towards a complex theory of learning', in A.M. Lesgold (Ed) *Cognitive Psychology and Instruction*. New York: Plenum.

Nye, B., Hedges, L.V. and Konstantopoulos, S. (2000) 'The effects of small classes on academic achievement: the results of the Tennessee class size experiment', *American Educational Research Journal* 37(1): 123–51.

Office for Standards in Education (Ofsted) (1997) *The Annual Report of Her Majesty's Chief Inspector of Schools: standards and quality in education 1995/6*. London: The Stationery Office (TSO).

——(1998a) *The Annual Report of Her Majesty's Chief Inspector of Schools: standards and quality in education 1996/7*. London: TSO.

——(1998b) *Setting in Primary Schools: a report from the Office of Her Majesty's Chief Inspector of Schools*. London: Ofsted.

——(2000) 'Small schools: How well are they doing?', Report by Ofsted based on the data from inspections and national test results. Online (Available: http://www.ofsted.gov.uk/assets/837.pdf).

——(2002) *Changing Schools: evaluation of the effectiveness of transfer arrangements at age 11 (HMI550)*. London: Office for Standards in Education.

Peverett, R. (1994) 'Teaching 9–11 year olds', in The Paul Hamlyn Foundation National Commission on Education (Ed) *Insights into Education and Training*. London: Heinemann.

Plummer, G. and Dudley, P. (1993) *Assessing Children Learning Collaboratively*. Chelmsford: Essex Development Advisory Service.

Prais, S.J. (1996) 'Class-size and learning: the Tennessee experiment – what follows?' *Oxford Review of Education* 22(4): 339–414.

Rice, J.K. (1999) 'The impact of class size on instructional strategies and the use of time in high school mathematics and science courses', *Educational Evaluation and Policy Analysis* 21(2): 215–29.

Sammons, P., Taggart, B., Smees, R., Sylva, K., Melhuish, E., Siraj-Blatchford, I. and Elliot, K. (2003) *The Early Years Transition and Special Educational Needs (EYTSEN) Project (RR431)*. London: DfES.

Sanders, D., White, G., Burge, B., Sharp, C., Eames, A., McCune, R. and Grayson, H. (2005) *A study of the transition from the foundation stage to Key Stage 1, Research Report SSU/2005/FR/013*. Nottingham: DfES/National Foundation for Educational Research (NfER).

Scottish Office HMSO (1996) *Achievement for All: a report on selection within schools*. Edinburgh: HMSO.

Simon, S., Erduran, S. and Osborne, J. (2002) 'Enhancing the quality of argumentation in school science', Annual conference of the National Association of Research in Science Teaching. New Orleans (April 7–10).

Slavin, R. (1987) 'Ability grouping and student achievement in elementary schools: a best evidence synthesis', *Review of Educational Research* 57(3): 293–336.

——(1995) *Cooperative Learning* (2nd edition). Boston: Allyn and Bacon.

Slavin, R., Hurley, E.A. and Chamberlain, A. (2003) 'Cooperative learning and achievement: theory and research', in W.M. Reynolds and G.E. Miller (Eds) *Handbook of Psychology: Educational Psychology* 7: 177–98. New York: Wiley.

Stanford, G. (1990) *Developing Effective Classroom Groups*. Bristol: Acora Books.

Sukhnandan, L. and Lee, B. (1998) *Streaming, Setting and Grouping by Ability: a review of the literature*. Slough: NFER.

Suppe, F. (1998) 'The structure of a scientific paper', Philosophy of Science 65(3): 381–405.

Sylva, K., Melhuish, E., Sammons, P., Siraj-Blatchford, I. and Taggart, B. (2004) *The Effective Provision of Pre-School Education (EPPE) Project: final report*. London: DfES.

Thacker, J., Stoate, P. and Feest, G. (1992) *Using Group Work in the Primary Classroom*. Crediton: Southgate Publishers Ltd.

Tizard, B., Blatchford, P., Burke, J., Farquhar, C. and Plewis, I. (1988) *Young Children at School in the Inner City*. Lawrence Erlbaum Associates.

Tolmie, A. and Howe, C.J. (1993) 'Gender and dialogue in secondary school physics', *Gender and Education* 5: 191–209.

Tolmie, A., Howe, C.J., Mackenzie, M. and Greer, K. (1993) 'Task design as an influence on dialogue and learning: primary school group work with object flotation', *Social Development* 2: 183–201.

Tolmie, A., Thomson, J., Foot, H., Whelan, K., Morrison, S. and McLaren, B. (2005) 'The effects of adult guidance and peer discussion on the development of children's representations: evidence from the training of pedestrian skills', *British Journal of Psychology* 96: 181–204.

Tuckman, B. (1965) 'Developmental sequence in small groups', *Psychological Bulletin* 63: 384–99.

Veenman, S. (1995) 'Cognitive and noncognitive effects of multigrade and multi-age classes: a best evidence synthesis', *Review of Educational Research* 65(4): 319–81.

Vulliamy, G. and Webb, R. (1995) 'The implementation of the national curriculum in small primary schools', *Educational Review* 47: 25–41.

Wang, M.C. and Finn, J.D. (2000) 'Small classes in practice: the next steps', in M.C. Wang and J.D. Finn (Eds) *How Small Classes Help Teachers Do Their Best*. Philadelphia, PA: Temple University Center for Research in Human Development.

Webb, N. and Farivar, S. (1994) 'Promoting helping behavior in cooperative small groups in middle school mathematics', *American Educational Research Journal* 31: 369–95.

Webb, N. and Mastergeorge, A. (2003) 'Promoting effective helping behaviour in peer directed groups', *International Journal of Educational Research* 39: 73–97.

Whitburn, J. (2001) 'Effective classroom organisation in primary schools: mathematics', *Oxford Review of Education* 27(3): 411–28.

Wilkinson, J. and Canter, S. (1982) *Social Skills Training Manual: assessment, programme design, and management of training*. Chichester: John Wiley and Sons.

Williams, J.M. and Tolmie, A. (2000) 'Conceptual change in biology: group interaction and the understanding of inheritance', *British Journal of Developmental Psychology* 18: 625–49.

Word, E.R., Johnston, J., Bain, H.P. and Fulton, B.D. (1990) *The State of Tennessee's Student/ Teacher Achievement Ratio (STAR) Project: Technical Report 1985–90*. Nashville, TN: Tennessee State University.

22 Primary schools

The built environment

Karl Wall, Julie Dockrell and Nick Peacey

THE PRIMARY SCHOOL AS A BUILT SPACE

Introduction

Children experience a key part of their childhood in their primary school and it forms one of their principal social spaces (Dudek 2000). The school site, its buildings and grounds, provides the infrastructure which supports learning and development. 'School buildings should inspire learning. They should nurture every pupil and member of staff. They should be a source of pride and a resource for the community' (Ministerial introduction to the Building Schools for the Future consultation, DfES 2003a). Nurturing pupils means examining the ways in which school buildings contribute to, or become a barrier to, accessing the curriculum and meeting the core principles of the *Every Child Matters* agenda (DfES 2004). The design, disposition and use of school buildings transmit educational and social values (Alexander 2001: 176); so does the value placed by society on the quality and appropriateness of the spaces it provides for children's learning, inside and outside of school. To understand the ways in which school buildings impact on children and teachers it is necessary to consider a number of key features of the built environment: the school's location; its size; the ways in which classrooms are lit, ventilated, heated and exposed to different types of noise.

The focus of this chapter is the impact of the interconnected spaces of the English primary school as an environment for living and learning. To address this question we begin by considering the primary school as a building and the ways in which various social changes and political directives have impacted on its development. The evidence base examining the effects of noise, ventilation, heating and lighting in schools is then considered. For each environmental variable we consider relevant outcome measures. These outcome measures include pupil educational attainment and pupil and teacher well-being and health. The limitations of the current data are discussed. The concluding section considers the factors that limit the 'future proofing' of schools and the impact of schools on environmental sustainability.

School design, pupil welfare and pedagogy

The quality of the built environment relates in part to the physical nature of its walls and roof (the built 'envelope') and the way these are constructed to create particular spaces, such as rooms and halls. Current school building stock necessarily embodies previous ideas of design, construction, purpose, maintenance and pedagogy. They also embody past assumptions and relationships between the communities served by the school and its staff and pupil body. Different perspectives and priorities have informed this basic view of the English school building as a 'used' space since the first great expansion in school building following the 1870 Act. The resulting building pro-grammes were coherent and used relatively standard technical and architectural approaches. Building proceeded quickly in part because standardised designs were used. Two interrelated strands impacted on school building development; a welfare-informed design strand and a pedagogy-informed design strand.

Pupil welfare has been an explicit feature of school design since the 1870s. The introduction of Board Schools in this period brought with it the provision of spaces in which pupils could be active, the provision of adequate latrines and the creation of a robust and safe environment (Dudek 2000). Edwardian school designs reflected wider concerns that children should have access to daylight (through the provision of large windows) and access to fresh circulated air (Lowe 2007). The 1931 Hadow Report (Board of Education 1931) took the view that buildings would be single storey with plenty of sunlight and fresh air where 'cross ventilation would be a prerequisite for classrooms expected to take 50 or more pupils' (MacLure 1984). After the Second World War this belief in the need for fresh air and light was linked to emerging ideas of the importance of making spaces outside a classroom 'healthy'; ideas of a 'vista' – an immediate view – and the nature of spaces adjacent to a classroom began to be important (Maclure 1984). This is apparent in more contemporary views, which also emphasise the importance of outdoor areas as an ideal vehicle for learning and socia-lisation across abilities and ages (Hayhow 1995).

Effective socialisation, which manages pupil learning, safety and well-being, needs to consider spaces both inside and outside the classroom. The recent Steer Committee Report (2005) noted that building layout affected pupil behaviour; that hidden spaces could prevent appropriate supervision of pupils and that narrow corridors encouraged jostling between pupils. The organisation of classrooms and offices and their relation to each other impacts on school atmosphere, potentially compromising a sense of focus and calmness. More broadly, the same committee suggested that school design should support members of a school community in feeling safe, motivated, valued and respected.

Concerns about the school environment have typically focused on the needs of children. More recently there has been equal concern for school staff, focusing on morale, effectiveness and well-being. Research has demonstrated that the school environment has perceived and identifiable effects, both positive and negative, on school staff (USA: Corcoran, Walker and White 1988; UK: PriceWaterhouseCooper (PwC) 2001; Steer Committee Report 2005; McIntyre 2006).

The ways in which school design factors impact on children's behaviour and school ethos is complex. Both direct and indirect effects need to be considered and, as we shall see in the later sections, it is often difficult to quantify these effects and how they interact with each other. Two examples serve to illustrate these points. School toilets have a clear and specific intended use. Poorly maintained and managed toilets are a concern to pupils and staff alike. Moreover, pupils may find them unwholesome and frightening places because of substantiated risks of bullying (Vernon, Lundblad and Hellstrom 2003). The need to balance privacy and pupil security and safety with appropriate supervision for pupils in relation to toilets is acknowledged in current guidelines (DfES: Building Bulletin 99, 2006: 45–47). Direct impacts on pupil health may occur if pupils refrain from using toilets for long periods during the day, leading to potential urinary and bowel problems, prolonged ill health and missed schooling (Vernon, Lundblad and Hellstrom 2003). By corollary if pupils perceive their school toilets to be unsanitary or risky places, absenteeism may be encouraged as pupils seek to go home to use the toilet.

School dining areas illustrate another dimension of the built environment. Primary halls are often the venue for physical education (PE), assemblies, drama, dance, and other activities, as well as being let out for community use in the evenings and used for dining at lunchtime. Typically these areas are compromise spaces, which have multiple functions during a working day or at different times of the academic year (DfES: Building Bulletin 99, 2006: 38–39). The Steer Committee Report (2005) suggests that communal areas such as dining areas need to be civilised and well-ordered places that motivate pupils to remain in school over lunchtime and make a positive contribution to a healthy eating lifestyle. Such spaces should offer opportunities for positive and relaxed social interactions between pupils and adults. Recent guidelines even suggest that dining does not need to take place in the main hall of a primary school: consideration of in-class dining offers an alternative approach, depending on how meals are provided in the school (DfES: Building Bulletin 99, 2006: 38–39).

Prior to the Board schools, teaching involved large numbers of pupils being taught in rows in large communal rooms. According to Dudek (2000), Robson, in the Board School Reforms, introduced the use of separate classrooms, with sufficient circulation space for a teacher to inspect each pupil's work. The arrangement allowed each child to leave its desk during the lesson. Classrooms also included a generous area at the front for display, presentation and general circulation. Many primary schools built in this period and informed by these pedagogic principles remain in use today. In Board Schools most knowledge was transmitted from teacher to pupil; post-First World War policymakers adopted a different stance. They increasingly viewed the curriculum in terms of promoting a variety of experience and activity. The implications of the pre-Second World War decision to separate primary and secondary schools was still being consolidated after the Second World War, spurred on by the many schools that had been damaged or destroyed in the war and the government's raising of the school-leaving age.

Pedagogy changed over the period: knowledge ceased to be just about what could be acquired and stored. This change in pedagogy influenced changes in school buildings. Spaces were created to facilitate the ideal of the pupil as the agent of their own learning, development and social being. Despite the rhetoric of changes in learning, the dominance of the 3Rs in the primary school was maintained by history and selection at age 11 with an overwhelming focus on literacy and numeracy and little else (Alexander 2001).

Maclure (1984) has identified four threads in the Plowden Report (CACE 1967) which had a direct bearing on building approaches: the teacher's authority moving from being 'autocratic' to 'facilitative'; the encouragement of vertical grouping in schools; the 'integrated' organisation of the day and a commitment to a wider range of areas of learning, beyond the three Rs. The link between school design and learning was apparent in the thinking of those advising the Department for Education and Science (DES). Eric Pearson (1975), a recently retired Her Majesty's Inspectorate (HMI) inspector, took the view, when advising the Architects and Buildings Branch of the DES, that learning was both personal and individual. In infant schools this could be accommodated, he felt, through the use of an integrated curriculum organised in the form of a 'free day' model, which allowed learning experiences to run on into each other instead of being restricted to regularly changing, fixed periods of time devoted to particular subjects. Synthesis and understanding were the goals of learning, implying a need for more flexible and adaptable spaces. These spaces could then accommodate different activities with minimal disruption to learning.

In practice these pedagogic impacts on design were also influenced by cost and were exacerbated by the poor financial state of English school-building authorities in 1950 (Saint 1987). The war had left many schools damaged and a large programme of rebuilding and new building was needed; that it be achieved quickly and at the lowest possible cost was critical. One response to these pressures was the introduction of 'systems' built schools, using lightweight frames and panel construction. This reduced costs and could be justified on the basis of flexibility and adaptability, but was not defensible for long. The system building approach was not without its critics. Four key criticisms were levelled against the system building approach: initial calculations failed to cover the likely cost of maintenance; the constructional stability of the buildings produced was in doubt; there were concerns about fire safety, in particular the ease with which flames could spread quickly through roof related spaces; and the quality and effectiveness of acoustic insulation and the possible impact of noise (Ward 1976).

Scarcity of resources in subsequent periods encouraged architects to develop new approaches. The 1960s and 1970s are often characterised as the period in which 'open-plan' classrooms, consequent on changes in educational theory, held sway. 'Open plan' classrooms may have had their origins in earlier developments. Maclure (1984) cites a Ministry of Education pamphlet from 1952, which compares primary schools of the early 1950s with those from the late 1940s. The former had 20 per cent of their space for circulation, the latter, 7 per cent. In effect this recreated the large spaces moved away from in the 1870s. The plan of the school therefore had fewer but larger class-rooms (for example 61 to 83 square metres). This can be compared with the most recent Building Bulletin (DfES: Building Bulletin 99, 2006: 31) on primary school space which suggests a 'standard classroom' of 56 to 63 square metres, 'with the top to mid range used for inclusive classrooms,' and 'large classroom areas' of 63 to 70 square metres.

System-building, with other measures, was successful in delivering the numbers of buildings required across much of the country. In 1976 (DES/WO 1977) there were 5.8 million (m) places in primary schools in England and Wales: 1.1m (20 per cent) were in buildings completed before 1903, 1m (17 per cent) in buildings completed between 1903 and 1945 and 3m (51 per cent) between 1946 and 1976 (0.6m places (11 per cent) were in 'temporary accommodation'). Though the last statistic is depressing, building had proceeded since 1945; 10,500 schools had been built between 1945 and 1975. In com-parison it should be noted that of the 17,504 schools forming England's primary school stock in 2006, 3,400 (19 per cent) were built before 1919 (Patel 2007). If this was the height of school building in the 20th century, its low point followed the loss of power of the Labour government in 1979.

The change of government in 1979 ushered in 25 years of neglect – the importance of the school environment ceased to be an issue. Effective learning and teaching was reported to occur despite adverse physical conditions and lack of resources (Rutter, Maughan, Mortimore and Ouston 1979). As there was no evidence that school build-ings made any difference to attainment there did not need to be much money spent on them. England reached a low point in its spending on school buildings (£600m a year) in 1996/1997. On the basis that the total number of school buildings in use at the time was approximately 23,000, £600m represented an allowance of £26,000 per school per annum. When Helen Clark published her review of the literature in 2002, she noted that:

> The neglect of school buildings in the past quarter of a century corresponds with a lack of educational research into their use. Investigation into the physical environment as influencing learning outcomes has been largely ignored in favour of research into pedagogical, psychological and social variables ... discussion ... has ignored the fact that schools are physical entities as well as organisational units.
>
> (Weinstein 1984, cited in Clark 2002: 3)

The First National Commission of Education report *Learning to Succeed* (1993) made no reference to school buildings or architecture in its index. The follow-up study into the basis of improvement in ten disadvantaged areas (National Commission on Education 1996) indicated that while physical environment might not be a necessary pre-condition for improvement in some schools it was nonetheless an important and necessary condition for effective learning. Where improvements were found these were associated with careful attention to the physical environment. A significant study of school buildings, in terms of its effects on attainment, found evidence of indirect rather than direct relationships between buildings and attainment (PriceWaterhouse-Coopers 2001). A similar conclusion was drawn in a more recent review (NRCNA 2007); however, in addition, the implications of many small effects in aggregation were highlighted.

Principles underlying school building in the future

A major programme of primary rebuilding and renovation is planned for England (Patel 2007). The question must be, however, the extent to which governments or other authorities now feel able to take the confident position of the Victorian builders and build schools, other than those which are not system-built, to a relatively standard pattern. The terms 'flexibility' and 'adaptability' have never been far from the thoughts of the builders of schools. Flexibility is normally taken as referring to a building's ability to be changed by its users; adaptability to refer to more major changes of use. The terms relate to architects' and other professionals' concerns to 'future-proof' their buildings, but also reflect a concern apparent in recent building guidance (DfES: Building Bulletin 99, 2006: 21–22).

School building design increasingly needs to take account of the actual uses to which the designed spaces will be put and the current costs. Learning needs change, and the spaces in which that learning takes place may also need to change. Two examples of impending change are illustrative. One is the acknowledged change in significance of the involvement of parents and carers in children's educational success (Desforges and Abouchaar 2003). Buildings that welcome and support parents' and carers' active involvement as partners in their children's learning are likely to be appreciated more than those that do not. A second example is the still developing impact of new communication technologies on classroom practice within and beyond the bounds of the physical space of a school in, for example, the use of wireless communication, text messaging and off-line and on-line interactive learning environments (BECTA 2007; DfES: Building Bulletin 99, 2006: 19).

Learning environments can have different implications for, and effects upon, different groups within the school population. Over the last ten years, it has become apparent that an education system can exclude or risk excluding pupils if it does not grow and adapt to remove barriers to their successful learning and participation. A drive to make buildings as supportive of inclusion as possible has developed alongside an increasing understanding of ways of removing barriers. The law (Disability Discrimination Act (DfEE) 1995; Special Educational Needs and Disability Act (SENDA) (DfES) 2001; Disability Discrimination Act (DfES) 2005) has reinforced this approach in relation to special educational needs and/or disabilities, supported by a series of Building Bulletins. This legislation has impacted powerfully upon contemporary approaches to school design and redesign because of its implications on provision for all, and in particular for those with a physical disability. The two areas of the school physical environment review that are showing the most rapid development are those relating to the acoustic and visual properties of learning spaces – both aspects that impact upon those with physical, behavioural and learning needs most directly. Many pupils identified as experiencing emotional and behavioural difficulties[1] have identified or unidentified communication impairments for whom the acoustic quality of classrooms is critical (Visser 2001).

More recently the government issued a consultation document, *Every Child Matters: primary capital programme* (DfES 2006b), which set out the government's intentions regarding the refurbishment of existing primary schools and the building of new ones. In this way, the government has targeted providing primary school settings that were 'fully equipped for 21st Century learning, at the heart of the community, with children's services in reach of every family' (DfES 2006: 4). These new and refurbished environments are to support national policy aims in raising standards, the *Every Child Matters* agenda, the development of inclusion, diversity and responsiveness and to foster extended services, including the personalisation agenda. To do this the government committed itself to 'Rebuild, remodel or refurbish at least half of primary schools: Targeted to address deprivation nationally and in every authority and responding to population changes' (DfES 2006: 4). This commitment has been linked to extensive funding (*ibid.*: 5 and 22–30) and represents a new and commendable focus by government on the funding of primary school buildings. The same document identifies how this programme will be informed by recent changes to primary school building regulations involving, for example, an increase of floor space per pupil and a commitment to sustainability in design and materials (*ibid.*: 37). Improving the school environment for learning is also a key element of the recent Children's Plan (DCSF 2007b).

This 2006 consultation was followed by the issuing of guidance to local authorities on how the programme would work in practice (DCSF 2007a). The guidance suggests that 'experience gained from the Building Schools for the Future programme' means 'that local authorities will need to plan for professional development for school leaders, staff, governors and other stakeholders to ensure that they can contribute effectively to, and get the most from, the programme' (DCSF 2007a: 15). It also provides summary links to related government polices such as the *Every Child Matters* agenda (*ibid.*: 30–40). However, it is not clear how this process will be informed by current research about the relationships between learning and the built environment, or how the experience of others involved in the same process will be shared so that an accumulation of experience and best practice may be achieved. It is also not clear how research about learning in schools influences or informs architectural design practice and training. Addressing these issues is critical if we are to move on from current concerns about the Building Schools for the Future programme, where an estimated 8 out of 10 designs for secondary schools were described as mediocre or not good enough (Commission for Architecture and Built Environment 2008), with few proposals addressing sustainability. The Commons select committee on education has now launched an enquiry into schools being built under the programme.

Sustainability, both environmental and social, is important for the future of the design and building of primary schools. Sustainable design involves the use of energy saving techniques such as intelligent lighting systems, automatically adjusted temperature systems keyed to changes in room use, anti-glare systems and the use of low emissivity glass coupled with efficient monitoring and maintenance systems (McIntyre 2006; National Research Council of the National Academies of the USA (NRCNA) 2007; DfES: Building Bulletin 99, 2006).

Current policy suggests that schools will move from being primarily a place of instruction and teaching towards being a broader-based centre for interaction, where many children's services will be focused and used by a wider and more age-diverse community (DfES: Building Bulletin 99, 2006: 19–21). This has implications for the way buildings are designed – it will no longer be relevant, as other guidelines suggest (for example DfES: Building Bulletin 87, 2003b) to view a school as only working between 8.30 am and 3.30 pm, or to assume that a large classroom will have four networked computers (DfES: Building Bulletin 99, 2006: 31) or be typically occupied by a group of 30 pupils (*ibid.*: 29). Room use parameters will need to be flexibly designed to accommodate their different uses.

Designs will also need to include provision for green spaces adjacent to, and as extensions of, buildings, as the government acknowledges (DfES 2006; DCSF 2007). These offer a variety of environmentally positive effects, for example cooling effects on air temperature in congested streets; interception of solar reflection; improved air quality by reducing airbourne pollutants; as well as social and psychological effects on people's moods, feelings and sense of well-being (McIntyre 2006).

Along with extended periods of use there will be a need to manage and maintain these settings, both through the year and in the course of a single day (NRCNA 2007; DfES: Building Bulletin 99, 2006). The importance of maintaining school buildings is identified as an issue by government as part of its recent commitment to school refurbishment and re-building (DfES 2006; DCSF 2007), developments which need to be located within an understanding of pedagogy and the impact of the built environment. School buildings' windows and doors not only permit access for people – they also allow light, sound and moisture-laden air to enter and leave. In physically entering school buildings, pupils and staff modify the environment they enter and are in turn affected by that environment. Parents, pupils, staff and others from the local community all move between larger community spaces and the specific spaces of the school, negotiated through corridors, doors and partitions and the way interior spaces and exteriors spaces are accessed and interconnected. Sustainable building in the future will need to take into account these movements and variations in use and activity.

There is now a growing research basis to support the design and organisation of primary schools. School building programmes and modifications need to draw on this evidence base. In the subsequent sections we examine data that address these issues. We consider the evidence that addresses (and challenges) the view that when 'minimal standards are attained, evidence of the effect of changing basic physical variables is less significant' (Higgins, Hall, Wall,[2] Woolner and McCaughey 2005).

NOISE[3]

Background and noise parameters

The ways in which classroom acoustics can impact on children's learning and attainments have been relatively neglected in education. Yet there is increasing evidence that poor classroom acoustics can create a negative learning environment for many students (Shield and Dockrell 2002), especially those with hearing impairments (Nelson and Soli 2000), learning difficulties (Bradlow, Krauss and Hayes 2003) or where English is an additional language (Mayo, Florentine and Buus 1997). Excessive noise in the classroom can serve as a distraction and annoyance for teachers and pupils alike (Dockrell and Shield 2004). To address these concerns many countries have recently introduced or revised legislation and guidelines relating to the acoustics of schools, for example 'Building Bulletin 93: Acoustic Design of Schools' in the UK (DfEE 2003) and ANSI standard S12.60 'Acoustical Performance Criteria, Design Requirements and Guidelines for Schools' (ANSI 2002) in the USA. The purpose of such guidelines is to improve the teaching and learning conditions for pupils and teachers in schools.

There are two main acoustical parameters to consider in classrooms that will affect speech intelligibility: noise and reverberation. Noise levels are recorded in decibels. The decibel is a logarithmic unit which means that a doubling of sound energy, caused for example by doubling the number of speakers in a room, results in an increase in noise level of 3 dB. Environmental noise is usually measured using the A weighted decibel, dB (A), which approximates to the response of the human ear to sound. Reverberation occurs when sound is reflected off surfaces. Reverberation (commonly known as an echo) is defined as the persistence of sound in a room after the source has stopped. In a reverberant space, successive syllables blend into a continuous sound, through which it is necessary to distinguish the orderly progression of speech. The level at which this sound persists is determined by the size of the space, the speech level and the interior finish materials. Reverberation time (RT), the time it takes for a sound to die off, is measured in seconds, with a low value, around 0.5 seconds or less, being optimum for a classroom seating of about 30 children. In general, the harder or more reflective a surface is, the greater the amount of sound that is reflected back into the room. Reverberation alone has detrimental effects on listeners' understanding of speech, even in a quiet environment. Research suggests that RTs in excess of 0.4 seconds may be unacceptable for verbal communication and verbal learning by all children, especially when they occur in the presence of background noise. Both reverberation and background noise should be controlled to ensure that acoustical barriers to communication and learning are minimised.

Background or irrelevant noise in classrooms can occur from both external and internal sources and can be divided into speech and non-speech. The predominant external noise source, particularly in urban areas, is likely to be road traffic (BRE 2002; Shield and Dockrell 2002) although both aircraft noise and railway noise can affect schools in specific locations. Internal sources include noise from building services (heating, lighting, ventilation systems), noise of teaching aids (overhead projector, computers) and noise from the children themselves and other adults. The effects of irrelevant sound on learning and performance are influenced by both these noise parameters and whether the noise is speech or non-speech.

Impacts

Speech intelligibility

A major effect of noise and poor acoustics in the classroom is the reduction of speech intelligibility. Speech intelligibility is related to the signal to noise (S/N) ratio, which is the difference between the signal (in this case, speech) and background noise in a room. If children are unable to understand the teacher then the major function of a classroom in providing an environment that enables the exchange of information between teacher and pupil and pupil-to-pupil is impaired. Young children are far more susceptible to poor acoustic conditions than adults (Elliott 2002). Children under the age of 13 are particularly vulnerable to irrelevant noise interference (Johnson 2000). The negative effects of combined poor S/N (signal-to-noise) ratio with long RT (reverberation time) affect children with hearing loss more than children with hearing within the average range. Even when the hearing loss is minimal (less than 20 dB), moderate levels of noise and reverberation may have a marked and detrimental effect (Crandell 1993; Nabelek 1992).

There are other groups of children for whom understanding their teachers and their peers can be difficult in the classroom, for example children who are not being taught in their first language (Mayo, Florentine and Buus 1997; Nelson 2003), children with disorders such as attention deficit/hyperactivity disorder (Breier 2002), and children with speech and language difficulties. These children may be easily distracted in poor acoustic conditions or may have general problems in processing language, which will be exacerbated in classrooms with poor acoustics. Given the high reported levels of middle ear problems in the early years (Bess, Dodd-Murphy and Parker 1998) and current reported levels of special educational need (DfES 2006), speech intelligibility in class-rooms is an important consideration.

Both background noise level and reverberation time affect speech intelligibility, although noise level appears to be the more critical factor (Bradley 1986; Hodgson 2002). In work with adults, Bradley, Reich, and Norcross (1999) found that noise, rather than reverberation, was the most significant factor in understanding speech and that the most important parameter for speech intelligibility is the signal (that is, speech) to noise ratio. As the levels of teachers' voices vary, this means that it is particularly important to reduce the background noise level in a classroom. As a result of these studies the general guideline is that 30 dB (A) is an appropriate background noise level, with optimum reverberation times of 0.4 to 0.5 seconds.

Cognitive processes

There are both theoretical and empirical reasons to predict that classroom noise from children and noise from the environment will influence learning and performance in different ways (Beaman 2005). Studies with adults of the effects of irrelevant noise have highlighted the importance of the variation in the sound sources heard in the disrup-tion of tasks (Hughes and Jones 2001; Jones, Madden and Miles 1992). In contrast, background speech is seen to have its most profound effect on performance on verbal tasks (Banbury and Berry 1997, 1998; Tremblay, Nicholls, Alford and Jones 2000). This would suggest that intermittent sources of sound, such as traffic, might be more disrupting to tasks requiring attention, while the noise from other children in the classroom may interfere, predominantly, with language-based tasks. Irrelevant speech effects have been shown to interfere with literacy tasks (Dockrell and Shield 2006) and younger children are more susceptible to irrelevant speech effects (Elliott 2002). The majority of the research into the effects of noise on children's performance in the classroom has examined the effects of environmental noise. Two major studies around airports in the 1980s and 1990s, involving children aged from 8 to 12, found impaired performance in noise-exposed children (Cohen *et al.* 1981; Hygge, Evans and Bullinger 1996). In these studies high noise exposure was associated with poor long-term memory and reading comprehension, and decreased motivation in school children. Significant effects of train and road traffic noise on reading and attainments have also been recorded (Bronzaft and McCarthy 1975). However, the introduction of noise abatement programmes has indicated significant improvements are possible. Of particular concern is the high correlation between a school's external noise level and levels of deprivation – thereby, arguably, resulting in a double disadvantage for children attending these primary schools (Shield and Dockrell 2008).

Children are not equally at risk from noise interference. Children without additional learning needs may function adequately in an acoustically marginal classroom whereas those with learning or language-based problems may be differentially disadvantaged. There is limited (Johansson 1983; Masser, Sorensen, Kryter and Lukas 1978), and equivocal evidence (Fenton, Alley and Smith 1974; Nober and Nober 1975; Steinkamp 1980) to support this view. In support of this contention Cohen *et al.* (1981) found that children who have lower aptitude or other difficulties were more vulnerable to the harmful effects of noise on cognitive performance. More specifically, early laboratory research indicated that only children with suspected learning disabilities had difficulties in tracking an auditory signal against a background of competing, irrelevant speech (Lasky and Tobin 1973). By corollary, sentence processing in white noise is more adversely affected for children with learning disabilities than children without such problems (Bradlow *et al.* 2003). There is an increasing evidence base that children who already have difficulties in learning may be subjected to a secondary impediment resulting from the environment in which they learn.

Children's voice

The most widespread and well-documented subjective response to noise is annoyance. Recent research has begun to consider children's annoyance due to noise. Children's annoyance may be an important factor in determining the impacts of noise in classrooms (Lundquist, Holmberg and Landstrom 2000). Children at school have consistently been found to be annoyed by chronic aircraft noise exposure (Evans, Hygge and Bullinger 1995; Haines *et al.* 2001a, 2001b, 2001c). However, children may be aware of noise without necessarily being annoyed by it. A recent survey of over 2000 London primary school children aged 7 and 11 years, in schools exposed to a range of environmental noise sources, found that children were aware of, and some were annoyed by, specific noise sources (Dockrell and Shield 2004). The older children were more aware of the noise, while the younger children found noise more annoying. The most annoying noise sources were trains, motorbikes, lorries and sirens, suggesting that it is intermittent loud noise events that cause the most annoyance to children while at school. Importantly it was only the older children who provided indicative evidence of strategies that might minimise the effect of noise on speech intelligibility.

Managing noise in classrooms: teaching and learning

The ways in which the potential impacts of noise in classrooms can be modified by approaches to classroom organisation and management have not been the focus of current research. There is evidence that monitoring and modifying noise levels in classroom is not a feature of initial teacher training (Dockrell, Shield and Rigby 2004). More experienced teachers report attempting to militate against the distracting effect of external noise by arranging quiet times. Although many teachers felt that noise levels impacted on most class activities (39.2 per cent), teachers also report a limited range of classroom strategies to combat the effect of external noise sources. These include raising voices (33.3 per cent); specific attention-gaining strategies (21.6 per cent); stopping teaching (17.6 per cent); and ignoring the situation (3.9 per cent) (Dockrell *et al.* 2004). There is, importantly, a range of strategies that could support the maintenance of classroom noise levels at an acceptable level for relevant activities. These include classroom layout, class grouping, using classroom spaces in strategic ways. At a school level, organisation of playtimes and the introduction of quiet times could all provide the potential to manage noise levels.

In addition to children's hearing concerns, the effect of trying to compete with an acoustically difficult environment creates a problem of severe vocal chord strain for many teachers. Voice strain is being recognised as a serious and potentially incapacitating problem for teachers. However, effective acoustical treatment of a classroom can create benefits.

Managing noise in the classroom: acoustic modifications

In parallel with studies of the effects of noise at school, there have been several surveys of classroom noise and acoustics, and investigations into the way in which the acoustics of classrooms may be improved (Canning and Peacey 1998). There are a number of classroom modifications that can be implemented to reduce noise levels in classrooms, although there have been few detailed studies to examine the effects on children and teachers. Reverberation times and potential noise in a classroom can be reduced by the use of acoustic ceiling tiles (Maxwell and Evans 2000), wall coverings, and carpets to absorb sound (Tanner and Langford 2002). An acoustical consultant can advise on the acoustic design of a school and on quietening the HVAC and other noise sources.

Speech reinforcement systems are an alternative or complementary approach (Smaldino and Crandell 2000). These systems amplify the teacher's voice through a portable microphone and feed it into the classroom via strategically located loudspeakers. Such systems are becoming more common for classroom situations. However, for primary schools, the two-way flow of information from teacher to pupil and vice versa may be affected. If the teacher has a microphone and is clearly heard the child's response might not be. Such systems also require high levels of maintenance and training which may not be available in all classroom situations.

Critical evaluation

Consideration of classroom acoustics offers scope for both improving learning and for providing more inclusive classrooms. It is important that teachers, parents and administrators understand the impact that a noisy classroom has on students' learning and work with noise control consultants and architects to create a quiet learning environment. Different areas of a school have differing acoustical requirements (DfES 2004), which depend to some extent on activities and types of teaching. Concern about the effects of noise on children's learning, and how they may be mitigated, is reflected in current work towards improving standards for classroom acoustics; standards which are often compromised. The new Evelina Hospital school serves as an example:

> The school suffers from being located within the atrium area. Ambient sound is totally inappropriate for a school environment. This can range from loud conversations, mobile phones, performance noise, ... sound rising from the ground floor. The installation of new sound absorbent screening and the carpeting of some areas would help but it may be necessary to carry out a **full acoustic survey** in order to consider the most appropriate measures required to resolve the problems.
>
> (Borough of Southwark, Evelina School review 2007)

TEMPERATURE, HEATING, HUMIDITY, AIR QUALITY AND VENTILATION

Background and key parameters

Temperature, humidity, air quality and ventilation comprise four key and inter-related dimensions of a classroom's physical environment. The nature of these parameters in relation to schools in England is contained in a series of guidance documents (DfES: Building Bulletin 87, 2003b) and advice regarding school design (DfES Schools Buildings and Design Unit 2004). These advise users of desirable temperature and humidity ranges associated with school buildings at different times of the year and for different activity purposes. Ventilation and air quality guidelines similarly link physical variables to assumptions about particular conditions and user activities, including the significance of ICT equipment and its impact on physical environment variables such as heating levels. Unlike adults and older children, young pupils in the classroom have limited opportunities to modify their immediate environment. Moreover, young children and adults may have different physiological responses and sensitivities to the same environmental factor (for example carbon dioxide levels: Corsi, Torres, Sanders and Kinney 2002).

How temperature, humidity, ventilation and air quality separately (reviewed by Weinstein 1979; Stevenson 2001; Clark 2002) and in combination (for example, Hygge and Knez 2001; Mendell and Heath 2003; NRCNA 2007) directly affect children's learning activity and attainments in the primary setting are not clear. Research that is available has tended to draw on data from other settings (Kimmel *et al.* 2000, in respect of ventilation and windows); or with other populations and activity contexts (for example adults and ventilation in offices); or the impact of performance on logical reasoning, typing and arithmetic (Wargocki *et al.* 1999); or in other countries, such as the USA (for example Schneider 2002; Mendall and Heath 2003; NRCNA 2007). The different pedagogic, activity foci and age of participants of these studies limit the application of these results to primary classrooms. In the absence of more specific work, such studies are indicative of the effects of classroom environments on primary school pupils and their teachers (Higgins *et al.* 2005).

Impacts

Temperature, heating and humidity

Among the limited research that may be related to primary school settings (for example Schneider 2002; Young *et al.* 2003), perceived links to the effect of physical factors have been reported: these draw on research in related areas (such as children's health) and make inferences about the effect of particular physical factors on the classroom. They have also considered room users' well-being.

Temperature, heating and air quality have all been associated with pupil achievement (Earthman 2004; Department of Education, Training and Youth Affairs (Australia) 2001) and perceived effects on pupil behaviour (Young *et al.* 2003).

Indicative research suggests that specific temperature ranges (between 20–23.3°C), have an impact on reading and mathematics learning, with negative learning effects above 23.3°C (Harner 1974). Current classroom heating guidelines for England suggest that 18°C is acceptable where there is a normal level of physical activity such as when teaching, engaging in private study or undertaking examinations and that excessive variation in heating should be avoided, particularly in the summer heating season (DfES: Building Bulletin 87, 2003b: 8–10). Task performance and apparent task-related attention span decrease as temperature and humidity increase (King and Marans 1979), with implications that heating and air conditioning affect learning conditions and so learning itself (McGuffey 1982).

Schneider (2002) suggests that individuals may show different sensitivities to the same temperature. Notions of a 'comfortable temperature' have informed classroom-heating debates, but Schneider (2002) queries whether it is possible to have a comfortable heating level that all in a room find comfortable. There is some specific evidence that changing heating levels is associated with altered levels of mental activity (Wyon 1991). Such studies, however, carried out in different locations (usually in the US), with different external climatic conditions, need to be evaluated in a UK context.

Heating levels also affect humidity as warmer air can hold a greater proportion of suspended water vapour than colder air. High humidity encourages the growth of bacteria and moulds, high levels of which are associated with effects on respiratory health – leading to illness and missed schooling (Schneider 2002; Mendell and Heath 2003). Humidity has been found to interrelate with perceptions of indoor air quality (IAQ) when schools in which humidity is actively controlled are compared to those where it is not. There are perceived health and learning effects (Bayer, Hendry, Crow and Fischer 2002). Humidity changes may also arise from other sources such as floor moisture problems, with associated links to ill health (Ahman, Lundin, Musabasic and Soderman 2000).

Air quality

Air quality research has focused on the effects of suspended materials, gaseous aerial pollutants and airborne pathogens on room users' health. In England, guidance relating to ventilation and IAQ are linked (DfES: Building Bulletin 87, 2003b: 15–17). Here carbon dioxide concentration is taken as a key IAQ indicator (acceptable carbon dioxide concentrations are given as 1000 ppm, equivalent to a ventilation rate of approximately 8 litres per second per person (DfES: Building Bulletin 87, 2003b: 16)).

Poor air quality leads to respiratory irritation symptoms, nausea, dizziness, headaches, fatigue or sleepiness – all of which reduce concentration and presumably affect cognitive activity (Schnieder 2002). Such effects would apply to teacher and pupils alike.

There is some indication that materials used in classroom flooring and furniture may contribute to levels of airborne irritants, including dust and fibres (Smedje and Norback 2001). These are thought to have an impact on young children's respiratory health (particularly asthma): poor air quality in terms of concentrations of airborne particles (dust, for example) may negatively affect learning by increasing the amount of absenteeism in nursery school settings (Rosen and Richardson 1999). The equivalent research for older pupils in primary settings appears not to have been undertaken yet.

Ventilation

Air quality is modified by how a room is ventilated. Ventilation is usually achieved through 'natural' ventilation (the opening and closing of windows) or 'mechanical' ventilation (using various forms of air conditioning), or by a combination of both. In England ventilation is assumed to be achieved by natural means alone for normal room occupancy, at a level of 8 litres per second per individual (DfES: Building Bulletin 87, 2003b: 16). This may vary however as room occupancy changes and, in the longer term, seasonally. Room ventilation alters the balance of respiratory gases, which may have an impact on general well-being as well as on learning activity through altered levels of concentration and perceived tiredness. A study of eight different European schools (Myhrvoid, Olsen and Lauridsen 1996) noted that elevated classroom carbon dioxide levels (that is to say above 1000ppm), arising through poor ventilation, were associated with decreased performance on concentration tasks when compared to classrooms with lower carbon dioxide levels.

Carbon dioxide levels may regularly exceed national indicative values in the UK (Coley and Beisteiner 2002) in the winter season, and even in the summer time when open windows might be expected to reduce carbon dioxide levels (Beisteiner and Coley 2002). Elevated carbon dioxide levels, above 2000ppm, were found to be associated with impaired cognitive function expressed in measures of task attention (Coley and Greaves 2004). Within the current research literature a carbon dioxide concentration of 1000ppm is increasingly taken as an indicator of inadequate ventilation (for example Lee and Chang 2000; Corsi *et al.* 2002). More direct physiological effects of low ventilation rates on pupil nasal congestion, as another factor and associated with increased absenteeism from school, have been reported in Sweden (Walinder *et al.* 1997).

Multiple effects and interactions

Opening windows (or altering air conditioning settings) does not just alter air flow: it may also modify room temperature, humidity and the extent to which particular pollutants or airborne pathogens are prevalent in the incoming and outgoing air. An open window may also bring in external noise; equally an air conditioning system may itself introduce additional noise (Shield and Dockrell 2004). In both cases this may affect pupil and teacher concentration or task activity. The impact of air conditioning is potentially more significant where localities have high external temperatures for all or part of the school year, but this is disputed (Higgins *et al.* 2005: 17). An important implication of these studies is that addressing the impact of one physical factor may compromise the optimising of the effects of another factor (Weinstein 1979; Higgins *et al.* 2005: 16).

Keeping a room comfortably warm in the winter may lead to the air becoming dry; this in turn may lead to both teacher and pupil tiredness. However, while differential effects on teachers and pupils do not seem to have been investigated directly, given that children breathe a larger volume of air in proportion to their body weight than do adults in the same conditions (for example Kennedy 2001; Moore and Warner 1998), they may be differentially and negatively affected. Smaller sized teaching rooms compared to offices, given the number of pupils in a classroom compared to adults in a typical office, will exacerbate this effect (Crawford 1998).

An elevated breathing level may make pupils more likely to lose water quickly (breathed out air is saturated with water and represents a body's largest continuous source of water loss), and so become dehydrated faster than adults. They will also be likely to experience dehydration-related tiredness more quickly. Higher levels of respiration lead to still higher levels of gas exchange, increased carbon dioxide levels and higher levels of water loss. Room humidity would increase as a result, allowing airborne bacteria and moulds to flourish, which, given elevated breathing rates, would be taken in by both children and adults to a greater extent. Such an environment would lead to reduced concentration, participation in the lesson and tiredness, and might, through increased exposure to infection, lead to missed schooling and intermittent learning experiences. Current understanding of the impacts of these factors on pupil learning and performance are based on inferences about what may be occurring (for example Rosen and Richardson 1999; Schneider 2002; Earthman 2004), and specific effects on learning have not yet been investigated.

Teachers and pupils

Classroom heat, humidity and ventilation affect teachers' workplace satisfaction, with a likely secondary effect on teacher effectiveness. Studies across different types of school buildings of different ages in one English county (Essex) identified heating, ventilation, lighting and acoustics as significant factors in affecting perceptions of the school environment (Cooper 1985). More recently in two American cities, Chicago and Washington, bad indoor air quality, uncomfortable temperatures, bad lighting and noisy facilities were identified as having negative impacts for teachers (Schneider 2003). These factors have also been identified as having a negative impact on teacher retention rates in US elementary schools (Buckley, Schneider and Yi 2004). Indirect effects may influence teachers who feel disempowered if they are unable to control the physical characteristics of the spaces they teach in (for example room temperature – Lowe 1990), believing that lack of control may affect pupil performance (Lackney 1999). As such, they suffer reduced morale and increased stress (Corcoran *et al.* 1988; Heschong-Mahone Group 2003a).

Critical evaluation

The physical characteristics of primary classrooms – temperature, heating, humidity, air quality and ventilation – have been little investigated as specific contexts for their effects on pupil learning and teacher activity. It must be noted that much of the research available focuses on perceptions, rather than on systematic measurements of any objective measures. The implications for the UK are uncertain since many studies are based in the USA. There is clearly a pressing need for research in the UK context, and this should be a priority in coming years given current government commitments to school building and maintenance.

Given the apparent complexity and inter-relatedness of the physical factors themselves, it is not surprising that linking them to specific effects on pupil concentration, pupil learning, motivation, performance and teachers' involvement in learning has been very difficult: there is little direct indication in the existing literature of any specific causal relationships among the factors discussed here. However, it may be that correlational studies offer the best possible indicators in the circumstances and a basis for future action. The lack of causal findings should not be used to justify research, funding, design or maintenance inaction – a view endorsed in the recent large-scale review by the NRCNA (2007).

Health effects associated with substantive and intermittent poor health or reduced learning readiness may be significant, as they reduce pupil and teacher learning focus in the classroom, day by day. Through episodes of missed schooling, this may lead to a reduced level of overall learning: such health related effects on learning are better supported in the literature, both for pupils and teachers.

Teachers, parents, administrators and designers should take into account that physical factors – temperature, heating, humidity, air quality and ventilation – may influence classroom activity by affecting pupil and teacher concentration, motivation and learning activity, and that this may be made manifest in pupil and teacher health and absenteeism. Poor maintenance and monitoring of the physical characteristics of established environments can have similar associational effects on classrooms, learners and teachers (see, for example, Young *et al.* 2003; Schneider 2002; NRCNA 2007).

LIGHTING

Background and key parameters

Light in the classroom serves three basic functions. First, it allows those in the room to perceive their immediate environment and thus retrieve environmental cues. Second, it allows pupils, teacher and other adults to engage with materials for learning purposes and, crucially, third, it allows pupils and adults to see each other, particularly for communicative purposes. This said, an explicit link between lighting and pupil performance has not been clearly demonstrated but a number of suggestive studies exist: Larson (1965) (elementary class children); Boyce, Hunter and Howlett (2003) (benefits of natural light); and Boyce (2004) (review of effects of daylight on productivity). Light informs what objects in the environment look like and how we interpret and process visual information (our visual performance).

Light has a number of physical characteristics. These inform its potential impact on the classroom and those in it. Key among these is its source, natural or artificial, and its background level, where the illumination level may be high (at around 1500 lux) or low (around 300 lux, as defined by Knez 1995). The colour spectrum of light is also important (Knez 1995), as are its distribution in the environment and its availability to particular users. Guidance on appropriate levels of these factors is contained in UK government building guidelines (DfES: Building Bulletin 87, 2003b) and varies according to designated room activity (teaching classroom, hall, gymnasium area and so on). However, light levels used in particular research studies vary *between* studies and *between* those conducted in the UK and USA. As much of the research informing this chapter is American, its implications for the UK setting can only be suggestive due, for example, to the different patterns of light availability in each geographical setting over the course of a typical year and different perspectives and practices about how spaces are illuminated.

Overhead lighting – which may be in the form of an illuminated ceiling (Spencer 2003), or discrete strips of light/suspended lamps – tends to generate fewer shadows and a more uniform distribution of light. Wall mounted lighting tends to produce localised sources of light. The dimensions of the space, higher ceilings being associated with reduced light intensity for the same level of illumination compared to lower ceilings, may also have an effect (for example Earthman 2004).

Impacts

Natural and artificial lighting as light sources

There is an extensive literature on different aspects of light, lighting and its various sources relating to classrooms. From this it is not clear which form of lighting – natural or artificial – is likely to have the most impact on pupils' learning, however the consensus seems to be that a mixture is inevitable and that the greater the amount of natural light the better (for example Earthman 2004; Higgins *et al.* 2005; NRCNA 2007). That lighting levels directly impact on pupil performance is hotly debated.

What constitutes *adequate* lighting necessarily depends on the task being undertaken and its context. UK building regulations (DfES: Building Bulletin 87, 2003b: 18) suggest that priority should be given to using natural lighting where possible, with overall lighting levels for teaching spaces being 300 lux, and, where visually demanding tasks are undertaken, such as reading a text, a set minimum maintained illuminance levels of 500 lux. Basic optimum levels of lighting have been researched. These studies suggest that task-appropriate lighting levels may be associated with improved test scores, more on-task behaviour and positive student attitudes (Dunn, Krimsky, Murray and Quinn 1985; Jago and Tanner 1999). A recent review of fifty-three studies suggested that higher levels of daylight exposure were associated with improved student achievement (Lemasters 1997).

However, the often-cited work by the Heschong-Mahone Group (1999, 2001, 2003a, 2003b) is contradictory (see, for example, Schneider 2002) in relation to light sources. The 1999 study, which focused on elementary school classrooms, appeared to show a correlation between the amount of daylight in a student's classroom and their performance on test scores for maths and English – it suggested that an increase in the amount of daylight would be associated with an increase in scores. However, Boyce's (2004) analysis of the regression data provided by the study suggests that only 0.3 per cent of the variance in the regression model was associated with daylight-related codes (a measure of daylight levels in a particular classroom), reflecting little impact on student performance. Subsequent research by the Heschong-Mahone Group (2003b) failed to find similar effects to those reported in their first study.

One compounding issue may be that of ceiling height, where, for the same level of background illumination, higher ceilings appear to reduce lighting and so adversely affect lighting levels. Earthman (2004) has argued that this may be a problem related, in turn, to the age of a school. This is relevant in a UK context as older, Victorian, schools have higher ceilings than those built more recently (Cooper 1985). On the other hand, higher ceilings may distribute light more uniformly and produce fewer shadows, particularly when such schools often have larger areas of window, admitting natural light from multiple directions.

The complexity of the issue of lighting and windows, ceilings aside, is also apparent in a later study by the Heschong-Mahone Group (2003b). This suggested that lighting-related effects were, in turn, related to physiological and psychological issues. The impact of different sources of glare; thermal discomfort linked to sunlight entering un-shaded windows; and being unable to control light entry through windows due to inadequate blinds or shades were all identified. All showed an effect on student performance; the more of each of these variables, the lower the student performance. However, the type of 'view' out of the window also had an effect. The more the 'view' was perceived to be poor, the more student performance declined.

Windows not only admit light but also allow the viewer to see outside of their immediate location into the world beyond. In any discussion of natural light effects, the issue of view may be a confounding variable. There is some literature on the effect of 'view outside a window' that suggests that the better the view, the better subject performance and affect for adult users of a room (for example Leslie and Hartleb 1990), including in a university context (Douglas and Gifford 2001). Financial and psychological effects in relation to views from buildings have also been noted (Kim and Wineman 2005). There is no current equivalent for children apart from that indirectly gleaned through the Heschong-Mahone Group (2003b) account. Rusak, Eskes and Shaw's review (1997) of links between human health and lighting suggested that apart from a year-long study by Kuller and Lindsten (1992), which indicated that a lack of window access altered children's cortisol levels (a stress-associated hormone), there was no current work establishing firm links between access to windows for light or 'view' and children's well-being. This remains the case today. Nonetheless, recent reviews (for example NRCNA 2007) and reports (for example McIntyre 2006) assert the importance of 'views' based on interviews and self reports.

Light spectrum

The spectrum of light available in classrooms is another issue to be examined. Daylight spectrum varies during the day, along with light level: in contrast, artificial lighting is usually static in both composition and level. One debate has been about the effects, or not, of using full spectrum fluorescent lighting (this includes ultraviolet light as a part of the emission spectrum of the lamp). The more 'blue-end' of the spectrum in the emitted spectrum the more it is perceived as 'cold', while a greater emphasis on the red end of the spectrum is associated with a perception of 'warmth'[4] (Knez 1995).

In terms of pupil affect, various colour-related effects have been reported. UK building guidance notes that colour appreciation is important in educational contexts and supports the accurate rendering of the real colour of objects. To achieve this, lamps with a colour-rendering index of not less than 80 are recommended. The colour appearance of light itself, specifically its 'coldness' or 'warmness', is also identified as an important variable. The guidelines suggest that lamps with a warm to intermediate colour temperature should be used (in the range of 2800K and 4000K) (DfES: Building Bulletin 87, 2003b; DfEE: Building Bulletin 90, 1999). Colour 'temperature' has been identified as having several effects on people; lighting 'coldness' makes people feel negative and is associated with a decline in performance (Knez 1995 – but see Veitch 1997, for a contrary view). Performance under different types of lighting shows variations in terms of age and gender (Knez and Kers 2000). Research suggests that females are more perceptive to light than males and that both males and females perform differently under different types of lighting, informed by perceived lighting warmth and level of illumination (Knez 1995, 2001). However, little comparable research involving primary-aged children is apparent in the literature. There is evidence that the perceived temperature of incident light has an effect on student long-term memory recall and that 'cool' light has more of a negative effect than 'warm' light (Knez and Hygge 2002). However, other researchers suggest little difference in effect between the use of full and limited spectrum lighting (Gifford 1994; Benya 2001).

Glare

Light reflecting off of surfaces that are highly polished or reflective (windows, computer monitors or interactive whiteboards, for example) or are light in colour creates 'glare'. UK guidance suggests that the overall glare index within a teaching space should not exceed 19 (DfES: Building Bulletin 87, 2003b: 18; DfEE: Building Bulletin 90, 1999). 'Disability glare' may be one outcome of excessive glare. Here, a burst of bright light interrupts visual performance and is associated with a loss of concentration and attention to the task in hand (Boyce 2003) – this effect varies with age, being more significant as a person grows older (Weale 1963, 1992). In a classroom context, different sensitivities for pupils and adults, and among adults of different ages may be an issue. Another type of glare is termed 'discomfort glare,' which appears to have a psychological origin such that in one context glare from a flash of bright light might be distracting (the classroom) but in another setting (at a party) it might be desirable (Boyce 2003). The issue of glare is increasingly significant as classrooms accumulate more computer-associated display technologies such as monitor screens and interactive whiteboards (see, for example, Barnitt 2003), but the more general issue of how glare impacts on children in a classroom context has yet to be examined in detail.

Light and colour in the environment

Related to the colour spectrum of background illumination is the perceived colour of the environment that it illuminates. UK guidance indicates that the accurate rendering of the real colour of objects supports colour appreciation. To achieve this, lamps with a colour-rendering index of not less than 80 are recommended (DfES: Building Bulletin 87, 2003b; DfEE: Building Bulletin 90, 1999). Interviews with pre-school and young children indicate that young children are sensitive to the colour of their classrooms (Read, Sugawara and Brandt 1999) and that it is an important issue for them, even if adults in the same setting are less conscious of it (Maxwell 2000).

Improvements in achievement were identified by Cash (1993) when pastel colours were used on walls instead of white and for the same background illumination. Age is a relevant factor, with younger children preferring bright colours and older children more subdued colours (Engelbrecht 2003). In contrast, Pile (1997) advocates using strong but warm colours (and not intense primary colours) for younger children. Colour preferences also exist for older students (Rosenstein 1985), and may be gender- and age-related among adults. Khouw (1995) and Radeloff (1990) claim differences exist between adult males and females in colour preferences (but see Ou, Luo, Woodcock and Wright 2004 for an opposing view).

Many of the studies looking at the impact of colour use brief exposure to limited areas of colour as part of their methodology. This may lack face validity given the large scale and more sustained exposure experienced by teachers and pupils in their classrooms. As a result, people's apparent preferences should be interpreted with caution (Sundstrom 1986). A similar caution should inform the interpretation of claims linking the effect of colour on perceptions of room space (light colours appearing to expand a space) and room temperature (warm colours, such as orange, being associated with a 'warmer' room – Sundstrom 1987).

Ceiling height may have additional effects not directly linked to light levels. One such effect is that they may affect teachers' and pupils' sense of space. However, the evidence is contradictory, with Ahrentzen and Evans (1984) claiming higher ceilings lead to a greater sense of space and well-being for younger children. In contrast, Read *et al.* (1999) suggest that lower ceilings support group work and higher ceilings hinder it among pre-school children. As noted earlier, ceiling height may affect overall illumination levels for the same amount of available light. This in turn may affect perceived colour intensity and shade.

Teachers and Pupils

For adults in the age range of 18–65, relationships between background luminance, target contrast, target size and age exist and can be calculated (Rea and Ouelette 1991). For adults, large classroom objects (such as desks) are quickly processed visually, even when light levels are low and contrast with the background is poor. However, for smaller targets, greater discrimination is required. Visual processing declines markedly if light levels are low. Poor contrast between target (some print, for example) and background (the page containing the print) also makes visual processing more difficult. The importance of appropriate light levels is recognised in current UK guidance on light levels (DfES: Building Bulletin 87, 2003b). A need for high background light levels and high contrast increases with age for adults (Rea 2000). No such visual performance calculations currently exist for evaluating school children's needs. Partly this is a result of the fact that, for young children in particular, the visual system is still maturing as they enter school.

However, adults and young people routinely overcome inadequate background lighting levels by changing their behaviour. They may hold a text nearer to them for reading or move the target closer to a bright source of light. They may also alter how they hold the target material or its position on the work surface (Rea, Ouellete and Kennedy 1985). Teachers should attend to such behaviours, as they may indicate that background light levels for the child concerned (or a colleague) are inadequate.

Poor lighting levels in the classroom may also compound the effect of poorly corrected eyesight in children and adults and will create varying degrees of difficulty for teachers and other adults depending on their age. A significant proportion of English school children use corrective lenses for everyday use on the basis of redeemed spectacle vouchers – 27.1 per cent for 2005–6 (NHS 2006). This is consistent with estimates in other countries such as the USA, where spectacle use is at 25.4 per cent among 6–18 year olds (Kemper, Bruckman and Freed 2004). However, many more may need to use spectacles as current use in the UK is regarded as an underestimate of need – a further 12 per cent of 5–16 year olds may need spectacles (Taylor Nelson Sofres 2002). The lenses prescribed for children's use may need to be supported by appropriate background lighting levels such as those associated with reading and working with classroom materials, and the use of materials with high contrast levels. Light distribution may be a further factor as even distribution of light reduces potentially distracting shadows. The effect of increasing the availability of natural light in this respect has not been investigated.

For teachers and other adults in the classroom, loss of refractive power in the eyes and the ability to accommodate to targets (such as books held close to the viewer) declines naturally with age (presbyopia), from about the age of 20 through to 65 years, with a marked decline more noticeable at approximately age 45 (Weale 1992). Lighting may therefore have differential effects on classroom adults of different ages, which may in turn impact on their access to task materials and task activity.

Full spectrum lamps are usually free of flicker and produce little or no glare, both factors identified as possible distracters in classrooms; Karpen (1993) has suggested that use of these lamps might lead to reduced levels of headaches, eyestrain and tiredness. Bad lighting has been identified by American teachers as one of the factors affecting their general classroom health (Schneider 2003). More general effects on health are not established however: pupil absenteeism has been examined with some researchers claiming a link with lighting (for example Hathaway 1994; Jago and Tanner 1999), and with others claiming the reverse (for example Heschong-Mahone Group 2001, 2003b).

Light further affects human activity by influencing an individual's underlying circadian rhythm, which cycles on an approximately 24-hour basis (NRCNA 2007). Natural light level and spectral composition are detected in the retina of the eye. Circadian effects occur at higher light levels than those needed for visual processing (McIntrye *et al.* 1989a, b) and need a longer period of exposure to be activated (Rea, Figueiro and Bullough 2002). Circadian processes are also more sensitive to the short wavelength component of the spectrum (Brainard *et al.* 2001). The sensitivity of the retina to these effects also varies during the day (Jewett *et al.* 1997). Seasonal variation in daylight exposure is associated with altered productivity and personal health (for example in the case of Seasonal Affective Disorder (SAD)), and has been linked to depression in various populations (Rosenthal *et al.* 1985).

Adults showing SAD symptoms report having had them as children (Rosenthal 1998), although there is little specific research relating to primary age children. Light/ dark balance is also linked to altered sleep patterns (Reid and Zee 2004), and inadequate sleep is known to impact on adults' learning activity (Heuer, Kleinsorge, Klein and Kohlisch 2004) and to affect older teenagers' school attendance patterns (Carskadon *et al.* 1998). As a result it may be hypothesised that access to daylight is important for adults and children across the age range, and that increasing this access in the classroom is desirable. It also indicates another area where further research is urgently needed.

Critical evaluation

The literature reviewed here indicates that light appears to have underlying physiological effects on the human body and specific effects on visual processing that may inform learning. These include the effects of background lighting level, contrast and colour. It may also have psychological effects through the perception of colour in relation to mood, and the impact of having a 'view' to look at and a person's sense of well-being.

Whether physiological or psychological, a person's health and productivity may be affected. These effects vary according to the age of the person in question, with most research having been conducted with young people and older adults. Where work has focused on young children and their classrooms, general effects have been noted and associations claimed between the amount and extent of exposure to daylight (and the balance of daylight to artificial light) and its impact on concentration and performance. The effects of glare as a potential source of distraction, of light spectrum and perceptions of comfort in the classroom have also been identified as important.

It has also been noted that there is conflicting evidence for saying that light has an effect on absenteeism and that colour preferences in the immediate environment are significant. The ways in which light is distributed in the classroom, and the impact of ceiling height and lighting design, may also be important. Overall it is not clear that light and its several characteristics have *direct* links to pupil performance. However, it is clear that, like the issue of heating and related factors discussed under 'Temperature, heating, humidity, air quality and ventilation' (p. 600), lighting may interact with a range of factors which will preclude the identification of clear-cut causal effects. Similarly, associational links may need to be sufficient.

DISCUSSION

Minimal standards?

The survey of evidence for this chapter has drawn on and examined a broad range of literatures, including contemporary research from the educational, built environment and health literatures as well as publicly available national data where relevant. The built environment for primary school children and their teachers has the potential to enhance well-being and attainment. The current evidence for individual environmental variables suggests that, in a range of different classroom contexts, minimal standards are not actually achieved. The extent to which physical variables impact on children and adults, beyond a set of minimal standards, is more contentious (Higgins *et al.* 2005).

To a large extent, drawing reliable and valid conclusions is limited by the paucity of large scale, systematic and rigorously controlled empirical studies that show a direct relationship between specific single environmental variables, pupil learning, and pupil and teacher health. Much of the larger scale research informing this survey has been carried out in the United States, and less frequently in Europe and Scandinavia, with the possible exception of noise research. Much of the other research is small scale, often case study-based and seldom comparative. Comparable measures across studies have generally not been used so it is very difficult to compare different studies, particularly to allow for different settings and contexts.

Diversity

Minimum standards are derived from a range of different methodologies and are typically the subject of debate between the relevant building professionals (BCSE 2007). The extent to which minimum standards meet the needs of all classroom users has been the focus of limited research. There is a need to think of those using primary school buildings not as groups (all the pupils of a school; all the staff at a school) but rather as a series of age-defined developmental groups, with each group having different needs and using the facilities in different ways. The same may apply to adults using particular facilities, such that what is appropriate visually for a young teacher may well be less so for older teachers. This necessarily involves a consideration of the range of pupils' learning needs and the range of teachers' needs, and how they are supported by environmental variables.

It is also apparent in the research to date that little account has been taken of the diversity of different forms of learning activity that can take place in primary school buildings, and their impact in relation to environmental factors. The diversity of geographical locations of the primary school buildings in this country has not been related to the question of whether or not minimum standards, if met in practice, are equally applicable to the diverse sites in question, or to the activities they play host to. These issues raise a range of methodological problems.

Methodology and practice

As we have argued, the current data sets are limited in their focus and consideration of the key variables. The absence of agreed standards and investigative practices, and the apparent lack of use of common definitions across researchers, makes the sharing and development of research more difficult and the application of research findings more complicated. Many of the sources examined were not drawn from a primary school context, and conclusions are drawn on generalisations for other relevant data. Moreover, it is important to establish not only that there is a significant effect of a key parameter but also the size of its effect – the variance accounted for. The data are also limited in their failure to calculate the effect sizes of various modifications. Thus it is currently unclear, for example, what effect a reduction of sound level might have on test success (but see Shield and Dockrell 2008).

Interconnectedness and modelling

Current research does not address the way in which primary school spaces are interconnected and influence each other, how they are used pedagogically, or how they are managed and maintained. This has meant that a particular learning space has tended to be examined in isolation rather than in the context of the learning environment. Contemporary pedagogical priorities and perspectives, affecting how those spaces are used and managed for learning, also affect environmental variables. For example, having the whole school together in one space may affect local air quality and heating, and may modify the acoustic properties of the space being used. This may in turn affect the attention of pupils, their ability to distinguish what is being said and constrain their overall behaviour. Thus the spaces available may affect their pedagogical use and influence the environmental variables of the space. These relationships have yet to be examined from a research perspective.

User health and learning

The materials reviewed strongly suggest that the nature of school environments impacts on the health and well-being of pupils and staff. Interactions between health and learning exist if only because ill health often means non-attendance at school, and this has been used – in various forms – as a key outcome indicator. Previous work has focused on whether particular environmental factors, such as heating, affect learning in a direct manner. An alternative and potentially more productive approach would be to note that many small effects might, in the aggregate, have substantial effects on pupil and teacher health. The focus would then shift to the impact of multiple factors working together.

Where more than one factor has been examined, small effects can be combined and the wider impact, in terms of broader outcome indicators, evaluated. This allows a focus on learning to be explicit as learning opportunities that are missed inhibit and dissipate pupil-learning progress. It may also impact on the development of social relationships with other pupils through the missing of shared learning experiences and events. Re-integration into the school's broader learning activity as a community, on returning to school after illness, may also impose learning losses on the returning child as they seek to 'catch-up' with their peers.

At the same time, staff absence through illness has impacts on children's learning opportunities; for example, the effect of a cover teacher on class learning. Teacher health may be compromised by infections arising outside of school but may also be influenced by the health environment of the school, in the form of more generalised stress, as indicated in the current review. Reduced physical (and arguably, mental) well-being is also, as has been shown here, itself exacerbated by poor air quality, over- or under-heating and inadequate ventilation, poor acoustics, limited access to natural light and the opportunity to take in 'a view'.

High humidity levels may create the conditions in which airborne infections can be exchanged more readily, affecting the health of pupils and staff alike. If pupil behaviour is adverse this can impact on teacher stress, and precipitate increased teacher tiredness and absenteeism from school. For pupils with particular learning and behavioural needs and for those teaching them, additional and specific effects have been identified.

Current research has restricted itself to mainstream schools with a small amount of research focusing on special school environments. Learning in pupil-offsite units or pupil-referral units where pupils would, by the nature of their needs and behaviour, be more sensitive to managed environmental factors has not been considered.

Decision makers

Those responsible for specifying the nature and detail of school building designs (for example at the individual school governor or head teacher level) need access to the limited but detailed information identified in this chapter. A 'one-stop shop' could inform those making school design decisions and might prevent the difficulties that are occurring with the Building Schools for the Future programme (CABE). It is therefore suggested that one priority should be the dissemination of existing knowledge through a range of accessible outlets, both on paper and electronically-based. There is an equal need to examine the ways in which architects and those advising school projects are trained and informed about links between physical environment variables, school design, teacher and pupil health and pupil learning. Where the design task is the redevelopment of an existing school, close attention to collaboration with those involved in using the new school or refurbishment is clearly of paramount importance.

This chapter has suggested that single variables may contribute relatively small amounts towards an overall impact of the built environment on learning and health.

However it may be at the level of interactions between, say, light levels, acoustic properties and pupil attention and learning progress those significant environmental impacts occur. Current research has not explored these interactive effects in primary school environments. Researchers and policy makers should be wary of drawing conclusions derived from adult studies or studies in different environments and then relating them to educational settings: the needs of young children are different and they do not respond to key variables in the same way as adults. While it may be easier to access the impact of environmental variables on young pupils' learning and well-being, the research leading to such understandings has yet to be conducted and suggests another agenda for future research.

Research implications

This chapter has highlighted the need for further research in a wide number of areas. In summary it suggests the following requirements for future research:

In relation to multiple variables

- Research should focus on the learning impacts of more than one physical variable at a time (and their interactions) on pupil learning and teacher teaching activity.

In relation to school users

- Research should be informed by a developmental perspective, which acknowledges that children of different ages in the same school may be affected differently by the same physical variables.
- Research should note that adults of different ages working in the same school may also be affected in different ways by key environmental variables.

In relation to teacher practice

- Research should take account of how pedagogic practices involving this age group relate to aspects of the physical environment.
- Research should examine teacher practices in controlling the physical characteristics of the classroom space and how these may affect pupil learning and teachers' sense of being able to influence learning.

In relation to building management

- Research should examine the relationship between the management and maintenance of physical environmental variables and how users experience that environment.

In relation to research methodologies

- Research should report effect sizes for the results they obtain and use these to assess the implication of their results.
- Research should clarify and state the definition and extent of particular variables it uses and their relation to other measures of the same variable.

- Research should, with both children and adults, including teachers, use a broader range of explicitly defined outcome variables as indicators of environmental impact. These should include: concentration in class; tiredness; respiratory unease; dehydration; time off task; time off school; absenteeism.
- Research should seek to undertake multi-site, multi-season and longitudinal research rather than single case study research.
- Research should consider and work towards the needs of establishing more sophisticated modelling procedures for the way real learning environments function and vary during the school day, school term and school year.
- Research should model the alternative uses to which school buildings are actually put in relation to the management of a school site and its impact on the learning use of the same site.

In relation to the consultation for, design and construction of, new schools and upgrading work

- Research should focus on the process of *how* schools are designed interactively through working with the communities who use them and have an interest in what goes on in them.
- Research should examine the extent that post-occupancy evaluations (and other forms of user evaluation, after completion of building) inform design, particularly in schools of a similar design or in schools in a particular locality.

NOTES

1 Usually categorised by the DfES/DCSF census term 'behavioural, emotional and social difficulties'.
2 Dr Kate Wall.
3 Professor Bridget Shield contributed to the evaluation of the evidence presented here.
4 The notion of the 'temperature' of light can be confusing: what is perceived as being 'cool' – light with a high proportion of the blue end of the spectrum in its output – is actually indicative of a higher physical temperature ~4000 K. 'Warmer' perceived light is actually generated at lower physical temperatures, ~3000K (Knez 1995).

REFERENCES

Ahman, M., Lundin, A., Musabasic, V. and Soderman, E. (2000) 'Improved health after intervention in a school with moisture problems', *Indoor Air* 10: 57–62.

Ahrentzen, S. and Evans, G.W. (1984) 'Distraction, privacy and classroom design', *Environment and Behaviour* 16(4): 437–54.

Alexander, R.J. (2001) *Culture and Pedagogy: international comparisons in primary education.* Oxford: Blackwell Publishing.

American National Standards Institute (ANSI) (2002) *ANSI Standard S12.60-Acoustical Performance Criteria Design Requirements and Guidelines for Schools.* Washington: ANSI.

Banbury, S. and Berry, D.C. (1997) 'Habituation and dishabituation to speech and office noise', *Journal of Experimental Psychology: Applied* 3(3): 1–16.

——(1998) 'Disruption of office-related tasks by speech and office noise', *British Journal of Psychology* 89: 499–517.

Barnitt, H. (2003) 'Lighting for the future', *Building Services Journal: the magazine for the CIBSE* 25(1): 38–39.

Bayer, C.W., Hendry, R.J., Crow, S.A. and Fischer, J.C. (2002) 'The relationship between humidity and indoor air quality in schools', *Proceedings of Indoor Air 2002*, The Ninth International Conference on Indoor Air Quality and Climate: Monterey, CA.

BCSE (2007) 'British Council for School Environments'. Online (Available: http://www.bcse.uk.net/menu.asp, accessed 01 May 2007).

Beaman, C.P. (2005) 'Irrelevant sound effects amongst younger and older adults: objective findings and subjective insights', *European Journal of Cognitive Psychology* 17: 241–65.

BECTA (2007) *Emerging Technologies for Learning* pages. Online (Available: http://partners.becta.org.uk/index.php?section=rh&catcode=_re_rp_ap_03&rid = 11380, accessed 18 April 2007).

Beisteiner, A. and Coley, D.A. (2002) 'Carbon dioxide levels and summertime ventilation rates in UK schools', *International Journal of Ventilation* 1(3): 181–88.

Benya, J.R. (2001) *Lighting for schools*. Washington DC: National Clearinghouse for Educational Facilities. Online (Available: http://www.edfacilities.org/pubs/lighting.html., accessed 09 January 2007).

Bess, F.H., Dodd-Murphy, J. and Parker, R.A. (1998) 'Children with minimal sensorineural hearing loss: prevalence, educational performance, and functional status', *Ear and Hearing* 19(5): 339–54.

Board of Education Consultative Committee (1931) *Report of the Consultative Committee on the Primary School* (the Hadow Report). London: HMSO.

Boyce, P.R. (2003) *Human Factors in Lighting* (2nd edition). London: Taylor and Francis.

——(2004) 'Reviews of technical reports on daylight and productivity'. Online (Available: http://www.lrc.rpi.edu/programs/daylighting/pdf/BoyceHMGReview.pdf, accessed 02 April 2007).

Boyce, P.R., Hunter, C. and Howlett, O. (2003) *The Benefits of Daylight through Windows*. Online (Available: http://www.lrc.rpi.edu/programs/daylighting/pdf/DaylightBenefits.pdf, accessed 02 April 2007).

Bradley, J.S. (1986) 'Speech intelligibility studies in classrooms', *Journal of the Acoustical Society of America* 80(3): 846–54.

Bradley, J.S., Reich, R.D. and Norcross, S.G. (1999) 'On the combined effects of signal-to-noise ratio and room acoustics on speech intelligibility', *Journal of the Acoustical Society of America* 106: 1820–29.

Bradlow, A.R., Krauss, N. and Hayes, E. (2003) 'Speaking clearly for children with learning disabilities: sentence perception in noise', *Journal of Speech Language and Hearing Research* 46(1): 80–97.

Brainard, G.C., Hanifin, J.P., Greeson, J.M., Bryne, B., Glickman, G., Gerner, E. and Rollage, M.D. (2001) 'Action spectrum for melatonin regulation in humans: evidence for a novel circadian photoreceptor', *Journal of Neuroscience* 21(16): 6405–12.

BRE (2002) *The National Noise Incidence Study 2000 (England and Wales)*. London: BRE.

Breier, J.L. (2002) 'Dissociation of sensitivity and response bias in children with attention deficit/hyperactivity disorder during central auditory masking', *Neuropsychology* 16: 28–34.

Bronzaft, A.L. and McCarthy, D.P. (1975) 'The effect of elevated train noise on reading ability', *Environment and Behaviour* 7(4): 517–27.

Buckley, J., Schneider, M. and Shang, Yi. (2004) 'The effects of school facility quality on teacher retention in urban school districts'. Online (Available: http://www.edfacilities.org/pub, accessed 03 February 2007).

Central Advisory Council for Education (CACE) (1967) *Children and Their Primary Schools: a report of the Central Advisory Council for Education (England)* (the Plowden Report). London: HMSO.

Canning, D. and Peacey, N. (1998) 'A sound education', *Education Journal* 27: 28–30.

Carskadon, M.A., Wolfson, A.R., Acebo, C., Tzischinsky, O. and Seifer, R. (1998) 'Adolescent sleep patterns, circadian timing and sleepiness at a transition to early school days', *Sleep* 21(8): 871–81.

Cash, C.S. (1993) 'Building condition and student achievement and behaviour', unpublished doctoral dissertation. Blacksberg, VA.: Virginia Polytechnic Institute and State University.

Clark, H. (2002) *The Role of the Physical Environment in Enhancing Teaching and Research.* London: Institute of Education, University of London.

Cohen, S., Evans, G.W., Krantz, D.S., Stokols, D. and Kelly, S. (1981) 'Aircraft noise and children: longitudinal and cross-sectional evidence on adaptation to noise and the effectiveness of noise abatement', *Journal of Personality and Social Psychology* 40(2): 331–45.

Coley, D.A. and Beisteiner, A. (2002) 'Carbon dioxide levels and ventilation rates in schools', *International Journal of Ventilation* 1(1): 45–52.

Coley, D.A. and Greaves, R. (2004) 'The effect of low ventilation rates on the cognitive function of a primary school class', *International Journal of Ventilation* 6(2): 107–12.

Cooper, I. (1985) 'Teachers' assessments of primary school buildings: the role of the physical environment in education', *British Educational Research Journal* 11(3): 253–69.

Corcoran, T.B., Walker, L.J. and White, J.L. (1988) *Working in Urban Schools.* Washington DC: Institute for Educational Leadership (ED299356).

Corsi, R.L., Torres, V.M., Sanders, M. and Kinney, K.A. (2002) 'Carbon dioxide levels and dynamics in elementary schools: results of the TESIAS Study', *Proceedings of Indoor Air 2002,* The Ninth International Conference on Indoor Air Quality and Climate: Monterey, CA.

Crandell, C.C. (1993) 'Speech recognition in noise by children with minimal degrees of sensorineural hearing loss', *Ear and Hearing* 14(3): 210–16.

Crawford, N.G. (1998) 'Going straight to the source', *American School and University* 70(6): 26–28.

DCSF (2007a) *Every Child Matters: primary capital programme – primary strategy for change.* London: DCSF.

——(2007b) *The Children's Plan: building brighter futures.* London: HMSO.

DES/Welsh Office (DES/WO) (1977) *A Study of School Building: report by an inter-departmental group.* London: HMSO.

Desforges, C. and Abouchaar, A. (2003) *The Impact of Parental Involvement, Parental Support and Family Education on Pupil Achievement and Adjustment: a literature review,* DfES Research Report 433. London: HMSO.

DfEE (1995) *Disability Discrimination Act 1995 (c. 50).* London: The Stationery Office (TSO).

——(1999) *Building Bulletin 90.* London: HMSO.

——(2003) *Building Bulletin 93 – Acoustic Design in Schools.* London: HMSO.

Department for Education and Skills (DfES) (2001) *Special Educational Needs and Disability Act 2001.* London: The Stationery Office.

DfES (2003a) *Building Schools for the Future: consultation on a new approach to capital investment.* London: DfES.

——(2003b) *Building Bulletin 87.* London: HMSO.

——(2004a) *Every Child Matters.* London: HMSO.

——(2004b) *School Building and Design Unit.* London: TSO.

——(2005) *Disability Discrimination Act 2005.* London: TSO.

——(2006a) *Building Bulletin 99–Briefing Framework for Primary School Projects* (2nd edition). London: TSO.

——(2006b) *Every Child Matters: primary capital programme, building schools at the heart of the community.* London: TSO.

——(2006c) *Schools and Pupils in England, January 2006* (DfES Statistical First Release, Ref: 38/2006).

Department of Education, Training and Youth Affairs (Australia) (2001) *Building Better Outcomes: the impact of school infrastructure on student outcomes and behavior.* Australia: Department of Education, Training and Youth Affairs (Australia).

Dockrell, J.E. and Shield, B.M. (2004) 'Children's perceptions of their acoustic environment at school and at home', *Journal of the Acoustical Society of America* 115(6): 2964–73.

——(2006) 'Acoustical barriers in classrooms: the impact of noise on performance in the classroom', *British Educational Research Journal* 32(3): 509–25.

Dockrell, J.E., Shield, B.M. and Rigby, K. (2004) 'Acoustic guidelines and teacher strategies for optimizing learning conditions in classrooms for children with hearing problems', in D. Fabry and C. DeConde Johnson (Eds) *Proceedings of the First International Conference. ACCESS: Achieving Clear Communication Employing Sound Solutions– 2003*: 217–29. Chicago, IL: Phonak.

Douglas, D. and Gifford, R. (2001) 'Evaluation of the physical classroom by students and professors: a lens model approach', *Educational Research* 43(3): 295–309.

Dudek, M. (2000) *Architecture of Schools: the new learning environments.* London: Architectural Press.

Dunn, R., Krimsky, J.S., Murray, J.B. and Quinn, P.J. (1985) 'Light up their lives: a review of research on the effects of lighting on children's achievement and behavior', *Reading Teacher* 38 (9): 863–69.

Earthman, G.I. (2004) 'Prioritization of 31 criteria for school building adequacy'. Online (Available: http://www.schoolfunding.info/policy/facilities/ACLUfacilities_report1–04.pdf, accessed 09 January 2007).

Elliott, E.M. (2002) 'The irrelevant speech effect and children. Theoretical implications of developmental change', *Memory and Cognition* 30: 478–87.

Engelbrecht, K. (2003) 'The impact of colour on learning', online. (Available: http://web.archive. org/web/20040218065036/http://www.merchandisemart.com/neocon/NeoConConfPro/W305.pdf, accessed 15 February 2007).

Evans, G.W., Hygge, S. and Bullinger, M. (1995) 'Chronic noise and psychological stress', *Psychological Science* 6: 333–38.

Fenton, T.R., Alley, G.R. and Smith, K. (1974) 'Effects of white noise on short-term memory of learning disabled boys', *Perceptual and Motor Skills* 39: 903–6.

Gifford, R. (1994) 'Scientific evidence for claims about full spectrum lamps: past and future', in J. Veitch (Ed) *Full Spectrum Lighting Effects on Performance, Mood and Health* (IRC Internal Report No. 659). Ottawa, Canada: Institute for Research on Construction.

Haines, M.M. and Stansfield, S.A. (2000) 'Measuring annoyance and health in child social surveys', *Inter-Noise 2000* (29th International Congress and Exhibition on Noise Control Engineering, 27–30 August). Nice, Italy.

Haines, M.M., Stansfield, S.A., Brentall, S., Head, J., Berry, B., Jiggins, M. and Hygge, S. (2001a) 'West London schools study: the effects of chronic aircraft noise exposure on child health', *Psychological Medicine* 31: 1385–96.

Haines, M.M., Stansfield, S.A., Job, R.F.S., Berglund, B. and Head, J. (2001b) 'A follow-up study of effects of chronic aircraft noise exposure on child stress responses and cognition', *International Journal of Epidemiology* 30: 839–45.

——(2001c) 'Chronic aircraft noise exposure, stress responses, mental health and cognitive performance in school', *Psychological Medicine* 31(2): 265–77.

Harner, D. (1974) 'Effects of thermal environment on learning skills', *The Educational Facility Planner* 12(2): 4–6.

Hathaway, W.E. (1994) 'Non-visual effects of classroom lighting on children', *Educational Facility Planner* 32(3): 12–16.

Hayhow, D. (1995) 'The physical environment in primary schools and successful differentiation: impressions from a development project', *Schools' Special Educational Needs Policy Pack: discussion papers.* London: National Children's Bureau.

Heschong-Mahone Group (1999) *Daylighting in Schools: an investigation into the relationship between daylighting and human performance.* Fair Oaks, CA: Herschong-Mahone Group.

——(2001) *Daylighting in Schools: re-analysis report*, Technical Report P500-503-082-A-3. Sacramento, CA: California Energy Commission.

——(2003a) *Re-analysis Report: daylighting in schools, additional analysis.* Sacramento, CA: California Energy Commission

——(2003b) *Windows and Classrooms: a study of student performance and the indoor environment*, P500-503-082-A-7. Fair Oaks, CA: Herschong-Mahone Group.

Heuer, A.T., Kleinsorge, T., Klein, W. and Kohlisch, O. (2004) 'Total sleep deprivation increases the costs of shifting between simple cognitive tasks', *Acta Psychologia (Amsterdam)* 117(1): 29–64.

Higgins, S., Hall, E., Wall, K., Woolner, P. and McCaughey, C. (2005) *The Impact of School Environments: a literature review.* Newcastle: Design Council.

Hodgson, M. (2002) 'Rating, ranking, and understanding acoustical quality in university classrooms', *Journal of the Acoustical Society of America* 112(2): 568–75.

Hughes, R.W. and Jones, D.M. (2001) 'The intrusiveness of sound; laboratory findings and their implications for noise abatement', *Noise and Health* 13: 35–74.

Hygge, S., Evans, G.W. and Bullinger, M. (1996) 'The Munich Airport noise study: cognitive effects on children from before to after the change over of airports', *Proceedings of Inter-Noise 1996*: 2189–92.

Hygge, S. and Knez, I. (2001) 'Effects of noise and indoor lighting on cognitive performance and self-reported affect', *Journal of Environmental Psychology* 21(3): 291–99.

Jago, E. and Tanner, K. (1999) *Influence of the School Facility on Student Achievement: lighting.* Department of Educational Leadership: University of Georgia.

Jewett, M., Rimmer, D.W., Duffy, J.F., Klerman, E.B., Kronauer, R. and Czeisler, C.A. (1997) 'Human circadian pacemaker is sensitive to light throughout subjective day without evidence of transients', *American Journal of Physiology*: 273. (RI1800-RI1809).

Johansson, C.R. (1983) 'Effects of low intensity, continuous, and intermittent noise on mental performance and writing pressure of children with different intelligence and personality characteristics', *Ergonomics* 26(3): 275–88.

Johnson, C.E. (2000) 'Children's phoneme identification in reverberation and noise', *Journal of Speech, Language and Hearing Research* 43: 144–57.

Jones, D.M., Madden, C. and Miles, C. (1992) 'Privileged access by irrelevant speech to short-term memory: the role of changing state', *Quarterly Journal of Experimental Psychology* 44A: 549–669.

Karpen, D. (1993) 'Full spectrum polarized lighting: an option for light therapy boxes', Paper presented at the 101st Annual Convention of the American Psychological Association, Toronto.

Kemper, A.R., Bruckman, D. and Freed, G.L. (2004) 'Prevalence and distribution of corrective lenses among school-age children', *Optometry and Visual Science* 81(1): 1–7.

Kennedy, M. (2001) 'Into thin air', *American School and University* 73(6): 32.

Khouw, N. (1995) 'The meaning of color for gender'. Online (Available: http://www.colormatters.com/khouw.html, accessed 02 February 2007).

Kim, J-J. and Wineman, J. (2005) 'Are windows and views really better? A quantitative analysis of the economic and psychological value of views'. Online (Available: http://www.lrc.rpi.edu/programs/daylighting/pdf/viewreport1.pdf, accessed 02 April 2007).

Kimmel, P., Dartsch, P., Hildenbrand, S., Wodarz, R. and Schmahl, F. (2000) 'Pupils' and teachers' health disorders after renovation of classrooms in a primary school', *Gesundheitswesen* 62(12): 660–64.

King, J. and Marans, R.W. (1979) *The Physical Environment and the Learning Process*, Report number 320-ST2. Ann Arbor, MI: University of Michigan Architectural Research Laboratory. (Ed177739).

Knez, I. (1995) 'Effects of indoor lighting on mood and cognition', *Journal of Environmental Psychology* 15(1): 39–51.

——(2001) 'Effects of colour of light on non-visual psychological processes', *Journal of Environmental Psychology* 21(3): 201–8.

Knez, I. and Hygge, S. (2002) 'Irrelevant speech and indoor lighting: effects on cognitive performance and self-reported affect', *Applied Cognitive Psychology* 16: 709–18.

Knez, I. and Kers, C. (2000) 'Effects of indoor lighting, gender and age on mood and cognitive performance', *Environment and Behaviour* 32(6): 817–31.

Kuller, R. and Lindsten, C. (1992) 'Health and behavior in classrooms with and without windows', *Journal of Environmental Psychology* 12: 305–17.

Lackney, J.A. (1999) *Assessing School Facilities for Learning/Assessing the Impact of the Physical Environment on the Educational Process.* Mississippi State, MS: Educational Design Institute.

Larson, C.T. (1965) *The Effects of Windowless Classrooms on Elementary School Children.* Ann Arbor, MI: Architectural Research Laboratory, Department of Architecture, University of Michigan.

Lasky, E. and Tobin, H. (1973) 'Linguistic and nonlinguistic competing message effects', *Journal of Learning Disabilities* 6: 243–50.

Lee, S.C. and Chang, M. (2000) 'Indoor and outdoor air quality investigation at schools in Hong Kong', *Chemosphere* 42: 109–13.

Lemasters, L.K. (1997) *A Synthesis of Studies Pertaining to Facilities, Student Achievement and Student Behavior*. Blacksburg, VA: Virginia Polytechnic and State University.

Leslie, R. and Hartleb, S. (1990) 'Some effects of sequential experience of windows on human response', *Journal of the Illumination Engineering Society* Winter: 91–99.

Lowe, J.M. (1990) *The Interface Between Educational Facilities and Learning Climate in Three Elementary Schools*. Unpublished dissertation. College Station, TX: Texas A&M University.

Lowe, R. (2007) 'The development of educational policy', Paper to the Victorian Society Conference, *Learning from the Past: The Future of Historic School Buildings*.

Lundquist, P., Holmberg, K. and Landstrom, U. (2000) 'Annoyance and effects on work from environmental noise at school', *Noise and Health* 2(8): 39–46.

Maclure, S. (1984) *Educational Development and School Building*. London: Longman Group Ltd.

Masser, A., Sorensen, P., Kryter, K.D. and Lukas, J.S. (1978) 'Effects of intrusive sound on classroom behavior: data from a successful lawsuit', Paper presented at *Western Psychological Association*, San Francisco, California.

Maxwell, L.E. (2000) 'A safe and welcoming school: what student, teachers and parents think', *Journal of Architectural Planning Research* 17(4): 271–82.

Maxwell, L. and Evans, G. (2000) 'The effects of noise on pre-school children's pre-reading skills', *Journal of Environmental Psychology* 20(1): 91–97.

Mayo, L., Florentine, M. and Buus, S. (1997) 'Age of secondary language acquisition and perception of speech in noise', *Journal of Speech, Language and Hearing Research* 40: 686–93.

McGuffey, C. (1982) 'Facilities', in H. Walberg (Ed) *Improving Educational Standards and Productivity*, Berkley, CA: McCutchan Publishing Co., Chapter 10.

McIntrye, I.M., Normal, T.R., Burrows, G.D. and Armstrong, S.M. (1989a) 'Human melatonin suppression by light is intensity dependent', *Journal of Pineal Research* 6(2): 149–56.

——(1989b) 'Quantal melatonin suppression by exposure to low intensity light in man', *Life Science* 45(4): 327–32.

McIntyre, M.H. (2006) 'A literature review of the social and economic impact of architecture and design', in *Scottish Executive Social Research*. Edinburgh: Information and Analytical Services Division, Scottish Executive Education Department.

Mendell, M.J. and Heath, G.A. (2003) *Do Indoor Environments in Schools Influence Student Performance: a review of the literature*. Indoor Health and Productivity Project. Berkley, CA: University of California.

Moore, D.P. and Warner, E. (1998) *Where Children Learn: the effects of facilities on student achievement*. Scottsdale, AZ: Council of Educational Facility Planners International.

Myhrvoid, A.N., Olsen, E. and Lauridsen, O. (1996) 'Indoor environment in schools: pupils' health and performance in regard to CO_2 concentrations', *Indoor Air 1996. The Seventh International Conference on Indoor Air Quality and Climate, International Academy of Indoor Air Sciences* 4: 369–71.

Nabelek, A.K. (1992) 'Communication in noisy and reverberant environments', in G. Studebaker and I. Hochberg (Eds) *Acoustical Factors Affecting Hearing Aid Performance*. Boston, MA: Allyn and Bacon: 15–28.

National Commission on Education (1993) *Learning to Succeed: a radical look at education today and a strategy for the future*. London: Heinemann.

——(1996) *Success Against the Odds: effective schooling in disadvantaged areas*. London: Routledge.

NHS (2006) 'General ophthalmic services: statistical bulletin–ophthalmic statistics for England 1996–97 to 2005–6', in *Information Centre for National Statistics*: National Statistics Office.

National Research Council of the National Academies, USA (NRCNA) (2007) *Green Schools: attributes for health and learning*. Washington DC: National Academies Press.

Nelson, P.B. (2003) 'Sound in the classroom–why children need quiet', *ASHRAE Journal* February: 22–25.

Nelson, P.B. and Soli, S. (2000) 'Acoustical barriers to learning: children at risk in every classroom', *Language, Speech and Hearing in Schools* 31(4): 356–61.

Nober, L.W. and Nober, E.H. (1975) 'Auditory discrimination of learning disabled children in quiet and classroom noise', *Journal of Learning Disabilities* 8(10): 656–59.

Ou, L., Luo, M.R., Woodcock, A. and Wright, A. (2004) 'A study of colour emotion and colour preference: colour emotions for single colours', *Colour Research and Application* 29(3): 232–40.

Patel, M. (2007) Paper to the Victorian Society Conference, *Learning from the Past: The Future of Historic School Buildings.*

Pearson, E. (1975) *School Building and Educational Change.* Paris: OECD.

Pile, J.F. (1997) *Color in Interior Design.* New York: McGraw-Hill.

PriceWaterhouseCoopers (PwC) (2001) *Building Performance: an empirical assessment for the relationship between schools' capital investment and pupil performance.* Research Report 242. London: DfEE.

Radeloff, D.J. (1990) 'Role of colour in perception of attractiveness', *Perceptual and Motor Skills* 71: 151–60.

Rea, M.S. (Ed) (2000) *IESNA Lighting Handbook: reference and application.* 9th Edition. New York: Illuminating Engineering Society of North America.

Rea, M.S. and Ouellette, M.J (1991) 'Relative visual performance: a basis for application', *Light Research Technology* 23(3): 135–44.

Rea, M.S., Figueiro, M.G. and Bullough, J.D. (2002) 'Circadian photobiology: an emerging framework for lighting practice and research', *Light Research Technology* 34(3): 177–90.

Rea, M.S., Ouellette, M.J. and Kennedy, M.E. (1985) 'Lighting and task parameters affecting posture, performance and subjective ratings', *Journal of the Illuminating Engineering Society* 15(1): 231–38.

Read, M., Sugawara, A.I. and Brandt, J.A. (1999) 'Impact of space and colour in the physical environment on pre-school children's cooperative behavior', *Environment and Behaviour* 31(3): 413–28.

Reid, K.J. and Zee, P.C. (2004) 'Circadian rhythm disorders', *Seminars in Neurology* 24(3): 315–25.

Rosen, K.G. and Richardson, G. (1999) 'Would removing indoor air particulates in children's environments reduce the rate of absenteeism? A hypothesis', *The Science of the Total Environment* 234: 87–93.

Rosenstein, L.D. (1985) 'Effect of colour of the environmental task performance and mood of males and females with high and low scores on the Scholastic Aptitude Test', *Perceptual and Motor Skills* 60: 550–59.

Rosenthal, N. (1998) *Winter Blues. Seasonal Affective Disorder. What it is and how to overcome it.* London: Guildford Press.

Rosenthal, N., Sack, D., Parry, B., Mendelsom, W., Tamarkin, L. and Wehr, T. (1985) 'Seasonal affective disorder and phototherapy', *Annals of the New York Academy of Sciences* 453: 260–68.

Rusak, B., Eskes, G.A., and Shaw, S.R. (1997) *Lighting and Human Health: a review of the literature.* Ottawa: Canada Mortgage and Housing Corporation.

Rutter, M., Maughan, B., Mortimore, P. and Ouston, J. (1979) *Fifteen Thousand Hours: secondary schools and their effects on children.* London: Open Books.

Saint, A. (1987) *Towards a Social Architecture: the role of school-building in post-war England.* New Haven and London: Yale University Press.

Schneider, M. (2002) 'Do school facilities affect academic outcomes?', National Clearinghouse for Educational Facilities. Online (Available: http://www.edfacilities.org/pubs/outcomes.pdf, accessed 11 January 2007).

——(2003) 'Linking school facility conditions to teacher satisfaction and success'. Online (Available: http://www.edfacilities.org/pubs/teachersurvey.pdf, accessed 11 January 2007).

Shield, B.M. and Dockrell, J.E. (2002) 'The effects of environmental noise on child academic attainments', *Proceedings of the Institute of Acoustics* 24(6).

——(2004) 'External and internal noise surveys of London primary schools', *Journal of the Acoustical Society of America* 115(2): 730–38.

——(2008) 'The effects of environmental and classroom noise on the academic attainments of primary school children', *Journal of the Acoustical Society of America* 123(1): 133–44.

Smaldino, J.J. and Crandell, C.C. (2000) 'Classroom amplification technology: theory and practice', *Language – Speech and Hearing Services in Schools* 31(4): 371–75.

Smedje, G. and Norback, D. (2001) 'Irritants and allergens at school in relation to furnishings and cleaning', *Indoor Air* 11: 127–33.

Spencer, D.E. (2003) 'Narrative luminous ceilings in the twenty first century. Non-imaging optics: maximum efficiency: light transfer V11', *Proceedings of the Society of Photo-Optical Instrumentation Engineers* 03–04, San Diego, CA.

Steer Committee Report (2005) *Learning Behaviour: the report of the practitioners' group on school behaviour and discipline, chaired by Sir Alan Steer*. DfES, London: HMSO.

Steinkamp, M.W. (1980) 'Relationships between environmental distractions and task performance of hyperactive and normal children', *Journal of Learning Disabilities* 13(4): 209–14.

Stevenson, K. (2001) *The Relationship of School Facilities Conditions to Selected Student Academic Outcomes*. South Carolina: Education Oversight Committee.

Sundstrom, E. (1986) *Work Places: the psychology of the physical environment in offices and factories*. Cambridge: Cambridge University Press.

——(1987) 'Work environments: offices and factories', in D. Stokols and I. Altman (Eds) *Handbook of Environmental Psychology*: 733–82. New York: Wiley.

Tanner, C.K. and Langford, A. (2002) 'The importance of interior design elements as they relate to student outcomes', online. (Available: http://www.coe.uga.edu/sdpl/research/SDPLStudiesInProgress/criann02elem.html, accessed 02.01.07).

Taylor, N.S. (2002) *Children's Eyesight Study: vision screening in schools*. London: Guide Dogs.

Tremblay, S., Nicholls, A.P., Alford, D. and Jones, D.M. (2000) 'The irrelevant sound effect: does speech play a special role?', *Journal of Experimental Psychology – Learning Memory and Cognition* 26(6): 1750–54.

Veitch, J.A. (1997) 'Revisiting the performance and mood effects of information about lighting and fluorescent lamps type', *Journal of Environmental Psychology* 17(3): 253–62.

Vernon, S., Lundblad, B. and Hellstrom, A.L. (2003) 'Children's experiences of school toilets present a risk to physical and psychological health', *Child Care Health Development* 29(1): 47–53.

Visser, J. (2001) 'Aspects of physical provision for pupils with emotional and behavioural difficulties', *Support for Learning* 16(2): 64–68.

Walinder, R., Norback, D., Wieslander, G., Smedje, G. and Erwall, C. (1997) 'Nasal mucosal swelling in relation to low air exchange rate in schools', in *Indoor Air '96. The Seventh International Conference on Indoor Air Quality and Climate, International Academy of Indoor Air Sciences*. 2: 198–205.

Ward, C. (1976) *British School Buildings: designs and appraisals 1964–74*. London: Architectural Press.

Wargocki, P., Wyon, D.P., Baik, Y.K., Clausen, G. and Fanger, P.O. (1999) 'Perceived air quality, SBS-symptoms and productivity in an office at two pollution loads', in *Indoor Air '99. The Eighth International Conference on Indoor Air Quality and Climate, International Academy of Indoor Air Sciences*. 2: 107–12.

Weale, R.A. (1963) *The Ageing Eye*. London: HK Lewis and Company.

——(1992) *The Senescence of Human Vision*. Oxford: Oxford University Press.

Weinstein, C.S. (1979) 'The physical environment of the school: a review of the research', *Review of Educational Research* 29(4): 577–610.

Wyon, D.P. (1991) 'The ergonomics of healthy buildings: overcoming barriers to productivity', in *IAQ'91: Post Conference Proceedings.* Atlanta, GA: American Society of Heating, Refrigerating and Air-Conditioning Engineers Inc. 43–46.

Young, E., Green, H.A., Roehrich-Patrick, L., Joseph, L. and Gibson, T. (2003) *Do k-12 School Facilities Affect Education Outcomes?* Tennessee: The Tennessee Advisory Commission on Intergovernmental Relations.

Part 7

Teaching in primary schools

Training, development and workforce reform

Continuing our exploration of the implications of recent research on primary teaching and teachers, the three chapters in this section examine research on the professional environment of primary schooling in the context of major changes over the past two decades in initial teacher education (ITE), teachers' continuing professional development (CPD), school leadership and workforce reform, all of which have had inevitable and often critical consequences for how teachers see themselves and how they are viewed by the public. Indeed, changing professional perceptions and status as well as professional practice was an explicit goal of many of the reforms. Inevitably, therefore, the surveys in this section discuss the balance of cost and benefit, judged in both educational and professional terms, of recent government interventions in the activities of those who work of primary schools.

No less inevitably, the picture conveyed by the considerable range of evidence surveyed for these three surveys is mixed, as during any period of transition it is bound to be. Thus, on the basis of its inspections, Ofsted records greatly improved standards of initial teacher training, especially in relation to government priorities, and talks of 'the best trained generation of teachers ever'; but other studies find that vital aspects of the primary teacher's work have been squeezed out, even supposing that Ofsted's claim is empirically sustainable, which it is not. The streamlining of CPD has effectively focused professional attention on the requirements of the national literacy and numeracy strategies; but it has not always served the needs of teachers with different skill levels and at different stages of their careers. Workforce reform initiatives are generally welcomed, though there are concerns about sustainability. Some studies report primary teachers feeling de-professionalised and de-skilled; others view this as an over-simplification when younger teachers are positive and enthusiastic and many of their more experienced colleagues successfully resist attempts to make them fit a particular professional mould.

The surveys here are a response to some of the remit questions for Cambridge Primary Review Theme 6, *Settings and Professionals:*

- How well are teachers and other professionals involved in this age-range trained?
- How effectively are they deployed?
- How well is their development supported at school, local and national levels?
- How can the nation secure and retain the best professionals for this phase of education?

- What balance of expertise, and of teachers, assistants and other para-professionals, should schools contain and how should they be used?
- What are the conditions for their success?
- What are the future workforce needs of the phase as a whole?
- How can these be met?

Primary Schools: the professional environment, by Liz Jones, Andy Pickard and Ian Stronach (Chapter 23), reviews research on the nature and changing character of professionalism in English primary schools, concentrating on the role of the primary teacher, and on developments in primary school leadership and management, placing these in the context of policy since 1988. The survey uncovers evidence of tensions between primary teachers' professional aspirations and beliefs and the assumptions and imperatives of policy over the past two decades, with a consequent perceived loss of professional autonomy and creativity; but it also detects considerable variation in teachers' responses to these, and signs of a return to a more open professional culture. Covering a period of rapid and substantial change as it does, the survey suggests that the period from 1988–2008 offers important lessons for both policy-makers and teachers in the handling of reform.

Primary Teachers: initial teacher education, continuing professional development and school leadership development, by Olwen McNamara, Rosemary Webb and Mark Brundrett (Chapter 24), moves from professional roles and identities to professional learning, training and development. The survey tracks initial teacher education (ITE) reforms since 1984, the point at which government sought to systemise provision and increase central regulation, control and monitoring with the establishment of CATE (1984–94), TTA (1994–2005) and, currently, TDA. It charts a shift in the focus of continuing professional development (CPD) from the needs and aspirations of individual teachers to the addressing of government priorities, noting problems posed by the new arrangements both logistically and in the way they may neglect broader and no less significant aspects of professional learning. Centralisation of ideas and provision is also the theme of research in the third area, school leadership. Overall, however, the report notes evidence of significant and innovative practice in the three areas surveyed, and improvements in professional quality as judged by Ofsted.

In *Primary Workforce Management and Reform* (Chapter 25), Hilary Burgess shows how the last twenty years have seen a profound change in the way primary schools have been managed and organised, alongside a fundamental restructuring of the professional school workforce. These changes have created both controversy and debate among policy makers, teachers and educational researchers. The chapter provides an overview of the impact of policies upon professional workforce management, reform and support and assesses recent developments in England and Wales and elsewhere in the UK. A brief comparison with the USA then offers an international context for understanding key issues that impact upon teachers and other professionals in primary schools.

Reforming the workforce

'Overall,' concludes Hilary Burgess in Chapter 25, 'the view from head teachers, teachers and teaching assistants on workforce reform in schools is supportive, although there are concerns about sustainability ... Teachers have been positive about the introduction of Planning and Preparation Time (PPA) and the increased deployment of teaching assistants in schools ... Teachers now view teaching assistants as crucial to their effective teaching [and] assistants [are] on the whole broadly satisfied with their role ... Evaluation of the Primary Leadership Programme found [that] pupil attainment at Key Stage 2 was improving, there were improvements in data analysis ... changes in teaching style ... [and] a stronger sense of team work ... Problems have been created through the speed at which the reform of the workforce agenda has been pushed out to schools. There are still issues to resolve such as the impact upon pupil learning, the impact upon school management and the linking with a wide range of external services.'

Reforming initial teacher training and CPD

McNamara, Webb and Brundrett (Chapter 24) report that the successes of the post-1984 training reforms must be set against adverse consequences for children as well as teachers: 'The last 25 years have seen a period of sustained and increasingly radical reforms to ITE as successive governments have progressively increased prescription and control through the regulation of courses, curriculum content and the assessment of standards ... The result has been to improve standards and increase the quality and preparedness of newly qualified teachers, as measured by the Ofsted inspection framework ... but leave little time for previously key aspects of curricular and professional learning such as non-core subjects [and] render peripheral many important debates about ITE ... In the "new professionalism" ... participation in CPD is recognised as important, albeit with the predominant purpose of equipping teachers to implement government reforms ... Teachers' access to CPD is constrained by lack of time, heavy workload, cost and distance from training opportunities [and] overemphasis on meeting system needs to the detriment of the career and development needs of individual teachers ... Leadership development activity has moved through phases of ad hoc provision under the aegis of LEAs ... to the development of national programmes for head teachers ... and the formation of a National College of School Leadership ... This has been a significant achievement but has raised concerns that ... the leadership development framework has too great an emphasis on standards-based approaches ... [and that] the structure is too detailed, prescriptive and detailed and is subject to manipulation by central government'.

A profession in transition

In Chapter 23, Stronach, Pickard and Jones assess the evidence for the claim, familiar during the 1980s but voiced with increasing frequency after 1997, that the Government's educational and professional reforms had eroded to excess the freedom of judgement and action on which claims to professional status usually depend. 'Commitment, morale and status all feed into perceptions of [professional] autonomy ... Across the research literature there is a preponderance of studies that point to the de-skilling of the primary teacher ... The National Curriculum decreased teacher autonomy in relation to content, the National Literacy Strategy and National Numeracy Strategy likewise in relation to pedagogy. Teachers were reported to be "proletarianised", de-professionalised, de-skilled and sometimes demoralised.'

This at the time was the prevailing view. 'But,' the authors continue, 'this bleak picture had exceptions. Younger teachers were much more likely to be positive about the job;

levels of enthusiasm were generally high amongst newly-qualified teachers, although teacher retention rates in urban areas remained a concern. In addition, not all teachers succumbed to government micro-management of their work ... On balance, we find that the claimed de-professionalisation of teachers is an over-simplification ... There needs to be a slower, more deliberative and consultative context of policy development ... The relation of research to policy and practice needs to be linked more systematically and enduringly to deep issues concerning learning and motivation, rather than tied to the evaluation of ephemeral initiatives in a naïve kind of "what works" rationale. Innovation is too often a matter of ill-considered policy borrowing. Research needs to consider not just outcomes within a rubric of effectiveness and efficiency but also the slower and deeper emergence of enduring excellence in classrooms and schools.'

As with the chapters on teaching, it is pertinent to draw attention to those other surveys in this collection which attend to the professional and organisational contexts of primary education. For example:

- the relationship between children's lives outside and inside school (Chapter 3);
- the relationship of teachers to parents and carers (Chapter 4);
- the relationship of schools to other agencies, especially in relation to *Every Child Matters* (Chapter 8) and children with special educational needs (Chapter 9);
- the relationship between the work of schools and the frameworks of national legislation, policy and strategy in which that work is set: Chapters 14, 15 and 10 on statutory requirements for ages, stages, aims and the curriculum; Chapters 17–19 on standards and testing; Chapters 26 and 27 (next section) on governance, funding and inspection; Chapters 17, 18 and (next section) 29 on the impact of the government educational reforms of 1988–2008.

23 Primary schools

The professional environment

Ian Stronach, Andy Pickard and Liz Jones

INTRODUCTION

The authors of this chapter for the Cambridge Primary Review were charged with presenting an assessment of the current state of the professional environment of the English primary school. We decided to overview the salient issues, and then to identify a number of central themes whose understanding seemed to us to be of central importance. It was clear also that sustained empirical research of life inside primary schools, or indeed any schools, of the kind published in the 1980s heyday of ethnographical sociology is now limited. We found that what empirical studies did exist had also become more theoretically impoverished over the years. Atheoretical and simplistically evaluational approaches tend to dominate contemporary academic published writing. This is not to deny that there is significant and critical work being done by the likes of Pollard and Alexander (see, for example, Pollard and Triggs 2001 and, in the international comparative field, Alexander 2001). Nevertheless, there seem to be large enclaves of sponsored research that did not seem able or willing to contest critically the realities of contemporary schooling.

Against this general backdrop, therefore, we have chosen to focus on two major themes in particular: teacher professionalism and the leadership of primary schools. Both, we would argue, dominate the recent history, current debate and future practices of primary schools. In that sense they provide a means of enculating the complexity of the contemporary professional environment of primary schools in a wholly dominant way. In addition, professionalism and leadership are central to the nexus between policy and practice in so far as primary teachers' and their co-workers' capacity to be or to become professional, and the capacity of head teachers to deliver change in primary schools, has been the crucible into which policy has been poured.

Our own position on policy in primary education is broadly this: policy in this sector has been as bedevilled by a combination of 'moral panics' and 'policy hysteria' as elsewhere in education and beyond. There have been too many initiatives; too much short-term response to media engendered scares, involving ever shortening cycles of reform, multiple innovations, frequent policy shifts, an increasing tendency for reforms to become symbolic in nature, a scapegoating of systems, professional and client groups, shifting meanings within the central vocabulary of reforms, an erosion of professional discretion, and untested and untestable success claims (Stronach and Morris 1994). These features were already present when the current government came to power in 1997 but they seem to have become a permanent feature of contemporary modernisation by New Labour. They relate to similar practices and theories developed in the US in relation to business philosophies and practices; hence our emphasis here on 'leadership styles'. Strang and Macy (2001), in their quantitative study of the Quality Control movement, write of 'fad theory'. They identify the following features of fads: a potentially extensive incubation period where a few firms utilise the innovation; a take-off period when popularity rises explosively; a short period of ascendancy marked by high levels of innovation usage; a period of rapid decline leading to a low equilibrium level of usage. Then, of course, the next fad comes along and the process is repeated. Particularly relevant to this chapter is Strang and Macy's finding that 'an artificial world of actors preoccupied with performance via success stories is a world of fad-like waves of adoption and abandonment' (2001: 162). They found that 'fadlike vicissitudes are most robust *not* when innovations are worthless but when they have identifiable but modest merit' [their emphasis] (*ibid.*: 172). It is precisely policy of possibly 'modest merit' which we would argue has disordered notions of professionalism and leadership within the primary sector, and it is that process which dominates this review of the professional environment of primary schools.

THE NATURE OF PROFESSIONALISM IN PRIMARY SCHOOLS

Our starting point is that the professional environment of primary schools cannot be understood without reference to the professional identities of the teachers and others who work in those schools, and their professionalism cannot be understood without at least some reference to the intense debate which now surrounds the issue of teacher professionalism. Thus this section of our chapter sets out to review some of the major parameters of the writing and research on teacher professionalism and to try to see where primary teachers sit within those configurations.

Issues of teacher professionalism and teacher professional identity are now evident in much research literature emerging from the USA, the UK and Australia. Recent educational reforms, and associated changes in working conditions and professional expectations, have meant that the issues of teacher professionalism and professional identity are being contested at the level of both policy and practice (Sachs 2001). Moreover, these contestations take place against an historical backdrop of doubts about the professional status of teachers, especially those working in primary schools or in an earlier era, elementary schools. As Katz somewhat cynically noted a generation ago, 'Few professionals talk as much about being professionals as those whose professional stature is in doubt'. (Katz, in Etzioni 1969, cited in Stronach *et al.* 2002: 109).

These long-standing debates about teacher professionalism have intensified in recent years as what counts as teacher professionalism has become the site of a struggle between various interest groups. Some would argue that it is in the best interests of government for teaching not to be seen as a profession, as it gives greater opportunity for regulative control of the (non-) profession. Others would suggest that, given the specialised knowledge base of teachers, the increased demands for professional standards and the greater demands for teachers to see themselves as knowledge workers, they have earned the status of being a profession in a more orthodox sense (Sachs 2001). Undoubtedly the extent of direct government intervention into the classroom has complicated teachers' own view of their profession as being about doing 'good in society' (Stronach *et al.* 2002). It is not just that professionalism implies a degree of autonomy and independent judgement, but that the 'goodness' of government policy itself can be contested. What can, for the politician, be a commitment to raising standards can, for their critics, be the imposition of a narrow, traditional curriculum.

PROFESSIONAL BINARIES AND BEYOND

Sachs (2001) identifies three paradoxes in relation to current teacher professionalism. Firstly, the call for greater professionalism is occurring at a time when there is evidence that teachers are being deskilled and their work intensified. Secondly, while it is acknowledged that classrooms are becoming ever more demanding places, fewer resources per capita are being put into teacher education either in its initial or post qualification form. Thirdly, the teaching profession is exhorted to be autonomous while at the same time it is under increasing pressure from politicians and the community to be more accountable and to raise standards. These paradoxes, we would argue, have produced an academic literature which constructs binary oppositions in the ways in which teacher professionalism can be understood. The dominant thesis is one of 'proletarianisation' (Ball 1990; Maguire and Ball 1994; Ozga 2000; Avis 2003). As a consequence of policy reform, teachers have experienced an intensification of workload with an emphasis on technical competence and performativity. Centralising reforms have been represented as giving greater freedom but are actually acting to deregulate and then re-regulate, a process which Du Gay and Hall (1996) term controlled de-control. Within this context teachers are represented and encouraged to think of themselves as enterprising neoliberals (Walkerdine 2003), yet they are managed according to an ideology of professionalism which has the effect of de- and then re-professionalising them (Ozga and Lawn 1981).

In contrast with these rather gloomy appraisals, Dawson (1994) has drawn upon on an older Aristotelian version of the virtuous person to emphasise the continued opportunities for teachers to exercise professional autonomy, rooted in the collective values of the profession. Here there is an echo of what might be described as the traditional view of a profession.

Dawson sees this as an 'inside out' professionalism to be distinguished from the 'outside in' professionalism. The latter refers to the policy and accountability impositions, the former to the ethical codes teachers have culturally created for themselves. Dawson argues that imposed codes can never be sufficiently comprehensive to drive out inside/out professionalism. Teachers will continue to identify with their own sense of what is ethically and educationally appropriate for their pupils.

Stronach *et al.* (2002) have developed this 'inside/out – outside/in' concept still further. They are critical of the ways in which professionalism has been deployed in the literature, arguing that the term is both a reduction and an inflation in that teachers (and nurses too) are 'victims' destined to deliver others' prescriptions, and agents for social good. Thus analyses of professionalism become caught in a series of simple polarities: state control versus professional autonomy; traditional versus progressive; art versus science; and audit culture versus collective values and solidarities. The narratives which emerge from such analyses display similar polarising qualities – de-professionalisation or redemption. Their own analysis turns away from the fixidity of such accounts into something altogether more fluid, more plastic, more dynamic, arguing for a more 'fissiparous emplotment' which keeps tensions and movement in play (Stronach *et al.* 2002: 114). They do this by 'reframing/unframing' professionalism ontologically (as an expression of an oscillating liberal self), as politically conflictual, as a symbolic hybrid of past and present, and as resistant to universalistic, essentialist and reductionist accounts.

The data they produce on the basis of this deconstruction of the theories of professionalism emphasise the ways in which teachers 'juggle' between professional goals, vocational commitments, and collectivist and external pressures, including the press for corporate identities. They characterise these as 'ecologies of practice' on the one hand, and 'economies of performance' on the other, but they resist the notion of a professional resolution of these dilemmas common to other accounts of professionalism. For them there is an inevitability about outside/in colonisation of educational discourses but there is an inevitability too in teachers' inside/out capacities to ridicule and ignore their school and classroom manifestations. Teachers work in an in-between world and that is to be encouraged and supported.

What these accounts of teacher professionalism tend to have in common is an indifference to the specific location of teachers within the system. There is little attempt to distinguish between primary and secondary teachers. Instead they are presented as a rather amorphous mass, subjected to the same external pressures and with the same opportunities for accommodation and resistance. This is somewhat surprising given that the timing and form of media- and government-led critiques of the values, practices and achievements of teachers have varied between sectors. Secondary teachers stand charged with, variously, inflating A-level grades, encouraging course work at the expense of examinations, neglecting Key Stage 3, and preferring to teach subjects at the expense of relevant vocational skills. Meanwhile primary teachers have favoured progressive teaching methods over more traditional ones, have adopted wrong approaches to the teaching of reading and mathematics, and have generally failed the nation by neglecting 'basics'.

It may be that at times the virulence of these onslaughts overwhelms distinctions between the professionalism of primary and secondary teachers. The level of prescription is such that the shared sense of crisis around teaching is more significant than age range differences. Certainly a recent review of teacher status using questionnaire, interview and media survey data suggested that there are only marginal differences between the status afforded to secondary and primary teachers, respectively (Hargreaves *et al.* 2006). Such was the finding from recent public opinion surveys (Everton *et al.* 2007). Linda Hargreaves found, in research conducted in 2006, however, that 48 per cent of her sample regarded secondary teachers as having superior status (Hargreaves *et al.* 2007): a judgement that was supported from within the profession, and also extended to the differential perceived status of secondary as opposed to primary head teachers. Status is not synonymous with professionalism, being concerned with occupational ranking. Nevertheless, the two concepts are linked in that status is likely to be afforded to those occupational groups who are perceived to display ethical qualities, linked to rigorous training and a demanding knowledge base. The research findings suggested secondary head teacher occupational status was marginally higher than that of primary head teachers (8th and 10th, respectively in a list of sixteen). Similarly, secondary teachers were ranked 12th and primary teachers 14th. In terms of occupational esteem (a measure of what occupational groups are deemed to deserve rather than their 'real' position), there was a similar differential with secondary head teachers moving to 3rd, primary head teachers to 4th, secondary teachers to 6th, and primary teachers to 7th. Possibly these differences reflect the higher regard for the professionalism of secondary teachers over that of their primary colleagues. The report authors, however, argue the opposite, seeing their findings as evidence of the erosion of the traditionally greater regard for secondary teachers. This in turn reinforces the implication of the literature on professionalism that teachers' sense of professional identity, including any feelings of crisis, is common to both our secondary and primary schools.

The research report also contains other findings of relevance to this chapter. On the whole, the general public afforded more status to teachers than teachers did themselves. This was especially true of parents, who tend to have a high regard for the profession. Neither the quality nor the popular press give space to teacher status, but the former provides coverage of employment issues and government targets while the latter focuses on teachers' personal lives, especially if they appear before the courts. Teachers themselves have a complex view of their own status. On the whole they believe that their status was at its lowest in the 1980s and that there may have been some recovery in recent years. Most significant of all was the difference between the attitudes of teacher trainees and recently qualified teachers, who were among the most positive of all respondents to the researchers, and long-serving teachers who were the most pessimistic group when it came to teacher status. It is possible to speculate on the basis of this research, therefore, that a school with a high proportion of newish teachers, which offers places to teacher training students and has close relationships with its parents, will have a different professional ethos from a school without these features.

It is tempting to extend the previous point to argue that children in a school with a staff with a robust and positive sense of their own professionalism will benefit educationally. While this seems not unrealistic, research into primary education warns against such simplistic reductionism. Robin Alexander (1990: 72) argues that discourses within the primary world are as 'problematic as communication between the inhabitants of that world and those outside it'. Discourses within primary schools tend to be oral, pragmatic, contingent, nuanced, and alert to the affective dimension. This contrasts with the language of academia and policy makers, which is typically written, apparently coherent and above all powerful. Again, there is a bifurcation in the professional languages of primary teachers. Alexander refers to their *public* representation of their world of the primary school as 'primaryspeak'. He contrasts the slogans and shibboleths of 'primaryspeak' with the more nuanced and dilemma-conscious private conversations of primary teachers where feelings matter – their own as well as the children's – where subtlety and realism puncture the notions of one-size-fits-all 'good primary practice'. Here Alexander draws on the classic Argyris and Schön distinction between 'espoused theory' and 'theory in use' (Alexander 1995).

Alexander's representation of the primary school is consistent with the views of teacher professionalism as set out by Stronach *et al.* (2002) and examined above. They replace the 'indefensible unitary construct' of professionalism with teachers as inevitably and invariably encountering dilemmas which are themselves a source of motivation. Ambiguity and uncertainty is at the heart of professional identity, with recollections of good teachers and good pupils; the pressured individual; the subject specialist; the kind of person as well as teacher the individual wants to be; the socialised apprentice; the coerced innovator; the convinced professional; the professional critic; and the sceptical pragmatist as 'shards' in which teachers can see themselves.

How then do these differing but inherently plural discourses contrast in ways of 'seeing' teachers and teaching measure up against the somewhat limited number of texts dealing with professionalism among those working with younger children? It is a genre which is dominated by the early years, which is hardly surprising given how recent policy initiatives (notably Every Child Matters, Sure Start and the commitment to 'professionalise' teaching assistants) have had their greatest impact on the early years sector.

As with the 'parent' genre of teacher professionalism in general, analysis is dominated by a sense of external control and loss of professional independence. Thus, like teachers everywhere, early years practitioners increasingly have to wrestle with demands for accountability, performativity and standardised approaches to their practice. This pronounced movement towards centralised control and prescription is seen as posing a potential threat to professional autonomy and morale (Mahony and Hextall 2001). Moreover, early years practitioners face these challenges from a position of some weakness in that the diverse nature of provision in the sector encourages practitioners to behave in diverse and isolated ways. There is a lack of unified identity or shared belief in themselves as a 'professional' group that is made especially difficult when faced, Osgood argues, with an exercise of power which is largely 'invisible'. This power is exercised through policy, workforce reform, constant surveillance and the normalisation of 'good' practice in ways so sophisticated and abstract that challenge or even negotiation becomes very difficult. Thus, Osgood (2006) argues, in a quest to conform to dominant constructions of professionalism, practitioners become regulated and controlled by disciplinary technologies of the self.

As if this was not enough for early years practitioners to face, Osgood (2004, 2005) also draws attention to the masculinist undertones of neo-liberalism and the economic rationale behind policy reforms in the early years. In recent policy reforms, the UK government has continued to state its intentions for early years practitioners to operate in entrepreneurial ways and to adopt commercial approaches to the management of provision (Sure Start Unit 2004). For Osgood, this neo-liberal discourse marginalises the ethic of care of central significance to early years practitioners, replacing it with a constructed professionalism which emphasises rationality, competitiveness, and individualism. Beliefs, it seems, no longer matter: it is output that counts, although teachers seek to hold onto the knowledge being displaced by the new orthodoxy. Interestingly, Osgood also suggests that this is not entirely a one-way street. The government itself has a fear of early years practitioners, whom it sees as hyper-feminine and therefore unmanageable, unquantifiable and hence impossible for the state to regulate. This, of course, has not prevented it from trying to do so.

As we move closer to the professional ethos of primary schools, therefore, albeit by riding on the back of early years, it seems that teachers in the sector have experienced the same state-led challenges to their professional identities as teachers elsewhere. The prescriptions offered are also familiar. Osgood (2005) calls for resistance to the regulatory gaze by reasserting the ethic of care and emotional labour, acknowledging the unique nature and complexity of the work of early years practitioners in order to establish a different kind of professionalism. However it may be that, given the analyses offered by Stronach *et al.* (2002) and Alexander's (1990) account of the complex nature of primary schools, both discussed earlier, a less cataclysmic and confrontational version of primary professionalism might be appropriate. Francis (2001) certainly advocates a new agency model for early years practitioners which sees professional identities as negotiated, ambiguous and shifting in accordance with personal experience, beliefs and values, and includes aspirations about the kind of professional the individual wants to be.

It is clear from this survey of the evidence that the professional ethos of primary schools in the recent past has been dominated by the government's project to reconstruct primary teachers in a form which is amenable to the need to demonstrate that an investment in education brings economic and social returns. Whilst teachers might not disagree with the policy ends, they have sometimes disagreed with the means – and the ways in which these means redefine teacher professional identities. Nevertheless, their rejection has never been total. Some aspects of policy and coerced change have been welcomed, and certainly the opportunities for professional diversity are sometimes welcomed.

Most accounts of these processes recognise the importance of primary school management to the tensions which surround the complexity of professionalism. Sachs (2001) sees professional identity as being shaped by the competing discourses of democratic professionalism and managerialist professionalism. The latter has been developed and mandated by the state on the basis of two claims: that efficient management can solve any problem; and that practices which are appropriate for the conduct of private sector enterprises can also be applied to the public sector. The former has been advocated, among others, by Apple (1996), who sees the alternative to state control not as traditional professionalism but as a democratic professionalism which seeks to demystify professional work and build alliances between teachers and excluded constituencies of children and their communities. How the leaders of primary schools respond to these competing possibilities is what follows in this chapter.

THE NATURE OF LEADERSHIP WITHIN THE ORGANISATION OF PRIMARY SCHOOLS

We begin by citing a former Secretary of State:

> The grit in the oyster ... is leadership. We need leadership at all levels – from the top of schools to every teacher and every member of the school team ... in helping every pupil get the best out of their time at school.
>
> (Charles Clarke 2002)

The statement carries important implications. The choice of the word 'leadership' rather than 'management' carries with it ideological and practical baggage, which reflects much of the contemporary positioning on primary school headship and its consequent impact on the school environment. It also implies some distinction between management and leadership that is ripe with the same kinds of polarities we have discussed in relationship to the wider issue of professionalism. It also accepts as given that leadership is a generic issue: whether the leader is a primary or secondary head, they are the 'grit'.

More immediately the statement raises questions of a meaning kind: just what is 'gritty' about being a leader within the context of primary schooling? Does leadership have to involve traits that might be associated with 'grittiness' including, for example, determination, tenacity, courage, fortitude and bravery? And what kind of pearl is embedded within an expression such as 'the best out of their time at school?' In this section we want to prize open the construct of leadership and, in so doing, detail why it is that that it seems characterised by the same polarities examined in the previous section. Thus, on the one hand, a Minister for Education not only reveres it but perceives it as key to a school's success (see also Mortimer *et al.* 1988; Fullan and Stiegelbauer 1991; Southworth 1998) whilst on the other, it seems that we are currently experiencing a 'leadership crisis' (see Hartle and Thomas 2003; NCSL 2004) where deputy heads are reluctant to apply for promotion (Hayes 2005).

As Gronn (2003) indicates, the field's understanding of 'leadership' is grounded in highly dubious and problematic assumptions – a concern shared by Hopkins who notes that commentators tend to ' ... conflate their own views about what leadership should be with their descriptions of what leadership actually is and fail to discipline either position by reference to empirical research' (2003: 57). So whilst the literature might well be problematic – a point we shall return to subsequently – this has not impeded its growth. Indeed Simkins describes it as an 'explosion of leadership literature' (2005: 9) and one, moreover, that in recent times has been considerably driven by the school effectiveness and school improvement agendas.

Educational leadership is surrounded by the same need to unscramble the intersections between language, policy and practice as the broader discussion of professionalism. The language is mostly opaque, and meaning rarely stands still long enough to clarify either policy or practice. Indeed the term 'leadership' has been adopted relatively recently. In the early 1980s educational 'administration' was the well-worn vocabulary, so terms such as 'educational leadership' and 'school leadership' were much more muted than is the case at present (Gronn 2003). For us a key question is what changes, if anything, when commentators begin to privilege words such as 'leader', 'leading' and 'leadership' as discursive modes for representing reality, instead of previously favoured terminology such as 'manager', 'management' and so forth? Some commentators have queried whether anything is gained by differentiating between 'leaders' and 'managers'. Nicholls (2002), for example, proposes that formal position-holders are employed as managers and that members of this cadre who manifest the behaviour typically associated with leadership need simply to be thought of as more high profile managers than their peers.

Others do want to claim a distinction. Southworth, for example, identifies leadership as being ' ... about behaviour; it is action orientated, and it is about improving the quality of what we do' (1988: 8). Leadership, therefore, requires having vision so as to establish goals, and additionally having the capacity to work with colleagues so as to secure these – particularly that of children learning. Within this model, effective delegation is key (Dean 1990). Meanwhile, management ' ... is about keeping the organisation going. Leadership is about ensuring the organisation – the school – is going somewhere' (Southworth 1998: 8). For Terry, leadership is the activity of 'influencing people to strive willingly for group goals' (Terry, cited in Smith and Piele 1996: 2; see also Lawlor and Sills 1999).

As we have noted, contemporary literature on educational leadership focuses on effectiveness, improvement and change (see, for example, Bennett *et al.* 2003; Harris *et al.* 2003; Riley and Seashore 2000; Gronn 2003). In this context the head teacher's leadership is commonly emphasised as 'crucial' (Sammons 1999; Chemers and Reezigt 1996; Harris *et al.* 1997; Mortimer 1998; Stoll and Fink 1996; Fullan 1993). It is highlighted as a means for securing sustainable school improvement. Hall and Southworth (1997), in discussing primary headship, make a historical distinction between manifestations pre- and post-1988. The pre-period is framed by centralisation, heads as central and pivotal figures in school who had also exercised hegemony over general school policy. They refer to Coulson (1985), who argued that power and influence were seen as personal and individual in primary schools.

If one examines a version of the role of head teacher as outlined in DfEE/DfES/DCSF documentation (for example, DfEE 1994) then its possible to discern how, from a governmental perspective at least, there are clear overlaps between the two locations of 'leader' and 'manager'. Thus the head's duties include actions that might be associated with 'leadership', including for example formulating the overall aims of the school. One can also see how other duties, including the appointment of staff, might well fit into the leader's vision. Other responsibilities are couched in language that is associated with management speak, including for example *reviewing* the work and organisation of the school, culminating in *strategic planning*; *evaluating* teaching and learning; *supervising* and *appraising* teachers in terms of *performance management*; as well as *accounting* for financial and material resources of the school (Osborn *et al.* 2000). Some commentators have identified how successful leadership also seems dependent on traits such as 'flexibility', 'willingness to take risks' and 'effective relationships,' all of which might be summarised as 'grit' (Caldwell and Spinks 1998: 31).

Different dimensions and concepts of 'leadership' have emerged so as to respond to different sets of interest. For example: transformational leadership and transactional leadership (see Leithwood, Leonard and Seashore 1999; Silins 1994; Hallinger and Heck 1996; Gronn 1999); 'post-transformational' leadership (Day *et al.* 2000); moral leadership (Sergiovanni 1992); instructional/pedagogical leadership (see Stalhammer 1994; Hopkins *et al.* 2003); and also leadership in relation to learning organisations and organisational learning (see Leithwood, Leonard and Seashore 1999; Leithwood and Seashore 1998; Dixon and Ross 1999).

We, however, are concerned with whether such studies have the capacity to provide insights into the actual practices that occur within the kaleidoscopic life of primary schools. As Heck and Hallinger note, there is a need to 'separate what moves the field intellectually from what continues to spin it in ideological or methodological circles' (2005: 239). Moreover, as terms, both 'leadership' and 'management' can mask or even render invisible other explanatory factors, including individual predispositions, the inherent nature of tasks, workplace processes and the kinds of relationships that are possible. To lead infers that others will follow. As such, leaders are constructed as causal agents of work outcomes. Alternative perspectives on the role, however, might be to begin the analysis at the opposite or rear end where the task would involve combing back through the range of explanatory possibilities of which leadership may (or may not) turn out to be just one. As inferred above, Southworth's (1998, 2004) research edges towards this – particularly where he focuses on the influence of school size and context on head teacher leadership. Additionally Grace (1995), Day *et al.* (2000) and Webb (2005) explore 'leadership' from the perspectives not only of head teachers but also of those within the school, but these aside there appear to be 'only a few studies which have increased our understanding of leadership in English primary schools' (Webb, 2005: 69).

CHANGING TIMES, CHANGING STYLES: BASH STREET KIDS, PLOWDEN'S CHILD, KEY STAGE CHILDREN AND EVERY CHILD MATTERS

In Figure 23.1 we have tried to summarise how significant shifts in educational policy have in turn provided the conduit along which various performances of leadership could be enacted.

Given such a map there might well be a temptation to 'read' the period from the mid-1940s through to the onset of the 1980s with rose-tinted spectacles, where a binary could be constructed between 'educative leadership' and 'instructional leadership' with the former being valorised over the latter. We are cautious of doing this, recognising that labels such as 'consensus', 'exemplary' and 'working relations' are not benign and that their presumed smoothness can work at concealing how traits such as manipulation and compliance might well be active (Gronn 2002, 2003). Moreover, as Webb

Policy document or phase	Implications for leadership
1944–1980 **1967 Plowden Report** • Child-centredness and learning by discovery • DES, LEAs and schools as partners. Change introduced by headteachers was evolutionary, involving serialised developments	• Consensus as a core principle. Each party could offer advice. Change through agreement. • Head teachers as 'educative leaders' involved in teaching and direct working relations with children and class teachers • Heads required to be 'exemplary' teachers
1986 Education Act • Surveillance and regulation operating both outside of and within schools • Marketisation of education	• Increased parental and community representation on governing bodies • Governors given power to modify the LEAs' curriculum policies to meet the needs of individual schools plus limited control of school budget • Governors accountable to parents through an annual report presented at an annual meeting
1988 Education Reform Act (ERA) • 'The Child' no longer referred to per se ; primary schools segmented into Key Stages 1 and 2 • Introduction of school league tables. • Cooperation replaced by competition.	• Increased responsibilities of governing bodies • Schools assume responsibilities for own budgets • Governors establish staffing levels • Governors could take school out of LEA control by applying for grant-maintained status
1988 The National Curriculum (NC) • Structural solutions through top–down regulations • Emphasis on systems, procedures and tasks to promote the efficient running of the school	• Emphasised the importance of curriculum management for all staff • Emphasised monitoring, reviewing and evaluating pupil performance • Placed the curriculum at the centre of management activity • 'Instructional leadership' seen as way to achieve compliance with government reforms • Raised question of whether NC stifled teachers' creativity and constrained school innovation.

Figure 23.1   Shifts in educational policy and implications for leadership.

1992–1994	
• Continuing emphasis on systems, procedures and tasks to promote the efficient running of the school • Ofsted inspections work at ensuring compliance – 'strong leadership provides clear educational direction for the work of the school'. • 'Performativity discourse' of assessment prevalent	• Only a minority of head teachers in other than small schools retain a regular teaching commitment • Curriculum leadership role delegated to deputy heads, senior management teams (SMTs) and curriculum co-ordinators
2003 The Primary Strategy (DfES 2003). • Standards for qualified teacher status; • Induction standards for beginning teachers; • Standards for crossing the performance pay threshold; standards for advanced skills teachers; • National standards for headship	• Pedagogical leadership = creativity and innovation in teaching.
2006–7 *Every Child Matters* • The child and the family identified as key in terms of economic prosperity and social stability. Education in conjunction with other agencies (multi-professionalism) perceived as instrumental in securing the normalisation of children and their families.	

Figure 23.1 (continued)

(2005) reminds us, leadership is a value-laden concept and a range of factors will determine its interpretation by individuals. So, a head teacher's notion of leadership will be fashioned in part by historical expectations (see, for example, Hallinger 1992). In addition, the local community will also require certain kinds of leadership performances (see, for example, Day *et al.* 2000). So, presumably, the fictitious community in which the Bash Street kids were growing up might well have looked to the school to discipline their unruly offspring. But they might also have had hopes that their children might better themselves or, to return to our opening quotation, 'get the best' in terms of education; within the comic strip this is signified by the mortarboard, an emblem associated with a 'classical' or academic education.

It is interesting to note that the ideology embedded within the Plowden report (CACE 1967) has crucial similarities with that around which the current *Every Child Matters* agenda (DfES 2003a) is located. The much-quoted sentence, 'At the heart of the educational process lies the child' enculates both the tone and the intent of the

Plowden report. Similarly, as the terminology suggests within the *Every Child Matters* agenda, the young child (and her family) are perceived as central in determining not only that every child gets 'the best' out of schooling but additionally that this 'best' will also work at ensuring economic prosperity, culminating in the overall well-being of society.

Clearly the materialisation of both the aims of the Plowden report as well as those of the *Every Child Matters* agenda depended, and will depend, on a number of factors and, as we have implied, leadership might well be one of them. In terms of Plowden, the translation of its embedded ideology was for the most part undertaken where the favoured style of leadership was 'educative'. Attempts have been made above to identify the salient features of this particular discourse. Crucially, heads were more 'hands on' and so as a consequence were extremely well-placed to combine theory and practice where the 'realisation of an educational culture' was a real possibility (Grace 1995: 123). Alexander *et al.* (1992) are of a similar opinion when they note that, 'Actions speak louder than words and the head teachers' teaching can and must exemplify their vision of what the school might become' (p.48; see also NCSL 2003). But to talk of 'their vision' does carry with it first the implication that they did indeed have a vision, and second they had the capacity to share this vision with colleagues. In some respects there appears to be an expectation that heads could operate as 'exceptional leaders' where, as a consequence of individual deeds, sometimes perhaps of heroic proportions, a 'vision' of what a school might become could be materialised.

Currently 'exceptional leadership' (Thrupp and Willmott 2003) is part of the discourse of 'transformation' that is put to work in order to turn around organisations, including primary schools, who are in 'special measures' (that is to say, failing) so as to revitalise their performance in terms of set standards. In returning to the materialisation of the tenets of the Plowden report one can see how in order for these to become practice there would have had to have been a need for individually 'focused' leadership (Gabriel 1997). Exceptional focused leadership, besides having some strengths, carries certain weaknesses (Harris 2003). In terms of the latter, two unhelpful consequences can be identified. First, while highlighting the presumed superiority of leaders, the idea of 'exceptionalism' serves to residualise non-leaders as 'followers' and can consequently contribute towards a culture of dependency. A second and potentially more damaging consequence in terms of organisational capability is that exceptionalism creates strong incentives for individuals to disengage from the pursuit of career roles that carry with them expectations of leadership. That is, if organisation members learn to associate leadership with the kinds of superlative, larger than life behaviour displayed by their high profile managers, they began to feel emasculated or disempowered (Gronn 2002). Such consequences, both in terms of trying to implement the ideas embodied in Plowden as well as roll out the *Every Child Matters* agenda, were and will continue to be toxic.

So how do you get teachers to sign up to a 'vision'? Whether it is a vision that is influenced by Plowden, where children are 'learning by acquaintance' or whether it is where children are perceived within a salvation narrative as exemplified by the *Every Child Matters* discourse it seems imperative that this is a collective endeavour where notions of 'distributed leadership' operate (Harris 2003). Indeed, as the national standards for head teachers (DEE 1999) note, a head teacher needs to understand the expectations of the staff 'in order to secure their commitment to her vision' (Smith 2002: 25). But, significantly, Smith also points out that problems are likely to occur when it is the head teacher's vision of the school's goals that prevails, and in so doing negates interaction between staff where aims could be formulated together. But what are the consequences when visions are instigated from above rather than from within? In part the answer is the 'Key Stage' child.

The 'Key Stage' child: the radical reconfiguration of the organisation of primary schools and leadership

Above we have been able to make tenuous links between ideological conceptualisations of the child, as manifested in Plowden and within the *Every Child Matters* agenda. An identifiable missing link is the 'Key Stage child' who emerged in consequence of the 1988 Education Reform Act (ERA) and was fully fashioned within the terms of the National Curriculum (NC). 'Children' disappeared from the vocabulary of teachers to be replaced with the lexicon of 'Key Stage', where Key Stage 1 refers to the infant department and Key Stage 2 the juniors. To separate children into Key Stages is part of the overall apparatus of regulation and normalisation. The NC, with its prescribed content, is premised on the idea that learning is linear, where regular national testing of pupils is used as a measure of school and teacher effectiveness as well as pupil performance (Aubrey 2003).

The NC was part and parcel of the marketisation of education that was augmented by Thatcher's Conservative government. Besides transforming teaching and learning within the primary school it significantly altered leadership patterns. As observed by Grace (1995: 21) and further compounded by Figure 23.1, 'expectations in the role of the head-teacher have now moved substantially from the cultural and pedagogic sector to the marketing, financial and presentational sectors of schooling'. In effect, two dimensions – professional/educational and executive/managerial – have to be straddled, with some commentators seeing a dangerous emphasis on the latter (Dennison and Shenton 1990; Bottery 1988; Alexander 1992; Bell and Rhodes 1996).

The implementation of the NC centralised education. With its introduction, the realisation of government education policy became less reliant on leadership skills. Through a battery of performance management mechanisms, including the regular testing of children, the publication of tests results, plus Ofsted inspections, the compliance of teachers was secured. Effectively they were placed under a regulatory gaze and as a consequence were predisposed towards what Perryman describes as 'panoptic performativity' (2006: 150). The issue of whether teachers felt committed or otherwise to the NC was immaterial (Mahony and Hextall 2001). As Bottery notes, given such a scenario, head teachers in England 'must see themselves as strategists for implementing external directives and as monitors, evaluators and managers of teacher and pupil standards which are defined elsewhere' (Bottery 2001: 210, cited in Hatcher 2005).

Given the unprecedented scale of interventions that primary schools had to endure following the Educational Reform Act, involving what Fullan describes as 'large scale tinkering' (1993: 2), it is unsurprising that leadership patterns were adjusted. In general, heads, whilst acknowledging the value and importance of a curriculum leadership role as advocated by Alexander *et al.* (1992) and reiterated by the National College for School Leadership (NCSL), found that it – together with a regular teaching commitment – could not be managed within the plethora of administration (Webb and Vulliamy 1996). It is not too surprising therefore that delegation became a key leadership strategy.

Following the publication of the *School Teacher's Pay and Conditions of Employment* document (DfES 1994), the role of deputy heads was more closely defined with part of their brief being to formulate the aims and objectives of the school, establish policies through which these could be achieved, manage staff and resources, plus monitor pupil progress. This policy document also stressed the management role of all teachers where, as an instance, there was now an expectation that teachers would participate at curriculum meetings and be actively involved in the overall administration and management of the school. Additionally, senior management teams (SMTs) were evolved and by 1994 were part of schools' administrative and management fabric. Furthermore, in 1996 The National Professional Qualification for Headship was introduced by the Teacher Training Agency (TTA), which was followed in 1999 by the National Standards for Head teachers. These formed the basis for various leadership development programmes, including one for newly appointed head teachers, the Head teacher Leadership and Management Programme (HEADLAMP). Thrupp (2005) expresses a number of concerns about the introduction of national standards for head teachers, where as an instance it is felt that heads are becoming concerned that accreditation works at conformity and that there is little critical thinking in relation to what is being taught. These training programmes are now under the auspices of the National College of School Leadership. Below we offer further details about this organisation.

Whilst one can see how it became necessary to delegate, there still remained the question of actually realising the NC within schools and the part leadership played in this. Webb notes that 'instructional leadership' (Hopkins 2003), was 'found to be effective for bringing about change in line with government requirements' (Hopkins 2003: 85). But she further notes that, '… the pressure for conformity that it exerted fostered a school climate of fear and dependence on external guidance that stifled creativity'. However, for some teachers this notion of 'dependence' seems to have been reconfigured where there appears to be a clear sense of them welcoming the structure that the NC provides. Webb (2005), drawing on interviews with a small sample of primary teachers, identified that they perceived structures – including identifying learning goals as well as assessment techniques and recording pupil progress – as contributing towards 'improvements' in their teaching (p.73).

Despite the climate of fear, or maybe even because of it, 'instructional leadership' has been favoured first by the Conservative government and then by New Labour – and in both instances this is because it is closely associated with raising standards (Leithwood *et al.* 1999). 'Instructional leadership' draws strength from, and is supported by, 'high reliability' systems to achieve their goals of improvement in pupil attainment (Hopkins 2003). Examples of a high reliability structure include the National Literacy Strategy (DfEE 1998) and the National Numeracy Strategy (DfEE 1999).

Winds of change?

Blair's New Labour government was elected in 1997. Those who had hopes that there might be some degree of relaxation in terms of centralised control of education would remain disappointed. One of the administration's first steps in terms of education was to introduce the 'Framework for Teaching' (DfEE 1998), of which a central element was the National Literacy Strategy. Both this and the National Numeracy Strategy, which followed closely behind, were directed towards raising standards. It is beyond our brief to go into close detail about either of these strategies but what is important to stress is that for some commentators they were clearly perceived as further erosions of teacher autonomy and expertise. As Gillard remarks, ' ... [the] Education Reform Act imposed a sterile, content based National Curriculum ... [and] just when we all thought things could only get better, along came Tony Blair's New Labour administrations. With their literacy and numeracy strategies, they've gone even further than the Tories, telling teachers not only what to teach but how to teach it' (Gillard 2007: 4). Similar complaints were found in teachers' responses documented between 1990 and 1996 in the Primary Assessment Curriculum and Experience project (Osborn *et al.* 2000). Additionally, there were very real concerns that a heavy emphasis on the core subjects (literacy, numeracy and science) was to the detriment of subjects that included art, drama, music and ICT. Moreover, training programmes for teachers' continuing professional development (CPD) were also skewed towards core subjects, where, as Webb (2005) notes, CPD programmes were aimed to ' ... ensure that teachers assimilate the knowledge and skills developed externally and to train them in the adoption of prescribed best practice' (p.22).

It is striking that government policy in relation to the primary curriculum and pedagogy has involved a kind of state nationalisation of curriculum, assessment and pedagogy, most notably of course through the numeracy and literacy strategies, but also through displacements that the basic curriculum inevitably involved. At first accountability was rigorously addressed to the 'standards' achieved by schools, expressed as enumerations of SATs, Ofsted scores and so on. Such dirigisme, as we saw, altered teachers' sense of identity and professionalism, but it also resulted in a much more subtle phenomenon. The job became less fun for teachers and pupils alike. The remorseless pursuit of grades had unhealthy effects on other educational goals; the impact of these degradations took a few years but by 2001 Secretaries of State were beginning to talk a new language of 'creativity', of 'emotional intelligence', 'personalisation' and 'self esteem'. 'Standards' were still important but there had to be more flexibility and less 'bog standard'. The displaced curricula of the 1960s and 1970s therefore began to creep back, transformed in interesting ways to a more neo-liberal incentivisation of pupils that would ensure 'global effectiveness' – a concern that had reached all the way down to early years as well as all the way up through higher education via the 2003 White Paper (DfES 2003b).

In Webb's (2005) views these shifts, as outlined above, could be accommodated within 'pedagogical leadership' (Sergiovanni 1998), which is characterised by leaders working with teachers so as to achieve shared commitments. It is reliant on the leader's capacity to build relationships and foster feelings of trust. However, the contradiction between the proclaimed intention of greater freedom for teachers and the continuing, and in some cases even stricter apparatus of centralised control over them has been noted by a number of commentators. Alexander, for example, refers to 'the Strategy's doublespeak on professional autonomy' as 'an ambiguity of intent – a desire to be seen offering freedom while in reality maintaining control' (Alexander 2004: 15; see also Richards 2004).

SUMMARY

Recently, the concept of 'teacher leadership' has emerged in England (Muijs and Harris 2002; Frost and Durrant 2003; Day and Harris 2003). Elsewhere it is more familiar; in the USA and Canada, for example, 'teacher leadership' is an accepted form of leadership activity where it has been demonstrated that the forms of teacher leadership and teacher collaboration have contributed towards school improvement (Harris 2003). Similarly Møller *et al.* (2005) found that leadership in Norwegian schools is almost entirely characterised by collaboration and team effort.

Within the context of English primary schools, however, the construct of 'teacher leadership' appears beset with a number of difficulties. A significant factor hampering its development as a model of leadership is the difficulty of viewing teachers as leaders within a hierarchical school system where leadership responsibilities are clearly delineated. Additionally, within schools the social exchange theory of leadership still prevails. Here, leaders provide services to a group in exchange for the group's approval or compliance with the leader's demands. The maintenance of the leader's power and authority rests on his or her continuing ability to fulfil follower obligations. Certain variations of this theory argue that, by empowering their followers, leaders can increase their own power (Kouzes and Posner 1995). In this sense, the leadership process is one of facilitating the personal growth of individuals or groups, which in turn brings greater benefit to the leader. This does however beg the question, if teachers were to be leaders, who would follow? What would the nature of the social exchange be and where would be the benefits? (Harris 2003)

Arguably questions such as these, plus others of course, should be encompassed within the work of the NCSL. This was established in November 2000 and is generously funded by the DfES. It currently runs some twenty-four different school leadership programmes. In its short life it has become a 'major influence, arguably the major influence, on school leadership, management and administration in England and beyond' (Bush 2004: 243). There has been surprisingly little academic interrogation of the NCSL. Work that has been undertaken has included tracing its historical development, looking at its international role, considering its organisational features plus trying to assess its likely impact (see journal *Educational Management, Administration and Leadership* (EMAL) 2004). Whilst useful in their way, such studies have had a mutual tendency to view the NCSL as a largely beneficial development. Weindling (2004) has shown that by 2002 the NCSL was funding 50 per cent of the UK research on educational leadership. Since a number of the contributors to the EMAL journal are strongly linked to the NCSL, the rather benign picture of the NCSL they paint may have partly resulted from a form of nepotism (Thrupp 2005). Similarly it was identified that school leaders who were surveyed in 2001 felt that the NCSL 'needed to show its independence and demonstrate that it was not simply another arm of the government or more specifically the DfES' (Earley and Evans 2004: 336).

It would appear that, as we write, primary schools in general have the potential to develop leadership models that are engendered from within individual organisations whilst simultaneously responding to external expectations. Certainly within the literature for educational leadership the discussions are located around the 'art of leadership', where inspiration, vision, non-hierarchical relationships, shared decision-making (see Anderson 2002; Harris 2003), collegiality (see Campbell 1996) and moral leadership have become prerequisites for success. Here leaders are regarded as capable in managing several competing tensions and dilemmas, and are above all people-centred and also 'invitational' (Stoll and Fink 1996). Such a leader is more likely to an 'enabler' rather than a 'controller'. There is cooperation and alignment between the values and visions of a leader and a follower. Webb's small-scale study (2005) has indicated that there are a few heads who are both evolving and testing out 'pedagogical leadership'. So, whilst standards still have to be met and targets have to be achieved, such work is done where trust in teacher competence and faith in their professionalism to do the job are privileged.

Certainly as we write the notion of 'teacher compliance' is key. The Department for Children, Schools and Families, the National College for School Leadership and the majority of academic theorists of educational management and leadership share the view that the compliance of teachers is most effectively accomplished by securing their commitment. Indeed, Hallinger and Heck (2003) state that 'achieving results through others is the essence of leadership' (p.229) and that the role of the leader is to 'help others find and embrace new goals individually and collectively'. The favoured strategy in the most recent of school management discourses is the notion of 'distributed leadership'. It is, as Gross perceives it, 'an idea whose time has come' (2000: 333). Woods (2004) defines distributed leadership as an emergent property of a group or network of interacting individuals engaged in concerted action, creating a new organisational culture, based on trust rather than regulation, in which leadership is based on 'knowledge' as opposed to 'position'. Fullan affirms that 'strong institutions have many leaders at all levels' (Fullan 1993: 64) and, additionally, Harris (2003) makes the point that 'this mode of leadership challenges the conventional orthodoxy of the single, individualistic leader' (p.75). As a form of management, distributed leadership also promises a way of coping with the immense amount of information that is generated and circulated in modern societies, and of maximising chances of identifying the most relevant information and new knowledge and turning these to practical effect. In short, it empowers the many eyes, ears and brains in the organisation rather than the few (Woods 2004). For Gronn (2000), distributed agency is not the agency of individuals but 'structurally constrained conjoint agency, or the concertive labour performed between followers by pluralities of interdependent organization members' (p.28). Distributed leadership can take the form of spontaneous collaboration, role sharing or institutionalised means of working together such as a committee or team structures. As such, the distinction between leaders and followers is blurred where leadership is more appropriately understood as 'fluid and emergent rather than a fixed phenomenon' (Gronn 2000: 324). It reflects the view that every person, in one way or another, can demonstrate leadership (Goleman, McKee and Boyatzis 2002). This does not mean that everyone is a leader, or should be, but it opens up the possibility for a more democratic and collective form of leadership so that 'leadership is present in the flow of activities in which a set of organisation members find themselves enmeshed' (Gronn 2000: 331). As such, leadership can be separated from an individual, or their role or notions of status, and is primarily concerned with the relationships and the connections among individuals within a school (Harris 2003).

REFERENCES

Alexander, R.J. (1990) 'Core subjects and autumn leaves: the National Curriculum and the languages of primary education', in B. Moon (Ed) *New Curriculum – National Curriculum.* London: Hodder and Stoughton.

——(1992) *Policy and Practice in Primary Education.* London: Routledge.

——(1995) *Versions of Primary Education.* London: Routledge.

——(2001) *Culture and Pedagogy: international comparisons in primary education.* Oxford: Blackwell.

——(2004) 'Still no pedagogy? Principle, pragmatism and compliance in primary education', *Cambridge Journal of Education* 34(1): 7–33.

Alexander, R.J., Rose, A.J. and Woodhead, C. (1992) *Curriculum Organisation and Classroom Practice in Primary Schools: a discussion paper.* London: DES.

Anderson, K. (2002) *The Antecedents and Influences of Teacher Leadership in Schools. An unpublished doctorial dissertation.* Ontario Institute of Studies in Education: University of Toronto.

Apple, M. (1996) *Cultural Politics and Education.* Boston: Teachers College Press.

Aubrey, C. (2003) 'Implementing the foundation stage in reception classes', *Child Education*: 36–37.

Avis, J. (2003) *Work-based Knowledge, Evidence-informed Practice and Education.* London: Blackwell.

Ball, S. (1990) *Politics and Policy-Making in Education: explorations in policy sociology.* London: Routledge.

Bass, B. (1990) *A Handbook of Leadership: theory, research and managerial applications* (3rd edition). New York: The Free Press.

Bell, C. and Rhodes, C (1996) *The Skills of Primary School Management.* London: Routledge.

Bennett, N., Crawford, M. and Cartwright, M. (Eds) (2003) *Effective Educational Leadership.* London: Sage.

Bottery, M.P. (1988) 'Educational management and ethical critique', *Oxford Review of Education* 14(3): 341–51.

——(2001) 'Educational leadership and political realities', *Educational Management and Administration* 30(2): 157–74.

Bush, T. (2004) 'Editorial; The National College for School Leadership', *Educational Management, Administration and Leadership* 32(3): 243–49.

Central Advisory Council for Education (CACE) (1967) *Children and Their Primary Schools: a report of the Central Advisory Council for Education (England).* London: HMSO.

Caldwell, B.J. and Spinks, J.M. (1998) *Leading the Self-Managing School.* London: Falmer Press.

Campbell, R.J. (1996) 'The National Curriculum in primary schools: a dream at conception, a nightmare at delivery', in C. Chitty and B. Simon (Eds) *Education Answers Back.* London: Lawrence and Wisehart.

Chemers, B. and Reezigt, G. (1996) 'School level conditions effecting the effectiveness of instruction', *School Effectiveness and Improvement* 7(3): 197–228.

Clarke, C. (2002) Quoted in *Education Guardian*, Wednesday 30th October, 2002, www.guardian.co.uk

Coleman, M. (2002) *Women as Head teachers: striking the balance.* Stoke on Trent: Trentham.

Coulson, A. (1985) 'The managerial behaviour of primary school heads', *CORE* 9: 2.

Dawson, P. (1994) 'Professional codes of practice and ethical conduct', *Journal of Applied Philosophy* 11(2): 169–83.

Day, C. and Harris, A. (2003) 'Teacher leadership, reflective practice and school improvement', in K. Leithwood and P. Hallinger (Eds) *Second International Handbook of Educational Leadership and Administration.* Dordrecht: Kluwer Academic.

Day, C., Harris, A., Tolley, H., Hadfield, M. and Beresford, J. (2000) *Leading Schools in Times of Change.* Milton Keynes: Open University Press.

Dean, J. (1990) *Managing the Primary School.* London: Routledge.

Dennison, W.F. and Shenton, K. (1990) 'Training professional leaders: the new school managers', *Oxford Review of Education* 16(3): 311–20.

Department for Education and Employment (DfEE) (1994) *School Teachers' Pay and Conditions of Employment Document.* London: DfEE.

——(1998) *The National Literacy Strategy: framework for teaching literacy from Reception to Year 6.* London: DfEE.

——(1999a) *National Standards for Head Teachers.* London: DfEE.

——(1999b) *The National Numeracy Strategy: framework for teaching mathematics from Reception to Year 6.* London: DfEE.

Department for Education and Science (DES) (1959) *The Schools' Regulations, 1959.* London: HMSO

——(1978) *Primary Education in England: a survey by HM Inspectors of Schools*. London: HMSO.

——(1982) *The New Teacher in School*. London: HMSO.

——(1988) *The Education Reform Act*. London: HMSO.

Department for Education and Skills (DfES) (2003) *Excellence and Enjoyment*. London: DfES.

——(2003a) *Every Child Matters*. London: Stationery Office.

——(2003b), *The Future of Higher Education*, Cm 5735, White Paper, London: HMSO

Dixon, N.M. and Ross, R. (1999) 'The organisational learning cycle', in P. Senge (Ed) *The Dance of Change*. New York: Currency/Doubleday.

Du Gay, P. and Hall, S. (1996) (Eds) *Questions of Cultural Identity*. London: Sage.

Earley, P. and Evans, J. (2004) 'Making a difference', *Education Management, Administration and Leadership* 32(3): 325–38.

Everton, T., Turner, P., Hargreaves, L. and Pell, T. (2007) 'Public perceptions of the teaching profession', *Research Papers in Education* 22(3): 247–65.

Francis, B. (2001) 'Commonality AND difference: attempts to escape from theoretical dualisms in emancipatory research in education', *International Studies in Sociology of Education* 11(4): 381–93.

Frost, D. and Durrant, J. (2003) *Teacher-led Development Work: guidance and support*. London: David Fulton Press.

Fullan, M. (1993) *Change Forces: probing the depths of educational reform*. Bristol: Falmer Press.

Fullan, M. and Stiegelbauer, S. (1991) *The New Meaning of Educational Change*. New York: Teachers College Press.

Gabriel, Y. (1997) 'Meeting God: when organisational members come face to face with the supreme leader'. *Human Relations* 50(4): 313–42.

Galton, M. (1995) *Crisis in the Primary Classroom*. London: David Fulton Publishers.

Gillard, D. (2007) Editorial, *Forum* 9 (1 and 2).

Goleman, D., McKee, A., Boyatzis, R.E. (2002) *Primal Leadership: realizing the power of emotional intelligence*. Boston, MA: Harvard Business School Publishing.

Grace, G. (1995) *School Leadership: beyond education management*. London: Falmer Press.

Gronn, P. (1999) *The Making of Educational Leaders*. London: Cassell.

——(2000) 'Distributed properties: a new architecture for leadership', *Educational Management and Administration* 28(3): 317–38.

——(2002) 'Distributed leadership as a unit of analysis', *Leadership Quarterly* 13(4): 423–51.

——(2003) 'Leadership: who needs it?' *School Leadership and Management* 23(3): 267–90.

Gross, M.L. (2000) 'Sustaining change through leadership mentoring at one reforming high school', *Journal of In-Service Education* 28(1): 35–49.

Hall, V. and Southworth, G. (1997) 'Headship', *School Leadership and Management* 17(2): 151–70.

Hallinger, P. (1992) 'The evolving role of American principals: from managerial to instructional to transformational leaders', *Journal of Educational Administration* 30(3): 35–48.

Hallinger, P. and Heck, R.H. (1996) 'Reassessing the head teacher's role in school effectiveness: a review of empirical research, 1980–95', *Educational Administration Quarterly* 32(1): 35–44.

Hallinger, P. and Heck, R. (2003) 'Understanding the principal's contribution to school improvement', in M. Wallace and L. Poulson (Eds) *Learning to Read Critically in Educational Leadership and Management*. London: Sage.

Hargreaves, L., Cunningham, M., Everton, T., Hansen, A., Hopper, B., McIntyre, D., Maddock, M., Mukherjee, M., Pell, T., Rouse, M., Turner, P. and Wilson, L. (2006) *The Status of Teachers and the Teaching Profession. Views from inside and outside the profession: interim findings from the Teacher Status Project*. DfES Research Report RR755. London: DfES.

Hargreaves, L., Cunningham, M., Hansen, A., McIntyre, D., Oliver, C. and Pell, T. (2007) *The Status of Teachers and the Teaching Profession in England: views from inside and outside the profession. Final report of the Teacher Status Project*. Research Report 831A. London: DfES.

Harris, A., Bennett, N. and Preedy, M. (Eds) (1997) *Organizational Effectiveness and Improvement in Education*. Buckingham: Open University Press.

Harris, A. (2003) 'Teacher leadership as distributed leadership: heresy, fantasy or possibility?', *School Leadership and Management* 23(3): 313–24.

Harris, A., Day, C., Hopkins, D., Hadfield, M., Hargreaves, A. and Chapman, C. (2003) *Effective Leadership for School Improvement*. New York: Routledge.

Hartle, F. and Thomas, K. (2003) *Growing Tomorrow's School Leaders*. Nottingham: NCSL.

Hatcher, R. (2005) 'The distribution of leadership and power in schools', *British Journal of Sociology of Education* 26(2): 253–67.

Hayes, T. (2005) 'Rising stars and sitting tenants: a picture of deputy headship in one London borough and how some of its schools are preparing deputies for leadership', *Summary Practitioner Enquiry Report*. Nottingham: NCSL.

Heck, R.H. and Hallinger, P. (2005) 'The study of educational leadership and management: where does the field stand today?' *Educational Management Administration and Leadership* 33 (2): 229–44.

Hopkins, D. (2003) 'Instructional leadership and school improvement', in A. Harris, C. Day, D. Hopkins, M. Hadfield, A. Hargreaves and C. Chapman (Eds) *Effective Leadership for School Improvement*. New York: Routledge.

Hopkins, D. and Jackson, B. (2003) 'Building the capacity for leading and learning', in A. Harris, C. Day, D. Hopkins, M. Hadfield, A. Hargreaves and C. Chapman (Eds) *Effective Leadership for School Improvement*. New York: Routledge.

Kouzes, J.M. and Posner, B.Z. (1995) *The Leadership Challenge: how to keep getting extraordinary things done in organisations*. San Francisco, CA: Jossey Bass.

Lawlor, H. and Sills, P. (1999) 'Successful leadership – evidence from highly effective head teachers', *Improving Schools* 2(2): 53–60.

Leithwood, K., Leonard, L. and Seashore, L.K. (1999) *Changing Leadership for Changing Schools*. Buckingham: Open University Press.

Leithwood, K. and Seashore, L.K. (1998) 'Organizational learning: an introduction', in K. Leithwood and L.K. Seashore (Eds) *Organizational Learning in Schools*. Lisse: Swets and Zeitlinger.

Maguire, M. and Ball, S.J. (1994) 'Researching politics and the politics of research', *International Journal of Qualitative Studies in Education* 7(3): 269–86

Mahony, P. and Hextall, I. (2001) 'Performing and conforming', in D. Gleeson and C. Husbands (Eds) *The Performing School*. London: Routledge Falmer.

Møller, J., Eggen, A., Fuglestad, O., Langfeldt, G., Prethus, A., Skrøvset, S., Stjerstrøm, E. and Vedøy, G. (2005) 'Successful school leadership: the Norwegian case', *Journal of Educational Administration* 43(6): 584–94.

Mortimer, P. (1998) *The Road to Improvement: reflections on school effectiveness*. Lisse: Swets and Zeitlinger.

Mortimer, P., Sammons, P., Stoll, L., Lewis, D. and Ecob, R. (1988) *School Matters: the junior years*. London: Open Books.

Muijs, D. and Harris A. (2002) *Teacher Leadership: principles and practice*. Online (Available: http://www.teachers.org.uk/resources/pdf/teacher-leadership.pdf).

National College for School Leadership (NCSL) (2003) *Sustaining Improvement in the Primary School: leadership programme for primary school leaders*. Nottingham: NCSL.

NCSL (2004) *Final Report*. Nottingham: NCSL.

Nicholls, J. (2002) 'Escape the leadership jungle: try high-profile management', *Journal of General Management* 27(3): 14–35.

Osborn, M., McNess, E., Broadfoot, P., Pollard, A. and Triggs, P. (2000) *What Teachers Do: changing policy and practice in primary education*. London: Continuum.

Osgood, J. (2005) 'Rethinking professionalism in the early years: perspectives from the United Kingdom', *Contemporary Issues in Early Childhood* 7(1): 1–4

——(2006) 'Deconstructing professionalism in early childhood education: resisting the regulatory gaze', *Contemporary Issues in Childhood* 7(1): 5–14

Ozga, J. (2000) *Policy Research in Educational Settings: contested terrain*. Buckingham: Open University Press.

Ozga, J. and Lawn, M. (1981) *Teacher Professionalism and Class: a study of organised teachers*. London: Falmer Press.

Perryman, P. (2006) 'Panoptic performativity and school inspection regimes: disciplinary mechanisms and life under special measures', *Journal of Education Policy* 21(2): 147–61.

Pollard, A. and Triggs, P. (2001) *What Pupils Say*. London: Continuum.

Richards, C. (2004) 'It's sharp, but is it clever?', *Times Educational Supplement*, 20.2.04: 21.

Riley, A.K. and Seashore, L. (2000) *Leadership for Change and School Reform*. London: Routledge.

Sachs, J. (2001) 'Teacher professional identity: competing discourses, competing outcomes', *Journal of Education Policy* 16(2):149–61

Sammons, P. (1999) *School Effectiveness: coming of age in the 21st century*. Lisse: Swets and Zeitlinger.

Sergiovanni, T.J. (1992) *Moral Leadership: getting to the heart of school improvement*. San Francisco: Jossey Bass.

——(1998) 'Leadership as pedagogy, capital development and school effectiveness', *International Journal of Leadership in Education* 1(1): 37–46.

Silins, H. (1994) 'Leadership characteristics and school improvement', *Australian Journal of Education* 38(3): 266–81.

Simkins, T. (2005) 'Leadership in education; "what works" or "what makes sense"?', *Educational Management, Administration and Leadership* 33(1): 9–26.

Smith, M. (2002) 'The school leadership initiative: an ethically flawed project?' *Journal of Philosophy of Education* 36(1): 21–39.

Smith, S. and Piele, P. (1996) 'Better preparation for educational leaders', *Educational Researcher* 25(9): 18–27.

Southworth, G. (1988) 'Looking at leadership: English primary school head teachers at work', *Education 3–13* 16(2): 53–56.

——(1998) *Leading and Improving Primary Schools: the work of head teachers and deputy head teachers*. London: Falmer Press.

——(2004) *Primary Leadership in Context*. London: Routledge.

Stalhammer, B. (1994) 'Goal-orientated leadership in Swedish schools', *Educational Management and Administration* 22(1):14–25.

Stoll, L. and Fink, D. (1996) *Changing our Schools*. Buckingham: Open University Press.

Strang, D. and Macy, M. (2001) 'In search of excellence: fads, success stories and adaptive emulation', *American Journal of Sociology* 107(1): 147–82

Stronach, I., Corbin, B., McNamara, O., Stark, S., Warne, T. (2002) 'Towards an uncertain politics of professionalism: teacher and nurse identities in flux', *Journal of Education Policy* 17(1): 109–38.

Stronach, I. and Morris, B. (1994) 'Polemic notes on educational evaluation in the age of "policy hysteria"', *Evaluation and Research in Education* 8(1/2): 5–19

Sure Start Unit (2004) *Childcare and Early Years Workforce Survey*. London: Sure Start Unit.

Thrupp, M. (2005) 'The National College for School Leadership: a critique', *Management in Education* 19(2): 13–19.

Thrupp, M. and Willmott, R. (2003) *Educational Management in Managerialist Times: beyond the textual apologists*. Buckingham: Open University Press.

Walkerdine, V. (2003) 'Reclassifying upward mobility: femininity and the neoliberal subject', *Gender and Education* 15(3): 285–301

Webb, R. (2005) 'Leading teaching and learning in the primary school: from "educative leadership" to "pedagogical leadership"', *Education Management, Administration and Leadership* 33(1): 69–91.

Webb R. and Vulliamy, G. (1996) *Roles and Responsibilities in the Primary School: changing demands, changing practices.* Buckingham: Open University Press.

Weindling, D. (2004) *Innovation in Head Teacher Induction: case study research carried out for the National College for School Leadership.* Online (Available: http://www.ncsl.org.uk/media/F7B/95/randd-innov-case-studies.pdf, accessed 03 January 2007).

Welch, G. and Mahony, P. (2000) 'The teaching profession', in J. Docking (Ed) *New Labour's Policies for Schools: raising the standards?* London: Fulton.

Woods, P. (2004) 'Democratic leadership: drawing distinctions with distributed leadership', *International Journal of Leadership in Education* 7(1): 3026.

Yukl, G. (1998) *Leadership in Organisations* (4th edition). New Jersey: Prentice-Hall.

24 Primary teachers

Initial teacher education, continuing professional development and school leadership development

Olwen McNamara, Rosemary Webb and Mark Brundrett

INTRODUCTION

This survey of the teacher education and training in England has been structured into three sections covering the key areas of initial teacher education (ITE), continuing professional development (CPD) and the training of education leaders. The final section looks across these and draws out some common themes. Each of the authors has chosen to work on one of the three areas reviewed and contributed to the analysis which gave rise to the themes and issues identified in the concluding comments. The survey covers an area so extensive as to make systematic review an unrealistic prospect; whole books, indeed entire series of books, have been written on each of these individual strands. The chapter thus does not therefore purport to be exhaustive but will present an overview of the professional learning landscape.

Even within these parameters, the challenge faced by the authors in mapping out the particular area in which they were working was considerable. Firstly, in terms of identifying appropriate navigational tools that would render the accounts accessible, not only to 'insiders' but also to a generalist audience with an interest in education. Secondly, in terms of identifying aspects of broad relevance within the field that could be meaningfully and coherently addressed in such a short treatise. Such constraints and the disparate nature of the areas meant that the authors each took a different approach, as is explained in the individual sections, to delineating the breadth and scope of their enquiry. However, having determined the parameters of the enquiry, carrying out the literature review itself brought its own challenges.

The main data sources that have been drawn on include academic research and professional literature together with official reports, databases and electronic publications. Searches certainly revealed a wealth of research evidence. However, obtaining a coherent overview from it was often challenging: none more so than in the case of evaluating the effectiveness and outcomes of CPD for primary teachers. For example, surprisingly in these days of financial accountability, no single organisation is responsible for publishing and collating such data in order that policy decisions can be informed and cost effectiveness evaluated. Bolam (2000) is critical of the inadequate knowledge base on CPD resulting in a lack of facts about 'the scale of provision, who does what, costs, numbers on courses, how the considerable sums now spent on CPD are actually spent and how value-for-money is measured' (2000: 275). The evidence base is very diverse and fragmented, and usually grounded in individual self-report that generally relates solely to the quality of the CPD experience. Much of the research occurs summatively, after the CPD experience, rather than formatively, and evaluation processes are not sophisticated enough to track multiple outcomes, both intended and unintended, and different levels of impact. Where outcomes are reported, the relationship between teacher, school and pupil benefits are not unpicked. Additionally, surveys and larger studies frequently focus on teachers in all phases of mainstream and special schooling and inadequately differentiate between them. Similar themes emerge in respect of ITE, where the lack of a systemic, robust and cumulative evidence base means we are as yet unable to answer many questions about the effectiveness of our teacher education programmes – questions such as those posed in the United States by Wilson *et al.* (2001) about: the content of course and instructional methods best suited for particular aspects of teacher preparation; the relative contributions of centre-based learning, assignments and teaching experience to trainees' progress; the importance of their particular school experience contexts on the outcome of their practice; and the importance of consistency between school and centre-based training. A data-rich environment in the US, supported by initiatives such as 'no child left behind', means that a number of high profile research programmes are beginning to attempt to answer such questions. The evidence base relating to primary leadership programmes is, surprisingly, little more comprehensive. Raw data on completion of leadership programmes was released by the National College for School Leadership (NCSL) on request but, beyond gender and phase, individual profile detail was not available to support a more sophisticated level of analysis. Furthermore, phase categories extended only to 'primary' and 'secondary'; no data was available for the 'special education' sector. Yet such fundamental information is vital to support strategic workforce planning, at a time when the age profile in special education is such that, overall, 60 per cent of classroom teachers are over 45 years of age and 40 per cent of these are over 50. Additionally, the career progress to headship positions of successful completers of the soon to be mandatory National Professional Qualification for Headship is not tracked, meaning the opportunity to gather systematic data on gendered and ethnic patterns in leadership appointments is lost.

INITIAL TEACHER EDUCATION (ITE)

Introduction

The last two decades have been a period of sustained and increasingly radical change to the structure, content and regulation of primary ITE in England. The utilitarian, practical and skills-based nature of the reforms reflects not just a rethink of the theory/practice ratio and the way the process of development and assessment of academic and professional competences are conceptualised, but a redefinition of 'good' practice in ITE. In this section of the chapter we locate primary teacher education in its historical context and examine the strategic, political, and in some cases ideological, drivers of its centralisation within the compass of political control. We examine the sector's relationship with its accrediting bodies and consider the nature of the regulation and inspection regimes. We map the impact of these central influences on the sector over the last twenty years, in respect of its 'core principle' partnership and the profiles and characteristics of the various training routes. Finally, we look at succession planning in the teacher education workforce.

In setting these parameters we realise that many important debates, particularly subject specific debates, are not addressed. Debates in respect of trainees' classroom performance and its relation to subject knowledge and pedagogic content knowledge are well documented and analysed in mathematics (for example Goulding *et al.* 2002; Rowland *et al.* 2005), science (for example Heywood 2005) and English (for example Twistleton 2000; Poulson 2003). Here we restrict ourselves to noting research in core subject areas, but much valuable work is, of course, undertaken in respect of foundation subjects – their absence reflects pragmatism, in response to the sheer volume and the impossibility of being inclusive, but is also perhaps symbolic of their current positioning in the ITE curriculum. Other debates, such as the appropriate curriculum balance between core and foundation subjects and the appropriateness of the primary generalist/specialist model (for example Thornton 1998), are highly relevant to ITE, but are located within primary education itself and will be covered elsewhere in this book. The general point to note, perhaps, is how policy over the last twenty years has been mobilised to align ITE with the primary curriculum and to advance the reform agenda. In acknowledging so many limitations, this section of the chapter mirrors a key challenge facing the sector as a whole: namely that the sheer weight and intrusiveness of policy requirements and accountability have rendered many fundamentally important debates about ITE peripheral. We will begin by tracing the historical trends that have led to such a positioning.

Historical context

Alexander (1984) documented the main developments in teacher education in the two decades following the seminal Robbins Report (1963) and identified two defining and still current influences on the sector: the culture and organisation of the teacher education institutions, and their relationship with the validating body. An even longer-term historical perspective (1876–1996) makes it clear that these comparatively contemporary influences have historical precedents (Gardener and Cunningham 1998). The 1963 Robbins Report instituted the four year concurrent BEd; prior to this the main route into primary teaching was the recently extended three year certificate course, while the degree and postgraduate certification was barely a player.

Subsequent to this, the James Report (DES 1972) was also a significant influence on the sector in respect of the structure and validation of teacher education courses. It recommended structural reform of the BEd, endorsed both cyclic and consecutive training, and encouraged colleges to seek validation under the Council for National Academic Awards (CNAA) regulations; prior to this, universities had validated all teacher education courses and overseen area training organisations. The post-war baby–boom had resulted in a teacher supply crisis which augured a dramatic expansion of postgraduate training. The expansion was largely situated in colleges of education, and brought cultural as well as purely volume changes. Before 1970 the postgraduate training routes (Diploma in Ed / PGCE) were largely run by university departments of education and were traditionally undertaken by the 10 per cent of teachers intending to enter the grammar or independent school sectors (Alexander 1984). The expansion was followed in the 1970s by the beginning of a contraction of the market, although the introduction of mandatory training for graduates teaching in primary (in 1969) and secondary non-shortage subjects (in 1973) mitigated the effect, to a degree.

The raft of institutional mergers of specialist teacher training colleges into polytechnics and universities during the 1970s/1980s and into the 1990s was in part a pragmatic response to the downsizing of the sector, but had been an ambition signalled in McNair's (1944) recommendations. The loss of autonomy of the colleges was balanced against what they, misguidedly as it transpires, thought to be increased protection against early centralising tendencies shown by the government. Yet establishing their niche, in terms of specialist knowledge, within the complex, internally competitive, and somewhat dismissive, academy was not easy. Initially accomplished through the practical application of the foundation disciplines of psychology, philosophy, history and sociology, from thence teacher education's warrant moved to practical professional knowledge (Alexander 1984; Nixon *et al.* 2000; Gardener and Cunningham 1998). The mergers, however, often proved a culture shock and occasionally 'traumatic' (Kirk 1999). 'Contradictions' and 'confusions' were reported as the closure programme, orchestrated by the National Advisory Board, proceeded. A leader in the *Times Educational Supplement* in 1985 (1st November) reflected, 'It's impossible not to feel somewhat sorry for teacher training institutions, caught up as they are in a double pincer movement between the Council for Accreditation of Teacher Education (CATE), the National Advisory Board (NAB), HM Inspectorate and Sir Keith Joseph. Troubles, these days certainly never come singly.' Things were, however, to get worse before they got better!

Politicisation

The establishment in 1984 of the Council for Accreditation of Teacher Education (CATE) (DES Circular 3/84, DES 1984) was a key watershed for ITE introducing, as it did, the notion of *accreditation* for the first time. The two decades since have been a period of sustained and increasingly radical reform as successive governments have progressively increased control mechanisms and regulatory prescription in respect of processes and curriculum (Furlong *et al.* 2000; Mahony and Hextall 2000; Whitty 2002). Perry (1985: 3–4), Chief Inspector of Schools and HMI assessor on CATE, claimed its functions were: 'to raise the academic standards and to raise the level of professionalism and professional partnership'. She invoked the metaphor of a 'clinical' model of training, later taken up by Hargreaves (1996) in a controversial Annual TTA Lecture. Others have ascribed the move of ITE from relative obscurity to strategic significance to an assumption on the part of the successive governments that ITE would be an effective mechanism for steering changes in the school curriculum and transforming teacher professionalism (Furlong 2001, 2005).

Alexander (1984) identifies the appointment of Keith Joseph as Secretary of State for Education in 1976, and the availability of increased evidence from HMI surveys of the impact of training on the competence of new teachers, as the catalysts for central government interest in the sector. A corpus of inspection evidence (HMI 1982, 1983, 1987, 1988a, 1988b, 1991a) indicated that all was not well: new primary teachers emerged as more competent in teaching skills than their secondary colleagues, but less so in curricular areas. Twenty five per cent of new primary teachers were deemed to demonstrate insecurity in subject teaching (HMI 1982), although whether in academic knowledge or its application in the classroom was not clear. Yet, under the direction of the government, CATE sought to make recommendations about the content of teacher education courses, the links between subject study and the needs of schools, and the academic background of candidates suitable to be admitted into training (Reid 1985).

CATE importantly sought to create more practically-based teacher education, which later of course was to develop into full partnership with schools. Circular 24/89 (DES

1989a) required the creation of Professional Committees to oversee course management, and prescribed minimum lengths of school-based training for different courses: 100 days for all undergraduate trainees and 75 days for postgraduate students. This target was met by all courses by 1991, and exceeded by some (Furlong *et al.* 2000), a fact also noted in the HMI (1991b) study of school-based training. This study recommended a 'measured' increase in the extent and formality of partnership in school-based training, whilst expressing caution about capacity and resourcing – particularly in the primary sector. 'School-based training' and 'partnership' were now the new mantras, promoted in 1992 by Kenneth Clarke, Secretary of State for Education, at the North of England (Southport) Conference. (Secondary) Circular 9/92 and (primary) Circular 14/93 (DFE 1992, 1993a, 1993b) rapidly followed, increasing the school-based component of primary courses to 90 days for postgraduate and 160 days for four-year undergraduate, and prescribing a competences-based assessment model of subject knowledge and classroom skills. The combined effect of these modifications increased the level of intensification of courses, rendered them over-full, and what had previously been key aspects of curricular and professional development were squeezed out (Furlong *et al.* 2000: 103). The new arrangements were condemned by others variously as 'political rape' (Gilroy 1992), 'time constrained', 'lacking flexibility', diluting the intellectual and professional foundation of ITE (Wilkin 1996; Bines 1994; Bines and Welton 1995) and 'eroding rigour' – largely against international trends in teacher education (Holyoake 1993; Judge *et al.* 1994). An additional impact of the changes was the apportioning of funds between higher education institutions and schools in respect of the latter's greatly increased role, which in turn increased financial pressures (Gilroy 1998). This change in funding caused a marked casualisation of the workforce, with the introduction of more part-time staffing and also, indirectly, increased pressure on the delivery of courses (Taylor 2000).

There was also a drive to diversify routes into teaching through establishing school-based Licensed and Articled Teacher Schemes (later to be renamed and relaunched under the umbrella Employment Based Routes) and School-Centred Initial Teacher Training (SCITT) (DES 1989b; DFE 1993c). However, Modes of Teacher Education (MOTE), the first national survey of training provision, showed that in 1991 99 per cent of student teachers were still trained on traditional programmes offered through higher education institutions (HEIs) (Barrett *et al.* 1992), and even a decade later the overall percentage of teachers trained through HEIs had not changed significantly (Furlong *et al.* 2000). Meanwhile, traditional provision itself was developing progressively more complex variants, designed to attract a wider range of candidates: three- and four-year primary undergraduate degrees (with QTS); one year PGCE for primary, with part-time and flexible variants.

Indications of further drastic reform came in the 1994 Education Act (DFE 1993b), with the establishment of the Teacher Training Agency (TTA) as a successor to CATE. The move from 'Council' to 'Agency' signalled a change in governance and the, now formal, redesignation of 'Teacher Education' as 'Teacher Training' augured a profound ideological shift (Wilkin 1999). The proposals attracted much opposition from all quarters (Edwards 1994), not least the retiring Chairman of CATE. The TTA's brief, more wide-ranging than that of CATE, was to include teacher recruitment, quality control/assurance and funding, and accreditation of training routes. Its central remit extended only to England, and it is arguable at this point that the three devolved administrations began to diverge significantly in their teacher training provision. The

Agency survived its first turbulent years, a change of government in 1997 and the establishment of a General Teaching Council in England (GTCE). It was even allowed to broaden its scope to include control of professional development. Feelings of 'alienation' and 'hostility' in the sector towards the TTA (Kane 1998, cited in Gilroy 1998) came to a head, however, when an impending teacher supply crisis and a national debacle over TTA's ill-conceived in-service education policy meant that, at its Quinquennial Review (DfEE 1999a) in 1999, TTA's portfolio was refocused on initial training and induction. A decade after its inception, however, its fortunes were to change again dramatically when the TTA was re-launched in the 2005 Education Act (DfES 2005) as the TDA (Training and Development Agency *for Schools*); its purpose being to raise children's standards of achievement and to promote their well-being by improving the training and development of the whole school workforce. ITE did not feature in the DfES 5 year strategy (DfES 2004), and in its 2002 counterpart (DfES 2002c) HE was not listed as a partner in the drive for standards. ITE was, it seems, taking a back seat again. As Furlong (2005: 132) reflected, 'the last 30 years may have been uncomfortable for many of us, but at least there was an arena in which to engage […] the end of the era is to be regretted'.

Regulation

The TTA's quality assurance remit extended not only to assessment but also to curriculum content, which now for the first time had become politicised and regulated. The most radical and comprehensive change with regard to the practice of training providers was heralded by the publication of the National Curriculum for Initial Teacher Training (DfEE 1997, Circular 10/97; revised DfEE 1998a, Circular 4/98) which prescribed requirements for courses including length, partnership arrangements, selection of trainees, and quality assurance and assessment processes. A thorough analysis of the procedures and reporting of the 1997 consultation process left Hextall and Mahony (2000: 323) 'concerned about the state of democracy in England'. Central to Circular 4/98 were the Standards for the Award of Qualified Teacher Status (QTS), which related to: trainees' knowledge and understanding; planning, teaching and classroom management; monitoring, assessment, recording, reporting and accountability in relation to subject knowledge, teaching studies and monitoring and assessment; and other professional requirements. Subject to much critique (for example, Richards *et al*. 1998), it set down in unimaginable detail around 100 standards.

In addition to these standards, Circular 4/98 also specified extensive knowledge (equivalent to at least National Curriculum level 7) in core subjects and ICT. These subject knowledge demands focused the curriculum on core areas (particularly English and mathematics – for undergraduate degrees even hours of study time were prescribed) but still maintained the requirement for at least one specialist subject (with subject knowledge expectation equivalent to A-level). This drive was linked to impending changes in the primary curriculum resulting from the introduction of the National Literacy and Numeracy Strategies in 1998 and 1999, respectively, and the revised National Curriculum in 2000 (Wyse 2003; Brown and McNamara 2005). The notion was to steer and support curriculum change through ITE (Furlong 2005), informed by TTA-funded research in the teaching of literacy (Medwell *et al*. 1998) and numeracy (Askew *et al*. 1997). Parallel to these developments, the (post-National Curriculum) on-going debate over whether to introduce subject specialist teaching into upper primary education had rapidly grown in momentum. The weight of opinion for once appeared to favour the status quo in that, since neither 'generalist' nor 'specialist' systems had 'a monopoly on effectiveness', there was not convincing enough evidence to warrant change (see Thornton 1998). Subject knowledge demands were, however, further increased in 2001 by the introduction of QTS skills tests in mathematics, English and ICT. These were controversial not least because they focused on professional knowledge, such as interpretation of data, rather than curricular knowledge; and there was evidence to suggest that certain minority constituencies were disadvantaged (Hextall *et al.* 2001; TTA 2002/06).

Circular 4/98 was superseded in 2002 by the slim line 'Qualifying to Teach' (DfES 2002a) and much weightier handbook of guidelines (DfES 2002b). The government having now explicitly abandoned attempts to prescribe pedagogy and detail subject knowledge, the new framework (containing about 40 QTS standards) was much more positively received by the profession (Simco and Wilson 2002). Its explicit focus on professional values and practice, informed by the GTCE Code of Professional Values and Practice (GTCE 2002, 2004), was much appreciated. Although addressing curriculum capacity problems, less well received by some was the fact that the requirements no longer necessitated providers to offer a subject specialism or full curriculum coverage (either history or geography, and either art and design or design and technology, were made optional). Inspection evidence indicates that primary provision continued to place strong emphasis on the teaching of core subjects, leaving little time for foundation subjects – particularly on the increasingly popular postgraduate routes (HMI 2005). The next manifestation of the Standards (DfES 2007), a refinement of the 2002 version foregrounding the Every Child Matters (ECM) agenda, reduced the number of standards still further (to 33) and, significantly, generated a coherent framework of National Professional Standards first mooted ten years earlier. It also increased flexibility in training pathways (now to be two or more of the 3–5, 5–7, 7–9, 9–11 age phases), including reintroducing the 'upper / lower junior' divide that had been lost in the Key Stage-focused model of the previous two manifestations.

If policy has been used in the last ten years to refocus the content of ITE to engage with subject knowledge as it is situated in primary classrooms and to more closely align with, and steer changes in, the primary curriculum, then the inspection regime has been mobilised to ensure that providers are 'on message'.

Inspection

The inspection of the quality of training provision, previously managed by Her Majesty's Inspectorate (HMI), was brought under the auspices of the Office for Standards in Education (Ofsted) in the 1994 Education Act. The first 'new style' inspection of all 67 primary providers was undertaken in 1995–96 and unofficially became known as the 'Primary Sweep'. A summary report of the strengths and weaknesses of overall provision was never published, and it was left to the sector to draw its own conclusions from the providers' reports. Furlong and Kane (1996) conducted just such an analysis on behalf of UCET and concluded that the sector was generally in good health. There was no evidence to indicate undue weakness in the teaching of reading or numeracy, the two foci for the 'primary follow up survey' (1996–98) of the, now 72, primary training providers (Ofsted 1999).

These first inspections were a considerable cultural shock to the community and judgements were fiercely contested. A system of grading, 1 (very good) to 4 (non-compliant), was used to measure standards, low grades incurred real penalties in terms of reduced allocation of training places and even worse non-compliance was notified at institution rather than course level. Campbell and Husbands (2000), in a case study of two primary inspections (1996–97 and 1997–98) at Warwick University, contrasted the 'informed connoisseurship' model, formerly deployed by HMI, to the new 'technicist' model adopted by Ofsted. The move from HMI to Ofsted heralded an era of 'surveillance and control' that professed greater transparency of criteria through the Framework for Assessment of Quality and Standards, and had the potential to lead to greater inter-inspector reliability of assessment and greater consistency of judgements across contexts. Lack of confidence was expressed however in the piloting, evaluation and rigour of the evidence-base for the criteria statements (the 1997–98 version contained about 160) (Gilroy and Wilcox 1997) and the validity and reliability of the process (Graham and Nabb 1999).

A subsequent round of 90 primary inspections (1998–2002) coincided with the introduction of the National Strategies and focused on English and mathematics. The inspections concluded that, over the four years, significant improvement had occurred in all provision, including SCITTs – although on the whole they performed less well than HEI providers (Ofsted 2003a). Evidence of this improvement is supported by data from inspection reports of NQTs during the years 1997 to 2001 (HMI 2002). The burden and high-stakes nature of inspection led to the Parliamentary Select Committee on Education and Employment recommending the introduction, as a priority, of a four year cycle with differentiated light-touch provision (HoC 1999). The latter, with a focus on management and quality assurance, was introduced in the 2002–5 Framework of Inspection (Ofsted 2002b); although the short inspection was not felt by providers to be markedly less onerous (UCET 2007). In 2006–7, under the 2005–11 framework (Ofsted 2005b), just under half of primary providers inspected were deemed to be 'outstanding' in management and quality assurance (Ofsted 2007a). Primary SCITTs were still performing less well than their HEI provider counterparts (2005–7) in terms of Ofsted gradings and entry qualifications, although trainees fared considerably better in terms of employment (Smithers and Robinson 2007). Evidence from the annual survey of NQTs supports the perception of continuous improvement, with some 88 per cent of the NQTs (n = 11,000) rating their training good or very good. In the primary sector, undergraduate routes were rated more highly (91 per cent good or very good) against postgraduate (84 per cent). Evaluation of assessment/feedback and support/guidance were also at a 5-year high, with 82 per cent and 80 per cent respectively rating the provision good or very good (TDA 2007).

By contrast to the inspection of traditional provision, the rapidly increasing Employment Based Route into teaching (now renamed Employment Based Initial Teacher Training: EBITT) has, since its (re)launch in 1998, been subject only to survey inspections. The most recent (2003–6) concluded that the management of training had improved considerably over the period but that there was room for further improvement. Primary provision was judged to be consistently better than secondary, but was found in the majority of cases not to offer good enough subject training (Ofsted 2005a, 2006a, 2007b) and generally there was an underlying weakness in the quality of mentoring (Brookes 2005). Primary NQTs trained on employment-based routes concurred with this evaluation, with 87 per cent rating it good or very good against 83 per cent for their secondary counterparts (TDA 2007). Half of the lessons observed in 2005/06 in EBITT inspections displayed strengths but 17 per cent still had significant weaknesses (Ofsted 2007b).

Inspection grades are now systematically and transparently being used to inform the allocation of training places for traditional provision, but ideological drivers can be deduced from the tolerance of the repeatedly less than favourable inspection reports on EBITT provision since its inception. The combined weight of the QTS standards and the Ofsted framework functioned as a quality assurance instrument for the assessment of training and trainees, and the weight of inspection and evaluation evidence cited above indicates an increase in quality measures. Mahony and Hextall (2000), however, reported that very few providers thought that the overall quality of their courses had improved and generally felt the whole assessment portfolio was a 'bureaucratic nightmare'. Reports indicate that workloads for the new short inspections, rather than lessen significantly, have shifted to fall more intensively onto course leaders (UCET 2007). That inspection is still being strategically planned to focus the primary sector on particular educational enterprises and nationally defined goals is evidenced by the survey inspection in September 2007 of initial training in early reading on the quality and impact of training in phonic work as reflected in the renewed Primary Framework, subsequent to the publication of the Rose (2006) review of early reading.

Partnership

The 1944 McNair report endorsed school-based training and, encouraged by CATE in the late 1980s, providers had voluntarily made considerable strides in the sector towards developing such formal models; the Oxford Internship Scheme (Benton 1990) was one such ground-breaking initiative. As the 'school-based training' evolved into 'partnership', a review of contemporary literature characterised it as a 'problematic concept' (Brown *et al.* 1993) and a 'slippery and imprecise word' (Crozier *et al.* 1990). It was soon to become much less 'imprecise' but, despite substantial international interest (Brisard *et al.* 2005), England and Wales still remain the only countries where 'partnership has become institutionalised at a national level as a core principle of provision' (Furlong *et al.* 2006a: 33).

Once partnership was mandated in legislation (DFE Circular 14/93, 1993a) and moved into its second era in 1993, many providers challenged what they saw as the government's simplistic depiction of the trainee's developing practical skills in schools and subject knowledge in the university (for example, Edwards 1995). They argued that the changes had reinforced 'hierarchical relations' and the 'demarcation of practice in schools from educational theory' (Dunne *et al.* 1996: 41). Taylor (2000: 55) speculated that 'specification of who does what, is less important than the existence of shared values based as far as possible on a common knowledge base'. However, he also expressed concern at the lack of acknowledgement of the additional costs or the equity of the relative distribution of resources, control, quality assurance, penalties and accountability.

Furlong *et al.* (2000) concluded that who actually did what, with regard to the substantive content of training courses, had changed little as a result of the introduction of the new arrangements. They identified a continuum in partnership models that extended from the HEI-led to the entirely school-led (SCITTS); they argued that neither extreme was a true partnership. They characterised ideal typical models of ITE partnerships as either 'complementary' or 'collaborative'. The former were a 'pragmatic response to limited resources' in which the partners had separate roles and responsibilities; the latter partners were deemed to have different, but equally legitimate, bodies of knowledge –

the Oxford Internship Scheme was posited as a classic example (Furlong *et al.* 2000: 78). Furlong *et al.* reported that in reality the most common model of partnership throughout the 1990s was still largely HEI-led, with contributions from school-based colleagues. There was little evidence in the literature that primary schools in particular harboured a desire to establish more independent school-based primary ITE (for example, the infamous government proposals for a 'Mum's Army' scheme (DFE 1993c)) (Williams and Soares 2002). However, there was an interest in restructuring the present arrangements to give primary schools a more significant role (Hannan 1995). The introduction of school-led SCITT provision and employment-based routes in the mid 1990s, however, opened up this possibility and in the process undermined the notion of partnership even further as collaboration with HEI stakeholders was not a requirement. Brisard *et al.* (2005: 50), comparing England to other parts of the UK in a review of partnership commissioned by the General Teaching Council in Scotland (GTCS), suggest that the 'detachment of some forms of entry away from the university sector perhaps reflects the relatively low standing of teaching within the English culture'. Furlong *et al.* (2006a: 41) argue that the key strength of the HEI partners 'is theorising the epistemological and pedagogical underpinnings of training', so in their absence '(the) complexity and contestability of professional knowledge is no longer seen to be at the heart of what partnership is about; professional knowledge becomes simplified ... it is essentially about contemporary practice in school'.

Evidence of what was actually happening in school-based training during the first decade of formal partnership is somewhat limited in scope. A TTA-funded EPPI Review (1992–2003) on school-based partnership practices supporting trainee teachers' professional development (Moyles and Stuart 2003) revealed a dearth of evidence across the UK, and only two studies (both, as it happens, primary) were found to be appropriate for in-depth reporting (Mills 1995; Baird 1996). The review concluded that trainee development was supported by regular constructive feedback; oral feedback offering a chance for constructive dialogue on issues of immediate concern or practical relevance; and written feedback linked to more long-term development objectives. Professional skills supported and developed on paired school placements found that significant drivers of professional learning included increased opportunities for developing communication and teamwork skills, a theme further developed by Smith (2004).

Of the burgeoning body of research literature into partnership that did emerge in the 1990s around school-based partners' roles, the vast majority focused on professional and affective dimensions of the mentoring, particularly mentors' perceptions, views and beliefs and reported on individuals / individual institutions (Moyles and Stuart 2003). The use of mentoring as a vehicle to encourage reflective practice featured largely in the literature in the early 1990s, although higher levels of reflection was generally held to be a much more productive exercise for mentors than trainees (McIntyre 1993; McNally *et al.* 1994). Moyles *et al.* (1998), conducting a review of primary mentoring for the Association of Teachers and Lecturers, concluded that professional, interpersonal and communication skills were important and that guidelines for selection and training of mentors were necessary. Primary school-based mentors tended to emphasise classroom management and professional issues and did not provide quality subject-specific feedback to support trainees in applying subject knowledge effectively (Brown and McNamara 2005; Ofsted 2007a). Mentors were also found not to take sufficient account of adult learning needs and not to understand the principles underpinning mentoring (Jones and Straker 2006). Edwards and Protheroe (2003), in a study of the school-based learning of 125 student teachers, concluded it focused on curriculum delivery and was heavily situated in a way that limited their understanding of learners. They also speculated that the participatory model of school-based training did not make the most of the strengths of mentors.

The professional learning gains offered by ITE mentoring in primary schools is a recurrent theme in the literature, particularly the need for leaders and managers to have greater awareness of its potential (Price and Willett 2006; Hurd *et al.* 2007); more effectively integrate it into school structures and processes (Menter and Whitehead 1995); and employ it as a mechanism for school improvement (Hurd *et al.* 2007). Chief HMI Perry (1985) identified links between ITE and teacher professional development (IT-INSET) as powerful. Two decades later, however, Hurd *et al.* (2007) in an analysis of all 13,202 primary Ofsted reports (1999–2005) found that fewer than 6 per cent made any reference to ITE, limited in the main to statements of involvement. Although all evaluative comments made were supportive, only one example was found of a report explicitly linking ITE mentoring to professional learning.

Partnership underwent renewed scrutiny with the introduction of Circular 4/98 (Annex I, DfEE 1998), and partnership (and school-based training generally) have formed a key element of subsequent inspection frameworks. During this same period a teacher supply crisis, and an ensuing planned rapid increase of 40 per cent overall (primary and secondary) in training numbers between 1998 and 2004, bought with it concerns about the capacity of the system to deliver the relatively new partnership model of training. A number of interventions were planned to bolster the enterprise, including a network of high quality Training Schools (DfEE 1998b) to develop and disseminate good practice in ITE, train mentors/school-based tutors and undertake research. The model was always in essence secondary (some 80 per cent of the existing 250 schools) and has now been subsumed under the specialist schools network (DfES 2004). By 2004, when the anticipated decline in pupil numbers precipitated a planned contraction in the secondary training sector, the placement crisis was perceived by TDA to be abating (Furlong *et al.* 2006a); albeit in shortage subjects that were not subject to cuts, and capacity issues still remained in some geographic areas. In the primary sector, however, Key Stage 1 placements were at an increasing premium (HMI 2005) owing to a considerable expansion in the Early Years sector and changes to the Qualifying to Teach requirements in 2002. In a UCET survey on school placements, virtually all responding institutions claimed to be experiencing difficulties – Early Years followed by modern languages, science and ICT were posing the greatest challenge (UCET 2005).

The major national intervention devised to address the school-based training crisis at the turn of the millennium was the high profile National Partnership Project (2001–5). Built on the government office regional infrastructure, it funded the nine regions in proportion to numbers of training places. Partnership, now in its third era, was to be commodified and marketed to schools by a TDA Regional Partnership Manager supported by devices such as a glossy magazine, 'Doing ITT'. The aim was to increase the capacity of the system, the quality of school-based training, and to enhance collaboration between partners and other stakeholders in the teacher training enterprise. Each region had a Regional Steering Group. Chaired by the partnership manager, it comprised representation from all stakeholders (HEIs, SCITTs, schools and LAs), and was a forum for discussion and management of projects funded centrally (from a national budget of £1.7 million per year) to meet the locally-agreed national objectives. At a national level the project portfolio included a web-based school usage survey (which attempted to map schools involved with ITE) and the newly created Partnership Promotion Schools initiative, which funded (mainly primary) schools doing outreach work to develop training capacity. The whole package was estimated by the evaluation team to amount to £6 million per year (Campbell *et al.* 2007). The project was terminated a year early because of a change in government priorities, driven perhaps by a perception that partnership was increasingly secure. The evaluation team concluded that the project met many of its objectives but much activity 'finding placements' and 'producing common paperwork' reduced teacher education to a 'technical-rationalist task'. Overall, the project was about 'making the existing model work, not developing a new model'. Partnership, the authors concluded, had moved to where it should have been five years ago (Furlong *et al.* 2006a: 41).

Routes into teaching

The historical background to the proliferation of ITE provision in England in the early 1990s has been documented above and, although the political significance was considerable, the relative uptake of non-traditional provision was extremely small even in the late 1990s. The ongoing debate about the introduction of subject specialists into primary education (Thornton 1998), aligned with the increasing focus on English and mathematics, was more significant in practical terms. Its relevance was thrown into sharp focus with the publication of the Sutherland Report (1997) (as part of the Dearing Committee of Enquiry into Higher Education), which recommended greater differentiation of ITE routes and questioned the effectiveness of the one year PGCE in preparing primary teachers adequately, whilst problematising inspection evidence which appeared to indicate that BEd trained NQTs out-performed them. All this had a marked impact on increasing concern about the vulnerability of the four-year BEd degree, which for many years had been unassailable as a primary training route (UCET 2004).

Even more significant, however, was the introduction of the HE tuition fee in 1998 and the £6000 postgraduate training bursary in 2002, which together triggered the rapid growth of the shortened three-year education degrees (with QTS) to capture 40 per cent of the undergraduate market in England by 2004/05 (cited Furlong 2006b). Practice across the UK is extremely varied in respect of undergraduate QTS provision: in Scotland and Northern Ireland virtually all primary undergraduate courses are still four years in duration, by contrast Welsh undergraduate provision (which accounts for over half of the Welsh primary training numbers) is virtually all of three years in duration. Furlong *et al.* (2006b), in their review of Welsh ITT provision, recommended that this route should be phased out in favour of a new, academically rigorous three year pre-professional degree designed to prepare students for a range of education-related careers.

Compared to the evolution of the undergraduate degree, the traditional PGCE has remained remarkably stable over its long history. In 2007, however, to accord with the Framework for HE Qualifications (QAA 2001), it branched into the M (masters) level Postgraduate Certificate of Education and the H (honours undergraduate) level Professional Graduate Certificate of Education. An enhanced Fast Track Programme, which included a lucrative package of incentives for postgraduate trainees, was launched in 2000 as part of the school improvement/workforce reform agenda. Its ambition was to attract into teaching able young graduates, identified as potential future leaders, and support them in developing the skills to progress rapidly into senior positions. Piloted for two years, the programme was rolled out to selected providers in 2003–4 only to be terminated in 2005–6.

Other changes in provision, already alluded to, have been the demise of the school-based Licensed and Articled Teacher Schemes in the late 1990s and their relaunch as the mainly post graduate Graduate and Registered Teacher Programmes. Now repackaged under the umbrella of employment-based routes (and commonly referred to as EBITT) they also encompass the Overseas Trained Teacher Programme and QTS-only assessment routes. Additional diversity in postgraduate provision was created by the introduction of primary SCITTs in the mid 1990s, and the last 5 years has seen their numbers grow rapidly to 28 (16 covering the full primary range). However, they still account for only around 4 per cent of training allocations.

Alongside these structural changes, contextual factors – such as the teacher supply crises which coincidentally followed the inception of the TTA – have had a marked impact on primary provision in the last decade. Rising school rolls, low teacher retention, and falling recruitment were exacerbated by the introduction of HE tuition fees and caused a shortfall in teacher numbers; especially significant in the period 1998–2001. The latter was felt most acutely in London and southern England, where it was overcome in the short term by recruiting overseas-trained teachers (McNamara *et al.* 2007). Ultimately the crisis led to an increase of 30 per cent in primary training numbers (50 per cent in secondary) and the introduction of the postgraduate bursary. Currently England is in a period of oversupply of primary teachers as a result of falling rolls (an estimated 600,000, 2003–13), in part offset by increases in Early Years provision, triggering a reduction of just 7 per cent in primary allocations (compared to 17 per cent in secondary) (TDA 2006). This temporary downsizing of the 'client base', however, should be read against the impending retirement of 25 per cent of female and 21 per cent of male primary teachers who are currently over 50 (DfES 2006b) and a greatly increased population growth estimate recently announced by the Office of National Statistics (ONS 2007), which is about to augur an increase in primary training numbers.

Marked shifts in the patterns of training have reconfigured the landscape of new entrants into the teacher workforce for the period 1998 to 2005. The data in Table 24.1 show DfES Workforce Recruitment Statistics disaggregated by training route. The

Table 24.1 Workforce recruitment by route and phase of education

	Year	*1998/ 1999*	*1999/ 2000*	*2000/ 2001*	*2001/ 2002*	*2002/ 2003*	*2003/ 2004*	*2004/ 2005*
Undergrad	Primary	7,370	6,580	6,390	6,490	6,600	7,030	6,990
	% all pri	*53%*	*47%*	*43%*	*40%*	*36%*	*36%*	*37%*
PostGrad	Primary	6,000	6,590	6,750	8,030	9,040	9,510	9,270
	% all pri	*43%*	*47%*	*46%*	*50%*	*50%*	*49%*	*49%*
EBITT	Primary	490	830	1,610	1,690	2,510	2,750	2,690
	% all pri	*4%*	*6%*	*11%*	*10%*	*14%*	*14%*	*14%*
Total	**Primary**	**13,860**	**14,000**	**14,750**	**16,210**	**18,150**	**19,290**	**18,950**
	% Total	48%	47%	44%	45%	45%	46%	46%

(Source: DfES Workforce statistics, Initial Teacher Training)

proportion of undergraduate-trained teachers has decreased from 53 per cent to 37 per cent and that of postgraduate-trained teachers has increased from 43 per cent to 49 per cent. The proportion entering though (postgraduate) EBITT has increased from 4 per cent to 14 per cent (secondary EBITT having increased to 21 per cent in the same period).

The data in Table 24.2 reveal marked shifts in the trends of primary allocations and trainee characteristics. It shows a 30 per cent decrease in undergraduate numbers and a 120 per cent increase in postgraduate numbers (including EBITT). A key issue with regard to primary recruitment has characteristically been a gender imbalance in the applicant pool, and despite a number of high profile national initiatives the proportion of men has remained at a consistently low 13–14 per cent (Harnett and Lee 2003). Data from Smithers and Robinson (2007) show that disaggregating the routes reveals marked variation in the proportion of male trainees, ranging from 13 per cent in traditional programmes to 20 per cent on EBITT. The effect on student teacher gender identities (Skelton 2003; Carrington 2002; Jones 2007) is well documented, although whether it impacts negatively upon pupil achievement or attitudes is contested (Thornton and Bricheno 2000, 2006; Skelton 2002; Carrington 2002). In respect of training, the government now presents 'males into primary' as an 'important but still relatively small area of TDA recruitment work' and instead emphasises the importance of 'high-quality confident and celebrated teachers, of whatever gender' (Watkins 2006: 37).

Table 24.2 shows that the overall trend in the proportion of mature trainees in the period 1998–2006 has increased quite significantly to nearly 50 per cent, but again this proportion ranges from 40 per cent on traditional provision to 88 per cent on EBITT (Smithers and Robinson 2007). Likewise the proportion of minority ethnic trainees shows a gradual increase across the sector from 5 per cent to 8 per cent.

Table 24.3 shows the characteristics of the primary training sector in 2005–6 disaggregated by Government Office Region, and evidences a number of key regional differences. In particular the proportion of minority ethnic trainees varies from 2 per cent in the north east to 20 per cent in London.

Ross (2002) reported that a survey of 22 LEAs (18 in London) found that less than 50 per cent of white teachers qualified in the 1990s, compared with 63 per cent of all black teachers, 69 per cent of Asian teachers and 62 per cent of mixed ethnic origin

Table 24.2 Primary sector training and employment data, disaggregated

Year	1998/ 1999	1999/ 2000	2000/ 2001	2001/ 2002	2002/ 2003	2003/ 2004	2004/ 2005	2005/ 2006
First year trainees	11,677*	11,552*	12,918	14,471	15,276	17,111	18,616	18,700
Final year trainees	13,079	11,035	11,682	12,767	14,741	15,660	17,127	16,999
UG final year	7892	5795	5443	5566	5891	5394	5338	5391
PG final year	5187	5240	6239	7201	8850	10,266	11,789	11,608
UG award of QTS	91%	92%	93%	93%	89%	93%	88%	89%
PG award of QTS	87%	86%	88%	89%	91%	89%	90%	87%
UG employment	80%	83%	87%	87%	80%	77%	78%	78%
PG employment	83%	83%	82%	82%	76%	76%	78%	79%
Females	87%	87%	87%	87%	87%	86%	86%	86%
Males	13%	13%	13%	13%	13%	14%	14%	14%
Age 25+	37%	38%	39%	48%	48%	50%	50%	47%
Minority ethnic	5%	6%	6%	6%	7%	7%	9%	8%

(Source: TDA Sector Level Data Performance Profiles.)

Table 24.3 Primary sector trainee characteristics disaggregated by region

	Primary			
	Total trainees	*% Male*	*% Minority ethnic*	*% aged 25+*
Eastern	1,779	14%	7%	54%
East Midlands	1,321	13%	6%	44%
London	3,703	15%	20%	62%
North East	889	14%	2%	42%
North West	3,167	15%	5%	38%
South East	2,696	12%	4%	49%
South West	1,555	18%	3%	42%
West Midlands	1,567	12%	12%	44%
Yorkshire and Humber	1,979	14%	5%	36%
Non-regional providers	70	16%	6%	64%

(Source: TDA Characteristics by region of 2005/06 intake.)

teachers. Twenty eight percent of all Asian teachers were aged under 30 years. There was also a marked increase in female Asian teachers in this period, particularly into the primary phase: 70.5 per cent of Asian women teachers had qualified since 1989. Once in training, however, there is still concerning evidence relating to the experiences of black and minority ethnic trainees both in school and university contexts (Basit *et al.* 2007; Carrington *et al.* 2001; Carrington and Tomlin 2000; Jones and Maguire 1998) and statistically they have been shown to have a significantly higher withdrawal rate (Basit *et al.* 2006).

The relative 'effectiveness', 'impact' and 'value for money' of the various training routes in the UK is unproven, and in some cases unresearched, although there is anecdotal evidence from inspection prior to the early 1990s about the relative performance of NQTs and self report from trainees/NQTs on perceived effectiveness of training (see below). Despite the cautionary note cited in the introduction (Wilson *et al.* 2001), the US is still a good way ahead of the UK in developing a research base on teacher preparation. A number of large scale initiatives such as the Teacher Pathways Project (2003–7), a multi-year data-rich analysis of programmes and routes into teaching and their impact on student achievement in the classroom, have been funded. Focusing on the New York City public school system, the study includes detailed programme information on fifteen public and private traditional teacher preparation programmes, and two alternative route programmes primarily serving the New York City area. It analyses and identifies the attributes of programmes and pathways into teaching that positively impact on student outcomes. In comparison, UK evidence often relates to single case studies or contexts, albeit some of extremely high repute such as the Leverhulme Primary Project, which tracked primary PGCE students through their training programme and into their first appointments (Bennett and Carré 1993). There have been a few exceptions such as 'Modes of Teacher Education' (Barrett *et al.* 1992) and 'Changing Modes of Professionalism' (Furlong *et al.* 2000) cited in this chapter. The current 'Becoming a Teacher Project' (BaT) (2003–9), co-funded by GTCE, TDA and DfES/DSCF, is tracking 5,000 trainee teachers for five years, charting their experience of training and early professional development and has so far published a number of extensive reports (Hobson *et al.* 2004, 2005, 2006, 2007) although they include only trainee self report comparative data relating to the 'effectiveness' of the routes.

Learning to teach

A number of different theoretical models have been used over the years to conceptualise the student experience of learning to teach, including 'apprenticeship of observation' (Lortie 1975); 'development of expertise' (Berliner 1988); 'rite of passage' (White 1989); 'performance theory' (McNamara *et al.* 2002); 'legitimate peripheral participation'/ 'community of practice' (Lave and Wenger 1991; Maynard 2001); 'activity theory' (Twiselton 2004; Edwards and Protheroe 2004). As a model of professionalism and pedagogy, however, the 'reflective practitioner' has been pre-eminent in ITE over the last quarter century. Empirical evidence from the 1991 Modes of Teacher Education survey of training providers indicates that over 80 per cent (218) of courses claimed to espouse a particular philosophy, which in over 70 per cent per cent of cases was the 'reflective practitioner'; only 6 per cent (mainly primary undergraduate) laid claim to a 'competency model' (Barrett *et al.* 1992). Yet Edwards (1995: 600) identified scant evidence in the literature to suggest that 'reflection on practice in ITT is an opportunity to connect any sort of pedagogical theory with practice'. In the late 1990s the 'reflective practitioner' was, to a degree, a casualty of the intensification of ITE. Furlong *et al.* (2000: 143) observed that 'while many teacher educators aspired to maintain the ideal of the reflective practitioner [...] in reality that was increasingly difficult'. The introduction of the M level postgraduate pathways in 2007 will undoubtedly cause reflection to once again move up the ITE agenda. A crucial area of immediate reflection for the new postgraduate trainee might be how the space to reflect can be created amongst all the other competing demands on their time, and what policies, practices and pedagogies are sanctioned as legitimate objects for reflection, given the competing discourses of 'audit' and 'standards'.

Learning to teach in the 21st century, notwithstanding an enduring focus on the core curriculum, involves demonstrating expertise in an ever-increasing curricular and pedagogic knowledge base and skill set, the latest impending addition being modern languages. Aspiring primary teachers are also required to broaden their key focus on the academic curriculum to encompass contribution to society, safety, health, and economic well-being. In addition, they need to develop an understanding of an extended range of professional contexts, from working with others in the classroom to working in multi-professional teams providing access to integrated and specialist services including childcare, parenting and family support, community facilities/ learning and, finally, to promoting community cohesion.

Even before the extended school and Every Child Matters (ECM) outcome agendas listed above were incorporated, Lunn and Bishop (2003) reported that trainees perceived the training curriculum as overly prescriptive and felt the need for space to develop their understanding of what it is to be an effective teacher. Brown and McNamara (2005) claim the transition to teacher, if it is to be effective, necessitates the student: unlearning their pupil perspective to develop a teacher identity; changing beliefs and attitudes; enhancing curricular knowledge; transforming subject knowledge into pedagogic content knowledge; and developing pedagogic and reflective skills. They conceptualise the transition in terms of students reconciling dichotomies between their own understanding of subject knowledge and the formal curriculum; their personal aspirations for teaching and learning and the official requirements; and their developing identity as teachers and representations of themselves as an aggregation of standards.

A substantive corpus of empirical evidence on how effective primary students perceive their training to be in terms of their preparedness, support and developing self efficacy compared to their secondary counterparts can be gleaned from the Becoming a Teacher Project, and it indicates overall that the latter are generally more positive about their experiences. This perhaps reflects the demanding nature of the challenge posed by primary training, particularly through the postgraduate route. Hobson *et al.* (2006) report that only 31 per cent of primary trainees thought the support they received very good, compared to 43 per cent of secondary trainees. Data indicate marked differences between primary routes: 46 per cent of trainees who had undertaken SCITT training rated it very good, followed by 43 per cent of GRTP, 34 per cent BEd, 31 per cent BA/BSC (with QTS) and only 21 per cent PGCE. Generally speaking, the older the trainee the lower they rated the support they received. Overall, however, 74 per cent of primary completers reported they would follow the same route with the same provider given their time again; variations between routes show primary SCITT completers to be the most positive again with 86 per cent content to follow the same training programme.

The Becoming a Teacher Project also explored the motivations that brought primary and secondary trainees into teaching and found significant differences: 72 per cent of primary trainees were motivated by wanting to work with children and young people compared to only 45 per cent of secondary trainees, and 82 per cent of primary trainees were strongly attracted to helping young people learn compared to 74 per cent of secondary trainees. Only 10 per cent of primary trainees were significantly interested in pursuing their subject specialism, compared to 41 per cent of secondary, but more surprisingly they were also significantly less interested in opportunities for career development, 15 per cent compared to 23 per cent of secondary trainees (Hobson *et al.* 2005). Exploring trainees' preconceptions about the effectiveness of their chosen training routes, prior to training, Hobson *et al.* (2005) reported that factors associated with increased confidence that would prepare them to be effective teachers were gender (being male), phase (being secondary) and age (being mature). Primary trainees were reported to be particularly concerned about managing their workload (74 per cent), coping academically (58 per cent) and managing financially (57 per cent) whilst secondary trainees were more concerned about discipline (74 per cent).

Regarding the content of primary courses Hobson *et al.* (2006) reported that BEd trainees were least satisfied with the theory/practice balance, 46 per cent thinking their programmes were too theoretical whilst GRTP trainees thought their programmes were too practical. SCITT trainees were clearest about the links between theory and practical elements of their courses and thought the balance about right by a significant margin. Whilst primary trainees were more positive than secondary trainees about relationships with their peers, regarding relationships with HEI staff primary trainees were again less positive than their secondary counterparts: 35 per cent of secondary trainees rated their relationship with HEI staff very good compared to only 24 per cent of primary. Within primary, BEd trainees were the most positive about HEI relationships and PGCE trainees the least positive. At the end of their training, primary trainees were more likely than secondary to identify maintaining classroom discipline as very important and it was more commonly cited for PGCE-trained students as a development point for induction than undergraduates. Overall, the ability to work with pupils with SEN was the most frequently mentioned as the area requiring further training.

That learning to teach cannot all be accomplished in ITE has been long recognised, and there have been various probationary schemes for newly qualified teachers over the years. The latest statutory induction period of three terms for NQTs in England was introduced in 1999 (DfEE 1999b) and revised in 2003 to align with the new QTS Standards. The induction policy has two main principles: firstly, the NQT's entitlement to support from a school-based induction mentor and a 10 per cent reduction in contact hours for professional development activities; secondly, the assessment of NQTs against defined national standards (monitored by LAs). From April 2001 schools had a funding allocation of £1000 per term per NQT for induction support, but in 2003 this was incorporated into standards funding.

Initial response from the sector was, on the whole, positive. A large-scale DfES-funded evaluation (Totterdell *et al.* 2002) reported that the vast majority of NQTs, head teachers, induction tutors and LEA representatives considered the process beneficial. Reports of the actuality falling short of intentions were in respect of entitlement for reduction in contact hours, access to professional development activities, mentoring, and funding (Kyriacou and O'Connor 2003; Heilbronn 2002; Jones *et al.* 2002); Bubb *et al.* (2005) developed a typology of 'rogue' schools. An Ofsted survey inspection of the induction of NQTs (Ofsted 2001) found that most schools were meeting their responsibilities but that in a small number of instances release time was not used effectively to support induction activities and that mentors needed further training in assessing against the standards. On the whole this training was better received by primary than secondary NQTs. It was also noted that large numbers of NQTs on short-term contracts had no entitlement to support and that 60 per cent of primary NQTs (compared to 30 per cent of secondary NQTs) were appointed on temporary contracts.

Six years later, according to Hobson *et al.* (2007), the situation had not improved. Primary NQTs got on average 2.7 hours of their statutory entitlement to non-contact time, compared to secondary NQTs who had an average of five hours. Of those in employment, 58 per cent of primary NQTs secured a permanent post compared to 76 per cent of secondary NQTs. Variation between routes showed that SCITT NQTs were most likely to secure a permanent post followed by GRTP, PGCE, BA/BSc (QTS) – BEd NQTs were least successful in this respect. Additionally, primary NQTs were more likely to have encountered difficulties in securing first appointments (32 per cent) compared to secondary (12 per cent), and of the primary NQTs those trained through undergraduate routes were again most likely to encounter difficulties (46 per cent).

Hobson *et al.* (2007) reporting NQTs' retrospective perception of their level of preparedness found variation between routes with PGCE trained NQTs feeling least well prepared (76 per cent good or very good) to be effective teachers and those trained in SCITTs best prepared (92 per cent good or very good). Rippon and Martin (2006) highlight the importance of the emotional as well as professional learning needs of NQTs as they are socialised into the teaching profession. Overall, however, NQTs were overwhelmingly positive about their chosen career virtually all agreeing they enjoyed working as a teacher and rating the relationships they established with their pupils as good or very good. Variations between routes show the most positive being NQTs trained through BEd routes, 97 per cent enjoying working as a teacher, and PGCE trained NQTs the least positive but with 91 per cent still enjoying being a teacher.

Teacher educators

The nature of the ITE curriculum, requirements and inspection framework in England has made it virtually essential that teacher educators have QTS. More recently non-managerial career development opportunities such as Advanced Skills Teachers, and the relatively poor remuneration levels in HE, have made a move to teacher education from a senior leadership position in a primary school financially unattractive. Additionally, the transition from teacher to teacher educator involves 'boundary-crossing' between two very different cultures and activity systems (Boyd *et al.* 2006), and individuals can take two or three years to establish their 'new' professional identities (Murray and Male 2005). The sheer range of knowledge and skills required in the role is challenging (Boyd *et al.* 2007), and having become teacher educators many new recruits are reported to receive inadequate induction (Boyd *et al.* 2006; Murray 2005a). Boyd *et al.* (2007: 7) observe that the literature (Boyd *et al.* 2006; Murray 2005b) identifies three immediate priorities for new teacher educators:

(1) 'survival';
(2) 'shifting the lens of existing expertise. ... [to] the differing pedagogic demands of working with adults'; and
(3) 'laying the foundations for scholarship and research activity'.

Recent initiatives aimed at building capacity and expertise include the allocation of £25 million over three years (2006–9) by HEFCE, through the Teaching Quality Enhancement Funding, to support the 'research informed teaching environment' in less research-intensive institutions. ESCalate (2003–9), an Education Subject Centre of the Higher Education Academy produces resources, organises conferences, and funds small-scale research and development projects with a focus on teaching and learning in education studies – including initial teacher education. Another such initiative is the TDA-funded Teacher Training Resource Bank (TTRB), which aims to increase the quality and range of resources available in ITE to support teacher educators and those training to teach. More recently still, a Teacher Education Reference Group (funded jointly by UCET/BERA/TLRP) with a focus on research support has been established to work alongside the TLRP Capacity Building Programme to produce an on-line bibliography (due to be launched in 2008) as a research training resource to contribute to capacity building in the field of teacher education. Boyd *et al.* (2007) identify the expectation that new teacher educators should engage in research and scholarly activity as an especially challenging aspect of their role.

In addition to the pressure on the individual, however, the impact of institutional research development strategies in the sector as a whole has also had significant structural effect upon education departments. The drive for increased research selectivity, particularly in research intensive universities, has made non research–active recruits from school less attractive to employ and more difficult to assimilate into the academic culture. The profile of staff in education departments who made a submission to the Research Assessment Exercise (RAE) in 2001 shows that, whilst research expertise was spread widely across these institutions, the spectre of a growing dislocation between teacher education and research was a worrying trend. For example, 50 per cent of staff reported in the RAE were employed in institutions that no longer received core QR research funding (rated 3a and below). Increased selectivity can be deduced, however, from inspection of the research profile and character of the institutions that do and do not receive core QR research funding. Departments with no core research designated on average 35 per cent of staff as research-active, attracted 22 per cent of the total UK external research grant income, focused their research on schools and directed it to the teacher audience. Those departments with core QR research funding also received nearly 80 per cent of total UK external research grant income, returned on average 70 per cent of staff as research active, researched areas such as curriculum, assessment, organisation, policy, management and inclusion and directed more of their research to other researchers and policy makers (Oancea 2004a, b). Profiling teacher education in 2004, Dadds and Kynch (2003) found that 80 per cent of teachers were trained in education departments with no core research funding. No data are available regarding the proportion of dedicated teacher educators amongst staff designated research-active in education departments but one can surmise that this will be even less.

Considering the profile of education against comparable disciplines, Mills *et al.* (2005) conducted a Demographic Review of the UK Social Sciences for the ESRC and concluded that the field of education was significantly different. In terms of research activity, at 42.5 per cent it had the lowest proportion of staff entered in the 2001 RAE, compared to an average of 64 per cent in the social sciences as a whole, and only 25 per cent of staff had PhDs in education, compared, for example, to 60 per cent in psychology. Education was three times more likely to attract funding from government than research councils and, as a result, 'tends to lack the research autonomy to enable it to engage policy debates confidently and critically' (Mills *et al.* 2005: 44). Education is the second largest unit of assessment in the social sciences, with some 5000 staff as compared to an average of less than 2000 in the social sciences as a whole (HESA staff record 2003/04). The age profile of education department staff is also older than that in the social sciences generally: in 2003–4 nearly 70 per cent of staff were over the age of 46, 50 per cent were over 50 and approximately 22 per cent over 56. One reason for this is that, because of the need to appoint teacher education staff with QTS, many enter HE later after a mid-career switch. In a survey of research interested/active BERA members conducted by the Research Capacity Building Network (Taylor 2002), just over a third of respondents began their research career aged over 38 years.

It is undoubted that the teacher education workforce succession planning will pose a very significant concern in the near future, and New Blood Schemes are under consideration (HEFCE/TDA). The reasons are complex as rehearsed above: the sheer scale of the problem in terms of the numbers involved; the age profile of the workforce; the age at which teacher educators typically commence their academic career; and the difficulty of recruitment of staff with QTS. Increasing research selectivity potentially poses even more of a threat if research/scholarly activity/doctoral studies are not seen as essential to underpin teaching and as a professional learning expectation for teacher educators. The HEFCE research-informed teaching funding has signaled that teacher educators in all institutions should be providing such an environment. In research intensive institutions the danger is that teacher education may be less attractive to research-active academics if conditions are not conducive to support them in undertaking research, and if teacher educators are not research-active then teacher education may not be valued sufficiently in such institutions to be sustained as core business.

CONTINUING PROFESSIONAL DEVELOPMENT (CPD)

Introduction

Continuing professional development (CPD) is the current terminology for what has been described as in-service education, in-service training, professional development and lifelong learning. The DCSF defines CPD as 'any activity that increases teachers' knowledge or understanding and their effectiveness in schools and can help raise children's standards and improve teachers' job satisfaction' (www.teachernet.gov.uk). However other definitions, such as that offered by Day (1997), interpret the nature and purpose of CPD much more widely and stress the crucial role of teachers in the transmission of values and the evaluation and development of educational policy for which they need the knowledge, skills and emotional intelligence essential to stimulate, sustain and develop professional thinking.

This section focuses predominantly on CPD from the perspectives and experiences of primary teachers. However, to set these in context a brief overview is provided of the trends that have given rise to current CPD provision in England. This is followed by a description of the centralisation of CPD under New Labour. Key issues are explored which relate to: the conceptualisation of CPD by the government and by teachers; the shifting focus from the needs of individual teachers to government priorities and system needs; the move to work-based learning in collaboration with others, culminating in the notion of schools as professional learning communities; and the relationship between CPD and teacher professionalism. Finally the factors constraining and facilitating future CPD development at the level of national policy, the school, and the individual teacher are identified and the implications of these examined.

Historical context

Since the James Report (DES 1972) emphasised the necessity for teachers to receive in-service education in order to develop their knowledge and skills, successive governments have increasingly recognised that not only is support for the ongoing education of teachers vital to the realisation of programmes of educational reform but it is also crucial for the educational, social and economic well-being of the country. From the 1960s to the early 1980s, initiatives and funding arrangements were geared predominantly to the pursuit by individual professionals of their own in-service interests and needs which were met predominantly through attendance at external courses provided by LEAs and HE institutions. As documented by Eraut and Seaborne (1984), who trace the changes in the structure, provision and conceptualisation of in-service teacher education over this period, provision was fragmented and uncoordinated, leading to an uneven distribution of opportunity. In the 1970s and early 1980s school-based curriculum development and school-focussed in-service training (INSET), such as that arising from government awarded Education Support Grants (ESGs), accorded greater attention to the needs of schools and the education system as a whole. However, teachers still retained responsibility for, and control of, their own development. Innovatory teacher-initiated INSET activities were developed in a few areas, such as those arising from curriculum development projects, but these activities were not available for the majority of teachers.

The Education Reform Act (ERA) (1988), which introduced the National Curriculum and its associated national testing, heralded considerable changes for CPD. The CPD agenda became increasingly determined by national priorities and the emphasis shifted from individual to school development. At the same time as central control tightened over the curriculum and assessment, the government decentralised through the delegation to schools and their governing bodies of school budgets, planning and management. Local management of schools (LMS) – initially involving primary schools of over 200 pupils but extended to all primary schools in 1991 – resulted in a substantial reduction in the capacity of local authorities to deliver training. It also brought about the demise of local teachers' centres and the redundancy and redeployment of advisory teachers – a professional group whose numbers expanded rapidly in the 1980s when such teachers played a major role in INSET provision (see, for example, Kinder and Harland 1991; Webb 1989).

Five compulsory training days for all teachers were introduced. Although these training days quickly evolved to provide opportunities for staff to work co-operatively and receive training on topics of importance to their schools, initially teachers were dissatisfied with their content – which was generally unrelated to previous or subsequent training programmes and was not part of any long-term strategy for either school or individual development (Cowan and Wright 1990). Curriculum coordinators (later known as managers and leaders) assumed a major role in the development of their subjects that included INSET provision for their colleagues (Webb and Vulliamy 1996). This consisted mainly of disseminating information from courses that they had attended, which varied in length from one-off 'twilight' sessions to attendance at DES 20-day courses in mathematics and science. However, the 'cascade' approach was fraught with problems and was perceived by staff as having minimal direct impact on classroom practice (Kinder and Harland 1991). Schools received annual funding through developments such as Teacher Related In-Service Training (TRIST), Grant Related In-Service Training (GRIST) and Grants for Educational Support and Training (GEST) to provide and buy training and consultancy services (see, for example Harland *et al.* 1993). These changes in the funding of CPD also gave rise to a substantial increase in the number of professional associations and unions, private trainers, consultants and other commercial agencies entering the CPD market.

Traditional relationships between primary schools and local authorities began to break down. This process was hastened by the introduction of Ofsted inspections and the subsequent change of role for many LEA advisors to that of inspectors. Also, in response to the government's standards agenda, they assumed a hierarchical and authoritative role in driving up pupil attainment in schools in order to satisfy LEA accountability and maintain their position in the tables of LEA performance. For example, LEA consultants for the National Literacy and Numeracy Strategies (NLS and NNS) were regarded negatively by teachers for their role in policing the implementation of the content and pedagogy of the Strategies (Webb and Vulliamy 2006). As argued by Jeffrey (2002), 'the performativity discourse changed teacher-inspector relations from one of partnership to one of subjugation' (p.54). Nevertheless, some LEA (now LA) advisors have continued to act as mentors and critical friends to teachers, often over considerable periods of time (Holden 1997). LAs continue to provide CPD with in-school training – cited by LEA respondents in research by Brown *et al.* (2001) as the activity most frequently provided for teachers, followed by one-off conferences, seminars and workshops. LA initiatives also continue to provide opportunities for teachers' professional development through opportunities to work with teachers from other schools.

The role of higher education (HE) institutions in providing for teachers' professional development has also been subject to considerable change, with expansion throughout the 1960s, 1970s and 1980s followed by much-reduced provision for local teachers by universities over the last two decades. Eraut and Seaborne (1984) chart the demand for, and growth of, long course provision for teachers by HE, including the one year supplementary courses for those trained on courses shorter than the three-year teaching certificate; retraining courses in shortage subjects; first degree courses for serving teachers as teaching became a graduate profession; diploma courses; and higher degrees. Since the 1990s the structure and nature of long courses provided by universities has altered as universities have become increasingly market driven. This has given rise to flexible, modularised masters courses enabling credit transfer and accumulation, accreditation of prior learning and experience, professional development profiles, distance and open learning programmes and a substantial increase in taught doctorates – especially the Ed.D. (Bolam 2000).

According to a survey by Ofsted (2004), about £23.5 million is awarded annually by the government to support the postgraduate training of around 25,000 teachers. The funds are distributed to INSET providers, including HE, through a triennial bidding process with bids being assessed against national priorities and their likely impact on raising standards in schools. This funding supports a range of postgraduate certificates, diplomas and higher degrees where the focus of the training and assignments is on the participants' own schools and on practical action to bring about change in accord with government initiatives. However, the linking by the TTA of the funding for university award-bearing INSET to national priorities has resulted in several programmes with different priorities losing funding. In addition, masters level provision in education, which often involved innovatory programmes of teacher research resulting in changes in teachers' attitudes and classroom practice (Vulliamy and Webb 1991), has lost out in the growing competition from vocational qualifications such as the NPQH. The fall in numbers of practitioners attending longer academic courses in HE can also be attributed to reduced opportunities for them to gain assistance with funding and lack of teacher time and energy owing to increased workloads. Universities have also increasingly turned to the provision of programmes recruiting overseas students or offering programmes in the students' own countries, both of which strategies are a great deal more financially lucrative than courses for local teachers studying part-time. In addition, HE staff under pressure to research and publish in an RAE-dominated university economy have less time to devote to supporting teachers in research and development activities.

New Labour's CPD strategy

The policy document *Teachers: meeting the challenge of change* (DfEE 1998b) set out New Labour's intentions to 'modernise' the teaching profession and have it embrace a 'new professionalism'. This new professionalism required recognition that 'the time has long gone when isolated unaccountable professionals made curriculum and pedagogical decisions alone without reference to the outside world' (DfEE 1998b: 14). It also signalled the increase in central control and prescription, not only of the school curriculum but also of teaching methods (for discussion of the debate on the impact of government reform on primary teachers' professionalism and their perspectives on the issues, see Vulliamy 2006). In the 'new professionalism', participation in CPD is recognised as important – albeit with the predominant purpose of equipping teachers to implement government reforms, and tightly circumscribed within progression through standards and competences for QTS, induction, post-threshold, advanced skills teacher, excellent teacher status and headship. Government policy characterises career progression as a linear process but, as found by Poulson and Avramidis (2003) in relation to the career histories of effective teachers of literacy, many primary teachers follow multi-faceted, non-linear pathways through professional development rather than conforming to such straightforward career trajectories. This is particularly the case for women, who often take a career break to raise children and on return to teaching are likely to specialise in different age groups and/or take on the coordination of different curriculum subjects to those experienced previously.

In September 2000 the General Teaching Council in England (GTCE, or GTC) was formally established and given a specific remit to promote teachers' professional development. In March 2001 the government's strategy for CPD was introduced (DfEE 2001a). Designed in consultation with the GTC, its aims were: to promote the benefits of CPD; to help teachers make the most of the choices available to them; and to integrate CPD with performance management and school improvement, so building schools' capacity for effective professional development. The strategy was then relaunched to reflect additional CPD initiatives such as e-learning and networked learning communities, and the Virtual Teachers' Centre. The GTC contributed to the strategy with its Teachers' Professional Learning Framework (TPLF) that sets out teachers' entitlement and responsibilities in relation to CPD with a view to facilitating individual and school 'learning plans'. It also hosts a range of conferences and events for teachers and has set up the Teacher Learning Academy (TLA) to provide professional and public recognition through a national system of accreditation for the learning and development that teachers undertake as part of their professional work. This accreditation spans six stages, from 'Associate' (entry-level) to 'Senior Fellow' (equivalent to an education doctorate). An NFER evaluation of pilot phases 1 and 2 (Moor *et al.* 2006) found of the 1,267 teachers joining the TLA 48 per cent taught primary age children. The strongest impacts of participation were the perceived improvements to pupils' learning, enrolees' teaching and the enhanced contribution made to their colleagues and schools. In common with other forms of CPD lack of time was a constraint, but understanding the submission requirements and process was also a chief concern that threatened TLA project completion. However, for those who did submit their work (non-submitting enrolees exceeded submitters) Moor *et al.* (2006) concluded the venture 'was highly valued' and 'they derived significant outcomes from their involvement' (summary, xi).

In 2005 the Training and Development Agency for Schools (TDA) assumed the responsibility from the DfES for the national coordination of CPD for all school staff. The CPD Partnership Project, which promoted the TPLF principles of collaboration, ownership, entitlement and responsibility, brought together the GTC, the TDA and schools and LEA personnel in the 26 participating LEAs to exert a positive coordinated influence on CPD provision (Moor *et al.* 2005). The Local Government Association (LGA) is also addressing what entitlement to CPD teachers should have throughout their careers and how the responsibility for this should be shared by individual teachers, schools, LAs and other institutions and agencies (Brown *et al.*2001). Increasingly, statements of CPD policy are posted on LA websites. At the level of policy rhetoric, teachers' CPD has a high profile.

The centralisation of CPD carried forward under New Labour was manifest particularly in the training of primary teachers to support the implementation of the NLS and the NNS, described by Earl *et al.*(2003) as 'the most ambitious large-scale educational reform initiative in the world' (p.11). An extensive infrastructure of regional directors and LEA staff for literacy and numeracy was set up to link schools to the central agencies and bring about change. Literacy and numeracy coordinators, following initial training, were responsible for disseminating the Strategies in their schools. In contrast to the situation when coordinators disseminated information on National Curriculum subjects, Earl *et al.* (2003) found many coordinators to be highly influential in supporting colleagues through assisting with planning, monitoring teaching and analysing assessment data. However, for coordinators to play a leading role successfully required support from the head teacher such as the provision of release time and opportunities to develop new skills.

Although primary teachers greatly resented the ways in which the Strategies were imposed on schools, their implementation resulted in greater consistency of practice in literacy and numeracy and across the curriculum, and brought about changes in practice that challenged teachers' beliefs and stimulated professional learning (Webb and Vulliamy 2006). However, such an approach to change is viewed as having important shortcomings because teachers may not develop adequate understanding of the rationale and principles underpinning the initiative in order to sustain and develop it. Thus Earl *et al.*(2003) conclude that 'some teachers may feel they have fully implemented the Strategies, but may lack awareness of the underlying principles', or owing to lack of subject knowledge 'will have made the easier changes required by the Strategies and may not recognise that many changes and more knowledge are still required' (Earl *et al.* 2003: 94). While research has identified considerable benefits for teaching and learning derived from the Strategies, it also substantiates Earl *et al.*'s (2003) conclusions by suggesting that, particularly in relation to the characteristics of interactive whole class teaching promoted by the Strategies, the changes are superficial (see, for example, Brown *et al.* 2003; Hargreaves, L. *et al.* 2003). In addition, Hargreaves, A. (2003: 189) warns that over time teachers who have become dependent on 'the external authority of bureaucrats, on scripted texts, or on "incontrovertible" results of research' will 'lose the capacity or desire to make professional judgements and become more reflective'.

Identifying and meeting CPD needs

In the third annual 2006 survey for the GTC (Hutchings *et al.* 2006) more than a third of the respondents identified CPD as a factor that had enhanced their career development while 12 per cent indicated that their career development had been constrained by insufficient or poor quality CPD. Responses differed according to the respondents' professional roles. Head teachers were the most satisfied that their needs were met, having engaged in the most different types of CPD activity. They were also the most confident that CPD was valued in their schools and taken into account in decision-making. By comparison, classteachers were less satisfied that their needs had been met, had experienced less variety in CPD activity, and were less confident that CPD was valued and taken into account in their schools. Supply teachers were the least satisfied group, especially those entering teaching in 2004–5.

A much higher proportion of teachers in each professional role in primary schools reported that their needs had been met (fully or to some extent) than in secondary. The generally more positive perception of CPD provision held by primary teachers in the GTC survey was consistent with the findings of Hustler *et al.* (2003) in a DfES-funded survey of teachers' perceptions of CPD and teachers involved in the VITAE project (Day *et al.* 2006). Both studies found most teachers were satisfied with their CPD over the last five years. Positive feelings about CPD for all but late career teachers were quite often associated with a sense of career progression possibilities to which CPD opportunities could be linked. Features of worthwhile CPD across all the studies drawn upon were that it should be focused, well-structured, presented by people with recent knowledge, included provision for active learning, and that it was relevant and applicable to school/classroom settings. However, notions of what constitutes relevance differ. Negative feelings were especially associated with 'one size fits all' standardised CPD provision (for example, much New Opportunities (NOF) ICT training), which did not take account of teachers' existing knowledge, experience and needs' (Hustler *et al*. 2003: ix).

Grundy and Robinson (2004) stress the importance of 'personal drivers' – the needs and concerns of teachers derived from life histories, personal circumstances and professional life trajectories which determine receptiveness to and enthusiasm for professional development – a finding which is echoed by Day *et al*. (2006). However, Hustler *et al*. (2003) found that most teachers felt that the principal drivers for CPD activity over the last five years had been school development needs and national priorities. Moreover, in many schools there appeared to be a compliant culture which discouraged teachers from pressing for CPD to meet their professional needs (Hustler *et al*. 2003). As observed by Burns (2005) in his case study of CPD within a group of rural primary schools, teachers identify their own personal professional needs with school training needs. This is because the current managerialist system projects external pressures of government requirements, league tables and Ofsted inspections onto individual teachers through school development/improvement plans and performance management. These pressures were so strong that some teachers felt guilty about having personal goals and ambitions different from, or even at odds with, school needs. A bottom-up approach whereby a whole school focus and specific staff training were built into the school improvement plan as a result of weaknesses identified through staff performance management and individual requests appears to occur less frequently (Burns 2005). The DfEE (2000: para.8) states that 'existing practice in many schools demonstrates that these three strands (i.e. individual, school and national needs) reinforce rather than conflict with each other', which is hardly surprising if school and individual needs are determined by, and subsumed under, national needs. The intention to focus on 'more closely integrating CPD, performance management and school improvement as key components of effective whole school policies on teaching and learning' (www.teachernet.gov.uk) seems likely to exacerbate the situation.

Research has established the effectiveness of CPD where teachers have ownership over their professional development and scope for identifying their own CPD focus (for example Cordingly *et al*. 2003; Downing *et al*. 2004; Moor *et al*. 2005). In response, the DfEE (2000) has given some acknowledgement of the importance of balancing system and individual needs by increasing investment in CPD for individual teachers. Thus, for example, the ongoing Teachers' International Professional Development (TIPD) programmes launched in 2000 provide 2,500 short-term study visits abroad a year. However, the professional bursaries that were paid directly to teachers to help them achieve their individual career goals, the £3 million that was allocated for individual Best Practice Research Scholarships for teachers to carry out research in partnership with a university and/or other schools, and the sabbaticals for experienced teachers working in challenging schools have ceased. This is despite evidence that they were a valuable form of professional development (for example Furlong *et al*. 2003; Downing *et al*. 2004). Clearly there needs to be greater government recognition of the importance of opportunities for individual professional and career development.

The nature of CPD activities

Hustler *et al.* (2003) found that, although thinking about CPD varied in relation to school context and career stage, most teachers held a traditional view of CPD as consisting of courses, conferences and INSET days. Reflecting government policy, in 2001 most CPD focussed on teaching skills and subject knowledge and was predominantly led by school staff. Although CPD activities, such as research, secondments, award bearing courses and international visits were highly valued by respondents, few teachers took part in them. Similarly, in the GTC 2006 survey the most frequently reported CPD activities over the previous 12 months identified from a list of CPD activities were 'courses held on school INSET days' (90 per cent) followed by 'being observed by colleagues' (83 per cent); 'taking part in school self-evaluation processes' (81 per cent); and 'collaborative learning with colleagues in my school' (80 per cent) (Hutchings *et al.* 2006: 62). The VITAE teachers had similar experiences of CPD, leading Day *et al.* (2006) to identify two key messages. The first concerns teachers' apparent lack of experience of the relatively recent extensive CPD initiatives taken at policy level. The second is that their schools did not seem to offer a wide range of CPD opportunities which focussed on both their professional knowledge and skills and their socio-emotional (well-being) needs (p.141).

The GTC emphasises that 'Evidence from school improvement research and testimony from teachers highlights how important it is to move from individual to collective professional development' (www.gtce.org.uk/TPLF). Collaborative working involving teamwork in schools, networking between schools such as in the NCSL/DfES Network Learning Communities, and collaboration with the wider community are advocated as the way forward for raising standards and promoting innovation in primary schools (DfES 2003a). Since the ERA (1988), largely as a result of teachers working together to implement government reform, the individualised culture of primary schools has changed to one which emphasises collegiality, even though the pace of change and pressures of accountability mean that teachers may be 'collaborating under constraint' (Woods *et al.* 1997) and forced into 'contrived collegiality' (Hargreaves 1994). Collaborative CPD interventions such as peer support, observation with feedback, the use of external expertise in school-based activity and professional dialogue have been found to be beneficial for teachers and pupils (Cordingley *et al.* 2003). Boyle *et al.* (2005) also report that time and opportunities for teachers to reflect on their own practice and to share this with colleagues were the most popular longer-term professional development activities that had an impact on the change of one or more aspects of a teacher's classroom practice. In the VITAE study, 'collaborative learning with colleagues within teachers' own schools as well as across schools was also rated as a highly important and useful form of CPD activity' (Day *et al.* 2006: 133). As shown by Webb and Vulliamy (forthcoming 2008), the introduction of planning, preparation and assessment (PPA) time in primary schools where teachers within a key stage or year group are released together has created additional opportunities for collaborative learning.

As argued by Clement and Vandenberghe (2000: 81) in relation to professional development and school improvement, collegiality has acquired the status of a panacea for all problems, whilst remaining ill-defined and underconceptualised. They suggest that autonomy and collegiality have tended to be polarised, with autonomy regarded negatively, whereas Poulson and Avramidis (2003) in their study of effective teachers of literacy found autonomous and collegial learning to be complementary. Their case-study teachers engaged in personal reading and study and solitary experimentation with the ideas encountered in their own classrooms and this often led to the sharing of their experiences with trusted colleagues and collaborative activity.

Day *et al.* (2006) found the need for collaboration and network support to be parti-cularly important for teachers in small primary schools. The geographic isolation of some small rural primary schools, the small pool of within-school expertise on which to draw for school-based training, and little flexibility in deployment of the school budget can pose constraints on access to CPD. However, as argued by Wilson and McPake (2000), head teachers of small schools usually work closely with staff, are involved in planning and implementing change and so have heightened awareness of the issues. In some areas, clusters of primary schools and pyramids of secondary schools and feeder primaries have reduced potential isolation and created opportunities for joint CPD (Webb and Vulliamy, forthcoming 2008). However, such co-operation can be adversely affected by competition for pupils, reduced LEA support and the individual management of school budgets (Ribchester and Edwards 1998).

Professional learning communities

The term professional learning community (PLC) has become a globally fashionable one for describing schools, with its realisation viewed as essential for bringing about substantial and successful change in school policy and practice (Webb *et al.* 2006). The ideal professional learning community is one 'where people continually expand their capacity to create the results they truly desire, where new and expansive patterns of thinking are nurtured, where collective aspiration is set free, and where people are continually learning how to learn together' (Senge 1990: 3). Such communities value, promote and are sustained by teachers' CPD. However, 'professional', 'learning' and 'communities' are all contested concepts that lend themselves to a variety of inter-pretations and can be fitted into differing and potentially conflicting agendas from narrow government concerns to meet national attainment targets to the kinds of heightened political awareness that could give rise to 'an activist teaching profession' envisaged by Sachs (2003). The idea of a PLC overlaps with, and is informed by, earlier work on schools as learning organisations and school improvement research (Stoll *et al.* 2003). The New Labour government's CPD strategy (DfEE 2001a) encouraged schools to become PLCs, and the notion is central to the DfES' Core Principles for Raising Standards in Teaching and Learning and the NCSL's revised National Standards for Headteachers. Guidance derived from DfES commissioned research (Bolam *et al.* 2005) on evaluating, planning and developing schools as PLCs and assessing their impact is available on the DCSF Standards Site (http://www.standards.dfes.gov.uk).

While PLCs put a premium on teachers working together, albeit for varying out-comes, Hargreaves states they must 'also insist that this joint work consistently focuses on improving teaching and learning, and uses evidence and data as a basis for inform-ing classroom improvement efforts and solving whole-school problems' (Hargreaves 2003: 184). The collection, analysis and use of attainment data, school-based self-evaluation and the use by teachers of externally generated research reflect the government's aspirations for evidence-based practice. The focus on teaching and learning is viewed as crucial to raising standards of pupil attainment. While as yet there is little research linking schools working as PLCs to student outcomes, there is evidence particularly from the USA that schools operating in the ways outlined above positively influence student achievement (for example Bryk *et al.* 1999).

An extended interpretation of a PLC is one incorporating not only members of the school staff but also pupils, parents and the local community, who all work together to identify for themselves shared aims, values and an agenda for action for their school. However, MacBeath's (2005) research on distributed leadership suggests that in many English schools there appears to be a considerable gap between these aspirations and reality, and that a major turn around in teacher attitudes will be required if parents and pupils are to become accepted contributors to school learning communities. Nevertheless, there are schools to point the way forward. Jeffrey and Woods in their in-depth study of Coombes Infant and Nursery school describe the involvement of the whole community in the school and argue that 'Coombes is a paradigm case of a learning community', and 'the heart of its success lies in that concept' (Jeffrey and Woods 2003: 123).

Factors promoting and constraining CPD

Ofsted (2006c) describes the CPD arrangements in schools with good practice in CPD management and use 'as a logical chain of procedures which entails identifying school and staff needs, planning to meet those needs, providing varied and relevant activities, involving support staff alongside teachers, monitoring progress and evaluating the impact of the professional development' (p.2). However, even in these schools concerns are raised regarding: the lack of rigour in identifying and meeting the CPD needs of individual teachers; inadequate identification at the planning stage of the intended outcomes of the CPD – and largely because of this few schools evaluated the impact of CPD successfully; and the inability of head teachers to evaluate the value for money of their CPD policy. Goodall *et al.* (2005) carried out a two year project to investigate the range of evaluative practices used by schools in relation to CPD, and to provide materials which could aid schools with evaluating CPD in the future. They found that the vast majority of evaluation practices were geared to collecting participants' reactions and views on their learning and on the use of new knowledge and skills. Surveys or questionnaires were the most widely used evaluation tool. In many cases the completion of a questionnaire was regarded as an end in itself. The most frequent second party means of evaluating the impact of CPD was observation of teaching, with only 25 per cent of schools engaging in practices to evaluate pupil learning outcomes such as pupil interviews and monitoring pupil work. Goodall *et al.* (2005) also discovered a high degree of confusion between dissemination (transference of knowledge to colleagues) and evaluation (including some attempted measurement of change as a result of that knowledge), resulting in a proliferation of low level dissemination that was equated with evaluation. They conclude that many schools appeared to collect data that could have been used to evaluate the effect on pupils of changes in practice as a result of CPD but they lacked the opportunity to relate the information back to CPD in general or particular CPD events.

Brown *et al.* emphasise the fundamental role in teachers' CPD played by the head teacher and/or the CPD co-ordinator. They were identified as 'the gatekeepers to staff's participation in external CPD activities, receiving external CPD information; suggesting/recommending CPD to staff; and ultimately governing whether staff could participate in CPD' (Brown *et al.* 2001: iii). It was their role 'to bridge the gap between individual and CPD needs.' The CPD coordinator role, which appears crucial in balancing and inter-relating national, school and individual needs, and that of other senior staff involved in shaping CPD policy and practice is underdeveloped (see also Hustler *et al.* 2003; Goodall *et al.* 2005). CPD coordinators and primary head teachers and deputies, who either assume or support this role, require guidance in identifying staff CPD needs, wider interpretations of CPD and greater awareness of the relationship of CPD to job satisfaction and career routes together with the need to evaluate CPD in relation to a range of factors in addition to meeting government targets.

Lack of time, heavy workload, financial cost and distance from training opportunities were important constraints on access to CPD (Day *et al.* 2006; Goodall *et al.* 2005; Hustler *et al.* 2003). In the GTC 2006 survey (Hutchings *et al.* 2006), 31 per cent of teachers agreed with the statement that 'in my school, the budget for supply cover is adequate for teachers' CPD needs', but 41 per cent disagreed with it. This reflects the finding of other studies, such as Webb and Vulliamy (forthcoming 2008), that lack of funds was a major barrier to professional development.

In 2003 the government, employers and most trade unions (with the exception of the National Union of Teachers) signed up to the *Raising Standards and Tackling Workload: a national agreement* (DfES 2003b) that aimed to raise standards and reduce teachers' workloads over a three-year timescale. The resulting increase in the size and nature of the primary schools' workforce, particularly the expansion in the numbers of teaching assistants employed, means that primary schools are having to cater for an even wider range of CPD needs than previously and will require additional resources and support in order to do this effectively (Webb and Vulliamy 2006).

As illustrated by Webb (2005), exceptional primary head teachers can practise forms of transformational leadership that create school climates promoting individual and collective learning, risk taking and innovation. However, the current climate of central control, managerialism and performativity makes it exceedingly difficult for head teachers to develop school communities where teachers can engage in a range of initiatives and developments that simultaneously lead to personal development, improvements in classroom practice and pupil learning and the confidence and willingness to engage in debate on primary education at local and national level. The discourse of derision vented on primary teachers; the approach to bringing about reform whereby through incentives, systems, routines and inspections teachers are pressured to embrace central recommendations and adjust their practice accordingly; and the lack of attention paid to teachers' expertise and perspectives have undermined teacher confidence and made them wary or unwilling to challenge imposed initiatives.

The GTC 2006 survey concludes that, owing to the diversity of needs and experience across the teaching population in relation to CPD, 'there is certainly no "one size fits all" solution possible' (Hutchings *et al.* 2006: 80). Like pupils, teachers benefit from personalised learning and require access to a diversity of differentiated provision to facilitate and promote their learning and careers. Government actions need to match the possibilities espoused in policy rhetoric by disseminating and promoting the broader lifelong learning characteristics of CPD and by alerting teachers to the range of opportunities for them to pursue and develop specific interests within and outside school, both in this country and abroad. In addition, CPD needs to be concerned not only to update teachers' content knowledge and pedagogical skills and improve pupil learning but also with the moral purposes of teaching, the political context of teaching and the quality of teachers' thinking. It also has the potential to play a much greater role in maintaining motivation and commitment to teaching and boosting morale. Currently, the government CPD strategy fails to recognise that teachers need more responsibility and control over the focus, structure and timing of their professional development and that this is fundamental to the development of professional learning communities that have the capacity to solve problems and to be creative. The 'new professionalism' requires a reconceptualisation of CPD.

SCHOOL LEADERSHIP DEVELOPMENT

Introduction

Recent decades have seen a growing interest in the ways in which schools are structured and administered as a method of enhancing pupil outcomes. Moreover, it is acknowledged widely that the shift to school-based systems of management, along with the increased regulatory and accountability requirements embodied in the 1988 Education Reform Act, created the need for enhanced leadership training for schools. During this period the term 'management' enjoyed dominance in the discourse on school administration, only to be replaced by the allied and sometimes overlapping conception embodied in the term 'leadership'. It is this latter term which is employed throughout this section. By far the most significant development in this field in the UK, and to some extent internationally, over this period has been the increasing intervention of national government agencies in the preparation and subsequent development of school leaders prior to appointment and post appointment to headship. However, it is important to point out that the conception of school leadership has increasingly come to encompass a broader conceptualisation that views leadership as an important element in the work of teachers at all levels in schools, and there is also a developing notion of pupils as leaders in their own right. Nonetheless, limitations of space require that the focus in this section is primarily on training of the most senior leaders in schools, although the section on 'Other leadership development programmes' (page 567) attempts to outline the wider work of the National College for School Leadership (NCSL). The parameters of the Primary Review and the dramatic expansion of interest in this area, and the consequent expansion in the literature on the topic, necessitate that the discussion and main references are limited to British, and more specifically, English developments in this field. The central line of argument adopted is that the creation of national leadership programmes and the allied construction of a National College has been profoundly impressive but has brought with it inherent dangers of bureaucratic intervention by the state, with allied challenges to the role of more traditional providers of leadership research and development such as Higher Education Institutions and Local Education Authorities.

A number of accounts of the development of school leadership programmes in England have been offered (see, for instance, Bolam 1997, 2003; Brundrett 2000, 2001), one of the most persuasive of which is that by Bolam (2004) which sees the development as having three phases, including: 'ad hoc provision' in the 1960s and early 1970s; 'towards coherence and coordination' in the 1970s, 1980s and 1990s; 'a national college' from 2002. Limitation of space precludes a detailed outline of all three phases and this analysis will concentrate on the period from the 1988 Act, especially the construction of a framework of 'national programmes' by the Teacher Training Agency (TTA) and subsequently by the National College for School Leadership (NCSL). However, it is apposite to point out that a series of reports dating back to the 1960s, including those by Robbins (1963), Franks (1967), Plowden (CACE 1967), and James (1972), identified the emerging need for more effective in-service training throughout the education sector. The Commonwealth Council for Educational Administration and Management (CCEAM) and the British Educational Management and Administrative Society (now British Educational Leadership, Management and Administration Society) were founded in 1971 and 1972 respectively. Co-terminously with such developments, Master of Education degree programmes began to proliferate in the 1960s (Shanks 1987: 122–23) and higher degree programmes with elements of Educational Management began to appear in the 1970s (Bush 1999: 239). Moreover, central government agencies intervened in leadership development as early as the 1980s when Department of Education and Science (DES) Circular 3/83 identified educational management training as one of four priorities for teacher training and introduced 'One Term Training Opportunities' (OTTOs) for head teachers. The 1980s also witnessed the creation of a National Development Centre for School Management Training (NDC), established at the School of Education at the University of Bristol to stimulate management training and research. By the end of the 1980s, however, the National Development Centre had been closed down and the government had set up a School Management Task Force with a remit to report on a more effective national strategy for training head teachers and school staff with management roles. Although the work of these initiatives had come to an end by the early 1990s their work undoubtedly influenced the subsequent development of national training initiatives.

Creating national programmes for leadership development

From the mid-1990s, the focus shifted from local and regional initiatives, increasingly supported and co-ordinated by central co-ordination, to the progressively more influential 'national programmes' which changed the power relationship between the governmental and regulatory authorities and the providers of in-service training significantly (Brundrett 2001: 237). The remit for the development and management of these programmes originally fell to the TTA. It was held briefly under the direct control of DfES and subsequently transferred to the NCSL, which commenced its activities in temporary premises at the University of Nottingham in 2000 before moving to purpose-built premises on the same site in 2002. The NCSL was established to ensure that our current and future school leaders develop the skills, the capability and capacity to lead and transform the school education system into the best in the world (DfEE 2001). The NCSL has subsequently played a pivotal role in the co-ordination of national programmes of school leadership development and now oversees the development and delivery of courses and qualifications in England. It aims to combine the intellectual, professional and practical development of school leaders, drawing on best practice, while supporting an ongoing discourse about school leadership that will inform its work (Earley *et al.* 2002). NCSL's corporate plan for 2002/06 put in place what was by 2004 the largest educational leadership development programme in the world (NCSL 2001b).

In 2001, NCSL produced the *Leadership Development Framework*, which outlined five areas of leadership development linked to a series of core and extension programmes. These included: emergent leaders – for people who are beginning to take on formal leadership roles; established leaders – experienced deputy and assistant head teachers who have decided not to pursue headship; entry to headship – for those aspiring to or embarking on their first headship; advanced leaders – head teachers with four or more years' experience able to attend the Leadership Programme for Serving Head teachers (LPSH); and consultant leaders – experienced head teachers and other leaders who wish to take on the responsibility for the future development of school leadership (NCSL 2001c). In essence this framework enculated and enlarged the construction that had emerged during the previous six years of development which had come to be based around preparatory, induction and further training for head teachers.

Early headship programmes

The Head teachers' Leadership and Management Programme (HEADLAMP) was the first of the headship development programmes to be introduced, and commenced operation in 1995. Its key aim was to provide funds 'to support the cost of developing the leadership and management abilities of head teachers appointed to their first permanent headship' (TTA 1995b). The HEADLAMP programme gave a considerable degree of flexibility to head teachers and governors in their choice of training and training provider (Busher and Paxton 1997: 121). Nonetheless, it was LEAs who became the major HEADLAMP providers (Blandford and Squire 1999: 7) and thus the scheme never fulfilled the purpose of opening up leadership training to a range of trainers chosen in an open market. The impact of the initiative is not to be underestimated since it prefigured other programmes. It was a centrally-controlled initiative based on a set of generic standards that defined the required leadership and management capabilities of school leaders. The HEADLAMP scheme came under review in 1998, but a report was not completed until three years later when it was found that there was insufficient focus on leadership in context and variability in the quality of programmes (Newsome 2001).

During this period, the programme was evaluated by Ofsted (2003b) which, while reporting how few of the providers had effective quality assurance procedures in place (p.6), made a number of further observations. Candidates received little objective guidance or advice about the full range of training that was available, and so they frequently opted to select from what was available locally. Only one of the six providers examined was judged to have good or very good provision across all aspects inspected, although each provider exemplified good practice in at least one area. Weakest areas were deemed to be the identification of needs and quality assurance, though the overall quality of the training was good or very good in all of the providers and the impact of the provision was considered to be good in most. The needs identification process was most effective when it enabled head teachers to analyse their development needs accurately against the National Standards for Head teachers, while the quality of individual training sessions was mostly judged to be good though their content was often insufficiently based on the particular needs of participants and explicit links were very rarely made with the National Standards (p. 5). Notably, the report indicated that there was little differentiation of the needs of head teachers from different sectors of education or from different contexts, such as those from small rural primary schools as opposed to those from large inner-city comprehensives (p. 5). Nevertheless Ofsted indicated that HEADLAMP training was felt by most participants to have been effective in increasing their confidence, helping them to address specific issues in their schools and developing their knowledge and understanding of leadership styles and management strategies. However, the lack of systematic evidence checking impact made it difficult to assess fully the impact that HEADLAMP training had since its inception on improving participants' ability to manage change, improve teaching and learning, and raise standards in their schools (p. 5).

The recommendations from the subsequent review were underpinned by the notion that programmes should be more tightly structured around a number of aims promoting clear links to National Professional Qualification for Headship (NPQH) and the professional development of new heads within the context of school improvement. A 'blended learning' approach was also promoted as being consistent with the *Leadership Development Framework* (NCSL 2001c). The findings and recommendations of the review have contributed to the new framework for entry to headship. The decision about replacement programmes was publicly announced by the NCSL in 2003 and the Head teachers' Induction Programme (HIP), designed to replace HEADLAMP, commenced in that year. The programme was subject to further review and revision and was replaced by the Early Headship Programme (EHP) in 2006, which was designed for a number of purposes. It was designed to support new head teachers in identifying and addressing their development needs as they followed their desired pathway through the early years of headship, providing access to a wide range of learning opportunities for new head teachers. It had to enable new head teachers to experience and understand the value of coaching and collaborative leadership learning and help them apply their learning in the contextual realities of their school and locality. It was meant to bring new head teachers from the periphery of headship to full membership and help new head teachers to recognise the impact that their leadership behaviours have on others and ultimately on pupils' learning in their schools (NCSL 2007e).

Headship qualifications

The second element of the governmental strategy to improve school leadership arrived in 1997 and was styled the NPQH. In its early form it was a complex, centrally controlled but regionally delivered programme of training and development with an allied, but separate, system of assessment (Brundrett 2001). The initiative has been attacked for its reliance on a competency system (Revell 1997), for its daunting nature (Downes 1996: 27), and for its lack of a centralised 'staff college experience' (Bazalgette 1996: 17). Others felt that there was a danger that the qualification might become too academically-rather than practically-focused (Pountney 1997: 4). Moreover, Bush (1998) identified three particular areas for 'further consideration and review'. Firstly, a distinction was made between 'leadership' and 'management'. Secondly, 'best practice outside education' was emphasised. Thirdly, the weak links between NPQH and specialist masters' degrees in educational leadership and management (Bush 1998: 328) were pinpointed. In response to such robust criticisms the NPQH was completely restructured in 2000 following a major review, with new contractors being appointed to offer the revised scheme which commenced in 2001 (NCSL 2001a). The new scheme is much more competency-based and is more focused on schools with a school-based assessment process which is more challenging, individualised and focused on school improvement. It has been acknowledged that the new model transformed the programme and made it 'genuinely and internationally cutting-edge' (Tomlinson 2004: 231), while these transformations enabled the DfES to make the qualification mandatory for all head teachers from 2004. This move towards mandatory status has undoubtedly presented a challenge to ensure sufficient throughput on the programme, in order that the required numbers of graduates would exist to fill headship vacancies. Total numbers undertaking NPQH are indicated in Table 24.4.

The programme is currently going through a further review with the aim of making it more specifically related to those intending to move into headship and linking it more closely to the Early Headship Programme. This revised version was trialled during 2007.

Advanced leadership programmes

The third rung in the ladder of qualifications and programmes came with the introduction of the Leadership Programme for Serving Head teachers (LPSH) (Green 1998). The LPSH scheme offered even tighter centralised control than had the NPQH programme. The contract to construct materials was awarded to the management consultancy firm Hay-McBer (with the NAHT and the Open University), although a number of consortia were successful in being permitted to deliver the resultant training package. The programme was designed to encompass a three-stage process. These included: self diagnosis; a four-day residential workshop; and follow-up support through Information and Communications Technologies (ICT), coaching and mentoring. Each head teacher was, somewhat contentiously, paired with a partner from business who contributed to the implementation of the action plan (Bush 1998: 330). The revised programme was underpinned by a Leadership Effectiveness Model, developed by the Hay Group, that encompassed the 'four circles': 'job requirements'; 'the context for school improvement'; 'leadership styles'; and 'individual characteristics'. The revised programme provided a very different model from the National Standards that underpin other NCSL activity. The model was one which concentrated on leadership effectiveness and performance, measuring leadership capacity through adapted psychological assessment techniques and 360 degree appraisal rather than by using the standards based model inherent in NPQH final assessment (Tomlinson 2004: 235). Total numbers undertaking the LPSH programme run into several thousands, as indicated in Table 24.5.

The programme came under further review in 2006 and a new programme entitled Head for the Future (HftF) was created in that year. The new programme was designed collaboratively between NCSL and the Hay Group Consortium, and retains what are

Table 24.4 Numbers undertaking NPQH 1997–2003

Phase	Status	New Model		Old Model		Totals	
		Male	*Female*	*Male*	*Female*	*Male*	*Female*
Primary	Completed	2,673	8,883	654	2,068	3,327	10,951
	In progress*	1,040	3,332			1,040	3,332
	Withdrawn	498	1,471	515	1,289	1,013	2,760
Secondary	Completed	4,016	3,492	1,182	915	5,198	4,407
	In progress*	1,737	1,551			1,737	1,551
	Withdrawn	530	401	655	419	1,185	820

*in progress included deferred, deferring, withdrawing, not started, frozen.
(Source: National College for School Leadership.)

Table 24.5 Numbers undertaking LPSH 1997–2003

		Male	*Female*
Primary	Enrolled/Completed	626	1,595
	Withdrawn/Deferred	15	29
Secondary	Enrolled/Completed	252	148
	Withdrawn/Deferred	7	5
Unknown	Enrolled/Completed	190	279
	Withdrawn/Deferred	15	13

(Source: National College for School Leadership.)

considered to be the best elements of LPSH including the feedback and diagnostics, the practical models of leadership and the debate with other head teachers. The new programme is designed to 'directly tackle emerging challenges for headship, particularly the need to collaborate with other schools and agencies' and 'asks each participant to challenge perceptions about the change and outcomes they require, keeping a clear view of what their distinctive context demands' (NCSL 2007a).

Other leadership development programmes

The functions and activities of the NCSL include not only the preparation, induction and development of headship initiatives but also include a wide number of other programmes. The comparatively recent (2003) inclusion of 'Leading from the Middle' in the NCSL portfolio is a highly significant development since it targets middle leaders in schools and is thus emblematic of a commitment to the development of leadership capacity at all levels in the teaching profession. In terms of numbers this is a major initiative, as can be judged from Table 24.6.

Other NCSL activities include: online learning and network information including Talking Heads and Virtual Heads; research and development projects; and the Networked Learning Communities scheme (Bolam 2004: 260). The NCSL also operated 'affiliated regional centres', which no longer exist, but the 'Leadership Network' now takes responsibility for developing the College's regional links and involves over 2000 schools organised in nine regions. This rapid expansion in activity can be perceived as

Table 24.6 Numbers undertaking 'Leading from the Middle' 2003–2006

		Male	*Female*
Primary	Enrolled/Completed	1,577	7,360
	Withdrawn/Deferred	172	799
Secondary	Enrolled/Completed	7,379	9,153
	Withdrawn/Deferred	867	1,161
Unknown	Enrolled/Completed	1,464	1,461
	Withdrawn/Deferred	95	151

(Source: National College for School Leadership.)

both an achievement and a weakness. An end to end review of the NCSL, presented in 2004, noted its 'very significant, even remarkable, achievements', but called for 'streamlining the NCSL's efforts to increase its impact through greater role clarity, outcome focus, goal clarity and efficiency' (DfES/NCSL 2004: 5). This was re-echoed by the Minister of Education, who called for 'greater precision, discipline, outcome-focus, and depth in the future work of the College' (Minister of State for Education 2004: 2). Nonetheless, at the time of writing, the NCSL website listed 29 programmes that address a diverse range of issues including Bursar development, developing the capacity for improvement, equality in promotion, the strategic leadership of ICT, and an influential research associates scheme that enables leadership practitioners to undertake systematic research funded by the College (NCSL 2007b).

For the purposes of this study it is notable that two of these programmes focus on primary school leadership specifically. The 'Leading Small Primary Schools' programme runs over two terms and involves four days of blended learning, including interactive workshops, a two-day residential visit, a series of structured inter-school visits and access to a dedicated online community.

The programme 'offers opportunities for school leaders and local authorities to work collaboratively together at both regional and local levels' and 'a framework of support and advice is provided by a network of head teacher and lead facilitators' (NCSL 2007c). The Primary Strategy Leadership Programme involves a working partnership between the DCSF, Primary Strategy, NCSL and local authorities. Approximately 1,900 Primary Strategy Consultant Leaders were trained and then deployed to work with nearly 10,000 primary schools across England between May 2003 and the end of 2006. The programme had a number of aims, including the following. It was designed to:

- strengthen collaborative leadership and responsibility for teaching and learning within a school;
- provide time for the leadership team of a school;
- bring together the expert support and guidance available locally to help address the particular issues identified within a school;
- help schools realise the benefits of remodelling and primary learning networks to improve learning and teaching and raise standards;
- make further improvements in Foundation Stage outcomes and Key Stage 1 and 2 results in English and mathematics over the period 2006–8; and
- include the 'Sustaining Success' programme from 2006, designed to analyse, embed and extend, successful activity (NCSL 2007d).

Critiques of leadership development programmes

An Ofsted review of leadership and management training for head teachers, published in 2002 (Ofsted 2002a), drew for its conclusions on inspections of all of the first seven cohorts of NPQH, inspection of the induction arrangements for head teachers in 43 LEAs, visits to 15 LPSH training events with follow-up visits to 33 course members in 23 LEAs, substantial evidence on the quality of leadership and management in schools from section 10 inspections, and focused surveys by HMI. The report thus provides some of the most detailed analysis of the efficacy of the main national programmes of leadership development. The report noted that leadership and management in schools was improving and that leadership and management were good or better in approximately three quarters of primary, special and secondary schools. However, there were still one in twelve primary schools, one in seventeen secondary schools and one in twenty special schools with unsatisfactory or poor leadership and management. In addition, even in schools where leadership and management were judged to be good overall, there were common areas of weakness across all phases to which training needed to respond. The report had a number of main findings. The quality of the NPQH programme improved significantly throughout the first seven cohorts. Much of the training was of good quality but there remained concerns about the selection of appropriate candidates and the capacity of the training to respond to a wide range of needs. There was inconsistency in the quality of support provided by LEAs for newly appointed head teachers and, while the quality of much of the LPSH training was good and was generally well received by head teachers, the programme did not always meet the needs of head teachers from a range of contexts and there was no effective monitoring of the outcomes. There was no clear progression in the content of the three national training programmes for head teachers. The various training programmes did not sufficiently meet the particular needs of participating head teachers, for example head teachers of schools facing particular challenges and head teachers of small rural primary schools. The monitoring of the impact of national head teacher training programmes was not well established (Ofsted 2002a: 5–6).

The development of national programmes of school leadership development has been subjected to sustained critique on a number of counts. Firstly, the leadership development framework has been underpinned by the National Standards for Head Teachers (DfES 2004a) thus establishing an emphasis on standards-based approaches in training and leadership development (Brundrett *et al.* 2006). Concerns exist that such a structure is too detailed, prescriptive and bureaucratic (Glatter 1997; Gronn 2003; Thrupp 2005). Secondly, the decline of university sector-accredited provision (Brundrett 1999) raises questions as to whether school leadership development may be impoverished by inadequate attention to explicit theoretical and conceptual groundings (Brundrett 1999, 2000, 2001; Ribbins 1997; Thrupp 2005). Thirdly, and finally, the sustainability of the leadership college model, which may be sensitive to political change, is open to question (Bolam 2004: 260). Nonetheless, the development of such a wide-ranging framework has meant that England has moved quickly towards coherent provision of leadership programmes in the period of a decade (Huber and West 2003).

A major review of school leadership conducted by PricewaterhouseCoopers (2007) concluded that there is a 'strong need to renew leadership capacity in the sector' in order to meet, embrace and deliver new policy objectives such as the ECM and 14–19 agendas – with one in ten heads claiming to have undertaken no professional development in the three years prior to the report (PricewaterhouseCoopers 2007: 148). Further, the report noted that there is mixed evidence from school leaders and stakeholders on the appropriateness of NCSL programmes such as NPQH and LPSH/Head for the Future and that aspects of these qualifications require reform in order to ensure that they are appropriate and fit-for-purpose (p.150). PricewaterhouseCoopers note that this suggests the need to widen the concept of leadership qualifications and draw on the best of what is already in the market in terms of other bespoke management and leadership qualifications for ongoing leadership development. Overall the report calls for the adoption of a new approach towards leadership qualifications whereby the DCSF and NCSL should give consideration to reforming key aspects of NPQH and Head for the Future (formerly LPSH), including:

- ensuring that the key needs articulated by school leaders in this research are given further prominence, in particular financial management, extended services and the associated implications for team working and people management;
- modernising the delivery vehicle to include, for example, e-learning solutions;
- a greater element of modularisation and tailoring to individual need; cross-sectoral inputs and participation; and less emphasis on what often comes across as a formulaic 'tick box' approach;
- ensuring that NPQH is fully 'joined up' with the outputs from secondments, exchanges and other CPD initiatives, so that participation in these initiatives can provide significant accreditation towards modules of NPQH. Ensuring also that this is the case, and understood to be so, in relation to relevant elements of other professional qualifications including, for example, Masters degrees and MBAs;
- ensuring that NPQH and Head for the Future are widely understood across the sector *not* as being one-off exercises, but rather part of an ongoing development process;
- ensuring that leadership training for support staff and senior support staff leaders (for example the Bursar Development Programme, delivered by NCSL) is accepted across the sector as being as important as leadership training for teachers; and,
- promoting ongoing mentoring and support programmes in order to increase the successful number of NPQH candidates who take up headship or other leadership positions in schools.

No doubt the findings of this influential report will impact significantly on future policy development in this general area of school leadership. For those operating in traditional higher education settings, the conclusion that some school leaders indicated that other qualifications such as MBAs and Masters degrees have proved, in their view, to be very useful in terms of helping them deal with leadership challenges, offers the possibility of a renewed role for the university sector (p.151).

For the purposes of this chapter it is also important to note that many of the plethora of national programmes in England, listed in the previous section, have developed as cross-phase initiatives and no specific provision has been developed for the particular professional requirements of primary school leaders. The individualised nature of many of the programmes, such as LfTM, HEADLAMP/ HIP/ EHP, and LPSH means that much of training is differentiated according to phase by means of personalised learning activities. Nonetheless, the question remains open as to whether primary leadership has developed a robust conceptual base in its own right. However, the most recent remit letter by the Secretary of State has asked the College to provide advice on the future leadership needs of those leading primary schools. This is a wholly welcome development. The Annual Report of Her Majesty's Chief Inspector of Schools 2005/06 (Ofsted 2006a) noted that good leadership and management remain crucial to the quality of schools and that 'the very large majority of primary schools inspected are led and managed at least satisfactorily' (Ofsted 2006a: 23). In the one in 10 primary schools in which leadership is outstanding, the management team as a whole, including subject leaders, is highly effective. Nonetheless, monitoring and evaluation, including the work undertaken by subject leaders, remain the weakest elements of leadership and management (*ibid.*).

CONCLUDING COMMENTS

From this relatively brief, and necessarily selective, snapshot of the professional train-ing landscape we have identified a number of examples of excellent practice but have also observed that they have been achieved at some cost to the respective sectors. We have organised our concluding comments thematically, identifying common issues that have emerged and where possible exemplifying them across the areas of initial training, in-service and leadership development.

1. Many examples of good and innovatory practice can be identified in England. In leadership development, for example, England is rapidly moving towards creating one of the most systematic portfolios of programmes for leadership in education in the world, a significant achievement in the period of a decade. The English model of ITE partnership has provoked much international interest, and there has been a qualitative improvement in the standard of provision and preparedness of newly qualified teachers and a refocusing of ITE to more closely engage with the curricu-lum as it is situated in primary classrooms. In the area of CPD, significant initiatives include increased opportunity for accrediting teacher's professional learning through the framework offered by the Teacher Learning Academy and a wide variety of M Level qualifications and Professional Doctorates in Education grounded in work-based learning.
2. The education climate over the last two decades has been characterised by an increased level of centralisation, monitoring and accountability. This has established a common framework of professional expectations and assessment which is parti-cularly apparent across the highly structured portfolio of programmes and qualifi-cations in leadership development and in ITE. The degree of bureaucratisation and accountability, however, has engendered a 'technical rationalist' approach to edu-cation outcomes and processes that has tended to restrict the nature of professional engagement and create a 'culture of compliance' in both staff and students.
3. Juxtaposed with this micro-managed environment is a rapidly growing sector char-acterised by greater deregulation. This is exemplified in the context of in-service development where the regulation of HE provision, through the triennial bidding and monitoring processes, contrasts sharply with the lack of accountability for how the considerable sums allocated through standards funding for CPD are actually spent, how outcomes are evaluated and how value-for-money is measured. Although the involvement of external consultants can bring fresh ideas and widen horizons, quality assurance mechanisms and evaluative processes are often not in evidence. In ITE over the last two decades the highly regulated training outcomes and processes of 'traditional' HEI provision have unfolded hand in hand with a proliferation of 'alternative' school-centred and employment-based routes that have not been subject to the same regulations in terms of performance and process measures.
4. Relationships between institutions and their accrediting bodies are of crucial importance, and never more so than in the prevailing culture of audit and accountability where performance indicators are linked with resourcing. This is the case with some of the NCSL-branded leadership programmes and TDA-funded PPD and ITE courses. In such circumstances, inspection regimes can be punitive and we see instances of this in the context of ITE where the established principle is to downsize or close provision when judgements of inadequacy are made. Yet here

again there are contradictions, such as the ideological commitment to the growth of EBITT even when, historically, inspection evidence has pointed to quality being compromised.

5. As noted, regulation has secured a good standard of provision and established a common framework of professional expectations and assessment. There remains, however, a lack of coherence, and at times transparency, in the educational principles underpinning developments across all three areas. The ITE sector, for example, despite working towards common outcome measures, has been subject to a number of contradictory ideological drivers and a lack of consistency is apparent in philosophies and models of professionalism. This is exemplified in the case of employment and school-based routes which are not required to work collaboratively in partnership with HEI. The same can be said of primary leadership, where we have pointed to the lack of a coherent conceptual base apparent across individual programmes which display overlapping, but different, conceptual models. Stark contrasts have also been apparent in the past decade in the principles and values underpinning the government's CPD strategy. Tensions between individual and national priorities have been mirrored in the disparity between the tightly structured, large-scale, top-down training implemented for the National Strategies and the more informal coaching/mentoring, bursaries/sabbaticals, Best Practice Scholarships and collaborative networks.

6. A problematic disarticulation exists between professional and academic qualifications across the sector and this has implications both in terms of the status of professional qualifications and the transferability of credentials. Weak links with specialist M Level degrees in leadership and management was a critique made of the prototype NPQH. Concerns were raised in relation to the locatedness of NPQH in the academic framework which, it was felt, should be at M level. There is now some reciprocal accreditation in individual universities, but this remains a complex and problematic relationship. The disjunction is also exemplified in postgraduate initial training between professional QTS-only employment-based routes and academic PGCE and QTS certification. The PGCE itself has just diverged into the M Level Post Graduate Certificate of Education and the H Level Professional Graduate Certificate of Education, which will potentially cause confusion in the sector. In the context of in-service development the increase in opportunities for the accreditation of work-based learning though M level awards, the Teaching and Learning Academy and the expansion in the Professional Doctorate market is to be celebrated. However, here again the Level 3 qualification in the Teaching and Learning Academy framework has been aligned at M Level without any clarity about how this will be achieved.

7. A loss of capacity in HE has reduced its capability to engage fully in the quasi education market place and innovation, where it is occurring, is often incoherent. A number of factors impact upon this loss of corporate energy: the ageing profile of staff in university education departments; the difficulty of recruitment in a labour market where the funding level of HEIs has been depressed for a number of years; and the effects of increased research selectivity determined by the Research Assessment Exercise (RAE). There are additional contextual factors such as concerns about the continuing capacity of HEI to provide high quality research and academic programmes in the area of management and leadership, given the fierce competition from the NCSL suite of programmes linked more directly to career progression. The

extensive professional development programmes that accompanied the implementation of the Numeracy and Literacy strategies had a similarly deflationary impact upon the uptake of award-bearing courses. In ITE loss of capacity is again a serious threat, although welcome strategies for capacity building are beginning to emerge.

8. Finally, the extent of the centralisation and politicisation in the three sectors has led to an inherent instability and uncertainty. Teacher education and development and leadership development are now subject to the vagaries of political whim, short-termism and change of ideology, leadership or government, resulting in vulnerability of organisations and programmes. In this respect the considerable cost of the NCSL central organisation and national infrastructure renders it especially vulnerable. In ITE the short-lived Fast Track route proved susceptible to a policy change, paradoxically at a time when succession planning for primary leadership was beginning to be seen as a significant concern.

REFERENCES

Alexander, R.J. (1984) 'Innovation and continuity in the initial teacher education curriculum', in R.J. Alexander, M. Craft and J. Lynch (Eds) *Change in Teacher Education: context and provision since Robbins*. London: Holt, Rinehart and Winston: 103–60.

Askew, M., Brown, M., Rhodes, V., Johnson, D. and Wiliam, D. (1997) *Effective Teachers of Numeracy*. London: Kings College.

Atkinson, D. (2004) 'Theorising how student teachers form their identities in initial teacher education', *British Educational Research Journal* 30(3): 379–94.

Baird, A. (1996) 'The Primary Partnership: the forgotten partner', *Welsh Journal of Education* 5: 66–79.

Barrett, E., Whitty, G., Furlong, J., Galvin, C. and Barton, L. (1992) *Initial Teacher Education in England and Wales: a topography*. London: Goldsmith's College.

Basit, T.N., McNamara, O., Roberts, L., Carrington, B., Maguire, M. and Woodrow, D. (2007) 'The bar is slightly higher: the perception of racism in teacher education', *Cambridge Journal of Education* 37(2): 279–98.

Basit, T.N., Roberts, L., McNamara, O., Carrington, B., Maguire, M. and Woodrow, D. (2006) 'Did they jump or were they pushed: reasons why minority ethnic trainees withdraw from initial teacher training courses', *British Educational Research Journal* 32(3): 387–410.

Bazalgette, J. (1996) 'Greater than a mere sum of skills', *Times Educational Supplement*, 31.05.1996: 17.

Bennett, N. and Carré, C. (Eds) (1993) *Learning to Teach*. London: Routledge.

Benton, P. (Ed) (1990) *The Oxford Internship Scheme: integration and partnership in Initial Teacher Education*. London: Calouste Gulbenkian Foundation.

Berliner, D. (1988) 'Implications of studies of expertise in pedagogy for teacher education and evaluation', in The Educational Testing Service (Ed) *New Directions for Teacher Assessment*, Proceedings of the 1988 ETS Invitational Conference. Princetown: New Jersey.

Bines, H. (1994) 'Squaring the circle?: government reform of initial teacher training for primary education', *Journal of Educational Policy* 9(4): 369–80.

Bines, H. and Welton, J. (Eds) (1995) *Managing Partnership in Teacher Training and Development*. London: Routledge.

Black, D.R., Ericson, J.D., Harvey, T.J., Hayden, M.C. and Thompson, J.J. (1994) 'The development of a flexible, modular MEd', *International Journal of Educational Management* 8(1): 35–39.

Blandford, S. and Squire, L. (1999) 'New light on HEADLAMP: an evaluation of the Teacher Training Agency Head Teacher Leadership and Management Programme', *Management in Education* 3(2): 27–31.

Bolam, R. (1997) 'Management development for head teachers', *Educational Management and Administration* 25(3): 265–83.

——(2000) 'Emerging policy trends: some implications for continuing professional development', *Journal of In-Service Education* 26(2): 267–80.

——(2003) 'Models of leadership development', *Leadership in Education*. London: Sage Publications.

——(2004) 'Reflections on the NCSL from a historical perspective', *Educational Management, Administration and Leadership* 32(3): 251–67.

Bolam, R., McMahon, A., Stoll, L., Thomas, S. and Wallace, M., with Greenwood, A., Hawkey, K., Ingram, M., Atkinson, A. and Smith, M. (2005) *Creating and Sustaining Effective Professional Learning Communities*. London: DfES.

Booth, M., Furlong, J. and Wilkin, M. (Eds) (1990) *Partnership in Initial Teacher Education*. London: Cassells.

Boyd, P., Baker, L., Harris, K., Kynch, C. and McVittie, E. (2006) 'Working with multiple identities: supporting new teacher education tutors in Higher Education', in S. Bloxham, S. Twiselton and A. Jackson (Eds) *Challenges and Opportunities: developing learning and teaching in ITE across the UK*, ESCalate 2005 Conference proceedings, Higher Education Academy.

Boyd, P., Harris, K. and Murray, J. (2007) *Becoming a Teacher Educator: guidelines for the induction of newly appointed lecturers in Initial Teacher Education*. Bristol: ESCalate.

Boyle, B., Lamprianou, I. and Boyle, T. (2005) 'A longitudinal study of teacher change: what makes professional development effective? Report of the second year of the study', *School Effectiveness and School Improvement* 16(1): 1–27.

Brisard, E., Menter, I. and Smith, I. (2005) *Models of Partnership in Programmes of Initial Teacher Training: a systematic review*. Edinburgh: General Teaching Council of Scotland.

Brooks, V. (2000) 'School-based initial teacher training: squeezing a quart into a pint pot or a square peg into a round hole?', *Mentoring and Tutoring* 8(2): 99–112.

Brookes, W. (2005) 'The graduate teacher programme in England: mentor training, quality assurance and the findings of inspection', *Journal of In-Service Education* 31(1): 43–62.

Brown, M., Askew, M., Millett, A. and Rhodes, V. (2003) 'The key role of educational research in the development and evaluation of the National Numeracy Strategy', *British Educational Research Journal* 29(5): 655–72.

Brown, S., Edmonds, S. and Lee, B. (2001) *Continuing Professional Development: LEA and school support for teachers*, LGA research report 23. Slough: NFER.

Brown, S., McNally, J. and Stronach, I. (1993) *Getting it Together: questions and answers about partnership and mentoring*. UK, Department of Education: University of Stirling.

Brown, T. and McNamara, O. (2005) *New Teacher Identity and Regulative Government: discursive formation of primary mathematics teacher education*. New York: Springer.

Brundrett, M. (1999) 'The range of provision of taught higher degrees in educational management in England and Wales', *International Studies in Educational Administration* 27(2): 43–59.

——(2000) *Beyond Competence: the challenge for educational management*. King's Lynn: Peter Francis.

——(2001) 'The development of school leadership preparation programmes in England and the USA', *Educational Management and Administration* 29(2): 229–45.

Brundrett, M., Fitzgerald, T. and Sommefeldt, D. (2006) 'The creation of national programmes of school leadership development in England and New Zealand: a comparative study', *International Studies in Educational Administration* 34(1): 89–105.

Bryk, A., Camburn, E. and Louis, K.S. (1999) 'Professional community in Chicago elementary schools: facilitating factors and organisational consequences', *Educational Administration Quarterly* 35 (supplement): 751–81.

Bubb, S., Earley, P. and Totterdell, M. (2005) 'Accountability and responsibility: rogue school leaders and the induction of new teachers in England', *Oxford Review of Education* 31(2): 255–72.

Burns, C. (2005) 'Tensions between national, school and teacher development needs: a survey of teachers' views about continuing professional development within a group of rural primary schools', *Journal of In-service Education* 31(2): 353–72.

Bush, T. (1998) 'The National Professional Qualification for Headship: the key to effective school leadership?', *School Leadership and Management* 18(3): 321–33.
——(1999) 'Crisis or crossroads? The discipline of educational management in the 1990s', *Educational Management and Administration* 27(3): 239–52.
Busher, H. and Paxton, L. (1997) 'HEADLAMP – a local experience in partnership', in H. Tomlinson (Ed) *Managing Continuing Professional Development in Schools and Colleges*. London: Paul Chapman Publishing: 120–34.
CACE (1967) *Children and Their Primary Schools: a report of the Central Advisory Council for Education (England)* (the Plowden Report). London: HMSO.
Campbell, J. and Husbands, C. (2000) 'On the reliability of OfSTED inspection of Initial Teacher Training: a case study', *British Journal of Educational Research* 26(1): 39–48.
Campbell, A., McNamara, O. Furlong, J., Lewis, S. and Howson, J. (2007) 'The evaluation of the National Partnership Project in England: processes, issues and dilemmas in commissioned evaluation research', *Journal of Education for Teaching* 33(4): 471–83.
Carrington, B. and Tomlin, R. (2000) 'Towards a more inclusive profession: teacher recruitment and ethnicity', *European Journal of Teacher Education* 23: 139–57.
Carrington, B., Bonnett, A., Demaine, J., Hall, I., Nayak, A., Short, G., Skelton, S., Smith, F. and Tomlin, R. (2001) *Ethnicity and the Professional Socialization of Teachers*, final report to the Teacher Training Agency. London: TTA.
Carrington, B. (2002) 'A quintessentially feminine domain? Student teachers' constructions of primary teaching as a career', *Educational Studies* 28(3): 287–303.
Clement, M. and Vandenberghe, R. (2000) 'Teachers' professional development: a solitary or collegial (ad)venture?', *Teaching and Teacher Education* 16: 81–101.
Cordingley, P., Bell, M., Rundell, B. and Evans, D. (2003) *The Impact of Collaborative CPD on Classroom Teaching and Learning: how does collaborative Continuing Professional Development (CPD) for teachers of the 5–16 age range affect teaching and learning?*, from Research Evidence in Education library. London: EPPI-Centre.
Cowan, B. and Wright, N. (1990) 'Two million days lost', *Education* 2 (February): 117–18.
Crozier, G., Menter, I. and Pollard, A. (1990) 'Changing partnership', in M. Booth, J. Furlong and M. Wilkin (Eds) *Partnership in Initial Teacher Education*. London: Cassells: 44–56.
Dadds, M. and Kynch, C. (2003) 'The impact of RAE 3B ratings on educational research in teacher education departments', *Research Intelligence* 84: 8–11.
Davies, B. and Ellison, L. (1994) 'New perspectives on developing school leaders', *British Journal of In-Service Education* 20(3): 361–71.
Day, C. (1997) 'In-service teacher education in Europe: conditions and themes for development in the 21st century', *Journal of In-service Education* 23(1): 39–54.
Day, C., Stobart, G., Sammons, P., Kington, A., Gu, Q., Smees, R. and Mujtaba, T. (2006) *Variations in Teachers' Work, Lives and Effectiveness*, Research Report 743. Nottingham: DfES.
Dearing, R. (1997) *Higher Education in the Learning Society: the National Committee of Enquiry into Higher Education:* Report of the National Committee (the Dearing Report). London: HMSO.
Department of Education and Science (DES) (1972) *The Education and Training of Teachers* (the James Report). London: HMSO.
——(1983) *Teaching Quality*. London: HMSO.
——(1984) *Initial Teacher Training: approval of courses (Circular 3/84)*. London: HMSO.
——(1989a) *Initial Teacher Training: approval of courses (Circular 24/89)*. London: HMSO.
——(1989b) *Licensed Teacher Regulation Circular 18/89*. London: HMSO.
Department for Education (DFE) (1992) *Initial Teacher Training (secondary phase) (Circular 9/92)*. London: DFE.
——(1993a) *The Initial Training of Primary School Teachers (Circular 14/93)*. London: DFE.
——(1993b) *The Government Proposals for the Reform of Initial Teacher Training*. London: DFE.

——(1993c) *School-centred Initial Teacher Training (SCITT)*. London: DFE.

Department for Education and Employment (DfEE) (1997) *Teaching: high status, high standards (Circular 10/97)*. London: DfEE.

——(1998a) *Teaching: high status, high standards (Circular 4/98)*. London: HMSO.

——(1998b) *Teachers: meeting the challenge of change*, Green Paper. London: HMSO.

——(1999a) *The Quinquennial Review of the Teacher Training Agency*. London: DfEE.

——(1999b) *The Standards for the Induction of New Teachers (Circular 5/99)*. London: DfEE.

——(2000) *Professional Development: support for teaching and learning*, London: HMSO.

——(2001a) *Learning and Teaching: a strategy for professional development*. London: DfEE.

——(2001b) *Schools Building on Success*. London: The Stationary Office (TSO).

——(2001c) *Learning and Teaching: a strategy for professional development*, DfEE 0071/2001. London: DfEE.

Department for Education and Skills (DfES) (2002a) *Qualifying to Teach: professional standards for Qualified Teacher Status and requirements for Initial Teacher Training (Circular 2/02)*. London: Teacher Training Agency (TTA).

——(2002b) *Qualifying to Teach: handbook of guidance*. London: TTA.

——(2002c) *Education and Skills: delivering results. A strategy to 2006*. London: DfES.

——(2003a) *Excellence and Enjoyment: a strategy for primary schools*. London: DfES.

——(2003b) *Raising Standards and Tackling Workload: a national agreement*. London: DfES.

——(2004) *Department for Education and Skills: five year strategy for children and learners*. London: DfES.

——(2006a) *The Five Year Strategy for Children and Learners: maintaining the excellent progress*. London: DfES.

——(2006b) *Statistics of Education: school workforce in England 2003 edition*. London: TSO.

——(2007) *The Revised Standards for Qualified Teacher Status*. Online (Available: http://www.tda.gov.uk/upload/resources/doc/draft_qts_standards_17nov2006.doc, accessed 20 April 2007).

DfES/NCSL (2004) *School Leadership: end to end review of school leadership policy and delivery*. London: DFES/NCSL.

DfES/TTA (2002a) *Qualifying to Teach: professional standards for Qualified Teacher Status and requirements for Initial Teacher Training (Circular 2/02)*. London: DfES/TTA.

——(2002b) *Qualifying to Teach: handbook of guidance*. London: DfES/TTA.

Downes, P. (1996) 'The deputy head's magic roundabout', *Managing Schools Today* 5(7): 27–28.

Downing, D., Watson, R., Johnson, F., Lord, P., Jones, J. and Ashworth, M. (2004) *Sabbaticals for Teachers: an evaluation of a scheme offering sabbaticals for experienced teachers working in challenging schools*. London: DfES.

Dunne, M., Lock, R. and Soares, A. (1996) 'Partnership in Initial Teacher Training: after the shotgun wedding', *Educational Review* 48(1): 41–53.

Earl, L., Watson, N., Levin, B., Leithwood, K., Fullan, M. and Torrance, N., with Jantzi, D., Mascal, B. and Volante, L. (2003) *Watching Learning 3, Final Report of the External Evaluation of England's National Literacy and Numeracy Strategies*. Toronto: Ontario Institute for Studies in Education, University of Toronto (OISE, UT).

Earley, P., Evans, J., Collarbone, P., Gold, A. and Halpin, D. (2002) *Establishing the Current State of School Leadership in England*. Institute of Education, University of London: Queen's Printer.

Edwards, T. (1994) 'The Universities Council for the Education of Teachers: defending an interest or fighting a cause?', *Journal of Education for Teaching* 20(2).

Edwards, A. (1995) 'Teacher education: partnership in pedagogy?', *Teaching and Teacher Education* 11(6): 595–610.

Edwards, A. and Protheroe, L. (2003) 'Learning to see in classrooms: what are student teachers learning about teaching and learning while learning to teach in schools?', *British Educational Research Journal* 29(2): 227–42.

——(2004) 'Teaching by proxy: understanding how mentors are positioned in partnerships', *Oxford Review of Education* 30(2): 183–97.

Eraut, M. and Seaborne, P. (1984) 'In-service teacher education: developments in provision and curriculum', in R.J. Alexander, M. Craft and J. Lynch (Eds) *Change in Teacher Education: context and provision since Robbins*. London: Holt, Rinehart and Winston.

Franks, O. (1967) *Report of Commission of Inquiry*. Oxford: University of Oxford.

Fuller, A., Hodkinson, H., Hodkinson, P. and Unwin, L. (2005) 'Learning as peripheral participation in communities of practice: a reassessment of key concepts in workplace learning', *British Educational Research Journal* 31(1): 49–68.

Furlong, J. (2001) 'Reforming teacher education, reforming teachers: accountability, professionalism and competence', in R. Phillips and J. Furlong (Eds) *Education, Reform and the State: 25 years of policy, politics and practice*. London: Routledge.

——(2005) 'New Labour and teacher education: the end of an era', *Oxford Education Review* 33 (1): 119–34.

Furlong, J., Barton, L., Miles, S., Whiting, C. and Whitty, G. (2000) *Teacher Education in Transition: re-forming professionalism?* Buckingham: Open University Press.

Furlong, J., Campbell, A., Howson, J., Lewis, S. and McNamara, O. (2006a) 'Partnership in English teacher education: changing times, changing definitions – evidence from the Teacher Training Agency National Partnership Project', *Scottish Education Review* 37: 32–45.

Furlong, J., Haggar, H. and Butcher, C., with Howson, J. (2006b) *Review of Initial Teacher Training provision in Wales. A report to the Welsh Assembly Government*. Oxford: University of Oxford.

Furlong, J. and Kane, I. (1996) 'Recognising quality in primary Initial Teacher Education: findings from the 1995–96 Ofsted Primary Sweep', *UCET Occasional Paper No. 6*. London: UCET.

Furlong, J., Salisbury, J. and Combes, L. (2003) *Best Practice Research Scholarships: an evaluation*. Nottingham: DfES.

Furlong, J., Whitty, G., Whiting, C., Miles, S., Barton, L. and Barrett, E. (1996) 'Redefining partnership: revolution or reform in initial teacher education', *Journal of Education for Teaching* 8(3): 275–304.

Gardener, P. and Cunningham, P. (1998) 'Teacher trainers and educational change in Britain, 1876–1996; "a flawed and deficit history?"', *Journal of Education for Teaching* 24(3): 231–55.

Gilroy, P. (1992) 'The political rape of teacher training in England and Wales: a JET rebuttal', *Journal of Education for Teaching* 18: 5–22.

——(1998) 'New Labour and teacher education in England and Wales: the first 500 days', *Journal of Education for Teaching* 24(3): 221–30.

Gilroy, P. and Wilcox, B. (1997) 'OfSTED, criteria and the nature of social understanding: a Wittgenstienian critique of the practice of educational judgement', *British Journal of Educational Studies* 45: 22–38.

Glatter, R. (1997) 'Context and capability in educational management', *Educational Management and Administration* 25(2): 181–92.

Goodall, J., Day, C., Lindsay, G., Muijs, D. and Harris, A. (2005) *Evaluating the Impact of CPD*, Research report 659. London: DfES.

Goulding, M., Rowland, T. and Barber, P. (2002) 'Does it matter? Primary teacher trainees' subject knowledge in mathematics', *British Educational Research Journal* 28(5): 689–704.

Graham, J. and Nabb, J. (1999) 'Stakeholder satisfaction: survey of OfSTED inspection of ITT 1994–99', *UCET Research Paper No. 1*. London: Universities Council for the Education of Teachers.

Green, H. (1998) 'Training for today's school leaders', *Education Journal* 21: 11.

Gregory, M. (1995) 'Implications of the introduction of the doctor of education degree in British Universities: can EdD reach parts the PhD cannot?', *The Vocational Aspect of Education* 47(2): 177–88.

Gronn, P. (2003) *The New Work of Educational Leaders*. London: Paul Chapman.

Grundy, S. and Robinson, J. (2004) 'Teacher professional development: themes and trends in the recent Australian experience', in C. Day and J. Sachs (Eds) *International Handbook on the Continuing Professional Development of Teachers*. Maidenhead: Open University Press.

GTCE (2002) *Code of Professional Values and Practice.* London: GTCE.

——(2004) *Code of Conduct and Practice for Registered Teachers.* London: GTCE.

Hallinger, P. (Ed) (2003) *Reshaping the Landscape of School Leadership Development: contexts of learning.* Lisse: Swets and Zeitlinger.

Hannan, A. (1995) 'The case for school-led Primary Teacher Training', *Journal of Education for Teaching* 21(1): 25–35.

Hargreaves, A. (1994) *Changing Teachers, Changing Times: teachers' work and culture in the postmodern age.* London: Cassell.

——(2003) 'Professional learning communities and performance training cults: the emerging apartheid of school improvement', in A. Harris, C. Day, D. Hopkins, M. Hadfield, A. Hargreaves and C. Chapman, *Effective Leadership for School Improvement.* London: RoutledgeFalmer.

Hargreaves, D. (1996) *Teaching as a Research-based Profession: possibilities and prospects.* London: Teacher Training Agency Annual Lecture 1996. London: TTA.

Hargreaves, L., Moyles, J., Merry, R., Paterson, F., Pell, A. and Esarte-Sarries, V. (2003) 'How do primary teachers define and implement "interactive teaching" in the national literacy strategy in England', *Research Papers in Education* 18(3): 217–36.

Harland, J., Kinder, K. and Keys, W. (1993) *Restructuring INSET: privatisation and its alternatives.* Slough: NFER.

Harnett, P. and Lee, J. (2003) 'Where have all the men gone? Have primary schools really been feminised?', *Journal of Educational Administration and History* 35(2): 77.

Heilbronn, R. (2002) 'School–based induction tutors: a challenging role', *School Leadership and Management* 22(4): 371–87.

Hextall, I. and Mahony P. (2000) 'Consultation and the management of consent: standards for Qualified Teacher Status', *British Educational Research Journal* 26(3): 323–42.

Hextall, I., Mahony, P. and Menter, I. (2001) 'Just testing?: an analysis of the implementation of "skills tests" for entry into the teaching profession in England', *Journal of Education for Teaching* 27(3): 221–39.

Heywood, D. (2005) 'Primary teachers' learning and teaching about light: some pedagogic implications for Initial Teacher Training', *International Journal of Science Education* 27(12): 1447–75.

Her Majesty's Inspectorate (HMI) (1982) *The New Teacher in School.* London: HMSO.

HMI (1983) *Teaching in Schools: the content of Initial Teacher Training.* London: DES.

——(1987) *Quality in Schools: the initial training of teachers.* London: DES.

——(1988a) *The New Teacher in School: a survey by HM Inspectors in England and Wales 1987.* London: HMSO.

——(1988b) *Initial Teacher Training in Universities in England, Northern Ireland and Wales.* London: HMSO.

——(1991a) *The Professional Training of Primary School Teachers.* London: HMSO.

——(1991b) *School–based Initial Teacher Training in England and Wales: a report by HM Inspectorate.* London: HMSO.

——(2002) *The Annual Report of Her Majesty's Chief Inspector of Education 2001/02.* London: TSO.

——(2005) *The Annual Report of Her Majesty's Chief Inspector of Education 2004/05.* London: TSO.

Hobson, A.J. and Malderez, A. (Eds), with Kerr, K., Tracey, L., Pell, G., Tomlinson, P. and Roper, T. (2005) *Becoming a Teacher: student teachers' motives and preconceptions, and early school-based experiences during Initial Teacher Training (ITT).* Nottingham: DfES.

Hobson, A.J., Malderez, A., Tracey, L., Giannakaki, M.S., Kerr, K., Pell, R.G, Chambers, G.N., Tomlinson, P.D. and Roper, T. (2006) *Becoming a Teacher: student teachers' experiences of initial teacher training in England.* Nottingham: DfES.

Hobson, A.J., Malderez, A., Tracey, L., Homer, M., Mitchell, N., Biddulph, M., Giannakaki, M.S., Rose, A., Pell, R.G., Chambers, G.N., Roper, T. and Tomlinson, P.D. (2007) *Newly Qualified*

Teachers' Experiences of their First Year of Teaching: findings from Phase III of the Becoming a Teacher project. Nottingham: DCSF.

Hobson, A.J., Tracy, L., Kerr, K., Malderez, M., Pell, R.G., Simm, C. and Johnson, F. (2004) *Why people choose to became teachers and the factors influencing their choice of initial teacher training route: early findings from the Becoming a Teacher Project.* Nottingham: DfES.

HoC (1999) *The Work of Ofsted: other inspection frameworks. Select Committee on Education and Employment, report from the Education sub-committee: June 1999.*

Holden, G. (1997) '"Challenge and support": the role of the critical friend in continuing professional development', *The Curriculum Journal* 8: 441–53.

Holyoake, J. (1993) 'Initial Teacher Training – the French view', *Journal of Education for Teaching* 19(2): 215–26.

Huber, S. and West, M. (2003) 'England: moving quickly towards a coherent provision', in S.G. Huber (Ed) *Preparing School Leaders for the 21st Century: an international comparison of development programs in 15 countries.* London: RoutledgeFalmer.

——(2005). 'Developing school leaders – a critical review of current practices, approached and issues, and some directions for the future', in P. Hallinger, K. Leithwood and M.D. Mumford (Eds) *International Handbook of Educational Leadership and Administration.* Kluwer Publications.

Hurd, S., Jones, M., McNamara, O. and Craig, B. (2007) 'Initial teacher education as a driver for professional learning and school improvement in the primary phase', *Curriculum Journal* 18(3): 307–26.

Hustler, D., McNamara, O., Jarvis, J., Londra, M. and Campbell, A. (2003) *Teachers' Perceptions of Continuing Professional Development*, Research report 429. London: DfES.

Hutchings, M., Smart, S., James, K. and Williams, K. (2006) *General Teaching Council for England Survey of Teachers 2006.* London: Institute for Policy Studies in Education, London Metropolitan University.

James, L. (1972) *Teacher Education and Training: report.* London: HMSO.

Jeffrey, B. (2002) 'Performativity and primary teacher relations', *Journal of Education Policy* 17 (5): 531–46.

Jeffrey, B. and Woods, P. (2003) *The Creative School.* London: RoutledgeFalmer.

Jenkins, A., Healey, M. and Zetter, R. (2007) *Linking Teaching and Research in Disciplines and Departments*, The Higher Education Academy.

Jones, C., Bubb, S., Totterdell, M. and Heilbronn, R. (2002) 'Reassessing the variability of induction for Newly Qualified Teachers: statutory policy and schools' provision', *Journal of In-service Education* 28(3): 495–508.

Jones, C. and Maguire M. (1998) 'Needed and wanted? The school experiences of some minority ethnic trainee teachers in the UK', *European Journal of International Studies* 9(1): 79–91.

Jones, D. (2007) 'Millennium man: constructing identities of male teachers in early years contexts', *Education Review* 59(2): 179–94.

Jones, M. and Straker, K. (2006) 'What informs mentors' practice when working with trainees and newly qualified teachers? An investigation into mentors' professional knowledge base', *Journal of Education for Teaching* 32(2): 165–85.

Judge, H., Lemosse, M., Paine, L. and Sedlak, M. (1994) *The University and the Teachers: France, the United States, England.* Wallingford: Triangle Books.

Kalous, J. (1977) *a kol.: Příprava řídicich pracovniků ve školství, /School management.*

Kinder, K. and Harland, J. (1991) *The Impact of INSET: the case of primary science.* Slough: NFER.

Kirk, G. (1999) 'Teacher education institutions', in T. Bryce and W. Humes (Eds) *Scottish Education.* Edinburgh: Edinburgh University Press.

Kyriacou, C. and O'Connor, A. (2003) 'Primary Newly Qualified Teachers' experience of the induction year in its first year of implementation in England', *Journal of In-service Education* 29(2): 185–200.

Lave, J. and Wenger, E. (1991) *Situated Learning: legitimate peripheral participation.* Cambridge, MA: Cambridge University Press.

Leithwood, K. and Jantzi, D. (1990) 'Transformational leadership: how principals can help reform school cultures', *School Effectiveness and School Improvement* 1(3): 249–81.

Lortie, D. (1975) *School Teacher*. Chicago, IL: University of Chicago Press.

Lunn, P. and Bishop A. (2003) '"To Touch a Life Forever": a discourse on trainee teachers' perceptions of what it means to be an effective teacher in the primary school', *Educational Studies* 29(2/3): 195–206.

Macbeath, J. (2005) 'Leadership as distributed: a matter of practice', *School Leadership and Management* 25(4): 349–66.

Mahony, P. and Hextall, I. (2000) *Reconstructing Teaching: standards, performance and accountability*. London: RoutledgeFalmer.

Maynard, T. (2001) 'The student teacher and the school community of practice: a consideration of "learning as participation"', *Cambridge Journal of Education* 31(1): 39–52.

McIntyre, D. (1993) 'Theory, theorizing and reflection in Initial Teacher Education', in J. Calderhead and P. Gates (Eds) *Conceptualising Reflection in Teacher Development*. London: Falmer: 39–52.

McNally, J., Cope, P., Inglis, B. and Stronach, I. (1994) 'Current realities in the student teaching experience: a preliminary enquiry', *Teaching and Teacher Education* 10(2): 219–30.

McNair, A. (1944) *Teachers and Youth Leaders* (The McNair Report). London: HMSO.

McNamara, O., Lewis, S. and Howson, J. (2007) '"Turning the tap on and off": the recruitment of overseas trained teachers in the UK', *Perspectives in Education* 25(2): 39–54.

McNamara, O., Roberts, L., Basit, N.T. and Brown, T. (2002) 'Rites of passage in Initial Teacher Training: ritual, performance, ordeal and the numeracy skills tests', *British Educational Research Journal* 28(6): 861–76.

Medwell, J., Wray, D., Poulson, L. and Fox, R. (1998) *Effective Teachers of Literacy*. Exeter: University of Exeter.

Menter, I. and Whitehead, J. (1995) *Learning the Lessons: reform in Initial Teacher Education*. Bristol: University of West of England, and the National Union of Teachers.

Mills, D., Jepson, A., Coxon, T., Easterby-Smith, M., Hawkins, P. and Spencer, J. (2005) *Demographic Review of the Social Sciences, Report to the Economic and Social Research Council*. Swindon: ESRC.

Mills, J. (1995) 'Partnership experiences for schools', *Mentoring and Tutoring* 3: 30–44.

Minister of State for Education (2004) *National College for School Leadership Priorities: 2005–06, Letter to the Chair of the National College for School Leadership*. London: DfES.

Moor, H., Lord, P., Johnson, A. and Martin, K. (2005) *'All Together Better': an evaluation of the GTC-DfES-LEA Continuing Professional Development Partnership Project*. Slough: NFER.

Moor, H., Lamont, E., Lord, P. and Gulliver, C. (2006) *An Evaluation of the Teacher Learning Academy: Phases 1 and 2*. Slough: NFER.

Moyles, J. and Stuart, D. (2003) 'Which school-based elements of partnership in initial teacher training in the UK support trainee teachers' professional development?', in *Research Evidence in Education Library*. London: EPPI-Centre, Social Science Research Unit, Institute of Education, University of London.

Moyles, J., Suschitzky, W. and Chapman, L. (1998) *Teaching Fledglings to Fly? Mentoring and support systems in primary schools*. London: Association of Teachers and Lecturers.

Muijs, D., Day, C., Harris, A. and Lindsay, G. (2004) 'Evaluating CPD: an overview', in C. Day and J. Sachs (Eds) *International Handbook on the Continuing Professional Development of Teachers*. Maidenhead, England: Open University Press: 291–310.

Murray, J. (2005a) *Investigating Good Practices in the Induction of Teacher Educators into Higher Education*. ESCalate.

——(2005b) 'Re-addressing the priorities: new teacher educators' experiences of induction into Higher Education', *European Journal of Teacher Education (CORE)* 26(3): 1–530.

Murray, J. and Male, T. (2005) 'Becoming a teacher educator: evidence from the field', *Teaching and Teacher Education* 21(2): 125–42.

National College for School Leadership (NCSL) (2001a) *What is the NPQH?* Nottingham: NCSL.

NCSL (2001b) *First Corporate Plan: launch year 2001–2002*. Online (Available: http://www.ncsl. gov.uk).

——(2001c) *Leadership Development Framework*. Nottingham: NCSL.

——(2007a) Head for the Future. Online (Available: http://www.ncsl.org.uk/programmes/head-forthefuture/index.cfm, accessed March 2007).

——(2007b) *A-Z list of Programmes*. Online (Available: http://www.ncsl.org.uk/programmes/ programmes-atoz.cfm, accessed March 2007).

——(2007c) *Leading Small Primary Schools: programme structure*. Online (Available: http:// www.ncsl.org.uk/programmes/small-schools/smallschools-structure.cfm, accessed March 2007).

——(2007d) *Primary Strategy Leadership Programme*. Online (Available: http://www.ncsl.org.uk/ programmes/plp/index.cfm, accessed March 2007).

——(2007e) *Early Headship Provision: benefits*. Online (Available: http://www.ncsl.org.uk/ programmes/ehp/index.cfm, accessed March 2007).

Newsome, P. (2001) *The Head teachers' Leadership and Management Programme (Headlamp) Review*. Nottingham: NCSL. Online.

Nixon, J., Cope, P., McNally, J., Rodrigues, S. and Stephen, C. (2000) 'University-based teacher education: institutional re-positioning and professional renewal', *International Studies in Sociology of Education* 10(3): 243–61.

Oancea, A. (2004a) 'The distribution of educational research expertise – findings from the analysis of RAE 2001 submissions (I)', *Research Intelligence* 87: 3–8.

——(2004b) 'The distribution of educational research expertise – findings from the analysis of RAE 2001 submissions (II)', *Research Intelligence* 87: 3–9.

Ofsted (1999) *Inspection of Initial Teacher Training Primary Follow-up Survey 1996–1998*, HMI 193. London: Ofsted.

——(2001) *Induction of Newly Qualified Teacher: implementation of DfEE Circular 5/99*, HMI 270. London: Ofsted.

——(2002a) *Leadership and Management Training for Head Teachers*, HMI Document No 457. London: HMI.

——(2002b) *Framework for the Inspection of Initial Teacher Education 2002–2005*, HMI 548. London: Ofsted.

——(2003a) *Quality and Standards in Initial Teacher Training*, HMI 547. London: Ofsted.

——(2003b) *Training for Newly Appointed Head teachers (Headlamp)*, HMI Document No 1763. London: HMI.

——(2004) *Making a Difference: the impact of award-bearing in-service training on school improvement*. London: Ofsted.

——(2005a) *An Employment-Based Route into Teaching: a report of the first year of inspection*, HMI 2406. London: Ofsted.

——(2005b) *Framework for the Inspection of Initial Teacher Education for the Award of Qualified Teacher Status 2005–2011*, HMI 2446. London: Ofsted.

——(2006a) *An Employment–Based Route into Teaching 2004–05*, HMI 2623. London: Ofsted.

——(2006b) *Annual Report of Her Majesty's Chief Inspector of Schools 2005–2006*. London: TSO.

——(2006c) *The Logical Chain: continuing professional development in effective schools*. London: Ofsted.

——(2007a) *Annual Report of Her Majesty's Chief Inspector of Schools 2006–2007*. London: TSO.

——(2007b) *An Employment-based Route into Teaching 2003–06*, HMI 2664. London: Ofsted.

Perry (1985) 'The system's response to the challenge of CATE', in C. Mills (Ed) *The Impact of CATE*. Report of Teacher Education Study Group, London (26.10.1985).

Poulson, L. (2003) 'The subject of English', in E. Bearne, H. Dombey and T. Grainger (Eds) *Classroom Interactions in Literacy*. Maidenhead: Open University Press.

Poulson, L. and Avramidis, E. (2003) 'Pathways and possibilities in professional development: case studies of effective teachers of literacy', *British Educational Research Journal* 29(4): 543–60.

Pountney, G. (1997) 'Moving towards NPQH', *Managing Schools Today* 7(1): 1–4.

Price, A. and Willett, J. (2006) 'Primary teachers' perceptions of the impact of initial teacher training on primary schools', *Journal of In-Service Education* 32(1): 33–45.

PricewaterhouseCoopers (PwC) (2007) *Independent Study into School Leadership: main report.* London: DfES/ PwC.

Raffo, C. and Hall, D. (2006) 'Transitions to becoming a teacher on an initial teacher education and training programme', *British Journal of Sociology of Education* 27(1): 53–66.

Reid, I. (1985) 'Hoops, swings and roundabouts in teacher education', in C. Mills (Ed) *The Impact of CATE.* Report of Teacher Education Study Group, London (26.10.1985).

Revell, P. (1997) 'Who said the TTA stands for totalitarian?', *Times Educational Supplement: Management Update*, June 6th: 13–14.

Ribbins, P. (1997) 'Editorial: twenty-five years of Educational Management and Administration', *Educational Management and Administration* 25(3): 211–12.

Ribchester, C. and Edwards, W. (1998) 'Co-operation in the countryside: small primary school clusters', *Educational Studies* 24: 281–93.

Richards, C., Simco, N. and Twiselton, S. (1998) *Primary Initial Teacher Education: High status? High standards?* London: Falmer.

Rippon, J.H. and Martin, M. (2006) 'What makes a good induction supporter?' *Teaching and Teacher Education* 22(1): 84–99.

Robbins, L. (1963) *Report of the Committee on Higher Education* (the Robbins Report). London: HMSO.

Rose, J. (2006) *Independent Review of the Teaching of Early Reading: final report.* London: DfES.

Ross, A. (2002) *Towards a Representative Profession.* Online (Available: http://www.multiverse. ac.uk/attachments/eade599f-5fd9–4d73–92ae-8beb3c817848.doc, accessed 15 July 2007).

Rowland, T., Huckstep, P. and Twaites, A. (2005) 'Elementary teachers' mathematics subject knowledge: the Knowledge Quartet and the case of Naomi', *Journal of Mathematics Teacher Education* 8(3): 255–81.

Sachs, J. (2003) *The Activist Teaching Profession.* Buckingham: Open University Press.

Sayer, J. (1995) 'The continuing professional development of teachers and the role of the University', *Oxford Studies in Comparative Education* 5(1): 65–70.

Senge, P. (1990) *The Fifth Discipline: the art and practice of the learning organisation.* New York: Doubleday.

Shanks, D. (1987) 'The Master of Education degree in Scotland', *Scottish Educational Review* 19 (2): 122–25.

Simco, N. and Wilson, T. (2002) *Primary Initial Teacher Training and Education: revised standards, bright future?* Exeter: Learning Matters.

Skelton, C. (2002) 'The feminisation of schooling or re-masculining primary education?', *International Studies in Sociology of Education* 12(1): 77.

——(2003) 'Male primary teacher and perceptions of masculinity', *Educational Review* 55(2): 195–209.

Southworth, G. (2004) 'A response from the National College for School Leadership', *Educational Management, Administration and Leadership* 32(3): 339–54.

Smith, J.D.N. (2004) 'Developing paired teaching placements', *Educational Action Research* 12(1): 99–126.

Smithers, A. and Robinson, P. (2007) *Teacher Training Profiles 2007.* University of Buckingham: Centre for Education and Employment Research.

Stoll, L. and Myers, K. (1998) *No Quick Fixes.* London: Falmer Press.

Stoll, L., Wallace, M., Bolam, R., McMahon, A., Thomas, S., Hawkey, K., Smith, M. and Greenwood, A. (2003) *Creating and Sustaining Effective Professional Learning Communities*, DfES research Brief RBX12–03. Nottingham: DfES Publications.

Sutherland, S. (1997) *Teacher Education and Training: a study for the Dearing Report into Higher Education.* London: DfEE.

Taylor, C. (2002) 'ESRC Teaching and Learning Research Programme Research Capacity Building Network', *The RCBN Consultation Exercise: survey report.* Cardiff: Cardiff University School of Social Science.

Taylor, W. (2000) 'The role of the providers', in I. Reid (Ed) *Improving Schools: the contribution of Teacher Education and Training: an account of the Joint UCET/HMI Symposium, Edinburgh, December.* London: UCET.

Teacher Pathways project (2003–7) Online (Available: http://www.teacherresearchpolicy.org, accessed 20 April 2007).

Thornton, M. (1998) *Subject Specialists: primary school* (UCET Occasional Paper No. 10). London: UCET.

Thornton, M. and Bricheno, P. (2000) 'Primary school teachers' careers in England and Wales: the relationship between gender, role, position and promotion aspirations', *Pedagogy, Culture and Society* 8(2): 187–206.

——(2006) *Boys to Men: teaching and learning masculinities in schools and colleges.* Birmingham: NASUWT.

Thornton, M., Bricheno, P. and Reid, I. (2002) 'Students' reasons for wanting to teach in primary school', *Research in Education* 67: 33–43.

Thrupp, M. (2005) 'The National College for School Leadership: a critique', *Management in Education* 19(2): 13–19.

Tomlinson, H. (2004) 'Head teacher', in H. Green (Ed) *Professional Standards for School Leaders: a key to school improvement.* Abingdon: RoutledgeFalmer: 225–45.

Totterdell, M., Heilbronn, R., Bubb, S. and Jones, C. (2002) *Evaluation of the Effectiveness of the Statutory Arrangements for the Induction of Newly Qualified Teachers.* London: DfES.

Training and Development Agency for Schools (TDA) (2000/2006) *ITT place allocations.* Online (Available: http://www.tda.gov.uk/partners/funding/allocations.aspx, accessed 13 March 2007).

TDA (2007) *Note from the Rewards and Incentive Group. Update on proposed changes to professional standards for teachers in England from September 2007.* Online (Available: http://www.tda.gov. uk/teachers/professionalstandards.aspx?keywords=professional+standards, accessed 15 May 2007).

Teacher Training Agency (TTA) (1995a) *A Survey of CPD.* London: TTA.

TTA (1995b) *Head Teachers' Leadership and Management Programme.* London: TTA.

——(1998) *The National Standards* ('Rainbow Pack'). London: TTA.

——(2002/2006) *QTS Skills Test in Numeracy, June and July 2000: National Results Summary for Initial Training Providers.* London: TTA.

Twistleton, S. (2000) 'Seeing the wood for the trees: the National Literacy Strategy and initial teacher education; pedagogical content, knowledge and the structure of subjects', *Cambridge Journal of Education* 30(3): 391–404.

——(2004) 'The role of teacher identities in learning to teach primary literacy', *Education Review* 56(2): 157–64.

Universities' Council for the Education of Teachers (UCET) (2004) 'The BEd – is it under threat?', *Minutes of the ITE Primary Committee, 04.11.2004.* London: UCET.

UCET (2005) *School Placement Survey.* London: UCET.

——(2007) *ITE Inspection Burdens.* London: UCET.

Vulliamy, G. (2006) 'Primary teacher professionalism', in R. Webb (Ed) *Changing Teaching and Learning in the Primary School.* London: Open University Press.

Vulliamy, G. and Webb, R. (1991) 'Teacher research and educational change: an empirical study', *British Educational Research Journal* 17(3): 219–36.

Watkins, M. (2006) *Boys to Men: teaching and learning masculinities in schools and colleges.* Birmingham: NASUWT.

Webb, R. (1989) 'Changing practice through consultancy-based INSET', *School Organisation* 9 (1): 39–52.

——(2005) 'Leading teaching and learning in the primary school, from "educative leadership" to "pedagogical leadership"', *Educational Management Administration and Leadership* 33(1): 69–91.

Webb, R. and Vulliamy, G. (1996) *Roles and Responsibilities in the Primary School: changing demands, changing practices*. Buckingham: Open University Press.

——(2006) *Coming Full Circle? The impact of New Labour's education policies*. London: ATL.

Webb, R. and Vulliamy, G. (forthcoming 2008) *'On a treadmill' but 'the kids are great': primary teachers' work and wellbeing*. London: ATL.

Webb, R., Vulliamy, G., Sarja, A. and Hämäläinen, S. (2006) 'Globalisation and leadership and management in primary schools: a comparative analysis of England and Finland', *Research Papers in Education* 21(4): 407–32.

White, J. (1989) 'Student teaching as rite of passage', *Anthropology and Educational Quarterly* 20: 177–95.

Whitty, G. (2002) *Making Sense of Educational Policy*. London: Paul Chapman.

Wilkin, M. (1996) *Initial Teacher Education: the dialogue of ideology and culture*. London: Falmer Press.

——(1999) *The Role of Higher Education in Initial Teacher Education* (UCET Occasional Paper No. 12). London: UCET.

Williams, A. and Soares, A. (2002) 'Sharing roles and responsibilities in Initial Teacher Training: perceptions of some key players', *Cambridge Journal of Education* 32(1): 91–107.

Wilson, S., Floden, R. and Ferrini-Mundy, J. (2001) *Teacher Preparation Research: current knowledge, gaps, and recommendations*. Seattle, WA: University of Washington, Center for the Study of Teaching and Policy.

Wilson, V. and McPake, J. (2000) 'Managing change in small Scottish primary schools', *Educational Management and Administration* 28(2): 119–32.

Wood, K. (2000) 'The experience of learning to teach: changing student teachers' ways of understanding teaching', *Journal of Curriculum Studies* 32(1): 75–93.

Woods, P., Jeffrey, B., Troman, G. and Boyle, M. (1997) *Restructuring Schools, Reconstructing Teachers*. Buckingham: Open University Press.

Wyse, D. (2003) 'The National Literacy Strategy: a critical review of empirical evidence', *British Educational Research Journal* 29(6): 903–16.

25 Primary workforce management and reform

Hilary Burgess

INTRODUCTION

The last twenty years have seen a profound change in the way primary schools have been managed and organised, alongside a fundamental restructuring of the professional and para-professional school workforce. These changes have created both controversy and debate among policy makers, teachers and educational researchers. This chapter provides an overview of the impact of policies upon professional workforce management, reform and support, and assesses recent developments in England and Wales and elsewhere in the UK. A brief comparison with the USA provides a global context for understanding key issues that impact upon teachers and other professionals in primary schools.

The time span for this survey is relatively short and focuses on the period from 1998, when the government published the Green Paper *Teachers: meeting the challenge of change* (DfEE 1998), to the present day. The survey is necessarily selective, and includes those policies and research studies deemed to have the most impact on the practice of the professional primary school workforce.

A number of research studies have been examined in detail. They include, in particular:

- NFER evaluation of the National Remodelling Team (Easton *et al.* 2006)
- Transforming the School Workforce Pathfinder Project (Thomas *et al.* 2004a)
- The impact of New Labour's education policies on primary school teachers' work (Webb and Vulliamy 2006)
- The deployment and impact of support staff in schools (Blatchford *et al.* 2004).

All research needs to take account of the political, educational, social and cultural emphases of the time in which it is conducted and this chapter will begin by providing a brief context for the research reports that are discussed.

CONTEXT

The Education Reform Act (House of Commons 1988) introduced a National Curriculum for all schools in England and Wales and began what was to be a succession of curriculum and other reforms that would have a major impact upon the primary workforce through curriculum specification, assessment of pupils at the ages of seven and eleven, the inspection of schools by the newly created Office for Standards in Education (Ofsted) and the introduction of specific standards for teachers and teaching assistants. The breadth of curriculum activity that teachers in primary schools had to undertake to meet the requirements of the new Act created an immense workload with associated stress (Dunham 1992) for the primary teaching workforce. This in turn led to major problems in terms of the recruitment of head teachers and the retention of teachers in some parts of the country, and initiated concerns among the teaching profession and teaching unions that these issues had to be addressed.

Studies by Ofsted (1993) and the National Curriculum Council (1993) both reported that the National Curriculum was severely overloaded and difficult to implement. Research into curriculum reform (Campbell and Neill 1994a) explored the amount of time spent on work by teachers at Key Stage 1. This study found teachers conscientiously trying to make the reforms work but discovered little curriculum change had occurred because of structural faults in the 'reformed' curriculum, confusion over assessment and working conditions that did not support the reform process in infant schools and departments. At Key Stage 2, research focussed on issues arising from the implementation of the National Curriculum and assessment procedures and argued for a curriculum framework that was both flexible and enabling, and for stronger partnership between the government and teachers (Pollard 1994). The Dearing review (1993) addressed some of these issues by reducing the statutory curriculum and introducing up to 20 per cent non-National Curriculum teaching time. In primary schools, methods of teaching remained the prerogative of teachers although reports advocated broadening the range of teaching roles to include specialists as well as generalist class teachers, various forms of grouping, including by ability, and a greater use of whole class teaching (Alexander *et al.* 1992; Ofsted 1995).

The National Literacy and Numeracy Strategies were introduced in 1998 and 1999 respectively, following international achievement studies that showed children in England were not performing as well as their peers in other countries (Second International Mathematics Study [SIMS] 1993; Third International Mathematics and Science Study [TIMSS] 1996). Ofsted reported that a majority of primary teachers welcomed the introduction of the National Literacy and Numeracy strategies (Ofsted 1999) as the statutory requirement to cover all the non-core foundation subjects in full was relaxed. However, these strategies had a wide-ranging impact upon methods of teaching in primary schools as they specified the amount of time to be spent on these subjects, while the lesson format for teaching the prescribed content resulted in more whole class subject teaching and for the first time a particular pedagogy was prescribed and rigorously enforced.

In 2003 the Primary National Strategy was launched with the aim of supporting teachers across the whole curriculum, offering teachers more control and flexibility and building up teachers' own professionalism and capacity to teach better. In essence, teaching excellence and pupil enjoyment were to be combined (DfES 2003a). The strategy covered issues impacting upon school character and innovation, excellent primary teaching, learning with a focus on individual children, partnership beyond the classroom, leadership in primary schools and the power of collaboration, managing school resources and workforce reform in primary schools. A key element of the workforce reform strategy, identified in the Primary Strategy launch document *Excellence and Enjoyment: a strategy for primary schools*, was the use of teaching assistants. The document states:

> The National Agreement aims to make sure that increasing numbers of support staff, and ICT, are used in a way which helps improve standards and also reduces teachers' workload so that they have more time to spend on their most important

tasks. Our survey showed that the way support staff were used strongly influenced the effect they had. Almost all head teachers thought that support staff used for learning and teaching raised standards. Over half the head teachers thought that more administrative staff helped reduce workload; and seven out of ten thought that staff supporting behaviour and attendance reduced teacher stress.

(DfES 2003a: 7.4)

Research that has examined the Primary Strategy has focussed on the emphasis on individual learning; for example, Brehony (2005) in his analysis of primary schooling under New Labour argues that the lexicon of progressivism is 'being re-appropriated by New Labour' (Brehony 2005: 40) through the emphasis on personalised learning and the individual child. However, as Alexander (2004) argues, the Primary National Strategy 'vision' of a curriculum that has breadth and balance and enshrines excellence and enjoyment is diminished through the embedding of the Literacy and Numeracy Strategies and national targets for pupil achievement in English and mathematics.

The Children Act and the publication of *Every Child Matters: change for children* and *Every Child Matters: next steps* (DfES 2003b; DfES 2004a) initiated changes in the reform process that would have a major impact upon the primary school workforce. The first report defined the relationship between well-being and educational achievement and paved the way for the development of extended schools, where there would be access to and liaison with external services (social services, health care, child care), thus creating coherent provision for the needs of children. There was also a proposal to develop a Children's Workforce Unit to develop a pay and workforce strategy to address recruitment and retention. The 'next steps' report set out the structure and remit of the UK Sector Skills Council (SSC) for Social Care, Children and Young People which would enable the reforms that had been proposed. A federated structure was proposed which would:

- Bring together those working in social care with other occupational groups who work with children;
- Be required as a condition of its licence to set up and maintain a UK Children's Workforce Network which would bring together all those who worked with children, young people and families;
- Allow each country within the UK to develop operational arrangements in line with their own policy. For England, this meant an approach to workforce planning and children's workforce that would be co-ordinated through a Children, Young People and Families Council.

The Children's Workforce Strategy (DfES 2005) is a significant document in the government's remodelling agenda as it incorporates New Labour's drive for social inclusion and its intention to tackle the tail of underachievement and child poverty. All of these policies are largely being directed through the remodelling of education and schools. In 2005, a prospectus for extended schools set out what was to be the 'core offer' of services accessible through schools by 2010. Underlying all these policies was the government's aim to raise standards and improve pupil achievement.

These policy developments in curriculum organisation and methods of teaching in primary schools provide the background in which proposals for remodelling the school workforce emerged.

The next section of this chapter focuses upon some of the key issues and research studies linked to workforce remodelling in terms of the early agreements and planned phases for the introduction of these changes.

THE CASE FOR MODERNISING THE TEACHING PROFESSION

The Green Paper *Teachers: meeting the challenge of change* (DfEE 1998) set out the case for modernising the teaching profession. The modernised profession was intended to provide

> good leadership, incentives for excellence, a strong culture of professionalism, and better support for teachers to focus on teaching to improve the image and status of the profession
>
> (DfEE 1998: 6)

The reforms had three objectives:

- To promote excellent school leadership by rewarding our leading professionals properly;
- To recruit, retain and motivate high quality classroom teachers by paying them more;
- To provide better support to all teachers and to deploy teaching resources in a more flexible way.

> (DfEE 1998: 6)

Achievement of these objectives was central to New Labour's reform agenda for schools. However, evidence gathered by the School Teachers' Review Body (STRB), which had commissioned surveys to examine teachers' workload in 1994, 1996 and 2000, revealed that there was growing concern about workload in the teaching profession and the impact this was having upon teacher morale. In February 2001 the STRB published a tenth report recommending that the DfEE should commission an independent report to review teacher workload. This task was undertaken by PricewaterhouseCoopers (PwC 2001). It was after the findings of this report confirmed that teacher workload was excessive that the STRB were asked to consider in detail teacher workload and conditions of service (STRB 2002, 2004).

The three objectives of the Green Paper were to have a wide-ranging impact as successive government policies sought to implement the proposed reforms. The increased pay levels proposed for teachers were linked to a system of performance management and performance-related pay, and in 1998 the new Advanced Skills Teacher posts were established. The framework of professional standards (TDA 2007) reflects the progression now expected (in England) as teachers develop knowledge, skills and understanding alongside their professional attributes.

The professional standards underpin the five key outcomes for children as set out in *Every Child Matters* (to be healthy; stay safe; enjoy and achieve; make a positive contribution; and achieve economic well-being) and the six areas of the Common Core of Skills and Knowledge for the children's workforce that everyone working with children should be able to demonstrate. The Common Core of Skills and Knowledge covers effective communication and engagement; child and young person development;

safeguarding and promoting the welfare of the child; supporting transitions; multi-agency working; and sharing information. Included within the framework for professional standards are the Training and Development Agency for Schools (TDA) review of the standards for teaching assistants and the professional standards for higher level teaching assistants in consultation with social partners, key stakeholders and a review of leadership standards. The standards now range from those for initial teacher training and induction to the National Professional Qualification for Headship. Normally, teachers reach the point of Threshold Assessment after five years and up to that time their salary increases by yearly increments. Those teachers who meet the Threshold standards receive a performance related promotion and transfer to an upper pay spine. Four further increments can be awarded by school governors on the advice of head teachers. In this way, teachers' working lives are divided into career stages which are linked to performance management in schools. (The standards for Post Threshold Teachers, Excellent Teachers and Advanced Skills Teachers are pay standards and apply to England and Wales.)

Mahoney *et al.* (2004) argue that this system transforms what was a national pay scale into one that is determined and managed locally. Their ESRC-funded research project found that teachers experienced difficulties when Threshold was introduced because of the technology of the form and many teachers found the standards to be repetitive and unclear. Head teachers, however, had a much more positive view of the process, claiming that passing through the Threshold gave teachers' professional identity a boost. Some research argues that the professional lives of teachers have been structured into a system of performance management, where they are dependent upon external definitions of quality, progress and achievement for their success and where there is pressure, particularly for younger teachers, to comply with 'competency based agendas' (Day 2002: 677).

In the document *Time for Standards* (DfES 2002), reform was sought by the government linked to four principles: standards and accountability; devolution and delegation; flexibility and incentives and expanding choice. To achieve these principles there was to be investment which would ensure that:

1. Our pupils are supported by a wide range of teachers and other adults working flexibly and differentiating their approaches to meet pupils' needs; and pupils are developing their own learning skills
2. Our teachers are using effective approaches to teaching and learning, are working in teams with other teachers and support staff, are committed to their own development and confident in exercising their professional judgement; and have higher status, proper remuneration and incentives, more responsibility and autonomy, more support and a better work/life balance
3. Our support staff are recognised for their contribution to raising standards and have more opportunities to take on wider and deeper roles in support of teaching and learning, supported by the right training and new career paths, with numbers growing to deliver reform
4. Our Heads and leadership teams are committed to innovation, leading the change to new, more flexible ways of working, and to better teaching not just within their own schools, but in partnership with other schools and institutions and with their LEA, are ensuring an appropriate work/life balance for their staff; and are embracing leadership responsibilities in the wider community, and

5. Our schools are making world class provision, supported by world class teaching and world class ICT with well designed and equipped premises which can adapt to modern approaches to teaching and learning, and where there is flexibility over the length and size of individual lessons and the school day.

(DfES 2002: 4)

To test the viability of the principles and aims of the proposed reforms, the DfES commissioned the *Transforming the School Workforce* (TSW) Pathfinder project which was launched in 2002. The aim of this project, carried out by a team from the London Leadership Centre and led by Dame Pat Collarbone, was to discover ways of making significant reductions in the hours teachers worked and to increase the proportion of teachers' time spent on teaching and teaching related activities. The aims were to be achieved through the provision of resources to support change in teachers' working practices and covered several areas:

- Providing schools with consultancy support (school workforce advisors)
- Training head teachers in change management
- Allocating funds for employing additional support staff
- Providing ICT and software
- Funding the bursarial training of school managers; and
- Providing schools with capital resources

(Thomas *et al.* 2004a: 1)

However, as Butt and Gunter (2005) report, although learning from the TSW Pathfinder schools was intended to be used to support remodelling in schools nationally from January 2004, the National Agreement (ATL *et al.* 2003) was signed and remodelling in all schools instigated (DfES 2004b) before the end of the project and the publication of the TSW evaluation findings.

THE NATIONAL AGREEMENT AND THE PHASES OF WORKFORCE REFORM

The National Agreement was set up between the government, employers and the school workforce unions. The Agreement promised joint action, designed to help every school in England and Wales to raise standards and tackle workload issues, and included a seven point plan for creating time for teachers and head teachers which included: a reduction in teachers' hours; changes to teachers' contracts to ensure the aims set out in *Time for Standards* (DfES 2002) could be met; a concerted attack on unnecessary paperwork and bureaucratic processes; reform of support staff roles to help teachers and support pupils; the recruitment of new managers including business and personnel managers; additional resources and national 'change management' programmes to help school leaders achieve the reforms; and monitoring of progress on delivery by signatories to the Agreement. Within the detail of the Agreement is a statement about strategies for managing cover, where it is stated:

high level teaching assistants will be able to cover classes, and should be able to ensure that pupils can progress with their learning, based on their knowledge of the learning outcomes planned by the classroom/subject teacher.

(ATL *et al.*: 7)

This is one of the statements within the Agreement that caused much controversy and debate among the teaching profession and elsewhere, as teachers were concerned that their job would be devalued if untrained staff were allowed to cover and thus maybe teach whole classes. Parents also raised concerns about the quality of staff who would be covering and teaching their children. This statement in the Agreement was a key reason that the National Union of Teachers (NUT), the largest of the teacher unions, refused to sign up to the Agreement (Butt and Gunter 2005).

To help implement the reforms a Workforce Agreement Monitoring Group (WAMG), consisting of government, employers and unions, was set up alongside an Implementation Review Group (IRU), which consisted of practitioners, to review policy initiatives from a school perspective. Change in schools was to be introduced in three stages:

Phase 1 – 2003
- Promote reductions in overall excessive hours
- Establish monitoring group
- Establish new Implementation Review Group
- Routine delegation of 24 non-teaching tasks
- Introduce new work/life balance clauses
- Introduce leadership and management time
- Undertake review of use of school closure days

Phase 2 – 2004
- Introduce new limits on covering for teachers

Phase 3 – 2005
- Introduce guaranteed professional time for planning, preparation and assessment
- Introduce dedicated headship time
- Introduce new invigilation arrangements

(DfES 2004c)

The National Remodelling Team (NRT), set up in 2003 and initially based in the National College for School Leadership (NCSL), moved in 2005 to the Training and Development Agency for schools (TDA) in order to support the extended TDA role to oversee provision of advice and support to schools.

It has been argued that remodelling has the potential to:

enable teachers and teaching to thrive in a reinvigorated public sector, where teachers can put emphasis on their core purpose of teaching, and work in productive networks with other adults to support learning.

(Butt and Gunter 2005: 135)

However, Butt and Gunter also suggest:

There is also the possibility that nothing much will change at all in relation to educational goals, and remodelling will be a make-over where the control of teachers and their work will remain outside of schools orchestrated by those at a distance from practice.

(Butt and Gunter 2005: 135)

The NFER conducted an evaluation each year of the National Remodelling Team (NRT) (Wilson *et al.* 2005; Easton *et al.* 2005). The third evaluation by the NFER (Easton *et al.* 2006) was set up to examine the effectiveness and the impact of the NRT in completing the third phase of the remodelling programme. It also sought to explore the effectiveness of the NRT in applying its model, tools and techniques to the extended schools programme. Data was collected through questionnaire surveys of:

- All Local Education Authority Remodelling Advisers (RAs)
- All Extended Schools Remodelling Advisers (ESRAs)
- All Extended Schools Remodelling Trainers (ESRTs)
- All extended school pilot schools.

The second strand of the evaluation involved telephone interviews with LEA RAs, ESRAs, and ESRTs in all nine government regions in England. Case study visits also took place to schools involved in the pilot of the extended schools programme.

The extended schools pilot programme aims to trial the implementation of an extended service in and around schools by providing: high quality child care on the school site or through other local providers, available ten hours a day from 8 am to 6 pm all year round and with supervised transport arrangements where appropriate; a varied programme of activities such as homework clubs, arts and music and enterprise activities; parenting support, particularly at key transition points; swift and easy referral to a wide range of specialist support services such as speech therapy and family support services; and wider community access to ICT, sports and arts facilities and adult learning.

Key findings from the evaluation in terms of the remodelling programme were that most schools were at the 'developing' stage (as defined by the NRT), although some schools had reached the sustainable stage. There was concern about the long-term sustainability of the programme as head teachers and teachers considered sustainability to be reliant on continuing levels of funding. Successes of remodelling as far as teachers were concerned included the introduction of Planning, Preparation and Assessment (PPA) time, meeting the requirements of the National Agreement, introducing the change management process and flexible team working.

Progress with other initiatives was also being made, specifically with *Every Child Matters* (ECM). However, it was evident from the questionnaire responses that it was thought more could be done to link the different agendas and show schools how they interrelate. The positive aspects of the remodelling programme were considered to be the training and support provided by the NRT and particularly the adaptability of the training materials to meet local demands.

Teachers and advisers involved in the extended schools pilot programme felt they needed additional support in sharing examples of good practice and in improving the understanding of the agenda among school staff and other service colleagues and developing multi-agency working. The RAs and ESRAs considered the management change process to be flexible and fit for purpose although schools were less positive and ESRTs thought it was too early to comment. Overall, the work of the NRT was thought to be effective and to be having a positive impact upon schools and the local communities.

LEADERSHIP AND MANAGING CHANGE IN SCHOOLS

The management of change in schools is crucial to the successful implementation of the school workforce agenda and good leadership of that process is essential for effective and smooth transitions to occur. The DfES was determined to make sure that every head teacher would do more than 'run a stable school' and that leadership would be transformed. Such a transformation requires leadership that can:

- Frame a clear vision that engages the school community
- Motivate and inspire
- Pursues change in a consistent and disciplined way; and
- Understands and leads the professional business of teaching

To achieve their full potential, teachers need to work in a school that is creative, enabling and flexible. And the biggest influence is the Head. Every teacher is a leader in the classroom. Every Head must be the leader of these leaders. And the Head's greatest task is the motivation and deployment of their key resource staff.

(DfES 2003a: 20)

Head teachers were encouraged under the remodelling agenda to review how staff should be deployed in their schools, how the school day, week and year was organised and encouraged to be creative in the use of school space so that new opportunities in the community and with business were opened up. Rayner and Gunter's research (2005) draws on the Transforming the School Workforce (TSW) Project to provide examples of the way in which head teachers responded to the management of workforce change in schools. They argue that remodelling has strengthened hierarchical leadership and this continued dominance is reinforced by a 'policy context that has reworked headship as organisational school leadership' (Rayner and Gunter 2005: 152–53). This approach assumes distribution of leadership is through formal organisational procedures such as line management and role descriptions. Delegation is the reallocation of one role to another and therefore delegation brings authorisation. The emphasis on role definition allows work previously done by teachers to be allocated to others such as teaching assistants. However, they also suggest such an approach to leadership does not recognise that:

remodelling grows out of how people think about and experience their practice, and how teachers strategically engage with the aims and what it means for them within their working and wider lives.

(Rayner and Gunter 2005: 153)

They argue that questions need to be asked about how remodelling is interpreted within schools and how teachers can 'accept, redefine and match' (Rayner and Gunter 2005: 155) the external definition of remodelling.

The TSW project evaluated the three official features of remodelling; the change plan, the change management team, and changes within the organisational culture. However, the research team also found within the data:

a discernible distributed practice associated with how people made sense of the relationship between professional practice and the work involved in the project.

(Rayner and Gunter 2005: 155)

The Project required all the schools taking part to produce a change plan that reflected the schools' intention to reform and innovate practice and this required the wider workforce to work through often complex issues concerning purposes and practice. The change management team (CMT) was also an area that demonstrated distributed practice. Supported by an external School Workforce Adviser, schools were able to engage in thinking about opportunities afforded by the project. One primary school support staff member reported:

> The management of the school has changed in a positive way the change management team has more positive ideas. Management has changed for the better, it is a more positive school. (Meadow School – Support Staff 1).
>
> (Rayner and Gunter 2005: 156)

The third element that Rayner and Gunter researched is the disposition to discuss and develop practice in school. Within their case study data they found an increased flexibility and renewed trust. One senior manager in a primary school reported:

> A mental shift in teachers was needed. They work long hours and are committed. Now because of the early opening of school we say: 'unless you need to be here, take your lap top and go' It is important to do this because our work never finishes, it is constantly in your head. (Meadow School – Senior Manager).
>
> (Rayner and Gunter 2005: 156)

In their research, Rayner and Gunter acknowledge that existing structural influences in the schools would also play a part in the change process and that sometimes the change idea might begin to work in ways that had not been envisaged. Occasionally, there were criticisms of the CMT in relation to the pace of change (this was largely due to external and political considerations forcing the pace) and that what came through clearly was how the Project required new and additional work in order for it to be successful. While reductions in workload were achieved in the short term, they consider the implications for educational leadership to be much more far-reaching.

As a key element of the Primary National Strategy, the Primary Leadership Programme (PLP) was set up in 2003. The PLP evaluation (Wade *et al.* 2007) focussed on the aims of the programme to evaluate if they had been achieved. The aims of PLP were:

- To strengthen collaborative leadership and responsibility for teaching and learning in primary schools
- To equip leadership teams with a greater understanding of expectations in English and mathematics and the expertise needed both to identify where improvements should be made and to take appropriate steps towards bringing about these improvements
- To develop and extend the use of management tools to inform effective leadership and to contribute towards improvements in the teaching and learning of English and mathematics
- For participating schools to make significant improvements in Key Stage 2 results in English and mathematics over the period 2004 to 2006.

(Wade *et al.* 2007: 2)

The evaluation team interviewed key staff at ten case study schools, sent a large scale questionnaire survey to 1000 randomly selected leaders involved in the programme and used statistical evidence from the KS1 and KS2 results. The key findings showed that pupil attainment at KS2 improved, in teaching and learning there were improvements in data analysis, changes to teaching styles and the adoption of identified good practice. In the PLP schools there was a widening of leadership with change management teams increasing in size. Leadership was deemed to have improved with a more widely shared vision for the school and a sharing of responsibility with middle management. Many respondents indicated a stronger sense of team work and increased opportunities for collaboration with other schools. Inputs from the Primary Strategy Consultant Leaders (PSCL) were viewed positively and many schools had improved their own monitoring and evaluation processes. While schools were doing their best to embed practice, the project team found that schools were encountering difficulties with sustainability. These difficulties included time constraints, staff turnover, changing priorities and the importance of funding to enable meetings to take place. Recommendations emerging from the project included the need to maintain contact with the PCSL (or someone in a similar role) and that there should remain a focus on distributed leadership as the sharing of responsibilities and a common vision shared across a number of staff was thought to work well.

RESHAPING THE WORKFORCE: TEACHERS

Teachers' work and roles in primary schools had begun to change considerably even before the National Agreement was introduced in response to the curriculum and assessment reforms introduced at the end of the twentieth century. The impact that these early reforms had upon primary teachers has been well documented in a number of research reports, for example impact upon teacher workload at Key Stage 1 (Campbell and Neill 1994a); impact upon primary teachers' work through the implementation of changes in curriculum and assessment (Campbell and Neill 1994b); teacher responses to escalating workloads and the new demands of their expanding roles (Webb and Vulliamy 1996a); the changes that have taken place in teacher practice and links to professional ideology and personal practice in terms of curriculum, pedagogy and assessment (Pollard *et al.* 1994; Alexander *et al.* 1996; Osborne *et al.* 2000; Galton *et al.* 1999; Moyles *et al.* 2003). More recently, research by Thomas *et al.* (2004) on transforming the school workforce (TSW project); Blatchford *et al.* (2006, 2007) on the deployment and impact of support staff in schools (DISS project); Webb and Vulliamy (2006) on the impact of policies on primary school teachers' work; Woodward and Peart (2005) on the role of the higher level teaching assistant; and Wilson *et al.* (2007) on the impact of support staff who have achieved HLTA status is of particular relevance for this chapter as the research draws attention to the impact of the remodelling initiative in primary schools.

Much of this research has a wider remit than workforce reform or focuses upon only one element of it. Gunter (2007) claims that 'there is no robust research evidence regarding school and workforce experiences of this reform' (Gunter 2007: 4), and states that the main evidence base comes from the TSW project.

Transforming the School Workforce (TSW Project)

The TSW pilot project (Thomas *et al.* 2004a) included thirty-two schools (4 special schools, 16 primary schools and 12 secondary schools) and nine comparator schools to compare change in these schools with that in the pilot schools. The project pilot schools were provided with consultancy support to give guidance in the management of change in schools and the schools were also asked to think radically about human and physical resources. Funds were provided to buy in additional support staff and to obtain hardware and software so that all teachers had access to a laptop computer. There was also access to training for certain groups of staff including teaching assistants. According to Thomas *et al.* (2004b) these elements would contribute to the pattern of change in the working practices of those employed in schools allowing the aims of remodelling to be fulfilled.

The teachers in the TSW project identified five areas that were problematic for them and created excessive workload. These included too much bureaucracy and paperwork, planning, government initiatives, unrealistic targets and discipline in schools. Teachers across all sectors stated the single most effective solution would be the employment of more support staff and additionally more non-contact time; reduction in paperwork; development of ICT and smaller classes. The study also reported that a case study of a cluster of four primary schools revealed a dominant focus for change was remodelling (although this covered a number of initiatives). These schools gave examples of not only appointing more support staff but also of changing the roles and status of such staff. The project team concluded that (at that time) there was no signal that teaching assistants would be appropriately rewarded in terms of improved salary and that greater attention needed to be paid to the training of teachers in the coordination of teaching assistants. More recently Gunter (2007) reported that the TSW project found

> that interventions that are now known better as Remodelling led to teachers reporting a reduction in their workload, change in culture and a better work-life balance, and they had begun to develop the role of support staff. However, the research also found that the changes needed substantial and sustained funding, and that reform is itself a time hungry process that adds to the burden of senior staff in particular.
>
> (Gunter 2007: 6)

The evaluation also found variation in the way that remodelling strategies were developed in different schools so that whereas one school reported a reduction in workload hours by 13 hours per week, another school reported a two hour increase in time spent on work per week. It would appear that the way in which strategies are developed within the local context is of key importance for remodelling in schools.

The findings from the TSW project concluded that an impact had been made in reducing teachers' working hours and there was a shift in role boundaries between teachers and other members of the school workforce enabling more effective support. The project research brief commented

> The schools give examples of appointing more support staff but, more importantly, changing the roles of many support staff and raising their status. It is apparent that support staff became a more visible and important part of school communities.
>
> (Thomas *et al.* 2004a)

The resource that increased ICT in schools had been beneficial, but the project concluded that levels of training and support in this area were not matched with the resources.

The project authors were also concerned about the sustainability of several of the initiatives that had been supported by additional funding without the continuation of these funds.

In terms of workload, teachers reported a reduction in hours worked and there was evidence of reduction in time devoted to tasks that could be done by others. The project report revealed there was a relationship between decline in hours and positive views among teachers on the quality of leadership, decision making and change management in primary schools. A consistent relationship was also identified between good quality ICT training and support and reduction in hours.

Research on the impact on teachers of New Labour's policies

The first detailed report on the impact of New Labour's education policies on primary school teachers' work (Webb and Vulliamy 2006a) focuses upon the effects on primary teachers' attitudes, values and experiences and their perceptions of the changes in their roles and responsibilities over the last decade. To conduct their research Webb and Vulliamy used a condensed fieldwork qualitative research strategy that involved classroom observation, teacher interviews and the collection of documentation from day-long visits to 50 schools in 16 local education authorities throughout England (most of these schools formed the research sample for their earlier report in the early nineties, see Webb and Vulliamy 1996b). The fieldwork took place over three years between 2003 and 2006, and in total 188 teacher interviews were recorded and transcribed. The analysis of the interviews was based upon the 'constant comparison' method advocated originally by Glaser and Strauss (1967). As in previous research such as Day (2002) and Osborne *et al.* (2000), differences have been found in teachers' responses between those who entered teaching before the 1988 Education Reform Act and those who entered afterwards; the project authors took note of those teachers who trained before 1990 (68 per cent) and those who trained after that date (32 per cent). In terms of assessing the outcomes of this project it is relevant to note that the teacher sample was drawn from experienced teachers who were often the most confident teachers in a school.

The data from the project provided research evidence of teachers' perceptions of the National Literacy and Numeracy Strategies (NLS and NNS); targets, testing and assessment; the impact of ICT; the role of teaching assistants; the Primary National Strategy and changing classroom practice. The project found that there were many criticisms of the NLS but that in contrast, apart from a few caveats, the NNS 'received overwhelming support' (Webb and Vulliamy 2006a: 5). Overall, the strategies were viewed positively by the primary workforce because they provided continuity and structure although teachers were very critical of the way they were imposed in schools and the implication that the government lacked trust in the teaching profession. The consequence of this was a lowering of teacher morale and reduced teacher self-confidence, and there was also resentment of the pressure to comply with the strategies from the LEA and Ofsted. Schools also found several ways to adapt the strategies to suit the needs of the children or take account of the strengths and weaknesses of the teaching staff. Overall though, and as a result of teaching methods promoted by the strategies, teachers considered that the methods had 'greatly improved the quality of their teaching' (Webb and Vulliamy 2006a: 5).

In terms of targets, testing and assessment the findings showed that staff in schools felt an 'unremitting pressure' to achieve the government's national literacy and numeracy targets and they described how this pressure was passed on to pupils. This still proved to be the case, even though ministers told schools in 2003 that they could set their own targets at KS2, as the head teachers in the research survey sample were still expected to fit in with LEA predictions. The report states that 'teachers held an overwhelmingly negative view of SATs and would like to see them abolished' (Webb and Vulliamy 2006a: 6). The majority of head teachers, however, did not hold this view as they considered the tests necessary to drive up standards, but they were all highly critical of performance tables and the problems associated with value added versions of these tables. The use of ICT aided schools in the collection and evaluation of their own data and analysis of the strengths and weaknesses in the coverage of literacy and numeracy. However, the report considered that judgements were being made about the performance of teachers according to their ability to enable pupils to meet attainment targets. A similar difference of perspective on SATs, between teachers and head teachers, emerged from the Primary Review Community Soundings witness sessions in nine regional locations during 2007 (Alexander and Hargreaves 2007: 28).

ICT use in the 50 schools was reported as having increased dramatically with the development of ICT suites and the installation of interactive whiteboards in classrooms. These developments, it was considered, had an impact on teachers and in turn on classroom pedagogy by promoting whole-class teaching, as the majority of teachers stood at the side of the whiteboard and talked to the whole class. Technical problems with ICT were reported as the most frustrating issue, creating pressure for ICT coordinators. Teacher use of ICT for both personal and professional use and the potential it holds for teaching and learning was improved in those schools that had been able to provide personal laptops, and there was increasing awareness about how to teach children and alert parents to the risks for children of using the internet.

RESHAPING THE WORKFORCE: TEACHING ASSISTANTS

The dramatic increase in support staff in schools lies at the heart of the government plans for a modernised workforce. It was reported that in 2004 there were 134,100 total support staff working in mainstream primary schools and nurseries in England, with a ratio of 2.08 teaching assistants to every teacher (DfES 2004c; Vincett *et al.* 2005). By 2007, there were 163,000 support staff in primary schools and nurseries: including 105,800 teaching assistants and 57,400 other support staff (DCSF 2007).

Research into the roles and relationships of Key Stage 1 teachers and classroom assistants (Moyles and Suschitzky 1997) urged greater involvement of teaching assistants in lesson planning and finding time to share knowledge so that better support could be provided for children. Ofsted (2002) concurred with this view, stating that while teachers valued the additional support more time had to be spent in planning and preparation. They also noted the role that teaching assistants might play in curriculum enrichment contributing to both curriculum quality and breadth. Usually, however, they found that teaching assistants were used to support the literacy hours, mathematics or to support children with special needs. This is confirmed by the research findings of Hancock and Eyres (2004) who suggest teaching assistants had been assigned a 'remedial' role in the teaching of literacy and numeracy and yet were barely visible in the reports that evaluated the implementation of the literacy and numeracy strategies (Earl *et al.* 2000, 2001, 2003).

The TSW Pathfinder project picked up on a number of issues relating to role definition, job specification and the development of skills for teaching assistants to carry out the work assigned to them (Butt and Lance 2005). In the project there was a major focus on expenditure to provide support for teachers through the employment and deployment of teaching assistants. Questionnaire and interview data from the 32 schools studied and the in-depth case study material revealed that teachers thought the teaching assistant role was an important one, and 78 per cent of primary teachers surveyed agreed that teaching assistants needed more training. The effective use of teaching assistants in schools and classrooms appeared to change considerably between 2002 and 2003, with 43 per cent of teachers considering teaching assistants were under-used in 2002. By 2003, 87 per cent of teachers agreed employing a teaching assistant allowed them more time to teach. The teaching assistants surveyed in the project were found to be broadly satisfied with their role, well motivated and positive about the ways they were being led and managed. The researchers surmised that, as a workforce, such a positive group might welcome changes in their roles and responsibilities if accompanied by appropriate recognition and remuneration.

Webb and Vulliamy (2006a) reported that, in terms of the recent expansion in teaching assistants in response to the government's workforce agenda, the number of adults working in the school community had increased considerably. Teaching assistants were perceived as 'promoting pupil's self-esteem, motivation and achievement' (Webb and Vulliamy 2006b: 9, Report summary) and many teachers regarded the teaching assistant as crucial to their effective management of pupils and teaching. The research found that by 2004 most schools had strategies in place to relieve teachers of the 24 administrative tasks cited in the workload agreement. However, it appeared that not all teachers took full advantage of these strategies to relieve their workload, preferring to use additional teaching assistant time to support children. This point coincides with the TSW finding that there was no systematic relationship between job satisfaction and hours worked. These findings suggest that moving a particular type of work from teachers to support staff might move the administrative/bureaucratic burden elsewhere but may not necessarily motivate teachers who place more emphasis on enjoying their job and caring for their pupils (Thomas *et al.* 2004b). A modest reduction in workload may not necessarily enhance job satisfaction and bring the corresponding hoped for improvement in recruitment and retention (Butt *et al.* 2005).

Webb and Vulliamy's research (2006a) found that most teachers disagreed completely with the notion that teaching assistants should take whole classes on a regular basis to provide planning, preparation and assessment time (PPA), and that in only 6 schools out of their whole sample were teaching assistants used in this way. In these 6 schools the use of teaching assistants for PPA time was dependent upon one or more teaching assistants achieving higher level teaching assistant (HLTA) status. The researchers reported that the increasing numbers of teaching assistants in schools and classrooms required teachers to develop new skills in cooperation, delegation and mentoring. Workforce remodelling was viewed as both a threat to teacher professionalism and as a means of enhancing it by opening up new possibilities.

Deployment and Impact of Support Staff in Schools (DISS) project

The Deployment and Impact of Support Staff in Schools (DISS) project is providing comprehensive information on support staff in England and Wales over a five year period (2003–8). Results from Strand 2 Wave 1 focus specifically on the Impact of the National Agreement (Blatchford *et al.* 2008). It describes findings on the deployment of all categories of support staff; the impact of support staff upon teachers and teaching and pupil learning and behaviour; and the impact of the National Agreement on pupils, teachers and support staff. The research methods included a survey in a sample of 76 schools (out of this, 33 Year 1 and 22 Year 3 classes were sampled), a systematic observation component and a case study component was carried out in 49 schools (this included 20 primary, 4 infant and 1 junior school in England, and 2 primary schools in Wales). In terms of deployment of support staff in primary schools, the research findings showed that the most common activity was working with a group of pupils. It also showed that all pupils seemed to benefit from support staff presence in terms of more individualised attention for pupils and more active pupil role interaction with adults, leading the research team to conclude that the presence of support staff is of particular benefit in improving the attention of children in most need. However, active interactions with teachers were reduced as more time was spent interacting with the support staff. The impact of support staff on pupils' approach to learning was shown to be most positive for the youngest age group in the study (Year 1).

As with Webb and Vulliamy's and Thomas' research, the 24 tasks cited in the National Agreement had largely been transferred to support staff. While some tasks were being retained by teachers for pragmatic and/or professional reasons, overall teachers reported an improvement in their work-life balance since the introduction of PPA time. Cover for absent teachers was found to be done mainly by support staff. However while these were perceived as advantageous by teachers, they had gained responsibility for their day-to-day deployment, line management and performance reviews, all tasks which were more demanding in terms of skills than the mainly administrative tasks removed by the National Agreement. Improvements in pupil behaviour, attitudes and attainment was a broad aim of the National Agreement but the research team found little hard evidence to support the achievement of this aim as:

> most of the evidence available was indirect, impressionistic and consequently hard to interpret. The view in schools was that support staff did have an impact on pupil attainment, behaviour and attitudes; the problem the head teachers faced was proving it.
>
> (Blatchford *et al.* 2008: 13)

Findings in terms of class-based support staff indicated that some worked in excess of their paid time as they became involved in planning and preparation with the teachers with whom they worked. The expanded role was welcomed by many but was not often matched with higher rates of pay, increased hours of paid work, inclusion in meetings and decision making, or opportunities for training in preparation for their new roles. The research team commented that '[i]n practice, the good will of the support staff was indispensable in making the policy work' (Blatchford *et al.* 2008: 13).

Many of the findings in these research projects were confirmed by Ofsted (2007) in their report on reforming and developing the school workforce. Their main findings reported positively on the way most schools had met the statutory requirements, resulting in a revolutionary shift in workforce culture with clear benefits to staff and pupils. Head teachers and teaching staff that had understood the principles underlying workforce reform had planned a coherent strategy, managed the changes well and implemented other initiatives successfully. A key principle of the National Agreement, to provide time for teachers to focus on teaching and learning, had been realised in nearly all schools. There had also been significant progress in terms of use of ICT for administration, teaching and learning. However, Ofsted were critical that many schools visited had not clearly understood messages from the government and external agencies about the desired outcomes of workforce reform as a means to improve the quality of education and raise standards. Most schools had not monitored and evaluated the impact of the reforms on pupil learning and had little firm evidence to show that standards were rising as a result. Slow progress was being made on making time for strategic leadership and management and dedicated time for headship, because the requirements were not clearly understood. The full potential of the wider workforce in raising achievement and standards was not realised when head teachers and leadership teams did not match skills and expertise sufficiently closely to staff and pupil needs and when insufficient attention was given to the performance management and career development of the workforce. Performance management of the wider workforce was not consistent as it was not always clear who should be conducting the performance review and how evidence would be collected.

OTHER COUNTRIES AND WORKFORCE REFORM: COMPARATIVE EVIDENCE

Workforce reform in other UK countries, for example Scotland, and elsewhere in the world may deepen our understanding of what is happening in the English context. Ozga (2005), drawing on evidence from the Education Governance and Social Inclusion and Exclusion in Europe (EGSIE) project, which compared nine European countries and Australia, focuses on the form that modernisation of the teaching workforce is taking in Scotland. Unlike England, which has focussed on a business model of best practice, Scotland has offered a 'revived public service partnership model of governance combined with new elements of public consultation and democratisation' (Ozga 2005: 209). Significant differences in Scotland hinge around the curriculum as Scotland has a national framework and not a national curriculum; there are differences in devolved school management, in qualification frameworks and in performance measurement which is based on school self-evaluation. These differences shape the policy framework within which the workforce operates and the way the teaching profession defines itself.

The McCrone inquiry into teachers' pay and conditions of service in 1997 resulted in a report (SEED 2000) with complex recommendations. The Scottish executive group, set up to implement the recommendations, produced the Agreement (SEED 2001) which resulted in considerable changes to the teaching profession in Scotland. In particular, salary was increased and teachers' contact hours reduced through the introduction of a 35-hour working week. A new career structure with only four levels across both primary and secondary schools was developed, consisting of teacher, senior teacher, management grade and head teacher, and there were also new arrangements for professional development. Chartered Teacher status offered recognition of excellence in teaching for those teachers who did not wish to become managers. To obtain Chartered Teacher status, teachers must follow a four-year programme of enquiry and research structured around professional values, professional knowledge, professional and personal attributes leading to professional action. Such a programme of professional development leads not only to Chartered Teacher status but also to the award of a Masters' degree.

Menter *et al.* (2004), drawing on their ESRC research project 'The Impact of Performance Threshold Assessment on Teachers' Work', contrast the policy issues underlying the Chartered Teacher programme and the Threshold Assessment in England. They focus on three areas: the problems lying behind the policy initiatives; the values and motivations underlying the policies and the processes of development and implementation. The first difference they identify in relation to each area is that the Scottish approach anticipates commitment while the English approach expects to motivate through incentives. Second, while each approach involves a stepped progression up the teacher career ladder in Scotland this is characterised as a series of achievements while in England:

> with the notable exception of the National Professional Qualification for Headship (NPHQ), they are rather a series of 'hoops and hurdles' through or over which teachers are judged at each stage to have jumped (or not).
>
> (Menter *et al.* 2005: 205)

Thirdly they identify the very different approaches to implementation, where in Scotland ownership of the policy process was broadened through serious attempts to discuss and negotiate at all levels and the involvement of the major teachers' union on the McCrone Committee. Unions and the GTCS had a major influence on the report produced, which established an induction year and an entitlement to CPD as an alternative to an appraisal-based system. In England the extensive involvement of the private sector and the different role played by the unions 'as negotiators of procedural justice' (Menter *et al.* 2005: 208) who work in partnership to provide guidance for teachers on how to apply to cross the 'Threshold' are examples of the differences in the process of implementation. Another significant difference is the role played by Her Majesty's Inspectorate (HMI). In England they have 'become detached from the policy process' (Menter *et al.* 2005: 209) while in Scotland they still have an influence upon policy development and implementation. In addition, the Scottish GTC (GTCS), established in 1965, has considerable influence and power in education in Scotland whereas the English GTC (GTCE) was only set up in 1999 and has neither the influence nor the power of its Scottish counterpart.

While additional classroom assistants have been employed in classrooms in Scotland, there are specific guidelines which ensure that the roles and responsibilities of teachers and assistants remain separate. In the Scottish context, teaching assistants only undertake tasks which do not arise directly from the process of teaching and learning (GTCS 2003) and this is a clear and distinct difference in the way classroom assistants are deployed when compared to the English context.

Another international context that provides interesting comparisons with England is that of the United States, a decentralised system where under the American Constitution the 50 states have control of educational funding and major aspects of policy, and many key decisions are devolved even further, to individual school boards. Each state department of education distributes funds, which account for about 50 per cent of school funding, and implements and interprets state laws on matters such as curriculum and assessment and certification. Within each state, district school boards and superintendents of schools are responsible for hiring teachers, maintaining school buildings and determining the curriculum within the state guidelines. There is no national curriculum or national assessment system, though these matters are subject to increasing intervention at state level, and the federal government can exert leverage through the distribution or withholding of substantial funds for earmarked support initiatives. Alexander (2001) comments that:

in the United States the last two decades of the twentieth century marked increased levels of state and federal intervention in educational matters. Nevertheless, the American system remained firmly rooted in the local community while in England the national government seized control, tightened it, and tightened it still further.

(Alexander 2001: 107)

However, there has been much concern about educational standards and achievement of pupils and in 2001 the *No Child Left Behind Act* (NCLB) was introduced. This Act places a requirement upon all schools and school districts that receive Title-1 federal funding to have a set of standards for improving student achievement, and detailed plans showing how these standards will be monitored and met. For the first time, testing was linked with school accountability. The Title 1 funding is distributed to approximately 90 per cent of school districts in the US (Smith 2005). Each state has now to assess performance annually in Grades 3–8 in language, arts, literacy and mathematics and in science. States were also to indicate how schools and school districts would demonstrate Adequate Yearly Progress (AYP) by 2014 and make their results public. While the Act is intended to make sure schools pay attention to all pupils, and specifically those groups who have consistently underperformed, it has been highly controversial among teachers and educationalists. Smith's (2005) research found that despite the equitable intent:

> some commentators fear that the high stakes testing and accountability-linked sanctions that underpin the Act could result in many otherwise successful schools being labelled as failing

(Smith 2005: 507–8)

Educationalists in the US have argued that since the introduction of the NCLB Act there are now competing visions of the public education system. For example, Nieto and Johnson (2008) comment:

> In spite of its limitations, the one thing that had been true of public education until now is that it largely was viewed as a beacon of hope by poor people, who saw it as the only option their children had. For many generations, public schools offered children of poverty-stricken and immigrant populations the opportunity to move into the mainstream of American society.

(Nieto and Johnson 2008: 17)

The teaching profession in the US faces challenges in terms of implementing the NCLB, and this challenge is increased when the composition and distinctiveness of the teacher labour market is taken into account. Teachers are nearly all graduates, largely female, highly unionised and working in non-profit settings (Belfield 2005). Belfield argues that reforms to the teaching profession will not be effective in a rigidly controlled school system. The NCLB stipulates that there should be a qualified teacher in every classroom and some states are pressing for reduced class sizes in all their schools. These requirements are only possible to meet if there is a large additional supply of teachers at current wage levels. He argues that there is no evidence that such a supply exists and that:

even where there is strong evidence on the relative ineffectiveness of uncertified, out-of-field teachers, there is no mechanism by which these teachers are replaced by certified teachers with a college degree in their field of instruction.

(Belfield 2005: 176)

The teacher perspective of the NCLB is also explored by Baghban and Li (2008), who argue that certified teachers now feel unable to use their full teaching skills:

> The practice that rankles teachers the most is the administration's imposition of highly scripted programmes that tell them exactly what to do and what to say; in short, not just what, but how, to teach. All teachers in New York State go through a rigorous certification process, which is one of the most demanding in the nation. All are holders of masters' degrees in their field of specialization and many continue onto postgraduate work. Yet, the rigid nature of New York city's mandated math and literacy programmes does not allow teachers to draw on their knowledge of child development, theories of cognitive awareness and affective behaviour, or learning styles and multiple intelligences. Nor are teachers able to respond to the needs, strengths, and weaknesses of the child as an individual. Rather, teachers are required to read verbatim from a scripted, prepared lesson and regurgitate it for the entire class.
>
> (Baghban and Li 2008: 108)

Those who do support the NCLB consider it to be 'landmark legislation demonstrating the government's commitment to educating underserved students and closing the achievement gap' (O'Day 2008). From whatever perspective the NCLB is viewed, there are clear comparisons to be made with the UK in terms of the introduction of the literacy and numeracy strategies, testing and the publication of league tables.

CONCLUSION

The research into educational policies and workforce reform presented in this chapter has raised issues around head teachers and the management of remodelling linked to workforce and curricular changes in primary schools, teachers' workload, and teaching assistants and their deployment in classrooms. While problems have been identified in several of the research studies, some of these are related to the number of policies and speed at which schools have had to implement them since 2002 – causing initiative fatigue amongst teachers in some cases. However, the overall perspective of teachers presented in the research reports is a positive one. At the beginning of this chapter the context in which the reforms were introduced and the objectives set out in the Green Paper *Teachers: meeting the challenge of change* were presented. So how far have the three objectives set out in the Green Paper been achieved, and what has research had to say about the implementation of those objectives?

The first objective aimed to promote excellent leadership by rewarding leading professionals properly. A system of performance management and performance-related pay has been implemented and there are now professional standards linked to every level in the different career stages for head teachers, teachers and teaching assistants. Research indicated that the new pay structure initially caused problems for some experienced teachers, who felt they were required to 'prove' their professional knowledge and skills all over again, and how deeply this was felt very often depended upon the way in which head teachers dealt with the process of implementation in their schools. Other teachers found the pay structure gave them something to aim for and received a boost when they achieved the new pay level through the linked standards. Head teachers generally held a more positive view of the process, and the researchers claim that there was considerable evidence that a system of performance management linked to further professional development was welcomed by both teachers and managers (Mahoney *et al.* 2004).

The second objective of the Green Paper was to recruit, retain and motivate high quality classroom teachers by paying them more. Research indicated that there was no systematic relationship between pay, hours worked and job satisfaction (Gunter 2007; Webb and Vulliamy 2006a). What motivated teachers more was enjoying their job and caring for their pupils. How teachers and teaching assistants engaged strategically with the aims of remodelling and changes in role definition and what it meant for them within their working and wider lives was thought to be of more relevance. Research into leadership and management (Thomas *et al.* 2004; Rayner and Gunter 2005) linked to remodelling (Easton *et al.* 2005) revealed there was a move towards innovation and role change, and that a diversity of initiatives had been developed revealing several forms of distributed leadership. Overall, leadership was thought to have improved with a sharing of responsibility with middle management. Reductions in workload were achieved, but a new and additional workload was created to carry out the remodelling agenda. Changes to teaching style and the adoption of good practice were noticeable in some schools and there was a stronger sense of flexible teamwork and increased collaboration with other schools. While there was occasional criticism from teachers of the change management team in schools at the pace of change, they recognised that this was largely due to external and political considerations driving the remodelling programme.

Research that focussed upon the remodelling teams found that most schools were still at the 'developing stage' and that only a few had reached the 'sustainable' stage. There was concern that future sustainability of workforce change in schools was reliant on future funding for additional teaching assistant posts. However, the introduction of PPA time to meet the requirements of the National Agreement and the change management process were thought to be successful by teachers and head teachers. Progress was being made with the *Every Child Matters* agenda, although the research found that more needed to be done to link the different agendas and show schools how they interrelated. An area that teachers still found stressful was the unremitting pressure to achieve the government literacy and numeracy targets.

The third objective was to provide better support to all teachers and to deploy teaching resources in a more flexible way. The increase in the numbers of teaching assistants and other staff in schools is significant, almost doubling the numbers of adults working in a school in some cases. Teaching assistants were found to be broadly satisfied with their role, well-motivated and positive. Teachers now regarded teaching assistants as crucial to the effective managing of teaching and learning, although most thought that teaching assistants should not be used to cover whole classes on a regular basis to provide PPA time (Webb and Vulliamy 2006a). Teacher use of ICT for both personal and professional reasons had improved considerably, and some research identified improvement in terms of pupil attainment at Key Stage 2 and improvement in data analysis to support teaching and learning. However, some evidence showed that teachers and head teachers had not evaluated the changes made through remodelling.

A number of areas emerge which would benefit from further research, including those that can be drawn from the comparison with Scotland and the USA. Models of leadership revealed that change had been implemented in a variety of ways and that distributed practice opened up new possibilities for educational leadership. Further research into how teachers have generated a shared understanding of practice would be useful. The changing role of teachers and teaching assistants, and the blurring of boundaries between these roles, is also a fruitful topic for further investigation. In particular, much greater attention needs to be paid in the training of teachers to the coordination of teaching assistants in classrooms and the mentoring of teaching assistants in schools. The Scottish context provides a comparison with the way teacher professional development and career progression is bound together in a more collegial system through the *Chartered Teacher programme*, and it will be interesting to see how the new Masters in Teaching and Learning in England will be perceived by teachers. Research into the management of workforce reform in primary schools demonstrates that there have been both difficulties and successes in terms of achieving the remodelling agenda, and the overall picture is one of teachers trying to make sense of a plethora of initiatives and turn policy into understandable practice.

REFERENCES

Alexander, R.J. (2001) *Culture and Pedagogy: international comparisons in primary education.* Oxford: Blackwell.

——(2004) 'Still no pedagogy? Principle, pragmatism and compliance in primary education', *Cambridge Journal of Education* 34(1): 8–33.

Alexander, R.J. and Hargreaves, L. (2007) *Community Soundings: the Primary Review regional witness sessions.* Cambridge: University of Cambridge Faculty of Education.

Alexander, R.J., Rose, J. and Woodhead, C. (1992) *Curriculum Organisation and Classroom Practice in Primary Schools: a discussion paper.* London: DES.

Alexander, R.J., Willcocks, J. and Nelson, N. (1996) 'Discourse, pedagogy and the National Curriculum: change and continuity in primary schools', *Research Papers in Education* 11(1): 81–120.

ATL, DfES, GMB, NAHT, NASUWT, NEOST, PAT, SHA, TGWU, UNISON, WAG (2003) *Raising Standards and Tackling Workload: a national agreement. Time for standards.* London: DfES.

Baghban, M. and Li, H. (2008) '"I thought I was a professional": teachers' and parents' reactions to NCLB in New York City', in H.L. Johnson and A. Salz (Eds) *What is Authentic Educational Reform? Pushing against the compassionate conservative agenda.* New York: Lawrence Erlbaum Associates: 105–20.

Belfield, C.R. (2005) 'The teacher labour market in the US: challenges and reforms', *Educational Review* 57(2): 175–91.

Blatchford, P., Bassett, P., Brown, P., Martin, C., Russell, A., Webster, R. and Heywood, N. (2006) *The Deployment and Impact of Support Staff in Schools: report on findings from a national questionnaire survey of schools, support staff and teachers (Strand 1, Wave 1, 2004)*, DCSF Research Report 776. London: DCSF.

——(2007) *The Deployment and Impact of Support Staff in Schools: report on findings from a national questionnaire survey of schools, support staff and teachers (Strand 1, Wave 2, 2006)*, DCSF Research Report 005. London: DCSF.

Blatchford, P., Bassett, P., Brown, P., Martin, C., Russell, A. and Webster, R., with Babayigit, S. and Heywood, N. (2008) *The Deployment and Impact of Support Staff in Schools and the Impact of the National Agreement. (Strand 2, Wave 1, 2005/06)*, DCSF Research Report 027. London: DCSF.

Blatchford, P., Russell, A., Bassett, P., Browne, P. and Martin, C. (2004) *The Effects and Role of Teaching Assistants in English Primary Schools (Years 4–6) 2002–2003. Results from the Class Size and Pupil-Adult Ratios (CSPAR) KS2 project*, Research report 605. London: DfES.

Brehony, K.J. (2005) 'Primary schooling under New Labour: the irresolvable contradiction of excellence and enjoyment', *Oxford Review of Education* 30(1): 29–46.

Butt, G. and Gunter, H. (2005) 'Challenging modernization: remodelling the education work-force', *Educational Review* 57(2): 131–37.

Butt, G. and Lance, A. (2005) 'Modernising the roles of support staff in primary schools: changing focus, changing function', *Educational Review* 57(2): 139–49.

Butt, G., Lance, A., Fielding, A., Gunter, H., Rayner, S. and Thomas, H. (2005) 'Teacher job satisfaction: lessons from the TSW Pathfinder Project', *School Leadership and Management* 25(5): 455–71.

Campbell, R.J. and Neill, S.R. St. J. (1994a) *Curriculum Reform at Key Stage 1: teacher commitment and policy failure*. London: Longman.

——(1994b) *Primary Teachers at Work*. London: Routledge.

Day, C. (2002) 'School reform and transitions in teacher professionalism and identity', *International Journal of Educational Research* 37: 677–92.

Dearing, R. (1993) *The National Curriculum and its Assessment, Final Report*. London: SCAA.

Department for Children, Schools and Families (DCSF) (2007) *School Workforce in England (including pupil: teacher ratios and pupil: adult ratios)*. London: DCSF.

DCSF (2007) *School Workforce in England (including pupil: teacher ratios and pupil: adult ratios)* (Revised). London: DCSF.

Department for Education and Employment (DfEE) (1998) *Teachers: meeting the challenge of change*. London: The Stationary Office.

Department for Education and Skills (DfES) (2002) *Time for Standards: reforming the school workforce*, London: DfES

——(2003a) *Excellence and Enjoyment: a strategy for primary schools*. London: HMSO.

——(2003b) *Every Child Matters: change for children*. Nottingham: DfES.

——(2004a) *Every Child Matters: next steps*. Nottingham: DfES.

——(2004b) *Raising Standards and Tackling Workload: implementing the National Agreement*. London: DfES.

——(2004c) *School Workforce in England (including pupil: teacher ratios and pupil: adult ratios). Revised*. London: DfES.

——(2005) *Children's Workforce Strategy: a strategy to build a world-class workforce for children and young people*. Nottingham: DfES.

Dunham, J. (1992) *Stress in Teaching* (2nd edition). London: Routledge.

Earl, L., Levin, B., Leithwood, K., Fullan, M. and Watson, N. (2000) *Watching and Learning: OISE/UT evaluation of the implementation of the National Literacy and Numeracy Strategies, summary*, First Annual Report. Ontario Institute for Studies in Education, University of Toronto: DfES.

——(2001) *Watching and Learning 2: OISE/UT evaluation of the implementation of the National Literacy and Numeracy Strategies*. Ontario Institute for Studies in Education, University of Toronto: DfES.

——(2003) *Watching and Learning 3: final report of the external evaluation of England's National Literacy and Numeracy Strategies*. Ontario Institute for Studies in Education, University of Toronto: DfES.

Easton, C., Eames, A., Wilson, R., Walker, M. and Sharp, C. (2006) *Evaluation of the National Remodelling Team: year 3*, Final report. Berkshire: NFER.

Easton, C., Wilson, R. and Sharp, C. (2005) *National Remodelling Team: evaluation and impact study (Year 1)*, Final Report. Berkshire: NFER.

Galton, M., Hargeaves, L., Comber, C., Wall, D. and Pell, T. (1999) *Inside the Primary Classroom: 20 years on*. London: Routledge.

General Teaching Council for Scotland (GTCS) (2003) *Classroom Assistants: a GTC position paper*. Edinburgh: GTCS.

Glaser, B. and Strauss, A. (1967) *The Discovery of Grounded Theory*. Chicago, IL: Aldine.

Gunter, H. (2007) 'Remodelling the school workforce in England: a study in tyranny', *Journal for Critical Education Policy Studies* 5(1): 1–11.

Hancock, R. and Eyres, I. (2004) 'Implementing a required curriculum reform: teachers at the core, teaching assistants on the periphery?', *Westminster Studies in Education* 27(2): 223–35.

House of Commons (1988) *Education Reform Act 1988: Chapter 40*. London: HMSO.

Mahoney, P., Menter, I. and Hextall, I. (2004) 'The emotional impact of performance related pay on teachers in England', *British Educational Research Journal* 30(3): 435–56

Menter, I., Mahoney, P. and Hextall, I. (2004) 'Ne'er the twain shall meet?: modernizing the teaching profession in Scotland and England', *Journal of Education Policy* 19(2): 195–214.

Moyles, J., Hargeaves, L., Merry, R., Paterson, F. and Esarte-Sarries, V. (2003) *Interactive Teaching in the Primary School: digging deeper into meanings*. Maidenhead: Open University Press.

Moyles, J. and Suschitzky, W. (1997) *'Jills of all trades? … ' Classroom assistants in KS1 classes*. London: ATL.

National Curriculum Council (NCC) (1993) *The National Curriculum at Key Stages 1 and 2: advice to the Secretary of State for Education*. York: NCC.

Nieto, S. and Johnson, H.L. (2008) 'The socio-political context of No Child Left Behind: hard times and courageous responses', in H.L. Johnson and A. Salz (Eds) *What is Authentic Educational Reform? Pushing against the compassionate Conservative agenda*. New York: Lawrence Erlbaum Associates: 15–24.

O'Day, J.A. (2008) 'NCLB and the complexity of school improvement', in A.R. Sadovnik, J.A. O'Day, G.W. Bohrnstedt and K.M. Borman (Eds) *No Child Left Behind and the Reduction of the Achievement Gap. Sociological perspectives on federal educational policy*. New York: Routledge: 25–52.

Office for Standards in Education (Ofsted) (1993) *Curriculum Organisation and Classroom Practice in Primary Schools: a follow-up report*. London: HMSO.

——(1995) *The Annual Report of Her Majesty's Chief Inspector of Schools, Part 1*. London: HMSO.

——(1999) *Primary Education 1994–98: a review of primary schools in England*. London: TSO.

——(2002) *Teaching Assistants in Primary Schools: an evaluation of the quality and impact of their work*. London: Ofsted.

——(2007) *Reforming and Developing the School Workforce*, Ref. 070020. London: Ofsted.

Osborne, M., McNess, E. and Broadfoot, P., with Pollard, A. and Triggs, P. (2000) *What Teachers Do: changing policy and practice in primary education, findings from the PACE project*. London: Continuum.

Ozga, J. (2005) 'Modernizing the education workforce: a perspective from Scotland', *Educational Review* 57(2): 207–19.

Pollard, A. (1994) *Look Before You Leap: research evidence for the curriculum at Key Stage Two*. London: Tufnell Press.

Pollard, A., Broadfoot, P., Croll, P., Osborne, M. and Abbott, D. (1994) *Changing English Primary Schools? The impact of the Education Reform Act at Key Stage One*. London: Cassell.

PricewaterhouseCoopers (PwC) (2001) *Teacher Workload Study*. London: PwC.

Rayner, S. and Gunter, H. (2005) 'Rethinking leadership: perspectives on remodelling practice', *Educational Review* 57(2): 151–61.

Scottish Executive Education Department (SEED) (2000) *A Teaching Profession for the 21st Century: report of the committee of inquiry into professional conditions of service for teachers* (the McCrone report). Edinburgh: HMSO.

SEED (2001) *A Teaching Profession for the 21st Century: agreement reached following the McCrone report*. Edinburgh: HMSO.

Second International Mathematics Study (1993) *The IEA Study of Mathematics.* (Ed) L. Burstein, Oxford: Oxford University Press.

School Teachers' Review Body (STRB) (2002) *Teachers' Pay Survey.* London: Office of Manpower Economics.

STRB (2004) *Teachers' Workloads Diary Survey.* London: Office of Manpower Economics.

Smith, E. (2005) 'Raising standards in American schools: the case of "No Child Left Behind"', *Journal of Education Policy* 20(4): 507–24.

Teacher Development Agency (TDA) (2007) *Professional Standards for Teachers: post threshold.* London: TDA.

Third International Mathematics and Science Study (1996) *Mathematical Achievement in the Middle Years: IEA's Third International Mathematics and Science Study.* (Eds) A. Beaton, I. Mullis, M. Martin, E. Gonzalez, D. Kelly and T. Smith. Boston, MA: Boston College.

Thomas, H., Butt, G., Fielding, A., Foster, J., Gunter, H., Lance, A., Rayner, S., Rutherford, D., Potts, L., Powers, S., Selwood, I. and Szwed, C. (2004a) *Transforming the School Workforce Pathfinder Evaluation Project*, Research Brief No: RBX03–04. London: DfES.

——(2004b) *The Evaluation of the Transforming the School Workforce Pathfinder Project, Research Report No: RR541.* London: DfES.

Wade, P., McCrone, T. and Rudd, P. (NFER) (2007) *National Evaluation of the Primary Leadership Programme*, Brief no: RB820. Nottingham: DfES.

Webb, R. and Vulliamy, G. (1996a) *Roles and Responsibilities in the Primary School: changing demands, changing practice.* Buckingham: Open University Press.

——(1996b) 'The changing role of the primary-school headteacher', *Educational Management Administration & Leadership* 24(3): 301–15.

Webb, R. and Vulliamy G. (2006a) *Coming Full Circle? The impact of New Labour's education policies on primary school teachers' work. A first report.* London: ATL.

——(2006b) *Coming Full Circle? The impact of New Labour's education policies on primary school teachers' work. A first report. Report Summary.* London: ATL.

Vincett, K., Cremin, H. and Thomas, G. (2005) *Teachers and Assistants Working Together.* Maidenhead: Open University Press.

Wilson, R., Easton, C. and Smith, P. (2005) *National Remodelling Team: evaluation and impact study (year 1). Final report.* Berkshire: NFER.

Wilson, R., Sharp, C., Shuayb, M., Kendall, L., Wade, P. and Easton, C. (2007) *Research into the Deployment and Impact of Support Staff Who Have Achieved HLTA Status*, Final Report. Berkshire: NFER.

Woodward, M. and Peart, A. (2005) *Supporting Education: the role of Higher Level Teaching Assistants.* London: ATL.

Part 8

Policy frameworks

Governance, funding, reform and quality assurance

The four research surveys in this final section relate to aspects of Cambridge Primary Review Themes 10 (*Funding and Governance*), 3 (*Curriculum and Assessment*) and 4 (*Quality and Standards*). What links them is their concern with the framework of policy and legislation within which contemporary English primary schooling is set. Three of the chapters note the relatively tight degree of control, compared with many other countries, which by 2008 the government exerted over the day-to-day work of English primary schools. In England, moreover, government policy does not merely frame or facilitate educational practice so much as seek actively to shape it via national initiatives, strategies, curricula, tests, teacher training standards and inspection arrangements. That being so, it is fair to say that in the matter of educational quality the decisions of ministers and the national agencies are in their way no less important than those of teachers themselves. This raises important questions about accountability, culpability and justice in the apportioning of credit and blame for what goes on in the nation's primary schools.

The relevant Review remit questions for this synoptic collection are:

(From Theme 10)
- How adequately is the system of primary education in England funded and how efficiently is it controlled and administered?
- Does it have the right balance of control and responsibility between national government, local government, local communities and schools?
- What has been the impact of the post-1988 drive to a more centralised system?
- Through what system of school governance are the interests of children, teachers, parents and local communities most effectively and equitably addressed?
- How might matters be differently ordered?

(From Theme 4)
- What are the most effective contributions to standards and quality of, for example, research, inspection, government initiatives, school and teacher self-evaluation, performance management, pre-service training and in-service training?
- What are the proper roles in the processes of systemic review and quality assurance of DfES, Ofsted, the other national agencies and Parliament?

(From Theme 3)

- Do the current national curriculum and attendant foundation, literacy, numeracy and primary strategies provide the range and approach which children of this age really need?
- What is the most helpful balance of national and local in curriculum and assessment?

The picture of England's increasingly centralised education system which these four chapters provide is enriched and sometimes qualified by other surveys in this book:

- Chapters 17–19 on trends in standards of pupil attainment, judged by reference to both national and international data, and the character and impact of the tests through which standards are monitored;
- Chapter 5 on the formal relationship of schools and other agencies, especially after the 2004 Children's Act;
- Chapters 10 and 11 on the aims set for primary education by successive governments and how these compare with those of other countries;
- Chapters 14 and 15 on the statutory frameworks of school starting and transfer ages, stages of schooling, national curriculum requirements and assessment procedures, again using comparisons with other countries;
- Chapters 23–25 on the disposition, training, professional development and leadership of the primary school workforce, and recent initiatives aimed at workforce reform.

The Governance and Administration of English Primary Education, by Maria Balarin and Hugh Lauder (Chapter 26), reviews the changing nature of educational governance, the new roles of national agencies, local authorities and school governing bodies, and the overall character of policy making under the current dispensation. It notes a fundamental change since 1988, accelerated since 1997, from a system based on local authority control to one where schools are nominally given greater autonomy but within very tight constraints imposed by central government. This system in effect amounts to what the authors call a 'state theory of learning'. The chapter also assesses alternative models encouraged by central government, such as Academies and Foundation Schools, and identifies problems resulting from the paradox of 'decentralised-centralism'.

The Funding of English Primary Education, by Philip Noden and Anne West (Chapter 27), reviews evidence on per pupil levels of funding for primary schools, how these have changed in recent years, and how they compare with expenditure on secondary education. It examines the funding assumptions and arrangements that underlie the expenditure and highlights variations between local authorities. It also compares funding and funding differentials between England and other OECD countries, thereby further extending the Review's now substantial array of international comparative evidence on English primary education. The chapter judges that the historic primary-secondary funding differential, which has regularly featured in official reports since the 1930s, should once again be re-assessed.

Quality Assurance in English Primary Education, by Peter Cunningham and Philip Raymont (Chapter 28), examines evidence on procedures for monitoring, assuring and maintaining quality in primary education at national, local and school levels. Placing its analysis in historical context it considers the developing role of Ofsted since it replaced the old HMI system in 1992, and records some of the controversies which have attended the work of the current body. The chapter considers the changing part played by local authorities in quality assurance following the reduction in their powers during the 1980s and 1990s, and it considers the possibilities for school and teacher self-evaluation. The chapter identifies issues which remain problematic despite the many changes: trust between the parties concerned; procedural credibility; reliability of data; distortion in educational provision resulting from excessive selectivity of focus in inspection.

The Trajectory and Impact of National Reform: curriculum and assessment in English primary schools, by Dominic Wyse, Elaine McCreery and Harry Torrance (Chapter 29), reviews evidence on major government efforts at reform which have attended the development of English primary education during the past four decades, concentrating particularly on the period since 1988 during which the pace of government-initiated reform in the areas of curriculum, assessment and teaching quickened considerably and effectively extended government control from what is taught (after 1988) to how (since 1997). Examining research and inspection evidence on the impact of the reforms on the quality of classroom practice and standards of pupil attainment (on which see also Chapters 17–19), the authors discover a contested and uncertain picture, with evidence of negative as well as positive impact.

A number of important themes emerge from these surveys.

Partnerships and markets: tensions arising from the current model

Chapter 26 shows how 'since the arrival of New Labour central control in key areas of educational action has been strengthened within a framework of administrative and fiscal devolution and a growing emphasis on "partnerships" aimed at bridging traditional private/public and market/state divides'. However, 'research suggests that the paradoxes involved in this model of "decentralised-centralism" are at the core of the application of government policies. The notion of partnership, too, is problematic and evidence suggests that private involvement has not produced the changes claimed by its advocates.'

Funding for primary education: has it risen and how does England compare with other countries?

Chapter 27 uses government figures to show that 'in real terms, spending per pupil in primary schools was relatively flat from 1992–98 and even declined during the latter half of that period. Spending then rose markedly from 1998–99 onwards'. Judged internationally, and 'taking into account the different costs of goods in different countries, the UK is ranked 12th out of the 29 OECD countries for which comparable data [on primary school funding] are available'. However, 'when expenditure is expressed relative to gross domestic product (GDP) per capita the UK appears 18th out of the 29 countries'.

Primary and secondary funding: a continuing anomaly?

The primary-secondary funding differential is deeply rooted historically, and is greater than in many other OECD countries. It reflects contrasting ways of organising teaching –

the primary generalist class teacher and the secondary subject specialist – and the assumption that these are inevitable, right and permanent. Both the generalist pattern and its associated educational and financial assumptions have been questioned in major national enquiries going back to 1931. Reviewing this matter once again, Chapter 27 concludes: 'Historically, in England primary schools have been less generously funded than secondary schools. It is by no means self-evident that this should be the case. Government should consider the potential benefits of improving levels of resourcing in the primary phase given that later progress and achievement are highly dependent on earlier attainment'.

A state theory of learning?

Chapter 26 shows how since 1997 'government has strengthened its hand through what may be called a "state theory of learning" … based on the idea that the repeated high stakes testing of pupils, a national curriculum, and in primary schools mandated pedagogy in numeracy and literacy, will raise standards … There is little doubt that the machinery of surveillance and accountability makes it difficult for schools to deviate from focusing on test performance'. Chapter 29 makes a similar point and both surveys raise obvious questions not just about whether the assumptions behind the 'state theory of learning' are correct, but whether it is right or sensible for governments to intervene to this extent in the detail of professional practice.

What has been the impact of the reforms on teaching?

Reviewing evidence from research, inspection and official evaluations, Chapter 29 offers its assessment of the efficacy of the reforms up to and including the literacy, numeracy and primary strategies and current policy on the teaching of reading. It concludes: 'All studies show clearly that change has occurred, and that in 2007 primary classrooms are very different places from the way they were in 1988, or even 1997. However, while one major study reported significant changes in teachers' practice, a much larger number showed that at the deeper levels of classroom interaction there had been little movement away from the cognitively-restricting kinds of interaction noted … during the 1970s and 1980s. At the same time, the range of teaching methods employed is probably narrower now than hitherto'.

Cause, effect and unintended consequence in educational reform: a note of caution

However, Chapter 26 warns that tracing causation between particular reforms and children's learning and attainment is 'extremely difficult' and that 'there is likely to be a range of tensions and contradictions between and across the various levels of management which have a bearing on outcomes … One of these tensions concerns the way that head teachers have to deal with multiple external agency requirements and relationships, while also conforming to test performance demands. This is clearly difficult and may explain the significant number of vacancies for headships'. In any case, Chapter 26 also asks 'whether these outcomes represent the sum of children's education or merely their ability in taking tests'.

Inspection: a question of stability and trust

Chapter 28 notes that 'constant change in quality assurance procedures has proved a great burden and cause for complaint by schools and teachers. While some change is inevitable to meet cultural and political expectations, the degree and pace of change have been exceptional in the last fifteen years ... The need to address poor provision and poor teaching is undisputed, but empirical studies have revealed flaws in the [Ofsted] inspection processes and possibilities for improvement. Some flaws have been addressed ... but these are not widely or openly discussed ... It is important that policy on quality assurance should inspire the maximum possible trust between politicians, parents and professionals'.

Inspection: relevance, selectivity and distortion

Chapter 28 argues from the evidence that 'national inspection procedures need more closely to address equality and equity in education, monitoring factors such as gender, race, poverty, deprivation and special learning needs for their impact on achievement' (see also Chapters 7 and 8). The report also warns that 'many research studies point to the tendency of narrowly-focused inspection to distort the curriculum. Inspection should therefore continue to cover the full range of provision and/or be alive to this danger where inspection is selective'.

26 The governance and administration of English primary education

Maria Balarin and Hugh Lauder

The governance, administration and control of primary education and of the school system in general is one of the policy areas that has undergone the deepest changes in recent decades. Since the rise of the Conservative government to power in the early 1980s there has been a move towards the idea of governance and more decentralised forms of decision-making and administration.

Paradoxically, and while the official rhetoric tends to emphasise autonomy and participation, the shift towards a governance model has been matched by the introduction of some measures of greater control, such as the National Curriculum and the more recent move towards a system of standards, targets and assessments. Lauder, Brown, Dillabough and Halsey (2006) have called this centralised system of 'learning' the 'state theory of learning' because it mandates for teachers modes of assessment, the curriculum and elements of pedagogy. Pedagogy is test driven where the criterion for pupil progress and school improvement turn on improvements in a battery of official tests at entry to primary school (baseline tests) and at the ages 7 and 11.

The tensions emerging from the coexistence of such differing tendencies are what characterise the governance arena in the present in what has been described as a new model of decentralised-centralism (Karlsen 2000). New roles have been devised for traditional agencies both at the central and local levels, while yet other instances have been created and new actors have become involved in policies of governance, administration and control.[1]

In the following pages a more detailed description of the current state of educational governance, administration and control will be presented. This will include an account of the transformations that have led to it, as well as a detailed look of the current role of different actors. Following this there will be a discussion of the main difficulties and possibilities of the current state of educational governance through the eyes of research findings.

FROM GOVERNMENT TO GOVERNANCE – RECONFIGURING THE BALANCE OF POWER

The current configuration of power and relations between different governance, administration and control agents can be traced back to the 1980's, and particularly to the introduction of the 1988 Education Reform Act (ERA). Up to this point school administration had been largely in the hands of Local Education Authorities (LEAs), and few forms of centralised control were in existence, with most government control taking place through legislature, rather than direct involvement in school matters

(Alexander 2001). The rise to power of the Conservative government led to the development of a discourse that stressed the need to make the public sector more efficient and this, it was argued, would be achieved through a reduction of the state.

In education, as in other policy areas, it was argued that 'provider capture' on the part of the state was the main cause of inefficiency, and that the monopoly of the state over education had to be broken down (Whitty 1997). The ensuing policies thus promoted the devolution of administrative capacities directly to schools, with the consequent reduction in the authority of LEAs. Not only were funds to go directly to schools, but the possibility of schools opting out of LEAs after a parental ballot and acquiring 'grant-maintained' status was also introduced. Such moves were justified under the rhetoric that school-autonomy was the best way to increase efficiency and generate better educational results.

The focus on efficiency stemmed from a New Public Management discourse which, together with the reduction of the state, led not only to the promotion of the self-management of schools, but also to growing private sector involvement and the introduction of market mechanisms in the administration and governance of schools. The latter refer specifically to the introduction of choice policies that would allow parents to act as consumers in a market that would have to adapt to their demands. Such measures included the opening up of school selection policies beyond traditional catchment areas, so that parents would be able to decide which school they wanted to send their children to, and also the promotion of wider diversity to provide more possibilities from which to choose.

Together with these measures there was a change in the constitution of school governing bodies. While all schools were already required to have individual governing bodies, the latter 'were reformed by removing the inbuilt majority of self-serving local politicians and increasing the representation of parents and local business interests' (Whitty 1997: 7).

In parallel, and largely in contrast, to this move towards a more 'fragmented' form of public service delivery (Dale 1997; Catherine Farrell 2005) the 1980's saw an unprecedented rise in government control measures. While this was different to direct intervention in the delivery of policies, the 1988 ERA introduced a compulsory National Curriculum – allegedly one of the policies that have most radically altered the British education system, at least since the 1944 Education Act – as well as a system of high-stakes assessments that aimed at regulating the operation of the educational market. Thereafter control of the curriculum and assessment would lie in the hands of independent agencies that are, nevertheless, appointed by government and directly accountable to it – initially the National Curriculum Council and the School Examinations and Assessment Council, which were then transformed into the School Curriculum and Assessment Authority and more recently into the Qualifications and Curriculum Authority (QCA).

Government intervention later extended to other areas such as teacher training and inspection with the creation of specific agencies such as the Council for Accreditation of Teacher Education (CATE, later renamed the Teacher Training Agency (TTA)), and the introduction of a curriculum for teacher training.

The tightening of central government control intensified with the creation of the Office for Standards in Education (Ofsted) in 1992, which came in to replace the traditional His/Her Majesty's Inspectorate. While Ofsted was set up as a non-ministerial government department its activities are 'closely tied to the implementation and validation of government policy', which indicate that 'England thus lost its independent inspectorate.' (Alexander 2000: 142).

The end of the Conservative era arrived with considerable criticism of its educational policies. Research evidence from the UK and other countries in which choice policies were being deployed suggested that the latter were contributing to the generation of considerable inequalities. Class variables were seen to affect the structure of the educational market, with the middle-classes acquiring considerable positional advantages in relation to their working class peers in terms of both access to educational opportunities and performance in the system (Lauder and Hughes 1999; Whitty 1997). There were also indications that the stronger central control measures that were being deployed were having negative effects on teachers' morale, while the notion of teacher professionalism was reconstructed (Lauder, Brown, Lupton, Castle and Hempel-Jorgensen 2007).

Furthermore, the Tory reliance on a strong critique of the comprehensive educational system which had led to the promotion of greater diversification in catering for students' needs was also under question. Evidence suggested that this was also leading to forms of selection that discriminated against children according to class characteristics. Besides, there appeared to be clear indicators that market choice was leading to homogenisation rather than diversity within schools as regards the pedagogy, the curriculum, and assessment (Whitty 1997).

The advent of New Labour brought some expectations of change, especially as the party had expressed criticisms of the 1988 ERA. However, rather than moving back in terms of decentralisation and control policies, the government moved towards an enhancement of the latter. In education, New Labour's main criticism of its predecessor focused on its failure to meet desirable standards of academic achievement. The main shift in the policy discourse thus proposed the need to focus on 'standards not structures' (Taylor, Fitz and Gorard 2005), a pledge that led to the introduction of specific targets for test performance which would have to be met by the year 2002 (Alexander 2000). This gave way to the prescription of the literacy and later the numeracy hours, which, 'while allowing for innovation and experimentation in selected areas' (Muschamp, Jamieson, and Lauder 1999: 107) mandated 'a single national formula' (Alexander 2001: 143) that was expected to produce desired outcomes. Such policy moves have been part of a discourse that emphasises the role of accountability in the improvement of public service delivery.

The tightening of central control is part and parcel of New Labour's move towards a governance model that emphasises collaboration and participation within a network – rather than hierarchichal-policy structure (see Dale 1997; Pierre and Peters 2000). The devolution of responsibilities for the provision and management of educational services to schools has been accompanied by a tightening of control through standard setting, assessments and the permanent scrutiny of school practices. This has led to a redefinition of the role of the various agencies involved in the delivery of educational services and to the formation of a new balance of power between and within the various levels of the system.

These changes are consistent with New Labour's emphasis on bridging traditional divisions such as those between left/right, public/private and state/civil society and have also led to the establishment and promotion of various forms of partnership and collaboration in educational governance and administration. These, it is argued, are the way towards more transparent, effective and efficient administration.

Some researchers have argued that many of these policy changes are a continuation, rather than a break, with the policies of the Conservative government (Cardini 2006), particularly in relation to private sector involvement, which is 'expanding as the obvious 'solution' to public sector difficulties (Ball 2007: 121). However, while such continuities might exist, the research also suggests that talk about 'enforced privatisation as an ideological strategy' should be avoided (Ball 2007). What is happening nowadays is much more complex: a reconstitution of public sector actors as 'entrepreneurial' together with an increasing incorporation of the private sector as an important part of the policy process.

More recently, the introduction of the Every Child Matters agenda has added a further degree of complexity to the above by somewhat challenging the 'corporatization of the public sphere' (Ranson 2008). Every Child Matters has emerged partly in reaction to the evidence about existing inequalities and their effects on learning, which it seeks to redress, and it challenges some of the standardisation agenda by raising awareness about the importance of supporting the individual needs of each child. Every Child Matters thus promotes coordination, adequate service provision and assigns a broader role to schools, which are now encouraged to provide extended services in partnership with other organisations. As Ranson (2008) argues, this new agenda of community and individual child needs is in tension with the previous one of private partnerships and standardised achievement, but it is still to be seen in which direction the system will actually go.

THE NEW ROLE OF CENTRAL AGENCIES, LEAS AND SCHOOL GOVERNING BODIES

Changes at the central level

The shift towards a governance model has brought about a 're-agenting' (see Jones, quoted in Hatcher 2006: 600) of the school system that has radically altered the role of traditional actors and the way in which policies are developed. A series of new agencies and actors have come to define the education policy arena. The government's Five Year Strategy (DfES, 2004a) makes an explicit case for the DfES to assume fewer responsibilities in terms of direct management and service delivery. By the same token, the more traditional actors in charge of policy development and implementation, such as LEAs and teachers, have been restructured with two new categories of actors becoming involved: on the one hand quasi non-governmental organisations which include the Office for Standards in Education (Ofsted), the Teacher Development Agency (TDA), the Qualifications and Curriculum Authority (QCA) and the Specialist Schools and Academies Trust; and on the other private companies (Hatcher 2006).

The changing role of LEAs

LEAs had been traditionally dedicated to the provision of educational services, a role that, since 1944, they began to partially share with central government and local institutions. By considerably devolving resources and decision making powers directly to schools the 1988 ERA radically altered the definition of LEA functions. The Conservative government saw LEAs as representing 'local bureaucracies', and as 'barriers to raising standards' because of their 'liberal' and 'child-centred' views; on the other hand, LEAs appeared to be 'the antithesis of the envisaged market-driven' reforms (Fitz, Gorard, and Taylor 2002: 376). Several policies were introduced to address this situation. As part of the move towards self-management, a large proportion of LEA budgets was to be handed directly to schools; policies of open enrolment meant that LEAs would have reduced decision making powers over this issue; at the same time LEA representation in governing bodies was also reduced; finally, the possibility of achieving grant-maintained status meant that some LEAs could further lose their powers over schools. With their role thus heavily curtailed, LEAs were left in a difficult position (see Bache 2003; Fitz, Gorard *et al.* 2002).

While New Labour kept the direction of policies in terms of devolved power to schools and strong central policy definition and monitoring, the role of LEAs became more clearly defined and somewhat strengthened in relation to policies of standard setting, school achievement and enrolment (Fitz, Gorard *et al.* 2002).

Several policy documents (DfEE 1998a, 2000; Her Majesty's Government 1998; Ofsted 2000, 2001a, 2001b) have contributed to redefining the role of LEAs. The 1998 School Standards and Framework Act (Her Majesty's Government 1998) aimed particularly at tackling issues of access and created new types of schools (community, foundation and voluntary-aided) open to different degrees of influence from their LEAs. The Act also increased LEA representation in governing bodies, and considerably tidied up the admissions confusion created by the previous governments, especially through the grant-maintained policy (see Fitz, Gorard *et al.* 2002 for a more detailed account of current admissions arrangements). The Code of Practice on LEA-School relations (DfEE 1998a) stresses the need to raise standards, it reinforces the self-management of schools and intervention in inverse measure to success, it highlights the importance of partnerships and cooperation, and it establishes a policy of zero tolerance to underperformance. A policy of fair funding has also been deployed which defines the four areas in which LEAs can allocate funds (that is, special educational needs, access, school improvement and strategic management). The LEA framework for inspection confirms that the government regards 'schools as the main drivers of their own development, with LEAs working in partnership with them to provide support and challenge as necessary' (Hatcher 2006).

Since 1997 LEAs themselves have become the target of government inspection, especially in relation to the meeting of targets and the development of planning strategies (Bache 2003). Inspection has led to the categorisation of LEAs according to whether they are fulfilling their role in a satisfactory or unsatisfactory way. When the latter has been the case, the government has deployed a policy of transferring school administration to local, usually private, partners – the case of the Leeds LEA being a somewhat exemplary one (Bush and Gamage 2001).

LEAs in general have been encouraged by central-government to engage in public-private partnerships which are expected to help towards the development of better planning and target setting strategies, and to school improvement in general. There is an expectation in relation to this that the business model of administration will generate more positive and efficient dynamics within LEAs.

The operation of school governing bodies

With LEA control reduced and the shift towards the self-management of schools, the role of governing bodies has become increasingly important. This is in line with an international trend underpinned by the idea that school autonomy will lead to better school management and achievement (Catherine Farrell 2005). It also fits the 'New Public Management' model, which moves away from bureaucratic organisation and towards more 'fragmented service delivery' (DfES 2004b). The underlying assumption of this model is that by incorporating leaders from the community and private organisations school management will become stronger and more efficient (Farrell 2005).

Since the mid-eighties governing bodies have been given control over major aspects of school management 'including strategic leadership, resourcing decisions, the employment of professional staff and the development of key policies within areas, including the school curriculum and disciplinary policies' (DfES 2004b). At the same time, participation in governing bodies has been opened up to include representatives from parents and the wider community, as well as from school teachers.

'Governing the School of the Future' (DfES 2004b) offers an official description of the role of school governing bodies as 'equal partners in leadership with the head teacher and senior management team'. In accordance with this the government's 'Five Year Strategy' (DfES 2004a) establishes a series of measures, particularly related to the reduction of red tape, which aim to enhance the role of governors, especially in relation to schools' performance management policy and the management of head teachers' performance.

Apart from the making of strategic decisions in the areas mentioned above, governing bodies are seen as having a fundamental role in promoting school accountability. In order to guarantee that governing bodies fulfil this role appropriately DfES established a Governor Support and Training Strategy which works with local authority Co-ordinators of Governor Services to deliver a national training programme for both new governors and for the clerks of school governing bodies (Farrell 2005).

Governing bodies broadly follow the private sector board of directors model, which is expected to have an especially positive effect on the development of more strategic forms of school management (Farrell 2005: 5). However, unlike business, school governing bodies have a stakeholder base that also seeks to grant representation and, through it, accountability. Governing bodies thus count with elected parent and teacher representatives as well as with co-opted members from the wider community (including business), and with nominated Local Authority governors, and they can also include sponsor, partnership or foundation governors – community and parent representatives having 'numerical dominance' (Farrell 2005: 6). In order to grant accountability governing bodies have 'legal responsibilities to LEAs, inspection authorities and to parents' (Taylor, Fitz *et al.* 2005) in relation to both administrative and pedagogic matters. This initially led to overburdening of governors, who were required, among other things, to produce an annual report to parents. More recently, however, some of these measures have changed in order to create a more flexible and 'intelligent' accountability framework that places less reporting burden on governors while seeking to generate transparent and more easy to access information, such as the 'school profile' (DfES 2004b; DfES/Ofsted 2005).

Alternative models of school administration

The government's encouragement of private-public partnerships in education has also led to the development of a series of initiatives that promote direct private sector involvement in the running of schools. While this continues the previous trend towards diversification, the models have varied. The Conservative government had introduced policies such as those of grant-maintained schools – schools that could opt out of LEA control to be administered by their own governing boards – and the assisted places scheme – through which high-performing students who wanted to go to an independent school, but could not afford the fees, would be subsidised with public funds. These initiatives did not yield the expected results. Only a few schools opted in or out of the grant-maintained scheme (Walford 2000) and the assisted-places scheme was seen to be elitist and not benefiting its target population (Fitz, Edwards and Whitty 1989).

New Labour decided to put an end to both these policies and initially seemed to be inclined towards the promotion of greater homogeneity, rather than diversity. However, in time the inclination towards specialisation in schooling remained strong (Hatcher 2006: 608). The new legislation identified three main categories of schools: community schools, which remain under LEA control; voluntary schools, which can be 'controlled' or 'aided', and are mainly faith-based schools; and foundation schools, which group most of the former grant-maintained schools (and the majority of primary schools) and are run by an independent governing body. At the secondary level other modalities such as the Specialist Schools and Academies were introduced, with the former accounting for the 'majority of business sponsorship' (Hatcher 2006).

The 2006 Education and Inspections Act (HMSO 2006) allowed for Foundation schools to become Trust schools by setting up a charitable foundation or trust that committed to support the school. Unlike in the case of Academies or Specialist Schools, Trust schools are completely state-maintained and sponsors are not required to give a financial donation, but are expected to establish a long-term relationship with their schools. The scheme seeks to promote the formation of partnerships as well as the grouping of schools to enhance collaboration and it is expected that in the future the majority of new schools will fall within this category.

The government has also shown a particular interest in promoting the expansion of faith-based organisations' involvement in school administration, as the latter are seen as particularly successful partners in running schools (Taylor *et al.* 2005: 57). While the government does not have any specific programmes for faith-based schools it clearly sees them as making 'a major contribution to offering a greater choice of schools and encouraging schools to have distinct identities and ethos.' (DfES 2002). This can be seen, for instance, in the government's support through the White Paper *Schools Achieving Success* (Church House Publishing 2001) of the Dearing report *The Way Ahead: Church of England schools in the new millennium* (Church House Publishing 2001), which proposes to increase the number of Church of England Schools.[2] While church involvement in schooling has traditionally been associated with Church of England and Roman Catholic schools, the government's White Paper also makes it clear that there needs to be equal expansion of other faith-based schools.

A different, more specific government initiative for promoting private-public partnerships can be seen in the case of Education Action Zones (EAZ). Following the private-public partnership model EAZs have been devised to run schools in difficult areas with particularly low educational results (DfES/Ofsted 2005: 5). The zones bring together a series of partners that include LEAs, the business and voluntary sector, and community representatives which are expected to work together in running these schools. More recently EAZs have been absorbed by the Excellence in Cities initiative, which has similar aims.

How educational policy is formulated and implemented

The shift towards a governance model has radically altered the way in which policies are formulated and implemented. While traditional actors such as LEAs and teachers were in charge of policy development and implementation, today the balance of power lies mostly between central government and local partners involved in the running of schools. While control is in the hands of the former, strategic decisions and the planning of school activities is largely in the hands of governing bodies. It is these non-traditional actors, including members from the community, the private business and voluntary sector and parents who are now in charge of the making, implementation and monitoring of most decisions.

Control takes place largely through standard setting and monitoring strategies, with Ofsted playing a central role through the development of mandatory assessments and inspections. In 2005 the government released *A New Relationship with Schools*, a policy document which outlined Ofsted's new inspection system. The latter is based on much shorter but more frequent inspections, and aims to rely more strongly on schools' self-evaluation. A system of School Improvement Partners is being implemented together with the new measures, and is expected to work directly with schools for improvement purposes. The aim of such changes is 'to lighten the burden for schools without losing any of the rigour of inspection' (Karlsen, 2000). The document also places considerable emphasis on improving communications with schools on the basis of more efficient data collection and delivery of inspection results with clear guidance to help schools' improvement.

The image of centralised-decentralisation is a clear description of the current situation, where administration lies in the hands of local actors and control is in the hands of central government agencies.

FINDINGS FROM EXISTING RESEARCH

Governance policies in context

Existing research shows that the trend towards the establishment of governance models has an international scope. Scoppio (2002) compares educational developments in England, California and Ontario and finds similarities in terms of the move towards standardization, accountability and devolution. At the same time, the author finds similarities in terms of the impact of quasi-markets in education, which in different contexts appear to increase inequalities through processes of 'skimming' good from bad students in the competition for increased funding.

These findings are in line with those of other international studies. Whitty (1997) compares the policies of the UK, New Zealand and the US in relation to the creation of quasi-markets in education. The author's review of existing research evidence is conclusive in relation to how such policies tend to deepen inequalities through processes of cream skimming the most able, typically from professional and managerial backgrounds. Moreover, the creation of quasi-markets in education tends to move schools towards greater homogeneity, rather than diversity, which is against the explicit aims of such policies. Whitty, Power and Halpin (1998), through a comparison of school reforms in England, Wales, USA, Australia, New Zealand and Sweden, show how devolution policies have generally been accompanied by a strengthening of state control through measures of standardisation, assessments and accountability. The authors suggest that the emphasis on consumer rights – seen in the move towards the establishment of quasi-markets in education – raises serious problems for social equality and citizenship formation.

While the direction and the effects of policies are similar, Scoppio (2002) highlights that there are considerable variations in the specific arrangements through which the policies are instantiated. In the case of California, for instance, the author highlights that together with the shift towards standards, assessments and performance-based funding, there has been a strong move towards the creation of charter schools. The latter generally emerge as community based initiatives and although they offer public access they are not responsive to most school district laws. In this sense they are similar to the UK grant-maintained schools. In the case of Ontario, on the other hand, the author shows that central government control includes also the allocation of funds to schools. In all cases, however, the author finds a common aim of increasing government control while at the same time reducing the power of local authorities by devolving capacities directly to schools.

Bush and Gamage (2001) also identify similar international trends in education policies and focus on the particular ways in which models of self-governing schools have developed in Australia and the United Kingdom. The authors highlight that the idea of self-governance refers generally to the management and allocation of resources, with the assumption being that schools will have better knowledge of their needs and will therefore be better able to allocate resources. The review of the research presented in the article suggests that the move towards self-governance is generally accepted by head teachers, who would not prefer to go back to older centralised models of administration.

Intra-national arrangements vary in terms of the composition of governing bodies, with Australia favouring more voluntary forms of partnership than the UK, where the emphasis has been on empowering parents and business partners. Existing research suggests that it is generally the working relationship between the head teacher and the chair of the governing body that determines the success of partnerships. There is also evidence of low parental participation in governance, as parents often feel they lack the capacities or the knowledge to contribute in useful ways. At the same time there often appears to be a divide between professionals and amateurs – with parents being included among the latter – that hinders better forms of participation.

In an article focusing on the issue of parental participation in schooling, Balarin and Cueto (2007) present a review of the current policy framework in Peru which shows that the move to governance models has spread also to the developing world. This is being promoted by international organisations such as the World Bank, which favour decentralization and school-based management.[3] On the basis of research carried out in Peru, the authors criticise the assumptions underlying the application of such reforms, which often overlook differences in national contexts which can seriously limit the ways in which increased parental and community participation can lead to educational improvements.

The idea that within country arrangements show considerable variations in relation to the broader policy frameworks is also explored by Phillips (2003) in the UK context. The author highlights how in Scotland and Wales strong traditions of autonomy and non-central intervention have led to the development of less intrusive forms of central control over educational matters. This echoes the findings of a study carried out by Ranson, Arnot et al. (2005) which also highlights the considerable variations between UK countries, and suggests that the actual ways in which policies have been implemented is culturally specific.

The role of centralised control in a devolved system of educational administration

On the basis of a study of governance policies and the changes in the role of LEAs, Bache (2003) highlights that the devolution of power to schools has not led to a reduction of state control over educational matters. On the contrary, control has been strengthened, although there has been a shift on its locus from the more traditional local authorities to central government.

Lauder *et al.* (2007) looked at a sample of schools to analyse the effects of current control measures and the emphasis of performativity on teachers' practices. The paper argues that where teachers are driven by targets and test results they are highly constrained in using their own criteria for judging student progress and this undermines their professionalism. The authors focus specifically on the issue of student setting, which is among New Labour's policies. They show that setting requires considerable professional autonomy and contextual knowledge, and that this is contradicted by 'the imposition of particular practices by external agencies'. The paper concludes that current policies of educational governance have a definitive impact on professional autonomy and judgement, and generate problems because of the often contradictory demands placed on different groups (i.e. teachers).

The changing role of LAs

As seen above, LEAs are probably the level most affected by the introduction of governance policies. Fletcher-Campbell and Lee (2003) carried out a study on how the new role of LEAs is impacting on school standards and achievement. The study showed that there is a strong degree of acceptance of government policies among LAs. Problems emerge from the different ways in which policies are being implemented. While, as seen above, there is a much clearer definition of the role of LAs in relation to raising standards there is still considerable scope for interpretation as to how the policies are to be implemented, with particular arrangements being a function of different variables such as LA size, organisational dynamics and community composition. Such differences are seen to affect particularly the establishment of partnerships. The latter, 'rather than being underpinned by cooperation and trust, seem to vary between sectors, indicating a variety of struggles for power and recognition' (Fletcher-Campbell and Lee 2003: 410). Such variations go from cooperative arrangements to more typical contractual ones 'where there is no evidence of trust between those involved' (Fletcher-Campbell and Lee 2003: 410).

The study also found that the 'strict performance targets that partnerships are supposed to meet' (Fletcher-Campbell and Lee 2003: 411) considerably constrain the kinds of organizations that can enter such partnerships, with those in the voluntary and community sectors having much more difficulties. This is in line with the research findings presented by Cardini (2006) who, in a survey of research into educational partnerships, found that the balance of power is considerably skewed in favour of business partners – making the partnership model much more similar to quasi-market policies than the official policy rhetoric seems to admit.

Complementing the above perspective, Farnsworth (2006) presents a critique of an official study carried out by the Confederation of British Industry on LAs that had outsourced their services to the private sector. The author compares the results of this study with findings from his own research to suggest problems with the interpretation of data in the CBI study which led to conclusions about positive effects of outsourcing. Farnsworth shows that many of the outsourced LAs had been under council control during much of the studied period, making changes attributable to LAs and not only to the new agents. Besides, improvements appear to have taken place faster in non-outsourced LAs.

Following from some of the paradoxes involved in the shift towards a model of centralised-decentralisation, Wallace (2000) reflects on research into large-scale reorganisation of schools in England (Wallace and Pocklington 1998) to highlight how the contradictory aims of reforms generate problems in LA practices. While LAs had responsibility for redeploying staff after schools were shut-down due to demographical changes, they lacked the authority to carry out this effectively. School heads and governing bodies often differed from LA views in relation to the redeployment of staff that had been displaced in the reorganization. And since schools now have autonomy from their LAs the latter were often caught between the different interests of displaced staff and school administrators. While the LA interest lay in redeploying staff, schools were more interested in selecting the staff that best matched their interest. The study thus shows how the move towards governance may have created 'partially incompatible interests' (p. 620) between such primary agents as LAs and school heads.

Further highlighting existing contradictions between different policies, a study carried out by Fitz, Gorard *et al.* (2002) suggests that while the 1998 *Schools Standards and Framework Act* considerably reorganized LAs and strengthened their role in relation to standards and school improvement, they proved to be considerably weak – particularly in view of coexisting types of school administration – to promote more equitable forms of access to educational services.

The operation of school governing bodies

The main area of research in relation to new governance arrangements appears to deal with the operation of school governing bodies. Ranson, Farrell *et al.* (2005) report on a study carried out in Wales to gauge the contribution of governance to school improvement. The authors suggest that the emphasis of existing research into governing bodies has focused on the latter's impact on decision-making and school management and not so much on how governors can impact school improvement. Their study revealed considerable variation in the organization of governing bodies, which have developed 'different kinds of structure and practice' on the basis of varying definitions of their purposes and responsibilities; different relations of power 'between the head teacher and the chair of governors; and 'the extent of corporateness of the governing body in its deliberations and decision-making' (p.310). This led the authors to develop a typology of governing bodies in terms of: governance as a deliberative forum; governance as a consultative sounding board; governance as an executive board; and governance as a governing body. The main differences relate to whether the body is a mere space for communicating information or whether it has a central role in school decisions.

The authors conclude that governance can have a positive impact on school improvement where governing bodies take the last two forms and show a greater degree of involvement in school decisions. The scrutiny function performed by governing bodies is seen as especially fruitful, particularly when it takes the form of a 'critical friendship' that does not undermine confidence and promotes reflection upon school practices.

A study carried out by Farrell (2005) on the basis of interviews with relevant actors found that governing board members are rarely involved in strategic planning, and that it is infrequent for them to challenge head teachers' decisions. The author concludes that governors tend to act in a reactive rather than in a proactive way, limiting themselves to making decisions, but not getting involved in shaping strategies. Moreover, the evidence suggests that school governors tend to get more involved in school activities which are not educational. This, it is suggested, seems to be the outcome of governors focusing more specifically in the areas where they are specialised, such as accounting or finance, leaving the more educational issues in the hands of school staff. On the other hand, as in other areas, there appears to be excessive government control, so while governors appear to have been strategically empowered to deliver policies they are 'effectively curtailed in their freedom of action' (Farrell 2005: 106). The author suggests that limitations to governors' involvement also stem from the fact that governing bodies have been modelled on the basis of business boards of directors, which are often not involved in strategic management. Finally, the author suggests that the leadership role of governing bodies has often been neglected in the literature, which tends to focus on the role of head teachers in this respect.

In another article, Farrell and Law (1999) explore the issue of the accountability of school governing bodies. The research carried out into this issue shows that governing bodies are not very accountable and, it is suggested, this has to do with the lack of clear guidance from central government in this respect. The research highlights that the role of governing bodies tends to be one of giving support and advice more than one of accounting for school decisions. While governing bodies appear to have to account to a variety of actors, it is not very clear to whom exactly they are accountable, or how they can perform such a role – this was the case among head teachers, as well as among co-opted members of governing bodies. Besides, accountability issues only appear to arise when something goes wrong, rather than being something permanent. While mandated annual reports and parent meetings offer a space for accountability, reduced attendance to the meetings suggests a lack of interest on the part of parents, which makes it difficult to establish relations of accountability, especially as the latter depend both on the willingness to account as on the interest of existing parties.

In line with other studies referred to above, research carried out by Ranson, Arnot *et al.* (2005) highlights the considerable variations in the way that governing bodies operate in relation to central government policies. While this is so, their study also found that there are some widespread problems in the composition of governing bodies, which tend to have low levels of parental participation. Moreover, the study showed that class tends to mediate volunteer recruitment, with women, ethnic minorities and disadvantaged classes tending to be under-represented on governing bodies. All this, they suggest, raises questions in relation to how democratic governing bodies really are.

On a more positive note, the authors highlight the ways in which volunteer members of governing bodies tend to progress from 'initial preoccupation with their own child to growing understanding of and commitment to the needs of the institution and the wider community' (Ranson, Arnott *et al.* 2005: 361). This, they suggest, indicates that when participation is achieved it generally has a positive impact. The authors thus conclude that while 'participation has developed to strengthen institutions in the official world of the public sphere, it remains incomplete' (p.370).

A further line of recent research has explored the role played by school governing bodies in areas of social deprivation, where some of the problems that affect school governance in general appear to be more acute – recruitment in particular. A study conducted by a team from the University of Manchester (Dean, Dyson, Gallannaugh, Howes and Raffo 2007) found that many of the problems that now affect school governance in disadvantaged areas stem from the different and sometimes contradictory discourses about it. They identify three different rationales for school governance that can be found in policy requirements: a managerial one that focuses on efficiency and standards (and requires managerial skills from governors); a localising rationale that emphasises adaptation to local needs (and requires governors with knowledge of the local community); and a democratising rationale that emphasises democratic partici-pation and active citizenship. The struggle to meet the demands of these different rationales means that very often governors recruited to enhance democratic account-ability or local adaptation will not have the right managerial skills to deal with 'the complex tasks they are required to undertake' (Dean *et al*. 2007: 46). The researchers highlight the need to clarify the role of governing bodies, and suggest that different alternatives could be followed which could either place more emphasis on the managerial or on the democratic role of governors. The latter, however, seems to be favoured.

Research into alternative models of school administration

As seen above, the involvement of key partners from the private and voluntary sectors is one of the central elements of New Labour's emphasis on the development of educational partnerships. While a variety of partnerships have developed, the case of the Education Action Zones, now included within the Excellence in Cities initiative, constitutes a paradigmatic case of public-private partnership directly promoted by central govern-ment to improve the quality of education in areas with low results. While EAZs have had considerable funding from central government, they are also meant to gather resources from private sponsorship. EAZs were generally composed of about 20 schools, and while they counted with an appointed director they were run by an Education Action Forum which had planning, implementation and monitoring responsibilities.

A study carried out by Power, Whitty *et al*. (2004) into the effects of EAZs showed that their achievements were far from those expected by the government. Their regression analysis of zone effects showed that 'if anything, a negative EAZ effect' could be perceived, 'with zone schools doing less well than the same LEA's non-zone schools' (p.460).

At the same time, the authors found that in terms of innovation – which was one of the zones' main aims – there was a tendency towards homogeneity rather than diversity among zone schools. This, the study argues, was partly because of the strong emphasis on meeting targets, which considerably reduced the scope for actual changes within zones – a suggestion that is in line with other studies mentioned above.

Moreover, the study showed that private investment in the EAZs had been reduced. The authors argue that this has to do with the limitations established by government for the establishment of for-profit investments in education, something that is not likely to change (see also Hatcher 2006). Apart from this, access to private funding seemed to depend on zones' location and proximity to sources. But, as the authors highlight, 'the most striking thing about business involvement was its banality (...) there was little evidence that business had the capacity, energy, creativity, and know-how to transform education in socially disadvantaged areas in the radical manner originally envisaged' (p.462).

As other studies have suggested, Power, Whitty *et al*. (2004) found that parental involvement was also rather weak, and tended to be limited to breakfast clubs and parent-as-educator schemes, which do not necessarily generate positive educational changes. On a more positive line, however, EAZs did appear to have desirable effects in terms of bringing the parental community closer.

One final issue highlighted by the study has to do with the role of teachers in the development of the EAZ initiative. Findings suggested 'a general trend towards fragmentation within professions' (Power *et al*. 2004), which was generally articulated around the issue of support or rejection of the reforms. The authors thus suggest that teachers have frequently been caught in the middle of the transformation agenda and with their role as insiders/outsiders remaining unclear.

While the EAZs constituted an 'attempt to rebuild collaboration in areas where the market-oriented reforms of previous Conservative administrations were clearly not working' (Power *et al*. 2004: 467), the study is not very positive in relation to the partnership policies of New Labour's Third Way government. The overall findings of the study suggest that the impact of EAZs has not been very important in achieving the aims that were originally set for them in terms of improving governance, innovation and learning. Some changes were found in terms of an erosion of traditional public/ private boundaries, but the effects of this were varied, and in many cases new boundaries emerged.

Voluntary sector partnerships

Given the failure of the grant-maintained scheme to attract more support New Labour halted the policy and replaced it with various initiatives such as the creation of the Voluntary Aided sector. The latter offers incentives for the establishment of voluntary-aided schools, most of which are church schools, and which are more subject to local authority and central government control than the GM schools were. Existing research suggests that these measures are still not enough to encourage the development of more voluntary aided faith-based schools. The main deterrent appears to be precisely the extent of central government control (Walford 2001). Voluntary-aided schools, while having considerable freedom of selection, have to submit to central government policies such as the National Curriculum and the Literacy and Numeracy Hours, while the private sector does not. The latter thus appears to be more attractive.

One of the main areas of research in relation to faith-based schools focuses on the issue of selection. Various studies suggest that one of the reasons behind the good performance of such schools is the freedom they have to select pupils, which leads to processes of skimming that raise serious questions in relation to the provision of equal opportunities (Fitz, Gorard *et al*. 2002; Fitz, Taylor and Gorard 2002; Muschamp *et al*. 1999; Power *et al*. 2004).

While the 1998 *School Standards and Framework Act* introduced considerable changes in relation to Conservative policies of open enrolment in schools, current research suggests that voluntary schools are still contributing to local patterns of segregation by having the possibility to expand their catchment areas as well as to deploy various measures of selection (Fitz, Gorard *et al*. 2002).

CONCLUSIONS

Throughout this chapter the reader will have found a descriptive account of the current situation of the governance, administration and control of primary education. The latter has fed from existing academic and policy literature, and includes an outline of the main changes that have taken place in this area over the past decades. This account shows how since the rise of New Labour to power there has been a clear move towards the establishment of a governance model in which the devolution of powers to schools has been complemented with a strong emphasis on the development of partnerships. The latter are part of the government's discourse of bridging traditional dichotomies such as those between private/public, market/state, or state/civil society. The move towards a governance model has thus entailed a shift from traditional actors, such as LEAs and teachers, to new ones, such as parents, and business and voluntary organisations, which are now involved in the making and implementation of policies. At the same time, however, government control has strengthened to a point never seen before. Such control takes place through policies of standard setting, assessments and inspections, and a strong emphasis on accountability and performativity.

The move towards a governance model thus constitutes a change from the policies of previous Conservative administrations, which were more geared to keeping government intervention reduced and placed much more explicit emphasis on the operation of market mechanisms in education. In recent years, central government control has intensified through a variety of performance measures that some argue are creating a culture of self-governed individuals (Lingard and Ozga 2007).

The research discussed shows that the move towards a governance model and the combination of decentralised administration and strong government control has an international scope. This is not only the case among developed nations, but also among developing ones, where international organisations such as the World Bank have been keen on promoting the governance model.

Existing research suggests that the paradoxes involved in a model of 'decentralized-centralism' (Karlsen 2000) are at the core of difficulties found in the application of governance practices. In the UK, the case of LEAs is particularly illustrative of the ambiguous role that this model sets for many actors, whose autonomous decisions are often curtailed by external demands and requirements to meet specific targets. The same is applicable to teachers, who have seen their professional autonomy increasingly limited by new governance policies.

One of the central findings encountered across various studies is the idea that the instantiation of policies tends to be context-specific, with some places showing positive changes in the direction expected by policies and others not. The same is applicable in the case of school governing bodies, which also appear to have developed in different ways, with some generating more positive working relations with schools than others.

The notion of partnerships that has been central to New Labour's governance policies appears to be problematic at the level of its definition, and some (see Cardini 2006) suggest that they are not at such a distance from Conservative marketisation policies as the official discourse asserts. At a more specific level, research findings suggest that private involvement in education has not brought about expected changes in terms of increased funding and innovation at both the administrative and pedagogic levels.

The operation of governing bodies is one of the main arenas for the operation of partnerships, and here, as in the case of LEAs, research suggests the existence of considerable variations in terms of how governance arrangements operate. While a good working relationship between head teachers and chief governors is seen as crucial, the governance partnerships can vary considerably producing different results. While research suggests that governance can definitely have a positive effect on school improvement, this is not always so, and will depend on a combination of variables. This suggests the need to provide better guidance for the operation of governing bodies.

Another issue in relation to this is the reduced participation of volunteer citizens and members from the parental and wider community in school governance, particularly in areas of social deprivation. Existing research points to a widespread divide between the professionals (teachers, head teachers, private business members) and amateurs (parents), which hinders more and better parental involvement.

The general idea that stems from this research survey is that while the governance model seems to be progressing and is generating positive results in many cases, there are still important improvements to be made in order to achieve the desired outcomes. There are already indications that some of the issues raised by the research might have started to be tackled, with central government recently proposing considerable changes in relation to school inspection and relations with schools more generally. However, progress is measured according to the State Theory of Learning, which in itself raises profound questions as to whether it provides the most appropriate structure for learning (Lauder, Brown, Dillabough and Halsey 2006).

NOTES

1 Such shifts are not exclusive to the education sector. On the contrary, they fit a predominant international or global discourse on the role of the state and civil society. While there have been some undeniable changes in the forms of this discourse over the past two and a half decades, there are also some evident continuities. Whereas the early eighties were pre-dominantly influenced by a neo-liberal perspective which highlighted the need to minimise the role of the state in favour of market dynamics, the rise of New Labour to power has involved a discourse on bridging the public/private divide.
2 The report refers specifically to secondary schools, but this reflects the government's general orientation towards faith-based and Church of England schools.
3 An account of these policies and case studies of their application in various countries can be found in the World Bank's Global Education Reform website: http://www1.worldbank.org/education/globaleducationreform/06.GovernaceReform/governace_ref.htm

REFERENCES

Alexander, R.J. (2001) *Culture and Pedagogy: international comparisons in primary education.* Oxford, Malden: Blackwell Publishers.

Bache, I. (2003) 'Governing through governance: education policy control under New Labour', *Political Studies* 51: 300–14.

Balarin, M. and Cueto, S. (2007) 'The quality of parental participation and student achievement in public schools in Peru', *Young Lives Working Papers Series (awaiting publication)*.

Ball, S. (2007) *Education plc: understanding private sector participation in public sector education.* Oxon, New York: Routledge.

Bush, A. and Gamage, D. (2001) 'Models of self-governance in schools: Australia and the United Kingdom', *The International Journal of Educational Management* 15(1): 39–44.

Cardini, A. (2006) 'An analysis of the rhetoric and practice of educational partnerships in the UK: an arena of complexities, tensions and power', *Journal of Education Policy* 21(4): 393–415.

Church House Publishing (2001) *The Way Ahead: Church of England schools in the new millennium.* London: Church House Publishing.

Dale, R. (1997) 'The state and the governance of education: an analysis of the restructuring of the state-education relationship', in A.H. Halsey, H. Lauder, P. Brown and A. Stuart Wells (Eds) *Education: culture, economy, society.* Oxford: Oxford University Press.

Dean, C., Dyson, A., Gallannaugh, F., Howes, A. and Raffo, C. (2007) *Schools, Governors and Disadvantage.* York: Joseph Rowntree Foundation.

DfEE (1998) *Code of Practice on LEA School Relations: draft consultation*. London: DfEE.
——(2000) *Code of Practice on Local Education Authority-School Relations*. London: DfEE.
DfES (2002) *Schools: achieving success*. London: DfEE.
——(2004a) *Five Year Strategy for Children and Learners*. London: DfES.
——(2004b) *Governing the School of the Future*. London: DfES.
DfES/Ofsted (2005) *A New Relationship with Schools: next steps*. London: DfES.
Farnsworth, K. (2006) 'Business in education: a reassessment of the contribution of outsourcing to LEA performance', *Journal of Education Policy* 21(4): 485–96.
Farrell, C. (2005) 'Governance in the UK public sector: the involvement of the Governing Board', *Public Administration* 83(1): 89–110.
Farrell, C. and Law, J. (1999) 'The accountability of school governing bodies', *Educational Management and Administration Quarterly* 27(1): 5–15.
Fitz, J., Edwards, T. and Whitty, G. (1989) 'The Assisted Places Scheme: an ambiguous case of privatization', *British Journal of Educational Studies* 37(3): 222–34.
Fitz, J., Gorard, S. and Taylor, C. (2002a) 'School admissions after the School Standards and Framework Act: bringing the LEAs back in?', *Oxford Review of Education* 28(2&3).
Fitz, J., Taylor, C. and Gorard, S. (2002b) 'Local Education Authorities and the regulation of educational markets: four case studies', *Research Papers in Education* 17(2): 125–46.
Fletcher-Campbell, F. and Lee, B. (2003) *A Study of the Changing Role of Local Education Authorities in Raising Standards of Achievement in School*. London: DfES.
Hatcher, R. (2006) 'Privatisation and sponsorship: the re-agenting of the school system in England', *Journal of Education Policy* 21(5): 599–619.
Her Majesty's Government (1998) *School Standards and Framework Act*. London: The Crown.
——(2006) *Education and Inspections Act*. London: The Crown.
Karlsen, G. (2000) 'Decentralized centralism: framework for a better understanding of governance in the field of education', *Journal of Education Policy* 15(5): 525–38.
Lauder, H., Brown, C., Castle, F., Lupton, A. and Hempel-Jorgensen, A. (2007) *Politics and Professionalism: the question of teacher autonomy in relation to grouping practices*. Online (Available: http://www.bath.ac.uk/research/harps/Resources/).
Lauder, H., Brown, P., Dillabough, J.A. and Halsey, A.H. (Eds) (2006) *Education, Globalization and Social Change*. Oxford: OUP.
Lauder, H. and Hughes, D. (1999) *Trading in Futures: why markets in education don't work*. Philadelphia, PA: Open University Press.
Lingard, B. and Ozga, J. (Eds) (2007) *The RoutledgeFalmer Reader in Education Policy and Politics*. London: Routledge.
Muschamp, Y., Jamieson, I. and Lauder, H. (1999) 'Education, education, education', in M. Powell (Ed) *New Labour, New Welfare State?* Bristol: The Policy Press.
Ofsted (2000) *LEA Support for School Improvement: framework for the inspection of Local Education Authorities*. London: Ofsted.
——(2001a) *Inspection of Local Education Authorities: grade criteria for inspection judgements*. London: Ofsted.
——(2001b) *Local Education Authority Support for School Improvement*. London: Ofsted.
Phillips, R. (2003) 'Education policy, comprehensive schooling and devolution in the disUnited Kingdom: and historical "home international" analysis', *Journal of Education Policy* 18(1): 1–17.
Pierre, J. and Peters, G. (2000) *Governance, Politics and the State*. London: MacMillan Press.
Power, S., Whitty, G., Gewirtz, S., Halpin, D. and Dickson, M. (2004) 'Paving a "third way"? A policy trajectory analysis of education action zones', *Research Papers in Education* 19(4): 453–75.
Ranson, S. (2008) 'The changing governance of education', *Educational Management Administration and Leadership* 36(2).
Ranson, S., Arnot, M., McKeown, P., Martin, J. and Smith, P. (2005) 'The participation of volunteer citizens in school governance', *Educational Review* 57(3).

Ranson, S., Farrell, C., Peim, N. and Smith, P. (2005) 'Does governance matter for school improvement?', *School Effectiveness and School Improvement* 16(3): 305–25.

Scoppio, G. (2002) 'Common trends of standardisation, accountability, devolution and choice in the educational policies of England, U.K., California, U.S.A., and Ontario, Canada', *Current Issues in Comparative Education* 2(2): 130–41.

Taylor, C., Fitz, J. and Gorard, S. (2005) 'Diversity, specialisation and equity in education', *Oxford Review of Education* 31(1): 47–69.

Walford, G. (2000) 'A policy adventure: sponsored grant-maintained schools', *Educational Studies* 26(2): 247–62.

——(2001) 'Evangelical Christian schools in England and the Netherlands', *Oxford Review of Education* 27(4).

Wallace, M. (2000) 'Integrating cultural and political perspectives: the case of school restructuring in England', *Educational Administration Quarterly* 36(4): 604–32.

Wallace, M. and Pocklington, K. (1998) 'Realizing the potential of large-scale reorganization promoting school improvement', *Educational Management and Administration* 26(3): 229–41.

Whitty, G. (1997) 'Creating quasi-markets in education: a review of recent research on parental choice and school autonomy in three countries', *Review of Research in Education* 22: 3–47.

Whitty, G., Power, S. and Halpin, D. (1998) *Devolution and Choice in Education*. Buckingham, Philadelphia: Open University Press.

27 The funding of English primary education

Philip Noden and Anne West

INTRODUCTION

In this chapter we examine the funding of primary education in England. We identify how much money is spent by schools on primary education per pupil and how this has changed in recent years. We also examine how that level of expenditure compares with per pupil expenditure on secondary level education. We then describe the funding arrangements that underlie this level of expenditure and, in particular, describe the changes in that funding system, noting the importance of historical patterns of expenditure in determining current allocations and also the recent shift to central control over expenditure on primary (and secondary) education. We go on to describe the scale of variation between local education authorities[1] (LEAs) in the balance of budget allocations per pupil between primary and secondary education. In the penultimate section, we compare figures for the UK with those relating to other Organisation for Economic Co-operation and Development (OECD) countries in the level of expenditure per pupil in primary education, the proportion of Gross Domestic Product (GDP) spent on primary education and the balance of funding between primary and secondary education. The final section concludes the chapter.

THE LEVEL OF SCHOOL-BASED EXPENDITURE IN PRIMARY EDUCATION IN ENGLAND

Figure 27.1 shows the change in school-based expenditure per pupil (taking inflation into account) from 1992–93 to 2004–5 (the underlying data are shown in the Appendix (Table 27.5)). Some difficulties of interpretation arise from changes in definitions during this period, and these are shown as breaks in the lines. For example, a figure for expenditure in primary schools only (not including pre-primary schools) is only available from 1999–2000 onwards. Nevertheless, Figure 27.1 suggests that, from 1992–93 to 1997–98, the level of school-based expenditure per primary school pupil was relatively stable, though in the latter half of that period it was declining. This was followed by an increase in school-based expenditure per pupil from 1998–99 onwards.

We also see in Figure 27.1 that school-based expenditure per pupil was consistently higher for secondary school pupils than for primary school pupils. This difference in per pupil funding reflects the different roots of primary education (which developed from the elementary system) and secondary education. In short, the elementary education system aimed to provide cheap, mass schooling based on a single generalist teacher instructing a large class. In contrast, the secondary system was organised around specialist

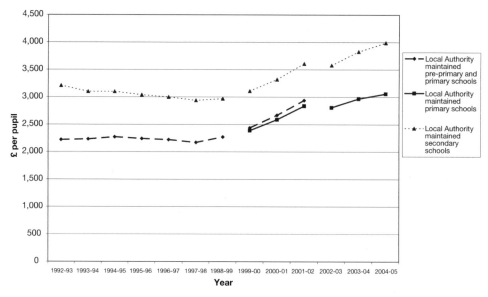

Figure 27.1 School-based expenditure per pupil in England in real terms in primary and secondary schools from 1992–93 to 2004–05. (Source: DfES 2006.)

teachers with smaller classes. The persistence of the concomitant difference in funding levels in primary and secondary schools was noted by the Education Select Committee in 1993–94 (House of Commons Education Committee 1994). It had also been criticised in the Hadow Report of 1931, the Plowden Report of 1967 and the government's 'three wise men' primary education enquiry of 1991–92 (Alexander, Rose and Woodhead 1992: paras 4 and 149).

Figure 27.1 also shows that there was a narrowing of the funding gap between primary and secondary schools each year from 1992–93 to 1998–99 (with the exception of 1997–98). Such a narrowing of the gap was recommended by the Select Committee report (House of Commons Education Committee 1994). Once again interpretation of the figures is impeded by changing definitions, although we can see that from 2002–3 to 2004–5 the gap began to widen once again.

THE FUNDING SYSTEM FOR PRIMARY SCHOOLS IN ENGLAND

In this section, we describe and discuss some of the changes to the funding system that have taken place during the last ten years. The level of funding received by primary schools in England is determined by decisions made both by central government and by local government. The current funding arrangements (intended to operate until 2010–11) are, in fact, relatively simple although these arrangements are currently under review.

It is consequently useful to understand not only the current funding model but also its predecessors. These comprise the Standard Spending Assessment (SSA) system which operated until 2002–3 and the Education Formula Spending Share (EFSS) system that operated between 2003–4 and 2005–6. When considering these funding arrangements it is useful to keep in mind three central issues in the funding arrangements for primary schools in England. First, we need to understand the particular allocation mechanisms from central government to local government and from local government to schools, as these determine levels and variations in school funding. Second, it is important to note changes in the balance of control over school funding between central government and local government. Third, we must note the crucial importance of stability in the levels of funding received by individual schools.

The Standard Spending Assessment system

About three-quarters of funding for local authority services comes from central government grants (Office of the Deputy Prime Minister 2005), with the remaining quarter funded from local taxation (council tax). From 1990 until 2002, the allocation of the bulk of central government funds for education to individual local authorities was determined by the Education Standard Spending Assessment (SSA).

The SSA was a funding formula that was supposed to identify the level of central government funding required by each local authority to achieve a standard level of service for the same rate of council tax (Department of the Environment 1990). Different service areas, such as education, were addressed by different blocks in the SSA calculation. In the case of education the main element in the calculations was simply the number of pupils, and approximately three-quarters of local authority funding for schools was determined on the basis of pupil numbers. In addition, the Education SSA included elements addressing variations in the local cost of living and also increased costs arising from population sparsity. The final element in the Education SSA was determined by 'additional educational needs' (AEN), acknowledging the fact that pupils with different characteristics (such as low level special educational needs or social deprivation) required different levels of support. However, the weighting given to this element was determined by identifying particular population characteristics (such as the proportion of children living in lone parent households as identified in the ten yearly census) that best predicted *past levels of expenditure* on education – that is, past expenditure was itself used as the indicator of need (see West *et al.* 1995).

Having received their funding through the SSA system, individual local authorities decided how much should then be spent on education – the funding was not hypothecated (or earmarked) so the *actual* level of expenditure could be higher or lower than the figure identified within the SSA allocation process.

From April 1999 the distribution of funds to schools by local authorities entailed local authorities setting a Local Schools Budget (LSB) and an Individual Schools Budget (ISB). Local authorities were able to retain funds centrally, via the LSB, to support four key areas: strategic management, access to schools (planning, admissions, transport, and so on), school improvement, and special educational provision. The ISB was then distributed to schools on the basis of a funding formula, and 80 per cent of that funding was to be distributed according to 'pupil-led' factors (non-pupil-led factors would include, for example, 'site specific' factors such as a school being on a split site) (see West *et al.* 2000). The 80 per cent rule was reduced to 75 per cent in 2002–3, and the requirement for a certain percentage of funding to be pupil-led was removed from 2006 onwards although funding formulae were required to take into account pupil numbers (see West, 2009). Nevertheless, throughout the period from 1990 to the present, local funding formulae were required to take into account pupil numbers with local authorities, importantly, free to determine their own *age weightings*. Individual schools then controlled how that budget was spent, for example by deciding on the balance between staffing and other expenditure.

The change to the Education Formula Spending Share system

Concerns about the indicators and methods used by the government to distribute resources to local authorities resulted in a review of funding (see West *et al.* 2000). Following this, from 2003–4, the methods used to fund local authorities for the provision of schooling changed. Formula Spending Shares (FSSs) replaced SSAs for education (and other service areas).

The Education Formula Spending Share (EFSS) was divided into two main funding 'blocks' – one for schools (the Schools Formula Spending Share or SFSS) and the other for local authorities' responsibilities for education (West, 2009). In effect, this split made explicit the division between the LEA budget and ISB which had operated previously. These blocks were divided into sub-blocks for pupils of different ages and pupils with 'high cost special educational needs'.[2] The formulae for the sub-blocks each had a basic per-pupil allocation and additional amounts for deprivation (described as 'additional educational needs') (DfES 2003).[3] In arriving at this model, the government commissioned PricewaterhouseCoopers to carry out empirical research to estimate the additional costs associated with supporting children with additional educational needs. The intention was that the allocation would meet most of the costs directly associated with social deprivation; the costs of supporting children with less severe special educational needs (without statements of special educational needs); and the costs of supporting children with English as an additional language (DfES/HM Treasury 2005; see also West, 2009).

The factors used in the primary additional educational needs index under the EFSS system were the proportion of children in families in receipt of Income Support/Job seekers allowance; the proportion of children in families in receipt of Working Families Tax Credit (WFTC) (all indicators of poverty); and the proportion of primary pupils with a mother tongue other than English, as recorded in the pupil level annual school census.

In summary, the indicators and formulae used changed when the EFSS replaced the ESSA. The measures introduced used pupil level administrative data collected by individual schools from January 2002. Measures derived from the census were no longer used. Furthermore, the new measures were more clearly associated with educational attainment. However, the *overall* amount of funding allocated via the AEN indicator was broadly similar. Table 27.1 gives the allocations under the last year of the SSA system and the first year of the FSS system (see also West, 2009).

Table 27.1 Allocations to AEN, sparsity and area cost adjustment in 2002–03 and 2003–04

	2002–03 *(Education SSA)* %	*2003–04* *(Education FSS)* %
Basic amount per pupil	75	75
AEN total	19	19
Sparsity	1	2
Area Cost Adjustment	4	4

Note: percentages do not add up to 100 because of rounding.
(Source: DfES 2003)

However, while the allocations for additional educational needs were, for the first time, largely based on empirical research into the costs associated with those needs, the basic allocations per pupil (and consequently the balance of funding for primary school pupils relative to pupils of other ages) were determined, once again, by historical patterns of spending (DfES 2003; Levačić 2005). Interestingly, in the course of designing the new funding arrangements, it was acknowledged that when efforts had previously been made by local authorities to determine a unit of funding per pupil based on the funding required to deliver the national curriculum rather than simply on historical patterns of spending, this tended to show that primary schools were relatively underfunded (Education Funding Strategy Group 2001).

Of course, even though the overall proportions of funding allocated by particular formula elements may be similar, as shown in Table 27.1, there was a degree of instability introduced into the system in 2003–4 by the shift to the EFSS system and, although the new formula included a 'damping mechanism' to ensure that every local authority saw an increase in funding of no less than 3.2 per cent and no more than 7 per cent per pupil, that turbulence was exacerbated by further changes to the funding system, and most notably the Standards Fund, in the same year (Audit Commission 2004).

Instability and the introduction of the Dedicated Schools Grant (DSG)

Neither the ESSA nor the EFSS were hypothecated; that is, the indicated amounts were not earmarked for expenditure on education. The result was that local authorities were not obliged to spend a specific amount on education: they could choose to spend more or less than the amount indicated (see also West, 2009). This has clearly been a source of tension between central and local government as central government was not able to ensure that its own priorities were reinforced by the decisions of individual local authorities.

One means by which central government *was* able to promote its own priorities was through a very substantial increase in the direct funding of schools by central government through mechanisms that by-passed local authority control – for example, through the Standards Fund which supported numerous government initiatives. In 1996–97, in real terms a total of £195 million was allocated by central government for schools via the Standards Fund; by 2004–5 this had increased to an estimated £1,612 million[4] (DfES 2005a) – an increase of over 800 per cent. Even though this figure was dwarfed by the funding distributed through the EFSS, the incorporation of much of this Standards Fund expenditure into the core allocation mechanisms in 2003–4, ironically with the intention of simplifying the funding system and creating greater stability, contributed to the instability in school budgets that precipitated the second major reform of this period.

The first year of the EFSS introduced considerable instability and, following the publicity given to schools that had seen cuts in their level of funding, even the Secretary of State for Education acknowledged: 'There is no doubt … that many schools have experienced real difficulties this year with their budget allocations' (House of Commons Hansard 2003, col. 454). In short, central government increases in funding for schools had not translated, for many schools, into increased school budgets. This precipitated a rapid response from central government which, as well as providing additional transitional funding, instigated two key reforms. The first was to introduce a 'minimum funding guarantee' (MFG) that ensured all schools would, in future, receive a specified minimum level of increase in their level of funding per pupil. Secondly, central government required that increases in the SFSS must be 'passported' to schools to ensure that they were not absorbed by increases in central expenditure by the LEA.

Following a promise in the 2005 Labour Party election manifesto to introduce a 'national schools budget set by central government' (Labour Party 2005: 33), the central government response to the problems of the EFSS was crystallised in the introduction of a new 'Dedicated Schools Grant' (DSG). The new funding arrangements restored stability in school and LEA budgets and, for the first time, introduced a ring-fenced schools budget – that is, it would no longer be permitted for local authorities' schools budgets to be smaller than the Dedicated Schools Grant that they received.[5]

Compared with its predecessors, allocations to local authorities under the DSG are simple to understand. The funding model is based on previous levels of spending within the local authority (for 2005–6) including any funds spent by the authority on schools over and above the level of their SFSS (DfES 2005b). The allocation mechanism operates in the following way: a baseline level of spending per pupil for 2005–6 is identified to which a national per pupil increase for the following year is then applied; to this are added allocations reflecting DfES priorities (including, for example, funding 'pockets of deprivation'[6] and implementing the personalisation agenda[7] – although this funding is not ringfenced). If the local authority spent less than its SFSS in 2005–6 then a proportion of the underspend is added to the notional allocation; and, finally, if the resulting local authority figure is then less than a minimum percentage cash increase from the previous year, it is topped up to reach this level (this element is to protect LEAs dealing with sharply falling rolls).[8]

Following a consultation on this funding arrangement, a statement to Parliament announced in June 2007 that the DSG 'spend plus' model would be retained until 2010–11. It also initiated a further review with the aim of developing a single formula to determine the distribution of the DSG from 2011–12 (see Department for Children, Schools and Families [DCSF] 2007).

Of course, the 'spend plus' funding model ties future allocations to the 2005–6 distribution rather than to, for example, any independent measures of need that may change over time. Similarly, a guaranteed school level funding increase each year reduces the opportunity to make changes to the historical pattern of expenditure including, for example, the balance between spending on primary and secondary schools. While local school forums do have the power to change to the level of the MFG, the current funding climate certainly emphasises stability of funding and severely limits the scope for allocating core resources in line with either measures of need or other policy priorities.

Thus we have seen that the last ten years have seen major changes in England's school funding system in which the balance of control between central and local government has ebbed and flowed, as has the importance of historical patterns of spending and also the degree of stability in school funding. The change from the ESSA system to the EFSS was intended to allocate funds on the basis of accurate measures of need and also to give schools greater budgetary stability and independence by incorporating funds for initiatives (previously supported through the Standards Fund) into the core allocation mechanism. Ironically, the reform introduced short-term instability in school budgets with the result that further reforms, to increase stability, reduced the autonomy of local authorities and tied funding to past expenditure levels rather than need.

VARIATIONS IN PRIMARY SCHOOL BUDGETS BETWEEN LOCAL AUTHORITIES AND BETWEEN SCHOOLS

Local authority and school-level budgets have been published in a consistent manner since 2000–2001 and the DCSF also now publishes budget allocations per pupil and the ratio of per pupil funding between primary and secondary pupils in the Individual Schools Budget (ISB) (see DfES 2007).

Interestingly, summary figures for the whole of England are produced for the total ISB for all maintained schools in England divided by the number of pupils in each Key Stage and for each year since 2000–2001. These indicate that there has been a *convergence* in the ISB per pupil between Key Stage 2 (ages 7 to 11) and Key Stage 3 (11 to 14), and also Key Stage 2 and Key Stage 4 (14 to 16), even for the years during which we saw a *divergence* in reported school-based expenditure between primary and secondary schools (shown in Figure 27.1). It should be noted that Figure 27.1 relates to all school-based expenditure (including, for example, funding from grants such as the Standards Fund) whereas Table 27.2 relates only to the ISB. We also see in Table 27.2 that relative to other Key Stages, ISB funding per pupil was consistently the lowest for Key Stage 2 pupils from 2000–2001 onwards.

Local authority level figures are also published, for 2005–6 and 2006–7, showing the ratio in the primary ISB per pupil to the secondary ISB per pupil (although, in contrast to Table 27.2, the ratio is expressed as primary / secondary). Tables 27.3 and 27.4 show, for 2006–7, the 15 local authorities with the highest level of primary ISB per pupil relative to the secondary ISB per pupil and the 15 local authorities with the lowest primary school allocations compared with local secondary schools. What is immediately apparent is the great variation in this ratio. In Table 27.3 we see that in Northumberland the primary ISB per pupil is 94 per cent of the size of the secondary ISB per pupil. In contrast, as Table 27.4 shows, in Middlesbrough the primary ISB per pupil is only 66 per cent the size of the secondary equivalent.

A high level of expenditure on primary relative to secondary education is associated with the presence of middle schools[9] in an LEA,[10] and also with the proportion of primary schools with very few pupils. It is nevertheless interesting to note the variety of LEA areas appearing in Tables 27.3 and 27.4. It is also noteworthy that six of the 'top 15' local authorities showing relatively high primary school expenditure are in London. Three of the 15 local authorities with the lowest level of ISB per pupil in primary schools (relative to secondary schools) are also located in London.

Table 27.2 Ratio of per pupil funding between primary and secondary pupils in ISB by Key Stage

	Key Stage 1	Key Stage 2	Key Stage 3	Key Stage 4
ISB Funding 00–01	1.02	1.00	1.27	1.49
ISB Funding 02–03	1.02	1.00	1.23	1.42
ISB Funding 03–04	1.03	1.00	1.17	1.35
ISB Funding 04–05	1.02	1.00	1.17	1.35
ISB Funding 05–06	1.02	1.00	1.18	1.37
ISB Funding 06–07	1.02	1.00	1.18	1.36

(Source: DfES 2007 – Section 52 Benchmarking archive.)

Table 27.3 Local authorities with the highest levels of spending on primary schools relative to secondary schools (2006–07)

Fifteen LAs with highest level of spending	Primary school expenditure per pupil as a percentage of secondary expenditure per pupil
Northumberland*	94
Suffolk*	90
Merton	90
Westminster	90
Isle of Wight*	90
Lambeth	90
Camden	89
Solihull	88
Rutland	87
Southwark	87
Bedfordshire*	86
Somerset*	85
Wakefield	84
Wandsworth	84
Kirklees*	84

*Local authority includes some middle schools.
(Source: DfES 2007 – Section 52 Benchmarking archive Additional information table.)

Table 27.4 Local authorities with the lowest levels of spending on primary schools relative to secondary schools (2006–07)

Fifteen LAs with lowest level of spending	Primary school expenditure per pupil as a percentage of secondary expenditure per pupil
Middlesbrough	66
Slough	67
Barking and Dagenham	69
Greenwich	70
Wirral	71
City of Bristol	71
Doncaster	72
Rotherham	72
Poole*	73
Reading	73
North Tyneside*	73
Lincolnshire	73
Torbay	73
Brent	73
Telford and Wrekin	74

*Local authority includes some middle schools.
(Source: DfES 2007 – Section 52 Benchmarking archive additional information table.)

There is also considerable variation between individual primary schools in the school budget share (that is, the school's share of the ISB) per pupil. As we see in Figure 27.2, there are a few schools in upper tier authorities (shire counties) with a very substantial budget share per pupil and these tend to be extremely small primary schools in sparsely populated areas. However, the median level of the budget share per pupil in upper tier authorities (shire counties) is lower than for the other types of authority, with schools located in London boroughs tending to have the largest budget shares per pupil. This is largely a function of the differing proportions of pupils with additional educational needs (as measured by the government funding formula) and area differences in costs (also reflected in the formula).

LEVELS OF FUNDING AND FUNDING RATIOS FOR PRIMARY SCHOOLING IN OECD COUNTRIES

The Organisation for Economic Cooperation and Development (OECD) produces comparative figures relating to the funding of primary education. Figure 27.3 shows the level of funding per pupil in different countries (data underlying the Figure are shown in Table 27.6, Appendix). As the same level of expenditure will purchase different quantities of educational resources in different countries, the comparison is expressed

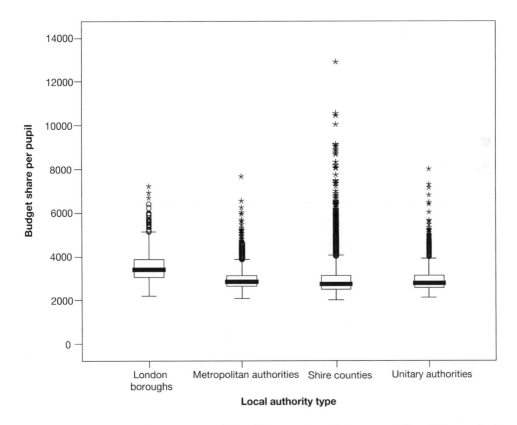

(Lines represent median school, boxes represent 25th and 75th percentiles, whiskers represent 5th and 95th percentiles)

Figure 27.2 Boxplot of primary school budget shares per pupil by local authority type. The box-plot does not include data for 'middle deemed primary' schools.

in US dollars in terms of purchasing power parity (PPP). With currencies converted in this way, $100 would then purchase the same basket of goods in each of the countries listed. We see that primary education is extremely well-funded in Luxembourg and that the level of funding in the United Kingdom is ranked in the middle of the OECD nations – 12th out of the 29 countries shown.

It may be that expenditure expressed in terms of PPP primarily reflects the relative wealth of nations rather than their particular commitment to primary education. Indeed, we see in Figure 27.3 that the lowest levels of funding are found among the least wealthy of the OECD countries. Figure 27.4 therefore shows countries' expenditure *relative to their GDP* (the data underlying the Figure are shown in Table 27.6, Appendix). In this array, the United Kingdom appears 18th out of the 29 countries shown. Italy and Portugal show the highest levels of expenditure in primary schools relative to their GDP. Interestingly, while some of the least wealthy countries again feature among the lower spending countries, the bottom quarter of countries also includes Ireland, Germany and France.

Figure 27.5 shows the relative level of expenditure on primary education per pupil expressed as a percentage of expenditure per pupil in secondary education (the data underlying the Figure are shown in Table 27.6, Appendix). Interestingly there is a wide variation in this ratio, showing a similar range to that which was noted earlier among English local authorities. In this array, the United Kingdom ranks in 14th place out of the 29 countries shown. In the national comparison, we see that in Iceland expenditure per pupil in primary education is reported to be higher than spending per pupil in secondary education. At the other end of the ranking, spending per pupil in primary education in the Czech Republic and France stands at less than 60 per cent of the level of spending per pupil in secondary education.

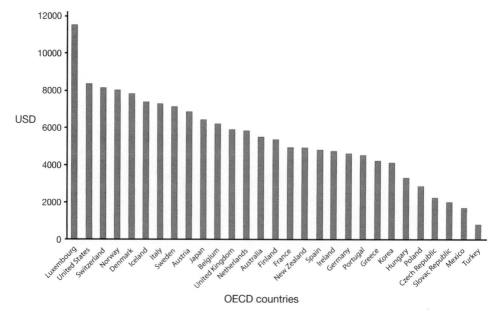

Figure 27.3 Annual expenditure on primary educational institutions per student (2003) (in equivalent US dollars converted using PPPs for GDP, based on full-time equivalents). (Source: OECD 2006 – Table B1.1a.)

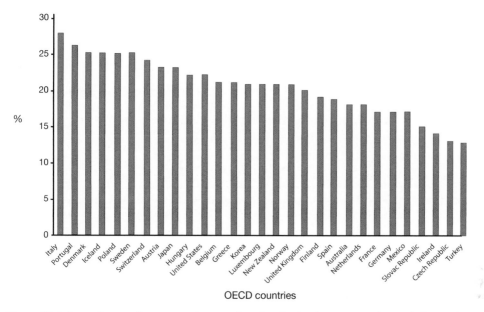

Figure 27.4 Annual expenditure on primary education institutions per student relative to GDP per capita (2003). (Source: OECD 2006)

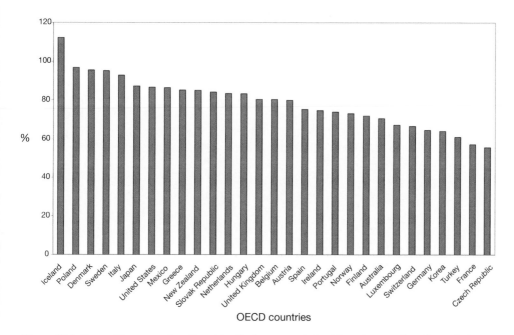

Figure 27.5 Expenditure on educational institutions per student in primary education relative to secondary education (2003). (Source: OECD 2006.)

It is interesting to note that of the four countries with the highest expenditure on primary education relative to secondary education, three are Nordic countries. All three have combined schools providing primary and lower secondary education. *Grunnskólar* in Iceland cater for pupils from 6 to 16 years of age, *folkeskole* in Denmark for those between 7 and 16/17 and *grundskola* in Sweden for those aged 6/7 to 15/16. However, there are also differences between these countries relating to the use of specialist teachers and the size of classes, each of which could be associated with greater levels of expenditure and account for some of the variation.[11]

CONCLUSIONS

School-based expenditure per primary school pupil has risen substantially in recent years. However, after a previous slow convergence with spending at secondary level, since 2002–3 the gap in spending per pupil has grown between primary schools and England's more generously funded secondary schools. Conventional forms of primary and secondary school organisation reflect this historical difference in funding. However it is not self-evident that there should be such a difference in funding levels – especially because later attainment is highly dependent on earlier attainment.

The funding arrangements underlying this expenditure are complicated and depend on decisions taken by central government and local government, and also on several funding streams. The current funding mechanism, the Dedicated Schools Grant, is largely driven by historical patterns of spending, and with its introduction, control over spending on schools became more centralised than ever. These changes were the consequence of a previous funding reform, the short-lived Education Formula Spending Share, which unintentionally created instability in school budgets. Ironically, the EFSS reform had been intended to introduce greater predictability in funding levels and a closer fit with levels of need rather than previous patterns of spending.

We have also seen that there is substantial variation between LEAs in the ratio of spending per primary pupil and spending per secondary pupil with spending per primary pupil at 66 per cent to 94 per cent of the level of expenditure per secondary school pupil.

Overall, however, the United Kingdom is a mid-ranking country among OECD countries in terms of the level of expenditure on primary schools, in the proportion of GDP spent on primary schools and also in the level of spending on pupils in primary education relative to secondary education.

APPENDIX

Table 27.5 School-based expenditure[i,ii,iii] per pupil[iv] in real terms[v] in England since 1992–93[vi]

Year	Local Authority maintained pre-primary and primary schools[vii]	Local Authority maintained primary schools[viii]	Local Authority maintained secondary schools	Local Authority maintained pre-primary, primary and secondary schools	Local Authority maintained primary and secondary schools
1992–93	2,150	..	3,110	2,540	..
1993–94	2,170	..	3,010	2,490	..
1994–95	2,200	..	3,010	2,500	..
1995–96	2,180	..	2,950	2,460	..
1996–97	2,160	..	2,910	2,440	..
1997–98[ix]	2,100	..	2,850	2,380	..
1998–99[ix]	2,200	..	2,880	2,460	..
1999–00[ii,x]	2,370	2,320	3,010	2,640	2,610
2000–01	2,590	2,520	3,220	2,860	2,820
2001–02	2,850	2,760	3,510	3,140	3,080
2002–03[ii,iii]	..	2,730	3,480	..	3,060
2003–04	..	2,880	3,710	..	3,250
2004–05	..	2,970	3,870	..	3,370

Notes:

i. School-based expenditure includes only expenditure incurred directly by schools. This includes the pay of teachers and school-based support staff, school premises costs, books and equipment, and certain other supplies and services, less any capital items funded from recurrent spending and income from sales, fees and charges and rents and rates. This excludes the central cost of support services such as home to school transport, local authority administration and the financing of capital expenditure.

ii. 1999–00 saw a change in data source when the data collection moved from the RO1 form collected by the ODPM to the Section 52 form from the DfES. 2002–03 saw a further break in the time series following the introduction of Consistent Financial Reporting (CFR) to schools and the associated restructuring of the outturn tables. The change in sources is shown by the dotted line. Comparable figures are not available prior to 1992–93.

iii. The calculation for 2002–03 onwards is broadly similar to the calculation in previous years. However, 2001–02 and earlier years includes all premature retirement compensation (PRC) and Crombie payments, mandatory PRC payments and other indirect employee expenses. In 2001–02 this accounted for approximately £70 per pupil. From 2002–03 onwards only the schools element of these categories is included and this accounted for approximately £50 per pupil of the 2002–03 total. Also, for some LAs, expenditure that had previously been attributed to the school sectors was reported within the LA part of the form from 2002–03, though this is not quantifiable from existing sources.

iv. Pupil numbers include only those pupils attending maintained establishments within each sector and are drawn from the DfES Annual Schools Census adjusted to be on a financial year basis.

v. Cash terms figures are converted to 2005–06 prices using September 2006 gross domestic product deflators.

vi. Figures are as reported by local authorities as at 18th October 2006 and are rounded to the nearest £10.

vii. School-based expenditure in nursery schools was not recorded in 2002–03 and comparable figures for nursery expenditure are not available from 2003–04 onwards.

viii. Expenditure was not distinguished between the pre-primary and primary sectors until the inception of Section 52 for financial year 1999–00.

ix. Spending in 1997–98 reflects the transfer of monies from local government to central government for the nursery vouchers scheme. These were returned to local government from 1998–99.

x. The 1999–00 figures reflect the return of GM schools to local authority maintenance.

(Source: DfES 2006 – data last updated by DfES on 18 October 2006.)

Table 27.6 Equivalent expenditure on primary educational institutions, expenditure relative to GDP and relative to expenditure on secondary education

	Annual expenditure on educational institutions per student (2003)[i]	Annual expenditure on primary education institutions per student relative to GDP per capita (2003)[ii]	Expenditure on educational institutions per student in primary education relative to secondary education (2003)
Australia	5494	18	70.5
Austria	7139	23	79.8
Belgium	6180	21	80.2
Czech Republic	2273	13	55.6
Denmark	7814	25	95.5
Finland	5321	19	71.9
France	4939	17	57.1
Germany	4624	17	64.5
Greece	4218	21	85.1
Hungary[iii]	3286	22	83.2
Iceland	7752	25	112.4
Ireland	4760	14	74.7
Italy[iii]	7366	28	92.8
Japan	6350	23	87.2
Korea	4098	21	63.9
Luxembourg	11481	21	67.2
Mexico	1656	17	86.3
Netherlands	5836	18	83.4
New Zealand	4841	21	85.0
Norway	7977	21	73.1
Poland[iii]	2859	25	96.9
Portugal[iii]	4503	26	73.9
Slovak Republic	2020	15	84.1
Spain	4829	19	75.2
Sweden	7291	25	95.2
Switzerland[iii]	8131	24	66.6
Turkey[iii]	869	13	60.9
United Kingdom	5851	20	80.3
United States	8305	22	86.6

Notes:

i. This is expressed in equivalent US dollars converted using PPPs for GDP, based on full-time equivalent pupils.

ii. This represents the expenditure figure per pupil as shown in the first data column, expressed as a percentage of the country's GDP per capita, in equivalent US dollars using PPPs. (Figures for GDP per capita are shown in OECD 2006, Appendix 1, 2, Table X2.1.)

iii. Public institutions only.

(Source: OECD 2006.)

NOTES

1 The term 'local education authority continues to be used by the Government in relation to the financing of school-based education, although the Education and Inspections Act 2006 includes a clause that allows for the renaming of LEAs as local authorities (LAs).

2 Within the schools block there were four main 'sub-blocks' covering children under 5 years of age; primary; secondary; and high-cost pupils (this block was intended to cover the costs of pupils who are high cost, in particular, those with special educational needs). Within the local authority block there were two sub-blocks: one for youth and community provision and one for local education authority central functions (DfES 2003).

3 As with the Education SSA there were other adjustments for areas where it costs more to recruit and retain staff (area cost adjustment) and, in the case of the primary school sub-block, for sparsity (DfES 2003).

4 These figures do not include capital allocations within the Standards Fund (which rose by more than 1600 per cent from 1998–99 to 2004–5).

5 The DSG in effect replaced the SFSS element of the EFSS system. That is to say, expenditure on LEA functions (strategic management, SEN provision, school improvement and access) continued to be funded through the local government settlement rather than the DSG. This was also the case for non-school expenditure on the youth service. Expenditure on schools and pupils covered by the DSG could nevertheless (with the consent of the local schools forum) be held centrally in order to cover specified activities which included providing for pupils with SEN, providing Pupil Referral Units and library services for primary and special schools.

6 This funding was introduced to support schools with disadvantaged intakes located in affluent LEAs because central government's deprivation funding review (DfES/HM Treasury 2005) had previously concluded that the element of central government funding to local authorities that was driven by measures of deprivation was not in turn being allocated to schools entirely on the basis of measures of deprivation.

7 Personalisation is described by the DfES as 'the key to tackling the persistent achievement gaps between different social and ethnic groups. It means a tailored education for every child and young person, that gives them strength in the basics, stretches their aspirations, and builds their life chances. It will create opportunity for every child, regardless of their background' (DfES 2005c: 50).

8 While the allocation mechanism is relatively simple, the process through which the base level of spending is identified is less so.

9 Middle schools cover varying age ranges from 8 to 14. Depending on their age range they are deemed either primary or secondary.

10 Some of these LEAs have large numbers of middle schools (Isle of Wight, Northumberland and Bedfordshire) while others have relatively few (for example Kirklees, Somerset and North Tyneside). The presence of 'middle deemed secondary' schools (age range 9 to 13) means that expenditure for the second half of Key Stage 2 (which is relatively poorly funded as shown in Table 27.2) would take place in secondary schools, so shifting the ratio of expenditure in favour of primary schools.

11 In Iceland, classes at primary level generally have one teacher for all subjects, whilst in lower secondary education pupils generally have separate subject teachers; class sizes are not prescribed. In Denmark, on the other hand, there are separate teachers for each subject throughout the folkeskole, and the number of pupils in each class must not exceed 28 – the average number of pupils per class in 2005/06 was 19.6. In Sweden, in the first three years pupils are generally taught by the class teacher (except in some cases for music, physical education and health); in classes 4 to 5 there are, in addition, specialist teachers for languages, mathematics, art and craft; from classes 6 to 7 all teachers are specialised to teach two or three subjects; class size is not centrally regulated but determined by the municipality and the school (Eurydice 2007).

REFERENCES

Alexander, R.J., Rose, J. and Woodhead, C. (1992) *Curriculum Organisation and Classroom Practice in Primary Schools: a discussion paper.* London: DES.

Audit Commission (2004) *Education Funding: the impact and effectiveness of measures to stabilise school funding.* London: Audit Commission.

Department for Children, Schools and Families (DCSF) (2007) *School Funding Settlement 2008–11*, Press Release 12 November. London: DCSF.

Department for Education and Skills (DfES) (2003) *Technical Note on the New Education Funding System.* London: DfES.

DfES (2005a) *Education and Training Expenditure Since 1995–96.* London: DfES.

——(2005b) *Dedicated School Grant 2006–07 and 2007–08: overview.* London: DfES.

——(2005c) *Higher Standards, Better Schools for All*, Cm 6677. London: The Stationery Office (TSO).

——(2006) *School Based Expenditure Per Pupil in Real Terms Since 1992–93 in England.* London: DfES.

——(2007) *Section 52 website.* Online (Available: http://www.dfes.gov.uk/localauthorities/section52).

DfES/HM Treasury (2005) *Child Poverty: fair funding for schools.* London: DfES/Treasury

Department of the Environment (1990) *Standard Spending Assessments: background and underlying methodology.* London: Department of the Environment

Education Funding Strategy Group (2001) *Per Pupil Funding – derivation and presentation, EFSG-9.* London: DfES.

Eurydice (2007) *Country Reports: Denmark, Iceland, Sweden.* Brussels: Eurydice.

House of Commons Education Committee (1994) *The Disparity in Funding Between Primary and Secondary Schools, Second Report of the House of Commons Education Committee Session 1993–94.* London: HMSO.

House of Commons Hansard (2003) *Statement made to the House of Commons by Secretary of State for Education and Skills*, Charles Clarke, 17 July 2003.

Labour Party (2005) *The Labour Party Manifesto 2005.* London: The Labour Party.

Levačić, R. (2005) *Decentralizing and Centralizing: the tensions between school autonomy and central government education policy initiatives in England 1988–2004.* Conference paper presented to the World Bank Conference, Washington DC, 13–14 January.

Office of the Deputy Prime Minister (2005) *Balance of Funding Review Report.* London: ODPM.

Organisation for Economic Cooperation and Development (2006) *Education at a Glance.* Paris: OECD.

West, A. (2009) 'Redistribution and financing schools in England under Labour: are resources going where needs are greatest?', *Educational Management, Administration and Leadership*, 37(2): 158–79.

West, A., Pennell, H. and West, R. (2000) 'New Labour and school-based education in England: changing the system of funding?', *British Educational Research Journal* 26(4): 523–36.

West, A., Pennell, H., West, R. and Travers, T. (2000) 'Financing school-based education in England: principles and problems', in M. Coleman and L. Anderson (Eds) *Managing Finance and Resources in Education.* London: Paul Chapman.

West, A., West, R. and Pennell, H. (1995) 'The financing of school-based education: changing the Additional Educational Needs Allowance', *Education Economics* 3(3): 265–75.

28 Quality assurance in English primary education

Peter Cunningham and Philip Raymont

INTRODUCTION

This chapter begins with a brief introduction highlighting two key recent works selected for their understanding of historical and comparative dimensions in the evolution of quality assurance. It goes on to outline the range of methodological approaches from critical analysis and empirical research at the national level, to smaller scale qualitative case studies of the impact of inspection locally, and on to international comparative studies. Following consideration of the cultural and political contexts of inspection, a representative selection of studies is then reviewed under headings defined by research focus and methodology: national policy and theoretical critique; empirical studies of national practice; case studies of local experience with particular regard to teachers; teachers, curriculum and emergent self-evaluation; and comparative international studies. Key findings and insights from the research are synthesised, implications for current policy and practice are considered, and suggestions for further research are made.

RESEARCH THEMES

Monitoring, assuring and maintaining quality in primary education are processes that are historically embedded in more than one respect. Firstly, there is an inherent chronological dimension in 'maintaining' or 'improving' standards, where current or past conditions are adopted as a benchmark, and secondly, the procedures for monitoring and assurance are cultural practices constantly subject to change over time. The evaluative overview of research below will be set in the context of a brief historical account of debate on policy and structure as it evolved up to and beyond the creation of Ofsted, and necessarily referring to political and media debates in order to highlight the contentiousness of the topic. The link between quality assurance and questions of standards also addressed in the Primary Review's Theme 4 (Chapters 17, 18 and 28) may appear self-evident, but a key issue for debate remains how far monitoring is on the one hand driven by concerns about national and international standards, or on the other hand provides the necessary credible data for charting progress and making international comparisons.

Two key works that emerge in the following chapter are characterised by an acute awareness of the historical dimensions. Learmonth's (2000) outstanding overview of inspection offers a perceptive and sensitive overview drawing on historical data that ranges from political angst to personal anguish. Through historical example we can graphically illustrate and begin to comprehend the high stakes entailed at national and local levels, and the interdependence on broad principle and detailed practice. Contrasting approaches in research of quality assurance are characterised both by philosophical and by technical perspectives and Learmonth provides a concise and accessible synthesis of both. MacBeath (2006) achieves a similar breadth of analysis, and like Learmonth, encompasses both historical and comparative international perspectives. As a leading researcher and critical developer of strategies for school improvement MacBeath has promoted self-evaluation in collaboration with the NUT through a succession of research projects. He has also networked internationally and the outcomes of these exchanges inform the arguments he brings to bear on the UK.

The present survey begins with a review of historical research, establishing the narratives that underlie and explain current theory and practice. Regarding the last two decades, the chapter provides a broad overview of published research, organised in distinct but overlapping themes: English national policies and practices; experiences at school level with regard to teachers, curriculum and the trend towards self-evaluation; international and comparative research. Whilst this chapter cannot be comprehensive it offers a detailed account of selected pieces of research in order to provide a representative picture of the kinds of enquiry that inform the continuing evolution of quality assurance in primary schools.

RESEARCH QUESTIONS AND METHODOLOGICAL TRENDS

National education policies in general from the mid-1970s onwards, and the creation of Ofsted in 1992 in particular, triggered a great deal of research into monitoring and school improvement. The macro level of government policy provoked theoretical critiques of the political and power relations embodied in systems of inspection and control, informed both by the immediate political contentiousness of the reforms and by trends in sociological and philosophical thought during the last quarter century. Historians have adopted longer time-scales in seeking to understand change in national school inspection since its origins, and especially over the last fifty years.

Concern for standards at the international level had been marked by large scale quantitative surveys, but despite the increasing quantity of available data for children's and schools' achievements, there has been less research associating these trends specifically with changing methods of quality assurance, where the variables may be too diverse to allow of convincing correlation. Notwithstanding, Ofsted has sought to evaluate and validate its own inspection procedures, and to demonstrate the effectiveness of inspection in securing school improvement. A lot of inspection data is freely accessible to independent researchers and some have also gained access to less public documentation and to key officials for interview in exploring the development and application of policies and practices.

Far more research on quality assurance and its impact is available at the meso and micro levels of Local Authority, schools, and classrooms, where qualitative rather than quantitative methods predominate. Most independent researchers appear motivated by their closer association with schools and with teachers than with national policy and administration, and many studies have focused on the impact of monitoring and evaluation on the quality of life in primary schools. Here the data is generated through questionnaire, interview and ethnographic methods, sometimes longitudinal over the period before, during and following inspection (or following failure and re-inspection). One perennial challenge for the researcher in these contexts is that of balancing critical distance with empathetic understanding; another is the problem of generalising from case studies. Where such empirical research investigates the effects of inspection on curriculum and teaching methods, researchers have also drawn on documentary evidence by analysing national frameworks and official guidance, as well as the texts of inspectors' reports. Documentary analysis may facilitate examination of the quality and consistency of prescriptive documents and feedback, and evaluation of the scope for implementing recommendations.

International comparison has been prominent in the discourse over standards that led to greater emphasis on quality control, so it is unsurprising that independent research on monitoring and evaluation has also been heavily influenced from overseas. International research offers an overview of global developments (as well as of educational provision that may transcend national boundaries), comparative analysis of two or more countries' policies or practices has also provided some insights, as have trans-national studies of the transfer of practices or 'policy borrowing'. Comparative research has been especially influential in the introduction of school self-evaluation as a model of quality assurance.

SELECTION OF LITERATURE

Our chapter is based on a search of relevant literature in available databases of educational research. The selection referred to below is representative of articles appearing in the principal educational research journals, and of book-length studies. Unpublished papers have not been included, nor has a category of literature comprising books of advice on inspection for teachers, from which a good deal of inference might be drawn but which do not in themselves constitute first-hand research of a formal kind. A further exclusion, with just one or two exceptions, is the considerable volume of published discussion by parliamentary committees, and responses from Ofsted; a lengthier review might have included more of this material as constituting a genre of 'research' that contrasts interestingly with the academic mode. A good deal of press comment that would not count as research has been excluded but one non-academic item referred to is a Channel 4 TV documentary, as a token reminder of the power of the media in popular dissemination of research. The selection is designed to be representative of four groups identified in terms of focus and research methodology, and may not therefore be either statistically representative of the whole field nor indicative of the level of influence that such studies have had.

QUALITY ASSURANCE AND RESEARCH, CULTURAL AND POLITICAL CONTEXTS

An excellent starting point for historical and philosophical consideration of quality assurance in schooling is provided by Silver (1994). He observed how defining a good school over the centuries and in different countries and localities, had been a question not only of the way a school operated but of the way its aims had been established, by whom, and with what intentions. The variety of purposes that schooling has had meant that judgements have been made from a range of competing viewpoints.

In the first half of the twentieth century, expert opinion began to play an influential role, and two features are significant: firstly, the expert and research community was by no means homogeneous, and over time pre-eminence was accorded variously to educational psychologists, sociologists, evaluators or curriculum developers amongst other specialists; secondly was the increasingly international nature of educational development and debate. Scientific approaches to evaluation of school performance are identified by Silver as emerging in the 1960s with the educational 'war against poverty' in Britain and the USA, but policy concerns distracted from the internal processes of schools, so that in Britain the focus was on school systems and access to secondary schooling, rather than on the specifics of curricula and teaching methods. School effectiveness research of the 1970s and 1980s however shifted attention away from social equity and concentrated on the correlation of detailed internal features.

Characteristic of the twentieth century also were changing systems of school organisation and control, in the role of state and public agencies and increasing opportunities for expression of public and media opinion.

Origins and tensions

Research on the origins and development of school inspection in Britain has been synthesised in a number of book-length studies (Lawton and Gordon 1987; Dunford 1998; Maclure 2000). Her Majesty's Inspectorate was conceived in 1839 for accountability, to monitor value for money as the state began to subsidise school buildings and teachers' salaries. A small number of men drawn from the upper echelons of society and with little personal experience of working class education were appointed to this role. As the century drew to a close and the elementary school system expanded, their growing numbers were reinforced by assistant inspectors drawn from elementary school teaching, and women who specialised in the housecraft curriculum for girls and in the education of infants. During the twentieth century Her Majesty's Inspectorate provided a career route for some outstanding elementary teachers, and following the 1944 Education Act with its creation of a universal primary sector, many HMIs had specialist expertise in that sector, as well as curriculum subject specialisms. Their work was increasingly supplemented by local education authorities' own inspectorates, and though the structure, organisation (and status) of national and local inspectorates were quite distinct, both bodies undertook increasingly a supportive role of curriculum and professional development with schools and teachers. HMI's principal function continued to be national reporting for the benefit of policy-makers; organised in geographical regions, they would individually make many short visits to individual schools according to need, and, working in teams, would undertake a very small number of 'full inspections' of schools each year as a basis for the annual reports compiled by the Senior Chief Inspector.

Though educationists have cited in positive terms the purpose of school improvement as uppermost in Sir James Kay-Shuttleworth's original instructions to inspectors, the notorious 'Revised Code' of 1862 instituted a system of testing children and 'payment by results' to ensure that schooling would be cost effective. Idealists such as HMIs Matthew Arnold (1822–88) and Edmond Holmes (1850–1936) vocally resisted utilitarian curriculum and mechanical teaching methods, however, and as centralised curriculum control was loosened HMI transformed its function to curriculum innovation and fostering professional development. Local Education Authorities, established in 1902, also began to provide forms of local inspection that through the middle decades of the century focused increasingly on providing curriculum support and in-service training for elementary and primary teachers (Cunningham 2002).

Lawton and Gordon (1987) have revealed how antagonism between elementary (later primary) teachers and HMI has been quite complex and ambiguous. The official

Suggestions of 1905 left a great deal of judgement and initiative to the teacher, yet teachers were often criticised by progressive inspectors for their 'cast-iron' methods and dull routines. Over the first half of the twentieth century however, HMI gradually built a more constructive relationship with the LEAs, schools and teachers (Dunford 1998). A developmental and supportive aspect of the inspector's role was implicitly endorsed by Plowden (1967) but at the same time HMI enhanced their research role. For the Plowden Committee HMI made a comprehensive survey of the 20,664 primary schools of England, for which they had, however, no objective measures of quality such as achievement in literacy and numeracy, but rather rated them subjectively (and often on flimsy evidence) in nine categories, the ninth (bad schools) comprising 0.1 per cent of the total, while a sixth were not very good, a half were more or less average, and about a third were pretty good (Maclure 2000).

In terms of inspection, or the monitoring of quality, practice by the middle years of the twentieth century had changed from the annual inspection and assessment made by Victorian inspectors, to occasional and often small-scale inspections for particular purposes of information gathering. Full inspections were relatively few – an inspection of every school in England and Wales was achieved between 1944 and 1960 (Dunford 1998). These inspections provided the data for advice to policy-makers and administrators, which constituted an important part of the HMI role. From 1988 onwards the Senior Chief Inspector was required to produce an annual report on teaching and learning which became a much publicised exposé of problems faced by the educational system, and this annual publication continued under the Ofsted regime to attract considerable attention as a platform for criticism of policies and practice.

Quality and policy

Maclure's detailed research of HMI in their contribution to educational policy-making from 1945 has drawn on swathes of documentary evidence, published and unpublished, formal and informal, as well as personal testimony of many key figures. HMI became closely involved in formulating policies in the aftermath of Labour Prime Minister Jim Callaghan's famous speech at Ruskin College (18th October 1976). They were increasingly deployed as an information-gathering service, their reports and surveys used to legitimize central intervention. This function was epitomised in the survey *Primary Education in England* (DES 1978) although it had been planned as a follow up to Plowden before the events of 1977. It broke new ground by combining the outcome of an HMI inspection programme (using a carefully constructed sample of schools) with a parallel testing programme devised by the National Foundation for Educational Research using standardised tests. Maclure noted that the decision to bring in the NFER was recognition of the growing need to provide quantitative evidence as well as the assessments of HMI; in the event the joint design was successful in presenting a complementary database from which to assemble a balanced assessment (Maclure 2000). By this time, the development of a three-tier system of compulsory schooling had been adopted by a significant number of LEAs, so the primary school survey was followed by others relating to First Schools (age ranges 5–8 and 5–9) in 1982, 9–13 Middle Schools in 1983, and 8–12 combined and Middle Schools in 1985. These surveys, and their earlier work for Plowden, are of particular importance in marking the confluence of routine inspection and methodical research in the work of the national inspection body. Targeted, thematic research constitutes at this point in its history an emergent mode of official engagement with quality and standards that is reflected in various discussions below.

Quality assurance in primary schools required attention to the quality of teacher training and this aspect received close attention from the mid-1980s. A Council for the Accreditation of Teacher Education established in 1984 was to assess individual providers' fitness for the task according to set criteria, the evidence provided by HMI inspections of institutions (Dunford 1998). Its successor in 1993, the Teacher Training Agency (later the Training and Development Agency), had responsibility for funding the courses and inspection became ever more detailed; sets of competencies or 'Standards' to be demonstrated by qualified teachers were determined, reflecting curricular priorities such as literacy and numeracy, and institutions continue to be judged according to both the trainees' demonstration of these Standards and also the accuracy of trainers' own assessments.

A key policy theme from 1991 became the 'Citizen's Charter' and subsequent 'Parent's Charter'; inspection was henceforth to act on behalf of the consumer, as a 'regulator' of standards and quality, so that HMI would have to accept new responsibilities towards parents and the Secretary of State, and rethink their relationship with schools. This aspect of public accountability through inspection had been pre-figured by the radical innovation of Secretary of State Keith Joseph who in 1982 had decreed an end to the traditional closely guarded confidentiality of school inspection reports (Dunford 1998). From 1983 reports were to be published (foreshadowing the later policy of New Labour's Secretary of State, David Blunkett in 1997, of 'naming and shaming' so-called 'failing schools'). These policy trends led to the Education Act of 1992 which had 15 of its 17 substantive clauses devoted to inspection. Its radical reconstruction of the mechanism and manner of school inspection created the Office of HMCI of Schools in England, whose task was to commission independent teams of inspectors, operating in a commercial market, to inspect all schools on a four yearly cycle. 'Ofsted' was the name and acronym coined by Professor Stewart Sutherland as first incumbent of the post.

Inspection and controversy

1992 also saw publication by the DES of a discussion paper that generated a highly polemical debate on primary curriculum (Alexander *et al.* 1992; Alexander 1997). In seeking to review available evidence and make recommendations for implementation of the National Curriculum at Key Stage 2, the paper drew on data accumulated from HMI inspections and shifted the debate on primary schooling from 'content' which had preoccupied discussion around the introduction of the National Curriculum, to 'method' as the critical issue of concern. It was followed one year later by a 'progress report' from Ofsted on the basis of inspections conducted in the intervening months and highlighting 'benefits' arising from the NC together with 'serious weaknesses' arising from a mismatch between the curriculum and its assessment, on the one hand, and the capabilities of primary schools and teachers on the other (Ofsted 1993). A further survey by inspectors of curriculum organisation and classroom practice in 49 schools identified specific factors underlying high achievement (Ofsted 1994); this was followed by a series of eight national conferences, the proceedings of which were published (Ofsted 1995a).

One of the 1992 discussion paper's co-authors, Chris Woodhead, was subsequently appointed in 1994 to lead Ofsted, where he initiated a controversial and campaigning role, especially aimed at attacking 'progressive' methods and exposing 'incompetent' teachers. In 1995 a revised *Framework for the Inspection of Schools* was issued, including guidance on the inspection of nursery and primary schools. From 1996 teachers were graded on their performance, and parental opinion became a significant source of data for school inspection. Considerable opposition was generated both from professionals and from educational researchers concerning the unreliability of Ofsted inspection methods and data and the uses to which it was put. By 1998 all primary schools had been inspected at least once under the new regime and 3000 inspection reports per year were published, creating an unprecedented database. The experience also generated a great deal of independent research into the process of inspection and school improvement generally.

An independent group, entitled the Office for Standards in Inspection (Ofstin), reviewed the practices of Ofsted (Duffy 1997). Here Carol Fitz-Gibbon argued that Ofsted's inspection methodology did not meet research standards, and that Ofsted had been allowed to operate without adequate validation, with potential to mislead and distress parents, pupils and teachers, and with apparent faith placed in its findings by politicians (Fitz-Gibbon 1997). Two major purposes of inspection, school improvement and accountability, were found to be confused but also further confused by two other purposes: maintenance of minimum standards of quality, and collection of standardised national data on school performance. The complexity of the inspection process was seen to put primary schools at a particular disadvantage.

In 1997 New Labour, building on earlier initiatives, established a Standards and Effectiveness Unit (SEU) at the DfES to encourage and monitor school improvement, with an ever increasing availability of data, and emphasis on 'value added' measures. Data and inspection evidence provided a foundation for HMCI advice to ministers and for public pronouncements. PICSI data (Pre-Inspection Context and School Indicators) were used in early Ofsted inspections, succeeded by PANDA (Performance and Assessment data) reports issued annually to all schools and Local Authorities. RAISEonline is now the web-based source for disseminating school performance data. This ability to monitor continuously through statistical data led in 1998 to increasing the interval of school inspection from 4 to 6 years. Ofsted also increasingly sought to monitor quality and standards through other means in addition to regular inspection. There were surveys on specific issues such as class size and the teaching of reading (Ofsted 1995b, 1996) and, following the change of government, evaluations of New Labour's National Strategies for literacy and numeracy (Ofsted 2002a, 2002b, 2005). Ofsted also engaged in significant collaboration with academic researchers following Woodhead's departure; one example was a highly structured international study of education for six year olds comparing England with Denmark and Finland (both examples of lightly inspected national systems offering considerable autonomy for teachers) but this kind of research was given less publicity in the policy-making process than international comparative statistics on standards of literacy and numeracy (Ofsted 2003).

Widespread concern with inspections and their place within a continuing programme of politically driven educational change led to a House of Commons Select Committee enquiry, whose report was published in 1999. Having heard a great deal of written and oral evidence, amongst many other conclusions it acknowledged the stress that the current programme placed on teachers and proposed reducing the period for notice of inspection from one year to four weeks; it recommended that inspectors take account of self-evaluation procedures used by the school, and that HMCI 'should be concerned to improve morale and promote confidence in the teaching profession'. Responses from the government and from Ofsted were subsequently published by the committee (House of Commons Education and Employment Committee 1999a, 1999b).

With the accession of David Bell as HMCI in 2003, research was commissioned in collaboration between Ofsted itself and an independent researcher to evaluate the impact of Ofsted's work (Matthews and Sammons 2004). Ofsted's 'New Relationship', following government policy initiatives to improve standards in all schools by giving greater autonomy and responsibility to schools within the context of more intelligent accountability and reduced bureaucracy, was launched in June 2004 followed by a new School Inspection Framework and guidance on self-evaluation in March 2005. Shorter, sharper school inspections began in September, and by October Ofsted had published the first new-style school inspections on its website.

Policy developments since 1992 have generated a great quantity of research into the inspection process in particular, closely related to the exponential growth of school effectiveness and school improvement research. Research projects can be broadly classified by focus and methodology, though clear boundaries are not always easily drawn; the present research review adopts four categories:

- National policy, critical theory;
- National practice, empirical studies;
- Local experience, empirical studies (with particular consideration of teachers, curriculum and self-evaluation);
- International policies and practices, comparative research.

NATIONAL POLICY, CRITICAL THEORY

The broader political role and significance of a national inspection body was subjected to examination by critical theorists. Smith (2000) addressed the developments that took place in respect of the relationship between inspection and research, over two decades as HMI transformed into Ofsted. As education policy had become central and contested, HMI had been increasingly called upon to provide data for policy-makers. Smith examined the similarities and contrasts between inspection and research, and how the two began to converge as HMI drew on research-like methods such as rating scales and other quantitative methods. The increasing attractiveness and sophistication of statistical data on school performance gradually overcame the reservations maintained by traditional HMI. Political pressure groups used statistical data gathered expressly to underpin particular policies, described by Smith as 'forensic research'. These tendencies informed Ofsted's way of working, with the establishment of a Research and Analysis section to handle the mass of data expected from the new inspection regime. Research Reports published by Ofsted that caused contention amongst education researchers included the class size study (Ofsted 1995b) and a report on reading standards in inner London (authoritatively but not uncontroversially criticised by Mortimore and Goldstein 1996), because of the political spin that they were given, leaked to the media, with high profile coverage and generating extensive public debate. In 1998 Ofsted published Tooley's critical assessment of the state of educational research, with a foreword by Woodhead attacking educational researchers (Tooley 1998).

Hartley (2003), like other observers, focused on Ofsted and its inspection methods, which effectively encouraged a pedagogy that conflicted with policies espoused in other areas of government. His critique was set in the context of a globalised economy, with its demand for flexibility and innovative thinking, contrasted with the traditional tea-cher-centred pedagogy prevalent in primary schools, as revealed not only by Galton's follow-up research to ORACLE (1999), but also greeted with approval by Ofsted in its review of English primary schools 1994–98. Hartley identified 'Ofsted-driven, subject-based' teaching as at odds not only with pedagogies advocated in some high-performing Asian economies, but also with directions advocated by other government departments such as that of Culture, Media and Sport, and the Department of Trade and Industry. Policy-makers were caught between pedagogies that might foster global competitiveness on the one hand, and those that are more 'cost-effective' on the other. A bias towards whole-class traditional pedagogy may reduce costs, standardise procedures and raise test scores, but economic benefits would be few in the long run (see also Hartley 2006). Brehony (2005) highlighted the significant role of Ofsted in the development of national strategies for literacy and numeracy, the report on reading in London primary schools as key to the former, and that commissioned from David Reynolds on international standards for the latter (Reynolds and Farrell 1996). Analysing education policy from the stand-point of political theory, Brehony focused specifically on curriculum and teaching in England. He noted that ability grouping was one particular New Labour policy implicitly supported by Ofsted who reported an increase in ability grouping for Maths and English at Key Stage 2 especially in their review of primary education 1994–98. Her Majesty's Chief Inspector's Annual Reports of 2002 and 2003, however, had subsequently con-firmed that concentration on literacy and numeracy were detracting from the enquiry, problem-solving and practical work that bring these subjects to life, and had observed that pressure on literacy and numeracy were producing a 'two-tier curriculum'.

International comparisons

Comparative studies made a contribution to critical research on the ideological and political contexts of new approaches to quality assurance, especially on New Zealand and the UK as the two national contexts in which the creation of 'quasi markets' had been taken furthest. Gordon and Whitty (1997) saw the restructuring and deregulation of state education in England, Wales and New Zealand as part of a neo-liberal project, but they held that the rhetoric of neo-liberal schooling was far removed from reality as governments confronted the classic tension between fiscal imperatives and the need for legitimation. Regarding accountability, they argued that even the neo-liberal state was unlikely to abdicate responsibility for the shaping of education to a fully 'marketised' public sector; in both countries the 'quasi market' had produced new and sometimes enhanced forms of accountability, based on a belief that state agents, bureaucrats and teachers, would act only in their own interest rather than that of the students. Deliberate separation of accountability from curriculum development agencies meant that both Ofsted and the New Zealand Education Review Office (ERO) were divorced from other national educational concerns, placing potentially conflicting rather than consistent demands on schools. Martin Thrupp (1998) examined how the ERO and Ofsted constructed blame for failure at school level in order to gain ideological power as agents of accountability. While these 'politics of blame' were contested in both countries by an alternative 'contextual' claim that took account of broader social constraints on schools, where New Zealand academics had been distrustful of ERO's agenda English researchers into school effectiveness had often provided support for Ofsted's 'politics of blame'; in fact, as 'failing' schools in both countries invariably served low socioeconomic communities, reasons for poor performance were unlikely to be so straightforward.

NATIONAL PRACTICE, EMPIRICAL STUDIES

Wilcox and Gray (1995) described the reactions of LEA chief inspectors to the Ofsted inspection model and *Handbook for the Inspection of Schools*. Methods and procedures were discussed, and although chief inspectors generally commended the thorough nature of the inspection process, substantial reservations were expressed about certain aspects, particularly the logistics including cost, time demands made on inspectors, and the availability of a sufficient pool of experienced inspectors, particularly in the primary field. A leading critic of external inspection as practised in the Ofsted model was Carol Taylor Fitz-Gibbon (1996) who argued that all-pervasive and simplistic politically driven concerns about performance evaluation, effectiveness, efficiency and appraisal had to be avoided. Instead she celebrated self-evaluating educational systems. Fitz-Gibbon argued that if we conceived of education as a highly complex system then simplistic attempts to describe 'good schools' or 'effective practices' were misjudged; what was required was a sensitive system of performance indicators used to feed back information to the providers of education at a local level, who could then advance their own development as they interpreted the data into their 'live' context. Her critique ranged from the philosophical to the basic statistical procedures for monitoring and the design of performance indicator systems or the impact of monitoring on other systems. Computers meant that monitoring systems were here to stay, so a major challenge was to get them working for the benefit of society as a whole, for staff and students in institutions, and for the advancement of knowledge. Stoll and Fink (1996) took the reality that school systems worldwide had come under political attack, with policies such as decentralisation, market based reform and high stakes testing, and attempted to describe a future that they believed both inevitable and desirable. They concluded, however, that the metaphor of a factory for a school, with its standardisation, control, compliance, and focus on deficits as opposed to quality, was no substitute for the metaphor of the school as caring family.

Meanwhile, Ofsted started to conduct research into its own procedures. Matthews *et al.* (1998) presented the results of the first study of the reliability and validity of judgements of teaching quality made by independent inspectors in the classrooms of primary and secondary schools in England. A total of 173 pairs of observations were received from 100 inspections representing about thirteen per cent of the inspections conducted during November and December 1996. Individual teachers' strengths and weaknesses identified by applying Ofsted evaluation criteria were shown to be agreed by the two inspectors, although there was more disagreement at the crucial 'satisfactory/unsatisfactory' boundary. It was concluded that Ofsted's Framework and related advice provided an effective means by which inspectors could judge teaching with considerable reliability, and the authors noted that their results were in keeping with similar findings by the Dutch Inspectorate. Much of Ofsted's own research, however, was discredited by independent scholars, and this particular research piece was criticised as flawed in the 1998 Channel 4 Despatches TV documentary, which also featured distinguished independent researchers and was aimed at a wide audience (Channel 4 Television 1998).

Cullingford (1999) edited an authoritative collection of chapters reporting a variety of research on Ofsted at the crucial turning point of 1999. In Cullingford's collection,

Winkley offered a critique of the inspection process, arguing that much of a school's and of children's achievements may be overlooked; from a survey of 200 recently inspected schools he found dislike of and opposition to the process amongst head teachers, and evidence of personal damage in terms of paranoia and self-doubt (Winkley 1999). He did acknowledge that it was better to have Ofsted proclaiming improving standards, based on evidence of whatever kind, to counter the continued and baseless claims of right wing pressure groups about 'falling standards'. Though much work in this volume was criticised by Goldstein (2000) for the poor quality of its research, it stands as an important collection of positions questioning the Ofsted regime (and Goldstein was equally critical of Woodhead's dismissive attitude to all research, and of Ofsted's failure to conduct any credible research of its own practices).

A significant change of tone in Ofsted's attitude to research came with David Bell's term of office, and the commissioning of an evaluative enquiry into the inspection process, conducted by Ofsted in collaboration with an independent partner from the University of London Institute of Education. Matthews and Sammons (2004) noted that the inspection system in England has attracted much international interest and generated a minor research industry. They referred also to Ofsted holding one of the world's largest longitudinal educational databases holding both qualitative and quantitative information by collating data from 4000 inspections per year since 1993. Following a steady rise in the later 1990s both in pupil performance at Key Stage 2 and in primary teaching of 'good or better' quality, they illustrated also the plateau that appeared from 1999. The revised *Framework* of inspection in 2003 was designed to address this problem. Significant improvements in leadership and management were demonstrable as a consequence of schools being placed in 'special measures', and this improvement was more marked in primary than in secondary. However, it proved more difficult to identify a general 'inspection effect'; some schools improved but just as many did not. This no effect finding had previously been shown by Shaw *et al.* (2003). Their conclusions regarding school improvement (both primary and secondary) were that the schools most likely to act successfully on inspection findings were those that were self-critical and capably led, often those already highly effective, but that weak schools also made substantial and rapid improvements through additional efforts following a poor inspection, and the incentive of a follow-up inspection. Their conclusions also addressed the dilemma that whilst professional education providers were typified by a desire for public accountability through self-evaluation, this entailed problems of credibility – with evident variability between institutions, public and parents wanted up-to-date reports on schools. Despite a general desire to reduce unnecessary stress and workload, especially for primary teachers, 'high stakes' were bound to lead to some apprehension. The thrust of government policy was to look for improvement *by* rather than *through* inspection with Ofsted *reporting* and not *advising*. The general conclusion of Matthews and Simmons' report was an evaluation of Ofsted's work as 'very good' on most counts, but as being only 'good' in respect of its contribution to improvement, its user perspective, and its value for money, and as being only 'fair' in its tailoring of inspection to the specific needs of individual schools or 'proportionate inspection'.

LOCAL EXPERIENCE, EMPIRICAL STUDIES

Local Education Authorities (LEAs) enjoyed a century or more of experience in monitoring and evaluating school quality, the ambivalence of their role however reflected in ambiguous role descriptions of adviser and inspector, in Winkley's terminology 'diplomats and detectives' (Winkley 1985). 'Progressive' LEAs secured their achievements through proactive advisory work with primary schools, but education policy has become more centralised at the same time as it has promoted delegation of powers to individual schools, which has left Local Authorities caught in between. Local government's role has frequently been contended and politically inconvenient for the state, but the need for some level of local or regional accountability in the provision of education has not disappeared. Whitbourn's authoritative analysis of LEA functions dedicates one chapter to statutory requirements and examples of best practice in monitoring and improving standards (Whitbourn 2004). The 1996 Act (Section 13) required authorities to meet the needs of its population in contributing to the spiritual, moral, mental and physical development of the community, which includes securing *efficient* primary education, and in particular to promote high standards (Section 13A). Specific funds have been made available to support *improvement*, latterly under the 2002 Act (Section 14). Until quite recently the basis of agreement between LEA and schools has been the DfEE (1999) *Code of Practice for School-LEA relations*, but much of the monitoring is now through continuous streams of ever more sophisticated data relating to pupil attainment, attendance, exclusion and so on, with value-added calculations.

Potentially well placed to reconcile conflicting requirements of both local knowledge and detachment in the evaluation of individual schools' performance, local inspectorates or advisory teams in the years before and after Plowden were central to provision of in-service education and training and in the modernisation of curriculum and teaching methods. With a more interventionist approach of central government from the mid-1970s, LEAs were called to account for their curriculum monitoring, an accountability that had been determined in the 1944 Act but had not been actively pursued. Influential research conducted at the local level included that of Peter Mortimore and others (1988) in London. In Leeds the local authority commissioned an evaluation of their £14 million project of primary school improvement over the late 1980s which identified specifically, amongst many other recommendations, the need for closer monitoring of schools' achievement (Alexander 1997). Although the relationship between local inspectorates and their schools was open to attack as too 'cosy', the continuing value of face-to-face work in evaluation and school improvement has been extensively researched. Learmonth (2000) has provided a concise account of significant initiatives and their merits, from the early work of the 'IBIS' ('Inspectors Based in Schools') scheme developed by the Inner London Education Authority.

Nixon and Rudduck (1993) addressed the role of professional judgement in the local inspection of schools, analysing the situation of LEA advisers/inspectors in a time of transition when professional judgement had become increasingly politicised and problematic; they concluded that although local inspectorates would continue to have a significant role to play, the production of public lists of criteria, driven by social and political considerations, would not resolve the tensions around local inspections. Local inspection was concerned primarily with the exercise of professional judgement, not with the measurement of school performance against pre-determined norms or standards. Ribbins and Burridge (1994) provided a critical reflection by practitioners and researchers into what they had attempted and achieved over a period of eight years in promoting the quality of schools in Birmingham. They concluded on a positive note recognising that the price of improvement was high but worth paying, while the path to it difficult but passable. In a final chapter the editors described the key purposes, principles and working practices of an approach that is based on the notion of supported self-evaluation. Stoll and Thomson (1996) adopted the concept of 'doors' to improvement in schools such as collegiality, research, self-evaluation, curriculum, teaching and learning, quality approaches, teacher appraisal and school development planning. Partnerships provide one such 'door' and, unlike others 'that are often operated alone and internally', partnerships encourage voluntary activities and projects that link schools with one or more external partners in pursuit of improvement. Their partnership between Lewisham LEA, its schools, and the London University Institute of Education was launched in 1993 with four aims blending school effectiveness and school improvement goals. After two years, researchers identified partnership elements that support the improvement process: shared values and beliefs; collaborative negotiation and planning; support; joint evaluation; and critical friendship. The authors concluded that whereas one of the difficulties of schools taking responsibility for their own improvement was insufficient rigour in self-evaluation, the partnership approach provided the necessary empowerment for real commitment to change, improvement and rigour. Several case studies collected by Earley (1998) and others (Ouston *et al.* 1997) drew attention to the value of LEA input in the context of national inspection.

Teachers – before Ofsted

Regarding the impact of the new inspection methods on schools, most of the research focuses on teachers, and this will be considered before turning to studies concerning particular aspects of the curriculum. Inspection and assessment of one's working practices is never a comfortable experience and, as noted earlier, a template for tension between teachers and inspectors was laid in the Victorian era of 'payment by results'. Learmonth (2000) records two tragic individual cases from the nineteenth and early twentieth centuries, of teacher suicides resulting from inspectors' judgements. For primary teachers in particular, power relations in various configurations over time have coloured their responses to inspection. But the tension needs to be understood in broader terms than any specific historical set of power relations. Elliot Eisner in *The Art of Evaluation* (1985, cited by Learmonth 2000) exposed the uncomfortable relationship between 'accountability defined in terms of specific operational objectives and precise measurement of outcomes' and the more incommensurate goals that teachers espouse, a contrast even starker in primary education than in secondary. A body of psychological research had already focused on 'investment of self' and consequent vulnerability even as the Teachers' Contract and the National Curriculum began to erode professional status and self-confidence (Steedman 1987; Nias 1989).

Ian Sandbrook's (1996) research was conducted mostly in the period immediately preceding Ofsted. His twelve case studies covered a variety of primary schools in seven different authorities, and revealed inspection to be much more than a singular event in the life of a school but rather a complex set of interactions between inspectors, head teachers, teachers and governors. With regards to the developmental consequences of inspections for the schools, views of participants were mixed and Sandbrook conceded that to track longer term effects would require further research. The measurement of development remained problematic however, with too many variables and too many qualitative factors. For benefits to outweigh costs in the inspection system, the process must be such as to lead to increased professional learning, confidence and self-esteem of teachers. Joan Dean (1995) analysed the reactions of teachers and head teachers in five local authorities after inspection during 1992 and 1993, including three primary schools, three junior and one middle. From her interview data, she concluded that Ofsted would be less than satisfactory in providing adequate teacher feedback and or follow-up advice and support. She noted that most head teachers saw Ofsted inspections as being about accountability.

Teachers and Ofsted

Continuing through the decade, a major research project was conducted on the effects of new organisation, curriculum and working practices, including the new Ofsted inspections, on English primary schools (Woods *et al.*1997; Jeffrey and Woods 1998; see also Hargreaves *et al.* 1998). An early article explored how the technicist approach of an Ofsted inspection conflicted with the holistic and humanistic values of teachers, producing a high degree of trauma (Jeffrey and Woods 1996). Long-term observation from three months before inspection to one year later was combined with continual semi-formal and informal interviewing of staff, and the study of documents. The trauma expressed was not a simple emotional response of the moment nor was it a product of school failure or lack of leadership. Professional uncertainty was induced, with teachers experiencing confusion, anomie, anxiety and doubt about their competence. Of three individuals who feature in the 1997 book, one female head teacher planned her inspection 'like a wedding', the successful outcome of which legitimated her management approach and boosted her confidence, one deputy head found the event 'cut deep into her being' but the 'negative trauma' reflected her energies back into teaching and away from managerialism, and she 'returned to her educational roots of active learning and pupil engagement', while a Year Two teacher reported having 'played safe' and quickly 'got back to normal'. Six years on from their original article, Woods and Jeffrey (2002) contended that primary teachers had had to reconstruct their identities in response to the reconstruction of the education system. Government attitudes and policies had thrown up dilemmas which Woods and Jeffrey contended had engaged teachers in identity talk and a number of emotional and intellectual strategies; the result had been a partitioning of the 'old Plowden self-identity' with the 'real self' largely withheld from the new personal identity and the sense of vocationalism set to one side. The new identity was of necessity more instrumental and situational in outlook and continued to change as teachers resolved how to relate to two or more competing discourses.

Ouston *et al.* (1997) were surprised at the level of satisfaction they found following inspection, especially where the process exposed issues that schools were aware of but hadn't faced. However they also perceived the danger of an audit culture imposing a way of working. In 1998 the NUT commissioned NFER to survey the impact of Ofsted, focusing on the effects on schools placed in special measures (Scanlon 1999). Effects to be surveyed included school monitoring, teachers' workload, health and stress, professional support and relationships between staff, LEA, governing body and parents, school improvement, staff morale and staff turnover. Most head teachers agreed with key problems identified – raising the question of whether inspections identified issues of which schools were already aware. Monitoring increased, a 'culture of inspection' was developed, but negative responses included loss of confidence, public humiliation, health, stress and an increase in bureaucratic workload precisely where more effort was needed in teaching. School monitoring addressed some problems but created others. Positive responses included greater solidarity amongst the teaching team, mutual support, and increased support from the LEA.

Case, Case and Catling (2000) argued, on the basis of a relatively small scale ethnographic study, that Ofsted was little more than a grand political gesture and classroom teachers understood themselves to be stage managing a performance for inspectors. Ethnographic methodology was used to collect data over a three year period, and the cumulative experience of respondents represented inspection of ten schools from three LEAs. Contextualising their research amidst the adoption of a managerialist discourse, their account drew attention to the effects of intensified control on the overall wellbeing of teachers and, by implication, the quality of children's classroom experience, and despite the evident intensity of the experience their study showed that there was no lasting impact upon what the teachers did in their classroom one year after inspection.

Other recent research articles have referred obliquely to the role of inspection, within a reform agenda, in teachers' understanding of their identity (Kelchtermans 2005; Burns 2005; Forrester 2005). Brunsden, Davies and Shevlin (2006), however, questioned explicitly the psychological effects of an Ofsted inspection, concentrating their quantitative study on a single primary school where stress and anxiety scales, as determined by two self-reporting personality measures, were administered not only to teachers but to all staff, governors and PTA committee members. These were administered three months and a fortnight before the inspection and ten weeks after it. The authors reported that unhealthy levels of anxiety were found to be present in teaching staff at all times and, by contrast to other participants, teachers also demonstrated symptoms of severe traumatic distress. Significantly, their data suggested that the inspection process rather than its outcome generated psychological distress with its potential impact on the children's schooling. The framework for Ofsted inspections subsequently changed in 2005 with schools now given less than a week's notice to prepare an inspection of no longer than two days.

Curriculum

The impact of inspection on curriculum subjects has attracted limited research, focusing on single subjects including mathematics, design and technology, physical education and religious education, and on cross-curricular issues such as spirituality, pastoral care, racial equality, and citizenship. Ofsted inspection generated a wealth of documentary and statistical data on which researchers have drawn, and interviews have been conducted with inspectors and key personnel.

Millett and Johnson (1998a, 1998b) reported ESRC-funded research to examine interpretations of Ofsted policy on primary mathematics through three levels of mediation. Ofsted facilitated access to senior personnel, allowed use of its database for sampling purposes, and provided anonymous textual data for a small set of schools. Analysis focussed on consistencies and inconsistencies of interpretation within and between those responsible for policy, primary inspectors, and key personnel in schools. Findings suggested evidence of a tension between 'experience and expertise' and 'baggage' at different levels of the process; some inspectors were less attuned to problems arising from lack of teachers' subject knowledge than to those arising from particular teaching styles. The researchers concluded that the greater the inspector's subject expertise, the more likely that judgements were made on mathematical criteria instead of general teaching criteria and subject knowledge. Documentary evidence was drawn on by Osler and Morrison (2002) to examine, for the Commission for Racial Equality, the effectiveness of school inspection in monitoring how schools address and prevent racism. Content analysis of sixty inspection reports and interviews with inspectors, head teachers and advisers provided the data. Osler and Morrison supported other research findings (Ouston *et al.* 1997; Fitz-Gibbon and Stephenson-Forster 1999) with doubts about reliability and validity of inspections. Reid (2006) analysed and evaluated comments on school attendance in Ofsted inspection reports for 2003, revealing a gap between inspectors' expectations and everyday reality. Sampling 200 of the 1,163 primary schools inspected by Ofsted in 2003, he found minimal allowance for socio-economic profile, location or pupil intake; the overall average score awarded for attendance was lower than for any other of the aspects of the school assessed; and inspectors interpreted the government's targets literally, taking no account of mitigating circumstances. Ofsted's annual national subject summary reports and individual primary school inspection reports on design and technology for the years 2000 to 2004 were analysed thematically by Alan Cross (2006a, 2006b): he found that, while inspectors say much about the teaching, their approach was neither systematic nor comprehensive, concluding that Ofsted needs to be clearer, more systematic and more thorough in its summary of good practice.

Questionnaire, interview and observation have been used to elicit both teachers' and inspectors' understandings in relation to particular curriculum areas. Ron Best (1997) was optimistic about the impact on pastoral care and PSE after a decade of educational policy change; his research based on a questionnaire survey of 159 members of a national association found respondents more positive than expected about Ofsted guidance, though divided as to the effect of inspections. Ofsted's inclusion of children's spiritual development in its inspection framework was examined by Sokanovic and Muller (1999); their interviews of a small sample of inspectors and teachers indicated a significant gap between the views and understandings of both groups as to what should be provided for the spiritual growth of children in schools, and in what they looked for as indication of children's spirituality. Hanlon's (2000) study of twenty-eight teachers from two LEAs found that inspections had a positive short-term effect on initiating change in religious education. In relation to inspection, children's views have been little researched, but in Flecknose's (2002) case study of one school, she interviewed eight pupils, five teachers and three co-professionals to explore democratic procedures. Analysing this data in the light of published official guidance (*Inspecting Citizenship*) she argued that HMI had defined citizenship in an unhelpfully narrow and academic way and that society's needs would be better served by inspecting citizenship through its influence on the structure of schools. Davies (1999) drew on his inspection experience in 35 schools and his own empirical research into PE standards, to conclude that Ofsted inadvertently generated practices unhelpful to the promotion of improved standards in PE; partly the result of greater emphasis on literacy and numeracy, and lack of specialist knowledge of PE by most primary teachers, it also reflected the limited knowledge of PE by most primary inspectors.

Self-evaluation

Self-evaluation as a mode of quality assurance evolved uncertainly from the 1970s, and in 1991 became embedded in Scottish practice. Its logic became all the more persuasive following Local Management of Schools (LMS) and School Development Planning (SDP) but was formally resisted in England until the election of New Labour in 1997. In 1995 the NUT commissioned a study of school self-evaluation to see if the kind of model developed in Scotland could be applied to the English and Welsh context, and the report *Schools Speak for Themselves* was published in 1996. In 1998 the union commissioned a follow-up study published by MacBeath (1999), offering case studies of developments at school and local authority levels, and the consequent self-evaluation framework was adopted by some LEAs – including Newcastle, where David Bell was director. Ofsted itself began to make gestures towards self-evaluation in its frameworks for inspection.

Ouston and Davies (1998) had found that schools most positive about school inspection were those that had high level of professional self-confidence and refused to allow the process of external inspection to intimidate them – demonstrating an incipient or well-developed self-evaluation culture. An NFER survey visited sixteen schools in nine LEAs using an explicit package or model as a self-evaluation framework; a mixture of models was used, but mostly models developed by the LEA itself (Davies and Rudd 2001).

INTERNATIONAL POLICIES AND PRACTICE, COMPARATIVE RESEARCH

Given the prominence of international comparisons in discourse over standards that underpinned arguments for rigorous and even punitive models of external evaluation, it is ironic to find that self-evaluation as a mechanism of quality control was also heavily influenced from overseas. Comparative research grew steadily in influence over the course of the last century; Bone (1968) drew on two large international surveys of school inspection undertaken by the International Bureau of Education in 1937 and the International Conference on Public Education in 1956, and found instructive the variety of ways in which inspectors' work was defined around the globe. Comparative work subsequently flourished and most particularly in relation to school improvement (Silver 1994, cited above). Watson's 1994 survey of 'School Inspectors and Supervision', for the *International Encyclopaedia of Education*, observed how all governments tried to ensure that their system of public schooling was not only regulated but controlled and monitored so that minimum standards of academic performance, teaching, administration and maintenance of physical plant were upheld; some or all of these functions might be roles for school inspectors. The more centralised the system and the more politically doctrinaire its governance, the more likely that school inspectors were seen as instruments of control over the system (Watson 1994).

International research and self-evaluation

A comparative study of curriculum change in English and Finnish primary schools (Webb, Vulliamy, Hakkinen and Hamalainen 1998) offered insights on external inspection and school self-evaluation. The two countries' policies on inspection and monitoring moved in opposite directions in the mid-1990s as Finland abandoned its national inspection system in favour of self-evaluation. Qualitative case studies were made of six English schools and six Finnish schools, a diverse sample in size, location and curriculum approach. Analysis of the interviews, classroom observations and documents revealed how in England the impact of Ofsted inspections had been mainly on policies and procedures rather than on classroom practice, and the effects on teacher morale had been debilitating. In Finland, although early attempts at school self-evaluation had lacked a whole school strategy, there was evidence of ownership of the evaluation process by teachers, together with inputs from parental feedback and pupil self-assessment. Together these contributed to positive changes in classroom practice.

MacBeath's (1999) wide ranging account of international practice indicated that many countries, whilst seeking stronger accountability, simultaneously respect the professionalism of teachers and the integrity of the school as a self-evaluating organisation. Norwegian Trond Alvik's three categories of internal/external evaluation – parallel, sequential and co-operative – are taken to describe how different countries attempt to accommodate school evaluation to the unique context and history of their own systems. MacBeath considered countries in Europe, Israel, Central Asian Republics, the 'Pacific Rim', Australia, and North, Central and South America. Learmonth (2000) followed MacBeath by analysing six examples of self-evaluation in the UK, including Scotland, the Channel Islands and the London Borough of Wandsworth, together with the USA, Netherlands and Victoria, the second largest state of Australia. Scotland was described as a system moving from parallel to the sequential with the hint of some genuinely co-operative evaluation. In the Channel Islands a process of 'validated school self-evaluation', which included a 'framework' for development and review, influenced by Ofsted but agreed by working parties, provided opportunities for teachers to develop evaluative skills in other schools and to exchange information or ideas about effective practice across the school system. In the Netherlands a distinctive feature of self-evaluation was the influence of a higher education institution; the University of Twente contributed to a sequential system in which the school conducted its own self-evaluation validated by external inspection. In Victoria the school charter, annual report and triennial review were key elements in the accountability framework and underpinned the planning, monitoring, reporting and performance review over a three year period. As in many English LEAs, Wandsworth included support for individual schools in self-evaluation in their Education Development Plans.

A European Socrates project, 'Evaluating Quality in School Education', and a large body of research literature provided data for MacBeath *et al.* (2000). A hundred and one schools in eighteen countries agreed to work with a common approach while at the same time developing thinking and practice within the context of their own cultures and histories. The authors recognised that a successful marriage between internal and external evaluation was, and remains, the goal for which European systems are striving: evaluation of quality must enhance the capacity of school and teachers and cannot progress without the commitment of teachers, students and parents who have their own personal stake in quality, standards and improvement; external expectations had to meet internal needs and pressure does not work without the push of some internal direction or vision. Within the UK, Learmonth (2000) noted experimental self-evaluation that incorporated 'pupil voice' in Scotland (Improving School Effectiveness Project) and in Northern Ireland (Making Belfast Work: Raising School Standards project) linking with the International School Effectiveness and Improvement Centre at the University of London Institute of Education. Potential for pupil voice has been identified at the primary stage especially in connection with citizenship education and 'practical democracy' in schools.

DEVELOPMENTS IN SELF-EVALUATION

The government's 'new relationship' from 2004 triggered further steps towards self-evaluation in the UK, including the allocation of critical friends or School Improvement Partners (SIPs) to every school. The SIP scheme for primary schools was to be completed nationally by 2008 and research so far has been limited, but MacBeath (2006) drew together some early evaluations. He related them to research in other countries, including experimental projects in new European countries. He provided a synthesis of findings that are both critical of national policy but also constructive and practical in exploring possibilities for implementation and continuing development according to sound principles of professional development and rigorous accountability. One such practical development is the ever more sophisticated software available to schools for self-evaluation (Target Tracker 2007). MacBeath did however identify a lack of realism in trying to inspect the broad agenda of Every Child Matters within a tightly constrained inspection framework.

Evaluations of the new inspection regime continue, both by Ofsted itself and by the NFER. The House of Commons Select Committee on Education and Skills suspended judgement on self-evaluation and on new shorter inspections in July 2007, with a need to be certain that inspection continues to identify both failing schools and schools that are coasting. NFER maintains a web-based resource for such evaluation and information (NFER 2007).

DIVERGENCE, DISAGREEMENT AND CONSENSUS

Fundamentally conflicting positions between a 'skills' and a 'culture' approach to curriculum, and the implications of these for monitoring performance and quality control, go back to the Victorians Robert Lowe and Matthew Arnold. Political and ideological differences are also fundamental regarding the propriety and effectiveness of public or privatised systems of school inspection, and the aggressive stance adopted by HMCI Woodhead not only in inspection of schools but also against independent educational research undoubtedly exacerbated the inevitable conflict and disagreement. These differences and disagreements are reflected in much of the literature cited above.

Also pertinent to the divergences emerging in published research is Silver's historical perception of competing interests that may be found reflected in divergences of ongoing research. The expert and research community is rooted in different intellectual traditions. Sociologists examining power relationships in the control of education may share concerns but diverge in their perspectives from social psychologists whose focus may be teachers' identities and working practices. The latter have interests in common but very different ways of working from curriculum evaluators or policy developers whose horizons are national levels of attainment.

Substantive disagreement emerges on the effects of inspection on standards: though there was clear evidence for improvement in schools placed in special measures, the question remained as to whether the particular methods of inspection adopted were necessary to achieve this end; in some cases the positive effects in individual schools were found to be short-lived. Regarding the impact of quality assurance procedures in raising standards nationally, researchers continue to disagree about relevant measures. Arguments between statisticians about validity of data and rigour of analysis are accompanied in some cases by broader disagreements on research method. Many researchers are aware of the multiple concurrent policy developments that make it almost impossible to isolate or assess the influence of any one factor in the decade and a half since Ofsted, let alone during the past thirty years or more of increased curriculum intervention and monitoring.

A formidable consensus accumulated on the negative effects of inspection at the school level, though some researchers identified ways in which it worked to teachers' advantage. Some agreement could also be found on the ways inspection distorted curriculum by concentrating on core subjects, and through lack of expertise across the curriculum amongst teams of inspectors. But wide consensus may also be found in the many studies of self-evaluation, from which positive effects on school culture and on professional development can be identified.

SYNTHESIS OF KEY FINDINGS

Quality assurance procedures have changed and continue to change, to meet shifting cultural and political expectations. National inspection has provided a means not only of monitoring, and thus generating considerable data, but also of raising standards and a means of effecting change through influencing curriculum and teaching methods. As a mode of achieving accountability for educational expenditure, it has been used more or less self-consciously as a means of controlling teachers as well as schools. Consequently the methods and findings of national inspection have not gone unchallenged and have provoked a good deal of critical independent research, which has, for example, revealed contradictions within national policy.

Research has been of variable quality, but has engaged with a wide range of aspects. Some research has challenged official conclusions drawn about standards based on inspection data, whilst other, often small-scale local studies, have revealed unintended effects such as distortions of the curriculum. A large body of research has focused on teachers, the effect of different patterns of inspection on their professional fulfilment and the compatibility of inspection frameworks, especially in primary schools, with broader concepts of the teacher's role and their commitment to the 'whole child'.

The need for identifying and addressing poor provision and poor teaching is undisputed but empirical studies revealed flaws in the inspection processes adopted, as well as indicating possibilities for improvement. That an important role evidently remains for the Local Authority in providing support to schools following poor inspection outcomes has been demonstrated, as have the merits of the 'advisory' role that can be more effectively supplied locally rather than nationally. A positive direction has been the development, through research, of self-evaluation, and identification of the ways in which this can be combined with sufficiently rigorous forms of accountability. Many valuable insights and possibilities have derived from comparative international studies.

Some implications

The research surveyed above underlines the need for a national education policy with regard to underlines quality assurance that inspires the maximum possible trust between politicians, people (parents, children, taxpayers) and professionals. Monitoring of standards has to be credible and transparent, to provide reliable data, and to be supportive of values that reflect both the wide aspirations of parents and the professional understandings about primary pupils' development. Inevitably this will entail embracing, if not resolving, competing and conflicting claims. That is the stuff of politics. But a healthy research culture in the field of quality assurance should contribute to informed and reasoned argument and the avoidance of doctrinaire posturing. National policies will also need to employ inspection procedures to address more effectively issues of equality, monitoring factors such as gender, race, poverty and deprivation, and special learning needs for their impact on achievement, and to provide a conduit for sharing good practice.

For national agencies such as Ofsted, one implication of the research surveyed above is that high profile partisanship in the conduct of its affairs is likely to forfeit the three-way trust advocated above. It needs to be seen as neutral and not campaigning, to gain the trust of the profession, to supply sound and credible data for policy-makers. Whilst undoubtedly its task will be to advise government and to help formulate policy, its energies must be focused on achieving the most effective and efficient mechanisms for maintaining quality in primary education. One evident possibility is that of proportionate inspection, avoiding the potential waste of resources in heavy inspection of good schools, but on the other hand addressing the problem of coasting schools. Inspection must generate positive outcomes for average schools. Many research studies point to the importance of continuing to foster the whole curriculum and to avoid distortion through narrow inspection.

Research appears to demonstrate self-evaluation as one of the most promising developments in squaring professional development of teachers with quality control. To foster collaboration between schools in this respect, Local Authorities are ideally placed. A level of administration that understands the nature and needs of the locality, and knows the strengths and weaknesses of neighbouring schools, can remain an effective broker for School Improvement Partners (SIPs). In their turn, primary schools have the capacity and scope to become mature in self-evaluation; they now have access to advanced software for school self-evaluation that can incorporate both qualitative and quantitative evidence. They are also the best placed to engage parents, and ultimately the Local Authorities and the schools can combine, using new technologies, to provide parents and local communities with good quality information about the character and achievement of their neighbourhood schools.

SUGGESTIONS FOR FURTHER RESEARCH

The need for research is never-ending. Research, like education, is conditioned by its time, and changing preoccupations of policy makers, practitioners and researchers themselves generate a constantly moving agenda. There is continuing need for research that critically scrutinises and challenges the principles on which quality assurance mechanisms are founded; this will research policy-making as it develops for a mature and contemporary understanding of the political dimensions of quality assurance. Developments in mechanisms of quality assurance need to be monitored constantly for their effectiveness and cost-effectiveness, and given the political contentiousness of education policy, this research and evaluation needs to be seen to be independent. Globalisation of education implies that international and comparative studies will continue to be desirable, not simply in comparing levels of attainment of school populations but also in drawing on the experience of alternative models of quality assurance.

Research may continue to inform the development of professional independence of teachers in evaluating the processes and outcomes of teaching and learning. In particular the role of ICT in school self-evaluation, with ever more sophisticated software packages, will accommodate a 'bottom up' as well as a 'top down' approach to the collection of data, and will be a topic for investigation. As 'pupil voice' will undoubtedly play a part in these 'bottom up' models, a useful topic of investigation would be the impact this mode of quality assurance might have on children and their families, especially in the exercise of school choice.

REFERENCES

Alexander, R.J., Rose, J. and Woodhead, C. (1992) *Curriculum Organisation and Classroom Practice in Primary Schools: a discussion paper.* London: Department of Education and Science.

Alexander, R.J. (1997) *Policy and Practice in Primary Education: local initiative, national agenda.* London: Routledge.

Best, R. (1997) 'The impact on pastoral care of structural, organisational and statutory changes in schooling: some empirical evidence and a discussion', *British Journal of Guidance and Counselling* 27(1): 55–70.

Bone, T.R. (1968) *School Inspection in Scotland 1840–1966.* London: University of London Press.

Brehony, K.J. (2005) 'Primary schooling under New Labour: the irresolvable contradiction of excellence and enjoyment', *Oxford Review of Education* 31(1): 29–46.

Burns, C. (2005) 'Tensions between national, school and teacher development needs: a survey of teachers views about continuing professional development within a group of rural primary schools', *Journal of In-Service Education* 31(2): 353–72.

Brunsden, V., Davies, M. and Shevlin, M. (2006) 'Anxiety and stress in educational professionals in relation to Ofsted', *Education Today* 56(1): 24–31.

Case, P., Case, S. and Catling, S. (2000) 'Please show you're working: a critical assessment of the impact of Ofsted inspection on primary teachers', *British Journal of Sociology of Education* 21 (4): 605–21.

Channel 4 TV (1998) *Inspecting the Inspectors (Dispatches Series)*, broadcast 19/3/1998.

Cross, A. (2006a) 'School inspectors' comments relating to teaching methods in Design and Technology in primary school inspection reports', *Research in Education* 75: 19–28.

——(2006b) 'Looking for patterns in Ofsted judgements about primary pupil achievement in Design and Technology', *Education 3–13* 34(2): 163–72.

Cullingford C. (Ed) (1999) *An Inspector Calls: Ofsted and its effect on school standards.* London: Kogan Page.

Cunningham, P. (2002) 'Progressivism, decentralisation and recentralisation: Local Education Authorities and the primary curriculum, 1902–2002', *Oxford Review of Education* 28(2/3): 217–33.

Davies, D. and Rudd, P. (2001) *Evaluating School Self-evaluation.* Slough: NFER.

Davies, H. (1999) 'Physical education at Key Stage 1 and Key Stage 2 in England and Wales. Inspections and long term standards', *British Journal of Physical Education* 30(3): 21–24.

Dean, J. (1995) 'What teachers and headteachers think about inspection', *Cambridge Journal of Education* 25(1): 45–52.

Department of Education and Employment (DfEE) (1999) *Code of Practice for School-LEA Relations.* London: DfEE.

Department of Education and Science (DES) (1978) *Primary Education in England: a survey by HMI.* London: HMSO.

Duffy, M. (Ed) (1997) *A Better System of Inspection?* Hexham, Northumberland: Office for Standards in Inspection.

Dunford, J.E. (1998) *Her Majesty's Inspectorate of Schools Since 1944.* London: Woburn Press.

Earley, P. (Ed) (1998) *School Improvement After Inspection.* London: Paul Chapman.

Earley, P., Fidler, B. and Ouston, J. (Eds) (1996) *Improvement Through Inspection? Complementary approaches to school development*. London: David Fulton.

Fitz-Gibbon, C.T. (1996) 'Official indicator systems in the UK: examinations and inspections', *International Journal of Educational Research* 253: 239–47.

——(1997) 'Ofsted's methodology', in M. Duffy (Ed) *A Better System of Inspection?* Hexham, Northumberland: Office for Standards in Inspection.

Fitz-Gibbon, C.T. and Stephenson-Forster, N.J. (1999) 'Is Ofsted helpful? An evaluation using social science criteria', in C. Cullingford (Ed) *An Inspector Calls: Ofsted and its effect on school standards*. London: Kogan Page.

Flecknose, M. (2002) 'Democracy, citizenship and school improvement: what can one school tell us?', *School Leadership and Management* 22(4): 421–37.

Forrester, G. (2005) 'All in a day's work: primary teachers "performing" and "caring"', *Gender and Education* 17(3): 271–87.

Goldstein, H. (2000) 'Review article – *An Inspector Calls* by Cedric Cullingford', *British Educational Research Journal* 26(4): 547–50.

Gordon, L. and Whitty, G. (1997) 'Giving the "hidden hand" a helping hand? The rhetoric and reality of neo-liberal education reform in England and New Zealand', *Comparative Education* 33(3): 453–67.

Hanlon, D. (2000) 'The effectiveness of primary Religious Education in-service training', *British Journal of Religious Education* 22(2): 103–14.

Hargreaves, A., Nias, J., Menter, I. and Webb, R. (1998) 'Review symposium of Woods *et al. Restructuring Schools, Reconstructing Teachers*', *British Journal of Educational Studies* 19(3): 419–31.

Hartley, D. (2003) 'New economy, new pedagogy?', *Oxford Review of Education* 29(1): 81–94.

——(2006) 'Excellence and enjoyment: the logic of a "contradiction"', *British Journal of Educational Studies* 54(1): 3–14.

House of Commons Education and Employment Committee (1999a) *Fourth Report* (8 June).

——(1999b) *Fifth Special Report* (26 July) (Government's Response and Ofsted's Response).

Jeffrey, B., and Woods, P. (1996) 'Feeling de-professionalised: the social construction of emotions during an Ofsted inspection', *Cambridge Journal of Education* 26(3): 325–43.

——(1998) *Testing Teachers: the effect of school inspections on primary teachers*. London: Falmer Press.

Kelchtermans, G. (2005) 'Teachers' emotions in educational reforms: self-understanding, vulnerable commitment and micropolitical literacy', *Teaching and Teacher Education* 21(8): 995–1006.

Lawton, D. and Gordon, P. (1987) *H.M.I.* London: Routledge.

Learmonth, J. (2000) *Inspection: what's in it for schools?* London: RoutledgeFalmer.

MacBeath, J. (1999) *Schools Must Speak for Themselves*. London: Routledge.

——(2006) *School Inspection and Self-evaluation: working with the new relationship*. London: Routledge.

MacBeath, J., Schratz, M., Meuret, D. and Jakobsen, L. (2000) *Self-evaluation in European Schools: a story of change*. London: RoutledgeFalmer.

Maclure, S. (2000) *The Inspector's Calling: HMI and the shaping of educational policy, 1945–1992*. London: Hodder and Stoughton.

Matthews, P., Holmes, J.R., Vickers, P. and Corporaal, B. (1998) 'Aspects of the reliability and validity of school inspection judgements of teaching quality', *Educational Research and Evaluation* 4(2): 167–88.

Matthews, P. and Sammons, P. (2004) *Improvement Through Inspection: an evaluation of the impact of Ofsted's work*. London: Ofsted. Doc ref. no. HMI 2244 (pdf format).

Millett, A. and Johnson, D.C. (1998a) 'Ofsted inspection of primary mathematics: are there new insights to be gained?', *School Leadership and Management* 18(2): 239–55.

——(1998b) 'Expertise or baggage? What helps inspectors to inspect primary maths?', *British Educational Research Journal* 24(5): 503–18.

Mortimore, P. and Goldstein, H. (1996) *The Teaching of Reading in 45 Inner London Schools: a critical examination of Ofsted research*. London: University of London, Institute of Education.

Mortimore, P., Sammons, P., Stoll, L., Lewis, D. and Ecob, R. (1988) *School Matters: the junior years*. Wells: Open Books.

National Foundation for Educational Research (NFER) (2007) *Education Management Information Exchange (EMIE)*. Online (Available: www.nfer.ac.uk/emie).

Nias, J. (1989) *Primary Teachers Talking: a study of teaching as work*. London: Routledge.

Nixon, J. and Rudduck, J. (1993) 'The role of professional judgement in the local inspection of schools: a study of six local education authorities', *Research Papers in Education* 8(2): 135–48.

Ofsted (1993) *Curriculum Organisation and Classroom Practice in Primary Schools: follow-up report*. London: Ofsted.

——(1994) *Primary Matters: a discussion of teaching and learning in primary schools*. London: Ofsted.

——(1995a) *Teaching Quality: the primary debate*. London: Ofsted.

——(1995b) *Class Size and the Quality of Education*. London: Ofsted.

——(1996) *The Teaching of Reading in 45 Inner London Primary Schools*. London: Ofsted.

——(2002a) *The National Literacy Strategy: the first four years 1998–2002*. London: Ofsted.

——(2002b) *The National Numeracy Strategy: the first three years 1999–2002*. London: Ofsted.

——(2003) *The Education of Six Year Olds in England, Denmark and Finland: an international comparative study*. London: Ofsted.

——(2005) *The National Literacy and Numeracy Strategies and the Primary Curriculum*. London: Ofsted.

Osler, A. and Morrison, M. (2002) 'Can race equality be inspected? Challenges for policy and practice raised by the Ofsted School Inspection Framework', *British Educational Research Journal* 28(3): 327–38.

Ouston, J. and Davies, J. (1998) 'Ofsted and afterwards? Schools' responses to inspection', in P. Earley *School Improvement After Inspection*. London: Paul Chapman.

Ouston, J., Fidler, B. and Earley, P. (Eds) (1997) *Ofsted Inspections: the early experience*. London: David Fulton.

Reid, K. (2006) 'An evaluation of inspection reports on primary school attendance', *Educational Research* 48(3): 267–86.

Reynolds, D. and Farrell, S. (1996) *Worlds Apart?: a review of international surveys of educational achievement (Ofsted Reviews of Research series)*. London: Ofsted.

Ribbins, P. and Burridge, E. (Eds) (1994) *Improving Education: promoting quality in schools*. London: Cassell.

Sandbrook, I. (1996) *Making Sense of Primary Inspection*. Buckingham: Open University Press.

Scanlon, M. (1999) *The Impact of OFSTED Inspections*. Slough: NFER for the National Union of Teachers.

Shaw, I., Newton, D., Aitkin, M. and Darnell, R. (2003) 'Do Ofsted inspections of secondary schools make a difference in GCSE results?' *British Educational Research Journal* 29(1): 62–75.

Silver, H. (1994) *Good Schools, Effective Schools: judgements and their histories*. London: Cassell.

Smith, G. (2000) 'Research and inspection: HMI and OfSTED 1981–96, a commentary', *Oxford Review of Education* 26(3–4): 333–52.

Sokanovic, M. and Muller, D. (1999) 'Professional and educational perspectives on spirituality in young children', *Pastoral Care in Education* 17(1): 9–16.

Steedman, C. (1987) 'Prisonhouses', in M. Lawn and G. Grace (Eds) *Teachers: the culture and politics of work*. London: Falmer.

Stoll, L. and Fink, D. (1996) *Changing Our Schools*. Buckingham: Open University Press.

Stoll, L. and Thomson, M. (1996) 'Moving together: a partnership approach to improvement', in P. Earley, B. Fidler and J. Ouston (Eds) *Improvement Through Inspection? Complementary approaches to school development*. London: David Fulton

Target Tracker 2007: a suite of applications to record, track and chart pupil progress during their time in school. Online (Available: http://www.targettracker.org/).

Thrupp, M. (1998) 'Exploring the politics of blame: school inspection and its contestation in New Zealand and England', *Comparative Education* 34(2): 195–208.

Tooley, J. (1998) *Educational Research: acritique.* London: Ofsted.

Watson, J. (1994) 'School inspectors and supervision', in T. Husen and T. Postlethwaite, *International Encyclopedia of Education.* Oxford: Pergamon.

Webb, R., Vulliamy, G., Hakkinen, K. and Hamalainen, S. (1998) 'External inspection or school self-evaluation? A comparative analysis of policy and practice in primary schools in England and Wales', *British Educational Research Journal* 24(5): 539–56.

Whitbourn, S. (2004) *What is the LEA for? An analysis of the functions and roles of the Local Education Authority.* Slough: NFER/ EMIE.

Wilcox, B. and Gray, J. (1995) 'The Ofsted inspection model: the views of LEA chief inspectors', *Cambridge Journal of Education* 25(1): 63–74.

Winkley, D. (1985) *Diplomats and Detectives: LEA advisers at work.* London: Robert Royce.

——(1999) 'An examination of Ofsted', in P. Cullingford (Ed) *An Inspector Calls: Ofsted and its effect on school standards.* London: Kogan Page.

Woods, P., Jeffrey, B., Troman, G. and Boyle, M. (1997) *Restructuring Schools, Reconstructing Teachers: responding to change in the primary school.* Buckingham: Open University Press.

Woods, P. and Jeffrey, B. (2002) 'The reconstruction of primary teachers' identities', *British Journal of Sociology of Education* 23(1): 89–106.

29 The trajectory and impact of national reform

Curriculum and assessment in English primary schools

Dominic Wyse, Elaine McCreery and Harry Torrance

INTRODUCTION

A vast amount of literature could have been included in this survey and we have had to be selective. After a brief introduction, setting the work in context, the chapter reviews key empirical studies of primary school teaching and learning which are widely regarded as central to the field, pre- and post-National Curriculum; these include particularly Galton *et al.*'s successive studies (1980 and 1999) and the Bristol 'PACE' project (an ESRC-funded longitudinal study of the introduction of the National Curriculum throughout the 1990s). These pivotal investigations are augmented by other individual studies exploring the impact of assessment and the impact of the National Literacy and Numeracy Strategies.

The criteria for selecting those studies to be discussed included their financial independence, scope and scale. The survey paid particular attention to observational studies in order to assess the impact of reform on classroom life and pupil experience.

HISTORICAL BACKGROUND

Before 1988 there was no statutory state control of the primary curriculum. Schools and teachers were able to implement a curriculum which they felt met the needs of the pupils they taught, although Local Education Authorities exerted considerable influence over curriculum development. The introduction of the National Curriculum in 1988 heralded statutory control of the curriculum and marked the culmination of changes that had been developing in education over many years. The 1944 'Butler' Education Act formalised the 'end-on' structure of primary education leading to the tripartite system of secondary education (grammar, modern and technical). Selection for grammar schools was usually via the 11 plus test.

Research evidence in the 1950s indicated that:

- coaching and practice could improve 11 plus scores, thereby undermining the theoretical case for selection (that is that IQ was inherited and stable and that early selection of those who would benefit from an academic grammar school education could be done with confidence (Yates and Pidgeon 1957),
- such selection benefited middle class children disproportionately and was essentially selecting on the basis of class acculturation to schooling rather than ability (Halsey, Floud and Anderson 1961).

These findings led to the introduction of comprehensive secondary education and the gradual abandonment of the 11 plus after the election of the Labour government in 1964. Even today, however, 10 local authorities in England retain selection at 11 plus and 10 others retain some grammar and/or secondary modern schools within ostensibly 'comprehensive' local systems (Levacic and Marsh 2007).

The Plowden Report (CACE 1967) attempted to discover exactly what sort of education the children of the country were receiving after these various changes. It advocated an approach to education which was child centred and based on enquiry, and which has been generally labelled as 'progressive'. However HMI evidence suggested such an approach was not widespread and later research evidence from Galton *et al.* (1980) suggests that 'progressive' classroom organisation and task presentation was not typical. A similar point was made in the so-called 'three wise men' report of Alexander, Rose and Woodhead (1992), which was commissioned by the then government to review available evidence from both inspection and research about 'the delivery of education in primary schools'. It covered some 90 sources, both published and unpublished, and concluded:

> The commonly held belief that primary schools, after 1967, were swept by a tide of progressivism is untrue ... The reality ... is rather more complex. The ideas and practices connoted by words like 'progressive' and 'informal' had a profound effect in certain schools and LEAs. Elsewhere they were either ignored or ... adopted as so much rhetoric to sustain practice which in visual terms might look attractive and busy but which lacked any serious educational rationale. Here they lost their early intellectual excitement and became little more than a passport to professional approval and advancement.
>
> (Alexander, Rose and Woodhead 1992: paras 19–20)

Nevertheless between the 1960s and the 1980s, there appeared to be a growth in focus on the curriculum among teachers, and a public perception of school autonomy, with the emergence of classroom based research and professional subject associations, and curriculum development projects, stimulated and supported by the government-funded Schools Council. Emerging interest in curriculum was also reflected in publications produced by the Department for Education and Science.

In parallel with this rise of autonomous teacher professionalism there also began to emerge a dissatisfaction among government ministers that schools were too free to do as they pleased, with little apparent accountability. Some were critical in particular of the supposedly too unstructured 'child-centred approach' (viz. the Black papers and the William Tyndale affair, cf. Ellis *et al.* 1976). This criticism culminated in the 1976 James Callaghan 'Ruskin Speech' in which schools' role in preparing the future generation to contribute to the country's economic success was articulated.

The origins of the Education Reform Act 1988 can be found in this debate about school autonomy, the response to the economic crises of 1970s and the increasing link being made between education and economic needs. The notion of 'accountability' emerges and the perceived need for governmental control over education, and in particular for control over expenditure related to 'value for money' in terms of the national investment in education.

The impact of the Education Reform Act 1988 began to be felt in schools when it was introduced to Key Stage 1 in primary schools in 1989. The 1988 Act (and subsequent legislation) introduced a range of changes at the same time and in many ways it is difficult to unpack the impact of the National Curriculum from the other changes that took place around the same time or shortly afterwards (including the introduction of national testing, publication of results and changes to school inspection).

The explicit aims of the National Curriculum were to raise educational standards and make schools more accountable to the public.

RESEARCH ON TEACHING AND LEARNING IN PRIMARY CLASSROOMS

One of the key issues that has been addressed by empirical work on primary education in the period from 1980 to 2006 is the nature of teacher–pupil interaction and its impact on the quality of pupil learning. The extent to which primary teachers' practice has changed over this period also continues to be of interest to researchers. Some studies have been replicated or partly replicated offering a longitudinal dimension to the field. Galton *et al.*'s (1980) ORACLE (Observational Research and Classroom Learning Evaluation) project is such a study. The selection of schools in the research was related to a wider programme of research on school transfer that the authors were carrying out at the time. Three Local Education Authorities (LEAs) were involved covering 58 classes in 19 schools. The study's main findings were that, contrary to media and political commentary, the primary curriculum had not been strongly influenced by the recommendations of the Plowden Report for cooperative group work of the investigational kind, and that primary classrooms had retained the general pattern of the traditional curriculum and classroom organisation (Galton *et al.* 1980: 155).

Galton *et al.* (1999a) replicated the earlier pre-National Curriculum study. The replication showed some clear differences from the earlier period. The timetable of the primary curriculum had become one which was similar to secondary schools with its identification of particular subjects and clear timeslots for these subjects. Class teaching (teaching delivered to the whole class) had increased from 19 per cent to 35 per cent of all teachers' interaction with pupils. A summary journal article reviewing both studies concluded:

> Teaching in today's primary schools at Key Stage 2 is very much a matter of teachers talking and children listening. Of this talk by far the largest amount consists of teachers making statements ... Open or speculative or challenging questions ... are still comparatively rare. Even in science, where the highest percentage of open questions was recorded, teachers were three times more likely to require a single correct answer than they were to invite speculation. The demands of the programmes of study in the various National Curriculum subjects, even after the Dearing (1993) review, still appear to place too heavy an imperative on teachers to cut down the amount of pupil participation in order to 'get through' the curriculum content.
>
> (Galton *et al.* 1999b: 33)

The emphasis on task and routine as part of pupil–teacher interaction was confirmed by Alexander's work. As part of an extensive data-set which was gathered to evaluate an ambitious curriculum and staff development initiative by Leeds LEA, Alexander (1997) included systematic observation of classroom practice. The observational study of classroom practice had a sample of sixty schools. The schedule for systematic classroom observation was based on Galton *et al.*'s (1980) work. Alexander found that 'work and associated routine interactions accounted for nearly two thirds of the total of teacher-pupil interactions ... Although there were large differences between classes, in general individual children ... were involved in very few interactions with their teachers' (p.82).

The study by Mortimore *et al.* (1988) is regarded internationally as a particularly strong example of school effectiveness research methodology (Teddlie and Reynolds 2000) and one of the few studies of its kind to address primary education. The study took place over four years and utilised a wide range of quantitative and qualitative data including: measures of the pupil intakes to schools and classes; measures of pupils' educational outcomes; and measures of the classroom and school environment. The sample was 2000 pupils from 50 schools selected randomly from the 636 schools in the Inner London Education Authority (ILEA). Data were collected in relation to cognitive and non-cognitive outcomes and included systematic observation of lessons using ORACLE study tools.

Mortimore *et al.* concluded that a number of features were indicative of effective primary teaching. In general the aims that teachers expressed for their pupils were deemed to be worthwhile but their implementation was less effective when teachers had low expectations of particular groups of pupils: 'Thus, the first implication for all classroom teachers must be the need to focus carefully on classroom practice and to challenge the existence of such differential expectations.' (p. 286) Effective teaching involved structured sessions which allowed pupils freedom to manage their own work within a framework which ensured that important aspects were not omitted, and that time was not wasted. Intellectually challenging teaching was desirable and 'more likely to arise from group or class sessions than from individual interactions, which tended to be preoccupied with classroom management issues' (p. 287). A work-centred environment and limited focus within sessions (with not more than two curriculum areas) was a feature of more effective teachers. Although 'most teachers preferred to unify as much of the curriculum as possible through project or topic themes, whilst retaining the distinct character of subjects such as mathematics, and to some extent, language work ... teachers tended to prefer teaching in one curriculum area at a time. Almost three-quarters of the observations took place during single subject lessons, the remainder occurring when the children were working in more than one curriculum area' (p. 80). Mortimore *et al.* also concluded that maximum communication between teachers and pupils was important. 'The main implication of this finding for classroom teachers is that, whilst organisation before the pupils arrive is important, once they are in the classroom, the emphasis should be on communication and interaction ... as noted earlier, whenever teachers engaged the attention of the whole class, they increased, vastly, the number of opportunities for communication and especially for higher-order questions to be posed or statements to be made' (p. 288). In common with the studies reviewed above Mortimore *et al.* identified the importance of the nature of teacher–pupil interaction as a significant feature of primary education.

The 'PACE' project 1989–97

In 1994 the first of four books from the Primary Assessment, Curriculum and Experience (PACE) project appeared. This project was an ESRC-funded longitudinal study designed to monitor the impact on primary schools of the 1988 Education Reform Act. Its initial aim was to: 'describe and analyse the responses of pupils and teachers in infant (and primary) schools and departments to the National Curriculum, to collect views from head teachers and teachers concerning what was being proposed and what they thought its likely impact would be, and to explore the kinds of strategies schools were evolving to manage the changes impacting upon them' (Pollard *et al.* 1994: 3).

The project sought to contribute to understanding the complex 'web of social forces' surrounding education and asked questions such as:

- Would the National Curriculum bring in more competition between children?
- Would it change children's attitudes towards learning?
- Would it affect teachers' practice?

The project continued to 1997 and was divided into three phases of data collection; October 1989–December 1992, January 1993–December 1994 and January 1995–August 1997. Its longitudinal nature meant that the first cohort of children experiencing the National Curriculum in the first year of their primary education could be followed until they reached Year 6. Thus the second book (Croll 1996) followed the children into Key Stage 2, and the final two books revisited them in Years 5 and 6 (Osborn *et al.* 2000; Pollard and Triggs 2000).

The 1989–92 project focussed on Key Stage 1 because the Act impacted on this age group first. Fieldwork included observations, questionnaires and interviews with 48 head teachers, 102 teachers and 54 pupils, in 48 schools across eight Local Education Authorities (LEAs). The second stage of the project followed the children from Key Stage 1 into KS2, Years 1–4. This involved the same schools and largely the same group of head teachers (though a few had changed); but it involved a different sample of teachers teaching the older classes. Some children also changed because they moved out of the schools.

Impact of the National Curriculum 1989–92

The first years of the National Curriculum reaffirmed the historical emphasis on Maths and English, with the new introduction of Science to the 'core'. Teachers felt that the 'broad and balanced' curriculum promised was not achieved. The National Curriculum generated a move towards stronger subject classification and a reduction of topic-based and thematic teaching. Teachers reported problems with the amount of content that was to be covered.

Teachers also reported they had had to change their teaching approach and classroom practice. By 1992 there was a sense of loss of individual autonomy (with less freedom to choose the curriculum and operate independently within individual classrooms) but also a new form of professionalism which involved collaborative and more rigorous curriculum planning within and across year groups, with more focus on progression, differentiation and coherence. However, this, coupled with curriculum overload and the demands of assessment, led to an intensification of teachers' work load. At the same time the teachers were taking more direct control over pupil work and organisation in the classroom; there was more teacher direction over pupil activity, more whole class teaching, more grouping by ability.

Pupils interviewed at Key Stage 1 showed strong preferences for activities that offered interest, success, activity and fun. Among the things they disliked were: activities that led to boredom, were perceived as difficult or involved extended periods of sitting, listening or writing, and the core subjects appeared to be less favoured than others. At the time the PACE authors commented: 'At face value, this would seem to suggest that pupil motivation regarding the most important subjects of the curriculum was a concern and that the curriculum as a "planned intervention" was proving inadequate to harness the interest of the children in support of the learning process' (Pollard *et al.* 1994: 146). They go on to suggest that this may have always been the case (prior to the introduction of the National Curriculum) and in fact they found: '... little evidence to suggest that the NC had made any substantial difference at all to the curriculum as it is actually experienced by pupils' (Pollard *et al.* 1994: 147)

The impact of the National Curriculum 1992–97

In 1993, in response to teachers' dissatisfaction with a curriculum which was characterised as 'a mile wide and an inch deep' (Daugherty 1995), and a related boycott of National Testing at Key Stage 3, the Dearing Review was commissioned and published. This was designed to respond to teachers' concerns about curriculum overload and recommended 'slimming down' the statutory curriculum to free up 20 per cent of curriculum time for teacher initiated activities (cf. Daugherty 1995). Various studies including PACE (also Galton 1999a and 1999b) report that the impact of this change was marginal, affording little more than an even greater concentration on the 'basics' of English and mathematics.

The ESRC-funded CICADA study (Alexander *et al.* 1996) also evaluated the impact of the national curriculum. The research focused on teacher-pupil discourse in primary classrooms, setting it in the wider contexts of (i) a national survey of teachers and (ii) classroom data from before the legislation which heralded the reforms in question. Fourteen LEAs agreed to take part in the national survey which had 536 respondents. Classroom observation was undertaken in 1986, 1988 and 1992 in Leeds, Bradford, Calderdale, Wakefield and Bury. Transcripts of sixty lessons were subjected to computerised discourse analysis.

While the survey data confirmed the findings of other studies – namely, a scenario of considerable change in curriculum planning, management, assessment and record-keeping – the computerised analysis of the discourse data (using the categories of *discourse, syntax, pedagogy, curriculum, participants* and *lexis*) showed this taking place against a backdrop of relative continuity at the level of pedagogy. Here, independently of the reforms, teacher–pupil discourse tended towards two clear-cut and widely-differing clusters. The first involved the teacher in much more formative feedback, directing and commanding than the second, which in turn entailed higher levels of explaining, exploring, questioning and eliciting. The study offers a useful counterpoint to those studies which, grounded more in teacher perceptions, see the National Curriculum as having induced a more fundamental pedagogic change.

The PACE project found that the early 1990s saw an emerging dominance of 'scheme' systems in maths, with teachers relying on published, structured material. Furthermore, approximately half of curriculum time was devoted to the basic skills of English and Maths. Recent research by Boyle and Bragg (2006) confirms this proportion has been maintained post-1997 with a further 10 per cent of teaching time at Key Stage 2 devoted to Science. Interestingly, however, Boyle and Bragg (2006) also report that while the figures for English and Maths continue to increase marginally at Key Stage 2, the figure for Science is in decline from 11.4 per cent in 1997 to 9.8 per cent in 2004.

Impact on curriculum content

By 1997 teachers were concerned with the move from an expressive to an instrumental view of the curriculum, in which they would be seen as 'technicians who "deliver" the curriculum. The focus on the 'core' was felt to be restrictive and while there had been an increase in time spent on science, technology and ICT, it was matched by a decrease in art, music and PE. Teachers also reported that an integrated or topic approach to teaching and learning was difficult to maintain.

Researchers' lesson observations confirmed the teachers' views, with core subjects taking up 60 per cent of curriculum time. Not much time was devoted to ICT and design and technology and the other foundation subjects were difficult to observe due to lack of curriculum time (estimated at 18 per cent).

Many teachers in the study felt that the Dearing report had not had much impact in reducing curriculum overload, 25 per cent saying it had made no difference at all: this finding accords with those of Galton *et al.* (1999b) reported above. Of those who said it had made space, 20 per cent said it did not appear to offer time for wider studies but did give some flexibility in approaching what had to be taught, including spending more time on the basics and 19 per cent used it for other activities such as assembly. Only 32 per cent said they used it to go into topics in more depth.

A further impact on the curriculum was the emergence of more specific subject teaching and classification of subjects, although there was some cross-curricular teaching in History and Geography. The majority of teachers seemed happy with this move, although some were concerned about their own lack of subject knowledge especially in ICT, science and technology. However, they did not want to give up their class to a subject specialist following the secondary school model, even though the primary curriculum has come to resemble that of the secondary school.

The pupils' views of the curriculum appeared to change little over the six years of the study, essentially recognising mathematics and English as dominant. Furthermore, attempts to redefine the balance within core subjects had not been perceived by pupils, and so English is seen as mainly literacy (with writing disliked, and with no awareness of the role of speaking and listening), and mathematics is perceived as 'sums', with little awareness of the role of discussion, practical application or problem-solving. Similarly, in science there was little awareness of investigation. Pupils recognised that the creative curriculum had been squeezed by the core subjects, by testing and the weight of subject content. Children's access to music and ICT appeared to be dictated by lack of time, lack of resources available and limited teacher expertise. The children in the study were also very aware of the bulk of content to be covered, the demand for writing and the pressure of outcomes: 'As children moved to the end of Key Stage 2 they reported a curriculum in which the core subjects were powerfully present and which they experienced mainly through sitting, listening and writing, rather than through activity' (Pollard and Triggs 2000: 84).

The PACE research also revealed pupils' views on different curriculum areas and over the six years of the study, radical changes were seen in children's stated preferences for curriculum subjects. In Year 1 the children preferred activity, play and stories. In Years 3 and 4, with their growing skills and confidence, the core subjects become more popular. However, by Years 5 and 6 there was a move away from the core and back to their Year 1 preferences, with PE, art, technology, watching television programmes and listening to stories the most popular. This demonstrates a preference for physical, expressive activity and entertainment where there is little demand for writing and assessment. The reasons children gave for their preferences included these being fun or active, or where they had some autonomy. The main reasons to dislike a subject included that it was hard, difficult to succeed at and associated with failure. However, achieving success in a subject was not necessarily linked to liking it – many high achievers still did not like core subjects, and even when children were interested in a subject, they were put off by the demand to recall and record and the lack of personal control. Furthermore, low achievers were often anxious and afraid of being exposed as failures. The researchers comment: 'It is difficult to avoid a sense of children in flight from an experience of learning that they found unsatisfactory, unmotivating and uncomfortable' (Pollard and Triggs 2000: 103). This accords with Reay and Wiliam's (1999) and Hall *et al.*'s (2004) reports of the narrowing and instrumental impact of National Testing on children's views of themselves and of what counts as educational success (see below).

Impact on pedagogy

By 1994, most teachers still seemed to be using a mixture of approaches to teaching relevant to subject and task, but the emergence of more individual work became apparent in Key Stage 2, relating to the demands of Standardised National Tests (SATs). The teachers reported 'considerable change' to their classroom teaching (52 per cent of teachers in Key Stage 1, 47 per cent in Key Stage 2), but by 1995 the Key Stage 2 figure drops, suggesting that they are getting used to the NC after the first few years. The core activities of teachers appeared to be focussed on the content of the curriculum, assessment and record-keeping.

Teachers reported that there had been an increase in whole class teaching (especially in Year 6 with SATS preparation) and lesson observations supported this. In a separate paper from the same project, McNess *et al.* (2001) report that:

> Whole class teaching and individual pupil work increased at the expense of group work ... [there was] a noticeable increase in the time spent on the core subjects ... [and] teachers ... put time aside for revision and mock tests ...
>
> (McNess *et al.* 2001: 12–13)

At Key Stage 1 the teachers mainly used collaborative group work, and individual and teacher interaction with children was mainly to do with instruction. At Key Stage 2 a mixture of strategies was used, but whole class and individual work dominated. A typical Key Stage 2 lesson consisted of a whole class teacher input followed by individual tasks. The reasons given for this strategy included a lack of resources, time, and differentiation. Collaborative group work including scientific investigation fell victim to these restraints. There was also a rise in direct instruction in Years 5 and 6 and one-to-one interaction was rare.

Teachers used a range of grouping strategies, mainly according to ability, although some used gender and friendship grouping. They felt that the National Curriculum had not changed their practice in this respect. Pupils in Year 6 appeared very aware of the ability grouping system and this similarly accords with the findings of Reay and Wiliam (1999) and Hall *et al.* (2004).

Positive outcomes of the changes included the development of the role of curriculum co-ordinators, who were able to support staff in relation to subject knowledge. There was also more detailed planning, more progression and continuity and improved practice in passing on information to the children's next teacher.

Impact on the pupils' experience

The 1997 PACE data reports on children's views of their teachers' teaching. The learning process did not appear to be discussed and there was a sense of simply 'getting through the task' (p. 178). This accords with Torrance and Pryor's (1998) findings that children often have great difficulty in understanding the purpose of tasks which they are given by teachers. Pupils simply get on with tasks as best they can, focusing on producing an acceptable outcome (that is, acceptable to their teacher), rather than the formative experience or the process of learning.

Possibly the most worrying findings of the PACE project are the effect of the changes on pupils' attitudes towards learning. By the end of Key Stage 2 the children recognised that the curriculum is very tightly framed around specific subjects, that there is little opportunity for 'free choice' and that although they value opportunities to make their own learning decisions, they rarely get the chance (found mainly in non-core subjects such as art and technology). The pressure of time and workload was very apparent to children. Their motivation to learn was affected by the boredom associated with many tasks, the degree of clarity or ambiguity, the confidence in their own skills, and whether the work was felt to be 'too hard'.

Impact on teachers' professionalism and teacher–pupil relationships

The third publication from the PACE project focused on the reactions of teachers to governmental initiatives. It was concerned to discover what impact teachers believed recent policies had had on their work. The book traces teachers' changing perceptions from the beginning of the project up to 1996. A key finding is the recognition that educational priorities had been increasingly imposed from outside the school: 'various policy initiatives have ensured that primary school teaching has become increasingly framed by requirements that are external to the school itself' (Osborn *et al.* 2000: 9). In some cases this had led to a feeling of loss of fulfilment and autonomy. However it was also noted that teachers' own professional confidence is a key factor in mediating change and that this can be affected by the teacher's biography, career path and how much support they receive from colleagues.

In the first phase of the PACE project, findings indicate that the National Curriculum may have had a positive impact on curriculum coherence and teacher professionalism as they collaborated to plan implementation. However, at the same time many teachers felt alienated from their work as they struggled to comprehend central prescription and implement curriculum content with which they might not agree. They also reported significant curriculum overload and work overload. In the later stages of the PACE investigation, a picture is drawn of a 'pressurised classroom context' (p. 140), which is more intense than hitherto and highly teacher controlled, with little scope for pedagogic flexibility and little pupil autonomy.

MORE RECENT RESEARCH EVIDENCE

Webb (1993, and 2006 with Vulliamy) also investigated the impact of the National Curriculum, but later brought the evidence up to date with specific reference to the introduction of the National Literacy and Numeracy Strategies. The sample for the first study consisted of 50 schools spread across 13 local authorities. Interviews with local authority advisors/inspectors from the 13 local authorities were conducted. Data from the schools were gathered during a one day visit to each school. This included: factual information; samples of planning and record keeping; an interview with the head teacher; observation of a Key Stage 2 class for a lesson; an interview with the observed class teacher; and informal conversations. The teachers in Webb's study most commonly expressed the following views:

1. There was support for the concept of a broad and balanced curriculum.
2. The planning for all subjects was exceedingly complex and time-consuming and there were particular problems for mixed age classes.
3. There was a conflict between an emphasis on 'the basics' and the aim of a broad balanced curriculum.
4. The teachers felt a need for stability, and time for critical reflection (p. 83).

By 2006, when the study was replicated, with 48 of the original 50 schools, the views of teachers had changed radically. Teachers viewed the core of their professionalism 'as their ability to motivate and develop children's learning' (p. 126). Webb and Vulliamy (2006) claimed that suggestions that the national strategies had 'deskilled' teachers were misplaced. However this conclusion is difficult to reconcile with the evidence presented earlier in their report which shows that the imposition of the literacy and numeracy strategies:

> ... challenged the one remaining area of teacher expertise not previously subject to government prescription and further undermined teacher competence and confidence. Notwithstanding the strong resentment of such government imposition still felt by many teachers, they expressed approval of aspects of the National Literacy Strategy and over half 'strongly liked' the National Numeracy Strategy.
> (Webb and Vulliamy 2006: 36)

Webb and Vulliamy (2006) concluded that 'the last five years or so have witnessed such extensive changes in Key Stage 2 classrooms that any notion of a wholesale return to earlier practices is out of the question' (p. 125). This finding needs careful interpretation in view of the findings from other studies (some reviewed above and others covered in the section below on the National Literacy Strategy) which show relative continuity in classroom interaction. Indeed Webb and Vulliamy make reference to the findings from systematic classroom observation studies and suggest that we should perhaps not be surprised that the hopes for interactive whole-class teaching have not been met, but they do not make clear why this should not be regarded as surprising. One possible explanation for the different arguments about the extent of change is that the political rhetoric advocating interactive teaching was not realised in action because it was contradicted by the more simple aim of introducing more whole class teaching *per se*.

The most extensive study of primary education in recent years is Alexander's *Culture and Pedagogy* (Alexander 2001). This was a macro-micro comparative study of the relationship between culture and pedagogy in England, France, India, Russia and the United States undertaken at three levels: national, school and classroom. It used a combination of methods within a historical and comparative framework: interview and documentary analysis (national level); interview, observation and documentary analysis (school level); interview, observation (two observers), videotape, still photography, documentary analysis (classroom level). The dataset derived from 30 schools in the main *Five Cultures* study, with reanalysis of earlier project data from a further 30 English schools and reference to 40 others. It included 98 interviews (audiotape recorded and transcribed); 166 lessons observed (comprising 106 in the main *Five Cultures* study, together with reanalysis of a further 60 from English schools in previous projects); videotape recordings (130 hours from main *Five Cultures* study; supplementary English data (mixture of videotape and audiotape); lesson transcripts; photographs (1500 from *Five Cultures* schools and classrooms); documents (such as national, regional, local and school policy documents, curriculum and lesson plans, assessment materials and examples of children's work).

The analysis of classroom practice was undertaken within a specially-devised framework which extended the scope of what was observed in studies such as ORACLE and PACE and which focused on what were defined as the 'cultural invariants' of teaching, using a model comprising (i) the immediate context or *frame* within which the act of teaching is set, (ii) the teaching *act* itself, and (iii) its *form*, and then a set of elements within each such category. Thus, the core acts of teaching (*task, activity, interaction* and *assessment*) were framed by *space, pupil organisation, time* and *curriculum*, and by *routines, rules and rituals*, and were given form, and were bounded temporally and conceptually by the *lesson* or teaching session.

It is very difficult to adequately summarise *Culture and Pedagogy* because of its breadth of focus. One of the main features is the way that the methodological framework enables us to reflect upon teaching in England through the international cultural context. For example at the systems level Alexander warned of the problems of over-centralisation and showed significant differences between the countries' extent of control revealed in their education systems. In England, it is argued, policy changes over at least a 20-year period have been based on a 'deficit pathology' as part of press and government collusion (p. 145).

At the classroom level, as part of a plethora of findings about classroom practice, Alexander cautioned against simplistic notions of *pace* that have been seen by some in England as the idea that quicker teaching unproblematically equates to more effective learning. The complexities of the variable 'time on task' were also explored:

> In both England and Michigan, especially the latter, we found pupils spending higher proportions of time than in France and Russia on routine matters and awaiting the teacher's attention. These differences could be illuminated by reference to certain characteristics of classroom organisation: the focus on groups and individuals; the considerable amount of time given to one-to-one monitoring (which left others expecting, and waiting for, the same degree of attention); variability and unpredictability in lesson routines; and the much greater extent of divergence between one pupil and another which the long, unitary central stages of lessons encourage (but which episodic structures discourage). Yet there were always exceptions, and in this and other matters it was therefore clear that organisational tendencies could be outweighed by cultural considerations and factors such as individual teacher competence.
>
> (Alexander 2001: 538)

Alexander (2001) shows that teachers in England interacted substantially with individuals and groups as well as the whole class but that there were also frequent disciplinary interactions. With regard to monitoring, teachers in England spent a great deal of time on this and it tended to be supervisory more than instructional.

Assessment

Following the abolition of the 11 plus, primary schools were not subject to any form of national testing or measurement-based accountability for more than 20 years (1964–88), though as we have seen, a minority of English local authorities (10) and Northern Ireland still retain selection at 11 plus (Levacic and Marsh 2007). As concerns about school standards and accountability grew, and policymakers looked for evidence of the quality and standards of primary education, they found none. The Labour government of 1973–79 had set up a sample-based measurement programme, the Assessment of Performance Unit (APU), to try to provide evidence of national standards at age 11 and 15 years, but such detailed research evidence proved far too arcane for public consumption, and in any case tended to highlight the difficulties of measuring change over time, rather than provide easy sound-bites for public debate (Torrance 2003). The 1980s Conservative government of Margaret Thatcher, with Kenneth Baker as Education Secretary, introduced a programme of National Testing at ages 7, 11, 14 and 16 (GCSE) to accompany the National Curriculum. The claim was that:

> A national curriculum backed by clear assessment arrangements will help to raise standards of attainment by:
>
> (i)   ensuring that all pupils study a broad and balanced range of subjects …
> (ii) setting clear objectives for what children … should be able to achieve …
> (iii) ensuring that all pupils … have access to … the same … programmes of study which include the key content, skills and processes which they need to learn …
> (iv) checking on progress towards those objectives and performance at various stages …
>
> (DES 1987: 3–4)

The testing arrangements have gone through many transformations as initial policy clashed with systemic reality (Daugherty 1995; Torrance 2003). National testing was originally envisaged to apply to all ten National Curriculum subjects, for all pupils, at four ages/stages of the National Curriculum (7, 11, 14 and 16 years). It was also originally envisaged to incorporate extensive teacher assessment and use of practical, 'authentic', 'Standard Assessment Tasks' (SATs), rather than traditional paper-and-pencil tests. By the mid-1990s it had become condensed into narrow paper-and-pencil tests of the 'core' subjects of English, mathematics and science, as the sheer scale of the enterprise defeated the original plans. A key policy lesson is that the larger the scope and scale of the assessment arrangements, the simpler and narrower must be the technology employed (Torrance 1995). And in this respect the political imperative of testing every child, at three key stages (plus GCSE), defeated the educational arguments about employing sophisticated 'authentic' classroom tasks.

In the early 1990s infant school teachers had little or no experience of formal assessment activities. Early research by Gipps *et al.* (1995) identified three broad categories of teachers' approaches to classroom assessment: *intuitives, evidence gatherers and systematic planners.*

> For [intuitives] assessment is a kind of 'gut reaction' … They rely upon their
> memory of what children can do and so, during the study, it was difficult for us to
> observe any ongoing teacher assessment or describe the processes they were
> using … [·] … Evidence gatherers … particularly like written evidence … 'trying to
> get as much evidence as I can' is the aim of many of these teachers, one of whom
> described herself as 'a hoarder' who 'keeps everything' … [·] … Systematic plan-
> ners … plan for assessment on a systematic basis and this has become part of their
> practice.
>
> (Gipps *et al.* 1995: 36–42)

This early reaction of 'hoarding everything' became particularly prevalent as teachers initially thought they had to be able to demonstrate pupil achievement on all
National Curriculum Statements of Attainment (SoAs). Such assumptions seemed to
be fed by local authority advisers insisting on such documentary evidence. Newspaper
reports quickly picked up on the fact that even with only the first few SoAs in each
subject being taught, and only the 'core' subjects of maths, science and English to be
reported on, infant school teachers would be dealing with 227 SoAs for each of child in
the class (approximately 30) totalling 6810 SoAs per teacher per year (see Daugherty
1995: 117). Gipps *et al.* (1995) report many such problems of curriculum and assessment overload, but equally note that for the first time in a generation primary school
teachers, and especially infant school teachers, had to identify evidence for their judgements about pupil attainment and progress, and not just rely on 'gut reaction', with
all its potential for social class, gender and racial bias.

Torrance and Pryor (1998) investigated the emerging rhetoric and practice of formative assessment in infant classrooms. Much was made of the potential of Standard
Assessment Tasks (SATs), coupled with classroom-based teacher assessment, to inform
teachers and pupils not only about pupil attainment and progress, but also about where
learning problems might arise and what might be done to address them. Torrance and
Pryor (1998) report on detailed classroom observations of 'assessment events', that
is to say teacher-pupil interaction in the context of assessment, and the very act of
teachers making judgements about pupil achievement, and how pupils understood
those judgements.

Table 29.1 Comparison of convergent assessment and divergent assessment

CONVERGENT ASSESSMENT	DIVERGENT ASSESSMENT
Assessment which aims to discover *if* the learner knows, understands or can do a predetermined thing.	Assessment which aims to discover *what* the learner knows, understands or can do.
This view of assessment might be seen as tied closely to the curriculum, and less as formative assessment, rather as repeated summative assessment or continuous assessment.	This view of assessment might be seen as more oriented to pupil needs and could be said to attend more closely to contemporary theories of learning, accepting the complexity of formative assessment.

(Adapted from Torrance and Pryor 1998: 153.)

They conclude that young pupils have very little understanding of what it is that teachers want them to do, or to achieve, in curricular terms, and spend most of their time trying to provide minimally acceptable products and avoid too much direct teacher attention. Where assessment was deployed more formatively, Torrance and Pryor identified teachers using it in 'convergent' and 'divergent' ways.

Torrance and Pryor conclude that:

- teachers need to be clear about their curriculum goals, shorter term learning intentions and the purpose of classroom tasks in relation to those learning intentions;
- communicate these intentions and the purpose of tasks to pupils – that is, what they want pupils to do and why they want them to do it – that is, communicate *task criteria*;
- similarly, communicate to pupils what it means to do tasks well – that is communicate *quality criteria*;
- make comments, mark work and give feedback relating to these criteria – indicating positive achievement as well as what and how to improve;
- but equally be alert to unanticipated learning outcomes and encourage them when encountered – that is, be alert to the possibilities for *divergent* as well as *convergent* assessment.

(Torrance and Pryor 1998, 2001)

Torrance and Pryor also report a variety of incidents in which it is apparent that pupils are struggling to understand the demands of schooling and very early begin to realise their position in the 'pecking order' of the classroom. (Pryor and Torrance 2000; Torrance and Pryor 2003). In this their work accords with the findings of Reay and Wiliam (1999) and Hall *et al.* (2004) and indeed that of the PACE project reported above. Reay and Wiliam conducted a detailed study of the impact of national testing in one south London primary school, focusing on Year 6. They describe the intense pressure of testing in Year 6 and the anxiety this generates, as more and more time is spent practicing for the tests. The curriculum is narrowed to the basics of test preparation, 'correct spelling and knowing your times tables' (p.346) and pupils come to value themselves and construct their emerging identities in relation to these narrow definitions of academic success.

Hall *et al.* (2004) conducted case studies of the impact of national testing in two primary schools in a Midlands city and London. They likewise identify the overwhelming impact of formal testing, especially in Year 6, reporting that:

assessment is synonymous with testing ... [and] assessment, narrowed to test-taking in preparation for SATs, is the main business of life in the last two terms of year 6 [p. 804].

Further:

The major theme in this article ... is the power of SATs ... to shape ... the way the school acts to position children, their parents and the teachers [p. 802].

They note the importance of SATs in the construction of success and failure for teachers and pupils alike, in the construction of notions of 'good' and 'bad' pupils, and indeed in the construction of 'happy' or 'angry' parents. They report a similar curricular narrowing to other studies reviewed above (Boyle and Bragg 2006, Osborn *et al.* 2000, Pollard and Triggs 2000), including an emphasis on literacy and numeracy in the mornings, with afternoons 'left for things like Art and PE' (p. 813). Perhaps most importantly however they identify the subjectification of pupil identity to SATs activities:

> SATs and the prospects of SATs are used as a policing mechanism to keep children attentive … [·] … pupils are relegated to the role of question-answerers … [and] … the ideal and most worthy pupil is someone who prioritises SATs success [and] who self-polices to this end …
>
> (pp. 805–9)

Harlen's earlier chapter in this volume (Chapter 19, and Harlen, 2007) confirms this focus on 'teaching to the test' (pp. 21–22), while Harlen and Deakin-Crick's (2002) systematic review found multiple evidence of the negative impact of high stakes testing and concluded that:

- After the introduction of the National Curriculum tests in England, low achieving pupils had lower self-esteem than higher-achieving pupils, whilst beforehand there was no correlation between self-esteem and achievement.
- When passing tests is high stakes, teachers adopt a teaching style which emphasises transmission teaching of knowledge, thereby favouring those students who prefer to learn in this way and disadvantaging and lowering the self-esteem of those who prefer more active and creative learning experiences [p. 4].

These are quite extraordinary findings when one thinks of research cited previously (such as Galton *et al.* and Mortimore *et al.*) indicating that the quality of teacher-pupil interaction is the most important factor in improving pupil learning experiences and raising attainment.

Reay's (2006) research further investigated how far children feel included in the classroom, their view of the curriculum and their view of themselves as learners. Her research context was part of the discussion about hearing pupils' voices in education. She undertook group interviews, observations of maths / English lessons and individual interviews in an inner city, multi-cultural primary school, with some social deprivation. In total 26 Year 6 children took part. Reay found a clear hierarchy in the class mainly based on achievement, although other factors were equally important. For example, some well-behaved clever girls were not popular because they were seen as not 'cool'. The top of the group were two able boys who were also good at PE and had university educated parents (though they had low status jobs as immigrants).

Reay suggests that children juggle their identities to find a place in the hierarchy of the classroom and she is particularly concerned about a group of quiet, poorly achieving boys at the bottom of the hierarchy. She argues that these children's views of learning and life in classrooms may never get heard due to their low status in the class. Reay suggests that the current exclusive focus on a narrowly defined form of academic achievement reproduces the status quo, giving some children a poor self-image as learner; the use of labelling, for example 'gifted and talented', and ability grouping reinforce this.

The Primary National Strategy and the teaching of literacy

Excellence and Enjoyment, England's Primary National Strategy (PNS) (DfES 2003), published in 2003, offered hope to many in education of a more flexible and creative approach to the curriculum. However Ofsted's report on the primary curriculum, the National Literacy Strategy (NLS), and the National Numeracy Strategy (NNS) based on visits between 2002 and 2004 (Office for Standards in Education (Ofsted 2005) noted that few schools had made significant progress in adopting more flexible and creative ways of managing the curriculum. They also found that, 'In English, teachers' planning focuses too much on covering the many objectives in the NLS Framework for teaching, instead of meeting pupils' specific needs. This inflexibility hinders improvements in the quality of English teaching' (p. 2). The claimed lack of progress by schools with regard to flexibility and creativity is perhaps indicative of the contradictions that are part of *Excellence and Enjoyment.* Although the PNS exhorts schools to be more flexible and creative, at the same time the emphasis on the literacy and numeracy strategies remained, and was intensified.

One of the key features of the NLS and NNS has been the organisation of learning as a sequence of teaching objectives. In the report on the first four years of the NLS based on inspection visits carried out during 1998–2002 (Ofsted 2002) it was noted in relation to the teaching of literacy that, 'There is more direct teaching, the lessons have a clearer structure and learning objectives are more precise' (p. 2). The encouragement by Ofsted in this and other publications, including school and teacher-training institution inspection reports, to focus on teaching objectives resulted in the practice of teachers' lessons being strongly objective-led, to the extent that objectives were written onto classroom boards and pupils were encouraged to write the objective of the lesson in their exercise books. Ofsted's change of emphasis from positive findings on precise objectives in 2002 to the criticism that teachers were focusing on them too much in 2005 could be seen as a reflection of government policy represented in the change of guidance from the NLS to the PNS rather than a rigorous and objective analysis of the evidence from inspection observations. A persistent problem with Ofsted national reports on the English and literacy curriculum has been the lack of consistent attention to particular main findings from one report to the next.

Earl *et al.*'s (2003) government-funded evaluation of the NLS and NNS included collection of data from schools as follows:

a) two postal surveys (in 2000 and 2002), each to two samples of 500 schools, one for literacy and the other for numeracy. Parallel questionnaires went to head teachers and teachers;
b) a postal survey to all literacy and numeracy consultants in LEAs across England in 2002;
c) repeated visits to 10 selected schools (with various sizes, locations, pupil populations, levels of attainment) and their LEAs: 4 to 6 days in each school. The research team interviewed head teachers and teachers, observed literacy and mathematics lessons, and analysed documents;
d) interviews with literacy and numeracy managers and consultants from LEAs of the 10 selected schools. The researchers also attended training sessions and staff meetings in some of those LEAs;
e) observations and interviews in 17 other schools (including special schools) and LEAs. Three of these were one-day visits to schools early in 2000, while the others

were single visits as part of shadowing regional directors or HMI, or attending meetings locally.

Earl *et al.* (2003) found that the strategies had altered classroom practice. In particular greater use of whole class teaching, more structured lessons and more use of objectives to plan and guide teaching. Teachers' views about the strategies were more variable than head teachers' who were more likely to be in favour. Head teachers and teachers were more supportive of the NNS than they were of the NLS. For the most part, both teachers and head teachers believed that NNS has been easier to implement and had had greater effects on pupil learning than the NLS. Overall Earl *et al.* report a wide range of variation in teachers' opinion of the NLS ranging from positive to negative.

A problem with the development of the NLS Framework for Teaching and its associated pedagogy was the questionable evidence base, something that was addressed in a series of publications (Wyse 2000, 2001; Wyse and Jones 2001; Wyse 2003 – Beard (2003), who was commissioned to write a review of evidence related to the NLS after its implementation published a response to this). Subsequent publications questioned the evidence base for the PNS and its literacy teaching requirements (Alexander 2004; Wyse 2006; Wyse and Styles 2007; Wyse and Jones 2008).

A series of research studies all reported that the recommended pedagogy of the NLS literacy hour was resulting in rather limited teacher-pupil interaction which was tending towards short initiation-response sequences and a consequent lack of extended discussion. Observation schedules were used in studies such as those by Hardman *et al.* (2003), English *et al.* (2002) and Mroz *et al.* (2000). Mroz *et al.* (2000) noted the limited opportunities for pupils to question or explore ideas. English *et al.* (2002) found that there was a reduction in extended teacher pupil interactions. Hardman *et al.* (2003) found that the NLS was encouraging teachers to use more directive forms of teaching with little opportunities for pupils to explore and elaborate on their ideas. Skidmore *et al.* (2003) used audio recordings of teacher-pupil dialogue combined with video of non-verbal communication to support their finding that teachers were dominating interaction during the guided reading segment of the literacy hour. Tymms and Merrell (2007, Chapter 17 in this volume) report similar findings (p. 19). Parker and Hurry (2007) interviewed 51 Key Stage 2 teachers in 2001 and videotaped observations of the same teachers in class literacy sessions focusing on teacher and pupil questions and answers. They found that direct teacher questioning in the form of teacher-led recitation was the dominant strategy used for reading comprehension teaching and that children were not encouraged to generate their own questions about texts.

Our synthesis of research in relation to the NLS Framework for teaching presents a picture which reveals some limited benefits but overall shows poor outcomes. However, Stannard and Huxford (2007) are more positive in their evaluation. John Stannard was the director of the NLS until 2000 and Laura Huxford was the training director from 1997 to 2004. Stannard and Huxford base their claims for the success of the NLS mainly on their perception of the rise in statutory test scores (we show an alternative perception of statutory test outcomes in this chapter). Although their account is weakened by lack of attention to relevant research and scholarship in the field, they make a number of significant points about the NLS, in particular how the process of implementation was made more difficult by strident critics of the NLS approach to reading, resulting in a disproportionate amount of time spent managing a rather narrow debate about reading at the expense of addressing a range of arguably more important factors that needed attention.

In October 2006 the new *PNS Framework for Literacy* was released with an expectation that 'the majority of schools and setting are likely to be making extensive use of the renewed Framework at some stage during this academic year' (DfES 2006: 6). The following evaluative comments about the new literacy framework are based on Wyse and Jones (2008). The first change from the NLS Framework for Teaching was that although paper copies of a reduced version of the framework were available, the full framework and guidance appeared on a PNS Frameworks website. Whereas with the NLS the names of those who developed the literacy framework were known, with the PNS Framework all the material is attributed to the DfES Standards Site and the PNS. The number of objectives in the new framework was drastically reduced in comparison with the old framework. The tendency to encourage one-off lessons was replaced with longer units of work. The division of objectives into word-level, sentence-level, and text-level was abolished.

In spite of the overall reduction in objectives the framework as a whole, which includes many guidance documents and hyperlinks to other government resources may prove to be unwieldy and prescriptive. The types of books children will study is prescribed, the types of writing that they will carry out is prescribed. The way that this is to be taught has been specified in even more detail than the NLS. It appears that a single teaching model, rather than encouragement to use a range of approaches, is still being applied: 1, analyse a text; 2, teacher models the text; 3, children evaluate their work 'against agreed criteria'.

The PNS objectives show a welcome reduction in the grammar objectives that were a feature of the NLS. However, as in most sections of the PNS Framework, a summary of NLS objectives is given for each section of planning to show that these are still being covered. There is also a continued recommendation to use the *Grammar for Writing* resource which explicitly addresses the objectives from the NLS. Wyse's (2001) review of empirical evidence showed that traditional grammar teaching did not enhance children's writing, something that the systematic review by Andrews *et al.* (2004) confirmed; hence it seems questionable that the emphasis on grammar through reference to the old objectives is still encouraged.

Following the Rose Report (Rose 2006) teachers were required to use the 'synthetic phonics' approach to the teaching of reading. This marked another significant shift with regard to control of the curriculum and pedagogy that began with the relative freedom for teachers prior to 1988, and ended with government prescribing teaching method in 2006. The Rose report was controversial as can be seen in the following examples from the range of publications which followed:

- Kershner and Howard (2006) – a special edition of *The Psychology of Education Review* which featured a paper by Morag Stuart, one of Rose's advisors, followed by responses from a range of researchers;
- Lewis and Ellis (2006) – Final chapter of the book includes a range of views about the Rose Report;
- Wyse and Styles (2007) – Questioned the evidence base for Rose's recommendation;
- Brooks (2007) – One of Rose's advisors responds to the article by Wyse and Styles (2007) (this is followed by a response by Wyse and Styles);

- Ellis (2007) – discusses the different ways that policy makers in Scotland and England responded to the Clackmannanshire research;
- Wyse and Goswami (2009) – questions Rose's use of evidence to reach the conclusion that synthetic phonics is the best way to teach reading.

The concerns expressed about Rose's review of early reading lead to some doubt that the government review of the primary curriculum, also being carried out by Rose, will be an objective review of evidence. One of the key difficulties centres on how Rose will resolve the differences in the conclusions made by previous government reviews of mathematics and reading. For example the report of mathematics says, '233. … effective pedagogical practice is not confined to any single approach. Rather it stems from a principled selection from a wide repertoire of techniques and organisational arrangements designed to match teaching to the developing learner' (Williams 2008: 64). This is in sharp contrast to the Rose Report on the teaching of early reading, which said '51. Having considered a wide range of evidence, the review has concluded that the case for systematic phonic work is overwhelming and much strengthened by a synthetic approach' (Rose 2006: 20). Wyse (2008) argues that the tension between these two views of pedagogy should be resolved in favour of the conclusion put forward in the maths review. The government's response to the interim reports of the University of Cambridge Primary Review, this and the other chapters of this volume, also prompts some pessimism that evidence will be a sufficient influence in recommendations and decisions to be made about primary education.

The National Numeracy Strategy

A National Numeracy Project was introduced to a sample of 200 pilot schools in September 1996 following critical discussion of English schools' performance in the Third International Maths and Science Study (TIMSS) and a critical Ofsted report on standards in Maths (Brown *et al.* 2000). This was extended to all primary schools via a full National Numeracy Strategy (NNS) in 1999. The key curriculum change was to emphasise a higher proportion of basic calculation skills (rather than understanding and application of procedures) and more mental arithmetic (rather than reliance on calculators), while at the same time introducing more whole class teaching.

The Strategy was claimed by government to be based on research on effective Maths teaching. However key reviews of research at the time reported that there was no evidence that whole class teaching or the privileging of basic calculation skills led to higher standards overall (Brown *et al.* 1998, 2000). Moreover the 'objectives-based' curriculum model which the NNS employed can be said to be helpful in providing clarity of content and sequencing for teachers, but does not reflect the many complex ways in which children learn, and researchers expressed concern that lack of differentiation in whole-class teaching could interfere with learning. Such a lack has been shown to leave both high and low achievers without appropriate tasks (Brown *et al.* 1998: 369). Reporting findings which echo those of Galton *et al.* (1999b) among others, reviewed previously, Brown *et al.* (1998) state that 'the quality of teacher-pupil interaction [is] a much more important factor than class organisation' (p. 371) with respect to attainment. They report that:

> Both international and English observational studies … [agree] on … the aspects of teacher quality which correlate with attainment … the use of higher order

questions, statements and tasks which require thought rather than practice; emphasis on establishing, through dialogue, meanings and connections between different mathematical ideas and contexts; collaborative problem-solving in class and small group settings; more autonomy for students to develop and discuss their own methods and ideas.

(Brown *et al.* 1998: 373)

Even the need for the National Numeracy Strategy has been questioned. Most primary schools already spent an average of an hour a day on Maths (Mullis *et al.* 1997: the 'TIMSS' study); and Ruthven (1997) reported in any case that 'the degree of calculator use remains modest in most schools' (p.18). Furthermore Brown *et al.* (2000) note that:

The only educational (as opposed to social) factor consistently correlated with test performance is that of 'opportunity to learn'. This means that, unsurprisingly, teaching more mental arithmetic is likely to improve performance in mental arithmetic

(Brown *et al.* 2000: 463)

Equally however, teaching more mental arithmetic means teaching *less* of something else, including investigation, application and problem solving; which rather sums up the dilemma of the National Curriculum overall. Extensive research evidence cited above reports initial problems of curriculum overload followed by intense focus on only those core subjects included in national testing. Such distortion of the curriculum has also been noted by Ofsted's former Chief Inspector, Mike Tomlinson:

In some primary schools the arts, creative and practical subjects are receiving less attention than previously. This risks an unacceptable narrowing of the curriculum …

(Commentary, Ofsted 2002: 1)

Tomlinson's successor as Chief Inspector, David Bell, similarly reported that:

One of the things inspectors find is that an excessive or myopic focus on targets can actually narrow and reduce achievement by crowding out some of the essentials of effective and broadly-based learning … I have a very real concern that the innovation and reform that we need to see in our schools may be inhibited by an over-concentration on targets.

(Bell 2003)

SO WHAT IS HAPPENING TO STANDARDS?

The research evidence cited above seems to indicate that the current intense focus on testing and test results in the core subjects of English, Maths and Science is narrowing the curriculum and driving teaching in exactly the opposite direction to that which research indicates will improve learning and attainment. That is, good quality teaching will employ a variety of methods and tasks, including small group work and investigative work, but currently teaching in the upper primary school comprises little more than whole class 'cued elicitation' (Edwards and Mercer 1987) and direct test preparation (cf. also Harlen and Tymms and Merrell in this volume).

Interestingly, National Curriculum test results would seem to bear out this analysis. While extensive discussion of how 'standards' can be measured over time, and whether or not standards are rising, is beyond the scope of this chapter (cf. Torrance 2003; Tymms 2004; Tymms and Merrell 2007; Meadows *et al.* 2007), a brief review of national test results at Key Stages 1 and 2 indicates an initial improvement followed by a long plateau, with results still not meeting the government's own targets.[1]

While the data have been presented in such a way as to accentuate and hence highlight the trend, clearly, results improved quickly and dramatically, from a relatively low base (especially at Key Stage 2, age 11) but then have largely levelled off since 2000 (see Table 29.1 and Figures 29.1 and 29.2). They have reached a plateau (below the targets that the government set for itself) that not even the NLS and NNS have been able to raise. Indeed, it is interesting to note that at Key Stage 2, results in Science started higher and have remained higher, without the benefit (or hindrance) of a National Science Strategy. Various technical explanations have been advanced as part of the explanation for this phenomenon (cf. Tymms 2004) but the most obvious explanation is that teachers were initially unprepared for National Testing, learnt very quickly how to coach for the tests, hence results improved, but any benefit to be squeezed from the system by such coaching has long since been exhausted. Interestingly such an explanation parallels similar research internationally where, for example, Klein *et al.* (2000) reviewing state-level results in Texas report 'score inflation and unwanted test preparation' (p. 17). Similarly a recently completed study of the implementation of the US *No Child Left Behind* legislation by Rand Education, funded by the US National Science Foundation, reported that:

> […] changes included a narrowing of the curriculum and instruction toward tested topics and even toward certain problems styles or formats. Teachers also reported focusing more on students near the proficient cut-score …
>
> (Hamilton *et al.* 2007, Summary: xix)

Table 29.2 Percentage of pupils gaining National Curriculum Assessment Level 2 or above at age 7 and Level 4 or above at age 11

Date	KS1 : Age 7		KS2 : Age 11		
	English	*Maths*	*English*	*Maths*	*Science*
1992	77[1]	78			
1995	76	78	48[2]	44	
1996	80	80	58	54	62
2000	81/84[3]	90	75	72	85
2002	84/82	90	75	73	86
2003	84/81	90	75	73	87
2004	85/81	90	77	74	86
2005	85/82[4]	91	79	75	86
2006			79	75	86

Notes:
1 1992 is the 'first full run' of KS1 tests.
2 1995 is the 'first full run' of KS2 tests.
3 From 2000, 'Reading' and 'Writing' were reported separately for KS1; the first figure is 'reading'.
4 From 2005, KS1 results derive from Teacher Assessments only and cannot any longer be said to be the results of 'National Tests'.

Similar findings are reported in Harlen (2007: 22) and even reflect research in business management about how innovation initially brings improvement, but tails off, as personnel are de-skilled then re-skilled by change, but then become accustomed to it (Strang and Macy 2001). The key problem with such a phenomenon in education however, is that it is by no means apparent that even such early improvements in scores denote any actual improvements in educational standards. Tymms and Merrell (2007) report on modest improvements in reading and mathematics. Comparative international evidence reviewed by Whetton, Ruddock and Twist (2007) for this volume

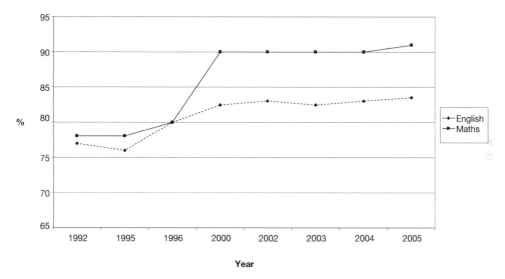

Figure 29.1 Percentage of pupils gaining National Curriculum Assessment Level 2 or above at age 7.

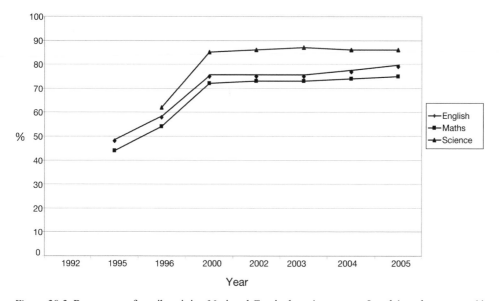

Figure 29.2 Percentage of pupils gaining National Curriculum Assessment Level 4 or above at age 11.

(Chapter 18) similarly notes a 'slight improvement' in maths and the likelihood of a more substantial improvement in reading. Whetton, Ruddock and Twist (2007) also note good comparative achievement in Science. However the various studies reviewed earlier in this chapter would indicate that coaching for the tests has restricted curriculum coverage and the quality of teaching and learning overall, and that as test scores have risen, educational standards, broadly conceived, may actually have declined.

NOTES

1 See Table 29.1, Figure 29.1, and Figure 29.2.

REFERENCES

Alexander, R.J. (1997) *Policy and Practice in Primary Education: local initiative, national agenda.* London: Routledge.

——(2001) *Culture and Pedagogy: international comparisons in primary education.* Oxford: Blackwell.

——(2004) 'Still no pedagogy? Principle, pragmatism and compliance in primary education', *Cambridge Journal of Education* 34(1): 7–33.

Alexander, R.J., Rose, J. and Woodhead, C. (1992) *Curriculum Organisation and Classroom Practice in Primary Schools: a discussion paper.* London: DES.

Alexander, R.J., Willcocks, J. and Nelson, N. (1996) 'Discourse, pedagogy and the National Curriculum: change and continuity in primary schools', *Research Papers in Education* 11(1): 81–120.

Andrews, R., Torgerson, C., Beverton, S., Locke, T., Low, G. and Robinson, A. (2004) 'The effect of grammar teaching (syntax) in English on 5 to 16 year olds' accuracy and quality in written composition', *Research Evidence in Education Library.* Online (Available at: http://eppi. ioe.ac.uk/cms/, accessed 5 February 2007).

Beard, R. (2003) 'Not the whole story of the national literacy strategy: a response to Dominic Wyse', *British Educational Research Journal* 29(6): 917–29.

Bell, D. (2003) Speech to the City of York's Annual Education Conference, 28 February 2003.

Boyle, B. and Bragg, J. (2006) 'A curriculum without foundation', *British Educational Research Journal* 32(4): 569–82.

Brooks, G. (2007) 'Rationality and phonics: a comment on Wyse and Styles', *Literacy* 41(3): 170–76.

Brown, M., Askew, M., Baker, D., Denvir, H. and Millett, A. (1998) 'Is the National Numeracy Strategy research-based?', *British Journal of Educational Studies* 46(4): 362–85.

Brown, M., Millett, A., Bibby, T. and Johnson, D. (2000) 'Turning our attention from the what to the how: the National Numeracy Strategy', *British Educational Research Journal* 26(4): 457–72.

CACE (Central Advisory Council for Education) (1967) *Children and their Primary Schools: a report of the Central Advisory Council for Education (England)* (the Plowden Report). London: HMSO.

Croll, P. (1996) *Teachers, Pupils and Primary Schooling: continuity and change.* London: Cassell.

Daugherty, R. (1995) *National Curriculum Assessment: a review of policy 1987–1994.* London: Falmer Press.

Dearing, R. (1993) *The National Curriculum and its Assessment: final report.* London: School Curriculum and Assessment Authority.

Department of Education and Science (DES)/Welsh Office (WO) (1987) *The National Curriculum 5–16: a consultative document.* London: DES/WO.

Department for Education and Skills (DfES) (2003) *Excellence and Enjoyment: a strategy for primary schools.* Suffolk: DfES.

DfES (2006) *Primary Framework for Literacy and Mathematics*. London: DfES.

Earl, L., Watson, N., Levin, B., Leithwood, K., Fullan, M. and Torrance, N. (2003) *Watching and Learning: Oise/ut evaluation of the implementation of the National Literacy and Numeracy strategies*. Nottingham: DfES Publications.

Edwards, D. and Mercer, N. (1987) *Common Knowledge*. London: Methuen.

Ellis, S. (2007) 'Policy and research: lessons from the Clackmannanshire synthetic phonics initiative', *Journal of Early Childhood Literacy* 7(3): 281–97.

Ellis, T., McWhirter, J., McColgan, D. and Haddow, B. (1976) *William Tyndale: the teachers' story*. London: Writers and Readers Publishing Co-operative.

English, E., Hargreaves, L. and Hislam, J. (2002) 'Pedagogical dilemmas in the national literacy strategy: primary teachers' perceptions, reflections and classroom behaviour', *Cambridge Journal of Education* 32(1): 9–26.

Galton, M., Hargreaves, L., Comber, C. and Wall, D. (1999a) *Inside the Primary Classroom: 20 years on*. London: Routledge.

Galton, M., Hargreaves, L., Comber, C., Wall, D. and Pell, T. (1999b) 'Changes in patterns of teacher interaction in primary classrooms 1976–96', *British Educational Research Journal* 25(1): 23–37.

Galton, M., Simon, B. and Croll, P. (1980) *Inside the Primary Classroom*. London: Routledge and Kegan Paul.

Gipps, C., Brown, M., McCallum, B. and McAlister, S. (1995) *Intuition or Evidence? Teachers' and national assessment of seven year olds*. Buckingham: Open University Press.

Hall, K., Collins, J., Benjamin, S., Nind, M. and Sheehy, K. (2004) 'SATurated models of pupildom: assessment and inclusion/exclusion', *British Educational Research Journal* 30(6): 801–18.

Halsey, A.H., Floud, J. and Anderson, C.A. (Eds) (1961) *Education, Economy and Society*. New York: Free Press.

Hamilton, L., Stecher, B., Marsh, J., McCombs, J., Robyn, A., Russell, J., Naftel, S. and Barney, H. (2007) *Standards-based Accountability Under No Child Left Behind*. Santa Monica: Rand Education.

Hardman, F., Smith, F. and Wall, K. (2003) 'Interactive whole class teaching in the National Literacy Strategy', *Cambridge Journal of Education* 33(2): 197–215.

Harlen, W. (2007) *The Quality of Learning: assessment alternatives for primary education* (Primary Review Research Survey 3/4). Cambridge: University of Cambridge Faculty of Education. (Chapter 19 of this volume).

Harlen, W. and Deakin Crick, R. (2002) 'A systematic review of the impact of summative assessment and tests on students' motivation for learning (EPPI-Centre Review, version 1.1)', *Research Evidence in Education Library. Issue 1*. Online (Available: http://eppi.ioe.ac.uk/cms/Default.aspx?tabid=108, accessed 9 January 2007).

Kershner, R. and Howard, J. (2006) *The Psychology of Education Review* 30(2): 1–60.

Klein, S., Hamilton, L., McCaffrey, D. and Stecher, B. (2000) 'What do test scores in Texas tell us?', *Education Policy Analysis Archives* 8(49).

Levacic, R. and Marsh, A. (2007) 'Secondary modern schools: are their pupils disadvantaged?', *British Educational Research Journal* 33(2): 155–78.

Lewis, M. and Ellis, S. (Eds) (2006) *Phonics: practice research and policy*. London: Paul Chapman Publishing.

McNess, E., Triggs, P., Broadfoot, P., Osborn, M. and Pollard, A. (2001) 'The changing nature of assessment in English primary schools: findings from the PACE Project 1989–97', *Education 3–13* 29(3): 9–16.

Meadows, S., Herrick, D., Filer, A. and the ALSPAC Study Team (2007) 'Improvement in national test reading scores at Key Stage 1: grade inflation or better achievement?', *British Educational Research Journal* 33(1): 47–60.

Mortimore, P., Sammons, P., Stoll, L., Lewis, D. and Ecob, R. (1988) *School Years: the junior years*. Wells: Open Books Publishing Ltd.

Mroz, M., Smith, F. and Hardman, F. (2000) 'The discourse of the literacy hour', *Cambridge Journal of Education* 30(3): 380–90.

Mullis, I., Martin, M., Beaton, A., Gonzales, E., Kelly, D. and Smith, T. (1997) *Mathematics Achievement in the Primary School Years: IEA's Third International Mathematics and Science Study (TIMSS)*. Chestnut Hill, MA: Boston College.

Office for Standards in Education (Ofsted) (2002) *The National Literacy Strategy: the first four years 1998–2002*. London: Ofsted.

Ofsted (2005) *The National Literacy and Numeracy Strategies and the Primary Curriculum*. London: Ofsted.

Osborn, M., McNess, E. and Broadfoot, P. (2000) *What Teachers Do: changing policy and practice in primary education*. London: Continuum.

Parker, M. and Hurry, J. (2007) 'Teachers' use of questioning and modelling comprehension skills in primary classrooms', *Educational Review* 59(3): 299–314.

Pollard, A., Broadfoot, P., Croll, P., Osborn, M. and Abbott, D. (1994) *Changing English Primary Schools? The impact of the Education Reform Act at Key Stage 1*. London: Cassell.

Pollard, A. and Triggs, P. (2000) *What Pupils Say: changing policy and practice in primary education*. London: Continuum.

Pryor, J. and Torrance, H. (2000) 'Questioning the three bears: the social construction of assessment in the classroom', in A. Filer (Ed) *Assessment: social practice and social product*. London: RoutledgeFalmer.

Reay, D. (2006) '"I'm not seen as one of the clever children": consulting primary school pupils about the social conditions of learning', *Educational Review* 58(2): 171–81.

Reay, D. and Wiliam, D. (1999) '"I'll be a nothing": structure, agency and the construction of identity through assessment', *British Educational Research Journal* 25(3): 343–54.

Ruthven, K. (1997) *The Use of Calculators at Key Stages 1–3*. London: School Curriculum and Assessment Authority.

Skidmore, D., Perez-Parent, M. and Arnfield, D. (2003) 'Teacher-pupil dialogue in the guided reading session', *Reading Literacy and Language* 37(2): 47–53.

Stannard, J. and Huxford, L. (2007) *The Literacy Game: the story of the National Literacy Strategy*. London: Routledge.

Strang, D. and Macy, M. (2001) 'In search of excellence: fads, success stories, and adaptive emulation', *American Journal of Sociology* 107(1): 147–82.

Teddlie, C. and Reynolds, D. (Eds) (2000) *The International Handbook of School Effectiveness Research*. London: Routledge.

Torrance, H. (1995) (Ed) *Evaluating Authentic Assessment*. Buckingham: Open University Press.

——(2003) 'Assessment of the National Curriculum in England', in T. Kellaghan and D. Stufflebeam (Eds) *International Handbook of Educational Evaluation*. Dordrecht: Kluwer.

Torrance, H. and Pryor, J. (1998) *Investigating Formative Assessment: teaching learning and assessment in the classroom*. Buckingham: Open University Press.

——(2001) 'Developing formative assessment in the classroom: using action research to explore and modify theory', *British Educational Research Journal* 27(5): 615–31.

——(2003) 'Investigating formative classroom assessment', in L. Poulson and M. Wallace (Eds) Learning to Read Critically in Teaching and Learning. London: Sage.

Tymms, P. (2004) 'Are standards rising in English primary schools?', *British Educational Research Journal* 30(4): 477–94.

Tymms, P. and Merrell, C. (2007) *Standards and Quality in English Primary Schools Over Time: the national evidence* (Primary Review Research Survey 4/1). Cambridge: University of Cambridge Faculty of Education. (Chapter 17 of this volume.)

Webb, R. (1993) *Eating the Elephant Bit by Bit: the National Curriculum at Key Stage 2*. London: Association of Teachers and Lecturers.

Webb, R. and Vulliamy, G. (2006) *Coming Full Circle? The impact of New Labour's education policies on primary school teachers' work*. London: The Association of Teachers and Lecturers.

Whetton, C., Ruddock, G. and Twist, L. (2007) *Standards in English Primary Education: the international evidence* (Primary Review Research Survey 4/2). Cambridge: University of Cambridge Faculty of Education. (Chapter 18 of this volume.)

Williams, P. and DCSF (2008) *Independent Review of Mathematics Teaching in Early Years Settings and Primary Schools*. Nottingham: DCSF Publications.

Wyse, D. (2000) 'Phonics – the whole story?: a critical review of empirical evidence', *Educational Studies* 26(3): 355–64.

——(2001) 'Grammar. For writing?: a critical review of empirical evidence', *British Journal of Educational Studies* 49(4): 411–27.

——(2003) 'The National Literacy Strategy: a critical review of empirical evidence', *British Educational Research Journal* 29(6): 903–16.

——(2006) 'Pupils' word choices and the teaching of grammar', *Cambridge Journal of Education* 36(1): 31–47.

——(2008) 'Primary education: who's in control?', *Education Review* 21(1): 76–82.

Wyse, D. and Goswami, U. (2009) 'Synthetic phonics and the teaching of reading', *British Educational Research Journal*.

Wyse, D. and Jones, R. (2001) *Teaching English, Language and Literacy*. London: Routledge Falmer.

——(2008) *Teaching English, Language and Literacy* (2nd edition). London: Routledge.

Wyse, D. and Styles, M. (2007) 'Synthetic phonics and the teaching of reading: the debate surrounding England's "Rose Report"', *Literacy* 47(1): 35–42.

Yates, A. and Pidgeon, D.A. (1957) *Admission to Grammar Schools*. London: Newnes.

Appendix 1
The Cambridge Primary Review
Remit and process

The Cambridge Primary Review is a wide-ranging independent enquiry into the condition and future of primary education in England. It was supported from 2006–10 by Esmée Fairbairn Foundation and based at the University of Cambridge. The Review was launched in October 2006. Between October 2007 and May 2008 it published as interim reports 28 research surveys and an account of the 2007 regional Community Soundings. In February 2009 it published a two-volume special report on the primary curriculum. Its final report was published in autumn 2009.

The launch of the Review was preceded by nearly three years of planning and by consultation with government, opposition parties, DfES/DCSF officials, the all-party Commons Education and Skills (now Children, Schools and Families) Committee, public bodies involved in the primary phase of education, the teaching unions and a range of other interested organisations.

The Review was initiated and directed by Professor Robin Alexander, Fellow of Wolfson College at the University of Cambridge and Professor of Education Emeritus at the University of Warwick. Its Advisory Committee was chaired by Dame Gillian Pugh, Visiting Professor at the University of London Institute of Education, Chair of the National Children's Bureau and formerly Chief Executive of Coram Family.

REMIT

The remit for the Cambridge Primary Review, as agreed between Esmée Fairbairn Foundation and the University of Cambridge in 2005–6, is as follows:

1. *With respect to public provision in England, the Review will seek to identify the purposes which the primary phase of education should serve, the values which it should espouse, the curriculum and learning environment which it should provide, and the conditions which are necessary in order to ensure both that these are of the highest and most consistent quality possible, and that they address the needs of children and society over the coming decades.*
2. *The Review will pay close regard to national and international evidence from research, inspection and other sources on the character and adequacy of current provision in respect of the above, on the prospects for recent initiatives, and on other available options. It will seek the advice of expert advisers and witnesses, and it will invite submissions and take soundings from a wide range of interested agencies and individuals, both statutory and non-statutory.*

3. *The Review will publish both interim findings and a final report. The latter will com-bine evidence, analysis and conclusions together with recommendations for both national policy and the work of schools and other relevant agencies.*

ESSENTIAL FEATURES

The Cambridge Primary Review:

- is financially and politically independent;
- focuses on the statutory primary phase, 4/5–11;
- is grounded in national and international evidence;
- has sought views across a wide range of professional, political and public con-stituencies;
- combines assessment of current provision with the development of a vision for the future;
- has produced interim reports and briefings, and a final report containing findings, conclusions and recommendations for future policy and practice.

PERSPECTIVES AND THEMES

The Cambridge Primary Review is conceived as a matrix of ten themes and four strands of evidence, overarched by three **perspectives**:

- The lives and needs of children and the condition of childhood today
- The condition of the society and world in which today's children are growing up
- The present condition and future prospects of England's system of primary education.

The **ten themes** addressed by the Review are:

1. Purposes and values
2. Learning and teaching
3. Curriculum and assessment
4. Quality and standards
5. Diversity and inclusion
6. Settings and professionals
7. Parenting, caring and educating
8. Children's lives beyond the school
9. Structures and phases
10. Funding and governance.

In respect of these themes, each of which is elaborated as the sub-themes and con-tributory questions listed in Appendix 2, the Review aims to address two fundamental questions:

- *Evidence:* how well is England's system of primary education doing?
- *Vision:* how can it best meet the needs of children and society over the coming decades?

EVIDENCE

The Cambridge Primary Review has four main strands of evidence:

Submissions. Following the convention in enquiries of this kind, written submissions were invited from all who wished to contribute. By March 2009, 1052 submissions had been received. They ranged from brief single-issue expressions of opinion to substantial documents of up to 300 pages covering several or all of the themes and comprising both detailed evidence and recommendations for the future. The majority of the submissions were from national organisations, but a significant number came from individuals.

Soundings. This strand had two parts. The *community soundings* were a series of nine regionally-based one to two day events, each comprising a sequence of meetings with representatives from schools and the communities they serve. They took place between January and March 2007, and entailed 87 witness sessions with groups of pupils, parents, governors, teachers, teaching assistants and heads, and with educational and community representatives from the areas in which the soundings took place. The *national soundings* were a programme of more formal meetings with national organisations both inside and outside education. Some of these, with government, statutory agencies, public bodies and unions, took the form of regular consultations throughout the Review's duration. Others, which included three seminars with specially-convened groups of teachers and two sessions with representatives of major non-statutory organisations, took place between January and March 2008 and explored issues arising from the Review's by then considerable body of evidence. The National Soundings helped the team to clarify matters which were particularly problematic or contested, in preparation for the writing of the final report.

Surveys. Several months before the launch of the Review, 28 surveys of published research relating to the Review's ten themes were commissioned, on the basis of competitive bidding and peer review, from 66 academic consultants in leading university departments of education and allied fields. The resulting research reports and their accompanying briefings and media releases were published in cross-thematic groups over several months, starting in autumn 2007. They provoked considerable media, public and political interest, and provided the top UK news story on several occasions.

Searches and policy mapping. With the co-operation of DfES/DCSF, QCA, Ofsted and TDA, the Review tracked recent policy and examined official data bearing on the primary phase. This provided the necessary legal, demographic, financial and statistical background to the Review and an important resource for its consideration of policy options.

The balance of evidence. The four evidential strands sought to balance opinion-seeking with empirical data; non-interactive expressions of opinion with face-to-face discussion; official data with independent research; and material from England with that from other parts of the UK and from international sources. This enquiry, unlike some of its predecessors, looked outwards from primary schools to the wider society, and made full but judicious use of international data and ideas from other countries.

Other meetings. In addition to the formal evidence-gathering procedures, the Review's director and other team members met national and regional bodies for the exchange of information and ideas. At the time of going to press (April 2009) 146 such meetings had taken place or were scheduled, in addition to the 92 community and national soundings, making a total of 238 sessions.

REPORTS

The Cambridge Primary Review has published both interim and final reports. The main series of 29 interim reports, which included 28 of the commissioned research surveys and the report on the community soundings, served a formative function, seeking to provoke further debate which then fed back into the Review. The interim reports were published on the Cambridge Primary Review's website (www.primaryreview.org.uk) together with a record of their extensive media coverage. Electronic and print versions of the reports and briefings were widely circulated.

The Cambridge two special reports on the primary curriculum were published in February 2009. Written as part of the Review's final report, they were brought forward and adapted as contributions to the formal consultation on the interim report of the government's Rose Review of the primary curriculum.

The Cambridge Primary Review final report draws on the various strands of evidence outlined above to address the ten listed themes and attendant questions. It combines findings, analysis, reflection and conclusions, together with recommendations for policy and practice. Its companion volume includes the commissioned surveys of published research, updated in light of the most recent research and policy.

OUTLINE TIMETABLE

Phase 1: **Preparation** (January 2004–October 2006)

Phase 2: **Implementation**

- Submissions (core submissions October 2006–April 2007, additional submissions to April 2009)
- Community Soundings (January–March 2007)
- Research Surveys (July 2006–January 2008)
- Policy searches (November 2006–April 2009)
- National Soundings (January–March 2008)
- Other consultations (October 2006–April 2009)

Phase 3: **Dissemination**

- Interim reports and briefings (October 2007–May 2008)
- Special report on the primary curriculum (February 2009)
- Final report (autumn 2009)
- Other dissemination events and activities (from summer 2009)

Phase 4: **Longer term evaluation and follow-up** (from late 2009)

- Programme to be agreed.

FUNDING

The Review was undertaken with the generous support of Esmée Fairbairn Foundation. To date (2009), the Foundation's Trustees have awarded the Review three grants: (i) the main Review implementation grant (Phase 2 and the first part of Phase 3 above), from 1 October 2006 to 30 September 2008; (ii) a supplementary implementation grant, from 1 October 2007 to 30 September 2008; (iii) a grant for dissemination (the second part of Phase 3), from 1 October 2008 to 30 September 2009.

LEAD PERSONNEL (FOR FULL LIST SEE THE FINAL REPORT)

Director of the Cambridge Primary Review: Professor Robin Alexander
Chair of the Cambridge Primary Review Advisory Committee: Dame Gillian Pugh
Chair of the Cambridge Primary Review Management Group: Hilary Hodgson, Esmée Fairbairn Foundation
Director of Communications: Dr Richard Margrave

The Cambridge team: core members

Professor Robin Alexander (2006–10)
Catrin Darsley (2006–9)
Christine Doddington (2006–8)
Julia Flutter (2007–10)
Dr Linda Hargreaves (2006–8)
Dr David Harrison (2006–8)
Ruth Kershner (2006–8)

Appendix 2
The Cambridge Primary Review
Perspectives, themes and questions

The coverage of the Cambridge Primary Review is expressed as a hierarchy of perspectives, themes and questions. We start with three broad *perspectives*: children, the world in which they are growing up, and the education which mediates that world and prepares them for it. These are the Review's core concerns and recurrent points of reference. Next, ten *themes* and 23 *sub-themes* unpack the education perspective in greater detail while remaining permeated by the other two. Finally, for every theme there is a set of *questions*.

PERSPECTIVES

P1 Children and childhood
P2 Culture, society and the global context
P3 Primary education

THEMES AND SUB-THEMES

T1   Purposes and values
T1a   Values, beliefs and principles
T1b   Aims
T2   Learning and teaching
T2a   Children's development and learning
T2b   Teaching
T3   Curriculum and assessment
T3a   Curriculum
T3b   Assessment
T4   Quality and standards
T4a   Standards
T4b   Quality assurance and inspection
T5   Diversity and inclusion
T5a   Culture, gender, race, faith
T5b   Special educational needs
T6   Settings and professionals
T6a   Buildings and resources
T6b   Teacher supply, training, deployment & development
T6c   Other professionals
T6d   School organisation, management & leadership

T6e   School culture and ethos
T7   Parenting and caring
T7a   Parents and carers
T7b   Home and school
T8   Beyond the school
T8a   Children's lives beyond the school
T8b   Schools and other agencies
T9   Structures and phases
T9a   Within-school structures, stages, classes & groups
T9b   System-level structures, phases & transitions
T10   Funding and governance
T10a   Funding
T10b   Governance

PERSPECTIVE 1 – CHILDREN AND CHILDHOOD

- What do we know about young children's lives in and out of school, and about the nature of childhood, at the start of the 21st century?
- How do children of primary school age develop, think, feel, act and learn?
- To which of the myriad individual and collective differences between children should educators and related professionals particularly respond?
- What do children most fundamentally need from those charged with providing their primary education?

PERSPECTIVE 2 – CULTURE, SOCIETY AND THE GLOBAL CONTEXT

- In what kind of society and world are today's children growing up and being educated?
- In what do England's (and Britain's) cultural differences and commonalities reside?
- What is the country's likely economic, social and political future?
- Is there a consensus about the 'good society' and education's role in helping to shape and secure it?
- What can we predict about the future – social, economic, environmental, moral, political – of the wider world with which Britain is interdependent?
- What, too, does this imply for children and primary education?
- What must be done in order that today's children, and their children, have a future worth looking forward to?

PERSPECTIVE 3 – PRIMARY EDUCATION

- Taking the system as a whole, from national policy and overall structure to the fine detail of school and classroom practice, what are the current characteristics, strengths and weaknesses of the English state system of primary education?
- To what needs and purposes should it be chiefly directed over the coming decades?
- What values should it espouse?
- What learning experiences should it provide?
- By what means can its quality be secured and sustained?

THEME 1 – PURPOSES AND VALUES

- What is primary education for?
- Taking account of the country and the world in which our children are growing up, to what individual, social, cultural, economic and other circumstances and needs should this phase of education principally attend?
- What core values and principles should it uphold and advance?
- How far can a national system reflect and respect the values and aspirations of the many different communities – cultural, ethnic, religious, political, economic, regional, local – for which it purportedly caters?
- In envisaging the future purposes and shape of this phase of education how far ahead is it possible or sensible to look?

THEME 2 – LEARNING AND TEACHING

- What do we know about the way young children develop, act and learn – cognitively, emotionally, socially, morally, physically and across the full spectrum of their development?
- What are the pedagogical implications of recent research in, for example, neuroscience, cognition, intelligence, language and human interaction?
- What is the relationship between children's physical health, emotional wellbeing and learning?
- What is the impact of gender on learning?
- What are the personal and situational circumstances for effective learning and what conditions are likely to impede it?
- As children move developmentally through the primary phase how do they learn best and how are they most effectively taught?
- Judged against all this evidence, how do current teaching approaches fare?
- How well do they capitalise on the findings of research?
- What is the proper place of ICT and other new technologies in teaching and learning?
- How can teaching, and the system as a whole, most appropriately respond to differences in children's development, ways of learning and apparent capacities and needs?
- In what ways might teaching, and the organisation of classrooms and schools, change in order to enhance young children's engagement and learning and maximise their educational prospects?

THEME 3 – CURRICULUM AND ASSESSMENT

- What do children currently learn during the primary phase?
- What should they learn?
- What constitutes a meaningful, balanced and relevant primary curriculum?
- What kinds of curriculum experience will best serve children's varying needs during the next few decades?
- Do notions like 'basics' and 'core curriculum' have continuing validity, and if so of what should 21st-century basics and cores for the primary phase be constituted?
- Do the current national curriculum and attendant foundation, literacy, numeracy and primary strategies provide the range and approach which children of this age really need?

- How are the different needs of children, including those with specific learning difficulties, currently diagnosed?
- How should their progress and attainment be assessed?
- What is the proper relationship and balance of assessment for learning and assessment for accountability?
- What are the strengths and weaknesses of current approaches to assessment, both national and local?
- What assessment information should be reported, and to whom?
- What is the most helpful balance of national and local in curriculum and assessment?

THEME 4 – QUALITY AND STANDARDS

- How good is English primary education?
- How consistent is it across the country as a whole?
- Have standards risen or fallen?
- How do they compare with those of other countries?
- How should 'standards' and 'quality' in primary education be defined?
- How should quality and standards be assessed?
- What is the available range of national and international evidence on these matters?
- How reliable is it?
- How well, and how appropriately, is it used?
- What are the most effective contributions to assessing and assuring standards and quality of, for example, research, inspection, government initiatives, school and teacher self-evaluation, performance management, pre-service training and in-service training?
- What are the proper roles in the processes of systemic review and quality assurance of DfES, Ofsted, the other national agencies and Parliament?

THEME 5 – DIVERSITY AND INCLUSION

- Do our primary schools attend effectively and equitably to the different learning needs and cultural backgrounds of their pupils?
- Do all children have equal access to high quality primary education?
- If not, how can this access be improved?
- How can a national system best respond to the wide diversity of cultures, faiths, languages and aspirations which is now a fact of British life?
- Of what is identity constituted in a highly plural culture, and what should be the role of primary education in fostering it?
- How can primary schools best meet the needs of children of widely-varying attainments and interests, including children with special educational needs and those who display or may have exceptional talents?
- How can schools secure the engagement of those children and families which are hardest to reach?

THEME 6 – SETTINGS AND PROFESSIONALS

- What are the physical and organisational characteristics of our best primary schools?
- How are they resourced and equipped?

- How are they organised and led?
- What are the lessons for school design and organisation of recent national initiatives?
- What balance of expertise, and of teachers, assistants and other para-professionals, should schools contain and how should they be used?
- What are the conditions for their success?
- What are the future workforce needs of the phase as a whole?
- How can these be met?
- How well are teachers and other professionals involved in this age-range trained?
- How effectively are they deployed?
- How well is their development supported at school, local and national levels?
- How can the nation secure and retain the best professionals for this phase of education?

THEME 7 – PARENTING, CARING AND EDUCATING

- What are the parenting and caring conditions on which children's welfare and their successful primary education depend?
- But what, too, should educational and other services do to support parents and carers in their work?
- How are the challenges of home-school relationships most effectively met?
- By what means can parents/carers, teachers and other professionals operate as far as possible in harmony and pursue goals which, while not identical, are not in such conflict that they damage the child's educational prospects?

THEME 8 – BEYOND THE SCHOOL

- What do we know about children's lives beyond school and the impact of those groups and influences – family, peers, community, media and so on – to which they are subject?
- What kinds of learning take place outside school?
- What is the current division of responsibilities between the people, institutions and agencies who are principally concerned with young children's education and those who are concerned with their upbringing and welfare – parents and carers especially, but also health services, social services and other statutory and voluntary agencies?
- How successfully does their work articulate and cohere?
- In the context of changing familial demographics and growing concern about young children's wellbeing, might these relationships, and the attendant responsibilities, be differently conceived?

THEME 9 – STRUCTURES AND PHASES

- How well do existing structures and phases – 'educare' and schooling, pre-school in its various forms, infant/junior/primary, first/middle, foundation/KS1/KS2 – work?
- What are the salient characteristics, strengths and weaknesses of the various institutions and settings in which primary education takes place?
- Are there problems of coherence, transition and continuity within and between phases?
- How can these be overcome?
- What can the primary phase profitably learn from developments in the phases which precede and follow it?

- How are children grouped within the primary phase and what are the advantages and disadvantages of the different grouping arrangements?
- When should formal schooling start, bearing in mind that many other countries start later than we do and conceive of the relationship of pre-school and formal schooling somewhat differently?
- Are there more effective alternatives to current structures?

THEME 10 – FUNDING AND GOVERNANCE

- How adequately is the system of primary education in England funded and how efficiently is it controlled and administered?
- Does it have the right balance of control and responsibility between national government, local government, local communities and schools?
- What has been the impact of the post-1988 drive to a more centralised system?
- What should be the position of faith schools?
- Through what system of school governance are the interests of children, teachers, parents and local communities most effectively and equitably addressed?
- How might matters be differently ordered?

Appendix 3
The Cambridge Primary Review
Research surveys

This was issued with the invitations to tender in June 2006. The list notes where each survey appears in this volume.

THEME 1 – PURPOSES AND VALUES

1/1: A discussion, across disciplinary boundaries, of representative literature on educational aims, purposes and values for national education systems in general and the primary phase in particular, and the problems of defining and implementing them. (Chapter 12)

1/2: A survey of the mainly descriptive and/or official literature on stated purposes, values and priorities in primary education: England, other parts of the UK and a representative range of other countries compared, drawing on historical as well as contemporary sources. (Chapter 13)

1/3: An analytical survey of literature on the changing national context of primary education: recent changes in the demographic, economic and social condition of England of relevance to primary education, and national prospects and projections for the next few decades. (Chapter 10)

1/4: The international counterpart of 1/3: an analytical survey of literature on the changing *global* context of primary education: emergent educational responses, both national and international, to globalisation and to projected geopolitical, social, climatic and environmental changes. (Chapter 11)

THEME 2 – LEARNING AND TEACHING

2/1: A survey of representative evidence on how children of primary age develop, think and learn, and how their motivation and engagement are most effectively secured and sustained, drawing on material from physiology, developmental and cognitive psychology, emergent brain research and other disciplines, and aiming to characterise the current consensus, if there is one. Note: part of this topic – children's development – was a central and influential theme in the Plowden Report of 1967, so it would be useful also to comment on how thinking on the topic has changed since then. (Subsequently reconfigured as surveys 2/1a and 2/1b: Chapters 6 and 7)

2/2: The teaching counterpart to 2/1: representative evidence on the nature of teaching and the conditions and characteristics of that teaching which most successfully promotes children's learning and understanding in the primary phase, and their capacity to continue to learn. The survey should draw on a wide range of studies and paradigms – quantitative and qualitative, process-product and ethnographic, systematic and impressionistic, national and international. It should also discuss the problems of defining and judging quality, productivity and effectiveness in teaching. (Some of this was covered by the additional survey 2/1b. The remainder was not completed in time to be issued as an interim report, and its material was fed directly into the final report.)

2/3: A subject-specific gloss on 2/1 and 2/2. Learning and teaching across the curriculum: comparative domain-specific evidence from the research literatures of different subjects, and its implications for the primary phase. (Not completed: issues treated directly in the final report.)

2/4: Special synoptic survey. Teaching and learning during the primary years and contingent phases: evidence and implications to date from the ESRC Teaching and Learning Research Programme. (Chapter 20)

THEME 3 – CURRICULUM AND ASSESSMENT

3/1: A descriptive comparison, mainly from official sources, of current national curricula and assessment arrangements in England, the rest of the UK and selected other countries. The other countries might be selected to include some others in the EC and major economic competitors of the UK; they might also be chosen to illustrate sharp contrast with English arrangements. (Chapter 15)

3/2: The trajectory of reform in primary curriculum and assessment: a descriptive and evaluative review. (i) a summary of the major English curriculum and assessment initiatives relating to the primary phase since Plowden, and the work of the agencies responsible for them, with particular reference to the post-1988 and post-1997 periods of centralisation and reform (e.g. national curriculum and assessment, the national literacy, numeracy and primary strategies); (ii) a review of evidence on the impact of these reforms on the character and quality of primary education, drawing on both official and independent sources. (Chapter 29)

3/3: Curriculum futures: a descriptive, analytical and discursive survey. Official and non-official alternative curriculum models for the future, from the UK and other countries, compared; curriculum variation for specific needs and contexts; the balance of national, regional and local in curriculum planning and provision. (Chapter 16)

3/4: Assessment alternatives: a description and critical discussion. The different purposes and uses of assessment in the primary phase; official and non-official patterns of assessment, from the UK and other countries, compared; the balance and character of national, local and classroom assessment. (Chapter 19)

THEME 4 – QUALITY AND STANDARDS

4/1: A survey of national evidence on standards and quality in English primary education over time, going back as far as the evidence safely allows; the strengths and limitations of such data, and implications for monitoring standards and quality in the future. This survey will need to consider both official data (for example, from the annual SAT results) and independent research studies. (Chapter 17)

4/2: The international counterpart to 4/1: international comparative evidence on standards and quality in primary education over time: England and other countries, drawing on IEA, PISA, TIMSS, PIRLS, OECD, World Bank and other data; strengths and limitations of the data, and future implications. The survey should concentrate on the primary phase but should also refer to the test data from other phases where these have implications for primary education. (Chapter 18)

4/3: A descriptive and evaluative survey of arrangements for monitoring, assuring and maintaining quality and standards in primary education. The nature, focus, efficacy and impact of school, local and national quality assurance and inspection arrangements in England, as revealed by both official enquiries and independent research; plus a comparative discussion of the lessons from arrangements in other parts of the UK and selected other countries. (Chapter 28)

THEME 5 – DIVERSITY AND INCLUSION

5/1: Gender, culture, ethnicity, class, faith and national origin and their bearings on primary education. A mainly demographic and descriptive account of the various groups represented in England's primary schools, together with a survey of evidence on their needs, opportunities, experiences and trajectories. Related issues of cultural identity, diversity and inclusion, and selective international comparisons of ways of responding educationally to these. (Chapter 8)

5/2: A descriptive, demographic and evaluative survey of the educational opportunities, experiences and trajectories of those primary-age children with different learning needs and difficulties in both mainstream primary schools and separate provision; issues in defining, identifying and providing for such children; recent national and international developments; alternative approaches and policies compared. (Chapter 9)

5/3: Special synoptic survey. Pupil voice and primary education: a survey of research on what primary pupils and former pupils think of their primary schooling – purposes, culture, organisation, learning, teaching, curriculum, assessment, etc. – and of their aspirations and preferences in respect of these and their own futures. Comparisons in pupil voice across different social and cultural groups. (Chapter 2)

THEME 6 – SETTINGS AND PROFESSIONALS

6/1: The physical environment of primary schools. A descriptive and analytical survey of the literature on changes and developments in primary school building design and on the physical organisation, equipping and resourcing of primary schools and classrooms, in relation to purpose, function and the well-being of pupils, teachers and other users. The survey to include historical changes, national variations and contrastive international comparisons. (Chapter 22)

6/2: The professional environment of primary schools. A descriptive survey of literature on primary school staffing (including teachers, assistants and other adults), demography, organisation, professional roles, staff deployment, and professional leadership, and on the nature of the professionals' work; plus an assessment of the evidence of the educational and institutional effectiveness of different staffing models and approaches; historical changes, national variations, international comparisons. (Chapter 23)

6/3: The training and development of primary teachers and other professionals; recent developments in initial training, induction and in-service development and support described and assessed, drawing on both official and independent evidence; the roles in professional training and development of the various providers (universities, colleges, local authorities, etc.) and accreditors/validators (CATE, TTA, TDA, etc.); the recent expansion of involvement of national agencies and government strategies in professional support and direction (e.g. DfES, NLS, NNS, PNS, NCSL); alternative UK and international approaches models compared and evaluated. (Chapter 24)

6/4: Policies for professional workforce management, reform and support: an account and assessment of recent developments in England, plus comparative evidence on developments in the rest of the UK and selected other countries. (Chapter 25)

THEME 7 – PARENTING, CARING AND EDUCATING

7/1: A demographic and analytical survey of variation and change in patterns of parenting and caring in the pre-adolescent years over the past few decades; demography, culture, custom and fashion; cultural and social differences; changes over time; future trends, possibilities and problems in relation to the tasks of primary schools. (Merged with 7/2: Chapter 4)

7/2: The roles and relationships of parents, carers and teachers; a descriptive account of changing patterns and procedures, both formal and informal, in home-school relations, together with a review of evidence on the efficacy and problems of the different approaches, and appropriate international comparisons. (Merged with 7/1: Chapter 4)

THEME 8 – BEYOND THE SCHOOL

8/1: A survey of evidence on children's lives outside school, and the influences of family, peer group, community, media and the wider culture on their development and education. Note: in the form of 'education and the environment' this, like child development, was another central theme of the Plowden Report of 1967, so a historical and critical perspective on changes in thinking about the topic will also be helpful. (Chapter 3)

8/2: A descriptive and evaluative survey of changes and developments in the responsibilities and relationships of schools and other agencies bearing on the lives of children of primary age, up to and including the most recent reforms; plus English, UK and international comparisons. (Chapter 5)

THEME 9 – STRUCTURES AND PHASES

9/1: System level structures. A descriptive/demographic account of the structure of the English primary education system as a whole and its various within-phase permutations (primary, infant, junior, first, middle, foundation/KS1/KS2/KS3, primary with/without pre-school, etc.); together with a review of evidence on the roles and relationships of pre-school and primary provision and on starting ages for formal schooling; and on the impact on learning and teaching of the different primary-phase structures described; together with appropriate UK and non-UK comparisons. (Chapter 14)

9/2: School-level structure and transition: a survey of evidence on the impact of internal primary school organisational structure and within-phase grouping on children and their education: pre-school to primary transition; grouping (classes, streams, sets and within-class groups); transition within the primary phase; transition from primary to secondary. (Chapter 21)

THEME 10 – FUNDING AND GOVERNANCE

10/1: Expenditure on and within primary education, using both official and independent sources: an account of the current position and change over time; expenditure on primary education relative to other aspects of educational and social policy; changes in the management and control of educational expenditure; international comparisons in primary education expenditure and its management; alternative models assessed. (Chapter 27)

10/2: Administration, control and governance of primary education: a description and analysis of the balance of power and responsibility between and within the various levels of the system; the roles of DfES and its predecessors, national agencies, local authorities and school governing bodies; the impact of centralised and decentralised control and decision making; how educational policy is formulated and implemented; the place of faith schools in a national educational system; changes since the 1960s; international comparisons; alternative models of administration, control and governance assessed. (Chapter 26)

Author Index

Subject Index